KU-548-555

N 0012995 X

Readings in
Personality Assessment

Readings in
Personality Assessment

Edited by
Leonard D. Goodstein
University of Cincinnati
Richard I. Lanyon
Northeastern University

John Wiley & Sons, Inc. New York · London · Sydney · Toronto

Library of Congress Catalogue Card Number: 77-149770

ISBN 0-471-31500-1

Printed in the United States of America

10 9 8 7 6 5 4 3 2 1

Preface

We have prepared this book of readings in personality assessment for two principal reasons: (1) as a useful source of original papers and writings that give a broad coverage of the field of personality assessment, and (2) as a companion volume to our textbook *Personality Assessment.* Although the organization and manner of presentation of these readings parallels that of the textbook, there are introductory remarks for each of the chapters in these readings that permit the independent use of this volume. The introductions provide a theoretical, conceptual, and historical overview of each of the chapters and discuss the salient issues in each of the readings. Also, there are brief biographical sketches of the authors included with the source of the readings, which puts each reading in context.

While editors of books of readings ordinarily attempt to avoid becoming embroiled in controversy, the very act of selecting certain authors as "representative" is frequently seen as a reflection of the editors' viewpoint on issues. Similarly, the amount of space devoted to various topics is judged to be an indication of the importance (or lack of importance) placed on these topics by the editors. Since we agree with this kind of interpretation, we cannot deny that this set of readings reflects our viewpoints and our biases. Indeed, we prefer to make these prejudices and positions somewhat explicit. The reader can then devote his efforts, if he is so inclined, to determining the degree to which we have been successful in presenting our position, rather than in attempting to ascertain where we stand by some complex interpretative process.

In general, this book of readings is intended to meet the learning needs of a rather wide audience who are potentially interested in personality assessment, including clinicians, researchers, and theoreticians. Consequently we have chosen articles that either deal with broad issues or are illustrations of generic problems. We believe that most readers will find the detailed reporting of some of the specifics of less importance than the general orientation, the methods, practices, and research findings that are presented in these readings. The details are of greater interest, of course, to the more advanced reader who already possesses an understanding of the field of personality assessment. We hope that a concurrent reading of this volume and the textbook will provide a solid background to the serious student and a comprehensive introduction on which to base the learning of practical skills in personality assessment. We believe that these applied skills can best be acquired in practical settings where, under careful supervision, the student can develop an adequate understanding both of the specific materials used in personality assessment and of the subject populations who are being assessed.

The major credit for this volume belongs, of course, to the many contributing authors, and our appreciation is expressed to them for their skillful efforts and their collective willingness to have their work reproduced here. We are particularly grateful to Loren and Jean Chapman, who prepared an original article for this volume, and to Paul Meehl and Raymond Fowler, each of whom, at their own suggestion, updated their work for inclusion.

Also, we especially thank Ellin L. Bloch for her help in preparing the biographical sketches that precede each reading. The burden of the vast amount of clerical work involved in collating and preparing these materials for publication was borne by Diane Burkhardt, Sherry Traub, and Sharon Vespie, and we are most appreciative of their help.

Leonard D. Goodstein
Richard I. Lanyon

September 1970

Organization of the Book

The organization of the book is revealed in the Table of Contents, although the reasons for this organization may not be clear. Because we firmly believe that the foundation for much contemporary concern is in the past, Chapter 1 provides a historical introduction to the field of personality assessment. With the exception of the final article in this chapter, all the material comes from an earlier era of psychology and illustrates the work and thought of some of the leading figures of psychology's past. Hopefully, the reader will note the similarities in viewpoints between these writers and our contemporary colleagues.

Chapter 2 presents several conceptual frameworks for understanding personality and personality assessment and it is here that the reader may begin to discern the great diversity of viewpoints that permeates this area, affecting both theory and practice. Chapters 3 and 4 are directly concerned with the several different approaches to the development of the standardized assessment procedures that are generally termed *personality tests.* The articles in these two chapters focus on the assumptions underlying different strategies in test development, their actual construction, and further attempts to contrast the differential usefulness of these strategies. Chapter 5 deals with the assessment of personality through the use of behavior sampling and biographical data, approaches that have gained considerable popularity in recent years.

Chapters 6 to 9 consider in detail a number of basic issues in personality assessment, almost all of which were raised in the first five chapters but which, because of their importance, require further elaboration. The readings in Chapter 6 deal with psychometric considerations of reliability and validity, concepts that are basic to all psychological tests. Chapter 7 surveys the literature on response distortion–those factors, other than personality *per se,* which affect an individual's responses to personality assessment instruments. Major emphasis is given to the response sets of social desirability and deliberate faking, the best understood of response distortions. Chapter 8 provides examples of research on the actual use of personality tests and how these devices can be made more effective in real-life settings. The criticisms of personality assessment are examined in detail in Chapter 9 with two major foci: (1) that some uses of personality assessment devices are invalid, and (2) that some uses are immoral. The final chapter discusses some approaches that we believe, and hope, will be increasingly important for personality assessment: an increasing emphasis on a more behavioral approach to personality assessment, the use of computers in assessment, and several statistical innovations such as the use of a decision-making model and the use of moderator variables.

Apart from the distinctly historical material, we have emphasized contemporary writings because we view the field of personality assessment as currently in great flux. We believe that it is important to provide an understanding of this flux, but we wish to do this in a historical context. As one index of our contemporary focus, notice that 40 of the 53 papers were published since 1960 and nearly half of the book of readings consists of materials originally published in the period between 1965 and 1970.

In any set of readings the articles finally selected must, of necessity, constitute only a very small proportion of the material initially considered. We were faced with the choice of covering a few topics in depth or of covering a larger number of topics more superficially. We chose the former course and even found difficulty in selecting the one or two articles that most cogently dealt with the covered issues from among the many that were available.

Clearly, a number of topics were excluded, some which may be regarded as having merited inclusion. We did not include any discussion of the use of physiological indices of personality, or of such topics as repression-sensitization, cognitive complexity, or field dependence-independence, nor did we include any case reports. Although we were most reluctant to exclude any relevant material, we feel that we have selected the topics and issues that are most critical for an adequate understanding of contemporary personality assessment and that the inclusion of such additional topics would have only modestly enhanced the value of this book. Our judgment in this regard has been supported by our use of many of these articles as supplementary materials in personality assessment courses at Rutgers University and the University of Pittsburgh. The reactions of successive classes of students were one basis for our decision about what material to include.

Because we felt that consistency in style was important for readability, a number of minor changes were made in several of the articles. The abstracts that preceded many of the recent articles were eliminated, some lengthy footnotes were deleted, and a single reference style was imposed. For the readers' convenience, one combined reference list appears at the end of the book instead of separate lists at the end of each article.

L. D. G.
R. I. L.

Contents

Readings in
Personality Assessment

Chapter 1

History of Personality Assessment

Man's concern with understanding and predicting the interpersonal behavior of others is an ancient one, probably stemming back to prehistoric times. In addition to the intuitive or nonspecified methods that presumably have always been used for personality assessment on an informal basis, there are many systematic procedures that have survived from pre-Biblical times. One such method is *astrology,* the attempt to understand and predict events on earth, including the behavior of individuals, through inferences based on the observation of the fixed stars and other heavenly bodies. Another method is *palmistry,* the determination of an individual's personality characteristics by interpreting the various irregularities and folds of the skin of the hands. While both of these methods are still practiced to some extent today, they are not regarded as acceptable procedures by scientifically oriented workers.

There are two reasons for the rejection of these procedures: first, the assumptions on which these techniques are based are contrary to our current scientific understanding, and, second, the predictions that emerge from these systems have not been shown to be accurate. Thus astrology is rejected because there is no scientifically acceptable reason to believe that the order of heavenly bodies at the time of one's birth should influence a person's psychological development and, also, the accuracy of astrological predictions has not been supported by empirical investigation. A similar indictment can be drawn against palmistry and many of the other pseudo-scientific approaches to personality assessment. Modern personality assessment procedures typically are based on assumptions that are congruent with modern science and rely on the empirical demonstration of the usefulness of their predictions.

In tracing the history of any scientific endeavor such as modern personality assessment, it is often found that the work of a few individuals stands out as being ahead of its time. In many cases these same individuals have contributed to knowledge in a number of diverse areas. Such a person was Sir Francis Galton, a famous British scholar and scientist of the nineteenth century. One of the important foundations of modern scientific psychology was the study of individual differences through the measurement and comparison of behavioral characteristics, and this effort was given considerable impetus by Darwin's work on evolution. Galton became interested in the hereditary aspects of individual differences, and was ultimately led into the study and measurement of the nonintellective aspects of behavior, now known as "personality" but known more commonly at that time as "character and temperament." In the first reading of this section, originally published in 1884, Galton discusses his ideas for the measurement of several such nonintellectual faculties of the mind. Galton's creativity and flexibility of thought is demonstrated in the methods that he discusses for the measurement of emotion and temper, using what today would be labeled as the behavior-sample approach.

Another of the early forerunners of modern personality assessment methods was *phrenology,* the determination of personality through the measurement of the external shape of the skull. Phrenology was given its major impetus late in the eighteenth century by Franz Joseph Gall, a German physician and anatomist, and it deserves scrutiny for several reasons. First, there were careful theoretical assumptions underlying the system; second, the system was completely empirical in basis, and thus open to scientific inquiry; and third, fairly complete documentation of the history of phrenology is available. One contributor to this history was Madison Bentley, whose scholarly account of the psychological and philosophical antecedents of phrenology, written in 1916, is our second reading. As interpreted by Bentley, Gall's analysis and integration of the psychological, philosophical, and anatomical knowledge of the time, although incorrect in several critical ways, should be considered no indictment of the quality of his scholarship.

One of the earliest personality assessment techniques that still finds some use today is the *word association* technique, and it often comes as a surprise to readers to learn that this procedure was developed around the turn of the century by none other than Carl G. Jung, the noted psychoanalyst. Jung made extensive use of the method, which he considered to "strike easily almost all complexes of practical importance." The third article in this section, written by Jung in 1910, gives his own account of the word association technique and demonstrates his considerable ingenuity in developing clinical applications of the procedure, including its use as a lie detector test. Jung paid attention not to the content of an individual's associations but to formal characteristics of the responses, such as variations in reaction time, failures to respond, and misunderstandings of the stimulus words. The antecedents of projective test methodology can clearly be seen in Jung's work.

By the 1920's, a significant proportion of psychologists in the United States were identifying themselves to some extent with the applied and professional aspects of their field, and they were attempting to gain recognition and status both within the psychology establishment and with the general public. This state of affairs provided first-class opportunities for frauds and charlatans to claim expertise in areas such as "character analysis," and a great many otherwise circumspect persons were gulled in the process. The flavor of this atmosphere is discussed by Knight Dunlap, whose paper, written in 1926, deplores the gullibility of the public and the greed and avarice of the character analysts. Dunlap also reviews, within the context of the state of psychological knowledge at that time, the possible legitimate bases for personality assessment based on physiological signs. While some of Dunlap's views, especially those on race, can no longer be supported, certainly not by the editors of this volume, there still is a certain contemporary ring about Dunlap's paper, and the problem of charlatanism in personality assessment is by no means resolved, even today.

Large-scale personality assessment programs, or multiple assessment methods, received their first real use in the 1940's as a result of their use by the British and U.S. governments in selecting personnel for key positions during World War II. Large-scale assessment methods involving multiple assessors and multiple assessment techniques have been steadily developed since that time, and now represent an important approach both to problems of personnel selection and to personality research. In our fifth and final reading in this section, Ronald Taft reviews the origins and development of multiple assessment methods, and gives practical advice on their implementation.

1. MEASUREMENT OF CHARACTER

Sir Francis Galton

I do not plead guilty to taking a shallow view of human nature, when I propose to apply, as it were, a foot-rule to its heights and depths. The powers of man are finite, and if finite they are not too large for measurement. Those persons may justly be accused of shallowness of view, who do not discriminate a wide range of differences, but quickly lose all sense of proportion, and rave about infinite heights and unfathomable depths, and use such like expressions which are not true and betray their incapacity. Examiners are not, I believe, much stricken with the sense of awe and infinitude when they apply their foot-rules to the intellectual performances of the candidates whom they examine; neither do I see any reason why we should be awed at the thought of examining our fellow creatures as best we may, in respect to other faculties than intellect. On the contrary, I think it anomalous that the art of measuring intellectual faculties should have become highly developed, while that of dealing with other qualities should have been little practised or even considered.

The use of measuring man in his entirety, is to be justified by exactly the same arguments as those by which any special examinations are justified, such as those in classics or mathematics; namely, that every measurement tests, in some particulars, the adequacy of the previous education, and contributes to show the efficiency of the man as a human machine, at the time it was made. It is impossible to be sure of the adequacy in every respect of the rearing of a man, or of his total efficiency, unless he has been measured in character and physique, as well as in intellect. A wise man desires this knowledge for his own use, and for the same reason that he takes stock from time to time of his finances. It teaches him his position among his fellows, and whether he is getting on or falling back, and he shapes his ambitions and conduct accordingly. "Know thyself" is an ancient phrase of proverbial philosophy, and I wish to discuss ways by which its excellent direction admits of being better followed.

The art of measuring various human faculties now occupies the attention of many inquirers in this and other countries. Shelves full of memoirs have been written in Germany alone, on the discriminative powers of the various senses. New processes of inquiry are yearly invented, and it seems as though there was a general lightening up of the sky in front of the path of the anthropometric experimenter, which betokens the approaching dawn of a new and interesting science. Can we discover landmarks in character to serve as bases for a survey, or

SOURCE. Sir Francis Galton (1822-1911) was an English scientist, anthropologist, and explorer. One of the early investigators of individual differences among people, he is also regarded as the initiator of the study of eugenics. This article originally appeared in the *Fortnightly Review* (of London), 1884, **42**, 179-185.

is it altogether too indefinite and fluctuating to admit of measurement? Is it liable to spontaneous changes, or to be in any way affected by a caprice that renders the future necessarily uncertain? Is man, with his power of choice and freedom of will, so different from a conscious machine, that any proposal to measure his moral qualities is based upon a fallacy? If so, it would be ridiculous to waste thought on the matter, but if our temperament and character are durable realities, and persistent factors of our conduct, we have no Proteus to deal with in either case, and our attempts to grasp and measure them are reasonable.

I have taken pains, as some of my readers may be aware, to obtain fresh evidence upon this question, which, in other words, is, whether or no the actions of men are mainly governed by cause and effect. On the supposition that they are so governed, it is as important to us to learn the exact value of our faculties, as it is to know the driving power of the engine and the quality of the machine that does our factory-work. If, on the other hand, the conduct of man is mainly the result of mysterious influences, such knowledge is of little service to him. He must be content to look upon himself as on a ship, afloat in a strong and unknown current, that may drift her in a very different direction to that in which her head is pointed.

My earlier inquiries into this subject had reference to the facts of heredity, and I came across frequent instances in which a son, happening to inherit somewhat exclusively the qualities of his father, had been found to fail with his failures, sin with his sins, surmount with his virtues, and generally to get through life in much the same way. The course of his life had, therefore, been predetermined by his inborn faculties, or, to continue the previous metaphor, his ship had not drifted, but pursued the course in which her head was set until she arrived at her predestined port.

The second of my inquiries was into the life-histories of twins, in the course of which I collected cases where the pair of twins resembled each other so closely, that they behaved like one person, thought and spoke alike, and acted similar parts when separated. Whatever spontaneous feeling the one twin may have had, the other twin at the very same moment must have had a spontaneous feeling of exactly the same kind. Such habitual coincidences, if they had no common cause, would be impossible; we are therefore driven to the conclusion that whenever twins think and speak alike, there is no spontaneity in either of them, in the popular acceptation of the word, but that they act mechanically and in like ways, because their mechanisms are alike. I need not reiterate my old arguments, and will say no more about the twins, except that new cases have come to my knowledge which corroborate former information. It follows, that if we had in our keeping the twin of a man, who was his "double," we might obtain a trustworthy forecast of what the man would do under any new conditions, by first subjecting that twin to the same conditions and watching his conduct.

My third inquiry is more recent. It was a course of introspective search into the operations of my own mind, whenever I caught myself engaged in a feat of what at first sight seemed to be free-will. The inquiry was carried on almost continuously for three weeks, and proceeded with, off and on, for many subsequent months. After I had mastered the method of observation a vast deal of apparent mystery cleared away, and I ultimately reckoned the rate of occurrence of perplexing cases, during the somewhat uneventful but pleasant months of a summer spent in the country, to be less than one a day. All the rest of my actions seemed clearly to lie within the province of normal cause and consequence. The general results of my introspective inquiry support the views of those who hold that man is little more than a conscious machine, the larger part of whose actions are predicable. As regards such residuum as there may be, which is not automatic, and which a man, however wise and well informed, could not possibly foresee, I have nothing to say, but I have found that the more carefully I inquired, whether it was into hereditary similarities of conduct, into the life-histories of twins, or now introspectively into the processes of what I should have called my own Free-Will, the smaller seems the room left for the possible residuum.

I conclude from these three inquiries that the motives of the will are mostly normal, and that the character which shapes our conduct is a definite and durable "something," and therefore that it is reasonable to attempt to measure it. We must guard ourselves against supposing that the moral faculties which we distinguish by different names, as courage, sociability, niggardness, are separate entities. On the contrary, they are so intermixed that they are never singly in action. I tried to gain an idea of the number of the more conspicuous aspects of the character by counting in an appropriate dictionary the words used to express them. Roget's *Thesaurus* was selected for that purpose, and I examined many pages of its index here and there as samples of the whole, and estimated that it contained fully one thousand words expressive of character, each of which has a separate shade of meaning, while each shares a large part of its meaning with some of the rest.

It may seem hopeless to deal accurately with so vague and wide a subject, but it often happens that when we are unable to meet difficulties, we may evade them, and so it is with regard to the present difficulty. It is true that we cannot define any aspect of character, but we can define a test that shall elicit *some* manifestation of character, and we can define the act performed in response to it. Searchings into the character must be conducted on the same fundamental principle as that which lies at the root of examinations into the intellectual capacity. Here there has been no preliminary attempt to map out the field of intellect with accuracy; but definite tests are selected by which the intellect is probed at places that are roughly known but not strictly defined, as the depth of a lake might be sounded from a boat rowing here and there. So it should be with respect to character. Definite acts in response to definite emergencies have alone to be noted. No accurate map of character is required to start from.

Emergencies need not be waited for, they can be extemporised; traps, as it were, can be laid. Thus, a great ruler whose word can make or mar a subject's fortune, wants a secret agent and tests his character during a single interview. He contrives by a few minutes' questioning, temptation, and show of displeasure, to turn his character inside out, exciting in turns his hopes, fear, zeal, loyalty, ambition, and so forth. Ordinary observers who stand on a far lower pedestal, cannot hope to excite the same tension and outburst of feeling in those whom they examine, but they can obtain good data in a more leisurely way. If they are unable to note a man's conduct under great trials for want of opportunity, they may do it in small ones, and it is well that those small occasions should be such as are of frequent occurrence, that the statistics of men's conduct under like conditions may be compared. After fixing upon some particular class of persons of similar age, sex, and social condition, we have to find out what common incidents in their lives are most apt to make them betray their character. We may then take note as often as we can, of what they do on these occasions, so as to arrive at their statistics of conduct in a limited number of well-defined small trials.

One of the most notable differences between man and man, lies in the emotional temperament. Some persons are quick and excitable; others are slow and deliberate. A sudden excitement, call, touch, gesture, or incident of any kind evokes, in different persons, a response that varies in intensity, celerity, and quality. An observer watching children, heart and soul at their games, would soon collect enough material to enable him to class them according to the quantity of emotion that they showed. I will not attempt to describe particular games of children or of others, nor to suggest experiments, more or less comic, that might be secretly made to elicit the manifestations we seek, as many such will occur to ingenious persons. They exist in abundance, and I feel sure that if two or three experimenters were to act zealously and judiciously together as secret accomplices, they would soon collect abundant statistics of conduct. They would gradually simplify their test conditions and extend their scope, learning to probe character more quickly and from more of its sides.

It is a question by no means to be decided off-hand in the negative, whether instrumental measurements of the magnitude of the reflex signs of emotion in persons who desire to submit themselves to experiment, are not feasible. The difficulty lies in the more limited range of tests that can be used when the freedom of movement is embarrassed by the necessary mechanism. The exciting cause of emotion whatever it be, a fright, a suspense, a scold, an insult, a grief, must be believed to be genuine, or the tests would be worthless. It is not possible to sham emotion thoroughly. A good actor may move his audience as deeply as if they were witnessing a drama of real life, but the best actor cannot put himself into the exact frame of mind of a real sufferer. If he did, the reflex and automatic signs of emotion excited in his frame would be so numerous and violent, that they would shatter his constitution long before he had acted a dozen tragedies.

The reflex signs of emotion that are perhaps the most easily registered, are the palpitations of the heart. They cannot be shammed or repressed, and they are visible. Our poet Laureate has happily and artistically exemplified this. He tells us that Launcelot returning to court after a long illness through which he had been nursed by Elaine, sent to crave an audience of the jealous queen. The messenger utilises the opportunity for observing her in the following ingenious way like a born scientist.

> Low drooping till he well nigh kissed her feet
> For loyal awe, saw with a sidelong eye
> The shadow of a piece of pointed lace
> In the Queen's shadow, vibrate on the wall
> And parted, laughing in his courtly heart.

Physiological experimenters are not content to look at shadows on the wall, that depart and leave no mark. They obtain durable traces by the aid of appropriate instruments. Maret's pretty little pneumo-cardiograph is very portable, but not so sure in action as the more bulky apparatus. It is applied tightly to the chest in front of the heart, by a band passing round the body. At each to-and-fro movement, whether of the chest as a whole, or of the portion over the heart, it sucks in or blows out a little puff of air. A thin india-rubber tube connects its nozzle with a flat elastic bag under the short arm of a lever. The other end of the lever moves up and down in accordance with the part of the chest to which the pneumo-cardiograph is applied, and scratches light marks on a band of paper which is driven onwards by clockwork. This little instrument can be worn under the buttoned coat without being noticed. I was anxious to practise myself in its use, and wore one during the formidable ordeal of delivering the Rede Lecture in the Senate House at Cambridge, a month ago (most of this very memoir forming part of that lecture). I had no connection established between my instrument and any recording apparatus, but wore it merely to see whether or not it proved in any way irksome. If I had had a table in front of me, with the recording apparatus stowed out of sight below, and an expert assistant near at hand to turn a stop-cock at appropriate moments, he could have obtained samples of my heart's action without causing me any embarrassment whatever. I should have forgotten all about the apparatus while I was speaking.

Instrumental observers of the reflex signs of emotion have other means available besides this, and the sphygmograph that measures the pulse. Every twitch of each separate finger even of an infant's hand is registered by Dr. Warner's ingenious little gauntlet. Every movement of each limb of man or horse is recorded by

Dr. Maret. The apparatus of Mosso measures the degree in which the blood leaving the extremities rushes to the heart and head and internal organs. Every limb shrinks sensibly in volume from this withdrawal of the blood, and the shrinkage of any one of them, say the right arm, is measured by the fall of water in a gauge that communicates with a long bottleful of water, through the neck of which the arm has been thrust, and in which it is softly but effectually plugged.

I should not be surprised if the remarkable success of many persons in "muscle-reading" should open out a wide field for delicate instrumental investigations. The poetical metaphors of ordinary language suggest many possibilities of measurement. Thus when two persons have an "inclination" to one another, they visibly incline or slope together when sitting side by side, as at a dinner-table, and they then throw the stress of their weights on the near legs of their chairs. It does not require much ingenuity to arrange a pressure gauge with an index and dial to indicate changes in stress, but it is difficult to devise an arrangement that shall fulfil the threefold condition of being effective, not attracting notice, and being applicable to ordinary furniture. I made some rude experiments, but being busy with other matters, have not carried them on, as I had hoped.

Another conspicuous way in which one person differs from another is in temper. Some men are easily provoked, others remain cheerful even when affairs go very contrary to their liking. We all know specimens of good and bad-tempered persons, and all of us could probably specify not a few appropriate test conditions to try the temper in various ways, and elicit definite responses. There is no doubt that the temper of a dog can be tested. Many boys do it habitually, and learn to a nicety how much each will put up with, without growling or showing other signs of resentment. They do the same to one another, and gauge each other's tempers accurately.

It is difficult to speak of tests of character without thinking of Benjamin Franklin's amusing tale of the "Handsome and the Deformed Leg," and there is no harm in quoting it, because, however grotesque, it exemplifies the principle of tests. In it he describes two sorts of people; those who habitually dwell on the pleasanter circumstances of the moment, and those who have no eyes but for the unpleasing ones. He tells how a philosophical friend took special precautions to avoid those persons who being discontented themselves, sour the pleasures of society, offend many people, and make themselves everywhere disagreeable. In order to discover a pessimist at first sight, he cast about for an instrument. He of course possessed a thermometer to test heat, and a barometer to tell the air-pressure, but he had no instrument to test the characteristic of which we are speaking. After much pondering he hit upon a happy idea. He chanced to have one remarkably handsome leg, and one that by some accident was crooked and deformed, and these he used for the purpose. If a stranger regarded his ugly leg more than his handsome one he doubted him. If he spoke of it and took no notice of the handsome leg, the philosopher determined to avoid his further acquaintance. Franklin sums up by saying, that every one has not this two-legged instrument, but every one with a little attention may observe the signs of a carping and fault-finding disposition.

This very disposition is the subject of the eighteenth "character" of Theophrastus, who describes the conduct of such men under the social conditions of the day, one of which is also common to our own time and countrymen. He says that when the weather has been very dry for a long time, and it at last changes, the grumbler being unable to complain of the rain, complains that it did not come sooner. The British philosopher has frequent opportunities for applying weather tests to those whom he meets, and with especial fitness to such as happen to be agriculturists.

The points I have endeavoured to impress are chiefly these. First, that character ought to be measured by carefully recorded acts, representative of the usual conduct. An ordinary generalisation is nothing more than a muddle of vague memories of inexact observations. It is an easy vice to generalise. We want lists of facts, every one of which may be separately verified, valued and revalued, and the whole accurately summed. It is the statistics of each man's conduct in small every-day affairs, that will probably be found to give the simplest and most precise measure of his character. The other chief point that I wish to impress is, that a practice of deliberately and methodically testing the character of others and of ourselves is not wholly fanciful, but deserves consideration and experiment.

2. THE PSYCHOLOGICAL ANTECEDENTS OF PHRENOLOGY

Madison Bentley

Dr. Franz Joseph Gall, a contemporary of the poet Goethe, was the founder of phrenology.[1] He is to be numbered among those brilliant and aggressive souls who create with like facility enemies and friends, who attract the reverent admiration of disciples as they attract the fires of denunciation, and who establish schools and creeds under the frown of emperors and flourish under the ban of episcopal authority.

Such men are difficult to measure. The emotional standards of their times either dwarf or exaggerate them. Only history can set them in just perspective; because history alone discovers their antecedents, traces their divergent course from the broad paths of tradition, and marks the impression which they leave upon men and upon knowledge. In the case of Gall we now know with some exactness how the man stood related to his own time, and we also know, in part, the influence which his doctrine has since exerted upon psychology, nervous anatomy, and the differential study of character. But the intellectual antecedents of his famous doctrine still remain in the obscure archives of science and philosophy. The elucidation of them is the task of the present essay.

I. The Foundation of Gall's System

To understand Gall, then, it is as necessary to go behind the contempt of those who place all phrenologists with the students of alchemy, palmistry, and astrology as it is to set aside the educational and moral constructions which have been shabbily built upon his doctrines of cerebral physiology.

The practitioners of phrenology have long been accustomed to invoke Gall's doctrine as a scientific sanction for their half-magical art of characterology; but

SOURCE. Madison Bentley (1870–1955), an American psychologist, was Professor of Psychology at Cornell University, an early editor of the *American Journal of Psychology* (1903–1951), and a past President of the American Psychological Association (1925). During his many active years in the field of psychology, Dr. Bentley was also Chairman of the Division of Anthropology and Psychology of the National Research Council (1930–1931) and a consultant for psychology to the Library of Congress (1938–1940). His published works include studies of social and experimental psychology. This article originally appeared in *Psychology Monographs,* 1916, 21 (Whole No. 12), 102–115. Reprinted by permission of the American Psychological Association.

[1]Gall was born in Tiefenbrunn in 1758; he died in 1828. P. J. Mobius (in "Franz Joseph Gall"; *Ausgewahlte Werke,* vol. vii, 1905) gives biographical sources and a short sketch of his life and writings.

their own popular expositions have, naturally enough, laid undue emphasis upon cranial peculiarities and the alleged significance of these in divining moral qualities and individual traits. These exaggerations and distortions of Gall we must ignore as we hope to do justice to the founder.

Gall was himself led in youth—so much we must acknowledge—to believe that certain facial and cranial features were symptomatic of mental traits. Moreover, he seems always to have been interested in the determination of character and of mental capacity. Nevertheless, these practical issues may reasonably be regarded as secondary to his scientific doctrine. And in our historical quest the main enquiry will be directed toward the principle of psychophysical dependence which underlay the founder's whole system—a principle which has steadily grown in importance with the empirical development of psychology and of the biological sciences.

As applied by Gall, this principle alleged the existence of a number of separate and distinct cerebral organs, which stood in functional relation to the several capacities and traits of the human and the animal mind. These organs, which exceeded twenty-five in number, were innate and heritable, although their development rested, in part, upon the exercise of function during the life-time of the individual.

Gall's method of investigation was empirical. He was a shrewd observer, and he seems to have been cautious in generalization. He examined the heads of men of talent and of genius, and the heads of the criminal, imbecile, and insane, making measurements or taking casts, and, if fortune favored him, adding the skulls to his large collection; he compared successive generations for common traits; he noted the mental and physical peculiarities of various animals, and he observed and dissected a great number of brains. He insisted—against many authorities and classical examples and on grounds of comparative physiology—that the neural pathways must be traced from below upward and not by slicing down from the vertex to the lower centres. By multiplying observations and experiment he sought to divide off the accidental from the essential and then, by generalization, to establish principles and laws.

So much by way of reference to the problem and the method of Gall is necessary if we are to view his work in the light of antecedent systems and doctrines. To his predecessors we now turn.

No one familiar with the history of psychology would seriously contend that the fact of the bodily dependence of mental phenomena awaited the discovery of an anatomist at the beginning of the nineteenth century. We readily trace psychophysical doctrines to the Greek physicians and philosophers, and we halt there, in all probability, only because we lose the thread of tradition. Were the historical gaps filled in, we should doubtless follow the uninterrupted lineage of these doctrines straight back to those early times in which men failed clearly to formulate a distinct difference between mental and physical existences. If our historical enquiry is to be significant, it must leave the paths of general psycho-physical history and discover the appropriate antecedents of the special and peculiar form of the principle of dependence which was adopted by the founder of phrenology. These appropriate antecedents we look for first among the French sensationalists of the eighteenth century, and secondly among rationalistic and empirical systems current in Germany during the same period.

II. The Influence of the French Sensationalists

The sensationalistic doctrine of the French school, with which Gall was familiar, was in the main an acceptance or a modification of Locke. Among the exponents of this view, those most often and most respectfully mentioned by Gall are Condillac, Bonnet, and Cabanis. Etienne Bonnet, Abbe de Condillac (1715-1780), the friend of Diderot and Rousseau, did most to establish in France the philosophy of Locke; although Locke's views had been introduced, in the first instance, by Voltaire. Charles Bonnet (1720-1790) was a scientist of note whom failing eye-sight drove to the solace of philosophical reflection. He follows Condillac in the doctrine of sensation, which they both owe to Locke, and he follows him also–independently, as it seems–in the famous use of the statue to illustrate the nature of sensation. Pierre Jean George Cabanis (1757-1808) was a French physiologist of considerable reputation, famous as physician to Mirabeau in his last illness.

In the formulation of sensationalism by these three contemporaries we find an important thread of Gall's psychology. Let us look first to Condillac, since Condillac is the first and most important of the three. In his "Essai sur l'origine des connoissances humaines" (1746), Condillac accepts Locke's explanation of the double source of knowledge in reflection and sensation. Sensation, he maintains, is the material of our knowledge, and reflection and the other operations organizing this material, are the instruments of knowledge. But in the most important of Condillac's philosophical works, the "Traite des sensations," we find the disciple turned critic, rejecting Locke's theory of reflection. Sensations alone, he contends, are sufficient to explain knowledge. He now maintains that "the principal object of this work is to show that all our knowledge and all our faculties derive from sense or–to speak with greater precision–from sensations." In further criticism of Locke, Condillac declares that much that is significant about judgments has escaped his predecessor, for Locke supposes that the activities of the soul participate in an innate quality, reflection, with no suspicion that they owe their single origin to sensations. In order separately to study sensation, Condillac imagines a statue equipped with a nervous organism which is ready to act but which has never acted. It is living, for it has a soul or mind, although it has never received an idea. Then upon the passive, waiting statue–an obvious elaboration of Locke's tabula rasa–the sensation of smell, the simplest of all sensations, is first allowed to play. This unmixed sensation of smell completely fills the psychic chambers as the light of a small wax taper may permeate an otherwise dark room–if we may interpret metaphor by metaphor. The sensation of smell, like the light, is the only thing present. By the addition, then, of other sensations, this follower of Locke proceeds to reconstruct, without the overt use of any other materials, the whole series of mental phenomena.

In abolishing "reflection" as an organizing principle among ideas, Condillac should, in logical consistency, have reached Hume's sceptical conclusion that there is no uniting principle, that mind is a mere "heap of impressions." Gall observing either with more acumen or from a different perspective saw this difficulty and offered a solution. It was that mind is not only compounded but also organized and that there exists a material basis for the organization of mind just as truly as there exists a material basis for the sensations themselves. Again he says: "Bacon, Locke, Hume, Helvetius and Condillac found themselves obliged, in order to comprehend in some manner the possibility of the functions of the understanding, to have recourse not only to the senses which certain of these authors have so greatly exalted, but to a recognition of the association of sensations, or to attention, or to experience, or to reflection, or to induction. Although they have at times contradicted each other, they have nevertheless perceived that none of the faculties which we have just enumerated could appertain to any one of the senses. But if, in this life, no faculty at all could exercise itself without a material condition–as we shall later prove beyond a doubt–then there must of necessity be presupposed a material basis for the exercise of the intellectual faculties. The investigation of those organs through which animals and men receive their material impressions of the external world has always been regarded as very important. Will it be less interesting, less noble, to try to discover the organs of the superior faculties of the spirit?" This quotation offers the key to Gall's whole system. It marks the point at which he breaks with this doctrine taken in its strictest form. Yet his purpose is clearly sensationalistic in its nature; it is to fill a gap in this doctrine and to answer a question which is distinctly sensationalistic in origin. He proposed to give to the functions of the brain the same degree of certitude as to the functions of the sensory apparatus. Much as we have seen Condillac explaining the growth of knowledge by the gradual addition of new senses, so we hear Gall declaring that the "faculties of the soul" develop in correspondence with the development of their appropriate organs in the brain. The doctrine of faculties appears, then, as something imposed upon the groundwork of Gall's sensationalism. He seems never to question that the sensationalists are giving an account which is correct so far as it goes.

In Bonnet's psychological works we find a resemblance closer–in some respects–than Condillac shows to the attitude of Gall upon the matter in question. Bonnet tells his readers again and again that man is a mixed being, in part physical and in part mental. Ideas come only by the intervention of the senses, and even the most abstract notions derive from the same source. It is in the body and by means of the body that the soul acts. We must, he says, always return in our consideration to the physical as the first cause of all the experiences of the soul. Gall is equally insistent upon explaining mind by reference to the body—or rather more insistent, since it is the very heart of his theory. Are we in a better position, he asks, to explain hunger and thirst than thought? Although we can find no physical substance to be called hunger and thirst in the digestive tract, we still maintain that they are inside of us. Then why not admit, when we can find no physical traces of houses and trees in the eye and still localize vision there, that thoughts and ideas are in a similar manner dependent upon the brain?

The empirical tendencies in French psychology appear quite as strongly in Cabanis, the surgeon and physician, as in Bonnet. Sensibility is, with Cabanis, the final term. The sense organs on the outside of the body furnish the materials for reason, the organs within, the materials for the instinctive life. Innate needs account for the faculties. The mental constitution is determined by the physical; although education is able to change both mind and body. The diverse functions of the brain are to combine and to rearrange impressions, to attach signs, and so to produce thought.

In these declarations we find the French sensationalists, as well as Gall, approaching the problem of mental organization. They seem, moreover, to be in essential agreement. The disagreement lies not in principle but in emphasis. The French sensationalists look to the structure of the brain and nervous system to account for what they call the diversity of sensations and the unity of consciousness, and they make attention, desire, volition, memory, and even judgment, the result of the combination in the brain of sensory excitations. Gall, on the other hand, does not rest in sensation but exalts those integrative functions which he calls the "higher faculties" and which possess, as he thinks, organs as strictly localized as are the organs of sense.

Gall himself was not unaware of his close relation to the sensationalists, and he believed, moreover, that they too were tending toward some theory of integrative faculties. Of Bonnet he says that his predecessor found in the brain fibres with particularized functions which could be likened to his own cerebral organs. Moreover, he recalls that Bonnet also held that any one who should thoroughly understand the structure of the brain would be able to read all that passed there "as in a book." Finally, he says, the time is not far distant when, convinced by the evidence, we shall agree with Bonnet, Condillac, Herder, Cabanis, Prochaska, Sommerring, Reil and others that all the phenomena of animate nature are based on the organism in general and all intellectual phenomena on the brain in particular.

That Bonnet at least was working in the direction of faculties appears in other instances than those noted by Gall. This trend is clearly seen in his exposition of the benefits of education, which, by the way, is almost identical with Gall's theory, of which the followers of phrenology today make capital. Both believe that by the exercise of the organs of the "higher senses"–fibres for Bonnet, cerebral areas for Gall–a superior power and strength will accrue to these organs and thus the "higher" nature will gain control over the lower.

III. The Influence of "Faculties" and of German Empirical Psychology

We come now to the "faculties" themselves, as they appear in Gall and in his predecessors. The criticism of faculties which has come to be a tradition in psychology complains that the doctrine confuses description and explanation, that it uses such class-terms as thought, memory and will to stand for the causes or at least the empirical conditions of observed mental phenomena. There is no doubt that the logic of the doctrine is faulty. That is a spurious explanation which refers a fact to its classname. A given instance of choice may be better understood as a fact when it is identified as an instance of will, but it is not thereby explained; and we know nothing further about the antecedents of an eristic outburst of temper after we have been told that the outburst is due to a faculty of combativeness.

Now the atmosphere in which Gall matured at Strassburg and Vienna was the atmosphere of faculties. Wolff had written his *Psychologia Empirica* in 1732, his *Psychologia Rationalis* in 1740, and among the defendants and critics of the Wolffian teachings had stood the names of Baumgarten, G. F. Meier, C. A. Crusius, and J. A. Eberhard. Gall spoke the language of faculties as naturally as we speak the language of organic evolution, of commercial barter, and of international strife. But notice also that Gall, the man of science, was constrained to use the doctrine of faculties in a manner that must seem to us peculiarly modern and familiar.

I mean that Gall-the-anatomist and Gall-the-follower-of-Condillac-and-Bonnet was bound to replace the empty causes of Wolff by the organic causes of anatomy and of sensationalism. Nothing is more evident in Gall's expositions of his doctrine than his attempt to realize Bonnet's hope that a thorough understanding of the structure of the brain should make that organ an open book to the psychologist–should provide, that is to say, a complete organic basis, not alone for sensations but for all the more involved and elaborate functions of mind.

In our search for the antecedents of Gall's theory, the strongly empirical trend in German psychology which appeared toward the close of the eighteenth century must not be overlooked. Crusius, who died (1775) just before Gall reached maturity, had rejected Wolff's potential faculties (Vermogen), the nudae agendi possibilitates, because they explained nothing. He substituted for them the forces (Krafte) of thought, judgment, imagination, and the like, which he conceived as empirical powers of mind. This revised conception of faculties, rather than Wolff's, seems to have been the view current in Gall's time. The physiological psychologist Karl Franz von Irwing (1729-1801) came a step nearer the position of the sensationalists in his declaration that the most abstract integration of ideas, as well as sensations themselves, found a basis in the fibrous structures of the brain. Over this "finer organization" the mind presided with its faculties of analysis, synthesis and comparison. Irwing's emphasis upon feelings and impulses, conceived as the springs of mental activity, leads naturally to Gall's doctrine that the faculties are innate, and that they appear throughout the development of the individual in the form of instincts, tendencies and aptitudes.

Gall's whole psychophysical system is plainly based upon heredity. The original nature of man furnishes his fundamental problem. It is natural, then, that both the Wolffian nudae possibilitates and the more empirical mental forces of his own day should have seemed, to Gall, to be vague and empty concepts. Putting together the crude psychophysics of Condillac, Bonnet, and the German physiologizing psychologists with his own superior knowledge of cerebral anatomy and of comparative physiology, Gall is led to insist that the sensory and motor centres in the cortex must be supplemented by other similar organs which provide the constitutional basis for the whole range of mind. It is, then, a logical consequence of his empirical methods which took Gall beyond will, attention, understanding, imagination, and the like general and abstract attributes of mind, and which prompted him to seek the particular and special impulses, memories, instincts, and capacities, actually to be observed in a given species or in a given individual.

IV. Gall's Doctrine and Modern Psychology

Surely no time could be more favorable than our own to the appreciation of a man who insisted that education had been overdone, that man is not, as current belief made him, a blank volume to be written full by the schoolmaster, that character is not the product of environment; who insisted, on the positive side, that the psychophysical constitution is innate and that the springs of experience are to be sought in heritable structures with their inclinations and functions impressed upon them by racial history.

So long as we are content, as Gall was not content, vaguely to use "habit," "instinct," "past experience," and "neural arcs" as speculative or undefined terms of explanation, so long we cannot, with good grace, set Gall aside as a fantastic master of cranial prominences.

It is, of course, evident to us, after a hundred years, that the faculties and forces of the eighteenth century were not based upon a proper classification of observed mental functions—the proper classification for which we still are searching. Some of them may indeed turn out to be inherited integers: we hear a good deal of "general intelligence," and geneticists have soberly affirmed that musical capacity represents a unit character; but the fate of faculties does not matter. The main point is that Gall took current psychology of both kinds, the German kind and the Anglo-French kind, and by conjoining it with a knowledge of the central nervous system which seems to have been decidedly superior to the neurology of his contemporaries, he tried to establish the bodily conditions of mental existence and of mental performance.

Surely we, in our day, can understand and applaud this attempt. So energetically do we try to do the same thing that we are prone—unless we are balanced by historical perspective—either to fabricate these organic conditions out of shreds of fact and speculation about arcs and synapses, or else, through biological and philosophical bias, completely to divest ourselves of psychological interests and to plunge headforemost into physiology and kinetic ecology.

Gall himself was zealous in his search for biological explanations; but his psychology, such as it was, he never forsook. His fixed conviction that mental processes and functions have a specific, not a general, dependence upon bodily processes running in heritable grooves we still maintain, although we now know (thanks to better scientific technique) that the brain does not show the kind of localizable functions that Gall—or, for that matter, that Paul Flechsig—believed in. But our own neurological knowledge is far from being adequate to the psychological facts. Current books and articles are full of neurological terms which give out, when sounded, a hollow ring. Whenever the weight of explanation is laid upon them there is danger that they, too, as much of Wolff's vis repraesentativa, will become mere names used to conceal ignorance.

To conclude, then, the founder of phrenology attacked the venerable problem of the organic conditions of mind. Mind, regarded from the more "active" side, he described in the terms of the native German psychology of his day, viewed from the more "passive" side (as the historical distinction runs), in the terms of the English and French sensationalists. Finding his clue in the organs of sense and their central correlates, he proceeded to dispose of the several functions or faculties, in a similar way. For Bonnet's specialized fibres, which had a transforming and integrative function, Gall substituted a large group of innate cerebral organs which corresponded—as he thought—to the mental talents and faculties. The historical importance of Gall touches not so closely the vagaries of his doctrine of phrenology as the fact that he sought empirically to integrate the psychological and anatomical knowledge of his time. Gall's problem is still in process of solution. At times it is evaded and at times it is distorted by the illicit use of mental or neurological faculties for which our own riper time offers no justification. Neither evasion nor distortion, however, is likely to advance the problem, which still requires a candid and empirical resolution.

3. THE ASSOCIATION METHOD[1]

Carl G. Jung

Ladies and Gentlemen: When I was honored with the invitation from Clark University to lecture before this esteemed assemblage, a wish was at the same time expressed that I should speak about my methods of work, and especially about the psychology of childhood. I hope to accomplish this task in the following manner:

In my first lecture I shall try to present to you the view points of my association methods; in my second lecture I shall discuss the significance of the familiar constellations; while in my third lecture I shall enter more fully into the psychology of the child.

I might easily confine myself exclusively to my theoretical views, but I believe that it will be better to illustrate my lectures with as many practical examples as possible. We shall therefore occupy ourselves first with the method of association, a method which has been of valuable assistance to me both practically and theoretically. The association method in vogue in psychology, as well as its history, is of course, so familiar to you that there is no need to speak of it. For practical purposes I make use of the following formulary:

1. head
2. green
3. water
4. to sing
5. dead
6. long
7. ship
8. to pay
9. window
10. friendly
11. to cook
12. to ask
13. cold
14. stem
15. to dance
16. village
17. lake
18. sick
19. pride
20. to cook
21. ink
22. angry
23. needle
24. to swim
25. voyage
26. blue
27. lamp
28. to sin
29. bread
30. rich
31. tree
32. to prick
33. pity
34. yellow
35. mountain
36. to die
37. salt
38. new
39. custom
40. to pray
41. money
42. foolish
43. pamphlet
44. despise
45. finger
46. expensive
47. bird
48. to fall
49. book
50. unjust
51. frog
52. to part
53. hunger
54. white

SOURCE. Carl C. Jung (1875-1961), Swiss-born psychiatrist, was an early student of Freud's and the founder of the school of analytic psychology. Not only was he the developer of the word association method, but his work on introversion-extroversion as a basic dimension of human personality has also been extremely influential in the development of modern psychology. This article originally appeared in the *American Journal of Psychology*, 1910, **21**, pp. 219-235 and is reprinted with the permission of the University of Illinois Press.

[1] Lectures delivered at the celebration of the twentieth anniversary of the opening of Clark University, September, 1909; translated from the German by Dr. A. A. Brill, of New York.

55. child
56. to take care
57. lead pencil
58. sad
59. plum
60. to marry
61. house
62. dear
63. glass
64. to quarrel
65. fur
66. big
67. carrot
68. to paint
69. part
70. old
71. flower
72. to beat
73. box
74. wild
75. family
76. to wash
77. cow
78. friend
79. luck
80. lie
81. deportment
82. narrow
83. brother
84. to fear
85. stork
86. false
87. anxiety
88. to kiss
89. bride
90. pure
91. door
92. to choose
93. hay
94. contented
95. ridicule
96. to sleep
97. month
98. nice
99. woman
100. to abuse

This formulary has been constructed after many years of experience. The words are chosen and partially arranged in such a manner as to strike easily almost all complexes of practical occurrence. As shown by the above formulary there is a regular mixing of the grammatical qualities of the words. This, too, has its definite reasons.[2]

Before the experiment begins the test person receives the following instructions: "Answer as quickly as possible the first word that occurs to your mind." This instruction is so simple that it can easily be followed by anybody. The work itself, moreover, appears extremely easy, so that it might be expected that any one could accomplish it with the greatest facility and promptitude. But contrary to expectation the behavior is quite different (Tables 1 and 2).

Table 1. An Example of a Normal Reaction Type

Stimulus Word	Reaction Time Unit 0.2 Second	Reaction	Reproduction
head	9	foot	part of the body
green	11	blouse	
water	14	clear	light
to sing	6	children	
dead	11	do not like	
long	6	short	I, tall
ship	7	forth	
to pay	9	bills	
window	9	room	
friendly	10	children	
table	9	chair	room
to ask	10	all kinds	
cold	7	warm	

[2]The selection of these stimulus words was naturally made for the German language only, and would probably have to be considerably changed for the English language.

Table 1. An Example of a Normal Reaction Type (continued)

Stimulus Word	Reaction Time Unit 0.2 Second	Reaction	Reproduction
stem	6	flower	
to dance	9	I	like
lake	8	Zurich	
sick	8	sister	
pride	6	people	
to cook	7	woman	
ink	5	black	
angry	10	children	people
needle	9	to prick	
to swim	10	healthy	
voyage	9	England	
blue	10	pretty	like
lamp	6	light	
to sin	8	much	people
bread	10	good	like, necessary
rich	9	nice	
tree	6	green	
to prick	9	need	

Table 2. An Example of an Hysterical Reaction Type

Stimulus Word	Reaction Time Unit 0.2 Second	Reaction	Reproduction
needle	7	to sew	
to swim	9	water	ship
* † voyage	35	to ride, motion, voyager	
blue	10	color	
lamp	7	to burn	
to sin	22	this idea is totally strange to me, I do not recognize it	
bread	10	to eat	
rich †	50	money, I don't know	possession
brown	6	nature	green
to prick	9	needle	
pity	12	feeling	
yellow	9	color	
mountain	8	high	
to die	8	to perish	
salt	15	salty (laughs) I don't know	NaCl
new	15	old	as an opposite
custom	10	good	barbaric

* Denotes misunderstanding. † Denotes repetition of the stimulus words.

Table 2. An Example of an Hysterical Reaction Type (continued)

Stimulus Word	Reaction Time Unit 0.2 Second	Reaction	Reproduction
to pray	12	Deity	
money	10	wealth	
foolish	12	narrow minded, restricted	?
pamphlet	10	paper	
despise	30	that is a complicated, too foolish	?
finger	8	hand, not only hand, but also foot, a joint, member, extremity	
dear	14	to pay (laughs)	
bird	8	to fly	
to fall	30	*tomber,* I will say no more, what do you mean by fall?	?
book	6	to read	
unjust	8	just	
frog	11	quack	
to part	30	what does part mean?	?
hunger	10	to eat	
white	12	color, everything possible, light	
child	10	little, I did not hear well, *bébé*	?
to take care	14	attention	
lead pencil	8	to draw, everything possible can be drawn	
sad	9	to weep, that is not always the case	to be
plum	16	to eat a plum, pluck what do you mean by it? Is that symbolic?	fruit
to marry	27	how can you? reunion, union	union alliance

The following curves (Fig. 1) illustrate the course of the reaction time in an association experiment in four normal test persons. The length of each column denotes the length of the reaction time.

The illustrations on pages 24, 25, and 26 (Figs. 2, 3, and 4) show the course of the reaction time in hysterical individuals. The light cross-hatched columns denote the locations where the test person was unable to react (so-called failures).

The first thing that strikes us is the fact that many test persons show a marked prolongation of the reaction time. This would make us think at first of intellectual difficulties—wrongly, however, as we are often dealing with very intelligent persons of fluent speech. The explanation lies rather in the emotions. In order to understand the matter comprehensively we must bear in mind that the association experiments cannot deal with a separated psychic function, for any psychic occurrence is never a thing in itself, but is always the resultant of the entire psychological past. The association experiment, too, is not merely a method for the reproduction of separated word couplets, but it is a kind of pastime, a conversation between experimenter and test person. In a certain sense it is even still more than that. Words are really something like condensed actions, situations, and things. When I present a word to the test person which denotes

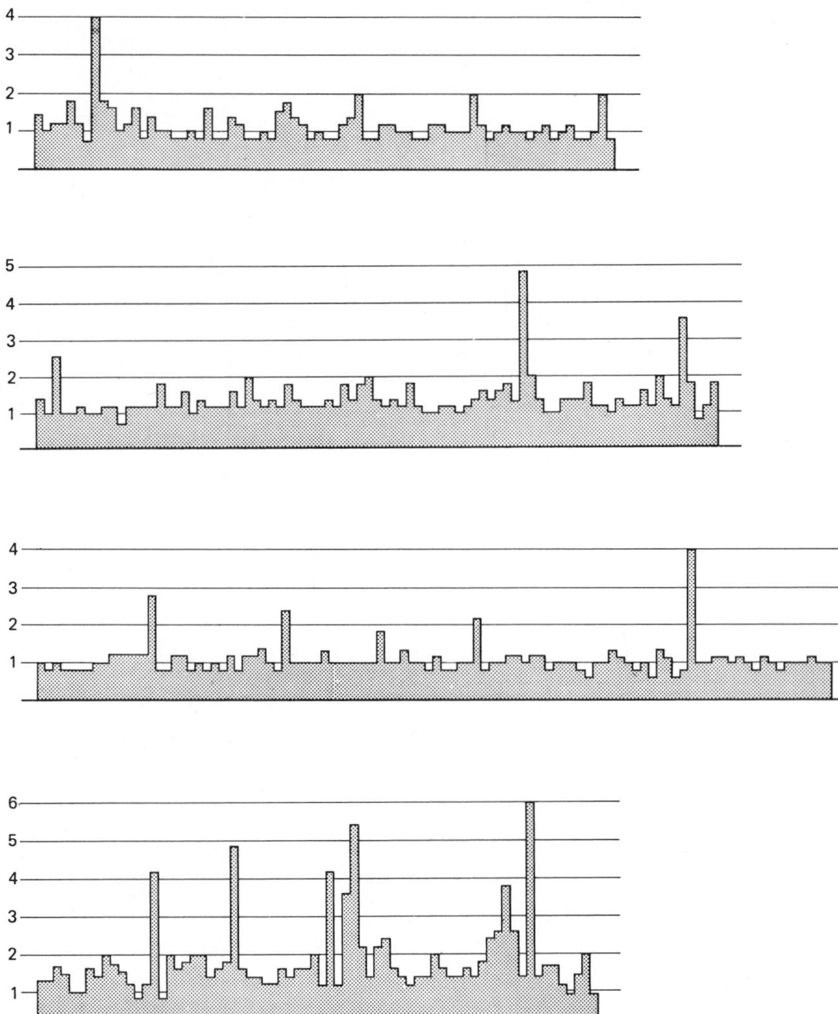

Figure 1

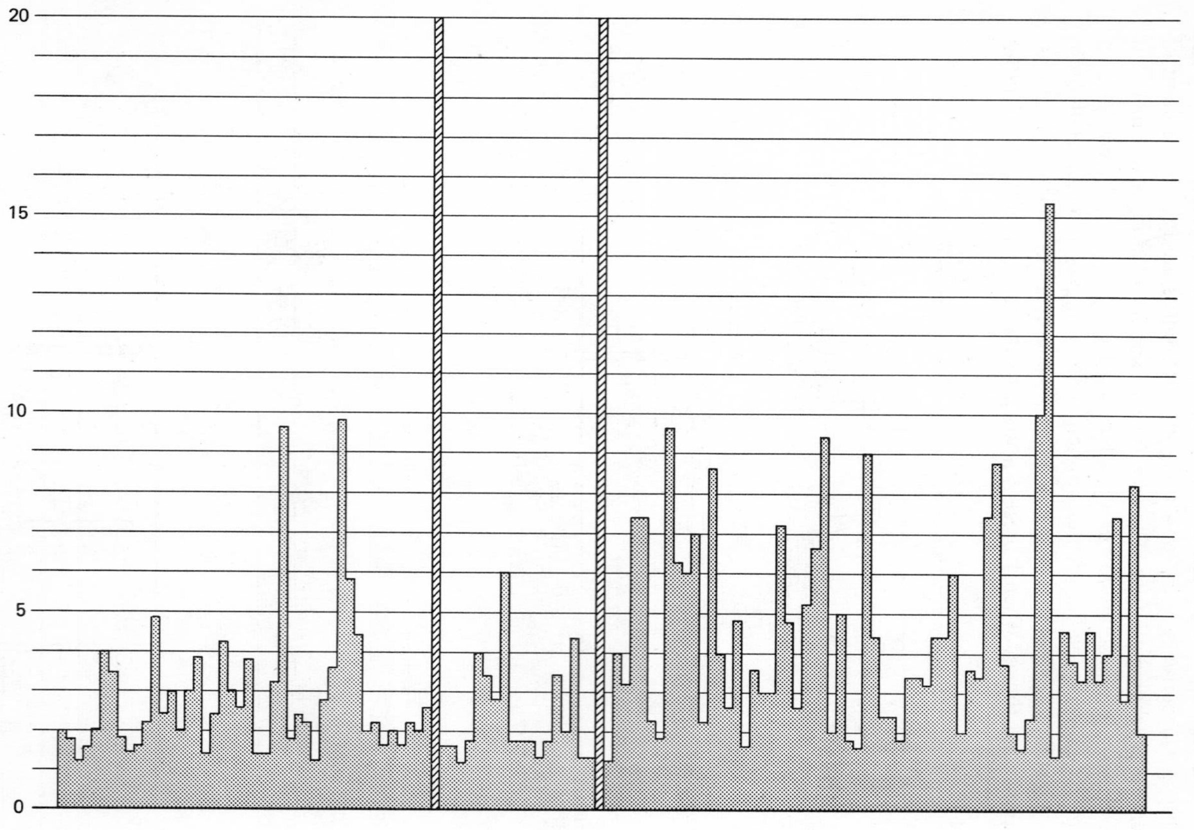

Figure 2

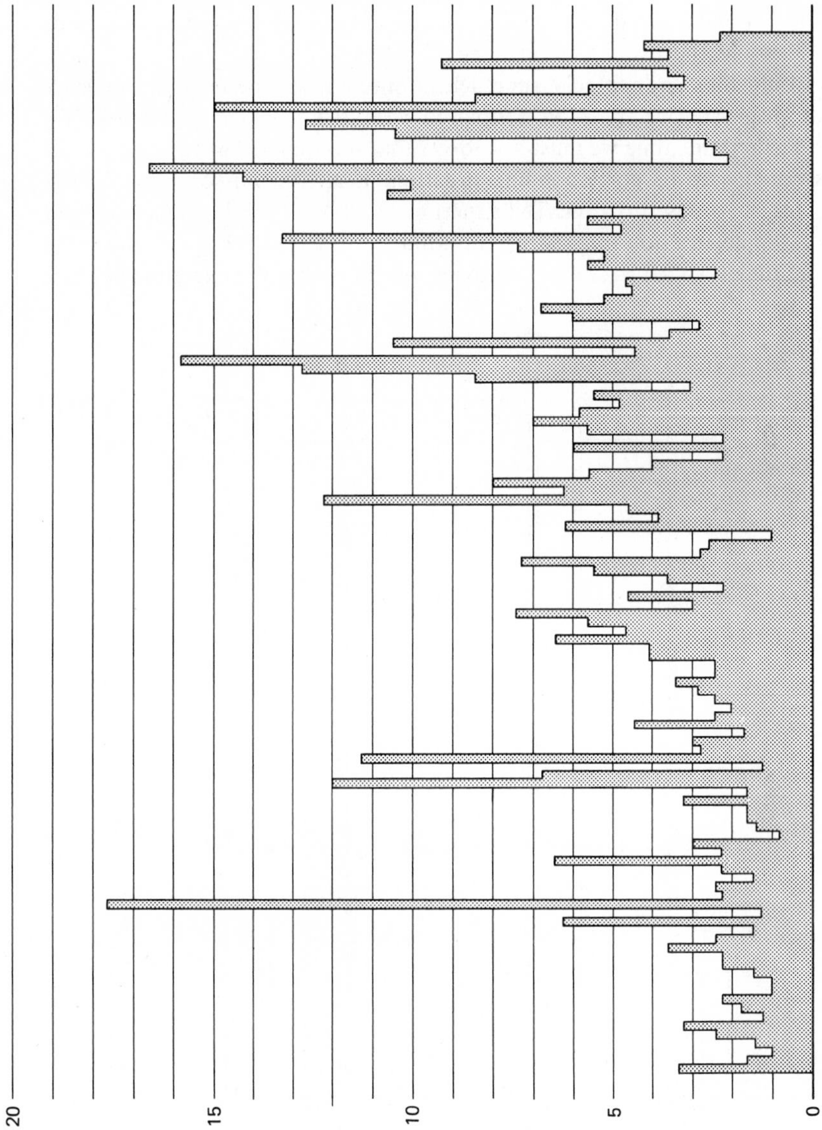

Figure 3

an action it is the same as if I should present to him the action itself, and ask him, "How do you behave towards it? What do you think of it? What do you do in this situation?" If I were a magician I should cause the situation corresponding to the stimulus word to appear in reality and placing the test person in its midst, I should then study his manner of reaction. The result of my stimulus words would thus undoubtedly approach infinitely nearer perfection. But as we are not magicians we must be contented with the linguistic substitutes for reality; at the same time we must not forget that the stimulus word will as a rule always conjure up its corresponding situation. It all depends on how the test person reacts to this situation. The situation "bride" or "bridegroom" will not evoke a simple reaction in a young lady; but the reaction will be deeply influenced by the provoked strong feeling tones, the more so if the experimenter be a

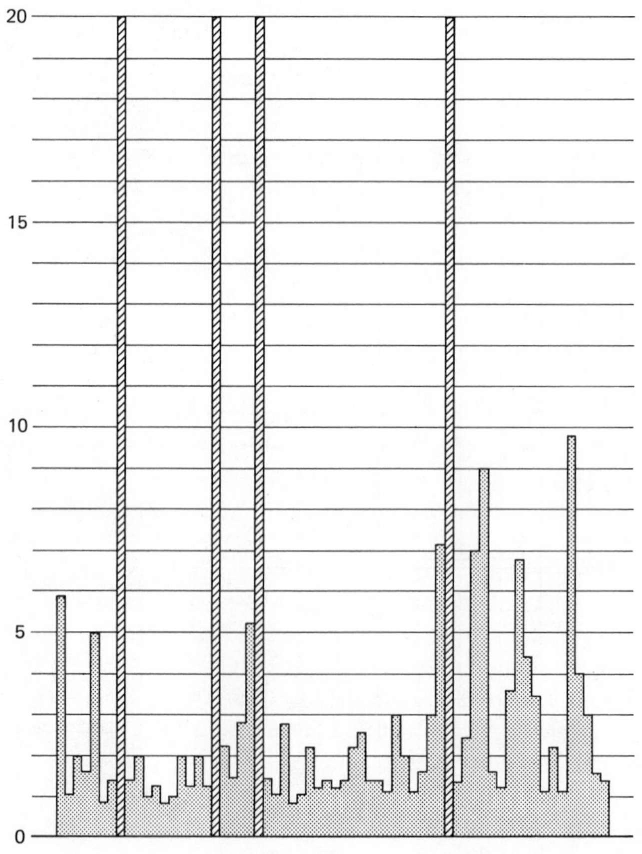

Figure 4

man. It thus happens that the test person is often unable to react quickly and smoothly to all stimulus words. In reality, too, there are certain stimulus words which denote actions, situations, or things, about which the test person cannot think quickly and surely, and this fact is shown in the association experiments. The example which I have just presented shows an abundance of long reaction times and other disturbances. In this case the reaction to the stimulus word is in some way impeded, that is, the adaptation to the stimulus word is disturbed. The stimulus words are therefore merely a part of reality acting upon us; indeed, a person who shows such disturbances to the stimulus words, is in a certain sense really but imperfectly adapted to reality. Disease is an imperfect adaptation; hence in this case we are dealing with something morbid in the psyche—with something which is either temporary or persistently pathological, that is, we are dealing with a psychoneurosis, with a functional disturbance of the mind. This rule, however, as we shall see later, is not without its exceptions.

Let us in the first place continue the discussion concerning the prolonged reaction time. It often happens that the test person actually does *not* know what to answer to the stimulus word. The test person waives any reaction; for the moment he totally fails to obey the original instructions, and shows himself incapable of adapting himself to the experimenter. If this phenomenon occurs frequently in an experiment it signifies a higher degree of disturbance in adjustment. I call attention to the fact that it is quite indifferent what reason the test person gives for the refusal. Some find that too many ideas suddenly occur to them, others, that not enough ideas come to their minds. In most cases, however, the difficulties first perceived are so deterrent that they actually give up the whole reaction. The example (Table 3) on page 28 shows a case of hysteria with many failures of reaction.

In example 3 we find a characteristic phenomenon. The test person is not content with the requirements of the instruction, that is, she is not satisfied with *one* word but reacts with many words. She apparently does more and better than the instruction requires, but in so doing she does not fulfill the requirements of the instruction. Thus she reacts: custom–good–barbaric; foolish–narrow minded–restricted; family–big–small–everything possible.

These examples show in the first place that many other words connect themselves with the reaction word. The test person is unable to suppress the ideas which subsequently occur to her. In doing this she also pursues a certain tendency which perhaps is more distinctly expressed in the following reaction: new–old–as an opposite. The addition of "as an opposite" denotes that the test person has the desire to add something explanatory or supplementary. This tendency is also shown in the following reaction: finger–not only hand, also foot–a limb–member–extremity.

Here we have a whole series of supplements. It seems as if the reaction were not sufficient for the test person, as if something else must always be added, as if

Table 3. A Case of Hysteria

Stimulus Word	Reaction Time Unit 0.2 Second	Reaction	Reproduction
to sing	9	nice	+
dead	15	awful	?
long *	40	the time, the journey	?
ship †			+
to pay	11	money	
window	10	big	high
friendly	50	a man	human
to cook	10	soup	+
ink	9	black or blue	+
angry			bad
needle	9	to sew	+
lamp	14	light	+
to sin			
bread	15	to eat	+
rich * †	40	good, convenient	+
yellow	18	paper	color
mountain	10	high	+
to die	15	awful	+
salt †	25	salty	+
new			good, nice
custom †			
to pray			
money †	35	to buy, one is able	+
pamphlet	16	to write	+
to despise †	22	people	+
finger †			
dear	12	thing	+
bird	12	sings or flies	+

* Donates misunderstanding. † Denotes repetition of the stimulus words.

what has been already said were incorrect or in some way imperfect. This feeling we may with Janet designate as the *'sentiment d'incomplétude,'* which by no means explains everything. I enter somewhat deeper into this phenomenon because it is quite frequently encountered in neurotic individuals. Indeed it is not merely a small and unimportant subsidiary manifestation in an insignificant experiment, but rather an elemental and universal manifestation which otherwise plays a role in the psychic life of neurotics.

With his desire to supplement the test person betrays a tendency to give the experimenter more than he wants, he even exerts the greatest efforts to seek further mental occurrences in order finally to discover something quite satisfactory. If we translate this elementary observation into the psychology of everyday life, it signifies that the test person has a tendency constantly to give to others more feeling than is required and expected. According to Freud, this is a sign of a reinforced object-libido, that is, it is a compensation for an inner unsatisfaction and voidness of feeling. In this elementary observation we therefore see one of the main qualities of hysterics, namely, the tendency to allow themselves to be carried away by everything, to attach themselves enthusiastically to everything, and to always promise too much and hence do little. Patients having this symptom, in my experience, are always hard to deal with; at first they are enthusiastically enraptured with the physician, for a time going so far as to accept everything blindly; but they soon merge into just as blind a resistance against the physician, thus rendering any educative influence absolutely impossible.

We see therefore in this phenomenon the expression of a tendency to give more than the instruction demands and expects. This tendency betrays itself also in other failures to follow the instruction:

to quarrel–angry–different things–I always quarrel at home;
to marry–how can you marry?–reunion–union;
plum–to eat–to pluck–what do you mean by it?–is it symbolic?
to sin–this idea is quite strange to me, I do not recognize it.

These reactions show that the test person gets away altogether from the situation of the experiment. For the instruction demands that he should answer only the word which next occurs to him. Here we find that the stimulus words apparently act with excessive strength, that they are taken as if they were direct personal questions. The test person entirely forgets that we deal with mere words which stand in print before us, and seeks in them a personal meaning; he tries to divine them and defend himself against them, thus altogether forgetting the instructions.

This elementary observation depicts another common peculiarity of hysterics, namely, that of taking everything personally, of never being able to remain objective, and of allowing themselves to be carried away by momentary impressions; this again shows the characteristics of the enhanced object-libido.

Another sign of impeded adaptation is the often occurring *repetitions of the stimulus words.* The test persons repeat the stimulus word as if they had not heard or understood it distinctly. They repeat it just as we repeat a difficult question in order better to grasp it before answering. This same tendency is shown in the experiment. The questions are repeated because the stimulus words act on hysterical individuals almost like difficult and personal questions. In principle it is the same phenomenon as the subsequent completion of the reaction.

In many experiments we observe that the same reaction constantly reappears to the most varied stimulus words. These words seem to possess a special reproduction tendency, and it is very interesting to examine their relationship to the test person. For example, I have observed a case in which the patient repeated the word "short" a great many times and often in places where it had no meaning. The test person could not directly state the reason for the repetition of the word "short." From experience I knew that such predicates always relate either to the test person himself or to the person nearest to him. I assumed that in this word "short" he designated himself, and that in this way he helped to express something very painful to him. The test person is of very small stature. He is the youngest of four brothers, who in contrast to him are all tall. He was always the *"child"* in the family, he was nicknamed "Short" and was treated by all as the "little one." This resulted in a total loss of self-confidence. Although he was intelligent, and despite long study, he could not decide to present himself for examination; he finally became impotent, and merged into a psychosis in which, whenever he was alone, he took delight in walking about in his room on his toes in order to appear taller. The word "short," therefore, signified to him a great many painful experiences. This is usually the case with the repeated words; they always contain something very important for the individual psychology of the test person.

The signs thus far depicted are not found arbitrarily spread throughout the whole experiment, but only in very definite locations; namely, in those stimulus words which strike against special emotionally accentuated complexes. This fact is the foundation of the so-called "diagnosis of facts" *(Tatbestandsdiagnostik);* that is, of the method employed to discover by means of an association experiment, the culprit among a number of persons suspected of a crime. That this is possible I should like to demonstrate briefly in a concrete case.

On the 6th of February, 1908, our supervisor reported to me that a nurse complained to her of having been robbed during the forenoon of the previous day. The facts were as follows: The nurse kept her money, amounting to 70 francs, in a pocketbook which she had placed in her cupboard where she also kept her clothes. The cupboard contained two compartments, of which one belonged to the nurse who was robbed, and the other to the head nurse. These two nurses and a third one, who was an intimate friend of the head nurse, slept in the same room where the cupboard was. The room was in a section which was regularly occupied in common by six nurses who had free access to this room. Given such a state of affairs it is not to be wondered that the supervisor shrugged her shoulders when I asked her whom she most suspected.

Further investigation showed that on the morning of the theft the above-mentioned friend of the head nurse was slightly indisposed and remained in bed in the room the whole morning. Hence, following the indications of the plaintiff, the theft could have taken place only in the afternoon. Of the other four nurses upon whom suspicion could fall, there was only one who regularly attended to the cleaning of the room in question, while the remaining three had nothing to do in this room, nor was it shown that any of them had spent any time there on the previous day.

It was therefore natural that these last three nurses should be regarded for the time being as less implicated, and I therefore began by subjecting the first three to the experiment.

From the particulars of the case, I also knew that the cupboard was locked but that the key was kept not far away in a very conspicuous place, that on opening the cupboard the first thing to be seen was a fur ornament (boa), and, moreover, that the pocketbook was between the linen in an inconspicuous place. The pocketbook was of dark reddish leather, and contained the following objects: one 50 franc banknote, one 20 franc piece, some centimes, one small silver watch chain, one stencil used in the insane asylum to mark the kitchen utensils, and one small receipt from Dosenbach's shoeshop in Zurich.

Besides the plaintiff and the guilty one, only the head nurse knew the exact particulars of the deed, for as soon as the former missed her money she immediately asked the head nurse to help her find it, thus the head nurse had been able to learn the smallest details, which naturally rendered the experiment still more difficult, for she was precisely the one most suspected. The conditions for the experiment were better for the others, since they knew nothing concerning the particulars of the deed, and some not even that a crime had been committed. As critical stimulus words I selected the name of the robbed nurse, plus the following words: cupboard, door, open, key, yesterday, banknote, gold, 70, 50, 20, money, watch, pocketbook, chain, silver, to hide, fur, dark reddish, leather, centimes, stencil, receipt, Dosenbach. Besides these words which referred directly to the deed, I took also the following, which had a special affective value: theft, to take, to steal, suspicion, blame, court, police, to lie, to fear, to discover, to arrest, innocent.

The objection is often made to the last species of words that they may produce a strong affective resentment even in innocent persons and for that reason one cannot attribute to them any comparative value. Nevertheless, it may always be questioned whether the affective resentment of an innocent person will have the same effect on the association as that of a guilty one, and that question can only be authoritatively answered by experience. Until the contrary shall be demonstrated, I maintain that even words of the above mentioned type may profitably be used.

I then distributed these critical words among twice as many indifferent stimulus words in such a manner that each critical word was followed by two indifferent ones. As a rule it is well to follow up the critical words by indifferent words in order that the action of the first may be clearly distinguished. But one may also follow up one critical word by another, especially if one wishes to bring into relief the action of the second. Thus I placed together "darkish red" and "leather," and "chain" and "silver."

After this preparatory work I undertook the experiment with the three above mentioned nurses. As examinations of this kind can be rendered into a foreign tongue only with the greatest difficulty, I will content myself with presenting the general results, and with giving somes examples. I first undertook the experiment with the friend of the head nurse, and judging by the circumstances she appeared only slightly moved. The head nurse was next examined; she showed marked excitement, her pulse being 120 per minute immediately after the experiment. The last to be examined was the nurse who attended to the cleaning of the room in which the theft occurred. She was the most tranquil of the three; she displayed but little embarrassment, and only in the course of the experiment did it occur to her that she was suspected of stealing, a fact which manifestly disturbed her towards the end of the experiment.

The general impression from the examination spoke strongly against the head nurse. It seemed to me that she evinced a very "suspicious," or I might almost say, "impudent" countenance. With the definite idea of finding in her the guilty one I set about adding up the results.

One can make use of many special methods of computing, but they are not all equally good and equally exact. (One must always resort to calculation, as appearances are enormously deceptive.) The method which is most to be recommended is that of the probable average of the reaction time. It shows at a glance the difficulties which the person in the experiment had to overcome in the reaction.

The technique of this calculation is very simple. The probable average is the middle number of the various reaction times arranged in a series. The reaction times are, for example,[3] placed in the following manner: 5,5,5, 7,7,7,7, 8, 9,9,9, 12, 13, 14. The number found in the middle (8) is the probable average of this series. Following the order of the experiment, I shall denote the friend of the head nurse by the letter A, the head nurse by B, and the third nurse by C.

The probable averages of the reaction are:

A	B	C
10.0	12.0	13.5

No conclusions can be drawn from this result. But the average reaction times calculated separately for the indifferent reactions, for the critical, and for those immediately following the critical (post-critical) are more interesting (Table 4).

From this example we see that whereas A has the shortest reaction time for the indifferent reactions, she shows in comparison to the other two persons of the experiment, the longest time for the critical reactions.

The difference between the reaction times, let us say between the indifferent and the critical, is 6 for A, 2 for B, and 3 for C, that is, it is more than double for A when compared with the other two persons.

[3] Reaction times are always given in fifths of a second.

Table 4. The Probable Average of the Reaction Time

For	A	B	C
Indifferent reactions	10.0	11.0	12.0
Critical reactions	16.0	13.0	15.0
Post-critical reactions	10.0	11.0	13.0

In the same way we can calculate how many complex indicators there are on an average for the indifferent, critical, etc., reactions (Table 5).

Table 5. The Average Complex Indicators for Each Reaction

For	A	B	C
Indifferent reactions	0.6	0.9	0.8
Critical Reactions	1.3	0.9	1.2
Post-critical reactions	0.6	1.0	0.8

The difference between the indifferent and critical reactions for A=0.7, for B=0, for C=0.4. A is again the highest.

Another question to consider is, in what special way do the imperfect reactions behave?

The result for A=34%, for B=28%, and for C=30%.

Here, too, A reaches the highest value, and in this, I believe, we see the characteristic moment of the guilt-complex in A. I am, however, unable to explain here circumstantially the reasons why I maintain that memory errors are related to an emotional complex, as this would lead me beyond the limits of the present work. I therefore refer the reader to my work *"Ueber die Reproductionsstörrungen im Associationsexperiment"* (IX Beitrag der Diegnost. Associat. Studien).

As it often happens that an association of strong feeling tone produces in the experiment a perseveration, with the result that not only the critical association, but also two or three successive associations are imperfectly reproduced, it will be very interesting for our cases to see how many imperfect reproductions are so arranged in the series. The result of computation shows that the imperfect reproductions thus arranged in series are for A 64.7%, for B 55.5%, and for C 30.0%.

Again we find that A has the greatest percentage. To be sure this may partially depend on the fact that A also possesses the greatest number of imperfect reproductions. Given a small quantity of reactions it is usual that the greater the total number of the same the more imperfect reactions will occur in groups. But in order that this should be probable it could not occur in so great a measure as in our case, where on the other hand B and C have not a much smaller number of imperfect reactions when compared to A. It is significant that C with her slight emotions during the experiment shows the minimum of imperfect reproductions arranged in series.

As imperfect reproductions are also complex indicators, it is necessary to see how they distribute themselves in respect to the indifferent, critical, etc., reactions (Table 6).

Table 6. Imperfect Reproductions Which Occur

In	A	B	C
Indifferent reactions	10	12	11
Critical reactions	19	9	12
Post-critical reactions	5	7	7

It is hardly necessary to bring into prominence the differences between the indifferent and the critical reactions of the various subjects as shown by the resulting numbers of the table. In this respect, too, A occupies first place.

Naturally, here, too, there is a probability that the greater the quantity of the imperfect reproductions the greater is their number in the critical reactions. If we suppose that the imperfect reproductions are distributed regularly and without choice among all the reactions there will be a greater number of them for A (in comparison to B and C) even as reactions to critical words, since A has the greater number of imperfect reproductions. Admitting such a uniform distribution of the imperfect reproductions, it is easy to calculate how many we ought to expect to belong to each individual kind of reaction (Table 7).

From this calculation it appears that the disturbances of reproductions which concern the critical reactions for A surpass by far the expected, for C they are 0.9 higher than the expected, while for B the real number is less than the one expected.

All this points to the fact that in the subject A the critical stimulus words acted with the greatest intensity, and hence the greatest suspicion falls on A. Practically one may venture to designate such a subject as probably guilty. The same evening A made a complete confession of the theft, and thus the success of the experiment was confirmed.

I maintain that such a result should be of scientific interest and worthy of consideration. There is much in experimental psychology which is less useful than the material treated in this work. Putting aside althogether the theoretical interest, we have in this case something that is not to be despised from a

Table 7. Imperfect Reproductions

	Which May Be Expected			Which Really Occur		
For	Indifferent Reactions	Critical Reactions	Post-critical Reactions	Indifferent Reactions	Critical Reactions	Post-critical Reactions
A	11.2	12.5	10.2	10	19	5
B	9.2	10.3	8.4	12	9	7
C	9.9	11.1	9.0	11	12	7

practical point of view, to wit, we have brought to light the culpable affair in a much easier and shorter way than is customary. What has been possible once or twice ought to be possible again in other cases, and it is well worth while to investigate the means of rendering the method increasingly capable of rapid and sure results.

This applicability of the experiment show it possible to strike a concealed (indeed an unconscious) complex by means of a stimulus word; and conversely we may assume with great certainty that behind a reaction which shows a complex indicator there is a hidden complex, even though the test person strongly denies it. One must get rid of the idea that educated and intelligent test persons are able to see and admit their own complexes. Every human mind contains much that is unacknowledged and hence unconscious as such; and no one can boast that he stands completely above his complexes. Those who persist in maintaining it do not see the spectacles which they wear on their noses.

4. THE READING OF CHARACTER FROM EXTERNAL SIGNS

Knight Dunlap

The relations between general psychology and individual psychology are important and not hard to grasp. Neither can be separated from the other in practice, but each has its set of problems and its complement of special methods.

SOURCE. Knight Dunlap (1875-1949) was an American experimental psychologist, best known for his early work on reaction time and for his contribution to the developemnt of experimental laboratory apparatus. His experimental studies of spontaneous facial expressions represented an early attempt to bring the study of human emotions into the psychological laboratory. This article originally appeared in *Scientific Monthly,* 1922, **15,** 153-165.

The problems of general psychology concern the determination of laws and principles applying to the human animal generally, which are either independent of individual peculiarities or inclusive of these idiosyncrasies as definite combinations of general factors, not as exceptions. The problems of individual psychology, on the other hand, concern the discovery of those factors of difference between individuals; thus, ultimately, the description of the important respects in which each individual varies from other individuals, and in as far as classification is useful, the assigning of each individual to the class or classes in which he belongs. The specific methods of general psychology are included under the general term *experiment;* the methods of individual psychology under the term *mental measurement.* The most obvious relation between the two branches is through the fact that reliable mental measures (commonly called *mental tests*) can be developed only through experimentation of the most rigorous kind, and the fact that general principles can be obtained only by taking into account the individual differences of the various reactors on whom experimental work is done. One of the most unfortunate and harmful details of the present enthusiastic movement in the individual psychology, in education, in industry, and in medicine, is the naïve assumption that persons ignorant of general psychology and untrained in experimental psychology can develop and apply mental tests in a useful way without the careful supervision of competent psychologists. The deleterious results of such bungling work on children, for example, are apparent not only in the harm to the children and needless trouble and expense to which parents are put, but also in the prejudices aroused in the public mind against mental measurements as a result of the mistake of amateurs. Equally unfortunate results are frequent in the legal, medical and industrial applications of amateur psychology. The general recognition of the need of individual psychology in commerce and industry in particular has led to the existence of a class of mere exploiters, many of whom reap large financial rewards from their practices, and whose eventual effect on the manufacturers and business men they victimize is to turn them against the application of real psychology.

Mental measurements have so far been developed to the point where effective determinations of general intelligence are made—determinations which are of value not only for schools and colleges, but also for commerce and industry. No psychologist claims that these measurements are completely satisfactory, and we all know that they are being constantly improved, and will be enormously improved in the future. On the other hand, no one but the psychologist knows the amount of time, labor and personal training required for the development and standardization of even the simplest test. The public, impressed by the apparent simplicity of the materials, assumes that any one can make up a test, and the public is right so far: any one *can* make up a test, and almost every one *does*, but the tests are not worth anything. The public either does not see this, or, if it does see it, assumes that the tests made up by the expert are also worthless. For some of the confusion the psychologists themselves are partly responsible. For example, the nomenclature of "mental ages" as established by intelligence tests, which should never have been allowed to escape from the laboratories, has very much confused and prejudiced the public.

In addition to tests of "general intelligence" (which may most safely be defined as that which standard intelligence tests measure), tests for special intellectual capacitites have been developed. We can now measure ability to sustain and to distribute the attention, ability to perceive accurately details of various kinds, ability to learn, ability to avoid learning, and many other special abilities of this class. The field of such measurements is rapidly being extended, and it now requires merely the application of the labor of the trained psychologist to develop systematic tests for the special combinations of intellectual abilities required in any branch of any trade or profession.

But this is the limit to which mental measurements so far have extended. Emotional and moral characteristics are not as yet measurable. Yet we know that these characteristics are of immense importance in all the divisions of life in which we are measuring intellectual capacity. Even as concerns the candidate for admission to college, while it is important to determine his intellectual capacity, emotional and moral factors ought to be known. There is many a man who goes down or barely survives in college, whose intellectual ability is sufficiently good, but who will not work, or who will get into trouble because of moral delinquency, or whose scale of values is inadequate.

I do not say that we shall never be able to measure these characteristics by the methods of individual psychology; in fact, I think that ultimately we shall compass such measurement. A number of us are now at work on the problem of moral measurements, and I think the prospects for development along this line are favorable. But at present we do not pretend to make standardized measurements of emotional and moral capacity.

Wherever there is a great need, attempts to fill it will be made; these attempts will not all be scientific, and not all made in good faith, especially if there is a prospect of fat remuneration. The historical development of medicine is an illustration of this fact. Medical practice developed long before there was any known basis for it and the bane of the medical profession today is the tendency to apply something in cases where there is really nothing to apply—a tendency against which Osler and other medical leaders have protested emphatically, and with some success.

The past lack of scientific means of measuring intelligence, and the lack of scientific means of measuring moral and emotional characteristics, together with the real need for such measures, has led to the development of unscientific methods of mental diagnosis which are popularly designated as *character analysis*. These methods are based on the assumption that there is a close relation between the anatomy of the individual and his mental characteristics, and that the details of this relationship may be discovered by casual examination, without the aid of statistical methods or experimental procedure, by persons ignorant not only of psychology but even of the rudiments of psychology.

The first systematic attempt at the development of character analysis was made by the phrenologists. The physiologist Gall early in the nineteenth century began to teach that the mental life is largely dependent upon the brain, especially upon the cerebral hemispheres. This fact was not widely recognized before the time of Gall, although it has become a commonplace since then, and Gall's work had a large influence in bringing this recognition about. But Gall and his disciples are also responsible for the introduction into psychology of several misleading conceptions concerning the relation of the brain to consciousness—conceptions which have retarded the development of psychology and which are being eliminated but slowly. Gall and his pupil Spurzheim developed a theory of the relation of the brain to mind which they called phrenology, which means literally the study of the intellect. These phrenologists believed that the different faculties or capacities of the mind were localized, each in specific portions of the cortex or outer surface of the cerebral hemispheres. They further believed that the relative development of each of these faculties depended upon the relative size of the portions of the brain in which the respective faculties were supposed to reside. Highly developed philoprogenitiveness, or love of children, for example, was supposed to depend upon a cortex relatively thicker in the philoprogenitive area than is the cortex in the same area of a person less strongly philoprogenitive. Finally, since they supposed the conformation of the skull to agree with the relative thickness of the cortex it encloses, they assumed the possibility of diagnosing the development of various cortical areas by examination of the outer surface of the cranium. The surface of the head was accordingly mapped off into a number of small areas, each associated with one of the faculties in the phrenological list; and from the relative depression or elevation of these areas the phrenologist attempted to read the "character" of the subject.

We need not dwell upon the series of bold assumptions involved in this system, since, from the scientific point of view, the system is of historical interest only. Quite aside from the further development of phrenology as a technique, it had a profound and on the whole unfortunate influence upon the course of psychobiology for many years. Physiologists and psychologists fell into the habit of assuming that consciousness is dependent upon brain activity in a remarkably simple way, ignoring the complicated interrelations of the various parts of the nervous system, and ignoring the fundamental function of the total nervous system in the control of movements through sensory stimulation. Moreover, both the psychologists and the physiologists accepted even the phrenological doctrine of the localization of conscious functions in specific parts of the cortex, although the functions as thus localized by the physiologists were not the "faculties" of the phrenologists, but a more generalized group, including the senses. It is only within the last fifteen years that psychologists have begun to reject the phrenological theory, and many physiologists still cling to it.

As an art, phrenology had a wide popular vogue and is still practiced lucratively in the United States, there being at least one school in which the system is taught. It has, however, sunk to a position of relatively minor importance, and has been largely supplanted by newer systems, in part derived from it, and in part derived from still older anatomical beliefs. In these newer systems little emphasis is placed upon the surface of the skull, the major stress being laid upon the contours of the face, upon the size and form of the nose, mouth, ears, brows and eyes, upon the color and texture of the hair, and upon similar anatomical traits.

In one of the most widely known systems, from which many other systems have been drawn, "conscientiousness" is indicated by a broad, bony chin; "benevolence" by a full, rolling, moist under lip; "love of home" by fullness of the soft part of chin just below the lip; "amativeness" by the thickness, moisture and redness of the central part of the upper lip; "cautiousness" by an extremely long nose; "judgment" by a broad, large nose; "observation" by a lowering of the brows at their inner ends and projection of the frontal bone at that point. Musical talent is indicated in this system by an ear of rounding form and fine quality, with a deep bell and perfectly formed rim. Mathematical ability is shown by squareness of the face bones, width between the eyes, and especially by the upward curve of the outer part of the eyebrow. The signs of acquisitiveness are a thick, heavy upper eyelid, with fullness and breadth of the nose just above the nostril. Sometimes an arched, curved or hooked nose indicates the same thing. But in this system the significance of many signs is modified by others; hence, the degree of development of a given characteristic is read, not from a single anatomical sign but from a group of anatomical details, to which I will apply the term *physiognomic pattern.* Thus, a certain relative form or size of one feature might indicate a certain mental trait, provided it is accompanied by certain other details of form, position and size of other features. Linguistic ability, for example, is shown by large bright convex eyes, fullness under the eyes, the rounding out of head above temples, full lips, full cheeks, full throat, wide mouth and chest, large nostrils, length from point of nose to tip of chin, with vertical, lateral and perpendicular width of concha of ear. The physiognomic pattern indicative of well-developed color sense is decided color of the complexion, eyes, eyebrows and hair, clearness of skin, and veins showing through.

By the use of patterns instead of single signs there is secured an elasticity of application of the system, which is of great importance, and to which I shall later refer.

The foregoing samples are drawn from a single system; but this system is one from which a number of variant systems have apparently been derived. There are many systems in use, all equally definite, all equally "successful." Some systems stick pretty closely to physiognomy; some add signs from the voice, posture, and the anatomical details of arms, leg and trunk. But all these systems agree in two points: They are in the main anatomical, and they are lucrative to their promoters.

The attempts to read character from anatomical signs have not, however, originated in modern times, nor have they been confined to professional character analysts. Evidences of popular associations between anatomical details and especially between facial and mental and moral traits are to be found in the literature of all peoples. "Let me have men about me that are fat," Shakespeare makes Caesar say. Confluent eyebrows have long been supposed to be evidence of a lecherous disposition; a long nose of meddlesomeness; red hair of passion; and so on *ad infinitum.* As an attempt made in all seriousness to evolve a scientific system of mentoanatomy, I may point to Lombroso's description of the criminal type. It is evident that we have here to deal with tendencies which are widespread, and which are by no means always operating in the interests of private profit. Yet it is the professional character analyst who forms the main problem, since it is his work which furnishes the most pernicious results.

It requires little investigation to convince us that the system of character analysis now in use have no scientific foundation, and that if any one of them were in part valid, it would be a most marvelous coincidence. None of the authors of the various modern systems shows any evidence of knowledge of physiology or psychology, to say nothing of genetics; nor do they attempt to apply even the simplest principles of statistics or experimental procedure in arriving at their conclusions. Naïve conclusions from selected cases at the best, mere guesses at the worst, are the sole means employed. A study of works on physiognomy strongly reminds the reader of the interpretations of the psychical researcher and the Freudians. Aside from this, the contradiction of system by system would give even the layman cause to doubt. If we consider the signs of the same character trait, such as "honesty," we find it indicated in different systems by quite different signs. If we consider the same sign, such as the shape of the nose, we find it indicating quite different traits in different systems. And yet the claims of any one system to practical success are as well substantiated as are those of any other system.

Nevertheless, the incompetence of the existing systems does not dispose of the question whether there might not be a valid system evolved. In spite of the futile efforts of various would-be flyers, the airplane was invented. We must inquire therefore what possible basis there is for a system of character analysis based on anatomical signs. And we find the answer that there is no known basis on which such a system might be constructed.

We know that the exercise of mental and moral capacities does not change the gross anatomical details of the human being. (Some of the systems of character analysis assume the contrary.) That a man can not, by taking thought, add to his height is true, and is an illustration of a more general law. No exercise of generosity, judgment, musical talent, malice or amativeness can change the form of the nose, or of the ear, or the setting of the eyes, or the form of the brows. If training can not develop anatomical signs, then the putative signs of character must be signs of inherited capacity only, showing the endowment of the individual in respect to capacities which he may or may not have cultivated and developed.

But the results of genetics to date give us no basis for assuming anatomical signs of inherited capacity, except in pure races or relatively homogeneous races. It is true that we may conclude from such signs as the shape of the eyes and the color and texture of the hair that a certain individual belongs to the Chinese race, and hence that he has traits of character common to the Chinese. But the Chinese race, although not an absolutely pure race, is one which is sharply distinct from the white races, and we may expect to find different racial characteristics, although as a matter of fact the characteristics usually imputed to the Chinese are probably due more to training than to heredity. A Chinese boy, brought up under white conditions, is surprisingly like a white boy mentally, although he retains his anatomical race characteristics. In the case of the negro and of other markedly inferior races definite racial mental differences may be admitted. But we must remember that these differences are racial, not individual.

The European races, however, are exceedingly mixed, being the products of the blendings of many stocks, and although it is possible that the original pure stocks may have had specific anatomical characteristics and also specific mental characteristics, we find no linkage of these characteristics in their hereditary transmission after mixture. A remote ancestor of a certain man may have belonged to a stock which had long noses and also had violent dispositions; another remote ancestor may have belonged to another stock, having snub noses and great amiability. The man under consideration may, however, have inherited the long nose from the one stock and the amiable disposition from the other. This fact comes out most clearly in the blendings of the white and negro races. The features of the mulatto or the octoroon give no indication of the relative mental inheritance of the individual from his white and colored progenitors, although statistically the greater the proportion of white ancestry, the greater may be the probability of white intelligence.

It is possible, although not probable, that our feeble-minded whites inherit their mental defect from certain original pure stocks of low mentality which unfortunately became mixed with the other European stocks, but there are no anatomical signs by which the feeble-minded may be identified. Nor are there any anatomical signs of the criminal, Lombroso to the contrary notwithstanding.

It is true that there are certain exceptions to the generalizations I have made. Cretins, microcephalic and macrocephalic individuals and other distinctly pathological cases show anatomical signs of their mental deficiences. So does a blind man show that he is deficient in the visual faculty and the legless man show his deficiency in the faculty of locomotion. But these cases are due to specific defects, and have no bearing on the attempts to analyze and classify the common run of humanity. These pathological cases may be easily segregated, and character analysis contributes nothing to our identification of them. In the remaining bulk of the population there is no discernible principle of linkage of the mental and the anatomical.

Finding no scientific basis for the anatomical character analysis, we are now thrown back upon the pragmatic problem. How is it that these systems apparently succeed? And we must admit that they do have at least financial success, for many of the character analysts are making money from their practice on commercial and industrial concerns.

For this success there are two outstanding reasons: first, the actual value of character readings is rarely checked up; second, a few, not many, of the professional analysts, when subjected to actual tests, can make surprisingly good guesses.

As an illustration of the way in which character reading may obtain the prestige of success without being checked up in regard to its accuracy, I may cite the case of a large industrial plant, in which several thousand employees were "analyzed" by a reputed "expert" at a good round price. This expert had a system devised by himself after the usual type, and apparently drawn either directly or indirectly from the older system from which my illustrations were taken and from which many other popular systems are drawn. This self-styled expert told me that in his opinion the systems of several other and better known fakers, whom he named, were defective because they were too rigid. "Now I," he went on to say, "have used in my system all that is worthwhile in psychology, phrenology and physiology; but I am not hide-bound like the others. When I find a case to which the system doesn't apply, I discard the system and use common sense." This expert spent several minutes in interviewing each employee, marking on a form card the characteristics of eyes, mouth, ears, hair, head form, etc. Then, combining these records, he decided upon the general mental and moral characteristics of the individual, and upon the particular line of work, if any, in the plant at which he should be put.

The "experting" of these employees was done at the instance of one of the directors of the corporation who had become interested in this sort of "efficiency" through the "success" obtained by it in certain other corporations. By the time the analyses were completed, this director had lost interest in this particular fad, and had become interested in another kind of "efficiency." The results were, of course, pigeonholed; the managers and foremen who were actually working with the employees knew too much to use the readings. But the "expert" went on to the next job with thousands of dollars in his pocket, and with the reputation of having successfully "experted" this corporation, whose directors, being cold, hard business men, obviously would not have put money in the scheme unless it were financially profitable. This corporation, of course, had been influenced by similar considerations. Other concerns had their employees "experted" "successfully," the success having been of the same imaginary sort.

"Success" under the conditions of an actual check up is another matter, and it is said that certain "experts" have, under test conditions, achieved a surprising measure of success. Such tests are made by submitting to the inspection of the "expert" a number of individuals of known and proven capacity in various lines, but who are unknown to the "expert." The "expert" is then required to make a written statement as to the mental characteristics of each person, and these statements are compared with previously prepared statements based on the established characteristics of the test-persons.

Now I can not guarantee that any such tests have actually been successful. I have to restrict my statement to the form "it is said." There are, of course, many chances of erroneous conclusions when the tests are not made under the rigid supervision of psychologists. We know from the alleged proofs of telepathy and of various forms of spirit manifestations that unskilled investigators commonly overlook the most vital points in the test conditions, because they do not know their importance. The records on most tests of this sort have a value of approximately zero, because they contain no reliable evidence on the vital points, however much detailed information is given on other points.

But suppose we assume (although we may have as yet no good grounds for the assumption) that tests of certain character-analysts have given positive results. This would not be surprising. In fact, I should expect to find that some "experts" could produce positive results. Few "experts" are willing to submit to real tests, but those few who are willing must be so because they are confident that they could succeed to some extent, even in a carefully checked test.

We may freely admit that certain persons, working in entire independence of any system, may be able to make some good guesses. Many of us think that we can make good guesses. Our guesses are probably very much less accurate than we suppose, yet they may have some validity. In many cases we have to entrust important matters to individuals as to whose honesty or intelligence we have no evidence except from our guesses based on brief observation of the visible appearance of the individual. There is no reason to suppose that professional character analysts should not be able to make as good guesses as any one else, provided these experts have the requisite native capacity, and provided that, like the one I quoted, they ignore their systems and use common sense.

It is actually a fact that we do make correct judgments about the transient mental processes of other persons without being able to identify the facts on which these judgments are based. If you are talking to someone, and you say something which offends or grieves or pleases him, you may recognize that fact at once, although it may be impossible for you to designate the exact change in his face or voice or posture which is the basis of your idea. You may even make similar judgments when carrying on a conversation over the telephone, in which case changes in the timbre and inflections of the voice alone could give you the clue. You know from the other person's voice that he is offended or pleased, although you may not be able to identify the exact change in his voice which is the important factor. When you have the visual clues from the other person's face, as well as the clues from his voice, your judgments are more definite and more secure.

This whole matter is but a special case of the more general phenomenon of perception and judgment by sign. It is a fact that in much of our perception we perceive meanings without perceiving the signs on which the perception is based. In some cases, the signs could be perceived, if attention were drawn to them; in other cases, the signs can not be discriminated even under the best conditions. I shall not go into this topic in an extended way, both because it is familiar to psychologists, and because it can not be briefly expounded to those without psychological training. I mention it only to show that on this point of character readings we are not dealing with a unique phenomenon, but with a particular manifestation of a general principle which runs broadly through our mental life.

As another illustration of the general principle, I may refer to certain cases of supposed "thought-reading" which are really cases of sign-reading. Many amateurs succeed in catching ideas from other persons, where there is physical relation of such sort that movements of the second person may actually stimulate receptors of the first person, either tactually, visually or acoustically. But these amateurs never succeed if they watch for the signs. They succeed only when they ignore the signs and attend to the meanings. In fact, if amateurs who succeed brilliantly in muscle reading tests become convinced that their performance really is muscle reading and nothing more occult, they can usually do the trick no longer, and this is precisely what we might expect. Similarly, if, instead of watching to see whether the person you are talking to is pleased or not, you watch for the facial changes which indicate pleasure, you will not catch his emotional changes unless the symptoms are extremely gross. The conditions here are not greatly different from those obtaining in the visual perception of depth, where, if you attend to the signs, convergence, accommodation, binocular disparity, and so on, you will lose the depth-effect which those signs would give if they were not attended to.

The important question, therefore, is: What are the signs which tell us something about the mental characteristics of other persons? In the case of fleeting, ideational and emotional changes, these signs are obviously not anatomical; and in the case of fundamental tendencies of mental and moral sorts, we have already shown that there are no known anatomical signs. We are, therefore, forced to the conclusion that in the one case as in the other, the signs are physiological. Changes in the complicated muscular system of the face do occur along with ideas, especially if these ideas are emotionally toned. Changes in the complex musculature of the vocal organs and changes in the arm, leg and trunk muscles also occur. There are, in other words, changes in voice, in features, in posture and in other bodily postures and movements which are perfectly competent to serve as indexes of ideational and emotional changes. Unfortunately, we have not yet succeeded in analyzing more than the most gross of these signs.

Fundamental tendencies in ideational and emotional reaction give rise to habitual modes of expression of the various sorts. Habitual modes of expression, moreover, leave their traces, especially in the face, even when the actual expression is not occurring. There would seem to be, therefore, a complex system of signs, not only of fleeting mental changes, but signs also of character traits, provided we can make use of them.

Signs of this sort are effective, prior to analysis. Habits of perception and of judgment are built up on signs, without necessitating any analysis or identification of such signs. Moreover, the development of the capacity to catch meanings in this way, if it be possible, depends upon native capacity as well as upon practice. We should, therefore, expect to find exactly what we do find, namely, that there is great individual variation in this apparent skill, and that in the absence of a really comprehensive and accurate analysis of signs, the attempt to attend to signs is a disturbing factor.

Character analysts, if successful under real test conditions, obviously make their guesses just as you or I do. "The systems" can be nothing but obstacles, since they have no real bearing on the problem. But, after having made a guess, the analyst can readily find in his system details which back up his guess, provided the system is elastic, depending upon sign patterns rather than upon hard and fast single signs. We need not assume that successful character analysts, if there are such, go through this sophistical process deliberately. The tendency to construe evidence to suit one's theory, and to recognize the data which may thus be construed, overlooking conflicting data, is too well known and too widespread to need demonstration. One of the important reasons why scientific procedure and scientific methods are necessary is that such procedure and methods are indispensable helps to the avoidance of arbitrary inferences, and even with the best of scientific aids the tendency will sometimes operate.

As a matter of fact, there is no reason to believe that the accuracy and reliability of such guesses as you and I and the character analyst make are very high. But there is reason to believe that if any character analyst does obtain even ten per cent of accuracy in certain special test cases, he very likely may not know how he gets his results, and may believe that he is getting them through his system, although he really is not.

I have no doubt that those mind-readers, such as Bishop and McIvor-Tyndall, who apparently attained striking results under test conditions, sincerely believed that they were reading minds directly, and not through physical signs. Certainly, they could obtain those results only by ignoring the signs, and it may well be that they would not have been successful if they had known the actual nature of the process. I may mention here the observation I have made that the most successful hypnotists are those who have no scientific comprehension of the hypnotic process, but who really believe that they are exercising an occult power, or that some "magnetic fluid" flows from their hands to the patient.

On the other hand, it is true that we do, in much of our perception and thought, make use of signs effectively, although we are fully aware of the nature of those signs. In visual depth perception, to which I have already referred, we lose nothing in the perception of depth in pictures and landscapes through an exact knowledge of the signs, provided we do not attempt to attend to those signs in the moment of perception. As another pertinent illustration I may point out that the knowledge that the thinking-process proceeds through muscular signs does not interfere with the vividness and the efficiency of thinking, provided we do not attempt to attend to those signs while thinking.

It is therefore entirely possible that a scientific system of character measurement may some day be developed. Such a system would be based on physiological, not on anatomical signs, and would necessarily be the result of extensive and prolonged experimental work. Even the development of such a system to the point of such relative efficiency as has been reached in mental measurements would require years of work by many and highly trained investigators, just as the development of mental measurements has required.

Although we do not know that it is possible to develop a science of character estimation, serious work in the attempt to find out is highly desirable. Even a definite negative result would be most valuable. In the meantime, a respectable name by which this field of investigation might be known would be practically useful. The term "analysis" and its derivatives can no longer be used in psychology, because, thanks to the efforts of the "psycho-analysts" and the "character-analysts," the terms "analysis" and "analyst" have come to connote superstition and quackery. In the meantime, in the interests of the gullible public as well as the interests of psychology, both pure and applied, we must carry on an educational campaign against "character analysis."

5. MULTIPLE METHODS OF PERSONALITY ASSESSMENT[1]

Ronald Taft

The term "personality assessment" refers to any procedure aimed at describing a person's characteristic behavior by categorizing him with respect to some communicable dimension or dimensions.[2] Since the OSS assessment procedures, however, the term has tended to be pre-empted for the procedure where several different types of assessment techniques are applied to the subjects and the final assessments are made by the combined judgments of several assessors concerning the subjects' predicted behavior outside of the assessment situation. These procedures are "multiple" in two senses: with respect to the techniques and with respect to the assessors.

Our treatment in this paper will deal with the basic logic of this type of assessment, and the discussion will be illustrated by the best known multiple personality assessments, details of which are outlined in Table 1.[3] Each one of these assessments has, in its own way, constituted a milestone in the history of multiple personality assessment.

The researches into personality conducted at Harvard in the 30's under the direction of Murray (1938) were the first to use the typical procedures of personality assessment—diagnostic committee assessments of personality based on interviews and a varied battery of objective, projective, and situational tests. However, unlike the later assessments, no outside criterion was used in these Harvard studies, and, therefore, no more than passing reference will be made to them. The same applies to the continuing series of studies of personality carried

SOURCE. Ronald Taft, an Australian psychologist, is Professor of Education at Macquarie University (New South Wales). Dr. Taft has contributed extensively to the American personality assessment literature, particularly in his major reviews and discussions of the theory of clinical interpretation, programmatic assessment, and interpersonal perception and judgment. This article originally appeared in *Psychological Bulletin,* 1959, **56,** 333-352. Reprinted by permission of the American Psychological Association and the author.

[1]The author expresses his thanks to the colleagues who have discussed various points in this paper with him, especially to James Lumsden; also to Saul B. Sells for his valuable comments.

[2]This is the same procedure as "instantiating a person object in a module or set of modules," a terminology which the writer has preferred in another context (Sarbin, Taft, and Bailey, 1960), but which is avoided here in the interests of communicability.

[3]Insofar as the assessments use multiple techniques, the problems of inferring the predictions and validating the tests are the same as those involved in other multi-variate procedures. See, for example, the treatment of these problems in Thorndike (1949). Our emphasis here will be mainly on the problems that arise from the combination of multivariate procedures and multiple assessors.

Table 1. Details of Milestone Assessment Programs
(Wide sample of techniques used: individual and multiple interviews; observation of group activities and situational tests; objective, projective, and performance tests; "made to measure" inventories)

Assessment	Date	Assessees	Primary Purpose	Strategies (In Order of Importance)
Harvard (Murray, 1938)	1934-37	Young men, mainly Harvard undergraduates (paid subjects)	Personality research	Analytic
WOSB (Harris, 1949; Morris, 1949)	1942-45	British officer candidates	Selection	Analytic Global
OSS	1944-45	U. S. Intelligence and espionage agent candidates	Selection	Analytic Global
Michigan, VA (Kelly and Fiske, 1951)	1946-49	Clinical psychology graduate students	Validation of techniques	Empirical Global
California IPAR (Various published reports, e.g., Barron, 1954; Gough, 1953)	1950-51	Advanced graduate students	Personality research; validation of techniques	Empirical Analytic Global
Chicago (Stern, Stein, and Bloom, 1956)	1952-54	Students in theology. education, and arts	Validation of techniques	Analytic Global
Menninger (Holt and Luborsky, 1958)	1946-52	Psychiatric training candidates	Selection, validation of techniques	Global Analytic Empirical

Assessors	Criterion Analysis Method	Method of Rating	Main Criterion	Some Selected Validities (Uncorrected for Selection of Groups)
Psychologists	–	Committee	No external criteria	–
Army officers, psychiatrists, and psychologists	Personal knowledge	1. Committee and 2. Final Review Board	Supervisors' reports	1. CISSB committee 0.13–0.25. 2. Review Board 0.23–0.41. (When corrected for selection the range of validities is 0.50–0.66.)
Psychologists, psychiatrists, and other social scientists	Intuitive and interview with experts	Committee	Field reports by the assessors and by field commanders on several molar traits	"Over-all" ratings 0.08–0.53 (varying with assessment group and criterion). Rating of "Effective Intelligence," 0.33–0.53
Psychologists (clinical and nonclinical)	Personal knowledge	Individual and pooled ratings	Ratings by clinical teachers and supervisors on several aspects of clinical work	"Over-all" rating and clinical competence, 0.37. Miller Analogies and clinical competence, 0.35. Strong Interest Key for Clinical Psychological and Research Competence, 0.35. Other validities lower
Psychologists	Personal knowledge	Committee	1. Teacher's prediction of student's professional potential. 2. Teacher's ratings of personal soundness	1. Cross-validated inventory with 1., 0.29 2. Committee ratings with 2., 0.41
Psychologists	Committee job analysis and interviews with teachers	Committee	Teacher's judgments and exam results	Very high validities
Psychiatrists and psychologists	Committee job analysis and success and failure	Individual and averaged ratings of interviewers	Supervisor's ratings (pooled) on specific and general competence	Interviews (global), 0.24. Interviews (analytic), 0.26. Tester's analytic ratings on projectives, 0.27. Objective scoring of projectives cross-validated at zero. Best interviewer (all data) 0.57

out by Cattell and his students (Cattell, 1957) which started to employ external criteria only at an advanced stage of its progress. The British War Officer Selection Boards (WOSB), which were inspired by the German officer multiple technique selection procedures (Farago & Gitler, 1941), pioneered the use of a quasi-natural social situation, including the leaderless discussion, as a basis for judging the potential social skills of the candidate. They also produced the first validation material on multiple assessment procedures as a means of selection. The British Civil Service Selection Boards (CISSB) continued this work, with more emphasis on the validation of individual techniques as well as the technique as a whole. The OSS assessment highlighted the psychological problems inherent in assessment and won many supporters for the value of combining multiple tests and observations by pooling the judgments of several assessors; the Michigan VA assessment program did much to upset that support while the Chicago and Menninger assessments reinstated some of it through their promising findings. The California Institute of Personality Assessment and Research (IPAR) differs from the other assessments in emphasizing research into personality to a greater extent.

The Orientation and Purpose of Personality Assessments

Three foci of assessment can be distinguished: human performance in some socially defined situation or situations (the criterion performance); performance in defined assessment situations, i.e., tests (the assessment performance); and the link between these two performances (test validation). Different assessment programs have been oriented towards one or more of these aspects depending on their primary purpose (see Table 1). The orientation towards criterion performance implies the primary purpose of assessing candidates with respect to the criterion in order to select or reject them. The orientation towards the assessment performance is concerned with the validation of the assessment techniques themselves, while the orientation towards the link between performances is concerned with research on the functioning of personality.

Selection was the original purpose for the WOSB, CISSB, and OSS assessments; in each case, the assessors were presented with the immediate problem of selecting from a given group of candidates those who would make the most adequate army, civil service, and secret service officers, respectively. After a consideration of the personality requirements of the positions for which they were selecting officers, the assessors judged the candidates on the basis of techniques chosen either because they appeared to have face validity for measuring these requirements or because the assessors were familiar with their use. At least in the case of wartime assessments, neither the time available nor the conditions permitted more scientific procedures than that, and it was hoped that accuracy would be achieved through weight of numbers (of techniques and of assessors).

Test Validation (and Construction). Some of the later assessments, notably the VA study, set as their short-run aim the task of developing and validating techniques for future use in selection. The validation studies were applied not only to the individual items and tests, but also to the purely subjective techniques, such as group observations and interviews. In some of them, e.g., Menninger, the individual judges were also validated as though their judgments were scores on a test. When we speak of the validity of assessment techniques it is important to include these judgments among the techniques, as they vary greatly in their accuracy.

The Harvard studies were the first to use multiple assessment techniques for *personality research,* and the outstanding recent example is the IPAR work at California. (The large-scale factor analytic studies of personality, e.g., Cattell and Eysenck [1947], did not use the combined judgments of several assessors.) The Harvard studies dealt with the correlations between different performances that were elicited in the test situation, whereas the IPAR studies were concerned, in addition, with the relationship between the assessment performances and criterion measures such as ratings by university teachers of the subject's professional potential, his originality, and his personal soundness. The Michigan studies of clinical psychologists were similar in orientation.

Most of the personality assessments have tried to pursue more than one of the above purposes at once, but there are drawbacks to such attempts at economy. For example, an attempt was made in the CISSB studies (Vernon, 1950) to combine selection and validation, but the validation indices were lowered and distorted by that attenuation of the sample through rejection of candidates. The low validities obtained became remarkably high (for that sort of prediction) when a correction for selection was applied, but such corrections are only arbitrary estimates. The use of assessment procedures for selection implies that the procedures have already been validated, but this has usually not been the case. The assessors have either had to use whatever prior knowledge they possessed about the validity of the techniques for the purpose at hand, or they have had to base their predictions on the relevant postulates in their theory concerning the link between the assessment and the criterion behavior of the subjects. For example, the assessors presume that the situational tests in the assessment program have what Cronbach and Meehl have termed "content" validity (1955). But in selection, this type of validity can be regarded only as a holding procedure for an ultimate "predictive" validity. Where the criteria are imprecise and not repeatable, or where selection is urgent, a separate validation study may not be practical, and under these circumstances there is no alternative to conducting selection without prior validation. It still may be possible, however, over a period of time, to utilize the imperfect validational material that becomes available in order to improve the existing selection procedures. This seems to have been the case, for example, in the OSS studies.

Validation studies of the assessment techniques also logically precede the use of those procedures for personality research, although techniques used in such research often are accepted on the basis of their face validity. To use the one and same study to validate the techniques and to use them to measure personality is lifting oneself up by one's boot-straps. In fact, however, the assessments which attempt to carry out this dual purpose obtain independent support for the "boot-strap lift" from already existing information regarding both validation and the functioning of personality. Even then, the interpretation of personality research projects that do not commence with a pilot study on the validity of the instruments is always subject to doubt. How do you know that expressed hostility to authority figures on the TAT measures suppressed rebellious tendencies? How do you know when the assessor X observes a subject to be dominant, that he is dominant? How do you know that observed "role empathy" in a role-playing test is a valid predictor of social skill? Such questions can be answered only by the progressive refinement of validity information and personality theory.

Assessment procedures usually rely on many unvalidated tests, and when the correlations between the tests are used as a means of studying personality—as in the case, for example, the Harvard and IPAR studies—it is necessary to decide whether these correlations are to be treated simply as validity indices, or whether the validity of the tests will be assumed and the correlations treated as throwing light on the relationships between different personality structures. The problem of simultaneous validation of tests and the study of personality is related to the problem of "concurrent" and "construct" validity. By setting up some of the behavioral measures made during the assessment as tentative criteria, it is possible to validate other assessment measures against these. Cronbach and Meehl call this concurrent validation, and it is one way of utilizing previous knowledge of validities by choosing criteria measures that have reasonably well-established reliabilities and validities. Then on the basis of all that is known about these measures, their implications for the understanding of personality can be explored further by a strategy of construct validation. The data collected during the assessment can be added to the "nomological nets" already used in thinking about the particular personality constucts and new hypotheses developed for investigation in later studies. Thus, even an assessment program that is aimed primarily at the purpose of selection can make a contribution to personality research through construct validation. (The place of construct validity in an assessment program is discussed more specifically below under the heading of *analytic strategy*.) This concept also enables an assessment program to avoid the problem of the priority of validation of instruments (versus conducting personality research) by conceiving both validation and personality research as two aspects of the one endeavor, both aspects gradually throwing light on each other as more and more data accumulate.

But this double-aspect approach of construct validation is an uneconomical process. Refinements may often be made more readily to our personality theory or to our knowledge of the validity of the techniques by a more direct approach to one or the other. In this case the problem of priorities which we have discussed cannot be avoided.

The Prediction Strategies In Assessment

The Criterion

All assessment programs involve studies of the link between two or more pieces of behavior, whether the primary purpose be selection, validation research on tests, or personality research. Some of this behavior is known as assessment behavior and some as criterion behavior. These concepts are analogous to the independent and dependent variables in experimental psychology, and it is an arbitrary decision by the experimenter which one is designated as which. Most of the reports of assessments have devoted some space to the criterion problem, especially the report of the Chicago assessments (Stern, Stein, & Bloom, 1956). Most of the problems are similar to those involved in the validation of multivariate objective techniques discussed, for example, by Thorndike (1949).

A special problem that arises in personality assessment is the frequent unreliability of the criteria which so often represent subjective judgments that vary from one criterion rater to another. This unreliability imposes a serious limitation on the potential validity of personality assessments, and it makes it difficult to evaluate some of the low validity coefficients reported.

The designation of the criteria of performance is determined by the circumstances of the assessment, and usually must be taken for granted by the assessors. Thus, in the Chicago study the assessors explicitly accepted the principle that the criterion rating represented the predilections of one or more supervisors with whom the subjects interacted in the criterion situation, and that the assessors' predictions of the subjects' success must be made in reference to the "psychological job requirements" implied by these predilections and interactions. The assessment strategy should be aimed at the criterion, once the latter has been established. Kelly (1957) did not accept this principle in his researches on medical school selection. In this study he analyzed the criterion measures and found that there were at least three, and possibly four, types of medical performance which could be predicted independently. In the long run, however, a selection program has to choose between the independent criteria, or the criteria have to be combined by some type of simple, weighted, or complex, interactional summation, or by taking account of one critical instance.

A complication that arises in criteria analysis, such as that of Kelly, is that an assessor can only predict to indices of the criteria, not to the actual criteria themselves. It may be possible in some instances for the assessor to demonstrate that an index used in assessment has a low correlation with some more satisfactory, although less accessible, criterion index; for example, that academic grades in medicine do not represent the doctor's subsequent service to the community as a practitioner. Assuming that the latter is accepted as the more fundamental in medical practice, the assessors should predict to it rather than to academic grades by trying to obtain some accessible index which more realistically measures this criterion of community service. Sometimes the assessors may be able to convince those who control the criterion ratings that the indices which the latter are using are not consistent with their fundamental criterion, but eventually the assessors and the criterion raters must agree on some criterion index in accordance with the policy of the organization. Otherwise it would be absurd to speak of the validity of the assessment.

Three types of strategies can be distinguished for predicting the criteria performance: *naive empirical, global,* and *analytic,* and we shall now consider each strategy in detail.

1. *Naive Empirical.* This refers to the classical method of test construction, adapted from aptitude testing, in which the inclusion in a selection program of a test—or test item, which may be treated for our purposes as a separate test—is determined mainly by its predictive validity, i.e., by the degree to which it correlates with or discriminates a specified criterion. Tests that are not sufficiently valid are either dropped from the program or amended and no consideration is given to the meaning of the test behavior, except as an afterthought. The naive empirical strategy, thus, is one in which inference proceeds directly from test to criterion without the mediation of intervening variable.

Not a great deal of use has been made of this empirical strategy in multiple personality assessment, partly because of intellectual resistance to atheoretical procedures on the part of personality researchers, and partly because of the absence of reliable criteria. The outstanding examples of the use of the naive empirical strategy are found in the IPAR studies, especially in the scales of the California Psychological Inventory and the Adjective Check List compiled by Gough. These scales, which give unit weight rather than beta weights to the tests, i.e., items, enable predictions to be made to quite complex behavioral criteria, for example, tolerance, delinquency, academic achievement, neurodermatitis, potential social status (Gough, unpublished bibliography, IPAR, 1955).

The naive empirical strategy has the advantage over other strategies of objectivity and also of enabling assessors to predict complex and little understood behavior. But it also has serious limitations: it can be used only where suitable criteria groups are available for validation and cross-validation, and the validities may "drift" owing to changes in significant aspects of the conditions–temporal, geographic, public attitudes and information, set of the subjects, etc. Either some understanding of the underlying theoretical factors is necessary to provide a warning system against "drift," or constant revalidation must be carried out.

The primary purpose served by the naive empirical approach is that of constructing, and validating assessment instruments, although the long-range purpose can be both selection and research on personality. Up to a point, the personality research aim can be served simultaneously with the validation aim, since the discovery of the intercorrelations between the tests themselves and the criteria can suggest personality constructs. But we are now back on the problem of priorities: we can use validation studies for personality research only if we already possess postulates about the significance for personality of the behavior tapped by the tests and the criteria.

In this reference we should briefly consider the sources of the test items that are used in the validation "try-outs." The sources may be naive empirical, or they may be theoretical. Empirical sources include: tests in the general area that are traditionally used, those that are readily available and can conveniently be given, tests whose title or item content bear a superficial relationship to the criterion, and tests which have previously been shown to relate to the criterion. Theoretical sources of tests, on the other hand, include the systematic or unsystematic sampling–usually the latter–of the areas of personality that are considered by the researcher to be relevant to the criterion behavior. The empirical outlook of the student who is developing personality assessment techniques is seldom so naive that it is entirely uninformed by theoretical considerations, so that the "naive empirical" approach in practice tends to become mediated by intervening structures and thus to approach the analytic strategy described below. The intervening structures, however, are not made explicit in this empirical approach.

2. *Global.* This is the second non-mediated strategy, in which the assessor relies on his intuition, empathy, and *verständnis* processes to provide the predictions, rather than using statistically established associations between assessment behavior and criteria. If any analysis is made of the criterion in a global strategy it is directed at the social role expectations for the criterion performance rather than at the required personal qualities for successful performance. (The latter is more appropriate to the analytic strategy discussed below.) Information may be given to the assessors about the subject's performance on objective tests, and even concerning the validity of these tests–for example, in the Menninger studies (Holt, 1958)–but the ultimate assessment is a global one. This procedure is the personality assessor's answer to some of the drawbacks of the empirical strategy. Intuitive predictions can be used when the assessors have only a vague

concept of the criterion conditions, but empirical methods require clear-cut criteria and expendable samples of trial subjects who have been rated on these criteria. Where this is impossible, as in the case of the OSS studies, the empirical strategy cannot be used, and intuition must be resorted to.

The distinction between empirical and global strategies also is analogous to the distinction between narrow- and wide-band techniques (Cronbach & Gleser, 1957), the former enabling comparatively more reliable but limited predictions. Supporters of the global strategy have claimed for it special adaptability to the vagaries of the conditions associated with both the assessment and criterion situations. Some writers also claim for it a special virtue in connection with personality research in that it avoids the violation of a "whole" person inherent in trait psychology; however, it is very doubtful whether it is correct to use the word "research" to describe a mode of study which, if it were applied in its pure form of global *verständnis,* would by definition preclude communication of the assessments.

The value of the claims of the global strategists to have improved on empirical validation as a basis for selection programs is limited. Subjective methods of making predictions have seldom been shown to be superior to objective methods where these are available, excepting in the case of especially competent assessors (see below). The relative competence of the assessors in making predictions about the subjects is analogous to the relative validity of the tests, and both can be established by the same type of validation techniques. In this way the empirical and the global strategies are similar in orientation: the proviso that incompetent assessors should either be eliminated from the assessment panel or trained to eliminate errors is analogous to the dropping or amending of an invalid test in the empirical strategy.

The "nonanalytic" techniques used in the global strategy are not necessarily nonmediated by personality constructs, even though these constructs may not be made explicit. The process of moving from observations of behavior to inferences about future behavior uses a set of postulates about personality and various derived premises; these premises involve certain personality constructs or categories into which the assessor places the behavior of the subjects, i.e., he "instantiates" the behavior. Intuitive inferences, even empathic ones, can be reduced to this formulation which provides a bridge between analytic and nonanalytic processes. This point is elaborated by Sarbin, Taft, and Bailey (1960).

3. *Analytic.* The analytic strategy makes explicit the role of mediating constructs in prediction. A two-stage inference is involved; first, there is an inference from the criterion requirement to the traits that are relevant to that performance (the "criterion analysis"); and, secondly, an inference from the subject's observed behavior and test performance to his status on the trait dimensions (the assessment). Research on the validity of these inferences re-

quires two separate studies: one of the validity of the analysis of the criterion requirements and the criterion indices, and one of the validity of the tests as predictors of the criterion. These validation studies should be based on independent samples of behavior and, for preference, on independent samples of subjects, the research on the criterion analysis to precede the validation of the instruments.

The importance of criterion analysis was recognized in each one of the "milestone" assessments, but the validity of the analysis is usually assumed. Two types of approach to the criterion analysis problem have been used: intuitive and empirical. The *intuitive* approach is the one usually used in personality assessment; typically the assessors have used either the testimony of "experts" or their own theoretical analysis to determine the criterion requirements. These analyses rest on a theory of personality, but the theory is usually not made explicit, nor is it subjected to empirical validation.

The empirical approach to criterion analysis can employ subjective or objective methods. The Menninger studies, for example, employed subjective rating methods to compare the characteristics of successful and unsuccessful psychiatrists.[4] The VA assessment program was, among other things, one big empirical criterion analysis using both subjective and objective methods. The study began with no explicit analysis of the requirements in clinical psychology and ended with an explicit description of some of the characteristics which relate to success in various aspects of that profession. In a sense, all preliminary validation tryouts of tests in a naive empirical strategy, such as those used in the VA and IPAR programs, constitute a criterion analysis. The cross-validation that follows may thus be regarded as testing a series of hypotheses about the criterion behavior. Referring once more to Cronbach and Meehl's contribution (1955), we see now that the analytic strategy is a type of construct validation which attempts to augment the "nomological net" surrounding the relevant constructs.

The main difficulty with the analytic method of assessment is that it requires a set of constructs which may not exist in our present state of psychological knowledge—although the assessment results may contribute to the development of such constructs. The difficulties which factor analysts often encounter in their attempts to label their factors leads one to sympathize with Cattell's preference for using reference letters and numbers rather than trying to find meaningful labels for his personality factors (Cattell, 1957). The analytic method, then, is limited by the current state of development of personality theory. A further drawback of a thoroughgoing analytic method of assessment is the practical consideration of economy of effort; the returns may be just as great,

[4] Knowledge of the results of this analysis did not improve the validity of the assessor's predictions, but this could have been caused by the assessors preferring to use a global rather than analytic strategy despite the analytic information which was supplied (Holt, 1958).

probably greater, in the first pilot assessments in a program, if we use an empirical or global strategy without trying to make explicit the underlying theoretical relationships. In addition, analytic assessments require a double inference and consequently the possibilities of error are increased; either the criterion analysis or the ratings of the candidate might be in error. In the analytic strategy, however, there is at least the hope that the sources of these errors will be discovered and corrected, whereas the sources are masked in the nonmediated strategies.

The analytic strategy is applicable to any of the three purposes, selection, validation research or personality research, but its greatest potential is in the latter; in fact, if the results of assessment are to be of any value in increasing our understanding of personality, it is essential that the data be expressed in terms of basic personality constructs underlying the subject's behavior so that the scores and observations on the subjects may become meaningful. This applies both to naive empirical strategies such as factor analysis or blind item validation, and to global strategies in which the mediating constructs are not made explicit.

To sum up: we have argued that both the naive empirical and the global strategies are actually mediated by analytic personality constructs, but that it is not always necessary, or even possible, to make those mediating variables explicit. This may apply both when the purpose of the assessment is validation of the techniques or the carrying out of an actual selection. But when the purpose is personality research, some explicit handling of the constructs is advisable. The concept of construct validation supports this requirement by merging the validation and the personality research orientations.

Each of the three strategies has its particular uses in assessment programs. Where mass screening is required, the empirical strategy is usually best, if possible; where the criterion situation is complex and unrepeatable, but familiar to the assessors, the global approach is to be preferred, and where the relevant personality theory has attained a sufficient level of development, the analytic strategy is indicated. Where none of the basic requirements is present—a repeatable and reliable criterion, familiarity of the criterion to the assessors, or appropriate personality theory—the assessors have to choose the strategy that seems best, although no strategy can really redeem such a hopeless situation. In general, personality assessors being what they are, they will prefer a largely intuitive approach, either analytic or global, as they did in the WOSB and OSS situations, but an increasing respect seems to be paid to the need for illuminating these intuitive methods by empirical analysis wherever possible.

Some Specific Issues in Assessment As a Method of Predicting

Clinical Versus Statistical Approaches

We have argued that there are occasions when intuitive methods of making predictions, i.e., "clinical" have their appropriate place. Statistical methods cannot be used where no prediction formula exists. But some personality assessors speak as if the clinical method is always to be preferred as it enables the assessor to be flexible in his use of the data in a way that is not possible with statistical techniques; for example, the clinician can give weight to obvious but rare and nonrepeatable factors in the subject's current situation which could not be validated empirically. Other advantages claimed for the clinical against the statistical approach are that it does not violate the essential unity of the subject's personality, and that it enables the use of empathy and recipathy in making the predictions. (Actually these subjective clues could also be used as data by the statistician along with other more objective data.)

Other assessors regard clinical techniques as only a last resort. A number of advantages can be quoted for statistical prediction over clinical, most of which boil down to the fact that the statistician has a far more efficient memory and a larger attention span than the clinician; he can "remember" the relevant data at the appropriate time and combine them with other data in order to obtain optimal weightings for future predications.

And so we have, on the one hand, the efficient but rigid and inhuman statistical prediction, and on the other, the flexible and humane but inefficient clinical. Which one is more useful in personality assessment? There are several discussions of this question available (e.g., Cronbach, 1956; Meehl, 1954; Holt, 1958; Sarbin, Taft, and Bailey, 1960; McArthur, 1954) so the points will not be elaborated fully here excepting in so far as they directly affect multiple personality assessment procedures.

The weight of the evidence clearly supports the accuracy of the statistical approach compared with the clinical. Meehl's notorious scoreboard (1954) recording the relative validity of clinical versus statistical prediction mounts grim evidence in favor of the latter. Holt (1958) criticizes Meehl's summary on the grounds that most of the studies pitted sophisticated, actuarial predictions against "naive clinical," while others (e.g., Wittman's) actually showed the superiority of "sophistical clinical" over naive clinical methods. But Meehl is quite clear about the rules of his contest: the rival methods start off with approximately the same objective and subjective data, although in some of the studies the clinician used additional subjective data. The important difference is that the reported statistical predictions were based on the naive empirical method of validation, while the clinical were either global or intuitively analytic. The statistical approaches were not concerned with the meaning of the correlations between the data and the criteria, although the use of cross-validation and statistical refinement meant that the empirical procedures were not as naive as it appeared, nor were they always uninformed by intervening personality constructs.

Holt pleads for the use of "sophisticated clinical methods," by which he means something similar to our analytic procedure, using intuition to make the final predictions. Among other things, he wants the clinicians to make preliminary studies of the criterion behavior in order to analyze the requirements for success. Holt does not take the step of requiring validation of the individual clinicians; but this is necessary to match fully the two sides in the contest. He reports that the best judges, using global clinical techniques, reached prediction validities of up to 0.57, whereas statistical treatment of the tests–regular Rorschach scoring (validated and cross-validated) and the Strong Interest Psychiatrist key–resulted in virtually zero validities. But Holt's contest is unfair to the statistical side. His experiment was a half-hearted affair; no attempt was made to develop objective tests that would be appropriate to the selection problem at hand, as was done in the VA and the IPAR studies, and on Holt's own admission the Strong key was validated a long time previously in an entirely different situation. Holt's report, as he himself indicates, does not provide us with a fair contest between sophisticated clinical and sophistical statistical approaches.

In recommending a sophisticated clinical approach, Holt argues that "there simply is no substitute for empirical study of the actual association between a type of predictive data and the criterion" (1958, p. 3). Despite this, the evidence of objective criterion analysis for the assessor (i.e., validation) is not promising. The assessors at Menninger were provided with "manuals" embodying validation material on the interview, TAT, Rorschach, and other assessment techniques that had been used in an earlier assessment of psychiatrists at Menninger. Holt's conclusion about their value reads as follows: "Of the six, two proved worthless . . . ; the other four all showed more or less promise, but *there was none that yielded consistently significant validities regardless of who used it*" (1958, p. 8, italics ours). Evidently, the assessors would not, or could not, use the validation data which were provided for them.

We are thus reminded once more that validation includes validation of the specific assessment task. Nearly all reports of personality assessments offer evidence that the assessors differ considerably in their predictive skill. These differences are made up of two types of variation; variation due to differences in general ability to judge people (Taft, 1955), and interaction effects between the assessor and the type of judgment called for (Crow & Hammond, 1957). The reports on assessments offer the hint that the highest validities are achieved by assessors who have the most familiarity with the criterion situations and with the type of person who is successful in those situations; for example, in the CISSB assessments, the Board of Review consisting of experienced civil service administrators made more accurate predictions than did the original CISSB selection committe. In the former, the most valid predictions were made by the chairmen who were also civil service administrators.

Accurate assessments are most likely to occur where the assessor uses the in-group stereotypes which are also held by the criterion raters; they are able to "play their predictions by ear" without any need to make the double inference involved in analytic techniques. In support of this method of predicting we can quote the comparatively high validities found for ratings of the "likeableness" of the candidates in the Michigan, Menninger, and IPAR assessments. For example, in the latter, the assessors were mainly university professors, and it is therefore not surprising that their ratings of "personal soundness" correlated as high as 0.52 with ratings made of the candidates on this quality by their own departmental professors (Barron, 1954). All other things being equal, the best assessors for predicting existing criteria are those who are partially contaminated with the same experience, standards, and outlook as the criterion raters and can thus rely on a global strategy to make their predictions. (The most accurate assessors are also more accurate than the most accurate, cross-validated tests.)

The validity of analytic methods is subject to the accuracy of the personality theory which the assessor uses, but psychologists usually possess fairly stable postulates, based on the lore of their discipline rather than behavior-oriented empirical research, and these are not readily changed in the light of actual empirical data. This is probably the reason why some of the Menninger assessors did not improve their accuracy with the help of the empirically-based "manual." The difficulty can be seen clearly if we consider the findings of the Minnesota starvation studies (Kjenaas & Brozek, 1952) that the Rorschach indices of adjustment had a negative validity in predicting ratings of the subject's adjustment after starvation. Could a typical clinical psychologist bring himself to reverse completely his normal interpretation of the Rorschach in order to predict the subject's adjustment under the criterion conditions? Not unless he were able to find an intervening variable between the Rorschach and the criterion that would enable him to understand the connection within the framework of his existing theory of personality.

Our discussion of clinical versus statistical methods of assessment has concentrated on one aspect of the procedure, the prediction-making stage. The contrast between these two approaches can be made in connection with a whole chain of decisions that must be made in the course of assessment: these decisions include determining the acceptable criteria, scoring the criterion analysis, determining the form of the tests and standard situations, observing and classifying the assessment behavior (i.e., scoring), combining the observations made by any single assessor into an assessment or prediction and combining the predictions made by different assessors. For example, should the individual assessments be combined subjectively by the chairman of an assessment board, by voting, or by averaging the individual predictions? Insufficient attention has been given to the relative merits of subjective and objective methods at each one of these stages.

The choice of method will depend on both the requirements and the over-all situation, including, sometimes, public relations considerations. The final selection of assessment techniques is likely to be a mixture of both subjective and objective, but the circumstances that will favor one or the other at any stage are rather vague, and the choice is usually made on subjective grounds, although it, too, could be made on the basis of objective, empirical investigation. In general, objective methods are to be preferred as far as possible as they maximize accuracy, but practical considerations of economy, convenience, and the limitations of the situation, dictate the wholesale use of subjective methods in personality assessment. These subjective methods may have high validity under favorable circumstances, and where the assessors are familiar with the criterion situation, clinical judgments may actually be more accurate than any objective methods are ever likely to be in predicting to criteria.

Conditional Variables in the Criterion

An old problem in evaluating the validity of prediction is set by variations in the criterion situation attributable to the surrounding conditions. For example, a prediction that a candidate will make a good officer may be invalidated through some contingency such as being posted to a commanding officer with whom he is incompatible. But these conditional factors do not stand on their own; there is an interaction between the person and the condition. Thus, Officer A may have the type of personality (or background) that makes it likely that he will be posted to a commanding officer with whom he will be incompatible; if, for instance, Candidate A is Jewish, he is more likely to have a CO who behaves uncongenially than is another candidate of a similar personality who is not Jewish. Further, Officer A may perform his duties better than otherwise when he has an uncongenial CO, while Officer B may perform his duties worse under the same circumstances. In most assessments, no specific reference is made to such conditional factors and there is an implicit assumption of "given normal conditions" attached to the predictions. The OSS reports a validity of only 0.19 for all cases from Station S compared with 0.39 for only the cases who were given assignments that were consistent with the ones for which they were assessed.

A further condition that is often ignored in assessment is that of effluxion of time; the predictions are usually made on the assumption that the status of the candidate on the relevant variables will remain constant over time. At a more sophisticated level, trends towards change may be observed in the candidate together with potential but as yet unrealized capacities, and the assessment may extrapolate these into the future. But it is virtually impossible to take into account subsequent learning, maturation and deterioration in the assessment prediction.

In this connection, Cronbach and Gleser (1957) have proposed a useful distinction between fixed treatment (the same conditions for all successful candidates) and adaptive treatments varying according to the candidate. Evidently the treatment of the OSS selectees was fixed rather than adaptive, and the predictions should have taken this into account. Five different types of solutions are suggested below for the problem of conditional factors in these treatments. Solutions 1 and 3 being particularly appropriate to fixed treatments, and the other three to adaptive. (These represent an expansion of the three solutions proposed in Horst, 1941, ch. 5.)

1. Adjust the criterion ratings ex post facto according to the ease or difficulty presented to the candidate by the criterion conditions and the effects of these conditions on him over the relevant period of time. This adjustment requires an intuitive judgment that takes into account the interaction between the conditions and the candidate, and this can be done only by the rater making a further, independent assessment of the candidate. For the validation to carry conviction, it is necessary that the adjustment to the criterion rating be made independently of the assessment.

2. Make the predictions to the ideal possible conditions so that they represent the candidate's fullest potential; the criterion ratings can then be made in accordance with the same standards. In other words, both assessment and prediction attempt to hold conditions constant in the form that is considered to be optimal for the candidate's performance. The actual conditions applying at the time of assessment and during the criterion performance are unlikely to be optimal no matter how hard this state is sought, so that the use of this solution rests very heavily on intuition.

3. Predict to the average or modal conditions that have prevailed in the past with respect to the criterion situation, or which are expected to prevail in the future. This is the usual orientation in assessments based on empirical validation since the correlations on which the validities are based are in effect averages. The empirical strategy automatically takes into account the variations in conditions as well as their average effect and maximizes the prediction to these average conditions. The conditions, thus, influence the assessment only through their effects on the criterion performance, without regard to their specific nature. It is practically impossible for a clinician to average all possible relevant conditions by an intuitive act, although it is common for a clinician to bear in mind the modal conditions which candidates face when these are prominent.

4. The future conditions may be predicted specifically for each candidate so that the interaction between the candidate and the criterion conditions may be anticipated in the assessment. The prediction to the future conditions may be made on the basis of inside knowledge of the treatment to be given to the candidates in the criterion situation, or by forecasting on general grounds the specific changes that will occur in the conditions before the criterion ratings are

made. Such predictions must be intuitive rather than empirical, and, by the nature of the complexity of man's environment, all such intuitive predictions must fall well short of perfect validity. In some complex situations, in which the criterion performance is highly dependent on the conditions, the inability of the assessors to predict the specific conditions that will operate for any particular candidate may render the assessments completely invalid.

5. The predictions themselves can be made in terms of specific conditions: "if *X* conditions occur, then the candidate will be successful." In this endeavor, the recent proposal by Cattell (1957, pp. 426ff.) for a taxonomy of situations might eventually supply a list of standard situations to be considered in conditional predictions.

Solutions 4 and 5 are both specific conditional solutions which can take into account the effects of conditions that are external to the candidate, as well as intrinsic conditions such as maturation. They require both a knowledge of the criteria requirements and a correct assessment of the candidate, but the first type of conditional prediction emphasizes the criterion situation, and the second, the candidate. Both of these latter methods of meeting the problem of conditions are adaptable to taking into account multiple conditions and also "adaptive treatments" such as provisions for training that are tailor-made for the candidate. They hold out the possibility of making more exact predictions than can be made by the other three attempted solutions to the problem. This is one of the reasons why the global strategy, or slightly analytic versions of it, have been so often favored in selection assessment programs. But these conditional predictions are also the most difficult to make, and only the best judges of personality or the ones who are most experienced with the criteria conditions are able to make them accurately, and then only in appropriate situations.

The decision as to the appropriate solution to the problem of varying conditions is closely related to the choice of strategy. In the long run the choice is one between elegance and the practical limitations that are imposed on the possibilities of accuracy.

The Assumption of Safety in Numbers

Personality assessment programs rely on numbers to improve their validity in two directions: multiple tests and multiple assessments. We shall treat the evidence concerning these two points separately.

Multiple Tests. Where the tests and other assessment measures are combined objectively, for example, in accordance with a multiple regression equation, even the most valid test can usually be improved upon by adding one or two further measures to it. It is often striking, however, how quickly the multiple Rs reach their ceiling; the common components of almost all available personality measures seem to be so high that we quickly exhaust the new elements that additional tests can bring to the predictions. The same applies when the combining of elements is carried out intuitively; even though the clinician may believe that the pieces of information about a candidate are independent of each other. It is doubtful whether a clinician can use more than a few pieces of data that are relatively independent, even if they can be found. Sarbin (1942), for instance, demonstrated that clinicians who were given a mass of data from which to predict the success of university students, gave most of the weight to two variables only.

Evidently, to give a clinician more than two or three pieces of data about an assessee is likely to be of little value. Some critics go even further, claiming that giving extra data actually reduces validities by confusing the allocation of subjective weights to the predictor variables, and by increasing the variability of the predictions, i.e., inducing the clinician to venture into making extreme judgments which increase the risk of making large errors. Kelly and Fiske (1950) claim that in the Michigan study validities declined as more data were given to the assessors. Holt challenges the accuracy of their interpretation of the findings (1958, p. 8) but even so there are other studies that suggest that more data do not always improve accuracy (e.g., Gage, 1953; Giedt, 1955; Kostlan, 1954; Soskin, 1954). In Giedt's study, for instance, the clinicians were able to make more valid predictions of mental patients' personalities from sound recordings than from sound movies.

But there are several studies affirming that, at least under some circumstances, more data do enable clinicians to improve their accuracy. We have already referred to Vernon's report (1950) that in the CISSB selections the Board of Review was able to improve on the assessment board's recommendations by combining these with their own interview impressions of the candidate. Increased validity with increased data is also reported for the California (Mackinnon, 1951), Chicago (Stern, Stein, & Bloom, 1956), and Menninger (Holt, 1958) assessments.

We must suspend our verdict on the value of multiple data at this stage. Evidently there are circumstances that can overcome the limitations on the ability of a single assessor to hold in mind data and to combine them. One suggestion worth testing is to combine data into subdecisions of an increasing degree of molarity, until the final molar decision is reached. This procedure can assist the clinician to consider all of the data in reaching his final decision and it is analogous to the use of structured schedules and rating forms that are used by interviewers to consolidate portions of the data as they go along. This technique as a general aid to clinical judgments seems worth experimenting with, although the danger must be avoided of giving too much weight to the data that are presented first. In this respect it would seem to be wise to seek out first the data that are believed to be the most valid.

Another way of handling the combining of data is to use several assessors, each responsible for one or two different techniques or areas of personality. This was the method adopted, for example, in the CISSB assessments. This proposal carries over to the general question of using multiple assessors and we shall consider it further below.

Multiple Assessors. The practice of using more than one assessor in selection work is an old one; the assumption has been that the more assessors there are, the more ideas will be thrown into the pool and therefore the more thorough will be the marshalling of data. Where ratings are pooled, it is also hoped that errors will cancel each other out. Very little experimental material is available on the relative value of group versus individual judgments in personality assessments, but evidence can be used from other work on other types of group performance (see Kelly & Thibaut, 1954; Klein, 1956, ch. 1; Argyle, 1957, ch. 5).

These findings suggest, among other things, that accuracy of judgments increases with the size of the group, but the optimum number in informal problem-solving groups is possibly five, since larger groups require formal structuring in order to ensure adequate communication of information; that compatible membership is important in problem-solving committees; that democratic groups produce more different ideas than individuals but fewer per person; that the quality of group decisions increases with an increase in the skill of the members; that groups are quicker at solving problems than individuals, although less economical in terms of man-minutes. However, these findings vary according to the type of task concerned, and before we can carry them over to personality assessment it is necessary to bear the type of task in mind.

Some of the questions that should be asked concerning group factors in personality assessment are: are group ratings more accurate than those of the individual members of the group; does group discussion by the assessors improve accuracy over pooled individual ratings; what is the relative value of means, modes, and medians as methods of pooling; the ideal size of committees; committee ratings versus averaging; authoritarian leadership of assessment committees versus democratic; should all of the committee members be given the same data; should both the observations and the interpretation be made by groups? These questions can be considered at three points in the assessment procedures: (*a*) in making subjective observations of the subjects; and (*b*) in eliciting data from the subjects; and (*c*) in integrating and intepreting the data, and making the decision.

(*a*) At the observation level, we should expect that the pooled ratings of several observers would be more accurate than individual ratings, since pooling reduces the error variance, provided always that the individual judgments have some validity in the first place (*cf.* Kelley & Thibaut, 1954, p. 739).

(*b*) The value of the group interview versus individual interviews as a means of eliciting data is equivocal (see the discussion in Oldfield, 1947). A recent study (Glaser, Schwarz, & Flanagan, 1958) on the selection of supervisors found that individual ratings based on group interviews by a panel of three were no more accurate than the ratings made by one interviewer per candidate. While it is true that the group situation may elicit a wider sample of behavior than an individual interview, it is more difficult for an interviewer to evaluate the significance of the group as the stimulus to which the candidate is responding. However, if the interviewing is conducted by the chairmen only, while the other assessors are simply observers, this may enable the assessors to make more unbiased judgments than when they are actually involved in the interviewing. This effect still remains to be tested empirically.

(*c*) The usual consideration of the value of group assessment versus individual deals with the integration of the available data. As in the case of group observations, pooled predictions are more accurate than most or all of the individual predictions (Klugman, 1947; Luborsky & Holt, 1957; Travers, 1941). In one study (Smith, 1932) of assessing the qualities of a child on the basis of behavioral data, the accuracy increased with an increase up to 50 of the number of assessors whose ratings were pooled (there were only 50 assessors available).

Does discussion prior to assessment increase accuracy? The evidence on this suggests that it does not (Rusmore, 1944; Taylor, 1947; Kelly & Fiske, 1951; Oldfield, 1947). As Oldfield puts it: "Discussion of the merits of candidates merely amounts to a somewhat clumsy method of averaging the individual judgments of the members" (1947, p. 129). Whether discussion aids accuracy or not appears to depend on the quality of the persons who dominate the discussion either through their position in the group, their personality, or their professional standing. Discussion is justified particularly when there is an "expert" as chairman, who will actually make the final decision in an autocratic manner, but who calls on the other members of the panel to give him the benefit of their opinions. An "expert" is defined, for this purpose, as a person who is experienced both in assessment and in the criterion situations.

Kelly and Fiske are quite pessimistic regarding the use of multiple assessors. "Until some of the major sources of error in predictions are eliminated, the replications of assessors and the use of staff conferences hardly seems justified for this type of prediction" (1951, p. 178). This conclusion is too sweeping. As we can see from Table 1, both pooled and committee (discussion) ratings have justified themselves in some studies.

Let us conclude this section on the "safety in numbers" assumption with a proposal to combine the advantages of both multiple techniques and multiple assessors. The suggestion is that each assessor be given a limited amount of information on which to base his assessment judgments about the candidates, each assessor to receive different information. The assessments will then be pooled arithmetically. The information supplied may be objective or subjective, atomistic or molar, and may range from one item of life-history, or a test result, to a projective test protocol, an interview or the observation of behavior in a miniature situation. This procedure would enable a vast amount of data to be integrated without problems of weighting since unit weights for each assessor's contribution would be adequate—this would be analogous to an inventory that gives unit weight to each item. With adequate organization of the assessment program, this would permit several assessors to contribute to the final assessment so that different viewpoints and personality theories can be represented. This approach seems to be at least worth experimenting with.

Even if it is found that increased numbers of assessors increases perceptibly the accuracy of the assessments, there is still a fine calculus of cost in human time and effort to be computed. The decision to augment the panel with additional assessors is a function, among other things, of the gradient of diminishing returns, the ability of available extra assessors, the cost of using them, the effects on the candidates, and the desire to allow executives in the institution to participate in the assessment. The proposal made above of having many assessors, who contribute small peices of information, may make it possible to conduct multiple assessments comparatively cheaply.

Summary

Multiple personality assessment procedures have been analyzed with respect to their primary purpose and the validation strategy used. Problems that arise in the attempt to use personality assessment for selection were discussed with respect to the problem of clinical versus statistical predictions, the problem of conditional factors that affect the criteria, and the value of using multiple tests and more than one assessor.

Some recommendations:

1. Use objective techniques as far as possible for analyzing the criterion, for scoring tests, and for making predictions.
2. Give careful consideration to requirements of the criterion and make empirical studies of the link between these requirements and both the test behavior and the criterion behavior. This is a step in construct validation.
3. As a preliminary to the above type of criterion analysis, nonmediate empirical or clinical methods of prediction may be used.
4. Subjective observations should be made by several observers whose opinions should be pooled arithmetically.
5. The assessors should be selected for proven ability to make accurate judgments in the assessment situation, i.e., they should be validated.
6. The assessors should be familiar with the criterion situation, and should take this situation into account when they make the predictions.
7. Each assessor should be given no more than two or three units of information; there should be a large number of assessors whose predictions are pooled arithmetically, and without discussion.

8. In selection assessments, if committee decisions are desired, the assessors who are particularly well-experienced in the criterion situation should be given special influence in forming the final decisions, provided they have been shown to possess good ability to judge persons.

Chapter 2

Definitions and Concepts

Most observers of the behavior of other people note that behavior occurs in recurring patterns. The individual who is fussy and crabby in one situation is likely to be fussy and crabby in other situations. The "life of the party" tends to be seen as generally exuberant and boisterous. Observations such as these have led most serious students of human behavior to posit some underlying, internal process to account for these regularities. This process, most often called "personality," is never directly observable and can only be known through the study of its products, overt behavior.

There are some recent critics, notably Mischel (1968), who argue that the persistence of these individual characteristics is more apparent than real and is more a function of our descriptive language for labeling behavior than any real similarity. Furthermore, Mischel argues that much of what appears to be regularities in human behavior are situationally rather than intrapsychically determined. Nevertheless, most psychologists have searched and will continue to search for an understanding of that elusive internal process, the functioning of the human personality.

Personality is one of the most confusing areas to study in contemporary psychology since it is a process that can only be inferred from observable behavior and psychologists tend to study different behaviors and have different ideas on how to make inferences about internal, human processes. The student of personality is often overwhelmed by a plethora of theories and concepts which are often vague, overlapping, and not readily translatable from one system to another.

With the study of personality functioning itself in a confused and confusing state, it is no surprise to discover that the field of personality assessment is in a similar, unsatisfactory state of development. The dimensions of personality functioning which are presumably measured by different instruments, are often difficult to relate to each other and the beginning student is often confused about how to proceed in the task of personality assessment or evaluation.

There are two general reasons for personality assessment: first, to assist in gaining an understanding of the behavior of another person, that is, for the clinical assessment of a single individual; and, second, in the context of psychological research and theory building, to advance our general understanding of human behavior. The most frequent application of personality assessment instruments has been in the first context, the clinical assessment of individuals.

While it is possible clearly to differentiate these two purposes, it must be noted that they are tightly interconnected. In order to understand the behavior of a single individual, one presumably should have some theory, or set of interrelated concepts, about personality functioning; otherwise there can be no way of integrating and understanding the observed data. As noted above, many such notions or approaches have been advanced, which accounts for much of the current confusion in the field of personality and personality assessment. While it may be argued that none of these approaches to personality functioning has reached the status of a theory in the strictest scientific sense, a number of these conceptualizations are worthy of more careful examination.

Before we turn to these more systematic approaches, however, it is worthwhile to recognize that all of us make personality interpretations about the people we meet in our daily lives, interpretations based on our informal observation of their behavior. These interpretations are most often made in a habitual and an unaware, if not unconscious, fashion. The first reading in this chapter, an excerpt from the writings of Philip Vernon, surveys these intuitive, informal, and largely unconscious, but well-developed, processes by which we perceive and interpret the behavior, motives, and personality of others. In Vernon's analysis people are not explicitly aware of the cues that they note in other people's appearance and expressions, but interpret these cues directly as expressing some underlying personality characteristics. Vernon also points out that it is typical for most of us to make some effort to create a favorable impression on others, while simultaneously attempting to penetrate the facade the others are presenting. A number of sources of error that normally operate in intuitive assessments of this nature, such as the tendency to oversimplify and overgeneralize, and distortions resulting from the perceiver's own motivations and needs, are also discussed by Vernon.

Turning to the more systematic approaches to personality, we find that most of the formal assessment methods in use tend to be oriented toward a relatively specific practical goal, and that they either utilize a minimum of explicit theory or are based in a framework that is poorly defined. As the study of personality becomes more sophisticated, however, at least some of the methods for personality assessment will tend to become more solidly based within theoretical frameworks. The next two readings present well-known but highly divergent viewpoints about the framework within which personality can most usefully be understood, and on which assessment procedures could be based. One, that of personality theorist Gordon Allport, argues for a much more concentrated study of *individual* persons and for the development of a science based on the study of particular individuals. Allport argues that frameworks for studying personality that are based on *general* dimensions and principles tend to obscure what is critical in the understanding of individuals, namely, the countless unique experiences and idiosyncracies from which the essential individuality of the person emerges. Although his approach is obviously oriented toward the clinical use of assessment procedures, Allport also feels that a greater emphasis on the individual is necessary for the advancement of the psychology of personality as a field of inquiry.

The other framework for the study of personality, presented by I. E. Farber, is a central statement of the social learning or behaviorist tradition, and this framework differs from Allport's in a number of critical ways. In Farber's view, there is no meaningful distinction between the study of personality and the study of behavior in general. Furthermore, the understanding of the individual can proceed only as general laws and principles of behavior are discovered and empirically validated. Thus, clinical assessment logically should await the development of theoretical bases for understanding behavior in general. In this deterministic framework for the study of personality, there is no discontinuity between the simple behavior of laboratory organisms and the complex actions of humans, though Farber, among others, notes that sufficient scientific knowledge to enable generalizations of clinical utility are simply not available at the present time.

After these excursions into differing theoretical viewpoints concerning the appropriate conceptual basis for personality assessment, we might inquire about the manner in which systematic personality assessment is actually carried out in contemporary psychological practice. Unfortunately, recent information is not available on this topic; some interesting trends, however, are revealed in an article by Norman Sundberg, who conducted a survey of psychological testing practices in 1959 and compared the results with previous data obtained in 1935 and 1946. Two of

Sundberg's findings are notable: the widespread use of personality tests and the sheer volume of their usage, and the heavy reliance on projective methods of assessment, whose interpretation is more intuitive and individualistic rather than based on general or formal norms. Since the time of Sundberg's writing, important advances have taken place in the development of empirical rules and "cookbooks" for personality assessment, and this work has undoubtedly had significant impact on more recent clinical assessment practices. It should be noted that these newer empirical procedures tend to be *less,* rather than more, theory-oriented than the projective methods and thus do not represent any advance toward Farber's criterion for sophisticated assessment procedures. The development of assessment procedures based on a behavior theory approach is presented in a later reading by Kanfer and Saslow.

1. PERCEPTIONS AND MISPERCEPTIONS OF PEOPLE

Philip E. Vernon

Our first task will be to study the processes whereby the ordinary man judges the personalities of those he meets. What theories of personality does he assume, and how can we account for his successes and his failures? This topic received comparatively little attention until the post-war years. In the 1920's and 30's psychologists were more concerned with the reliability and accuracy of the interview, of ratings or of judgments of expressions. And they demonstrated repeatedly the fallibility and bias of our judgments of ourselves and others. Much ingenuity, also, went into investigations of the characteristics of the "good" or "poor" judge of personality. However, in the 1950's there began a spate of publications on *how* we judge, under the headings "person perception" or "social perception." The suitability of these terms might be queried in so far as we interpret, judge, analyse and evaluate, over and above seeing or perceiving people's characteristics. It is not only in Britain that the problem was neglected until fairly recently. Its popularization in America was due largely to immigrants from Europe, including Heider and Ichheiser, W. Wolff and Arnheim, and the leading Gestalt psychologists.

SOURCE. Philip E. Vernon is a British psychologist, currently Professor of Psychology at the University of London's Institute of Education. Dr. Vernon previously was chairman of the Department of Psychology at Londanhill Training College, Glasgow, Scotland. His research contributions have included the psychology of music appreciation, cultural and environmental factors in intellectual development, personality assessment, and selection and guidance. This article originally appeared as Chapter 2 of *Personality Assessment,* London: Methuen, 1964, pp. 25-45. Reprinted by permission of Methuen and the author.

Our Ignorance of How We Interpret

The ordinary adult or child cannot formulate explicitly how he interprets, any more than he can explain how he walks or reads; though if pressed he could mention some of the signs or *cues* he uses: that when people blush they are embarrassed, if they yawn they are tired or bored, and so on. And he can often produce saws or generalizations which, he believes at least, guide his understanding: "children should be seen but not heard," "you can't teach an old dog new tricks," "most actors and actresses are unstable," "Jews are clever but unreliable," and so forth. Much as a child learns and applies grammatical rules without having been taught grammar, when he says: "I eated my dinner," so we shall find that A judges B, and B judges A, according to quite systematic though implicit (i.e., largely unconscious) principles. At the same time, much of what we have to say in this chapter must seem platitudinous if it is to describe correctly something we are doing all the time.

Our unsophisticated Mr or Mrs A does not think of interpretation as a problem. He or she *sees* B as "irritated," "looking for something," "domineering," just as he or she sees them "walk," or hears them "shout," and sees a chair as solid and brown and 3 feet tall. True, B is more variable, complicated and unpredictable than things are, but that is because B is regarded as a person with thoughts and feelings like A's. He is a self-activating being, and he is not entirely unpredictable if A understands him aright. A thinks of himself as consistent and logical, and expects B to be the same. Note that "being a person" is a matter of degree rather than of kind, depending on the extent to which people affect us personally. The teeming millions of China, India and Africa tend to seem more "object-like," less human than dwellers in our own slums, than even our pet dog. And slum-dwellers, or strangers seen in a bus, have less person-quality than our acquaintances.

Now a moment's thought will show that B's "domineeringness" or his subjective states cannot be physical stimuli which are directly seen, that they are somehow inferred from B's behaviour. But thinking a stage further, we realize that perhaps this is not so different from the perception of physical objects. The "solidity" of the chair is not given either; it is an inference from A's past experience of touching and handling chairs. In both instances A assigns "dispositional qualities" to the percept (Heider, 1958). The chair looks comfortable–it possesses the quality or trait of comfortableness; B looks amiable–he has a disposition or trait of amiability. And just as A's judgment of the chair is usually borne out when he subsequently sits in it, so his readings of B's dispositions, thoughts and feelings normally seem to be confirmed. At the same time, these qualities are definitely referred to the object or person. If A is pricked, the sensation of pain is subjective–it happens to him; but he regards the sharpness of the pin as objective. So too is B's amiability.

Behaviour Is "Explained" by References to Intentions

Dispositions and traits, intentions, motives and attitudes, interests and abilities play a crucial part in our interpretations of people, since it is these that give consistency and stability to what might otherwise be a chaotic series of actions. If an observer from another planet saw B preparing a meal or arguing with his teenage son, the successive bits of behaviour might seem fragmentary, arbitrary and inexplicable; but to A, who realizes the underlying intention, they fall into line. A similar observation was made by Hebb (1946) when studying chimpanzees, namely that records of their specific actions were meaningless, but they became intelligible when grouped into general categories and related to preceding actions. It was impossible to give a complete description without resorting to anthropomorphic interpretations of the animals' wants and feelings. Others have shown that certain sequences of physical stimuli readily evoke animistic impressions of causation and motivation.

> In a long series of experiments on the perception of moving squares, Michotte (1946) found that one square was seen as "launching" or "pushing" or "carrying along" a second one, and concluded that we have an innate disposition to perceive mechanical causality directly. In other situations, purpose or "intentionality" might be inferred. Similarly, Heider and Simmel (1944) presented a short film in which two triangles and a circle moved in or out of a rectangle with a door in it (Fig. 1). Almost all his observers described one triangle as "chasing" or "hitting" the other, the circle as "hiding to escape." The large triangle was "aggressive," the smaller "heroic," the circle "timid and feminine."

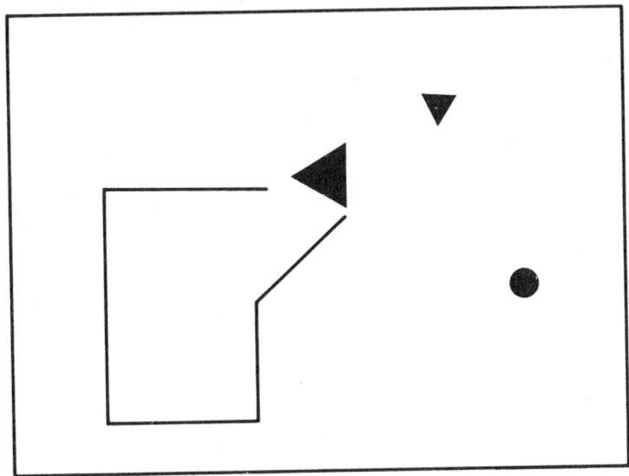

Figure 1. Apparent behavior geometrical figures. (From Heider and Simmel, 1944)

From (1960) goes so far as to claim that it is impossible for us to perceive behaviour as such; what we think we see always depends on the intention that we ascribe to the person. And if he should act in some unexpected fashion, we say that he has made a mistake or changed his mind, not that we were wrong in our interpretation.

Invariance of Dispositional Qualities

Behaviour is variable also in the sense that many different actions seem to stem from the same disposition. B's amiability may be shown at one time by his facial expression or tone of voice, at other times by the opinions he states in a discussion, or by various kindly acts that he performs towards C or D. The same end may be achieved by diverse means. Likewise there is no one definable pattern of behaviour which is always recognized as a cue for amiability, or other such traits, but rather a kind of theme with variations. Indeed the significance of any one cue depends a good deal on the circumstances. An action which is kind to C, who is a weak and undeserving person, might be taken to imply currying favour if performed for D, who is a popular and powerful person. Note, moreover, that dispositional qualities—traits, abilities, interests and the like—are assumed to persist in the individual whether or not he is displaying them at the moment. We recognize that, under conditions of stress, he may behave out of accord with these qualities.

This invariance or stability in the trait or intention, despite variable appearances and temporary lapses, is particularly striking in the interpretation of people; but it occurs also in our identification of objects, for example in so-called phenomenal regression and the "constancy phenomenon." A circular white dinner-plate, a foot across, is seen as such whether it constitutes a large stimulus close to the eyes, or a tiny stimulus 30 feet away, when it is a narrow ellipse seen on its side, and even when the illumination is so dim that it reflects no more light into the eye than a dull grey surface. Similarly a person's physical characteristics are perceived as highly constant. When he walks from a spot 10 feet away to another 20 feet away, he certainly does not appear to halve his size. However, constancy is limited; for if we see people from the top of a tall building, they tend to lose this human or person quality, and look like ridiculous ants. Again, while constancy of colour can be demonstrated, and is certainly a dispositional quality of the object, yet a blue dress will become greenish in yellow illumination, and a human face looks ghostly in the light of mercury vapour lamps.

> Ittelson and Slack (1958) and Cantril (1957) report experiments in which perceptual distortions were induced by wearing aniseikonic lenses, or by viewing people in an Ames distorted room. They claim to have found greater stability or freedom from distortion in perceiving familiar people

than strange people, and greater for persons in authority than for less important people, though the differences were fairly small.

A number of other parallels between Gestalt characteristics in visual perception and characteristics of person perception have been pointed out, e.g. by Heider (1958) and MacLeod (1960). True, considerable caution is needed before assuming that the perception of personal qualities is essentially identical with the perception of meaningless shapes. Yet equally it might be questioned whether perceptual phenomena observed under controlled laboratory conditions fully cover the normal perception of objects and occurrences in our everyday environment.

Cues and Their Interpretation

What are the cues or stimuli on which our judgments of people are based? The following list is modified from Ichheiser (1949):

1. *Static or physical factors:* facial appearance, physique, also such modes of expression as clothes, personal adornment, furnishings of home, etc. Although, as we shall see, these are quite inaccurate as indicators of enduring personality traits, they do enable A to classify B's social *roles.* By identifying his sex, age, often his nationality and social class, or his job, he can anticipate the patterns of behaviour and attitudes associated with these categories, and adapt his own behaviour accordingly.
2. *Dynamic or expressive factors:* movements of the features and limbs, vocal and speech qualities. These allow A to judge temporary moods with some facility, but he is also likely to extrapolate and interpret such enduring dispositional qualities as energy, vivacity, caution, seriousness, insincerity, etc.
3. *Content factors: What* he does rather than how he does it. In this and the preceding category, it may be possible to specify just what cues are operating. They may influence A subconsciously, or produce an affective rather than a cognitive response. Rommetveit (1960) provided an experimental demonstration of this process of "discrimination without awareness." But this feature too is not peculiar to the interpretation of persons. We are seldom aware of the bases of our judgments of spatial characteristics such as distance and solidity. The tennis player would find it hard to specify how he tells what kind of shot his opponent is playing; still less could he analyse all the components that make up his responses, i.e. his own strokes.
4. *Situational factors:* the context in which the behaviour occurs, whether realized or not.
5. *Communications from other people:* what A has previously heard about B.
6. *Communications from the person himself:* This category is usually regarded as the least trustworthy, not to be taken at its face value, unless it is backed up by previous knowledge of B's sincerity, by evidence of behaviour (No. 3) and judgments of expression (No. 2), for example, the

definiteness and clarity of his speech and its relevance, the keenness and interest he displays. Indeed, in contacts between persons other than close friends and relatives, the participants normally take it for granted that each is "playing a part," that the visible expressions, actions and speech are chosen to create a favourable impression and to ward off, as far as possible, any revelation of the "real" self or Ego.

Much as perception of the world around us is inextricably entangled with inferences based on past experience, so too, even in quite casual social contacts, we carry out elaborate analyses of, and inferences from, the cues that others present. Heider (1958) provides a detailed description of the components which seem to enter into these judgments.[1]

As an example, let us suppose that A is visiting B's home and observes him adjusting the television set for a ballet programme. He weighs up *situational factors* that help or hinder (age of set, positioning, etc.) and may ascribe B's success or failure in part to *luck* (e.g. interference conditions). He also tends to differentiate between "can," "tries," "wants," and "why." Failure may be due to lack of skill–he *cannot;* or to lack of persistence and keenness–he does not *try* and this is because he does not *want* it sufficiently. But in addition "want" is complex. The reason "why" or the goal may be:

(i) B's own wish, or interest in ballet. This may be subdivided into intrinsic attractiveness–the ballet is "good" in the same way as sugar is sweet; and idiosyncratic attraction–B's particular taste.

(ii) Some temporary feeling rather than an enduring disposition, e.g. he is tired, or upset by some extraneous circumstance.

(iii) Some secondary motive–e.g. to appear cultured, although he will be bored.

(iv) He is asked to by the other guests or knows they would appreciate it, i.e. the degree of provocation as distinct from personal responsibility. If, in A's estimation, B would not find the action *personally satisfying,* then he is absolved, and this forms one of the most crucial elements in any judgment. Thus, if A had said that he would prefer to watch a political broadcast, he would be angered by B's action, unless he believed that B was not *at fault,* or realized that he had *tried,* but *could not* through lack of skill or situational handicaps.

A similar analysis might be made of the interviewer's interpretation of a candidate's motivations in an employment interview. Indeed, the good interviewer will try to establish much more explicitly the parts played by luck, opportunity, ability, superficial and deeper motives, in exploring the candidate's previous successes or failures.

[1]Both Heider's account, and our own brief summary, consist too largely of 'armchair' speculation, and more empirical data on the kinds of analyses that different judges carry out are badly needed.

Types of Social Interactions

However, the components that A looks for, and his interpretations, may vary considerably with the type of social interaction between A and B, i.e., with the situation or context (cf. Sarbin, Taft and Bailey, 1960; Jones and Thibaut, 1958). We may distinguish the following:

1. Giving and receiving information, e.g. a social survey interview, a purchase in a shop, etc. Here, A is particularly on the lookout for B's reliability, candour, his objectivity, prejudice, his relevant knowledge and experience. In the survey situation, B is suspicious of any threat to his values, intrusions on his personal affairs, and therefore attempts to assess A's role and his motive for making the inquiry.
2. Social rituals, e.g. meeting people at a cocktail party. These might well be compared to dogs sniffing each other's tails, the object being simply to assess status or dominance and role. A looks for cues which will tell him who B is, in order to behave appropriately, while also striving to maintain his own position in the social hierarchy. Each also avoids expressing any attitudes strongly, being reluctant to give away cues to his own personality until he knows that the other will not disapprove.
3. Obtaining support for one's attitudes and values. A wishes to know if B thinks as he does; if not, he will tend to devaluate B as a person. Is he compatible as a friend or work-mate; does he flatter A's self-esteem and help or hinder his needs? In most ordinary social intercourse between acquaintances the approach is strongly normative; each is assessing the other in terms of good or bad.
4. Persuading people to do a job, buy something, etc. Here A looks for evidence of B's competence and dependability, his persuasibility and willingness, and his interest in his (A's) goals. Conversely, B is concerned with A's reliability in describing the proposition and his personal disinterestedness.
5. Directing people and being directed, e.g. the employer-employee, parent-child, or other such situations. A is primarily concerned with B's responsibility and his values or standards which he wishes to modify. But he usually takes careful account also of abilities and personal dispositions so as to avoid antagonizing B against the values he wants to communicate. Likewise, B assesses which approach to A will placate him and minimize the extent of the blow to his self-esteem.
6. Purposive analysis, as by a doctor, psychologist, social worker, counsellor, teacher, lawyer, novelist. This is a more logical and deliberate, if less evaluative, study of B's motives. Here, even more than in No. 1, B is on the alert to reveal only those cues which he is willing that A should know, and is concerned about A's trustworthiness and approval of him.

Note that in all these contacts there is an interplay; they are not just a matter of B providing stimuli for A. By addressing or answering someone, and letting him see us perform any action, we are revealing ourselves to his evaluation and, in a way, laying ourselves open to potential attack. Thus, we seldom look directly at another, or like to be looked at, for long, and are apt to become paralysed with stage-fright if, at a public function, large numbers of people are able to attack us with their eyes.

Many social situations, of course, contain two or more of these types. Thus the selection interview falls primarily under No. 6, but would include much of Nos. 2, 3 and 4. As Oldfield (1941) points out, the interviewer's main object should be to stimulate the candidate to display his "attitudes,"[2] through first establishing good rapport, then introducing a series of topics on which he will talk spontaneously, sometimes by arguing or stating his own attitudes, or by a variety of other tactics.

The Synthesis of Impressions

So far we have been concerned with the analytic aspects of interpreting people. But it should be stressed that the observer always tends to see the subject as a unitary whole, however fragmentary the cues. He is not a sum of his physical, dynamic and other qualities any more than a chair is perceived as an addition of certain dimensions and colours. At first sight (or on first hearing about him from others) he is an individual, and the information about more detailed qualities which is obtained from subsequent cues is integrated into this whole. Inconsistencies, variability or unintegratedness may indeed be perceived, but these tend to make us search for deeper motives or traits which reconcile them. As Bartlett (1932) described in his work on perception of, and memory for, complex drawings and stories, there is an "effort after meaning," a striving towards an integrated structure or good Gestalt. Links are more readily established because any one cue often carries multiple meanings and implications. Thus, if A sees that B is a cripple or a negro, or is told that B is a professor, he at once expects a whole series of qualities which he associates with these roles.

> This is illustrated by an experiment in which Haire and Grunes (1950) presented the following list of items to a group of college students, and asked them to describe what sort of person this man was:
>
> > "Works in a factory, reads a newspaper, goes to movies, average height, cracks jokes, strong and active."
>
> To a second similar group the same list was presented, but with the insertion of an additional word: "intelligent."

[2] It is not entirely clear what Oldfield means by attitudes; they are not just sentiments, beliefs and values (as in common American usage), but appear to include more general personal dispositions such as cautiousness, domineeringness, introversion, etc. They are both states of mind in the candidate and qualities of his behaviour.

> The first group had little difficulty in picturing the man, usually in rather patronizing tones, but the second group found it much harder to integrate the qualities. Some subjects denied the intrusive item, e.g. "He is intelligent, but not too much so, since he works in a factory," others promoted him to foreman, i.e. denying that he was a worker; and others qualified it so as to render it harmless, e.g. "He is intelligent but doesn't possess the initiative to rise above his group."

Asch (1946) showed that the significance of any one trait is affected by others with which it is associated. As in visual or auditory perception the whole is more than the sum of its parts. For example, to two groups he presented lists of traits differing in one item:

> intelligent, skilful, industrious, warm, determined, practical, cautious.
> intelligent, skilful, industrious, cold, determined, practical, cautious.

asking them to write "a characterization" of the person. He found that this alteration of one term produced a basic change in the subjects' impressions, and went on to show by similar experiments that some traits are more influential or central, while others are more peripheral and easily altered.

Asch's work has been justly criticized by Luchins (1948) on the grounds of the artificiality of experimental technique and poor control of conditions. Luchins points out that we do not normally perceive discrete qualities in people and then integrate them, nor even necessarily make use of the notion of traits at all in arriving at our impressions (unless told to by an investigator). However he does not deny the tendency to organize our impressions, though the structure may be looser and more inconsistent as between different judges than Asch and others have claimed.

In another study with adjectives, similar to Asch's, Wishner (1960) pointed out that those traits are most affected which correlate most highly with the altered item. In other words, this type of experiment does not necessarily support the view that A's synthesis of B's characteristics constitutes an unique Gestalt (cf. also Bruner *et al.*, 1958).

> An experiment by H. H. Kelley (1950) seems to bear a closer resemblance to real-life situations. A new instructor was introduced to a group of students by means of a brief sketch which included the words, either "a warm person" or "a cold person." After a class discussion period with him they rated him on a series of traits, and those whose preliminary cue was "warm" assessed him as more considerate, informal, social, popular, and humorous than those whose cue was "cold." Moreover, 56% of the former judges actually participated in the discussion as against 32% of the latter. However, ratings on intelligence, generosity, dominance, and getting ahead, were little affected by this cue. It did not merely raise or lower the

judges' all-round halo, but mainly influenced their perception of a cluster of related personality traits.

What we seem to arrive at is a mental image or model of the person, or as Oldfield calls it, a *homunculus,* which guide our reactions to him in any future situation. Thus, if A's first impression of B includes the idea of "pushingness," he will behave differently to him throughout that meeting, or at subsequent meetings. And though he will modify, clarify and expand his image as further cues are received, the initial judgment often remains dominant. The homunculus may or may not incorporate verbalized labels or names of traits, attitudes, etc., or visual images. Indeed it is as much an affective concept or sentiment towards the person (in McDougall's sense–a crystallization of feelings) as a cognitive picture. If A is asked for an opinion of B, he refers to it in formulating his answer, and if A is a job interviewer, he will try to match this "working model" (cf. Wilson, 1945) against what he considers to be the job requirements. We should note, too, that the homunculus is not usually constructed by conscious deliberation–it forms itself; and just because it is a synthesis, it would be very difficult for A to state on just what cues any particular feature is based. However, the scientifically minded vocational or clinical interviewer will often do his best to "validate" or test out his analysis of B's motivations by seeking additional evidence. For example, he will suspend judgment on B's "pushingness" until he has probed further into his past career and present relations with people.

Personality Displays

Complementary to the process of interpretation is the process whereby each participant attempts to influence the other's judgment by displaying an acceptable and impressive personality (cf. Goffman, 1956). Not only in important situations like the selection interview, but in trivial social contacts, B impersonates, or puts on what he considers an appropriate front or façade for A. Indeed it might be said that we change our personalities to suit the occasion as women change their clothes, but much more rapidly and with less conscious deliberation. To some extent B may calculate or plan to create a particular effect on A, but it is largely an automatic adjustment to the particular social situation and to B's assessment of A's expectations. Note also that we have taboos against discussing this;it would be as impolite to admit that we are not behaving "naturally" as it would be to talk about our private sexual or excretory functions. Moreover, the barriers against all these topics tend to be raised or lowered simultaneously; we behave more naturally and are more willing to discuss both impersonations and sex with our wives or with a psychotherapist than with a stranger. (A particularly interesting social phenomenon, analysed in great detail by Goffman, is the assumption of mutual "fronts" by two or more people, as when husband and wife back one another up at a party, or the sales staff in a shop combine to impress the customer.) Yet at the same time the participants are generally aware of what is going on, and do their best to penetrate the other's disguise.

Young children, of course, are not conversant with these rituals, and have to be kept out of adult functions because they are apt to give away information about their parents' private behaviour. However, they become indoctrinated remarkably early. Even at 3 years they are being taught to behave more circumspectly when visitors arrive. By 7 years they are displaying different personalities when the teacher is present or absent, and soon they are putting on "fronts" to other children appropriate to their own age. For example, they despise certain games or toys as babyish in front of their peers, though liking to play with them privately.

Two important points must be held over for later discussion. First: is there a real, natural or undisguised personality? Even when B is performing before a completely trusted friend or psychotherapist, or before no one at all, is he not his own audience, putting on behaviour which approximates to his internal standards and values, in just the same way as he adapts to others' expectations? And secondly, despite the variations with different audiences, is there not a fair degree of consistency—a personal style which he cannot readily disguise? Clearly, some traits, e.g. abilities and interests, are less modifiable than others. Some people, also, are less willing to modify and more rebellious against putting on conventional displays than others are.

Misinterpretations of Personality

Oversimplification

Let us consider now the main sources of errors and biases that are only too apt to arise in so complex a process as the interpretation of personality. A useful account is given by Ichheiser (1949), and at the head of his list is the tendency to oversimplify people, to exaggerate their consistency or invariance.

In our perception of the physical world, we usually assume that the mind's eye, as it were, somehow mirrors or photographs external reality directly. But it would be more correct to say that we merely use the incoming stimuli to construct a picture or model of the world which best serves our practical needs. M. D. Vernon (1952) points out that the essential function of perceiving is to maximize its stability and consistency, to see (and hear or feel) it as a world of familiar and enduring objects, while also developing sufficient sensitivity to be able to respond to any unfamiliarities or changes that might be potentially harmful or significant to us. Similarly, it is of the utmost importance to us personally, and to the stability of society, that people should be consistent and simple beings, who stay the same in different surroundings or at different times.

Both in object perception and personality interpretation we do not like ambiguity, complexity or unusualness, and therefore simplify down to what is essential from our standpoint. Hence the well-known tendency to see people in blacks *or* whites, as goodies or baddies, to overestimate their unity and to ignore their subtler variations. Normally A meets B only in a limited context, and extrapolates, assuming that B will be the same in other circumstances. The teacher sees a boy as badly behaved in school, and imputes his mother's favourable opinion of him at home to prejudice; and the mother reciprocates. Even the novelist or biographer, who appeals to us through his sensitivity to motives, is apt to simplify his characters down to a single theme (for example, Dickens and Emil Ludwig). The writer such as Boswell, who gives us the rich unintegratedness of a personality, is the exception (cf. Allport, 1961a). Most of us simply cannot hold the innumerable cues that a person provides in mind, and therefore have to select and over-generalize.

In so far as we ignore situational variations, we tend to overweight "personal responsibility" in analysing the sources of people's actions. Oversimplification is often associated with the kind of animism which Piaget has described in children's thinking–the tendency to attribute natural occurrences to human agencies rather than to physical factors. In children, this probably arises because their basic experiences of movement occur when *they* push or pull things. To quote an example from Watts (1944): if a young child is asked–"The clock stopped because . . . ?," he is likely to give such answers as, "Because father dropped it." Not until 7 or 8 years or later will impersonal, mechanical causes be invoked. As adults we are less anthropomorphic about physical events, but we are still apt to attribute complex social and economic occurrences to the personalities of certain individuals: for example the rise of fascism and all that it entails to the personal qualities of Mussolini and Hitler, or the difficulties of a commercial firm to the inefficiency of the manager, and so on. Similarly in everyday affairs, we are usually satisfied with imputing the behaviour of those we meet to a few stock motives or dispositions.

Rigidity

The exaggeration of personal consistency implies, too, that we are remarkably impermeable to contradictory evidence. Often we simply do not see behaviour, or hear speech, which does not fit in with our conception of a person, much as we don't see an object placed in an unusual context in the game of Hunt-the-Thimble. When tape recordings are made of vocational or social-survey interviews, it is often found that the interviewer, A, so largely anticipates what he is expecting B to say that he either does not allow him to complete, or even ignores, his answers (Kahn and Cannell, 1957). And if B gives qualified, uncertain or reluctant answers, A tends to sharpen or improve them in his recollection. Obviously this is a serious difficulty in inquiries into people's opinions on political, social and moral issues, since more often than not their attitudes *are* confused, ambiguous and inconsistent.

> In an experiment by Stanton and Baker (1942), five experienced interviewers were told to find out from a group of students which of a series of geometrical designs they had been shown previously. The interviewers were working from keys which supposedly gave the "correct" responses for each student. But even when the keys were false, they still tended to obtain positive results; i.e. they unwittingly recorded the students as recognizing the designs which they, the interviewers, believed to be correct.

Often, again, we resist admitting changes in the personalities of our acquaintances, as when our children grow up, or a friend alters markedly through going to university, getting married, or moving to a new job. We are not, of course, entirely impervious to contradictory evidence; indeed, with children, we expect them to change to some extent with growth. However, Ichheiser points out that what we perceive "in principle" may differ from what we interpet "in fact." A may acknowledge *theoretically* that B differs from what he thought, and yet *effectively* behave towards him as before. Often, indeed, we are genuinely unaware of our effective attitudes and would indignantly disclaim our snobbishness or our prejudice against negroes. This distinction may be related to that drawn earlier between the affective and the more cognitive, verbalizable aspects of the homunculus.

To a large extent people back us up in our interpretations, since they show us these aspects of their personalities of which they think we will approve. A does not realize that he himself is an important element in the situation to which B is reacting. This happens in the selection interview, where the candidate is extremely sensitive to what he thinks the interviewer wants, and chooses his answers in the light of any hints he can get from the interviewer's questions, tone of voice, manner, even pauses (the "frigid silence"), and other expressions of which the interviewer may be quite unaware. But the same is true of everyday social intercourse and of long-term contacts. The boy who is regarded as a delinquent at school tends to live up to his reputation. The unemployed man realizes that many think of him as unemployable (they attribute his position to his "own fault" rather than to situational factors), and this lowers his security and self-esteem until he accepts their judgment and actually becomes more and more unemployable.

Egocentricity and Projection

Experimental studies of personality ratings show that a major component in our judgments of almost any trait is the "halo" – a general good or bad impression. In part this derives from oversimplification, or failure to recognize that people can be high in some desirable traits, low in others. But in addition there is a strong tendency to evaluate people along the single dimension of how they affect us, and to assume egocentrically that most of their actions are directed towards helping or harming us. We dislike ambiguity also, and are apt to polarize people; they must be for us or against us, not qualified in their approval. If one is harmed by a person one doesn't know or whom one dislikes, e.g. if he steps on one's toe on a bus, it is a sign of his malignancy (personal responsibility), whereas if a friend does the same action, it is excused and attributed to situational factors or luck.

Again, we expect people's attitudes, beliefs and habits to be similar to our own; and if this is falsified we regain our peace of mind by concluding that there is something wrong with them–they are queer, outsiders, etc. This assumption that all right-minded people think as we do has been called "projection." However, as Cattell (1951) and Murstein and Pryor (1959) point out, the term projection has been variously interpreted. The present phenomenon should be distinguished both from Freudian projection–the attribution to others of our repressed impulses, and from the influence of personal factors on the perception of ambiguous stimuli, which occurs in projection tests. Note that our values are another example of constancies or absolutes, which we regard as independent of people's wishes. Meat *must* be eaten with cutlery, boys *should* fight for dominance and girls *shouldn't,* royalty *is* to be respected, just as grass *is* green, and a plate seen sideways on *is* circular.

This egocentricity in interpreting others is more marked among young children, as Piaget has shown, and among less educated people. The more sophisticated and insightful, possibly because they themselves have richer personalities, are better able to differentiate their evaluations from mere personal compatibility. For example they are more tolerant of foreigners, less apt to devaluate introverts if they themselves are extraverted, or conservatives if they are radicals, and vice versa.

> Howard and Berkowitz (1958) set up an experimental situation in which college students heard a number of evaluations of their performance at a complex task, and assessed these for accuracy. It was found that they regarded both over- and under-evaluations as inaccurate; i.e. they did not accept praise which exceeded their own levels of aspiration.
>
> This experiment suggests that Heider and Ichheiser (whom we have largely followed in analysing personality interpretation) tend to exaggerate our egocentricity. However, the conditions of the experiment were rather different from those of everyday social interactions. The students were well educated and it was not their values which were being approved or disapproved. Thus it is hardly surprising that they put more trust in their own internal standards of performance than in the evaluations by onlookers.

Frameworks of Interpretation

A number of lines of evidence indicate that it would be a mistake to reduce our guiding principle of judgment to a single dimension of congeniality-uncongeniality, or goodness-badness. Osgood's work (1957) on the "semantic differential," and George Kelly's (1955) studies of personal constructs show that different people have varied "frames of reference," or attitude systems.

Osgood took a series of concepts: "My father, Confusion, Lady, Sickness, Hatred, etc.," and had them rated by groups of subjects on a number of adjectival scales such as rough vs. smooth, thick vs. thin, large vs. small, etc. The subjects did not find this unduly difficult and gave fairly consistent judgments.

When correlations were calculated between the adjectival scales, there was considerable overlapping; and by factor analysis it was shown that they could be reduced to three main dimensions:

I. Evaluative: good-bad, beautiful-ugly, clean-dirty, fair-unfair, etc. In numerous investigations this has always proved to be the most outstanding factor.

II. Potency: large-small, strong-weak, heavy-light, etc.

III. Activity: fast-slow, active-passive, excited-calm, etc.

In other words, our classificatory system, either for people's traits or for other abstract concepts, though largely evaluative, does recognize other aspects and dimensions.

> A later analysis by Osgood (1962) of a more heterogeneous set of 40 epithets, applied to 40 concepts about people, yield a larger number of significant factors, at least six of which could be identified as follows:
> 1. Moral evaluation; 2. Rationality; 3. Uniqueness or Unusualness; 4. Excitable-calm; 5. Sociable-introverted; 6. Tough-sensitive.

These dimensions still represent the average attitudes of many judges, and one may doubt the adequacy of Osgood's technique for revealing the richness of individual frameworks, despite his demonstration of a high degree of consistency, even among judges of different ethnic backgrounds. A combination of his approach with that of Kelly, where each individual chooses his own effective dimensions might be more fruitful. One might expect different individuals to have widely varying conceptions of "good." For example, the rebellious intellectual looks for unconventionality rather than conformity, and the schoolboy who is unconcerned about his mother's dimension of social respectability instead refers the actions and speech of other boys to his own value of "good at football, rags the teacher, vs. bookworm." Again people who are strong in Spranger's aesthetic, theoretical or religious, values will judge others according to different criteria.

The 'New Look' in Perception

Recent years have seen a spate of work on affective or motivational factors influencing our perception of objects, pictures, words, etc. (cf. Blake and Ramsey, 1951; Jenkin, 1957). People tend to recognize more readily words that refer to their values than those that don't, and to set up defences against stimuli that arouse unpleasant associations. If hungry, they are more apt to see images of food in weakly structured perceptual situations. These phenomena are more complex than was originally assumed, and their explanation more controversial (cf. W. P. Brown, 1961). Other writers, including M. D. Vernon (1955) and Gibson (1951), point out how small and inconsistent are the effects in contrast to the effects of perceptual constancy, or of variations in the experimental instructions. They can generally be demonstrated only in situations where it is difficult to perceive realistically. But for this very reason we might expect them to assume importance in interpreting people. If Mr A has had a tiring and frustrating day at work and has to entertain Mr and Mrs B as guests in the evening, he is likely to regard them with a more jaundiced eye. Perhaps it would be difficult to prove here that A really perceives the B's differently—that he is not merely feeling and reacting differently. However, it has been shown, for example, that people prejudiced against negroes actually misperceive pictures or incidents involving whites and negroes (Allport & Postman, 1947). Similarly, Murray (1933) found that children who had just experienced a frightening situation—a game of "Murder"—tended to interpret pictures of people as being more malicious than normally. It is probable, then, that our attitudes and values arouse expectations and sensitize us to certain cues from people or make us repress other cues.

Naïve Personality Theories And Stereotypes

More generally, each of us, in the course of his lifetime, seems to build up a rough-and-ready set of theories or schemata of human nature, of how and why various kinds of people react to various situations. We possess a considerable repertoire of concepts about motivation and personality, although much of it is but weakly formulated or verbalizable. Probably our schemata are based largely on analysing ourselves and observing others, but also on discussions about people and on what we were taught in childhood, at school and elsewhere, on novels, stories and newspapers, cinema films, plays, and television. All these help to develop categories for interpreting others which will, of course, differ from one judge to another despite a fair amount of consensus attributable to common cultural values and mutual discussions. Among other things our theories tell us that certain traits go with others—that a well-educated person is likely to be more intelligent, reliable, perhaps more interested in books and less in sports, than an ill-educated, and so on. These theories guide our understanding of people's intentions and enable us to anticipate their behaviour—so much so that when people from foreign countries or from a different social class do not fulfill our expectations we are apt to think them peculiar, aimless, or even immoral.

Another prominent feature of our theories is what social psychologists call "stereotyping"—that is we see a person as a specimen of a certain group and attribute to him all the characteristics that we associate with that group. If A has heard that B is a Jew, or rightly or wrongly identifies him as Jewish, he tends to expect various traits and attitudes and consequently usually finds evidence of these. We have stereotypes or expected roles for people of different ages, for the two sexes, for many occupational groups—doctors, ministers, teachers, army officers, etc., for interest groups—athletes, aesthetes, socialists, and for various personality types—the hen-pecked husband, the shy intellectual, the efficient organizer, etc.

Normally, on first meeting, as pointed out above, we try to fit a person into one or more of our pigeon-holes or stock personalities, on the basis of physical cues or previous communications, and these do indeed allow us to go quite a long way in adjusting our behaviour to suit them and in making predictions about them. Social psychologists have too often given the impression that stereotypes are fictitious and biased. But while it is true that they are always over-simplified, often irrational or based on hearsay or other unreliable fragments of evidence, and thus lead us, for example, to misinterpret foreigners, negroes, and other "out-groups," yet at least as often they help us to get to know people more quickly, and promote common reactions among members of the in-group who share the same stereotypes. For example, social intercourse would become chaotic if we did not straight away react differently to a 60-year-old and a 6-year-old, to a society hostess and a prostitute. Moreover, stereotypes are misnamed in that we habitually use them as starting points, when we have nothing else to go on, and are often willing to modify them—to recognize that B differs from "the typical" Jew, etc.

Nevertheless, they do often act as barriers to understanding, particularly because the process of stereotyping is reciprocal. Not only may the secondary school teacher oversimplify and misinterpret a pupil through thinking of him as "a teen-ager," but the pupil likewise pigeon-holes the teacher, and each tends to react in accordance with the other's expectations until some measure of trust and recognition of individuality is built up between them. One of the reasons for the unsatisfactoriness of the short selection interview is that it is seldom able to progress much beyond this exchange of stereotypes, particularly since the role of employer (or personnel officer) and candidate are strongly demarcated. Wide differences in social class, age, interests, speech patterns and so forth obviously make for difficulty in the interpretation of cues. For example, the style of haircut is interpreted very differently by the teen-ager and the teacher.

Perceptual Styles

A factor neglected so far is differences in "perceptual styles." Several references have been made to intolerance of ambiguity. Frenkel-Brunswik (1949) claims that this is a perceptual and personality variable; that people who show rigidity and insistence on definite categories in their perceptions and thinking also tend to show authoritarian prejudice and ethnic intolerance, usually due to insecurity in their own personality make-up. The work of Klein (1951) has suggested a distinction between sharpeners and levellers—those who tend to accentuate unusual features, say in perceiving a diagram, and those who level down such features so as to make the perception more conventional and acceptable. It may be that sharpeners are more aware of inconsistencies in others' personalities and more interested in probing their sources. However, this is purely hypothetical: there is as yet little convincing evidence that the way we see and interpret people is linked with the way we see objects.[3] Indeed it is by no means certain that these styles are consistent or general over a wide range of visual phenomena.

Nevertheless we do find individual differences in methods of viewing personalities. Some appear to be satisfied with describing people in terms of relatively superficial traits and interests: others look for deeper motivations, perhaps because they have a strong, neurotically based, need to analyse people (cf. Taft, 1960). There are variations also in the treatment of cues, some obtaining a more synthetic or global impression, others inferring particular traits from particular impressions or behaviour. And Oldfield (1941) points out that interviewers vary widely in the use they make of different kinds of evidence. Rosenzweig's (1945) classification of reactions to frustration may also be relevant, though again we know of no direct evidence. He suggests that, in a frustrating situation, some people tend to blame others or the environment (extrapunitive); some find fault with themselves (intropunitive); while some tend to evade or minimize the frustration (impunitive). These might conceivably be connected with the tendency, noted above, to underestimate situational factors in favour of personal responsibility, also the attribution of malignancy to those who step on our toes, literally or metaphorically.

Finally, we should not forget Jung's four types of mental function—thinking, feeling, sensation and intuition; though there is little experimental proof that these operate as consistent "styles." The thinker would try to understand people logically, the sensation type would perceive literally in terms of concrete actions; the feeling type values others with reference to effects on himself, and the

[3]Harvey *et al.* (1961) claim that persons whose conceptual structure falls at different developmental levels from the concrete to the abstract show characteristic differences in interpreting others.

intuitive person tries to perceive their essential nature through non-analytic processes. Jung believes that when one type of function is strongly developed in an individual, another would be repressed. Thus one might expect considerable discrepancies in the way different individuals perceive a mutual acquaintance, as also between psychologists who interpret personality from different theoretical standpoints, such as the empirical-psychometric, and the subjective-clinical.

Interpretations of Self

It would be premature at this stage to discuss fully our self-concepts or analyses of our own motives. But it should be pointed out how largely self-perception follows the same lines as interpretations of others. One's homunculus is, of course, much more vivid and of more consuming concern than anyone else's, and it is based on direct awareness of one's feelings rather than on the physical and expressive cues listed above (Nos. 1 and 2).[4] However, a person certainly weighs the significance of his own actions, the situational factors and others' opinions (Nos. 3, 4 and 5) in judging himself. We overestimate the constancy of our own personalities more than that of others, but allow for greater temporary variations with mood, fatigue, etc; and rather than over-simplify, we seem to over-elaborate our motives. We give far more credit to situational factors in adverse situations, instead of blaming "can," "tries," or personal responsibility, and correspondingly more credit to the latter, less to the environment, when things go well.

Belief in the Correctness of Our Interpretations

Finally, in this chapter, it should be asked why we remain generally satisfied with our interpretations of people we meet, despite all the variations and possibilities of error, and despite our realization that people are playing a part and are trying to impress or deceive us, as we do to them. The fact is that to a large extent it works; in so many instances it is confirmed by later evidence. We can tell when our child is hurt, a shop salesman is helpful, a neighbour lowbrow and so forth. Normally there is a lot of feed-back; B indicates to A by his subsequent behaviour that A has read him aright, or if not A is quickly able to correct or cover up minor misjudgments. Not only our experience shows us that we are often justified, but also there is "consensual validation"—that is, others arrive at the same judgments. A group of cronies quickly agree that the new family across the street is snobbish. The group forgets, however, that their own attitudes are

[4]The work of Wolff (1943) and Huntley (1940) shows that we are often not consciously aware of our own expressive cues, e.g., we do not recognize our own voices, while also evincing strong affective attitudes towards them.

likely to be fairly similar, otherwise they would not be friendly, and that, therefore, they may all have made the same misinterpretation. Again, we have seen that personality interpretation is closely bound up with our self-esteem. We cannot afford to be wrong since this would mean that we do not know who is for us, who against us. Thus we are likely to rationalize or repress any evidence that we have misjudged another person. If A_1 and A_2 disagree about B, each tends to ascribe it to the other's bias or ignorance.

2. THE GENERAL AND THE UNIQUE IN PSYCHOLOGICAL SCIENCE[1]

Gordon W. Allport

Let me take my text from the opening sentence of *Ethical Standards of Psychologists,* the official code set forth by the American Psychological Association (1959). This sentence defines a psychologist as a person "committed to increasing man's understanding of man." The code itself makes it abundantly clear that both *man in general* and *man in particular* are objects of our concern. Thus the psychologist, as psychologist, can properly make two sorts of statement; he can say:

(1) the problem of human personality concerns me deeply;
(2) the problem of Bill's personality concerns me deeply.

Although superficially similar the two statements are poles apart. In the second we are speaking of one and only one person; in the first we are abstracting elusive properties from all of the three billion inhabitants of the earth. Both statements are true; both appropriate; and both fall squarely within the domain of psychological science.

Some people, to be sure, object to this broad coverage. Artists, literati, some psychiatrists, perhaps a few clinical psychologists, would say that to generalize about personality is to lose it. Bill, as an integral datum, we are told, cannot belong to scientific psychology. He can be represented only by the methods of

SOURCE. Gordon W. Allport (1897-1970) has been identified with an emphasis on the uniqueness of the person in psychology. He is widely known for his study of the mature, well-functioning person as well as for his study of the "abnormal personality." Allport stressed the importance of examining expressive behavior, personal documents, and case studies in individual personality assessment. This article originally appeared in the *Journal of Personality,* 1962, **34**, 405-422 and is reprinted by permission of Duke University Press.

[1] An earlier (and considerably different) version of this paper appeared in the *Festschrift* published in honor of the 75th birthday of Professor Wolfgang Köhler.

biography, drama, or other artistic portraiture. Bill himself might say to the psychologist, "If you think those pockmarks on your silly IBM card represent *me,* you have another guess coming."

Among scientific psychologists the objection takes a somewhat different form. Usually we repress one half of the APA definition, and say that our job is to reach only generalized formulae–propositions that hold across the board for all mankind, or at least for some identifiable section of the population. We recognize the single case as a useful source of hunches–and that is about all. We pursue our acquaintance with Bill long enough to derive some hypothesis, and then spring like a gazelle into the realm of abstraction, drawing from Bill a "testable proposition" but carrying with us no coordinated knowledge of him as a structural unit. We tolerate the single case only as a take-off point. We forgive Ebbinghaus for performing 163 experiments on himself, since almost immediately his findings were confirmed on other subjects. Luckily these subjects, like him, displayed a logarithmic relationship between the percentage of material forgotten and the time elapsing after the original act of learning. We forgive Köhler and Wallach for intensive work on their own figural after-effects, for it was soon confirmed that others too show a displacement of the percept, after long stimulation, away from the retinal area stimulated.

But imagine the consternation if some deviant psychologist (perhaps I myself) were to say, "Can't we linger longer with Ebbinghaus and discover in his life what relationships might exist between his memory functions and *his* motives and *his* cognitive style and *his* aspirations?" The objection would be: "Of what use is that? Even if we find the relationship we'd have to generalize to other people or else we'd have nothing of any scientific value."

Such is the prevailing "response set" of our specialty. The intricacy of internal structure in concrete lives seldom challenges or detains us. Our concern is with commonalities and comparabilities across individuals.

This response set is undoubtedly derived from our submissiveness to the goals and procedures of natural science. And this submissiveness is not in itself a bad thing. Up to now it has taught us much. The question is whether we have become so enslaved that we overlook an important half of our particular professional assignment which is "increasing man's understanding of man."

It does no good to argue that every individual system in nature is unique; every rat, every porpoise, every worm; and that it is only the general laws of their functioning that lead to comprehension. No, we can't take this easy way out of the dilemma. The human system, unlike all others, possesses a degree of openness to the world, a degree of foresight and self-awareness, a flexibility and binding of functions and goals that present a unique structural challenge far more insistent than that presented by any other living system. It is because of their essential stereotype and lack of variation that psychologists like to draw their generalizations from lower animals. But for my part I venture the opinion that all of the infrahuman vertebrates in the world differ less from one another in psychological functioning and in complexity of organization, than one human being does from any other.

And so I wonder whether the time has not come for students of personality to shake themselves loose from a too-rigid response set, and perhaps even to reverse it. Instead of growing impatient with the single case and hastening on to generalization, why should we not grow impatient with our generalizations and hasten to the internal pattern? For one thing we should ask, are our generalizations really relevant to the case we are studying? If so, do they need modification? And in what ways is this individual the asymptote of all our general laws?

Or to state the procedure more simply: Why should we not start with individual behavior as a source of hunches (as we have in the past), and then seek our generalizations (also as we have in the past), but finally come back to the individual—not for the mechanical application of laws (as we do now), but for a fuller, supplementary, and more accurate assessment than we are now able to give? I suspect that the reason our present assessments are now so often feeble and sometimes even ridiculous, is because we do not take this final step. We stop with our wobbly laws of personality and seldom confront them with the concrete person.

The Dimensional and The Morphogenic

The issue before us is not new. More than a hundred years ago John Stuart Mill proposed that we distinguish sharply between psychology, the science of mind-in-general, and ethology, a science of character (having no relation to what is called ethology today). To his mind ethology should trace the operation of psychological laws in specifically individual combinations—such as the pattern of the single person or of a single culture or nation. Somewhat similar was Dilthey's proposal to distinguish between "explanatory" and "understanding" psychology. Said Dilthey, "We explain nature, but we understand human beings." Windelband too would recognize two classes of science: the nomothetic (seeking general laws) and the idiographic (dealing with structured pattern).

In confronting this same problem William James almost threw up his hands in despair. It is well known that after writing his textbook, he concluded that general psychological laws are poor stuff. He declared that psychology has not produced "a single law in the sense in which physics shows us laws. . . . This is no science, it is only the hope of a science" (1961 ed., p. 335). Perhaps the ensuing half-century of intensive research would have strengthened his faith in general laws; but I doubt it. At any rate he not only questioned the validity of general laws but, champion of the individual though he was, he seemed to feel that the concrete person must also inevitably elude psychology. In his *Memories and Studies* (1912) he wrote,

> . . . in every concrete individual, there is a uniqueness that defies all formulation. We can feel the touch of it and recognize its taste, so to speak, relishing or disliking, as the case may be, but we can give no ultimate account of it, and have in the end simply to admire the Creator (pp. 109 f.).

And so at the end of his career James seems to despair of psychology as a science of either the general or the concrete.

The problem has not yet been solved, but I for one detect signs of progress. For one thing it increasingly haunts us, in our dual roles as experimenter and clinician, as theorist and practitioner. Nearly a decade ago Meehl (1954) wrote a distinguished treatise on the subject entitled *Clinical vs. Statistical Prediction.* His own position he declared to be "ambivalent." Some called it middle-of-the-road (but only those, I think, whose own adaptation level was somewhere to the right of Sarbin and Lundberg).

Meehl's book draws an important distinction. It points out that in comparing so-called clinical with so-called statistical procedures we may be talking about (*a*) the methods we employ and the type of data we use, or (*b*) about the way we piece together these data and reach a final assessment. Thus the data, on the one hand, may be percentile scores or other quantifiable dimensional data; or they may be looser types of information, case records, free associations, and the like. Further, in reaching a conclusion from these data we may use statistical procedures with mechanical regularity, or we may—as Dilthey advises—simply try to "understand" the pattern. Meehl's chief concern is with the latter issue. Does one handle the data (whatever they be) more successfully through using the statistical cookbook, or through global comprehension? While this issue is surely central, it is not the focus of my interest in the present paper. Here I am concerned rather more with Meehl's first problem: the type of data that should go into our assessments.

More recently a German author (Graumann, 1960) puts the problem this way: shall our units of analysis in the study of personality be derived from general psychological concepts, or from lives as actually lived? Another statement of the issue is found in the presidential address of L. S. Hearnshaw (1956) to the British Psychological Society. He first calls attention to the strain that exists between the demands of conventional scientific method and "the appreciation of the richness of human individuality." He pleads for "a constant search for concepts which while capable of scientific definition and employment, nevertheless possess humanistic implications" and reflect patterned structure accurately.

It would serve no good purpose here to review the long-standing debate between partisans of the nomothetic and idiographic methods, between champions of explanation and understanding. Indeed, to insure more rapid progress I think it best to avoid traditional terms altogether. For the purposes of our present discussion I shall speak of "dimensional" and "morphogenic" procedures. Let me explain the latter term.

The science of molecular biology shows us that life-substances are identical across species. The building blocks of life–vegetable and animal–turn out to be strikingly uniform in terms of nucleic acids, protein molecules, and enzymatic reactions. Yet an antelope differs from an ash tree, a man from an antelope, and one man is very unlike another. The challenge of morphogenesis (accounting for pattern) grows more rather than less acute as we discover the commonalities of life. Yet biologists admit that morphogenic biology lags far behind molecular (or dimensional) biology. So too does morphogenic psychology lag far behind dimensional psychology.

The commonalities in personality are the horizontal dimensions that run through all individuals. We focus our attention chiefly upon these commonalities: for example, upon the common traits of achievement, anxiety, extraversion, dominance, creativity; or upon the common processes of learning, repression, identification, aging. We spend scarcely one per cent of our research time discovering whether these common dimensions are in reality relevant to Bill's personality, and if so, how they are patterned together to compose to Billian quality of Bill. Ideally, research should explore both horizontal and vertical dimensions.

I have already rejected the easy solution that assigns the general to science and the unique to art. I should like also to dispose of another proposed solution. Some psychologists would say that Bill, our individual, is known primarily by his conformity to, or deviation from, universal norms or group norms. His private and unique qualities are only the residual peculiarities left over when we have accounted for most of his behavior in terms of general norms. My colleagues, Professors Kluckhohn, Murray, and Schneider (1953, p. 53) have expressed the thought by saying every man is in certain respects:

a. like all other men (universal norms)
b. like some other men (group norms)
c. like no other men (idiosyncratic norms).

Now it is certainly true that we often wish to use universal and group norms. We want to know whether Bill, relative to others, is high or low in intelligence, in dominance, in affiliativeness. But although Bill can be compared profitably on many dimensions with the average human being or with his cultural group, still he himself weaves all these attributes into a unique idiomatic system. His personality does not contain three systems, but only one. Whatever individuality is, it is not the residual ragbag left over after general dimensions have been exhausted. The organization of Bill's life is first, last, and all the time, the primary fact of his human nature.

Since we cannot brush our problem aside we do well to ask how a truly morphogenic psychology (sadly neglected up to now) can become a scientific asset. To become such it will have to learn certain lessons from dimensional empiricism, and from positivism—most of all the lesson of observer reliability. It is not sufficient to "intuit" the pattern of Bill or Betty. All of their friends do this much, with greater or less success. A science, even a morphogenic science, should be made of sterner stuff. The morphogenic interpretations we make should be testable, communicable, and have a high measure of predictive power.

My purpose is to suggest certain procedures that seem to me to be morphogenic in nature, or at least semi-morphogenic, and yet to be at the same time controlled, repeatable, reliable. Before I do so, let us look more closely at the question of successful prediction, which, we are told, is the acid test of a valid science.

Prediction: Dimensional And Morphogenic

Prediction based on general or dimensional information is called actuarial. For many purposes it is surprisingly accurate. One marvels, for example, at the correctness with which insurance companies predict the number of deaths that will occur by highway accidents, from cancer, or from suicide. The changes of a hypothetical average man for survival or death are all the insurance business wants to know. Whether Bill himself will be one of the fatal cases it cannot tell—and that is what Bill wants to know.

The situation is exactly the same in psychology. Actuarial prediction enables us, with fair success, to predict what proportion of boys, having a certain type of physique and family history, will become delinquent; what percentage of engaged couples, having various types of background, will enjoy successful marriage. Actuarial prediction can tell approximately what the average student's university record will be on the basis of his elementary school record or I.Q. It can advise industry concerning crucial cutting points on psychological tests by designating the score below which most applicants would probably fail on the job.

Note please that these actuarial predictions are far more useful to insurance companies, school authorities, police, and industrial management than to Bill himself. As a person he is frozen out, for although statistical generalizations hold with small error for large populations they do not hold for any given individual. And as practitioners we have fully as much responsibility to Bill as to his employers or to the public. Nay, if we follow our own professional code of ethics, we have more.

Suppose we take John, a lad of 12 years, and suppose his family background is poor; his father was a criminal; his mother rejected him; his neighborhood is marginal. Suppose that 70 per cent of the boys having a similar background become criminals. Does this mean that John himself has a 70 per cent chance of delinquency? Not at all. John is a unique being, with a genetic inheritance all his own; his life-experience is his own. His unique world contains influences unknown to the statistician: perhaps an affectionate relation with a certain teacher, or a wise word once spoken by a neighbor. Such factors may be decisive and may offset all average probabilities. There is no 70 per cent chance about John. He either will or will not become delinquent. Only a complete understanding of his personality, of his present and future circumstances, will give us a basis for sure prediction.

It was this line of argument, I believe, that led Meehl (1954) to say, "Let us see what the research evidence is regarding the relative success of dimensional and morphogenic prediction." Surveying such relevant studies as were available, Meehl concludes that morphogenic (what he calls "clinical") prediction seems to be actually inferior. More successful are predictions made mechanically with the aid of a standard formula. Best to keep strictly to our Rorschach diagnostic signs, to our I.Q. measures, to our profile on the Minnesota Multiphasic Personality Inventory, and to other standard predictive indexes. We can, of course, weight the signs, but we must do so according to rule. We may give one sign twice as much weight as another, just as a cook uses two cups of flour but only one of sugar. Meehl appropriately calls the procedure he advocates the "cookbook" method.

The point is that whenever we deal with well-defined variables, possessing a known relation to a pathological type, or to success in occupation or in school, we are usually safer in following the cookbook method of combining scores according to a formula known to have a good average validity. If strictly followed the logical outcome of this procedure would be the early elimination of the clinician or practitioner as assessor or diagnostician. A computing machine could handle the data more accurately than a fallible psychologist. In coming years we shall, no doubt, increasingly encounter IBM diagnoses and IBM predictions in psychological practice. It does no good to shudder at such a *lèse majesté* to human dignity. It will surely come to pass. But already we can sense its limitations.

Limitations of the Cookbook

In the first place, as Meehl (1957) himself has pointed out, the cookbook is usable only under restricted circumstances. The dimensions studied must be objectively defined, reliably measured, validly related to the target of prediction (e.g., to vocational success), clearly normed for a population to which the subject belongs. Most of the dimensions we employ have not attained this level of objective perfection.

The question of weighting signs gives us special difficulty. Suppose John has a good engineering profile, but also scores high in aesthetic interests; suppose he is introverted, but has high ego-strength; and with all this suffers some physical disability—what then does the final pattern signify? Cookbook enthusiasts might say a computer could tell us. But could it? In all the world there are not enough cases of this, or of any other, personal pattern to warrant assured actuarial prediction.

Again, by keeping within a previously established dimensional frame the cookbook procedure rules out insights peculiarly relevant to the individual. True, the computer can tell whether Sam should be diagnosed as schizophrenic. But whether Sam's love for his sister and her way of dealing with him are such as to effect his recovery, the computer cannot tell. A dimensional frame is a rigid thing. It is like giving to the cook ingredients that will produce only dumplings while imagining that she has the freedom to produce a cake.

Further, the dimensions imposed on the individual are dimensions of interest to the investigator, or to the hospital, school, or firm. For this reason they may not be relevant in guiding John. The most salient features of his life—his aspirations, his sense of duty, his existential pattern, may be left untouched. In every dimensional analysis there are inevitably many "empty cells."

Finally, as for the discovery that clinical or morphogenic predictions are in fact poorer than cookbook predictions, I can only say, "What a pitiful reflection on the inventiveness and sensitivity of psychologists!" The findings—which, by the way, are not necessarily the last word on the matter—prove only that we do not yet know how to maximize clinical skill through training. I suspect that our present emphasis on tests and cookbooks may actually be damaging the potential skill of young clinicians and advisers. There are studies that indicate that clinicians grow confused when they have too many data concerning an individual life, and that for this reason their predictions are better when they fall back on a mere formula (Sarbin, Taft, & Bailey, 1960, pp. 262-264). But this finding, too, points chiefly to our neglect in inventing and training in sensitive morphogenic methods.

Recently, Meehl (1959) has shown that under certain circumstances a combined actuarial and clinical—a kind of "configural"—procedure is superior in predictive power to either method used alone. This is progress indeed. But I would raise two objections: (1) the level of success achieved is still too low; (2) the diagnostic instruments employed in the first instance are too one-sided. The original instruments on which the predictions are based are nearly always of a dimensional or horizontal order (extending across people) and seldom of an intensive vertical order (within the person).

My point is that while dimensional diagnostic methods are an indispensable half of the psychologist's tools of trade, the other half of the tool box is, up to now, virtually empty. I recall that a few years before his death I was discussing this matter with the beloved psychologist, Edward Tolman. He said to me with his characteristic twinkle, employing the then-current terminology, "I know I should be more idiographic in my research, but I just don't know how to be." My reply now, as then, is, "Let's learn!"

Morphogenic Methods

To start simply: it is worth asking whether we ought to seek only objective validation for our measuring instruments. Why not demand likewise, where possible, subjective validation by asking our subject what he himself thinks of the dimensional diagnosis we have made? (If the subject is a child, a psychotic, or manifestly defensive, this step, of course, has no point.) Too often we fail to consult the richest of all sources of data, namely, the subject's own self-knowledge. During the war psychiatrists were assigned the task of screening candidates for the armed services. While they employed various dimensional tests, it is said that the best predictive question turned out to be, "Do you feel that you are emotionally ready to enter military service?" The men themselves were often the best judges—although, of course, not infallible.

One might think that the existential outlook in psychology (now spreading at considerable speed) could logically be expected to bring a revolution in methods of psychological assessment. Its basic emphasis is upon the individual as a unique being-in-the-world whose system of meanings and value-orientations are not precisely like anyone else's. Hence an existential psychologist, be he conducting research, assessment, or therapy, would seem to need procedures tailored to each separate case. But up to now followers of this school of thought have not been as inventive as their own basic postulate requires. There is a methodological lag.

It is true that psychiatrists and clinical psychologists have long known that they should take the patient's own story as a starting point. But almost immediately they redact this story into general categories, dismembering the complex pattern of the life into standard dimensions (abilities, needs, interest inventories, and the like), and hasten to assign scores on their favorite variables. One notes too that therapists who claim to be existential in their orientation also tend to employ standard procedures in treatment. Their techniques and even their interpretations are sometimes indistinguishable from orthodox psychoanalysis (G. W. Allport, 1961a).

Our conceptual flexibility is greater than our methodological flexibility. Let me illustrate the point by reference to the valuable and extensive bibliography of nearly 500 items prepared by Ruth Wylie (1961). Most of these items deal with empirical studies of the self concept. (The very fact that the self in recent years has been readmitted to good standing in psychology is proof of our conceptual flexibility.) A close inspection, however, shows that virtually all the studies approach the self concept only via general dimensions. We encounter such descriptions as the following: "this test infers self-esteem from scores on an anxiety questionnaire"; or "nine bipolar semantic differential scales are employed"; or "self ratings on 18 trait words on a five-point scale from which self-acceptance is inferred." I am not objecting to these studies but point out that they are methodologically stereotyped.

But let us turn now to what at present lies available in the morphogenic half of our tool box. My inventory will be illustrative rather than exhaustive. I shall be brief in describing each method, hoping that the array as a whole will help to make clear what I mean by morphogenic method, and, best of all, may stimulate further invention.

1. Familiar is the method of matching, used with profit by both German and American investigators (see G. W. Allport, 1961 (b), pp. 387 f. and 446 f.). This method invites us to fit together any record of personal expression, however complex, with any other record. We test our skill in seeing that this case record must fit such-and-such a test profile; or that this handwriting goes with that voice. It is a good way to discover how much of a perceptible form-quality saturates separate performances. Although the method gives us no insight into causal relationships it is, so far as it goes, a good example of a 100 per cent morphogenic procedure.

2. Another wholly morphogenic technique was devised by Baldwin (1942) who made use of a long series of personal letters written by one woman, Jenny by name. Her unique thought-structure, i.e., associative complexes, was the object of interest. If she talked about women, money, or nature, with what feeling-tone did she mention them? If she mentioned her son what else did she mention in the same context? This technique, called by Baldwin "personal structure analysis," is highly revealing, and is carried through without reference to any general or dimensional norms.

3. Somewhat similar, and wholly morphogenic, is the procedure recommended by Shapiro (1961) for psychiatrists. On the basis of a five-hour intensive interview with a patient he constructs a questionnaire which from that time on is standard for this patient but not directly relevant to any other patient. Administered over intervals of months or years, the instrument will show the course of development, including improvement or deterioration in health.

4. A somewhat more ambitious attempt, still wholly morphogenic, would be to attempt to discover the number and range of all the major structural foci a given life possesses. Many years ago in his *Experiment in Autobiography*, H. G. Wells asserted that there were only two major themes in his life: interest in world government and in sex. Elsewhere I have explored the possibility that a life may be understood almost completely by tracing only a few major themes or intentions. Probably two is too few for most lives (perhaps especially for H. G. Wells), although it is said that Tolstoy after his conversion had only one major theme: viz., the simplification of life. More typical, I believe, would be the case

of William James, who, according to his biographers, R. B. Perry (1936, chaps. 90-91), had eight dominant trends. In some preliminary explorations with my students (G. W. Allport, 1958), I find that they regard it possible to characterize a friend adequately on the average with 7.2 essential characteristics, the range falling for the most part between 3 and 10.

What to call these central motifs I do not exactly know. They are "essential characteristics," for the most part motivational in type although some seem to be stylistic. F. H. Allport (1937) has proposed the term "teleonomic trends" and suggests that we proceed to regard them as life-hypotheses held by the individual, and count carefully how many of his daily acts can accurately be ordered to one or more of these trends. The idea has merit but it has not yet been systematically tried out. One question is whether we can obtain sufficiently high observer-reliability (i.e., reliable judgments of the fit of specific acts to the hypothesized trend). At present it is only one of the avenues of research needing exploration.

5. Suppose we are interested in an individual's value system. Direct questioning is useful, of course. "What would you rather have than anything else in the world?" "What experiences give you a feeling of completeness, of fully functioning, or of personal identity?" "What," in Maslow's terms, "are your peak experiences of life?" Elsewhere I have argued strongly for the use of such direct questions as these, for in important matters we should grant our client the right to be believed. Projective methods should never be used without direct methods, for we cannot interpret the results of projective testing unless we know whether they confirm or contradict the subject's own self-image (see G. W. Allport, 1960, chap. 6).

But how can we grow more precise in this type of work, benefitting from lessons learned from objective dimensional procedures? One such technique is the "self-anchoring scale," devised by Kilpatrick and Cantril (1960). It consists of a simple diagram of a ladder, having 10 rungs. The subject is asked first to describe in his own terms the "very best or ideal way of life" that he can imagine. Then he is told that rung 10 at the top of the ladder represents this ideal. Similarly he is asked to describe the "worst possible way of life" for himself. This he is told is the bottom of the ladder. Now he is asked to point to the rung on the ladder where he thinks he stands today—somewhere between the bottom and top rungs. He can also be asked, "Where on this scale were you two years ago? Five years ago? Where do you think you will be five years hence?"

This device has considerable value in personal counselling. It is also used by the authors to study rising or falling morale in different countries, e.g., in those having undergone recent revolution as compared with those living in a static condition. In this case, a curious thing happens, a completely morphogenic instrument is adapted for use as a tool for nomothetic research. Ordinarily, of course, the situation is reversed: it is a nomothetic mold that is forced upon the individual.

All these various examples suffice to show that it is possible to examine the internal and unique pattern of personal structure without any dependence whatsoever on universal or group norms. All the methods I have mentioned up to now are completely morphogenic, although they are seldom explicitly recognized as such.

Semi-Morphogenic Methods

Let us turn our attention to certain procedures that are highly useful for exploring individuality even though they are in part also dimensional.

6. First, there is the common dimensional instrument, the rating scale. Many years ago Conrad (1932) asked teachers to rate pupils on 231 common traits. The teachers were thus forced to make the assumption that all children did in fact possess all 231 traits in some degree. Proceeding on this assumption the teachers agreed poorly, as reflected in a median reliability coefficient of .48. After this nomothetic orgy, the same teachers were asked to star *only* those traits that they considered to be of "central or dominating importance in the child's personality." On this part of their task the teachers agreed almost perfectly, their judgments correlating .95. This result shows that low reliability may be due to the essential irrelevance of many of the dimensions we forcibly apply to an individual. On well-configurated prominent dispositions there is likely to be good agreement.

A related method is the simple adjective check list. Here the rater is confronted with perhaps hundreds of common trait-names (which are, of course, common linguistic dimensions). But he is required to use only those that seem to him appropriate to the primary trends in the individual life.

Both the method of starring and the use of the check list have the advantage of permitting us to discard irrelevant dimensions—a feature lacking in most other dimensional procedures.

7. Another half-way method is the Role Construct Repertory Test, devised by Kelly (1955). The method asks the subject to tell in what way two concepts are alike and how they differ from a third. The concepts might, for example, be *mother, sister, wife.* The subject could, for instance, reply that mother and sister are alike because both are comforting; and the wife different because she is demanding. Not only is the particular response revealing of his family attitudes, but over a long series of comparisons it may turn out that the subject has a characteristic cognitive style in which the polarity of comfortableness vs. demandingness may recur time and time again. This method is not wholly morphogenic since it prescribes for the subject what "significant others" he shall characterize, and in other ways limits his spontaneous choices, but it allows none the less for a certain amount of morphogenic discovery.

8. Certain other devices for approaching cognitive style likewise move in a desirable direction. I have in mind Broverman (1960) who employs standard tests with his subjects, but makes his interpretations entirely in terms of the subject's tendency to do well or poorly on a given type of test relative to his own mean for all tests. By the use of such ipsative scores he is able to determine which responses are strong or weak with respect to other responses within the same individual.

If this line of thought were extended we would be moving toward a psychophysics of one person—a desirable advance indeed. We would at last know, so to speak, the relation between Bill's sensory acuity and his interests, between his cognitive style and his tempo, between his respiration and extraversion. To what extent it is necessary to start, as Broverman does, with standard dimensional measures, is a question for the future. I doubt that we can answer it a priori.

9. Another mixed method is the Allport-Vernon-Lindzey *Study of Values* (1960), devised to measure the relative prominence of each of the six Spranger *Lebensformen* within a particular person. The resulting profile does not tell how high or low a given person stands on the economic, theoretic, or religious value in the population at large, but only which value is relatively most, or next most, or least prominent in his own life. This type of profile is semi-dimensional, semi-morphogenic.

10. Sometimes the *Q* sort (Stephenson, 1953) is said to be an idiographic technique. Yet it, like other devices we are now considering, goes only part way. It has the merit of making use of self-report, and can be used for measuring changes in the self concept. As ordinarily used, however, only a standard set of propositions is employed, thus creating for the subject little more than a standard rating scale. And if the subject is forced, as he often is, to produce a quasi-normal distribution among his sorts he is further restricted. In short, the method can be rigidly dimensional. Yet it is a flexible method, and some variants are highly promising, perhaps especially when combined with inverse factor analysis.

11. For example, Nunnally (1955) studied one therapy case over a two-year period, using 60 statements selected for their unique relevance to this person (and this, I think, is a great improvement over the use of uniform lists). The patient made her sorts under many different sets of instructions on many occasions. Using an inverse factor analysis it was possible to find three fairly independent factors that comprised her total self concept. During therapy these factors showed only a moderate change.

It strikes me as curious that out of the thousands and thousands of factor-analytic studies that smother us today, scarcely any are carried through in such a manner as to discover the internal, unique, organizational units that characterize a single life. Even inverse factor analysis does not fully achieve this goal unless the initial information employed is selected for its morphogenic relevance. A good deal of creative work still lies ahead for factor analysis. It has potentiality,

I think, for discovering the main foci of organization in a given life, but has not yet moved far enough in this direction.

Final Word

This survey of possible relevant methods is not complete, but may indicate that by a deliberate shift of procedures we can bring the laggard end of our science up to a more flourishing level. To effect the shift we shall have to restrain to some extent our present dimensional debauch.

In this paper I have introduced the term "morphogenic psychology," borrowed from, but not identical with the usage in, biology. It is, I think, a good term, better than "idiographic" which so many students of personality misuse and misspell. I hope the concept "morphogenic" catches on, but even more do I hope that the types of research to which I have ventured to apply the label will flourish and spread. Already we know that personality (in general) is an interesting topic for study. But only when morphogenic methods are more highly developed shall we be able to do justice to the fascinating individuality that marks the personalities of Bill, John, and Betty.

3. A FRAMEWORK FOR THE STUDY OF PERSONALITY AS A BEHAVIORAL SCIENCE

I. E. Farber

Whether any behavior system or theory can be at once comprehensive enough and detailed enough to encompass the mysteries of personality and personality change is still an open question. One reason why some psychologists are skeptical is that such formulations do not seem to refer at all to a special class of concepts or phenomena called "personality," but rather to behavior in general, or to predispositions inferred from behavior in general. I believe this observation to be quite accurate. Behavior theorists ordinarily do not distinguish between the task of explaining or predicting personality and that of explaining or predicting behavior. To be sure, in discussing personality they are likely to stress

SOURCE. I. E. Farber is Professor in the Department of Psychology at the University of Illinois, Chicago Circle. This article reflects Dr. Farber's continuing interest in the relationship between personality dynamics, motivational variables, and the principles of learning. This material is excerpted from a chapter which originally appeared in P. Worchel and D. Byrne (Eds.), *Personality Change,* New York: John Wiley & Sons. 1964, pp. 3-31. Reprinted by permission of John Wiley & Sons and the author.

certain processes or concepts such as learning and motivation, but this is characteristic of their general approach to psychology. In their typical view, the study of personality is essentially coterminous with the study of behavior.

I must confess to a certain puzzlement concerning some other views of personality, especially in regard to the distinctions between those behaviors or processes that are supposed to comprise or reflect personality and those that are not. Statements such as "Personality is what a man really is" are simply not helpful, since any kind of behavior or hypothetical variable that might reasonably be used to account for behavior, e.g., habit, libido, press, or positive self-regard, seems equally realistic. Nor does the following amplification seem more satisfying: "Personality is the dynamic organization within the individual of those psychophysical systems that determine his unique adjustments to his environment" (Allport, 1937, p. 48). Except for the term "unique," which is better calculated to reassure people than enlighten them (cf. Eysenck, 1952; Meehl, 1954), this statement does not appear to exclude from consideration any aspect of behavior or a single variable of which behavior in general may be considered a function.

Still, discussions of personality do not, as a rule, cover every aspect of behavior, though some, even of a non-behavioral sort (e.g., Murphy, 1947), come close. Most frequently, as Hall and Lindzey (1957) observe in their excellent text, they concentrate on motivational variables, i.e., those used to account for the apparently purposive, striving, goal-directed aspects of behavior. Thus, performance on an intelligence test may not be regarded as an index of personality unless there is reason to suppose it is affected by such variables as boredom, achievement needs, anxiety, or hostility toward the tester. Since any kind of behavior, including that involved in taking an intelligence test, running the hundred-yard dash, or whatever, might conceivably be affected by such variables, there seems no clear basis for excluding any kind of behavior from consideration.

I would maintain, therefore, that any relatively comprehensive theory of behavior, especially if it includes variables of a motivational sort, qualifies as a theory of personality. The relative adequacy of the various behavioral approaches in accounting for the complexities of human behavior is, of course, another question.

The basic assumption of behavioral scientists is that behavior is a function of its antecedents. These antecedents are natural events in the natural world, and the laws relating behavior to its antecedents can be discovered in the manner of other natural sciences, by the observation and analysis of empirical events. These laws of behavior are, at least in principle, susceptible of discovery. Not all will, as a matter of fact, be known at any given time, since they are exceedingly complex, and new information tends to uncover new complexities. But this is merely a recognition of pragmatic difficulties. It does not make a virtue of obscurantism nor elevate ignorance of ultimate causes to the status of a scientific principle. Once the laws of behavior, or enough of them, are known, the behavior can be predicted. And if the determinants, or enough of them, are manipulable, the behavior can be controlled.

One might suppose that these assumptions, which involve little more than the denial of transcendental or supernatural causation, would be accepted as a matter of course, but, in fact, they seem to arouse intense dissatisfaction. One reason is that, for some, lawfulness implies fatalism, and a second is that, for some (usually the same people), lawfulness implies coercion.

These objections are not usually among those voiced by psychologists, and can be quickly disposed of. In the fatalistic view, certain consequences are inevitable regardless of the antecedent conditions. The antecedents may change, but the consequence does not. This, of course, is exactly the opposite of a deterministic view, which considers consequences to be a function of their antecedents, i.e., if the antecedents change, the consequences change. In the one view, behavior is lawful; in the other, it is unlawful.

The notion of scientific laws as mandatory or coercive results from confusing scientific laws with judicial or legislative laws. If one does not obey a judicial law, one is punished; but if one does not obey a scientific law, the law is inaccurate and must be modified. Scientific laws do not make anything happen. They are merely statements of what does happen under certain conditions. Natural phenomena do not depend on scientific laws. Rather, the converse is true—the statement of the law depends on the nature of the observed phenomena.

Although psychologists do not usually object to determinism on the foregoing grounds, many join the humanists in the protest, on related grounds, that it relegates man to the level of a robot, a senseless and purposeless machine reacting to every fortuitous change in the external and internal environment. Instead, they insist, men actively select the environmental changes to which they respond, and actively decide what responses they shall make.

This position certainly has a strong emotional appeal, as evidenced by the storm of protest raised against both Watson and Freud, in part because of their insistence on a thorough-going determinism. Most people not only do not want to believe they are mere robots; they do not actually feel that they are. Whether there is any autism in this self-perception may be a moot question. Practically, anyone who regards himself as a machine is likely to be subjected to therapeutic treatments aimed at modifying this view. Certainly, normal phenomenological experience runs counter to the notion that people are helpless victims of inexorable circumstances. Rogers (see Murray et al., 1961) has recently affirmed both his acceptance of this position and his conviction of its untenability: "I prefer to live with what seems to me to be a genuine paradox, . . . that in our pursuit of science, we are fools if we do not assume that everything that occurs is a portion of a cause-and-effect sequence, and that nothing occurs outside of that. But I also feel that if we adopt that point of view in our living as human beings, in our confrontation with life, then that is death" (p. 575).

It seems to me this statement epitomizes a rather widespread attitude, that the rules of the scientific game are all very well on the home grounds—in the laboratory, in dealing with insentient objects—but ought not be applied to the study of real persons in the real world. By contrast, behavioral scientists insist on attempting to apply these rules under all conditions, even in the face of the complexities of human personality.

It is important, at this point, to distinguish between the contention on phenomenological grounds that behavior is unlawful, and the possible role of an analysis of mental events in constructing psychological concepts. To the best of my knowledge, no one these days denies the existence of mental events. Watson did on occasion, but in Bergmann's perspicuous phrase, "Watson's particular mistake was that in order to establish that there are no interacting minds, which is true, he thought it necessary to assert that *there are no minds,* which is not only false but silly" (1956, p. 266). To follow Bergmann's analysis, no one doubts that there are such things as mental contents, awarenesses, cognitive states, percepts, etc. However, to any statement containing such terms it is possible, at least in principle, to coordinate another ". . . which mentions only behavioral, physiological, and environmental items, such that they are either both true or both false. Otherwise one would have to maintain that we can, literally and not metaphorically speaking, directly observe other people's states of mind" (p. 270). Thus, mental events exist, and in a commonsense way we know what we mean when we refer to them, but it is unnecessary to appeal to them in a thorough-going account of behavior.

Causation, Finalism, and Explanatory Fictions

The preoccupation of personality theorists with motivation, the apparently purposive, striving, goal-directed aspects of behavior referred to earlier, has sometimes led to the adoption of a finalistic or teleological view of behavior. The biological counterpart of this view has been aptly summarized by Simpson (1950):

> The distinctive finalist belief is that of progression toward a goal or end. The end is not reached, the finalist believes, because of what goes before, but what goes before is but a means for reaching the end. The end, although later in time, is, then, the cause and the preceding course of history is the effect. The history of life is thus to be viewed as purposeful, and (it almost goes without saying) finalists usually consider man as the essential feature of that purpose (pp. 126-127).

The degree of conviction with which this belief has been held by some theorists is indicated in the following quotation from Adler's (1930) chapter in the *Psychologies of 1930:*

> Individual Psychology insists absolutely on the indispensability of finalism for the understanding of all psychological phenomena. Causes, powers, instincts, impulses, and the like cannot serve as explanatory principles. The final goal alone can explain man's behavior (p. 400).

To the typical non-scientist man-in-the-street this view seems not only reasonable but self-evident. Asked why an acorn planted in the ground grows as it does, he is likely to reply, "So that it can become an oak tree." Or, if he has had the benefit of a liberal education, asked why people sleep, he may answer, "To restore homeostasis." Even psychologists who know better fall into the habit of explaining one kind of behavior or another by referring to the goals to be attained.

Quite apart from the reversal of the order of materialistic cause and effect, such explanations tend to account for either too little or too much. They account for too little when the expected goal is not reached. Not all acorns become oak trees. Some rot and others are eaten by hogs. People and animals who have suffered injury to the anterior portion of the hypothalamus may be unable to sleep. And people all too frequently fail to achieve goals or achieve them by the most diverse means. Such explanations are too comprehensive when they are used to account for every conceivable kind of eventuality. To explain all behavior in terms of "adjustment" or "satisfaction of the pleasure drive," for instance, explains nothing, since one must still account for the different kinds of behavior.

I must confess to the belief that some constructions of the concept of self-actualization, which in one form or another appears to have wide currency in personality theories, suffer from this defect. Rogers, for instance, assigns to human beings only a single motive, the actualizing tendency. "This is the inherent tendency of the organism to develop all its capacities in ways which serve to maintain or enhance the organism" (1959, p. 196). It includes the concepts of tension reduction, growth motivation, differentiation of organs and functions, enhancement through reproduction, autonomy, and indeed, so far as I can tell, almost any predisposition one can think of that results in the expanded effectiveness of the organism. This seems equivalent to saying that organisms tend under all conditions to do those things that are "good" for them, in a vague sense of the word "good." Unfortunately, even if one adopts this optimistic view of man, one still does not know what a given individual will do, or why one individual differs from another. To know this, one would have to identify the particular factors, whether hereditary or environmental, that occasion different behaviors. This is not to say that the postulated correlates of the actualizing tendency, e.g., originality, creativity, and spontaneity, are fictitious or unimportant. On the contrary, precisely because they are important, a behavior science ought to be adequate to their prediction and explanation. And this can be done, not by defining them as the culminating aspects of a universal *élan vital,* but by discovering their particular determinants. In the present view, if we knew the independently defined variables of which such behaviors or behavior characteristics are a function, we would dispense with such overarching concepts as self-actualization.

It is interesting to contemplate the number of concepts that might be dispensed with in psychology, if we only knew more about the determinants of given kinds of behavior. For instance, behavior theorists, like everyone else, occasionally talk about the phenomenon of "choosing." It is notable, however, that the term "choice" usually refers to nothing more than the descriptive fact that an organism behaves in one way rather than another. Suppose we know that a person has repeatedly heard a tone just before receiving an air puff on the cornea of his eye. If we then note that he blinks when the tone is presented, we add nothing to our explanation by saying he chose to blink. Similarly, when after prolonged food deprivation, a person identifies an ambiguous picture as a steak rather than something else, it is trivial to say this is because he decided to say "steak." Since the evidence of the decision is the behavior itself, attributing the behavior under these circumstances to choice is exactly as useful as attributing it to demons. Note should be made of the qualification, "under these circumstances." If the definition of choice is made independently of the behavior it is supposed to explain, this concept may, of course, be useful.

In general, the frequency of appeals to such explanatory fictions is an index of our ignorance of the antecedents of the phenomenon under consideration. All too often, the sole evidence for the supposed cause is the very behavior it is supposed to explain. Thus, as Skinner (1961, p. 535) has observed, it is useless to say that forms of life that have survived did so because they had survival value, if all we know is that they survived. And it is useless to argue that people adjust to their environment because of some special capacities such as intelligence, if these are defined in terms of their adjustive value. Similarly:

> When we say that a man eats *because* he is hungry, smokes a great deal *because* he has the tobacco habit, fights *because* of the instinct of pugnacity, behaves brilliantly *because* of his intelligence, or plays the piano well *because* of his musical ability, we seem to be referring to causes. But on analysis these phrases prove to be merely redundant descriptions (Skinner, 1953, p. 31).

The Control of Behavior

It was stated earlier that, if the determinants of behavior were known, and if enough of them were susceptible to manipulation, then it would be possible to control behavior. It was also noted that this proposition arouses the most intense annoyance and anxiety in many people, including psychologists, who for good reasons, abhor the idea of a totalitarian technocracy (Bergmann, 1956). In its superficial aspects, one can rather readily understand why the concepts of "control" and "despotism" are sometimes equated. If behavior can indeed be controlled by manipulating its determinants, then individuals with the requisite knowledge could and very possibly would exercise this control. In this light, any deterministic view of behavior may be suspect. For instance, psychoanalytic theory, which on other grounds does not perhaps qualify as a behavioral approach, has, because of its thorough-going determinism, also been accused of sinister and exploitative advocations.

The reaction against the proposition that behavior is susceptible of manipulation tends to take two different and rather contradictory forms. At one extreme, it emerges as a flat denial—the use of the Freudian term is not unintentional—that behavior, particularly implicit behavior, is controllable or even predictable. According to this view, the deterministic thesis, as applied to human behavior, is simply false. At the other extreme, it consists of the condemnation and proscription of attempts to discover the laws of behavior. According to the latter view, behavior is not only lawful and predictable, but the laws are already well-known and the techniques for their effective application all-too-readily available. Couched in less extreme terms, the two arguments, oddly enough, frequently appear in a single context, without recognition of their inconsistency.

Some aspects of the first objection concerning the essential unpredictability of behavior have already been referred to. Beliefs to the contrary rest on philosophical assumptions not subject to empirical proof or disproof. It might be commented, not altogether frivolously, that anyone who sincerely believes *as a matter of principle* that behavior is unlawful and unpredictable ought to complain about the expenditure of his tax dollar for such things as schools and mental hospitals, since they are established on the supposition that at least some behaviors are somewhat amenable to control.

The second reaction, that the laws of behavior are well-known, and are even now being applied in one or another program of exploitation, is, despite allegations from the best-seller list, unwarranted by the facts. The facts are that, at present, much human behavior is unpredictable because its laws, though discoverable, are as yet largely unknown. This is not exactly news to informed individuals, and affords psychologists scant basis for self-congratulation. It may conceivably comfort those who regard the acquisition and application of psychological knowledge as a threat to human welfare, including, paradoxically, some psychologists who appear to see in the advancement of behavioral science only the grim prospect of 1984. As Skinner (1955) observes:

> Such predictions of the havoc to be wreaked by the application of science to human affairs are usually made with surprising confidence. They not

> only show a faith in the orderliness of human behavior: they presuppose an established body of knowledge with the help of which it can positively be asserted that the changes which scientists propose to make will have quite specific results–albeit not the results they foresee (p. 61).

The essential ingredient in such views is a distrust of science. Those who bemoan our lack of knowledge concerning the factors governing intersocietal and interpersonal relations are frequently the same people who condemn the use of those procedures best calculated to achieve that knowledge–the methods of science. If these forebodings were taken seriously, we should have to conclude that even if we knew how to make our educational system more effective, even if we knew what kinds of conditions in our homes would increase the probabilities of our children's becoming responsible and useful citizens, we nevertheless ought to refuse to establish such conditions on the grounds that this would constitute undesirable control; even if we knew how to allay those suspicions and change those motives or cognitive structures of individuals, the consequences of which threaten our country with racial upheaval or the world with nuclear disaster, we ought not act because this would violate men's freedom.

Surely, few persons would care to push the argument for the inviolability of human freedom so far. Nevertheless, the issue is not a simple one, and will certainly not be resolved here. I merely wish to point to the illogicality of an automatic rejection of any plan calculated on the basis of scientific knowledge to modify the behavior of individuals or societies.

On the one hand, we must recognize that different societies and different individuals have different goals. What is desirable or reinforcing for one may be frustrating and punishing for another. We are only too liable to the delusion that our own goals are the only reasonable ones. Thus, when I try to change a person's behavior or attitudes, I am appealing to his better judgment; when you try to do so, you are using propaganda; and when "they" do so, they are brainwashing. To complicate matters further, this multiplicity of motives and goals extends to the intrapersonal sphere. The behavior that is instrumental to the satisfaction of one motive may frustrate the satisfaction of another.

On the other hand, our respect for the rights of others to their particular goals and the instrumental acts whereby they are achieved should not lead us to the romantic delusion that these are spontaneous products of unfettered choice. No one escapes control by the physical environment short of death; and no one escapes control by his social environment short of complete isolation. Almost the entire period of childhood is given over to the acquisition of new behaviors, goals, and motives, under the guidance of parents, family, and teachers. Be it wise or unwise, deliberate, impulsive, or unconscious, such guidance inevitably has its effects. It is difficult, in fact, to think of any kind of social interaction that has absolutely no effect on behavior. That the effects are unintentional or unwanted does not negate them. There is some feeling among those who read popular discussions of persuasive techniques that frank and open appeals to frank and open motives such as hunger and thirst may be tolerable; but disguised and subtle appeals to disguised and possibly disreputable motives such as sex or dominance are illegitimate. This reaction probably results from the belief that behavior related to the first class of motives is more liable to self-control and less liable to control by others. This is extremely doubtful. But, in any event, those who would proscribe the use of such techniques on the grounds that they constitute unwarranted control are usually not nearly so concerned with the ethical implications of their own proposal to control the attitudes and behavior of others. The plain fact is, the obdurate refusal to arrange circumstances for influencing others, on ethical or moral grounds, may simply serve as a mask for indecision and irresponsibility. Furthermore, such refusal ignores the evident fact that we influence others in unintended and unplanned ways.

Even non-directive psychotherapists adopt their procedures on the assumption that they have certain behavioral consequences. If refusing to say or do something produces given effects, this constitutes control no less than does active intervention. Which of these kinds of antecedents is more closely related to the desired behaviors is an empirical matter, not to be decided on a priori philosophical grounds. Advocates of a non-interventionist approach to psychology know this, of course, since they frequently refer to empirical evidence indicating that their procedures are more effective than some others.

It seems to me there is much more agreement concerning the kind of world most of us want and the kinds of people we should like to have in it than one would suppose from the interminable arguments about such matters. The disagreements among social scientists or, for that matter, between social scientists and humanists, relate not so much to goals as to the means by which they can best be achieved. For example, in a recent symposium (Murray et al., 1961), Rogers suggests that an alternative to control is the release of potentialities and capacities, leading to "... behavior that is more variable, more spontaneous, more creative, and hence in its specifics, more unpredictable" (p. 575). Surely no one would question the desirability of such behavior. We might question whether the optimal conditions for creativity and spontaneity are those of laissez-faire or accident. And we might question whether such conditions do, as a matter of fact, constitute an alternative to control, since some sorts of controls by parents, teachers, and many other individuals and institutions are inevitable. Whether such fortuitous controls are likely to encourage or stifle creativity needs to be investigated, not taken for granted.

There may be some who would deny the desirability of such empirical investigations, presumably on the principle that ignorance is bliss. But if, as a result of investigations such as those Rogers himself has inspired, there was good reason to suppose that certain conditions have a greater likelihood than others of eliciting behavior upon whose worth almost all can agree, then I doubt that one could reasonably argue against the deliberate institution of such conditions on the grounds of ethical propriety. We are mainly ignorant about the controls that now exist, so we can only be sure they are man-made and far from perfect. It seems inconceivable and, indeed, a contradiction in terms to suppose that controls based on scientific knowledge would be worse. Unfortunately, influential writers, including some psychologists in the field of personality, seem otherwise persuaded.

Prediction versus Understanding

It is possible that we have been setting up a straw man, since relatively few individuals in our time would condemn the pursuit and application of empirical knowledge, though not many years ago a congressional committee investigating the social sciences heard such complaints. However this may be, there are certainly differences of opinion concerning the criteria whereby knowledge may be verified. In one aspect, they relate to the foregoing discussion of prediction and control. Thus, Maslow, in the aforementioned symposium (Murray et al., 1961), suggests that the testing of scientific hypotheses in terms of prediction and control implies an "overactive and interfering conception of science" (p. 572). He prefers a conception whose "key characteristics are receptivity to knowledge . . . , understanding as the main goal of science, rather than prediction and control . . . , the freer use of intuition, empathy, and identification with the object of study, a greater stress on experiential knowledge, a less pragmatic attitude" (p. 572).

This statement addresses two somewhat independent problems which may be easily confused. The one has to do with techniques or modes of acquiring knowledge; the other with procedures for verifying knowledge.

In respect to the first, one may note that we frequently do not know the circumstances that yield useful hunches concerning the determinants of behavior in specific instances. The context of discovery, to use Reichenbach's (1938) excellent term, is uncertain. This is so, not because the determinants of useful hunches are in principle unknowable, but because we are as yet relatively ignorant about them. We do know that many hunches, including those asseverated by psychologists, turn out to be mistaken. Citing the conclusion of one investigator, that non-psychologists appear to be able to judge others more accurately than do clinical psychologists, Allport suggests that the present training of psychologists merely ". . . leads them to a *knowledge about*, rather than an *acquaintance with,* human nature in its concrete manifestations" (1961, p. 543). This may be so, and we may be training our students badly. This should not be surprising, since psychologists, like other educators, know less than they should about the conditions of effective training for various purposes. Though I very much doubt that psychological training generally impairs one's ability to judge others, it is unquestionably true that others can do a better job than psychologists of predicting behavior under some circumstances.

Sometimes the reasons for this are perfectly evident. On occasion, my neighbor, who is a dentist, can predict the behavior of my dog—understands its personality, if by that one means its behavioral tendencies—much better than I, because, for good reasons, it spends its time around his garden bed and garbage cans. On the other hand, I can occasionally predict the condition of my children's teeth better than he, because I am in a better position to control their predilection for sweets. In these instances, as in all others, successful prediction depends on the amount and kind of information available. Psychologists, including personality theorists, simply do not predict behavior in general. They can only say, given such and such conditions, a given behavior should ensue. As Dollard and Miller (1950) nicely point out in respect to the cultural determinants of behavior, they may not always be in a position to know just what these conditions may be in specific instances.

In this regard, we may frequently be impressed with the perceptiveness of politicians, salesmen, and animal trainers. Many of the more highly educated in our society are even more likely to be impressed with the insights of novelists, poets, biographers, and the great religious and social essayists who have written so well and wisely about the nature and condition of man. We should certainly not disparage such insights as these persons may have. Psychologists have no monopoly of access to the cues that may serve as the basis for successful prediction and evaluation of behavior.

But this recognition of the variety of sources of possible knowledge, that is, the diverse contexts of discovery, should not blind us to the second problem, the necessity for verifying knowledge. The context of justification (Reichenbach, 1938) has its own ineluctable requirements. The accuracy of statements by those whose writings appear to embody the wisdom of the ages must, like those by dentists and psychologists, be evaluated in the light of their predictive value.

The deficiencies of speculative wisdom, as of intuition and empathic understanding generally, lie not in their inaccuracy. They may be quite accurate. Their fault is that they give no adequate basis for knowing whether or not they are accurate. As Campbell (1959) has observed, the speculative wisdom of the ages has often proposed contradictory resolutions of the same problem. The insights of classical wisdom, in contrast to scientific knowledge, are notoriously equivocal and non-cumulative. The reason is that science insists that insights and hypotheses be tested and sets up a machinery for this purpose, whereas classical wisdom is content with the mere experience of certitude. Even the putative wisdom of Allport's commonsensical homespun philosopher must be tested, else we should never know when he is truly being wise and when, like the rest of us, he is merely a victim of undisciplined conviction.

Sources of Information Concerning the Determinants of Behavior

We know, of course, that the variables influencing behavior are many, and their interactions extremely complex. For this reason, if one wants to know whether a given kind of behavior is some function of one, or, at most, a restricted set of these variables, one must either construct or find situations such that the effects of the one variable or the particular set of variables may be isolated. This can be done by eliminating the other relevant variables, holding them constant, or in some way measuring their effects.

This does not imply the expectation that in other combinations the variable(s) under consideration will invariably affect behavior in ways clearly evident from their relatively isolated effect on behavior. It merely presupposes that the study of the effects of restricted sets of variables on the behavior of relatively simple organisms may lead to useful hypotheses concerning their effects in more complex combinations and in more complex organisms. This method of science is usually necessary because "it is seldom possible to proceed directly to complex cases. We begin with the simple and build up to the complex, step by step" (Skinner, 1953, p. 204).

Now, nothing is more certain than the fact that relations found in such simple instances will sometimes, perhaps usually, fail to hold in more complex instances. No one would deny that changes in the combinations of variables may affect behavior. But unless one has fairly precise notions about the conditions under which a given kind of behavior occurs, it seems exceedingly unlikely that one can decide with any certainty what particular aspects of different or more complex conditions are responsible for a change in that behavior.

Generalizing from the Laboratory to Real Life

Those who argue that the observation of behavior under the artificial and highly controlled conditions of the laboratory has no predictive value for behavior under "real life" conditions sometimes appear to fail to understand the necessity for doing more than simply pointing to the change. What we wish to know is the nature of the variables of which that change is a function. In any event, there is universal agreement on one point: before one generalizes from observations of behavior in the laboratory to real-life situations, one had better consider very carefully the differences between the laboratory conditions and those in real life.

In the light of this recognition of the necessity for considering the variables involved, it is puzzling why anyone who objects to generalizations from laboratory findings should consider it safe to generalize from behavior in one complex, uncontrolled situation to behavior in another. Obviously, circumstances change from one uncontrolled situation to another. When one does not know what variables have changed, generalizations from one real-life situation to another are at least as uncertain as those from controlled situations to real-life situations. An added disadvantage lies in the relatively greater difficulty of disentangling the particular variables that have changed. This is not easy, whether one deals with either controlled or uncontrolled conditions, but under any circumstances the lack of control or information concerning the effects of specific variables can hardly be regarded as a positive aid to understanding and prediction.

Generalizing from Animals to People

In view of the well-known differences between rats, which are non-social and non-verbal, and human beings, who are exceedingly social and verbal, it is not surprising to find a good deal of skepticism concerning the applicability of rat laws to human behavior. Occasionally, there is an autistic element in such criticisms. Some people consider it degrading to be compared with rats, just as some consider it insulting to be compared with infants, as in psychoanalytic theory. But most criticisms of this sort are based on the objective fact that rats and people differ in many and possibly crucial respects. Koch (1956) has expressed in eloquent detail his disbelief in the probability of generating the *essential* laws of human behavior from rat data. He points out that one may not even be able to generate decent laws concerning rats by observing rats, especially if they inhabit different laboratories.

In regard to the latter observation, that one cannot generalize from rats to rats without risk, one can only agree that animal experimenters ought perhaps to describe their experimental conditions more adequately, or to try harder to discover those conditions whose variation is responsible for the reported inconsistencies. I do not believe animal psychologists are generally regarded as unusually deficient in their specification of the variables they know about or in their zeal to discover the ones they do not know about. But perhaps they ought to be doing a more careful job. It is important to note that this calls for more analytic precision, not less.

In regard to the former observation, that one cannot generalize from rats to human beings, it seems fair to repeat that frequently one also cannot generalize from human beings to human beings. Koch (1956) for instance, in describing his own "B states," i.e., his experiences while deeply engrossed in work, maintains that despite the importance of such states, despite their exemplification of behavior in its most organized, energized, and motivated form, current psychological theories are inadequate to the recognition of such states, let alone their explanation. "Subtle and organized descriptive phenomenologies of B states are badly needed by science—but not from individuals whose B-state products are 'creative' only by extravagant metaphor" (p. 68). Whatever one thinks of this pronouncement, it is certain that B-states cannot be observed in rats, and unlikely that they could be even partially accounted for in terms of principles based on rat behavior. But, as Koch himself suggests in the foregoing quotation, it would be rash to suppose that all human beings share these experiences. And in view of the restriction imposed, even among those who might have such experiences, very few could claim the privilege of attempting to communicate them. This is not to say that B-states do not exist, nor that they are unimportant. It does suggest the uncertainties of attempting to generalize from what may be discovered about Koch's B-states to the experiential states of people whose phenomenological descriptions may be limited to a phrase such as "Man, it's the most!" There is grave risk in generalizing from both rats and human beings when important variables differ.

Despite these cautionary notes, I think it possible to point to some instances of successful generalizations from animal as well as other human behavior, i.e., to hypotheses that have turned out to be fruitful. Instead, I should like to tell of an "Aha!" experience I recently had while listening to Frank A. Logan describe some of his animal experiments at Yale, in which delay of reward was balanced against amount of reward in simple choice situations. The experimental results showed that, within limits, rats will choose a longer delay, if the reward is large enough, in preference to shorter delays with lesser rewards. Probably because of obtuseness, it had never before occurred to me in quite the same way that the morality of human beings in giving up the pleasures of this world for the sake of eternal salvation may have something in common with the morality of rats in giving up an immediate reinforcement for the sake of a bigger piece of Purina dog chow. Now, this is undoubtedly a specious analogy at best. It ignores the many disanalogies in the two instances, and may be utterly foolish. But until this has been demonstrated, it suggests some, not by any means all, of the variables of which even such sublime sentiments may be a function. Of course, it goes without saying that no matter how intriguing this notion may appear in the context of discovery, it must make its scientific way in the context of justification.

The distaste of some psychologists for animal studies frequently extends to conditioning studies as well, in part because the conditioned reflex appears characteristic of subhuman or subnormal behavior. Again, we might attempt to show how the laws of conditioning have been used as a basis for predicting some relatively complex human activities, such as verbal learning. Instead, we can point to a curious inconsistency in our treatments of such concepts. According to the earlier Gestalt psychologists, insight, or perception of relations, is also a primitive process, altogether characteristic of animals. Yet we seldom hear the argument that this concept is, therefore, useless for the understanding of human behavior. Unfortunately, judgments of what is scientifically useful are all-too-frequently confounded with judgments of what is good or bad. Thus, the successful efforts of Communists to modify beliefs and actions are likely to be attributed to the use of Pavlovian conditioning techniques, which work only if men are reduced to the level of witless automatons (cf. Farber, Harlow, and West, 1957); our own successful efforts, on the other hand, are likely to be attributed to methods engaging the higher mental processes. It seems just possible, does it not, that many of the same determinants may be operative in both instances?

Proponents of a behavioral approach are likely to answer this question affirmatively because, for the most part, they distrust the doctrines of emergentism. While the variables influencing animal behavior are certainly different and less complex than those influencing human behavior, most behavioral scientists, nevertheless, prefer to look for continuity in the explanatory principles involved. Similarly, they look for continuity between the laws of child and adult behavior, between social and non-social behavior, and between normal and abnormal behavior. Whether this sort of search is useful may be open to question. At this stage of the game there appears to be no way of deciding this to everyone's satisfaction.

General Laws and the Individual Case

The foregoing discussion has dwelt on two apparently contradictory principles. The one stresses the necessity for caution in generalizing from one circumstance to another, in the face of inevitable changes in the variables represented. The second holds to the optimistic belief that generalization is frequently possible, even in the face of changes in some of the variables affecting behavior. Behavioral scientists, like others, differ in their relative emphases on these two principles, depending in part on the relative strengths of their empiricist or theoretical predilections; but they are likely to agree that the question whether one can successfully predict from one context to another can be answered only by empirical test.

Some personality theorists, however, appear to consider this a methodological rather than an empirical issue. They may deny, for instance, even the possibility of applying general laws to the prediction of individual behavior. Since, they argue, the variables influencing a given individual's behavior are not exactly duplicated for any other person, and since these variables interact in complicated ways, it is simply not possible to predict anything about one person from laws based on the observation of others. Since each individual is unique, the only legitimate predictions concerning any given person must be based on what is known about that person. Curiously enough, this reasoning is ordinarily not extended to the intraindividual case. If it were, we would have to deny the possibility of predicting an individual's behavior even on the basis of what is known about that person, since the variables influencing his behavior at one time can never be exactly duplicated at any other time. At the very least, the ordinal positions of the two occasions differ.

Most behavioral scientists believe that general laws can be reasonably and usefully applied to individuals (Eysenck, 1952; Meehl, 1954). At the same time, they can readily agree that predictions about a given individual will frequently be more precise if they are based on the observation of his own past behavior. Perhaps the main reason for this is that many of the important determinants of his past behavior are likely to persist as determinants of his future behavior. Individuals carry such determinants around with them, so to speak, in the form of their inherited and learned predispositions. Nevertheless, if there is reason to suppose that present conditions are quite different from those in the individual's past, predictions are likely to be more successful if they are based on the behavior of others for whom we know these conditions have obtained. It is gratuitous to say so, but this merely means it may be more useful, in predicting the effects of aging on a given person, to look at old people than at that person at age two; or it may be more useful, in predicting the effects of a certain drug on a person's behavior, to observe other people drunk than that person sober. Of course, the more nearly alike the reference group and the individual in question, the more accurate the prediction. This simply means that the probability of successful prediction from one instance to another is some positive function of the communality of their behavioral determinants (cf. Meehl, 1954).

We should note that this formulation of the issue does not dispose of the empirical question whether general laws can at present be usefully applied to a particular individual in any given instance. The hard job of ascertaining just what the important variables are in any given context, and when a change in one variable changes the significance of another, must still be done. We may hypothesize to our hearts' content about such matters. But we should not mistake the hypothesis, no matter how firmly held, for empirical proof.

4. THE PRACTICE OF PSYCHOLOGICAL TESTING IN CLINICAL SERVICES IN THE UNITED STATES[1]

Norman D. Sundberg

Which tests are most used in clinical work these days? How do practices compare with earlier times? In what ways do clinical services differ? These questions come to mind in considering the practice of testing in hospitals and

SOURCE. Norman D. Sundberg is Dean of the Lila Acheson Wallace School of Community Service and Public Affairs and Professor of Psychology at the University of Oregon. A clinical psychologist by training, he has worked in the areas of personality assessment, creativity, and person perception. This article originally appeared in the *American Psychologist,* 1961, **16**, 79-83 and is reprinted by permission of the American Psychological Association and the author.

[1]This study was partially supported by Public Health Service Grant M-2825(A).

clinics in the United States. If one is to evaluate clinical practice, one must know what is going on. Yet the literature is very scanty. The most recent survey of clinical testing practices was done by Louttit and Browne (1947). Their 1946 study was based on returns from 43 institutions which were mainly college clinics. They also refer to a survey done in 1935. A few studies report on tests in special settings: Darley and Marquis (1946) surveyed practices in veterans guidance centers shortly after World War II; Swenson and Lindgren (1952) reported on the use of psychological tests in industry. Other than the studies reported by Louttit and Browne, there has been no general survey of clinical testing for at least 25 years.

Procedures and Sample

The survey form consisted of a questionnaire about the agency and its testing practices and a check list for reporting the usage of specific tests. The check list included the most used tests from the Louttit and Browne study, tests with a high number of publications (Buros, 1953), and spaces for adding other tests. For each test, the respondent made a rating on the frequency of usage like that used in the Louttit and Browne study: 0 (never used), 1 (used occasionally), 2 (used frequently), or 3 (used with the majority of cases). The first survey request and one follow-up were conducted in the spring of 1959. Of the total of 304 agencies and hospitals, usable responses were obtained from 185 or 61%.

The intent of the sampling procedures was to obtain a broad selection of clinical agencies and hospitals from all over the United States. To this end, five different kinds of clinical services were selected from four different sources of information (American Board of Professional Standards in Vocational Counseling, 1958; American Psychological Association, 1959; Moore, 1958; and the National Association for Mental Health, 1955). Each state was sampled and additional random selections were made for every multiple of eight agencies listed. The respondents totaled 10% of all the agencies and institutions listed in the directories, and the original sample was 16% of the total. The numbers in the final sample on which this analysis is based were as follows: 27 Veterans Administration stations (all hospitals except for 3 clinics), 66 hospitals and institutions (including 39 state mental hospitals and 13 institutions for mental defectives), 53 outpatient clinics (37 of which were primarily child clinics), 23 counseling centers (of which one-third were affiliated with universities and most of the rest were community counseling agencies sponsored by organizations), and 16 university training clinics. In the total sample there was almost an exact balance between outpatient and inpatient services, and between adults and children (including adolescents) seen for testing.

Findings and Comments

As might be expected from such a heterogeneous sample, testing practices differed greatly. The number of tests used by any single agency varied from 5 to 82 different tests. The median number of different kinds of tests was 26. The total number of tests administered in a year ranged from 18 in one small outpatient clinic to 14,230 in a large counseling center. The median number was 868 test administrations per year. The average number of persons tested annually varied from 153 for outpatient clinics to 578 for counseling centers. Table 1 presents 62 tests used by 10% or more of the respondents. The Total Mentions column refers to the number of agencies mentioning the given test, and the Weighted Score column is the total of the ratings multiplied by the frequency with which agencies checked these ratings. The rank-difference correlation between the two is high (.96 for the 62 tests). Among the leading 10 tests there are 4 projective techniques and 5 intelligence tests. The other test is the MMPI. The Rorschach outstrips its competitors very clearly both on number of places using the test and on amount of usage. A number of interesting tests which are rather new do not appear on Table 1 but were mentioned among the 375 different tests listed by the total group.

Table 2 presents data on the 20 most used psychological tests in each of three decades. The data from 1935 to 1946 were taken from the Louttit and Browne report (1947). Among the 40 tests listed there were 13 tests that have appeared on all of the test lists in the three decades. Of these the leader in all-time use in the clinic has been the Stanford-Binet. The Goodenough Draw-A-Man Test also has enjoyed a high position. The instability of testing preferences is indicated by the turnover rate in the top 20 tests. Between 1935 and 1946 there was a turnover of 60%. Between 1946 and 1959 there was a turnover of 38%. Between 1935 and 1959 there was a turnover of 76%. This figure means that among the tests which undoubtedly account for the majority of clinical test administrations in the United States, three-fourths of the tests have changed in 25 years. There are, however, some differences in samples which would be likely to affect the results. The earlier ones were smaller and at least the 1946 sample had relatively few psychiatric hospitals. The present sample is much more representative of clinical services of all kinds.

It is interesting to see the shift in kinds of tests used in the three decades as revealed by the complete lists. Intelligence tests dropped from 55% of the totals listed for 1935 by Louttit and Browne to 24% of the tests in use in 1959. The other striking change has been in the number of projective techniques starting with almost none in 1935 and rising to 23% of the total in 1959. Other percentages have remained almost constant. There has been a general increase in adult testing as compared with tests for children and a slight decrease in performance testing.

Table 3 shows the testing practices of the different psychological services with the 31 leading tests. The percentage of the given psychological agencies which are using the test is given, and also the rank of the Frequent Usage Index (FUI), which is an attempt to provide a more pure measure of usage by eliminating the distorting effect of the checking of tests which were rarely used. FUI uses only the ratings for frequent usage and usage with a majority of cases. The differences among the agencies on some tests are quite distinct. For instance, notice the counseling center column as compared with the outpatient clinics and hospitals and institutions columns in the usage of the Rorschach and the Kuder. Table 4 presents the intercorrelations on the FUI ranks among the different kinds of psychological services. The figures which stand out most prominently are the correlations between counseling centers and the two predominantly psychiatric organizations. This table gives support for a real difference between counseling psychology and psychiatry-affiliated clinical psychology. The vocational and educational problems facing counseling psychologists require different kinds of tests. VA services and university training clinics occupy intermediate postions.

Discussion

Psychological testing is a large activity in the United States. It is interesting to see what this sample implies if the numbers are extrapolated on the assumption of a 10% sampling of clinical services in the country. The picture would be as follows: nearly 7,000 clinical and counseling psychologists are seeing 1,300,000 people every year for all kinds of psychological service; of these; psychological tests are administered to 700,000 persons. Even this large number is only a fraction of the total figure on psychological testing if one would bring in industrial, military, educational, and private clinical work.

Such a survey as this raises many questions. Why are some tests widely used and others ignored? Levy and Orr (1959) have shown that institutional affiliation affects the kind of research psychologists do with tests. The social psychology of test usage would be equally interesting to explore. What is the relation between test usage and the number of publications? The most widely used test, the Rorschach, also has the largest number of publications (Buros, 1959). Its rate has remained at almost three publications in English per week for a decade (Sundberg, 1954). For the tests listed in Table 1, the rank-difference correlation between FUI and Publication Rate for the last 7 years as taken from Buros (1959), was .46. This matter assumes greater importance since number of publications probably reflects highly the amount of research. Some tests are much published and others are underpublished. In the latter category is the Draw-A-Person Test which is much used but has very few publications and little

Table 1. Tests Used by Ten Percent or More of the Total Sample ($N = 185$)

Name of Test	Usage Rating Totals*			Total Mentions	Weighted Score	TM Rank	WS Rank
	1	2	3				
Rorschach	24	36	110	170	426	1	1
Draw-A-Person (Machover)	37	46	77	160	360	2.5	2
Thematic Apperception Test	50	63	47	160	317	2.5	4
Visual Motor Gestalt Test (Bender)	33	58	67	158	350	4	3
Stanford-Binet	69	46	31	146	254	5	6
WAIS	33	46	53	132	284	6	5
MMPI	55	42	26	123	217	7.5	8
Wechsler-Bellevue	64	30	29	123	211	7.5	9
Draw-A-Man (Goodenough)	67	29	23	119	194	9	10
WISC	33	34	47	114	242	10	7
Kuder Preference Record	66	26	16	108	166	11	12
House-Tree-Person	60	23	21	104	169	12	11
Goldstein-Scheerer Tests of Abstract & Concrete Thinking	74	18	1	93	113	13	16
Sentence Completion Tests (of all kinds)	(44)	(26)	(21)	(91)	(159)	(13–14)	(12–13)
Vineland Social Maturity Scale	42	32	8	82	130	14	13
Otis Self-Administering	52	21	7	80	115	15	14.5
Gray Oral Reading	61	14	3	78	98	16	18
Vocational Interest Blank for Men (Strong)	42	23	9	74	115	17	14.5
Porteus Maze Test	63	6	3	72	84	18	22
Rosenzweig Picture Frustration Study	60	10		70	80	19	25
Arthur Point Scale of Performance Test	62	5		67	72	20.5	28
Kohs Blocks	49	16	2	67	87	20.5	20.5
Kent Series of Emergency Scales	52	9	4	65	82	22.5	24
Make-A-Picture Story	52	13		65	78	22.5	26
Minnesota Clerical	44	15	3	62	83	24	23
Minnesota Paper Form Board	39	18	4	61	87	25.5	20.5
Sentence Completion (unnamed)	31	16	14	61	105	25.5	17
Kent-Rosanoff Word Association	52	8		60	68	27.5	29

Test of Mechanical Comprehension (Bennett)	34	24	2	60	88	27.5	19
Vocational Interest Blank for Women (Strong)	40	11	5	56	77	29	27
Gesell Developmental Schedule	42	9		51	60	30	31.5
Concept Formation (Hanfmann Kasanin)	42	3		45	48	31	40
Ishihara Color Blindness	42	2		44	46	32.5	42
Purdue Pegboard	36	6	2	44	54	32.5	34
Differential Aptitude Test (Bennett)	28	13	2	43	60	34.5	31.5
Hunt-Minnesota Test for Organic Brain Damage	42	1		43	44	34.5	44
Stanford Achievement	30	10	2	42	56	36	33
Shipley Institute of Living Scale	26	10	5	41	61	37	30
Meier-Seashore Art Judgment	39	1		40	41	39	45
Minnesota Rate of Manipulation	34	5	1	40	47	39	41
Szondi Test	30	7	3	40	53	39	35.5
Study of Values (Allport-Vernon-Lindzey)	28	7	3	38	51	41	38
Minnesota Spatial Relations Test	29	5	2	36	45	42.5	43
Mooney Problem Check List	24	9	3	36	51	42.5	38
Primary Mental Abilities (Thurstone)	31	4		35	39	44	46.5
Children's Apperception Test	16	16	1	33	51	45	38
Personality Inventory (Bernreuter)	27	1	2	30	35	46	52.5
Blacky	22	6	1	29	37	47.5	50
Pseudo-Isochromatic Plates for Color Perception	27		2	29	33	47.5	55
Adjustment Inventory (Bell)	23	1	4	28	37	50	50
Cattell Infant Scale	22	5	1	28	35	50	52.5
Wide Range Achievement	12	7	9	28	53	50	35.5
Healy Picture Completion, II	23	4		27	31	53	56.5
Leiter International Performance	18	7	2	27	38	53	48
Wechsler Memory Scale	17	10		27	37	53	50
California Test of Personality	20	4	1	25	31	55	56.5
General Aptitude Test Battery	19	4	1	24	30	56.5	58
MacQuarrie Test for Mechanical Ability	21	3		24	27	56.5	59
Babcock Test of Mental Deterioration	20	2		22	24	58.5	61
Symond's Picture Story Test	12	8	2	22	34	58.5	54
Monroe Diagnostic Reading	21			21	21	61	62
Rotter Sentence Completion	8	8	5	21	39	61	46.5
SRA Mechanical Aptitudes	16	5		21	26	61	60

* Usage Ratings: 1. Occasionally; 2. Frequently; 3. With Majority of Cases.

Table 2. Summary of the Twenty Most Used Psychological Tests in Each of Three Decades
N (1935) = 49 N (1946) = 43 N (1959) = 185

Name of Test	Total Mentions			Total Mention Order			Weighted Scores		Weighted Score Order	
	1959	1946	1935	1959	1946	1935	1959	1946	1959	1946
Arthur Performance	67	29	26	20.5	15.5	3	72	58	28	7.5
Bell Adjustment Inventory	28	26	—	50	18.5	—	37	42	50	19.5
Bernreuter Personality Inventory	30	25	11	46	20	19.5	35	41	52.5	21
Binet-Simon	—	—	11	—	—	19.5	—	—	—	—
Draw-A-Man (Goodenough)	119	36	17	9	3.5	12	194	74	10	3
Draw-A-Person (Machover)	160	—	—	2.5	—	—	360	—	2	—
Gesell Developmental	51	24	20	30	22	8.5	60	45	31.5	17
Goldstein-Scheerer	93	4	—	13	97.5	—	113	4	16	100
Gray Oral Reading	78	32	7	16	8	34.5	98	63	18	6
Healy Picture Completion, I	—	19	17	—	35	12	—	28	—	38.5
Healy Picture Completion, II	27	30	24	53	12	4	31	44	56.5	18
Herring-Binet	—	7	16	—	77.5	14	—	7	—	90
House-Tree-Person	104	—	—	12	—	—	169	—	11	—
Ishihara Color Blindness	44	30	—	32.5	12	—	46	42	42	19.5
Kent EGY	65	30	—	22.5	12	—	82	50	24	12.5
Kent-Rosanoff Free Association	60	27	6	27.5	17	43	68	36	29	28
Kohs Blocks	67	26	6	20.5	18.5	43	87	47	20.5	15
Kuder Preference Record	108	23	—	11	25	—	166	46	12	16
Kuhlmann-Anderson	—	15	20	—	47.5	8.5	—	25	—	40.5
Kuhlmann-Binet Revision	1	11	19	—	61	10	1	14	—	65.5
Merrill Palmer	18	22	22	—	28.5	6	26	40	—	22
MMPI	123	29	—	7.5	15.5	—	217	50	8	12.5
Otis Intelligence	—	21	12	—	31.5	17.5	—	38	—	23.5
Otis Self-Administering	80	33	12	15	7	17.5	115	55	14.5	10
Pintner-Patterson Performance	—	12	22	—	54	6	—	20	—	53
Porteus Mazes	72	30	27	18	12	2	84	48	22	14
Rorschach	170	34	—	1	5.5	—	424	68	1	4
Rosenzweig Picture Frustration Study	70	—	—	19	—	—	80	—	25	—
Stanford Achievement	42	34	22	36	5.5	6	56	58	33	7.5
Stanford-Binet	146	43	49	5	1	1	254	112	6	1
Stenquist Mechanical Aptitude	—	13	17	—	50	12	—	21	—	48.5
Strong VIB (Men)	74	31	7	17	9	34.5	115	57	14.5	9
TAT	160	36	—	2.5	3.5	—	317	64	4	5
Terman Group	—	11	15	—	61	15	—	13	—	68.5
Thurstone Personality	—	10	14	—	66	16	—	11	—	74
Vineland Social Maturity	82	30	—	14	12	—	130	54	13	11
Visual Motor Gestalt (Bender)	158	12	—	4	54	—	350	15	3	60.5
WAIS	132	—	—	6	—	—	284	—	5	—
Wechsler-Bellevue	123	41	—	7.5	2	—	211	103	9	2
WISC	114	—	—	10	—	—	242	—	7	—

*N*s : Veterans Adm. Stations 27
Hospitals and Institutions 66
Outpatient Clinics 53
Counseling Centers 23
University Affiliated Clinics 16
185

Name of Test	UAC		CC		OPC		H & I		VA		Total	
	%[a]	FUI Rank[b]	%	FUI Rank	%	FUI Rank	%	FUI Rank	%	FUI Rank	%	FUI Rank
Rorschach	69	1	57	10	100	1	100	1	100	1	92	1
Draw-A-Person (Machover)	75	3	57	13.5	94	2	91	3	93	5	86	2
TAT (Murray)	69	2	61	12	100	3	83	7	100	6	86	4
Visual Motor Gestalt Test (Bender)	56	9	43	15	94	4	97	2	93	3	85	3
Stanford-Binet	56	6.5	70	13.5	87	6	91	6	56	27.5	79	7
WAIS	50	4	65	7.5	58	9	80	4	93	2	71	5
MMPI	75	12.5	74	10	43	11	73	11	85	4	66	8
Wechsler-Bellevue	56	11	83	7.5	51	13	71	8	78	8	66	9
Draw-A-Man (Goodenough)	56	9	48	16.5	66	7	80	9	41	22	64	10
WISC	50	5	48	16.5	72	5	85	5	4	27.5	62	6
Kuder Preference Record	69	9	87	1	40	22	52	17.5	82	7	58	12
House-Tree-Person	44	16.5	22	19	60	8	64	10	67	12	56	11
Goldstein-Scheerer Tests of Abstract & Concrete Thinking	50	16.5	22	21.5	38	22	55	15	89	14.5	50	23.5
Sentence Completion Tests (Combined)	(38)		(17)		(43)		(50)		(93)		(49)	
Vineland Social Maturity Scale	31	14	39	18	70	10	39	12	19	27.5	44	13
Otis Self-Administering	38	24	83	3	26	29.5	35	20.5	67	9	43	16
Gray Oral Reading	38	24	35	21.5	60	12	33	22.5	37	27.5	42	23.5
Vocational Interest Blank for Men (Strong)	56	12.5	78	2	21	22	26	27.5	70	11	40	15
Porteus Maze Test	38	29	13	28	38	22	47	17.5	44	17	39	34.5
Rosenzweig Picture Frustration Study	50	20	17	28	40	17.5	33	27.5	56	19.5	38	38
Arthur Point Scale of Performance Test	38	29	26	28	45	29.5	45	20.5	4	27.5	36	51
Kohs Blocks	44	29	13	21.5	30	15.5	44	16	44	17	36	23.5
Kent Series of Emergency Scales	6	24	26	21.5	21	29.5	53	14	44	22	35	27.5
Make-A-Picture Story	44	24	9	28	34	15.5	41	19	41	22	35	32
Minnesota Clerical	25	20	87	10	13	26	15	25	78	17	34	20.5
Minnesota Paper Form Board	25	16.5	91	4.5	8	26	20	29.5	70	14.5	33	18
Sentence Completion	31	6.5	17	28	19	14	42	13	52	10	33	14
Kent-Rosanoff Word Association	31	29	17	28	23	22	39	22.5	48	19.5	32	44
Test of Mechanical Comprehension (Bennett)	19	20	87	4.5	6	26	20	29.5	78	12	32	17
Vocational Interest Blank for Women (Strong)	50	16.5	74	6	23	19	21	31	19	27.5	30	20.5
Gesell Developmental Schedule	19	24	22	24	40	17.5	32	25	4	27.5	28	41
Concept Formation (Hanfmann-Kasanin)	31	29	4	28	9	29.5	27	25	59	27.5	24	56.5

[a] % = Percent mentioning using the test (Total Mentions divided by *N*).
[b] FUI Rank = Rank on Frequent Usage Index (Weighted Score minutes Total Mentions).

Table 4. Intercorrelations Among Different Kinds of Psychological Services on Frequent Usage of Tests

	VA	H & I	OPC	CC
H & I	.46			
OPC	.30	.78		
CC	.51	.04	.08	
UAC	.47	.68	.74	.50

research; there is much criticism of the test (Swenson, 1957) which needs answering (Arbit, Lakin, & Mathis, 1959). Another question is the implication of these findings for training. Certainly popularity does not mean validity. This survey does not mean that these tests should be used. It does say which tests are the leading ones, and it seems that students should be familiar enough with them to read the literature critically and evaluate the clinical testing practices that they are bound to meet.

Chapter 3

Rational-Theoretical Approaches to Assessment

The term *personality tests* tends to be reserved for personality assessment procedures that meet several criteria. Included among these criteria are the demands that the test stimulus materials should always be identical and presented in the same manner; norms should be available; and useful correlates should be known for the responses typically given to the test stimuli. In those cases where these criteria are not met, the procedure may be termed a personality assessment "technique" rather than a "test."

Personality tests or techniques may be characterized by a number of dimensions. For example, these devices vary widely in the degree of restriction, or structure, that is placed on the responses. Thus, some procedures limit the respondent to a simple "yes" or "no," while others encourage him to say absolutely anything that may occur to him. Another dimension in personality assessment devices is the degree to which formal norms are available, and a third is the amount and variety of the established validity evidence. But perhaps a more basic characteristic of personality tests lies in the rationale used to select the stimuli, such as self-descriptive statements, inkblots, or pictures.

In this chapter we examine the method that has been most widely used for selecting the basic stimuli for personality tests—the *rational-theoretical* approach. This term is offered as a kind of compromise between those psychologists who believe that many personality tests are based on simple face validity or common-sense considerations, and those, willing to use a looser definition of what constitutes a theory, who would identify these same approaches as "theoretical." In this category would be placed virtually all the assessment devices traditionally known as *projective techniques,* and it will be recalled from Sundberg's paper that, at the time of his writing, these represented the most widely used personality assessment procedures.

There has never been a satisfactory single theory or framework to "explain" the operation of projective techniques. A general introduction to this strategy was given in Lawrence K. Frank's classic paper, written in 1939, which formulates in detail a complete and sufficient explanation of projective technique methodology, at least for that time. According to Frank, the stumbling block to further advances in understanding personality at that time was an inability to gain entry to an individual's "private world." In presenting his position, Frank drew on analogies from several of the more fully developed branches of science, and the critical analogy was his likening of the projective technique to a mental X ray, which reveals the components and organization of the mind in much the same way as the X ray does for the physical body.

Thirty years of research, clinical practice, and theorizing have led us to conclude that this "X ray concept" of projection is much too simplistic to merit serious consideration. And, in spite of the ubiquity of projective techniques in clinical use, research psychologists have still not established entirely satisfactory empirical support for these techniques. The last three papers in this section deal in detail with problems in establishing such validity through research.

A possible exception to this statement regarding lack of validity is found in the *sentence completion* technique, as shown by the recent detailed review by Phillip Goldberg, our second paper. This review dates the use of sentence completion for personality assessment as early as 1928. Since that time, the sentence completion method has been put to a wide variety of uses, and in the majority of cases the individual's responses have been interpreted in a subjective and impressionistic manner for whatever they might reveal about the person. However, Goldberg's review illustrates that the best demonstrated validities are achieved when standardized and objective scoring systems are used to derive scores from the completed sentences. Paradoxically, some writers have considered that the use of structured scoring systems robs the sentence completion method of whatever intrinsic merit it has as a projective technique.

Of all projective techniques, and indeed of all personality tests, the Rorschach inkblot test has been the most widely used and also the most widely researched. The extent and complexity of the manner in which the Rorschach test has influenced the development of personality assessment practice cannot adequately be conveyed in the space available here. Yet, as indicated above, the use of the Rorschach could never be substantiated on the basis of the research designed to examine its validity, for all the great volume of this work. In attempting to account for th the Rorschach, some psychologists are now consid reasons, some involving statistical complexities, in research design, and some of which examine artifacts su correlation" phenomenon presented by Chapman and Cl 9 of this book.

A careful account of the research efforts that ha demonstrate validity for the Rorschach has been presented in a volume by Zubin, Eron, and Schumer, and a selection of their writings is reproduced as our third reading. These authors survey the wide range of research methods employed: "blind analysis," matching studies, the use of differential diagnosis and contrasted groups, laboratory validation studies, studies of prediction, of screening, and of prognosis, studies of specific signs, developmental studies, and factor analysis. In spite of this multitude of work, they conclude that satisfactory validity has simply not been shown, and they conclude that it is probably wisest to regard the Rorschach technique as a complex standardized interview and to base one's analysis on the overall *content* of this interview situation.

Many of the Rorschach studies reviewed by Zubin, Eron, and Schumer have been criticized as being naive in conception, poorly designed from a statistical viewpoint, and as failing to provide controls for important factors in determining an individual's responses. The same criticisms have been commonly leveled at the research done on other projective techniques and have often been used to explain the equivocal results. Sophisticated validity research on projective techniques does exist, however, and the fourth reading, a validity study on the Thematic Apperception Test by Bernard Murstein, provides an illustration of such sophistication. Murstein set out to examine the validity of the TAT in assessing hostility. Complexity is at once introduced when one learns that there are nine different scoring systems for hostility that merit consideration. Murstein investigated the relationship of TAT hostility, as defined in each of these nine ways, to three important variables in projective testing: the amount of hostility that is objectively present in the stimulus picture, the test-taking attitude of the subject (whether neutral or defensive), and the amount of hostility possessed by each subject as rated both by himself and by his peers. While the complexity of Murstein's results make his paper difficult to follow closely, the basic findings are clear. The more hostility that is objectively present in the pictures, the more is reported by the subjects in their stories. Second, a person's expression of hostility depends much more on whether he sees himself as hostile than on whether his peers see him that way. A variety of more complex findings and interactions in the results serves to emphasize the care and caution that must be observed in making interpretations from projective test responses.

Clifford Swenson's paper, the fifth and final in this section, reviews the validity evidence for another widely used projective technique, human figure drawings. Once again, there are shown to be certain basic problems in the interpretation of an individual's responses, such as the fact that wide variation in overall quality of drawings may mask meaningful patterns and that the reliability of individual signs is generally too low for meaningful interpretation. Swenson, however, is able to conclude that the quality of recent reseach on figure drawings represents a substantial improvement over earlier efforts, and that some empirical support does now exist for certain clinical uses of this technique.

1. PROJECTIVE METHODS FOR THE STUDY OF PERSONALITY

Lawrence K. Frank

An initial difficulty in the study of personality is the lack of any clear-cut, adequate conception of what is to be studied. The recent volumes by Allport (1937) and by Stagner (1937), and the monograph by Burks and Jones (1936), may be cited as indicators of the confusion in this field, where as they show, there are so many conflicting ideas and concepts, each used to justify a wide variety of methods, none of which are wholly adequate.

A situation of this kind evokes different responses from each person according to his professional predilections and allegiances. Obviously pronouncements will be resisted, if not derided, while polemics and apologetics will only increase the confusion. The question may be raised whether any light upon this situation can be obtained by examining the *process* of personality development for leads to more fruitful conceptions and more satisfactory methods and procedures.

Specifically, it is suggested that we reflect upon the emergence of personality as an outcome of the interaction of cultural agents and the individual child. In the space here available only a brief summary statement is permissable of the major aspects of this process in which we may distinguish an individual organism, with an organic inheritance, slowly growing, developing, and maturing under the tutelage of parents and teachers intent upon patterning him to the culturally prescribed and socially sanctioned modes of action, speech, and belief.

The child is not passive clay but a reacting organism with feelings, as are the parents, nurses, and teachers who are rearing him. He therefore receives training

SOURCE. Lawrence K. Frank (1890-1968) was one of America's most distinguished psychologists at the time of his death. A prolific author for both the professional and popular literature in child development and personality, he held a number of important research, teaching, and administrative positions during his productive professional lifetime and, most recently, was Lecturer in the Department of Planning at the Massachusetts Institute of Technology. This article originally appeared in the *Journal of Psychology,* 1939, 8, 389-409, and is reprinted by permission of the Journal Press.

in the prescribed cultural and social norms of action, speech, and belief, according to their personal bias and feelings, and he accepts this training with varying degrees of observance, always idiomatically and with feelings toward these instructors. What we can observe then is the dual process of *socialization,* involving sufficient conformity in outer conduct to permit participation in the common social world, and of *individuation,* involving the progressive establishment of a private world of highly idiosyncratic meanings, significances, and feelings that are more real and compelling than the cultural and physical world.

The foregoing does not imply any subjective duality or other traditional dichotomy; it is an attempt at a simple statement of the well-known and generally accepted view that in all events we may observe both similarities or uniformities and also individual deviations. We may concentrate upon the larger uniformities and ignore the individual components that are participating, as we do in measuring the temperature, pressure, and other properties of a gas or we may look beyond the aggregate uniformities to the individual, discrete molecules and atoms and electrons which, as we now are realizing, are highly erratic, unpredictable, and far from that uniformity of behavior described statistically. Thus, we may observe a similar antithesis between the group uniformities of economic, political, and social affairs and the peculiar personal conduct of each of the citizens who collectively exhibit those uniformities and conformities.

Culture provides the socially sanctioned patterns of action, speech, and belief that make group life what we observe, but each individual in that group is a personality who observes those social requirements and uses those patterns idiomatically, with a peculiar personal inflection, accent, emphasis, and intention. Strictly speaking, there are only these individuals, deviating from and distorting the culture; but with our traditional preoccupation with uniformities we have preferred to emphasize the uniformity of statistical aggregates of all activities as the real, and to treat the individual deviation as a sort of unavoidable but embarrassing failure of nature to live up to our expectations. These deviations must be recognized, but only as minor blemishes on and impediments to the scientific truths we seek!

Those ideas flourished in all scientific work up to about 1900 or 1905 when x rays, quantum physics, relativity, and other new insights were developed that made these earlier ideas obsolete, except in a number of disciplines which still cling to the nineteenth century. Thus it is scientifically respectable, in some circles, to recognize that uniformity is a statistical group concept that overlays an exceedingly disorderly, discontinuous array of individual, discrete events that just won't obey the scientists' laws! It is also respectable to speak of organization and processes "within the atom," although it is recognized that no direct measurements or even observations can be made within the atom; inferences being drawn from activities and energy transformations that are observable and frequently measurable.

For purposes of discussion it is convenient to see individuals (*a*) as organisms existing in the common public world of nature, (*b*) as members of their group, carrying on their life careers, in the social world of culturally prescribed patterns and practices, but living, (*c*) as personalities in these *private worlds* which they have developed under the impact of experience. It is important to recognize these three aspects of human behavior and living because of their implications for scientific study.

As organisms reacting to the environmental impacts, overtly and physiologically, human activity presents a problem of observation and measurement similar to that of all other organisms and events. The human body moves or falls through geographical space, captures, stores, and releases energy and so on. As members of the group, individuals exhibit certain patterns of action, speech, and belief that may be aggregated into larger categories of uniformity or cultural and group norms; at least we find certain pronounced, often all inclusive modes in their observed activities in which they tend to conform to social and cultural prescriptions.

When we examine the personality process or *private worlds* of individuals we face a somewhat peculiar problem, because we are seeking not the cultural and social norms of the uniformities of organic activity, but rather the revelation of just that peculiar, individual way of organizing experience and of feeling which personality implies.

In this context we may emphasize then that personality is approachable as a *process* or operation of an individual who organizes experience and reacts affectively to situations. This process is dynamic in the sense that the individual personality imposes upon the common public world of events (what we call nature), his meanings and significances, his organization and patterns, and he invests the situations thus structured with an affective meaning to which he responds idiomatically. This dynamic organizing process will of necessity express the cultural training he has experienced so that until he withdraws from social life, as in the psychoses, he will utilize the group sanctioned patterns of action, speech and belief, but as he individually has learned to use them and as he feels toward the situations and people to whom he reacts.

If it were not liable to gross misunderstanding, the personality process might be regarded as a sort of rubber stamp which the individual imposes upon every situation by which he gives it the configuration that he, as an individual, requires; in so doing he necessarily ignores or subordinates many aspects of the situation that for him are irrelevant and meaningless and selectively reacts to those aspects that are personally significant. In other words the personality process may be viewed as a highly individualized practice of the general operation of all organisms that selectively respond to a figure on a ground, by reacting to the configurations in an environmental context that are relevant to their life careers.

It is interesting to see how the students of personality have attempted to meet the problem of individuality with methods and procedures designed for study of uniformities and norms that ignore or subordinate individuality, treating it as a troublesome deviation which derogates from the real, the superior, and only important central tendency, mode, average, etc. This is not the occasion to review these methods and the writer is not competent to assess them critically, but it is appropriate to point out some aspects of the present methodological difficulty we face in the accepted quantitative procedures.

Since individuals, as indicated earlier, learn to conform to the socially sanctioned patterns of action, speech, and belief (with individual bias and flavor of their own), it is possible to establish the social norms appropriate for *groups* of like chronological age, sex, and so on and to construct standardized tests and to calculate statistically their validity, i.e., do they measure or rate what they are expected to measure or rate for each group, and their reliability, i.e., how well or reliably do they measure or rate the performance of the groups (Frank, 1939)?

While standardized tests are generally considered to be measurers of individual differences, it would be more appropriate to say that they are ratings of the degree of likeness to cultural norms exhibited by individuals who are expected, as members of this society, to conform to those group patterns. In other words, the standardized test does not tell very much about the individual, *as an individual,* but rather how nearly he approximates to a normal performance of culturally prescribed tasks for which a more or less arbitrary, but internally consistent, scheme of quantitative ratings is utilized. By the use of an all-over total figure for an individual, it becomes possible to assign numerical evaluations to individuals in various categories of achievement, skill, conformity, and so forth, such as accelerated, average, or retarded mentally; manual or verbal proficiency, etc. Having assigned him to a rank order in a group or class according to the standardized test, the individual is disposed of and adequately explained. The history of the use of standardized tests shows how they are used to place individuals in various classifications that are convenient for administration, for remedial work and therapy, or for segregation for purposes of social control, with little or no concern about understanding the individual so classified or placed, or discovering his characteristics *as an individual.*

It would seem fair to say, therefore, that standardized tests offer procedures for rating individuals in terms of their socialization and how nearly they approximate to the acceptance and use of the culturally prescribed patterns of belief, action, and speech for which statistical norms can be calculated from actual observations of performance of *groups* of individuals, according to age, sex, etc.

In order to apply these and more recently developed quantitative methods to the study of personality it has been necessary to adopt a conception of the personality as an aggregation of discrete, measurable traits, factors, or other separable entities which are present in the individual in differing quantity and organized according to individual patterns. But since the personality is more than overt activity, some way of getting at the underlying personality is necessary. The need for quantitative data has led to the use of the culturally standardized, socially sanctioned norms of speech and belief and attitudes in and through which the individual has been asked to express his personality, as in questionnaires, inventories, rating scales, etc.

If time allowed, it would be desirable to examine more fully the implications of this procedure which attempts to reveal the individuality of the person by using the social stereotypes of language and motives that necessarily subordinate individuality to social conformity, emphasizing likeness and uniformity of group patterns. This point becomes more significant when we recall that almost identical actions and speech may be used in extraordinarily different senses by each individual using them; while conversely the widest diversity of action and speech may have almost identical sense and significance for different individuals exhibiting them. Moreover the conventional traits and motives and objectives derived from traditional concepts of human nature and conduct, carry meanings often alien to the investigator using them as data. Words are generalized symbols, are usually obscuring of, when not actually misleading about the individual idiomatic personality using them (Willoughby and Morse, 1936).

It should be further noted that many procedures for study of personality rely upon the subject's self-diagnosis and revelation of his *private world* of personal meanings and feelings which the social situation compels the individual to conceal, even if, as is unusual, he had any clear understanding of himself. When we ask an individual to tell what he believes or feels or to indicate in which categories he belongs, this social pressure to conform to the group norms operates to bias what he will say and presses him to fit himself into the categories of the inventory or questionnaire offered for self-diagnosis. Moreover, as Henry A. Murray has observed, the most important things about an individual are what he cannot or will not say. The law has long recognized testimony as unreliable, to be accepted only after many checks and tests as formulated in the law of evidence.

At this point there may be a feeling of dismay, if not resentment, because the discussion has led to a seeming impasse, with no road open to study the personality by the accepted methods and procedures of present-day quantitative psychology. Moreover, the insistence upon the unique, idiomatic character of the personality appears to remove it from the area of scientific study conceived as a search for generalizations, uniformities, invariant relationships, etc. It is proposed, therefore, to discuss a few recent developments in scientific concepts and methods and the new problems they have raised in order to indicate a way out of this apparent impasse.

It is appropriate to recall that the uniformity and laws of nature are statistical findings of the probable events and relationships that occur among an aggregate of events, the individuals of which are highly disorderly and unpredictable. Theoretical physics has adjusted itself to the conception of a universe that has statistical regularity and order, and individual disorder, in which the laws of aggregates are not observable in the activity of the individual making up these aggregates. Thus quantum physics and statistical mechanics and many other similar contrasts are accepted without anxiety about scientific respectability. The discrete individual event can be and is regarded as an individual to whom direct methods and measurements have only a limited applicability. We can therefore acknowledge an interest in the individual as a scientific problem and find some sanction for such an interest.

Another recent development is the concept of the *field* in physics and its use in biology. The field concept is significant here because it offers a way of conceiving this situation of an individual part and of the whole, which our older concepts have so confused and obscured. Instead of a whole that dominates the parts, which have to be organized by some mysterious process into a whole, we begin to think of an aggregate of individuals which constitute, by their interaction, a field that operates to pattern these individuals. Parts are not separate, discrete, independent entities that get organized by the whole, nor is the whole a superior kind of entity with feudal power over its parts, e.g., a number of iron filings brought close to a magnet will arrange themselves in a pattern wherein each bit of iron is related to the other bits and the magnet and these relations constitute the whole; remove some bits and the pattern shifts as it does if we add more filings, or bits of another metal. Likewise, in a gas, the gas may be viewed as a field in which individual molecules, atoms, and electrons are patterned by the total interactions of all those parts into the group activity we call a gas. Ecology studies this interaction of various organizations in the circumscribed life zone or field which they constitute.

This field concept is highly important because it leads to the general notion that any "entity" we single out for observation is participating in a field; any observation we make must be ordered to the field in which it is made or as we say, every observation or measurement is relative to the frame of reference or field in which it occurs.

There are many other far-reaching shifts in concepts and methods that should be discussed here, but the foregoing will suffice to indicate that the study of an individual personality may be conceived as an approach to a somewhat disorderly and erratic activity, occurring in the field we call culture (i.e., the aggregate interaction of individuals whose behavior is patterned by participation in the aggregate). Moreover, the observations we make on the individual personality must be ordered to the field of that individual and his life space. We must also regard the individual himself as an aggregate of activities which pattern his parts and functions.

Here we must pause to point out that the older practice of creating entities out of data has created many problems that are unreal and irrelevant and so are insoluble. In by-gone years it was customary to treat data of temperature, light, magnetic activity, radiation, chemical activity, and so on as separate entities, independent of each other. But the more recent view is to see in these data evidences of energy transformations which are transmitted in different magnitudes, sequences, etc., and so appear as heat, light, magnetism, etc. This has relevance to the study of personality since it warns us against the practice of observing an individual's actions and then reifying these data into entities called traits (or some other discrete term), which we must then find some way of organizing into the living total personality who appears in experience as a unified organism.

With this background of larger, more general shifts in scientific procedures, let us examine some more specific developments that are relevant to our topic.

Within recent years new procedures have been developed for discovering not only the elements or parts composing the whole, but also the way those parts are arranged and organized in the whole, without disintegrating or destroying the whole. The x rays are used, not merely for photographs or to show on a fluorescent screen what is otherwise invisible within an organism or any object, but also for diffraction analysis, in which the x rays are patterned by the internal organization of any substance to show its molecular and atomic structure. Spectrographic analysis reveals the chemical components qualitatively, and now quantitatively, and in what compounds, by the way light is distributed along a continuous band of coarse and fine spectral lines, each of which reveals a different element or isotope. The mass spectroscope offers another exceedingly delicate method for determining the composition of any substance that gives off radiations whereby the electrons or their rate of travel can be measured and the composition of the substance inferred.

X rays, however, are only one of the newer methods whereby any complex may be made to reveal its components and its organization, often quantitatively, when approached by an appropriate procedure. Recently, it has been found that the chemical composition of various substances, especially proteins, can be ascertained by the reflection of a beam of light upon a thin monomolecular film of the protein substance spread on a film of oil on water over a metallic surface. Again it has been found that metallic ores and coal may be analyzed, i.e., be made to reveal their chemical composition and other properties by the "angle of wetability," the angle of reflection, or the color of the light reflected from a liquid film that adheres to the surface of the unknown material.

Polarized light has also become an instrument for revealing the chemical composition of substances without resort to the usual methods of disintegration or chemical analysis. Electrical currents may also be passed through substances, gaseous, liquid, or solid, and used to discover what they contain and in what form. Indeed, it is not unwarranted to say that these indirect methods that permit discovery of the composition and organization of substances, complexes, and organisms, seem likely to become the method of choice over the older destructive analytical procedures, because these methods do not destroy or disturb the substance or living organism being studied.

In this connection reference should also be made to the development of biological assays, whereby a living organism, plant, or animal, is used for assaying the composition of various substances and compounds and determining their potency, such as vitamins, hormones, virus, drugs, radiation, light, magnetism, and electrical currents (including electrophoresis for separating, without injury or change, the different sub-varieties of any group of cells, chemical substances, etc.). In these procedures the response of the living organism is utilized as an indicator, if not an actual measurement, of that about which data are sought, as well as the state, condition, maturation, etc., of the organism being tested. It is appropriate to note also that physicists are using such devices as the Wilson Cloud Chamber and the Geiger Counter to obtain data on the *individual* electrical particle, which reveals its presence and energy by the path traced in water vapor, or by activation of the Counter, although never itself observable or directly measurable.

These methodological procedures are being refined and extended because they offer possibilities for ascertaining what is either unknowable by other means or is undeterminable because the older analytic methods destroyed part or all of that which was to be studied. They are being accepted as valid and credible, primarily because they are more congruous with the search for undivided totalities and functioning organisms and are more productive of the data on organization on which present-day research problems are focussed. They are also expressive of the recent concepts of whole-and-parts and their interrelations, which no longer invoke the notion of parts as discrete entities upon which an organization is imposed by a superior whole, but rather employ the concept of the field. Finally they offer possibilities for studying the specific, differentiated individuality of organized structures and particulate events, which are ignored or obscured by the older quantitative determinations of aggregates.

Since the threshold task in any scientific endeavor is to establish the meanings and significances of the data obtained by any method of observation and measurement, it should be noted that these indirect methods for revealing the composition and organization of substances and structures rely upon experimental and genetic procedures to establish reliability and validity, not statistical procedures. That is to say, these newer procedures establish the meaning of any datum by employing the procedure upon a substance or structure of known composition, often made to order, so that it is possible to affirm that the resulting bending, patterning, arrangement of light, radiation, and so on, are reliable and valid indicators of the substance or structure when found in an unknown composition. These methods for establishing reliability and validity are therefore genetic in the sense of observing or tracing the origin and development of what is to be tested so that its presence or operation may be historically established: they are also dependent upon the concurrent use of other procedures which will yield consistent data on the same composition which therefore are validated by such internal consistency and congruity of findings.

Psychology developed the statistical procedures for establishing reliability and validity because the only data available were the single observations or measurements taken at one time on each subject. Since no other data were available on the prior histroy and development of the subjects, reliability had to be determined by statistical manipulation of these test data themselves; also since no other data were available on the subject's functions and activities only statistical validity could be established. It would appear that these tests of reliability and validity devised to meet the difficulty presented by absence of other data now act as barriers to the use of any other procedures for personality study in which reliability and validity for each subject is tested through these other non-statistical methods.

Methods of *temporal validation* offer great promise because they permit testing of the validity of data for a *specific subject* over a period of time, and the method of congruity among data obtained by different procedures from the same subject offer large possibilities for testing the reliability of any data for a *specific subject*. It is appropriate to recall here that the accepted methods for testing reliability and validity of tests, inventories, etc., offer indices only for the *group*, not for any individual subject in that *group*.

We may therefore view the problem of personality in terms of these more recent ideas and conceptions and consider the application of these indirect procedures for revealing the composition and organization of substances and energy complexes.

As indicated earlier the personality may be viewed as a dynamic process of organizing experience, of "structuralizing the life space" (Lewin) according to the unique individual's *private world.* This conception may be made precise and operational by seeing the individual and his changing environment as a series of fields which arise through the interaction of the individual personality with his selective awareness, patterned responses, and idiomatic feelings, with the environmental situations of objects, events, and other persons. A field organization or configuration arises out of this interaction wherein, as suggested, the personality distorts the situation, so far as it is amenable, into the configurations of its *private world,* but has to adjust to the situation in so far as it resists such distortion and imposes its necessities upon the personality. What we have called personality and fumblingly have tried to formulate as the total responses of the whole individual and similar additive conceptions becomes more understandable and approachable for investigation when conceived as the living process in this field created by the individual and the environing situation.

The objective world of objects, organisms, and events likewise may be seen as fields of interacting object-situations, upon which cultural patterns operate in the conduct of human beings who, by very reason of behaving in these learned patterns, create the cultural fields of interacting human conduct. What is highly important to note is that every observation made must be ordered—given its quantitative and qualitative interpretation—to the field in which it occurs, so that the idea of pure objectivity becomes meaningless and sterile if it implies data not biased, influenced, relative to the field in which observed. Likewise the conception of a stimulus that may be described and measured apart from the field and the organism in that field is untenable. The "same" stimulus will differ in every field, and for every field and for every organism which selectively creates its own stimuli in each situation. Indeed, this dynamic conception of the personality as a process implies that there are no stimuli to conduct (as distinct from physical and physiological impacts) except in so far as the individual personality selectively constitutes them and responds to them in its idiosyncratic patterns. In other words the stimuli are functions of the field created by the individual interacting with the situation.

Thus the movement in various areas of scientific work is toward recognition of the field concept and the devising of methods that will record not merely data but the fields in which those data have been observed and find their significance. Those who are appalled by the seeming anarchy thus threatening scientific work may be reminded that the present-day standards of scientific work and of methods are part of a development that will inevitably make today's ideas and procedures obsolete. It is well to recall how proud (justly so) chemistry was to achieve quantitative determinations of the composition of substances and now, how crude those early quantitative methods and findings now appear, when they now are seeking to find out not merely what and how much, but the spatial arrangement of the constituents as in stereochemistry where the same atoms in the same quantity produce different substances according to their spatial arrangement. It is likewise worth recalling, that about 1900, young physicists could find no problems except the more precise measurement of the pressure, temperature, etc., of a gas and were content with such crude quantitative findings. Furthermore, biologists today are accepting as commonplace that the same nutritive components, amino-acids, carbohydrates, fats, minerals, and vitamins are selectively digested, assimilated, and metabolized in different ways by each species and by each individual. Moreover, it is conceded that the proteins of each species are different as are those of each individual with the possibility of an almost unlimited number of different protein molecules, in which the same basic elements are organized into unique spatial-temporal configurations appropriate to the organic field of the individual organism.

Coming directly to the topic of projective methods for personality study, we may say that the dynamic conception of personality as a process of organizing experience and structuralizing life space in a field, leads to the problem of how we can reveal the way an individual personality organizes experience, in order to disclose or at least gain insight into that individual's *private world* of meanings, significances, patterns, and feelings.

Such a problem is similar to those discussed earlier where indirect methods are used to elicit the pattern of internal organization and of composition without disintegrating or distorting the subject, which is made to bend, deflect, distort, organize, or otherwise pattern part or all of the field in which it is placed—e.g., light and x rays. In similar fashion we may approach the personality and induce the individual to reveal his way of organizing experience by giving him a field (objects, materials, experiences) with relatively little structure and cultural patterning so that the personality can project upon that plastic field his way of seeing life, his meanings, significances, patterns, and especially his feelings. Thus we elicit a projection of the individual personality's *private world* because he has to organize the field, interpret the material and react affectively to it. More specifically, a projection method for study of personality involves the presentation of a stimulus-situation designed or chosen because it will mean to the subject, not what the experimenter has arbitrarily decided it should mean (as in most psychological experiments using standardized stimuli in order to be "objective"), but rather whatever it must mean to the personality who gives it, or imposes upon it, his private, idiosyncratic meaning and organization. The subject then will respond to *his* meaning of the presented stimulus-situation by some form of action and feeling that is expressive of his personality. Such responses may be *constitutive* as when the subject imposes a structure or form or configuration (Gestalt) upon an amorphous, plastic, unstructured substance such as clay, finger paints, or upon partially structured and semi-organized fields like the Rorschach cards; or they may be *interpretive* as when the subject tells what a stimulus-situation, like a picture, means to him; or they may be *cathartic* as when the subject discharges affect or feeling upon the stimulus-situation and finds an emotional release that is revealing of his affective reactions toward life situations represented by the stimulus-situation, as when he plays with clay or toys. Other expressions may be *constructive* organizations wherein the subject builds in accordance with the materials offered but reveals in the pattern of his building some of the organizing conceptions of his life at that period, as in block-building.

The important and determining process is the subject's personality which operates upon the stimulus-situation as if it had a wholly private significance for him alone or an entirely plastic character which made it yield to the subject's control. This indicates that, as suggested earlier, a personality is the way an individual organizes and patterns life situations and effectively responds to them, "structuralizes his life space," so that by projective methods we are evoking the very process of personality as it has developed to that moment. Since the way an individual organizes and patterns life situations, imposes his *private world* of meanings and affectively reacts upon the environing world of situations and other persons and strives to maintain his personal version against the coercion or obstruction of others, it is evident that personality is a persistent way of living and feeling that, despite change of tools, implements, and organic growth and maturation will appear continuously and true to pattern.

When we scrutinize the actual procedures that may be called projective methods we find a wide variety of techniques and materials being employed for the same general purpose, to obtain from the subject "what he cannot or will not say," frequently because he does not know himself and is not aware what he is revealing about himself through his projections.

In the following statement no attempt has been made to provide a complete review of all the projective methods now being used, since such a canvass would be beyond the present writer's competence and intention. Only a few illustrations of projective methods are offered to show their variety and their scope, in the hope of enlisting further interest in, and creating a better understanding of, their characteristics and advantages (Horowitz and Murphy, 1938).

The Rorschach ink blots, to which the subject responds by saying what he "sees" in each of a number of different blots, are perhaps the most widely known of these procedures. They have been utilized in Europe and in the United States, frequently in connection with psychiatric clinics and hospitals, for revealing the personality configurations and have been found of increasing value. In so far as life histories and psychiatric and psychoanalytic studies of the subjects who have had the Rorschach diagnosis are available, the ink blot interpretations are being increasingly validated by these clinical findings. Such comparative findings are of the greatest importance because they mutually reinforce each other and reveal the consistency or any conflicts in the different interpretations and diagnosis of a personality.

Another similar procedure is the *Cloud Picture* method, developed by Willhelm Stern, to evoke projections from a subject upon more amorphous grounds, with advantages, he believed, over the Rorschach blots. The more amorphous or unstructured the ground, the greater the sensitivity of the procedure which however loses in precision as in most instruments. Hence the Rorschach may be less sensitive than *Cloud Pictures* or clay but more precise and definite. Both the ink blots and the *Cloud Pictures* offer a ground upon which the subject must impose or project whatever configural patterns he "sees" therein, because he can only see what he personally looks for or "perceives" in that ground. The separate detail of the responses, however, are significant only in the context of the total response to each blot and are meaningful only for each subject. This does not imply an absence of recurrent forms and meanings from one subject to another but rather that the same letters of the conventionalized alphabet may recur in many different words and the same words may be utilized in a great variety of sentences to convey an extraordinary diversity of statements, which must be understood within the context in which they occur and with reference to the particular speaker who is using them on that occasion.

Play techniques are being increasingly employed for clinical diagnosis and for investigation of the personality development of children. As materials almost any kind of toy or plaything or plain wooden building blocks may be presented to the subject for free play or for performance of some designated action, such as building a house, sorting into groups, setting the stage for a play or otherwise organizing the play materials into some configuration which expresses for the subject an affectively significant pattern. In children, it must be remembered there are fewer disguises and defenses available to hide behind and there is less sophisticated awareness of how much is being revealed in play. The investigator does not set a task and rate the performance in terms of skill or other scale of achievement, since the intention is to elicit the subject's way of "organizing his life space" in whatever manner he finds appropriate. Hence every performance is significant, apart from the excellence of the play construction or activity, and is to be interpreted, rather than rated, for its revelation of how the subject sees and feels his life situations that are portrayed in the play constructions and sequences. The question of how to decide whether a particular activity is or is not meaningful is to be decided, not by its frequency or so-called objective criteria, but by the total play configuration of that particular subject who, it is assumed, performs that particular action or uses that specific construction, as an expression of his way of seeing and feeling and reacting to life, i.e., of his personality. But the degree of relevance is to be found in the context, in what precedes and what follows and in the intensity of feelings expressed. If these criteria appear tenuous and subjective and lacking in credibility, then objections may be made to the use of various methods for discovering the composition and structure of an unknown substance through which light, electric current, or radiations are passed, to give patterned arrangements or a spectrum photograph in which the position, number, intensity of lines and the coarse and fine structure indicate what the unknown substance is composed of, how organized internally, and so on. Personality studies by projective methods have not, of course, been as extensively studied nor have the patterns used by subjects been so well explored. The important point is that the way is open to the development of something similar to spectroscopic and diffraction methods for investigation of personality.

If the foregoing appears far-fetched it may be recalled that the lines on the spectroscopic plate were established, not by statistical procedures, but by experimental procedures through which a known chemically tested substance was spectroscopically tested so that its identifying line could be precisely located and thereafter confidently named. In much the same fashion it is being established that a child who is known to be undergoing an affective experience will express that feeling in a play configuration that can be so recognized. Thus, children who have lost a beloved parent or nurse, who have been made anxious by toilet training, are insecure and hostile because of sibling rivalry, etc., will exhibit those feelings in their play configurations. Experimentally produced personality disturbances can be established and their severity investigated by subsequent play forms and expressions. Moreover, the insights derived from play configurations yield interpretations that are not only therapeutically effective but often predictive of what a child will show in the near future.

Not only play toys and objects are utilized but also various plastic amorphous materials such as modelling clay, flour, and water, mud and similar substances of a consistency that permits the subject to handle freely and manipulate into various objects. In these play situations the subject often finds a catharsis, expressing affects that might otherwise be repressed or disguised, or symbolically releasing resentments and hostility that have been long overlaid by conventionally good conduct. Dolls, capable of being dismembered, can be used to evoke repressed hostility and aggression against parents and siblings. Dramatic stage play with toy figures and settings have also provided occasions in which a subject not only revealed his personality difficulties but also worked out many of his emotional problems. Clay figures are modelled by child patients in which they express many of their acute anxieties and distortions. Reference should be made to eidetic imagery, which, as Walther Jaensch in his constitutional studies has shown, indicates one aspect of the subject's way of expressing what enters into his personality make-up or way of organizing his life space.

Artistic media offer another series of rich opportunitites for projective methods in studying personality. Finger-painting has given many insights into child personality make-up and perplexities. Painting has been found very fruitful for study of personality make-up and emotional disturbances. Other clinical uses of painting have been reported that indicate the way paintings and drawings supplement the clinician's interviews and evoke responses, that are exceedingly revealing, often more so than verbal responses. Puppet shows elicit responses from child patients that are both diagnostic and therapeutic because the intensity of the dramatic experience arouses the child to a vehement expression of his feelings toward authority and toward parents and of his repressed desires to hurt others. Rôles have been assigned to individuals who are then asked to act out those rôles, impromptu, thereby revealing how tangled and repressed his or her feelings are and how release of pent-up emotion leads to insight into one's personality difficulties. Dramatic teachers are finding clues to personality in the way individuals portray the characters assigned them in a play. Music offers similar and often more potent possibilities for expression of affects that are revealing of the personality. It is interesting to note that as psychotherapy proceeds to free the patient, his art expressions, painting, modelling, music, and dramatic rendition become freer and more integrated.

As the foregoing indicates, the individual rarely has any understanding of himself or awareness of what his activities signify. In the Thematic Perception methods this unawareness offers an opportunity to elicit highly significant projections from subjects who are asked to write or tell stories about a series of pictures showing individuals with whom they can identify themselves and others of immediate personal concern. Likewise the subjects project many aspects of their personality in the completion of stories and of sentences, in making up analogies, sorting out and grouping objects, such as toys, and similar procedures in which the subject reveals "what he cannot or will not say."

Expressive movements, especially handwriting, offer another approach to the understanding of the personality who reveals so much of his characteristic way of viewing life in his habitual gestures and motor patterns, facial expressions, posture and gait. These leads to the study of personality have been rejected by many psychologists because they do not meet psychometric requirements for validity and reliability, but they are being employed in association with clinical and other studies of personality where they are finding increasing validation in the consistency of results for the same subject when independently assayed by each of these procedures. In this group of methods should be included observations on tics of all kinds and dancing as indications of tension, anxiety or other partially repressed feelings.

If we will face the problem of personality, in its full complexity, as an active dynamic process to be studied as a *process* rather than as entity or aggregate of traits, factors, or as a static organization, then these projective methods offer many advantages for obtaining data on the process of organizing experience which is peculiar to each personality and has a life career. Moreover, the projective methods offer possibilities for utilizing the available insights into personality which the prevailing quantitative procedures seeem deliberately to reject.

Here again it may be re-emphasized that the study of personality is not a task of measuring separate variables on a large group of individuals at one moment in their lives and then seeking, by statistical methods, to measure correlations, nor is it a problem of teasing out and establishing the quantitative value of several factors. Rather the task calls for the application of a multiplicity of methods and procedures which will reveal the many facets of the personality and show how the individual "structuralizes his life space" or organizes experience to meet his personal needs in various media. If it appears that the subject projects similar *patterns* or *configurations* upon widely different materials and reveals in his life history the sequence of experiences that make those projections psychologically meaningful for his personality, then the procedures may be judged sufficiently valid to warrant further experimentation and refinement. In undertaking such explorations the experimenter and clinicians may find reassurance and support in the realization that they are utilizing concepts and methods that are receiving increasing recognition and approval in scientific work that is today proving most fruitful.

2. A REVIEW OF SENTENCE COMPLETION METHODS IN PERSONALITY ASSESSMENT[1]

Philip A. Goldberg

The sentence completion method has its origins in the work of Ebbinghaus (1897), Kelley (1917), and Traube (1916) who used the method to measure intellectual variables. Though there have been more recent attempts to use the test to investigate intellectual capacity (Copple, 1956; Piltz, 1957; West, 1958), it has been used primarily in recent years as a device for personality assessment. Payne (1928) and Tendler (1930) are generally credited with being the first to use sentence completions for personality assessment.

Since that time, sentence completion methods have become increasingly more popular and the sentence completion has become a regular part of standard clinical test batteries (cf. Carr, 1958; Peskin, 1963). The essence of the method is to present the subject with a sentence fragment or stem which he is asked to complete. The instruction, content and structure of the stems vary from form to form as does the manner of categorizing the responses, but the method has generally attractive features. The content of the stems may be adapted to meet specific clinical and research purposes, and the method lends itself to group administration.

These two features of flexibility and economy seem to have been of paramount importance in gaining the sentence completion the wide popularity it currently enjoys. Sundberg (1961) found that of all the psychological tests and instruments used in clinical services, the sentence completion ranked 13 in frequency of use, and among the group personality instruments the sentence completion was second only to the MMPI.

The flexibility and popularity of the method have led to a proliferation of sentence completion forms, the origins of which are often obscure (cf. Rohde, 1948; Stein, 1949).The sentence completion method has been used to assess a variety of attitudes: attitudes toward Negroes (Brown, 1950), attitudes toward old people (Golde and Kogan, 1959), attitudes toward school life (Costin and Eiserer, 1949), attitudes toward peers and parents (Harris and Tseng, 1957),

SOURCE. Philip A. Goldberg, Associate Professor of Psychology at Connecticut College, is a clinical psychologist whose special areas of interest are person perception, schizophrenic deficit, and personality theory. This selection by Dr. Goldberg presents a thorough review of the research on one technique for the assessment of personality. This article originally appeared in the *Journal of Projective Techniques and Personality Assessment,* 1965, **29,** 12-45. Reprinted by permission of the Journal and the author.

[1]The author is indebted to his colleague, Dr. Bernard I. Murstein, for his aid and encouragement throughout the development of this paper, and to Dr. Bertram R. Forer for his generous bibliographic assistance.

attitudes toward career choice (Getzels and Jackson, 1960), attitudes toward mental hospitals (Souelem, 1955), and attitudinal change (Lindgren, 1954).

The sentence completion method has often been used to predict achievement for specialized groups. The OSS (1946) used a sentence completion form to evaluate its candidates. The sentence completion has been used to predict the success of graduate students in clinical psychology (Kelly and Fiske, 1950,1951; Samuels, 1952), and to predict the success of flight cadets (Holtzman and Sells, 1954).

The sentence completion has been used to assess differences between a wide variety of contrasted groups. Touchstone (1957) used a sentence completion test to investigate Negro-white differences. Smith (1952) compared stutterers to non-stutterers, MacBrayer (1960) investigated sex differences in sex perception and Farber (1961) used a sentence completion to assess differences in national character.

The sentence completion has proved to be useful in virtually all areas of clinical psychological research. The method has been used to examine schizophrenic language (Cameron, 1938a, 1938b; Ellsworth, 1951), and to examine the adjustment of patients to hospital routines (Luft, Wisham, and Moody, 1953). The sentence completion method has been used to evaluate counselor training (Kirk, 1956), and it has also been used in a case study of a mass murderer (Kahn, 1960).

In the bulk of these studies, the sentence completion methods used were "custom" tests, devised specifically for the particular research project. The ease of constructing sets of stems, the content of which bears a *prima facie* relationship to the variables under investigation, has encouraged a wide variety of research. Consequently, the development of a systematic and parametric body of information relevant to any one sentence completion method has been retarded. Additionally, in light of the number of sentence completion forms extant, general statements made about the method must be viewed with caution. The inter-changeability of these various forms across populations and for different purposes is unknown.

There have, however, been several attempts to construct and present "standard" forms (Holsopple and Miale, 1954; Sacks and Levy, 1950; Rohde, 1946, 1957; Stein, 1947; Forer, 1950, 1957, 1960a). Special standard sentence completion forms for use in the armed services were developed by Bijou (1947), Flanagan (1947), Trites, Holtzman, Templeton and Sells (1953), and Willingham (1958). The attempt at standardizing a sentence completion form, which has probably been most rigorous, had most impact, and provided most stimulation for further research has been that of Rotter and his associates (Rotter, 1946; Rotter, Rafferty and Schachtitz,1949; Rotter and Rafferty, 1950, 1953; Rotter, 1951; Rotter, Rafferty and Lotsof, 1954).

The Rotter Incomplete Sentences Blank (ISB) was developed out of earlier work done by Rotter and Willerman (1947), Shor (1946), Hutt (1945), and

Holzberg, Teicher and Taylor (1947). Though stemming from work done in the army, Rotter has extended the ISB for use with college and high school populations as well as the general adult population. The ISB consists of forty stems ranging in structure from "I . . . " to "My greatest worry is . . . . ". The general aims of the ISB are to provide an economical instrument for group use in assessing general psychological adjustment. A discussion of the theoretical rationale underlying the ISB, its structure, its scoring methods, and its weaknesses and strengths will be presented after a consideration of more general issues.

What Is The Sentence Completion?

The sentence completion is a method. Its status as a test or as a projective technique varies with the psychometric criteria used and with the specific sentence completion method. For Cronbach, "a test is a systematic procedure for comparing the behavior of two or more persons" (1960, p. 21). None of the available sentence completion methods would have any difficulty in meeting this criterion. If, however, the criteria are made somewhat more demanding as in Anastasi's definition that "a psychological test is essentially an objective and standardized measure of a sample of behavior" (Anastasi, 1954, p. 22), then the words *objective, standardized,* and *measure* in combination are sufficient to eliminate most sentence completion methods from further consideration as tests.

The decision as to whether the sentence completion method is or is not a test may perhaps be evaded safely as a matter of little pragmatic concern. The question as to the status of the sentence completion as a projective device is a matter of an entirely different magnitude that goes beyond taxonomic nicety. The data yielded by sentence completion methods can have no intelligibility unless there is a clear understanding of the psychological processes involved in the production of the data.

Are sentence completion responses to be treated as signs or samples? Is the response controlled by the subject and shaped by consciously maintained attitudes and beliefs devoid of deeper psychic meaning? Or, does the sentence completion response tap deeper psychic levels, involving urges and desires of which the subject is, at best, but dimly aware? Is the sentence completion a projective test and will the projection hypothesis[2] serve as an adequate

[2]The projection hypothesis, which generally serves as the theoretical rationale underlying the use of projective tests, was made most explicit by L. K. Frank (1939; 1948). Presented simply, the projection hypothesis states: when an individual is forced to impose meaning or order on an ambiguous stimulus complex, his response is a "projection" of his "feelings, urges, beliefs, attitudes, and desires . . . " (Frank, 1948, p. 66). The general relevance and validity of the projection hypothesis has been critically examined and questioned by several authors (Bellak, 1950; Cattell, 1951; Murstein, 1963).

theoretical rationale for the use of the method? What a test can or can not do involves notions of validity and implies a relatively advanced stage in the development of a psychometric instrument. A prior stage is the determination of what a test ought to, in principle, be able to do. These questions concerning the nature of the sentence completion method need answering if this prior stage is to be successfully negotiated.

Few tests have so resisted consensual typological classification as has the sentence completion. There are those who are decisive in their appraisal of the sentence completion as a projective device. Rohde states that, "In unconstrained response to sentence beginnings, the subject inadvertently reveals his true self, since there is no way in which he can anticipate the significance of his answers for personality study" (Rohde, 1946, p. 170). Holsopple and Miale (1954), Sacks and Levy (1950) are all in substantial agreement with Rohde that the sentence completion is a projective technique and that the projection hypothesis serves as the theoretical rationale for its use.

Others have expressed reservations though still regarding the sentence completion as a projective technique. Campbell (1957), in an attempt at test classification, believes the sentence completion to be a projective test, but one that differs from the Rorschach and TAT in that "rarely is the respondent unaware that he has been revealing his own attitudes" (Campbell, 1957, p. 208). Lindzey (1959) similarly regards the sentence completion as a projective test, but one that is most like the Rozenweig P-F. Forer (1950) regards the sentence completion as a "controlled projective test" (Forer, 1950, p. 3).

Still others are apparently not at all sure of what to make of the test. Hanfmann and Getzels (1953) regard it as "half way between a projective technique and a questionnaire" (p. 294). Rotter and Rafferty (1950) are similarly perplexed: "The sentence completion method of studying personality is a semi-structured projective technique . . . as in other projective devices, it is assumed that the subject reflects his own wishes, desires, fears and attitudes in the sentences he makes" (Rotter and Rafferty, 1950, p. 3). Such a statement is entirely consistent with the view that the sentence completion is a bona fide projective test. The following statement made by the same authors is not: "The responses tend to provide information that the subject is willing to give rather than that which he cannot help giving" (Rotter and Rafferty, 1950, p. 3). The juxtaposition of these two statements helps to highlight the difficulties involved in attempting to assess the sentence completion, its limits and its potential.

One of the major theoretical controversies in the field of projective testing which has special relevance for the sentence completion revolves around the "levels hypothesis." Stated most simply this approach conceptualizes personality as arranged at various and different levels of psychic functioning and organization. Different tests tap different levels and "the expression of a motive in one context or at one level of psychological organization is not highly correlated with its manifestations at another psychological level or in another stimulus context" (Forer, 1957, p. 359). Carr (1954, 1956, 1958) advances the levels hypothesis to explain the lack of congruity among data derived from different projective techniques.

Accepting the level hypothesis forces us to raise the same question in a slightly different context: Where do we position the sentence completion? What level of personality does it tap? Sacks and Levy help us very little when they say, "The SSCT (Sacks Sentence Completion Test) may reflect conscious, preconscious, or unconscious thinking and feeling" (Sacks and Levy, 1950, p. 375). Carr (1954, 1956) and Hanfmann (1947) agree that the material elicited by the sentence completion comes from a personality level closer to awareness than material elicited by either the Rorschach or the TAT. Hanfmann and Getzels (1953) are but a bit more precise: "The test (sentence completion) elicits material from a range of levels but with the bulk of it being fairly close to awareness" (Hanfmann and Getzels, 1953, p. 290). Fitzgerald (1958) in accepting this position also points out that a less "deep" test is not therefore a less valuable one. Where inferences about overt behavior are to be made, he believes that a highly structured, behaviorally-oriented projective test, such as the ISB may be more appropriate than the TAT, which he believes is better than the ISB as a "source of inferences about conflict in a given need" (Fitzgerald, 1958, p. 202).

Considering the significance of the levels hypothesis, there is unfortunately relatively little hard supporting empirical evidence. Murstein (1963) says in this regard "although the 'levels' approach appears intuitively tenable, no conclusive demonstration of the existence of discriminable levels has been made through experimental research" (Murstein, 1963, p. 67).

Stone and Dellis (1960) have conducted what is probably the most specific empirical test of the levels hypothesis. Stone and Dellis hypothesized an inverse relationship between level of personality tapped by psychological tests and the degree of stimulus structure inherent in each of the tests. The authors gave the WAIS, The Forer Sentence Completion Test, TAT, Rorschach and Draw-a-Person to a group of 20 patients hospitalized for psychiatric conditions. The tests, in the order named, were evaluated by the authors as possessing decreasing amounts of stimulus structure, and were thus hypothesized to reach increasingly less conscious levels of personality organization.

Stone and Dellis submitted the protocols to judges for "blind" ratings of amount of psychopathology. The results of the study were in striking agreement with the hypotheses. The test protocols were rated for psychopathology in the precise order predicted by Stone and Dellis. The authors conclude: "If supported by future observation and research, the Levels Hypothesis could conceivably affect the entire concept of validity in regard to projective techniques" (Stone and Dellis, 1960, p. 339).

Stone and Dellis' work has, however, been criticized by Murstein (1963) for not having a necessary control. Murstein points out in reviewing Stone and Dellis' results that, "The results might be explained on the grounds that most projective scoring systems emphasize unhealthy traits, and that projective responses are more likely to reflect frustrations than positive thought. Accordingly, the more a test permits projection in the responses made to it, the more likely it is to be scored as 'unhealthy' " (Murstein, 1963, p. 67). We believe Murstein's point to be well taken. Tests may vary in the degree to which they *permit* projection to occur without such demonstrated differences in tests' potential being related to structural differences in personality organization.

Murstein's suggested control we believe, however, to be less well considered. He suggests that Stone and Dellis should have obtained protocols from a group of normal subjects as well. It is to be expected that a group of normals would have produced protocols with less rated psychopathology. The *relationship* among the five tests, however, should be the same as obtained with the psychiatric population. This would be the expectation whether one accepts Stone and Dellis' Levels Hypothesis or Murstein's suggestion that tests differ in the degree of projection allowed.

A reconciliation of these views, at least for purposes of positioning the sentence completion, is entirely possible. A position vis-a-vis the levels hypothesis is not really necessary in order to understand the potential limits of the sentence completion. Although, as already discussed, there exists some disagreement as to the nature of the material elicited by sentence completion methods, it does seem to be the general view that the sentence completion is truly a projective test. Beyond that, most theorists apparently agree that the material elicited by the sentence completion is typically less dynamic than the material elicited by such tests as the Rorschach, TAT, and projective drawings. All this may be so whether personality is viewed as layered in different levels of psychic functioning, or whether tests are arranged in a hierarchy according to degree of permitted possible projection.

Often implicit in the levels hypothesis is the notion that tests which tap deeper layers of personality organization are better or more valid than tests which tap less deep layers. This position has, however, failed to receive empirical support. Deep levels are not necessarily better predictions of various validity criteria than less deep levels. In fact, the sentence completion is probably better substantiated than the TAT, Rorschach and DAP. Both reliability and validity tend to vary inversely with depth of level.

One further and final observation concerning the levels hypothesis; the levels hypothesis is too easily, and has been too often, abused. Accepting such a theoretical orientation in no way alters the standards for scientific rules of evidence. Though the levels approach may explain inconsistency in projective test findings, it is clearly not an alternative to an empirical test of validity. It continues to be the researcher's task to provide a behavioral referent to substantiate his claim of test validity, irrespective of the level at which he presumes to be operating.

The Effects of Instruction and Set

The instructional set given the subject varies from one sentence completion form to another. The instructions used with the ISB are as follows: "Complete these sentences to express *your real feelings*. Try to do every one. Be sure to make a complete sentence" (Rotter and Rafferty, 1950, p. 5). The emphasis of these instructions is on truthful rather than immediate responding. The instructions to the Miale-Holsopple test are even less demanding; they neither ask for quick responses nor for truthful responses. The subject is told to "complete each sentence in whatever way you wish." Rotter and Willerman (1947) and Rotter and Rafferty (1950) claim that the instructions that emphasize speed tend to produce short responses similar to responses typically obtained by word association methods. However, Sacks and Levy (1950), Stein (1947), Forer (1950), Murray, *et al.* (1948) all stress speed of responding.

There is no clear evidence that instructional emphasis on quick responding produces more immediate responding than instructions lacking such emphasis. Carter (1947) found that neurotics produce longer latencies than normals. A study by Cromwell and Lundy (1954), comparing the effects of instructions stressing speed to instructions emphasizing real feelings, found no significant differences in speed attributable to the differences in the instructions.

However much instructions may differ, it is safe to say that all of these authors wish to achieve essentially the same goal; namely, honest, non-censored responding, thereby eliciting material which will be differentially and predictively useful. If instructions vary, it is only because each author believes his instructions to be most efficient. The paucity of research findings relevant to the effects of different types of instructions on sentence completions encourages the continuation of this often gratuitous variation. Benton, Windle and Erdice (1957), in reviewing the procedural differences among sentence completion forms, conclude that "The cumulative effect of these many procedural variations is a presumptive lack of comparability among studies" (Benton *et al.*, 1957, p. 6).

It might be expected that the sensitivity of sentence completion responses to variations in the preparatory instructions would vary with the purposes of the respondents taking the test. Certainly, where the test is used in an industrial research project to measure employee attitudes (Miller and Gekoski, 1959; Friesen, 1952) the respondents' orientation might be expected to be quite different from the orientation of the patient voluntarily seeking psychotherapeutic help at an adult outpatient clinic (Hiler, 1959). It is not unreasonable to speculate that such presumed differences in test-taking attitudes would either obliterate or intensify or, in any event, interact with differences attributable to variations in instructions. Whatever the test constructor might think of his test instructions, the crucial question is what does the subject taking the test think of them?

A study by Meltzoff (1951) emphasizes the importance of mental set in response to sentence completion tests. Meltzoff hypothesized that the subject's set, as determined by a) test instructions and b) stimulus tone, directly affects the tone of the sentence completion response. To test these hypotheses, Meltzoff randomly assigned an equal number of a population of 120 college students to one of four treatment categories. All subjects were required to take a sentence completion test designed specifically for this study by the author. The test consisted of 30 of each of three types of stems: positive (e.g. He loves . . .), negative (e.g. He hates . . .) and neutral (e.g. He is usually . . .). The test was the same for all subjects, but the instructions given to the subjects varied with the treatment condition. One group of subjects worked anonymously and was asked to produce an impression of good emotional adjustment. A second group was required to sign their names to the tests and was told that the results would be discussed with the university authorities; a third group took the test anonymously and was told that it was the test that was being investigated; the fourth group also worked anonymously and was asked to try to produce emotionally disturbed protocols.

The test responses were rated by experienced judges for adjustment, and the results supported both of the main hypotheses. The degree of threat inherent in the instructional set correlated with the frequency of positively toned responses and correlated inversely with negatively toned responses. Further, Meltzoff found that negatively toned stems produced more negatively toned responses, and that there were several significant interactions between mental set and stimulus tone on the quality of the responses. "The mental sets imposed by variations of instructions had most differential effect with neutral stimuli, and least with negative stimuli. Negative stimuli tended to evoke negative responses regardless of the test condition, and in general exhibited the strongest effect among the three types of stimuli" (Meltzoff, 1951, p. 184).

From these findings Meltzoff concludes that subjects can censor their responses to the sentence completion to a considerable degree. His incidental finding that subjects who experienced more threat took more time to complete the test supports the view that subjects are able to manipulate consciously their responses to the test in a manner consistent with the image of themselves that they wish to present. Meltzoff's conclusions are consistent with Rotter and Rafferty's (1950) speculation that the test provides information which the subject is "willing" to give. Rhode (1946), however, on purely theoretical grounds, denies that the subject is able to control his responses to the sentence completion method. Further, she believes that it is "immaterial" whether the subject is telling the truth or not; he reveals himself in either event.

The importance of Meltzoff's findings is considerable. It directly challenges the tenability of the projection hypothesis as applied to the sentence completion, and raises questions about its validity with other projective devices. Meltzoff's findings would seem to require of the sentence completion user that he understand the subject's approach to the test if he is to understand the subject's responses.

One note of modification is, perhaps, in order. There is, of course, a very real question as to the generalizability of these findings from a normal group of college students to the clinical populations for which the sentence completion is most generally intended. Additional research is needed.

The Effects of Variation of the Sentence Stem

The flexibility of the sentence completion method, as noted previously, has led to a proliferation of sentence completion tests, many of which were designed for a single and limited research purpose. The research purposes have determined the stem content and form, which typically have reflected sophistication at the level of face validity. Many researchers have assumed that structuring the stem with regard to content or need would elicit responses pertaining to the same content and, or, need. There is, therefore, a considerable literature involving the use of widely different stems.

There are, unfortunately, no definite experimental studies which have systematically investigated the effects of variation in stem structure or form. What work there has been investigating the effects of stem variation has tended to fall into one of two categories; a) investigations dealing with stem structure or ambiguity and b) investigations dealing with the person of reference in the stem, i.e. self or other reference.

Stem Structure

The structure of a sentence stem is defined by the determining power of the stem's content. Nunnally's definition, "If there is an agreed-on public meaning for a stimulus, it is referred to as a *structured* stimulus" (Nunnally, 1959, p. 339), would probably be acceptable to most people working with the sentence completion method. Structure is high if the content of the stem tends to establish narrow response classes.

The content of sentence stems varies in kind and degree from one sentence completion test to another. Forer (1950) believes his test to be "fairly highly structured" whereas Rotter and Rafferty (1950) characterize their own test as "unstructured." On inspection, the two tests do seem to differ, and Rotter's ISB does seem to be less highly structured than Forer's test. The first stem on Forer's test is "When he was completely on his own, he . . . ;" the first stem on the ISB is "I like . . .". There does, however, appear to be at least some overlap between the two tests. "Men . . . " is a stem from the Forer test, and "My greatest worry is . . . " is a stem from the ISB.

The use of structured items generally reflects the test constructor's desire to direct the responses of the subject to areas pre-determined by him to be of special psychological significance. Such an approach has been exemplified by Forer (1950; 1960a). Forer reasons that if we wish to use projective test stimuli to predict behavior we must establish a stimulus equivalence between the test stimuli and the social stimuli in which we are predictively interested. Consequently, the stems in Forer's test were designed to correspond with limited areas of life in which the clinician is likely to be most interested.

The areas sampled by Forer's sentence stems are a) various important interpersonal figures, b) dominant needs, c) environmental pressures, d) characteristic reactions, e) moods, f) aggressive tendencies, and g) affective level. Forer (1950) specifies which stems were designed to elicit material from each area and he provides the user of his test with a check sheet which permits him to note the responses as well as the areas to which the responses relate. Forer says of such a procedure: "Systematic interpretation and critical diagnostic inferences are thereby encouraged and the phases of the diagnostic process can more easily be examined and systematized. In addition, quantitative norms become a distinct possibility" (Forer, 1950, p. 29).

Other sentence completion test constructors have endorsed the use of structured, content determining items. Stein (1947) in his development and extension of the OSS test, similarly used *a priori* content categories, and the sentence stems selected for use in the final form of the test had to meet criteria of category relevance and low response stereotype. Stein's categories are a) family, b) past, c) drives, d) inner states, e) goals, f) cathexes, g) energy, h) time perspective, and i) reactions to other.

All the stems in Sacks's test (SSCT) are similarly clustered in specific clinically significant content categories. The four categories chosen by Sacks are a) family, b) sex, c) interpersonal relationships, and d) self-concept. These four areas are further subdivided into fifteen sub-categories, each of which is represented by four sentence stems.

Shaping the content of stems to elicit material in specific areas of clinical interest is not, however, a universal approach. Rotter and Rafferty (1950) and Holsopple and Miale (1954) do not position their stems within specified categories. Holsopple and Miale say of their selection procedure: "For many items, the only criterion of selection which can now be identified is that they seemed to be a good idea at the time, and we suspect that some of them remained in the series because we liked them" (Holsopple and Miale, 1954, p. 5).[3]

Though Holsopple and Miale's candor has a certain amount of charm, Nash's (1958) discussion of this problem of content selection is, perhaps, more cogent:

> Variations in response to a sentence fragment should be concentrated along a limited number of dimensions, preferably along a single dimension. Simultaneous variation along a variety of dimensions dissipates the information in the responses, leaving little information available in any given dimension which is of interest to *E*. There is, then, an optimum heterogeneity in *S's* responses: this optimum is characterized by maximum heterogeneity along a limited number of dimensions and by maximum homogeneity along all other dimensions (p. 570).

Nash suggests that in order to achieve this optimum and to increase the predictive efficiency of a sentence completion test, stems should be arranged in a "tight cluster." A tight cluster of stems in one in which the constituent stems are intimately interrelated in content and structure. Nash suggests that when stems have a specified and common content, the responses to these stems are less ambiguous and more easily interpretable.

Forer (1950; 1960b) and Nash are thus in substantial agreement. Forer similarly believes that unstructured stems produce responses which are more difficult to interpret. "The interpreter lacks sufficient information regarding the stimulus situations to determine what the response means. The less the interpreter knows of the stimulus situation the less able he is to determine the role of the response in the total personality and the less able to predict behavior" (Forer, 1950, p. 17). Additionally, Forer believes that unstructured stems make it easier for the subject to avoid getting involved. Structured items, however, force the subject to respond without evasion to areas the items were designed to tap.

The construction of sentence stems with content specifically designed to elicit "significant material" seems intuitively to be a reasonable approach. Unfortunately, support for this approach has remained largely at the level of intuition, and as Rotter and others have shown, intuitions differ. There is no clear evidence to demonstrate that creating stems to conform to specific content areas increases the likelihood of eliciting responses which are significant as well as relevant to these areas. It is conceivable, in fact, that such content structuring may threaten the subject. Holsopple and Miale believe that highly structured stems do indeed constitute an obvious threat which in turn leads the subject to evade by giving responses which merely reflect conscious attitudes. Clear experimental support for this position is similarly not available.

[3]Thalland (1959), in his review of Holsopple and Miale's monograph, has some biting comments to make about such selection procedures.

It must be understood that the issue is not between stems with content and stems without content. There is nothing contentless about the stems in the ISB. The difference between the Forer, Stein, and Sacks tests is that the authors of the more structured tests have explicitly prescribed the content areas for which they wish to elicit information. As for the unstructured tests, their stems are likely to have less obvious content structure, but to assume that there is no structure would require that every stem would have an equal probability of eliciting material in any given area. There is no experimental evidence demonstrating the existence of such stems, and it is unlikely that such stems could be constructed.

In the absence of evidence that structure facilitates assessment, the decision as to which approach to use will probably be answered by preference and purpose. As the aims of Rotter's test and Forer's test are quite different, it is possible that each has adopted the approach most valid for his purpose. The ISB was designed to be a group screening device that would provide a summary score of general psychological adjustment. Forer was more concerned with devising an aid to clinical personality analysis and description.

Dole and Fletcher (1955) present the most specific principles as to the effects of stem structure on sentence completion responses reported in the literature. The principles presented by Dole and Fletcher are based on an analysis of 500 protocols of the *Dole Vocational Sentence Completion Blank* (DVSCB) (Dole, 1958). Though the authors' specificity is impressive, the principles presented are largely grammatical ones: e.g., "When the stem is a coordinate clause, the completion is usually a subordinate clause" (Dole and Fletcher, 1955, p. 107). Similar precision involving principles of a somewhat more dynamic nature are to be hoped for.

Trites (1955, 1956) found that structured unambiguous stems tend to elicit responses which are unambiguous. Peck and McGuire (1959) similarly found that well defined sentence stems yield less ambiguous data then relatively unstructured stems. King (1958) used a sentence completion form developed for his study to investigate sexual identification in a group of college males. He found that the responses which indicated "sexual confusion" were normatively tied to specific stems, and he concluded that the responses were, at least in part, a function of the stimulus properties of the specific stems. Rozynko (1959) correlated the rated social desirability of sentence completion responses obtained from 50 psychiatric patients. He found that "the social desirability of the sentence stem performs the function of establishing the direction of the response. A socially desirable stem tends to evoke a socially desirable response and *vice versa*" (Rozynko, 1959, p. 280).

Based on the available evidence there seems little doubt that the *content* of a response can be controlled to a considerable degree by the structure of the stem. "My mother . . . " leads obviously to more predictable response content than the stem "My . . . ". The question is, what is the effect on the *significance* of the content as the structure of the stem increases. It is possible that increasing stem structure provides the tester with greater control over less significant material. Advocates of structured stems have tended to stress the advantages of content control. Advocates of unstructured stems have tended to stress the advantages of honest responding, which is presumed to be facilitated by relatively unstructured stems. Research is needed which will investigate the relationship of content control and response significance to varying degrees of stem structure.

Person Reference

Two of the sentence stem properties that have generated most interest have been the person of the pronouns used and the effects related to variations in the personal reference of the stem. Logically consistent with the projection hypothesis is the assumption that a subject is more likely to reveal himself when talking about another person, and more likely to manifest defensive behavior when talking about himself. Many workers have accepted this assumption and have cast their stems in the third person. Here too, however, agreement is far from complete.

Rotter and Rafferty (1950) and Sacks and Levy (1950) use stems that are neutral or cast in the first person. Forer (1950) and Stein (1947) use stems cast in both the first and third person. Stein, interestingly, refers to first person as "personal" and third person stems as "projective." Forer believes that third person stems supplement first person stems in eliciting material that would be too threatening in response to the more charged first person construction. Holsopple and Miale (1954) use two first person stems; the rest of their list of 73 stems is either in the third person or neutral.

Trites *et al.* (1953) employed a variation not so easily categorized. Their sentence completion form was intended for use as a screening device with Air Force flying personnel. The cadets taking the test were shown a large sketch of an aviation cadet and instructed to complete the sentences "by writing what the cadet in the picture is saying" (Trites *et al.*, 1953, p. 7). Once again, though the purposes and aims of the test constructors are essentially the same, the procedures used to achieve the goal vary in almost all possible ways. Given the fact that this variability is not occurring among grossly different techniques, but rather within the limits of a single method, the variability is remarkable. It is hard to imagine a sound scientific model that would legitimatize all these approaches.

There has fortunately been a fair amount of work investigating the effects of person reference. The first and most important study dealing with this problem is one by Sacks (1949). Sacks developed two forms of a 60 stem sentence completion which were identical except that one form had stems that were all cast in the first person, whereas in the other form the stems were in the third person. Both forms were given to 100 neuro-psychiatric patients. Three psychologists rated the subjects for disturbance on the basis of the sentence completions and the psychiatrists treating the patients rated them for disturbance on the basis of clinical impressions.

The results of the study clearly indicated that the first person form manifested greater agreement with the psychiatric ratings than did the third person form. An additional finding was that six of the seven psychologists who took part in the study preferred the first person form for clinical use.

Sacks' study is an interesting and important one. Nonetheless, questions might be raised about the criterion used to evaluate the two sentence completion forms. It might be suggested that the psychiatrists in their ratings were responding to the more peripheral aspects of personality; that they were in fact responding mainly and merely to what the applicants chose to tell them. If this were so, and if it is further assumed that first person stems lend themselves to greater conscious control, Sacks' findings would assume a quite different significance. The congruence of the ratings based on the first person form with the psychiatric ratings would only demonstrate an equal lack of profundity. The lack of agreement between ratings based on the third person form with the psychiatric ratings would be consistent with the assumption that such a form taps the projective core of personality.

There is no wish to defend this highly speculative argument, but rather to merely present it. There is no direct empirical support for such a position, but a study by Morton (1949) is interesting and suggestive. Morton found that the ISB correlated .40 with the Mooney Problem Check List. This check list (Mooney and Gordon, 1950) consists of a number of statements, each of which refers to a specific problem. The subject is asked to check the problems which concerns him. As is obvious, the information generated by the check list is limited by the subject's willingness to reveal the information. The significant correlation of the ISB (a first person form) with such an instrument raises questions about the degree of conscious control the subject has and uses in responses to the ISB and other tests of this kind. It would be of some interest to know the correlation of a third person form of the ISB with the Mooney.

Arnold and Walter (1957) corroborate Sacks' finding that the person reference of the sentence stem is an important determinant of the response. They used the ISB as a self-reference form and a variation of the ISB as an other-reference form. They gave these forms to 120 female college students and found that the two forms correlated r=.55. The authors concluded that first and third person forms are not interchangeable.

Cromwell and Lundy (1954) do, however, support Sacks' contention that first person stems are superior to third person stems. Thirty-nine clinical psychologists made personality inferences about 60 VA neuro-psychiatric patients on the basis of data obtained from a sentence completion form designed for the study. The author had the clinicians make specific hypotheses about the subjects and additionally asked the clinicians to indicate the specific sentences which had contributed to their evaluations. By this method the authors were able to assess the differential productivity of the stems, and they found that first person stems were clinically more productive than third person stems. No attempt, it should be noted, was made to validate the clinical inferences.

In a study by Forer and Tolman (1952) it was found that clinicians asked to make judgments about the potential clinical value of each stem in the Forer Structured Sentence Completion Test showed no preference for either first or third person constructions. Though these results are not consistent with the findings of Cromwell and Lundy, it should be noted that the clinicians made their judgments using a blank form. It is entirely possible that had the clinicians seen what the stems could "do," they would have, as in the study by Cromwell and Lundy, shown a similar preference for first person stems.

A study by Hanfmann and Getzels (1953) offers some support for the use of third person stems. Using third person stems, the authors tested a group of white and Negro high school girls with a specially constructed sentence completion form. A special procedure termed by the authors, the *Self-Reference Technique,* was used. This technique consisted of reviewing each of the responses with the subject and asking her whether or not the responses to the test were true of herself. Hanfmann and Getzels found that the subjects identified 70% of the responses as personally relevant. On the basis of these data, the authors suggest that third person stems elicit self-revelatory responses, the bulk of which tap a level of personality organization fairly close to consciousness. This study did not provide a direct comparison of the efficacy of first person versus third person stems. Consequently, these findings are, at best, suggestive.

In summary, there is considerable variability in the treatment of the stem relative to the person of reference. This variability seems to be related to theoretical assumptions that are largely untested, unstated, or both. What empirical evidence there is does seem to favor the first person construction of sentence stems. The evidence is, however, far from being definitive.

Treatment of the Response

There are a variety of ways of treating sentence completion responses reported in the literature, and several authors use more than one method of analysis. Basically, however, responses are either subjected to a) formal analysis, or b) content analysis, and content analysis methods may be further classified as semi-objective or impressionistic.

Formal analysis refers to the assessment of the non-meaningful properties of the sentence completion response. Benton, Windle, and Erdice (1957) classify some of the formal analyses that have been reported:

(a) Length of completion (Carter, 1947; Wilson, 1949).
(b) Use of personal pronouns (White, 1949).
(c) Time for reaction and for completion (Carter, 1947; Meltzoff, 1951; White, 1949).
(d) Absolute and relative frequencies of parts of speech, such as verb/adjective ratio (Ellsworth, 1951; Mann, 1941).
(e) Range of words used in relation to number of words used (Mann, 1941).
(f) Grammatical errors, nonsensical responses, or neologisms (Cameron and Margaret, 1949: White, 1949).
(g) First word used (Benton, Windle, and Erdice, 1952).

Guertin (1959), in a factor analytic study of errors (e.g. misspelling) made on the ISB, found four factors which related to other clinically significant material. Wilson (1949), however, found that analyses of sentence completion data for misspellings, use of sentence fragments, response length and other formal characteristics did not discriminate groups of well adjusted and groups of maladjusted school children, and she suggests that a content analysis approach would be more discriminating. This recommendation, whatever its merits, does seem to be consonant with general practice. The treatment of sentence completion responses most typically involves the analysis of content.

Content analysis, however, is anything but a monolithic procedure. Approaches to the content analysis of sentence completion responses have been many and varied, but they have tended to polarize on a dimension of objectivity. Many authors have used highly subjective impressionistic methods. These methods have had historical priority in the development of the sentence completion and they continue to be widely endorsed.

In contrast, there have been a number of attempts to develop objective scoring procedures for the analysis of content. It should be understood, however, that even the most objective methods of scoring sentence completion responses involve a high degree of subjectivity. Free-response tests defy clerical scoring, and though there have been variants of the sentence completion method that lent themselves to greater objectivity, these have typically involved the imposition of response limits (Grigg and Kelley, 1960; Izard, Rosenberg, Bair, and Maag, 1953; Shay, 1950). It is doubtful, as Benton, Windle, and Erdice (1957) point out, that these variants are comparable with the traditional free-response forms.

Impressionistic Methods

Holsopple and Miale (1954) are probably, of all the sentence completion test constructors, the ones who are most committed to a clinically impressionistic method of coping with sentence completion responses. They maintain:

> This desire to achieve a scoring system which would provide for a more "objective" handling of the data sounds like a reasonable desire, but we believe that an effort in this direction at the present time would be premature. . . For the time being, however, we believe that more and better material can be acquired by a process of interpretation sentence by sentence until an acceptable global description is achieved (Holsopple and Miale, 1954, p. 6).

In order that the reader might gain a truer understanding of the clinical interpretation of the sentence completion, Holsopple and Miale present their clinical interpretation of a sample protocol, taken response by response. Toward this same end, the interpretation of the response "they are right" given to stem 1 *Children are usually certain that . . .* is presented in full:

> It did not occur to the subject to say that children are usually certain that they are loved or that they can have their own way. On the basis of our observation that adults here often ascribe certainty to children in areas of their own more important uncertainties, the question raised at the outset is 'How right am I?' The implication is that being right is important, and the subject has some doubts about his judgment (Holsopple and Miale, 1954, p. 45).

Stein (1947) similarly regards the sentence completion as a method of generating useful data to which the clinician may respond interpretively. The validity of the clinician's interpretations are presumably correlated with his experience, sensitivity and general clinical expertise. Sacks and Levy (1950) also believe that a non-quantitative or clinical approach is called for. Such an approach has greater flexibility which they believe is required, considering our primitive understanding of human personality. Forer (1960a) rejects the quantitative scoring systems of Rotter *et al.,* (1949) and Rohde (1957) as having limited clinical utility. Elsewhere, (Forer, 1960b) in discussing objective quantitative scoring systems for the sentence completion, Forer says:

> While such neatness facilitates validation, the evidence in the research literature is that the sheer occurrence of magnitudes of drives or traits has little predictive utility. Particularly does this appear to be the case because such labeling or quantification of needs provides no evidence of the likelihood or conditions or forms of expression of these needs. Rather a growing focus in description of the personality deals with the enduring organizing aspects, often conceptualized as the ego or the self (Forer, 1960a, p. 215).

There is meager empirical support for the impressionistic approach to content analysis. Dean (1957) used the ISB in combination with other tests to assess the adjustment of blind subjects. Rotter's quantitative scoring system was unable to discriminate well adjusted subjects from poorly adjusted subjects. Dean concluded that a qualitative approach would be more useful. Unfortunately, he did not put his faith in a qualitative approach to an empirical test. Stein (1947), Holsopple and Miale (1954), and Forer (1960a) all offer clinical, non-quantitative data to support impressionistic analysis. Beyond this, there is little firm experimental evidence to support the impressionistic approach to content analysis.

Further, even Sacks, Stein, and Forer are apparently not entirely willing to submit their tests to completely free impressionistic analysis. These authors arrange their stems, as previously noted, in specified content categories and they direct users of their tests to organize their clinical efforts within these categories. And though it is certainly true that these authors permit clinicians considerable latitude in the interpretation of the responses, they do offer relatively pointed interpretive guides.

Sacks, in fact, uses a rating procedure similar to the one devised by Rotter and Willerman (1947). He clusters his sentence stems within each of his categories and rates the subject on a four point scale for degree of disturbance in each of the fifteen clinical areas. These ratings are achieved through clinical acumen and no attempt is made to treat the ratings statistically. Sacks' method seems to be but a step away, albeit a good size step, from being an objective, quantitative method of content analysis. There is also an attempt, reported in the literature, to apply Rotter and Willerman's rating procedures to Forer's stems. Karen (1961) reports reliability coefficients ranging from .90 to .96 for this method. Unfortunately, this work was based on only eight items, and no attempt was made to validate the procedure.

Stein eschews the use of ratings, but he does cluster his stems, and he presents seven principles to sensitize clinicians to critical responses. Forer, too, clusters his stems and presents the potential user of this test with a number of interpretive tips. These attempts to make the bases for clinical impression more public and consensual, coming as they do from people committed and sympathetic to the clinical approach, seem to emphasize the ultimate desirability of the clinical cookbook (Meehl, 1956). The issue is, however, as it has always been, the feasibility and not the desirability of a cookbook approach. Is an acturial approach theoretically possible? And if it is theoretically possible, are we, at out present level of sophistication, ready for it?

These questions will not be answered here, but ready or not there is considerable evidence in the general clinical literature and in the sentence completion literature specifically, that clinical impressionistic methods involve a too full measure of risk and uncertainty.

In a study by Masling (1957), eight clinical psychology graduate students were required to give and interpret ISB's obtained from female undergraduates. Unknown to the graduate students, the testees were accomplices who had been instructed to assume either a "warm" or "cold" role toward the examiner according to a predetermined schedule. Masling defines the roles as follows:

> In the warm role the accomplice was told to act friendly and interested in both the testing situation and the examiner, the goal being to make him feel comfortable and accepted. In her cold roles she was to act in a formal, disinterested way and her object was to make him feel awkward and incompetent (Masling, 1957, p. 378).

Each examiner saw one "cold" and one "warm" testee. The protocols, though different in content, had been prepared so that they were equal in rated adjustment. The examiner-subjects were asked to write clinical interpretive reports for the two protocols. After all references to the examiner-testee relationships had been deleted, the reports were analyzed for number of positive and negative statements made about the testee. The ratings were done blind, and the results were as predicted in that "warm" subjects were perceived more positively than "cold" subjects.

In evaluating the significance of these findings it must be remembered that the examiners were relatively inexperienced graduate students. Nonetheless, the study is intriguing and the results provocative. The sentence completion method may be even more of a projective device than its adherents had ever intended. It is, moreover, unfortunate that Masling did not also have the examiner rate the ISB's using Rotter and Rafferty's procedure which is alleged to involve a high degree of objectivity. It would have been of considerable interest to know if "objective" scoring procedures are similarly sensitive to the effects of "warm" and "cold" interactions.

A study by Horowitz (1962) attempted to assess the accuracy of clinical judgments based on projective test data. The clinicians were asked to predict to Q sort descriptions made by patients' psychotherapists. *Michigan Sentence Completion Test* protocols were part of the projective data available to the clinicians. The major finding was that the clinical judgments were no more accurate than base rate predictions.

In a study by Luft (1950) experienced clinicians and physical scientists were asked to identify patients' true responses to the OSS sentence completion test from among lists of five alternatives. The judges were presented with tape recordings of the patients' diagnostic interviews as a basis for their identifications. The clinicians and non-clinicians were equally unable to predict the sentence completion responses.

There have been a number of studies which have questioned the efficacy of the impressionistic approach.[4] A number of studies by Fiske and his associates,

[4]For a broader discussion of this issue, the reader is advised to consult Meehl (1954), Holt (1958), and Schafer (1949).

however, suggest that the problem may not be with the clinical method *per se,* but rather with the instability of the data. Fiske and Van Buskirk (1959) had clinicians do a Q sort of 30 need variables using sentence completion protocols. Three protocols obtained at different points in time were obtained from each of eight subjects. This procedure permitted Fiske and Van Buskirk to answer the question: "Are the differences between the interpretations of protocols from the same person less than the differences between interpretations of protocols of different persons?" (Fiske and Van Buskirk, 1959, p. 177). The authors found that "in 25% of the comparisons, the agreement was higher with protocols for different subjects than with other protocols from the same subject" (Fiske and Van Buskirk, 1959, p. 180).

This study developed from a more general interest in the problem of intra-individual response variability, reviewed by Fiske and Rice (1955). In other studies (Osterweil and Fiske, 1956; Fiske, 1957) it was found that sentence completion responses showed great variability on repeat-testing. Of special significance was the finding by Osterweil and Fiske that those responses which were most individuating and useful to the clinician were the ones which were least stable over time.

Stephens (1960) reported that "the stems with lowest retest reliability were those which were rated by judges as being most likely to be sensitive to change in adjustment" (Stephens, 1960, p. 333). Such a finding tends to support the results obtained by Osterweil and Fiske, but in at least one important sense it alters the interpretation of Osterweil and Fiske's data. If Stephens' data are valid, then the instability of the sentence stems is a function of *true* personality change rather than random variability. Further, these results question the legitimacy of traditional notions of test-retest reliability as applied to a personality test like the sentence completion. This old and thorny problem has been discussed at length by MacFarlane and Tuddenham (1951) and others. The general conclusion seems to be that the projective test user must find other non-temporal methods of coping with the problem of reliabilty.

Nonetheless, however achieved, there does appear to be considerable intra-individual response variability; a fact which presents the actuary and the clinician alike with a problem of considerable magnitude.

Semi-Objective Methods

The validity and power of sentence completion test analyzed impressionistically can be no greater than the skill of the clinician using the instrument. In general practice the validity of the test and the astuteness of the tester are non-independent. As methods of analysis become more objective, the analytic role of the clinician decreases. Whether this relationship is viewed with alarm or delight, the relationship as such is incontestable.

The most rigorous and objective system of scoring the content of sentence completion responses has been presented by Rotter and Rafferty (1950). Each completion is scored on a 7 point scale from 0 to 6 for degree of conflict (C). There are three classes of C responses, three classes of positive (P) responses, and a class of neutral (N) responses. The scoring of the responses is guided by examples provided in the test manual with separate scoring manuals provided for males and females. The ISB user compares the response to the examples provided in the appropriate manual, and assigns the rating given to the example which is most similar to the one he has obtained. The list of examples contained in the manual is not intended to be exhaustive, and the authors provide general scoring principles to be used in combination with the specific examples.

As an illustration, item 10, "People . . ." is presented with the examples of scoring weights given in the male manual:

(6) C3 disturb me; worry me; never understand me; frighten me; have it in for me; are hateful
(5) C2 annoy me (strong criticism of people in general—e.g., destroy what they build; have a deplorable sense of value); (indication of unfavorable attitude toward subject—e.g., think that I am a snob)
(4) C1 can be got along with if you try; do not cooperate enough; run around in circles most of the time
(3) N are sometimes good, sometimes bad; who are truthful will be rewarded; work to achieve something; inherit the world; are interesting to study; (stereotypes—e.g., are funny; are crazy)
(2) P1 are interesting; are fascinating; are nice
(1) P2 are good; are basically good; I like
(0) P3 are fun; I like them all; are wonderful; are the salt of the earth; touch wet paint in spite of wet paint signs (Rotter and Rafferty, 1950, p. 58)

After the responses are rated individually, the weights are totaled to produce an over-all "adjustment" score. The higher the score, the greater the degree of maladjustment.

In a validation study by Rotter, Rafferty and Schachtitz (1949), it was found that a cutting score of 135 correctly identified 68% of maladjusted female college students, 69% of maladjusted male students, 80% of well-adjusted females and 89% of well-adjusted males. In light of the simplicity of the scoring system and the relative homogeneity of the population, these results are impressive. A cross-validation study by Churchill and Crandall (1955) yielded results in essential agreement with the original findings, and the authors suggest that the ISB norms may be applicable in a variety of college settings. Arnold and Walter (1957), however, found that for another college population the cutting score of 135 seemed to be pegged too low.

If the "objectivity" of an objective test is simply defined in terms of its ability to be scored with perfect agreement by a number of judges, then based on a number of empirical studies, it is clear that the ISB *approaches* being an objective test. Rotter, Rafferty and Schachtitz (1949) report interscorer reliabilities of .91 and .96 for male and female protocols respectively. Using the high school form of the ISB, Rotter, Rafferty and Lotsof (1954) report interscorer reliabilities of .96 and .97 for the boys' and girls' manuals. Studies by independent researchers report interscorer reliabilities for the ISB that are comparably high. Jessor and Hess (1958) report an interscorer reliability of .97; Churchill and Crandall (1955) for a sample of female subjects report interscorer reliabilities ranging from .94 to .98; Bieri, Blancharsky and Reid (1955) found interscorer reliability to be .95; Arnold and Walter (1957) found interscorer reliability to be .97; Chance (1958) obtained an interscorer reliability of .89; and Cass (1952) reports an interscorer reliability of .90.

The success achieved by Rotter and his associates in developing reliable scoring methods has encouraged other attempts at objectifying the content analysis of sentence stems through the use of manuals of scoring examples. Sechrest and Hemphill (1954) devised a manual of scoring examples to be used specifically with Air Force personnel which proved to be sensitive to motivational variables involved in the assumption of combat responsibility.

Trites *et al.* (1953) report the development of a scoring manual based on the protocols of 1,038 flight cadets. The manual contained principles and examples that permitted the assignation of a response to one of thirteen categories. Each category had two properties: a) it referred to a particular attitude, and b) it had either a positive or a negative tone. An example of one of Trites *et al.*'s categories (Category L, *Sexuality Attitudes*) as defined in their manual is, "Expresses positive, mature, heterosexual attitude toward dating, courtships, love, marriage, sexual and marital relations" (Trites *et al.*, 1953, p. 21). Using a scoring manual to assign responses to such categories, judges achieved interscorer reliabilities ranging from .80 to .94. These reliabilities are quite respectable and are comparable to the reliabilities reported by Rotter and Rafferty (1950).

Rychlak, Mussen and Bennett (1957) believe that objective methods of scoring sentence completion responses are more appropriate for research purposes than more impressionistic methods. Accordingly, in a study using a sentence completion test to measure social adjustment in native Japanese students enrolled at an American university, the authors attempted to construct a scoring manual that would facilitate the objective scoring of the sentence completion.

They made hypotheses about ten personality variables presumed to be related to social adjustment. Their scoring manual defined each of these variables, gave examples of responses that related to them, predicted the relationship of each variable to social adjustment, and presented the theoretical rationale underlying each prediction. Each response was scored on all appropriate variables, and the score for each variable was the number of responses which had been relevant to the particular variable. The percentage of interscorer agreement for this scoring procedure was .80.

In their study, Rychlak *et al.* correlated the sentence completion adjustment scores on each of the ten personality variables with social adjustment ratings based on interview data. Six of the ten correlations were significant at $p < .05$ or better. The authors concluded that the sentence completion test scored by their procedures "proved to be a remarkably efficient predictor of the quality of the individual's social relationships" (Rychlak *et al.*, 1957, p. 28).

Perhaps the most elaborate and ambitious scoring system is reported by Rohde (1946, 1957). Responses to each one of her 65 sentence stems are analyzed in terms of Murray's theory of needs and presses. She employs 38 categories of needs, inner integrates, inner states, and general traits, each of these variables being scored for strength. The criteria for assessing the strength of a variable are frequencey and intensity. "Frequency is obtained by counting the number of occurrences of the variable. Intensity is estimated on a 1 to 3 scale: (1) low, (2) medium, (3) high. The determinant is the vividness and potency with which the variable is expressed. For example, a suggestion of annoyance is rated 1, and outright expression of dislike is rated 2, while intense hatred is rated 3 in reference to *n* Rejection" (Rohde, 1957, p. 63).

Rohde (1946) conducted a validation study of her test using the scoring procedures described above. One hundred high school students, 50 boys and 50 girls, were given the *Rohde-Hildreth Sentence Completion Technique,* and each of 33 variables abstracted from the test was rated on a ten point scale. On the basis of interviews with teachers and school supervisors, another set of ratings for the subjects was obtained to serve as the criterion measure for the validation of the test. The correlations between these two sets of ratings were impressively high, .79 for the girls and .82 for the boys. However, as both Rotter (1951) and Zimmer (1956) note, the experimenter was involved in the rating of the criterion measure as well as the scoring of the test responses. The possibility of bias confounding the data is clear and unfortunate.

In studies by Jenkins and Blodgett (1960) and Jenkins (1961), attempts were made to quantify the *changes* in sentence completion responses on repeat testing. Using the Miale-Holsopple test, the authors paired responses given to the same stems at two different times. Judges were asked to compare the second response to the first and rate the response for improvement (+) or worsening (–). The pluses and minuses were summed to give an over-all improvement score. These scores were used to predict or postdict improvement for a group of juvenile delinquents (Jenkins and Blodgett, 1960) and for a group of schizophrenics (Jenkins, 1961). These scoring methods did have some success in predicting improvement and are considered by the authors to have considerable promise.

The scoring procedures used by Jenkins and Blodgett and Rotter are characterized not only by features of objectivity and quantification, but by emphasis on a single score whether it be "improvement" (Jenkins and Blodgett) or "adjustment" (Rotter). This approach is quite different in procedure and purpose from other semi-objective methods, such as the one used by Trites *et al.* and Rychlak *et al.* who attempted to assess a number of variables.

Scoring all responses from a given sentence completion test for a single variable rather than for a number of variables has the obvious effect of increasing the test's length and reliability. The increasing monotonic relationship between test length and reliability is well known and accepted (Guilford, 1954). In a study by Mishler (1958) there is empirical support, specific to the sentence completion test, for the value of increasing the number of sentence stems in order to decrease instability.

Zimmer (1956) shares this view: "The attempt to derive only a single variable, rather than several from a test record may increase the likelihood that an adequate number of responses relevant to all aspects of the variable can be obtained, and may thereby contribute to the stability and accuracy of prediction" (Zimmer, 1956, p. 67). In his review of sentence completion validation studies, he concludes that an objective scoring system is a more promising method than a global impressionistic evaluation. Most promising of all, he believes, are approaches that combine objective scoring systems with single variable analysis.

Such an approach would seem to be the most generally useful method of treating sentence completion responses for research purposes. A single variable orientation is likely to maximize data relevance, and objectification facilitates replication, which is, after all, the corrective that distinguishes the scientific enterprise. Is the single variable-objective scoring system treatment of responses an equally valuable method for general clinical purposes?

Merely raising the question tends to furnish the answer. Clinical purposes are typically different from research purposes. Data relevance and procedural replicability are, of course, important to the clinician. His purpose in using projective techniques for personality assessment, however, reside in the power of these tests to generate hypotheses which will help him to describe and understand the particular patient with whom he is confronted. A single summary score of psychological adjustment, however sophisticated psychometrically, is likely to be regarded by the clinician as limited at best.

Problems in the Assessment of Validity

In Table 1, some 50 studies bearing on the validity of the sentence completion method are summarized. Even a cursory inspection of the table suggests that there can be no unequivocal claim for the validity of the sentence completion method. Many tests, scored in many ways, using a variety of criteria, applied to a variety of populations, have yielded a variety of data.

Standard and Custom Tests

Research with 26 different sentence completion forms is reported in Table 1. Of these 26 forms, 11 have been presented by their authors as standard forms; the others, referred to as *custom* tests, were by and large designed for the study of specific variables. Of the 50 studies summarized, the ISB has 15 citations with the next most cited test having four. No claim is made that this table is a perfect reflection within any of its categories of the nature and amount of work done with the sentence completion method. Nonetheless, whatever the true proportions, it is clear that the ISB has received more research attention than any other standard sentence completion form.

It is entirely possible, however, that sentence completion forms designed for more general clinical purposes like the Forer, SSCT, Miale-Holsopple, and the Rohde are in wider clinical use than the research literature suggests. It is not entirely unlikely, though it would be unfortunate, that clinical instruments with least research support are most "used," and that instruments such as the ISB are most researched because they lend themselves to research purposes irrespective of pragmatic virtue.

One further note about the various completion forms. Many of the standard sentence completion tests available have their roots in work done during World War II (c.f. Holzberg, Teicher and Taylor, 1947; Hutt, 1945) and most of the others are also at least a decade old. It is not suggested here that new tests are best. Certainly, any test that could be of value ten years ago in the assessment of personality is very much up to date. It is interesting to note, however, what might be referred to as the sociology of test construction. Shortly after the War a spate of sentence completion tests were made available, but more recently other tests appear to have caught the creative fancy of people in the field.

A notable exception to this trend is provided by a sentence completion form constructed by Stotsky and Weinberg (1956). In follow-up studies by Stotsky (1957), Connors, Wolkon, Haefner, and Stotsky (1960), and Wolkon and Haefner (1961) the Stotsky-Weinberg Sentence Completion Test has appeared to be a sensitive and useful instrument for assessing ego-strength in psychiatric subjects.

Subjects

Captive groups have traditionally been the major source of subjects for psychological experimentation. So, too, has it been the case with sentence completion research. Three groups have been most used; college students, psychiatric patients, and armed forces personnel. The last-named group may

Table 1. A Summary of 50 Representative Sentence Completion Validity Studies

Test	E	Method of Analysis	N	*S*s	Criterion	Results
Forer	Meyer & Tolman (1955)	Rated for attitudes toward parental figures	20	Therapy patients	TAT & interview data	r = N.S. (value of r not reported)
Forer	Carr (1956)	Rated for 4 affect categories	50	Male patients in a mental hygiene clinic	Rorschach variables	χ^2: 13 significant relationships at $p < .10$ or better
Forer	Stone & Dellis (1960)	Rated on Menninger Health-Sickness Rating Scale for amount of psychopathology	20	Schizophrenics	WAIS, TAT, Rorschach, DAP	Difference in amount of pathology between SCT & Rorschach; SCT & DAP $p < .01$
ISB[1]	Rotter & Willerman (1947)	Ratings on a 7 point scale of conflict using a scoring manual of examples	200	AAF convalescent hospital patients	Evaluation of severity of disturbance based on tests, case history, & interview data	Tri-serial r = .61
		Global clinical evaluation of disturbance	148		Presence or absence of psychiatric complaints	bis. r = .41 & .39
ISB	Morton (1949)	Rotter & Willerman's procedures	28	College students	Adjustment ratings Mooney Problem Check List	r = .53 r = .40
					Adjustment, therapy–non-therapy	bis. r = .50
ISB	Rotter, *et al.* (1949)	Rotter & Willerman's procedures	82f[2] 214m	College students	Adjustment ratings	bis. r = .64, $p < .01$ bis. r = .77, $p < .01$
ISB	Barry (1950)	Rotter & Willerman's procedures	38	College students in counselling	Adjustment ratings	bis. r = .67, $p < .01$
ISB	Rotter & Rafferty (1950)	Rotter & Willerman's procedures	299	College freshmen	Ohio State Psychological Examination	r = .11

ISB[3]	Rotter, *et al.* (1954)	Rotter & Willerman's procedures	48f 45m 70f 68m	High school students	Adjustment ratings Adjustment ratings Sociometric choice Sociometric choice	r = .37, $p<.05$ r = .20, N.S. r = .32, $p<.05$ r = .20, N.S.
ISB	Sechrest & Hemphill (1954)	Rated on 16 scales relevant to air crew adjustment	340	Air crew members	Assumption of combat responsibility	*t* test: 4 of 16 scales sig. at $p<.05$ or better
ISB	Bieri, *et al.* (1955)	Rotter & Willerman's procedures	40	College students	Taylor MAS Accuracy of prediction of other *S*'s MAS	r = .46, $p<.01$ r = .19, N.S.
ISB	Churchill & Crandall (1955)	Rotter & Willerman's procedures	188f	College students	Application for psychol. couns.	bis. r = .42, $p<.01$
			156m	College students	Application for psychol. couns.	bis. r = .37, $p<.01$
			44	Mothers	Adjustment ratings	r = .49, $p<.01$
ISB	Berger & Sutker (1956)	Rotter & Willerman's procedures	199m 154f	College students	Academic achievem't. Academic achievem't.	r = .01, N.S. r = .01, N.S.
ISB	Dean (1957)	Rotter & Willerman's procedures	54	Blind *S*s	Adjustment ratings	r = –.16, N.S.
ISB	Chance (1958)	Rotter & Willerman's procedures	52	College students	Prediction of other *S*'s EPPS	r = –.26, $<.10$
ISB	Fitzgerald (1958)	Rated for n dependency using a scoring manual of examples	60	College students	Sociometric ratings of dependency Interview ratings of dependency	r = .25, $p<.05$ r = .28, $p<.05$
ISB	Jessor & Hess (1958)	Rotter & Willerman's procedures	41	College students	Rotter Level of Aspiration Board	White's test $p<.10$
ISB	Denenberg (1960)	Rotter & Willerman's procedures	40 21	College students	Kinesthetic maze	r = .39 tris. r = .46

[1] Preliminary form. [2] Where results are broken down by sex, N is reported by sex. [3] High school form.

Table 1. A Summary of 50 Representative Sentence Completion Validity Studies (continued)

Test	E	Method of Analysis	N	*S*s	Criterion	Results
Miale-Holsopple	Jenkins & Blodgett (1960)	Rated re-test improvement	92	Delinquent boys	Recidivism	χ^2 for 3 judges; $p < .005$, $p < .01$, $p < .025$
Miale-Holsopple	Jenkins (1961)	Schizophrenics	30	Schizophrenics	Improvement as measured by Lorr Multidimensional Scale	t test = $p < .05$
Michigan	Kelly & Fiske (1950)	"Blind" prediction of criteria based on global ratings	78	Clinical psychol. grad. students in VA training	Success in clinical psychology evaluated by clinical staff members	4 of 8 r's: $p < .05$ or better
Michigan	Hiler (1959)	Intensity ratings on 25 pers. variables	70	VA psychotherapy patients	Continuation in psychotherapy versus termination	71% agreement with criterion
		Clinical impression to predict criterion	95			68% agreement with criterion
OSS	Hardy (1948)	Scored for dominance, submission	25	Grad. students in course in non-directive counsel	Non-directiveness of counseling statements	Rho = .26, N.S.
OSS	Hadley & Kennedy (1949)	Modified Rotter & Willerman procedures (3 point scale)	157	College students	High versus low grade point averages	Critical ratio $p < .04$; of 12 $\overline{X}$ ratings 6 $p < .05$ or better
Peck	Peck & McGuire (1959)	Re-test changes rated positive/negative	69	College students	Lefkowitz Ridgidity Scale	r = .11, N.S.
					Worchel Self-Activities Index	r = –.02, N.S., .67 $p < .01$
					McGuire Q-Check	r = .00, .06, .19, .03 (all N.S.)

Rohde	Rohde (1946)	Ratings based on Murray's need system	50m 50f	High school students	Combined ratings of teacher judgments & interview data relative to Murray's need system	$\bar{r}$ = .82, p<.01 $\bar{r}$ = .79, p<.01
SAM	Trites, *et al.* (1953)	Scoring manual used to rate 13 personality variables	100 413 539 639	Flight cadets	Success vs. failure in flight cadet training	bis. r = .32, p<.005 bis. r = .21, p<.001 bis. r = .13, p<.001 bis. r = .18, p<.001
SSCT	Sacks (1949)	Impressionistic ratings on 3 point scale for disturbance	100	VA neuropsychiatric outpatients	Psychiatric adjustment ratings	Agree. on 8/15 variables, p<.001 (1st person form); agree. on 3/15 variables, p<.001 (3rd person form)
SSCT	Sacks & Levy (1950)	Ratings for disturbance Interpretative summaries	100 50	VA neuropsychiatric outpatients	Psychiatric ratings of disturbance Agreement with clinical findings	r = .48 to .57 77% agreement
SSCT	McGreevey (1962)	Pooled rankings on 4 personality traits using TAT & SSCT	40	Student nurses	Ego-threatened vs. non-ego-threatened	r's for non-ego threat. group N.S.; 5/8 r's for ego-threat. group p<.05 or better
Stein	Locke (1957)	3 point scale of disturbance	100	Naval Personnel	Imprisonment vs. non-imprisonment	6/12 *t* tests p<.05
Stein	Howard (1962)	Rank ordering of 10 of Murray's needs	10	VA psychiatric patients	Rorschach & TAT	$\bar{X}$ interjudge agreement between tests, r = .05, N.S.
Stotsky & Weinberg	Stotsky & Weinberg (1956)	Rated for positive or negative tone relative to 9 ego-strength dimensions	80 80	Psychiatric patients	Work performance ratings Work progress ratings	X^2 p<.05 or better on 8/9 vars. X^2 p<.05 or better on 8/9 vars.

Table 1. A Summary of 50 Representative Sentence Completion Validity Studies (continued)

Test	E	Method of Analysis	N	*S*s	Criterion	Results
Stotsky & Weinberg	Stotsky (1957)	Rated on 9 ego-strength dimensions	32	Normals I	Subject characteristics	I & II differed ($p < .05$) on 2/9 vars.; I & III differed ($p < .05$) on 8/9 vars. (X^2)
		Positive treatment outcome	39	Schizophrenics II		
		Negative treatment outcome	39	Schizophrenics III		
Stotsky & Weinberg	Wolkon & Haefner (1961)	Stotsky & Weinberg procedures	48	Psychiatric patients	Behaviorally improved group vs. unimproved group	*t* test: on 6/8 variables $p < .10$ or better
Custom	Wilson (1949)	Rated for grammar, spelling, and other formal aspects	22	High school students	Maladjusted children vs. well-adjusted children	no significant relationships observed
Custom	Cameron & Magaret (1950)	Frequency of response "scatter"	45	College students	Card-sorting test Guilford Inventory Guilford-Martin Inventory	r = .08 to .14 (all N.S.) 2/10 r's $p < .05$ 1/10 r's $p < .05$
Custom	Rosenberg (1950)	Rated for attitudes toward parents	72	Psychoneurotic patients	Therapists' judgments of patients' attitudes	58% agreement on attitudes toward father; 69% agreement on attitudes toward mother
Custom	Harlow (1951)	Scored for dominance-submission on a 4 point scale	40	Weight-lifters & non-weight-lifters	Weight-lifters vs. non-weight-lifters	7/11 *t* tests $p < .05$
Custom	Lazarus *et al.* (1951)	Rated for expression of hostility and sexuality	35	Psych. patients	Percept. acc. of hostile & sexual stimuli	r = .45, $p < .01$; r = .55, $p < .01$
			25	Repressors & Intellectualizers	Repressors vs. Intellectualizers	*t* test $p < .05$

Custom	Cass (1952)	Rated for parent-child conflict using a scoring manual of examples	42	Well-adjusted & maladjusted children	Well-adjusted vs. maladjusted children	*t* test $p < .001$
Custom	Kimball (1952)	Rated for attitude toward father Rated for aggression	117	Prep school students	Academic under-achievement vs. normal achievement	Critical ratio $p < .05$ (father); Critical ratio $p < .01$ (aggression)
Custom	Dorris *et al.* (1954)	Rated for ego-threat, passivity and masculinity	21	College freshmen	High vs. low authoritarians	12/16 hypotheses supported at $p < .05$ or better (*t* test)
Custom	Zimmer (1955)	Prediction of criterion based on clinical impression	73	AAF crew members	Sociometric rankings on 8 personality variables	$r = .10, .10, .21$ (all N.S.)
Custom	Burwen *et al.* (1956)	Rated on 5 point scale of superior-subordinate cluster	312	Air Force Cadets	Test of leadership knowledge Superior-subordinate cluster Scale of alienation	$r = .27, p < .001$ $r = .32, p < .001$ $r = -.45, p < .001$
Custom	Walter & Jones (1956)	Ratings on a 4 point scale of positive and negative attitudes	33	Psychiatric patients	O.T. ratings of behavior	$r = .50, p < .01$
Custom	Rychlak *et al.* (1957)	Ratings of inclusion with 10 personality categories based on scoring manual	18	Japanese-born college students in USA	Social adjustment ratings based on interview data	6/10 r's $p < .05$ or better
Custom	Willingham (1958)	Rated for acceptance of environment	164	Naval Aviation Cadets	4 morale tests	$\bar{r}$ with 4 tests = .27
Custom	Ebner & Shaw (1960)	Rated for activity-passivity	48	Psychiatric patients & normal *S*s	Psychiatric patients vs. normals	*t* test $p < .05$
Custom	Efron (1960)	Rated for suicide potential	92	Psychiatric patients	Expression vs. non-expression of suicidal thoughts	Correct identification = 43% & 30% (both N.S.)

indeed reflect the captivity of the psychologist as well as the subject. The danger in this restriction of subject populations is obvious. If we wish to know something about other people in the world, we are going to have to bring such specimens into our laboratories.

The problem of population restriction has been exacerbated in sentence completion research by the tendency for specific sentence completion forms to be used with specific populations. Of the sixteen studies cited in the summary table that used college students as subjects, eleven of them involved the ISB, though the ISB was used in less than a third of all the studies cited. (A chi-square for independent samples, as outlined by Siegel, 1956, was computed, yielding a chi-square value of 711, d.f. = 1, p. < .001). This finding indicates that the ISB has been primarily a "college" test. Only in the Rotter and Willerman (1947) study was the ISB used with a psychiatric population. On the other hand, all three of the studies cited using the Forer, all three of the Stotsky-Weinberg studies, and two of the three studies cited using the SSCT, employed psychiatric populations. Whatever the reason for such narrow usage, it is undeniably the case that cross-validation and generalizability have been thereby inhibited.

Criteria

Often in the history of psychological testing, tests have been devised to replace inadequate assessment techniques only to be validated against these very same techniques. Though these bootstrap operations have, on occasion, appeared to work, they can hardly be regarded as the method of preference. The establishment of appropriate validation criteria has often been regarded as an especially difficult problem for projective tests:

> Criteria can be obtained for overt, observable behavior. But that is not the forte of projective instruments. Their special attraction and most frequent use lies in the description of personality dynamics, which are mostly covert and inaccessible. How is one to establish criterion measures for such variables as confused sexual indentification, inner emotional resources, or castration anxiety? At best, ways may be found by which these inner states can be inferred from observable or recordable behavior. The value of such behavior as criterion measures is qualified by the imperfect and sometimes undefinable relationship of the behavior to the inner states proper (Zimmer, 1956, p. 59).

This argument is both appealing and traditional, and as such needs to be examined closely. All behavior presumably is tied to inner states, and in this regard the behavior of most interest to the projectivist is not special. What tends to distinguish the projective test user is his concern for inner states *per se.* The achievement test user, by contrast, though he may recognize the desirability of knowing the correlative intra-psychic forces, is primarily concerned with behavior and the implications of one set of behaviors for another set of behaviors.

Covert personality dynamics either relate in some predictable and orderly fashion to an observable, behavioral referent, or they are indeed untestable. There is, fortunately, no good theoretical reason to suppose that personality dynamics are without behavioral referent. Certainly, a psychoanalytic position would suggest otherwise:

> Mental phenomena are to be regarded as the result of the interplay of forces pressing respectively toward and away from motility. The organism is in contact with the outside world at the beginning and at the end of its reaction processes, which start with the perception of stimuli and end with motor or glandular discharge. Freud (1927) looks at the mental apparatus as modeled after an organism floating in water. Its surface takes up stimuli, conducts them to the interior, whence reactive impulses surge to the surface (Fenichel, 1945, p. 15).

The problem then for the projective test user becomes one of deducing a theoretically logical behavioral referent or outcome for the inner state under investigation. The measurement of this behavioral referent constitutes the criterion against which the projective test may be validated. Such procedures demand of the experimenter that his conceptual tools be valid if he is to assess the validity of his psychometric instruments. Given the complexity of personality and the primitiveness of personality theory, the task is formidable. There have, however, been researchers who were equal to the task.

Lazarus, Eriksen and Fonda (1951) classified psychiatric patients according to their characteristic defense mechanisms. They isolated groups of intellectualizers and repressers, and they predicted that intellectualizers would express significantly more sex and hostility related responses on a specially devised sentence completion test than repressers. The data supported their predictions.

Harlow (1951) used a sentence completion test to test hypotheses derived from psychoanalytic theory concerning masculine inadequacy. Harlow speculated that weight lifting involves an excessive amount of narcissism and that weight-lifters suffer from feelings of masculine inadequacy, have failed to identify with an adequate male object, and are attempting to obscure their underlying feelings of dependency and masculine inadequacy by the development of a strong masculine physique. Harlow gave groups of weight-lifters and athletes who were not weight-lifters sentence completion tests, which were scored for dominance and submissiveness. The two groups differed on seven of eleven variables; all differences were statistically significant at the .05 level, and were in the predicted direction.

In Harlow's study, two groups known to differ on X (weight lifting) were tested to see if they also differed on Y (feelings of masculine adequacy). The X variable was the criterion for the test and the Y variable was the major focus of interest. This, basically, is the experimental form where the attempt is to go beyond simple empirical differences. Other research models are available. The experimenter might wish to determine whether his sentence completion test is useful in predicting academic success and failure. Two groups, a success group and a failure group, (X variable) could be tested and the relationship between the test scores and the known group difference determined. Such a procedure need not involve the additional step of attributing a more "basic" determining difference distinguishing the two groups. This latter form is essentially the design used by Sechrest and Hemphill (1954), Hiler (1959), Hadley and Kennedy (1949), and many others. In the former case the criterion is made to do double duty; it serves as a standard for test validation, and additionally, it indicates another psychological event or process, which is typically of greater interest to the researcher.

Which research tactic is to be preferred must obviously be answered in the context of research goals. Clearly, the use of criteria as indicants is demanded when "inner states" are to be assessed; the use of single-purpose criteria is probably in order where "practical" psychometric goals are to be achieved. Both approaches have their uses and both have inherent dangers; one, the danger of confusion and unjustified extrapolation, the other, the danger of sterility and triviality.

The choice of criteria is not only restricted by research purpose, but is restricted as well by differences in sentence completion test structure and scoring procedure. Scoring procedures that yield a single variable summary score, as does the ISB for example, have less plasticity and are likely to narrow relevant criteria more than a test like the Miale-Holsopple which is analyzed impressionistically. Which test and what criteria to use, is again a problem to be resolved by individual research interests. Where the interest is in validating a specific test, the researcher will look for appropriate criteria; where the interest is in a given psychological process, the researcher will look for the appropriate test.

Matching test with criteria is, however, a task that requires greater sophistication than has often been given to this problem. As Zimmer (1956) points out: "When test and criterion are formulated and organized within different conceptual frameworks, the categories into which their materials have been arranged may not correspond to each other. If this is the case, it will be difficult to obtain a reliable estimate of the association between test and criterion. Any existing association may be obscured by the organization of the categories" (p. 59).

The Utility of the Method

Having noted repeatedly the dangers involved in making generalizations about a method as variable as the sentence completion, it is nonetheless in order that some general assessment of the method's validity be attempted.

Inspection of Figure 1 reveals that the power of the method is clearly related to the area of investigation. Sentence completion methods have been relatively unsuccessful in a number of research areas. The method has, so far, been insensitive in the measurement of variables associated with social perception. The one reported correlation of a sentence completion test with a test of intelligence yielded a non-significant correlation of .11. The method has been used to predict the achievement of a variety of criteria, and in general, the results have not been encouraging.

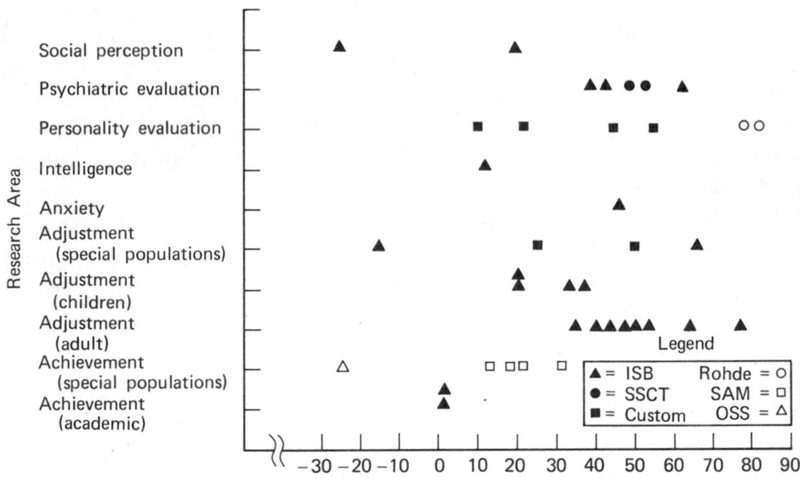

Figure 1. Distribution of validity coefficients abstracted from Table 1 and presented according to research area and S-C test used.

Sentence completions have been only moderately successful in evaluating psychological adjustment in children. The use of the method to evaluate the adjustment of special, homogeneous groups, and for global personality assessment has yielded data of considerable variability. Rohde (1946), reports validities of .79 and .82 using the test for global personality evaluation. However, as noted previously, Rohde's methodology is open to criticism, and her findings are without corroboration.

Sentence completion tests, the ISB in particular, have, however, had consistent success in certain areas of psychological investigation. In the assessment of psychological adjustment in adults, and in the evaluation of severity of psychiatric disturbance, sentence completion methods have proven to have considerable sensitivity and utility.

The differences between the areas in which the method has and has not been successful are not surprising. Sentence completion tests, like all other tests, are most successful when they are used to measure the variables they were constructed to measure. The ISB, for example, was designed to be a measure of psychological adjustment and its standardization groups were male and female college students. Used as such a measure with such groups, the reliability, validity and usefulness of the instrument has received impressive support from a considerable research literature. That the ISB is unsuccessful when used with other groups, such as the blind, or when used for other purposes, such as to predict academic success, serves to determine the useful limits of the test. These negative findings do not, however, call into question the validity of the test which is always specific to a given, stated criterion or set of criteria.

This principle is, of course, obvious. It is also obvious that this principle has too often been ignored. Projective test adherents have too frequently allowed themselves and their techniques to be used inappropriately. There is no logical reason to believe that clinicians can use sentence completions or a Rorschach to predict the success of flight cadets. The inability of the clinician to do so, however, has been taken as proof of the general invalidity of these techniques (c.f. Holtzman and Sells, 1954).

The sentence completion method, again like other tests, has been relatively unsuccessful in making discriminative predictions for homogeneous groups. The sentence completion, for example, was not especially successful in predicting the success of graduate students in clinical psychology (Kelly and Fiske, 1951). It might be noted, however, that in the Kelly and Fiske study, the sentence completion, though not efficient by absolute standards, was relatively among the most successful predictors.

The sentence completion has not often been placed in direct competition with other projective devices, but when it has, it seems to have more than held its own. Murray, *et al.,* (1948) report that a sentence completion test was added to their evaluative techniques as an after-thought. After examining the performance of all tests, it was the only projective device they believed was worth retaining in their program. Certainly, if one compares the findings of standard reviews of the validity of other projective techniques, the support for the validity of the sentence completion method becomes even more impressive.[5]

Conclusions

Having reviewed much of what has been reported about the sentence completion method, several conclusions emerge.

[5]The reader is advised to consult Swenson (1957), Harris (1960), and Murstein (1963). These authors offer authoritative reviews of the DAP, Rorschach, and TAT respectively. This author's view is that the sentence completion compares favorably to these other methods in reliability, validity, and utility.

1. The sentence completion is a valuable instrument in the assessment of personality that compares favorably to other standard instruments. A considerable, generally favorable, research literature tends to justify its wide clinical and research use.

2. Why the method works, and how it works are not as clear. The relevance of the projection hypothesis to the sentence completion seems questionable, but alternate hypotheses of any conceptual power have yet to be advanced.

3. Most researchers, using the sentence completion, have seemed little bothered by the absence of a theoretical rationale underlying the use of the sentence completion method. A too general research practice involves the construction of custom tests with little more than face validity. These tests are then correlated with criteria, the validity of which are similarly suspect. Many of these studies, reported as though they were in final form, could more legitimately be regarded as pilot studies awaiting cross-validation. The lack of cross-validation, the absence of normative data, and the often gratuitous variations in procedure and structure, have combined to retard standardization of the sentence completion, and has tended to make development diffuse and disorderly.

4. There have been sentence completion forms that have been developed more systematically, most notably the Rotter ISB. Critics of the ISB, while noting its psychometric advantages, have tended to regard it as undynamic and of relatively little use for general clinical purposes.

The objections to the ISB have tended to focus on two aspects of the test: 1) the quantification of its scoring system; and 2) the use of a single-variable method of analysis. Proponents of the ISB have tended to endorse the test precisely because of these two features. There does appear to be essential soundness in both positions, and it is probably the case that the ISB sacrifices scope for efficiency.

5. The number of problems involved in the sentence completion method and the significant success it has achieved, should both require and encourage additional research with the method. Much research has suggested that subjects can exercise considerable conscious control over their responses. One obvious research need, then, would be for the development of measures of dissimulation and defensiveness appropriate to the sentence completion. More systematic investigations of the interaction effects of variations in instruction, set effects, stem structure, stem reference, and test length across populations should prove to be a valuable research contribution. Though the problem of context effects is obvious and would need to be explored, it might be possible to develop not only standard sets of stems, but standard individual stems. Such standardization would provide normative data for the association value of individual stems.

6. But, perhaps, the greatest research need in regard to the sentence completion would be the refinement and extension of already available sentence

completion forms. Specific tests have become almost traditionally associated with specific subject populations and validity criteria. Extending these tests to new subject populations, utilizing new classes of criteria, would promote greater interresearch comparability, so that an already considerable research literature could be better integrated, better used, and better understood.

3. THE EXPERIMENTAL VALIDATION OF THE RORSCHACH TECHNIQUE

Joseph Zubin, Leonard D. Eron, and Florence L. Schumer

There are those who believe that traditional, empirical validation procedures, employing the use of a criterion and single Rorschach scores, should be followed. We have previously noted some of the difficulties attached to the single Rorschach score itself. But, as noted in connection with problems of assessing reliability, patterns or configurations of these scores, unreliable as they may or may not be, form the basis of an interpretation—not single scores.

It has been suggested, therefore, that instead of validating single scores against a simple quantitative criterion, scores can be combined and weighted in various ways and then validated against a quantitative criterion. The second approach does not "violate" the global, wholistic and gestalt aspects of interpretation deemed so important by clinicians, whereas the first one does. (But as attractive as this second possibility is, a technique such as the Rorschach does not guarantee or insure a sufficient or stable number of responses in various scoring categories.) Meehl (1950) has discussed this "patterned" approach (configural scoring) to scores, mostly with respect to the MMPI; but there are many implications for Rorschach validity procedures. After all, this is the way most clinicians do predict! Configural scoring, according to Meehl, is nothing more than the use of validity coefficients based on an item analysis using two or more items at the same time. Items with little or no validity in themselves may be quite discriminating when the pattern of other items is considered at the same time. Unfortunately, there has been only a minimum of research to date, using

SOURCE. Joseph Zubin is Professor of Psychology at Columbia University. His clinical interests and areas of specialization are diverse and have included physiological and comparative psychology, the psychopathology of aging, and clinical evaluation and interview techniques. Projective techniques in clinical assessment have been focal interests of both Leonard D. Eron (University of Illinois, Chicago Circle) and Florence L. Schumer (Institute of Developmental Studies, New York University). This material is excerpted from *An Experimental Approach to Projective Techniques.* New York: John Wiley & Sons, 1965. Reprinted by permission of John Wiley & Sons and the authors.

configural scoring principles applied to the Rorschach as well as to other instruments. Loevinger (1959), in a review of theory and techniques of assessment, has noted that pattern analysis and configural scoring has failed, or at least, it superiority to linear methods has not been demonstrated. What the future will disclose in terms of the rich (and logical, from a clinician's point of view) potential of configural validation, is hard to say.

But the picture is even more complicated. Clinicians do not utilize, in the process of writing a Rorschach report, a "set" series of interpretations for a particular pattern or configuration. Were this so, validity coefficients could be based on the relationship of a *pattern* of scores to a particular criterion. The situation, simplified, perhaps, amounts to this: most clinicians base their interpretations on a series of implicit and sometimes explicit "hypotheses" (differing ones, of course, are used by different clinicians) as to the meaning of a particular response, score, group of scores, configuration of scores, or the "quality" of a particular record–sometimes weighting one or the other of these in accordance with the "flavor" of the whole record, or the intensity or "vividness" of the ratio, response, score, etc., involved. Not only does this interpretative process vary from clinician to clinician, but clinicians may also vary in this procedure from record to record.

A third approach to Rorschach validation noted by MacFarlane and Tuddenham (1951) involves discarding quantitative scoring categories altogether, in favor of interpretative statements based on subjectively combined scores. Of this latter approach, they have said:

> If it should turn out that the interpretation of certain skilled clinicians has greater predictive significance than that of the other methods, then the research attack would have to be shifted to the interpreter of the test. Experiments would have to be designed to find the relative weights he gives to the various cues (his subjective categories) by some such procedure as having him predict at each step of an additive exposure to the protocols (p.46).

Others have suggested that the *interpretative hypotheses* extant in the field should be validated. Does the M-C ratio relate to certain personality types? Do movement responses reflect "inner, stable aspects of the S's fantasy?" Is the color response a reflection of the manner with which S handles the outer would in terms of his emotionality?

We shall soon see that Rorschach validation procedures have taken many paths, following one or another of the many possible avenues. Sometimes it appears that the form the research takes is not dictated by conviction as to the most appropriate validation procedure, but rather by convenience, availability of records, and the like. We agree that single score validity research does not necessarily reflect clinical usage, nor the manner in which results, predictions, and personality descriptions are constructed. On the other hand, validating on the basis of interpretations and traditional clinical usage introduces a host of other problems: clinical usage based on which clinicians? What are the implicit hypotheses? Not the least of these problems is the fact that validating or substantiating a particular hypothesis tells us little about *other* hypotheses or the test as a whole.

Rorschach Validity Studies

In the last analysis, a test cannot be valid unless it is reliable. We have already cast doubt on the reliability of the Rorschach. Thus, an examination of the present status of the Rorschach with regard to validity is most important. In 1954, Zubin discussed this problem and came to the following conclusions: *(a)* global interpretations of Rorschach protocols seem to work, that is, are positively correlated with independent evaluations of personality; *(b)* global as well as atomistic evaluations based on Rorschach content scales seem to work; *(c)* atomistic evaluations based on Rorschach perceptual variables alone are not successful; and *(d)* factor analysis of scores based on content scales as well as perceptual scores seems successful. Zubin explained these conclusions by hypothesizing that the Rorschach is essentially an interview. As such, the most appropriate analysis of Rorschach variables, as in any interview, should be based on an evaluation of content.

What is the status of the technique today, some time later? Before answering this question, let us examine the variety of ways in which the validity of the Rorschach technique has been investigated. First we will describe the global methods consisting of such procedures as blind analysis, matching techniques, and overall correspondence between the Rorschach and clinical evaluations. Then come the more specific approaches: evaluation of individual scores or signs in differentiating groups; evaluation of patterns or specific syndromes of signs; testing the alleged significance of a sign or syndrome against clinical evaluations or other criteria.

Cutting across the global vs. specific procedures are laboratory approaches to the evaluation of specific signs, as exemplified by correlations between Rorschach performance and physiological indicators or as exemplified by manipulation of the human organism by such techniques as hypnosis and surgical and other somatic intervention (e.g., lobotomy, shock therapy, etc.). Then come developmental studies in which the changes in performance are related to developmental changes that occur with maturation and learning. Prognostic and predictive studies in personnel selection and training or in therapeutic outcomes, and methodological approaches such as factor analytic investigations are discussed; illustrations of the validation of specific interpretative hypotheses, studies with normals and several content analysis approaches, constitute the final considerations in the area of validity.

It is interesting to note that validity studies are relatively new to the Rorschach scene, the first one of any importance appearing as recently as 1938 (Benjamin & Ebaugh). It should be remembered that the Rorschach technique appeared in protest against the alleged lack of validity which characterized personality inventories. The specific predictions made possible by these instruments proved their own undoing when it was discovered that despite their standardization, objectivity, and reliability, they produced validity coefficients ranging from zero to the .30's and .40's only. Projective techniques arose to remedy this failure. How well has the Rorschach met this challenge?

Blind Analysis.

An early method of demonstrating validity of the Rorschach was "blind analysis" in which the Rorschach expert analyzes the S's personality from the Rorschach record without seeing him. The correctness of the diagnosis, interpretation, or personality description is judged either by the expert himself or by other judges or the patient himself. In this method, the looseness of the terms and labels used, the generality of many of the statements made, as well as the implicit familiarity with the base rates for diagnostic groupings in the sample with which he is working, may yield what appears to *E*, "evidence" that his test is valid.

Blind analysis is one of the spectacular aspects of the Rorschach technique and has probably been the most important factor in the acceptance of the Rorschach by psychiatrists. These techniques have been popularly used in the context of diagnostic studies. Benjamin and Ebaugh (1938), for example, using diagnoses arrived at in clinical conferences as the criterion, were able to show surprisingly good agreement between most of their "blind," independent analyses of Rorschach protocols and ultimate diagnoses. Blind analysis has also been purported to be quite successful in anthropological research—see for example, DuBois and Oberholzer, (1942), who worked with the Alorese, in the Dutch East Indies. The method commonly used was to search for congruencies between the expert's blind interpretations of Rorschach protocols (at times, only a meager handful of records was used) and a description of personality "type" derived from other (non-test) sources such as observations, interviews, records, etc. Hallowell (1956, pp. 512-516) has summarized some of these "pioneer" anthropological studies. The successful studies reported were presumably not only a confirmation of Rorschach validity, but evidence that ideal "cultural types" exist.

One would wish that the method of blind analysis could be made more explicit and more public, and that the enthusiastic proponents of this method were as ready to report their failures as their successes. (One exception is a blind diagnosis study reported by Dawson [1949] which had disappointing results.) Successful "blind diagnosis" cannot be accepted as scientific evidence, even though it is impressive at first glance. Until this method becomes more open to public scrutiny, it has to be placed in the doubtful category, as far as validity is concerned.

Signs: Clinical and Statistical Uses

Some clinicians arrive at a belief in the trustworthiness of the results of a Rorschach analysis from their own experience with clinical cases. Often, this consists of administering and scoring the test, collecting data on S's subsequent behavior—sometimes randomly and subjectively—and then going back to the protocol, in which are "found" signs which "unmistakably" foretell such behavior. Unless cross-validation of these post-dicted signs is undertaken in another study with many cases and in different types of sampling situations, it is fruitless to accept them as indicative of future behavior, because with sufficient imagination and exertion of effort through trial-and-error, pseudosignificant signs can be found in any test. Unfortunately, such cross-validation is rarely encountered in the context of this type of "clinical sign construction." Even among more research-minded clinical psychologists, the use of signs and cutting points for frequency of a given score (determinant or locale, etc.) for predictive purposes has long held some fascination. Here too, the failure to cross-validate, the problem of base rates, and the lack of appraisal of situational, chance, and sampling problems, have introduced much confusion and contradictory evidence.

A number of sign studies are designed to establish useful criteria for differentiating groups. Even when such studies have essentially a practical and utilitarian orientation, such as developing a cutoff point for separating part of the sample for purposes of employee or student selection, etc., this particular use of signs should also be cross-validated.

Some sign studies make use of this approach as an aid in diagnostic classification, often comparing and contrasting various groups, and sometimes examining one group alone, in order to compile a group of signs, presumably not only to aid in the subsequent diagnoses of individual cases, but as a means for assessing and attesting to the validity of the instrument.

Weiner (1961) reported the results of a "sign" study which consisted of (*a*) an exploratory phase, during which three Rorschach signs (tendency to give 1 or 2 CF, have a Sum C' between 1.5 and 3.0, and give at least 1 CF or C response with no C' response) emerged—the signs showing a relationship to degree of pathology; and (*b*) two successful attempts to cross-validate these signs—these three indicators being associated significantly more frequently with the schizophrenic groups than with the others (neurosis and character disorder).

The influence of response totals, as well as of age and sex were determined to be negligible, and several other possible sources of error were controlled. Despite the seeming success of this research, however, a number of additional features might be noted. Contamination of original diagnosis and Rorschach protocols was present. The Rorschachs themselves apparently made some contribution to the diagnosis with which the patient was labeled. This motivated the investigator to explore whether or not the psychologists felt that they had actually utilized the indicators under consideration in diagnosing the *S*. Although the psychologists indicated that the three signs did *not* influence them in making a diagnosis of schizophrenia—and we are not informed as to whether or not they knew about the nature of the study—we do not know the statistical relationship between these signs and those that they *did* indicate as influential. Furthermore, the author himself states that ". . . it would seem in many cases that the psychologists, sometimes of necessity and sometimes of choice, had based their diagnostic impressions on indicators other than those they endorsed in the checklist" (p. 438). Another consideration is that the cultural, educational, social, etc., characteristics of the samples are unspecified; cross-validation, however, was based on an almost identical population to that used in the exploratory phase, all being drawn from the files of a general hospital. Would the signs "hold up" with other samples of schizophrenics? The author's conclusion that ". . . it is felt that the data recommend these signs for inclusion among Rorschach criteria for the presence of schizophrenia" (p. 439) overlooks the essential point that the particular clinic population with which he was working may not be at all representative of schizophrenia as defined elsewhere, and may, in fact, represent a biased sample, with unknown characteristics. These signs, perhaps potentially quite utilitarian, are for the time being meaningless, without knowledge of their efficacy with other populations. Auld and Eron (1953), for example, reported a dramatic shrinkage of correlation when a Rorschach scoring formula, worked out and cross-validated on samples of Boston patients, was applied to a fresh sample in New Haven.

One type of criticism leveled at the "sign approach" stems from clinicians who are opposed to the mechanical, analytic, formalistic procedures involved in constructing signs (e.g., Klopfer & Spiegelman 1956). The Rorschach technique, such workers claim, is a global, wholistic technique, and validity approaches should be firmly rooted in such a context. They point out the fact that even "proven" signs are useless when the clinician is confronted with the individual case.

There is some research support, as a matter of fact, to indicate that "global" approaches are more adequate than "sign" approaches. Zamansky and Goldman (1960), for example, have shown that global Rorschach evaluations were much better indicators of actual changes in social adjustment in the ward than were eleven quantitative Rorschach indices. Crumpton (1956), in a study of signs of "color shock," has reported that although statistical use of the usual signs failed to discriminate records based on an achromatic and a chromatic (standard) Rorschach series (judges did not know whether or not the records were based on the chromatic or achromatic series), the use of clinical, global ratings of the protocols did result in a statistically significant, valid, differentiation of the records. But the record of success of global evaluations is not encouraging. Furthermore, unless we find out the basis of the global evaluation, we are no further ahead, scientifically.

Subsequent sections of this chapter consider the utility of signs when their use in prognosis is discussed. Suffice it to say that the general picture concerning use of signs is not hopeful.

Matching

Early clinical attempts to validate the Rorschach technique were based on matching operations–often with the use of "independent blind analysis" (see previously). In general, the technique involves matching the Rorschach expert's findings with those of a psychiatrist or other expert. Specifically, methods used may involve the matching of sketches or descriptions from Rorschach protocols with those based on other sources such as case histories, and interviews. Matching might be based on specific interpretative statements, or more wholistic personality descriptions, or diagnoses. In any event, independent judgments must be obtained with respect to both Rorschach judgments and criterion judgments–that is, the Rorschach expert must base his description on the Rorschach protocol, and on that alone, uncontaminated by knowledge of *S*, the population from which *S* was drawn, or various biographical factors. The criterion judge, similarly, must have no prior knowledge of *S*'s test responses. There are too many possibilites, however, for unconscious collusion.[1] Furthermore, in the case of matching of diagnostic statements, the degree of correspondence between Rorschach interpretation and diagnosis is hardly a suitable measure, since diagnosis itself is not too stable or objective a criterion, and when the Rorschach worker "learns" to know his psychiatrist or criterion judge, the diagnosis could have really been based on the same type of "non-Rorschach" evidence that the criterion judge might have used. It is also quite apparent that

[1]Many of the earlier successful studies reported, it seems, did not make explicit the means by which collusion between clinician and diagnostic expert (usually psychiatrist) was prevented. Benjamin and Ebaugh (1938) were outstanding exceptions. In their report they indicated the care they took to avoid foreknowledge or collusion.

the choice of patients or subjects within a given research setting (clinic, institution, hospital, university, school, etc.) is often very restricted, and the mere presence of the S in the particular research setting is often self-diagnostic. (In many research hospitals, for example, only patients of a certain type are admitted.) Moreover, "styles" and preferences in diagnostic choices and labels vary, often significantly, with the particular clinical setting–a factor which might well contribute to a spuriously high congruency in matches. The Rorschach expert, under such conditions, need consciously or unconsciously pay little, if any, attention to basic and intrinsic Rorschach factors in the protocols themselves. This discussion, it might be noted, again raises the problem of base rates and population differences.

Matching techniques in which Rorschach protocols or scores are matched against personality sketches or case histories in groups of five or more have also been used, not always with findings favorable to the instrument. There are certain basic objections to the procedures involved, an important one of which is that the determination of the precise grounds on which successful pairing is made is virtually impossible. Psychiatrists' or other experts' criterion judgments are not always infallible, and there is little knowledge as to the correctness or incorrectness of even perfectly matched statements. There are many inadvertent and tangential characteristics of this method, not germane to validity, which may influence the outcome. Successful matching is frequently effected on the basis of minor details or coincidences rather than essential equivalance. Heterogeneity of matchees also makes the task too easy; similarly, complete failure in matching may be due to homogeneity of the sample. Another point is that the words, phrases, and content of the responses are often diagnostic in themselves. Some of the successful inferences made by the Rorschach expert depend not on the Rorschach technique *per se,* but on the interview-like material which the protocols provide. Thus, intellectual level can be estimated from the vocabulary level of the responses, bizarre thinking from the outlandish responses given by S, and perseverative tendencies from the actual repetition of responses. These are not basically Rorschach factors in the same sense as are W, M, and FC. Moreover, the generality, sterotypes, and "jargon" of clinical statements used in the matching study may create a picture which is specious. Terms such as sexual problems, anxiety, conflict, etc., are found both in Rorschach interpretations as well as in statements based on non-Rorschach material and can be applied with equal "validity" to many individuals in our culture! Another difficulty in matching studies involves the nature of the descriptive categories used. Anastasi (1954) had this to say about the latter point:

> If the personality descriptions given in the case history and in the test protocol are couched in the terminology of different personality theories, behavioral similarities may be concealed by semantic discrepancies. On the other hand, if the same descriptive concepts are utilized in both, observed

> correspondences may be an artifact resulting from the broadness and looseness of the concepts. Such pseudo-congruencies would of course be detected in the control data from randomly paired records. But the use of control data is no real solution, since it might only mean that the results would have to be discarded as inconclusive (p. 627).

There has been much criticism of matching techniques (Cronbach [1948]; Meehl [1959]) with the overall conclusion that matching techniques are not adequate as validation methods. Meehl, stressing the necessity for construct validity, stated that blind-matching, globally, is not justified. What are the components? How do we know what contributed to what? Meehl prefers the Q-sort technique, which he feels is both quantifiable and global. Cronbach has proposed a trenchant methodology for freeing the matching methods from its many defects, but it is quite intricate and has not proved to be very popular.

Although successful matches have often been obtained, most of the results indicate that the matching is only better than chance, an insufficient criterion for validity (see Newton [1954] for an illustration of an unsuccessful matching study, and Krugman [1942], for an illustration of a successful study). The only general conclusion that may be drawn from some of the successful matching studies described in the Rorschach literature, is that there is some connection between Rorschach technique results and personality description from other sources. But the all-important problem of the nature of this connection cannot be investigated through matching techniques of the type now used.

Content Approaches

The content category as used by Hermann Rorschach was one of three types of classifications of responses–location and determinants are the other two. These last two categories were traditionally regarded as the formal categories. The content categories involved a simple classification of the response into one of several groups–human, animal, anatomical, object, etc.

In the past several years there has been increased attention to content considerations, but with considerable extension of Rorschach's simple classification. Included are not only many additional considerations as to the content of *S*'s responses, but there has also been some focus on more "dynamic" or psychoanalytic aspects of the response and its symbolic referent. The point is that contemporary content analysis has gone beyond a simple designation as to whether or not a response is "animal," "vegetable," or "mineral"!

Our own content scales, described in our text, cover many aspects of the response not regarded as "perceptual" or formal, and touch, as do other content-analysis systems, on the quality and nature of *S*'s verbalizations and interpretative attitudes. The inclusive quality of our scales, plus the fact that their reliability and validity, for various purposes, are open to public inspection and use, contrast this approach to those preferred by some clinicians who are concerned with what they claim to be more clinically meaningful and provocative schemes.

Some history of success with content analysis has been found, a consideration which bears keeping in mind, when an overall evaluation of the Rorschach method is made. For example, note has already been made of successful factorial studies utilizing content (Sandler & Ackner [1951], and Sen [1950]). Elizur (1949) found that an analysis of content in relation to hostility yielded significant correlations with ratings of hostility. Using the Harrower Group Rorschach slides, Rychlak and Guinouard (1960) reported confirmation of their hypothesis that certain measures of content would be related to independent measures of personality and popularity. Watkins and Stauffacher (1952) constructed a series of indices for "deviant verbalizations" based on content considerations, and found that these indicators had a high reliability (.774) between two raters, and that they distinguished normals from neurotics and the latter from psychotics. McCall (1951) found that certain psychometrically weighted nonperceptual categories related significantly to outcome in psychosurgery, either pre- or postoperatively, or both. Chief among these were ascendance-submission, plant importance, dehumanization, reaction time, and popularity. Of these, the ascendance-submission scale was the most "senstive," although no rationale was provided for the fact that those destined for eventual improvement showed a consistent tendency to see more submissive human figures in the Rorschach cards.

But it should be borne in mind that while psychometrically oriented researchers were turning to developing objective methods for scoring and evaluating various types of content scales, some clinicians, especially those with experience and background in psychoanalysis, or psychoanalytic therapy, were also fascinated by the possibilities that content offered for interpretative purposes. Among these men was Lindner (1946, 1947, 1950), who was convinced that *what* S perceived is as important as *how* he perceived it. He felt that if Rorschach had lived, he would most certainly have explored this avenue. On the basis of his own clinical experience, Lindner "isolated" certain responses as reflections of basic personality, and as characterizing different types of diagnostic groupings. Confirmation of these significant responses, he believed, could be found by "pragmatic" means based on his own experience, as well as that of other clinicians. A few examples of such significant responses are:

Card I. Lower central D: normal males–"female torso"; homosexuals–"male torso" or "mannish female."

Card X. Reverse position, middle blue dd: "Extracted tooth" seen by chronic masturbators and those with severe conflicts in this area.

Experienced clinicians and Rorschach workers will be familiar, no doubt, with some of the foregoing. What is more, frequent use of such interpretations is common practice. But despite his strong feelings with respect to the validity (based on his own clinical experiences) of the interpretations of his "significant" responses, Lindner has cautioned:

> It cannot be too often stressed nevertheless that the conclusions from content analysis have to be treated cautiously and with scientific circumspection. An attitude of objective skepticism is the one best suited to the content analyst. The forty-three responses thus far isolated should be subjected to the severest tests–statistical and empirical–before they are accepted fully and integrated wholly into the compendium of Rorschach knowledge (1950, p. 90).

Finally, note should be made of Schafer's volume (1954) which was devoted mostly to an examination of the total Rorschach situation, from a psychoanalytic point of view. The principles, "rules-of-thumb," and skills presented here are based largely on insightful, undoubtedly wise, but not necessarily "public" procedures, in that they are derived almost entirely from the author's own clinical background and experience. In the chapter on thematic analyses, the author illustrates his psychoanalytic method of thematic (content) analysis. He does caution, however, that it is important not to be too "wild" in psychoanalytic interpretations; the clinician is urged to corroborate interpretations by turning to other tests to see if the same themes recur. The general methods for content analyses Schafer proposes may be extremely helpful, clinically, but they await validation through more advanced methodological and theoretical developments than are now available, in addition to more precise knowledge as to the validity of psychoanalytic theory and methods.

In general then, content approaches offer some promise, and the validity picture is not dim. Two main streams have been delineated in manner of approach to problems and procedures, research and clinical uses: *(a)* psychometric and objective, and *(b)* generally psychoanalytic and clinical. We can only wait hopefully for some welding of ideas, and for continued research efforts.

4. EFFECT OF STIMULUS, BACKGROUND, PERSONALITY, AND SCORING SYSTEM ON THE MANIFESTATION OF HOSTILITY ON THE TAT[1]

Bernard I. Murstein

It has long been acknowledged that the projective response is multiply determined including the individual's idiosyncratic methods of dealing with the testing situation and the influence of nonprojective determinants. Despite verbal acceptance of this fact, little research has attempted to focus on more than one of these determinants at a time. There are many reasons for this state of affairs. The early adherents of projective techniques tended to presume that the subject's personality was the key determinant of his response and paid scant attention to the context in which the test was administered or to the stimulus characteristics of the projective instrument. Moreover, the lack of concern with quantitative methodology would, in any event, have assured the inability to measure these components and their interaction.

In recent years, the importance of the stimulus (Eron, 1950; Murstein, 1963) and situational factors (Masling, 1960) have been heavily emphasized. At the same time, numerous quantitative measures have been derived (Murstein, 1963) with respect to the Thematic Apperception Test (TAT), and the analysis of variance technique has been found to be much more robust and useful with many kinds of skewed data than was formerly suspected. This technique is particularly suitable for the measurement of the interaction of variables, and it is, therefore, most useful in the investigation of the determinants of the projective response.

The immediate purpose of this study was to attempt to measure several of the determinants of responses and their interaction in a projective test situation. These determinants are classified as stimulus, background, and personality. In addition, since the meaning of a projective response is often contingent upon the

SOURCE. Bernard I. Murstein, Professor of Psychology at Connecticut College, has contributed extensively to personality and social psychological research, to the study of interpersonal influences on behavior, and to both the study of conceptualization and measurement of projection. This article originally appeared in the *Journal of Consulting and Clinical Psychology,* 1968, **32,** 355-365. Reprinted by permission of the American Psychological Association and the author.

[1]This study was supported in part by a Public Health Service Grant (M-4698) from the National Institute of Mental Health and by a Faculty Research Grant from Connecticut College. Thanks are gratefully tendered to the following persons who bore the brunt of the countless hours of computation involved: Judy Foldes, Edward Lepinski, Edith Marsden, Martyn Spitzer, Sally Tehan, David Winer, and especially Rena L. Rimsky.

scoring system employed (whether crude or sophisticated, covert or overt, content-centered or reflecting the style of the response), nine scoring systems also were investigated.

The more far-reaching purpose was to demonstrate the usefulness of the field-interaction methodology employed herein in ultimately predicting the character of response to the TAT. Such knowledge would be extremely useful in tracing the relationship of various need tensions impinging upon the individual to the expression of these needs on projective techniques. Through knowledge of the subject's responses, the stimulus pull of the cards, the background in which the test is administered, and the subject's trait behavior, one could better understand the ego mechanisms which sometimes allow a need to be manifested directly in thematic expression, at other times permit no trace of the need to be expressed, and, on yet other occasions, show no apparent relationship between need and response.

The determinants examined in this study were as follows:

Stimulus. The stimulus refers to the visual impact of the test on the subject. The TAT was chosen for the present study because it had earlier been scaled in its entirety for the dimension of hostility by the author and colleagues (Murstein, David, Fisher, & Furth, 1961). Three levels of judged hostile value involving nine cards were employed: low (10, 13B, 13G), medium (7GF, 6GF, 9GF), and high (13MF, 18BM, 3GF). These nine cards were selected on the basis of their ability to discriminate between college students in the upper and lower quartiles of total judged hostile values, as well as on the basis of their ability to represent the entire gradient of hostility. All other aspects of the stimulus were ignored for the purposes of this study.

Background. Background refers to the environment or context in which the administration of the test occurs. There are a multitude of these factors in any testing situation, such as influence of examiner, locale, and purpose of the testing. Practically speaking, however, present resources permitted the use of only one such variable. Since the test was to be group administered, the influence of the examiner was minimal. The use of students involved only one locale, that of school classrooms. The background variable which was maximized, therefore, was "purpose of the testing." This condition was achieved by presenting two sets of instructions, one calling for an impersonal "scientific" approach on the part of the subjects, the other calling for the person to appear at his best on the thematic protocol.

Personality. The personality component was subdivided into two dimensions. One represented the objective assessment of the subject's possession of the trait of hostility, whereas the other represented his phenomenological self-concept. Both of these measures were to be obtained for each individual.

Scoring System. The TAT literature is replete with contrary findings on the projection of hostility. Part of these contradictory findings, no doubt, may be attributed to the failure to adequately understand and control for the influence of the stimulus, background, and personality. Yet another crucial factor, the kind of scoring system employed, has failed to elicit the research attention its importance merits. Purcell (1956), working with a select population of overtly antisocial and nonantisocial soldiers, provided an excellent beginning, but there has since been a dearth of research in this area. The strengths and weaknesses of the content-centered approach, as opposed to formalistic measures, and the efficacy of measuring drive directly, as opposed to using approach-avoidance measures, have not been thoroughly studied.

The trait of hostility was chosen because it has been the object of considerable research in studies with thematic cards. In addition, it is a trait which is of paramount concern in the assessment of personality. A variety of forms was investigated to determine overall usefulness and also to discover whether some might prove more useful than others for specific kinds of analyses. The various kinds of scores will be discussed in greater detail under the heading "Scoring Systems."

Hypotheses. Since the author had previously done work investigating how objective possession of hostility and the self-concept regarding this trait influence the projection of hostile content on the Rorschach (Murstein, 1956), several predictions could be made regarding the function of the determinants in the present situation. From the earlier study it was concluded that objective possession of a trait such as hostility does not predispose towards the manifestation of that trait unless the subject's self-concept is in accord with the objective possession of the trait. If, then, a comparison is made between a group of extremely hostile persons and a group of extremely friendly ones, holding self-concept constant, there is no reason to expect a significant difference with regard to the thematic expression of hostility.

Further, the findings of the earlier study indicated that the self-concept was of more crucial significance in determining the content of a projective response than the objective possession of the trait. It is readily deducible from the above that the average college student should be able to control the content of his responses to the TAT or Rorschach so as to keep it in accord with his perceived self rather than his objective expression of behavior. These beliefs led to the formulation of two hypotheses:

1. Despite the use of extremely hostile and extremely friendly persons, there are no significant differences between these two groups with regard to the manifestation of TAT hostility.
2. Persons who perceive themselves as very hostile project more hostility than persons whose self-concepts are friendly. The hypotheses were extended to the first (Hostility) and the ninth scoring systems to be analyzed (Stimulus Discrepancy), both of which employ the same content scale of hostility as described in Hafner and Kaplan (1960).

Regarding the TAT scores other than these two, the author did not believe that sufficient evidence existed to warrant the formulation of further hypotheses. Thus, the analyses undertaken with the seven other measures of hostility are essentially descriptive.

Method

The *S*s were fraternity, sorority, or dormitory members from three western colleges. Prior to a regularly scheduled meeting, sheets of paper were given to all individuals present who had been members of the group for at least 3 months, thus assuring that each person had some acquaintanceship with the other members. The names of these individuals were written down, and they then read the following instructions:

> Put a 1 in the small column to the right of the name of the person whom you consider to be the most friendly of those taking the test with you. By "most friendly" is meant that person who is the most cooperative, easiest to get along with, and least hostile in the fraternity. Put a number 2 next to the second most friendly person, and so on, until you have a different number for each person currently taking the test. Remember to rate yourself and to make sure that your name is also at the top of the page. Also, do not rate any member who is not taking the test with you.[2]

The ranks were converted to normalized scores, using Hull's table (Guilford, 1954, p. 182). The students were paid for their participation and were also informed that a smaller "representative" group would be subsequently contacted and paid for further work.

From the 802 students participating (321 men and 481 women), 48 men and 48 women were chosen on the basis of group and self-judgments which seemed to place them in one of four groups: hostile-insightful, hostile-noninsightful, friendly-insightful, and friendly-noninsightful.[3] A hostile-insightful person, for example, had been judged very hostile by his peers and also perceived himself as very hostile. To ensure that *S*s chosen for the four experimental groups were either very hostile or very friendly, criterion scores based on consideration of the standard error of measurement of each group's judgments and the pooled self-judgments were established. The criterion was that the risk of error in calling a person hostile or friendly who was not actually so would be no greater than .05.

[2] In a previous pilot study the trait of hostility had been used. The use of this trait, however, met with considerable resistance on the part of *S*s, who were reluctant to term any of their fraternity brothers as hostile. Consequently, the trait deemed at the other end of the continuum, friendliness, was employed with the assumption that those *S*s who were the least friendly were the most hostile.

[3] One man from the hostile-noninsightful group failed to keep his appointment on three occasions and was replaced by an alternate who also met the criteria for selection of this group.

The selection procedure is described in greater detail in other studies (Murstein, 1956, 1961). Last, equal numbers of men and women were employed so that sex differences might be noted.

The design used was a Type III analysis of variance (Lindquist, 1953) with the "between" conditions being sex (2), instructional set (2), group judgments of a person (2), and self-concept (2). Six *S*s were assigned to each cell, making a total of 96 *S*s. The "within" effects consisted of the stimulus levels (3) and the interactions of the stimulus with the other variables.

Within a few weeks after the ranking procedure, the students were administered the nine TAT cards in groups numbering from two to six persons. The clusters were so arranged that half of the students received the "impersonal" (Imp) instructions, while the other half received instructions urging them to "look your best" (LYB). The Imp instructions were as follows:

> The purpose of this study is to obtain norms for college students taking the TAT. Your serious cooperation is necessary if the results are to be meaningful.

The instructions intended to arouse a set of "looking one's best" were as follows:

> The purpose of this study is to obtain norms for college students taking the TAT. In addition, I should mention that this test is very sensitive to personality disturbance and personality strengths, which is why it is so widely used in psychological clinics throughout the country. In a sense, the test has been said to give an X-ray of the person's personality. Accordingly, in addition to providing norms, we are using the results to select persons who would be competent to deal with other students in an adequate interpersonal manner. Two such persons (one man and one woman) will be chosen to participate in a further test at their convenience at the rate of $5.00 per hour.

The TAT instructions for the nine-card series were the usual group-slide instructions as described by Atkinson (1958, p. 837) and modified by Murstein (1965) so as to be more useful for analyzing specific components of the story. Each slide was presented for 20 seconds, and then 4 minutes were allotted for writing the story. The complete instructions may be found in Murstein (1965), which represents an analysis of one of the nine hostility systems with the present sample.

The slides were projected onto the screen in a randomized order, except that every consecutive set of three cards had to contain one card of low, medium, and high stimulus pull for hostility. This arrangement provided a rough control for the order of presentation of the three stimulus levels. The order of presentation was 7GF, 13MF, 10, 6GF, 13B, 18BM, 9GF, 13G, 3GF.

Scoring Systems

1. *Hostility (H).* This approach is the most common one applied to the TAT and involves assigning a score to the TAT story based on the degree of hostility expressed by the characters. Inhibitions, guilt, or anxiety experienced by the characters are not scored except as they may actually affect the expression of a hostile action. The 5-point scale employed, from Hafner and Kaplan (1960), extends from 0 for no expression of hostility to 4 for themes involving direct physical expression of hostility between people. Interscorer reliability is reported by the authors as .87. Similar scales by Stone (1956) and Purcell (1956) have been shown to be valid in differentiating overtly hostile persons from those not overtly hostile.

2. *Internal Punishment (IP).* This score presumes that the extent to which hotility is directed inward as internal punishment may differentiate groups varying in degree of hostility, and that the more hostility is turned inward, the less it is expressed outward. The scale used is taken from Purcell (1956, p. 450).

Internally based punishment included suicide, self-depreciation, and feelings of guilt, shame, or remorse. Since a broad definition of punishment encompasses "injury to a loved object," instances of death, illness, or accident to parents or other loved objects were recorded in this category of internal punishment. When the hero of the story was the direct agent of aggression, for example, husband striking his wife, internal punishment was not scored unless there was a clear expression of remorse or shame. By contrast, accidental injury, death, or illness of a loved one always received a score of internal punishment unless the hero specifically denied anything resembling guilt feelings. The reliability for this scale is reported by Purcell as .89.

3. *External Punishment (EP).* This score is concerned with the extent of aggression, physical violence, or domination directed towards the hero. Possibly, it may reflect the mechanism of projection whereby hostility on the part of *S* is projected onto the "other." The scale is used here as described by Purcell (1956, p. 450).

An external punishment score was obtained by summing the frequency of such themes as the following when they were directed toward the hero: assault; injury; threat; quarreling; deprivation of some privilege, object, or comfort; domination; physical handicap such as blindness, etc.; rejection. Scoring reliability was .81.

4. *Remoteness of Hostile Expression (RHE).* One way of avoiding personal responsibility for the thematic expression of hostility is to remove responsibility for the hostile action from oneself by having it occur on another planet, with imaginary people, in a play, or even by substituting animals for humans as the objects of aggression. It is assumed that the higher the *RHE* score, the less likely *S* is to express aggression in an overt manner. The scale used is taken from Purcell

(1956, p. 450), with some modification. As used in the present study, four of Purcell's five factors were considered: *(a)* object of aggression (person, society, animal, inanimate object); *(b)* time (present, past, future); *(c)* place (customary habitat, other countries, other planets); *(d)* level (behavior, wish, memory, daydream, night dream, special states of consciousness such as intoxication, dissociation, drug addiction, insanity).

Each of these factors was scored on a 5-point scale when some degree of hostility was present; 1 represented the least remote possibility and 5 the most remote expression of hostility. The score range was thus from 0 (no expression of hostility) to 180 (maximum expression of hostility for all factors on all nine cards). Purcell reported a reliability of .96 for the scale.

5. *Internal Punishment/Hostility (IP/H).* Recent workers such as Purcell (1956) and Lesser (1958) have argued that simple content scores depicting aggression are of little use unless they consider the inhibitions present in the story which vitiate or entirely prevent the complete or successful expression of hostility. One type of inhibition involves feelings of guilt, shame, or remorse. If, in addition to expressing thematic aggression, a person exhibits a great deal of internal punishment in his stories, he is presumably less likely to express aggression in overt behavior than is a person without these internal constraints. The higher the *IP/H* ratio, therefore, the less likely it is that the overt manifestation of hostility will occur. Purcell (1956)[4] also reported that the *IP/H* ratio significantly differentiated among three groups of soldiers classified according to degree of antisocial behavior, which ranged from little or no military or civilian delinquency to long histories of truancy and assault.

6. *External Punishment/Hostility (EP/H).* This ratio score may reflect the acceptability of perceiving oneself as a hostile individual. In Purcell's (1956) study, normal soldiers tended to perceive more EP/H than did the antisocial individuals.

7. *Internal Punishment/External Punishment (IP/EP).* This ratio is said by Purcell to reflect the ability to inhibit expression of aggression. The higher the ratio, the less apt the aggression of the individual is to be expressed overtly.

8. *Remoteness of Hostile Expression/Hostility (RHE/H).* Another mechanism for avoiding personal responsibility for the thematic expression of hostility, *RHE,* also was tested in conjunction with *H.* The use of the *RHE/H* ratio was based on the belief that the higher the ratio, the less likely the individual is to express aggression in overt behavior. This ratio significantly differentiated three groups of soldiers varying in antisocial behavior in a study by Purcell (1956), although it should be noted that Purcell's scale of fantasy aggression was unweighted, unlike the present scale.

[4]The present score is roughly equivalent to what Purcell has called "fantasy aggression."

9. *Stimulus Discrepancy (SD) Score.* The rationale for the development of this score is as follows:

Suppose, using a simple hostile content score *(H)*, that Individuals A and B obtain the same overall score. Are we justified in assuming that A and B are equally hostile? Hardly! On further inspection, we might find that A's score stemmed from his telling hostile stories to cards with highly hostile stimulus pull and friendly stories to cards with little apparent hostility. Individual B, on the other hand, might tend to tell hostile stories to nonhostile cards and nonhostile stories to hostile cards. Perhaps, then, the similarity of overall scores obtained, without attention to the nature of the stimulus properties of the card eliciting the story, masks considerable personality differences in the two hypothetical *Ss.* Could a scoring system based on the discrepancy between the degree of hostility represented in the picture and that evinced in the thematic story differentiate various personality groups? Are persons who are relatively unconcerned about the expression of hostility apt to show less discrepancy than those concerned about hostile expression? In an attempt to answer these questions, an *SD* scoring system was constructed as follows:

In a previous study (Murstein, *et al.*, 1961), the nine TAT cards employed in the present experiment had been scaled for hostility by the Thurstone equal-appearing interval method. These scaled values were transformed into standardized *Z* scores. In addition, *Z*-score equivalents for the Hafner-Kaplan TAT *H* scores were obtained from the raw scores of several hundred college students of both sexes in response to projected slides of these TAT pictures. These *Z*-score equivalents were used in transforming the raw scores of the present sample. A person's total *SD* score, thus, consisted of the sum of the *Z*-score discrepancies, without regard to sign, between the scaled values of the nine cards and the *Z*-score values for the Hafner-Kaplan scores.

Results

To prepare the ratio scores for statistical treatment, all raw scores employed in ratios were first converted to standard scores and then combined in ratio form. For the single scores, the original data were not transformed. Inspection of the frequency distributions for the nine variables revealed no gross departure from normality which would prevent the use of these scores in an analysis of variance according to the criteria set forth by Boneau (1960).

The Type III design used analyzes "between" effects for comparisons of independent subjects as well as "within" effects for comparisons between various sets of cards using the same subjects. In addition, since stimulus pull was a primary concern in this experiment, the between-effects part of the analysis also was computed for the low-hostile, medium-hostile, and high-hostile three-card subsets, respectively. For each of the 9 scoring systems, there were, thus, 4 analyses, making a total of 36. The results are categorized by scoring system. To conserve space, the significant *F* values for the overall analyses and for the subanalyses are condensed into Table 1. Omission of a particular subset from the table signifies the absence of any significant *F*s. Likewise, only those variables and interactions are included in which at least one significant value appeared.

Hostile-Content Score

Both hypotheses were substantiated, in that no significant differences were found between hostile and friendly persons, but a significant self-concept difference resulted, with hostile self-concept subjects projecting more thematic hostility than persons with friendly self-concepts. A significant Sex x Instructions interaction resulted from the fact that women projected more hostility than men under the Imp condition, with the situation reversed under the LYB condition.

By far, the most outstanding determinant of the thematic response (as it was for each of the nine scoring systems) was the stimulus value of the cards which accounted for half of the total variability and showed a high association between hostile stimulus structure and hostile projection. The significant Cards x Group x Instructions finding stemmed from the fact that hostile persons in the LYB condition projected more hostility to the low-hostility cards and friendly persons projected more to the medium cards.

Concerning the subanalyses, the low cards repeated the significant self-concept effect found in the overall analyses and also elicited a Group x Instructions interaction, with hostile persons projecting more hostility in the Imp condition than in the LYB condition, whereas friendly persons did the reverse. The medium cards Instructions x Sex interaction showed women projecting more hostility than men for the Imp condition and less for the LYB condition.

Internal Punishment

Persons with hostile self-concepts projected more than those with friendly self-concepts. Subjects in the Imp condition projected more than those in the LYB condition, and the significant cards effect showed those with hostile self-concepts projecting more *IP* than friendly self-concept individuals to low- and high-hostile cards, but not to the medium cards.

The low cards elicited a Group x Self effect, with insightful persons (group hostile, self hostile; group friendly, self friendly) projecting less *IP* than either of the noninsightful groups. The high cards showed a self effect similar to that found in the overall analysis.

Table 1. Significant F Values for the 36 Analyses of Variance for the Nine Scoring Systems of Hostility

Source of Variance	Hostility			Internal Punish-ment			External Punish-ment		Remote-ness of Hostile Expression			Internal Punish-ment/ Hostility			Ex-ternal Punish-ment/ Hos-tility		Internal Punish-ment/ External Punish-ment			Remoteness of Hostile Expression/ Hostility			Stimulus Dis-crepancy		
	O	L	M	O	L	H	O	H	O	M	H	O	L	H	O	L	O	L	H	O	M	H	O	L	M
Between																									
Group (G)																	*								
Self (S)	*	*		**		***			**		***			**						*		**	*		
Instructional set (I)				*						*															
G × S					*		*	*				**	**	*			**	**	**						
G × I		*								*						*					**		*	*	
G × Sex										*															*
S × I										**															
I × Sex	**		*							*										*	**				
I × S × Sex																					*				
Within																									
Cards (C)	***			***			***		***			***			***		***			***			***		
C × S				**					*			**					*								
C × G × S															*					*			*		
C × G × I	**																			*					
C × I × Sex																									
C × S × I × Sex																				*					

Note–Abbreviated; O = overall, L = low, M = medium, H = high.
* $p < .05$.
** $p < .01$.
*** $p < .001$.

External Punishment

Few significant findings occurred, with the exception of the ubiquitous cards effect, in accordance with stimulus pull, and the Group x Self interaction, suggesting that insightful persons manifest more *EP* than noninsightful ones (hostile-hostile > hostile-friendly; friendly-friendly > friendly-hostile). The only significant subanalysis effect (Group x Self for the high cards) repeated the overall Group x Self effect.

Remoteness of Hostile Expression

The self effect again proved significant, with the friendly self-concept subjects outscoring the hostile self-concept ones. The perennial cards effect showed highest scores for low, high, and medium cards, in that order. The Cards x Self effect resulted from friendly self-concept persons outscoring hostile self-concept persons for high and low cards, with no differences existing for medium cards.

The medium cards dominated the subanalyses. The LYB subjects manifested more *RHE* than the Imp subjects. The Group x Instructions interaction showed hostile persons manifesting more *RHE* for the LYB condition than for the Imp condition and friendly persons reversing this finding. The Self x Instructions effect resulted from the fact that hostile self-concept persons projected slightly more in the Imp condition than in the LYB condition, whereas friendly self-concept individuals showed a great deal more projection to the latter than to the former condition.

The Sex x Instructions interaction indicated that men manifested more *RHE* than women in the Imp condition and less than them in the LYB condition. Finally, the Cards x Self effect found hostile men projecting less than hostile women and friendly men more than friendly women. The high cards showed the significant self effect found in the overall analysis.

Internal Punishment/Hostility

The significant cards effect resulted from the greater projection to the low cards, with little difference found between the medium and high ones. The Group x Self interaction showed noninsightful persons as having the higher ratio (*IP/H*) and insightful ones the lower scores. The Cards x Self effect found hostile self-concept subjects manifesting considerably higher scores to the high cards with little difference in the others.

In the subanalyses, high hostile self-concept individuals scored higher than friendly self-concept persons on the high cards. These cards also evinced a significant Group x Self effect, with friendly-hostile persons outscoring all other groups. The Group x Self effect for low cards was the same as for the overall analysis.

External Punishment/Hostility

The cards effect showed the highest scores for low, medium, and high cards, in that order. The Cards x Group x Instructions interaction showed hostile subjects in the Imp condition and friendly ones in the LYB condition scoring highest to low cards, but hostile persons in the LYB condition and friendly ones in the Imp scoring highest to medium ones. The only significant subanalysis effect (Group x Instructions) occurred for low cards, with hostile persons scoring higher than friendly ones in the Imp condition and the reverse occurring in the LYB condition.

Internal Punishment/External Punishment

The group effect showed hostile subjects outscoring friendly ones, and the cards effect showed high cards eliciting highest scores followed by low and medium ones. The highly significant Group x Self effect occurred because insightful persons scored much lower than noninsightful ones, with the group-friendly-self-hostile ones outscoring all others. Because this effect occurred primarily with low and high cards, a significant Cards x Group x Self interaction resulted.

The subanalyses showed an instructions effect for low cards, with Imp subjects scoring higher than LYB ones. The significant Group x Self finding in the overall analysis was duplicated also for low and high cards, but not for the medium ones.

Remoteness of Hostile Expression/Hostility

The omnipresent cards effect showed highest scores to low, medium, and high cards, in that order. A self effect occurred when friendly self-concept individuals outscored hostile self-concept ones. The Instructions x Sex interaction resulted when men outscored women in the Imp condition and reversed their standing to the LYB. The Cards x Group x Instructions interaction reflected the fact that friendly persons outscored hostile ones to low cards in the LYB condition, but hostile persons outscored friendly ones for medium cards. The Cards x Self x Instructions x Sex effect, the only fourth-order interaction to reach significance, may well have been a chance occurrence and will not be discussed.

Turning to the subanalyses, three significant *F*s occurred for the medium cards. In the Instructions x Sex interaction, men scored higher than women in the Imp condition and lower than them in the LYB. The Group x Instructions effect found hostile persons scoring lower than friendly ones in the Imp condition and doing the opposite in the LYB. The Instructions x Self x Sex interaction saw little difference between conditions for both male groups and the hostile self-concept women's group. The friendly self-concept women, however, showed extremely elevated LYB scores compared to their Imp scores. The only high-cards effect (self) was a repetition of the overall self effect.

Stimulus Discrepancy

Both hypotheses were supported, with no differences found for group judgments and a significant F found for self-scores when friendly self-concept persons showed less discrepancy between the hostile stimulus value and content than hostile self-concept persons. The Group x Instructions effect resulted in hostile persons showing a greater discrepancy in the LYB condition and friendly persons outscoring the hostile ones in the Imp conditon.

The cards F value was significant, the low cards eliciting the greatest discrepancy, followed by high and medium ones. The Cards x Group x Instructions effect saw hostile persons manifesting greater discrepancies in the LYB condition and smaller ones in the Imp to the low cards than did friendly persons, with little difference existing for the other cards. The Cards x Instructions x Sex interaction also was a function of the low cards, with women showing higher scores than men in the Imp condition and the reverse in the LYB condiition.

The subanalyses revealed that the low card's significant Group x Instructions effect repeated the overall Group x Instructions finding. The medium cards showed an instructions effect, LYB subjects adhering to the stimulus properties more than Imp subjects. The Group x Self effect for medium cards indicated that hostile women showed a greater discrepancy than hostile men, whereas friendly men and women reversed this finding.

Discussion

The differences between the stimulus properties of the cards seem to outweigh all other determinants of the thematic response. Of the nine scoring systems tested, the cards effect proved significant at the .001 level nine times. No other determinant manifested a comparable record, and it is noteworthy that this performance occurred not only for the simple content scores, but also for the more sophisticated ratio scores as well. In view of this finding, the fact that much clinical practice is undertaken in which the content is analyzed without respect to, or with only a crude awareness of, the stimulus impact seems unfortunate. Even in research studies with more than a modicum of sophistication, glaring omissions seem to have been made in this regard. In the Kelly and Fiske (1951) study on clinical psychology students in the Veterans Administration, for example, one learns only that 10 TAT cards were used and receives neither information as to which cards they were nor on what basis they were chosen. Such an approach vitiates the significance of conclusions drawn regarding the utility of the TAT.

The second most important determinant after cards in the overall analyses of the scoring systems, ignoring the analyses of the separate stimulus levels, was self-concept. In the nine overall comparisons, it was significant five times (twice at the .01 level and three times at the .05 level). Somewhat surprisingly, none of the other variables, considered without regard to interactions, proved of much consequence. Despite the fact that the author had chosen either very hostile or very friendly persons, as judged by their social stimulus values, on only one occasion *(IP/EP)* did the group variable prove significant ($p < .05$). Likewise, the instuctional sets elicited but one significant *F*, and the sex variable educed none at all. Apparently, only the self-concept, considered of itself, is of much importance in determining the nature of the response. It should come as no surprise, therefore, that psychiatric diagnosis, which usually does not take into account the self-concept of the patient so much as his external behavior, has proven so unfertile a ground through which to demonstrate the validity of the TAT.

If one turns to the interactions of the overall analyses, however, many of the other variables appear to play a more important role. Here, recording the number of times each of the variables appeared in significant interactions by summing over nine scoring systems, it is found that cards were involved in significant interactions 10 times; group and instructions, which appeared in only 1 significant main effect, each showed 9 significant interactions; self reached significance 8 times; and sex showed 4 significant findings.

If one focuses on the subanalyses and asks whether any of the stimulus levels proved superior to the others over all scoring systems, one reaches a negative conclusion. Summing all significant *F* tests over nine scoring systems for three stimulus levels each (27 analyses), 11 significant *F*s are noted for the moderately hostile cards, 8 for the low-hostile ones, and 7 for the high-hostile cards.

Certain stimulus levels, however, favored some variables at the expense of others. Thus, of the eight significant *F*s found over the nine analyses of the low-hostile subsets, six involved the group variable in interaction with either self or instructions. Sex played no significant role either individually or in conjunction with another variable. On the other hand, the medium subset with 11 significant *F*s had nine involving instructions as a main effect or in an interaction, and sex, which had not appeared in a significant role with the low cards, now appeared in six significant interactions. Group appeared four times, but self was significant in only two interactions.

Of the seven significant *F*s for high cards, all involved the self variable: four times as a main effect and three times in conjunction with group. No other variables played a role with these cards.

In sum, roughly speaking, it is noted that low cards proved most sensitive to the objective amount of hostility possessed by the subject in conjunction with his self-concept or the TAT instructions he received. The instructional set, however, was by far the most important variable for medium cards, with the effect of the self-concept being most pronounced on high cards.

While no main-effect sex differences appeared in any of the tests, there were several significant Sex x Instructions interactions involving *RHE, H,* and *RHE/H.* In each case, women showed a tendency to be freer in giving the less-adjusted response than men in the Imp situation, but they surpassed men in the production of "good" responses in the LYB situation. In scanning the literature on predicting others' responses, it appears that women show more accuracy in predicting men's responses than men show in predicting women's responses. Further, Witkin, Lewis, Hertzman, Machover, Meissner, and Wapner (1954) have shown that women are more field dependent or more sensitive to the environment with regard to their perceptual responses. It is tempting to conclude, therefore, that the greater flexibility of women in adjusting their responses to the conditions further supports this thesis. While such a conclusion is plausible and, in fact, may be true, the present data cannot be used as supporting evidence. This is because it cannot be assumed that the concept of adjustment is the same for men as for women.[5] In fact, it is likely that men would see the LYB condition as involving more aggressive masculine responses than would women.

The important personality concept of insight seems to be measured by the variables *EP* and *IP/EP.* Insightful persons (group and self-concepts in agreement) tended to score higher than noninsightful ones on *EP* and lower on the ratio *IP/EP.* Friendly persons who perceived themselves as hostile tended to show a very elevated *IP,* indicating that this score may be an excellent measure of inwardly turned aggression.

None of the scoring systems seems to show a marked superiority over the others, their efficacy varying with different variables. If all significant *F* values from the total of 36 analyses are considered it is found that the range is from three (*EP, EP/H*) to nine (*RHE, RHE/H*). If the two scoring systems involving *EP (EP, EP/H*), which fared the poorest, are excluded, the remaining seven show a narrow range, from six to nine significant findings.

Epstein (1962) has hypothesized that cards which have low stimulus relevance for a particular dimension are most sensitive to measures of drive on that dimension, whereas cards high on the dimension are more suitable for measuring inhibition. Insofar as present measures may be interpreted, after the fact, as essentially drive sensitive or inhibition sensitive, this hypothesis may be somewhat roughly investigated.

H and *SD* are clearly measures of drive, since they involve the expression of hostility directed outward without consideration of inhibitory or displaced methods of expression. *IP,* on the other hand, involves hostility directed inward,

[5]This possibility was first suggested by Frederick H. Kanfer in a discussion with the author.

and *RHE* involves the creation of socially acceptable rationales for the expression of hostility, as in a play or science-fiction story. These scores and the ratio scores of which they form a component (*IP, IP/H, RHE, RHE/H*) are considered measures of inhibition. Judgment involving the measures of external punishment (*EP, IP/EP, EP/H*) is ambiguous, since, conceivably, *EP* could represent a perception of aggression as stemming from others or a projection of it from oneself onto others. Hence, these scores will not be considered in evaluating Epstein's hypothesis.

From results involving the subanalyses it is clear that Epstein's hypothesis is strongly supported for the drive measures. The low cards show several significant *F*s, whereas the high cards show none. Regarding the inhibition measures, the majority of significant *F*s are found for the high cards. This was particularly true of the self-concept measure, which was significant in every one of the four measures of inhibition for the high cards, but never for the low and medium cards. Epstein's hypothesis for measures of inhibition is thus confirmed. If further research also confirms this finding, such information may be of considerable value to the clinician in the assessment of personality.

In closing, it should be emphasized that the ubiquity of the stimulus properties of the TAT cards employed here makes it unlikely that many, if any, scoring systems could be devised which would function independently of the stimulus. There is no reason to be alarmed by this fact, for the structure or lack of structure of the cards may be usefully harnessed for purposes of personality assessment if one but uses the proper scoring system.

The clinician who uses the knowledge of the scaled properties of the cards and familiarizes himself with the various scoring approaches reviewed here should be able to select the particular cards and scoring system to best answer the question with which he is confronted. It has been seen that certain personality types respond fairly reliably to certain kinds of cards in a consistent manner when scored by certain scoring systems. This is not meant to imply that the findings in the present study, which was largely descriptive, should be taken as clearly validated data. It has been observed, moreover, that the Epstein hypothesis was largely supported by present findings, though this support must be tempered by the fact that the designation of what constitutes an inhibition and a drive measure was not stated prior to the study. Still, it appears to the author that, despite this shortcoming, the evidence in favor of Epstein's hypothesis warrants further research with predictions in lieu of postdictions. In a similar vein, because of the numerous significance tests computed with non-independent scoring systems, it is quite probable that some of the present significant findings are chance occurrences. It is believed, nevertheless, that if this study has any contribution to make it is not in validating a particular system. Rather, the intention has been to demonstrate that a field approach emphasizing the measurement of stimulus, background, and personality, assessed through a variety of scoring approaches, can enrich the armamentarium of the clinician in his constant quest for the improvement of personality assessment.

5. EMPIRICAL EVALUATIONS OF HUMAN FIGURE DRAWINGS: 1957–1966

Clifford H. Swensen

In the 10 years that have elapsed since the publication of the author's original (1957) review of the literature on figure drawings a substantial amount of research on the topic has been published.

The original review was organized around Machover's (1949) theory that the figure drawn represented the subject's view of his own body. Not much of the research reported in the earlier review supported the Machover theory, nor had it been designed to provide much evidence to indicate the psychometric properties of the human figure drawing as a measuring device. The research published in the past 10 years has been conducted at a substantially higher level of sophistication, and thus has provided more support for the Machover theory, and for the use of the human figure drawings as a diagnostic instrument.

The original review also posed several questions that future research should attempt to answer. Most of these questions, as the review that follows will show, have been answered.

This review follows much the same organization as the original review, with some departures that seem indicated by the nature of the material reviewed. The first sections deal with reliability and the body image hypothesis, and the later sections deal with specific aspects of the validity of signs in drawings. The material reviewed was published between January 1957 and December 1966.

Conditions Affecting Performance In Drawing Figures

Several studies have attempted to assess the effect extraneous variables have upon the drawings. Some of these variables affect specific aspects of the

SOURCE. Clifford H. Swensen, Professor of Psychology at Purdue University, is a clinical psychologist whose areas of interest include interpersonal relations, psychotherapy, and personality measurement. In this article, Dr. Swensen supplements and extends his earlier review of research on human figure drawings to systematically evaluate recent work in this area of personality assessment. This article originally appeared in the *Psychological Bulletin,* 1968, **70**, 20-44. Reprinted by permission of the American Psychological Association and the author.

subject's performance, and will be discussed in the appropriate sections later in the article. Those factors having more general effects will be discussed first.

Some researchers have developed techniques to circumvent the effect of defensiveness upon drawing performance. Cassel, Johnson, and Burns (1958) studied the performance of subjects with the examiner either present or absent while the subject was drawing, and found that more deviant signs were present when the examiner was absent from the room. The subjects were "normal" job applicants. Ponzo (1957) asked the subjects to draw the figures "as an idiot would," and found the "idiot" drawings were more primitive and careless. He interpreted this to indicate that the subjects were less inhibited under the "idiot" conditions. West, Baugh, and Baugh (1963) found that under hypnosis subjects drew smaller, more primitive drawings.

Shanan (1962) felt that the ambiguity of the instruction "draw-a-person" resulted in more variation in drawings, so he gave his subjects clear and specific instructions on how to draw a teacher, after they had completed the Draw-A-Person Test (DAP) under the usual instructions. He retested the subjects 6 months later, and found less variability in size for those figures drawn with specific instructions.

Reliability

Machover (1949) stated that "structural and formal aspects of drawing such as size, line, and placement, are less subject to variability than content, such as body details, clothing, and accessories [p. 6]." Prior to 1957 only two studies, (Bradshaw, 1952; Gunderson & Lehner, 1949) attempted to assess the reliability of the DAP. Both analyzed their data largely through the percentage of agreement in the presence or absence of signs on two separate administrations of the DAP. Their results did not support Machover's opinion, with the consistencies for both structural and content aspects of the drawings falling in the 70% to 80% range. However, their attempts to assess reliability by percentage of consistency were criticized, since they failed to specify the base rate for the presence or absence of the signs they were assessing, thus making it impossible to determine whether or not the consistencies reported were a function of the reliability of the method or an expected function of the base rate, and thus not significantly different from chance expectation.

Since 1957 seven studies of various aspects of the reliability of drawings have been reported. These studies have largely taken into account the criticisms leveled at earlier studies. The results are contained in Tables 1, 2, and 3.

Cassel *et al.* (1958) and Strumpfer (1963) reported interjudge reliabilities. Cassel *et al.* reported that after three training sessions the judgments of judges on the presence or absence of signs correlated with each other above .90. In the first sesssion the correlations averaged only .33. Strumpfer assessed interjudge correlations on six different measures of general aspects of figure drawings such as overall quality, adjustment, sexual differentiation, maturity and body image disturbance. His interrater correlations ranged from .79 to .97 with most being above .90. These two studies suggest that with explicit instructions, or some training, judges can judge figure drawings with satisfactory reliability.

Seven studies have assessed the reliabilities of the quality and content of the drawings themselves. Three of these studies used adult subjects and four used children.

Starr and Marcuse (1959) assessed the reliability of seven aspects of figures, taking into account the base rate problem. They had three groups of college students: Group A drew on two separate occasions 1 month apart with the same examiner, Group B drew on two separate occasions 1 month apart with two different examiners, and Group C drew two sets of drawings on the same occasion with the same examiner. They found no differences among the three groups. They found that the following signs were consistent beyond the .01 level of confidence: placement of the figure on the page, sex of the first drawn figure for male subjects, perspective (direction figures faced on page), incompletions, height of figure, and ratio of head size to figure size. They found that the sex of the first drawn figure for female subjects, and the presence of sex symbols for both male and female subjects were not significantly consistent. None of their statistics was impressively large, however. The largest reported ratio of the obtained phi to the maximal phi correlation coefficient (phi/phi_{max}) was .54 for incompletions.

Strumpfer (1963) assessed the reliability of six standardized methods of judging overall aspects of the drawings, and found the following test-retest reliabilities: overall drawing quality–.89; adjustment–.84; sexual differentiation–.79; maturity–.85; body image disturbance–.74. The subjects were psychotics of varying ages.

Guinan and Hurley (1965) asked judges to match the drawings obtained on one testing occasion to the drawings obtained on another occasion 5 weeks later. They had three groups of judges: a group of PhDs, a group of graduate students, and a group of college freshmen. The drawings were by a group of 20 college students. They found that the judges were able to match the drawings significantly at the .001 level, but the most encouraging result of this study was the finding that the PhDs were correct on an average of better than 19 out of a possible 20 correct matches while the freshmen were correct on an average of only 12 out of a possible 20 correct matches.

Hammer and Kaplan (1964a, 1964b, 1964c, 1966) reported the reliability of children's figure drawings. Their subjects were more than 1,200 children in the fourth, fifth, and sixth grades. Hammer and Kaplan calculated reliability by chi-square, taking into account the base rates of the signs they were assessing. In the first reported study (1964c) they assessed the reliability of the size of the figures by categorizing the drawings into three groups: large (over 7 inches height), medium (3–7 inches), small (under 3 inches). They reported that drawings at the extremes in size are not very reliable, that children who drew small drawings tended to draw larger drawings on a second administration of the DAP. They reported that children who drew their own sex first tended to continue to draw their own sex first on subsequent administrations of the DAP, but children who drew the opposite sex first were likely to change and draw their own sex first on subsequent administrations of the DAP (1964b). Litt & Margolies (1966) repeated the Hammer and Kaplan study, administering the DAP three times to a group of 341 children and found much variability in the sex of the first-drawn figure. The unreliability of the sign "opposite sex drawn first" would explain why research has frequently failed to relate any particular pathology to the sex of the first-drawn figure on the DAP.

Hammer and Kaplan (1964a) found that the reliability of the direction the figure was facing varied, depending upon the direction the figure faced. They found that the drawing of the figure facing the front was highly reliable for both boys and girls. The left-facing profile was reliable for boys, but not for girls. Right-facing profiles were not reliable for either boys or girls. Most boys and girls drew front-facing profiles, but boys significantly more often than girls drew right-facing profiles.

Finally, they assessed a series of signs and found the following to be reliable: omission of fingers, drawing only the head, shading of hair and body, erasures, and open versus closed mouth. They found the following indices were not reliable: omission of hands, feet, and nose; placement on page; teeth; and buttons (Hammer & Kaplan, 1966).

These reliability studies indicate that global ratings, based upon the drawings as a whole, achieve levels of reliability that would generally be considered satisfactory for most psychometric purposes. However, single signs such as line quality or presence or absence of certain body parts are less reliable. This is true of structural aspects of drawings as well as the content of the drawings. Hammer and Kaplan's results suggest that normal drawings tend to be reliable, but drawings containing certain indices of pathology tend to be unreliable.

Finally, it should be pointed out that these more recent studies of reliability have taken into account the criticisms of earlier reliability studies. These results are summarized, for signs, in Tables 1, 2, and 3.

The "Body Image" Hypothesis

The basic hypothesis underlying human figure drawing interpretation is the "body image" hypothesis, which states that when a person draws a human figure

Table 1. Summary of Studies of Reliability and Significance of Global Measures of Figure Drawings

Measure	Number of studies		Interjudge (I-J), test-retest (T-RT) reliability range[a]			
	Significant (<.05)	Not significant	Correlation		Significance of other measures	
			I-J	T-RT	I-J	T-RT
Sexual differentiation (Swenson)	5	2	.94–.97	.79		
Overall quality (Wagner & Schubert; Nichols)	5	5	.74–.95	.89	.001	.001
Summed anxiety indicators (Hoyt & Baron)	1					
Adjustment (Albee & Hamlin)	1	1	.74–.90	.90		
Maturity (Dunn & Lorge)	2	1	.91–.95	.85		
Body Image Disturbance (Fisher)	1	2	.79–.88	.74		
Weighted flaw (Buck)	1			.86		
Weighted good (Buck)	2			.78		
Net weighted (Buck)	1			.85		
% Raw Good (Buck)	1			.75		
Sexual differentiation (Haworth & Worthington)	1					
Aggression		1	.59			
Self-concept (Bruck & Bodwin)	1					

[a] Only one figure is listed when only one study was available reporting reliability.

he draws a picture of himself as he views himself. Machover (1949) stated it thus:

> the human figure drawn by an individual who is directed to "draw a person" relates intimately to the impulses, anxieties, conflicts, and compensations characteristic of that individual. In some sense, the figure drawn is the person, and the paper corresponds to the environment [p. 35].

Hammer (1958) supported this view by expressing it through a quotation from Elbert Hubbard, who stated "When an artist paints a portrait, he paints two, himself and the sitter (Hammer, 1958, p. 8)."

The earlier survey of the research (Swenson, 1957) cited studies that provided some minimal research in support of the hypothesis, but the conclusion was "that definitive research on the basic meaning or significance of human figure drawings is lacking [p. 437]." In a sense, it could be said that a definitive test of the hypothesis is impossible. To determine what human figure drawings are "really" reflecting is a problem of measurement validity, and is thus heir to all of the problems that are associated with the problem of validity in personality measurement.

The concept of "body image" is a construct, which is defined by a variety of behavioral or self-report measures. Which measure is a "true" index of a person's image of his own body? Is it a photograph, or a verbal self-description, or is the body image a function of the interaction between a person's physical appearance and his self-concept? Or is it something else, or some combination of something elses? The question is, of course, unanswerable, and perhaps Ebel (1961) is correct in stating that the question should not even be asked. In a sense, the question is not even important. We could define a person's drawing of a human figure as indicating his "true body image" and validate all other purported measures against his drawing of the human figure. But even this approach would be meaningless since the only value of the human figure drawing, in the clinical setting at least, is its usefulness in predicting certain kinds of behavior in certain kinds of situations. The intellectual structure that rationalizes the process of this prediction is of value only insofar as it provides a parsimonious, reasonable explanation of the relationship which relates human figure drawing performance to other kinds of performance in a meaningful way.

Thus, the problem is basically one of determining construct validity. Therefore, all research related, even in a tangential way, to the relationship between the human figure drawings of subjects and their bodies, or their concepts of their bodies, or their self-concept, is applicable to the validity of the body image hypothesis. This would include most of the research reported on the DAP. Therefore, this section is restricted to reporting the results of research that seems to be more directly related to body image, self-concept, and human figure drawings.

Apfeldorf and Smith (1966), using a balanced lattice design, had two groups of judges match the same-sex drawings of 25 female subjects with full length photographs of the subjects. One group of judges was composed of 30 male graduate students and the second group was composed of 30 female art students. The two groups matched drawings with photographs significantly beyond chance, at the .01 level.

Kamano (1960) related performance on the DAP to subjects' concepts of themsleves. The subjects were 45 hospitalized schizophrenic women. The self-concept was determined by a rating on the semantic differential for 15 concepts. Judges rated these same concepts based upon the figure drawings. The self-concepts were determined for the subjects' concept of their actual self, their ideal self, and their least-liked self. The three self-concept measures were correlated with human figure drawing performance. The highest correlation, .59, was between the DAP and actual self-concept. The correlation between DAP and ideal self was .35, and the correlations between least-liked self and the DAP was .36.

Fisher (1959) related figure drawing performance to GSR body gradients. His subjects were 34 men and 16 women. He obtained the GSR from the right and left arms, hands and fingers. The DAPs produced by the subjects were measured for arm and leg size and scored for presence of Machover's body image disturbance signs (erasure, transparency, lack of body part, nose indicated by two dots, mouth only a line, one or more arms behind the back, nude or peculiar clothing, lack of breasts on the female, shading on the body, delimiting lines on the body, figure off balance, figure small, unusual shading of the crotch, opposite sex drawn first). Fisher also measured the height of the male and female figures. He found there was a significant relationship between GSR directionality and the body disturbance score. He split the group at the median of the body disturbance score, and found that those scoring below the median more often had the highest amplitude of GSR responses on the right side or had equal amplitude on both sides. He also found that those who drew the male figure larger had the highest GSR response on the left side.

Craddick (1963) asked 23 male and 23 female fifth-grade children and 23 male and 23 female college students to draw a person, then asked them to draw a picture of themsleves. He compared the two sets of drawings on size, sex of the drawing, position on the page, and the frequency of correct pairing of the drawings by a male and a female judge. On the basis of the results, he concluded that the body image hypothesis was confirmed, presumably because there was no significant difference between the two drawings in size, most subjects drew the same sex on both tasks, and 69 of the 92 subjects had both drawings placed on the same part of the page. However, the difference between the page placement on the two administrations was significant, and there was a significant difference between the males and the females on the sex of the first drawn figure. All subjects drew their own sex on the self drawing, but only 47.9% of the college girls and 60.9% of the fifth-grade girls drew their own sex on the first drawing.

Armstrong and Houck (1961) hypothesized that: (*a*) subjects drawing the opposite sex first have a different self-concept (measured by the Interpersonal Check List) from subjects who draw their own sex first; (*b*) subjects drawing the opposite sex first have a greater similarity of self-concept with their concept of the opposite sex parent; (*c*) subjects drawing the opposite sex first show a greater discrepancy between their self-concept and their ideal self-concept; and (*d*) if hypothesis *c* was supported, subjects drawing the opposite sex first will have an ideal self-concept that resembles their concept of the same sex parent to a greater degree than subjects who draw their own sex first. The subjects were 57 male and 57 female college students. The subjects produced the DAP and filled out the Interpersonal Check List for self, ideal self, mother and father. The Interpersonal Check List is scored for two factors, dominance and love. The only significant results obtained were that both males and females who drew the opposite sex first resembled the opposite sex parent for dominance, and the females who drew the opposite sex first resembled the opposite sex parent on love. The authors suggested the results provided some support for the Machover hypothesis, but conceded that the significant results could have been due to chance.

Bodwin and Bruck (1960) developed and validated the DAP as a self-concept scale. They defined self-concept as (*a*) self-confidence, (*b*) freedom to express appropriate feelings, (*c*) liking for one's self, (*d*) satisfaction with one's attainments, and (*e*) a feeling of personal appreciation by others. Self-concept was rated by a judge on the basis of an interview. The DAP was scored for shading, reinforcement of lines, erasures, detail in the figure, sketchy lines, transparency, asymmetry, distortion, incompleteness, mixed age of figures, opposite sex drawn first, primitive figure, and immature figure. They had 60 subjects between 10 and 17 years of age. They found that the DAP scores and the judge's ratings correlated .61. They also split the group into a top and a bottom 27%, and compared for DAP signs. They found that there was a significant difference between the top and bottom group on all of the signs except asymmetry, detail in figure, shading, and mixed age of the figures.

Silverstein and Robinson (1961) correlated the estimated height and weight of 30 boys and 30 girls in the sixth grade with the children's estimated height and weight of figures drawn by the children. They found a low negative correlation, although the children were fairly accurate in their estimation of their own height and weight.

McHugh (1965) had 312 girls and 287 boys in grades one through six assign ages to the figures they had drawn on the DAP. She found that the boys assigned ages in the twenties to the male figure, and an age in the late teens to the female figure. The girls tended to assign an age in the middle teens to the male figure, and an age to the female figure that was about four years older than the subjects were. Since the children uniformly assigned ages to their figures that were substantially higher than their own ages, McHugh concluded that the data did not support the Machover hypothesis.

Bennett (1964, 1966) found no relationship between self-concept as determined by the *Q* sort and the DAP for sixth grade children.

Hunt and Feldman (1960) related Machover scoring indices to scores on the Secord-Jourard Body Cathexis Scale, and found no relationship between the subjects' ratings of 25 body parts on the Body Cathexis Scale. Interjudge correlations for DAP ratings correlated between .74 and .86. Subjects were 39 male and 26 female college students.

To conclude from the data cited above that the DAP does or does not reflect a subject's concept of his own body would be difficult, and perhaps not necessarily meaningful. But the data does indicate that scores on various aspects of the DAP are significantly related to some other measures that would be expected to reflect a subject's image of himself. One interesting regularity is that all of the studies using adult subjects, with the exception of the Hunt and Feldman study, found some significant relationship between the DAP and some other measure of body image or self-concept. However, that one study by Hunt and Feldman did directly relate body concept to figure drawing performance. Aside from the Hunt and Feldman study, all of the studies cited that produced negative results used children as subjects. This suggests that performance on the DAP reflects one thing for adults and something else for children. In any case, the results of the last 10 year's research provides more evidence in support of the body image hypothesis than the previous 10 years had produced.

Global Judgments of Drawings

In her original monograph, Machover (1949, p. 21) stressed that patterns of signs should be considered in the interpretation of the DAP. Unquestionably this is what the clinician is doing, somewhere below the level of conscious awareness, when he judges the drawings as a whole. In recent years several methods have been developed for evaluating the drawings globally. This research will be reviewed in this section.

Adjustment or Artistic Ability?

Occasionally an impudent skeptic suggests that perhaps human figure drawings reflect nothing more profound than the subject's ability to draw. Hammer (1958) dismissed this suggestion. However, it is a question that needs to be considered, particularly since some published research bears upon the point. It could be argued that even those with artistic talent differ in the art they produce, as the briefest visit to any gallery will attest, and it seems reasonable to assume that these differences among artists are related to differences in personality.

If the overall quality of a drawing is asserted to be related to, or a sign of, adjustment, and if this characteristic of drawings is to be used to make decisions concerning the individual clinic case, then it must be assumed that artistic ability and training either bear little relationship to overall quality, or that the number of cases in which it bears a relationship is small enough to be disregarded for practical purposes.

Whitmyre (1953) did an early investigation of the topic, and found that there was a significant relationship between psychologists' ratings of drawings for adjustment and art teachers' ratings of the same drawings for artistic quality.

Sherman (1958a, 1958b) obtained drawings for 26 Veterans Administration hospital inpatients and a control group of 26 male nursing assistants, and found that there was a significant relationship between psychologists' ratings of adjustment and artists' ratings of the drawings for artistic quality. He also found a significant relationship between sexual differentiation as measured by the Swensen scale (1955) and artistic excellence.

But the Whitmyre and Sherman studies only prove that judgment of artistic excellence and judgment of adjustment are correlated. Since there was no significant difference between the judged adjustment and artistic excellence of the drawings by the patients and the nursing assistants, Sherman concluded that human figure drawings only demonstrate artistic ability. But these studies did not necessarily support that hypothesis. Anyone with much experience around a mental hospital would hesitate to assert with confidence that the aides were necessarily better adjusted than the patients.

Three studies get closer to the issue. Bieliauskas and Bristow (1959) had the drawings of a group of art majors and a control group of nonart undergraduates, matched for ACE scores, scored for IQ by the Buck system. He found that the mean IQ for the group with art training was significantly higher for Buck's raw G, net weighted score, good score, and flaw score.

Feldman and Hunt (1958) had two art instructors rate the various body parts for drawing difficulty, and had three psychologists rate the drawings of 65 students for signs of disturbance. He found a correlation of –.53 between the rated difficulty of a part to draw and frequency of signs of disturbance exhibited in the drawings of the part. The more difficult a part is to draw, the more likely a subject is to demonstrate some sign of disturbance in drawing that part.

Marais and Strumpfer (1965) controlled for artistic quality of drawings by using only drawings rated of median quality on the Wagner-Schubert Scale (1955). Subjects were 104 female undergraduates. The drawings were scored for the Fisher Body Image Disturbance Score (BIDS), and the upper and lower 25% compared. They found that those subjects with a high BIDS score attributed significantly more disturbance to undisturbed figures on a tachistoscopic test than subjects with a low BIDS score.

These results indicate that drawing ability and drawing quality is a source of variance that should be considered in interpreting drawings. The difficulty of drawing a particular part should be considered when interpreting signs of disturbance in that part. Finally, research on the personality traits or conflicts related to drawing performance should control for drawing ability.

Basic Factors Underlying Drawing Performance

The earlier review of the research suggested that the various scoring categories for figure drawings should be factor analyzed in an effort to determine the basic dimensions underlying the drawing. One factor-analytic study has been reported in the literature, that of Nichols and Strumpfer (1962).

Nichols and Strumpfer obtained figure drawings from 107 male college students, 30 Veterans Administration patients with a diagnosis of neurosis, and 30 Veterans Administration patients with a diagnosis of psychosis. The drawings were scored by a variety of global measures, including adjustment, drawing quality, and sexual differentiation, and also for a large number of specific signs. They found the reliabilities of the global measures were in the .80's and .90's with the highest reliability .95 for artistic quality. The reliabilities for the individual indices were much lower, ranging from .26 for transparencies to .51 for lack of body part.

They obtained four rotated factors. Factor A accounted for most of the variance, and was composed largely of measures of global quality of the drawing. This factor did not load on gross behavioral deviancy. Factor B was negatively correlated with Factor A, and was related to a tendency to draw "big, bosomy figures." Factor C was loaded on a tendency to leave parts out of drawings and to draw the hands behind the back, and was generally related to defensiveness, and drawing constricted figures. Factor D was related to gross behavioral adjustment. The global measure of sexual differentiation (Swensen, 1955) was loaded positively on this factor.

The authors concluded that the largest single factor in the drawings was the overall quality of the drawing, and suggested that investigations of the meaning of particular signs on the DAP should include control of the quality of the drawings.

Studies of Global Characteristics

The global characteristics of human figure drawings have been evaluated and related to various symptoms of psychopathology, with some success, for 20 years (Swensen, 1957). Inspection of Table 1 indicates that the global aspects of drawings have quite high interjudge and test-retest reliabilities. Since the reliabilities of global measures are, for the most part, over .80, and since they are higher than for any other aspect of drawings, it would be expected that global measures would correlate significantly with a variety of variables of interest to the clinical psychologist. As the studies described below indicate, this prediction is substantiated.

Lewinsohn (1965) correlated the overall quality of drawings with several personality and behavioral measures. His subjects were 42 male and 47 female psychiatric hospital inpatients with various diagnoses who produced the DAP both at admission to the hospital and discharge from the hospital. The quality of their drawings was correlated with a variety of personality measures and behavioral rating scales. For the men he found that quality correlated significantly with the MMPI Ego Strength scale (.32), Sexual Deviation scale (−.29), and the F scale (–.28). For the females quality correlated significantly with MMPI Anxiety scale (.25), Control (.31), Lie scale (–.32), Psychopathic (.27), and Feminine Interest (.25). He also found that it correlated significantly with ratings of occupational therapy creativity, and negatively with a personality trait rating of irritability. High quality drawings were significantly related to the patient being single, having fathers with high occupational ratings, being younger in age, and having high vocabulary scores. Good quality drawings were also positively, significantly related to good adjustment following discharge from the hospital and to cooperating while taking the tests.

Bruck and Bodwin (1963) developed a method of rating self-concept from the DAP and found that it correlated significantly with school grades for children in the third grade (.54) and the eleventh grade (.72). It did not correlate significantly with grades for sixth-grade subjects (.38).

Kahn and Jones (1965) used global ratings of drawings to predict whether or not the tested subjects would be admitted to a psychiatric hospital. Their sample was composed of 104 subjects applying for admission to the hospital, of whom 60 were subsequently admitted. They had their judges rate the drawings, globally, for nine areas of pathology. The ratings for severity of illness and impulsivity were significantly related to subsequent admission to the hospital. The prediction of subsequent admission to the hospitals made by the judges on the basis of globally rating the drawings, was significant at the .0001 level.

Silverstein (1966) induced anxiety by having some of his subjects tested by a "tough" examiner and others tested by a "tender" examiner. From the 80 hospitalized mental defectives, those tested by the "tough" examiner produced drawings of significantly poorer quality than those tested by the "tender" examiner.

A promising development in drawing analysis has been the technique of comparing the drawings of neutral objects, such as an automobile, with the drawing of the person which presumably is more anxiety arousing. Both Handler and Reyher (1966) and Lair and Trapp (1960) have used this technique.

Lair and Trapp hypothesized that maladjusted subjects would deteriorate more in their drawing of a person, compared with their drawing of the house on the House-Tree-Person (H-T-P) than would normal subjects. They found that subjects did produce person drawings that were inferior to their house drawings, but found no significant difference between adjusted and maladjusted subjects.

Handler and Reyher used the automobile as the neutral drawing, and used the Hoyt-Baron (1958) summed anxiety indicators and the GSR as measures of anxiety. They found significant differences between the drawing of the automobile and the same sex drawing on both the summed anxiety indicators and the GSR.

The Sexual Differentiation Scale (Swensen, 1955) was originally developed to assess the sexual differentiation between the male and female drawings on the

DAP. It was hypothesized that poor sexual differentiation of drawings might indicate sexual pathology. The original review failed to report evidence to support this hypothesis. Since then Armon (1960) failed to find a significant relationship between sexual differentiation and female homosexuality. Rabin and Limuaco (1959) hypothesized that since sex roles are more clearly differentiated among Filipinos than Americans, Filipino children would produce drawings with significantly greater sexual differentiation than American children. They found that among 10- and 11-year-old children, Filipino boys and girls differentiated significantly better than American boys and girls. Haworth and Normington (1961) confirmed an earlier finding that among children sexual differentiation improves with age. Among adult subjects having little formal education Murphy (1957) found that the women differentiate significantly better than men. Nichols and Strumpfer (1962), in their factor analysis of the DAP, found that the Sexual Differentiation Scale loaded higher on Factor D, gross behavior adjustment, than any other scale. Since their Factor A, quality of drawing, was not loaded highly by variables measuring gross behavioral maladjustment, but the Sexual Differentiation Scale did load highly on Factor A as well as Factor D, it would appear that the Sexual Differentiation Scale is largely a measure of drawing quality, but is also tapping some added element that is related to deviant behavior. Sherman (1958b) found that sexual differentiation was significantly related to rated artistic quality of drawings, thus providing additional evidence indicating that rated sexual differentiation is largely a measure of the overall quality of the drawings.

Global ratings of drawings are more reliable than other aspects of drawings, therefore it would be expected that they would be more likely to be significantly related to a variety of personality and behavioral ratings. This expectation is confirmed by the results of the studies cited above. Global ratings do not significantly detect specific kinds of pathology, however. It would appear that global ratings, by whatever name they are called, are mostly measuring the overall quality of a drawing, and for the most part, the variables to which they significantly relate are variables that are reflections of gross maladjustment. In the earlier review it was concluded that drawings rated globally are useful screening devices. That conclusion is confirmed by the subsequent evidence summarized here.

Structural and Formal Aspects of Drawings

Structural and formal aspects of drawings include general characteristics such as size, position upon the page, and the quality of the lines of the drawing. The reliabilities of these various indicators, contained in Table 2, vary mostly

Table 2. Summary of Results of Studies of Reliability and Significance of Structural Aspects of Figure Drawings

Sign	Number of studies		Interjudge (I-J), test-retest (T-RT) reliability range[a]			
	Significant (<.05)	Not significant	Correlation		Significance of other measures	
			I-J	T-RT	I-J	T-RT
Height	1	2	.52	.21–.85		
Shading	3	11	.31			.01–.05
Erasure	2	3	.46			.05
Line heaviness	3	2				
Placement	9	6	.43			.05
Omission	7	5	.51	.54	.01	.05
Line discontinuity	2	2				
Line emphasis	2	1				
Size	17	8	.51			
Head/body ratio	2	4	.23			
Head length		1				
Head size	2	4				
Transparency	2	4	.26			
Distortion	10	2				
Delineation line	3					
Stance	5	3	.38			
Line pressure	3	1				
Perspective	1	3	.31–.43			.05–.05
Reinforcement	2	3				
Detail in figure	2	2				
Asymmetry	1	3				
Line sketchy	1	1				

[a]Only one statistic reported when only one report of reliability was available.

between .30 and .50. Since the reliability of these indicators is lower than the reliability of global measures of the drawings, it would be expected that they would less consistently relate significantly to other measures of personality or behavior. A survey of the research evidence would be expected to produce contradictory results. The earlier survey of the literature (Swensen, 1957) found this to be true, with conflicting evidence cited for such structural characteristics as size, stance, perspective, and type of lines. As Table 2 indicates, the same result was obtained from the present review of the literature. A review of anxiety indicators in the DAP (Handler and Reyher, 1965) also found conflicting results for such structural characteristics as shading, erasures, size, placement, and line quality. Since the reliability of these indicators is lower than the reliability of global ratings, the appropriate conclusion would appear to be that these conflicting results are a function of the relative unreliability of these aspects of drawings.

Drawing Size

Both the Swensen and the Handler and Reyher reviews reported conflicting results, and the research reviewed here produces the same results. The reliability of drawing size reported is on the order of .51. With a reliability of this magnitude, the research results would be expected to be contradictory. Hammer and Kaplan (1964c) provided evidence that identifies some of the problems of drawing size as a psychometric device. They found that among 1316 school children, drawings that were deviant in size tended to be unreliable. Children who drew either large or small figures on the DAP tended, one week later, to draw average sized figures. This instability of deviant size must be kept in mind in analyzing the results of research on the meaning of the size of the figure drawn.

Both Machover (1949) and Hammer (1958) asserted that size is related to self-esteem and energy level, with high energy–high self-esteem subjects drawing larger figures and low self-esteem subjects drawing smaller figures. Hammer adds, however, that the size of the drawing may also reflect "fantasy self-inflation."

Gray and Pepitone (1964) experimentally manipulated self-esteem by giving their subjects a series of personality tests, then reviewing the test results with the subjects in a way that would either enhance or deflate the subjects' self-esteem. They found that high self-esteem subjects' drawings covered significantly more area than low self-esteem subjects' drawings. Lakin (1960) hypothesized that institutionalized aged subjects would have lower self-esteem than noninstitutionalized aged, and therefore would draw smaller drawings. His hypothesis was confirmed, with the noninstitutionalized aged drawing larger and taller figures than the institutionalized aged.

McHugh (1963a) hypothesized that Negro and Puerto Rican children would have less self-esteem than white children and thus would draw smaller drawings than white children, but found that only the Puerto Rican children drew significantly shorter figures. Bennett (1964, 1966) found no significant relationship between figure size and self-esteem as measured by the *Q* sort for sixth-grade children.

In short, there is some evidence to suggest that the size of the figure reflects self-esteem, but the evidence is not consistent.

Three studies relating figure size to pathology, which could be pertinent to a consideration of self-esteem, did produce positive evidence. It seems reasonable to suggest that shy children and depressed adults would have low self-esteem, and therefore would draw small drawings. Koppitz (1966c) found that shy children drew small figures, and Lewinsohn (1964) found that depressed patients also drew small figures.

Hammer (1958), as has already been indicated, suggested that drawing size can be related to fantasy self-inflation as well as realistic self-esteem. It would be expected, then, that abnormal populations that would be expected to exhibit fantasy self-inflation, such as paranoids and behavior disorders, would draw large drawings. McHugh (1966) found that children suffering from conduct disturbances did draw larger figures than neurotic children from a mental health clinic. Rosenberg (1965) obtained a series of drawings from a paranoid male, and found that as the patient improved his drawings, which were initially large, became smaller. On the other hand, Exner (1962) found no relationship between size and diagnosis of character disorder. Reznikoff and Nicholas (1958) found no relationship between size and carefully determined behavioral indications of paranoid pathology. Craddick (1962) found no relationship between size and criminal psychopathy, and Goldstein and Rawn (1957) found no tendency to increase the size of the drawings in subjects affected by experimentally induced aggressiveness.

A variety of other studies found size related to such things as: father being present in the boy's home (Lawton & Sechrest, 1962); presence of brain tumor (Mabry, 1964); mental age (Zuk, 1962); being a well-adjusted child (Koppitz, 1966b).

On the other hand, size has been found to not be related to: diagnostic categories of mental illness or chronicity of illness (Strumpfer, 1963; Strumpfer & Nichols, 1962); school achievement (Koppitz, 1966a; Lourenso, Greenberg, & Davidson, 1965); dominance (Shry, 1966), or seeking a furlough from a Veterans Administration domiciliary center (Apfeldorf *et al.,* 1966).

The size of the head relative to the size of the body has been found related to regressed schizophrenia (Baldwin, 1964), but not to school achievement (Lourenso *et al.,* 1965) or organic problems (Bieliauskas & Kirkham, 1958).

To summarize, the size of the drawings does seem to reflect self-esteem, and probably fantasied self-inflation, but with an inconstancy that is the reflection of the relative lack of reliability of the size of the drawings.

Placement

Hammer and Kaplan (1966) did not find, for 1300 school children, that the placement of the figure on the page was beyond chance reliability. Starr and Marcuse (1959) also failed to find it reliable for college students. Perhaps some of the significance of placement is revealed in studies by Dennis (1958, 1960) who found that handwriting training was significantly related to where a subject placed the drawing on the paper, with subjects who were taught to write from left to right (e.g., Americans) tending to draw on the left side of the page, and subjects who were taught to write from right to left (e.g., Arabs) tending to draw on the right side of the page. With questionable reliability, it would be expected that significant relationships between placement on the page and other measures of behavior or personality would be rather inconsistent and unpredictable. The earlier survey of the research (Swensen, 1957) found that the hypotheses concerning placement were not supported. Handler and Reyher (1965) reported seven studies supporting the hypotheses concerning placement and eight studies either not supporting the hypotheses or producing conflicting evidence. The current review reports nine studies reporting significant findings, and six reporting nonsignificant findings. With such questionable reliability, however, such findings as are reported should be accepted with caution.

Machover (1949) suggested that a figure placed on the right side of the page indicates a person who is self-oriented. Placement high on the page indicates optimism, while placement low on the page indicates pessimism. Hammer (1958) suggested that placement high on the page indicates striving, and drawing near the center indicates more self-centeredness, with placement on the left indicating impulsiveness, and placement on the right indication impulse control.

Two studies suggest that a tendency to place the figure in the upper left is related to anxiety (Handler & Reyher, 1964; Hoyt & Baron, 1958). Handler and Reyher induced experimental anxiety, and confirmed the presence of anxiety with a change in the subjects' GSR, while Hoyt and Baron correlated the DAP with scores on the Manifest Anxiety scale. However, an attempt by Mogar (1962) to replicate the Hoyt and Baron study was not successful, and Exner (1962) failed to find placement significantly affected in subjects in whom anxiety was induced.

McHugh (1963a, 1966) reported that Negro children tended to draw figures farther from the right margin than white children, and children with conduct disturbances tended to draw figures closer to the bottom of the page. Bradfield (1964) found that withdrawn, acting-out, and underachieving children tended to place drawings on the left side. Crippled children (Wysocki & Whitney, 1965) draw at the extremities of the page, noninstitutionalized aged subjects drew figures closer to the center of the page; and Apfeldorf *et al.* (1966) reported that institutionalized aged subjects who took furloughs from the hospital also significantly more often drew figures in the center of the page than aged patients who did not take furloughs.

However, Gray and Pepitone (1964) found no relationship between self-esteem and placement, Exner (1962) found no relationship between neurosis or character disorder and placement, Craddick (1962) found criminal psychopathy unrelated to placement, and Taylor (1960) failed to find a difference between students and patients in the placement of experimental figures on the page.

The evidence suggests that for every study finding a significant relationship between placement and some other behavioral characteristics, there exists a study relating similar kinds of data without significant results. The reliability of placement suggests these results are precisely what should be expected.

Perspective

The reported reliability of perspective, or the direction the figure faces, is between .31 and .43, which is rather low. With this level of consistency, contradictory results would be expected from studies relating perspective to other aspects of behavior. This is what the earlier review (Swenson, 1957) reported, and this is the finding of the current review.

Drawing the figure in profile is hypothetically related to evasiveness (Machover, 1949). However, the research suggests that it is more related to sex and handedness. Most subjects draw figures facing forward (Crovitz, 1963; Hammer & Kaplan, 1964a; Starr & Marcuse, 1959) but females significantly more often draw the figure facing forward than males. Of those subjects who draw profiles, right-handed subjects are more likely to draw profiles facing left, while left-handed subjects draw the profiles facing equally in both directions. Exner (1962) found that neurotics and character disorder patients drew profiles more often than normals, but McHugh (1966) found it unrelated to recovery in tuberculosis patients, and Wysocki and Whitney (1965) found it unrelated to crippling defects.

Stance

The stance taken by the figure, that is, whether the figure is relatively vertical and appears balanced or not, has a reported reliability of .38, which would suggest that the results of research on stance should be inconclusive. The earlier review (Swensen, 1957) found this to be the case, but the literature of the past ten years has produced more research reporting significant results than nonsignificant results.

Stance is supposed to indicate perceived stability, with insecure subjects drawing figures that are falling down or floating (Machover, 1949). The evidence summarized here tends to support that interpretation. Mabry (1964) reported a clinical case of malignant brain tumor in which the figure became more and more reclining as the tumor progressed. Kahn and Jones (1965) found stance related to judged severity of illness great enough to predict admission to a mental hospital. Koppitz (1966a, 1966b) found stance differentiated significantly between normal children and children with behavior problems, and that it was significantly related to school achievement. Handler and Reyher (1966) found stance significantly affected by induced anxiety. On the negative side, Bieliauskas and Kirkham (1958) failed to differentiate between normal and disturbed children on the basis of stance, and Hiler and Nesvig (1965) failed to distinguish between normal and disturbed adolescents on the basis of stance. It may be significant that all the reported negative studies used children and adolescents as subjects.

Line Quality

Although line pressure is reported as being a reliable measure (Hammer, 1958), adequate assessment of line quality is lacking. Since line quality is a structural variable, it would not be inaccurate to guess that its reliability would be comparable to that of other structural variables. The distribution of significant findings, in both the earlier and more recent literature, follows the same pattern as that of most of the other structural variables. The earlier review (Swensen, 1957) reported conflicting findings relative to line quality, and the present review also finds conflicting findings, although more are significant than not. Handler and Reyher (1965) also reported conflicting findings, but with substantially more significant than insignificant results reported.

Heavy lines indicate assertive, aggressive individuals who wish to erect a strong barrier between themselves and the environment, while light lines are drawn by passive, meek persons who are unable to differentiate themselves from the environment (Machover, 1949; Hammer, 1958). Faint, "ectoplasmic" lines are drawn by schizophrenics, while lines that vary in pressure are drawn by hysterics. Angular and jagged lines are masculine and indicate aggressiveness while curving lines are feminine.

Glatter and Hauck (1958) tested the symbolic significance of lines and found that the lines rated "male" were dark and angular while the lines rated "female" were light and curving.

Handler and Reyher (1964) observed that under induced stress line pressure increased. Reznikoff and Nicholas (1958) found that heavy line emphasis significantly discriminated patients who had exhibited paranoid signs from patients who had not exhibited such signs. Bodwin and Bruck (1960) found adolescent subjects with low self-concepts, as determined by interview, were more likely to draw figures with sketchy lines than subjects with high self-concepts. Exner (1962) found that patients with character disorders drew lighter lines than other subjects, and that neurotics and character disorders drew sketchy lines. Kahn and Jones (1965) found that among patients being examined for possible admission to a mental hospital, those who drew figures with firm outer bondary lines were less likely to be admitted.

Goldstein and Rawn (1957), on the other hand, induced stress in subjects, but found it had no effect on line pressure. Hoyt and Baron (1958) failed to find a relationship between line quality and scores on the Manifest Anxiety scale. McHugh (1966) found no difference between children with neuroses and conduct disturbances in line quality of figures drawn. Hiler and Nesvig (1965) found no difference between normal and hospitalized adolescents in sketchiness of lines.

The one consistency is the inconsistency. The two studies (Goldstein & Rawn; Handler & Reyher) that carefully provided a base line of line pressure, then induced stress and measured the concomitant change in line pressure, obtained contradictory findings.

Shading

Shading is the use of light lines to accentuate a particular part of the figure drawn. It is most commonly used in drawing the hair and in delineating body contours. The reported reliability for shading is significant, but lower (.31) than for most other structural aspects of drawings. Therefore, the probability is that significant findings would conflict. Handler and Reyher (1965) reported equal numbers of studies reporting significant, nonsignificant, and conflicting results. The earlier review (Swensen, 1957) reported nonsignificant results, and the present review found nonsignificant results predominating. Shading is supposed to indicate anxiety.

Koppitz (1966b) found that children with adjustment problems drew significantly more figures with shading than well-adjusted children. Wysocki and Whitney (1965) reported that crippled children shaded more than noncrippled children. Handler and Reyher (1964) found significantly more shading on the drawing of the male figure by male subjects than on the drawing of an automobile, which was hypothetically less anxiety arousing.

On the other hand, Handler and Reyher (1965) reported shading significantly negatively correlated with GSR, which presumably should have indicated the presence of anxiety. Reznikoff and Nicholas (1958) found no relationship between shading and paranoid symptoms. Bodwin and Bruck (1960) found no relationship between shading and self-concept. Craddick (1962) found a negative relationship between shading and criminal psychopathy. Exner (1962) found a nonsignificant trend toward shading among patients with character disorders and an induced anxiety group. Hoyt and Baron (1958) and Mogar (1962) found no relationship between shading and scores on the Manifest Anxiety scale. McHugh (1966) found no difference in shading between normal children and children with conduct disturbances. Hiler and Nesvig (1965) found no difference in shading between disturbed and normal adolescents. Grams and Rinder (1958) found no relationship between shading and homosexuality. Craddick, Leipold, and Cacavas (1962) found a significant relationship between shading and anxiety as rated by judges from the drawings, but found no relationship between either shading or the judges' anxiety ratings and scores on the Manifest Anxiety scale.

One problem with shading is that it is a sign usually found in drawings of good quality. Drawing quality is positively related to adjustment. Consequently, even though shading may indicate anxiety, the fact that its presence is limited to drawings of good quality, confounds it with the adjustment variable.

Erasures

Erasures have a test-retest reliability significantly above the .05 level, and an assessed interjudge reliability of .46. Swensen (1957) and Handler and Reyher (1965) reported nonsignificant results for erasures. The current review found the significant and nonsignificant studies about evenly divided.

Erasures, like shading, are supposed to indicate conflict, and are most often found in drawings of better quality, produced by subjects who are able to evaluate critically their artistic productions.

Mogar (1962) failed to find erasures related to Manifest Anxiety scale scores in psychiatric patients, but did find a small but significant relationship between erasure and intelligence. Handler and Reyher (1964) found significantly more erasures on the male and female figures drawn by male undergraduates than on the more affectively neutral drawings of an automobile. Bodwin and Bruck (1960) found erasures one of the indicators that significantly differentiated adolescents with a high self-concept from those with a low self-concept.

Omissions

Omissions appear to be somewhat more reliable than other structural indicators, with a reported test-retest reliability of .54. The earlier survey (Swensen, 1957) did not summarize the results of omissions per se, but Handler and Reyher (1965) reported 22 out of 24 studies indicating significant results for omissions, and the present review found a majority of studies reporting significant results for omission.

Omitting significant details in drawings (Hammer, 1958) is related to using defenses of withdrawal, and feelings of emptiness. Omissions are found in relatively primitive drawings, and thus are more likely to be noted in the drawings of psychotics, organics, and young children.

Koppitz (1966a, 1966b, 1966c) found disturbed children more likely to omit various items from their drawings than normal children, and found omissions or the lack of them related significantly to tested intelligence. Handler and Reyher (1964) found male undergraduates were more likely to omit details from their drawings of the male figure when they were subjected to stress. Hiler and Nesvig (1965) found that disturbed adolescents were more likely to omit essential details from their drawings than were normal adolescents. Kahn and Jones (1965) found that patients omitting details on an intake screening examination were more likely to be admitted to a psychiatric hospital. Lorge, Tuckman, and Dunn (1958) found that only 25% of the residents of a home for the aged drew intact drawings. Vane and Eisen (1962) found that poorly adjusted kindergarten children were more likely to omit essential body parts from their drawings than were well-adjusted children. Baldwin (1964) found regressed schizophrenics were more likely to omit parts of the figures they drew. Mogar (1962) found a small but positive relationship between scores on the Manifest Anxiety scale and omissions. Rosenberg (1965) reported that a paranoid schizophrenic omitted the pelvic area in his drawing of a woman, but as the patient improved his drawings improved.

However, Hoyt and Baron (1958) found no significant relationship between omissions and Manifest Anxiety scale scores. McHugh (1966) found no significant differences between normal children and children with conduct disturbances in omissions. Exner (1962) found no differences between normals and patients with diagnosed neuroses or character disorders on omissions, and no difference between normal control subjects and subjects undergoing stress in omitting details from their drawings. Grams and Rinder (1958) reported no differences between normals and homosexuals in omissions. Bieliauskas and Kirkham (1958) found no increase in omissions among children with organic disorders. Omissions are not related to crippling disabilities (Wysocki & Whitney, 1965). Santorum (1960) found no differences between tuberculosis patients who were discharged and patients who were not discharged in omissions.

Too many significant studies relating omissions to other aspects of behavior have been produced to dismiss omissions as an unreliable and questionable sign. The nonsignificant studies have generally related normals to out-patients, or have related omissions to measures of anxiety. It seems probable that omissions are characteristic of severely regressed patients, and thus do distinguish between normal, or relatively normal subjects and severely disturbed subjects, but fail to distinguish between normals and other patient groups, such as homosexuals or character disorders, who are not suffering from an overwhelmingly severe disorder. Omissions among children would probably be a relatively sensitive indicator among the very young, as the Vane and Eisen study suggests, but lose this sensitivity as the children grow older and their drawing skills improve. It must be concluded that, in general, omission of significant body parts is a fairly dependable indicator of severe pathology.

Transparency

A drawing contains a transparency when a body part shows through the clothing or internal organs show through the skin. Fairly common transparencies are the arms and legs showing through sleeves and trousers.

The reported reliability with which judges can assess the presence of transparency is rather low (.26), so relationships between transparency and other aspects of behavior would tend to be nonsignificant. Handler and Reyher (1965) reported half of the studies they reviewed obtained significant results for transparencies. The current review found about the same proportion of studies reported significant results.

Hiler and Nesvig (1965) found transparencies almost exclusively in the drawings of disturbed adolescents, who were compared with adjusted adolescents. Bodwin and Bruck (1960) found that transparency was among the signs significantly related to a negative self-concept. Koppitz (1966b) found children with behavior problems tended to draw figures with more transparencies than well-adjusted children.

However, Handler and Reyher (1964) failed to find a relationship between induced anxiety and transparency. McHugh (1966) was unable to differentiate normal children from children with neuroses and character disorders on the basis of transparencies. Grams and Rinder (1958) found no relationship between homosexuality and the drawing of figures with transparencies.

Distortion

Distortion is considered to indicate a subject suffering a severe emotional upheaval (Hammer, 1958), and is characterized by body parts being drawn out of proportion, parts not connected to the body, and parts drawn in inappropriate areas of the body. Handler and Reyher (1965) found a majority of studies reporting significant relationships between distortion and other behavioral measures and the present review found the same.

Hiler and Nesvig (1965) found distorted figures significantly more frequently drawn by disturbed adolescents than normal adolescents. Bodwin and Bruck (1960) found that adolescents with low self-concept more often drew distorted figures than adolescents with a high self-concept. Koppitz (1966a, 1966b) found that disturbed children were more likely to draw distorted figures than normal children, and that children who drew poorly integrated figures had lower achievement in the first grade. Handler and Reyher (1964) found that subjects in whom anxiety had been induced were significantly more likely to draw distorted drawings than under nonstressful conditions. Kahn and Jones (1965) found that among subjects being screened for admission to a psychiatric hospital those who drew distorted drawings were more likely to be admitted. Lorge *et al.* (1958) found that 55% of a group of institutionalized aged tended to draw distorted figures. Vane and Eisen (1962) found that well-adjusted kindergarten children could be significantly differentiated from poorly adjusted children on the basis of distortions.

However, Bieliauskas and Kirkham (1958) found no difference between organic and nonorganic children in drawing distorted drawings, and Hoyt and Baron (1958) found no relationship between distortion and Manifest Anxiety scale scores.

The cited evidence overwhelmingly indicates that distorted drawings differentiate between severely disturbed subjects and other kinds of subjects. Distortion of the drawings is the external manifestation of severe emotional disruption.

Symmetry

Symmetry is the extent to which the two sides of the figure are symmetrical. Presumably a drawing which stresses bilateral symmetry of the figure indicates rigidity and obsessive-compulsiveness (Hammer, 1958). The earlier review of the research (Swensen, 1957) failed to find studies testing the significance of symmetry. The present review found three of four reported results nonsignificant.

Koppitz (1966b) found that asymmetry of limbs tended toward but did not reach significance in differentiating normal children from children with conduct disturbances, but that (1966c) there was a tendency for aggressive children to draw asymmetrical figures. McHugh (1966) failed to find a difference between normal children and children with neuroses and conduct disturbances in drawing asymmetrical figures, and Bodwin and Bruck (1960) failed to find a relationship between symmetry and self-concept.

Significance of the Content of Drawings

The clinical literature on human figure drawings has frequently dwelt upon the significance of a subject's rendering of a particular body part. Unfortunately, the research literature has not generally supported the usual interpretations attached to particular kinds of artistic rendering of a particular body part. The earlier review of the literature (Swensen, 1957) summarizing this research reported either that most of the hypotheses concerning the significance of a particular kind of treatment for a particular body part were not supported by the evidence, or the hypotheses had not been tested. Table 3, which summarizes the results of the studies surveyed in this paper, indicates that the empirical evidence supporting a significant relationship between the treatment of a particular body part and some behavioral measure is either conflicting or negative. One clear exception to this statement is the sex of the first-drawn person, which will be discussed separately later.

It will be noted that Table 3 also indicates that for most of the body parts acceptable reliability information is either not available, or that the rendering of a particular part in a particular manner is not consistent. Subjects' drawings of body parts are not reliable. This should not be surprising, since the drawing of a particular body part is a very small sample of behavior. Global ratings of the drawings encompass all of the behavior sampled by a drawing, and have relatively high reliabilities. Structural aspects of the drawings sample a smaller amount of the universe of the figure drawing behavior, and have reliabilities that are somewhat lower than the global ratings. The drawing of a particular body part samples an even smaller sample of the subject's figure drawing behavior, and thus would be expected to have still lower reliability. Low reliabilities would be expected to result in few or no consistent relationships between the rendering of a particular body part, and a particular psychological symptom.

Figure drawing analysts (e.g., Machover, 1949) stress the importance of analyzing patterns of signs, rather than an individual sign. The evidence summarized here should reinforce that injunction.

Table 3. Summary of Results of Studies of Reliability and Significance of Content of Figure Drawings

Sign	Number of studies		Interjudge (I-J), test-retest (T-RT) reliability range[a]			
	Significant (<.05)	Not significant	Correlation		Significance of other measures	
			I-J	T-RT	I-J	T-RT
Mouth	3	3				.05
Nude	1	1				
Limb size		1				
Hair	2					.05
Sex symbols or organs	1	3				.01
Sex drawn first	12	6				.01–.05
Neck		2				
Hands	2	4				.05
Feet		4				.05
Head	1	3				.05
Arms	3	3				
Face		3				
Eyelashes		2				
Eyes	2	4				
Nose	1	2				.05
Legs	1	2				
Teeth	2					.05
Buttons	1	2				.05
Earrings		1				
Ears	1	3				
Heels		1				
Body	2					
Fingers	1	1				
Shoulders	1					
Toes	1					
Hips and buttocks		1				
Belt		1				
Breasts	1					
Knee	1					
Elbow	1					

[a] Only one figure is listed when only one study was available reporting reliability.

Sex of the First-Drawn Figure

Since the first figure drawn by a subject was presumed to be, in fact, the subject's drawing of his unconscious perception of himself, it was hypothesized that if the first figure the subject drew was of the opposite sex, then the subject was indentified with the opposite sex. This hypothesis lent itself to relatively easy empirical tests, which failed to produce significant evidence (Swensen, 1957). The evidence presented here suggests that the sex of the first-drawn figure is a more complex phenomenon than the simple sexual identification hypothesis would suggest. The sex of the first-drawn figure is significantly related to a variety of behavior deviancies, as the evidence will demonstrate. The proportion of subjects drawing the opposite sex on the first drawn figure varies with both age and sex, suggesting that this particular sign needs to be interpreted with some consideration of the specific subject producing the drawing.

Hammer and Kaplan (1964b) assessed the reliability of the sex of the first-drawn figure for fourth-, fifth-, and sixth-grade children. They found that 84% of the boys and 80% of the girls drew their own sex first. Upon retest one week later they found that those subjects who had drawn their own sex first on the first administration continued to draw their own sex first on the second administration, but the subjects who drew the opposite sex first on the first administration were equally likely to draw their own sex first on the second administration. Litt and Margolies (1966) replicated the Hammer and Kaplan study, but had their subjects repeat the figure drawings three times. They reported a substantial amount of variability of the sex of the first-drawn person. Starr and Marcuse (1959) assessed the reliability of the sex of the first-drawn person for college undergraduates, using both immediate and one month delay test-retest method. They report significance at the .01 level of confidence, using chi-square, but noted that 10% of the male subjects varied from the first to the second administration, and 42% of the females varied.

Butler and Marcuse (1959) found that through grade school, both boys and girls predominantly drew their own sex first, with the boys' percentage varying from 75% to 95%, and the girls' percentage varying from 70% to 88%. During the teenage years the boys' tendency to draw their own sex first remains above 90% while the girls' percentage drops, with only 36% drawing their own sex first at age 18. Craddick (1963) confirmed this downward trend for girls, reporting that 95.6% of college boys drew their own sex first, but only 47.9% of college girls drew their own sex first. Gravitz (1966) summarized the sex drawn first for presumably normal job applicants of both sexes between the ages of 17 and 59. The males varied between 82% and 100% drawing their own sex first, and the females varied between 60% and 68% drawing their own sex first. There was a clear trend for men to draw their own sex first in higher proportions than women, and this trend was more accentuated in adults than school children.

Whitaker (1961) related homosexuality to the sex of the first figure drawn in a group of male subjects. He added a third drawing in which the subject could choose the sex of the figure he drew. Whitaker concluded that his results varied little from the base rate, but he did find that 93% of the subjects drawing a female on both the first figure and the third, free, figure were adjudged either homosexual or effeminate. Grams and Rinder (1958) failed to differentiate between homosexuals and normal boys in a state training school on the sex of the first-drawn figure. Armon (1960), however, differentiated between normal and homosexual women at the .10 level on the basis of the sex of the first-drawn figure. Brown and Tolor (1957) reviewed the literature on the sex of the first-drawn figure, and failed to produce any significant results.

Davids and DeVault (1960) compared women who had had complications in delivering children with women who had had normal deliveries, and found the normal women significantly more often drew their own sex first. He also found pregnant women significantly more often drew the female figure first. The normal delivery women drew their own sex first 84% of the time, and 87% of the pregnant women drew their own sex first. Fisher (1961) found that of male adolescents who drew nude figures, a significantly greater number also drew the opposite sex first. Kurtzberg, Cavior, and Lipton (1966) reported that drug addicts significantly more often draw the opposite sex first and larger than a group of nonaddicts. Laird (1962a, 1962b) failed to find a significant difference between female normals and alcoholics in the sex of the first-drawn figure, but did find a significant difference between male alcoholics and normals. Wisotsky (1959) also reported a significant difference between male alcoholics and normals on the sex of the first-drawn person. Pollitt, Hirsch, and Money (1964) found that men suffering irreversible impotence following priapism tended to draw the opposite sex first.

McHugh (1966) reported that neurotic children significantly more frequently drew the opposite sex first than normal children, that girls tended to draw their own sex figure larger at all ages (1963b), and that boys drew their own sex figure larger at ages 8 and 11. Phelan (1964) found no relationship between sex drawn first and adjustment for sixth-grade boys.

Kahn and Jones (1965) found that applicants for admission to a mental hospital who were subsequently admitted were more likely to draw their opposite sex first.

Armstrong and Hauck (1961) tested several hypotheses concerning the self-concept and the sex of the first-drawn person, but the only one that was supported by their data was that subjects who drew the opposite sex first were similar in self-concept to their concept of the opposite-sex parent on the dominance scale of the Interpersonal Check List. Bodwin and Bruck (1960) found that subjects with low self-concept drew the opposite sex first. Richey (1965) found that fifth-grade children drew their own sex figure with significantly greater accuracy and detail than the opposite sex figure.

The research reviewed has produced enough significant results to suggest that the sex of the first-drawn figure is related to self-concept, but in a complex manner that is not yet clear. The attempts to relate the sex of the first-drawn person to symptoms of pathology have also produced significant results, but the proportions of abnormal persons drawing the opposite sex first do not deviate sharply enough from the base rates of normals drawing the opposite sex first to warrant using it as a diagnostic sign in individual cases. The Brown and Tolor (1957) review found that proportions of male college students drawing their own sex first ranged from 85% to 95%, while homosexuals ranged from 75% to 92%. Althoug Laird (1962) found a significant difference between alcoholics and normals on the sex of the first-drawn person, 81% of the alcoholics drew their own sex first, while 94.7% of the normals drew their own sex first. Assuming Laird's percentages are fairly representative, they would result in 43% wrong diagnoses if used as definitive sign of pathology.

Discussion and Conclusions

The earlier review (Swensen, 1957) made six recommendations for future research. In the past 10 years, all six have been fulfilled. The DAP has been factor analyzed (Nichols and Strumpfer, 1962); reliability has been assessed, taking into account the criticism of percentage of agreement as a measure of reliability (Guinan & Hurley, 1965; Hammer & Kaplan, 1964a, 1964b, 1966; Litt & Margolies, 1966; Starr & Marcuse, 1959; Strumpfer, 1963); extended drawing techniques have been used (Berryman, 1959; Craddick, 1963; Handler & Reyher, 1964; Kamano, 1960; Whitaker, 1961); clinical studies have reported the results of drawings obtained serially during the course of an illness (Mabry, 1964; Rosenberg, 1965); patterns of signs of psychopathology have been assessed (Grams & Rinder, 1958; Griffith & Payman, 1959; Hoyt & Baron, 1958; Koppitz, 1966a, 1966b, 1966c; Ribler, 1957; Wildman, 1963); and specific hypotheses concerning psychopathology and figure drawings have been tested (Armstrong & Hauck, 1961; Baldwin, 1964; Davids & DeVault, 1960; Fisher, 1959; Gray & Pepitone, 1964; Kurtzberg *et al.,* 1966; Lawton & Sechrest, 1962; Orgel, 1959). The research published in the recent past is clearly more sophisticated than the studies reported prior to 1957. A large proportion of the studies reported some attempt to assess the reliability of the measures they used, and many studies were designed to test specific hypotheses. As a consequence, a higher proportion of the studies report positive results.

Two classes of studies have appeared in the past 10 years that were not dealt with in the earlier review, and which have not been explicity discussed previously in this paper. One class might be termed "figure drawing methodology" and the other "experimental manipulation of variables."

Methodology Studies

Several studies have attempted to assess the process by which the clinician derives conclusions from figure drawings. Hiler and Nesvig (1965) paired DAPs from 21 male and nine female disturbed adolescents and 20 male and 10 female normal adolescents. They presented these drawings to six clinicians, one pair at a time, and asked the clinician to determine which pair was from a disturbed subject and which from a normal. A few days later each clinician was shown each pair again, told of his previous decision and asked to state the criteria by which he arrived at his decision. The number of correct and incorrect decisions for each stated criterion was noted, and those criteria leading to correct decisions significantly beyond 50% were retained. The criteria that distinguished beyond the .01 level of confidence were "definitely bizarre," "incomplete," and "nothing pathological." They also had eight nonpsychologists rate the drawings, and found that they did as well as the psychologists.

Schaeffer (1964) obtained DAP's from 10 normal subjects, 10 neurotics, and 10 psychotics and had the drawings rated by 17 clinical psychologists, 17 Veterans Administration trainees, and five nonpsychologists. He found no differences among the three groups of judges in accuracy of their ability to pick out the drawings by patients.

Murray and Deabler (1958) attempted to assess the effect experience had upon judges' accuracy in assessing drawings. They obtained a pair of drawings from 20 patients in each of five carefully diagnosed categories: character disorder, anxiety neurosis, undifferentiated schizophrenia, paranoid schizophrenia, and normal. The drawings were divided into 20 sets of 5 drawings each, with the drawings of one subject in each category in each set. Fifteen psychologists judged the drawings. After each judgment the psychologist was told the correct diagnosis for the person who had drawn the drawing just previously judged. They found that judgment improved with experience, with a correlation of .80 between the number of errors in judgment for a drawing and the drawing's position in the order of presentation. They found much variation in improvement among the judges, with the correlations between errors and position on the list ranging from −.12 to .63. They found that improvement was not related to previous experience. Their data suggest that some judges cannot learn to interpret drawings, and that careful assessment of judges is necessary in figure drawing research.

Arbit, Lakin, and Mathis (1959) asked 32 experienced clinicians to rate 26 items of DAP assessment for the extent to which they were used in assessing the DAP. The authors concluded that most sophisticated clinicians use the DAP to determine general rather than specific characteristics.

These studies suggest that formal training is not particularly related to success in interpreting the DAP, probably because some individuals learn from experience, but some do not. They reinforce the efficacy of global judgment rather than interpretation of specific signs on the DAP.

A final study related to DAP methodology, is that of Feldman and Hunt (1958), who related signs of maladjustment on a particular part of the figure drawn to the difficulty of drawing that part. They had clinicians rate drawings for indications of conflict on each body part, and had artists rate the difficulty of drawing each body part. They obtained a correlation of −.53 between signs of disturbance and rated difficulty of drawing a particular part, indicating that the more difficult a part is to draw, the more likely a subject is to exhibit a sign of disturbance in drawing that part.

Experimental Studies of Emotional State and Figure Drawings

Several studies have induced an emotional state in the subjects and studied the effect this emotional change had upon the figures drawn by the subjects. Cassel *et al.* (1958) assumed that the examiner had an inhibiting effect upon the subject, so had the examiner leave the room while the subject drew. They found more deviant signs were present in drawings drawn while the examiner was absent. Handler and Reyher (1964) found a significant increase in number of indicators of anxiety when the subjects were placed in a stressful situation. Goldstein and Rawn (1957) found an increase in signs of aggression when their subjects, who were state hospital attendants, were told that they would have to work longer hours without an increase in pay. Exner (1962) found that a group of normals in which fear was induced by puncturing their fingers for a blood sample drew as much shading in their drawings as a group of neurotics.

The induction of anxiety, fear, or aggression appears to produce a significant change in the figure a subject draws.

Conclusions

Three conclusions suggest themselves, at the end of this rather lengthy review of 10 years accumulation of studies. The first is that the value of a particular sign on the DAP is directly related to the reliability of that sign. The reliability of a particular sign is a direct, linear function of the amount of drawing behavior included to assess that sign. Since global ratings include all of the drawing behavior contained in a given DAP, global ratings are the most reliable, and therefore the most useful aspect of the DAP. The other signs on the DAP, such as structural and content variables have reliabilities that are probably too low for making reasonably reliable clinical judgments. This suggests that if content signs are to be used with any expectation of success, then the task must be extended to include several drawings so that the clinical judgment is based upon a larger sample of drawing behavior.

The second conclusion is that if content and structural signs are assessed, the quality of the drawing and the difficulty of drawing the particular body part should be taken into account in the assessment. Research has repeatedly demonstrated that: (*a*) better adjusted subjects produce drawings of higher quality, and (*b*) the higher the quality of the drawing the more conflict indicators it contains. Drawings of good quality contain more details and a more accurate rendering of the figure, which results in more frequent erasures, more shading, and use of a wider variety of kinds of lines. There is a positive correlation between the quality of a drawing and the number of conflict indicators that are present in that drawing. Further, one study indicates that the more difficult a part is to render the more likely it is to contain signs of conflict. If the psychodynamic significance of a particular sign, such as shading the hair, is to be assessed with any hope of producing a stable, significant result, the study must control the quality of the drawings. Otherwise the presence or absence of the sign is confounded with the quality of the drawing itself, which in turn is related to the overall adjustment of the subjects studied.

The third conclusion is that there has been substantial increase in empirical justification for the use of the DAP as a clinical tool. Unfortunately, aside from global judgments of the DAP, the base rates would suggest that the use of the structural and content signs on the DAP for clinical assessment is not likely to provide any improvement in the clinicians' judgmental accuracy.

Chapter 4

Empirical and Internal Consistency Approaches

There are two additional basic approaches to the selection of stimuli for personality assessment devices besides the rational-theoretical approach already discussed: the *empirical* method and the *internal consistency* method. It is convenient to describe the three approaches separately from each other; in modern test construction technology, no single approach is typically employed. Rather, in a sophisticated test development program, aspects of all methods are generally utilized in some fashion.

Meehl's (1945) paper presents the classic argument for the strict empirical approach to personality test construction. In this approach, as distinct from the traditional (rational) viewpoint which regards inventories and questionnaires as short-cut, if inaccurate, methods of gathering direct information about a respondent, the test responses are treated in their own right as behavior, whose correlates must be discovered by empirical research. The fact that there might not be an adequate theoretical rationale for the content of many inventory items that discriminate, let us say, psychopaths from people in general, does not deter users of the strict empirical approach. Meehl, in his prefatory comments prepared especially for this volume, indicates that he, himself, has moved away from this extreme empirical position. Meehl also questions the viewpoint that inventories are inherently limited in their ability to explore the "depths" of personality.

The strict empirical approach to personality test construction, if taken to its logical extreme, would hold that literally any stimulus materials whatsoever may be used for personality assessment, provided that one can find useful empirical correlates of the responses. The *content* of the stimulus materials and their logical relationship to what is being assessed becomes totally irrelevant. This position is a variant of a viewpoint known as the "deviation hypothesis," put forward in 1955 by Irwin Berg. A major potential advantage of the strict empirical approach, of course, is that the stimuli proposed can be "subtle," that is, not easily amenable to faking, because of the lack of a rational connection between the possible responses and their personality interpretation.

A number of psychologists, unable to accept the claim that the materials used in personality assessment need have no direct connection with the "contents" of personality, have produced research findings to demonstrate that stimulus content of personality assessment materials *is* in fact of considerable importance. More specifically, it has been shown that valid "subtle" items are very difficult to find, and also that such subtle items tend to lose their validity over time. One direct demonstration of the contention that content-relevant personality assessment stimuli result in more valid prediction than do content-irrelevent stimuli was obtained by Goldberg and Slovic, whose paper is the second in this section. These authors examined the validity of personality prediction scales built empirically from either "relevant" verbal items, "irrelevant" verbal items, or "irrelevant" nonverbal items (preferences among geometric designs). Their findings support the position that content relevancy may be a necessary (though not necessarily sufficient) condition for test validity. Thus, the approach to building fakeproof tests through the use of empirically valid but content-irrelevant items may not be as promising as was once thought.

The MMPI, the most widely used of all personality inventories, is often considered to be the prototype of empirically based tests, and the third paper constitutes the original "statement of intent" in 1940 by authors, Hathaway and McKinley, to construct this multiphasic personality schedule. They could hardly have foreseen the enormous influence their instrument would have on objective approaches to personality assessment during subsequent years. It is important to note that the original pool of more than a thousand items (refined to 504) was essentially based on the content of psychopathology in general. Thus, the stage was set for including on MMPI scales items that were both directly relevant to the diagnostic category being assessed and items that were irrelevant to the specific category but not totally irrelevant for personality or psychopathology in general.

The MMPI soon found its way into use for assessing variations in personality among nonpsychiatric individuals, a task for which it was not originally intended. Also, the large pool of items assembled by Hathaway and McKinley was utilized by other psychologists in constructing additional scales for assessing a wide variety of personality-related concepts. One such person was Harrison Gough, the author of the California Psychological Inventory or CPI. Gough began his work using the MMPI item pool, and later developed additional items. The 18-scale CPI was designed to fulfill the specific function of assessing normal variation in personality, and inferior adjustment is represented by lower rather than higher scores (as on the MMPI). The fourth paper, by Goodstein, Crites, Heilbrun, and Rempel, gives a clinical "feel" for its use in a college counseling service, a feel based on research evidence.

The majority of the CPI scales were developed by the empirical or criterion-groups method. Several of the scales, however, were based on *internal consistency* procedures, the third basic approach to the construction of personality assessment devices. In this approach, the test constructor identifies a preliminary set of items that bear a rational or face-valid relationship to the concept being assessed, and then employs statistical procedures to select those items that are most centrally related to the concept as defined by the preliminary items. A more complex internal consistency procedure involves the use of factor analysis to identify statistically meaningful clusters of related items. In either case, the use of empirical validity is also necessary in order to demonstrate that the selected items have meaning in more than just a statistical sense. A simple example of an internal consistency procedure is seen in the paper by Lanyon in the next chapter.

Which of the methods of selecting stimuli for personality assessment devices leads to the most valid instruments–rational-theoretical, empirical, or internal consistency? In the final paper of this section, Hase and Goldberg attempt to throw some light on this question. Regarding the rational and the theoretical as separate approaches, and utilizing the factor-analysis method of internal consistency, they constructed parallel sets of 11 scales by each of the four methods. Their findings showed that each method yielded the same empirical validities, suggesting that none has any obvious advantages in this respect. As we have already stated, in modern test construction technology elements of all approaches would probably be used in developing and refining a personality assessment device.

1. THE DYNAMICS OF "STRUCTURED" PERSONALITY TESTS

Paul E. Meehl

PREFATORY COMMENT. This paper–my first publication–appeared a quarter-century ago, and I like to think that I have learned a little something since then. I consented to its reprinting because I still believe it has a message, and of course it was an influential contribution to its time. (Professor Wiggins, before proceeding to make his impressive case *contra,* flatteringly calls it "Meehl's now classic empirical manifesto," Wiggins, 1969, p. 127). In 1945, a clinician or counselor who used structured verbal tests based on empirical keying against psychiatric or occupational criteria (MMPI, SVIB) was on the defensive against two dissimilar groups of opponents. The first group were academic psychologists in the "Bernreuter-Inventory" tradition, who tended to combine (a) unjustified trust in face-validity, (b) relative lack of psychiatric experience and clinical orientation, and (c) psychometric reliance upon fairly crude internal-consistency approaches in test-building. The other group were clinicians identified with the Rorschach and other projective techniques, who were (as subsequent critical research has shown) overly intoxicated with the "projective" idea, insufficiently aware of the unavoidable normative problem (having bought the fallacious X ray analogy in L. K. Frank's famous 1939 paper) and ideologically tendentious with respect to all "structured" instruments. In that situation, my 1945 paper was probably needed, and I do not have to apologize for its exaggerations. Being a neo-Popperian in my philosophy, I view the growth of science as a series of errors and corrections, of "conjectures and refutations." But I cannot consent to the paper's reprinting without at least indicating–no convincing arguments being intended–the respects in which I now disagree with it. Mainly, I see it as overly "dust-bowl empiricist," insufficently theoretical, and psychometrically simplistic. For example, the validity shrinkage we see in moving to new populations ("validity generalization" problem, not soluble by mere calculation of a random sampling error statistic) is, I am sure, partly a result of the presence of items that appeared in the criterion analysis mainly because they were correlates of unrecognized nuisance-variables. I now believe that "blind empirical keying," where we retain an

SOURCE. Paul E. Meehl is Regents Professor of Psychology at the University of Minnesota. A past president of the American Psychological Association, he has written extensively on current issues involved in clinical inquiry, clinical prediction, and the communication of assessment information. This article is based upon one that originally appeared in the *Journal of Clinical Psychology,* 1945, **1**, 296-303. Reprinted by permission of the *Journal of Clinical Psychology* and the author.

item whether it makes any sense or not, is conducive to this lack of generalizability. (As I reread it today, the 1945 paper shows an interesting ambivalence regarding theoretical interpretability!) My present views are, on the whole, closer to the position of Loevinger (1957), Campbell and Fiske (1959), and Wiggins (1969), Jackson (1969) or, for that matter, of Cronbach and Meehl (1955), than to the extreme position espoused in this paper. But this is not the place to expound them. The optimal strategy in structured test construction is currently being creatively researched (see, for example, Hase and Goldberg, 1967, which also is reprinted in this chapter) but one can safely predict that matters will remain pretty murky for some time to come. I am reasonably confident that two major components of that optimal strategy will be the external criterion keying so vigorously advocated in my 1945 paper, and its recognition that a person's response to a structured verbal item may be a probabilistic indicator of his psychological makeup in a variety of ways—some of them quite complex psychodynamically (for example, as indirect reflections of his preferred mechanisms of defense). Hence—*caveat lector*—I am still glad I wrote it, and pleased that Professors Goodstein and Lanyon have judged it worthy of reprinting.

In a recent article Max L. Hutt (1945) has given an interesting discussion of the use of projective methods in the army medical installations. This article was part of a series describing the work of clinical psychologists in the military services, with which the present writer is familiar only indirectly. The utility of any instrument in the military situation can, of course, be most competently assessed by those in contact with clinical material in that situation, and the present paper is in no sense to be construed as an "answer" to or an attempted refutation of Hutt's remarks. Nevertheless, there are some incidental observations contained in his article which warrant further critical consideration, particularly those having to do with the theory and dynamics of "structured" personality tests. It is with these latter observations rather than the main burden of Hutt's article that this paper is concerned.

Hutt defines "structured personality tests" as those in which the test material consists of conventional, culturally crystallized questions to which the subject must respond in one of a very few fixed ways. With this definition we have no quarrel, and it has the advantage of not applying the unfortunate phrase "self-rating questionnaire" to the whole class of question-answer devices. But immediately following this definition, Hutt goes on to say that "it is assumed that each of the test questions will have the same meaning to all subjects who take the examination. The subject has no opportunity of organizing in his own unique manner his response to the questions."

These statements will bear further examination. The statement that personality tests assume that each question has the same meaning to all subjects is continuously appearing in most sources of late, and such an impression is conveyed by many discussions even when they do not explicitly make this assertion. It should be emphasized very strongly, therefore, that while this perhaps has been the case with the majority of question-answer personality tests, it is not by any means part of their essential nature. The traditional approach to verbal question-answer personality tests has been, to be sure, to view them as self-ratings; and it is in a sense always a self-rating that you obtain when you ask a subject about himself, whether you inquire about his feelings, his health, his attitudes, or his relations to others.

However, once a "self-rating" has been obtáined, it can be looked upon in two rather different ways. The first, and by far the commonest approach, is to accept a self-rating as a second best source of information when the direct observation of a segment of behavior is inaccessible for practical or other reasons. This view in effect forces a self-rating or self-description to act as surrogate for a behavior-sample. Thus we want to know whether a man is shy, and one criterion is his readiness to blush. We cannot conveniently drop him into a social situation to observe whether he blushes, so we do the next best (and often much worse) thing and simply ask him, "Do you blush easily?" We assume that if he does in fact blush easily, he will realize that fact about himself, which is often a gratuitous assumption; and secondly, we hope that having recognized it, he will be willing to tell us so.

Associated with this approach to structured personality tests is the construction of items and their assembling into scales upon an *a priori* basis, requiring the assumption that the psychologist building the test has sufficient insight into the dynamics of verbal behavior and its relation to the inner core of personality that he is able to predict beforehand what certain sorts of people will say about themselves when asked certain sorts of questions. The fallacious character of this procedure has been sufficiently shown by the empirical results of the Minnesota Multiphasic Personality Inventory alone, and will be discussed at greater length below. It is suggested tentatively that the relative uselessness of most structured personality tests is due more to *a priori* item construction than to the fact of their being structured.

The second approach to verbal self-ratings is rarer among test-makers. It consists simply in the explicit denial that we accept a self-rating as a feeble surrogate for a behavior sample, and substitutes the assertion that a "self-rating" constitues an intrinsically interesting and significant bit of verbal behavior, the non-test correlates of which must be discovered by empirical means. Not only is this approach free from the restriction that the subject must be able to describe his own behavior accurately, but a careful study of structured personality tests built on this basis shows that such a restriction would falsify the actual relationships that hold between what a man says and what he *is.*

Since this view of question-answer items is the rarer one at the present time, it is desirable at this point to elucidate by a number of examples. For this purpose one might consider the Strong Vocational Interest Blank, the Humm-Wadsworth Temperament Scales, the Minnesota Multiphasic Personality Inventory, or any structured personality measuring device in which the selection of items was done on a thoroughly empirical basis using carefully selected criterion groups. In the extensive and confident use of the Strong Vocational Interest Blank, this more sophisticated view of the significance of responses to structured personality test items has been taken as a matter of course for years. The possibility of conscious as well as unconscious "fudging" has been considered and experimentally investigated by Strong and others, but the differences in possible interpretation or *meaning* of items have been more or less ignored—as well they should be. One is asked to indicate, for example, whether he likes, dislikes, or is indifferent to "conservative people." The possibilities for differential interpretation of a word like *conservative* are of course tremendous, but nobody has worried about that problem in the case of the Strong. Almost certainly the strength of verbs like "like" and "dislike" is variably interpreted throughout the whole blank. For the present purpose the Multiphasic (referred to hereinafter as MMPI) will be employed because the present writer is most familiar with it.

One of the items on the MMPI scale for detecting psychopathic personality (Pd) is "My parents and family find more fault with me than they should." If we look upon this as a rating in which the *fact* indicated by an affirmative response is crucial, we immediately begin to wonder whether the testee can objectively evaluate how much other people's parents find fault with them, whether his own parents are warranted in finding as much fault with him as they do, whether this particular subject will interpret the phrase "finding fault" in the way we intend or in the way most normal persons interpret it, and so on. The present view is that this is simply an unprofitable way to examine a question-answer personality test item. To begin with, the empirical finding is that individuals whose past history and momentary clinical picture is that of a typical psychopathic personality tend to say "Yes" to this much more often than people in general do. Now in point of fact, they probably should say "No" because the parents of psychopaths are sorely tried and probably do not find fault with their incorrigible offspring any more than the latter deserve. An allied item is "I have been quite independent and free from family rule" which psychopaths tend to answer *false*—almost certainly opposite to what is actually the case for the great majority of them. Again, "Much of the time I feel I have done something wrong or evil." Anyone who deals clinically with psychopaths comes to doubt seriously whether they could possibly interpret this item in the way the rest of us do (*cf.* Cleckley (1941) "semantic dementia"), but they *say* that about themselves nonetheless. Numerous other examples such as "Someone has it in for me" and "I am sure I get a raw deal from life" appear on the same scale and are significant because psychopaths tend to *say* certain things about themselves, rather than because we take these statements at face value.

Consider the MMPI scale for detecting tendencies to hypochondriasis. A hypochondriac says that he has headaches often, that he is not in as good health as his friends are, and that he cannot understand what he reads as well as he used to. Suppose that he has a headache on an average of once every month, as does a certain "normal" person. The hypochondriac says he often has headaches, the other person says he does not. They both have headaches once a month, and hence they must either interpret the word "often" differently in that question, or else have unequal recall of their headaches. According to the traditional view, this ambiguity in the word "often" and the inaccuracy of human memory constitute sources of error, for the authors of MMPI they may actually constitute sources of discrimination.

We might mention as beautiful illustrations of this kind of relation, the non-somatic items in the hysteria scale of MMPI (McKinley and Hathaway, 1944). These items have a statistical homogeneity and the common property by face inspection that they indicate the person to be possessed of unusually good social and psychiatric adjustment. They are among the most potent items for the detection of hysterics and hysteroid temperaments, but they reflect the systematic distortion of the hysteric's conception of himself, and would have to be considered invalid if taken as surrogates for the direct observation of behavior.

As a last example one might mention some findings of the writer, to be published shortly, in which "normal" persons having rather abnormal MMPI profiles are differentiated from clearly "abnormal" persons with equally deviant profiles by a tendency to give statistically rare as well as psychiatrically "maladjusted" responses to certain other items. Thus a person who says that he is afraid of fire, that windstorms terrify him, that people often disappoint him, stands a better chance of being normal in his non-test behavior than a person who does not admit to these things. The discrimination of this set of items for various criterion groups, the intercorrelations with other scales, and the content of the items indicate strongly that they detect some verbal-semantic distortion in the interpretation and response to the other MMPI items which enters into the spurious elevation of scores achieved by certain "normals." Recent unpublished research on more subtle "lie" scales of MMPI indicates that unconscious self-deception is inversely related to the kind of verbal distortion just indicated.

In summary, a serious and detailed study of the MMPI items and their interrelations both with one another and non-test behavior cannot fail to convince one of the necessity for this second kind of approach to question-answer personality tests. That the majority of the questions seem by inspection to require self-ratings has been a source of theoretical misunderstanding, since the stimulus situation seems to request a self-rating, whereas *the scoring does not assume a valid self-rating to have been given.* It is difficult to give any psychologically meaningful interpretation of some of the empirical findings on MMPI unless the more sophisticated view is maintained.

It is for this reason that the possible differences in interpretation do not cause us any *a priori* concern in the use of this instrument. Whether any structured personality test turns out to be valid and useful must be decided on pragmatic grounds, but the possibility of diverse interpretations of a single item is not a good *theoretical* reason for predicting failure of the scales. There is a "projective" element involved in interpreting and responding to these verbal stimuli which must be recognized, in spite of the fact that the test situation is very rigidly structured as regards the ultimate response possibilities permitted. The objection that all persons do not interpret structured test items in the same way is not fatal, just as it would not be fatal to point out that "ink blots do not look the same to everyone."

It has not been sufficiently recognized by critics of structured personality tests that what a man says about himself may be a highly significant fact about him even though we do not entertain with any confidence the hypothesis that what he says would agree with what complete knowledge of him would lead others to say of him. It is rather strange that this point is so often completely passed by, when clinical psychologists quickly learn to take just that attitude in a diagnostic or therapeutic interview. The complex defense mechanisms of projection, rationalization, reaction-formation, etc., appear dynamically to the interviewer as soon as he begins to take what the client *says* as itself motivated by other needs than those of giving an accurate verbal report. There is no good *a priori* reason for denying the possibility of similar processes in the highly structured "interview" which is the question-answer personality test. The summarized experience of the clinician results (one hopes, at least) in his being able to discriminate verbal responses admissible as accurate self-descriptions from those which reflect other psychodynamisms but are not on that account any the less significant. The test analogue to this experience consists of the summarized statistics on response frequencies, at least among those personality tests which have been constructed empirically (MMPI, Strong, Rorschach, etc.).

Once this has been taken for granted we are prepared to admit powerful items to personality scales regardless of whether the rationale of their appearance can be made clear at present. We do not have the confidence of the traditional personality test maker that the relation between the behavior dynamics of a subject and the tendency to respond verbally in a certain way must be psychologically obvious. Thus it puzzles us but does not disconcert us when this relation cannot be elucidated, the science of behavior being in the stage that it is. That "I sometimes tease animals" (answered *false*) should occur in a scale measuring symptomatic depression is theoretically mysterious, just as the tendency of certain schizophrenic patients to accept "position" as a determinant in responding to the Rorschach may be theoretically mysterious. Whether such a relation obtains can be very readily discovered empirically, and the wherefore of it may be left aside for the moment as a theoretical question. Verbal responses which do not apparently have any *self*-reference at all, but in their form seem to request an objective judgment about social phenomena or ethical values, may be equally diagnostic. So, again, one is not disturbed to find items such as "I think most people would lie to get ahead" (answered *false*) and "It takes a lot of argument to convince most people of the truth" (answered *false*) appearing on the hysteria scale of MMPI.

The frequently alleged "superficiality" of structured personality tests becomes less evident on such a basis also. Some of these items can be rationalized in terms of fairly deep-seated trends of the personality, although it is admittedly difficult to establish that any given depth interpretation is the correct one. To take one example, the items on the MMPI scale for hysteria which were referred to above as indicating extraordinarily good social and emotional adjustment can hardly be seen as valid self-descriptions. However, if the core trend of such items is summarily characterized as "I am psychiatrically and socially well adjusted," it is not hard to fit such a trend into what we know of the basic personality structure of the hysteric. The well known *belle indifference* of these patients, the great lack of insight, the facility of repression and dissociation, the "impunitiveness" of their reactions to frustration, the tendency of such patients to show an elevated "lie" score on MMPI, may all be seen as facets of this underlying structure. It would be interesting to see experimentally whether to the three elements of Rosenzweig's (1944) "triadic hypothesis" (impunitiveness, repression, hypnotizability) one might add a fourth correlate—the chief non-somatic component of the MMPI hysteria scale.

Whether "depth" is plumbed by a structured personality test to a lesser extent than by one which is unstructured is difficult to determine, once the present view of the nature of structured tests is understood. That the "deepest" layers of personality are not verbal might be admitted without any implication that they cannot therefore make themselves known to us via verbal behavior. Psychoanalysis, usually considered the "deepest" kind of psychotherapy, makes use of the dependency of verbal behavior upon underlying variables which are not themselves verbalized.

The most important area of behavior considered in the making of psychiatric diagnosis is still the form and content of the *speech* of the individual. I do not mean to advance these considerations as validations of any structured personality tests, but merely as reasons for not accepting the theoretical objection sometimes offered in criticizing them. Of course, structured personality tests may be employed in a purely diagnostic, categorizing fashion, without the use of any dynamic interpretations of the relationship among scales or the patterning of a profile. For certain practical purposes this is quite permissible, just as one may devote himself to the statistical validation of various "signs" on the Rorschach test, with no attempt to make qualitative or really dynamic personological inferences from the findings. The tradition in the case of structured personality tests is probably weighted on the side of nondynamic thinking; and in the case of some structured tests, there is a considerable amount of experience and clinical subtlety required to extract the maximum of information. The present writer has heard discussions in case conferences at the University of Minnesota Hospital which make as "dynamic" use of MMPI patterns as one could reasonably make of any kind of test data without an excessive amount of illegitimate reification. The clinical use of the Strong Vocational Interest Blank is another example.

In discussing the "depth" of interpretation possible with tests of various kinds, it should at least be pointed out that the problem of validating personality tests, whether structured or unstructured, becomes more difficult in proportion as the interpretations increase in "depth." For example, the validation of the "sign" differentials on the Rorschach is relatively easier to carry out than that of the deeper interpretations concerning the basic personality structure. This does not imply that there is necessarily less validity in the latter class of inferences, but simply stresses the difficulty of designing experiments to test validity. A very major part of this difficulty hinges upon the lack of satisfactory external criteria, a situation which exists also in the case of more dynamic interpretations of structured personality tests. One is willing to accept a staff diagnosis of psychasthenia in selecting cases against which to validate the Pt scale of MMPI or the F% as a compulsive-obsessive sign on the Rorschach. But when the test results indicate repressed homosexuality or latent anxiety or lack of deep insight into the self, we may have strong suspicions that the instrument is fully as competent as the psychiatric staff. Unfortunately this latter assumption is very difficult to justify without appearing to be inordinately biased in favor of our test. Until this problem is better solved than at present, many of the "depth" interpretations of both structured and unstructured tests will be little more than an expression of personal opinion.

There is one advantage of unstructured personality tests which cannot easily be claimed for the structured variety, namely, the fact that falsehood is difficult. While it is true for many of the MMPI items, for example, that even a psychologist cannot predict on which scales they will appear nor in what direction certain sorts of abnormals will tend to answer them, still the relative accessibility of defensive answering would seem to be greater than is possible in responding to a set of ink-blots. Research is still in progress on more subtle "lie" scales of MMPI and we have every reason to feel encouraged on the present findings. Nevertheless the very existence of a definite problem in this case and not in the case of the Rorschach gives the latter an advantage in this respect. When we pass to a more structured method, such as the T A T, the problem reappears. The writer has found, for example, a number of patients who simply were not fooled by the "intelligence-test" set given in the directions for the T A T, as was indicated quite clearly by self-references and defensive remarks, especially on the second day. Of course such a patient is still under pressure to produce material and therefore his unwillingness to reveal himself is limited in its power over the projections finally given.

In conclusion, the writer is in hearty agreement with Hutt that unstructured personality tests are of great value, and that the final test of the adequacy of any technique is its utility in clinical work. Published evidence of the validity of both structured and unstructured personality tests as they had to be modified for convenient military use does not enable one to draw any very definite conclusions or comparisons at the present time. There is assuredly no reason for us to place structured and unstructured types of instruments in battle order against one another, although it is admitted that when time is limited they come inevitably into a very real clinical "competition" for use. The present article has been aimed simply at the clarification of certain rather prevalent misconceptions as to the nature and the theory of at least one important structured personality test, in order that erroneous theoretical considerations may not be thrown into the balance in deciding the outcome of such clinical competition.

2. IMPORTANCE OF TEST ITEM CONTENT: AN ANALYSIS OF A COROLLARY OF THE DEVIATION HYPOTHESIS[1]

Lewis R. Goldberg and Paul Slovic

In a series of articles dating back to 1955, Irwin Berg has repeatedly stated what he calles the deviation hypothesis (e.g., Berg, 1955, 1957, 1959, 1961). A "corollary" of this hypothesis has been formulated by Berg (1957) as follows:

> Stimulus patterns of any type and of any sense modality may be used to elicit response patterns; thus particular stimulus content is unimportant for measuring behaviors in terms of the Deviation Hypothesis. This means that . . . we should be able to produce a Bernreuter Personality Inventory, an MMPI, a Strong VIB, etc., by using sights, sounds, tastes, smells, etc., in any combination for item content [p. 160].

SOURCE. Lewis R. Goldberg, Professor of Psychology at the University of Oregon, is also Senior Research Associate at the Oregon Research Institute. Paul Slovic also is a Research Associate at the Oregon Research Institute. Both authors have contributed extensively to the literature on personality assessment. The article originally appeared in the *Journal of Counseling Psychology*, 1967, 14, 462-472. Reprinted by permission of the American Psychological Association and the authors.

[1]This study was supported by Grants G-25123 and GS-429 from the National Science Foundation to Lewis R. Goldberg at Oregon Research Institute and by Grant MH 12972 from the United States Public Health Service. The authors wish to thank Leonard G. Rorer for his invaluable help and Jacob Kind, Patricia Taylor, Richard Hammersley, William Johnson, and George McCarger, who served as research assistants on this project. The authors are also indebted to Warren T. Norman for his thoughtful comments on an earlier draft of this article.

"Indeed, any content which produces deviant response patterns will serve, judging from the available evidence. . . . Accordingly for personality and similar tests a particular item content is unimportant [Berg, 1959, p. 95]."

To test this proposition, Berg and his co-workers developed the Perceptual Reaction Test (PRT), which consists of 60 abstract designs of the sort that could be drawn with ruler and compass; subjects are required to choose one of four response options for each design: "like much," "like slightly," "dislike slightly," or "dislike much." The PRT has been presented as a "contentless" item pool, from which personality scales can be empirically constructed.

A number of studies using the PRT have been reviewed by Berg (1961). They have shown that some PRT items discriminate between such grossly dissimilar criterion groups as *(a)* psychiatric patients and normals (Adams, 1960; Barnes, 1955; Hesterly & Berg, 1958; House, 1960); *(b)* mental retardates and normals (Cieutat, 1960); and *(c)* children, young adults, and the elderly (Boozer, 1961; Hawkins, 1960; Hesterly, 1960; Hesterly & Berg, 1958; Roitzsch & Berg, 1959). Of questionable success were attempts to discriminate tubercular and cardiac patients from non-patients (Berg, 1961; Engen, 1959). Admittedly unsuccessful were attempts to discriminate delinquents from nondelinquents (Berg, 1961), children from neurotic adults (Roitzsch & Berg, 1959), as well as attempts to discriminate the degree of schizophrenia (Harris, 1958) and the degree of emotional disturbance (House, 1960). None of these reports present validity coefficients between PRT scales and a criterion index. Instead, they present only the number of PRT responses that differentiated between the criterion groups at some level of statistical significance. In addition, the fact that almost half of the studies are in need of cross-validation (and few, if any, have been replicated in other settings) adds to the difficulty of comparing the PRT with other inventories.

While the deviation hypothesis, itself, has been shown to have very limited utility on strictly logical grounds (Norman, 1963a; Sechrest & Jackson, 1963), Berg's corollary asserting the unimportance of item content has such great implications for personality assessment that it certainly demands a careful empirical examination. If the MMPI could have been constructed using 550 abstract designs as items, then two decades of experimental work aimed at the detection and prevention of faking on personality inventories would have been unnecessary and advice to cheat on personality inventories (e.g., Whyte, 1957) would be muted. While the MMPI item pool was explicity assembled from statements reflecting psychiatric symptoms, Berg's corollary seems to assert that a miscellaneous collection of statements (or nonverbal stimuli) would have produced an equally effective inventory.

Berg's statements of his deviation hypothesis are ambiguous enough that a number of interpretations are logically possible (Norman, 1963a; Sechrest & Jackson, 1963). One interpretation, for instance, is that the *type* of stimulus is "unimportant," that scales could be constructed equally well using nonverbal or verbal items, though within any type of stimuli only a subset of "content specific" items are valid. Recently, however, data illustrating the relative invalidity of nonverbal items have been presented by Norman (1963a), who found that scales empirically developed from the Welsh Figure Preference Test had virtually no cross-validity for predicting peer ratings of personality characteristics, while scales constructed from adjectives that had at least moderate face validity had statistically significant cross-validities for the same criteria.

Another interpretation of Berg's corollary would posit that our present knowledge of the underlying relationships between item content and item validity is so sketchy that one type of content can substitute equally well for another type as an *initial* item pool from which scales may be developed. That is, Berg may simply be questioning the relationship between the "face validity" of an item and its empirical validity. While no psychologist would argue that this relationship is perfect, Berg seems to have implied that there is no relationship at all!

In a recent study, Duff (1965) investigated the relationship between the face validity and the empirical validity of the items in the *Hy, Pd,* and *Sc* scales of the MMPI. As an index of empirical validity, Duff used the item's discriminating efficiency in separating psychiatric patients from normal controls; the pooled judgments of 58 advanced graduate students in psychology provided an index of face validity. Duff found that the correlations between face validity and empirical validity were positive and statistically significant in all three item pools (*Hy* = .48; *Pd* = .38; *Sc* = .22). McCall (1958) carried out a similar study of the items in the *D* scale of the MMPI. Using a group of 41 depressive patients and a matched group of nondepressive psychotic patients, McCall found that 26 *D* scale items previously classified as "face valid" were considerably more discriminating than 22 items classified as "congruent" and that items from both of these sets were significantly more valid than 12 items previously classified as "irrelevant." Both Duff's (1965) and McCall's (1958) studies complement an earlier study by Brozek and Erickson (1948), who investigated the effects of experimental semistarvation upon responses to items in the *Hs, D,* and *Hy* scales of the MMPI. Brozek and Erickson found that items classified as "subtle" tended to show less response change under the experimental conditions than did all other items.[2]

The results of these three studies, when considered in connection with the findings of Norman (1963a) and the relative success of rational scales (and self-ratings) in the Hase and Goldberg (1967) study, suggest the following "revision" of Berg's corollary: The greater the face validity of the items included

[2]For additional studies of the concept of face validity, see Fricke, 1957; Gough, 1954; Kimber, 1947; Mehlman and Rand, 1960; Seeman, 1952, 1953; Stone, 1964, 1965; and Wiener, 1948.

in an initial item pool, the smaller will that pool have to be in order to provide the stimuli for the development of scales with some fixed level of external validity. Conversely, the more "subtle" the items included in an initial item pool, the larger must that pool be. If the "efficiency" of an initial item pool is defined as the proportion of its items which will add to the validity of a scale constructed from it, then face valid item pools should be more efficient than all pools of similar size made up of items lacking face validity.

The present study was designed as a direct test of this proposition. The experimental design permits an evaluation of the relative importance of various kinds of item content, verbal and nonverbal, for the prediction of nonpathological criteria. Thus, this study provides an empirical test of two competing viewpoints: Berg's corollary asserting the unimportance of item content versus the present suggestion relating face validity to predictive efficiency.

The need to understand more clearly the nature of the relationship between face validity and actual validity is a vital one for at least two reasons: *(a)* Theoretically, such knowledge is critical for the establishment of a "rational psychometrics" (e.g., Loevinger, 1957); *(b)* practically, such knowledge is of great importance for test constructors in the choice of initial item pools. For if item content is unimportant (in either of the senses of Berg's corollary), then subtle items (such as those in the PRT) would typically be preferable, since such items would obviate the need for concern about response dissimulation and/or image enhancement (e.g., Edwards, 1957).

Method

Subjects

From a freshman dormitory at the University of Oregon, 173 coeds volunteered as paid participants for this study. The mean age of the *Ss* was 18.0 years, with a standard deviation of .4 years.

Criteria

Two broad classes of criteria were used in this study, academic performance in college and social affiliation, each measured by a number of criterion indexes. For a more detailed description of the criteria, see Hase and Goldberg (1967).

Grade-point Average (GPA). The *Ss* were divided on the basis of first semester GPA into high-GPA (n = 88) and low-GPA (n = 79) criterion groups. GPAs were not available for six *Ss*.

Achievement (ACH). A prediction equation using high school GPA and aptitude test scores is used to predict academic achievement at the University of Oregon. The *Ss* in the present study were divided into criterion groups of high achievers (n = 83), defined as those with high GPA relative to predicted GPA, and low achievers (n = 70), defined as those with low GPA relative to predicted GPA. GPAs and/or predicted GPAs were not available for 20 *Ss.*

Sorority Joining (SOR). The first criterion of social affiliation contrasted sorority girls with "independents." The criterion groups consisted of 68 coeds who belonged to or were pledging a social sorority and 72 coeds who had not joined a sorority and had indicated that they did not intend to join one. Uncertain as to whether they would join a sorority, 33 *Ss* were not classified on this variable.

Yielding (YLD). A criterion of social conformity was obtained from shifts in responses to a double administration of a 45-item Opinion Questionnaire (Hastorf & Piper, 1951) previously used for the same purpose by Jackson (1964). The *Ss* were asked to indicate the amount of their agreement or disagreement with each statement on a nine-point scale. For the second administration of the Opinion Questionnaire, each of the 45 questions was followed by a number described as the average response given by the *Ss* on the first administration. For the 25 questions with the smallest dispersions of group ratings on the first administration, the reported mean value was obtained by shifting the actual mean three points toward whichever end of the scale was most distant. The mean values of the 20 questions with the largest dispersions were reported accurately. During the second administration, 5 weeks after the first, the *Ss* filled out the questionnaire using the same rating scale used previously. The criterion index of yielding was computed by averaging (across the 25 items for which spurious mean values were reported) the discrepancy between the *S's* average distance from the reported mean at Administration 1 and her average distance at Administration 2. The reliability of this index was .79 (a split-half reliability estimate corrected by the Spearman-Brown formula). A more complete description of this yielding index is given in Goldberg and Rorer (1966). By dichotomizing *Ss* on the yielding index, criterion groups of 78 "yielding" and 82 "non-yielding" coeds were obtained. Yielding scores were not available for 13 *Ss.*

Sociometric Status. Since all *Ss* in this experiment were coeds living in the same dormitory, it was possible to get sociometric ratings of each girl from her peers. Each *S* rated all of the coeds on her floor (approximately 15 girls), whether they were in the study or not; consequently, for each *S* the mean rating of 8-12 close associates could be obtained. Each girl rated her peers and herself on six personality traits, two of which (sociability and dominance) were relevant to the criterion of social affiliation. Ratings were made on a five-point scale, with instructions to assign one third of the targets to Categories 1 and 2, one-third to the middle category, and one-third to Categories 4 and 5. The raters were given detailed descriptions of each personality trait and were instructed to rate all the girls on one trait before proceeding to the next. The mean ratings of each of the

173 *S*s on sociability (SOC) and dominance (DOM) were dichotomized at the median for each trait in order to produce approximately equal sized criterion groups of *(a)* social versus retiring and *(b)* dominant versus submissive coeds.

Predictor Items

All *Ss* were administered the PRT and a 180-item inventory, the Statement Reaction Test (SRT). To insure comparability of the formats of the PRT and SRT, *Ss* were instructed to respond to each item in the SRT using one of the following options: "agree much," "agree slightly," "disagree slightly," "disagree much." The SRT included three sets of 60 items, each set presumably tapping a different area of verbal content. Items from each of the following three content areas were randomly arranged in the SRT.

Achievement. Sixty items, which on rational grounds reflected content relating to college achievement, were included. Some achievement items were selected from the alternatives scored on the n Achievement scale of the Edwards Personal Preference Schedule (EPPS), and others were rewritten from the Oregon Instructional Preference Inventory (Goldberg, 1963; Shiman, 1966). Additional items were written especially for this study. Some examples of achievement items are "I expect to get very good grades in college," "I work much harder in courses that I like," "I do most of my schoolwork just before it is due."

Affiliation. A second group of 60 items was selected to tap the broad dimension of social affiliation. This item pool included the alternatives scored in the n Affiliation, n Abasement, n Autonomy, and n Dominance scales from the EPPS. Some examples of affiliation items are "I like to be loyal to my friends," "I like to be self-sufficient," "In matters of conduct, I conform to custom."

Content-irrelevant Verbal Items. The remaining 60 SRT items were chosen at random from the Kuder Preference Record. Kuder items were chosen as examples of content-irrelevant verbal items, to be contrasted with the 60 PRT items characterized as content-irrelevant nonverbal items. Consequently, this experimental design makes possible a comparison between content-relevant and content-irrelevant items, and among the latter between verbal and nonverbal items.

Examination of the items from the SRT indicated that some of the items in the achievement pool could also have relevance for the affiliation criteria (e.g., "I would rather be a good student than have an active social life") and vice versa. Similarly, some Kuder items could be construed as having subtle affiliation or achievement themes. Therefore, an evaluation of each of the SRT items was carried out in order to allow for the possibility that an item might be relevant to more than one criterion or that a Kuder item might have high face validity. From an undergraduate course in general psychology, 29 male and 27 female judges were each given a list of the 180 SRT items and the six criterion variables, with detailed descriptions of the latter. Each judge was then asked to indicate for each item and each criterion variable whether he thought the two criterion subgroups would have responded differently to that item; in this way he categorized each item as either a valid or a nonvalid predictor for each of the six criteria. An index of face validity was obtained for each item and each criterion by calculating the proportion of judges who thought the item would be a valid predictor for that criterion. Since the correlations between the face validity scores calculated from the males and the scores calculated from the females averaged .92 across the six criteria, the male and female judgments were combined into a single index. The 180 SRT items were divided, for each criterion, into three pools containing, with respect to face validity, the 60 highest, 60 middle, and 60 lowest items.

Analyses

The two contrasting groups for each criterion were split into random halves for purposes of a double cross-validation study. Empirical scoring keys were developed separately from each of the four 60-item subsets (high, middle, and low face validity and PRT) to predict each of the six criteria. Keys derived from Sample A were cross-validated on Sample B, and keys derived from Sample B were cross-validated on Sample A.

The method used to key items was identical to the one recommended by Berg (1961, pp. 342-349) for evaluating the validity of the PRT and the deviation hypothesis. Each of the 60 items in a subset had four response options, and the responses were tabulated separately for each item and each option. Item options that discriminated between a pair of criterion groups at a prescribed level of statistical significance were selected for the key for that particular criterion. Empirical keys were first developed by selecting options that discriminated at the .10 level of significance or better; a second set of keys employed options discriminating at the .20 level or better. Since the stringency of the significance level had no important effect upon the size of the validity coefficients, the results to be reported below are based upon the average cross-validities for both significance levels.

Results

Table 1 presents the percentage of items from each of the three 60-item SRT content subpools falling into each of the three face validity categories for each of the six criteria. Note that, in general, most of the achievement items had relatively high face validity for the GPA and achievement criteria, while few of the affiliation items fell in the high face validity categories for these two criteria. Conversely, most of the affiliation items had relatively high face validity for the

Table 1. Percentage of SRT Items from Each Content Pool in Each of the Three Face Validity Categories

Criterion	Category	Initial Content Pool		
		Achievement[a]	Affiliation[a]	Kuder[a]
GPA	Highest 60	85	0	15
	Middle 60	15	38	47
	Lowest 60	0	62	38
ACH	Highest 60	80	10	10
	Middle 60	18	32	50
	Lowest 60	2	58	40
SOR	Highest 60	22	68	10
	Middle 60	45	25	30
	Lowest 60	33	7	60
YLD	Highest 60	22	75	3
	Middle 60	46	20	34
	Lowest 60	32	5	63
SOC	Highest 60	10	62	28
	Middle 60	18	38	44
	Lowest 60	72	0	28
DOM	Highest 60	28	60	12
	Middle 60	30	28	42
	Lowest 60	42	12	46
College performance[b]	Highest 60	83	5	12
	Middle 60	16	35	49
	Lowest 60	1	60	39
Social affiliation[b]	Highest 60	21	66	13
	Middle 60	34	28	38
	Lowest 60	45	6	49

[a] $n = 60$.
[b] Average.

four affiliation criteria, while the achievement items tended to fall in the low face validity categories.for these criteria. As expected, most Kuder items fell in the middle or lowest categories of face validity for all six criteria. Interestingly, Kuder items were perceived as having their highest face validity for the sociability (SOC) criterion and their lowest face validity for the yielding (YLD) criterion.

The average cross-validated point-biserial correlations for the three face validity pools of the SRT and the average cross-validities for the PRT are shown in Table 2. For five of the six criterion variables, only scales built from items of

Table 2. Average Validity Coefficients for Scales Constructed from Three SRT Face Validity Categories and the PRT

Item Pool	Criteria						*M*
	College Performance		Social Affiliation				
	GPA	ACH	SOR	YLD	SOC	DOM	
High FV SRT[a]	.29 (.58)	.14 (.66)	.35 (.68)	.11 (.62)	.35 (.61)	.18 (.56)	.24 (.62)
Med. FV SRT[a]	−.12 (.57)	−.13 (.61)	.06 (.65)	.14 (.70)	.08 (.58)	.03 (.54)	.01 (.61)
Low FV SRT[a]	.12 (.63)	−.05 (.62)	.12 (.60)	.15 (.57)	.05 (.65)	.02 (.45)	.07 (.59)
PRT[a]	.04 (.62)	.04 (.62)	.08 (.62)	−.04 (.58)	.07 (.59)	−.04 (.47)	.02 (.56)

Note. The average cross-validated coefficients are based on the mean of the two cross-validation samples; average coefficients from the derivation samples are in parentheses. Abbreviated: FV = face validity, SRT = Statement Reaction Test, PRT = Perceptual Reaction Test.

[a] $n = 60$.

the highest face validity had significant cross-validity, although all scales had almost equally high correlations with the criteria in the derivation samples. The only criterion not best predicted by the most face valid items was the YLD index, which was predicted about equally poorly by all three categories of verbal items and not predicted at all by the PRT items. It is important to note that the average derivation correlations shown in parentheses in Table 2 were quite high and did not differ across item pools. Had this study used Berg's method of keying responses, *without* benefit of cross-validation, the results would have mistakenly implied that the PRT was a good predictor of the six criterion indexes and that item content was unimportant.

The results presented above have focused on the relationship between face validity and predictive validity for scales composed of sets of items. In order to understand more fully the nature of this relationship, additional analyses were carried out at the level of the individual item. The validity of each of the 180 SRT items against each of the six criteria was assessed. All validity coefficients were based on the 2 x 4 table (two criterion groups by four response options) for all subjects. A high validity coefficient indicated that the distribution of responses to that item differed between the two criterion groups.

Six indexes of item validity were computed for each of the 180 SRT items: χ^2, $\sqrt{\chi^2}$, ϕ', C, H, and λ (See Hays, 1963, pp. 578-614). The six different validity coefficients turned out to correlate almost perfectly with one another (e.g., the intercorrelations among the first five ranged from .93 to 1.00, median = .96). Since the correlations of the six indexes with other variables were all virtually identical, the results for only one of them (χ^2) are reported here.

Table 3 presents the correlations across items between validity coefficients and face validity scores. Note that the correlations are, in general, positive and that they are rather high within a few of the item subpools that were presumably more homogeneous with respect to content. Inspection of the scatter plots which are summarized by these correlations revealed that items of low face validity generally had low validity coefficients, while items of high face validity had validities that were distributed over the entire range of the distribution (e.g., some presumably relevant items actually were valid discriminators, while others were not).

Table 3. Correlations between Face Validity Scores and Item Validity Coefficients

Criterion	Achievement Pool[a]	Affiliation Pool[a]	Kuder Pool[a]	Total SRT[b]
GPA	.49**	.03	.07	.24**
ACH	.04	.23*	.28*	.19**
SOR	.53**	−.02	.15	.13*
YLD	−.06	−.20	.16	.06
SOC	.38**	.26*	.01	.26**
DOM	−.02	.49**	−.20	.24**
M	.23**	.13*	.08	.19**

[a] $n = 60$.
[b] $n = 180$.
* $p < .05$, one-tailed test.
** $p < .01$, one-tailed test.

Examination of items that received high face validity scores for a particular criterion revealed subtle content differences between items which may have mediated their relative discriminating power. This is illustrated by the pairs of items shown in Table 4. The items within each pair are matched with respect to face validity for one of the six criteria, but for each of these matched pairs, one item was a valid discriminator while the other was not. Items were paired so as to be as closely related as possible in terms of the underlying behavior to which they referred. Thus, pair a_1 and a_2 both refer to the importance of achievement in the classroom, though they differ in that one item emphasizes examination performance, while the other is less specific. On the other hand, pair b_1

and b_2 both deal with the effect of achievement upon one's state of mind, though they also differ in a subtle way.

One possible explanation for the differences in validity among items of equally high face validity is that the judges did not know the response variance of each item and thus could not take this parameter into account when making their ratings. Thus, in Table 4, items e_1 and e_2 both had high face validity for the criterion of sociability, presumably because both dealt with friendship. However, virtually all subjects strongly agreed to item e_2, whereas there was a relatively uniform distribution of responses to item e_1. To evaluate the possibility that item variance might moderate the relationship between face validity and empirical validity coefficients, an index of response variance was computed for each item. The squared discrepancy between the frequency of responses falling in each response category and $N/4$ (the frequency that would have been obtained if all responses were equally divided among the four possible categories) was summed across all four response categories. Scores on this index were then reflected. Therefore, the highest response variance scores were elicited from items with a uniform response distribution (e.g., .25, .25, .25, .25) and the

Table 4. Matched Items of High Face Validity Differing Markedly in Actual Validity

	Item	Criterion	Validity	
			Face[a]	Actual
a_1	It is important for me to be among the best in the classroom.	GPA	84	High
a_2	It is important for me to do well on exams.	GPA	84	Low
b_1	I enjoy relaxing only after completion of work well done.	GPA	55	High
b_2	I feel that my future peace depends upon my accomplishment.	GPA	62	Low
c_1	I would rather be on social probation than on academic probation.	GPA	75	High
c_2	I would rather have fun than be an outstanding student in college.	GPA	68	Low
d_1	I like doing things my way, disregarding what others think.	YLD	39	High
d_2	It is important for me to feel free to do and say what I want.	YLD	39	Low
e_1	I like to make as many friends as I can.	SOC	95	High
e_2	It is important for me to have close friendships.	SOC	79	Low

[a]Percentages.

lowest response variance scores were elicited from items to which all responses were given to the same response option (e.g., 1.00, .00, .00, .00).[3]

Examination of the variance indexes for the items in Table 4 revealed that for every pair (e.g., a_1 and a_2) the item with the higher validity also had the more uniform distribution of responses. This seems to document the effect of subtle differences in content upon item variance, an effect which may have produced, at least in part, the substantial differences in item validity. However, when item variance was correlated with item validity on the one hand and with face validity on the other, the resulting correlations (reported in Table 5) were so low that partialing out the effect of item variance did not change the correlations between face validity and empirical validity.

Table 5. Correlations among Actual Validity, Face Validity, and Response Variance for 180 SRT Items

Correlation	Criterion						*M*
	GPA	ACH	SOR	YLD	SOC	DOM	
AV vs. Va	.11	.16*	.18**	.18**	.19**	.07	.15*
FV vs. Va	.12	.10	−.05	.03	−.03	.11	.05
AV vs. FV	.24**	.19**	.13*	.06	.26**	.24**	.19**
AV vs. FV[a]	.24**	.19**	.13*	.06	.26**	.24**	.19**

Note. Abbreviated: AV = actual validity, FV = face validity, Va = variance.

[a] Partial correlation; variance partialed out.

* $p < .05$, one-tailed test.

** $p < .01$, one-tailed test.

To provide another view of the effect of item response variance as a moderator of the relationship between face validity and predictive validity, the 180 SRT items were ranked on response variance; six variance-homogeneous subpools of 30 SRT items each were formed, and the correlations between face validity and empirical validity were computed within each subpool. The results are presented in Table 6. Note that while the 30 items of highest response variance (the top row in Table 6) had the highest correlations ($\bar{r} = .32$) and the 30 items of lowest response variance (the bottom row in Table 6) had the lowest correlations ($r = .06$), the moderating effect of response variance was neither

[3]The computing formula used to calculate item response variance was

$$\sigma^2 = -\Sigma_{i=1}^{4} \; [n_i - (N/4)]^2$$

where σ^2 = item response variance, N = the total number of subjects, and n_i = the frequency of cases falling in the ith response category ($\Sigma_{i=1}^{4} \times n_i = N$). See Walker and Lev (1953, p. 28).

Table 6. Correlations between Actual Validity and Face Validity for Six SRT Subpools of Differing Response Variance

Variance Items	GPA	ACH	SOR	YLD	SOC	DOM	*M*
Highest	.44*	.26	.49*	−.01	.51*	.21	.32*
High	.03	.37*	.21	−.12	.07	.27	.14
High–medium	.26	.07	.19	−.10	.27	.34	.17
Low–medium	.52*	.45*	.06	−.06	.39*	.16	.25
Low	.09	−.20	.29	.34	.38*	.35	.21
Lowest	.13	.30	−.25	.19	−.05	.05	.06

Note. All n's = 30.
* $p < .05$.

strong nor linear. For the trait of dominance, in fact, the highest correlation (r= .35) occurred within a subpool of items with a rather unimodal response distribution (i.e., low response variance). In general, the results appear to indicate that item response variance is, at best, a weak moderator of the relationship between face validity and predictive validity for items of this type.

Discussion

The findings from the present study are highly congruent with those of Norman (1963a), who also used nonpathological personality characteristics as criteria. Apparently the PRT can best discriminate among such dissimilar groups as psychiatric patients and normals, though it has not been established that the PRT can make even such gross kinds of discriminations more accurately or efficiently than other inventories. Evidence that the PRT can validly predict more subtle individual differences has yet to be presented.

In the history of structured inventory measurement, some assumptions about the relationships between face and empirical validity have been implicit in each new strategy of scale construction that has been proposed (Hase & Goldberg, 1967). The earliest personality inventories (composed of rationally developed scales) were predicated on the assumption that face validity and empirical validity were nearly isomorphic—that self-statements reflect honest appraisals of actual behavior tendencies (Buchwald, 1961). Over the years, this assumption began to be questioned, at first by critics proposing to substitute projective approaches to personality assessment (e.g., Frank, 1939) and soon by the proponents of structured inventories themselves. Modifications of the isomorphic assumption gave birth to two new strategies of scale construction: the empirical group-discriminative (or "criterion group") strategy (e.g., Meehl, 1945) and the variants of internal consistency (homogeneity) maximization strategies, of which the factor analytic strategy is typical (e.g., Cattell, 1946; Eysenck, 1947). Proponents of the empirical group-discriminative strategy argued that personality theory had not reached the stage where face validity could be expected to mirror actual validity (even to the most sophisticated of test constructors) and, therefore, that only the empirically determined effectiveness of each item should legitimately influence the decision whether an item belonged in a scale. Moreover, if criterion groups of subjects who fell at the polar extremes of a trait could be located, then the empirically determined differential response frequency of the two groups to each item could provide an external (nonsubjective) index of item validity. Berg's statements of his deviation hypothesis and its corollary represent an extreme position stemming from this stream of thought.

Proponents of the factor analytic strategy of scale construction appear to have been using a more complex correspondence assumption than either rational or group-discriminative strategists. While, on the one hand, factor analysts may have used relatively nonsubjective criteria for determining which items should be included in a factor scale ("items that hang together belong together"), nonetheless, they often invoke a near isomorphic correspondence assumption for scale labeling purposes. Even Cattell, who has proposed a factor naming system of "universal index numbers" (so as to leave to an unprejudiced posterity the task of determining the "meaning" of each factor uncovered), is not immune to peeking at item content to propose a first approximation of the trait purportedly measured by the factor scale.

Neither the empiricists nor the factor analysts have spelled out very clearly their expectations regarding the relationship between face validity and actual validity. For example, the MMPI item pool was initially assembled explicitly with "content" considerations in mind. Hathaway and McKinley (1940) state:

> The individual items were formulated partly on the basis of previous clinical experience. Mainly, however, the items were supplied from several psychiatric examination direction forms, from various textbooks of psychiatry, from certain of the directions for case taking in medicine and neurology, and from the earlier published scales of personal and social attitudes [p. 249].

Implicit in this statement is the assumption that such items were more likely to differentiate psychiatric patients from normals than were miscellaneous assortments of verbal items (or nonverbal PRT-type items). A similar implicit assumption seems to have guided Gough in writing the initial items for the CPI, as well as Cattell in initially selecting items to begin the factorial development of the Sixteen Personality Factor Questionnaire. The results of the present study indicate that these choices were probably wise ones.

However, for many kinds of personality scales (e.g., those to be used in selection situations) it may be necessary to begin scale development using less efficient item pools in order to ultimately develop more valid scales (see Campbell, 1950; Loevinger, 1955). That is, the use of face valid item pools could serve to purchase validity (among relatively honest subjects) at the price of increasing the transparency (and the fakability) of the resulting scale. While Berg's corollary aims investigators towards nonverbal questionnaire items of the sort found in the PRT and the Welsh Figure Preference Test, the results of both the present investigation and that of Norman (1963a) indicate the folly of following this road. Consequently, future personality scale developers must either develop more sensitive procedures for handling individual differences in impression management (e.g., Norman, 1963b) or they must find items which are valid under relatively diverse conditions (see Fiske & Butler, 1963). For this latter purpose, the search could lead away from subjective questionnaire items of all sorts and, as Cattell has repeatedly suggested, towards the development of "objective" or "maximum performance" tests of personality traits.

3. A MULTIPHASIC PERSONALITY SCHEDULE (MINNESOTA): I. CONSTRUCTION OF THE SCHEDULE[1]

S. R. Hathaway and J. C. McKinley

For several reasons it has seemed that a multiphasic personality schedule might be constructed which would be of greater value in the medical or psychiatric clinic than is true of personality inventories already available. It is desirable that more varied subject matter be included to obtain a wider sampling of behavior of significance to the psychiatrist, rather than to utilize independent sets of items for special purposes such as one might use in studying any particular reaction type. Then, too, in dealing with clinic patients, there seemed to be a need for simpler wording and a simpler method of presentation than is usually the case, in order to stay within the comprehension of those individuals who are

SOURCE. Starke R. Hathaway is Professor and Head of the Division of Clinical Psychology at the University of Minnesota Medical School. Together with J. C. McKinley (1891-1950), who was a neuropsychiatrist at the University of Minnesota Medical School, they are most widely known for their development of the empirically derived assessment technique, the Minnesota Multiphasic Personality Inventory (MMPI). This article originally appeared in the *Journal of Psychology,* 1940, **10,** 249-254. Reprinted by permission of the *Journal* and Dr. Hathaway.

[1] Prepared on Works Progress Administration Official Project No. 665-71-3-69. Subproject No. 262. Supported in part by a research grant from the Graduate School of the University of Minnesota.

not of high intellectual or cultural level. Finally, it seemed desirable to create a rather large reservoir of items from which various scales might be constructed in the hope of evolving a greater variety of valid personality descriptions than are available at the present time.

The individual items were formulated partly on the basis of previous clinical experience. Mainly, however, the items were supplied from several psychiatric examination direction forms, from various textbooks of psychiatry, from certain of the directions for case taking in medicine and neurology, and from the earlier published scales of personal and social attitudes. The original list consisted of more than one thousand items. By deletion of duplicates and of those items which seemed to have relatively little significance for the purposes of this study, the inventory finally contracted to its present form of 504 items.

The separate items were formulated as declarative sentences in the first person, singular. The majority were placed in the positive, the remainder in the negative. Interrogative sentences were not used. Simplified wording constituted the language of the items, the words used being selected as far as possible from those in most frequent use according to standard word frequency tables. Also, the statements were restricted to matters of "common knowledge." Idiomatic expressions were included when the idioms were common in the English language. Grammatical form was occasionally sacrificed in the interests of brevity, clarity, and simplicity. Each item was printed with its number in large type (16 point boldface) on a 3- x 5-inch card.

As a matter of convenience in handling and in avoiding duplication, the items were arbitrarily classified under 25 headings, though it was assumed that an item was not necessarily properly classified merely because it had been placed under a given subdivision. The arrangement was as follows:

I. General Health (9 items).
II. General Neurologic (19 items).
III. Cranial Nerves (11 items).
IV. Motility and Coördination (6 items).
V. Sensibility (5 items).
VI. Vasomotor, Trophic, Speech, Secretory (10 items).
VII. Cardiorespiratory (5 items).
VIII. Gastrointestinal (11 items).
IX. Genitourinary (6 items).
X. Habits (20 items).
XI. Family and Marital (29 items).
XII. Occupational (18 items).
XIII. Educational (12 items).
XIV. Sexual Attitudes (19 items).
XV. Religious Attitudes (20 items).

XVI. Political Attitudes–Law and Order (46 items).
XVII. Social Attitudes (72 items).
XVIII. Affect, Depressive (32 items).
XIX. Affect, Manic (24 items).
XX. Obsessive, Compulsive (15 items).
XXI. Delusions, Hallucinations, Illusions, Ideas of Reference (31 items).
XXII. Phobias (29 items).
XXIII. Sadistic, Masochistic (7 items).
XXIV. Morale (33 items).
XXV. Items modeled after suggestions of Hartshorne, May and Shuttleworth (1930) to indicate whether the individual is trying to place himself in an improbably acceptable or unacceptable light (15 items).

For purposes of recording and subsequent interview with the patient, a separate mimeographed booklet of the items in classified form with their appropriate code was constructed.

Since a considerable number of the statements were in the negative, an answer by the subject of *"False"* would produce a double negative. Our subjects report that they experienced little difficulty in dealing with these double negatives.

The pack of 504 cards was split into two sections, each approximately one-half of the total. Each section was placed in a separate box and marked respectively Section 1 and Section 2. Three guide cards were placed in each box marked *"True," "False,"* and *"Cannot say."* The following directions were pasted into the inner side of the cover of the box and these directions were called to the patient's attention by reading them to him at the time of handing him the cards for sorting.

Directions

Take the cards out from the front, one at a time and decide whether each is true or not.

If it is *mostly* true about you, put it *behind* the card that says TRUE.

If it is not mostly true about you, put it *behind* the card that says FALSE.

If a statement does not apply to you, or is something that you don't know about, put it *behind* the card that says CANNOT SAY.

There are no right or wrong answers.

Remember to give *your* opinion of *yourself.*
There are two boxes in this set.
In order that we may use your results, both boxes must be completed.

After the cards are sorted by the subject into the three categories, the responses are recorded on a tabulation sheet. The left-hand lower corner of each card bearing a statement which is significant if filed as *"False"* is clipped, whereas the right-hand lower corner is clipped in the case of cards with significance if filed as *"True."* Thus, in each of the true or false categories it becomes possible by breaking the deck over these clipped corners to separate the psychiatrically significant from the nonsignificant responses. Only the significant and the *"Cannot say"* responses need be recorded. Each section of cards is marked by a distinctively colored ink stripe along the top side of the pack from front to back. Thus, it becomes possible to locate at a glance a card which has crept into the wrong deck, been reversed or turned upside down. After each administration of the inventory the sections are weighed to demonstrate whether or not all of the cards for that section are still in the box. Before administration to another subject, each section is thoroughly shuffled so that the items come to the attention of the subject in random order. In this way no item has a constant effect on a subsequent item through any series of individual administrations. Theoretically, therefore, it should be possible either to delete old items or add new ones without producing any constant effect in the subsequent use of the inventory.

Subjects for standardization and development of scales are being obtained from several sources:

1. A normal group from the University hospital and out-patient department (724 cases). These are individuals who themselves are not ill but are bringing relatives or friends to the clinic. They constitute the bulk of our so-called normal cases. The assumption is made, of course, that these people are in good health, which may not always be the case. To help establish them as real normals we ask them whether or not they are receiving treatment for any illness. Only those who say they are not under a physician's care are accepted in this group.

2. A normal group from the University Testing Bureau (265 cases). These are mainly pre-college high school graduates who came to the Testing Bureau for pre-college guidance, but there are a number of representatives from various college classes as well.

3. A group of normals whom we were able to contact through the courtesy of the local *WPA* Administration (265 cases). These are all skilled workers from local projects.

4. Patients in the general wards of the University Hospital (254 cases). These are individuals mainly on the medical service but also in lesser numbers from other services of the hospital whom we have contacted through the courtesy of

the various members of the staff of the University Hospital. Of course, most of these patients are in the hospital for one or another physical disease. Some of these were suffering acute illnesses such as upper respiratory infections, jaundice and the like; others were chronically ill with carcinoma, gastric ulcer, leukemia, and a variety of other conditions. All of these have been checked so that they do not include obvious psychiatric conditions.

5. Patients in the psychopathic unit of the University Hospital and out-patient neuropsychiatric clinic (221 cases). All of the inpatients who are not too disturbed or otherwise unusable become subjects of the inventory regardless of the diagnosis.

On all normal groups the person's identity is withheld if the subject does not care to reveal his name, but information is obtained on age, sex, school level reached, occupational level, marital state, and children. The subjects report upon the presence of mental deficiency or of psychoses in the family. On the hospital patients one of two procedures is used. For those patients not seen and diagnosed by the neuropsychiatric staff, the hospital record is carefully read and an independent judgment is made as to the presence of mental disorder. If a disorder is present, a tentative diagnosis is made; if not present the case is classified "physical normal." This indicates a relatively normal mental state in a patient with a physical disease.

For those who have received full clinical work-up by the neuropsychiatric staff, the responsible clinician fills out a mimeographed symptomatic tabulation sheet of the essential symptoms and problems of the patient and writes the diagnostic summary.

Separate item tabulations are being made on these subjects, divided into convenient subgroups. The groupings and the present state of the records as they relate to Groups 1 and 2 are indicated in Table 1.

Table 1. Normals

		Male		Female	
	Age	Single	Married	Single	Married
Out-patient Department and Hospital (Group 1)	16-25	62	45	70	28
	26-43	39	194	26	123
	44-54	8	61	5	38
	55-65	2	14	0	9
Testing Bureau (Group 2)	16-25	152	–	113	–

Some of these groups are still much too small to afford adequate norms or standards, but the general normals and hospital classes are being enlarged daily. The tabulations being made show the percentage frequencies of each of the three possible answers.

It is the author's ultimate intention to publish the complete list of items with all the frequency statistics for the various normal groups when the number of cases becomes sufficiently large to provide adequate samples. We also plan to establish a series of scoring keys so that differential quantitative scales can be made available as an aid in differential psychiatric diagnosis. The problem of reliability and validity of each scale to be developed will receive special attention so that the strengths and weaknesses of this multiphasic personality schedule will be disclosed. Continued research will then make possible continued refinements and the overcoming of weaknesses.

4. THE USE OF THE CALIFORNIA PSYCHOLOGICAL INVENTORY IN A UNIVERSITY COUNSELING SERVICE

Leonard D. Goodstein, John O. Crites, Alfred B. Heilbrun, Jr. and Peter P. Rempel

An important problem which faces the college counselor is to find a valid personality inventory applicable to the relatively stable (nonpsychiatric) population of college students who seek counseling assistance. The widely-used Minnesota Multiphasic Personality Inventory (MMPI) is available, and there is some favorable research evidence on its value as a predictor of client behavior in counseling (Drake & Oetting, 1959). However, since it was specifically designed to provide diagnostic information on the pathological aspects of personality, most of the validity data pertain to its use with patients in mental hospitals and psychiatric clinics. Other standard inventories, such as the Bell Adjustment Inventory, the Bernreuter Personality Inventory, and the Minnesota Personality Scale, purportedly measure personality characteristics important for client appraisal, but research indicates that they actually have only very limited usefulness in counseling (Super, 1949). And, the recently developed Edwards Personal Preference Schedule and California Psychological Inventory are relatively unstudied with clients as subjects. As a result, there is a definite need for research on measures of normal personality variables which may have utility for counseling and adjunct activities.

SOURCE. Leonard D. Goodstein is Professor of Psychology and Director of Professional Training at the University of Cincinnati. Dr. Goodstein has contributed extensively to the professional literature on counseling and clinical psychology. John O. Crites is Professor of Education and Director of the Counseling Service at the University of Iowa. Alfred B. Heilbrun is Professor of Psychology and Director of Clinical Training at Emory University. Peter P. Rempel is on the staff of Counseling Center at the University of Alberta, Edmundton. This article originally appeared in the *Journal of Counseling Psychology,* 1961, **8,** 147-153 and is reprinted by permission of the American Psychological Association and the authors.

Problem

Designed to evaluate the positive aspects of personality which are important for social living, social interactions, and academic success, the California Psychological Inventory (CPI) is an instrument which appears to have considerable promise for use in "clinics and counseling agencies whose clientele consists mainly of socially-functioning individuals" (Gough, 1957, p. 7). Most of the CPI scales were developed empirically by differentiation of criterion groups and hence have some validity as a result of the initial standardization. Questions remain, however, as to the value of the CPI for the analysis and diagnosis of client problems, prediction of response to counseling, evaluation of counseling effectiveness, etc. The purpose of the present study, which is one in a planned series of investigations, was to determine the diagnostic usefulness of the CPI in a university counseling service.

Hypotheses

Gough (1957) suggests three methods for the interpretation of scores on the profile sheet: (1) the mean of the scores on all scales, or the over-all elevation of the profile; (2) the patterns of scores on pairs of scales, or the shape of the profile; and, (3) the magnitude of scores on individual scales. If these methods of interpreting CPI scores are diagnostically useful in a university counseling service setting, then each of them should:

1. Discriminate reliably between students who apply for assistance (clients) and those who do not apply (nonclients).
2. Differentiate significantly between clients with vocational-educational problems and those with more severe difficulties of a personal-social nature.

Procedure

The California Psychological Inventory

The CPI consists of 480 items which the respondent answers as either "true" or "false" of himself. The item content primarily samples experiences of the respondent in the area of social interaction, but also covers attitudes toward achievement and authority. The items are scored for 18 scales which are grouped into four general categories, based upon the psychological and psychometric clusterings Gough observed during the standardization of the test. The categories or classes, the scales which comprise them, and the standard abbreviations for the scales are as follows:

Class I. Measures of poise, ascendance, and self-assurance

1. Dominance *(Do)*
2. Capacity for status *(Cs)*
3. Sociability *(Sy)*
4. Social presence *(Sp)*
5. Self-acceptance *(Sa)*
6. Sense of well-being *(Wb)*

Class II. Measures of socialization, maturity, and responsibility

7. Responsibility *(Re)*
8. Socialization *(So)*
9. Self-control *(Sc)*
10. Tolerance *(To)*
11. Good impression *(Gi)*
12. Communality *(Cm)*

Class III. Measures of achievement potential and intellectual efficiency

13. Achievement via conformance *(Ac)*
14. Achievement via independence *(Ai)*
15. Intellectual efficiency *(Ie)*

Class IV. Measures of intellectual and interest modes

16. Psychological-mindedness *(Py)*
17. Flexibility *(Fx)*
18. Femininity *(Fe)*

The test manual (Gough, 1957) gives a more detailed description of the scales and a fuller description of how they were developed.

Subjects

The subjects of the study included both clients and nonclients. Two types of clients, Personal-Adjustment (PA) and Vocational-Educational (VE), were identified, according to the nature of the problem they presented. The PA clients were those individuals who checked the following category on an application card at the University Counseling Service at the State University of Iowa: "Would like to discuss my feelings about myself and others; some personal problems which are bothering me." The VE clients were those persons who upon application for counseling endorsed either or both of these statements: (1) "Would like to discuss my abilities, interests, aptitudes; my occupational plans for the future," and (2) "Would like to discuss my courses, grades, classes, study techniques; my progress here at the University." *Following initial application for counseling,* but preceding any interviews with a counselor, the CPI was routinely administered to all clients as part of an ongoing program of research begun in January, 1958. At the time of the study over 1,000 CPI profiles were available for analysis, from which four random samples were drawn. These included 100 male PA, 100 male VE, 100 female PA, and 100 female VE clients. In addition, CPI's on a comparable student group were collected. The nonclients (controls or C) were members of a sophomore and junior level psychology course, who were tested during a regular class period. A review of case records indicated that none of these students was a former or current client of the University Counseling Service. Moreover, this sample of nonclients had class standing, a variable related to CPI scores, comparable to that of the clients. There were 100 male and 100 female *S*s in the control groups.

Results

To test for differences in CPI profile elevation and shape, six subgroups of 30 profiles each were randomly selected from the larger groups of profiles for a

Type I analysis of variance (Lindquist, 1953), as suggested by Block, Levine, and McNemar (1951). In this statistical model, which was applied separately to males and females, the Blocks, Columns, and Rows effects correspond to differences between the PA, VE, and C groups, the 18 CPI scales, and the *S*s within the groups respectively.

Profile Elevation

The over-all elevation of the CPI profiles for males differed significantly between the client and nonclient groups ($F = 11.50$, $df = 2$ and 87, $p < .01$). Similarly, the profile elevations for females varied systematically from one group to another ($F = 9.67$, $df = 2$ and 87, $p < .01$). According to Gough (1957), these differences in average CPI profiles indicate differences in level of general adjustment.

Profile Shape

The male client and nonclient groups had dissimilar profile shapes on the CPI. The interaction between scales and PA, VE, and C groups was highly significant ($F = 4.00$, $df = 34$ and ∞, $p < .01$). Likewise, the female PA, VE and C groups varied significantly in the shapes of their CPI profiles ($F = 4.19$, $df = 34$ and ∞, $p < .01$). Following Gough's (1957) interpretation, these differences in CPI profile shapes indicate differences in modes of adjustment.

Individual CPI Scales

Table 1 presents the *T*- score means and *SD's* on the various CPI scales for the six male and female PA, VE, and C groups. An inspection of these data indicated that the direction of the differences in profile elevation for both males and females is from poorer to better adjustment. In general, the mean scores of the C groups are the highest and those of the PA groups the lowest, with the VE groups intermediate. Further support for this trend comes from a consideration of the mean differences on the CPI scales for the various combinations of the PA, VE, and C groups (Table 2). For males and females, who exhibit striking profile similarities within each of the three groups, the most reliable mean differences exist between the PA and C groups: 15 out of 18 comparisons for males and 16 out of 18 comparisons for females were significant. The differences between the VE and C groups were less extensive with 12 out of 18 comparisons for males and 9 out of 18 comparisons for females statistically significant. The VE and PA groups were the most similar, differing in only 7 out of 18 comparisons for males and 10 out of 18 comparisons for females.

Table 1. Means and *SDs* in T-score Units on the 18 CPI Scales for the Six Groups of *S*s. (N = 100 in Each Group)

CPI Scales	Males						Females					
	Pers. Adj.		Voc. Educ.		Control		Pers. Adj.		Voc. Educ.		Control	
	Mean	*SD*	Mean	*SD*	Mean	*SD*	Mean	*SD*	Mean	*SD*	Mean	*SD*
Do	47.3	12.8	50.6	12.4	55.8	12.3	47.7	11.8	49.7	12.3	54.1	10.4
Cs	51.4	10.8	50.2	10.5	53.1	11.1	49.0	10.0	51.1	10.1	54.7	10.8
Sy	45.1	11.0	51.3	9.5	56.0	9.8	44.7	11.0	48.7	11.0	54.5	10.8
Sp	50.2	13.8	51.9	11.1	58.6	11.9	48.4	11.0	50.2	11.3	56.1	10.9
Sa	55.6	12.2	56.8	10.9	61.4	11.1	53.2	9.7	54.4	11.1	57.7	10.2
Wb	39.9	15.9	46.1	12.6	50.8	10.7	40.6	12.6	45.8	11.5	48.7	9.5
Re	44.9	10.9	48.7	8.7	47.8	11.4	47.1	10.1	50.6	7.6	51.3	7.8
So	40.5	10.9	48.6	10.5	51.7	10.7	40.1	11.5	47.7	10.2	49.4	8.9
Sc	40.7	12.9	42.8	11.2	43.9	10.6	39.8	11.8	46.2	9.9	44.6	9.4
To	45.2	11.6	46.3	9.7	49.1	10.8	46.5	13.4	49.9	9.9	53.6	11.6
Gi	41.0	11.4	42.5	9.2	45.2	11.4	40.8	9.6	45.2	10.3	44.5	9.6
Cm	48.2	8.9	54.3	7.7	52.8	11.7	46.6	10.5	49.5	8.5	50.9	7.7
Ac	42.0	11.7	45.0	10.0	49.4	11.0	41.5	10.5	46.2	11.4	47.3	10.2
Ai	54.3	10.1	48.6	9.7	53.3	10.8	52.9	11.7	52.5	10.2	55.3	9.4
Ie	44.0	13.2	42.6	14.6	50.8	13.0	46.0	11.9	48.1	10.4	54.0	9.6
Py	46.0	12.9	42.6	11.9	50.9	9.4	45.7	12.1	44.4	12.2	51.4	10.1
Fx	61.0	10.2	52.5	10.8	54.2	10.8	59.2	12.1	56.3	10.3	55.5	10.8
Fe	53.8	10.6	51.3	10.6	47.7	9.7	49.5	10.5	50.6	9.8	48.5	10.5

Table 2. Mean Score Differences on the 18 CPI Scales for the Several Group Comparisons

CPI Scales	Males			Females		
	Pers. Adj. vs. Voc. Educ.	Pers. Adj. vs. Control	Voc. Educ. vs. Control	Pers. Adj. vs. Voc. Educ.	Pers. Adj. vs. Control	Voc. Educ. vs. Control
Do	–0.10	13.00**	14.00**	3.26*	8.80**	5.54**
Cs	2.24	8.44**	6.20**	3.60**	8.33**	4.73**
Sy	4.43*	12.17**	8.13**	2.87	9.97**	7.10**
Sp	3.07	11.80**	8.73**	6.30**	12.36**	6.06**
Sa	1.24	9.14**	7.90**	–0.93	5.84**	6.77**
Wb	5.53**	11.83**	6.30**	9.50**	11.67**	2.17
Re	2.20	2.93	0.73	1.90	1.33	–0.57
So	8.54**	14.57**	6.03**	6.84**	7.34**	.50
Sc	5.77**	5.83**	0.06	5.86**	4.63**	–1.23
To	3.90*	9.30**	5.40**	7.06**	12.03**	4.97**
Gi	4.80**	4.63*	–0.17	4.60**	4.37**	–0.23
Cm	3.37	3.77*	0.40	2.60	3.03*	0.43
Ac	4.30*	14.50**	10.20**	4.00**	6.73**	2.73
Ai	–1.67	7.10**	8.77**	–0.14	4.93**	5.07**
Ie	2.90	14.16**	11.26**	5.00**	11.80**	6.80**
Py	–2.36	10.87**	13.23**	0.10	9.07**	8.97**
Fx	–2.60	–1.24	1.36	–0.30	0.90	1.20
Fe	–1.43	–4.07*	–2.64	–2.00	–2.36	–0.66

* Significant at the .05 level. ** Significant at the .01 level.

Pairs of Scales

Since the over-all groups by scales interactions were significant, separate *t* -tests for differences in profile shape on every possible pair of scales for all combinations of groups were made. This analysis resulted in the data reported in Table 3 for males and Table 4 for females. The interpretation of these data involves an initial reference to Table 3 or Table 4 and a subsequent use of Table 1. As an example, consider the 3 in the *Do* by *Cs* cell of Table 3. This indicates that the male VE and C groups have differential patterns on the Dominance and Capacity for status scales, which are significant at the .05 level. The direction and absolute values of the pattern differences can then be determined from

Table 3. Significant Differential Patterns on Pairs of CPI Scales for the Several Male Group Comparisons

CPI Scales	*Cs*	*Sy*	*Sp*	*Sa*	*Wb*	*Re*	*So*	*Sc*	*To*	*Gi*	*Cm*	*Ac*	*Ai*	*Ie*	*Py*	*Fx*	*Fe*
Do	3				1,3	2,3	1,3	1,2,3	3	2,3	2,3					2,3	2,3
Cs							1			3					2,3		2,3
Sy						2,3		2,3		2,3	2,3				1	1,2,3	2,3
Sp						2,3		3		2,3	2,3					2,3	2,3
Sa						3	1			3	3					2,3	2,3
Wb						2				3			1		1,3	1,2	1,2,3
Re							2				2	3	3	2,3	2,3		2
So								2		2	2		1,2		1,3	1,2	1,2,3
Sc												3	1,23	2,3	1,3	1,2	1,2
To															1,3	1,2	2,3
Gi												2,3	1,3	2,3	1,2,3	1	2
Cm												2,3	3	2,3	3		2
Ac													2		1	1,2,3	2,3
Ai														2		2,3	2,3
Ie																2,3	2,3
Py																2,3	2,3
Fx																	

Note. The numbers in the table above refer to the following group comparisons:
1 = personal adjustment vs. vocational-educational
2 = personal adjustment vs. control
3 = vocational-educational vs. control

The italicized numbers refer to differences significant at the .01 level; non-italicized numbers at the .05 level.

Table 4. Significant Differential Patterns on Pairs of CPI Scales for the Several Female Group Comparisons

CPI Scales	*Cs*	*Sy*	*Sp*	*Sa*	*Wb*	*Re*	*So*	*Sc*	*To*	*Gi*	*Cm*	*Ac*	*Ai*	*Ie*	*Py*	*Fx*	*Fe*
Do						2		3								*2*	*2*
Cs						2										*2*	*2*
Sy					1	*2,3*	3	*3*		3	3		2			*2*	*2,3*
Sp				2		2,3		2,3		2	*2*		2				1,2,3
Sa					*1*	3	1	1	1	3							2,3
Wb						1,2		2		2	1,2		*1,2*		*1,3*	*1,2*	*1,2*
Re									*2*					2,3	2,3		
So													1		1,3	1	*1,2*
Sc												*1*	3	3	*3*		1,2
To										2	2		2		1	1,2	*1,2*
Gi														2,3	*3*		2
Cm														2,3	*3*		
Ac																	*2*
Ai														2			2
Ie																*2*	1,2,3
Py																2,3	*2,3*
Fx																	

Note. The numbers in the table above refer to the following group comparisons:
1 = personal adjustment vs. vocational-educational
2 = personal adjustment vs. control
3 = vocational-educational vs. control
The italicized numbers refer to differences significant at the .01 level; non-italicized numbers at the .05 level.

Table 1. In this example, the means on the *Do* and *Cs* scales, respectively, are 50.6 and 50.2 for the VE group and 55.8 and 53.1 for the C group. Thus, although the former *Ss* tend not to differ in their scores on these scales, the C *Ss* tend to score higher on *Do* than on *Cs.*

A comparison of Tables 3 and 4 indicates that there are a greater number of pattern differences on pairs of scales between the male groups than between the female groups. Out of the 365 possible comparisons, 145 yield significant differences for males, whereas only 94 are significant for females. The trend in shape differences between the client and nonclient groups, irrespective of sex, was quite similar to the trend in variations of profile elevation across the groups: the comparisons of the PA and VE groups with the C group produced more differences in profile shape than the comparisons of the PA and VE groups with each other. For males the number of significant differences were as follows: PA vs. C = 58; VE vs. C = 61; and, VE vs. PA = 26. The comparable results for females were: PA vs. C = 46; VE vs. C = 26; and, PA vs. VE = 22. From an inspection of Tables 3 and 4, it is apparent that most of these differences in profile shape involve either the measures of socialization, maturity, and responsibility (Class II) or the measures of intellectual and interest modes (Class IV). There were 92 and 76 significant differences in Class II and IV, respectively, for males, and 58 and 46 significant differences in these classes for females.

Discussion

Both the over-all profile elevation of the CPI, which reflects an individual's general adjustment level, as well as patterns of scores on pairs of scales, which indicate dominant adjustment mechanisms, differentiate reliably and extensively between groups of clients and nonclients. The results provide considerable support, therefore, not only for Gough's suggested approaches to interpretation of the CPI, but also for the use of these methods in a university counseling service setting. In the typical counseling center, for example, individuals with long-standing personal-social difficulties, who require more extensive treatment than the usually available short-term adjustive counseling, are generally referred to the other campus or community agencies for service. If included as a part of the intake procedure, the CPI can aid in this type of referral, since profile elevation and shape vary with adjustment status. Again, if used as a screening instrument in the student personnel program, the CPI can identify potential counseling cases for possible referral to the counseling service. Moreover, it can specify whether an individual's problem is more likely personal or vocational-educational in nature.

One restriction upon the use of the CPI and the generality of the results of this study concerns the differences between college samples from various institutions. The mean scores reported in Table 1 for the male and female C groups vary considerably from those published by Gough (1957, pp. 34-35) for presumably comparable groups of college students. The differences in scale means between these independent college samples were tested for statistical significance by Lindquist's (1947) trend test. The analysis indicated that the observed differences between the two sets of college profiles were highly significant ($F = 4.21$ for males, $F = 2.93$ for females, with 17 and 493 *df*, both exceeded the .01 level), which suggests that some caution is necessary in the extension of the present findings to other college settings. The nature of the differences between the groups of this study and Gough's norm group is noteworthy, since the latter resemble the PA and VE groups much more than the C groups. Whether these differences are a function of inadequacies in Gough's norms or a result of some special bias in the selection of the C groups is not determinable from the available data. Additional research is needed to clarify this issue.

Further research is also necessary to substantiate the elevation and shape patterns which differentiated the PA, VE, and C groups. The findings agree with those of Dahlstrom and Craven (1952) who found that personal adjustment clients appear less well adjusted on the MMPI than vocational-educational clients and controls and that vocational-educational clients are more poorly adjusted than controls. But the results disagree, at least in part, with the findings of Gaudet and Kulick (1954), who used the Minnesota Personality Scale to compare vocational-educational clients with an unselected norm group and with personal adjustment clients. They concluded that "Individuals who seek vocational and educational guidance have problems of emotional, social, and familial adjustment similar to others composing a normative sample. Persons seeking personal-social guidance are more poorly adjusted socially, emotionally, and in their family relationships than those requesting educational-vocational guidance" (Gaudet & Kulick, 1954, p. 214). Replication of the present study at different university counseling centers should provide answers to two questions: (1) how stable are the CPI patterns which differentiated the client and nonclient groups, and (2) are vocational-educational clients actually different from nonclients?

Summary

To evaluate the diagnostic usefulness of the California Psychological Inventory (CPI) in a university counseling service, six groups of 30 male and female personal adjustment clients, vocational-educational clients, and nonclients, were compared on over-all CPI profile elevation, profile shape, individual scales, and pairs of scales with an analysis of variance technique appropriate for the study of multidimensional personality instruments. The findings indicated consistent, psychologically meaningful differences between the various groups in all aspects of the profile comparisons. More specifically, with respect to profile elevation there was a definite ordering of the groups along the adjustment continuum from personal clients to vocational-educational clients to controls, with the latter being best adjusted. Similarly there were differences between the typical adjustment modes of the groups, with the greatest differentiation occurring between the clients and nonclients. Implications of the findings for use of the CPI in a university counseling service and for future research were discussed.

5. COMPARATIVE VALIDITY OF DIFFERENT STRATEGIES OF CONSTRUCTING PERSONALITY INVENTORY SCALES[1]

Harold D. Hase and Lewis R. Goldberg

Given a large pool of personality items, by what strategy might item subsets be assembled to form a multiscale inventory that would be maximally efficient in predicting a diverse array of important social criteria? While the approaches available for this task vary widely, personality inventories have typically been developed from one of three general strategies: (*a*) *Internal* (e.g., factor analytic), (*b*) *External* (e.g., group discriminative), or (*c*) *Intuitive* (e.g., rational). Factor analysis is the most popular variant of the first strategy, which includes all approaches aimed at maximizing internal consistency through homogeneous keying. The second strategy has alternatively been called the empirical or criterion group strategy, and the third the logical or theoretical strategy.

To construct scales by the factor-analytic strategy, the items are administered to a large number of subjects, the interitem correlations are factor analyzed, and the factor matrix is typically rotated to some criterion of simple structure. Items loading most highly on the factors so derived are selected for the scale measure of the factor. Only the internal structure of the initial item pool determines item selection and keying, though the labeling of the scales developed by this strategy rests on the test constructor's personal judgment. Three major proponents of the factor-analytic strategy—Guilford, Cattell, and Eysenck—have generated such

SOURCE. Harold D. Hase received his doctoral degree at the University of Oregon and is currently chief clinical psychologist at the Memorial Mental Health Center is Bismarck, North Dakota. Lewis R. Goldberg is Professor of Psychology at the University of Oregon. Personality assessment and tests and measurement have been major areas of their professional interest. This article originally appeared in the *Psychological Bulletin*, 1967, **67**, 231-248. Reprinted by permission of the American Psychological Association and the authors.

[1]This study was supported by National Science Foundation Grant G-25123 (GS-429) to Lewis R. Goldberg at the Oregon Research Institute. Data analyses were carried out through the facilities of the Western Data Processing Center at the University of California at Los Angeles, the University of Oregon Computer Center, and the Computer Center at the University of California at Berkeley. Special thanks are due to Robert Tryon who made available the BC TRY Computing System and to James Cameron who carried out the BC TRY analyses. The authors also wish to thank Leonard G. Rorer and Jerry S. Wiggins for their valuable advice and suggestions. This article, adapted from a doctoral dissertation carried out by the first author (Hase, 1965) under the supervision of the second author, is a preliminary report of a much larger project on personality inventory construction. A more complete report of the research in this project—including factor analyses of each scale set and canonical correlations among all pairs of scale sets—can be obtained from the second author.

inventories as the Guilford-Zimmerman Temperament Survey, Cattell's 16 Personality Factor Questionnaire, and the Eysenck Personality Inventory.

While factor analysis is a scale construction strategy purportedly optimizing properties arising from the *internal* structure of the initial item pool, a second strategy, the group discriminative approach, attempts to align scales optimally with some *external* criterion. In constructing an inventory by the empirical group discriminative (or criterion group) strategy, the test constructor initially attempts to locate two distinct groups of subjects who differ in some significant manner (e.g., psychotics vs. normals, lawyers vs. men in general, males vs. females) or who fall at each pole of a personality trait he seeks to measure. The test items are then administered to members of both criterion groups. Differences in the response of these groups to each item are examined, and those items discriminating between the groups at a desired level of significance are retained for the scale. Only the empirically discovered discriminating power of the item determines item selection for a scale, and the scale is typically labeled in terms of the criterion groups used. Most of the standard scales of the MMPI and CPI were constructed by the group discriminative strategy.

The third general strategy of test construction, the intuitive, rational, or logical approach, can be subdivided into two types. In the intuitive-rational strategy, the investigator has some dimension or personality trait in mind, and he attempts to select items which he believes will relate to this dimension. The test constructor depends upon his intuitive understanding of the dimension to be assessed, and no formal psychological theory is explicitly followed. Item selection could stop here, but more likely the scale is refined by selecting items of highest internal consistency. For example, the test constructor may administer a preliminary version of the scale to a group of subjects and then correlate each item with the total scale score; items correlating most highly may then be retained for the revised scale. The Woodworth Personal Data Scheet, the forerunner of all adjustment and personality inventories, was constructed by rational, logical means, and many other inventories have been devised in a similar fashion.

A second intuitive approach can be called the theoretical strategy. The main distinction between the two intuitive strategies is whether or not a formal psychological theory is used as a guide to test construction; subsequent procedures of scale refinement may be identical. The original Study of Values (Allport & Vernon, 1931), which was based on Spranger's personality typology, is an example of an inventory constructed by this strategy. Another example is the Edwards Personal Preference Schedule, based upon Murray's (1938) need system.

Significantly, though arguments on the merits of the major strategies have peppered the psychometric literature for decades (e.g., Butler, 1954; Cattell, 1950; Flanagan, 1951; Guilford, 1954; Jessor & Hammond, 1957; Loevinger,

1957; Meehl, 1945; Meehl & Hathaway, 1946; Peak, 1953; Travers, 1951; Vernon & Allport, 1931), the major strategies of scale construction have never received a systematic experimental comparison! While a few studies comparing two or three strategies have been reported (e.g., Berkeley, 1953; Gee, 1955; Heilbrun, 1962; Schumacher, 1959), these studies each utilized only a single type of criteria. To investigate the differential validity of the major strategies of scale construction, sets of scales constructed by each strategy from the same item pool must be compared against a *diverse* array of important external criteria.

While it might be argued that it is inappropriate to test a group discriminative scale on any criterion other than the specific one for which it was constructed, this is a legitimate objection only if one presumes that empirically derived personality inventories are not of general applicability. But the CPI, for example, was specifically intended to be a general-purpose inventory, which would be useful for the prediction of a variety of personality criteria. Furthermore, the advocates of empirically constructed inventories have themselves argued against the use of single scales and have stressed the importance of using composite sets of scales as predictors (e.g., Gough, 1964; Gough & Fink, 1964; Gough & Hall, 1964).

The purpose of the present investigation was to compare the major strategies in a more systematic manner than had been attempted before. This study, intended to investigate which of the strategies of inventory construction is most useful, utilized sets of scales rather than merely a single scale. That is, the principal question under consideration was not which type of single scale is most predictive of a single criterion, but rather the broader question of which strategy of inventory construction yields a set of scales which are most effective in predicting a variety of important criteria. Six sets of scales, four of which represented the factor-analytic, group discriminative, and each of two intuitive strategies, were used to predict a diverse set of criteria. The findings from this experimental comparison have important implications for issues which had previously been left solely to rhetoric.

Procedure

Scales

A common item pool, that of the California Psychological Inventory (Gough, 1957), was used for all scales. Six sets of 11 scales, each set constructed by a different strategy, were compared. Four sets were constructed by each of four major strategies of test construction: *(a)* factor analytic, *(b)* group discriminative, *(c)* intuitive-theoretical, and *(d)* intuitive-rational. In addition, two control sets of scales were used; they included a set of stylistic-psychometric scales and a set of scales generated by random selection and keying of items. These latter two sets of scales were included to provide a base line of predictive utility for scales generated from the CPI item pool. For convenience in further presentation, these six scale sets will be referred to as: *(a)* factor, *(b)* empirical, *(c)* theoretical, *(d)* rational, *(e)* stylistic, and *(f)* random scales. All scales were constructed from the 468 items in the CPI item pool (12 of these items are repeated in the CPI booklet, but only responses to the first appearance of these items were used in this study). The construction of each of the six scale sets will be briefly described.

Factor Scales. To develop homogeneous or factor scales for the CPI, one could attempt to carry out an analysis of the complete item pool. There are two problems, however, with this apparently straightforward attack. The first is the practical problem of computer capacity, since such an analysis would require working with a 468 x 468 correlation matrix–a demand which far exceeds the capacity of current computer programs. A second drawback to dealing with the complete item pool involves a theoretical problem relating to differences in item endorsement. Some items are answered true by approximately half of the subject group and false by the other half, while other items may be answered in the same direction by nearly everyone; correlations among items are attenuated by such differences in item extremeness. Fruchter (1954), among others, has pointed out that differences in item extremeness can cause problems in factor analyses, and important items may be lost or spurious factors may arise: "The phi coefficient (fourfold point correlation) should not be used [in factor analysis] unless some correction is made to avoid spurious factors due to differences in splits of the dichotomized variables [p. 192]."

To deal with both problems simultaneously, the 468-item pool of the CPI was divided on the basis of item extremeness into four subpools of approximately 117 items each. Items in the middle range of endorsement (40-60% endorsement) were grouped in Subpool Level A; slightly less balanced items (26-39% and 61-74%) were grouped in Subpool Level B; more extreme items (15-25% and 75-85%) were grouped in Subpool Level C; while the most extreme items (0-14% and 86-100%) were grouped in Subpool Level D. The responses of 179 University of Oregon freshman girls were used to calculate the extremeness of each CPI item.

A set of 11 factor scales was developed, using the BC TRY System for multidimensional analysis (Tryon & Bailey, 1966) on the CPI item responses of the same 179 University of Oregon freshman girls used to establish item-extremeness levels. By using the item groupings described above, problems related to differences in item extremeness were reduced; at the same time, a sequential procedure permitted an analysis of all items within the CPI. The feature of the BC TRY System which allows the analysis of a large number of variables is called BIGNV; its general logic is as follows:

> You draw successive samples of 120 variables in such a fashion that

> V-analyses on these samples increasingly converge upon the results of a hypothetical super single V-analysis performed on all variables. The V-analysis on the final sample of 120 variables is designed, in short, to depict the structure of all *n* variables, however large *n* may be; that is, it *is* the solution, we would expect, that would have been discovered in one run on all *n* variables by a hypothetical super-BC TRY System (Tryon, 1964, p. 84).

A factor analysis of Level A items was the starting point for the first stage of analysis. The items identified by a Varimax rotation of a principal axis analysis were augmented by cluster structure analysis. This program identified additional items which loaded on the factors as initially defined and added to the internal consistency of the factor. The items thus selected for each of 14 initial factors were then retained as definers or "markers" while unused items from Level A were excluded. Next, 60 items from Level B were added to the item pool. Items loading on the original factors were retained, as were any items that appeared to define new dimensions. The same procedure was carried out using the remainder of the Level B items, then the Level C items, and finally most of the Level D items.

The final stage of analysis involved the selection and refinement of the 11 most salient dimensions. Items which increased the reliability of the scale and had sufficiently high factor loadings ($\geqslant .29$) were retained for the final form of the scales. These 11 factor scales were provisionally titled Extraversion-Introversion (fEx), Harmonious Childhood (fHa), Surgency (fSu), Conformity-Rebelliousness (fCo), Ascendence-Submission (fAs), Neuroticism (fNe), Orthodoxy-Flexibility (fOr), Self Confidence (fSc), Amiability-Irritability (fAm), Serenity-Depression (fSe), and Psychoticism (fPs). The number of items per scale ranged from 9 to 27.

Empirical Scales. In the CPI manual, Gough (1957) described 11 of the standard CPI scales as having been originally constructed by the empirical group discriminative strategy. In constructing these 11 empirical scales, Gough relied on college or high school samples. In forming his criterion groups, he typically used nominations by peers or authorities to select persons considered high or low on a trait (e.g., dominance, responsibility). Naturally existing criterion groups (e.g., males vs. females, delinquents vs. nondelinquents) were also used, as were criterion groups selected by their standing on another questionnaire (e.g., authoritarians vs. nonauthoritarians). These 11 CPI scales, used in this study to represent scales constructed by the empirical strategy, were Dominance (Do), Capacity for Status (Cs), Sociability (Sy), Responsibility (Re), Socialization (So), Tolerance (To), Achievement via Conformance (Ac), Achievement via Independence (Ai), Intellectual Efficiency (Ie), Psychological-Mindedness (Py), and Femininity (Fe). The number of items per scale ranged from 22 to 54.

Theoretical Scales. The development of a set of theoretical scales raised a number of important considerations. The first of these was the demand that the theory selected be one that had gained some recognition in the personality area.

The theories surveyed by Hall and Lindzey (1957) meet this requirement and so were selected for further consideration. Since judges were to be asked to match particular items to theoretical concepts, it was necessary that the concepts be well explicated, preferably by the theorist himself. Of those theories considered, the need system of Murray (1938) best met this criterion.

To develop the theoretical scales tapping Murray needs, three judges participated in the item-selection process. The judges were all advanced graduate students in clinical psychology at the University of Oregon. The judges read Murray's description of the need system and were asked to refer to it continuously as they selected CPI items to tap each of the needs. Only those items whose placement had been argreed upon by at least two of the three judges were retained. Scales were constructed to measure each of the following 11 needs: Achievement (nAc), Affiliation (nAf), Autonomy (nAu), Deference (nDe), Dominance (nDo), Exhibition (nEx), Infravoidance (nIn), Nurturance (nNu), Order (nOr), Play (nPl), and Understanding (nUn). The number of items in the theoretical scales ranged from 11 to 20.

Rational Scales. Of the 11 rational scales, four are in the standard version of the CPI: Social Presence (Sp), Self-Acceptance (Sa), Self-Control (Sc), and Flexibility (Fx). For these four CPI scales, items were selected by Gough (1957) to tap each trait; the items were then administered to a sample of subjects, and from this group extreme scorers on the scale were identified. Those items which most adequately differentiated between the two extreme subgroups were retained for the final version of the scale. The number of items in these four CPI scales ranged from 22 to 56.

Seven additional rational scales were constructed for this study by the first author to measure each of the following traits: Dominance (Dom), Sociability (Soc), Responsibility (Res), Psychological-Mindedness (Psy), Femininity (Fem), Academic Achievement (Ach), and Conformity (Con). The 468 CPI items were judged on criterion relevance for each of the seven traits, the initial number of items per scale ranging from 52 to 66. The preliminary scales were then scored on a sample of 108 University of Oregon female sophomore and junior students. The total scale scores for each subject were correlated with the responses to each item, a procedure analogous to that employed by Gough. Items correlating significantly with the total scale score at the .05 level were retained for the final form of the scale. The number of items in the final seven new scales ranged from 27 to 45.

Stylistic Scales. Certainly the most active present debate in assessment circles centers on the relative influence of response styles (e.g., acquiescence) and sets (e.g., social desirability) in determining responses to structured personality inventories. In a frequently quoted review of the evidence for response styles and sets, Jackson and Messick (1958) stated:

> In the light of accumulating evidence it seems likely that the *major common factors in personality inventories of the true-false or agree-*

> *disagree type,* such as the MMPI and the California Psychological Inventory, are *interpretable primarily in terms of style rather than specific item content* (p. 247).

Jackson (1960), addressing himself specifically to the CPI, concluded that *(a)* "acquiescence is a major source of variance in the CPI" and *(b)* "the tendency to respond consistently in a socially desirable or undesirable direction is also an important response determinant in the CPI (pp. 345-346)." Spurred on by the hypothesis that measures of "acquiescence" and "social desirability" might account for almost all of the variance in structured inventories (e.g., Edwards & Walker, 1961), a number of investigators have constructed "stylistic scales" based solely on various psychometric properties of the items (e.g., Jackson & Messick, 1961).

Jackson and Pacine (1961) and Lovell (1964) extended Jackson and Messick's (1961) scale construction procedures to the CPI item pool. Lovell plotted the joint functional relationship between endorsement percentage and mean social desirability rating for each item from the CPI; then each of the two variables, endorsement percentage and social desirability mean rating, was trichotomized to yield a 3 x 3 division of the joint space. Items falling into each of the nine cells were grouped into a scale, and all items in each scale were keyed true; the scales were therefore necessarily nonoverlapping.[2] The number of items per scale ranged from 15 to 187. All nine of Lovell's scales were utilized in the present study, although Lovell's two longest scales, Deviance and Hyper-Communality, were reduced in length by the random elimination of some items.

Two other stylistic-psychometric scales were also included in the present study: *(a)* the Communality (Cm) scale of the CPI (Gough, 1957), composed of 28 items with extreme response splits, all keyed in the direction of the popular response; and *(b)* the 32-item social desirability (Dsd) scale of Dicken (1963), constructed from items in the middle range of endorsement, keyed in the desirable direction.

Random Scales. Eleven 25-item scales were constructed from the CPI item pool by selecting items randomly; keying was also random. The random scales provided a predictive base line against which *all* other strategies could be compared.

Table 1 lists the scales used to represent each of the six scale construction strategies. The scale names and abbreviations are presented, along with the

[2]Lovell's nine scales have the following names and properties: Deviance (PM1; low endorsement, low desirability), Non-Communality (PM2; low endorsement, medium desirability), Deviant Favorability (PM3; low endorsement, high desirability), Unfavorability (PM4: medium endorsement, low desirability), Acquiescence (PM5; medium endorsement, medium desirability), Favorability (PM6; medium endorsement, high desirability), Unfavorable Communality (PM7; high endorsement, low desirability), Communality (PM8; high endorsement, medium desirability), and Hyper-Communality (PM9; high endorsement, high desirability).

number of items in each scale, a test-retest reliability coefficient, and two estimates of internal consistency: *(a)* r_{tt} or Kuder-Richardson Formula 20 (Cronbach's coefficient Alpha), and *(b)* r_{ii} or an internal consistency estimate for the average item in the scale.

$$r_{ii} = \frac{r_{tt}}{n - [(n-1)\, r_{tt}]}$$

where n equals the number of items in the scale (a reversal of the Spearman-Brown correction). The test-retest correlations were computed from double administrations of the CPI to 179 University of Oregon freshman women; the interval between test and retest was 4 weeks. The r_{tt} and r_{ii} values were computed from the responses of the same 179 subjects to the first administration of the CPI.[3]

Table 2 summarizes some psychometric properties for the 11 scales representing each strategy. Included in Table 2 are the average number of items in the scales, the average amount of item overlap among pairs of scales, the average intercorrelation among pairs of scales, the average test-retest reliability coefficient, the average r_{tt}, and the average r_{ii}. As Table 2 indicates, the three reliability estimates were highly related, though the test-retest coefficients were generally higher than the r_{tt} (KR 20) values. Even though the factor scales had relatively few items on the average, their reliabilities were higher than scales constructed by all other strategies. The theoretical scales were also relatively short, and while their average test-retest and r_{tt} coefficients were lower than those for the rational and empirical scales, their r_{ii} values were higher. Although the stylistic scales appeared to possess some degree of reliability (especially Lovell's Deviance and Unfavorability scales), the average reliabilities of these scales were nonetheless considerably lower than scales constructed from all strategies other than random (where the average reliabilities were, as expected, the lowest of all). As the last two columns in Table 2 indicate, the empirical scales showed the greatest amount of average interscale correlation, followed closely by the rational scales; scales constructed by these two strategies were the only ones for which any substantial degree of item overlap occurred. Interestingly, the theoretical scales had relatively low mean intercorrelations, and the random scales—as would be expected—had virtually no communality whatsoever.

[3]A table of the intercorrelations (and amount of item overlap) among all pairs of scales, within and between scale sets, is available from Lewis R. Goldberg (Oregon Research Institute, P. O. Box 5173, Eugene, Oregon 97403) and has been deposited with the American Documentation Institute. Order Document No. 9301 from ADI Auxiliary Publications Project, Photoduplication Service, Library of Congress, Washington, D. C. 20540. Remit in advance $1.25 for microfilm or $1.25 for photocopies and make checks payable to: Chief, Photoduplication Service, Library of Congress.

Table 1. Some Psychometric Properties of the Eleven Scales Constructed by Each of Six Strategies

Scale Name and Abbreviation	Number of Items	Reliability		
		Test-retest r	KR 20 r_{tt}	r_{ii}
Factor scales				
Extraversion-Introversion (fEx)	23	.92	.90	.28
Harmonious Childhood (fHa)	9	.88	.72	.22
Surgency (fSu)	14	.88	.82	.25
Conformity-Rebelliousness (fCo)	17	.86	.84	.24
Ascendence-Submission (fAs)	15	.90	.85	.27
Neuroticism (fNe)	22	.89	.85	.20
Orthodoxy-Flexibility (fOr)	27	.90	.85	.17
Self Confidence (fSc)	11	.88	.82	.29
Amiability-Irritability (fAm)	10	.78	.67	.17
Serenity-Depression (fSe)	19	.83	.85	.23
Psychoticism (fPs)	22	.87	.81	.16
Empirical scales				
Dominance (Do)	46	.89	.80	.08
Capacity for Status (Cs)	32	.79	.59	.04
Sociability (Sy)	36	.90	.80	.10
Responsibility (Re)	42	.83	.67	.05
Socialization (So)	54	.88	.78	.06
Tolerance (To)	32	.88	.74	.08
Achievement via Conformance (Ac)	38	.81	.65	.05
Achievement via Independence (Ai)	32	.81	.63	.05
Intellectual Efficiency (Ie)	52	.85	.72	.05
Psychological-Mindedness (Py)	22	.74	.44	.03
Feminnity (Fe)	38	.71	.30	.01
Theoretical scales				
Need for Achievement (nAc)	17	.75	.61	.08
Need for Affiliation (nAf)	11	.86	.63	.13
Need for Autonomy (nAu)	18	.81	.63	.09
Need for Deference (nDe)	14	.82	.62	.10
Need for Dominance (nDo)	16	.91	.85	.26
Need for Exhibition (nEx)	14	.82	.64	.11
Need for Infravoidance (nIn)	20	.90	.86	.23
Need for Nurturance (nNu)	11	.64	.25	.03
Need for Order (nOr)	12	.81	.71	.17
Need for Play (nPl)	12	.85	.65	.13
Need for Understanding (nUn)	12	.73	.56	.10
Rational scales				
Social Presence (Sp)	56	.89	.78	.06
Self-Acceptance (Sa)	34	.81	.63	.05
Self-Control (Sc)	50	.88	.83	.09
Flexibility (Fx)	22	.87	.74	.11
Dominance (Dom)	45	.94	.88	.14
Sociability (Soc)	40	.92	.88	.15

Table 1. Some Psychometric Properties of the Eleven Scales Constructed by Each of Six Strategies (continued)

Scale Name and Abbreviation	Number of Items	Reliability		
		Test-retest r	KR 20 r_{tt}	r_{ii}
Rational scales (continued)				
Responsibility (Res)	37	.86	.75	.08
Psychological-Mindedness (Psy)	29	.84	.75	.09
Femininity (Fem)	27	.81	.48	.03
Academic Achievement (Ach)	38	.82	.72	.06
Conformity (Con)	29	.87	.74	.09
Stylistic scales				
Deviance (PM1)	50	.88	.78	.07
Non-Communality (PM2)	30	.74	.48	.03
Deviant Favorability (PM3)	21	.77	.46	.04
Unfavorability (PM4)	47	.86	.80	.08
Acquiescence (PM5)	25	.75	.30	.02
Favorability (PM6)	45	.82	.70	.05
Unfavorable Communality (PM7)	15	.73	.59	.09
Communality (PM8)	15	.63	.30	.03
Hyper-Communality (PM9)	42	.76	.59	.03
Communality (Cm)	28	.67	.48	.03
Social Desirability (Dsd)	32	.77	.61	.05
Random scales				
R1	25	.53	−.23	−.01
R2	25	.56	−.06	.00
R3	25	.55	−.17	−.01
R4	25	.69	.26	.01
R5	25	.55	−.27	−.01
R6	25	.46	−.40	−.01
R7	25	.59	−.01	.00
R8	25	.60	−.02	.00
R9	25	.65	.11	.00
R10	25	.57	.08	.00
R11	25	.52	−.36	−.01

Subjects

As part of a larger research project conducted by Goldberg and Rorer (1966), 201 freshman women, all residents of one dormitory at the University of Oregon, were paid to participate in a 6-week program of psychological testing. Testing sessions of approximately 1 hour's duration occupied one evening per week. Among the tasks completed by most of the subjects were test and retest administrations of the CPI.

Table 2. Average Values of the Properties of Scales Constructed by Each of Six Strategies

Strategy	Mean Number of Items in Scale	Reliability			Mean r (Absolute Value) Among Scale Pairs	Mean Number of Overlapping Items Among Scale Pairs
		Mean Retest r (4 Weeks)	Mean KR 20 r_{tt}	Mean r_{ii}		
Factor	17	.87	.82	.23	.24	0
Empirical	39	.83	.65	.06	.33	2.7
Theoretical	14	.81	.64	.13	.19	0
Rational	37	.86	.74	.09	.29	2.9
Stylistic	32	.76	.55	.05	.25	.6
Random	25	.57	−.10	.00	.07	0

Criterion Measures

Thirteen criteria, intended to tap a broad range of variables which psychologists have sought to predict from personality inventories, were assessed. These 13 criterion measures may be grouped into five major areas.

Social Conformity. Two indices of social conformity were included in this study: a Sorority Joining Index (SOR) and a Yielding Index (YLD). The Sorority Joining Index was based on the subject's reported interest in sorority affiliation. Coeds indicated whether they: *(a)* were pledges or members of a sorority, *(b)* were uncertain as to whether they would join a sorority, or *(c)* intended *not* to join a sorority. The validity of this index is indicated by the results of a follow-up study on 80 subjects enrolled at the University of Oregon 2 years later. Eighty-six percent of the girls in Category *a* were members of a sorority 2 years later, while 96% of the Category *c* coeds were not members. Category *b* coeds were approximately evenly split between sorority members and independents. For the *a* and *c* groups alone, the resulting phi coefficient was .83.

The Yielding Index, an experimental measure of conformity, was described in detail by Goldberg and Rorer (1966). The measure was obtained from shifts in responses to a double administration of a 45-item Opinion Questionnaire (Hastorf & Piper, 1951) previously used for the same purpose by Jackson (1964). Subjects were asked to indicate the amount of their agreement or disagreement with each statement on a nine-point scale. On the second administration of the questionnaire, 5 weeks after the first, each of the 45 questions was followed by a number described as the average response given by the subjects on the first administration of the questionnaire. For the 25 questions with the smallest dispersions of ratings on the first administration, the reported mean value was obtained by shifting the actual mean three points toward whichever end of the scale was most distant. The mean values of the 20 questions with the largest dispersions were reported accurately. The criterion index of yielding was computed by averaging (across the 25 items for which spurious mean values were reported) the discrepancy between the subject's average distance from the spurious mean at Administration I and her average distance at Administration II, divided by her distance at Administration I. This statistic estimated the extent to which the subject yielded in relation to her opportunity to yield. The reliability of this score was .79 (a split-half reliability coefficient corrected by the Spearman-Brown formula).

Peer Ratings. All subjects were rated by 8 to 12 peers on five trait dimensions, using a five-point forced-distribution rating scale. Subjects were rated only by those coeds living on the same floor of their dormitory wing. The traits rated were Dominance (DOM), Sociability (SOC), Responsibility (RES), Psychological-Mindedness (PSY), and Femininity (FEM)—all traits for which Gough had developed corresponding group discriminative scales for the CPI. The rating instructions were adopted from Gough's CPI scale descriptions. Each subject's mean rating on each of the five traits was used as the criterion index. The test-retest reliabilities of these five criteria over a 5-week interval in a sample of 77 high school girls were: DOM = .91, SOC = .88, RES = .89, PSY = .77, and FEM = .93 (Neilson, 1965). Each subject also rated herself on the same rating scale for each of these five traits.

Personal Popularity. Two criteria of personal popularity, How Well Known (HWK), and Dating Frequency (DAT), were used. the HWK criterion was the mean rating made by the same peers who provided the other peer ratings, using the same rating scale. The test-retest reliability of this criterion over a 5-week interval in a sample of 77 high school girls was .84 (Neilson, 1965). The DAT criterion was based on the subject's reported average number of dates per month.

Academic Achievement. Two measures of academic achievement were utilized: first-term Grade Point Average (GPA), and Achievement (ACH)—actual GPA minus GPA predicted by the University admissions office from a college aptitude test plus high school grades. Since the GPA measure represented attainment after only the first term of college work, a follow-up study was made to determine the stability of the measure. Data was obtained on 96 subjects who had completed their sophomore year. For these subjects, a correlation of .80 was obtained between first-term GPA and cumulative (2-year) GPA.

Academic Interest and Perseverance. Choice of Major (MAJ), a dichotomy between liberal arts versus non-liberal-arts majors, was included in the present study. Follow-up information obtained on 94 of these coeds during their junior year indicated that 79% were still in the same criterion category (phi = .58). The final criterion, College Dropout (CDO), was a follow-up measure providing an indication of the subject's diligence (and ability) in pursuing her academic goals.

Thirty-six percent of the original subjects left the University after their freshman year; an additional 21% left the University after their sophomore year, while 43% were still enrolled in their junior year. The CDO criterion indicated whether the coed had been enrolled in the University for one, two, or three academic years.

It would be difficult to argue that these 13 criteria represent a random sample of all that might be of interest to psychologists. They are, however, meant to be a representative sample of important and diverse criteria related to problems that have been of interest to many investigators.

Method of Analysis

The study utilized a double cross-validation design. For *each* of the 13 criteria, multiple regression equations were developed for each set of 11 scales on one half of the sample and applied to the other half. Likewise, a multiple regression equation was developed on the second half of the sample and applied to the first. This design produced two original (derivation) multiple correlation coefficients and two cross-validated coefficients for each of the 13 criteria, for each of the six sets of scales. The pairs of cross-validation multiple *Rs* formed the main data of the study.

Results

Members of each criterion group were randomly divided into two equal subgroups, for purposes of the double cross-validation design. Table 3 presents the means and standard deviations of each subsample for each criterion, as well as the intercorrelations among the 13 criteria for those 153 subjects for whom all criterion measures were available. Note that (*a*) the mean scores of the two random subsamples were very similar on each of the 13 criteria, and (*b*) the criterion measures were, in general, remarkably uncorrelated. Only GPA and Achievement, Dominance and Sociability, Responsibility and Psychological-Mindedness, and Sociability and How Well Known had as much as 30% of their variance in common.

Table 4 summarizes the basic findings of this study. The table presents the average cross-validated multiple correlation coefficients obtained by each scale group for each criterion, as well as the average derivation sample coefficients. In addition to the individual cell entries, the mean *Rs* for rows and columns are reported. Calculation of the means was based on z transformations of the individual multiple *Rs*.

Differences in row means indicate the extent to which the criteria differed in predictability. As Table 4 reveals, some criteria were well predicted by several strategies while others were virtually unpredictable. The column means indicate the differential effectiveness of the six strategies of scale construction in predicting the 13 criteria. The means for the factor, empirical, theoretical, and rational strategies were essentially identical. The mean multiple R for the

Table 3. Intercorrelations Among the Thirteen Criterion Measures

	SOR	YLD	DOM	SOC	RES	PSY	FEM	HWK	DAT	GPA	ACH	MAJ	CDO
Sorority Joining (SOR)[a]		−.01	.17	.37	−.15	−.14	.28	.08	.23	−.14	−.06	−.14	−.21
Yielding (YLD)[a]			−.20	−.03	.04	.03	.15	.10	.05	−.20	−.14	−.25	.10
Dominance (DOM)[b]				.60	.24	.24	.00	.38	.20	.16	.17	.17	−.10
Sociability (SOC)[b]					.19	.34	.39	.62	.30	−.15	−.08	.01	−.08
Responsibility (RES)[b]						.63	.32	.18	−.24	.36	.09	−.14	−.05
Psy-Mindedness (PSY)[b]							.29	.50	−.10	.15	.02	−.07	.13
Femininity (FEM)[b]								.27	.16	−.02	−.01	−.20	−.05
How Well Known (HWK)									.24	−.09	−.03	.00	.12
Dating Frequency (DAT)										−.16	.06	.03	−.02
Grade Point Average (GPA)											.64	.14	−.21
Achievement (ACH)												.13	−.08
Choice of Major (MAJ)													.06
College Dropout (CDO)													
n: Sample A	87	87	95	95	95	95	95	95	95	84	84	87	95
n: Sample B	87	87	95	95	95	95	95	95	95	84	84	87	95
M: Sample A	2.1	.29	3.1	3.3	3.1	3.0	3.2	3.2	6.6	2.4	1.0	.43	2.1
M: Sample B	2.2	.26	3.1	3.2	3.1	3.0	3.1	3.1	7.2	2.4	1.0	.52	2.0
σ: Sample A	.82	.18	.58	.69	.61	.50	.69	.45	5.0	.56	.41	.49	.89
σ: Sample B	.78	.20	.60	.65	.62	.48	.65	.53	5.7	.57	.43	.50	.88

Note N = 153.
[a]Index.
[b]Rating.

Table 4. Average Multiple Correlation Coefficients for Scales Constructed by Each of Six Strategies

Criterion	Strategy						Mean
	Factor	Empirical	Theoretical	Rational	Stylistic	Random	
SOR	.42 (.54)	.31 (.44)	.26 (.52)	.32 (.43)	.31 (.43)	.13 (.38)	.29 (.46)
YLD	.21 (.44)	.34 (.47)	.25 (.42)	.28 (.47)	.20 (.35)	−.08 (.39)	.20 (.42)
DOM	.34 (.50)	.35 (.53)	.38 (.49)	.43 (.50)	.21 (.38)	.27 (.43)	.33 (.47)
SOC	.57 (.63)	.44 (.59)	.51 (.61)	.49 (.58)	.35 (.50)	.12 (.40)	.42 (.55)
RES	.27 (.49)	.31 (.51)	.40 (.53)	.37 (.57)	.19 (.43)	.02 (.32)	.26 (.48)
PSY	−.01 (.36)	.09 (.36)	.20 (.43)	.16 (.40)	.08 (.34)	−.02 (.28)	.08 (.36)
FEM	.36 (.53)	.31 (.47)	.30 (.44)	.32 (.48)	.23 (.35)	.11 (.28)	.27 (.43)
HWK	.36 (.50)	.27 (.51)	.38 (.47)	.36 (.53)	.18 (.40)	.18 (.41)	.29 (.47)
DAT	.29 (.58)	.26 (.49)	.38 (.52)	.36 (.55)	.03 (.37)	.30 (.44)	.27 (.49)
GPA	.26 (.39)	.20 (.36)	.13 (.37)	.26 (.55)	.03 (.35)	.02 (.35)	.15 (.40)
ACH	.04 (.36)	.12 (.27)	.02 (.37)	.05 (.43)	−.07 (.39)	.00 (.34)	.03 (.36)
MAJ	.20 (.44)	.30 (.48)	.07 (.43)	.11 (.36)	.11 (.40)	.21 (.39)	.17 (.42)
CDO	−.05 (.36)	.04 (.36)	.01 (.26)	−.08 (.30)	.05 (.37)	.06 (.28)	.00 (.32)
Mean	.26 (.48)	.26 (.45)	.26 (.45)	.27 (.48)	.15 (.39)	.10 (.36)	.22 (.46)

Note. The means of the two cross-validation *R*s are listed above the means of the derivation *R*s (in parentheses).

stylistic scales was substantially lower than those for the four major strategies, while the mean for the random scales was the lowest. The column means suggest that *the four principal scale types were equivalent in predictive effectiveness*, and that each of the four was better than both groups of control scales (stylistic and random).[4]

The multiple correlation coefficients presented in Table 4 were based on regression equations with all 11 scales utilized as variables. Since cross-validated multiple *Rs* typically tend to approach a maximum value upon the inclusion of only a few variables, a significant proportion of error variance may have been forced into the equations, thus obscuring possible differences among the four major strategies. To test this hypothesis, all regression analyses were recomputed by a step-wise procedure, with the provision that only scales significantly increasing the predictable criterion variance in the derivation sample be included. Significance was defined as accounting for at least 1% of the criterion variance; typically only three to five scales were included in these regression equations. This variation in procedure failed to produce any substantial change in the results previously reported. The means for the six scale groups across all 13 criteria were virtually identical to those presented in Table 4.

While linear regression analyses provide one major approach to prediction, the use of regression equations is typically a rather cumbersome and technically complicated procedure. Moreover, since beta weights in regression equations are notoriously unstable as one moves to differing populations, less precise prediction approaches have often been shown to be as useful as regression analyses (e.g., Goldberg, 1965). One such approach to prediction involves the search for single scales to predict each criterion. The design of the present study allows a comparison of the six strategies of test construction when the goal is the development of a set of scales, each one of which is to be used *individually* to predict some important nontest criterion.

Table 5 summarizes the findings from this analysis. The correlations between each criterion and each of the 11 scales constructed by each strategy were examined separately for Samples A and B. Within each set of 11 scales, the one scale which correlated most highly with the criterion in Sample A was selected, and its correlation in Sample B was used as a measure of cross-validity.

[4]To attach additional confidence to these findings, some simple statistical analyses were carried out. A Friedman two-way analysis of variance of ranks for related samples (Siegel, 1956) was used, based on the rankings of the scale groups for each criterion. Rank assignments were based on the average cross-validated *Rs*, and apparent ties were broken by carrying computations to the third decimal place. The analysis of variance of ranks was highly significant ($p < .001$), indicating that significant differences existed in column effects, that is, strategies. Next, a series of comparisons among all possible strategy pairs was carried out. Differences between pairs were assessed by applying the sign test to the ranks. While there were no significant differences among the four primary scale groups, all of the four were significantly more valid than the two sets of control scales. The stylistic scales were not significantly more valid than the random scales.

Table 5. Average Cross-Validation Correlation Coefficients for the Highest Correlating Single Scales Constructed by Each of Six Strategies

Criterion	Strategy					
	Factor	Empirical	Theoretical	Rational	Stylistic	Random
SOR	.39	.12	.22	.29	.04	.12
YLD	.16	.15	.18	.28	.13	.03
DOM	.34	.35	.37	.41	.08	.08
SOC	.54	.44	.53	.49	.23	–.02
RES	.28	.39	.27	.42	.16	.06
PSY	.19	.11	.14	.17	.09	–.08
FEM	.23	.21	.22	.23	.20	.16
HWK	.36	.31	.39	.39	.05	.12
DAT	.29	.19	.41	.36	.09	.21
GPA	.17	.16	.18	.28	–.02	–.02
ACH	.07	.01	.04	.11	.06	.00
MAJ	.17	.18	.10	.24	.23	.14
CDO	.06	.04	–.01	–.01	–.01	.00
Mean	.25	.21	.24	.28	.10	.06

Note. The values listed are the means of the two cross-validation *r*'s. Signs were disregarded when consistent from the derivation to the cross-validation sample. Negative signs indicate that the signs of the coefficients reversed on cross-validation.

Conversely, the one scale correlating most highly with the criterion in Sample B was selected, and its correlation in Sample A was used. The values reported in Table 5 are the averages of these two cross-validated single-scale correlations; they indicate the average validity on a new sample of the most valid single scale from the derivation samples.

Note that the single-scale validity coefficients were virtually identical to those found in the multiple regression analyses. The stylistic and random scales were least valid in predicting the 13 criteria, while the four other scale groups had significantly higher cross-validities. In fact, the column means are remarkably similar to those reported in Table 4. An inspection of the individual cell entries in Tables 4 and 5 reveals that in about one-third of the cases the average cross-validated single-scale *r's* were higher than the cross-validated multiple *Rs.* Again certain criteria were more predictable than others. The "social" criteria—Dominance, Sociability, How Well Known, and Dating Frequency—were quite well predicted. In contrast, College Dropout was poorly predicted by all of the single scales, just as it was by the multiple regression techniques.

Discussion

The principal finding from this study was that sets of scales constructed by each of the four primary strategies of scale construction—factor analytic, empirical, theoretical, and rational—were equivalent in their validity across 13 diverse criteria. Moreover, since all four outperformed the two scale groups (stylistic and random) used for control purposes, their uniformity in predictive validity cannot be considered a function of chance-level prediction.

This finding, that strategies make little difference, may have profound implications for personality assessment. On the one hand, it indicates that dogmatic assertions of the superiority of one strategy over another are premature. In addition, the findings from this study suggest that procedures of item grouping are probably *not* a cause of the relatively low validity coefficients typically reported in the psychometric literature, and therefore that the guilty culprits might well be the inventory items themselves (Goldberg, 1963). While it is, of course, possible that scale construction strategies more novel than any investigated in this study (e.g., Horst, 1965; Loevinger, Gleser, & DuBois, 1953) might outperform those compared here, it is up to their proponents to prove their relative superiority. Meanwhile, efforts to maximize the validity of structured inventories should now begin to center on the investigation of individual item properties.

The failure of the stylistic-psychometric scales to cross-validate at a higher level than the random scales adds still another blow to the current thesis that stylistic variables are of paramount importance in structured inventories. Recent work at Oregon Research Institute (e.g., Rorer & Goldberg, 1965a, 1965b) as well as in other laboratories (e.g., Dicken, 1963; McGee, 1962a, 1962b) indicates that "acquiescence" is of negligible significance in determining responses to inventories such as the MMPI and the CPI.[5] For recent reviews of this evidence, see McGee (1962c) and Rorer (1965).

In addition, the findings from the present study have implications for the extremely important—and certainly quite complex—question of the relationship between content relevance and predictive validity (e.g., Berg, 1959). Table 6, a summary of the major findings from this study, presents some evidence related to this question. For each of the 13 criteria, Table 6 lists *(a)* the highest

[5]Some additional evidence against an extreme form of the acquiescence hypothesis can be seen from some other analyses in the present study. Two sets of scales were independently developed by selecting items randomly. "Nonoverlapping" scales were developed by selecting items randomly without replacement, while "overlapping" scales were constructed by selecting items randomly with replacement. Each set was keyed *(a)* randomly and *(b)* uniformly true. The average cross-validities obtained from multiple regression analyses applied to these four sets of random scales across all 13 criteria were as follows: nonoverlapping, keyed randomly=.10; nonoverlapping, keyed true=.15; overlapping, keyed randomly=.04; overlapping, keyed true=.09. Note that the nonoverlapping scales were slightly (though not significantly) more valid than the overlapping scales. While the cross-validity of the random scales tended to increase very slightly when the items were all keyed true, the differences between the means of the true-keyed and random-keyed scales were not significant. The failure of the random scales keyed true to predict these 13 criteria thus provides additional evidence that whatever valid personality variance can be extracted from CPI scales is certainly *not* simply a function of individual differences in acquiescence.

Table 6. Summary of the Relationships Between the Thirteen Criteria and the Four Major Scale Construction Strategies

Criterion	Highest Cross-Validation Multiple R (from Table 4)	Highest Cross-Validity for Single Scales (from Table 5)	Validity of "Best" Scale Constructed by Each Strategy			
			Factor	Empirical	Theoretical	Rational
SOR	.42 Factor	.39 Factor	.39 fSu	.24 Sy	.31 nPl	.29 Soc
YLD	.34 Empirical	.28 Rational	.26 fOr	−.24 Cs	.24 nDe	.28 Con
DOM	.43 Rational	.41 Rational	.34 fSc	.35 Do	.37 nDo	.41 Dom
SOC	.57 Factor	.54 Factor	.54 fSu	.44 Sy	.53 nAf	.49 Soc
RES	.40 Theoretical	.42 Rational	.30 fHa	.39 So	.40 nOr	.42 Res
PSY	.20 Theoretical	.19 Factor	.19 fHa	.23 So	.22 nNu	.19 Res
FEM	.36 Factor	.23 Factor	.32 fOr	.31 So	.26 nDe	.31 Con
HWK	.38 Theoretical	.39 Theoretical	.36 fSu	.31 Sy	.39 nAf	.39 Soc
DAT	.38 Theoretical	.41 Theoretical	.37 fSu	.29 Sy	.41 nPl	.38 Soc
GPA	.26 Rational	.28 Rational	−.18 fSu	.21 Ai	−.20 nPl	.28 Ach
ACH	.12 Empirical	.11 Rational	−.20 fEx	.12 Do	.17 nIn	−.19 Soc
MAJ	.30 Empirical	.24 Rational	−.28 fOr	−.23 So	−.22 nDe	−.24 Con
CDO	.06 Random	.06 Factor	.13 fPs	−.15 So	−.07 nDo	−.08 Sc

cross-validated multiple $\overline{R}$, using the 11 scales constructed by each strategy, *(b)* the highest cross-validity coefficient for the best single scale generated by each strategy, and *(c)* the single scale (within each of the four major scale sets) with the highest criterion correlation, averaged across both samples (and thus *not* cross-validated). Inspection of this summary table allows some inferences regarding the prediction of the criteria used in the present study, each of which will be briefly discussed in turn.

Sorority Joining (SOR)

For this criterion, one for which no empirical or rational scale has been specifically constructed, the best prediction came from the multiple regression equations using the 11 factor scales ($\overline{R} = .42$), while the individual factor scale of Surgency (fSu) performed almost as validly ($r = .39$). Note that the empirical and rational Sociability (Sy and Soc) scales ($r = .24$ and $.29$) as well as the theoretical Need for Play (nPl) scale ($r = .31$), were also relatively valid predictors of sorority affiliation. In line with the common stereotype, the sorority girl tended to be more surgent and sociable and expressed a greater need for play than did the nonsorority coed.

Yielding (YLD)

In previous studies relating scores on the standard CPI scales to yielding in Asch-type conformity situations (e.g., Harper, 1964; Tuddenham, 1959), Gough's Capacity for Status (Cs) scale has been shown to have a low negative relationship with yielding. In the present study, Cs turned out to have the highest correlation with this criterion ($r = -.24$) of the standard CPI scales, though the rationally constructed Conformity (Con) scale was slightly more valid ($r = .28$). While Cs and Con share no common items, their correlation in this sample was −.34. The best prediction of yielding in this study came from the multiple regression equations utilizing the 11 empirical scales ($\bar{R} = .34$), only a slight improvement over that achieved by the rational Con scale alone. Among the scales constructed by other strategies, the factor Orthodoxy-Flexibility (fOr) scale ($r = .26$) and the theoretical Need for Deference (nDe) scale ($r = .24$) achieved the highest validity coefficients, indicating that the yielding coed tended to describe herself as relatively orthodox, conventional, and deferent in her views and behavior.

Peer Ratings: Dominance (DOM), Sociability (SOC), Responsibility (RES), Psychological-Mindedness (PSY), and Femininity (FEM)

Table 7 summarizes the relationships between CPI scales and each of the five peer rating criteria. Included in Table 7 are the validity coefficients for the five standard CPI empirical scales against the corresponding five trait ratings the scales were built to predict, as well as the validity coefficients for each of the five rationally constructed trait scales against these same criteria. Also included in Table 7 are validity coefficients for two factor and two theoretical scales which on logical grounds might be highly associated with a specific trait rating. In addition, Table 7 includes the correlations between the subjects' self-ratings on each trait and their mean peer ratings on the same trait.

Table 7. Prediction of Five Peer Rating Criteria

Criterion	Empirical	Rational	Factor	Theoretical	Self-ratings
DOM	.35 (Do)	.41 (Dom)	.30 (fAs)	.37 (nDo)	.47
SOC	.44 (Sy)	.49 (Soc)	.54 (fSu)	.53 (nAf)	.56
RES	.29 (Re)	.42 (Res)			.41
PSY	−.12 (Py)	.05 (Psy)			.23
FEM	.24 (Fe)	.28 (Fem)			.46
Mean r	.24	.33			.43

While the peer rating criteria were relatively well predicted by a number of scales in this study, in every case the rational scales yielded higher validity coefficients for their respective trait ratings than did Gough's empirical CPI scales! Moreover, in almost every case, the subjects' self-ratings were more predictive of their peer ratings than *any* of the scales, and typically even more predictive than the best linear regression equations using an optimal combination of 11 scales. The mean validity coefficient for the five Gough empirical scales was .24, while the mean for the five rational scales was .33, and the mean for the five self-ratings was .43. This somewhat paradoxical finding—that peer ratings are better predicted by simple self-ratings than by scales specifically designed to predict these criteria—substantiates an earlier finding by Carroll (1952). Carroll (see Campbell & Fiske, 1959, Table 11) utilized peer ratings of five traits purportedly measured by five factor scales in the Guilford-Martin battery. In every case, self-ratings were more predictive of peer ratings than were test scores, the mean validity coefficient for the five Guilford-Martin scales being .33, as compared to a mean correlation of .39 for the self-ratings. Additional evidence for the superiority of self-ratings over scale scores can be found in Peterson (1965).

For Dominance ratings in the present study, the best predictor was self-rated Dominance ($r = .47$). The best multiple regression equations (rational scales) yielded a cross-validated $\bar{R}$ of .43, essentially the same as the validity coefficient of the rational Dominance (Dom) scale ($r = .41$). Both Dom and the theoretical Need for Dominance (nDo) scale ($r = .37$) were slightly more valid than Gough's empirical Dominance (Do) scale ($r = .35$). The Do and Dom scales, which share 25 items (one of which is keyed oppositely), correlated .89 in this sample.

Sociability ratings were the most predictable criterion used in this study. The multiple regression equations for the 11 factor scales ($\bar{R} = .57$), the self-ratings ($r = .56$), the factor Surgency (fSu) scale ($r = .54$), and the theoretical Need for Affiliation (nAf) scale ($r = .53$) all performed at about the same level, somewhat higher than the rational Sociability (Soc) scale ($r = .49$); all outperformed Gough's empirical Sociability (Sy) scale ($r = .44$). The empirical Sy and rational Soc scales turned out to share only 13 items, yet correlated .85 in this sample.

Ratings of responsibility provided the single instance where the validity of all scales was not surpassed by self-ratings; the rational Responsibility (Res) scale ($r = .42$), the self-ratings ($r = .41$), the theoretical Need for Order (nOr) scale ($r = .40$), and the multiple regression equations for the 11 theoretical scales ($\bar{R} = .40$) all performed at approximately the same level of validity. Gough's empirical Responsibility (Re) scale ($r = .29$) was surpassed by a number of scales, including the empirical Socialization (So) scale ($r = .39$). Re and Res shared only 11 items and correlated .71 in this sample.

Psychological-Mindedness ratings were not well predicted by any scale or set of scales, probably because the trait itself is less commonly articulated in our culture—and therefore much more difficult for peers to assess—than the other traits under study. This was the only trait for which a Gough empirical scale, Psychological-Mindedness (Py), correlated negatively ($r = -.12$) with the criterion ratings. However, the empirical Socialization (So) scale ($r = .23$), the theoretical Need for Nurturance (nNu) scale ($r = .22$), the rational Responsibility (Res) scale ($r = .19$), and the factor Harmonious Childhood (fHa) scale ($r = .19$) all performed at approximately the same level, about as well as the multiple regression equations using theoretical scales ($\bar{R}$ = .20). Py and Psy shared only two items and correlated .47 in this sample.

Femininity ratings were best predicted by self-ratings (r = .46), with no scale or set of scales even approaching this level of validity. The multiple regression equations using factor scales yielded a multiple $\bar{R}$ of .36, while single-scale validities for the factor Orthodoxy-Flexibility (fOr) scale (r = .32), the rational Conformity (Con) scale (r = .31), the empirical Socialization (So) scale (r = .31), and the theoretical Need for Deference (nDe) scale (r = .26) were slightly lower; the most feminine girls tended to rate themselves as highly socialized, orthodox in their views, conforming, and deferent. Fe (r = .24) and Fem (r = .28) shared only nine items and correlated .50 in this sample.

How Well Known (HWK) and Dating Frequency (DAT)

When the subjects rated how well they knew each other, How Well Known ratings were predicted moderately well by many scales and scale sets. The theoretical Need for Affiliation (nAf) scale (r = .39), the rational Sociability (Soc) scale (r = .39), the factor Surgency (fSu) scale (r = .36), and the multiple regression equations using theoretical scales ($\bar{R}$ = .38) were all approximately equal in validity, slightly more valid than the best empirical scale, Sociability (Sy), with a validity coefficient of .31. The best known coeds tended to describe themselves as sociable, surgent, and needing to affiliate with others, a fact which comes as no great shock or surprise.

Interestingly, the coeds' average number of dates per month, a self-rating, was equally well predicted, by almost the exact same predictors as the peer rating of How Well Known. The only difference between these two rows of Table 6 occurs among the theoretical scales, where the best predictor of dates was Need for Play (nPl), while Need for Affiliation (nAf) held this role for How Well Known.

Grade Point Average (GPA) and College Achievement (ACH)

First-term GPA was certainly not as well predicted by *any* of the scales derived from the CPI item pool as might be expected by using the more traditional academic predictors (e.g., college aptitude tests and/or high school GPA); for an important summary of the validity of the traditional predictors of GPA in all of the colleges in one state, see Hills (1964). While there is evidence (Gough, 1964; Gough & Fink, 1964) that the standard CPI scales can be used to make relatively valid predictions of high school GPA, there is by now equally compelling evidence that the predictive validity of the standard CPI scales for college GPA is usually rather low (e.g., Holland, 1959). For example, while

Gough's Achievement via Independence (Ai) scale has been shown to be a significant predictor of college GPA in a number of studies, the actual validity coefficients reported—for example, .20 (Jackson & Pacine, 1961) and .23 (Griffin & Flaherty, 1964)—are quite low compared to those achieved by the more traditional predictors. Moreover, when ability is partialled out, Ai tends to add little valid predictive variance (Jackson & Pacine, 1961). In the present study, Ai correlated .21 with GPA; and while it was more valid than any of the other standard CPI scales for this criterion, the rationally devised Academic Achievement (Ach) scale was even more valid for this sample (r = .28). Interestingly, Ai and Ach share only seven items, one of which is keyed oppositely, and the correlation between the two scales in only .32.

In fact, as Table 6 indicates, scales constructed from the CPI item pool are not likely to be good predictors of college GPA, no matter by what strategy they are constructed, and their ability to predict college achievement (aptitude partialled out) is even worse. The most promising CPI predictor of this latter criterion turned out to be the factor scale of Extraversion-Introversion (fEx) and the rational scale of Sociability (Soc); more introverted, less sociable coeds tended to achieve higher GPAs, relative to their predicted GPAs, than did more extraverted and sociable girls.

College Major (MAJ) and College Dropout (CDO)

The two last criteria were rather poorly predicted by all scales and scale sets, probably because they represented too gross a distinction, incorporating within a single category persons with very different types of personalities. For example, in constructing the CDO criterion index, coeds who left the University because of financial difficulties or because they wished to transfer to another college were grouped together with those who were dropped for academic reasons; and girls representing a very large number of different college majors were grouped together to form the liberal arts versus non-liberal-arts Major (MAJ) criterion. Nonetheless, multiple regression equations using the empirical scales did manage a cross-validated multiple $\bar{R}$ of .30 for the Major criterion, and the factor Orthodoxy-Flexibility (fOr) scale achieved a validity coefficient of −.28 for this same criterion. None of the scales was able to predict the CDO criterion, however.

Need for Replication

The present study, while providing the first full-scale experimental comparison of the major test construction strategies, certainly needs replication and extension. Specifically, the work needs to be extended to *(a)* different item pools, *(b)* different sets of criteria, *(c)* different types of subjects (e.g., males) and *(d)* different test-taking situations. It would indeed be remarkable, for example, if self-ratings continued to outperform test scores in predicting peer ratings when both the tests and the self-ratings were administered under applicant conditions. A replication of the present study under such test administration conditions could provide an important advance in personality assessment technology.

Chapter 5

Behavior Samples and Biographical Data

It would seem obvious that the most direct and presumably the most effective way to gain information about an individual's personality would be to observe him in real-life situations in which personality-related behaviors are present. In such an approach we would gather samples of a person's actual patterns of behavior, and generalize from these.

Although an inviting procedure in many respects, this *behavior sample* approach has a number of difficulties which, until recently, have made its use the exception rather than the rule in personality assessment. One such difficulty involves the representativeness of the observed behavior. If the observations are to be useful, a systematic schedule of observation periods must be worked out, and a sufficient number of observations must be made to ensure that the behavior sample has been both comprehensive and representative. Another effect, more difficult to control, has been variously termed the "guinea pig effect" and the "reactive effects of measurement." We are referring to the case in which an individual's behavior might change simply because he is being observed. For example, a student teacher or a budding clinician seemingly would perform differently when he is being observed by a supervisor and when he is not.

One method of unobtrusively obtaining a rather complete record of a person's verbal behavior is to have him wear a miniature wireless microphone-transmitter, or "bug." The obvious problem accompanying such a procedure is that the knowledge that a recording is being made would certainly have an effect, at least on some people. The first paper in this section reports a recent study by Rudolf Moos, who attempted to find out just how serious these reactive or "guinea pig" effects were in making continuous observations of psychiatric patients. Trained observers watched patients during routine hospital activities, both while the patients were wearing the transmitters and while they were not. In general, the differences between the two conditions in amount of verbalization were relatively small. What is important to note, however, was the wide variety of reactions among the different patients, some of whom did show substantial effects as a result of being observed.

One way of avoiding reactive effects of measurement would be to use "nonreactive" measures, that is, to measure behaviors that are not affected by the process of observation. In this sense, certain historical data might be regarded as providing behavioral observations, for example, official school records, yearbooks, and medical or military records. In the second reading in this section, Barthell and Holmes report using such a nonreactive measure in an attempt to "post-dict" the onset of schizophrenia in individuals by examining the number and variety of activities in which they had engaged in during high school as reported in their school yearbook. As predicted, the number of activities of various kinds reported for persons who later become schizophrenic was smaller than that for a randomly selected control group of "normal" students, indicating the beginnings of behavioral withdrawal before hospitalization actually occurred.

The third paper, in which J. Conrad Schwarz offers a methodological critique of the Barthell and Holmes study, provides a graphic illustration of the problem of deciding what constitutes an appropriate control or comparison group. Essentially, Schwarz argues for the possibility that there may be one or several more basic variables that are causally related to both nonparticipation in high school activities and predisposition toward schizophrenia—intelligence, social class, and academic achievement. Although not explicitly discussed by Schwarz, research using historical data is usually more vulnerable to difficulties in achieving adequate control over the data than is research in which the observations are arranged for and made by the researcher himself. Finally, it is worth noting that such methodological criticisms are quite frequent in personality assessment research, which should temper one's enthusiasm for initial findings.

Rather than simply follow an individual about and observe his spontaneous behavior, a more elegant and more useful procedure would be to place him in a situation where the behaviors of interest can be deliberately elicited. Naturally, some ingenuity may be required to arrange a suitable situation, and there is once again the problem of the reactive effects of being observed. For assessments where these problems can be worked through, however, systematic and controlled observation of behavior offers the advantages of actually obtaining samples of the critical behaviors, of convenience, and a greater degree of standardization. The fourth paper, by Mills, McDevitt, and Tonkin, describes a series of situational tasks administered under controlled conditions for the selection of police cadets. An important point, often overlooked, is that personality assessors should have a clear understanding of exactly what behaviors are of interest, so that the assessment task used can be selected for its clear relevance. In this paper, one of the tasks is a "clues" test, a situational exercise in police detection. It cannot be too strongly emphasized that most failures in assessment and selection programs have been due to a lack of a meaningful relationship between the behaviors involved in the assessment process and the behaviors involved in the criterion situation.

As noted above, biographical data can be regarded as a historical report of behavior samples, which could extend over a period of some years. Personnel psychologists have long made use of such data in their attempts to predict highly practical criteria such as specific job success. In the next reading, Scott and Johnson make use of routine information given by applicants for unskilled jobs as a basis for predicting which of the applicants will be most likely to stay with the company for a reasonable length of time. As with much personnel work, their approach was initially strictly empirical; once the items have been selected, however, the authors perform further psychometric analyses to evaluate whether or not the predictor variables are reasonable from a common-sense viewpoint.

In introducing the next reading we may first observe that tests of ability and achievement can be regarded as behavior samples. For example, the Wechsler Adult Intelligence Scale can be considered a device for gathering samples of an individual's general intellectual behavior, which is divided somewhat arbitrarily into a number of subcategories. Using a similar approach to the assessment of psychopathological behavior, Burdock and Hardesty developed their *Structured Clinical Interview* (SCI), an individual interview schedule which an examiner administers while simultaneously checking a 179-item true/false inventory in order to record the individual's behavioral responses. The resulting ten scale scores are plotted on a clinical profile of observed psychopathology, somewhat analagous to an MMPI profile. In constructing the SCI, Burdock and Hardesty attempted to include only items that called for judgments about the presence or absence of concrete behaviors and attitudes, thus requiring a minimum of inference on the part of the examiner.

The use of questionnaires to assess personality-related concepts has been discussed in Chapters 3 and 4, and it was indicated that psychometric procedures employed with such data are often empirical in nature. In the final article in this section, Richard Lanyon presents a step-by-step account of the development and validation of a measure in which questionnaire data are treated entirely as *factual* information. Thus, the measure (of social competence) is based on biographical data, tempered by the respondent's willingness to give a truthful report. Previous research has suggested that questions about specific actual events, as asked in this study, are quite likely to receive factually accurate answers, as compared with more ambiguous items about attitudes and feelings. It is important to note that biographical questionnaires contain items of two kinds: those referring to past irrevocable events (for example, mother's age at time of marriage), and those referring to current status (for example, church attendance). A scale composed entirely of the first kind of items would necessarily result in a static score; obviously, careful thought must be given to the nature of the concept to be assessed with biographical data before constructing the item pool.

1. BEHAVIORAL EFFECTS OF BEING OBSERVED: REACTIONS TO A WIRELESS RADIO TRANSMITTER[1]

Rudolf H. Moos

There has been a recent upsurge of interest in naturalistic observational studies of both animals and man (Barker & Wright, 1954; DeVore, 1965; Webb, Campbell, Schwartz, & Sechrest, 1966; Wieck, 1968; Zinner, 1963). The importance of the direct observation of social and interpersonal behavior in naturalistic settings is being reemphasized, especially by those investigators who are interested in ecological approaches and therefore wish to observe the behavior of their subjects in a wide variety of different environmental settings.

Direct observation of naturally occurring behavior immediately raises the question of what effects the observers have on the behavior which they are supposed to observe. The observer is typically a fixture in any observational setting and his impact on the events must be determined systematically if the

SOURCE. Rudolf H. Moos is associate professor in the Department of Psychiatry and also research associate in the Political Science Department at Stanford University. Learning theory, personality theory, and psychotherapy are Dr. Moos' current fields of research specialization. This article originally appeared in the *Journal of Consulting and Clinical Psychology,* 1968, **32,** 383-388. Reprinted by permission of the American Psychological Association and the author.

[1]The author wishes to acknowledge his appreciation to Eleanor Levine and Phyllis Nobel, who served as the behavior observers, to Bert Kopell and William Wittner, without whose openness to experimental approaches this research would not have been possible, to Mark Abramson, John Adams, and Sheldon Starr, who actively tolerated the intrusion into their individual and group therapy, and to William Lake, who provided valuable help in data analysis.

implications drawn from observational studies are to have their full value. There is little argument that the observer, in watching an event, may affect its course. The empirical issue is how extensive the impact is and which settings and individuals are most vulnerable to its effects. Ultimately the determination of these effects depends on validating studies, few examples of which are currently available. Webb et al. (1966) have pointed out that behavior observed under nonreactive conditions must be compared with corresponding behavior in which various potentially reactive conditions are introduced.

There have been several articles in the psychotherapy literature on the effects of recording and/or filming of psychotherapy on the patient and the therapist (Bellak & Smith, 1956; Cohen & Cohen, 1961; Gottschalk & Auerbach, 1966; Lamb & Mahl, 1956; Roose, 1960; Shakow, 1960; Sternberg, Chapman, & Shakow, 1958). Colby (1960), in an imaginative study, found that the presence of an observer served to raise the total activity of the image system (as measured by the amount of talk about people) and also produced a process change in the form of a drift toward a preponderance of talking about male figures. Roberts and Renzaglia (1965) studied eight counseling trainees, each of whom discussed adjustment problems for at least three sessions with two different clients. Each counselor conducted one of the three sessions under each of the following conditions: tape recorder visible and running (TR); mike only (MO); and, not recorded (NR), a condition in which the client and counselor were told the session would not be recorded, but in which it actually was recorded. The quantity of talk and the ratio of client-counselor talk did not differ under these three conditions. However, clients did make significantly more positive self-statements under the TR than the MO or NR conditions, and significantly more negative self-statements in the NR condition. Counselors made signficantly more interpretive statements under the TR than under the MO and NR conditions.

Haggard, Hiken, and Isaacs (1965), in what may be the most detailed empirical effort in this area, analyzed the direct and indirect references to being observed, as well as the durations of these references, in the first 40 hours of four cases and in one set of eight supervisory sessions. Three cases were recorded and filmed and the fourth was a "control" case the data from which were obtained from the therapist's extensive written notes. They found that patients differed widely in the extent to which they made direct and indirect references to being observed, and in the timing of these references, that is, whether the majority occurred in the beginning, middle, or end of the 40 hours. Patients also differed in the style or manner of expressing their concerns about being observed, that is, in the proportion of direct versus indirect comments.

There have been at least two previous studies which utilized a wireless radio transmitter in order to record naturalistically the behavior of human subjects. Neither of these studies, however, actually compared behavior under different observational conditions. Soskin and John (1963) reported on the use of this technique as a data-collecting medium using two husband-wife pairs in a vacation setting initially unfamiliar to the subjects. They note that it was difficult to evaluate the extent to which behavior was influenced by the fact of wearing the transmitter. However, they gained the impression that the subjects did accept and habituate to the continuous recording of their personal lives.

Purcell and Brady (1966) used a transmitter to monitor a vocal behavior of 13 young adolescents in a cottage environment for 1 hour a day on 10 different days. The subjects appeared to behave naturally after 2-4 days, as judged by *(a)* a marked decrease over time in tape-recorded references to the research context; *(b)* subjective reports of the subjects; *(c)* observations by adult observers; *(d)* analysis of the amount of talking and the amount and types of interpersonal behavior shown by the subject and by others; *(e)* the spontaneity and freedom of language and interaction.

Purpose

The purpose of the present study was the investigation of the wireless microphone transmitter as a technique for the collection of naturalistic data on the behavior of psychiatric patients on a psychiatric inpatient ward.

The study was concerned with four major questions: *(a)* What are the behavioral effects of wearing a wireless microphone? *(b)* Do some subjects react differently to the microphone than others, that is, is there an interaction between individual patients and observation conditions? *(c)* If behavioral effects occur, do they adapt, that is, do they tend to decrease with more experience in being recorded? *(d)* Are there correlations between personality characteristics of individual patients and the extent of their reactions to the observation conditions?

Method

The study was completed as part of a larger research project studying the behavior of psychiatric patients on an inpatient unit by the use of behavior observers and a miniature wireless radio transmitter. The plans for the use of the radio transmitter were discussed in both staff and patient-staff meetings and the patients participated in putting up TV antennas around the ward, including bedrooms, dayroom, visitors' room, dining room, etc.

The question to be investigated was whether the patients would behave differently when they had the microphone on than when they did not. Patients explicitly knew that when they had the microphone on, they were being observed by a behavior observer and what they said was being recorded.

The design of the study is summarized in Table 1. Patients were observed with and without the microphone on during both group therapy and community meetings. Group therapy took place in the visitors' room which had a one-way vision mirror. The practice on the ward initially was to draw the patients' attention to the one-way vision mirror and to explain that the group therapy might or might not be observed at any time.

Table 1. Design

Set of Observations	Group Therapy		Community Meeting	
	With Mike	Without Mike	With Mike	Without Mike
1	$N = 16$	$N = 16$	$N = 13$	$N = 13$
2	$N = 10$	$N = 10$	$N = 10$	$N = 10$

Sixteen patients were each observed twice in this group therapy setting. On one occasion they had the microphone on and knew that what they said was being recorded and that what they did was being observed. On the other occasion they did not have the microphone on, that is, they were not being singled out for observation; however they did know that they might be observed through the one-way vision mirror.

Thirteen of these 16 patients also were each observed twice in the community meeting setting, once with and once without the microphone. The community meetings on the ward always took place in a large dayroom. Patients knew that staff might observe them at any time; however, this observation had to be done by somebody in the room since there was no one-way vision mirror. Ten of the 16 patients were each observed twice more in both the community and group therapy settings. The first set of observations occurred during the first 2 weeks after the patient was hospitalized and the second set of observations occurred during the week or two before the patient was discharged. Since this was part of a larger study in which patients were observed in several other settings, these 10 patients had experienced a number of hours of being observed by the time the second set of observations was done, and thus adaptation effects would have had time to take place.

The behavior observations were done by two observers. The patients knew that they would be observed by one of these observers during the time they had on the microphone. The observers had been trained to categorize and note patient behavior in terms of 16 relatively simple behavior categories.[2]

For group therapy observations the behavior observers sat in back of the room with everyone else and recorded behaviors in full view. The explanation

[2]The 16 categories were: talking, smoking, nodding head yes, shaking head no, looking at speaker, smiling, coughing, playing with an object, scratching or rubbing parts of the body, general shifting, hand movement, clasping hands, talking with hands, arm movement, foot movement, leg movement.

that was given for having two observers recording in the community meeting (since only one patient was wearing the microphone at any one time) was that they were checking their coding reliability.

Subjects

The 16 patients used in this study were selected on the basis of several criteria: *(a)* Their conversation had to be easily understandable. *(b)* They had to be able to cooperate in wearing the microphone and also to be willing to answer a questionnaire about their affective reactions in each setting. *(c)* They had to be on the ward long enough for there to be an opportunity for systematic behavioral change to occur. The average age of the patients was 38.8 years (*SD* = 7.1) and their average education was 13.4 years (*SD* = 1.1). The median length of hospitalization was approximately 3 months and the number of previous hospitalizations ranged 0-5. Eight of the patients carried a primary diagnosis of neurosis; seven carried a primary diagnosis of schizophrenia and one carried a primary diagnosis of character disorder.

Results

Reliability of Behavior Category Observations

The reliability of the observations was established by having the two behavior observers observe and rate for 16 reliability sessions after the period of initial training which included discussion and definition of categories. Behavior rating sheets were made up and the observers' tasks were merely to note when any coded behavior occurred. Coded behaviors were noted only once for each minute of observation.

The 16 reliability sessions were all approximately 20 minutes in length and the two raters' scores were intercorrelated across the 16 settings separately for each category. These reliability correlations were very acceptable, ranging from a low of .77 to a high of .99.

The data were analyzed by utilizing an analysis of variance design. Separate analyses were done for each behavior category for each of the four sets of observations, that is, first and second sets of observations for group therapy and community meeting. Thus there were 64 separate analyses of variance. The between conditions sum of squares gave the variation which was due to whether or not the patients had the microphone. The Conditions X Individuals interaction measured the degree to which the observation conditions had differential effects on different individuals.

Table 2 summarizes the results for the two sets of observations in the group therapy setting. Only one of the 16 categories shows significant observation

Table 2. Summary of Results of Analyses of Variance in Group Therapy and Community Meeting Settings

Behavior Category	Group Therapy				Community Meeting			
	Set 1		Set 2		Set 1		Set 2	
	Observation Condition	Patient × Observation Condition	Observation Condition	Patient × Observation Condition	Observation Condition	Patient × Observation Condition	Observation Condition	Patient × Observation Condition
1. Talking		**	*	**				
2. Smoking								
3. Nodding yes								*
4. Shaking head no		*						
5. Look at speaker		**		**			**	*
6. Smiling		*		**	*	*		
7. Coughing	**	**						
8. Play with object				*		**		
9. Scratch or rub body			**	**	*			
10. General shifting		**		**	*	*		
11. Hand movement			**			*		**
12. Clasping hands		*				*		**
13. Talking with hands		**		**		**		
14. Arm movement				**	*		**	
15. Foot movement		**		**		**		
16. Leg movement		**			*	*		

* $p < .05$.

** $p < .01$.

condition effects for the first set of observations and only three categories show significant effects for the second set of observations. On the other hand, 10 and 9 of the 16 categories, respectively, show significant Observation Condition X Individual Patient interaction effects.

Table 2 also summarizes the findings for the community meeting setting. Five of the 16 categories showed significant Observation Condition effects in the first set of observations and only two showed significant effects in the second set of observations. There were eight significant Patient X Observation Conditions interaction effects in the first set of observations and only four in the second set of observations.

There were two further questions which were investigated. First, what were the actual differences related to the effects of the microphone for those behavior categories which showed statistically significant differences? The results for group therapy indicate that there is a tendency for the amount of hand and finger movement, the amount of talking, and, to a lesser extent, coughing, to increase significantly when the microphone is on, and conversely, for the amount of scratching and rubbing parts of the body to decrease when the patient has the microphone on. The results for community meeting indicate that the amount of leg movement, arm movement, general shifting, scratching or rubbing parts of the body, smiling, and looking at the speaker all tend to decrease when the microphone is on. The general effect of the microphone appears to be to constrain the individual to be somewhat less free to move about, and especially to engage in what might be regarded as purposeless movements. The major exception to this is that in group therapy, where talking is considered to be the most important activity, the number of minutes in which talking occurs increases significantly when the microphone is on. A similar but nonsignificant rise in talking with the microphone was seen in community meeting.

Second, the question arose as to whether the change in behavior from microphone on to microphone off conditions might be related to personality variables. Thus, the absolute change scores (change scores regardless of direction of change) for behavior categories showing significant interaction effects for the first set of observations were correlated with the MMPI scales. There was a tendency for high absolute change scores to correlate negatively with the *K* scale and positively with the *Pd, Pa, Sc,* and *Ma* scales. For example, absolute change scores for leg movement in group therapy correlated – .35, .41, .42, .58, and .67 with these five scales respectively, whereas for the category general shifting in group therapy the correlations were –.41, .58, .50, .61 and .62. These correlations suggest that there may be some tendency for more disturbed individuals to show greater effects of being observed.

Discussion

The results indicate that the average differences between the observation conditions were very small. The majority of behavior categories showed no significant differences between the two observation conditions. These results are consistent with those of Bales (1950), who found no differences in group behavior under different observation conditions, and those of Purcell and Brady (1966), who found that subjects appeared to behave naturally after 2–4 days experience (at only 1 hour per day) with a microphone transmitter. On the other hand, in psychotherapeutic settings, Colby (1960) found significant increases in talk about male figures when a male observer was present, and Roberts and Renzaglia (1965) found differences in clients' positive and negative self statements under three different observation conditions. It is important to note that in the latter study there were no differences in the quantity of talk and the ratio of client-counselor talk under the three conditions. Also, Colby's situation is somewhat artificial since the observer was the only person with whom the subject could attempt to interact, and therefore in this particular situation the observer would be more likely to make an appreciable difference. In general, however, average differences between observation conditions thus far studied tend to be rather small and therefore it may be concluded that they probably do not affect significantly studies in which group comparisons are made. The effects which do occur appear to result in subjects participating more in purposeful and less in purposeless activity.

Even though the average effects of observation conditions are small, individual differences in reaction to being observed are large. Almost half of the Observation Conditions X Individuals interaction effects were significant in this study. In addition, both Haggard, Hiken, and Isaacs (1965) and Purcell and Brady (1966) suggested the possibility of large individual differences. Clearly, different subjects react quite differently to the experience of being observed with a wireless microphone, and therefore it is not possible to draw simple generalizations about the effects of observations on individual behavior. It is likely that individual differences in the new and unfamiliar situation of being observed are related to the individual's characteristic adaptation reactions to new experiences. The phenomenon of individual differences in reaction to different observation conditions will need much further study, especially since it suggests that observational case studies of individual subjects may show large observation effect contaminations.

The suggestive evidence relating to personality characteristics indicates that sicker, more acutely disturbed patients may be more likely to react to wearing the microphone and to being observed. These tentative findings provide one important guideline to identification of the specific characteristics which may relate to individual differences in reaction to observation conditions.

The potential applications of the wireless microphone transmitter as a data-gathering technique already have been discussed in detail by Purcell and Brady (1966). Naturalistic observations with this technique could be utilized systematically to test hypotheses about the actual behavioral and interpersonal correlates of psychological test results, the effects of environmental transitions (for example, transfer from one ward to another) and adaptations to new environments, the effects of various kinds of experimental manipulations, the effects and correlates of different social atmospheres, and the behavioral effects of particular drug dosages or interpersonal relationships, etc. Importantly, experience with the wireless microphone technique in this study indicates that it is definitely a feasible technique for observational studies of psychiatric patients. In order fully to use this and other useful new devices to study behavior naturalistically, it will be important to assess systematically their behavioral effects.

2. HIGH SCHOOL YEARBOOKS: A NONREACTIVE MEASURE OF SOCIAL ISOLATION IN GRADUATES WHO LATER BECAME SCHIZOPHRENIC

Charles N. Barthell and David S. Holmes

Of the numerous hypotheses relating early social experience to the development of schizophrenia, none has been more frequently stated than that of "social isolation" (Faris, 1934; Kohn & Clausen, 1955). This hypothesis suggests that the preschizophrenic personality attempts to avoid painful exposure of his low level of self-esteem by reducing interpersonal contact or by rigidly controlling the nature of the interaction (Auerback, 1959; Sechehaye, 1956; White, 1956; Wolman, 1965). The individual consequently shuts himself off from communicative feedback and thus avails himself of fewer opportunities for reality testing. The avoidance of participation with others makes social participation progressively more difficult and the individual falls further and further behind his peers in the development of social skills. It has been specifically suggested that "at adolescence, when various new social skills are required, such

SOURCE. Charles N. Barthell, at the time of publication of this article, was a graduate student in psychology at Northwestern University. David S. Holmes, who was formerly on the faculties of Northwestern University and the University of Texas, is now a member of the Personality and Social Behavior Group at the Educational Testing Service in Princeton, New Jersey. Dr. Holmes' interests are in the area of personality, personality assessment, and psychopathology. This article originally appeared in the *Journal of Abnormal Psychology,* 1968, **73,** 313-316 and is reprinted by permission of the American Psychological Association and the authors.

individuals are likely to drop fatally out of step and still further restrict their future development" (White, 1956, p. 530).

A number of studies have been conducted to determine the extent of social isolation among preschizophrenics while in high school (i.e., during adolescence). Schofield and Balian (1959) found that preschizophrenics when compared with a "normal" control group could be characterized by "higher rates of social withdrawal, lack of social adeptness and poise, and narrow interests." Further support for the social isolation hypothesis is provided by Bower, Shellhamer and Daily (1960) who found that with few exceptions preschizophrenics could be characterized as "tending toward the shut-in, withdrawing kind of personality." Finally, Kohn and Clausen (1955) found that roughly one-third of their schizophrenic sample reported a sufficient lack of activities and friendship patterns to lead the authors to classify them as isolates or partial isolates, whereas only 4 per cent of the normals reported such patterns.

Although the above studies provide support for the social isolation hypothesis, an equal number of studies throw some doubt on its tenability. Bellak and Parcell (1964) found that in their study of the prepsychotic personalities of 100 cases diagnosed dementia praecox, "35 had distinctly extrovert prepsychotic personalities, 28 had distinctly introvert prepsychotic personalities, and 37 had to be considered ambivert, or a mixture between extroversion and introversion." Morris, Soroker and Burrus (1954) evaluated the current adjustment of 54 individuals who when seen in a clinic 16 to 27 years previously had been described as "internal reactors." They found that these individuals were "relatively free of overt mental or emotional illness and getting along quite well." Lastly, in the follow-up study of Michael, Morris and Soroker (1957), only one of the ten *Ss* who carried the diagnosis of schizophrenia as an adult had been classed as an introvert from the social history collected at childhood.

It is clear then that there are inconsistencies and points of disagreement in the literature on the relationship between schizophrenia and social withdrawal in the prepsychotic personality. One criticism of the previous studies, and a possible source of the inconsistencies, lies in the fact that in most studies the patient's social history was compiled by interviewing relatives and acquaintances after the patient had become psychotic, i.e., retrospectively. This leaves the studies subject to a number of errors. First of all, inaccuracies may result from the fact that reliable informants may be difficult if not impossible to find and their reports may have been distorted or changed with the passage of time. Secondly, if the *S* had been identified as a patient (either as an adult or as a child who was later followed up), informants may have been influenced in their reporting by what they had heard about mental disorders. Lastly, those studies in which information was gathered from patients may suffer from the disadvantage of information being unreliable due to the patient's disorder and feelings about hospitalization.

Webb, Campbell, Schwartz and Sechrest (1966) have recently outlined the value of using "nonreactive measures" such as archival material which would not be distorted by the passage of time or by the measurement process. With these measures there is no masking or sensitivity as there may be when the producer of the data knows he is being studied by some social scientist. According to Webb et al. (1966), "this gain by itself makes the use of archives attractive if one wants to compensate for the reactivity which riddles the interview and the questionnaire." In the present study, the activity summaries found in high school yearbooks were used as a means of determining the relative social isolation of the preschizophrenic and prepsychoneurotic individual.

Method

Subjects

A group of 20 hospitalized schizophrenics (14 males and 6 females) and a group of 20 hospitalized psychoneurotics (14 males and 6 females) were selected from the medical records of the Illinois State Psychiatric Institute. The criteria applied in subject selection were the following: (1) All *S*s were born between the years 1934 and 1944; (2) All *S*s graduated from Chicago area high schools between the years 1952 and 1962; (3) No *S* was selected who had been hospitalized within two years following the date of his high school graduation; (4) No schizophrenic patient was selected whose hospital stay was less than three months. The two year period following graduation and prior to hospitalization was thought necessary in order to insure the fact that *S*s were not overtly or incapacitatingly schizophrenic or neurotic while attending high school at which time the data was recorded. Schizophrenic *S*s hospitalized for less than three months were excluded on the grounds that their schizophrenic break was more likely to be of a reactive nature, and less likely to be the culmination of a long-term developmental process.

A "normal" control group was selected using the method introduced by Bower, Shellhamer and Daily (1960). At the time that data was being recorded from the yearbooks of the schizophrenic and psychoneurotic *S*s, data was also collected for the student pictured next to him. This rule was followed unless the student pictured next to the patient *S* was of a different sex, of a different race, or of the same name indicating the possibility of a family relationship. In such cases, the next student pictured was selected as the control *S*. Thus, for every schizophrenic or psychoneurotic *S* from a given high school, there was a control *S* from the same high school, graduating in the same year, and free to choose from the same number and types of activities offered by the high school at that time.

Procedure

A list of all of the activities engaged in by each *S* was taken from the index and/or the senior summary of each *S*'s senior yearbook. Only high school graduates were used in this study since it is only in the senior year of high school that any extensive record is set down of the students' activities in school. At the time of the data collection, the *E* knew to which group any one *S* belonged. Therefore, for each *S* the entire list of activites was copied verbatim and was later analyzed blindly. Following the collection of the data, each *S*'s activities were classified into one of the following categories; (1) social activities, (2) service activities, (3) performance activities, and (4) athletic activities. Those activities classified as social included all clubs, organizations and activities whose primary purpose was a social one. Examples of activities classified as such included student council or student government organizations, language, academic or special interest clubs, and student publications. Those activities classified as service activities included activities in which some service was performed for the high school. Such activities were of the type that necessitated very little social interaction. Examples of activities classified under this heading included: hall guard, office helper, library assistant, teacher's aide and the like. Performance activities included musical or dramatic organizations, while athletic activities included all individual and team sports as well as intramurals and athletic associations. There was a 95 per cent agreement between two independent judges on the classification of all of the activities into the above categories.

Results and Discussions

Number of Activities

An analysis of variance was performed to test the significance of sex, diagnostic category, type of activity and the interaction of these variables as related to number of activities participated in by *S*s. The results of this analysis are presented in Table 1. Both the variables of diagnostic category and type of activity were significant ($p < .01$). In light of the significant F for diagnostic categories, Kramer's Multiple Range Test (1956) for means based on unequal Ns was used to test the mean differences over all activities for the three diagnostic groups. The results of this analysis are presented in Table 2. This analysis indicated that the mean number of activities participated in by schizophrenics, as well as psychoneurotics, differs significantly from the mean number of activities for the control group ($p < .01$). There was, however, no significant difference found between the mean number of activities for the schizophrenic and psychoneurotic groups, although the difference was in the expected direction.

Table 1. Analysis of Variance Summary Table

Source of Variation	*df*	*SS*	*MS*	*F*
Sex	1	10.29	10.29	2.32
Diagnostic Category	2	44.41	22.21	5.01*
Sex x Diagnostic Category	2	1.32	.66	.15
*S*s / SD Groups	74	327.60	4.43	X
Type of Activity	3	102.08	34.03	17.54*
Activity x Sex	3	14.66	4.89	2.52
Activity x Diagnostic Cat.	6	4.99	.83	.43
Activity x Sex x Diag. Cat.	6	7.70	1.28	.66
Activity x *S*s / SD Groups	222	430.82	1.94	X
Total	319	943.87		

* $p < .01$

Table 2. Significant Ranges for Kramer's Extension of Duncan's New Multiple Range Test

Mean Number of High School Activities

Group:	Schizophrenic	Neurotic	Normal
Means:	3.75	4.00	6.95

Mean Number of Social Activities

Group:	Schizophrenic	Neurotic	Normal
Means:	1.60	1.95	2.83

Mean Number of Service Activities

Group:	Schizophrenic	Neurotic	Normal
Means:	.75	.85	1.55

Mean Number of Performance Activities

Group:	Schizophrenic	Neurotic	Normal
Means:	.65	.40	1.20

Mean Number of Athletic Activities

Group:	Schizophrenic	Neurotic	Normal
Means:	.75	.80	1.80

Note. Any two means not underlined by the same line are significantly different at the .01 level. Any two means underlined by the same line are not significantly different.

While schizophrenic subjects were found to differ significantly from "normals" in the mean number of activities in which they participated, it is of interest to note that the mean number of activities for the schizophrenic group did not differ significantly from that of the psychoneurotic group. On the basis of these findings, one is forced to conclude, then that both hospitalized groups showed a tendency toward withdrawal and isolation when compared to the control group. It is important to remember, however, that the psychoneurotics used in this study were all hospitalized. Since psychoneurotics do not as a general rule require hospitalization, it might be that the psychoneurotics in this sample could be considered more severely disturbed than psychoneurotics in general. This fact might explain the similarity found between the two patient groups.

Type of Activity

A number of analyses on the mean differences between social, service, performance and athletic activities for the three *S* groups were performed, again using Kramer's Multiple Range Test. The results of these analyses are presented in the lower part of Table 2. Significant differences were found between the mean number of social activities for the schizophrenic and normal groups ($p < .01$) while the mean of the psychoneurotic group fell between those of the schizophrenics and normals but did not differ significantly from either. There were no significant differences found between the means of the three groups on any of the other activity classifications: service, performance, or athletic activities.

From this data, it would appear then that social activity level forms a continuum with schizophrenics and normals falling at the extreme ends while psychoneurotics fall in the middle. It is important to note that there were no significant differences between the groups on any of the other types of activities considered. That is, it was only when *social* activities per se were considered that schizophrenics were found to fall behind their peers in level of participation. This fact seems an important finding and lends support to those investigators who hypothesize that the individual who becomes schizophrenic is socially withdrawn and introverted during adolescence.

In general the results of this research which employed a nonreactive measure offered support for those studies which have found that individuals who became schizophrenic were less active in the social realm prior to being diagnosed as schizophrenic. Social isolation may not, however, be unique to schizophrenics; for in the present study, psychoneurotics evidenced a similar trend.

3. COMMENT ON "HIGH SCHOOL YEARBOOKS: A NONREACTIVE MEASURE OF SOCIAL ISOLATION IN GRADUATES WHO LATER BECAME SCHIZOPHRENIC"[1]

J. Conrad Schwarz

The article by Barthell and Holmes (1968) on social isolation in high school students who later became schizophrenic stated clearly the advantages of non-reactive archival measures in studies attempting to elucidate the behavioral antecedents of schizophrenia. However, the study itself, while employing dependent variables and data coding procedures which were free of many potential sources of bias, lacked crucial and customary precautions in the selection of a control group. The control group consisted of those individuals pictured next to each schizophrenic *S* in his high school yearbook, provided that the next pictured individual was like the schizophrenic *S* in sex and race and unlike in family name. While it can be argued that this procedure constituted an essentially random method of selecting control *S*s from the respective high schools, the basic question is whether a random sample is an adequate control group. It would seem not, in view of the fact that the schizophrenic *S*s were clearly not a random sample of the individuals who had attended the respective high schools.

There is good reason to expect that the schizophrenic sample would differ from the control sample on variables other than those uniquely associated with schizophrenia. First, the higher incidence of schizophrenia and of long-term hospitalization for schizophrenia among the lowest social classes (Hardt & Feinhandler, 1959) suggests that the social class level of the schizophrenic group, all of whom were hospitalized more than 3 mo., may have been lower than that of the control group. Second, there is evidence of intellectual inferiority among preschizophrenics during the elementary and secondary school years, long before the appearance of clinical symptoms of schizophrenia (Albee, Lane, & Reuter, 1964). Third, the schizophrenic *S*s were selected from those hospitalized in the Chicago area who also attended Chicago area high schools. The limited mobility of

SOURCE. J. Conrad Schwarz received his doctoral degree in psychology at Ohio State University. He is currently Associate Professor of Psychology at Syracuse University, with specialized interests in the fields of social learning theory, personality development, and psychopathology. This article originally appeared in the *Journal of Abnormal Psychology,* 1970, **75,** 317-318. Reprinted by permission of the American Psychological Association and the author.

[1]The author wishes to express his appreciation to Norman F. Watt of Harvard University for his helpful comments on a prior draft of this note.

the schizophrenic sample may be associated with a lower educational, intellectual, and social class level than found in the control sample which had no mobility restriction. (See Mednick & McNeil, 1968, for a discussion of problems associated with the "childhood records method.")

In view of the activities classified in the study as "social," namely, participation in "student council or government organizations; language, academic, or special-interest clubs; and student publication [Barthell & Holmes, p. 314]," it is all the more important that the authors either provide evidence that participation in social activities is independent of intelligence, academic achievement, and social class or show that the schizophrenic and control groups did not differ on the latter variables. Of course, if evidence for either of these conditions were provided, the current interpretation of their findings would be greatly strengthened. However, if one of the variables of intelligence, social class, or achievement were found to be related to social participation and the two groups also differed on that variable, a re-analysis of the data incorporating either statistical or classificatory controls for that variable would be desirable. Hopefully, the investigators may still be able to obtain the additional information which would permit a more definitive test of the hypothesis under investigation.

4. SITUATIONAL TESTS IN METROPOLITAN POLICE RECRUIT SELECTION

Robert B. Mills, Robert J. McDevitt, and Sandra Tonkin

The emerging profession of law enforcement, as it is perceived in municipal police departments, has started to place greater emphasis upon selection of recruit material. Although the problem of attracting qualified candidates for law enforcement careers in sufficient numbers persists, the emphasis upon care in initial selection reflects recognition of the critical and complex demands placed upon the modern metropolitan police officer. The complexity of the challenge of competent law enforcement in our cities has, in turn, stimulated interest in the psychological procedures used to predict productive police performance.

A recent survey of assessment procedures used in 55 cities of the U.S. having populations greater than 150,000 revealed that all cities utilized some type of

SOURCE. Robert B. Mills is Professor and Head of the Department of Enforcement and Corrections in the new College of Community Services of the University of Cincinnati. Robert J. McDevitt is a practicing psychiatrist and Head of the Psychiatry Service at Good Samaritan Hospital in Cincinnati. At the time of publication of this article Sandra Tonkin was a graduate student in psychology at the University of Cincinnati. This article originally appeared in the *Journal of Criminal Law, Criminology, and Police Science,* 1966, **57,** 99-106. The article is reprinted by special permission of the *Journal,* the Northwestern University School of Law, and the authors.

psychological test(s); in addition, 16% of the cities also added a psychiatric interview of some type (Narrol & Levitt, 1963). Of the police departments surveyed, 85% reported use of an objective test specifically intended to assess aptitude for police work. However, analysis of 12 typical "police aptitude" tests showed them to be little more than unstandardized intelligence tests. A typical finding was that 90% of the score variance in a policeman test was attributable to general intelligence (Pounian, 1959). Only 12 cities reported use of any personality tests, and psychiatric interviews were often limited to a single interview, and then only with questionable candidates. Research was reported by only one city, according to the Narrol and Levitt survey.

Certainly the multiple responsibilities of the metropolitan police officer have made it increasingly difficult to define his field performance as a unitary function. But to limit selection procedures to measures of general intelligence, either in standardized form or disguised as "police aptitude" tests, may be an inadequate response to the assessment challenge. It seems likely that tests which include a general intelligence factor will continue to correlate with most measures of police performance, and will therefore continue to serve a useful function as a screening device. Their so-called "objectivity" and face validity recommended them to Civil Service Boards and similar hiring bodies.

However, the sole reliance upon paper-and-pencil intelligence-type tests leaves much to be desired. Critical motivational-emotional-personality dimensions are untapped. Whether these personality dimensions can be adequately sampled by the addition of standardized personality inventories to the test battery is questionable, despite the ingenuity of our test-makers. Since most personality tests were standardized on different populations from police recruits, a questionable extrapolation to the recruit group must be attempted. In addition, the police candidate seems even more guarded than the average job applicant, so that his test responses are hard to interpret, and hardly typical of his usual functioning. At best, objective personality inventories seem best suited for preliminary screening to pinpoint rather obvious pathology.

It would seem, therefore, that a technique(s) for assessment of non-intellectual functioning which has demonstrated relevance to police performance in the field is needed.

There is also reason to suspect that not every police candidate can translate his intelligence, as measured by paper-and-pencil tests, into equally intelligent decision-making in a field situation. Under stress some men are known to become paralyzed by anxiety, while others may flee, and some indulge in ill-advised impetuous behavior. This quality of clear-headed intelligent action under pressure was termed *"effective"* intelligence by the evaluation staff of the O.S.S. in WWII (O.S.S., 1948).

Other personality variables assessed by the O.S.S. staff are worth nothing because of their relevance to police field performance. They include *motivation for assignment, emotional stability, social relations, energy and initiative, leadership, observing and reporting, physical ability, propaganda skills, and maintaining security.* In the book, *Assessment of Men,* written by the O.S.S. staff, a wide variety of situational tasks are reported used to select personnel for military intelligence duties.

The unique advantages of situational-type tests were summarized by Cronbach in his book, *Essentials of Psychological Testing,* as follows:

> The greatest advantage of the test observation is that it makes possible the observation of characteristics which appear only infrequently in normal activities . . . characteristics such as bravery, reaction to frustration, and dishonesty. A single situational test may reveal more about such a trait than weeks of field observation. Second, the subject's desire to make a good impression does not invalidate the test. In fact, just because he is anxious to make a good impression, he reveals more about his personality than would normally appear . . . The third advantage of the situational test is that it comes closer than other techniques to a standardized measure of typical behavior . . . Situational and projective tests may be the only truly valid testing approach to personality.

Chenoweth (1961) has advocated the adoption of situational testing programs in police selection, and reported use of a test adapted from the O.S.S. in a police training program in Anchorage, Alaska. However, no other published reports of use of situational tests in police selection have appeared.

The Cincinnati Recruit Selection Program

It was decided to include in the test battery, on an experimental basis, several situational tests for the police recruit selection program in Cincinnati. Such tests were an addition to objective and projective tests of personality, and a separate prior program of intelligence examination, physical examination, oral interview, polygraph, and character investigation, which has been described elsewhere (Mills, McDevitt, & Tonkin, 1964). The situational tests, except for the Bull Session, did not enter into consideration of the overall final ratings of candidates. Situational tests were administered in the course of an intensive 5-6 hour psychological evaluation session conducted in small groups of 8-10 candidates. The intent of the situational tests was to create a microcosm of a "natural" field problem an officer might encounter, and to observe closely the candidate's reaction and performance under stress.[1]

[1]The assistance of Col. Stanley R. Schrotel, Chief, Cincinnati Police Division; W. Donald Heisel, City Personnel Officer; and Lt. Col. Robert Klug, Asst. Chief & Personnel Director, is gratefully acknowledged for administrative support and facilities to carry out the program.

In designing the behavior sample for the tests, the following criteria were relevant:

(a) The tasks should have a close relation to an activity in which an officer might commonly be engaged in the typical performance of his duties.

(b) The tasks should present a standard stimulus situation to each candidate. Conditions should not vary, if possible.

(c) Each situational task should have several alternate solutions.

(d) The accomplishment of the tasks should not require very specialized abilities, so that no candidate will be handicapped by lack of experience.

(e) The tests should be complex and difficult enough to engage the candidate, and stressful enough to produce a variety of emotional reactions. In short, the level of complexity and stress should differentiate between candidates. At the same time, care must be exercised not to harm or alienate candidates, since these young men are voluntarily presenting themselves as police candidates.

(f) If possible, some measure involving group activity should be included. While difficulties in measuring performance are greatly increased, the competition to achieve, the leadership qualities which emerge, and the capacity for teamwork make a group task extremely illuminating.

(g) Techniques should be devised for both quantitative and qualitative measurement, and for direct measures of performance from the candidate, as well as behavior ratings by a staff observer.

(h) A "de-briefing" session should be provided in order to establish an emotional climate of high morale, to encourage expression of anger or anxiety, and to help restore emotional equilibrium in a friendly atmosphere. This chance to "blow off steam" is quite valuable in providing clues to typical modes of relieving anxiety.

(i) Staff observers should have ample opportunity to confer after completion of a testing session. This gives the staff time to synthesize observations on behavior, reconcile differences, and arrive at final overall ratings of the candidates with a maximum of information on each man.

The initial trial of situational tests in the Cincinnati program included three tasks, which have been termed the Foot Patrol Observation Test, the Clues Test, and the Bull Session. They can be described as follows:

I. Foot Patrol Observation Test.

Candidates were instructed to report, at staggered intervals, to a location in City Hall. A sheet of instructions was then given to the candidates which required them to proceed on foot, unaccompanied, to the Police Administration Building. They were advised to observe closely everything along the route, since questions might be asked about anything they may have observed along the way. The prescribed route was marked with chalked arrows on the sidewalk at each intersection, but this fact was omitted from the instruction sheet, since it was one of the points of inquiry after arrival (almost 50% of the candidates failed to note the arrows). The route proceeded for about 6 blocks through a busy, downtown, predominantly Negro business section. Upon arrival at the Police Administration Building, where the balance of the testing was carried out, the elapsed time of their "patrol" was noted, and a two-part questionnaire administered. The first part consisted of 25 multiple-choice questions of fact concerning number of intersections traversed, location of key stores, type of street lights, color of plugs, type of paving in street, and similar observations. Two typical questions were as follows:

24. The flag pole before Police Headquarters bears the inscription
    a. "Commemorating those who have given their lives in the performance of their sacred duty"
    b. "Cincinnati Police"
    c. "Police Division Headquarters, City of Cincinnati"
    d. the flag pole bears no inscription at all
12. The fire lane designated along Central Avenue (due to fire station located on Court Street) is located
    a. in the right hand curb lane
    b. in the left hand curb lane
    c. in the center lane
    d. there is no fire lane on Central Avenue

Candidates were asked to complete these 25 questions, without guessing, and the number of correct answers became their score on the test.

The second part of the questionnaire was an open-ended essay designed to tap latent attitudes about law enforcement, minority groups, and motivation for a police career, as well as provide a written sample of grammar, spelling, and ability to express oneself. For example, candidates were asked to describe their impressions of the persons living in the neighborhood through which they had passed, and to describe their feelings about "keeping the peace" in this section. These replies were qualitatively evaluated by the staff, discussed informally with the candidates, and deviant replies marked for later comment during the Bull Session.

II. Clues Test

This situational test was adapted from the "Belongings" test described in *Assessment of Men.* A work area was roped off, consisting of a desk, chair, calendars, and miscellaneous office equipment. Within this area a carefully selected set of "clues" were planted which suggested certain hypotheses about the personality, habits, whereabouts, and possible flight of a hypothetical City employee who was supposed to have worked at the desk. Race-track sheets,

Scotch bottles, tranquilizers and aspirins, "cold" checks, dunning letters from local jewelry stores, perfumed love letters, a pay voucher, a passport application, and a memo from the City Manager requiring audit of accounts were included.[2]

Candidates were instructed to investigate the mysterious disappearance of this hypothetical employee. They were given 10 minutes, and encouraged to take notes. A staff member, working quietly in another part of the room, observed the candidate's approach to the task, and encouraged inquiries and expressions of attitude about the test.

Each candidate then filled blank spaces in a questionnaire requiring information ranging from simple factual data which could be taken from notes, to hypotheses (more heavily weighted) on whereabouts, motives for leaving job, probable mental state, and possible basis for prosecution. Alternative inferences could be developed from false leads which were included. A final score from 0-60 points was derived from the Clues Test.

III. Bull Session

The so-called "Bull Session" was a group diagnostic procedure adapted from a technique practiced by one of the authors (R. McD.) for several years in screening applicants for a religious missionary organization. The Bull Session borrows heavily from the principles of group psychotherapy. It is believed to possess unique advantages over the conventional one-to-one interview, in that it frees up inhibitions and defenses, spurs competitive participation with other group members while offering group support for greater self-revelation. The Bull Session also provided an opportunity for observing interaction of candidates with their peers, an important feature in police work. Lastly, it provided a "de-briefing" effect, where candidates could ventilate their reactions to the arduous psychological testing session preceding, and restore their emotional equilibrium.

All candidates from each testing session, 8 to 10 in number, were assembled following a dinner break, and offered coffee and cigarettes during the two-hour Bull Session. Seats were offered randomly around a large table in a comfortably furnished conference room in Police Headquarters. The evaluation team,[3] consisting of two group leaders and two observers, had been briefed previously on each candidate, with special attention to weaknesses spotted during testing. Observers were instructed not to be drawn into discussion, so that possible paranoid reactions to their presence could be elicited.

The group leaders initiated discussion by going around the table asking for introductions, present occupation, and reasons for choosing a police career.

[2]The guidance of Lt. Stanley Carle, Crime Bureau, was utilized in assembling the "clues".

[3]In addition to the author, John Schengber, M.D. and Kenneth Kuntz, M.A. served on the evaluation team.

Generally, discussion proceeded spontaneously from that point, with the group leaders raising key issues of police work, calling upon silent candidates from time to time, and occasionally pointing out that participation by each candidate was necessary in order to understand his point of view. A typical session might include discussion of use of force, the handling of fear, alcoholism, use of narcotics, mental illness, prostitution, homosexuality, administration of justice through the courts, minority groups, and the use of authority. Questions were usually posed in terms of personal experiences or hypothetical situations of a practical, concrete nature sometimes faced by a patrolman.

On some occasions candidates expressed fear of self-incrimination which might be prejudicial to their future careers with the Police Division. At such times the evaluation teams' policy of confidentiality was carefully emphasized. Information generated during psychological testing was used only to report an "acceptable" or "recommended for rejection" opinion to the Civil Service Commission, with no "feedback" to the police organization. This policy served to reassure the candidate during evaluation, and maintained the independence of our confidential predictions of future police performance made by the evaluation team. These predictions are being validated against future performance data, and will be reported later.

No separate set of ratings was derived from the Bull Session. However, immediately after each of these diagnostic sessions, the entire team met to make Overall Performance Prediction ratings (OPP) on each recruit. Group participation was evaluated, and synthesized with a summary of all previous testing procedures. Differences between evaluation staff members were discussed and resolved, and a final rating assigned. Occasional disagreements or personal predictions about some aspect of performance were separately recorded.

The OPP ratings, which included intelligence examination, objective and projective personality tests, the Bull Session, and behavior notes, were classified on a five-point rating scale as follows:

Rating	*Performance Prediction*	*Action Recommended to Civil Service Commission*
4	Superior	Acceptable (4–1)
3	Above Average	
2	Average	
1	Below Average	
0	High Risk	Rejection

Results

The situational tests, as part of a comprehensive screening program, were initially administered in 1964 to a group of 62 Cincinnati police candidates. Of this group, 42 eventually completed their recruit training in the Police Academy, and were termed the "success" group; 20 did not accomplish police training, and were termed the "failure" group.[4] The Army General Classification Test, Civilian Edition, which is routinely administered to all candidates by the City Personnel Dept., was included as a reference measure, since it is a standardized test known to correlate with police performance. The Foot Patrol and Clues Tests were not included in OPP ratings in order to test their possible value as independent predictors.

Results are shown in Table 1. As can be seen, the successful candidates scored somewhat higher on all measures, as might be anticipated. However, differences between the groups failed to reach statistical significance, when a t ratio was computed to assess mean differences.

The completion of Police Academy training by the 42 "successful" candidates (Group A) afforded the first opportunity to test the predictive validity of the situational tests. AGCT scores were again included as a reference measure. Two performance measures were derived from Police Academy records: The first was the final rank of each candidate in his class, a weighted measure based upon weekly examinations and notebooks during the training period; the second was his rank based upon scores in the Cincinnati Combat Course (CCC), a pistol markmanship trial. The CCC can be visualized as a situational test in its own right, and is therefore of interest as a comparative measure with other situational tests. Scores on Foot Patrol, Clues, and AGCT were ranked for the 42 candidates, and Spearman rank-order correlations computed to determine possible relationships between these measures.

Results are shown in the correlation matrix of Table 2. It was demonstrated that AGCT scores, as a measure of general intelligence, correlated rather highly with final Police Academy standing, and this was significant at the .01 level of

Table 1. Test Performance of "Success" and "Failure" Candidates (Group A)

	"Success" Group Mean (N = 42)	"Failure" Group Mean (N = 20)	Mean Diff.	t ratio	Signif.
Foot Patrol	14.7	14.0	.7	.17	NS
Clues	31.2	26.2	5.0	.597	NS
AGCT	125.5	122.5	3.0	.09	NS

[4] 12 were recommended for rejection by our evaluation team; 6 were acceptable but not appointed as recruits; and 2 resigned before completing the Police Academy.

Table 2. Rank-order Correlations of Successful Candidates on Situational, Intelligence, and Performance Measures (Group A)

	Foot Patrol	Clues Test	AGCT	CCC	Pol. Acad. Standing
Foot Patrol	–				
Clues Test	.099	–			
AGCT	.211	.105	–		
CCC	–.153	–.063	–.052	–	
Pol. Acad. Standing	.137	.375*	.595**	.093	–

N = 42
* Significant at .05 level
** Significant at .01 level

probability. The Clues Test also correlated positively with Police Academy standing, significant at the .05 level of probability. Neither Foot Patrol nor CCC correlated with final Academy grades, and none of the three situational measures correlated signficantly with each other. Tests of situational measures against field performance are not yet available.

In order to cross-validate results of the initial trial, an identical test battery was administered to a second group of 25 candidates (Group B). Fifteen candidates completed Police Academy training, and 10 did not accomplish this goal.[5] As Table 3 indicates, mean differences on AGCT scores were almost identical with Group A, but the failure to replicate mean differences on the Clues Test was disappointing. No mean differences were of statistical significance.

Table 3. Test Performance of "Success" and "Failure" Candidates (Group B)

	"Success" Group Mean (N = 15)	"Failure" Group Mean (N = 10)	Mean Diff.	Signif.
Foot Patrol	15.1	14.8	.3	NS
Clues	30.7	30.7	–	NS
AGCT Score	125.3	122.4	2.9	NS

The performance of the second recruit group (Group B) in the Police Academy substantially confirmed findings on the first group regarding predictive efficiency of tests: the AGCT score correlated .708 with final standing in the

[5] 3 were recommended for rejection by our evaluation staff; 6 were acceptable but not appointed as recruits; and 1 withdrew before completing Academy training.

Police Academy, which is significant at the .01 level of probability; the Clues Test correlated .425 with final standing, which just missed the .05 level of significance; the Foot Patrol Test again failed to show any relationship with Police Academy performance. These results are seen in Table 4. On the second trial, Foot Patrol and Clues correlated .522 with each other, which is significant at the .05 level of probability, a finding which did not appear on the first trial.

Table 4. Rank-order Correlations of Successful Candidates on Situational, Intelligence, and Performance Measures (Group B)

	Foot Patrol	Clues Test	AGCT	Pol. Acad. Standing
Foot Patrol	–			
Clues Test	.522*	–		
AGCT	.025	.340	–	
Police Acad. Standing	.159	.425#	.708**	–

N = 15
* Significant at .05 level
** Significant at .01 level
#Significant at .10 level; just misses .05 level

Bull Session Results

Evaluation of the Bull Sessions must be indirect, since no separate measurement resulted from these sessions. However, staff members agreed that the Bull Session was the single most valuable technique used in recruit selection, and weighted it heavily in the Overall Performance Prediction ratings (OPP) made by the team. Therefore, the correlation between our predictions and the recruit's actual performance in the Police Academy might be used as an estimate of the efficiency of the Bull Session as a predictor. For this purpose, the Kendall rank-order correlation (*tau*) was used owing to the restricted ranks on the 5-place OPP ratings. Results were converted to z scores, and level of significance read from a table of normal distribution (See Siegel, 1956).

For the initial recruit group a Kendall rank-order correlation of .359 was obtained between OPP ratings and final standing in Police Academy, which has a probability beyond the .0005 level. For the second group a correlation of .473 was obtained, which is significant beyond the .007 level of probability. It was concluded that the evaluation team's overall ratings were highly efficient at predicting Police Academy performance. By implication, the Bull Session accounted for a rather large proportion of the accuracy of prediction.

Unsuspected character traits and attitudes which had not been noted during previous tests and one-to-one interviewing sometimes emerged during the Bull

Session. For example, a group leader proposed a hypothetical situation in which a patrolman, working alone in a "rough" neighborhood, encountered several men fighting in a cafe. The question was asked, "If you were that patrolman, what would you do?" As general discussion developed around this theme, a consensus was quickly reached that the lone officer should summon aid before committing himself to stopping the fight, even though it might mean walking away from the scene to summon assistance.

One candidate vociferously disagreed with this solution, insisting that "You'd never be able to show your face again on that beat if you walked away." When he was challenged by several candidates with previous Military Police experience, he became red in the face and sat glowering with clenched fists. Another group member finally offered the comment, "I'd never want to be on patrol with you, buddy, that would be a good way to get myself killed." At this point, the isolated candidate exploded, "I think all of you guys are a bunch of yellow-backs!" This explosive outburst was a valuable clue in establishing the poor judgment and emotional instability of this candidate under stress; the stubborn pseudomasculinity he displayed within the group was almost a promise of inappropriate behavior in Police service.

On another occasion a candidate displayed very rigid and dogmatic attitudes on every issue and as the group began to warm up, he commenced to orate in an almost evangelical manner. This man, quietly referred to as "the preacher" by another group member, began to set everyone's teeth on edge, and they attempted to stop him by sarcasm and talking over him. However, this candidate, apparently insensitive to the reactions of the men around him, continued to rant about his pet religious beliefs, and to moralize about the duty of the policeman to correct moral injustices in the community. This candidate's reaction formation against his own unrecognized hostile impulses toward his fellow-citizens would have made him an unreliable and sadistic officer, and the other candidates quickly sensed how difficult it would be to work alongside this fellow.

In some cases a candidate was encountered who appeared to be unable to organize his thoughts in any coherent fashion during the group sessions. Some of these men had previously performed adequately on paper-and-pencil tests, but in the Bull Session became disorganized, rambling, and circumstantial. They were unable to react in a realistic and appropriate fashion to the other group members, and displayed completely inadequate social judgment in their responses to questions about practical matters. The evaluation team suspected that these candidates were making a borderline psychotic social adjustment, and sought a police career to give themselves a firmer self-identity and to move toward a more assertive role in life.

These examples have been given to illustrate the usefulness of the Bull Session in confirming psychological test signs whose meaning may have been somewhat tenuous, and in ferreting out behavior not revealed by conventional methods.

Discussion

It appears promising that a simple situational task (Clues) could be constructed on *a priori* basis, and on its initial trials manage to correlate with a performance measure (Police Academy standing). The correlations (.595 and .708) of an intelligence test with Police Academy performance are not unexpected, since the AGCT and similar instruments are widely used for police selection, and have regularly proven their usefulness. However, the failure of the Clues Test and AGCT to correlate with each other (.105 and .340) significantly, despite their demonstrated relationship to Police Academy success, raises some interesting speculations. It seems reasonable to infer that situational tests of the Clues type may be sampling behavioral dimensions not represented in paper-and-pencil intelligence tests.

It may be premature to speculate further on just what behavioral constructs are sampled by situational measures. It is characteristic of situational tasks to require a broad spectrum of skills for their solution. In fact, their life-like quality comes from this breadth. If situational tests can be devised within a setting of continuous research and cross-checks with eventual performance, they can be an interesting supplement to more conventional techniques.

The failure of the Foot Patrol Test to correlate with other measures may represent the narrow range of scores obtained or other inadequacies of test construction, and illustrates the pitfalls of attempting untried tests without reliability or validity checks. The selection process occurred with a highly homogeneous, pre-selected group from an original pool of more than 600 applicants, which places a severe task upon any unverified test instrument.

The limitations of using final grades in a Police Academy training program must also be recognized. It is not necessary to document here the disappointing patrol performance of some men who showed promise during the training period. And later, even the most painstaking rating system in the field is subject to multiple biases. For example, it is common practice to start "rookie" patrolmen with rather low ratings of efficiency, so that adequate differentiation between field performance of starting patrolmen becomes quite difficult. A weighted measure of activity level based upon systematic reports of arrests, citations, etc. is under study by the authors, and this activity field measure may ultimately vindicate the situational test approach to selection.

It may be important to note that, despite the rigor of the selection process, no candidate has yet withdrawn or failed to complete the psychological evaluation phase of selection. Candidates have reported that they enjoyed the life-like quality of the situational tests, thought this type of test "made sense" to them, and apparently preferred the action-centered tests to the conventional paper-and-pencil approach. Some candidates have expressed the feeling that the careful evaluation reflected the importance of the position they were seeking, and that finalists must be a hand-picked "elite" group, which is true. The group spirit generated during the Bull Session, with its overtones of competition and camaraderie, tended to counteract any anger or anxiety caused by the protracted testing session. The teasing and joking with examiners was an emotional catharsis which seemed to be helpful in restoring emotional equilibrium.

Summary

Three situational tests, analogous to tests used to select OSS personnel in WWII, were devised as part of an overall psychological evaluation program for Cincinnati police candidates. Tests were termed Foot Patrol Observation Test, Clues Test, and Bull Session. These tests were administered to two groups of candidates, and correlated with final rank in class after completion of Police Academy training. The Clues Test was significantly correlated with Police Academy performance, but not with an intelligence measure (AGCT), which suggested that non-intellectual traits important to police performance may be tapped with situational tests. The Bull Session, indirectly measured by its close tie with successful predictions by the evaluation team of Police Academy performance, was also judged to be an important measure of emotional-motivational traits predictive of superior police performance in the field. The third situational task, Foot Patrol Observation Test, did not appear to be predictive of later success in training.

Further validation of the situational test technique is necessary to establish its value in police candidate assessment, and a weighted activity rating of field performance of patrolmen is under study for later report. However, situational testing shows promise as a supplement to conventional paper-and-pencil procedures for police selection, if adequate reliability and validity studies can establish its usefulness.

5. USE OF THE WEIGHTED APPLICATION BLANK IN SELECTING UNSKILLED EMPLOYEES[1]

Richard D. Scott and Richard W. Johnson

Although the weighted application blank (WAB) has frequently been used to hire office and sales personnel, it appears to have been used relatively little in selecting unskilled employees. Dunnette and Maetzold (1955) report one study in which the WAB was used to select unskilled workers; however, their study was concerned only with seasonal employees.

The primary purpose of this study was to develop a WAB which would be successful in selecting permanently employed workers at the unskilled level. Two related purposes were *(a)* to compare the effectiveness of the WAB with a multiple-regression equation based upon the same data in predicting employee turnover, and *(b)* to describe by means of factor analysis the personal history items associated with long-term employment.

Method

Subjects

A survey was made of the records of all full-time, permanently employed, unskilled workers hired by a small canning factory in western Massachusetts during the past 4 yr. The unskilled jobs consisted of such tasks as cleaning and bottling pickles. From this subject (*S*) pool, 75 long-tenure *S*s (6 mo. or more) and 75 short-tenure *S*s (1 mo. or less) were selected on the basis of completeness in filling in the job application form.

Biographical Items

The 19 biographical items listed on the application form were used as the predictor variables.

SOURCE. Richard D. Scott, at the time of publication of this article, was a graduate student is psychology at the University of Massachusetts. Richard W. Johnson, Associate Professor of Psychology at the University of Massachusetts, has interests in the areas of vocational counseling, psychological measurement, and counselor education. This article originally appeared in the *Journal of Applied Psychology*, 1967, **51**, 393-395. Reprinted by permission of the American Psychological Association and the authors.

[1] Based upon a master's thesis completed by Richard D. Scott under the supervision of Richard W. Johnson. The helpful suggestions of Stanley M. Moss and J. Alfred Southworth, thesis committee members, are gratefully acknowledged.

Procedure

According to the procedures described by England (1961), two weighting groups (a long-tenure and a short-tenure group) of 50 *S*s each were randomly selected from the larger sample of employees. Item responses for these *S*s were compared for the purpose of assigning weights to the items. Differential weights (0, 1, or 2) were assigned as outlined by England.

The remaining 25 *S*s in each group were placed into two holdout (cross-validation) groups to check the effectiveness of the item weights in discriminating between long- and short-term employees.

Tenure, which was of vital concern to the management, was selected as the criterion of worker effectiveness. Thousands of dollars in unfilled contracts were lost each year as the result of labor shortage due to rapid employee turnover.

The 100 *S*s in the two weighting groups were also used to compute the multiple-regression equation between the application-blank items and the criterion. A sequence of multiple-linear-regression equations was calculated in a stepwise manner by means of the Control Data 3600 computer. The relative success of the two weighting techniques (WAB versus multiple regression) in predicting job tenure for members of the holdout groups was determined both by *(a)* percentage of correct classification, and *(b)* product-moment correlation coefficient.

The intercorrelations among the predictor items for the 100 members of the two weighting groups were factor analyzed by the method of principal components.[2] The factor matrix was graphically rotated to yield simple structure on the criterion variable. Only those factors which produced significant factor loadings ($p < .05$) on this variable were interpreted.

Results

Of the 19 items, 12 were assigned differential weights through the use of the WAB technique.[3] When these weights were applied to members of the holdout groups, 72% correct classification of *S*s was obtained by using a cutting score of 14 (the point of maximum differentiation). This percentage of "hits" was significantly different from chance (50:50 base rate) at the .01 level of probability ($CR = 3.10$).

[2]The factor-analysis and multiple-regression programs were obtained from the series of biomedical computer programs developed at the University of California, Los Angeles (Dixon, 1965).

[3]Tables reporting the assigned weights, means, standard deviations, intercorrelations, and factor loadings for all variables may be found in R. D. Scott's (1966) master's thesis on file in the University of Massachusetts library.

Table 1 presents the quartiles, means, and standard deviations for members of both holdout groups. The difference between the means was statistically significant ($t = 6.38$; $p < .01$). The product-moment correlation coefficient between the scored application blanks and months on the job was .45 ($p < .01$) for the 50 members in the holdout groups.

Table 1. Quartiles, Means, and Standard Deviations of WAB Scores for Long- and Short-Term Employees (Holdout Groups)

Group	Q_1	*Mdn*	Q_3	*M*	*SD*
Short term	5	8	12.5	9.32	4.42
Long term	11	14.5	16	13.88	3.85

Note: $N = 25$ in each group

The multiple correlation between the 12 significant items and the criterion was .71. Nearly as high a multiple R ($R = .69$) was obtained using just six items. The multiple-regression equation based upon these six items is shown below:[4]

$$Y' = .30\ (\text{age}) + 8.82\ (\text{sex}) - .69\ (\text{miles from plant}) + 5.29\ (\text{type of residence}) + 2.66\ (\text{number of children}) + 1.08\ (\text{years on last job}) - 1.99.$$

When the application forms for members of the holdout groups were scored by means of the multiple-regression equation, the percentage of correct classification (based on a cutting score of either 9 or 10) fell slightly from 72% to 70%. The size of the correlation between the weighted scores and the criterion dropped from .45 to .31. (Neither of these differences was significantly different from chance at the .05 level.) Both indexes suggest that the WAB was as efficient as, if not more than, the multiple-regression equation in assigning weights to the variables.

Because the optimal cutting scores were established after inspection of the data (as suggested by England), accuracy of classification was also compared at several arbitrary cutting levels. The relative success of the two techniques in predicting tenure status for the holdout *S*s at the twenty-fifth, fiftieth, and seventy-fifth percentile points is shown in Table 2. While the WAB appears to hold a slight edge in accuracy of prediction, the differences which exist may best be explained in terms of chance alone.

Factor analysis produced two rather-clear-cut factors which loaded high on the criterion variable: *(a)* "family responsibility" accounted for 16% of the variance in the criterion, and *(b)* "convenience" accounted for 31% of the variance. Only 4% of the variance was accounted for by the remaining factors

[4]The discontinuous variables were coded as follows: sex: 0=male, 1=female; type of residence: 0=live with parents or in room, 1=live in own home.

Table 2. Comparison of WAB and Multiple Regression in Predicting Tenure Status for Holdout Subjects at 3 Arbitrary Cutting Levels

Percentile	Cutting-point Score		Accuracy of Classification	
	WAB	Multiple Regression	WAB	Multiple Regression
Twenty-fifth	7.5	5	70%	62%
Fiftieth	12	11	70	66
Seventy-fifth	15.5	16	66	66

Note: None of the differences between the percentages at the three cutting levels was significantly greater than chance expectancy ($p > .05$). $N = 50$.

($h^2 = .51$); 49% of the variance was unaccounted for by any of the factors in the factor analysis.

Discussion

The WAB proved to be an effective technique in selecting long-term unskilled workers. The higher the individual's score on the WAB, the greater the likelihood of his staying with the company a reasonable length of time. While the cutting score of 14 maximally differentiates between the long-term and the short-term employees, the company in practice would use as high a cutting score as the available labor market permitted.

It is surprising that weighting by the multiple-regression technique was not more effective than the WAB. Two explanations appear to be most plausible: *(a)* the use of a fairly large number of predictor variables (initial $n = 19$) with a relatively small N ($N = 100$) may have yielded unstable weights, and *(b)* several of the variables (e.g., age, education, distance lived from plant, and years lived in the state) appeared to be nonlinearly related to the criterion.

Future comparisons of the two weighting procedures may profit by the use of a larger N and the application of curvilinear multiple-regression techniques. Until such comparisons can be made, however, the WAB, which is much easier to develop and apply, stands as the recommended weighting procedure.

The two factors isolated by means of the factor analysis, "convenience" and "family responsibility," appear reasonable. The one, convenience, suggests that unskilled females who live fairly close to work are likely to stay on the job. The other, family responsibility, describes the long-term employee as older, married, providing for one or more dependents, living in his own home, and as having worked a relatively long period of time on his last job.

The convenience factor agrees well with Dunnette and Maetzold's (1955) findings that females make good seasonal, unskilled employees and that in general, workers who live near the plant are more likely to continue on the job. The family responsibility factor, however, is missing in Dunnette and Maetzold's data. Presumably, the unskilled worker who is employed only seasonally is less likely to hold large-scale family responsibilities. The long-term seasonal worker, described as young (under 25) or old (over 55), married, but with no children, and possessing 10 yr. or more education, suggests a young college student or semiretired individual in search of summer employment. This same person would be unlikely to seek unskilled employment on a permanent basis.

Conclusion

The WAB developed in this study successfully differentiated between long-term and short-term employees in the cross-validation study. The WAB technique appeared to be as effective as, and certainly simpler than, the multiple-regression technique in weighting the item responses.

Factor analysis of the data suggested that two dimensions, convenience and family responsibility, could adequately account for most of the variance in the criterion tapped by the variety of biographical items. The family responsibility factor appeared to differentiate between the permanently employed and the seasonally employed long-term unskilled workers.

6. PSYCHOLOGICAL TEST FOR PSYCHOPATHOLOGY[1]

Eugene I. Burdock and Anne S. Hardesty

There is a need for a standardized psychological method for evaluation of psychopathology comparable to the standardized psychological methods for evaluation of intelligence. Such an evaluation has to be based on the accumulated clinical knowledge about abnormal behavior, but must select a

SOURCE. Eugene I. Burdock is Professor of Psychology at the New York University School of Medicine and formerly was an associate research scientist in biometric science at the New York State Department of Mental Hygiene. Dr. Burdock has contributed to the professional literature on conceptual frameworks and research methods for the assessment of personality and psychopathology. Anne S. Hardesty is Research Assistant Professor of Psychiatry (biometric) at the New York University Medical School. This article originally appeared in the *Journal of Abnormal Psychology,* 1968, 73, 62-69. Reprinted by permission of the American Psychological Association and the authors.

[1]This investigation was supported in part by Public Health Service Research Grant No. 11117 from the National Institute of Mental Health.

representative sample of molecular behaviors which can be reliably assessed in an individual testing session and which lead to quantitative determinations. The resultant scores can be employed as independent indexes and, when standardized against norm groups, can be used to make comparisons among groups and among individuals, as well as to detect changes in an individual over the course of time. Individual intelligence tests such as the WAIS and the Stanford-Binet have made important contributions to the understanding of mental abilities. A quantitative method for evaluating psychopathology would facilitate systematic studies of diagnosis and of response to treatment.

The Structured Clinical Interview (SCI; Burdock & Hardesty, 1962, 1964, 1965) is a technique which provides a quantitative evaluation of an individual for psychopathology. The SCI consists of an interview schedule, together with an inventory of 179 items which are incorporated as an integral part of the protocol to be marked *True* or *Not True* by the examiner during the interview on the basis of *S*'s responses and behavior. The interview usually takes about 20 min. The examiner records his judgments during the interview, so that no additional time is required for completion of the inventory after *S* has departed.

The SCI is intended for use both in screening and for determination of changes in psychopathology. It incorporates design features derived from psychological research:

1. A structured-interview protocol contains the stimulus input for the examiner with a preselected set of behaviors on which *S* is assessed as the examination progresses, similar to the WAIS and the Stanford-Binet.
2. A relatively mild tone of inquiry is set by stimulus questions which focus on specific content areas relevant for evaluation of psychopathology, but without insisting on detailed disclosures so as to avoid the effect of pressure.
3. Somewhat ambiguous open-ended input questions require *S* to construct his own responses, which thus tend to reflect his, rather than the examiner's, intentions.
4. Any response tendency to be communicative is reinforced by display of sympathetic interest and by avoidance of a judgmental attitude. The examiner is trained to accept *S*'s value judgments impartially, and to encourage a hesitating respondent by asking in a tone of friendly interest: "Can you tell me more about it?"
5. The examiner is also trained to modify his own behavior as necessary in order to set the stage for a significant response. For example, a miniature psychological experiment is embedded in the interview to determine *S*'s capacity for positive affect. At a predetermined point in the interview, after *S* has completed his response to: "What about your sense of humor?" the examiner smiles and, if *S* has smiled, says: "You haven't *forgotten* how to smile." But if *S* has failed to display a spontaneous smile, the examiner seeks to evoke one by smiling and asking: "You haven't forgotten how to *smile?*"

6. Inventory items are juxtaposed with the stimulus material where the corresponding behaviors are most likely to be elicited, so that the examiner can complete the inventory during the interview, a technique which retains the quantitative feature of the questionnaire as well as its immediacy, but which reflects a professional judgment rather than a self-evaluation.

7. An effective compromise is struck between detail and brevity by the 20-min. average length of the interview, so as to make the procedure suitable for screening in a wide variety of situations.

8. A concentration on current status, rather than on historical or dynamic source material, makes possible repeated applications for assessment of changes in pathology over time.

9. The inventory is a record of the judgments of a specially trained psychologist carrying out observations in a controlled setting. While a professional actor could learn to conduct the interview in a highly competent manner, the value of the judgments depends intrinsically on the experience and training of the psychological observer.

The comparatively neutral stimuli used in the SCI are intended to minimize any tendency of *S* toward acquiescence or disavowal. It is, therefore, desirable that the SCI be administered before any more probing inquiries, so as to avoid possible after effects of reinforcement of such response tendencies.

The inventory was constructed by identifying in the psychological and psychiatric literature areas of psychopathology generally recognized as having symptom significance. Each of these areas was then broken down into molecular items which reflect pathological verbalizations, attitudes, and behaviors displayed during the interview. The interview, in turn, was constructed so as to provide a uniform stimulus context in which to direct *S*'s attention toward these areas of adaptation, and to give him an opportunity to exhibit ideation and behavior from which the psychologist can judge the presence or absence of psychopathology. In order to minimize any tendency by the examiner to project premature diagnostic conclusions into his judgments, the SCI has been designed with items calling for molecular judgments of presence or absence of concrete behaviors and attitudes. In addition, the examiner in his training is inoculated for objectivity by the stress laid on the importance of assuring that his specific item judgments remain uncontaminated by diagnostic preconceptions so that they may serve as an independent criterion. The approach to areas of potential pathology is oblique rather than direct, but questions are nevertheless phrased in such a way as to preclude simple "yes" or "no" responses. The interview thus resembles a projective technique in that the interviewer's statements or questions serve as ambiguous stimuli which *S*, to some extent, invests with his own meanings. Although the stimuli are ambiguous, the responses are evaluated with explicit reference to the preselected behavioral items of the inventory.

The items of the inventory have been printed opposite those interview questions which, as experience has shown, are most likely to elicit the relevant behavior. This ordering of the items is intended to facilitate the examiner's task of locating relevant behaviors, but he is trained to be alert to record a significant item when it occurs earlier or later in the interview. Table 1 shows some typical sections of the SCI.

Table 1. Specimen Sections from the Structured Clinical Interview

Question	Item
"How is your eyesight?"	49. Indicates that he experiences visual perceptions in the absence of an adequate or appropriate stimulus.
"What happens when you close your eyes?"	50. Indicates that objects or people look unusually large or small.
	51. Indicates that people or things look weird or distorted.
"How is your hearing?"	52. Indicates that he experiences auditory perception in the absence of an adequate or appropriate stimulus.
"How does your head feel?"	53. Says that he gets creeping or crawling sensations on his body.
	54. Speaks of attack of palpitations, faintness, dizziness or unsteadiness.
(55) "How do you enjoy eating?"	55. Says that he has lost his appetite or the capacity to enjoy food.
("How does your food taste to you?")	56. Reports that his food tastes or looks suspicious or that he is being poisoned.
(57) "How is your sense of smell?"	57. Indicates that he notices smells in the absence of an adequate or appropriate stimulus.
	58. Claims that he just has a physical ailment in spite of evidence of psychological disturbance.
(62) "How is your memory?"	62. Mentions that his memory is impaired or that he keeps forgetting things.
	63. Reports difficulty in recalling important details of past experience.
	64. Tells of fit, seizure or lapse of consciousness.
(65) "Tell me about your imagination."	65. Reports that he engages in wishful thinking instead of working.
"What kinds of things have you been thinking about?"	66. Reports that he broods over a certain unpleasant thought or feeling.
	67. Reports or expresses weird or bizarre thought.
	68. Reports that a certain irrelevant thought intrudes on his consciousness.
	69. Reports that things seem unreal or dreamlike.
	70. Says that he feels as if he is outside of his body, or as if his body does not belong to him.
	137. Pitch of voice shows no variation (i.e., completely monotonous).
	138. Speaks extremely rapidly and with infrequent pauses.
	139. Speech is both slow and full of pauses.
	140. Speech is blurred or inarticulate.
	141. Stutters or stammers.
	142. Speech is at times inaudible or incoherent.
	143. Makes menacing gesture or physical attack.
	144. Throws something.
	145. Bangs fist on table or stamps foot.
	146. Deliberately tears or breaks something.

Internal Consistency

Initially, before the items had been segregated into subtests, a total score was computed by simply summing the items of maladaptive behavior observed. The internal consistency of the SCI was determined by point-biserial correlations between items and total on a sample of 870 mental patients. One hundred thirty-four items showed significant positive correlations with total, that is, had 95% confidence bands which did not include zero.

The items of the SCI have been clustered into 10 nonoverlapping subtests by the following procedure: (1) Initially items were constructed so as to represent significant areas of psychopathology on the basis of clinical and theoretical criteria. (2) Point-biserial correlations were then computed between items and subtest areas. (3) Frequency of occurrence of each item was balanced against magnitude of correlation in order not to exclude rare but critical items. (4) Stability of correlation was determined by replication of the point-biserial correlations in samples of chronic resident patients, of new admissions, and of normals. The authors examined each item in the light of the four criteria, and reassigned items on the basis of discussion and agreement. After several reshufflings of items and recomputations of the point biserials, when no further improvement could be obtained, the final assignments of items to subtests were cross-validated on a fresh sample, and intercorrelations among the subtests were determined. Correlations between subtests and total score averaged about .50; average intercorrelation among the subtests was about .10. Table 2 shows these intercorrelations.

Table 2. Intercorrelations Among 10 Subtests and Total of the Structured Clinical Interview on a Sample of 870 Mental Patients

Subtest	1	2	3	4	5	6	7	8	9	10	Total
1		.25	.10	.20	.35	.10	−.02	.06	.18	.19	.51
2			−.08	.38	.41	.20	.12	.01	−.01	.10	.61
3				.07	.04	.09	.09	.26	.54	.17	.47
4					.29	.19	.08	.01	.09	.11	.55
5						.01	.13	0	.09	.14	.53
6							.01	.02	.09	.08	.50
7								.11	.03	−.03	.16
8									.14	.01	.24
9										.34	.52
10											.38

A great deal of confusion has been engendered in the psychological literature by the loose application to various empirically derived scales of diagnostic terms which imply a medical judgment. Thus, the label "anxiety" has been applied to: (1) a set of items selected from the MMPI which reflect an *S*'s self-report; (2) a low threshold of response to stimulation of the sympathetic branch of the automatic nervous system in laboratory experiments; (3) an inferred inner state which is reflected in poor performance on an intellectual task (see, e.g., Mowrer, 1948). While it may be argued that one or all of these three are correlated with clinical anxiety as judged by a psychiatrist, the degree of correlation may vary, and they are certainly not operationally identical with the meaning of anxiety in clinical psychiatry. In order to avoid suggesting any specific diagnostic implications, the subtests have been assigned neutral but psychologically descriptive names. Brief descriptions of the item content of the 10 subtests follow:

1. *Anger-Hostility* (27 items) is sometimes reflected in verbalization, sometimes in action: fit of anger; trouble with the law; irritable; jealousy, bitter envy; hatred for relative or associate; angry when criticized; people push him around; does not care if he harms other; hits or attacks people; expresses resentment; accuses interviewer; acts contemptuous; belligerent; shouts, yells; menacing gesture; throws something; bangs or stamps; tears or breaks; looks angry; turns away.

2. *Conceptual Dysfunction* (28 items) is concerned with disturbances of concept formation, concept retention, or concept evocation which interfere with cognitive functioning, and which express themselves in defects of communication, orientation, memory, attention, and concentration: fails to give name, date, place; assumes false role; does not remember how he came; gives implausible or incomplete account; difficulty in recall; tells of fit, seizure; does not recognize behavior; misidentifies; obscure or cryptic explanations; mechanical repetitions; gibberish; aimless talk; minute elaborations; contradictory explanations; forgets what he is talking about, distractable; becomes preoccupied; pressure of speech; blurred speech; inaudible or incoherent.

3. *Fear-Worry* (12 items) reflects the apprehensions that *S* voices or displays: bothered by feelings of nervousness or anxiety; periods of depression; worries a lot or cannot stop; lots of fears or fears of different things; fear of insanity or of losing control; irrational fear; concern about panic; depressed or despondent; broods; irrelevant thoughts; sense of humor lost; weeps.

4. *Incongruous Behavior* (25 items) indicates modes of expression which seem contradictory to one another or which are anomalous and unusual ways of doing usual things: drags feet; hand is clammy; face dirty; hair unkempt; dirty or bizarre clothes; smells of urine or feces; tells of compulsive acts; incongruous emotional response; gesticulates; frenzied excitement; fleeting expressions; frightened expression; attack of panic; stands up; rubs, scratches, picks; pulls or tugs; rituals; writhes; restless; poses; tic; fidgets; giggles; belches, clucks, grunts; tremor.

5. *Incongruous Ideation* (28 items) consists of items reflecting contradictory emotions, strange or bizarre notions incompatible with reality, outright delusions, or ideas which are uncoupled from the socially expected emotional

toning (i.e., ideation with inappropriate affect or without affect): blames others; tells of period of elation; nothing bothers him; enjoys cruelty; "possessed"; enjoys tragic events; says he feels "high"; has uncorroborated disease; body changing in size or shape; body rotting; has fatal illness or is about to die; people or things look weird or distorted; food suspicious or poisoned; weird thoughts; things unreal or dreamlike; being punished for sin; harmed by stranger; mistreated by authority; ideas of reference; harassed or persecuted; mind controlled; has unknown enemy; superhuman power or knowledge; worldwide fame; *idée fixe;* expresses extreme elation.

6. *Lethargy-Dejection* (17 items) is reflected in physical as well as in emotional expression: feels tired; does not smile; no interests; enjoys nothing; no plans; flat affect; says little; faint voice; monotone; slow speech; sad expression or dejected posture; sighs; immobile; eyes closed or head averted; impassive expression; slow movements; hardly talks.

7. *Perceptual Dysfunction* (6 items) is comprised of what appear to be hallucinatory experiences: visual hallucinations; micropsia or macropsia; auditory hallucinations; tactile hallucinations; olfactory hallucinations; somatic hallucinations.

8. *Physical Complaints* (7 items) contains reports of somatic problems: motor or sensory dysfunction; dissatisfied with size or strength; palpitations, faintness, dizziness; anorexia.

9. *Self-Depreciation* (20 items) is made up of items in which *S* tells of his frailties or denigrates himself: feelings dried up; alcoholic or drug addict; rash; difficulty in decision making; afraid of acting out; getting nowhere; dissatisfied with appearance; suicidal thoughts; suicidal intentions; masochistic; impaired memory; wishful thinking; people avoid him; feels distant from people; no friends; guilt feelings; inferiority feelings; negative attitude toward future; intense regret.

10. *Sexual Problems* (9 items) groups together items indicative of problems stemming from sexual attitudes or behavior: uncomfortable when asked about opposite sex; has difficulty with opposite sex; impotent or frigid; sexual habits get him into trouble; worried about masturbation; homosexual, nymphomaniac; exposes genitals; sexual suggestion; sexual advance.

Interobserver Agreement

The reliability of the interviewer's observations has been studied by comparing the results of two or more simultaneous but independent observers by intraclass correlation (Burdock, Fleiss, & Hardesty, 1963). Reliabilities for total scores extended from .83 to .92, for groups of patients ranging in size from 26 to 83. Interobserver reliabilities for the subtests ranged in the .70s or .80s with one exception, Perceptual Dysfunction, which has since been revised (Burdock & Hardesty, 1966).

Stability

Determination of stability by test-retest presents special problems for a technique like the SCI which is sensitive to short-term fluctuations in behavioral adaptation. However, since continuously hospitalized chronic psychotics might be expected to show relatively little change in adaptation over time, a small sample of nine chronic resident patients from a study of chronic schizophrenics (Burdock & Hardesty, 1966) was reinterviewed after 6 mo. These patients were drawn from a group who had been transferred from the regular continued treatment services of a large state mental hospital to a special intensive treatment unit and had been returned to the regular services because of failure to show sufficient improvement to warrant release. A correlation of .84 was obtained between total scores for the two occasions. Fisher's z transformation provided 95% confidence limits as follows: $.40 \leqslant r \leqslant .97$.

Validity

Justification for use of a total score as a gross index of severity (or acuteness) of psychopathology was based on experience with the Ward Behavior Inventory (WBI; Burdock, Hakerem, Hardesty, & Zubin, 1960), an instrument developed by the present authors prior to the initiation of work on the SCI. The items of the WBI are molecular, and call for naturalistic observations by a psychiatric nurse or attendant, who, however, avoids direct contact with the patient. In the development of the SCI, relevant items from the WBI were adapted for use in the interview situation. The WBI was 1 of 21 instruments chosen to assess the efficacy of phenothiazines for the treatment of acute schizophrenia in a nine-hospital collaborative study under the direction of the National Institute of Mental Health Psychopharmacology Service Center. A multiple discriminant function analysis of the data showed the WBI total pathology score "to be the single measure most efficient in discriminating between the drugs and placebo . . . [Cole, 1964, p. 25]."

Some evidence for validity of the SCI total score has been obtained by correlating the SCI with the WBI. Significant correlations, .35 and .68, were found between the SCI and the WBI for samples of 73 and 16 patients, respectively, while for an unstructured psychiatric interview with 73 patients the correlation with the WBI was insignificant, only .22 (Burdock & Hardesty, 1964).

Scoring

Because the frequency distributions of scores for both total and subtests follow exponential decay curves, transformations were applied to the raw scores in order to reduce skewness and stabilize the variance. The determination of an appropriate transformation followed Bartlett's (1947) criteria for minimizing the dependence of the variance on the mean.

The 10 subtests contain different numbers of items. Therefore, the transformed scores of the normals were converted to standard form with mean of zero so as to facilitate profiling of an *S*'s scores on the different subtests, and to allow for comparisons among individuals and groups. Although total raw score is actually the sum of the subtest scores, it was standardized independently to obtain a measure of overall level of psychopathology. The 10 subtests, in turn, provide standard scores for pattern analysis. A study of the relation between SCI patterns and diagnosis has been carried out on a sample of 361 hospitalized mental patients (Burdock & Hardesty, 1966).

Figure 1 illustrates certain systematic differences among normals, outpatients, and inpatients. The sample of 870 inpatients includes 272 chronic resident schizophrenics from the study just cited who were interviewed in state hospitals. Most of the remaining inpatients were interviewed at time of admission or readmission to an acute service. With the exception of the chronic schizophrenics, the interviews were carried out by interviewers who knew only that *S*

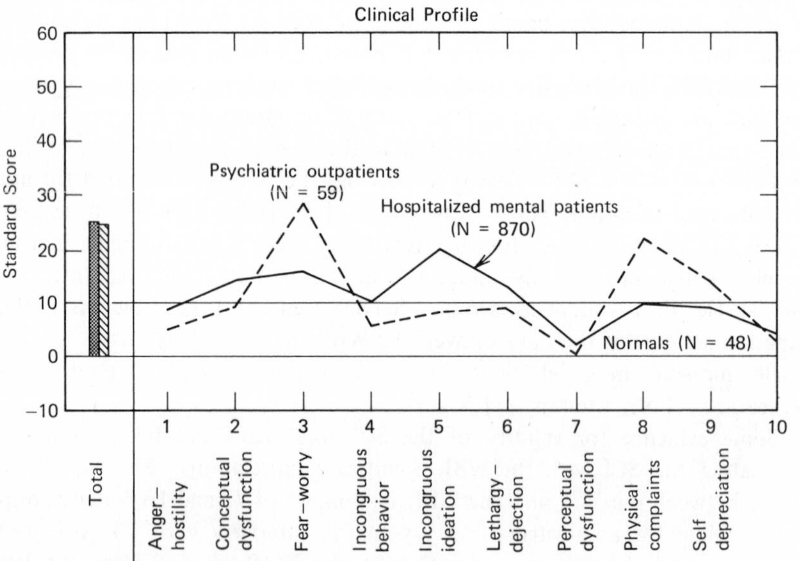

Figure 1. Comparison of mean scores on the SCI of three groups of *S*s.

was a psychiatric patient. The outpatients were a sample of applicants to a psychiatric clinic. The diagnoses recorded on the individual cases described below were obtained by independent examination of the case records after completion of the interviews. With normals as a reference base, outpatients and inpatients show about the same average levels of pathology; that is, mean total score for each group is 2½ standard deviations above the mean of the normals. However, while the inpatients tend to exceed the outpatients on most of the subtests, the latter score higher than the inpatients on Fear-Worry, Physical Complaints, and Self-Depreciation. Since clinic patients tend to include more neurotics, while inpatients are mostly psychotics, it is not surprising that the inpatients show more Conceptual Dysfunction, Incongruous Behavior, Incongruous Ideation, Lethargy-Dejection, and Perceptual Dysfunction, while the outpatients are highest on Fear-Worry, Physical Complaints, and Self-Depreciation.

Figure 2 illustrates how the technique can be used to compare individual *S*s. The base line represents the mean scores of a norm group of nonpsychiatric *S*s. Total scores are set off at the extreme left, followed by the profile of subtests. The three organics represented here were interviewed at time of admission to hospital. The overall level of pathology is about the same for the three patients, about 1½ to 2 sigmas above the mean of the normals. All three patients show a lack of Anger-Hostility and Incongruous Ideation, but elevated scores on Conceptual Dysfunction and Lethargy-Dejection. These features are consistent

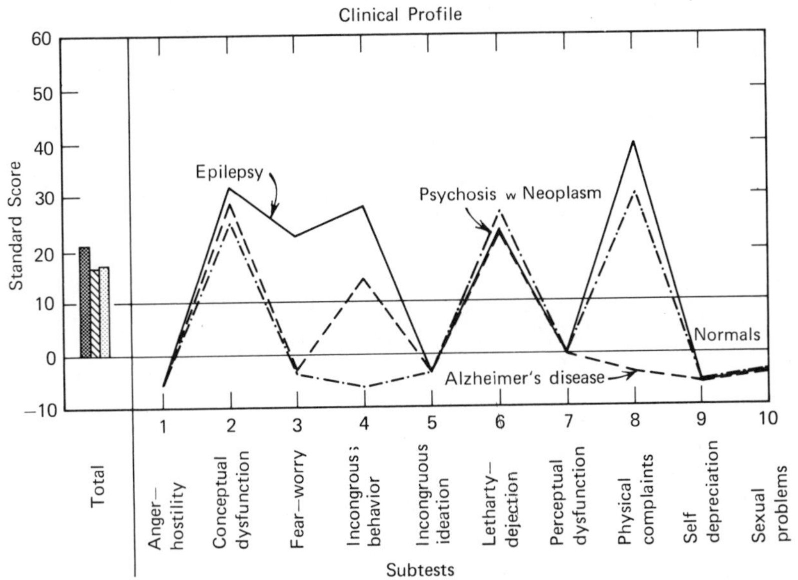

Figure 2. SCI profiles of three organic patients.

with expectancies expressed in the clinical literature. Other common features of the three profiles are low scores on Perceptual Dysfunction and Self-Depreciation.

Figure 3 presents successive profiles of a female manic-depressive patient who was interviewed three times at intervals of 2 mo. The first interview took place on admission to hospital, the second interview 2 mo. later at the request of the psychiatrist because of a marked change in the patient's behavior. The third interview was held 2 mo. after the second, on a follow-up visit by the patient who had been released in the interim. The three total scores show a progressive decline in overall level of psychopathology from a high of 2 sigmas above normal to less than 1 sigma above. The profile of subtest scores shows two features which remain relatively high on all three occasions: Anger-Hostility and Self-Depreciation. In her manic phase at time of admission, the patient showed extreme Incongruous Ideation and had numerous Physical Complaints. She also manifested considerable Conceptual Dysfunction, Incongruous Behavior, and Fear-Worry. Two months later, in a depressed phase, Incongruous Ideation, Conceptual Dysfunction, and Incongruous Behavior together with Physical Complaints had all declined to normal, but Lethargy-Dejection had risen. By the time of the follow-up interview, Fear-Worry had returned to normal, but Conceptual Dysfunction had increased again to a significant extent and, together with Anger-Hostility and Self-Depreciation, reflects the persistency of deviation from the normal reference group.

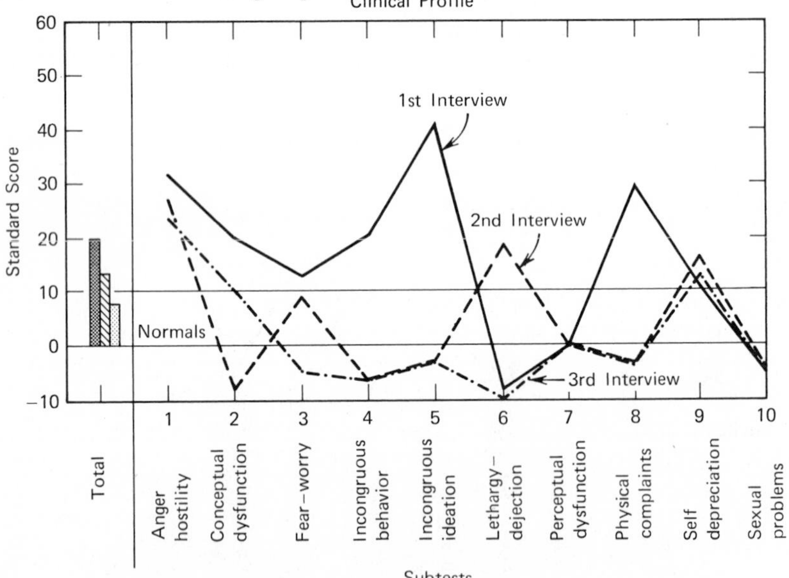

Figure 3. SCI profiles of a manic-depressive patient interviewed three times at bimonthly intervals.

Figure 4 illustrates the potentiality of the SCI for screening. Profiles of two normals are shown side by side. One of these, a relatively low normal, has a total score within half a standard deviation above the mean, and shows some elevation on Anger-Hostility and Lethargy-Dejection. The other *S* has a total score more than 1½ standard deviations above the mean. Her profile shows extremely elevated scores on Anger-Hostility, Fear-Worry, Self-Depreciation, and Lethargy-Dejection, together with suspiciously high amounts of Conceptual Dysfunction and Incongruous Behavior. In any screening program the latter *S* might well be referred for a detailed psychiatric evaluation.

In summary, the SCI has been designed to serve as an individual test for manifest psychopathology. It can provide reliable scores when it is administered and evaluated by a specially trained clinical or counseling psychologist. It may be used to compare patients with one another, to follow up changes in individual patients, or to detect *S*s with potential pathology in the community. The interview has been carefully arranged so as to move sequentially by a systematic, but apparently casual, progression from one area to another of the *S*'s life situation. Because the interviewer is trained to avoid applying any pressure, the scores obtained from the SCI offer a conservative estimate of potential psychopathology. While the technique may fail to uncover a well-masked psychopath or to detect a carefully concealed character defect, or even to identify a compensated neurotic, it is less likely to err in the direction of suggesting pathology when there is no basis for it.

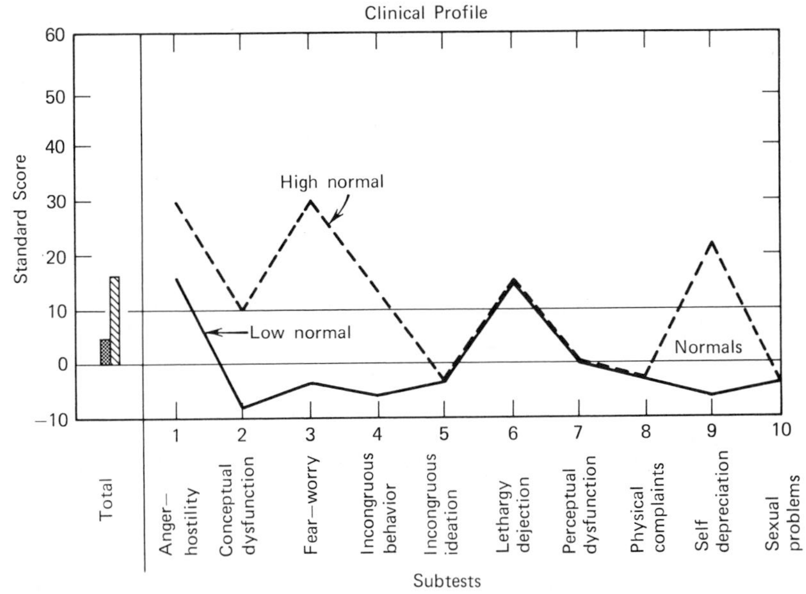

Figure 4. SCI profiles of two normals.

In the development of the SCI, the authors have intentionally adopted an empirical bias by focusing on those features of psychopathological behavior which are commonly recognized as significant for screening and for the management of patients. The avoidance of a specific theoretical point of view will, it is hoped, make the technique more generally acceptable to psychologists of various theoretical persuasions.

7. MEASUREMENT OF SOCIAL COMPETENCE IN COLLEGE MALES[1]

Richard I. Lanyon

Recent views of mental health (e.g., Jahoda, 1955; Lazarus, 1961, pp. 21-23) have tended to discard the traditional "avoidance of stress" approach in favor of more positive concepts such as social adequacy, interpersonal competence, achievement, and mastery of one's environment. One advantage of the newer approach is that the concepts used are fairly operational and thus amenable to measurement. Several instruments to define and measure these concepts have been constructed—for example, Doll's (1953) Vineland Social Maturity Scale, for the assessment of retardation, and the Worcester Scale of Social Attainment (Phillips & Cowitz, 1953), for assessing social competence in psychiatric patients. The competence or achievement approach to mental health has the further advantage of emphasizing the use of biographical and behavioral data in psychological description and prediction. There are indications (e.g., Fulkerson & Barry, 1961; Little & Shneidman, 1959) that such an approach to measurement is more valid in many cases than the use of traditional psychological testing procedures.

The present paper describes the construction of a scale to measure social competence in college males, using only biographical and behavioral data which involve verifiable statements of fact. Subjects were considered socially competent to the extent that their backgrounds and/or present lives showed behaviors or characteristics which indicated social participation, interpersonal

SOURCE. Richard I. Lanyon received his doctoral degree at the University of Iowa. He is currently Associate Professor of Psychology at Northeastern University and has contributed to the professional literature on the clinical applications of learning theory, personality assessment, and experimental psychopathology. This article originally appeared in the *Journal of Consulting Psychology*, 1967, **31**, 495-498. Reprinted by permission of the American Psychological Association and the author.

[1]This study was supported in part by a grant from the Rutgers Research Council. Thanks are extended to Carol Hamilton and Richard Knolblauch for their assistance.

competence, achievement, and environmental mastery. The following list of characteristics was drawn up as a working definition of social competence:

1. History of frequent and positive social interaction with both sexes.
2. Participation in organizing and directing group activities.
3. Better than average academic interest and achievement.
4. Acceptance of authority, ability to discipline oneself, and no history of legal difficulties.
5. An unbroken and secure family background, but with definite indications that personal freedom and responsibility have been encouraged.
6. Participation in athletic activities.
7. Some participation in socially desirable adult behaviors such as church attendance, drinking, and interest in world affairs.

The list describes a kind of cultural-ideal stereotype for a college student. It suggests a socially sophisticated, responsible, outgoing, friendly, and somewhat aggressive young man who was reared by loving yet wise parents and who hopes to become a respected and influential member of society.

Method

A set of 46 items was written to represent the above characteristics. An effort was made to have each topic represented to the extent of its intuitively judged relevance to social competence. Some of the items were written in multiple-choice form, while the remainder required a numerical response. This 46-item preliminary form of the Biographical Survey (B-I) was administered to 45 males in an undergraduate psychology class. As a result of their answers and comments, ambiguities in the questions were removed and multiple-choice foils were adjusted appropirately. Married students and those over 20 years old were excluded from this sample and from the two following samples.

The revised form (B-II) was administered to 135 introductory psychology students, and their responses were analyzed in the following manner. Frequency distributions were made of the responses to each item. Two judges (the author and a senior graduate student in clinical psychology with 2 years of college counseling experience) independently designated the direction and manner of scoring each item for social competence. Agreement was reached on 36 items, and the remainder were discarded. The cutoff point in the response distribution of each item was placed at what was considered the borderline of social competence. Such a procedure resulted in 70-80% of the responses to each item being defined as competent. One point was assigned for each answer in the direction of social competence. Thus, the maximum possible score was 36.

An internal consistency analysis was next carried out. Point-biserial correlation coefficients were determined between each item and the total score. The

20 items which were found to correlate with the total score beyond the 5% level in the predicted direction were retained for the final scale.

The 20-item final scale (B-III) was administered to a new sample of 195 introductory psychology students. The mean score was 14.9, and the standard deviation was 2.6. The 2nd, 10th, 50th, and 90th percentiles were 8.4, 11.5, 15.2, and 18.0, respectively.

The items and key are given in Table 1. The content is a fairly even representation of the initial list of characteristics (and thus of the initial 46 items), except that the items about dating are perhaps more heavily represented in the final form. Thus, if it can be assumed that the *S*s were honest in their responses, the high scorers corresponded essentially to the description given above—active and energetic, decisive, socially extroverted, well emancipated from parental control, and with a sense of basic social conformity.

Validation

The generality of the assumed differences between high and low scorers on the B-III was examined using group MMPI scores. The *S*s in the normative group who scored more than one standard deviation above the mean were contrasted on the 13 usual MMPI scales with *S*s scoring more than one standard deviation below the mean. It was predicted that compared with low B-III scorers, the high scorers' MMPIs should indicate greater interpersonal competence and social involvement (lower *Si* score), less anxiety and indecision (lower *Pt* score), and more conforming thought patterns (lower *Sc* and *F* scores).

These predictions were generally supported. Of the 13 comparisons 4 were significant beyond the .05 level. There was a mean difference of 13 *T* scores on the *Si* scale ($p < .001$), 10 on the *D* scale ($p < .001$), 8 on the *Pt* scale ($p < .01$), and 5 on the *F* scale ($p < .02$).[2] The difference of 5 *T* scores on the *Sc* scale failed to reach significance at the .10 level. In each case, higher B-III scores were associated with lower MMPI scores.

The greatest differences in the opposite direction were four *T* scores on the *Ma* scale, two on the *Hy* scale, and two on the *Pd* scale, none of which reached significance at the .05 level.

Further validation was carried out with the assistance of a local fraternity ($N = 43$). These students were asked to fill out the B-III and then to list the names of the five members with whom they would most prefer to double-date and the five with whom they would least prefer to do so. In this manner it was hoped to identify the most and least socially competent members of the fraternity. Strictest confidence was assured, and all members returned their responses in a sealed envelope. The *S*s who received five or more "most prefer" votes were considered to be most competent ($N = 17$), while those who received five or

[2]Two-tailed significance tests were used.

more "least prefer" votes were considered least competent ($N = 10$). The mean B-III scores of these two groups were 16.94 and 15.80, respectively. They differed from each other beyond the .05 level and were both greater (each $p < .05$) than the mean of the normative sample (14.91). Thus the validity of the B-III was again supported.

Discussion

The present scale was constructed from the responses of male college freshmen and sophomores, a sample highly restricted in age, education, intelligence, and, to some extent, socioeconomic level. The restricted nature of the sample permitted the use of some items which would be inappropriate for other populations and reduced the variance due to the factors listed above. On the other hand, the scale is clearly unsuitable for use with anybody but college males.

What do the B-III items and the validity evidence suggest about social competence among college males, as measured in the present manner? Emphasis appears to be placed on extroversion, activity, and decision making at the expense of thinking and reflection. It is noteworthy that the fraternity members who were rated least competent nevertheless scored higher than the classroom sample. It can be concluded that the B-III emphasizes the somewhat superficial or salesmanlike aspects of competence at the expense of the introspective aspects.

This paper does not answer the question of whether the kind of social competence measured here is healthy in the traditional sense of mental health. It has simply outlined a consistent set of behaviors and personality characteristics which were judged to bring social approval to their possessors. Whether such people will be regarded as possessing a high degree of traditional mental health in the long run is a question for further research.

Table 1. Biographical Survey III

1. How old was your mother when your parents married? 18–26
2. How many *different* girls did you date *up to the end* of your senior year in high school? 2 and more
3. What is the total number of dates you had during your senior year in high school? 10 and more
4. How frequently do you date at present? more often than once a month
5. How old were you when you began to date regularly? up to and including 17
6. How many serious physical illnesses have you had during your lifetime (those that have incapacitated you for 2 weeks or more)? 0 or 1
7. If you felt you were getting some illness while here at school, what would you do?
   ____ Try to ignore it as long as possible
   ____ Consider going home to your parents' place
   ____ Go home to your parents' place
   __*x*__ Go directly to Student Health or another doctor in town
   ____ Other (Specify)
8. Have you ever made a trip as much as 200 miles away from home (without your parents or other guardian) where you stayed overnight, *other than* visiting relatives? yes (yes or no)
9. Have you ever made such a trip as much as 1,000 miles away from home without a parent or other guardian? yes (yes or no)
10. How do you approach your school assignments?
   __*x*__ Get them done ahead of schedule
   __*x*__ Do them in the last few days, but always get them in on time
   ____ Rush them at the last minute, and sometimes get them in late
   ____ Have habitual problems with getting them done on time, in spite of adequate ability
11. How many times, in your lifetime, have you been spoken to by a policeman for any possible *traffic* offense, except parking? 0–3
12. Do you cook your own meals?
   ____ never
   __*x*__ rarely; perhaps an occasional piece of toast
   __*x*__ sometimes; it is not unusual for me to prepare my own meal
   __*x*__ frequently; I do this as often as not, when I have the opportunity
13. Who usually buys (i.e., selects) your clothes?
   __*x*__ I do
   ____ my mother does (or similar person)
   ____ sometimes I do; sometimes my mother does
14. With how many social, recreational, or organizational activities were you affiliated during your last year in high school? 2 and more
15. Of the activities in No. 14 above, in how many of these (if any) did you hold an office? 1 and more
16. With how many social, recreational, or organizational activities are you affiliated now? 1 and more
17. Do you drink at all now? yes (yes or no)
18. Do you participate frequently and regularly (once a week or oftener) in some non-organized athletic activity (e.g., play handball with Joe on Thursdays)? yes (yes or no)

Table 1. Biographical Survey III (continued)

19. How often do you go to church? <u>any response other than "never"</u>
20. How much freedom do you have (when home) with an automobile?

 __*x*__ I have my own car
 __*x*__ I can always (or nearly always) get the car from my parents
 __*x*__ I can sometimes get the car
 _____ I can occasionally get the car
 _____ I don't drive

Note. Criterion answers are checked or inserted. No more than 1 point is scored for any one question.

Chapter 6

Reliability and Validity

The readings in this section deal with the statistical or psychometric basis for evaluating the adequacy of personality assessment instruments. A satisfactory grasp of these basic psychometric and statistical considerations is considered essential for anybody who desires more than a superficial understanding of the issues involved in personality measurement. While this particular chapter is somewhat briefer than others in this volume, it is not because of any lesser importance attached to these issues or because of any lack of availability of adequate materials dealing with these problems, but rather because many of the other papers that are included in this book do deal substantively with the psychometric aspects of the particular topics that they discuss. The five papers that we have chosen make rather basic and general points, some of which have been fairly well integrated into contemporary assessment technology, and some of which are not yet accepted in wide practical use.

The psychometric considerations in the understanding of psychological tests are traditionally grouped under two central rubrics: *reliability* and *validity.* Reliability concerns the degree to which the same measurement or observation can be reproduced (repeated, verified) under a number of different circumstances: from time to time, with equivalent forms of the same assessment instrument, and under different conditions of measurement (place, type of examiner, time of the day, physical surroundings, etc.). Validity typically refers to the degree to which an assessment procedure has achieved its stated aims or purposes. Validity also may be defined in terms of the degree to which an assessment procedure can be shown to be related to other indices of the same behavior, especially nontest indices.

The importance of establishing the reliability of assessment devices has been raised earlier. Swensen's review and analysis of the usefulness of human figure drawings as an assessment technique reported that the limited reliability of individual signs in drawings constitutes a major obstacle to efforts to discover personality meaning for these signs. Swensen's suggestion for improving reliability was to have the respondent produce not one, but several drawings.

The same issue is involved in the attempts to evaluate the personality significance of formal scoring categories on the Rorschach test. Scores such as the ratio of human movement to color responses, for example, are quite unreliable, and it would be unrealistic to expect an adequate demonstration of validity when an individual's score may vary significantly from testing to testing. Recent researchers have begun to attend to different conditions of test administration, characteristics of examiners, etc., not merely as they affect reliability but also from the viewpoint that these are significant factors affecting an individual's performance on a test, and that they must be understood and taken into consideration in making interpretations from test data. It may be recalled that Murstein, in his article on the validity of assessing hostility from TAT stories, compared the effect of two kinds of orienting instructions that made the subjects either "defensive" or "objective" in their attitude toward the test. Test-taking attitude was found to interact with other factors in a complex manner in determining the amount of hostility that the subjects gave in their stories.

In the first reading in this section, Edward Cureton demonstrates once again that a strict empirical approach in selecting items for a personality assessment might well result in a meaningless measure. After taking the reader through an apparently legitimate series of steps in test construction, Cureton reveals that he has selected the items for his "Projective Psychokinesis Test" by a purely chance procedure, capitalizing on the fact that if a large enough pool of items is tried, some will correlate with the criterion purely by accident. An examination of test reliability immediately exposes this methodological flaw and reveals the purely chance nature of the resulting scale. An attempt to demonstrate cross-validity by seeing whether the test "works" on a new sample of subjects would also reveal the fallacy. In fact, given the statistical criterion that Cureton used in selecting his items (those that were more than one standard error distant from the mean), one would have expected slightly *more* than 24 out of 85 items to have been identified simply by "chance."

Forer's article, the second in this section, neatly demonstrates the fallacy of relying for validity on the subject's own evaluation of the adequacy of a test interpretation. One is reminded of the earlier paper by Knight Dunlap and his concern with essentially this same issue. Forer introduces us to what has been termed the "Barnum effect," namely, the use of personality interpretation statements that would be true of practically anybody. If the statements are written so that they tend to refer to socially desirable behaviors and qualities, we are practically guaranteed that the majority of persons will accept them as "true" about themselves and will further believe that they represent their unique personal description. The lesson to be learned from Forer's study is that personal testimony, no matter how frequent, has no necessary relationship to validity, and is largely inadmissible as scientific evidence of the validity of personality assessments.

When a personality test is used in clinical assessment, it is usually part of a series or battery of tests. In fact, the use of a "test battery" has been a tradition that has persisted despite the fact that it is frequently not the most efficient approach to take. In the third paper, Lee Sechrest draws attention to a specific way of approaching this issue, by considering the *incremental* validity of a test within a battery—that is, the overall increase in accuracy that would accrue from including the test compared with not including it. The paper by Sines in Chapter 8 gives a specific illustration of the incremental validity approach to assessing the utility of the various components of a personality assessment procedure in a clinical setting.

In our introduction to Chapter 2, we stated that increasing attention has recently been given in personality assessment to finding objective rules for personality description and for predicting personality-related events. With this emphasis has come the recognition of the critical importance of a previously overlooked factor in personality assessment methodology—the frequency, or *base rate,* of the characteristic to be predicted. Simple logic will show that if a characteristic occurs very infrequently in the population under study, the use of a test with somewhat less than perfect accuracy will result in an incorrect identification of a considerable number of people who do *not* possess the characteristic, in addition to correctly identifying most of those few who do have the characteristic. If we were to evaluate the test's success in terms of hits-and-misses, we would often find that we could have been more accurate overall by not using the test at all. Albert Rosen, in the fourth reading, takes up this problem in detail as he examines the psychometric limitations inherent in any attempt to predict the very infrequent event of suicide.

The philosophy of evaluating a test's usefulness by examining its overall hit-and-miss rate has been criticized from a variety of sources. Basically, the criticism has been the same: in actual practice the usefulness of a test does not depend on its absolute accuracy, but on its contribution in enabling the necessary decisions to be made effectively and at minimum cost, all things considered. For example, a failure to identify one suicidal person would be much more costly, in social terms, than making the error of misidentifying a nonsuicidal person as suicidal. In attempting to quantify these decision processes, David Rimm, in our final paper of the section, points out that the critical information needed is the relative costs of making the two kinds of errors. By making use of this information and also the base rate of persons possessing the characteristic of interest, Rimm shows how it is possible to decide whether it is economically worthwhile to use the test, and he also provides a formula for computing the relative amount of money that would be saved by doing so. To these costs must, of course, be added the costs of conducting the testing procedure itself.

1. VALIDITY, RELIABILITY, AND BALONEY[1]

Edward E. Cureton

It is a generally accepted principle that if a test has demonstrated validity for some given purpose, considerations of reliability are secondary. The statistical literature also informs us that a validity coefficient cannot exceed the square root of the reliability coefficient of either the predictor or the criterion. This paper describes the construction and validation of a new test which seems to call in question these accepted principles. Since the technique of validation is the crucial point, I shall discuss the validation procedure before describing the test in detail.

Briefly, the test uses a new type of projective technique which appears to reveal controllable variations in psychokinetic force as applied in certain particular situations. In the present study the criterion is college scholarship, as given by the usual grade-point average. The subjects were 29 senior and graduate students in a course in Psychological Measurements. These students took Forms Q and R of the *Cooperative Vocabulary Test,* Form R being administered about

SOURCE. Edward E. Cureton is Professor of Psychology at the University of Tennessee, where he was formerly chairman of the Department of Philosophy and Psychology (1950-1959) and chairman of the Department of Psychology (1959-1963). Dr. Cureton's fields of professional specialization include statistics, test construction, and factor analysis. This article originally appeared in *Educational and Psychological Measurement,* 1950, **10,** 94-96. Reprinted by permission of Duke University Press and the author.

[1]This paper was presented in Denver, Colorado, September 7, 1949, at a meeting sponsored jointly by the Division on Evaluation and Measurement of the American Psychological Association and the Psychometric Society.

two weeks after Form Q. The correlation between grade-point average and the combined score on both forms of this test was .23. The reliability of the test, estimated by the Spearman-Brown formula from the correlation between the two forms, was .90.

The experimental form of the new test, which I have termed the "B–Projective Psychokinesis Test," or Test B, was also applied to the group. This experimental form contained 85 items, and there was a reaction to every item for every student. The items called for unequivocal "plus" or "minus" reactions, but in advance of data there is no way to tell which reaction to a given item may be valid for any particular purpose. In this respect Test B is much like many well-known interest and personality inventories. Since there were no intermediate reactions, all scoring was based on the "plus" reactions alone.

I first obtained the mean grade-point average of all the students whose reaction to each item was "plus." Instead of using the usual technique of biserial correlation, however, I used an item-validity index based on the significance of the difference between the mean grade-point average of the whole group, and the mean grade-point average of those who gave the "plus" reaction to any particular item. This is a straightforward case of sampling from a finite universe. The mean and standard deviation of the grade-point averages of the entire group of 29 are the known parameters. The null hypothesis to be tested is the hypothesis that the subgroup giving the "plus" reaction to any item is a random sample from this population. The mean number giving the "plus" reaction to any item was 14.6. I therefore computed the standard error of the mean for independent samples of 14.6 drawn from a universe of 29, with replacement. If the mean grade-point average of those giving the "plus" reaction to any particular item was more than one standard error *above* the mean of the whole 69, the item was retained with a scoring weight of *plus one.* If it was more than one standard error *below* this general mean, the item was retained with a scoring weight of *minus one.*

By this procedure, 9 positively weighted items and 15 negatively weighted items were obtained. A scoring key for all 24 selected items was prepared, and the "plus" reactions for the 29 students were scored with this key. The correlations between the 29 scores on the revised Test B and the grade-point averages was found to be .82. In comparison with the Vocabulary Test, which correlated only .23 with the same criterion, Test B appears to possess considerable promise as a predictor of college scholarship. However, the authors of many interest and personality tests, who have used essentially similar validation techniques, have warned us to interpret high validity coefficients with caution when they are derived from the same data used in making the item analysis.

The correlation between Test B and the Vocabulary Test was .31, which is .08 higher than the correlation between the Vocabulary Test and the grade-point averages. On the other hand, the reliability of Test B, by the Kuder-Richardson Formula 20, was –.06. Hence it would appear that the accepted principles previously mentioned are called in question rather severely by the findings of this study. The difficulty may be explained, however, by a consideration of the structure of the B–Projective Psychokinesis Test.

The items of Test B consisted of 85, metal-rimmed labelling tags. Each tag bore an item number, from 1 to 85 on one side only. To derive a score for any given student, I first put the 85 tags in a cocktail shaker and shook them up thoroughly. Then I looked at the student's grade-point average. If it was B or above, I projected into the cocktail shaker a wish that the students should receive a high "plus" reaction score. If his grade-point average was below B, I projected a wish that he should receive a low score. Then I threw the tags on the table. To obtain the student's score, I counted as "plus" reactions all the tags which lit with the numbered side up. The derivation of the term "B–Projective Psychokinesis Test" should now be obvious.

The moral of this story, I think, is clear. When a validity coefficient is computed from the same data used in making an item analysis, this coefficient cannot be interpreted uncritically. And, contrary to many statements in the literature, it cannot be interpreted "with caution" either. There is one clear interpretation for all such validity coefficients. This interpretation is—

"Baloney!"

2. THE FALLACY OF PERSONAL VALIDATION: A CLASSROOM DEMONSTRATION OF GULLIBILITY

Bertram R. Forer

This paper is concerned with some of the methodological errors which can affect estimations of the validity of personality interpretations and measuring instruments. Of prime significance is the nature of the interpretations themselves. Personality evaluations can be, and often are, couched in such general terms that they are meaningless in terms of denotability in behavior. Or they may have "universal validity" and apply to everyone. Bobertag (1934) refers to the universally valid personality trait as *Universalscharakteristik.*

Possession of two eyes is a characteristic of all vertebrates, hence is of no value as a differentiating factor among vertebrates. The opposing thumb does

SOURCE. Bertram R. Forer has been a test and measurement specialist and an executive editor of the *Journal of Projective Techniques and Personality Assessment.* He is currently in private practice in Los Angeles, California, and senior attending psychologist at the Los Angeles Psychiatric Service. This article originally appeared in the *Journal of Abnormal and Social Psychology,* 1949, **44**, 118-123. Reprinted by permission of the American Psychological Association and the author.

not distinguish one human being from another. At the psychological level the acceptance of some cultural taboos appears to be universal among human beings who live within social groups. Virtually every psychological trait can be observed in some degree in everyone. For the purpose of characterizing a particular individual, stipulation of those traits which he demonstrates is a meaningless procedure. It is not in the presence or absence of a trait that individuals differ. The uniqueness of the individual, as Allport (1937) amply documents, lies in the relative importance of the various personality forces in determining his behavior and in the relative magnitude of these traits in comparison with other persons. Thus the individual is a unique configuration of characteristics each of which can be found in everyone, but in varying degrees. A universally valid statement, then, is one which applies equally well to the majority or the totality of the population. The universally valid statement is true for the individual, but it lacks the quantitative specification and the proper focus which are necessary for differential diagnosis. In a sense a universally valid statement is a description of a cultural group rather than a personal psychological datum.

A universally valid personality description is of the type most likely to be accepted by a client as a truth about himself, a truth which he considers unique in him. Many, if not most, individuals are able to recognize the characteristics in themselves—when it is not to their disadvantage—while oblivious to their presence in others. An example is the tendency for students to perceive their own problems in textbooks of abnormal psychology. In such cases the individual lacks the quantitative frame of reference necessary for a critical comparison of the printed description and his own self-evaluation.

At times confirmation by a client or by some other person familiar with his history is used as a criterion in the validation of diagnostic inferences and procedures (Crider, 1944). Test results may suggest certain problems and characteristic modes of behavior which therapists or the client, himself, can confirm or deny. Testing the correctness of inferences about a client by requesting his evaluation of them may be called "personal validation." When the inferences are universally valid, as they often are, the confirmation is useless. The positive results obtained by personal validation can easily lull a test analyst or a therapist into a false sense of security which bolsters his conviction in the essential rightness of his philosophy of personality or his diagnostic prowess. Such false validation increases his comfort in using what may have been a dubious instrument. A great danger arises when the confirmation of a prediction is extended uncritically to the instrument or conceptual system or person making the prediction. Such uncritical extensions occur too frequently in the clinical field.

Confirmation of a prediction does not necessarily prove the validity of the propositions from which the prediction was inferred. An identical prediction may be made from a group of propositions which contradict the original ones.

Taylor (1947) has shown empirically that judges of case histories may arrive at identical predictions for different reasons. Confirmation of a variety of predictions which will differentiate among a number of clients is necessary if validation is to be accepted with any degree of confidence.

The crystal-gazer is likely to be aware of some of these points and other pseudo-diagnosticians, though they may be unaware of the fallacies inherent in their procedures, make effective use of "universal validity" and "personal validation" in deceiving their clients. Allport (1937, p. 476) states that "one way in which character analysts secure a reputation for success is through the employment of ambiguous terms that may apply to any mortal person." A naive person who receives superficial diagnostic information, especially when the social situation is prestige-laden, tends to accept such information.[1] He is impressed by the obvious truths and may be oblivious to the discrepancies. But he does more than this. *He also validates the instrument and the diagnostician.* Crider's students (1944) found surprisingly accurate the analyses they received from a pseudo-diagnostician. Crider, himself, seems to have been beguiled by the results and decries a priori rejection of the claims of these persons. While the use of matching procedures has revealed fairly high validity for inferences derived from projective tests by trained clinicians, it has not supported the claims of persons employing non-standardized graphological techniques (Pascal and Suttell, 1947).

Recently the writer was accosted by a night-club graphologist who wished to "read" his handwriting. The writer declined and offered to administer a Rorschach to the graphologist. An amiable discussion ensued, during which the

[1] D. G. Paterson, in a personal letter to the writer, describes and includes a universally valid personality sketch which he uses in luncheon club lectures. It is reproduced here with his permission.

"Above average in intelligence or mental alertness. Also above average in accuracy—rather painstaking at times. Deserves a reputation for neatness—dislikes turning out sloppy work. Has initiative; that is, ability to make suggestions and to get new ideas, open-mindedness.

"You have a tendency to worry at times but not to excess. You do get depressed at times but you couldn't be called moody because you are generally cheerful and rather optimistic. You have a good disposition although earlier in life you have had a struggle with yourself to control your impulses and temper.

"You are strongly socially inclined, you like to meet people, especially to mix with those you know well. You appreciate art, painting and music, but you will never be a success as an artist or as a creator or composer of music. You like sports and athletic events but devote more of your attention to reading about them in the sporting page than in actual participation.

"You are ambitious, and deserve credit for wanting to be well thought of by your family, business associates and friends. These ambitions come out most strongly in your tendency to indulge in day-dreams, in building air-castles, but this does not mean that you fail to get into the game of life actively.

"You ought to continue to be successful so long as you stay in a social vocation. I mean if you keep at work bringing you in contact with people. Just what work you pick out isn't as important as the fact that it must be work bringing you in touch with people. On the negative side you would never have made a success at strictly theoretical work or in pure research work such as in physics or neurology."

graphologist ventured proof of the scientific basis of his work in that his clients affirmed the correctness of his interpretations. The writer suggested that a psychologist could make a blindfold reading and attain the same degree of verification.

Experiment

The following experiment was performed in the writer's class in introductory psychology to demonstrate the ease with which clients may be misled by a general personality description into unwarranted approval of a diagnostic tool. The writer had discussed his Diagnostic Interest Blank[2] (hereafter referred to as DIB) in connection with the role of personal motivational factors in perceptual selectivity. Class members requested that they be given the test and a personality evaluation. The writer acquiesced. At the next meeting the 39 students were given DIB's to fill out, and were told that they would be given a brief personality vignette as soon as the writer had time to examine their test papers. One week later each student was given a typed personality sketch with his name written on it. The writer encouraged the expressed desire of the class for secrecy regarding the content of the sketches. Fortunately, this was the day on which a quiz was scheduled; hence it was possible to ensure their sitting two seats apart without arousing suspicion. From the experimenter's point of view it was essential that no student see the sketch received by any other student because *all sketches were identical.*[3] The students were unsuspecting.

The personality sketch contains some material which overlaps with that of Paterson, but consists of 13 statements rather than a narrative description. A further difference lies in the fact that this sketch was designed for more nearly universal validity than Paterson's appears to have been. The sketch consists of the following items.

1. You have a great need for other people to like and admire you.
2. You have a tendency to be critical of yourself.
3. You have a great deal of unused capacity which you have not turned to your advantage.
4. While you have some personality weaknesses, you are generally able to compensate for them.

[2]The DIB consists of a list of hobbies, reading materials, personal characteristics, job duties, and secret hopes and ambitions of one's ideal person. The test is interpreted qualitatively and personality dynamics are inferred along lines similar to projective tests.

[3]These statements came largely from a newsstand astrology book. The writer was not aware of Paterson's sketch at the time this problem was formulated and carried out.

5. Your sexual adjustment has presented problems for you.
6. Disciplined and self-controlled outside, you tend to be worrisome and insecure inside.
7. At times you have serious doubts as to whether you have made the right decision or done the right thing.
8. You prefer a certain amount of change and variety and become dissatisfied when hemmed in by restrictions and limitations.
9. You pride yourself as an independent thinker and do not accept others' statements without satisfactory proof.
10. You have found it unwise to be too frank in revealing yourself to others.
11. At times you are extroverted, affable, sociable, while at other times you are introverted, wary, reserved.
12. Some of your aspirations tend to be pretty unrealistic.
13. Security is one of your major goals in life.

Before the sketches were passed to the students, instructions were given first to read the sketches and then to turn the papers over and make the following ratings:

A. Rate on a scale of zero (poor) to five (perfect) how effective the DIB is in revealing personality.

B. Rate on a scale of zero to five the degree to which the personality description reveals basic characteristics of your personality.

C. Then turn the paper again and check each statement as true or false about yourself or use a question mark if you cannot tell.

In answer to their requests students were informed that the writer had another copy of their sketch and would give it to them after the data were collected. After the papers had been returned to the writer students were asked to raise their hands if they felt the test had done a good job. Virtually all hands went up and the students noticed this. Then the first sketch item was read and students were asked to indicate by hands whether they had found anything similar on their sketches. As all hands rose, the class burst into laughter. It was pointed out to them that the experiment had been performed as an object lesson to demonstrate the tendency to be overly impressed by vague statements and to endow the diagnostician with an unwarrantedly high degree of insight. Similarities between the demonstration and the activities of charlatans were pointed out. That the experience had meaning for them was indicated by the fact that at least one-third of the class asked for copies of the sketch so that they might try the trick on their friends.

Results

The data show clearly that the group had been gulled. Ratings of adequacy of the DIB included only one rating below 4. Thus the instrument received a high degree of personal validation. In the evaluation of the sketch as a whole there were five ratings below 4 (Table 1). While a few students were more critical of the sketch than of the DIB, most of them were ready to admit that basic personality traits had been revealed.

Table 1. Distributions of Ratings

Rating	0	1	2	3	4	5	N
A (DIB)	0	0	0	1	25	13	39
B (Sketch)	0	0	1	4	18	16	39

The number of specific items accepted as true varied among the group from 8 to 13 except for one individual who accepted only 5 (Table 2). This same individual rated the test at 4 and the sketch at 2. Mean acceptance was 10.2 items.

Table 2. Distribution of "True" Responses

Number True	5	6	7	8	9	10	11	12	13	N
Frequency	1	0	0	5	5	10	9	7	2	39

No significant relationships were found between any of the ratings and sex, age, occupational background, or grades on the subsequent quiz.

In addition to the high ratings of the DIB which indicate a degree of gullibility or fallacious judgment, further evidence can be seen in the degree to which ratings were made on other than evidential grounds or contrary to the evidence. If the individual accepts all of the items as applying to himself, he is somewhat justified in accepting the instrument; if he rejects all of the items in the sketch, he is justified in rejecting the DIB.

The chi-square test indicates a degree of association, significant at the 1-percent level, between ratings of the sketch (rating B) and the number of items checked as true. However, the operation of other factors in judgment from part to whole is clearly indicated. For some individuals the presence of 8 true statements among the 13 was considered sufficient evidence for acceptance of the sketch as perfect. For others, high, but imperfect, validity was indicated by the acceptance of 12 of the 13 items. It may be said, then, that among this group of students individuals varied in the degree to which they weighted the truth and falsity of the descriptive items in arriving at an overall evaluation.

Ratings of the DIB as a diagnostic instrument (rating A) and number of items accepted as true show no significant relationship (the probability value of the chi-square is .4). On the one hand, estimation of the adequacy of the personality sketch was partially dependent upon the amount of confirmatory evidence. On the other hand, the degree of approval of the test was independent of the degree to which test results agreed with self-evaluations. That is, validation of the test instrument was an all-or-none affair depending on a certain minimum amount of evidence. The amount of confirmatory evidence set up as a standard varied among the students.

All of the students accepted the DIB as a good or perfect instrument for personality measurement. Most of them can be accused of a logical error in accepting the test on such scanty evidence. Those who accepted the test with a rating of 5 while accepting fewer than all of the 13 statements have demonstrated a disregard for the evidence of their own criticisms. The same can be said for those who rated the test higher than the personality sketch. It is interesting that the student most critical of the personality sketch, as indicated in an overall rating of 2 and acceptance of only 5 items, at the same time rated the DIB at 4.

The degrees of group acceptance for the 13 items are indicated in Table 3. None of the items attained complete universal validity, though more than half of them were close to complete group acceptance.

Table 3. Group Acceptance of Sketch Items

Response	Item Number												
	1	2	3	4	5	6	7	8	9	10	11	12	13
True	28	38	23	31	18	35	38	37	34	35	34	12	28
False	4	0	1	0	9	3	0	1	3	2	1	9	7
Uncertain	7	1	15	8	12	1	1	1	2	2	4	18	4

Recall of Ratings

Since many of the class had indicated their embarrassment at having been "taken in," the writer suspected that the dynamics of the memory process would operate in the direction of healing the results of this assault to self-esteem. The class had been informed of the distributions of ratings. Three weeks later the students were told that the writer had erased the names from their rating sheets as he had promised. Unfortunately he would have liked to compare their ratings with their grades on the quiz. Perhaps they would be willing to jot down from memory the ratings they had made of the DIB and the sketch. The rating scales were written on the blackboard. The students were understandably skeptical at first, but ultimately cooperative. Only 32 of the students were present who had taken the DIB and received the sketch.

Results were more or less as expected. In the case of rating A (of the DIB) no general trends were noted: two students raised their ratings from 4 to 5 and three others lowered their ratings from 5 to 4. On the other hand, rating B (of the sketch) tended to be lowered. Seven ratings of 5 were lowered to 4 and one rating of 5 was lowered to 3. None was raised. The two distributions of ratings on the sketch are shown in Table 4. The *t*-test for differences between related means indicates significance at the 1-per-cent level. Thus, there is confirmation of a significant lowering in the level of acceptance of the sketch among those who had been most credulous.

Table 4. Rating B, Original and Recall

Rating	2	3	4	5	N
Original	1	3	12	16	32
Recall	1	4	19	8	32

Conclusions

1. Claims of validity for their methods and results by pseudo-diagnosticians can be duplicated or surpassed in the laboratory *without* the use of a diagnostic instrument. Blindfold personality estimates can be shown to be valid when the method of personal validation (confirmation by the client) is used for descriptive items of approximate universal validity.

2. Validation of a test instrument or of a personality sketch by means of personal validation is a fallacious procedure which presupposes objectivity of self-evaluation and an understanding of other persons on the part of the client.

3. Using the method of personal validation, a fictitious personality sketch can easily deceive persons into approving a diagnostic device even when there is incomplete acceptance of the sketch itself. A minimum degree of correspondence between the sketch and self-evaluation appears to engender an attitude of acceptance of the total sketch and this attitude of acceptance is carried uncritically to the test instrument.

4. The personal validation procedure is likely to yield more fallacious results in the case of overall evaluations of a personality sketch than when specific statements are evaluated individually.

5. When self-esteem is threatened, memory functions operate in such a manner as to avert the threat and enhance self-esteem. Such memory changes are defensive distortions of recall rather than simple forgetting.

6. Clinical psychologists and others who make inferences about personality characteristics may be led into ascribing an excessively high degree of signifi-

cance to these inferences. There is pressing need for clinicians to submit their own procedures, presuppositions, and, perhaps, projections to experimental scrutiny.

3. INCREMENTAL VALIDITY: A RECOMMENDATION[1]

Lee Sechrest

The 1954 publication *Technical Recommendations for Psychological Tests and Diagnostic Techniques* established minimum standards to be met in the production and promotion of psychometric instruments. Since that time there have appeared a considerable number of articles elaborating or extending the considerations involved in developing tests (e.g., Cronbach & Meehl, 1955; Jessor & Hammond, 1957; Loevinger, 1957; Campbell & Fiske, 1959; Bechtoldt, 1959; Campbell, 1960). In one of the most recent developments, Campbell and Fiske (1959) have suggested that a crucial distinction is to be made between convergent and discriminant validity. It is necessary to demonstrate not only that a measure covaries with certain other connotatively similar variables, but that its covariance with other connotatively dissimilar variables is limited.

Campbell (1960) has suggested several possible additions to recommended validity indicators, all of which focus on the problem of *discriminant* validity, i.e., the demonstration that a test construct is not completely or even largely redundant with other better established or more parsimonious constructs. He has suggested, for example, that correlations with intelligence, social desirability and self-ratings should be reported since these variables are likely to be conceptually and theoretically simpler than most of our constructs. If a new test proves to be reducible to an intelligence or social desirability measure, its *raison d'etre* probably vanishes.

It is the purpose of this note to suggest an additional validity construct and evidence which should be presented in the basic publications concerning *any test which is intended for applied, predictive use.*

SOURCE. Lee B. Sechrest is presently Professor of Psychology at Northwestern University and was formerly Senior Specialist on a project for the Center for Cultural and Technical Interchange between East and West, Honolulu, 1965-1966. Dr. Sechrest has written many professional articles on psychological measurement, cognitive processes, and culture and personality. This article originally appeared in *Educational and Psychological Measurement,* 1963, **23,** 153-158. Reprinted by permission of Duke University Press and the author.

[1]The writer wishes to thank Donald T. Campbell and Douglas N. Jackson for helpful suggestions on an earlier version of this manuscript.

Incremental Validity

Almost without exception evidence which is presented to support the validity of a psychological test is presented in the form of some improvement over results which would be expected by chance. However, in *clinical* situations, at least, tests are rarely, if ever, used in a manner consistent with the chance model. Almost always Rorschachs are interpreted after interviews, reading of case reports, conferences and the like. The meaning of a report that some Rorschach variable will predict better than chance becomes obscure under those circumstances. It seems clear that validity must be claimed for a test in terms of some *increment* in predictive efficiency over the information otherwise easily and cheaply available.

Cronbach and Gleser (1957, pp. 30-32) and, as they point out, Conrad (1950), have both discussed the problem of the base against which the predictive power of a test is to be evaluated. Cronbach and Gleser declare, "Tests should be judged on the basis of their contribution over and above the best strategy available, making use of prior information" (1957, p. 31). They do indicate that tests may be valuable in spite of low correlations if they tap characteristics either unobservable or difficult to observe by other means. Shaffer (1950, p. 76) also suggested, "One can . . . study the degree to which the clinician is valid with and without the aid of a certain technique, and thereby assess the value of the test indirectly." We are not so sure that such an assessment is completely indirect.

In light of the above argument it is proposed that the publications adduced as evidence for the utility of a test in a clinical situation–and probably for most other uses–should include evidence that the test will *add to* or *increase* the validity of predictions made on the basis of data which are usually available. At a minimum it would seem that a test should have demonstrated incremental validity beyond that of brief case histories, simple biographical information and brief interviews. A strong case can also be made to demand that a test contribute beyond the level of simpler, e.g., paper and pencil, tests. As a matter of fact, Campbell's recommendation that new tests be correlated with self-ratings is quite akin to some aspects of incremental validity.

Adequate Statistical Evidence

When a test is added to a battery, the usual way to express its contribution is either by a partial correlation or by an increment to a zero order or multiple correlation. There is, perhaps, one objection to the partial or multiple correlation as a demonstration of incremental validity. That is, the increase, even if significant, is of somewhat undetermined origin and obscures the exact nature of the increment achieved.

Consider the matrix of correlations:

	1	2	0
1		60	40
2			40
0			

in which 1 and 2 are predictors of criterion 0. The multiple $R_{12.0} = .45$ and the partial $r_{20.1} = .22$. Both values might be considered to represent improvements over the zero order correlations, And yet, without knowing the reliabilities of 1 and 2 we will be unable to discern whether 2 contributes to the prediction of 0 because it represents a theoretical variable distinct from 1 or whether 2 has only the same, and informationally redundant, effect of increasing the length and, hence, the reliability of Test 1. It will often be important to know whether an increment results from a Spearman-Brown prophecy operation or from some contribution of theoretical importance. Kelley (1927) suggested quite a number of years ago that when correlations between intelligence and achievement measures are properly treated the two measures prove to be almost completely overlapping. Thus, in his view, the two kinds of measures only combine to form a longer and more reliable measure of a single variable.

One solution to the problem might be the correction of inter-test correlations for attenuation. If the reliabilities are so low that the corrected correlation approaches unity, no increment to R nor a significant partial correlation will ensue. In the above example, given reliabilities for 1 and 2 of only .60, the correlation between them would become unity, the multiple would be .40, and the partial r .00. On the other hand, if both variables had reliability coefficients of .90, the correction for attenuation would have little effect on either R or partial correlation.[2]

Exemplary Instances of Incremental Validity Research

Demonstrations of incremental validity are not common in research literature except in prediction of academic performance. Unfortunately, where they occur the data often are discouraging. Winch and More (1956) used a multiple correlation technique in an attempt to determine the increment produced by TAT protocols over a semi-structured interview and case history material. Their results provide no basis for concluding that the TAT contributes anything beyond what is given by interviews or case histories. Sines (1959) discovered

[2]It is to be noted that correction for attenuation of the validity values is *not* suggested and should not be done.

that the Rorschach apparently did yield better than chance predictions, but it seemingly not only did not add to other information obtained from interviews and a biographical data sheet, but it actually produced a net *decrement* in predictive accuracy. This in spite of *better than chance* "validity." Kostlan (1954) found that judges made better than chance inferences about patients' behavior from only "minimal data" (age, occupation, education, marital status and source of referral). When test results were used to make the same judgments, only the social history yielded more accurate inferences than those made from simple biographical facts.

In the general area of prediction of academic success, data are widely available indicating the increment over previous grades afforded by predictions based on psychometric data. Even in predicting academic performance, however, it is not always clear that the use of test data accomplishes anything beyond increasing the reliability of the ability measure based on grades. If treated as suggested above, it might be possible to determine whether a test contributes anything beyond maximizing the reliability of the general ability measure afforded by grades. Ford (1950) has presented data concerning the prediction of grades in nursing school making use of, among other measures, the Cooperative General Science Test (CGST) and high school point average (HSPA). The correlation matrix between these variables is:

	CGST	HSPA	Grades
1. CGST		.33	.57
2. HSPA			.51
0. Grades			

The multiple correlation $R_{12.0}$ is .66 and the partial $r_{10.2}$ is .50. The split-half reliability of the CGST has been reported to be .88. While no reliability estimate for HSPA is known to the writer, several researchers have reported reliabilities for college grades (Anderson, 1953; Bendig, 1953; Wallace, 1951). If we take the median value of the three reported values of .78, .80, and .90 as a likely estimate for HSPA and then correct the r_{12} for attenuation, the .33 becomes .40. The multiple correlation then drops only to .65 and the partial correlation only to .46. It is obvious that for the prediction of grades in nursing courses the use of the Cooperative General Science Test results in an *increment* in validity over high school grades and that the increment may be regarded as more than a contribution to reliable measurement of a single factor.

Summary

It is proposed that in addition to demonstrating the *convergent* and *discriminant* validity of tests intended for use in clinical situations, evidence should be produced for *incremental* validity. It must be demonstrable that the addition of a test will produce better predictions than are made on the basis of information other than the test ordinarily available. Reference to published research indicates that situations may well occur in which, in spite of better than chance validity, tests may not contribute to, or may even detract from, predictions made on the basis of biographical and interview information. It is further suggested that, when correlations for a given test are entered into a multiple correlation or partial correlation, the inter-predictor correlations be corrected for attenuation to determine whether an increase in the multiple or partial correlations is to be attributed to a mere increase in reliability of measurement of the predictor variable.

4. DETECTION OF SUICIDAL PATIENTS: AN EXAMPLE OF SOME LIMITATIONS IN THE PREDICTION OF INFREQUENT EVENTS

Albert Rosen

Since the detection of suicidal patients is an important responsibility of clinical psychologists, a number of investigators have proposed or evaluated certain signs, configurations, and items from psychological tests for their identification. The purposes of this paper are (*a*) to suggest modifications in the classification of patients in suicide research, (*b*) to emphasize some of the limitations inherent in the prediction of suicide, and (*c*) to indicate the general applicability of such limitations in the prediction of any other behavior or event of infrequent occurrence.

Classification of Patients In Suicide Research

The term "suicidal" has been used to describe patients demonstrating heterogeneous kinds of behavior, such as (*a*) suicide thoughts, (*b*) suicide threats, (*c*) suicide attempts, and (*d*) severe depression. In previous research on suicide

SOURCE. Albert Rosen is a co-director of the White Oak Psychological Center in Silver Springs, Maryland. He was previously Director of the Counseling Center and Professor of Psychology at Gallaudet College for the Deaf in Washington, D. C. He has written and done extensive research on problems of personality assessment, selection, and psychological aspects of deafness. This article originally appeared in the *Journal of Consulting Psychology,* 1954, 18, 397-403 and is reprinted by permission of the American Psychological Association and the author.

predictors, a common practice has been the combining of test data from such individuals with data from those who actually committed suicide.

Differentation of "Suicidal" Subgroups

The need for more precise classification in suicide research has been indicated by Farberow (1950) and by Rosen, Hales, and Simon (1954), who demonstrated that "suicidal" subgroups can be differentiated by means of psychological tests. The two studies closely agreed in indicating that, as a group, patients who express suicide thoughts or suicide threats are much more severely disturbed than either patients who have made a suicide attempt or patients-in-general, and that patients in the latter two categories are similar to each other.

Suicide Rates

Additional evidence of the need for greater refinement in the classification of patients in suicide research is provided by statistics on the incidence of suicide. Suicide is an extremely infrequent event, and very few of those patients who are severely depressed or who express suicide thoughts or threats actually commit suicide. Thus, data from such patients should not arbitrarily be grouped under the class term "suicidal." Examination of the following data on suicide rates provides substantiation of these statements.

Suicide Rate for the General Population. In the United States, the suicide rate for the general population is 11.4 in 100,000 (U.S. Dept. of Commerce, 1953). Reliable statistics for the frequency of suicide *attempts* in the general population are unavailable because of the difficulty of determining objectively what is an "attempt." Data on the incidence of suicide among psychiatric patients are sparse; they may be classified in two ways, according to occurrence: (*a*) after termination of treatment and (*b*) during hospitalization.

Posttreatment Suicide Rates Among Former Psychiatric Patients. Only four published studies could be located which reported data on the incidence of suicide among patients after termination of treatment. The authors of these reports obtained their data primarily by correspondence. The first three deal with psychoneurotics followed up for periods of from 2 to 20 years. Coon and Raymond (1940) found 6 suicides among 1060 cases, a rate of .0057. Ross (1936) reported 4 suicides among approximately 1186 neurotics, a rate of .0034. Denker (1939) discovered 3 suicides among 707 cases, a rate of .0042. Denker's cases had not been psychiatric patients, but had been diagnosed as neurotic. A fourth study, by Holt and Holt (1952), reported 2 suicides among a mixed diagnostic group of 141 patients (a rate of .0142) within a period of 30 years after hospitalization. A third patient in this group committed suicide while under treatment subsequent to his initial hospitalization.

Suicide Rates for Hospitalized Psychiatric Patients. The rate of suicide among patients undergoing psychiatric treatment is apparently lower, probably because these patients are under close observation. Ross (1936, p. 98) reported 3 suicides among 1186 neurotic patients, a rate of .0025. Two of these patients committed suicide during the period of treatment, and the other immediately after termination. Levy and Southcombe (1953) found 21 suicides among 6509 admissions (a rate of .0032) in a large state hospital for the period from 1936 to 1949.

For the sake of the present discussion, a rough estimate of .0033 will be used to represent the suicide rate among psychiatric patients undergoing treatment. Although the rate may be slightly higher in some hospitals and clinics, it is evident that suicide occurs very infrequently among psychiatric patients.

Suggested Classification Of Suicidal Patients

The need for more precise classification in research on suicide detection is thus emphasized both by the data on the low incidence of suicide and by the evidence earlier cited that "suicidal" subgroups can be differentiated by means of psychological tests. In the development and validation of a suicide detection device, one criterion group should consist exclusively of patients who committed suicide. Moreover, since a patient may undergo marked personality changes in the interval between test administration and the act of suicide, it is probably advisable to use data obtained only a relatively short time before the suicide. The most desirable time interval cannot be determined until more information on the stability of test responses of suicidal patients is available. The low incidence of suicide, of course, makes it extremely difficult to obtain presuicide data from an adequate number of cases for the development of a detection instrument.

Limitations of Suicide Predictors

A suicide detection instrument, to be effective, must identify a fairly large proportion of suicidal patients (true positives) and should not misclassify a large number of nonsuicidal patients (false positives). The low incidence of suicide is in itself a major limitation in the development of an effective suicide predictor, for in any attempt at prediction of infrequent behavior, a large number of false positives are obtained. To illustrate this point, a hypothetical suicide detection index will be devised.[1]

[1]The writer is indebted to Dr. Paul E. Meehl for indicating the importance of an inverse probability approach to the problem of suicide detection.

Development of a Hypothetical Suicide Detection Index

Assume that a suicide detection index was developed from test data obtained from a psychiatric patient population divided into two groups: patients who committed suicide during treatment (Suicide population), and patients who did not commit suicide during treatment (Nonsuicide population). Suppose that the steps in the development and validation of the index were as follows: (*a*) A random sample of patients was selected from each of these populations; (*b*) an index was devised which consisted of test data which significantly differentiated the two criterion samples; (*c*) all of the cases in the two samples were scored on the index; (*d*) a cutting line was established so that an equal percentage, say 80%, of the patients in each sample were correctly classified; (*e*) for the purpose of cross-validating this cutting line with new Suicide and Nonsuicide samples, every psychiatric patient over a period of years was scored on the index, and these scores were not divulged so that they could have no influence on the treatment of the patients.

Cross-validation of the Index. On the basis of the estimated suicide rate of .0033, there would be approximately 40 suicides among 12,000 patients. Assume that, in cross-validating the predetermined cutting line, only a slight amount of shrinkage occurs so that 75% of the patients in each of the two populations can be correctly indentified.[2] Table 1, Part A, indicates the number of patients in each population who are identified by the index. In the Suicide population, only those patients whose scores are above the stipulated cutting line are correctly identified (true positives), whereas in the Nonsuicide population, only those whose scores are below this line are accurately classified (true negatives). The effectiveness of the index must be evaluated in terms of the number of correct identifications, in both populations, among all the patients predicted to be suicides.

It can be seen that with the use of the index 30 of the 40 suicides could have been correctly predicted. However, of the 11,906 patients in the Nonsuicide population, 2990 would also have been predicted suicides (false positives). Since every patient scoring above the cutting line would have been predicted to commit suicide, 2990 out of 3020, or 99% of such patients are misclassified. Obviously, such a suicide detection index would have no appreciable value, for it would be impractical to treat as suicidal the prodigious number of misclassified cases.

[2]The figure of 75% is used because it probably represents the maximum effectiveness generally achieved with cross-validated prediction and classification devices. For example, Ellis and Conrad [1948, p. 406], in evaluating the effectiveness of the personality inventories used for screening "maladjusted" from "normal" servicemen during World War II, found that, in general, roughly 75% of each group were identified.

Table 1. Number of Patients in the Suicide and Nonsuicide Populations Identified by a Hypothetical Suicide Detection Index with Three Different Cutting Lines

Behavior Predicted by Index	Actual Behavior				Total with Predicted Behavior
	Did Commit Suicide		Did Not Commit Suicide		
	Number	%	Number	%	
A. 75% True Positives; 75% True Negatives					
Will commit suicide	30	(75%)	2990	(25%)	3020
Will not commit suicide	10	(25%)	8970	(75%)	8980
Total with actual behavior	40	(100%)	11960	(100%)	12000
B. 60% True Positives; 90% True Negatives					
Will commit suicide	24	(60%)	1196	(10%)	1220
Will not commit suicide	16	(40%)	10764	(90%)	10780
Total with actual behavior	40	(100%)	11960	(100%)	12000
C. 2.5% True Positives; 99.5% True Negatives					
Will commit suicide	1	(2.5%)	60	(.5%)	61
Will not commit suicide	39	(97.5%)	11900	(99.5%)	11939
Total with actual behavior	40	(100.0%)	11960	(100.0%)	12000

Type of Prediction Made with the Index. In planning the initial development or cross-validation of any psychological instrument, it is essential to consider the kind of decision which is to be made with the test results. In the prediction of suicide, the test results must be evaluated solely in terms of the number of correct classifications among those patients predicted to be suicides. In Table 1, Part A, there were only 1% of such correct classifications. Among all the patients in the Suicide and Nonsuicide populations, however, 9000 out of 12,000, or 75% were correctly classified. It is not appropriate or meaningful to evaluate the index in terms of the latter percentage, for there is no need to identify the patients in the Nonsuicide population. In fact, without any test or other information, all patients could be predicted to be nonsuicidal, and the prediction would be correct in 99.67% of all cases.

Cross-validation of an Elevated Cutting Line. For a suicide detection index to have any conceivable value, the number of false positives must be drastically reduced. This could have been effected in the original development of the index (step *d*) if a much higher cutting line had been established. Assume, for example, that when this elevated cutting line was cross-validated (step *e*), only 10% of the nonsuicide cases scored above the line (i.e., were false positives). Assume also that the new cutting line reduced to 60% (still a liberal estimate) the number of correctly classified suicide patients. Table 1, Part B, illustrates the results of applying the index to the Suicide and Nonsuicide populations. Of the 40 patients who did commit suicide, 24 could have been identified by the index. There would still be 1196 false positives, however, so that if every patient who scored above the cutting line were called suicidal, the number of correct classifications would be only 24 out of 1220 or 2%. The index, therefore, would still be an impractical instrument because of the large number of false positives.

Further Reduction of the Number of False Positives. With every elevation of the cutting line for the purpose of reducing the number of false positives, there will be a decrease in the number of correct predictions for the Suicide population (true positives). If the original cutting line were raised so that in the cross-validation procedure almost all false positives were eliminated, it might still be possible to detect one or two cases in the Suicide population by means of the index. Table 1, Part C, illustrates such a hypothetical situation. Although only 1 in 61, or less than 2% of the predicted suicides, is correctly identified, the important consideration is that the *number* of false positives has been reduced to a relatively manageable figure. The writer can think of no other event of relevance to clinical psychologists for which one might settle for such a low level of psychometric prediction. The attitude of hospital administrators, however, is that suicides must be prevented at almost any cost. Therefore, if the items comprising the index could be administered to all patients without undue expenditure of clinical time, the results in this apparently unique type of problem might be considered of some use.

Prediction within a Population Restricted To Certain Diagnostic Groups

It can be seen that it is very difficult to predict effectively any event with an extremely low *rate* of occurrence because of the large number of false positives. Another approach to the problem of reducing the number of false positives might be the development of an index within a population consisting only of those diagnostic groups with the highest rates of suicides. The advantage of this procedure, of course, is that the rate of suicide within this restricted population would be higher than that in the entire psychiatric patient population. Two immediate obstacles to the use of this approach are: (*a*) There is virtually no published information on suicide rates for given diagnostic categories. The writer could locate only one report [Dublin and Benzel, 1933, p. 311] which provided adequate data of this kind. (*b*) As a smaller *number* of suicides occur within a restricted population than in an entire psychiatric patient population, many years would have to elapse before a sufficient number of cases with presuicide data could be collected. It would be necessary, therefore, to conduct a coordinated research program in many installations.

Additional Limitations of the Restricted Population Approach. It would eventually be possible to obtain information on suicide rates within diagnostic groups, and it is also conceivable that a sufficient number of cases with pre-suicide data could be collected. Even if these two difficulties were surmounted, however, the procedure of developing and applying an index within a population restricted to one or several diagnostic groups has several limitations: (*a*) The rate of suicide would still be low; probably no group could be found with a suicide rate higher than .02, and there would still be an excessive number of false positives. (*b*) A considerable proportion of suicidal patients would not be included in the restricted population because of (*i*) the limited reliability of diagnosis, and (*ii*) the occurrence of suicide in diagnostic categories not included in the restricted population. (*c*) Variables differentiating suicide and nonsuicide patients would be more difficult to obtain within a somewhat homogeneous subgroup than within the whole psychiatric population.

Prediction Based On Clinical Judgment

The same kinds of difficulties which occur in psychometric prediction of suicide are encountered in prediction based on "clinical judgment." In clinical practice a large number of false positives are also obtained. The clinician, in referring to a patient as "suicidal," is willing to err on the safe side and treat a great many patients as though they were very likely to commit suicide.

Necessary Basic Research

It has been shown that the effectiveness of a suicide detection instrument is a function of (*a*) the *rate* of suicide within a given patient population (complete or restricted), and (*b*) the *percentage* of correct classifications both in the suicide and in the nonsuicide subgroups of the given population. Other things being equal, a given index will be most effective in the population with the highest suicide rate. Also, within a population with a given suicide rate, that index will be most effective which correctly classifies the highest percentage of cases in each of the population subgroups.

An essential prerequisite to the development of an effective detection device is the acquisition of a large body of information concerning the distinguishing characteristics of patients who commit suicide. To obtain such information, patients must be studied intensively by means of comprehensive social histories, behavior ratings, and psychological tests. The differentiating data thus collected may be utilized in either or both of the following ways: (*a*) to exclude from consideration as potential suicides a large proportion of psychiatric patients in order to obtain a restricted population with a higher suicide rate; (*b*) to find a large number of discriminating predictor variables which will correctly classify a high percentage of each of the suicide and nonsuicide subgroups.

Limitations in the Prediction of Other Infrequent Events

Clinical psychologists deal with virtually no other events as infrequent as suicide. One exception might be the prediction of homicide, for the incidence of homicide in the general population is about half that of suicide. The limitations of prediction discussed in this paper, however, apply in lesser degree to any other behavior as its rate approaches .50 in a population dichotomized according to the presence or absence of the behavior.

The problem of suicide detection provides an effective illustration of the importance of considering the rate of occurrence within a given population of *any* event which is to be predicted. Ellis and Conrad (1948) emphasized this point in their critical review of personality inventories used for screening purposes in the military services. They indicated that a large number of false positives were unavoidable because of the relatively small proportion of "maladjusted" individuals. They listed some studies which were misleading because the false positives were reported only in terms of percentages rather than the actual number of cases. Moreover, they reported some investigations in which the normal and abnormal samples were equal in number, and which were evaluated as though the proportions in the population were also equal, i.e., .50 rather than roughly .95 and .05. Ellis and Conrad indicated that such studies provide a spurious underestimate of the number of false positives in the population. Hunt (1950, p. 214), in reviewing the Ellis and Conrad article, further elaborated on these points because they are generally overlooked.

In the clinical psychology literature, population rates of the events under study are rarely reported or considered. However, the effectiveness of any method for the prediction of the behavior of *individuals* cannot be evaluated properly without at least a rough estimate of the frequency of the behavior in the population being studied.

Summary

A number of investigators have proposed certain signs and configurations from psychological tests for the detection of suicidal patients. The purposes of this paper have been (*a*) to suggest greater refinement of the classification of patients in suicide research, (*b*) to emphasize some of the limitations inherent in the prediction of suicide, and (*c*) to indicate the general applicability of such limitations in the prediction of any other behavior or event of infrequent occurrence.

Classification of Patients in Suicide Research. The need for more precise classification of patients in suicide research was emphasized both by (*a*) evidence that "suicidal" subgroups can be differentiated by means of psychological tests, and (*b*) data on the low incidence of suicide. Suicide is an extremely infrequent event, and very few of those patients who are severely depressed or who express suicide thoughts or threats actually commit suicide. Thus, data from such patients cannot arbitrarily be grouped under the class term "suicidal." It was suggested that in the development and validation of a suicide detection device, one criterion group should consist exclusively of patients who committed suicide and for whom test data were obtained a relatively short time before the suicide.

Limitations of Suicide Predictors. The low incidence of suicide is in itself a major limitation in the development of an effective suicide detection device, for in the attempt to predict suicide or any other infrequent event, a large number of false positives are obtained (patients incorrectly classified as suicides). To illustrate this point, a hypothetical suicide detection index was developed and cross-validated within a psychiatric patient population. It was demonstrated that such an index would have no practical value, for it would be impossible to treat as potential suicides the prodigious number of false positives. With elevations of the cutting line of the index so as to reduce the number of false positives to a practical level, it was estimated that the number of correctly identified suicidal patients (true positives) would also be drastically reduced, perhaps to zero.

Another approach to the problem of reducing the number of false positives is the development of an index within a population consisting only of those diagnostic groups with the highest rates of suicide. The major limitations in the procedure of studying a population restricted to one or a few diagnostic groups are as follows: (*a*) The suicide rate would still be so low as to produce an excessive number of false positives. (*b*) A considerable proportion of suicidal patients might not be included within the population because of both the limited reliability of diagnosis and the occurrence of suicide in many other diagnostic groups. (*c*) It would be more difficult to obtain variables differentiating between suicidal and nonsuicidal patients within one or a few diagnostic groups than within the whole psychiatric population.

The difficulties in predicting events of low incidence are not restricted to psychometric prediction, but are likewise encountered in prediction based on "clinical judgment." A suicide detection device is not feasible until much more is learned about the differential characteristics of patients who commit suicide.

Limitations in Prediction of Other Infrequent Events. The problem of suicide detection provides an effective illustration of the importance of considering the frequency within a given population of any behavior or event which is to be predicted. The limitations of prediction discussed in this paper apply in lesser degree to any behavior as its rate approaches .50 in a population dichotomized according to the presence or absence of the behavior. The effectiveness of any method for the prediction of behavior for *individuals* cannot be evaluated properly without at least a rough estimate of the frequency of the behavior in the population being studied.

5. COST EFFICIENCY AND TEST PREDICTION

David Rimm

In an informative and thought-provoking article, Meehl and Rosen (1955) considered the effectiveness of the more traditional assessment technique (i.e., standardized test) in comparison with a selection procedure involving the assignment of all subjects to the same class or category. One of the main points of their paper was that quite frequently even the better selection instruments are inferior, in terms of total correct decisions, to the procedure of simply passing everyone. The purpose of the present paper is to specify further the value or efficiency of a given selection test by taking into account the cost of the two possible types of errors. Thus, false positives may be considerably more costly, in terms of dollars, or man-hours, than false negatives, or vice versa.

As an illustration, suppose a psychiatric test is set up in order to screen out all potential neuropsychiatric "washouts" in a flight training program. Suppose that, on the average, it costs $10,000 to put a man through flight training. If, at the close of such training a man presents signs of a neuropsychiatric breakdown, he will immediately be discharged. The price for such a selection error (a false negative) is $10,000 (less if the breakdown occurs prior to the conclusion of training). On the other hand, suppose that the cost of recruitment and induction is approximately $1,000. An individual who is rejected at this stage, but who is actually quite resistant to the types of stress one experiences in flight training (a false positive), represents the second type of selection error, the price of this mistake being $1,000. The ratio of the cost of these two types of errors is 1:10. In other words, it is much better to reject a fit individual than to accept or pass a man who is, in reality, unfit for such training.

Consistent with Meehl and Rosen, the following notation will be used throughout this presentation:

p_1 is the proportion of sick people called "sick" by the test (i.e., the proportion of *true positives*).

p_2 is the proportion of healthy people incorrectly labeled "sick" by the test (i.e., the proportion of *false positives*).

P is the actual proportion of sick people in a given population (i.e., the *base rate*).

SOURCE. David C. Rimm is Associate Professor of Psychology at Arizona State University. A clinical psychologist by training, Dr. Rimm is interested in personality assessment and the investigation of the process of clinical prediction. This article originally appeared in the *Journal of Consulting Psychology*, 1963, **27**, 89-91. Reprinted by permission of the American Psychological Association and the author.

For N individuals, NP of them will actually be sick, and $NP(1 - p_1)$ will incorrectly be labeled "well" by the test. Thus there will be a total of $NP(1 - p_1)$ false negatives. For the same N individuals, $N(1 - P)$ will actually be healthy and $N(1 - P)p_2$ will incorrectly be labeled "sick." There will thus be a total of $N(1 - P)p_2$ false positives.

Let "A" be the cost of each false negative, and "B" equal the cost of each false positive error. The total cost, for both types of errors for any sample of size N is then given by:

$$\text{Total Cost} = ANP(1 - p_1) + BN(1 - P)p_2$$

If, instead of using a selection test, *all* individuals are passed or called "healthy," there will be a total of NP selection errors (all false negatives), and the cost for these errors will be given by:

$$\text{Base Cost} = APN.$$

We can now define "Cost Efficiency" as the proportion decrease in cost when a selection test is introduced. Thus:

$$\text{Cost Efficiency} = \frac{\text{Base Cost} - \text{Total Cost}}{\text{Base Cost}}$$

$$\text{Cost Efficiency} = p_1 - \frac{B(1 - P)p_2}{AP}$$

If the ratio of the cost of a false positive to the cost of a false negative is set equal to R, then:

$$\text{Cost Efficiency} = p_1 - \frac{R(1 - P)p_2}{P}$$

A few examples should aid in the interpretation of the Cost Efficiency. In the hypothetical flight training example "R" was equal to 1/10 or .1. Suppose that on the average 25% of the men "wash out" during the critical last week of training. Suppose that a screening procedure is now introduced which enables one to identify correctly 60% of the potential washouts. But at the same time this procedure incorrectly labels 20% of the potentially qualified men as unfit for training. From the above formula, the Cost Efficiency for this selection test would be equal to:

$$.6 - \frac{.1(1 - .25).2}{.25} = .54$$

This means that for every dollar that would have been spent paying for errors resulting from the procedure of accepting each applicant, .54 dollars will be *saved* as a result of using the screening test. To put it another way, for each dollar spent as a result of errors associated with passing everyone, only 1 – .54 = .46 dollars will be *spent* if the screening test is used instead.

There may be situations where the cost of training is low in comparison with the cost of recruitment. This might be the case when a company is confronted with the task of hiring semi-skilled construction workers for an extremely undesirable job overseas. Here individuals might be selected on the basis of whether or not they would remain on the job for a certain period of time, since every applicant is assumed to possess enough skill to handle the job. Suppose that on the average 50% of the men quit the job before they have completed 2 years work. Now suppose that a selection procedure is introduced which is capable of correctly identifying 70% of the "quitters" but mislabels 25% of the "nonquitters." Finally, suppose that in the long run, rejecting a nonquitter will be four times as expensive as accepting a quitter.

The Cost Efficiency for this selection test would be equal to:

$$.7 - \frac{4\,(1 - .5)\,.25}{.5} = -\,.30$$

A negative Cost Efficiency has the same interpretation as a positive index. In this instance, for each dollar spent due to errors resulting from hiring every man, 1 – (–.30) or 1.30 dollars will be spent if the screening procedure is used instead. In this example it would be much more economical simply to accept every applicant.

If "R" is set equal to unity, then the comparison which the Cost Efficiency measure makes would be reduced, in effect, to the sort of comparison Meehl and Rosen considered in their paper. In our flight training example an R of 1 would have resulted in a Cost Efficiency of 0.00. Since a zero Cost Efficiency implies no differential advantage, the test would have been rejected, because administering any instrument costs a certain amount of money. In the second example, an "R" of unity would have resulted in a Cost Efficiency of .45, so that the test would probably have been accepted as part of the standard induction procedure. Note that in both examples, ignoring relative error costs leads to a decision which is *opposite* to that which would have been made had cost been considered.

As has been indicated, whenever the Cost Efficiency for a given instrument is positive, the instrument has the advantage over base rate prediction. The maximum value of the Cost Efficiency is unity, possible only when the proportion of true positives is equal to 1 and when either the base rate is equal to 1 or there are no false positives. The minimum value for the index is negative infinity, with the index tending toward this value as the base rate approaches zero. Since the slope of the curve relating Cost Efficiency and base rate is always positive (see Fig. 1), an increase in base rate will necessarily mean an increase in Cost Efficiency, all other things being equal.

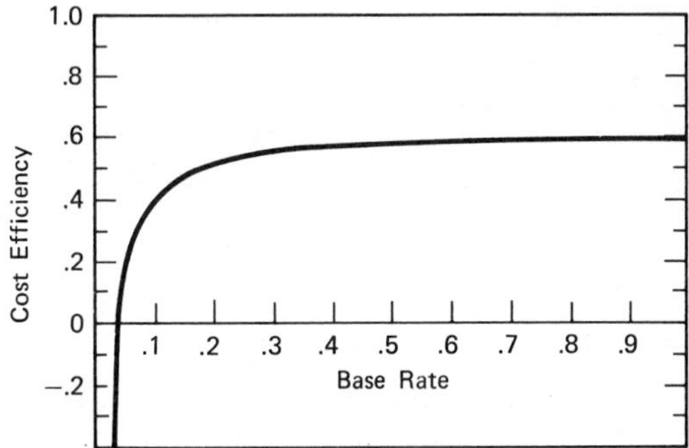

Figure 1. Cost Efficiency as a function of base rate, *P*. (The slope is given by Rp_2/P^2; the P intercept equals Rp_2/p_1Rp_2. This particular curve is for the flight training example.)

Discussion

Through this development we have made certain implicit assumptions. One such assumption is that the cost of administering a screening test is negligible. In most instances this would probably be true. Another assumption is that all individuals who pass the test will be accepted. In many cases a selection ratio is involved such that only a certain fixed number of openings is available. Since the Cost Efficiency would tend to vary with the number of applicants, this index would have to be adjusted so as to take this into consideration. This might be accomplished by expressing both p_1 and p_2 as functions of the cutting score.

Whenever these assumptions can be met, the Cost Efficiency can be calculated, providing of course that knowledge of the base rate and error costs is available. Unfortunately, as Meehl and Rosen have pointed out, this sort of information is frequently nonexistent. In many situations, the cost of errors could never be measured in dollars and cents (e.g., an unfit pilot dying in a plane crash, or a mental patient being refused therapy, though in fact he is quite ill and experiencing considerable anguish). However, some sort of relative valuation of the types of errors will almost always be possible. If this judgment can somehow be translated into a number (R), no matter how cold-blooded this procedure may seem, it would most certainly be better than assuming that all types of mistakes are equally bad.

Chapter 7

Response Distortions

There are several variables, including the respondent's personality characteristics, which determine his responses to personality assessment techniques. Among the other variables that affect or distort these test responses we would include the desire, conscious or unconscious, to appear well or poorly adjusted, a need to conform or agree with the test conditions or the examiner, a tendency to choose a particular position alternative in a multiple-choice format, and a variety of recent immediate experiences such as viewing a dramatic film or failing to perform well on a task. In both the development of and the practical use of personality assessment procedures, it is important to understand how such distortions have affected or can affect the subjects' responses and, hopefully, to keep such distortions to a minimum, so that the respondent's personality characteristics can be fairly evaluated.

Prior to the 1950s, little systematic attention was paid to these response distortions in personality assessment. During that decade, however, many psychologists became interested in this problem and an important distinction between two kinds of response distortion was introduced: *response styles,* or the tendency to distort responses in a particular direction regardless of the content of the test stimuli (to say "yes" on self-report items, to make animal responses to ink blots, etc.), and *response sets,* or the need of the respondent to answer in such a way as to produce a certain image of himself, such as well-adjusted, conforming, or dominant. With the rise of interest in response distortion as an important source of variance in personality measurement it was not uncommon to encounter the extreme position that scores on personality inventories reflected little else beside response distortions. The question of interest often only was to determine the kind of distortion that was operative. Within the last decade, however, a number of writers have been able to put the topic into clearer perspective.

The particular response style that has been subjected to the deepest research scrutiny is *acquiescence,* the tendency to respond "yes" on yes/no or "true" on true/false self-report questionnaires, regardless of the content of the items. Unless one takes the extreme position that item content plays no role in determining an individual's response to these items, one can assume that the influence of acquiescence should be greatest on those items that are somewhat ambiguous in content. Even further, acquiescence should be most easily investigated in tests whose items are free of content entirely. In our first reading in this section, the late Theodore Husek reports on one effort to devise such a test. The subjects believed that they were undergoing a test of extra-sensory perception in which they were trying to read the examiner's mind by responding "agree" or "disagree" to the items whose number the examiner called out. Husek's ESP measure of acquiescence, although reliable, showed no meaningful relationships either with intelligence or with a variety of personality traits, and showed only small and insignificant correlations with other measures of acquiescence. In general, it was felt that there is no unitary concept of acquiescence, and that the effects of acquiescent responding in personality assessment tend to be small in most instances. The same conclusion has been reached with respect to other response styles.

Response sets, the tendency to slant one's responses in a particular direction, have always posed a problem in personality assessment, and no really satisfactory method has ever been devised for countering the more deliberate efforts of this kind. A great deal of research attention has been paid to the response set of *social desirability,* the widespread and largely unconscious tendency to slant one's answers in a socially desirable direction rather than responding with complete candor. We distinguish between social desirability, as a more or less unconscious characteristic of a respondent, and the more deliberate efforts to slant response, which we will call *faking.*

Systematic research on social desirability was initiated in the early 1950s by Allen Edwards, who discovered a high correlation between the social desirability of an inventory item and the frequency with which respondents endorsed it. Since that time, Edwards has reported much research on this topic, and most of it is summarized in his 1964 paper which is our second reading. Edwards points out that many common personality inventory scales, particularly those assessing psychological adjustment-maladjustment, show substantial correlations with measures of social desirability, and he argues that they are more appropriately regarded as assessing social desirability response set than degree of psychological adjustment. A variety of evidence is brought to bear on this question, including cross-cultural research, analysis of the factor structure of MMPI scales, and an examination of various scales measuring social desirability.

In the third paper, Alfred B. Heilbrun, Jr. presents a detailed argument against Edwards' position concerning the basic significance of social desirability response set as a distorting variable in personality assessment. Central to Heilbrun's argument is his identification with social learning theory and its approach to explaining psychopathology. In this view, children are consistently reinforced for engaging in socially conforming (or desirable) behaviors. Social expectations of what is desirable become closely allied with what is regarded as good psychological adjustment; also, children learn to experience anxiety when their behaviors do not conform to social expectations. Thus, Heilbrun is essentially arguing that good adjustment tends to be *defined* as that which is socially desirable, so that there will necessarily be a high correlation between the two.

Edwards, reasoning that a person's tendency to give socially desirable responses on an inventory tends to mask his expression of actual personality characteristics, devised an inventory (the Edwards Personal Preference Schedule or EPPS) in which he arranged the items in pairs matched for degree of social desirability. Respondents, asked to endorse only one item from each pair, are thus obliged to make their choices on a basis other than social desirability. This *forced-choice* method, when originally proposed, was greeted enthusiastically as a possible solution to many of the problems engendered by the "obviousness" of inventory items. Later research, however, has shown that this optimism was not justified. In our next reading, Charles F. Dicken demonstrates that college students can easily slant their responses on the EPPS, when specifically requested to do so, in order to make a more favorable impression in general and also to demonstrate a greater amount of three of the EPPS needs or scores: order, dominance, and change. Thus, even if it were necessary to restrict test-takers' efforts to respond on the basis of social desirability, the EPPS does not appear to succeed in providing this control, and in any event, it provides no control against deliberate efforts to slant responses in the direction of particular traits.

Most of the research on response distortions has been in the context of personality inventories, and little attention has been given to the topic in projective techniques. Traditionally, projective techniques have been regarded as "subtle" in nature and therefore not amenable to the influence of response sets such as faking. Examination of the research, however, shows that this is not the case, and that an individual can deliberately distort his responses to a projective technique if he desires to do so, although the extent to which this is possible has not yet been fully investigated. In the final reading of this section, Martin F. Kaplan and Leonard D. Eron report a study in which subjects were asked to fake hostility on the Thematic Apperception Test, that is, to respond as though they were very hostile and aggressive. In general, subjects were able to do so, and those subjects who were sophisticated in projective techniques tended to do a better job of faking than naive subjects.

1. ACQUIESCENCE AS A RESPONSE SET AND AS A PERSONALITY CHARACTERISTIC[1]

T. R. Husek

Psychological tests are intended to measure human abilities and personality characteristics apart from the influences and distractions of the testing situation, per se. Insofar as the "natural" judgments and feelings of the people taking the test are distorted, the precision of the measuring instrument is reduced. However, it has long been recognized that people bring to the testing situation certain test-taking habits which influence their scores. Numerous investigators have reported on the presence and influence of such test-taking habits (Cronbach, 1950; Jackson & Messick, 1958).

The research reported here is primarily concerned with one type of test-taking habit, which is referred to as "acquiescence." Acquiescence supposedly concerns individual differences in the tendency to agree with assertions of all kinds. It is thought that with items with answer alternatives of agree-disagree, true-false, yes-no, and the like, there are individual differences in the tendency to say "agree" which interact with knowledge of and feelings about the content of the items.

The interaction of content and acquiescence effects involve the experimenter in a difficult problem. For example, in a study of acquiescence with such

SOURCE. Theodore R. Husek (1931-1970) received his doctoral degree at the University of Illinois and at the time of his death was Associate Professor of Education at UCLA. Measurement, educational evaluation, and quantitative research methodology had been Dr. Husek's major areas of professional interest. This article originally appeared in *Educational and Psychological Measurement,* 1961, **21,** 295-307. Reprinted by permission of Duke University Press and the author's estate.

[1]This paper is adapted from part of a dissertation submitted to the Department of Psychology, University of Illinois, in partial fulfillment of the requirements for the Ph.D. degree. The author would like to express his gratitude to his thesis chairman at the beginning of the research, Charles E. Osgood, to his thesis chairman at the conclusion of the research, Lee J. Cronbach, and to his committee members, Donald Burkholder, Franz Hohn, Jum C. Nunnally, and Ivan Steiner for their valuable assistance during the study.

statements as "Roosevelt was an excellent president—agree-disagree," he must try to separate the acquiescence effects from the subject's actual feelings about Roosevelt. Since subjects differ, not only with respect to acquiescence tendencies but also with respect to their feelings about the material in the question (i.e., Roosevelt), the various effects are not easy to separate.

The Measurement of Acquiescence

Many attempts have been made to partial out acquiescence effects from other aspects of a test. These attempts include, for example, "phony language examinations" (Nunnally & Husek, 1958), extremely difficult questions (Gage, Leavitt & Stone, 1957), guessing games, and scoring techniques for obtaining an acquiescence score from attitude tests (Frederiksen & Messick, 1958). All of these attempts have had to face the problem of separating out the various determinants of a subject's responses.

The present paper suggests a measure which is free of content effects and seems to be a pure measure of acquiescence. The measure (ESP acquiescence test) involves giving agree-disagree answer alternatives to a set of subjects and asking them to read the experimenter's mind and answer questions he is purportedly thinking of. However, the experimenter is not thinking of items, but merely counting from 1 to 10 over and over again. There are no questions on the test, only answer alternatives.

A similar measure was developed independently by Bass (1956). Bass had his subjects guess whether the experimenter was thinking yes or no, and he found that only 12 items with 24 subjects resulted in a corrected split-half reliability estimate of .57.

Relationship with Ability. In addition to the attempted development of a "pure" measure of acquiescence, the research examined acquiescence effects on an ability test. Gage, *et al.* (1957) hypothesized that acquiescence and intelligence tend to correlate negatively and cited a study by Crutchfield (1955) as evidence. Intuitively, one might reason as follows: A person of low ability is placed in more situations where others know more than he does. Consequently, he develops a habit of saying "yes," "agree," etc. However, an unpublished study by Nunnally[2] found essentially zero correlations between intelligence and the number of "true" scores on a phony German language examination similar to one that he and Husek had used in previous work (1958).

Relationships with Personality Variables. Although, as Cronbach (1950) has said, "It is scarcely necessary to marshal further evidence that reliable individual differences in response sets (including acquiescence) exist," evidence of the relation of acquiescence to personality variables is neither substantial nor conclusive.

[2]Personal communication.

Bass has obtained a number of significant correlations between a test of social acquiescence which he developed and certain personality variables. Because the traits are in themselves of interest in a study of acquiescence and because Bass obtained significant correlations between these traits and his test, Bass's measures were modified and used in the present study.

In two pilot studies done by the author, acquiescence was measured by the number of "agree's" on miscellaneous ambiguous items. It was found to relate slightly, but significantly, to self-ratings on the Semantic Differential on "potency" scales with 144 subjects of mixed sex, but not to relate to self-ratings on "potency" scales with 58 subjects who were almost all females. This suggests that there may be a sex difference in acquiescence behavior.

Lastly, it has been suggested (Jackson & Messick, 1958) that the Edwards scale of social desirability is confounded with acquiescence; however, Edwards's recent publication (1957) indicates that they should be independent.

Other Issues. Although the primary concerns of this paper are mentioned above, certain other content and response effects have been measured by the tests used in this study; and since certain relationships among these variables are pertinent to any study of test-taking behavior, some of them will be reported here. Some points of interest include: a replication of parts of the Bass research, the relation of the Bass social acquiescence test to the Edwards social desirability scale, and the relationships of the uncertainty expressed by the subjects on the acquiescence-loaded ability test to the personality measures obtained in the study.

Method

Subjects

The subjects in this experiment were 231 high school students, 121 males and 110 females. Ten classes were used—three senior classes, two sophomore classes, two junior classes, and three mixed classes.

One experimenter administered all of the tests to all of the subjects.[3]

The Tests

Eight tests were administered to the subjects.

Measure 1: The "Pure" Acquiescence Measure. This was a 120-item test in which the subjects thought they were reading the mind of the experimenter and answering questions he was purportedly thinking of. The instrument contained 24 pages; each page had five items. An item was a pair of words, "agree" and

[3]Two experimenters were used in one of the pilot studies mentioned in the introduction. No significant differences in acquiescence were found between the groups tested by each of the experimenters. The difference between the means of the two groups had a probability under a null hypothesis of no difference of approximately .55.

"disagree." The subjects were asked to mark whether they agreed or disagreed with items that the experimenter was purportedly thinking about. The experimenter sat in the back of the classroom during the testing sessions and announced the item numbers. The subjects heard only the numbers of the items. They could not see the experimenter during the session.

Measure 2 and 3: The Vocabulary Tests. To measure ability, two vocabulary tests were used. They were adapted from a standard vocabulary test (Durost-Walter Word Mastery Test, 1950). One of the tests was cast in a multiple-choice form to eliminate acquiescence effects, and the other was constructed as a "yes-no" test to maximize acquiescence effects.

The second test also had a "?" among the answer alternatives. Subjects were instructed that they should always answer either "yes" or "no", but that, in addition, they could also circle the "?". The subjects were told that questions marked "?" would only count one-half of a point. Since the subjects believed that the correct score was the number of rights minus the number of wrongs, it was felt that the instructions would allow them to indicate the items about which they were uncertain. Cronbach (1950) has indicated that a subject's tendency to acquiesce has a higher probability of affecting his score on items which are ambiguous or difficult for him than on other items. By allowing subjects to indicate items of uncertainty, it was thought possible to separate out those items which were appreciably affected by acquiescence.

Measure 4 and 5: The Bass Test and the Edwards Scale. The subjects also took the Bass Social Acquiescence Test (1956) and the Edwards Social Desirability Scale (1957).

Measure 6, 7 and 8: Self-Ratings, Ratings by Others, and Ratings of the Experimenter. The subjects were also asked to rate certain persons in the classroom. The ratings were done with 7-step, bipolar rating scales, a modified form of the Semantic Differential (Osgood, Suci & Tannenbaum, 1957). The person to be rated was named at the top of the page and nine scales were used. The scales (in the order and wording used on the form) were: person with initiative–person without initiative; sociable person–person who is not sociable; ignorant–intelligent; person who is not cooperative–cooperative person; strong-willed person–weak-willed person; independent-minded person–person who is not independent minded; person who does not like to help others–person who likes to help others; good student–bad student; follower–leader. Each subject rated himself and seven other persons. In some cases, one of the other persons was the experimenter.

Procedure

The tests were administered to the subjects in their classroom during the regular class periods, two class periods being required for the testing. The teachers were not present during the testing sessions.

After the study was completed, the experimenter returned to the classes, explained the nature and purpose of the study, and answered frankly any questions the students had.

Analysis and Results

Reliability estimates were computed for the various scores used in the study. The estimates are listed in Table 1. Most of them need no explanation; however, the method used to obtain the reliability estimates for the ratings by others should be described.

Table 1. Reliability Estimates for the Measures Obtained in the Study

Measure	Type of Reliability Estimate	Number of Subjects	Reliability Coefficients
ESP Acquiescence	Odd-even corrected[a]	231	.87
ESP Acquiescence	Test-retest (2 weeks)	60	.75
Bass social acquiescence	Odd-even corrected	231	.84
Number of "?" on yes-no vocabulary	Odd-even corrected	60	.88
Number of "yes's" on yes-no vocabulary	Odd-even corrected	60	.61
Edwards social desirability	Odd-even corrected	231	.79
Multiple-choice vocabulary	Odd-even corrected	231	.96
Yes-no vocabulary	Odd-even corrected	231	.94
Ratings by others:			
Person with initiative	Split-half corrected[b]	50	.68
Sociable person	Split-half corrected	50	.54
Intelligent	Split-half corrected	50	.71
Cooperative person	Split-half corrected	50	.52
Strong-willed person	Split-half corrected	50	.58
Independent-minded person	Split-half corrected	50	.69
Person who likes to help others	Split-half corrected	50	.50
Good student	Split-half corrected	50	.78
Follower	Split-half corrected	50	.81
Ratings of self:			
Person with initiative	Test-retest (2 weeks)	32	.45
Sociable person	Test-retest (2 weeks)	32	.38
Intelligent	Test-retest (2 weeks)	32	.48
Cooperative person	Test-retest (2 weeks)	32	.40
Strong-willed person	Test-retest (2 weeks)	32	.46
Independent-minded person	Test-retest (2 weeks)	32	.51
Person who likes to help others	Test-retest (2 weeks)	32	.38
Good student	Test-retest (2 weeks)	32	.54
Leader	Test-retest (2 weeks)	32	.58

[a] All coefficients reported as corrected have been corrected by the Spearman-Brown prophecy formula.

[b] These coefficients are reported as "split-half" because there were no "odd" or "even" items.

Each subject was rated by a number of his classmates. As a reliability estimate, a measure of consistency of these ratings was obtained by correlating, for 50 subjects, one half of the ratings they received with the other half. It should be noted that the reliabilities of the ratings by others are higher than those of the self-ratings.

The intercorrelations among the scores, along with their means and standard deviations, are presented in Table 2.

It was thought that subjects would acquiesce more often on the vocabulary test on items about which they stated they were uncertain than on other items. The data do not support this supposition. The mean proportion of "yes's" on the question-marked items of the "yes-no" vocabulary test was .47. The mean proportion of the "yes's" for the nonquestion-marked items was .56.

It was suggested in the introduction that the "pure" measure of acquiescence might be related to the measures of intelligence. The obtained correlation between the multiple-choice vocabulary test and the "pure" acquiescence was .008. None of the other measures of acquiescence has appreciable correlations with the multiple-choice test. The suggestion was not substantiated.

The measure of "pure" acquiescence was related by a small but significant amount ($r = .24$, p less than .001) to the Bass social acquiescence test, but not ($r = -.05$) to the Edwards scale for social desirability.

The obtained correlations between the "pure" acquiescence measured and the various ratings were quite small. The largest correlation was −.13. There seems to be little relationship between the acquiescence test and the personality ratings obtained in the study.

Another question concerns whether the Bass test of social acquiescence is related to the ratings given to the subjects by others. The largest of the nine relevant correlations obtained was .09.

The Edwards scale of social desirability was related to the ratings obtained by the subjects. Of the 18 correlations computed to examine this question, ten were significant at the 5 per cent level. The Edwards scale has the following significant relationships to the ratings: Ratings of self–"Intelligent," .21; "Cooperative person," .20; "Strong-willed," .20; "Good student," .25; "Leader," .23; Ratings by others–"Person with initiative," .14; "Intelligent," .17; "Good student," .17; "Leader," .16. The Edwards scale does have small but significant relationships with the ratings obtained in this study.

Since the ESP acquiescence score, the Bass test, and the number of "yes's" on the yes-no vocabulary test were all related, even though the relationships were small, it was decided that these tests be combined and a general over-all measure of acquiescence be obtained. None of the correlations obtained between this new combined acquiescence score and the ratings by others was above .08. The summed acquiescence score correlated .20 with self-ratings on "Person who likes to help others," .17 with self-ratings on "Sociable person," and .14 with

Table 2. Means, Standard Deviations, and Intercorrelations of the Measures[a] ($N = 231$)

	Possible Range	$\overline{X}$	S_X		2.	3.	4.	5.	6.	7.	8.	9.	10.	11.	12.
1.	120	65.60	11.30	ESP acquiescence	24	–14	–05	–07	–01	–02	–11	–03	22	23	08
2.	56	32.84	8.46	Bass soc. acquiescence		–51	–15	–10	–14	–16	–13	–07	26	24	15
3.	56	6.22	6.70	Bass "?"			–01	10	17	06	18	–15	–14	–05	–05
4.	39	27.33	5.33	Edwards soc. desirability				13	13	18	03	06	–06	–02	13
5.	1	.52	.53	Sex (male high)					–07	–02	–02	–03	–11	–15	–04
6.	50	23.67	8.50	Multiple-choice vocab.						78	–05	–05	01	–02	02
7.	100	60.00	9.32	Yes-no vocab.–#correct							–09	–11	00	–08	03
8.	100	20.55	16.53	Yes-no vocab.–#of "?"								91	–59	01	–04
9.	100	8.74	8.20	Yes-no vocab.–#of yes's "?"									–49	18	–04
10.	100	44.69	12.57	Yes-no vocab.–#of yes's non "?"										77	08
11.	100	53.43	11.14	Yes-no vocab.–total yes											06
12.	6	2.62	1.41	Me–initiative											
13.	6	1.89	1.15	Me–sociable											
14.	6	5.21	1.13	Me–intelligent											
15.	6	6.05	1.18	Me–cooperative											
16.	6	2.31	1.36	Me–strong willed											
17.	6	2.07	1.32	Me–independent minded											
18.	6	6.35	1.13	Me–helpful to others											
19.	6	2.75	1.35	Me–good student											
20.	6	4.39	1.64	Me–leader											
21.	6	3.11	1.11	By others–initiative											
22.	6	2.69	.97	By others–sociable											
23.	6	5.07	.93	By others–intelligent											
24.	6	5.11	.93	By others–cooperative											
25.	6	3.10	.89	By others–strong willed											
26.	6	2.86	.90	By others–independent minded											
27.	6	5.13	.82	By others–helpful to others											
28.	6	2.92	1.05	By others–good student											
29.	6	3.97	1.16	By others–leader											

[a] An r of .13 is significant at the .05 level of confidence
An r of .17 is significant at the .01 level of confidence.

Table 2. Means, Standard Deviations, and Intercorrelations of the Measures[a] ($N = 231$) (Continued)

	13.	14.	15.	16.	17.	18.	19.	20.	21.	22.	23.	24.	25.	26.	27.	28.	29.
1. ESP acquiescence	11	−07	03	13	00	09	00	03	−01	05	−03	03	04	06	06	−04	−09
2. Bass soc. acquiescence	15	−04	04	03	−05	17	12	07	−05	−02	−09	−07	−01	−05	−04	−07	−07
3. Bass "?"	01	−05	04	−02	−06	−10	−12	−03	−05	−03	00	01	−09	−04	−01	−01	−04
4. Edwards soc. desirability	09	21	21	20	00	12	25	23	14	05	17	15	10	12	10	17	16
5. Sex (male high)	−08	−09	03	−04	−07	−21	−14	10	−22	−15	−23	−22	−16	−20	−23	−26	−12
6. Multiple-choice vocab.	−19	30	06	05	15	−07	13	15	42	12	47	31	31	36	27	44	44
7. Yes-no vocab.–#correct	−19	30	00	07	11	−04	08	14	30	02	45	24	24	25	16	32	31
8. Yes-no vocab.–#of "?"	−11	02	−01	−01	03	09	01	−06	03	04	06	03	02	00	02	09	00
9. Yes-no vocab.–#of yes's "?"	−10	01	−03	01	01	15	04	−04	04	03	04	02	02	01	03	07	01
10. Yes-no vocab.–#of yes's non "?"	15	02	04	07	−10	05	02	04	−06	−05	−05	−06	−04	−04	−07	−09	−06
11. Yes-no vocab.–total yes	10	03	03	09	−11	16	06	02	−04	−03	−02	−05	03	−04	−06	−05	−06
12. Me–initiative	33	36	32	30	22	20	44	32	24	23	19	20	30	21	22	22	21
13. Me–sociable		12	39	21	12	35	19	20	01	14	06	01	04	−01	02	−02	02
14. Me–intelligent			36	26	16	12	44	25	21	07	26	13	23	15	08	28	31
15. Me–cooperative				23	22	35	43	22	10	09	07	07	06	01	10	12	09
16. Me–strong willed					32	24	36	29	10	12	14	09	19	15	10	13	16
17. Me–independent minded						08	22	23	21	14	17	08	23	16	09	23	21
18. Me–helpful to others							32	09	13	02	10	14	07	05	09	14	08
19. Me–good student								22	29	13	28	15	23	20	14	31	28
20. Me–leader									17	12	15	02	22	14	10	16	28
21. By others–initiative										62	84	69	77	78	63	83	77
22. By others–sociable											58	66	65	61	63	55	59
23. By others–intelligent												71	72	72	66	87	75
24. By others–cooperative													66	61	69	73	61
25. By others–strong willed														81	61	77	75
26. By others–independent minded															58	70	68
27. By others–helpful to others																68	60
28. By others–good student																	75
29. By others–leader																	

self-ratings on "Person with initiative." None of the other correlations between the summed acquiescence score and self-ratings was above .12.

From 121 subjects, ratings of the tester were obtained. These ratings were summed over all of the scales in order to obtain a general "positiveness" score for each subject with respect to the tester. That is, a score was obtained to measure the reactions of the subjects to the tester. The obtained correlation between these ratings of the tester and the ESP acquiescence test is .12. This correlation is not statistically significant.

Discussion

One of the aims of this study was to develop a reliable measure of acquiescence. A reliable measure of *something* was developed in what is called the ESP acquiescence test. On the face of it, this test would seem to measure acquiescence; at least it is difficult to see what else it might be measuring. It was designed to be free of content effects, and it seems to be a measure of what might be called "pure" acquiescence, the general tendency in the subject to say "yes." One of the arguments against its being a "pure" measure would be to say that it is measuring acquiescence to the experimenter. However, the small correlation between ratings of the tester and scores on the acquiescence test reasons against this conclusion.

The relation of the acquiescence test to other variables does not suggest that general acquiescence is an important personality variable. Its correlations with the ratings given to the subjects are trivial; it is not related to the sex of the subjects; and its correlation with vocabulary is not evident unless the coefficient is carried out to three decimal places.

None of the other measures of acquiescence relates to the personality indices. The Bass social acquiescence test, the number of "yes's" on the yes-no vocabulary test, the proportion of "yes's" on the question marked items of the yes-no vocabulary test–all have extremely small correlations with the sex of the subjects, their intelligence, and the ratings given to them.

The correlations obtained with the sums of three of the acquiescence variables mentioned above give little support to the role of acquiescence as a general personality variable. The summed acquiescence variable correlates .14 with ratings of self on "Person with initiative," .17 with ratings of self on "Sociable person," and .20 with ratings of self on "Person who likes to help others." None of the correlations with ratings by others is above .08. Thus the relationship of the summed measure with the personality variables is so small that it is of little or no practical importance.

There is at least one conclusion which might be drawn from the findings in this study about acquiescence–that it is not a meaningful general concept. For although a highly reliable content-free measure was demonstrated, it does not seem to have meaningful relationships with other traits. Perhaps one must talk about some specific material when discussing acquiescence; that is, one should study it with reference to specific content materials rather than as a response effect. Acquiescence may still be an important variable, but there may be many stable traits of acquiescence. Since the traits of acquiescence in this study are largely independent of each other, such a conclusion seems consistent with the findings of the study.

Other Issues

Bass (1956) has reported significant correlations between his test of social acquiescence and variables similar to those used in this study. Therefore, it was to be expected that his findings would be replicated. They were not. Although some of the personality ratings were obtained partially in an attempt to duplicate and generalize Bass's findings, the personality ratings obtained in this study may have been sufficiently different from those Bass utilized to prevent a direct comparison of the two studies.

The results obtained with the Edwards social desirability scale are more positive. It is interesting to note that the Edwards scale has positive correlations —small, but significant at the 5 per cent level—with both the multiple-choice vocabulary test and the yes-no vocabulary test. Does this mean that the tendency to check socially-desirable items is related to intelligence, perhaps through the connection that intelligent people have more in their makeup that is socially desirable than people of less intelligence?

A partial check on some of the facts in this matter is available. The Edwards scale has significant (5 per cent level) correlations with a number of the rating scales. For ratings of self, they include: "Intelligent," .21; "Good student," .25; "Leader," .23; and for ratings of others, they include: "Person with initiative," .14; "Intelligent," .17; "Good student," .17; "Leader," .16. All of this suggests that the Edwards variable is not independent of intelligence. People who tend to check socially-desirable items also obtain better scores on vocabulary tests, and they rate themselves and are rated by others as possessing traits related to intelligence.

The fact that the correlations among the self-ratings are generally much lower than the correlations among the ratings by others might lead to the conclusion that the subjects are more discriminating in their use of rating scales when they rate themselves than when they rate others. However, the reliability of the self-ratings is lower than the reliability of the ratings by others, and this probably accounts for much of the difference between the two sets of correlations.

Summary

An attempt was made to develop a reliable measure of general acquiescence, to examine its relationship to personality traits, and to investigate its influence on a paper-and-pencil test. A reliable test was developed, but it did not relate to personality traits or to scores on a vocabulary test. It is suggested that acquiescence does not seem to be a fruitful general concept, but rather must be examined with reference to some specific material—perhaps in order to give the subjects something to which they may acquiesce. Some relationships among social desirability, acquiescence, and personality traits were also investigated.

2. SOCIAL DESIRABILITY AND PERFORMANCE ON THE MMPI[1]

Allen L. Edwards[2]

I

Given a set of statements of the kind ordinarily found in personality scales and inventories, it is possible to have judges rate each statement in terms of how socially desirable or undesirable they consider the content of the statement to be. The distributions of ratings assigned to the statements can then be used to find the social desirability scale values of the statements. Once the social desirability scale values of the statements have been obtained, we have a basis for ordering the statements on a psychological continuum of social desirability ranging from highly socially undesirable, through neutral, to highly socially desirable.

There is now considerable evidence to show that when a representative or random set of personality statements is rated for social desirability by different groups of judges, the relative ordering of the statements on the social desirability continuum is much the same from group to group. The product-moment

SOURCE. Allen L. Edwards, Professor of Psychology at the University of Washington, is perhaps best known for his development of the self-report personality inventory, the Edwards Personal Preference Schedule. Dr. Edwards has contributed to the professional literature on the topics of test construction, psychological measurement, and social desirability. This article originally appeared in *Psychometrika,* 1964, **29,** 295-308. Reprinted by permission of the Psychometric Society and the author.

[1]Presidential address delivered at the annual meeting of the Psychometric Society, Los Angeles, California, September 8, 1964.

[2]Preparation of this paper was supported in part by Research Grant M-4075 from the National Institute of Mental Health, United States Public Health Service.

correlations between scale values derived from the judgments of two different but comparable groups of judges are typically .90 or greater (Edwards, 1957; Edwards and Diers, 1963; Edwards and Walsh, 1963; Messick and Jackson, 1961). Even when social desirability scale values are derived from the judgments of such diverse groups within our own culture as high school students (Klett, 1957), Nisei (Fujita, 1957), psychotic patients (Cowen, Davol, Reimanis, and Stiller, 1962), sex offenders (Cowen and Stricker, 1963), alcoholics (Zax, Cowen, Budin and Biggs, 1962), novice nuns (Zax, Cowen, and Peter, 1963), and a geriatric sample (Cowen, Davol, Reimanis, and Stiller, 1962), the correlations between the scale values are generally found to be .85 or higher.

Cross-culturally, it has been found that scale values based upon the judgments of Norwegian students correlate .78 with those based upon the judgments of American students (Lovaas, 1958). Scale values based upon the judgments of students at the University of Beirut in Lebanon were found to correlate .86 with those based upon the judgments of American college students (Klett and Yaukey, 1959). Iwawaki and Cowen (1964) found that scale values based upon the judgments of students at the Japanese Defense Academy correlated .90 with those based upon the judgments of American college students. Cowen and Frankel (1964) have reported a correlation of .95 between the scale values derived from the judgments of French students and those derived from the judgments of American students. Furthermore, they found that the French scale values correlated .85 with the Japanese scale values. It is of some social-psychological significance that cultural norms of what is considered desirable and undesirable in the way of personality traits and characteristics are so similar in such countries as Norway, Japan, Lebanon, France, and the United States, despite other differences which may exist between these nations.

II

If a set of personality statements is administered to a group of subjects with instructions to describe themselves by answering each statement True or False, we can find for this sample the percentage answering each statement True. I refer to this percentage as the probability that an item will be endorsed in self-description under the *standard* instructions ordinarily used in administering personality scales and inventories. If the social desirability scale values of the statements are also known, then it is possible to determine the relationship between probability of endorsement and social desirability scale value.

For a set of 140 personality statements, I found that probability of endorsement was a linear increasing function of social desirability scale value, the product-moment correlation between the two variables being .87 (Edwards, 1953). A correlation of this magnitude might be considered an artifact, either of the particular set of statements investigated or of the particular group of subjects tested, but subsequent research has shown that the relationship holds for all of the sets of statements which have been investigated provided the statements do not have a restricted range of social desirability scale values (Cowen and Tongas, 1959; Cruse, 1963; Edwards, 1957; Edwards, 1959; Hanley, 1956; Kenny, 1956; Taylor, 1959). The largest population we have studied consists of 2,824 descriptive statements of personality. For a serial sample of 176 statements drawn from this larger population of 2,824 statements, James Walsh and I found a correlation of .92 between probability of endorsement and social desirability scale value (Edwards and Walsh, 1963).

There is evidence to show that the relationship observed between probability of endorsement and social desirability scale value is not uniquely characteristic of American college students, but that it holds true for other diverse groups within our own culture as well (Cruse, 1963; Taylor, 1959). In fact, there is reason to believe that probability of endorsement should be substantially correlated with social desirability scale value in cultures other than our own (Edwards, 1964).

III

If we know the social desirability scale value of a statement, then it is possible to define the concept of a *socially desirable response* to the statement. I originally defined a socially desirable response as a True response to a statement with a socially desirable scale value or as a False response to a statement with a socially undesirable scale value, leaving the concept undefined for statements with precisely neutral scale values of 5.0 on a 9-point social desirability rating scale (Edwards, 1957). I regard the tendency to respond True to statements with socially desirable scale values and False to statements with socially undesirable scale values as a general personality trait.

A scale designed to measure the tendency to give socially desirable responses in self-description under the standard instructions ordinarily employed with personality scales and inventories is called a Social Desirability (*SD*) scale (Edwards, 1957). In an *SD* scale all of the items are keyed for socially desirable responses. Since the concept of a socially desirable response is, of necessity, undefined for items with precisely neutral scale values, items of this kind would not be included in an *SD* scale. In fact, we have found that responses to items falling within the neutral interval, 4.5 to 5.5 on a 9-point scale, are, in general, less consistent than and not highly correlated with responses to items falling outside the neutral interval. The various *SD* scales we have developed have thus consisted of items with scale values falling to the left of 4.5 or to the right of 5.5 on the 9-point rating scale.

Figure 1 shows the social desirability scale values and probabilities of endorsement for a 39-item *SD* scale, based on items from the Minnesota Multiphasic Personality Inventory (MMPI), which I have used in much of my research. The 30 items with scale values falling to the left or socially undesirable end of the continuum are keyed False and the 9 items with scale values on the socially desirable end of the continuum are keyed True. Scores on this 39-item *SD* scale have a test-retest reliability of approximately .87 and the internal consistency of the scale, as measured by the Kuder-Richardson Formula 21 (K-R 21), is approximately .82.

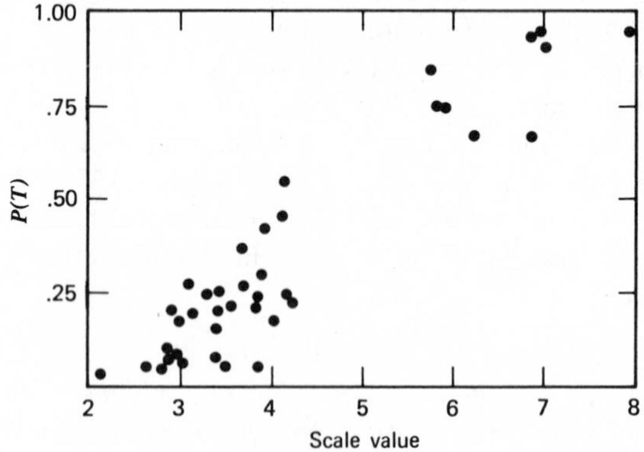

Figure 1. Social desirability scale values and probabilities of endorsement for the 39 items in the *SD* scale.

IV

Consider now one of the existing personality scales designed to measure some personality trait such as, for example, hostility, cooperativeness, dominance, rigidity, introversion, neuroticism, or the like. For each of these scales there is a scoring key which indicates whether the trait response to an item is keyed True or False. Presumably, individual responses to the items in these scales are content or trait oriented so that individuals who have a high degree of the trait are assumed to have a higher probability of giving the trait response to each item than individuals who have a low degree of the trait. Thus, if an individual obtains a high score on one of these scales he has given many trait keyed responses and, in this case, it is assumed that he did so because he has a high degree of the trait which the scale was designed to measure. If he obtains a low score he has given few trait keyed responses, and it is assumed, in this instance, that he did so because he has a low degree of the trait which the scale was designed to measure.

If we obtain social desirability scale values for the items in each of these trait scales, then it is also possible to determine whether the trait response to an item is a socially desirable or a socially undesirable response. If all of the items in a given trait scale are keyed for both trait and socially desirable responses, then, obviously, the trait keying and the social desirability keying of the items in the scale are completely confounded. It may be argued that individuals who obtain high scores on the trait scale are responding to the items in terms of the trait which the scale was designed to measure, but it is equally plausible that they are responding to the items in terms of a trait which the scale was *not* designed to measure, namely, the tendency to give socially desirable responses. If the latter is the case, then scores on the trait scale should be positively correlated with an independently constructed measure of the tendency to give socially desirable responses such as the *SD* scale.

Similar considerations apply to trait scales in which the trait keying is identical with the social undesirability keying. If all of the items in a scale are keyed for both trait and socially undesirable responses, then low scores may be obtained by individuals who have little of the trait which the scale was designed to measure. But, if the tendency to give socially desirable responses is also operating, then low scores on the trait scale should also be characteristic of individuals who have strong tendencies to give socially desirable responses. In this case, scores on the trait scale should be negatively correlated with scores on the *SD* scale.

Consider three examples from the MMPI. First, let us take a scale in which the trait keying is confounded with the social undesirability keying. The Psychasthenia (*Pt*) scale of the MMPI is a good example because it contains 48 items of which 47 are keyed for socially undesirable responses. Thus, individuals with strong tendencies to give socially desirable responses, as indicated by high scores on the *SD* scale, would be expected to obtain low scores on the *Pt* scale and the correlation between the two scales should be negative. It is. For a sample of 150 college males, the correlation between the *Pt* and *SD* scales was found to be –.84.

Second, let us take a scale in which the trait keying is confounded with the social desirability keying. An example is the Leadership (*Lp*) scale of the MMPI. This scale contains 50 items with 44 of the 50 items keyed for socially desirable responses. In this instance, we would expect high scores on the *Lp* scale to be associated with high scores on the *SD* scale and the correlation between the two scales should be positive. It is. The obtained correlation between the two scales for the same sample of college males was found to be .77.

As a third example, let us take a scale in which the number of items keyed for socially desirable responses is approximately the same as the number of items keyed for socially undesirable responses. The Masculinity (*Mf*) scale of the MMPI contains 60 items of which approximately half or 28 are keyed for socially desirable responses and approximately half or 32 are keyed for socially undesirable responses. Since the trait keying of the items in this scale is fairly well balanced for socially desirable and for socially undesirable responses, the scale should have a fairly low correlation with the *SD* scale. It does. For the sample of college males the correlation was –.16.

The three examples I have cited are not isolated cases. For a set of 43 MMPI scales, I found that the correlation between the MMPI scales and the *SD* scale was directly related to the proportion of items in the MMPI scales keyed for socially desirable responses. The product-moment correlation between the proportion of items keyed for socially desirable responses and the observed correlation of the scale with the *SD* scale was .92 (Edwards, 1961).

With a correlation of this magnitude, it is obvious that we could predict quite accurately the correlations of MMPI scales with the *SD* scale from knowledge of the proportion of items keyed for socially desirable responses in the scales. And, similarly, we could predict the proportion of items keyed for socially desirable responses in the scales from knowledge of the correlations of the scales with the *SD* scale. Does it make sense, in this instance, to regard one of these two variables as the independent variable and the other as the dependent variable? I suggest that it does and that it is the proportion of items keyed for socially desirable responses which should be viewed as the independent variable.

For each scale, for example, the proportion of items keyed for socially desirable responses is fixed and known and is not, therefore, something to be predicted. The correlation of a scale with the *SD* scale, on the other hand, is unknown, is free to vary, and is subject to sampling error. It thus remains to be predicted. Furthermore, we can experimentally manipulate the proportion of items keyed for socially desirable responses in scales, in much the same way that we can manipulate any other independent variable, and we can observe whether the correlations of the scales with the *SD* scale vary as a result of this experimental manipulation. At the same time, I do not see how we can experimentally vary the correlations of scales with the *SD* scale unless, of course, we change the proportion of items keyed for socially desirable responses. But to do this would again make the proportion of items keyed for socially desirable responses the independent variable and the correlation of the scale with the *SD* scale the dependent variable.

V

I suggested previously that items with scale values falling within the neutral interval of the social desirability continuum are relatively insensitive stimuli for eliciting the tendency to give socially desirable responses. If this is the case, then we would expect scales which contain a large proportion of items with scale values in the neutral interval on the social desirability continuum to have lower correlations with the *SD* scale than scales which have only a small proportion of items falling within the neutral interval. To test this hypothesis, the proportion of items falling within the neutral interval was obtained for each of 60 True-False personality scales. These proportions were then correlated with the absolute values of the correlations of the 60 scales with the *SD* scale. The resulting product-moment correlation coefficient was –.52 (Edwards, Diers, and Walker, 1962). In this study, the average or mean proportion of neutral items in the 60 scales was .24 and the largest proportion was only .53. I would expect a somewhat higher correlation between the proportion of neutral items in a scale and the absolute value of the correlation of the scale with the *SD* scale, if there were less restriction in the range of the proportion of neutral items.

The results of this study suggest that we may occasionally find a scale which has either a large or a small proportion of items keyed for socially desirable responses and yet the scale may have a relatively low correlation with the *SD* scale. If the scale values of the items in a scale deviate only moderately from the neutral point, then we would expect the scale to have a lower correlation with the *SD* scale than a scale in which the items have more extreme social desirability scale values, despite the fact that both scales may have the same proportion of items keyed for socially desirable responses. This hypothesis has been tested and confirmed in a study which James Walsh and I did on the intensity keying of MMPI scales (Edwards and Walsh, 1963).

VI

Consider a scale in which some of the items are keyed for trait *and* socially desirable responses and other items are keyed for trait *and* socially undesirable responses. To be more specific, take the case of two items, both of which are keyed for trait responses, but such that one of the items is keyed for a socially desirable response and the other is keyed for a socially undesirable response. The joint distribution of responses to these two items can be shown by means of a 2 X 2 table, Fig. 2.

		Item 2	
		SD Nonkeyed	*SUD* Trait keyed
Item 1	*SD* Trait keyed	*a*	*b*
	SUD Nonkeyed	*c*	*d*

Figure 2. Joint distribution of responses to two personality items. For Item 1 the trait response is a socially desirable response, whereas for Item 2 the trait response is a socially undesirable response.

If the trait is the only important determiner of responses to the two items, then we would expect the entries in cells *b* and *c* to be large relative to the entries in cells *a* and *d* and the trait responses to the two items should be positively correlated. But suppose that the tendency to give socially desirable responses is also operating. In this instance, we would expect the entries in cells *a* and *d* to be increased and those in cells *b* and *c* to be decreased relative to what we would have observed in the absence of any tendency to give socially desirable responses to the items. Obviously, if the tendency to give socially desirable responses is operating, then the increased frequencies in cells *a* and *d* will serve to lower the correlation between the trait responses to these two items.

The number of item correlations of the kind shown in Fig. 2 is maximized when a scale contains an equal number of items keyed for socially desirable and for socially undesirable responses, that is, in a scale which has a *balance* in its social desirability keying. Since these correlations contribute to the *average* intercorrelation of the items in a scale, we would expect the average intercorrelation to be lower for scales in which there is a balance in the social desirability keying of the items than for scales in which all of the items are keyed for either socially desirable or for socially undesirable responses, provided subjects are to some degree responding to the items in terms of social desirability tendencies. It is also obvious that if all of the items in a trait scale are keyed either for socially desirable responses or for socially undesirable responses and if the tendency to give socially desirable responses is operating, then this tendency will serve to increase the trait correlations between all possible pairs of items.

As a somewhat crude test of the prediction that the magnitude of the average intercorrelation of the items in a scale is a function of the imbalance in the social desirability keying of the items in the scale, we obtained K-R 21 values for each of 61 personality scales and correlated the K-R 21 values with the imbalance in the social desirability keying of the items in the scales. The resulting product-moment correlation coefficient was .62 (Edwards, Walsh, and Diers, 1963). This finding is consistent with the social desirability prediction that scales which have either a large or a small proportion of items keyed for socially desirable responses will tend to have higher K-R 21 values than scales which are more balanced in their social desirability keying. We also found, consistent with a prediction based upon social desirability considerations, that scales which have a large proportion of neutral items tend to have lower K-R 21 values than scales which contain only a small proportion of neutral items.

VII

I believe that scores on various trait scales are correlated with scores on the *SD* scale to the degree to which the trait scales are measuring the same common factor or personality dimension as that which I believe the *SD* scale to be measuring, namely, the tendency to give socially desirable responses in self-description. A standard technique for determining the degree to which different scales are measuring a common factor is to intercorrelate the scores on the scales and to factor analyze the resulting correlation matrix. To do this, of course, it is necessary to have available scores on a number of personality scales. Furthermore, if we wish to demonstrate that scores on all of these scales are measuring in varying degrees the common or general trait which I describe as the tendency to give socially desirable responses, it would be of value if each scale included in the analysis had been developed to measure some trait which the other scales were not designed to measure.

One source for a variety of personality scales is the MMPI. When the MMPI was first published the authors (Hathaway and McKinley, 1951) provided scoring keys for only a limited number of clinical and validity scales. But, over the years, many investigators must have felt that the original scales did not tap the full potentialities of the MMPI item pool. I say this because they proceeded to develop additional MMPI scales which, presumably, they believed would measure some personality trait not already being measured by one of the existing MMPI scales. By 1960 there were, according to Dahlstrom and Welsh (1960), scoring keys for a minimum of 212 MMPI scales, and there is no reason to believe that the end is yet in sight.

Factor analyses have been carried out with as few as 11 and with as many as 58 of these MMPI scales. Since there are only 566 items in the MMPI, there is item overlap in the different MMPI scales, even when only the clinical and validity scales are factor analyzed. This is a confounding variable and one to which I shall return later. However, regardless of the number of MMPI scales included in the factor analysis, there is general agreement that there is one dominant bipolar factor which accounts for the major proportion of the total and common variance. This factor, depending on which pole of the factor the investigator has chosen to emphasize, has been variously labeled as anxiety (Welsh, 1956), psychoticism (Wheeler, Little, and Lehner, 1951), general maladjustment (Tyler, 1951), ego-strength (Kassebaum, Couch, and Slater, 1959), acquiescence (Messick and Jackson, 1961), deviance (Barnes, 1956), and, last, but not least, social desirability (Edwards and Diers, 1962; Edwards, Diers, and Walker, 1962; Edwards and Heathers, 1962; Fordyce, 1956).

What basis do we have for choosing among these various interpretations of the first MMPI factor? The choice cannot be made solely on the basis of the names of the scales which have high loadings on the factor. For example, consistent with the social desirability interpretation of the first factor is the fact that the *SD* scale has a high loading on the factor. But, then so also does a scale designed to measure anxiety and so also do a number of other scales which were, presumably, designed to measure still other personality traits. Thus, if I suggest to you that the first MMPI factor is a social desirability factor, I must have more compelling evidence than the mere fact that the *SD* scale has a high loading on the factor. I do. Let me cite to you the results of a study which Carol Diers and I did (Edwards and Diers, 1962).

We obtained MMPI records from subjects under three sets of instructions: standard instructions, instructions to give socially desirable responses, and instructions to give socially undesirable responses. We intercorrelated and factor analyzed 58 MMPI scales for each set of instructions. The first-factor loadings for all three sets of instructions were highly correlated, the lowest correlation being .97. We also obtained the proportion of items keyed for socially desirable responses in each of the 58 MMPI scales. We then correlated the first-factor loadings under standard, socially desirable, and socially undesirable instructions with the proportion of items keyed for socially desirable responses in the scales. These correlations were .89, .92, and .94, respectively.

It is obvious that with correlations of this magnitude the first-factor loadings can be predicted quite accurately from knowledge of the proportion of items in the scales keyed for socially desirable responses. Scales with high loadings at one pole of the factor tend to have a large proportion of items keyed for socially desirable responses and scales with loadings at the opposite pole of the factor tend to have a large proportion of items keyed for socially undesirable responses. Since the loadings of the scales on the first factor vary directly in terms of the proportion of items keyed for socially desirable responses, and since this is precisely what the social desirability interpretation of the first factor would predict, I see no need to resort to such concepts as anxiety, ego-strength, and the like, in describing or interpreting the first factor. In fact, I see no way in which these concepts could be used to predict the loadings of MMPI scales on the first factor.

VIII

It may still be argued that because the 39-item *SD* scale is based upon items from the MMPI, an instrument that was designed primarily to measure various aspects of psychopathology, scores on the *SD* scale are reflecting content or trait oriented responses of some sort such as denial of psychopathology or affirmation of psychological health. The argument goes something like this: If one examines the content of the 39 items in the *SD* scale, it is possible to find a cluster or subset of items such that the items in the cluster will be judged homogeneous in content by a clinical psychologist. If a subject gives the keyed and socially desirable response to these items, he would be described by the same clinical psychologist as free from anxiety, as adjusted, and as a person with a feeling of well-being. If he gives the nonkeyed and socially undesirable response to these items, he would be described as chronically tense and anxious. Thus, responses to this subset of items and hence scores on the total *SD* scale may very well reflect a specific and content oriented trait rather than, as I believe, a general tendency to give socially desirable responses. In addition, the fact that the *SD* scale has a high loading on the first MMPI factor is regarded as further evidence that the *SD* scale is measuring the same content oriented trait as the first factor which is, of course, interpreted in terms of anxiety or ego strength or one of the other clinically significant labels which have been used to describe the first MMPI factor. This argument, although plausible, is one which I believe can easily be answered.

SD scales are rational scales and it is possible to build any number of them, provided we have a large pool of items with known social desirability scale values. We have obtained social desirability scale values for the 2,824 personality statements I mentioned previously. These items were developed to describe normal aspects of personality and there are no items in the pool which were specifically designed to relate to mental illness or psychopathology.

From the pool of 2,824 items, I constructed six *SD* scales by selecting items on the basis of their social desirability scale values and without regard to the content of the items. These six *SD* scales were included in a factor analysis along with the MMPI *SD* scale and a number of other experimental scales. In these scales there were no overlapping items. All of the *SD* scales, including the MMPI *SD* scale, had their highest loadings on a common factor, the lowest loading being .85 (Edwards, 1963).

In a second study, a number of trait or content oriented scales, including MMPI scales, were factor analyzed together with another set of six *SD* scales and the MMPI *SD* scale. Again there was no item overlap in any of the scales and again the *SD* scales all had their highest loadings on a common factor, the lowest loading being .85 (Edwards and Walsh, 1964).

In view of the nature of the item pool from which the items in these *SD* scales were drawn along with the fact that the items were selected on the basis of their social desirability scale values and without regard to content, it does not seem reasonable to me that the items in these distinct *SD* scales could have a common and homogeneous content. What the scales do have in common is a consistency in their social desirability keying.

The results of these two studies show, I believe, that there is a general trait, the tendency to give socially desirable responses to personality statements, which can be measured by any one of a variety of *SD* scales and which is not dependent on homogeneity of content of the items in the *SD* scales.

IX

I pointed out previously that there is item overlap in MMPI scales. Some of the MMPI scales we have investigated have items in common with the *SD* scale and it is possible that the correlations of these scales with the *SD* scale are, in part, the result of scoring common items. I therefore selected from the pool of 2,824 non-MMPI items a set of 39 items to form a new *SD* scale. Each item in the MMPI *SD* scale was matched with a non-MMPI item in terms of social desirability scale value and probability of endorsement and without regard to item content. This new *SD* scale I shall refer to as a non-MMPI *SD* scale.

Scores on the non-MMPI *SD* scale and 58 MMPI scales were intercorrelated and factor analyzed. Figure 3 shows the first-factor loadings of the MMPI scales as a function of the zero-order correlations of the scales with the non-MMPI *SD* scale. It is obvious that the first factor loadings are linearly and highly related to the correlations of the MMPI scales with the non-MMPI *SD* scale. Since the non-MMPI *SD* scale contains no items in common with any of the MMPI scales, the correlations cannot be attributed to overlapping items, and yet they predict quite accurately the first factor loadings.

I emphasize that the first-factor loadings of the MMPI scales and the correlations of the scales with the non-MMPI *SD* scale are both linear functions of the

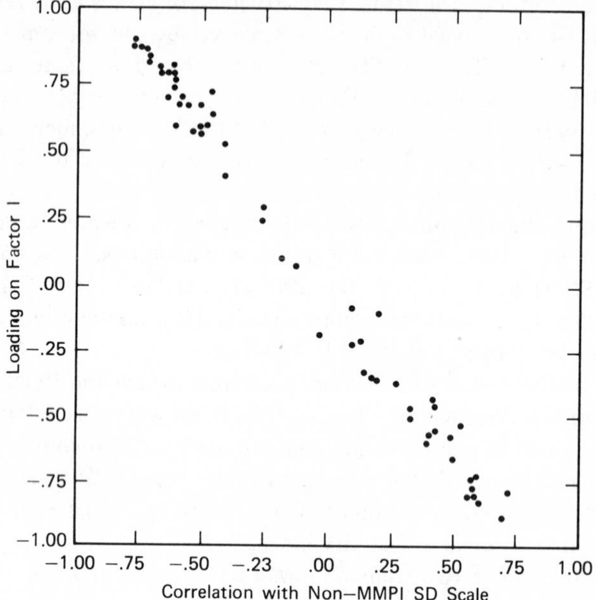

Figure 3. The relationship between first-factor loadings of MMPI scales and the correlations of the MMPI scales with a 39-item non-MMPI *SD* scale.

proportion of items in the scales keyed for socially desirable responses. In other words, we could predict either the first-factor loadings of the scales or the correlations of the scales with the non-MMPI *SD* scale in terms of the proportion of items keyed for socially desirable responses in the scales and do so quite accurately.

X

Is it possible to develop True-False scales which will measure psychologically significant traits and such that scores on these scales will be relatively independent of scores on the *SD* scale? I believe that it is possible and elsewhere I (Edwards, 1964) have described some techniques which may prove useful in the process. We know, for example, that if a scale has a balance in its social desirability keying and/or if the items are not too extreme in their social desirability scale values, then either of these two conditions tends to be characteristic of MMPI scales which have low correlations with the *SD* scale.

We are currently applying these and other prinicples in an attempt to develop rational scales which are trait and content oriented, which have a high degree of internal consistency, and which are also relatively independent of one another and of the *SD* scale. Our objective, in other words, is to try to maximize what

Philip DuBois (DuBois, 1962), in his presidential address to this society, described as redundancy within each scale and, at the same time, to minimize redundancy across or between scales.

Whether our efforts will be successful or not remains to be seen. But I hope that we are going to be able to develop scales which will measure traits other than the tendency to give socially desirable responses in self-description. As I have tried to show we already have, within the MMPI, an ample abundance of scales which are excellent measures of this trait.

3. SOCIAL-LEARNING THEORY, SOCIAL DESIRABILITY, AND THE MMPI

Alfred B. Heilbrun, Jr.[1]

Early in the development of the MMPI the test developers recognized that the item responses were susceptible to deception and considerable effort went into establishing special scales to detect (*L* and *F*) and correct for (*K*) dissimulation (Meehl & Hathaway, 1946). Since that time there have been a great many published studies investigating the question of how much performance variance on the MMPI can be attributed to level and type of psychopathology and how much to dissimulation. It is surprising that with as much accumulated evidence as there is, the issue is still a controversial one. In the opinion of the writer, some clarification may result from expanding the psychometric question to include the more basic issue of the relationship between socialization and psychopathology. The first purpose of this paper is to present a review of those studies in which the effect of deception upon MMPI performance has been investigated. The second goal is to present an interpretation of the old evidence from the standpoint of social-learning theory and to muster some relatively new evidence in behalf of the interpretation.

SOURCE. Alfred B. Heilbrun Jr., Professor of Psychology and Director of Clinical Training at Emory University, includes among his professional fields of specialization parental child rearing, objective personality measurement, and psychotherapy. This article originally appeared in *Psychological Bulletin,* 1964, **61,** 377-387. Reprinted by permission of the American Psychological Assoication and the author.

[1]The author would like to extend his gratitude to Leonard D. Goodstein for his helpful criticism of the proposals presented in this paper.

Review of the Literature

Effect on MMPI Performance Of Instructed Simulation

When the MMPI has been administered with instructions to simulate normal or psychopathologic performance, inconsistent results have been obtained. Hunt (1948) found that college students were able to alter their profiles when told to fake good or fake bad. Wiggins (1959) and Wiggins and Rumrill (1959) report moderate correlations between MMPI scales and a scale derived by social-desirability role-playing instructions to college subjects. Cofer, Chance, and Judson (1949) report that pattern differences were obtained, relative to standard instructions, when college subjects were asked to simulate normal or abnormal performance. Greater shifts followed from the abnormal test-taking set. When psychiatric patients were given the MMPI under instructions to simulate normalcy, Grayson and Olinger (1957) found a general tendency to change their profile patterns in the appropriate direction. However, wide individual differences between patients in the ability to simulate normalcy were observed and only 11% obtained normal simulated profiles. Gough (1954) requested college subjects to respond to the MMPI like psychoneurotics, and he found that their responses failed to correspond to those of neurotics. Even when professionally trained clincians were employed as subjects, Gough (1947) reports a failure to simulate psychoneurotic and psychotic profiles.

The general conclusion suggested by these studies is that MMPI responses can be modified under instructed simulation conditions so that the resultant test profiles appear more adjustive and, especially, more maladjustive; however, specific types of psychopathology are far less susceptible to simulation.

Special Dissimulation Scales

Of the three MMPI scales originally devised as measures of dissimulation (*Lie*, *F*, and *K*), *K* has received the greatest research attention. The *K* scale was developed as a measure of test-taking defensiveness by contrasting the MMPI responses of psychopathic hospital patients who presented normal profiles with the responses of subjects from the original norm group. Five of the nine clinical scales showed improved discrimination between normal and psychiatric criterion groups when *K* was added as a suppressor variable.

Despite the empirical derivation of *K*, some studies have reported a failure to improve MMPI prediction by its use (Hunt, 1948; Schmidt, 1948; Tyler & Michaelis, 1953). Others have found *K* useful in detecting positive malingering (Cofer *et al.*, 1949; Hanley, 1956) and in improving discrimination between normal and disturbed college groups (Heilbrun, 1963). Smith (1959) challenged the interpretation of *K* as a measure of defensiveness by finding a negative relationship between *K* and peer ratings of defensiveness in his normal groups. He suggested that *K* should be regarded as an index of psychological health, not defensiveness, in a normal population. The positive correlation between *K* and a measure of self-acceptance (Zuckerman & Monashkin, 1957) can be interpreted as supporting Smith's contention. Further support for a differential interpretation of *K* as a function of the population tested was provided by Heilbrun (1961) who found decreasing correlations between *K* and an independent defensive measure with more satisfactory adjustment of the college samples studied. One clear implication is that the denial of psychopathology implicit in keyed responses on the *K* scale is less likely to represent defensiveness when the respondent is within the normal range of adjustment; studies employing grossly normal subjects might, consequently, find *K* to be a less-effective suppressor variable.

Several scales have been constructed to measure the tendency to endorse socially desirable responses on the MMPI. Hanley's *Ex* scale (1957) included items of average popularity and neutral in social desirability; zero to moderate correlations with the MMPI scales were found. Wiggins (1959) employed social desirability role-taking procedures to develop his *Sd* scale, low to moderate relationships to the MMPI scales being reported. The *SD* scale, rationally derived by Edwards (1957), has been repeatedly found to be highly related to scores on the MMPI (Crowne & Marlowe, 1960; Edwards, 1961; Edwards, Heathers, & Fordyce, 1960; Fordyce, 1956; Wiggins, 1959). In addition, ratings of social desirability have also been shown to be highly related to MMPI scale scores (Rosen, 1956; Taylor, 1959).

The studies involving measures of social desirability leave little room for doubt that substantial negative covariance exists between social desirability and the MMPI. The greater the probability that a subject responds in a socially desirable direction on the MMPI, the more normal will his test profile appear. There remains, however, the question of interpretation of this psychometric relationship which will be discussed at some length later in this paper.

Factor-Analytic Studies Of the MMPI

Factor-analytic studies reported before 1960 have been consistent in finding that from one to three (usually two) major factors have accounted for most of the MMPI scale interrelationships whether the samples studied were drawn from normal or neurospsychiatric populations (Abrams, 1950; Cook & Wherry, 1950; Cottle, 1950; Kassebaum, Couch, & Slater, 1959; Little, 1949; Stout, 1949; Tyler, 1951; Welsh, 1956; Wheeler, Little, & Lehner 1951; Winne, 1950). Interpretation of factor meanings has been more variable but even in this regard fair agreement exists. Factor 1 with high loadings on the *Sc* and *Pt* scales has been labeled "psychotic" (Cottle, 1950; Wheeler, 1951), general maladjustment (Welsh,

1956), "tendency to personality maladjustment" (Cook & Wherry, 1950), and "ego strength versus ego weakness" (Kassebaum *et al.*, 1959). A more inclusive Factor 1, interpretable as a general maladjustment factor, was obtained by Stout (1949) and Tyler (1951). A second neurotic factor, with high loadings on the neurotic triad (*Hs*, *D*, and *Hy*), has also been commonly extracted (Cook & Wherry, 1950; Cottle, 1950; Tyler, 1951; Wheeler *et al.*, 1951).

More recent factor-analytic investigations of the MMPI have proposed that the two primary factors should be interpreted in terms of the test-taking habits of the respondent rather than in terms of adjustment level. Edwards and Heathers (1962) were able to show a correlation of –.985 between the *SD* scale and loadings of the MMPI scales on the primary factor, and suggested that the major source of variance on the MMPI is the tendency to give socially desirable responses versus the tendency to give socially undesirable responses to true-false type personality items. Messick and Jackson (1961) have proposed that the first MMPI factor is better interpreted in terms of acquiescence, but Edwards and Diers (1962) have provided additional evidence that loadings on the first factor can be predicted from the proportion of items keyed for socially desirable responses on MMPI scales or from zero-order correlations of the scales with the *SD* scale. In the latest study by Jackson and Messick (1962), results were obtained which they felt substantiated Edwards' contention that the primary factor is interpretable in terms of social desirability.

Implications of the Literature Review

That performance on the MMPI can be intentionally manipulated, given simulation instructions, so that the respondent will appear poorer or better adjusted is reasonably well established, although the extent to which dissimulation affects performance under standard instructions is left as a matter for conjecture.

Scales especially devised to detect dissimulation share the common problem of distinguishing between socially desirable but factual responses of well-adjusted subjects and the desirable but false and defensive responses of psychopathologic subjects. Crowne and Marlowe (1960) have criticized the Edwards *SD* scale in this regard, since they contend the keyed responses on the *SD* scale confound socially desirable behavior and psychopathologic behavior. If such confounding exists, then the correlations reported between dissimulation scales and MMPI scales are essentially uninterpretable. Covariance between both types of scales could be just as well attributed to the psychopathology implicit in each as to the effects of dissimulation upon endorsement of pathology.

Factor-analytic evidence is not sufficient to settle the question of the MMPI's vulnerability to dissimulation. The level of pathology interpretations of the major factor for one array of investigators are left to stand against the social-desirability interpretation of other investigators. The purpose of the next section is to consider the alternative interpretations of the primary MMPI factor which have been proposed (i.e., a level of adjustment factor versus social desirability), present some additional evidence, and hopefully provide a better rapprochement between personality measurement and social-learning theory.

Social-Learning Theory, Social Desirability, and the MMPI

Theory of Social Development

Although it is not yet possible to talk about a single stimulus-response theory of social development, there are certain broad principles which most stimulus-response psychologists would accept. Certainly the most basic principle would be that social behaviors which characterize an individual are primarily learned responses. Regardless of which learning-theory model one accepts, there seems to be general agreement that what is learned is contingent in some way upon the rewards and punishments which accrue as a function of our acts. Thus, in his social development the child learns to perform certain social behaviors and to avoid others, depending in large measure upon the nature of reinforcement imposed by the parents. The parents, in turn, share a common core of standards with the larger social group, and their reinforcement schedules as well as their own behaviors, which serve as a model for the child, reflect these common standards. These familial learning experiences and concurrent experiences with peers and other nonfamilial adults serve to provide the person with a relatively stable set of standards of social behavior. Some social behaviors are "bad" (premarital coitus, unprovoked aggression) and their occurrence or even the impulse to their occurrence elicits anxiety; other social behaviors are "good" (friendliness, dependability) and social rewards have been and continue to be associated with their occurrence. Still other social behaviors have been neither highly rewarded nor highly punished in the child's social history and are best described as neutral. Mussen, Conger, and Kagan (1963) list deviation from cultural expectations as one of the major sources of anxiety for the child. They state:

> Every culture has an unwritten list of valued traits that it expects its members to possess. . . . The individual's concept of himself is, to a large extent, a function of how closely his characteristics approximate the valued traits. When the individual perceives a great discrepancy between his own skill, traits, and temperamental qualities, and those he feels he *should* possess, anxiety is generated. The intensity of the anxiety is related

> to the degree to which the person perceives himself as deviating from his own and the culture's ideal standards (p. 147).

Individual differences in personal standards exist, needless to say. Factors such as social-economic class, sex of the child, identification model for the child, and unique events introduce variable patterns of antecedent conditions for their development. Yet within a social-economic class, like the American middle class, there is also a striking communality in social standards among its members. There is general consensus as to which behaviors are socially desirable and which are socially undesirable.

These broad outlines of social development are generally accorded the name socialization, and this aspect of the social development process involves learning the rules governing the behavior of some larger group. Social desirability of behavior, as perceived by the individual, is a function of the magnitude of positive or negative reinforcement imposed by the larger group as these have been filtered through familial and other learning experiences.

SD Test Response Set

Cronbach (1946, 1950) defined a test response set as a systematic response to items independent of item content and suggested that such sets contribute principally to error variance. When Edwards (1959) developed his own Personal Preference Schedule, he accorded the tendency to endorse socially desirable characteristics the status of a response set based upon the high correlation (.87) between the mean social desirability attributed to social behaviors by college subjects and the proportion of such subjects endorsing these behaviors as self-characteristic in a "yes-no" test format (Edwards, 1953). In a more recent statement (Edwards & Walker, 1961), "simple psychometric considerations" were considered adequate to account for the *SD* scale MMPI correlations rather than such "dynamic" interpretations as psychoticism versus normality. Characteristically, Edwards and his colleagues have refrained from going beyond the operational definition of social-desirability response set provided by the *SD* scale scores in considering performance variance on the MMPI. Other investigators (Jackson & Messick, 1958) have taken a middle ground, preferring to consider such attributes of test performance as acquiescence and social-desirability set as "styles" of response which may have more enduring and generalized behavioral effects. A response style is not necessarily a source of testing error, since it may have criterion relevance. Still others (Crowne & Marlowe, 1960; Heilbrun, 1962; Heilbrun & Goodstein, 1961; Wiggins, 1959) have taken a stronger stand in asserting that social-desirability responding on tests does have predictive relevance to nontest behavior and should not be considered a source of testing error. Marlowe and Crowne and their associates have provided rather convincing evidence that high and low *SD* test performers do show differential sensitivity to social approval in a wide array of experimental tasks (Barthel & Crowne, 1962; Crowne & Liverant, 1963; Crowne & Strickland, 1961; Marlowe & Crowne, 1961; Strickland & Crowne, 1962).

A positive relationship must be anticipated between social desirability of responses and actual social behaviors if one concurs with the theory of social development outlined above. The correlation of .87 between social desirability and endorsement of social behaviors on a questionnaire could legitimately be interpreted as reflecting the strength of this positive relationship in middle-class college students. The crucial question here would seem to be whether bright college subjects can and will provide veridical self-descriptions when afforded the opportunity. If one believes affirmatively, then the high correlation is best interpreted as demonstrating the influence of the socialization process; otherwise, the relationship is best interpreted as a reflection of a test-induced defensiveness.

Social Desirability And Psychopathology

Since psychopathological behaviors are almost invariably deviant behaviors and social standards serve to elicit conformity from members of a group, it follows that disordered behaviors are socially undesirable and normal behaviors are socially desirable. Szasz (1960) and Mowrer (1960) have previously emphasized the importance of deviation from ethical standards in defining mental illness.

Inspection of the 39 MMPI items included in the Edwards *SD* scale provides remarkable support for the proposed relationship between social desirability and psychopathology. Each item is keyed for the socially desirable alternative and without exception greater social desirability appears to be associated with endorsement of the more-adjustive behavior option. Crowne and Marlowe (1960) report that judges in their study also considered the socially undesirable options on the *SD* scale to be indicative of maladjustment. Perhaps more conclusive evidence can be extracted from two studies by Heilbrun (1960) and Goodstein and Heilbrun (1959). Fifteen personality variables were rated by 26 PhD psychologists with regard to their adjustive consequences in male and female college undergraduates in the former study, whereas the latter paper presents the personal (in oneself) desirability of these same behaviors as judged by college undergraduates.[2] Table 1 gives the rank order of the 15 variables both with regard to rated adjustment value and personal desirability. Social (in others) desirability ranks, using Edwards original statement values, are also provided for these behaviors. The rank-order correlations between rated adjustment value of

[2]The personal desirability values assigned to the personality variables represent the average values assigned to the nine statements measuring each variable. The statement values were obtained by scaling procedures identical to those used by Edwards in estimating the social desirability values of the statements.

Table 1. Rated Adjustment Value, Personal Desirability, and Social Desirability of 15 Personality Variables

Personality Variable	Adjustment		Personal Desirability	Social Desirability
	Value[a]	Rank	Rank	Rank
Achievement	2.75	2	1	3
Deference	2.32	8	11	9
Order	2.54	4.5	8	5.5
Exhibition	1.77	11	12	14
Autonomy	1.70	12	9	12
Affiliation	2.88	1	2	1
Intraception	2.33	7	10	8
Succorance	1.54	13	13	10
Dominance	2.19	9	6	13
Abasement	1.25	15	14	11
Nurturance	2.49	6	3	2
Change	1.96	10	5	4
Endurance	2.54	4.5	4	5.5
Heterosexuality	2.58	3	7	7
Aggression	1.30	14	15	15

[a]Values may range between 1.00 (highly maladjustive) and 3.00 (highly adjustive).

these behaviors and personal desirability is .82; the adjustment-social desirability correlation is .78. Both rho values are highly significant (t = 5.20 and 4.48, respectively, $df = 13, p > .01$). These data show a positive and substantial relationship between what college students consider desirable behavior and what experts consider adjustive behavior.

It has been argued (Wiener, Blumberg, Segman, & Cooper, 1959) that even expert judges in a rating task like that used in the Heilbrun study simply employ sterotypes of social acceptability of behavior in making their ratings rather than the adjustive consequences of demonstrating these classes of behaviors. If so, the correlations of .82 and .78 would be more parsimoniously considered coefficients of agreement between two ratings of desirability. It should be noted, however, that in the Heilbrun study, maladjusted college students were also psychometrically compared to adjusted students on measures of the same 15 personality variables, using the Adjective Check List (Gough & Heilbrun, 1965). The personality differences between the adjusted and maladjusted groups corresponded with what would be predicted from the adjustment ratings of the experts. As an illustration, of the 17/30 male and female scale comparisons for which significant group differences were obtained, the 10 traits which were more characteristic of the adjusted groups had a mean-rated adjustment score of 2.59. The seven variables more characteristic of the maladjusted groups showed a mean score of 1.51. Since the adjustment scores could range only from 1 (maladjustive) to 3 (adjustive) and there was no overlap between the two adjustment-score distributions, the correspondence between expert judgment and empirical finding is striking. These data suggest that the adjustment ratings were in accord with actual personality correlates of adjustment level rather than responses to desirability stereotypes.

Social Desirability and the MMPI As a Measure of Psychopathology

The clinical scales of the MMPI were developed by empirically determining differences in item performance between clearly pathological groups and normals. Accordingly, it has been assumed that an appreciable amount of the performance variance on the test is attributable to degree and type of psychopathology. It is appropriate at this point to reconsider the basic question of whether the major source of variance for the MMPI is attributable to psychopathology or to social-desirability response tendencies.

Heilbrun (1963), in a study of an optimal *K*-weighting system for prediction of maladjustment in a college population, determined the biserial correlations between each of the 10 MMPI clinical scales and membership in normal or psychologically disturbed groups. Heineman (1952), using college subjects, has provided desirability values for the MMPI items from which mean desirability values have been determined for the same clinical scales. Table 2 presents the rank order of these 10 scales from least to most socially desirable and two sets of biserial correlations ranked in order of magnitude. One set represents the ordered average correlations for college males and females, where the discrimination was between normal subjects ($N = 900$) and acutely disturbed psychopathic hospital patients ($N = 100$). Averaging was performed to be consistent with the social-desirability rankings which were obtained independent of sex. The second set of correlations represents the extent to which the clinical scales discriminated male college normals ($N = 270$) from maladjusted counseling service clients ($N = 30$). Maladjusted females were not included because the MMPI proved to be nonpredictive for this type of subject. The rank-order correlation between social desirability and the discriminatory power of the clinical scales was .75 for the acutely disturbed versus normal subjects and .77 for the maladjusted male versus normal subjects. Both rho values were significant ($t = 3.21$ and 3.41, $df = 8$, $p < .02$, $.01$). The more socially undesirable the keyed responses on a scale of the MMPI, the more successfully that scale distinguished the self-descriptions of psychologically disturbed and normal subjects. Since the pathological groups invariably received the higher scale scores, it follows that they were endorsing the keyed, socially undesirable, and psychopathological behaviors more frequently. Therefore, the more socially undesirable the behaviors endorsed by an individual, the more likely he will evidence a manifest psychological disturbance.

Table 2. Social Desirability Rank and Discriminatory Power of the 10 MMPI Clinical Scales

MMPI Scale	SD Rank[a]	Biserial r[b]		Biserial r[c]	
		r	Rank	r	Rank
Hs	2	.26	6	.38	1
D	4	.48	1	.31	2
Hy	7	.38	4.5	.29	4
Pd	5	.40	3	.20	6
Mf	10	.12	10	.17	7
Pa	8	.24	7.5	.12	9
Pt	3	.38	4.5	.25	5
Sc	1	.42	2	.30	3
Ma	9	.13	9	.04	10
Si	6	.24	7.5	.16	8

[a]Least to most.
[b]Psychiatric cases versus normals.
[c]Counseling cases versus normals.

That psychologically disturbed people tend to admit to being psychologically disturbed by their responses to the MMPI is an empirically demonstrated fact. That their admitted psychologically disturbed behavior is socially undesirable behavior is also beyond question. There remains, however, one missing link before this chain of reasoning will reach back to social-learning theory. Need the behavioral self-descriptions obtained on the MMPI bear any relationship to the same behaviors as they occur or have occurred in the natural (nontest) environment of the individual? If a person answers "false" to the item, "I loved my mother," is it any more likely that he failed to love his mother than the person who answers "true"? Hathaway and McKinley (1956) avoided this question by rendering it irrelevant. Empirical derivation of the items for the *Sc* scale required only that schizophrenics answer it differently than normals; in this case, schizophrenics answered it "false" with greater frequency. There was no need to show or even be interested in whether schizophrenics "really" failed to love their mothers more frequently than normals.

The point of view to be presented here is that given a "false" response to the mother item, two alternative answers to the question of test-response-actual-response equivalence are most reasonably entertained. One, those individuals who provide a socially undesirable "false" response to the statement, "I loved my mother," are in fact more likely to have behaved in this socially undesirable way than "true" responders; further, they are more likely to be psychologically disturbed than "true" responders. Two, those individuals who provide a socially undesirable "false" response to this item are not in fact more likely to have behaved in this particular socially undesirable way than "true" responders, but they will be characterized by other socially undesirable behaviors (such as answering "false" to the mother item); they are still more likely to be psychologically disturbed. Veridicality of response is not, therefore, a necessary assumption since either alternative is consonant with the social-learning theory presented earlier; namely, that psychopathology represents a deviation from socially desirable standards of behavior and its corollary, the greater the psychopathology, the greater the deviation.

Conclusions

The proposition set forth in this paper and explicated by theory and evidence is that the dimensions of psychological health and social desirability are in large measure one and the same. If true, then many of the research findings bearing upon the relationships of social desirability to psychological test performance have lacked adequate interpretation. The positive contingency of social behavior adjustment value upon the degree to which these behaviors elicit social approval has been unduly neglected, paving the way for misconstruing the *r*'s between test-based measures of social behavior and social desirability as necessary indications of test invalidity.

It is important to point out that some of the performance variance on personality tests is quite likely attributable to specific test-taking attitudes describable as "faking good" and "faking bad." The former attitude should lead to the endorsement of socially desirable responses and the latter to those which are socially undesirable. Thus, it becomes important to distinguish between the tendency to behave in socially desirable ways, which must be mirrored in test performance to the extent veridical self-appraisal is achieved, and the tendency to respond to test items without regard to fact but only with regard to the social appearance which the person wishes to create by his test performance. Block (1962) recently has also aligned himself behind the conclusions of this paper. After pointing out the necessary relationship between psychological health and socially desirable behavior, he distinguished between a facade or superficial brand of socially desirable behavior and socially desirable behavior which is a correlate of adjustment. The former seems to describe the "fake good" set on a test and the latter the basic product of social learning experiences.

4. SIMULATED PATTERNS ON THE EDWARDS PERSONAL PREFERENCE SCHEDULE[1]

Charles F. Dicken

An important problem in the use of inventories of interest and personality is the susceptibility of the scores to simulation. At least three forms of conscious attitude may result in scores which fail to represent accurately the characteristics of the individual: (*a*) deliberate "faking" with intent to deceive the test user, (*b*) response in terms of an ideal self concept rather than a candid self-appraisal, and (*c*) response in terms of an "honest" but inaccurate or uninsightful self-assessment.

One line of approach to the simulation problem has been concern for item selection and item subtlety (Gough, 1954; Meehl, 1945; Seeman, 1952; Wiener, 1948). Another approach has been the development of validity scores for detecting or counterbalancing bias introduced by test-taking attitude (Gough, 1952; Humm, Storment, & Iorns, 1944; Meehl & Hathaway, 1946).

Simulation has been investigated experimentally by asking *S*s to assume a specified role in responding to test items. Reviews (Gough, 1950; Meehl & Hathaway, 1946) of the extensive literature on role playing of the "fake good" and "fake bad" dimensions identified by Meehl and Hathaway (1946) indicate that the validity score approach, when available, is reasonably efficient in detecting these forms of simulation. Role-playing studies of structured inventory scales or patterns relating to specific personality traits or interest attributes (Bordin, 1943; Gough, 1947; Kelly, Miles, & Terman, 1935; Longstaff, 1948; Sundberg & Bachelis, 1956; Sweetland, 1948; Wesman, 1952) have consistently found substantial alterations in the scores of *S*s instructed to simulate. Validity scores have ordinarily been unavailable in studies of this type, although there is some evidence that they can be effective (Gough, 1947).

The most recent line of attack on the problem of the descriptive accuracy of structured inventory scores concerns what Jackson and Messick (1958) have termed "stylistic" determinants of item response. Tendencies to acquiesce and to respond in terms of the social desirability of the item are two major instances

SOURCE. Charles F. Dicken received his doctoral degree at the University of Minnesota and is presently Professor of Psychology at San Diego State College. Personality assessment, psychotherapy, and personality theory are among Dr. Dicken's current fields of specialization. This article originally appeared in the *Journal of Applied Psychology,* 1959, **43,** 372-378. Reprinted by permission of the American Psychological Association and the author.

[1]The author gratefully acknowledges the assistance of Ralph Granneberg in obtaining and testing the *S*s and of John Black in the data analysis.

of stylistic determinants. Jackson and Messick reviewed the experimental evidence and concluded, " . . . stylistic determinants . . . as distinct from specific content, account for a large proportion of response variance on some personality scales, particularly the California F scale, the MMPI, and the California Psychological Inventory" (1958, p.250).

The Edwards Personal Preference Schedule (EPPS) (Edwards, 1957) was constructed to measure a set of personality variables drawn from Murray's (1938) list of manifest needs.[2] The unique feature of the Schedule is an attempt to control the social desirability (*SD*) factor by means of a forced-choice format in which paired items scored for different variables are equated for independently judged *SD*. Control of *SD* would presumably eliminate one means by which a test *S* can obtain scores which are not truly characteristic of him, that of responding in the socially desirable direction.

Recent evidence on the EPPS casts doubt on the success of the control of *SD* and on the resistance of the Schedule to simulation. Corah, Feldman, Cohen, Grune, and Ringwall (1958) found that 20 of 30 item pairs sampled from the EPPS differed significantly in intrapair *SD* when judged *as pairs,* and found a high correlation between these differences and the probability of endorsement of the items. Borislow (1958) studied the EPPS response changes in *S*s who were first tested under standard instructions and then asked to role-play social desirability or personal desirability. Both role-playing groups differed significantly in number of item responses altered and in test-retest profile correlations from a control group retested under standard instructions. Neither the consistency score nor profile stability coefficients discriminated simulated profiles from controls. Borislow interpreted his findings as indicating susceptibility of the EPPS to faking, but his small *N*s prevented a descriptive analysis of score changes for the two role-playing samples, and he rejected the hypothesis of a differential effect of the two role-playing conditions.

The present study investigated the qualitative properties of EPPS score changes under four different role-playing instructions. The hypotheses were: (*a*) Subjects motivated to simulate a personality trait are capable of inducing substantial changes in their EPPS scores. (*b*) Substantial score changes will occur under the role-playing of a "good impression," in spite of the attempted control of the SD factor. (*c*) Subject groups that role-play different personality variables will obtain different simulated patterns. (*d*) The consistency score is not an effective index of simulation.

[2]The names of the EPPS variables are as follows: Achievement (ach), Deference (def), Order (ord), Exhibition (exh), Autonomy (aut), Affiliation (aff), Intraception (int), Succorance (suc), Dominance (dom), Abasement (aba), Nurturance (nur), Change (chg), Endurance (end), Heterosexuality (het), Aggression (agg). A consistency score (con) is also computed, based on the number of identical choices made in two sets of the same 15 items.

Method

The EPPS was administered with standard instructions to 75 students in five introductory psychology classes at the City College of San Francisco. The *S*s for the experiment ranged in age from 18 to 30. They were permitted to identify their records by code numbers to preserve anonymity.

The sample was then divided into four role-playing groups: *need order* (ORD), 8 males, 9 females; *need dominance* (DOM), 8 males, 11 females; *need change* (CHG), 13 males, 7 females; and *good impression* (GI), 8 males, 11 females. The first three roles were chosen to represent a variety of the EPPS variables and to correspond roughly to three variables under investigation in a parallel study of simulation of the California Psychological Inventory. The fourth role relates to Hypothesis *b*.

Each group was retested separately with instructions to simulate for the purpose of winning an imaginary but highly desirable college scholarship. Subjects in each of the first three groups were told to suppose a hypothetical "scholarship committee" used the EPPS to select individuals with a particular kind of personality trait. The name of the need variable and a three- or four-sentence description based on Murray (1938) and reproduced below were read to the group and printed on a blackboard visible throughout the session.

Need for Order. A person with a need for order wants to achieve organization, neatness, and precision. This kind of person aims for perfection in details, attempts to keep possessions and work in careful order, and is exact and precise in speech and manner. Persons with a need for order behave in an organized, restrained, and careful manner in whatever they do.

Need for Dominance. A person with a need for dominance wants to influence, persuade, or direct other people by suggestion, persuasion, or command. This kind of person tries to get others to cooperate with him and to convince them of the rightness of his opinions. Persons with a need for dominance desire to lead, influence, guide, govern or supervise other people. Note that a person with a need for dominance need not necessarily be domineering or unpleasant in his conduct.

Need for Change. A person with a need for change seeks variety, newness, and adventure in personal experiences. This kind of person avoids regularity or repetition in habits of living, attempting instead to experiment and to do things differently. Persons with a need for change are flexible and adaptable and enjoy changing their methods, habits, and preferences.

The GI group was told to respond so as to give the most favorable possible impression of themselves to the scholarship committee, without further specification of role. One week elapsed between the first and second test administrations for all groups.

Results

Tables 1–4 show the means and standard deviations of the EPPS scores of the four role-playing groups for standard and simulation conditions. The mean difference scores (simulation condition minus standard condition) are also shown.[3] The means for the standard condition are comparable for the four samples and are, in the main, reasonably close to those of Edwards' normative sample.

The *t* test for correlated measures was used to compare the mean differences with a null hypotheses of zero difference. The effect of the forced-choice format of the EPPS on score changes in simulation should be noted in interpreting the outcomes of the significance tests for individual scales. An altered item response which increases an *S*'s score on one variable also decreases his score on some other variable. Thus while the increases in any sample are independent of each other, and while the set of decreases is similarly internally independent, the increases and the decreases are not independent. A conservative interpretation would consider the significance of the changes for a single direction only (increases being probably of greater interest here), and would treat the remaining changes (e.g., decreases) in terms of relative magnitude only.

The effect of the role instructions on the similarity of individual EPPS profiles within each sample is shown in Table 5. Score patterns of individuals show little concordance in the standard conditions, but have a highly significant level of concordance in every simulation condition. This indicates a shift from an "individual" pattern of responses to a "role-characteristic" pattern when the *S* simulates. Borislow's (1958) concordance values for his simulated social desirability (*SD*) and personal desirability (*PD*) groups are included in the table for comparison. The present good impression group appears to have simulated in a more homogeneous fashion than the earlier *SD* group.

The large and statistically reliable mean changes in all samples and the consistent concordance shifts confirm Hypotheses *a* and *b*. The differences in the mean simulated patterns and the between-condition correlations of mean changes (Table 6) confirm Hypothesis *c* with one exception. The three trait-simulation conditions induced mean changes in the 15 variables which are either essentially uncorrelated or negatively correlated. In each case the pattern of prominently elevated scores is different, and the peak score is on the relevant variable. However, conditions ORD and GI yielded changes which are highly correlated, and mean simulated profiles which are for practical purposes indistinguishable.

[3]The raw scores were converted to *T*-score values appropriate to the sex of the *S*. Preliminary analysis of the four samples indicated no substantial sex differences in either standard or simulation conditions. There were no male-female reversals of the direction of mean change scores where both change score means differed significantly from zero. Data for male and female *S*s were combined for the main analyses.

Table 1. Means, Standard Deviations, and Mean Differences of EPPS Scores under Standard (Std) and Simulated Need Order (ORD) Conditions ($N = 17$)

Scale	Std		ORD		
	M	*SD*	*M*	*SD*	*D*
ach	53.5	10.6	64.2	11.2	10.7**
def	52.6	8.8	68.1	7.2	15.5**
ord	53.2	11.9	83.9	8.7	30.7**
exh	50.9	8.2	44.2	11.5	−6.8**
aut	46.4	6.6	37.8	6.2	−8.6**
aff	45.2	8.1	39.3	7.6	−5.8**
int	46.5	11.1	49.9	8.0	3.4
suc	46.5	8.8	45.9	8.2	−0.6
dom	50.6	9.3	47.8	15.0	−2.8
aba	50.1	9.6	48.8	10.6	−1.2
nur	46.3	8.7	40.8	8.3	−5.5**
chg	52.9	11.9	31.9	10.5	−21.0**
end	53.6	9.2	72.3	4.0	18.7**
het	48.6	12.3	35.9	8.5	−12.7**
agg	51.5	7.6	42.4	9.1	−9.1**
con	51.6	8.6	49.7	9.9	−1.9

*Differs from zero at .05 level.
**Differs from zero at .01 level.

Table 2. Means, Standard Deviations, and Mean Differences of EPPS Scores under Standard (Std) and Simulated Need Dominance (DOM) Conditions ($N = 19$)

Scale	Std		DOM		
	M	*SD*	*M*	*SD*	*D*
ach	52.0	10.1	62.7	9.5	10.7**
def	53.8	8.8	46.3	14.8	−7.6**
ord	52.7	10.6	50.2	9.9	−2.5
exh	47.0	10.3	63.8	11.7	16.8**
aut	51.6	12.3	49.4	9.5	−2.3
aff	43.4	9.0	49.5	8.1	6.1**
int	51.6	10.2	46.5	8.8	−5.2**
suc	49.1	11.2	44.7	8.1	−4.4**
dom	46.0	10.7	68.7	7.0	22.6**
aba	48.6	7.7	35.4	6.4	−13.3**
nur	47.3	8.6	49.2	15.0	1.9
chg	52.5	9.6	36.7	8.2	−15.8**
end	53.6	7.7	50.0	8.1	−3.5*
het	49.8	13.2	42.4	11.2	−7.4**
agg	49.7	10.2	58.9	8.7	9.3**
con	53.8	8.6	46.5	10.1	−7.3**

*Differs from zero at .05 level.
**Differs from zero at .01 level.

Table 3. Means, Standard Deviations, and Mean Differences of EPPS Scores under Standard (Std) and Simulated Need Change (CHG) Conditions (N = 20)

	Std		CHG		
Scale	*M*	*SD*	*M*	*SD*	*D*
ach	49.0	10.3	47.2	12.9	−1.9
def	52.1	7.6	47.0	8.4	−5.2*
ord	53.7	10.7	43.3	9.9	−10.4**
exh	47.7	9.1	57.7	12.8	10.0**
aut	46.8	9.1	60.4	10.1	13.6**
aff	46.6	9.1	43.0	7.6	−3.6
int	46.7	7.9	46.1	6.6	−.6
suc	49.4	10.4	48.6	7.4	−.8
dom	44.8	11.1	51.7	8.7	6.9**
aba	53.2	8.2	42.8	8.7	−10.4**
nur	51.7	10.5	43.0	10.1	−8.7**
chg	52.8	10.1	65.1	10.2	12.3**
end	51.7	12.9	45.0	10.2	−6.6*
het	50.8	12.6	50.0	7.9	−.8
agg	52.6	9.5	59.5	8.2	7.0**
con	47.3	10.0	43.3	14.4	−4.0*

*Differs from zero at .05 level.
**Differs from zero at .01 level.

Table 4. Means, Standard Deviations, and Mean Differences of EPPS Scores under Standard (Std) and Simulated Good Impression (GI) Conditions (N = 19)

	Std		GI		
Scale	*M*	*SD*	*M*	*SD*	*D*
ach	52.0	8.1	63.0	8.0	11.0**
def	47.8	8.4	68.6	7.2	20.8**
ord	54.5	12.5	71.8	8.7	17.3**
exh	52.4	14.4	44.7	10.0	−7.7**
aut	50.3	9.7	38.3	10.7	−12.0**
aff	47.0	6.6	42.9	7.1	−4.1*
int	47.9	10.0	50.4	6.7	2.5
suc	50.4	10.0	42.5	7.3	−8.0**
dom	51.2	10.3	52.4	9.8	1.2
aba	48.2	9.7	46.9	7.4	−1.2
nur	48.5	8.4	45.9	10.1	−2.5
chg	50.4	11.5	42.2	8.9	−8.2**
end	51.7	11.5	67.8	7.8	16.1**
het	46.5	11.7	34.6	8.5	−11.8**
agg	51.0	7.8	41.6	9.1	−9.4**
con	47.8	11.5	47.5	11.9	−.3**

*Differs from zero at .05 level.
**Differs from zero at .01 level.

Table 5. Kendall Coefficients of Concordance (*W*) of EPPS Profiles in Standard (Std) and Stimulation (S) Conditions for Four Role-Playing Samples and for Borislow's SD and PD Samples

Sample	Std	S
ORD	.11*	.64**
DOM	.04	.43**
CHG	.08	.30**
GI	.04	.61**
Borislow PD		.26**
Borislow SD		.38**

* *W* Significant at .05 level.
** *W* Significant at .01 level.

Table 6. Between-Condition Spearman Correlations of Ranks of Mean Change Scores for Fifteen Need Variables

Condition			
DOM	−.02		
CHG	−.67*	.22	
GI	.90*	−.02	−.48
	ORD	DOM	CHG

*Rho differs from zero at .01 level (no values significant at .05 level).

Edwards found relatively low intercorrelations of the EPPS variables in the normative sample. However, the simulation instructions in the present experiment induced significant changes in scales other than the "primary" scale for which the instructions were written. One hypothesis which might account for the changes in the "nonprimary" scales is that these changes relate to the size of the correlations of the nonprimary scales with the primary scale, even though the correlations are of a generally low order. The rank difference correlations between the amount of change in nonprimary scales and the magnitude of the normative sample correlations of these scales with the primary scale are positive and significant in conditions ORD (rho = .85) and DOM (rho = .55), but there is no association in condition CHG (rho = .03). There is no immediate explanation for the failure of the hypothesis in the CHG condition, although it may be noted that the score changes and the concordance shift are least in this condition.

Hypothesis *d* is confirmed by the data from all four conditions. Although the mean *con* score decreased in all conditions, the decreases are not significant in two groups, and the overlap of *con* scores for simulation and standard conditions is large in all groups. Even if a liberal cutting score of 10 or less raw score points on *con* is used as a simulation index (which would identify as "simulated" 15%

of the records in the normative sample), only the following relatively small proportions of the simulated records would be detected: ORD, 5/17; DOM, 6/19; CHG, 8/20; and GI, 5/17. Unsimulated records from these samples misidentified by this cutting score would be seven, two, seven, and four cases respectively.

Discussion

One of the most important findings is the failure of the social desirability pairings of items to control the distorting effect of test-taking attitudes. The changes in the GI condition tend to support the conclusion of Corah *et al.* (1958) that *SD* is not equated in some of the pairs. Even if the item format partly controls social desirability bias, which seems likely, the role-playing data suggest that distortion of the EPPS by simulations of characteristics other than *SD* remains a distinct possibility.

Since the *S*s in the three trait-simulation conditions were given descriptions of the variables they were to simulate, the question arises whether these experimental distortion sets are meaningfully related to conscious or unconscious role taking in a normal testing situation. The reader may verify the degree of similarity of the role instructions to the content of the EPPS items by reference to the scoring keys. Some correspondence was unavoidable because of the "obvious" character of the items. In general, however, the role instructions make a broader and more abstract reference to the need variables than do the items, suggesting that to some degree true role taking rather than information on specific item content determined changes. The success of the essentially uninstructed "scholarship applicants" in Condition GI in simulating traits (order, achievement, endurance, and deference) which are both relevant and "desirable" with respect to the goal they sought argues rather cogently against assuming that simulation could not occur except in *S*s with specific information about the instrument.

The evidence for susceptibility to distortion gives cause for question of the feasibility of constructing an instrument for variables of this type without a systematic procedure for determining item and scale validities. The Manual makes no reference to item selection other than for social desirability values. The nature and arrangement of the items suggests that the questions of subtlety and of comprehensiveness of content were similarly neglected. Scores for each scale are determined by endorsement of a very small number of statements (nine), because statements are repeated in identical form in the sets of 28-item pairs scored for each scale. The statements for each variable appear highly "face valid" and are strikingly similar in content. The effect of face validity and content homogeneity in facilitating selective endorsement of a particular kind of item is probably augmented by the arrangement of the test booklet. More than half the statements scored for each scale appear in "runs" of five consecutive item pairs.

The effect of conscious distortion, the limitations in content and subtlety of the items, and the inadequacy of validity data[4] suggest there is relatively little basis at present for regarding EPPS scores as measures with properties other than those of a self-report. If this conclusion is correct, interpretation of a score as a measure of an examinee's actual characteristics rests on the assumption that he is both (*a*) able to perceive his own characteristics accurately and (*b*) willing to report these perceptions candidly. Meehl's rationale for empirically constructed scales, "the scoring does not assume a valid self-rating to have been given" (1945, p. 299), cannot be used. In selection problems, (*a*) is usually unknown and (*b*) often false. In counseling, (*b*) may often be assumed, but if (*a*) is correct the need for a personality inventory may be vitiated. The usefulness of earlier personality inventories dependent on validity of self-report has been disappointing (Ellis, 1946).

A final and important practical implication of the findings is that the lack of effective validity indices for detecting distorting attitudes is one of the most crucial weaknesses of the EPPS in its present form.

[4]The Manual contains no validity data other than low correlations of the scales with other personality scales and mention of some inconsistent correlations with self-ratings. Subsequent studies of concurrent validity of the EPPS have given partly positive (Zuckerman, 1958), and partly negative (Dilworth, 1958; Himmelstein, Eschenbach, & Carp, 1958) findings. Construct validity studies have given mixed positive and negative findings (Bernardin & Jessor, 1957; Gisvold, 1958; Zuckerman & Grosz, 1958).

5. TEST SOPHISTICATION AND FAKING IN THE TAT SITUATION[1,2]

Martin F. Kaplan and
Leonard D. Eron

Subjective definition of the test situation has for some time been recognized as a variable in performance in "projective" assessment situations (Sarason, 1954). In order to provide structure and give meaning to relatively ambiguous stimuli, the subject must rely upon cues in the present situation as well as residuals from past experience. Not the least of these situational variables is that of subjective definition of the purpose of the test and conscious altering of test behavior in response to such definitions.

There exists a large body of evidence concerning the effect of experimentally induced sets to "fake" upon Rorschach performance (Abramson, 1951; Carp & Shavzin, 1950; Feldman & Graley, 1954; Fosberg, 1938, 1941, 1943; Hutt, Gibby, Milton & Pottharst, 1950). Few studies relevant to "faking" sets have been attempted with the TAT, however, perhaps due to the general lack of a systematic and established scoring system in its everyday use.

Leuba & Lucas (1945) hypnotically induced attitudes of happiness, criticalness and anxiety in their subjects, and found that the criticalness set influenced descriptions of magazine photographs. More relevant to the present study is one by Weisskopf & Dieppa (1951). Three TAT cards were administered to a group of neurotic males under three instructional sets: standard, faking the "best possible impression," and faking the "worst possible impression." Several differences were found between the three administrations on judges' ratings of a number of traits. The criticism may be raised that the same subjects received all three administrations; responses made to the standard administration very likely influencing later responses. Lubin (1958) found instructional sets toward free use of imagination, and "mastery of feelings," to be related to the extent of sexual, aggressive and creative expression as rated by judges.

SOURCE. Martin F. Kaplan received his doctoral degree at the University of Iowa. He is currently Associate Professor of Psychology at Northern Illinois University and psychological consultant to Elain State Hospital. Leonard D. Eron is Professor of Psychology at the University of Illinois, Chicago Circle. Both authors have extensively contributed to the research literature on personality assessment, particularly the TAT. This article originally appeared in the *Journal of Projective Techniques and Personality Assessment,* 1965, **29,** 493-503. Reprinted by permission of the *Journal* and the authors.

[1]The authors wish to express their appreciation to Dr. Dee W. Norton for his helpful advice in the design and statistical analysis of this study.

[2]This study was, in part, supported by U.S.P.H.S. Predoctoral Fellowship MH-16, 942-02, awarded to the first author.

Knowledge of the purpose of the test (i.e., test sophistication) may also be a factor in altering of test responses. Summerwell, Campbell & Sarason (1958) found that differential instructions concerning the purpose of the TAT affected ratings of emotional tone and tone of the outcome. Similarly, Henry & Rotter (1956) found Rorschach responses to be altered by information as to the nature of the test.

The present study is concerned with the effects of conscious altering of test responses (faking) upon a number of TAT response measures. Furthermore, the interaction of test sophistication with faking of responses is investigated to determine the effect of psychological sophistication and prior knowledge of the TAT upon faking.

Method

Subjects

Seventy-two subjects were placed into one of four groups. Thirty-six undergraduate students in an introductory psychology course at the University of Iowa were randomly assigned to either group "E" or group "C", the "naive" groups. There were 12 males and six females in each group. The criteria for inclusion in the sophisticated groups (S) was a minimum of graduate standing in clinical psychology and previous enrollment in at least one graduate course in projective techniques. Thirty-six "sophisticated" subjects were placed in either group "ES" or "CS", the two groups being equated on the basis of professional experience. Each sophisticated group also contained 12 males and six females.

Procedure

All 20 TAT cards of the male (or female) series were administered to each subject, and the subject was asked to write his stories. Each group received the following written instructions:

Groups C, CS:

You are participating in a study designed to determine the typical stories told to pictures by college students.

You will be given a number of pictures. Your task is to make up as dramatic a story as you can for each. You are to tell *what led up to the event shown in the picture, describe what is happening at the moment, what the characters are feeling and thinking, and then give the outcome.*

Write your thoughts as they come to your mind; literary master-pieces are not required.

You are allowed a maximum of FIVE MINUTES on each card. If you are through with a card before the five minutes are up, wait for instructions to begin the next card. You will be warned when four minutes have elapsed so that you can wrap up your story. When the five minutes are up, you must turn to the next card.

Look at the cards one at a time, in the order furnished, and do not look at the next until instructed to do so. Turn each card face down when you are through with it.

Do not compare stories with your neighbors.

Groups E, ES:

You will be given a number of pictures. Your task is to make up as dramatic a story as you can for each. You are to tell *what led up to the event shown in the picture, describe what is happening at the moment, what the characters are feeling and thinking, and then give the outcome.*

Literary masterpieces are not required.

You are allowed a maximum FIVE MINUTES on each card. If you are through with a card before the five minutes are up, wait for instructions to begin the next card. You will be warned when four minutes have elapsed so that you can wrap up your story. When the five minutes are up, you must turn to the next card.

You are asked to take this test pretending that you are an AGGRESSIVE, VERY HOSTILE PERSON. *In other words, you will be writing the stories you believe an* AGGRESSIVE, VERY HOSTILE *person would write.* A *hostile* person is generally considered to be one who is *unfriendly, antagonistic, characterized by aggression, and encroaches upon others.* He will have *difficulty with control over aggressive urges.* A *hostile* person tends to *feel anger toward, and seeks to inflict harm upon, others,* and may also attempt to *destroy or appropriate others' possessions.*

Look at the cards one at a time, in the order furnished, and do not look at the next until instructed to do so. Turn each card face down when you are through with it.

Do not compare stories with your neighbors.

Analysis

Scores were obtained for the following measures: 1. Emotional tone rating (ET). 2. Outcome rating (O). 3. Perceptual distortions (D). 4. Unusual formal characteristics (UFC). 5. Number of aggressive themes. 6. Frequency in a normative sample of the most common theme in each story as determined by reference to an earlier normative study (Eron, 1950). Full descriptions of these measures may be found in Eron (1950, 1953) and Eron, Terry, & Callahan, (1950). Protocols were randomized and all stories given in response to any one picture were scored at one time. The interscorer reliabilities, based on ten randomly selected protocols (200 stories) are reported in Table 1.[3] These are of the same order as reliabilities obtained in previous studies by other authors using these scales (e.g., Bernstein, 1956; Liccione, 1955; Murray, 1959; Murstein, 1960; Sarason & Sarason, 1958; Summerwell, *et al.,* 1958; and Waxenberg, 1955). Data were analyzed by means of analysis of variance in a 2 x 2 factorial design (Lindquist, 1953).

Table 1. Interrater Reliabilities

Measure	r	% Agreement
1. Emotional Tone	.89	
2. Outcome	.81	
3. Distortions		74
4. Unusual Formal Characteristics		88
5. Aggressive Themes		84
6. Frequency of Common Theme		78

Results

For the most part, results are presented here with males and females combined. Combination seemed justified where males and females did not differ significantly within each group. Similarity between the sexes was true of all analyses except for UFC and frequency of common theme. Table 2 presents pertinent data; Tables 3–8, the analyses of variance.

Table 2. TAT Scores

Measure	Group			
	Control		Experimental	
	Naive	Sophisticated	Naive	Sophisticated
Mean Emotional Tone[a]	1.338	1.524	.705	.651
Mean Outcome[a]	1.866	2.033	.785	.905
Total Distortions[b]	21	18	30	9
Total U F C[b]	41	78	62	46
Total Aggressive Themes[b]	175	159	471	584
Mean Frequency (%)[a]	21.90	27.25	21.24	27.01

[a]Per Subject
[b]Per Group

[3]The authors wish to express their appreciation to Dr. Charles W. Day for his scoring of the protocols which furnished the basis for the interscorer reliability coefficients.

With respect to the first response measure, emotional tone (ET), Table 3 reveals a significant treatment effect; i.e., emotional tone under the faking conditions is lower than under standard conditions. In addition, there is a suggestion, although it falls short of significance at the .05 level of confidence, of an interaction between sophistication and faking under instruction. The sophisticated *S*s presented stories with more positive emotional tone than naive *S*s under standard conditions but their ET scores dropped further than did those of the naive *S*s under faking instructions.

Table 3. Analysis of Variance of Emotional Tone Scores

Source	df	Ms	F
Between Groups	3		
Sophistication (S)	1	.08	.96
Instructions (I)	1	10.21	123.01****
S X I	1	.27	3.25*
Within Groups	68	.083	
Total	71		

*$p < .10$.
****$p < .001$.

Outcome scores also were lower under experimental instructions for both naive and sophisticated *S*s (Table 4). Although sophisticated *S*s had slightly happier outcomes under both conditions, the latter tendency was not significant.

Table 4. Analysis of Variance of Outcome Scores

Source	df	Ms	F
Between Groups	3		
Sophistication (S)	1	.371	2.65
Instructions (I)	1	21.959	156.85****
S X I	1	.009	.064
Within Groups	68	.14	
Total	71		

****$p < .001$

Analysis of distortions (Table 5) reveals both interaction and sophistication effects.[4] Sophisticated and naive subjects produced a comparable number of distortions under standard conditions, but the effect of experimental

[4]Although the number of perceptual distortions, unusual formal characteristics and themes are frequency data, the distributions were such that every *S* could be assigned a score representing the total number of instances of each of these variables. Thus the data could be considered continuous and analysis of variance appropriately employed.

instructions was to reduce distortions in the sophisticated groups, and to increase distortions in naive subjects. The sophistication effect seems to be due almost entirely to responses under experimental conditions.

Table 5. Analysis of Variance of Perceptual Distortions

Source	df	Ms	F
Between Groups	3		
Sophistication (S)	1	8.00	10.67***
Instructions (I)	1	.00	.00
S X I	1	4.50	6.00**
Within Groups	68	.75	
Total	71		

**p $<$.025
***p $<$.005

Interaction effects were also apparent with UFC as the response measure (Table 6), but these effects were due entirely to the male *S*s. The sophisticated males exhibited more UFC's under standard conditions than did the naive males, and this relationship was reversed under faking conditions, the sophisticated males reducing UFC scores under the latter condition, while the naive males increased their scores. Sophisticated females produced more UFC's than did their naive counterparts. A sex difference appeared among the naive subjects, the females showing less UFC's under experimental instructions than under standard procedures, the males reversing this trend.

Table 6. Analysis of Variance of U F C

Source	df	Ms	F
Females			
Between Groups	3		
Sophistication (S)	1	18.38	4.47*
Instructions (I)	1	9.38	2.28
S X I	1	.04	.01
Within Groups	20	4.11	
Total	23		
Males			
Between Groups	3		
Sophistication (S)	1	.00	.00
Instructions (I)	1	.33	.06
S X I	1	56.33	9.39***
Within Groups	44	6.00	
Total	47		

*p $<$.05
***p $<$.005

Table 7 indicates that total number of aggressive themes increased when subjects were asked to fake hostility. Sophisticated subjects tended to increase their output more than did naive students, but this tendency does not approach statistical significance.

Table 7. Analysis of Variance of Total Aggressive Themes

Source	df	Ms	F
Between Groups	3		
Sophistication (S)	1	7220.02	73.32****
Instructions (I)	1	130.69	1.33
S X I	1	231.11	2.35
Within Groups	68	98.47	
Total	71		

****$p < .001$.

Instructions to fake hostility had no effect upon Ss' inclusion of popular themes in their stories, but sophistication did, the male sophisticates using more common themes than their unsophisticated counterparts (Table 8). There were no such differences among the females.

Table 8. Analysis of Variance of Mean Frequency of Common Themes

Source	df	Ms	F
Females			
Between Groups	3		
Sophistication (S)	1	.05	.005
Instructions (I)	1	.00	.00
S X I	1	9.54	1.04
Within Groups	20	9.168	
Total	23		
Males			
Between Groups	3		
Sophistication (S)	1	821.71	55.9****
Instructions (I)	1	6.00	.41
S X I	1	.81	.06
Within Groups	44	14.70	
Total	47		

****$p < .001$.

Discussion

In general, it would appear that a conscious set to fake affects scores on several TAT response measures, a fact consistent with findings with the Rorschach.

Research with the Rorschach has indicated that personality variables, most notably personal adjustment, are determinants of how the person will alter his responses (Fosberg, 1943; Carp & Shavzin, 1950; Hutt, *et al.,* 1950; Feldman & Graley, 1954). Similarly, personality factors have been found to affect conscious alteration of responses in a thematic technique (Van Lennep & Houwink, 1953). The present study has demonstrated that both test sophistication, and sex, are also variables affecting the direction and intensity of shifts in some thematic response measures under faking conditions.

In a sense, sophisticated subjects faked more effectively, in that they had less UFC's and perceptual distortions when faking than did undergraduates. While attempting to fake, naive subjects did more violence both to the stimulus demands of the cards and the story telling demands of the situation. It would be interesting to compare how accurately the two groups approximate the responses of a known clinically hostile group.

Aside from sex differences noted in attempting to fake, females in general exhibited verbal styles differing from those of males, as reflected in UFC scores. Also sophisticated males relied more on their experience with the TAT by producing the more common themes, than did the opposite sex.

Under standard conditions, the emotional tone and outcome scores of the naive groups were comparable to those of normative samples (Eron, 1950; 1953). Sophisticated subjects, however, tended to tell happier stories with happier outcomes. Whether this is due to adjustment or experience factors remains to be seen.

One last point may be made in reference to stimulus "pull." Eron (1948), Murstein (1963), and Zubin, Eron, & Schumer (1965) have stressed the importance of the stimulus cue value of a picture as a determinant of thematic material. This position has been supported in the present study. Inducing a peripheral set to fake did not eliminate the presence of the more common themes associated with a specific card. This finding is consistent with Summerwell, Campbell & Sarason (1958), using emotional tone and outcome as response measures under varying sets of instructions.

Chapter 8

Problems of Application

There are a number of issues and problems that arise when assessment instruments are used in practice, for either clinical or research reasons, some of which may surprise the reader upon first encountering them. For example, there is no standardized or formal approach to the assessment of individuals, even in the single setting such as a psychiatric hospital or clinic. Most psychologists have their own preferred techniques and instruments for assessing others, procedures that they may or may not vary as they attempt to deal with different individuals and different settings. Thus one psychologist may use the Rorschach rather exclusively for personality assessment, regardless of the kind of individual to be assessed or the setting in which the assessment is to occur, while another psychologist might prefer the MMPI or the Draw-a-Person technique for precisely the same situations. Still another psychologist might use the Rorschach only for patients who are being considered for psychotherapy and the MMPI on a routine basis. There is little or no research evidence on the relative effectiveness of different instruments in different settings or with different populations and it would seem that the choice of the procedure to be utilized by the psychologist is a function more of tradition or familiarity than actual appropriateness.

Another problem involved in the actual use of personality assessment instruments is how the data obtained from these instruments are used to understand and predict the behavior of the respondent. Research in this area of clinical prediction is of recent origin and interest in this field is largely a result of Paul E. Meehl's (1954a) seminal volume, *Clinical Versus Statistical Prediction.* Among other things, this book reviews all of the then available studies that contrast two different approaches to the problem of behavioral prediction: the clinical approach, in which the available data are studied by an expert and are integrated in an intuitive and subjective manner, and the actuarial approach, in which the data are combined according to some clearly specified and objective fashion, typically by means of some mathematical equation. Meehl's conclusion, which was largely unanticipated, was that clinical prediction procedures neither equalled nor exceeded the accuracy of the actuarial or statistical approach. This finding was far from a popular one, especially with Meehl's clinical colleagues, and a storm of criticism arose, directed both at the quality of the research surveyed by Meehl and the manner in which Meehl had advanced his argument.

The topic was reviewed once again in 1966 by Jack Sawyer, and his paper is the first reading in this chapter. Pointing out that the clinical-statistical dimension could also be applied to the manner in which the data were *collected* as well as the way in which they were combined, Sawyer employed an expanded framework to include an analysis of the method of data collection used as well as the methods of data combination. His conclusions, however, are in essential agreement with those of Meehl; but, in addition, he concluded that clinical skill can be used to unique advantage in the data collection process, by the making of skilled judgments of complex characteristics that may have importance in the prediction task. Once the data are thus expressed in objective form their combination or integration is better carried out according to preestablished objective rules than by clinical judgment.

It is obvious that in most situations encountered in the practice of personality assessment there are relatively few opportunities to use statistical prediction, and that such a procedure would be possible only when the situation can be standardized sufficiently to permit the development of objective rules. In 1960 Meehl published the paper, which is our second reading, containing a variety of thoughtful speculations and pilot studies about ways in which personality assessment procedures, of an objective type, might contribute in the highly "artistic" work of the expert clinical psychologist in his routine assessment tasks. Although certain concepts employed in Meehl's paper may be beyond the scope of some readers, his thoughtfulness and creativity is clearly apparent in this work. In addition to his experiments with the use of quantitative procedures in clinical work, Meehl also indicates an interest in a slightly different question—whether traditional assessment procedures can be shown to contribute to clinical practice in a concrete and useful manner. Meehl is somewhat less than satisfied with the answer to which his ruminations lead him, and he adopts a rather gloomy view of the future of psychodiagnosticians.

The third paper, written by Lewis Goldberg some eight years later, presents another survey of research and ideas about the utility of objective assessment procedures in clinical practice. However, in marked contrast to Meehl, who had studied the clinician in his natural working environment, Goldberg turned his attention to simple "elemental" assessment tasks that might be conveniently handled in the laboratory, in the hope of learning about some of the more basic aspects of personality assessment and prediction. Summarized in Goldberg's paper are studies of the relationship between assessor experience and assessment accuracy, ways in which assessment skill can be taught, mathematical models underlying the assessment behavior, and optimal approaches to statistical prediction. While in basic agreement with Meehl concerning clinicians' poor showing on many assessment tasks, Goldberg takes a much more optimistic stance, giving the reader the impression that research of the type which he has initiated will ultimately provide a sound basis for personality assessment and prediction, though the methods to be developed in this manner might not bear much resemblance to traditional approaches.

Meehl's pioneer work in the development of techniques for standardized or "cookbook" interpretations of response patterns on personality tests led to the development of two noteworthy books on interpreting the MMPI: (1) by Marks and Seeman (1963) and based entirely on statistical data, *The Actuarial Description of Abnormal Personality,* and (2) by Gilberstadt and Duker (1965), clinically based but objective in approach, *A Handbook of Clinical and Statistical MMPI Interpretation.* Both volumes present a series of MMPI profile "types" found to be most common among psychiatric patients. Each profile type is defined by a specific set of objective rules and is accompanied by a wide variety of information found to be applicable to such persons either through statistical analysis or on the basis of extensive clinical experience. For each "cookbook," the series of profile types developed was sufficiently comprehensive to cover the majority of patients in the research population. Studies of the generality of the profile types, however, have tended to show that only a relatively small proportion of patients from other institutions and clinics can be fitted into these typologies. In the fourth paper, Payne and Wiggins attempt to determine the extent to which the population of a state psychiatric hospital can be fitted by the "types" of both books in combination, and also to see what the improvement in applicability would result if one or more of the rules defining each type were relaxed. Their findings are reasonably encouraging—about one-half of the patients in the sample produced MMPI profiles that fitted exactly one or another of the profile types, and the rate rose to about three out of four when Payne and Wiggins allowed the relaxation of any one of the rules defining a profile type (with the exception of the first major rule in each case).

Perhaps more important than studying the range of application of personality assessment cookbooks is the study of the validity, or accuracy, of the interpretations or prediction emerging from their use. The original pilot work on this question, reported by Meehl in 1956, was quite encouraging in this respect; unfortunately, however, direct validity research on the above-mentioned cookbooks is not yet available. A series of related validity studies, on the relative contributions of different kinds of data to accuracy in personality assessment, lead to a less encouraging conclusion. The reader should recognize this approach as one of incremental validity, a concept introduced in Chapter 6. Typical of these studies is that by Lloyd Sines, which is the final reading in this chapter. In his examination of the relative contributions of Rorschach, MMPI, and interview information to the accurate assessment of psychiatric patients, Sines found that neither the Rorschach nor the MMPI added much over and above what was already available from biographical data. Although there may be some methodological criticisms of Sines' and similar studies, they point up the very important fact that tests should not be used indiscriminately; rather, a determination should be made as to whether the additional information yielded by the test will justify the costs of giving it. Also emphasized is the relatively large contribution made in assessment by biographical data, and the comment that personality assessment experts in the future might well find it profitable to develop and utilize objective instruments based much more directly on biographical information.

1. MEASUREMENT *AND* PREDICTION, CLINICAL *AND* STATISTICAL[1]

Jack Sawyer[2]

"Clinical vs. statistical prediction," by concerning itself mainly with different methods of combining already-collected data, has largely ignored the initial part of the problem–the clinical or mechanical collection of data in the first place. Much more attention has been given, for example, to evaluating the clinician as an integrator of data than to determining his sensitivity as a measuring instrument. Yet because his sensitivity in collecting data influences his accuracy in prediction, these two aspects cannot be assessed independently. In general, the accuracy of any prediction depends upon modes both of collecting and of combining data–and upon their interaction. Thus a complete assessment of methods must consider measurement as well as prediction.

Neglect of the measurement part of the problem may help explain why the clinical-statistical question remains unresolved despite the substantial attention it has received (e.g., Holt, 1958; McArthur, Meehl, & Tiedeman, 1956; Meehl, 1954a; Sanford, McArthur, Zubin, Humphreys, & Meehl, 1956; Sarbin, Taft, & Bailey, 1960). To let this question depend mainly upon methods of combining data not only ignores differences that result from modes of collecting data, but permits such differences to obscure the comparison it does seek to make. Even worse, the failure to fully recognize the many possible "clinical," "statistical," and combined methods has produced much disagreement that results mainly because the words have different meanings for different persons.

Failure to resolve the clinical-statistical problem does not, on the other hand, mean that it is new, of only specialized interest, or of small theoretical or practical concern. On the contrary, the problem has been prominent for a long time and in areas other than abnormal psychology, as illustrated by Burgess's

SOURCE. Jack Sawyer received his doctoral degree at Purdue University. He has been on the faculty of the University of Chicago and is currently Associate Professor of Psychology at Northwestern University. Dr. Sawyer's fields of research specialization include social interaction and multivariate models. This article originally appeared in the *Psychological Bulletin,* 1966, **66,** 178-200. Reprinted by permission of the American Psychological Association and the author.

[1]For helpful comments on an earlier version of this paper, the author is grateful to Gordon W. Allport, Lee J. Cronbach, Edward E. Cureton, Otis Dudley Duncan, Donald W. Fiske, Lewis R. Goldberg, David R. Heise, and Robert R. Holt.

[2]This formulation was initiated during the author's tenure as a Rockefeller postdoctoral fellow in the department of statistics at the University of Chicago.

(1928) comparison of psychiatric diagnosis with objective psychological and sociological factors in predicting parole violation. Earlier still, Viteles (1925) and Freyd (1925) exchanged viewpoints on the appropriate place of clinicians and statisticians in industrial personnel selection.

Both clinical and statistical procedures have been used to predict physiological reactions, small group interaction, bureaucratic change, voting behavior, economic cycles, population growth, and war—to cite only a few behavioral phenomena. In these studies, as in general, the question of clinical and statistical prediction has been important for the same reasons that prediction itself is important—theoretically, because it underlies explanation, and practically, because it permits individuals, groups, and societies to operate more effectively.

Though both clinical and statistical methods have been widely employed, their most typical comparison lies in the prediction of individual performance in selection situations like those of special duty military personnel (Office of Strategic Service, 1948), Air Force personnel (Flanagan *et al.,* 1947-48), graduate students in clinical psychology (Kelly & Fiske, 1951), and psychiatric residents (Holt & Luborsky, 1958a, 1958b). The present comparison concentrates upon predicting individual behavior, as does the most prominent analysis of the clinical-statistical problem to date: Meehl's (1954a) *Clinical vs. Statistical Prediction.*

The conclusion of that extensive analysis would seem to have promptly laid the question to rest, for Meehl (1954a) concluded that there exist,

> depending upon one's standards for admission as relevant, from 16 to 20 studies involving a comparison of clinical and actuarial methods, *in all but one of which the predictions made actuarially were either approximately equal or superior to those made by a clinician* (p.119).

(Even the one apparent exception was later reported by Meehl, 1965, to have been a misclassification.) Thus it seems fair to conclude that clinicians in similar situations, given the same data as a multiple regression equation, are unlikely to produce better predictions.

Yet, despite this result, controversy has in fact increased rather than decreased. Holt (1958) reported that

> Clinical students in particular complain of a vague feeling that a fast one has been put over on them, that under a great show of objectivity, or at least bipartisanship, Professor Meehl has actually sold the clinical approach up the river (p. 1).

Such feelings may in part stem from Meehl's decision to focus upon the problem of clinical and mechanical modes of combining the same data, without systematically considering clinical and mechanical modes of measurement themselves. This exclusion continues to be the general practice, and is illustrated by Gough's

(1962) definition in his extensive review of the literature. Specifically disregarding different modes of collecting data, he considered that "The defining distinction between clinical and actuarial methods is instead to be found in the way in which the data, once specified, are combined for use in making the prediction (p. 530)."

The problem in only comparing modes of combining the same data is that this restriction excludes many crucial procedures—even the clinical interview. When the clinician has interviewed the individual as well as examined the test results, there are necessarily more data available for the clinical combination than for the mechanical, which can only use data that can at least be described by preestablished categories. The clinician, however, may observe behavior that does not fall into these categories, and his prediction may even be influenced by subtle cues he is quite unable to specify. Hence, for comparing clinical and mechanical modes of combining the same data, the clinical interview is inadmissible.

Nonetheless, a full comparison of clinical and statistical methods should show each method at its best. Even if a clinician were demonstrated to be a poor replacement for the prediction of a multiple regression equation, this should not disqualify him for the other major role, of measurement. The clinician, through his special ability to elicit responses, may obtain data that would otherwise be inaccessible. In any event, the full range of possibilities, for both clinical and statistical approaches, should be evaluated. The general purpose of this paper is not to enter a special plea for any particular method, but rather to provide a framework for the fair and complete comparison of all.

To conduct a comprehensive evaluation, the present analysis first develops a classification of methods that considers modes of collecting as well as combining data, and then applies this classification to 45 studies that include both clinical and mechanical modes. The result, however, of this extensive systematic analysis is less conclusive than might be expected—largely because of various methodological problems. (For example, in more than half of the 45 studies, the clinician was neither a psychologist nor a psychiatrist, but instead a physician, military officer or enlisted man, student, or someone else whose training did not necessarily include assessing or predicting individual behavior.) Hence, to encourage more definitive comparison than has been possible so far, the final part of this paper specifies several methodological considerations.

To focus the present analysis as sharply as possible, certain related considerations, discussed elsewhere in the literature, are taken as given. Specifically, this analysis is not directly concerned with examination of (*a*) the nature of the data, although Coombs' (1960) distinction between "behavior," "raw data," and "data" is relevant; (*b*) the process of clinical inference, as described, for example, by Meehl (1954a) or Sarbin, Taft, and Bailey (1960); or (*c*) details of statistical techniques. Two added considerations further define the present study:

First, the focus is upon the prediction of behavioral outcomes, rather than assessment of traits. Second, it is assumed that optimal prediction is usually multivariate, utilizing more than a single datum—for only in this context does the problem of combining data arise.

A Framework for Comparison

Whether *prediction* is called clinical or mechanical typically depends on how the data were *combined;* correspondingly, the present analysis calls *measurement* clinical or mechanical depending on how the data were *collected.* Thus, measurement, like prediction, is called clinical if a clinician must be involved. This standard relates directly to the concern suggested by Kelly and Fiske (1951), Meehl (1954a), and Sarbin, Taft, and Bailey (1960): How should a clinician allocate his time between diagnosis and other activities?

Extending the clinical-statistical distinction to modes of measurement suggests replacing the term "statistical" by the term "mechanical," which fits both data collection and data combination. Thus, "clinical" and "mechanical" here correspond, more or less, to distinctions made elsewhere between nonmechanical and mechanical, clinical and statistical, subjective and objective, case study and actuarial, qualitative and quantitative. The crucial point, of course, is not what the distinction is called, but that the concept can be applied to measurement as well as to prediction.

Modes of Data Combination. Nearly 50 years ago, Thorndike (1918) noted that one might consider as analogous the weighting of data by a mechanical formula and its judgmental integration by a clinician. This remains the major distinction psychologists make between clinical and mechanical methods of prediction. As Meehl (1954a) put it, "by *mechanical* (or statistical), I mean that the prediction is arrived at by some straight-forward application of an equation or table to the data. . . . The defining property is that no juggling or inferring or weighting is done by a skilled clinician (pp. 15-16)." The present formulation incorporates the same distinction.

Sarbin, Taft, and Bailey (1960), however, in specifying the bases of the two methods, made a slightly different distinction:

> The crux of the difference lies in the way in which new premises are formed from postulates and from combinations of the conclusions from previous inferences. The major premises in actuarial predictions are empirically based, their combination of previous conclusions utilizes optimal weights based on the experience, and they permit the explicit specification of the probability that the predicted event will occur. On the other hand, clinical predictions may utilize premises derived from non-inductive postulates, such as psychological theory, and thus may use data

for which experience tables would be impractical, if not impossible, to draw up (p. 245).

Thus Sarbin, Taft, and Bailey, in their "actuarial prediction," insist upon a rule that is mechanical not only in application but also in *derivation.* The present analysis is less restrictive: "mechanical combination" includes any set of rules whose application is objective, whatever mixture of experience and intuition their derivation involves. For example, Meehl and Dahlstrom (1960), working with MMPI profiles of patients with known diagnoses, used both theory and experience to devise 16 complex but completely mechanical rules for scoring the MMPI to differentiate psychotics from neurotics. A general procedure for transforming clinical judgment into formal rules was suggested by Kleinmuntz (1963), who illustrated how a clinician's taped comments while diagnosing MMPI profiles could be used to construct a computer program that would approximate his decisions.

Modes of Data Collection. For Meehl (1954a), the fact that clinical and mechanical modes of combination may employ different data was a confounding factor. In the present analysis, however, the variation that was troublesome to Meehl's evaluation is instead analyzed for its own sake.

Modes of data collection are distinguished by the same question that differentiates modes of data combination: Is the clinician involved? The answer produces the same dichotomy: mechanical or clinical. Data collection is mechanical if rules can be prespecified so that no clinical judgment need be involved in the procedure. Thus, on the one hand are all the self-report and clerically obtained data: psychometric tests, biographical data, personnel records, etc.; on the other hand are the usual clinical interview and observation. There are also intermediate cases, such as data that must be collected by interview, but for which a standard schedule and a nonclinical interviewer suffice. Actually, the *extent* of clinical involvement forms a continuum, varying between poles defined by the pure clinical and pure mechanical modes.

Clinical Versus Mechanical Data Collection provides a distinction that directly parallels the distinction in the data combination step that follows it. Meehl's (1954a) *psychometric versus nonpsychometric data* offers no such parallel, since nonpsychometric data can be collected either mechanically (from personnel files) or clinically (by interview). The special properties of psychometric data (standard conditions; immediate, categorical recording of responses; norms) neither require nor preclude their future use in either clinical or mechanical combination. However, whether or not a clinician must be involved in data collection is often highly consequential.

There is good reason to think that incorporating a clinician into data collection might improve prediction. The psychometric test may fail to provide an appropriate response alternative, or may fail to ask the most crucial question in the first place. The clinician, though subject to similar errors, is favored by feedback; in effect collecting and analyzing data at the same time, he can adjust as he goes. If one approach fails to elicit the desired data, he can try another, and if an area is particularly informative, he can probe it further. Of course this means that he will not have exactly the same data as the mechanical mode—or indeed, for one respondent and the next.

Far from being disqualifying, however, this flexibility constitutes the clinician's potential advantage; he can observe an individual's unique characteristics, which Allport (1961) suggested may cause morphogenic prediction to surpass actuarial. It remains to be seen, of course, whether these potential advantages of clinical data collection produce prediction that is superior, and enough so as to outweigh any added cost. Designs to evaluate such contributions are specified later.

Classification of Methods

Data can be collected in three ways (clinically, mechanically, or by both modes) and combined in two ways (clinically or mechanically). This creates six distinct prediction methods, one to six in Table 1; synthesis of some of these produces Methods 7 and 8. (The names of the methods in Table 1 are meant only to suggest typical illustrations of each.) It would be possible, of course, to distinguish procedures more finely than does this eightfold classification; further differentation could be made within each method. Nonetheless, this classification permits much finer distinction than the common practice of merely labeling a procedure clinical or statistical. It permits asking more than simply which is better, "the" clinical or "the" statistical method—a comparison that neglects many important variations. Instead, particular comparisons can evaluate the contribution of specific components of clinical and mechanical procedures.

Table 1. Classification of Prediction Methods

Mode of Data Collection	Mode of Data Combination	
	Clinical	Mechanical
Clinical	1. Pure clinical	2. Trait ratings
Mechanical	3. Profile interpretation	4. Pure statistical
Both	5. Clinical composite	6. Mechanical composite
Either or both[a]	7. Clinical synthesis	8. Mechanical synthesis

[a]Plus, for the clinical synthesis, the prediction of Method 2, 4, or 6; or, for the mechanical synthesis, the prediction of Method 1, 3, or 5.

1. *Pure clinical: Clinically collected data, clinically combined.* Here the clinician predicts behavior from an interview or other direct observation, without having any test or other objective information. In making his prediction, the clinician may take the intermediate step of constructing an explicit assessment of personality characteristics, then predict from these rather than directly from the observed behavior. Whether or not the clinician specifies an intermediate assessment, it seems likely that there exists at least a set of intervening variables between behavior and prediction.

2. *Trait ratings: Clinically collected data, mechanically combined.* Here the clinician collects data just as in the pure clinical method, then always explicitly assesses the individual on certain prespecified characteristics. He does not proceed, however, to predict future behavior; instead, the combination of his assessments into a prediction is performed mechanically. Restricting the clinician to assessment of elemental personality traits rather than prediction of behavioral outcomes corresponds to the distinction that Sarbin, Taft, and Bailey (1960) made between the process of instantiation ("the conversion of the occurrence into an instance of a general class [p. 47]") and the combining of such instantiations into a prediction. The value of this distinction was illustrated by Blenkner (1954), who found that although direct overall predictions by social caseworkers failed to relate to client progress, a mechanical combination of five ratings correlated .52 upon cross-validation.

Although in the trait-ratings method the clinician does not combine data to predict outcomes, he nonetheless does combine data in making his intermediate assessment (and in his ability to do this lies part of his potential advantage over mechanical data collection). In fact, he may make more than one level of nonfinal inference, as Schafer (1949) implied. In the Rorschach, for example, clinical judgment might first be employed in the scoring, then be employed again in making ratings on personality traits from the scores. It would be possible, of course, to incorporate such distinctions into a classification scheme. For the present analysis, however, the crucial combination is the final one into a behavioral prediction.

The trait-ratings method requires that the intermediate assessments of individual characteristics be objective. This problem has been attacked by much psychological research in rating methodology, but its connection with clinical and statistical prediction has not been emphasized. Sociological research, on the other hand, has extensively compared what have been called "statistical and case history methods." This problem, although it sounds like "clinical and statistical prediction," actually treats the comparison, between measurement modes, that psychologists have neglected—while itself neglecting the comparison, between combination modes, that psychologists have emphasized.

There is a long history of the development of rating procedures and of their comparison with other measurement modes. Cavan, Hauser, and Stouffer (1930) reported high agreement among their independent judgments of nine social and emotional factors on 117 autobiographical case histories. Stouffer (1930) found that judgments of subjects' attitudes toward prohibition from autobiographical accounts correlated .86 with responses to a Thurstone scale. Burgess (1941) and Wallin (1941) developed procedures that added further completeness and objectivity to the analysis of case study materials. Extensive suggestions on the use of case history materials produced by the subject were given by Allport (1942), who more recently (Allport, 1962) described 11 procedures for systematically obtaining information about characteristics unique to the individual.

The use of clinical measurement with mechanical combination has probably been insufficiently exploited, for at least two reasons: First, interviews and observations, as typically performed, often fail to yield data meeting the minimum scaling requirement for use in mechanical prediction–measurement of at least the nominal level, with standard, predetermined classifications. Second, a clinician who collects the data appears likely to feel that he is also best qualified to combine it into a prediction–a conclusion that usually substitutes for the actual determination. Nonetheless, trait ratings warrant added attention: As Meehl (1959b) noted,

> It is also possible that interview-based judgments at a minimally inferential level, if recorded in standard form (for example, *Q*-sort) and treated statistically, can be made more powerful than such data treated impressionistically as is currently the practice [p. 124].

3. *Profile interpretation: Mechanically collected data, clinically combined.* A typical example of this method is the clinician's use of a set of test scores to make a prediction about an individual he has not seen, as in the frequently cited profile interpretation of the MMPI (e.g., Meehl, 1956b). It was comparison of this method with the pure statistical method that Meehl (1954a) emphasized in his review of empirical studies as the only comparison in which the data used by the two modes of combination can be presumed to be exactly the same.

4. *Pure statistical: Mechanically collected data, mechanically combined.* A standard illustration is the use of biographical information and test scores in a multiple regression equation to predict job performance. Meehl (1956a) established a dichotomy between this and all other methods, saying, "in general, any genuinely *mixed* method is non-actuarial; because the defining property of the pure actuarial method is that it is unmixed [p. 137]." For present purposes, however, it is appropriate to recognize that there exists a continuum of the amount of clinical participation, and hence of the costs, which are often the critical consideration.

5. *Clinical composite: Both modes of data, clinically combined.* This is perhaps the most frequent clinical situation, where results of interview, observation, test scores, and biographical information are all integrated by the clinician in making his prediction.

6. *Mechanical composite: Both kinds of data, mechanically combined.* Like the clinical composite, this method uses data collected by both modes (such as objective test scores and a clinician's *Q* sorts), but integrates them mechanically, as in a multiple regression equation.

The above six methods result from merely a first-order cross-classification of three modes of collecting data and two modes of combining them; the next section examines some higher-order combinations.

"Syntheses"

A number of psychologists have expressed the need for a "synthesis" of clinical and statistical methods. As Holt (1958) stated the case,

> The real issue is not to find the proper sphere of activity for clinical predictive methods and for statistical ones, conceived in ideal type terms as antithetical. Rather we should try to find the optimal combination of actuarially controlled methods and sensitive clinical judgment for any particular enterprise [p. 12].

Holt then proceeded to propose a particular synthesis between clinical and statistical methods. The present paper extends consideration to alternative syntheses, to permit their comparison.

The syntheses proposed here differ from the previous six methods simply by incorporating a second stage, permitting the prediction of the first stage to be used as data in the second. Such higher-order combinations of methods let the clinician incorporate the statistical prediction and let the mechanical prediction incorporate the clinical judgment.

To construct a synthesis of both modes of data combination involves a sequential consideration, since the two modes cannot be employed simultaneously. One must first apply the clinical mode of combination, and then the mechanical mode, or vice versa; the question of which mode governs the final combination creates two cases:

Method 7. Clinical synthesis: Take a prediction, produced by *mechanical* combination, and treat it as a datum to be combined *clinically* with the other data.

Method 8. Mechanical synthesis: Take a prediction, produced by *clinical* combination, and treat it as a datum to be combined *mechanically* with the other data.

Clinical Synthesis. This synthesis gives the mechanically combined prediction from Method 2, 4, or 6 to the clinician along with the rest of the data and lets him integrate it all judgmentally. There is, after all, no inherent reason to withhold from the clinician any relevant information—even the actuarial prediction itself—as long as the validity of the resulting procedure is compared to that of others. (Two reasons sometimes advanced for withholding actuarial information are that this keeps comparison fair and keeps clinical reasoning pure; but both, as DeGroot, 1961, pointed out, are specious.) The "sophisticated clinical" approach suggested by Holt (1958) falls within this first general type of synthesis, although the present procedure goes somewhat further in that it gives the clinician the actual combining weights used in statistical prediction.

There are actually nine cases subsumed in the clinical synthesis. The mechanically combined predictions from Methods 2, 4, or 6 (Table 1) could each be made available to the clinician along with the data collected either clinically, mechanically, or by both modes. "Clinical synthesis," as used here and in Table 1, refers to any or all of these. In practice, however, the most common and reasonable synthesis may well be the pure statistical prediction of Method 4 plus both modes of data. For any clinical synthesis, the test of its value is whether its predictive ability exceeds that of the mechanical combination that enters into it; such comparisons should answer Meehl's (1957) query: "When shall we use our heads instead of the formula?"

Mechanical Synthesis. The other general type of synthesis consists of taking a clinically combined prediction of Method 1, 3, or 5 and treating it as an additional variable, to be mechanically combined with the other data.

Here, also, there are actually nine cases, that is, the prediction from Method 1, 3 or 5 plus data collected mechanically, clinically, or in both ways; and again the general term, "mechanical synthesis," refers to any or all of these. The most likely combination is the clinical composite combined with mechanical data, the synthesis employed by Sarbin (1943) in predicting college grades. He compared the pure statistical method based upon high school rank and college aptitude, a clinical composite based upon the same two measures plus several others and an interview, and the mechanical synthesis of the two measures plus the prediction of the clinical composite. (His hypothesis in including the clinical composite was that even if clinicians generally predicted no more successfully than did the mechanical composite, their successes might still involve different individuals, and so add to overall prediction. This turned out not to be so.)

An ultimate comparison, yet to be made, between the most general case of clinical and mechanical syntheses would pit the clinical combination of all the data including the mechanical composite against the mechanical combination of all the data including the clinical composite. The studies by Holt and Luborsky (1958a, 1958b) and by Sarbin (1943) represent special cases of this general comparison; they are, indeed, among the very few that have employed syntheses of both clinical and mechanical modes of data combination in a single procedure. However, proponents of a mechanical synthesis have not generally acknowledged the existence of a clinical synthesis, nor suggested comparison against it, and the same can be said for proponents of a clinical synthesis. There are, of course, arguments that can be advanced for each of these methods. But what is needed is a systematic, empirical comparison, the considerations of which are outlined in the third and concluding part of this paper.

The Framework Applied

Given the eightfold classification just described, existing empirical studies can be made to provide considerably more information than when viewed only by the gross distinction, clinical or mechanical (Meehl, 1954a). In addition, there are now available more than twice as many pertinent studies as in 1954, several of them performed with the clinical-statistical prediction problem particularly in mind. In assessing the relative effectiveness of the eight methods, the second section of this paper analyzes 45 such studies.

Empirical Comparisons

Table 2 summarizes the most essential elements of each of these 45 studies: the subjects, criterion, prediction methods, data, clinician, mechanical combination, validities and conclusion.[3] (Tabulation incidentally effects a great compression; half of this number of studies occupy 30 pages in Meehl's (1954a) volume without including all the information given here). This tabular summary, of course, does not fully describe these studies; its value, rather, is that from the perspective of clinical versus statistical prediction, it greatly facilitates their comparison and contrast. It makes apparent not only the conceptual similarity of these studies, but also their contextual variation, which the table shows to be great indeed.

Standards for Inclusion. Whatever their diversity of context, however, each of the 45 studies (*a*) predicted values for individuals on a prespecified criterion (except 1 that predicted group behavior–of a football team), (*b*) presented quantitative information about the relation of the predictors to the criterion, (*c*) employed more than one prediction method, and (*d*) included, for purposes of mechanical combination, more than one predictor. Exception to the last standard occurred when it was clear that addition of another predictor would not have changed the conclusion: that is, with only one predictor, the method was already superior.

From Table 2 it is possible to characterize systematically the population of 45 studies these four standards produced; the following paragraphs, in the course of defining the characteristics on which the studies are described, give the frequency distributions for type of subjects, criteria, etc.

[3]Most of the studies in Table 2 were summarized with the assistance of Robert F. Priest, whose efforts contributed not only to a more comprehensive empirical analysis, but to the conceptual framework as well. For comments on the adequacy of these summaries, resulting in several useful modifications, the author is grateful to the following: Frank Barron, John A. Bath, Joseph M. Bobbitt, Henry Chauncey, Rosemary Cliff, Herbert S. Conrad, Jack W. Dunlap, Daniel Glaser, E. Lowell Kelly, Richard S. Melton, Bernard M. Meltzer, William M. Lepley, Norman A. Polansky, Ned A. Rosen, Daniel Sydiaha, Arne Trankell, Morey J. Wantman, and Robert D. Wirt.

Table 2. Abstracts of 45 Clinical-Statistical Prediction Studies

Author	Subjects	Criterion	Prediction Method and Data[a]	Clinician	Mechanical Combination[b]	Validity[c]	Conclusion[d]
Barron	33 Psychoneurotics	Improvement during therapy	3. MMPI 4. MMPI	8 MMPI experts –	– All scales normal	62% 73%	3=4
Blenkner	63 Social work clients	Judged case "movement"	1. Int record 2. 5 ratings from int	2 Caseworkers 2 Caseworkers	– Configural	"nil" .62	2 > 1
Bloom & Brundage	37,862 Navy enlisted men	Training school grades	4. 9 apt, ach tests 5. 9 tests, bio, int	– Interviewer	Regression[e] –	.55[f] .23[g]	4 > 5
Bobbitt & Newman	1900 Coast Guard officer candidates	Final class standing	4. Quan, verb, spat tests 5. Tests, interview 8. Tests, pred (5)	– P'gist, p'trist –	Mean std score – Mean std score	.44[h] .37[h] .42[h]	4=5=8
Borden	261 New Jersey parolees	Parole success (5 obj. steps)	5. Bio, int 8. Bio, int, pred (5)	Psychologist –	– Regression[e]	.16 .41	8 > 5

[a] The most frequent abbreviations are int (interview), bio (biographical data), obs (observation), and pred (prediction).

[b] Unless otherwise noted, mechanical combination procedures were not derived from the same sample for which the validity is reported.

[c] Unless otherwise noted, %'s represent percentage hits (number of persons predicted to be high on a dichotomous criterion who actually were, plus the number predicted to be low who actually were, divided by the total number of persons), and decimals represent product-moment correlations with the criterion.

[d] See Conclusion section in "The Framework Applied" for standards by which the present conclusion was reached.

[e] Weights obtained on same sample used for validation.

[f] Median of 49 two-predictor regressions, involving all possible pairs of 9 tests, in different schools (Tables 3-XII, 6-XII, 9-XII, 12-XII).

[g] Tetrachoric correlation between pass-fail and high or low rating (Table 13-XII).

[h] From Figures 1, 2, 3.

Table 2. Abstracts of 45 Clinical-Statistical Prediction Studies (continued)

Author	Subjects	Criterion	Prediction Method and Data[a]	Clinician	Mechanical Combination[b]	Validity[c]	Conclusion[d]
Burgess (1941)	1000 Illinois parolees	Parole violation	5. 21 bio, int 8. 20 bio, pred (5)	2 Psychiatrists –	– Unit weights[e]	61%[i] 73%[i]	8 > 5
Burgess & Wallin	226 couples	"Marriage success score"	2. 9 case hist ratings 4. 24 engagement items	Grad. students –	Weights: 0,1[e] Unit weights	.42[j], .39 .32, .38	2=4
Chauncey	100 Harvard entrants	Freshman grades	4. HS rank, Col Bd tests 5. (4), refs, statement	– 3 Stud pers adm	Regression –	".60's" ".60's"	4=5
Cliff	150 Naval officer candidates	OCS grades	2. 16 traits from obs 4. 2 tests: verb, arith 5. Tests, bio, int 8. (2), 8 tests, pred (5)	Sup. officer – Officer board –	Mean Mean std score – Regression[e]	–.17 .79 –.29 .83	4=8 > 2=5
Conrad & Satter	3246 Navy enlisted men	Electrical school grades	4. 2 tests: arith, elec 5. 2 tests, int, bio	– Interviewer	Regression[e] –	.50 .41[k]	4=5
Doleys & Renzaglia	183 College freshmen	Two-quarter grades	5. Self-estimate 6. SCAT total 8. (6), pred (5)	Subjects – –	– One score only Regression[e]	.41 .63 .65	6=8 > 5
Dunham & Meltzer	505 Psychotics	Length of hospitalization	5. Bio, int 6. Duration, insight, marital status	Psychiatrists –	– Unit weights	58%[l] 58%	5=6

[i] Combining figures reported separately for successes and failures, assuming these groups to be of equal size, and ignoring, for the clinical composite, an unknown proportion of the cases in which the psychiatrists rendered a judgment of "doubtful."

[j] The first column gives validities for males, the second for females.

[k] Correlation ratio eta.

[l] Assuming, for 217 cases unpredicted by the psychiatrist, chance accuracy of 50%.

Table 2. Abstracts of 45 Clinical-Statistical Prediction Studies (continued)

Author	Subjects	Criterion	Prediction Method and Data[a]	Clinician	Mechanical Combination[b]	Validity[c]	Conclusion[d]
Dunlap & Wantman	CAA pilot trainees: 50-69 Harvard; 26-49 Ohio St	Rated post-training pilot potential	1. "Flight trng fitness"	Same as (6),(8)	–	.30[m] –.04	4=6=8 > 1
			4. Mech comp, bio	–	Regression[e]	.53 .35	
			6. Mech comp, pers rating	P'gist, aviator, pers officer	Regression[e]	.41 .32	
			8. Mech comp, pred (1)	P'gist, aviator, pers officer	Regression[e]	.46 .33	
Glaser	2693 Illinois parolees	Parole violation	5. Bio, int	Sociologist	–	.32[n]	6 > 5
			5. Bio, int	Psychiatrist	–	.16[n]	
			6. Bio, pers rating	–	Unit weights	.43[n]	
Glaser & Hangren	190 Illinois probationers	Satisfactory termination	4. 6 bio	–	Unit weights	84%	4=5
			5. Bio, int	Probation officer	–	84%	
Grebstein	30 VA patients	Wechsler-Bellevue IQ	1. 10 Rorschach scores	5 Psychologists	–	.68	1=2
			2. 10 Rorschach scores	–	Regression	.56	
Gregory	201 Female naval officers	Indoctrination school grades	4. Abil test, col grades	–	Regression[e]	.57	4=8 > 5
			5. Bio, int	2 Interviewers	–	.15	
			8. (4), rat's on int, refs	2 Interviewers	Regression[e]	.58	
Hallblower	8 Mental patients	Therapist *Q* sort of 154 traits	3. MMPI, 4 bio	Psychologists	–	.52[o]	4 > 3
			4. MMPI	–	Profile match[p]	.70[o]	

[m] The first column gives validities for Harvard, the second for Ohio State.

[n] MCR (Duncan, Ohlin, Reiss, & Stanton, 1953).

[o] Between predicted and actual *Q* sorts over the 154 traits, computed separately for each subject for each of 2-5 clinicians, and averaged.

[p] Patients grouped into 4(exclusive but nonexhaustive) classes on basis of MMPI profiles. All patients within a class were predicted to have the same criterion *Q* sort, based upon average *Q* sorts made for other persons having similar MMPI profiles.

Table 2. Abstracts of 45 Clinical-Statistical Prediction Studies (continued)

Author	Subjects	Criterion	Prediction Method and Data[a]	Clinician	Mechanical Combination[b]	Validity[c]	Conclusion[d]
Hamlin	501 Reformatory inmates	Adjustment in institution	5. (6), int 6. 100 bio, tests 8. (6), pred (5)	Psychiatrist – –	– Not combined Unit weights	.28[q] .25–.35[q,r] .55	8 > 5
Harris	244 Football games	Winner	2. Previous scores 5. Reporter's usual info 7. Pred (2), weather, etc.	– Sportswriter E.E. Litkenhaus	"Formula 1" – –	72% 73% 71%	2=5=7
Hovey & Stauffacher	47 Student nurses	Rated personality traits	3. MMPI 4. MMPI	Psychologists –	– Configural	74% 63%	3=4
Husén	834 Swedish enlisted men	Superior's rating	2. Ratings from obs 4. 2 tests: intel, mech 5. Tests, int	Sup. officer – 13 Interviewers	Unit weights Unit weights –	.52 .42 .54	2=4=5
Kelly & Fiske (1950)	53-93 VA clinical trainees	10 ratings, 2 exams	3. Tests, bio 4. 101 tests 5. Tests, bio, int, obs	Psychologists – Psychologists	– Not combined –	.29[s] .34[t] .34[u]	3=5
Lepley & Hadley	405 Pilot trainees	Completion of training	4. Tests 5. Tests, int	– P'gist, physician	Multiple cutoffs –	31%[v] 27%[v]	4=5

[q] Contingency coefficient.

[r] Range for 20 best items of 100.

[s] Median of correlation of ratings on each of 12 criteria.

[t] Median of best correlation with each of 12 criteria (excluding liking) (p. 158).

[u] Median of correlations for final pooled ratings, on each of 12 criteria (p. 168).

[v] Percentage of those predicted to be high on the criterion who actually were.

Table 2. Abstracts of 45 Clinical-Statistical Prediction Studies (continued)

Author	Subjects	Criterion	Prediction Method and Data[a]	Clinician	Mechanical Combination[b]	Validity[c]	Con-clusion[d]
Lewis & MacKinney	70 Engineering graduates	Job satisfaction	3. 7 tests, 7 bio, grades	6 Counselors	–	.10[w]	4 > 3
			4. Strong Grp IV, Fa occup	–	Regression[e]	.56	
Lindzey	40 Male undergrads	Overt homosexuality	1. TAT protocol	Psychologist	–	95%	1=2
			2. 20 TAT scores	–	Unit weights	85%	
			2. 20 TAT scores	–	Configural[e]	85%	
Lindzey	30 Prison inmates	Overt homosexuality	1. TAT protocol	2 Psychologists	–	70%	1=2
			2. 20 TAT scores	–	Unit weights	57%	
			2. 20 TAT scores	–	Configural[e]	57%	
Meehl (1959a)	350 patients	Psychosis vs. neurosis	3. MMPI	21 Psychologists	–	69%	3=4
			4. MMPI	–	Linear disc func	66%	
			4. MMPI	–	Lykken technique	x	
			4. MMPI	–	Hathaway code	x	
			4. MMPI	–	Meehl-Dahlstrom	74%	
			4. MMPI	–	Taulbee-Sisson	x	
Melton	U. Minnesota entrants: 543,35[z]	Freshman grades	4. HS rank, ACE	–	Regression	.40[y]	4=5=7
			4. HS rank, ACE	–	Regression	.35[y]	
			5. (4), int, 3 tests	Psych grad stud	–	.47[y]	
			7. (5), pred (4)	Psych grad stud	–	.45[y]	

[w] Median for six counselors.

[x] Between 66% and 74%.

[y] Mean absolute error in predicting grade point, which ranges from 0 to 3.0; differences, though statistically significant, judged of near practical significance.

[z] $N = 543$ for Methods 4 and 5; $N = 35$ (a nonoverlapping sample) for Methods 4′ and 7.

Table 2. Abstracts of 45 Clinical-Statistical Prediction Studies (continued)

Author	Subjects	Criterion	Prediction Method and Data[a]	Clinician	Mechanical Combination[b]	Validity[c]	Conclusion[d]
Oskamp	100 VA patients	Psychiatric vs. medical	3. MMPI	42 Psychologists	–	72%[aa]	3=4
			3. MMPI	14 Undergrads	–	73%[aa]	
			4. MMPI	–	Configural[bb]	65%[aa]	
Parrish, Klieger, & Drucker	1000 Army officer candidates	Rated OCS leadership performance	2. Learning potential	Superior NCO Officers	–	.35	2=4[oo]
			2. Board int ratings		–	.40	6 > 4
			4. Bio	–	Unit wgt items	.29	2=6
			6. (2), (2), (4)	–	Unit weighted	.47	
Pierson	228 College students	Freshman grades	1. Classroom obs	HS teachers	–	.48	4=8 > 1
			4. High school grades	–	Average	.65	
			8. HS grades, pred (1)	–	Regression	.67	
Polansky	3 Harvard College students	12 Behaviors, attitudes	3. 6 pers, intel tests	36 Judges[dd]	–	37%[ee]	3=5
			5. Tests, int, bio, obs[cc]	36 Judges[dd]	–	48%[ee]	
Rosen & Van Horn	255 scholarship applicants	First semester grades	3. (4), tests, refs, bio	Award committee	–	30%[gg]	3=4
			4. High school rank[ff]	–	One score only	35%[gg]	

[aa] Median of nine counselors.

[bb] Mean of 16 variations of Meehl, Dahlstrom, Peterson, Taulbee-Sisson, and Oskamp rules.

[cc] From these data, author wrote Allport-type "structural analyses," from which judges predicted.

[dd] Both sexes, varying age and amount of psychological training.

[ee] Each of the 12 behaviors has five categories; chance is 20%.

[ff] Adding to high school grades either of two pairs of verbal and quantitative tests raised the correlation with college grades from .56 to not more than .59.

[gg] Proportion of highest 89 (out of 225) on predictor achieving B average.

[oo] See footnote to Table 3.

Table 2. Abstracts of 45 Clinical-Statistical Prediction Studies (continued)

Author	Subjects	Criterion	Prediction Method and Data[a]	Clinician	Mechanical Combination[b]	Validity[c]	Con-clusion[d]
Sarbin	73 Male,	First quarter	4. HS rank, apt test	–	Regression	.45[j] .70	4=5
	89 female	college	5. Tests, bio, int	5 Counselors	–	.36 .69	
	students	grades	4. HS rank, apt test	–	Regression[e]	.57 .73	4=8
			8. (4), pred (5)	–	Regression[e]	.56 .68	
Schiedt	500 Bavarian	Criminal	4. 15 bio (from Burgess)	–	Unit weights	79%[hh]	4 > 5
	ex-prisoners	recidivism	5. 15 bio, int	Physician	–	63%[hh]	
Schneider	200 Former	Military	1. Bio, int	Psychiatrist	–	84%[ii]	
et al.	delinquents	offense	6. 5 bio, rated traits	–	Prob. of offense	85%[ii]	1=6
Sydiaha	90; 77 Canad.	Acceptance	2. 67 *Q* sorts from int	Pers. officer	Weights: 1-9	.85 .80	–jj
	army appl'ts	by officer	4. 13 tests, bio	–	Mean std score	.39 .33	
Trankell	191 SAS copilot	Retention	4. 5 tests	–	Regression[e]	.84[kk]	4=5
	trainees		5. 5 tests, int, obs	3 Psychologists	–	.88[kk]	
Truesdell	100 Freshman	Attrition from	3. 20 tests, 1st qtr grds	9 Counselors	–	71%[aa] .42[aa]	3=4
& Bath	engr students	engineering	4. 5 tests, 1st qtr grds	–	Disc function[e]	75% .50	
Watley &	100 Minn. male	Grades	3. Grades, tests, bio	12 Coun. p'gists	–	70%[ll] 64%	3=4=7
Vance	undergrads		4. HS rank, 1 test score	–	Regression	75% 69%	
			4. HS rank, 21 scores	–	Regression	79% 71%	
			7. (3), stat. pred.	12 Coun. p'gists	–	71% 65%	

hh From p. 55 and Table III.

ii Of those committing offense; percentages for nonoffenders unreported.

jj The same officer who interviewed a man and made *Q* sorts also determined whether he was accepted; because of this contamination, no decision is assigned.

kk Biserial correlation.

ll First column gives hits in predicting success or failure in achieving a C average during first year; second column does same for all 4 years.

Table 2. Abstracts of 45 Clinical-Statistical Prediction Studies (continued)

Author	Subjects	Criterion	Prediction Method and Data[a]	Clinician	Mechanical Combination[b]	Validity[c]	Conclusion[d]
Westoff, Sagi, & Kelly	145 Engaged couples	Number of live births 20 yrs later	4. 2 tests, 3 bio 5. Desired number child. 8. 3 tests, 5 bio, pred (5)	– Couple –	Regression[e] – Regression[e]	.49 .30 .52	4=8 > 5
Wirt	38 Therapy patients	Rated improvement	3. MMPI 4. MMPI Ego strength	8 MMPI experts –	– One score only	54%[mm] 79%	4 > 3
Wittman	343 Schizophrenics	Improvement after shock	5. Int, bio, obs 6. 28 traits, 2 bio	Physicians –	– Weights: 1-9	44%[nn] 81%[nn]	6 > 5
Wittman & Steinberg	960 Psychotic inpatients	Improvement in 1-3 years	5. Int, bio, obs 6. 28 traits, 2 bio	Physicians –	– Weights: 1-9	41%[nn] 68%[nn]	6 > 5

[mm] Average of eight experts.
[nn] Predictions and criterion trichotomous.

Subjects. Thirteen of the studies employed college students; 10, military servicemen; 9, mental patients; 8, present or former prisoners or delinquents; and 5, other populations.

Criterion. Studies were sought that employed as criterion a behavioral outcome, rather than a personality assessment or diagnostic classification. Six studies with assessment-like criteria are included, however, because they are either well-known or otherwise of particular interest. Seventeen studies, 9 in colleges and 8 in military service schools, employed training criteria, usually grades; 6 employed measures, usually ratings, of adjustment, or improvement in therapy; 6 employed parole violation or other criminal offense; the 10 others employed various performance measures ranging from retention as copilot to the number of children a couple had 20 years later.

Prediction Method and Data. Each prediction method is classified into one of the eight combinations of Table 1, though occasionally the decision was based upon a presumption rather than a certainty; for example, when some data were collected clinically and others mechanically, it was sometimes unclear whether the clinician had access to both kinds of data, or only to those collected clinically.

The data themselves are identified as tests, biographical information, interview, other observation, or other materials. When possible, the number of separate data is given, to approximate the quantity of information available to each method; for trait ratings, the number of traits is given. If all the data from one method, say Method 1, were used again in a later method, this is indicated in the latter method by "(1)." If Method 7 (or 8) employed, simply as added data, the prediction from, say, Method 1, this is indicated by "pred (1)."

Clinician. For any method where the data were either collected or combined clinically, the occupation of the person who did so is given. In 16 of the 45 studies, psychologists acted as the clinicians; in 6, psychiatrists; in 4, other psysicians; in 4, military "interviewers" (probably enlisted men); in 5, military officers; and in 16, graduate students, social workers, counselors, the subjects themselves, or others. Thus the level of experience in psychological assessment is by no means uniformly high—a problem that will be relevant later in evaluating this summary.

Mechanical combination. In combining the predictors, 16 studies employed multiple regression, 16 applied equal weights (to raw or standard scores), 13 used configural or other combination, and 4 did not combine scores mechanically at all. Multiple regression, more often than not in these studies, employed weights derived from the same sample on which the validity was assessed; consequently, it overestimated the replicable relation—to an extent varying directly with the number of variables and inversely with the number of subjects. On the other hand, the various configural methods mostly represent a priori combinations, and thus they avoid the substantial overfitting that results when these methods are applied a posteriori.

Validity. The present summary employs two different validity coefficients —correlation and percentage—depending upon the predictor and criterion metrics. About half of the studies used an essentially continuous measure for both predictors and criterion, and almost all of these reported results by product-moment correlation. A few studies used continuous predictors and a dichotomous criterion; these did not always report correlations, and coefficients were sometimes specially computed for this analysis. (Any such instance of analysis additional to that by the original author is footnoted in Table 2. The other footnotes indicate, for particular studies, special features that might influence comparison; the presence of these many footnotes, necessary to accurately represent the studies, further illustrates their diversity.)

The remainder of the studies, where both predictor and criterion are categorical, employed a variety of summary measures. Thus, for these studies, the present analysis required recomputing a single measure on which comparison could be made. The measure computed, which possesses both simplicity and direct operational meaning, is the percentage of correct predictions: the number of subjects predicted to be high on the criterion who actually were high, plus the number predicted to be low who actualy were low, divided by the total number of subjects. Before this computation, any categorical predictor or criterion not originally dichotomous was made so, as near a 50-50 split as possible. Doing this minimized bias that might have resulted if different predictors in the same study had varying base rates; in general, however, large differences in base rate were infrequent since many studies had already dichotomized their variables near the median.

Conclusion. The last column of Table 2 gives the conclusion the present analysis draws about the methods compared in each study, taking into account both the magnitude and statistical significance of the differences.

For those comparisons using the percentage of correct predictions as their standard, methods whose percentage differences exceeded the .05 significance level were called unequal, and all other comparisons were called equal. The smallest difference thus favoring one method over another was 12% for 1000 subjects, while the largest difference indicating equality was 13% for 30 subjects.

When correlation was used, two methods were called equal if their correlations were not significantly different at the .05 level; the largest difference thus judged as indicating equality was .13 for 232 subjects. In addition, five other differences—all smaller than .13—were also called equal, even though their large number of subjects (averaging over 2000 each) made them statistically significant. All other statistically significant differences—the smallest being .18—were considered as indicating inequality of the two methods.

The cutting lines for correlation and for percentage of correct predictions are roughly equivalent, since for dichotomous predictors and criteria, divided at the median, a 10% difference corresponds to a difference of .20 in the correlation (consistent with a zero correlation representing 50% accuracy). For both correlations and percentages, significance tests were based upon the assumption of zero correlation between the two methods, since the actual correlation is rarely available. If, however, the correlation between methods within a study is in fact positive, which seems likely, the significance of the observed differences is underestimated.

Combined Results

The 45 studies (many including more than two methods) produced a total of 75 comparisons, classified in Table 3 by the two methods compared. Each cell in the table totals the conclusions for all the studies comparing that particular pair of methods: the three numbers indicate the number of studies in which (*a*) the first (lower-numbered) method surpassed the second, (*b*) the two were judged equal, and (*c*) the second surpassed the first. This table shows the remarkable consistency of these studies: *not one single conclusion directly opposes another*—that is, there is no pair of methods for which one study found one method better while a second study found the other method better.

The consistency goes even further, however, than the lack of directly opposing conclusions when the same pair of methods is compared. Considering *all* comparisons for each method, there is, with the exception of just two comparisons, no method that is superior in some comparisons and inferior in others. To find such a consistent distribution among these comparisons would of course be extremely improbable if methods differed only by chance. Moreover, the differences show consistency by mode of combination: all four methods that are never superior combine data clinically.

The above consistencies reflect the results of the 28 comparisons in which one method was found to be definitely superior to another; only in such comparisons would it be possible for one result to directly contradict another. In the other 47 comparisons—almost two-thirds of the total—the two methods compared were found to be approximately equal. This means that although differences, when they appear, are consistent, their appearance itself is unlikely. Of course, it is useful to be able to say, for example, "*If* differences appear between modes of combining data, they will favor the mechanical mode." But this statement would be *more* useful if differences occurred more than an unpredictable one-third of the time. The unreliability of these differences reflects the presence of other, unspecified influences and illustrates that we do not fully know under just what conditions one prediction method surpasses another.

Even if the relative merits of these methods are not altogether clear, some methods are employed (at least in this set of 45 studies) much more frequently than others. When only mechanically collected data are available, their combination, reasonably enough, is usually mechanical (28 studies to 12); with

Table 3. Conclusions from 45 Clinical-Statistical Prediction Studies

	Number of Comparisons in Which the Row Method Surpassed, Equalled, and Was Surpassed by the Column Method								Number of Studies	Number of Comparisons	Percentage of Comparisons		
Method	1	2	3	4	5	6	7	8			Superior	Equal	Inferior
1. Pure clinical	---	0-3-1	0-0-0	0-0-2	0-0-0	0-1-1	0-0-0	0-0-2	7	10	0	40	60
2. Trait ratings		---	0-0-0	0-3-1	0-3-0	0-1-0	0-1-0	0-0-1	9	14	7	79	14
3. Profile interpretation			---	0-7-3	0-2-0	0-0-0	0-1-0	0-0-0	12	13	0	77	23
4. Pure statistical				---	5-9-0	0-1-1	0-2-0	0-7-0	28	41	27	71	2
5. Clinical composite					---	0-1-4	0-2-0	0-1-7	25	34	0	53	47
6. Mechanical composite						---	0-0-0	0-2-0	8	12	50	50	0
7. Clinical synthesis							---	0-0-0	3	6	0	100	0
8. Mechanical synthesis								---	11	20	50	50	0

Note. The original version of this article in *Psychological Bulletin* erroneously reported the second and third conclusions in the Parish, Klieger, and Drucker study as 6>2 and 4=6. Table 2, as it appears in this reprinting, reports the correct conclusions. The reprinted Tables 3 and 4 consequently show slightly altered figures for methods 2 and 4. No general conclusions are affected.

clinically collected data, combination by either mode is about equally likely. However, when data are collected by both modes, combination is usually clinical (25 studies to 8). The apparent preferences thus favor mechanical combination for simpler data and clinical combination for more complex data. But, in fact, it is precisely when both kinds of data are available that the advantage of mechanical combination is greatest. This suggests that preferences among methods reflect something other than efficacy of prediction.

The clearest and most summary comparison of methods can be made when they are arranged by modes of data collection and combination and the efficacy of each is given by a single number, as in Table 4. There the standard is the percentage of the comparisons in which the method was superior, plus one-half the percentage of the comparisons in which it was equal. (This procedure weights each comparison equally, though it is obvious that some conclusions are firmer than others. Yet, it would be difficult to demonstrate that any particular alternative weighting is superior. Nor does it seem likely that any plausible alternative weighting would change the general conclusions.)

Table 4. Summary of Conclusions from 45 Clinical-Statistical Studies

Mode of Data Collection	Mode of Data Combination	
	Clinical	Mechanical
Clinical	1. Pure clinical 20%	2. Trait ratings 46%
Mechanical	3. Profile interpretation 62%	4. Pure statistical 62%
Both	5. Clinical composite 26%	6. Mechanical composite 75%
Either or both[a]	7. Clinical synthesis 50%	8. Mechanical synthesis 75%

Note. In each cell is the percentage of the comparisons in which the method surpassed, plus one-half the percentage of the comparisons in which it equalled, the other method.

[a]Plus, for the clinical synthesis, the prediction of Method 2, 4, or 6; or, for the mechanical synthesis, the prediction of Method 1, 3, or 5.

From the single standard of Table 4, the following may be observed:

1. Within each mode of data collection, the mechanical mode of combination is superior, by margins of 26, 24, 49, and 25%. This not only replicates Meehl's (1954a) conclusion, but shows that it holds independently for each mode of collection.

2. Within each mode of data combination, the clinical mode of collection by itself is inferior, by margins ranging from 6 to 29%.

3. With the exception of a single method, the difference between modes of combination depends very little upon the mode of collection, and vice versa. This gives little reason to prefer particular modes of data combination for particular modes of collection—even though the choice of methods in these 45 studies in fact shows such preferences strongly.

4. The one exception to this low interaction is the clinical composite, which is about 24% lower than the other seven values would indicate in the absence of interaction. Thus, when combination is mechanical, it is better to have both kinds of data than either alone; but when combination is clinical, having both kinds is little better than having only clinically collected data and not as good as having only mechanically collected data.

5. The clinical synthesis, where the clinician knows the mechanical prediction, surpasses the clinical composite (though mainly, it appears, because the latter is so low). The mechanical composite, however, is better than either, and is *not* improved by adding to it the clinical prediction. Thus, in these studies, neither synthesis appears promising.

Like Meehl's (1954a) review, the present analysis finds the mechanical mode of combination always equal or superior to the clinical mode; moreover, this is true whether data were collected clinically or mechanically. Clinical combination actually predicts less well with data collected by both modes than with only mechanically collected data, and clinical combination that includes a mechanical prediction is inferior to the mechanical composite alone. These results appear consistent with the analysis of components of clinical judgment by Hoffman (1960), Hammond, Hursch, and Todd (1956), and Tucker (1964); together they suggest that the valid portion of clinical judgment is largely duplicated by mechanical combination.

In the *measurement* part of the clinical-statistical question, the comparison is by no means as clear. The best method from Table 4—the mechanical composite—includes data collected both clinically and mechanically. (So does the mechanical synthesis, which predicts as well but requires more data.) This suggests that the clinician may be able to contribute most not by direct prediction, but rather by providing, in objective form, judgments to be combined mechanically.

Altogether, the findings of these 45 studies indicate that, whatever the data, clinical combination never surpasses mechanical combination; nonetheless, clinical skills may contribute through data collection, by assessing characteristics that would not otherwise enter the prediction. Moreover, it seems likely that inaccurate prediction usually results less from inappropriate combination than from lack of valid predictors to start with. If this is so, then improvement should result from devising better ways for the clinician to report objectively the broad range of possibly relevant behavior he perceives.

The present analysis, though it compares a larger number of studies more comprehensively than any prior treatment, by no means firmly resolves the various questions of "clinical versus statistical prediction." This lack of resolution stems largely from various methodological problems, which the final portion of this paper considers in proposing means for more definitive comparison.

Methodology for Future Comparisons

Analysis of the studies just reviewed reveals several crucial methodological considerations affecting comparison of clinical and mechanical methods. Among the most important are these: By what standard is comparison to be made? Exactly what comparisons are to be made? Under what conditions is comparison to be made? The next three sections treat these questions.

Standards

It might appear that by now no one questions that the ultimate standard for comparison must be accuracy of prediction. Twenty-five years ago, even such an eloquent proponent of the case study approach as Gordon Allport (1942) squarely acknowledged this standard by recommending that "Studies should be made of the relative success of actuarial and case study prediction [p. 160]." Yet Meehl (1954a) found it still advisable to emphasize that comparison should be based strictly upon the "hit-and-miss" frequency, even if the clinician is especially confident of a particular prediction—since that, too, can be checked. Even more recently, Sarbin, Taft, and Bailey (1960) included a case for predictive, rather than consensual or congruent, validity. Perhaps by the next review of clinical and statistical prediction it will be unnecessary to reiterate this standard.

It is, however, necessary to add to this standard of accuracy the standard of efficiency. Clinical-statistical comparisons have seldom treated efficiency at all, let alone considered it systematically. But deciding how prediction should be made involves the allocation of scarce resources like clinical skills (or computer time); hence comparison should include cost as well as predictive ability—that is, methods should be compared on their *utility*. This means considering, as Cronbach and Glaser (1957) noted, not only the correlation with the criterion, but also the cost of testing, and the mean and variance of the payoff associated with performance on the criterion.

When methods are compared against the same criterion, payoff mean and variance are constant, making cost (aside from the correlation itself) the major variable. And although it may frequently be difficult to specify costs precisely, it is better to estimate than to ignore them.

To estimate costs of tests or interviews for data collection should be relatively easy. To estimate costs of data combination, an empirically derived prediction could be made, perhaps in the form $C = an^k + b$, where n is the number of elements to be combined, a reflects costs that depend upon the number of elements, k (by being greater or less than 1) reflects increasing or decreasing cost per element as their number increases, and b represents fixed costs.

Values in this equation need not be grossly different for each prediction situation. For example, one set of constants a, b, and k might apply for a multiple regression equation, and another for a clinician combining data someone else had collected (here n might represent length of time rather than number of elements). A formula such as this would show clearly the wide relative differences between initial and operating costs for various methods. Mechanical combination probably has larger fixed cost b (from the initial validation study) than clinical combination, but lower unit costs a. Thus, when the frequency of any single kind of prediction problem is small, clinical combination costs less, but above some crucial frequency, mechanical combination is cheaper.

Studies that evaluate comparisons by a measure, like correlation, that does not incorporate cost necessarily attack mainly the theoretical question "Which method predicts better?" The operational question "Which method should be used in practice?" is better answered by considering utility. Since most studies ignore cost, mainly the theoretical question has been attacked. Of course, if the most predictive method is also cheapest, then its efficiency is greatest; but if the more predictive methdos are also more expensive, relative efficiency is unclear. Employing the concept of utility removes such ambiguity.

Comparisons

As the classification of methods in Table 1 shows, the question is not as simple as "Which is better–clinical or statistical prediction?" These eight methods permit 28 comparisons, almost all of which might be said to compare "clinical versus statistical" methods. Thus, it is crucial to distinguish these various possible comparisons, and to get the right one for the question one wants answered.

Five prominent kinds of comparisons may be considered: those in which (*a*) both methods use clinical combination, (*b*) both methods use mechanical combination, (*c*) the two methods use the same mode of data collection, (*d*) both methods use both modes of data collection, and (*e*) the two methods vary both in mode of collection and in mode of combination. The following summary shows exactly what question is answered when two particular methods (indicated by their numbers) are compared:

Using clinical combination:

1-5 (Method 1 vs. Method 5): Is prediction improved (i.e., is utility increased) by knowledge of test scores, in addition to an interview?

5-7: Is prediction improved by knowledge of the mechanical composite, in addition to test and interview data?

Using mechanical combination:

4-6: Is prediction improved by weighting clinical ratings, in addition to test scores?

6-8: Is prediction improved by weighting the overall clinical prediction, in addition to test scores and clinical ratings? (Sarbin, 1943.)

Using the same mode of data collection:

3-4: Given only a set of scores, is prediction better from clinical or mechanical combination? (Meehl's, 1954a, ideal comparison.)

1-2: given only an interview, is prediction better from mechanical combination of ratings or from direct clinical inference?

Using both modes of data collection:

5-6: Given both scores and interview data, is prediction better from mechanical or clinical combination?

7-8: Which predicts better: an overall clinical integration that includes the mechanical composite, or the reverse? (Ultimate comparison of two syntheses.)

6-7: Can the clinician modify the mechanical composite to make it predict better than the latter alone? (Holt's 1958 "sophisticated clinical" method.)

5-8: Can mechanical combination weight the clinical composite to improve prediction over that of the latter alone?

Using different modes of data collection and combination:

1-4: Which predicts better: mechanical combination of a set of scores or clinical judgment from interview alone?

4-5: Which predicts better: mechanical combination of a set of scores or clinical judgment from both scores and interview?

Most of the above comparisons, as Table 3 shows, have in fact been employed. No wonder, then, that there is no general agreement on "the" answer to the clinical-statistical prediction question—it depends upon *which* question is asked.

Conditions

The answer to any comparison also depends strongly on the particular conditions under which it is made. As Table 2 shows, these conditions range widely; their variation constitutes the most conspicuous reason why the results of the 45 studies cumulate less than they might. The variety does serve, however, to identify those conditions that need to be considered. Of these, the most prominent are the criterion situation, the data, the sample of subjects, the clinician, and the statistical method. Comprehensive comparison of prediction methods should systematically vary these conditions—ideally, perhaps, in a four-way factorial design, separately for each criterion situation—and so find the relative effectiveness of each method for each set of conditions.

1. *Criterion situation.* It seems reasonable that predicting a student's college grades might require a different mixture of clinical and mechanical procedures than predicting his popularity among his peers. But the mixture that best

predicts science grades might not differ much from the mixture that best predicts other grades; even though the optimal weights for the specific tests would probably differ, the relative balance of clinical and mechanical modes might be similar. Thus, to determine what combinations of clinical and mechanical modes are likely to be better for given criteria may not require separate assessment in each criterion situation. Instead, certain characteristics of the criteria (e.g., simple vs. complex, short-term vs. long-term, school vs. job) can be combined to create criterion classes; then it may be found that most of the criteria in a given class are best predicted by about the same mixture of clinical and mechanical modes.

2. *Data.* Different data are likely to call for different modes of collection and combination. Which methods are optimal may depend, for example, upon whether the data are meant to reflect ability or motivation, conscious motivation or unconscious. The most obvious and probably most important characteristic, however, is simply the gross quantity of data. Comparison of a pure statistical method based upon 2 test scores with a pure clinical method based upon 50 therapy sessions should produce a different result than comparison based upon 50 test scores and 2 therapy sessions. Not that the amount of data available to the two modes of collection should be equal (this is often impossible); rather that the amount of data, and its costs, should be considered. This, of course, is what the concept of utility does, and is why it was advanced as the appropriate standard for comparison.

Examining utility as a function of the amount of data raises the question of the marginal utility of added data. This may depend upon how the data are combined; Estes (1957) suggested that as the amount of data increases the clinician may find it increasingly difficult to use more than merely the first-order relations between predictors and criteria. This agrees with Kelly and Fiske's (1951) finding that "In general, assessment [clinical] predictions based on the credential file plus the objective test profile tend to be almost as accurate as those based on more materials including an autobiography, projectives, tests, interviews, and situation tests [p. 160]." Earlier, Kelly and Fiske (1960) had hypothesized that added information might even decrease the clinician's predictiveness, by leading him to weight, in his prediction, information that had little, if any, validity.

Even when added information does have substantial validity, it may not contribute much to overall prediction, and this is true with mechanical as well as clinical combination. What matters is not simply how well a new variable predicts, but how much it adds to the prediction of the previous variables, as indicated, for example, by the partial correlation coefficient. This agrees with what is found in practice: even if it is possible to keep adding predictors of some validity, it is usually not possible to increase overall prediction substantially beyond a given level. Further, examining utility may reveal that a small increase in overall prediction fails to raise the payoff on the criterion enough to meet the cost of the added data.

3. *Sample of subjects.* It is important to know if a method that predicts for one group will work as well for another. At the very least, any method should predict in a second random sample from the same population. For mechanical modes of combination, however, even this minimal requirement is not always met, since the predictor-criterion relations in the sample from which the mechanical weighting is derived will differ somewhat from the relations in the second random sample. (Of the 16 studies using multiple regression, 11 reported validities for the same sample used to derive the equation; 3 of these 11 had at least 1000 subjects and so their weights were little affected by sampling error, but the rest ranged from 26 to 261 subjects and could be considerably affected.)

Another influence, in addition to the size of the sample, affects how well weights derived from one random sample predict in another: the *number* of weights that are determined from the relations in the first sample. The more variables that are weighted, the greater the loss in prediction is likely to be: if in the derivation sample, the best $m + n$ variables predict little better than the best m alone, it is possible that in another sample, the m variables alone may predict better.

Having smaller samples and weighting more variables contribute to a loss of prediction in a second random sample only when the combination scheme is constructed from the specific predictor-criterion relations in the first sample itself. Any scheme, mechanical or clinical, devised independently of the specific predictor-criterion relations in a given sample would not be expected to suffer a loss when applied to a second random sample. Thus clinical modes of combination are generally not subject to this decrease since clinicians do not usually weight variables according to how they correlate with the criterion in the sample at hand.

Consequently, the actual application of weights derived in one sample to a second random sample from the same population is a procedure (cross-validation) usually restricted to methodological checks on mechanical combination schemes. In practice, one rarely wants to apply a prediction scheme to another random sample from the very same population. Instead, two other cases also treated by Mosier (1951) are more common: validity generalization, where prediction is made in a sample from a different population; and validity extension, where prediction is made to a different criterion.

Predicting in a population different from the one in which experience was derived offers a possible relative advantage to the clinician, for clinical combination, unlike mechanical, can adjust to the altered situation. Now successfully the clinician adjusts depends, of course, upon his ability to recognize the differences in the two samples and to anticipate their effect on the relation between predictors and criterion. Use of theory may help the clinician to anticipate such effects and so "to extrapolate into a region where we have sparse actuarial entries, or none at all," but as Meehl (1954b) also notes, "the advantage of using 'theory' depends upon its being *correct* (p. 208)."

4. *Clinician.* Holt and Luborsky (1958a), in their report on selection for the Menninger School of Psychiatry, illustrated the marked differences that frequently exist among clinicians: of four judges, one consistently predicted more accurately on all criteria, while two others usually predicted no better than chance. Such differences indicate the need for validation procedures that differentiate among individual clinicians. It should not be necessary, however, to validate each clinician separately. Variables like type of training, amount of experience, and personality may identify groups of clinicians, who, in particular situations, can predict more accurately.

To identify clinicians who assess individuals similarly, a modification of the multitrait-multimethod analysis of Campbell and Fiske (1959) might be useful. Meehl (1960) suggested having different clinicians perform Q sorts on two or more patients, then correlating over the Q sort items. In the resulting matrix, Q sorts by two clinicians on the same individual should correlate more than Q sorts by the same clinician on two individuals, and decidedly more than Q sorts by two different clinicians on two different individuals.

Results to date on the effect of psychological training on assessment are not encouraging. Taft (1955) reported that

> physical scientists, and possibly other non-psychologists, e.g., personnel workers, appear to be more capable of judging others accurately than are either psychology students or clinical psychologists. . . . There is also evidence that suggests that courses in psychology do not improve ability to judge others and there is considerable doubt whether professional psychologists show better ability to judge than do graduate students in psychology (p. 12).

Later, Sarbin, Taft, and Bailey (1960) found that of 14 studies comparing the accuracy of psychologists and nonpsychologists, 6 showed no difference, 5 favored psychologists, and 3 favored nonpsychologists; of 10 studies comparing students with more and less psychological training, 6 showed no difference, 2 favored those with more training, and 2 favored those with less.

5. *Statistical methods.* Just as different clinicians should be evaluated, so should different statistical methods. The question is how fully a specific statistical method can use the information available in the original data. In particular, the occurrence of a nonlinear relation between predictor and criterion, or of a patterned relation of several predictors with the criterion, is frequently said to constitute an advantage to the clinical mode of combination. Yet, as Stouffer (1941) pointed out 25 years ago, the statistician, too, can predict by "analyzing the unique dynamic configuration of traits within the individual (p.352)."

A mechanical combination, like multiple regression, can easily include, in addition to the predictor variables themselves (x, y, and z, say), higher powers of these variables (x^2, x^3, y^2) and so examine nonlinear relations. By also including cross-products (xy, yz, xyz), it can examine patterned relations as well. (When the criterion is categorical rather than quantitative, the same can be done for multiple discriminant analysis.) Horst (1954) illustrated how the use of cross-products in multiple regression is formally identical with the configural problem posed by Meehl (1950) and with the H-technique for improving Guttman scales (Stouffer, Borgatta, Hays, & Henry, 1952). Lubin and Osburn (1957) presented a technique of pattern scoring that, in predicting a quantitative criterion, employs all possible combinations of categorical predictor variables; they also showed (Osburn & Lubin, 1957) how to determine how closely a particular mechanical combination approaches maximum validity.

Patterned relations can also be examined by performing separate analyses for different subgroups; Sarbin (1943), for example, found he could predict college grades much better for males than for females. Thus, separate subgroups like these may represent "contingency factors" (Horst *et al.*, 1941) which alter the weights accorded various predictors. Correspondingly, when these factors are quantitative rather than qualitative, they may be treated as "moderator variables" (Saunders, 1956).

Relatively little use of these methods has been reported, and it is consequently not known in general how much, if any, is added to prediction by consideration of nonlinear and patterned relations. One extensive assessment (Goldberg, 1965), however, found that including higher powers and cross-products of MMPI scales added nothing to prediction from a linear composite of the scales alone. Clinician's judgments also failed to exceed simple linear composites, suggesting that diagnosis from the MMPI need not be so highly configurated as has commonly been thought.

Altogether, then, there exist several readily available mechanical procedures that consider both nonlinear and patterned relations with the criterion, and—thanks to electronic computers—do so quickly and economically. Like many other useful and feasible methodological features, however, they have experienced limited use; nonetheless, they illustrate the potential for further and more definitive prediction research.

The clinical-statistical problem is far from being solved, and a general solution appears likely to result only from carefully conceived and conducted empirical comparison, under a wide range of relevant conditions, of representative combinations of clinical and mechanical modes, both of measurement and prediction.

2. THE COGNITIVE ACTIVITY OF THE CLINICIAN

Paul E. Meehl

Somebody has described psychotherapy as "the art of applying a science which does not yet exist." Those of us who try to help people with their troubles by means of that special kind of conversation are uncomfortably aware of the serious truth behind this facetious remark. The clinical psychologist has been able to assuage some of his therapeutic anxiety, and to refurbish his sometimes battered self-image, by keeping one foot planted on what seemed like comparatively solid ground, namely, psychodiagnosis. In recent years, some clinicians have been making a determined effort to assess the validity of our currently fashionable diagnostic instruments, and the findings are not very impressive. The cumulative impact of validation studies is reflected, for example, in Garfield's excellent textbook (1957), where one does not need a highly sensitive third eye to discern a note of caution (or even pessimism?). E. L. Kelly finds that 40% of young clinicians state that they would not go into clinical psychology if they had it to do over again. One suspects that at least part of this professional disillusionment springs either from awareness of the weaknesses in our psychodiagnostic methods or from the chronic intrapsychic (and interprofessional!) strain exacted of those who ward off such a confrontation. Who, for example, would *not* react with discouragement upon reading the recent monograph by Little and Shneidman (1959) where, in an unbiased and well-designed study, we find a very low congruency among interpretation of psychological test data, the test interpreters having been chosen as "experts" on four widely used instruments? Any tendency I felt to rejoice at the slight superiority of the MMPI over the three projective techniques with which it was competing was counteracted by the finding that my favorite test, like the others, does not do at all well when judged in absolute terms.

The cognitive activity of the clinician can be separated into several functions, which I have discussed in a recent paper (Meehl, 1959a). Setting aside for the moment that special kind of cognitive activity which goes on within the therapeutic interview, we can distinguish three classes of functions performed by the psychodiagnostician: *formal diagnosis* (the attachment of a nosological label); *prognosis* (including "spontaneous" recoverability, therapy-stayability,

SOURCE. Paul E. Meehl, Regents Professor of Psychology, University of Minnesota, has contributed to the professional literature a number of important articles on the processes of clinical inquiry and inference, and on the nature of clinical prediction. This selection is representative of Dr. Meehl's work in this area. This article originally appeared in the *American Psychologist,* 1960, **15**, 19-27. Reprinted by permission of the American Psychological Association and the author.

recidivism, response to therapy, indications for differential treatment); and *personality assessment* other than diagnosis or prognosis. This last may be divided, somewhat arbitrarily, into *phenotypic* and *genotypic:* the former being the descriptive or surface features of the patient's behavior, including his social impact; the latter covering personality structure and dynamics, and basic parameters of a constitutional sort.

Quite apart from the validity of current techniques for performing these various cognitive functions, their pragmatic value is open to question. It is commonly believed that an accurate pretreatment personality assessment of his patient is of great value to the psychotherapist. It is not known to what extent, if at all, this is true. However, what do psychotherapists themselves have to say about it? Bernard C. Glueck, Jr. and I have recently collected responses from 168 psychotherapists (both medical and nonmedical, and representing a wide spectrum of orientations: e.g., Freudian, neo-Freudian, Radovian, Sullivanian, Rogerian, eclectic, "mixed") to a questionnaire dealing with 132 aspects of therapeutic technique. One of our items reads: "It greatly speeds therapy if the therapist has prior knowledge of the client's dynamics and content from such devices as the Rorschach and TAT." While the self-styled groups differ significantly in their response to this item (ranging from a unanimous negative among Rogerians to a two-thirds affirmative among George Kelly disciples), all groups except the last tend to respond negatively. The overall percentage who believe that such prior knowledge of the client's personality greatly speeds therapy is only 17%. This low figure, taken together with the fashionable deemphasis upon nosology and the feebleness of most prognostic studies, at least raises doubts about the practical value of our diagnostic contribution.

Although they do not bear directly upon this question, we have some other interesting results which suggest considerable skepticism among therapists as to the significance of causal understanding itself in the treatment process. For example, 43% state that "Warmth and real sympathy are much more important than an accurate causal understanding of the client's difficulty." Over one-third believe that "Literary, dramatic, aesthetic, or mystical people are likely to be better therapists than people of a primarily scientific, logical, or mathematical bent." Four out of five believe that "The personality of the therapist is more important than the theory of personality he holds." About half believe that "Interpretation as a tool is greatly overrated at present." Two out of five go as far as to say that "Under proper conditions, an incorrect interpretation, not even near to the actual facts, can have a real and long-lasting therapeutic effect." Time does not permit me to read other examples of items which, in the aggregate, suggest minimization of the importance of the therapist's forming a "correct" picture of the client's psyche.

Setting aside the pragmatic question of the therapeutic value of assessment, let us look briefly at the inductive structure of the assessment process. The epistemological rock bottom is a single, concrete, dated slice or interval in the behavior flux, an "episode," identified by certain physical or social properties. Having observed one or more episodes of a given kind, we make an inductive inference as to the strength of low order *dispositions* which these episodes exemplify. Such dispositions are grouped into families, the justification for this grouping being, as Cattell (1946, 1950) has emphasized, some kind of covariation (although not necessarily of Type R) among the members of the disposition-family. It is perhaps possible to formulate the clinician's decision making behavior entirely in terms of such disposition-classes. In such a formulation, clinical inference involves probabilistic transition from episodes to dispositions, followed by the attribution of further dispositions as yet unobserved. Ideally, such inferences would be based upon an extensive actuarial experience providing objective probability statements. Given a particular configuration of dispositions present in a patient, the statistical frequencies for all other dispositions of practical import would be known within the limits of observational and sampling errors. In practice, of course, this ideal is rarely achieved, the conditional probabilities being subjectively judged from clinical experience without the benefit of an actual tallying and accumulation of observations, and the probabilities being expressed in rough verbal form, such as "frequently" and "likely," rather than as numerical values.

I am still of the opinion (McArthur, Meehl, & Tiedeman, 1956; Meehl, 1954, 1956, 1957) that the practical utility of this approach has been insufficiently explored, and I think that many clinicians are unaware of the extent to which their daily decision making behavior departs from such a model not by being qualitatively different but mainly by being less explicit and, therefore, less exact. However, we must recognize that a purely dispositional approach is not the *only* way of proceeding. An alternative, more exciting (and more congenial to the clinician's self-concept) is to view the clinician's cognitive activity as aiming at the assessment of hypothetical inner states, structures, or events which cannot be reduced to dispositions but which belong to the domain of theoretical entities, crude though the theory may be. Episodes and dispositions are here treated as "signs" or "indicators" of the postulated internal states. These states should not be spoken of as "operationally defined" in terms of the dispositions, because the logical relationship between propositions concerning theoretical entities and those describing dispositions is not one of equivalence, but merely one of degrees of confirmation. The inference *from* dispositions *to* states of theoretical variables is again only probabilistic, partly because statistical concepts occur within the causal model itself (i.e., probability appears, as in the other sciences, in the object-language) and partly because the theoretical network is incomplete and imperfectly confirmed.

A fundamental contribution to the methodology of inference from multiple indicators is the "multitrait-multimethod matrix" of Campbell and Fiske (1959). These authors show that in order to support a claim of construct validity, we must take into account more kinds of correlational data than have been traditionally provided and that it is just as important for some correlations to be low as it is for others to be high. Consider two or more traits (e.g., dominance and sociability), each of which is allegedly measured by two or more methods (e.g., MMPI scores and peer group ratings). Computing all possible intercorrelations, we construct a multitrait-multimethod matrix. The relationships within this matrix may or may not lend support to the claim of construct validity. The monotrait-heteromethod coefficients should be not only statistically significant and respectable in size, but should exceed both the heterotrait-heteromethod and heterotrait-monomethod coefficients. For example, if MMPI dominance and sociability correlate higher than does MMPI dominance with peer group dominance or than MMPI sociability with peer group sociability, we ought to be nervous about the relative contribution of methods factors versus traits under study. Campbell and Fiske point out that the individual differences literature is very weak in this respect, usually failing to provide the necessary data and, when it does, usually showing unimpressive results.

An interesting adaptation of the Campbell-Fiske technique arises if we substitute "persons" for "traits" and deal with Q correlations rather than R correlations. Suppose that a therapist provides us with Q sort descriptions of two patients. From the MMPI profiles these patients are then Q sorted independently by two interpreters. This set up generates a modified Campbell-Fiske matrix of 15 Q correlations, in which the validity diagonals (i.e., heteromethod-mono*patient* coefficients) represent how similarly the same patient is perceived by the therapist and the two MMPI readers; the monomethod-heteropatient and heteromethod-heteropatient values reflect the projections, sterotypes, and other idiosyncratic sorting biases of the therapist and of the two interpreters, the extent to which such stereotypes are shared by all three, and the unknown true resemblance of the particular patient pair. Robert Wirt and I have been running a series of such matrices, and thus far our results are as unencouraging as those of the Little and Shneidman study. I have decided to spare you the data, faintly hoping that the pairs thus far completed will turn out to be atypically bad.

The situation is not much improved by selecting a small subset of "high confidence" items before Q correlating. One disadvantage of Q sort is that it requires the clinician to record a judgment about every trait in the deck. The technique has the advantage that it presents the judge with a standard set of dispositions and constructs and therefore gets judgments which he is able to make but would often fail to make in producing a spontaneous description. But, for this advantage in coverage we have to pay a price. Such a situation is clinically unrealistic: whether we are starting with test data, history, or interview impressions, the particular facets which stand out (whether high or low) will not be the same for different patients. It may be that the meager results of recent validation studies are attributable in part to the calculation of hit frequencies or Q correlations over the entire range of traits, only a minority of which, variable in composition, would willingly be judged by the clinician on any one patient.

I cited earlier the statistic that only one psychotherapist in six believes that he is greatly helped in the treatment process by having advance knowledge of the patient's psychodynamics. One relevant consideration here is the rate at which the psychotherapist's image of his patient coverages to a stable picture. John Drevdahl, Shirley Mink, Sherman Nelson, Murray Stopol, and I have been looking into this question. So far, it seems that the therapist's image of his patient crystallizes quite rapidly, so that somewhere between the second and fourth therapeutic hour it has stabilized approximately to the degree permitted by the terminal sort-resort reliabilities. Let me show you a couple of typical results. Figure 1 shows the Q correlations between Stopol's phenotypic sort after the twenty-fourth hour and his successive sorts after the first, second, fourth, eighth, and sixteenth hours. "S_t" indicates the correlation of his stereotype with the twenty-fourth-hour sort. "Rel" is sort-resort reliability. (The phenotypic and genotypic ratings are made separately.) Figure 2 shows results for the genotypic pool. I do not mean to suggest that the therapist's perception at the end of 24 hours is "the criterion," which would involve a concept of validation that I reject (Cronbach and Meehl, 1955, pp. 284-285, 292-294). But presumably his perception after 24 contacts is more trustworthy than after only one. Or, if we (*a*) assume that some information gained early is subsequently lost by forgetting, erroneous revisions, and the like; (*b*) take as our standard of comparison the average value of ratings over all six sortings; and (*c*) treat this as a kind of "best combined image," the essential character of the situation remains as shown.

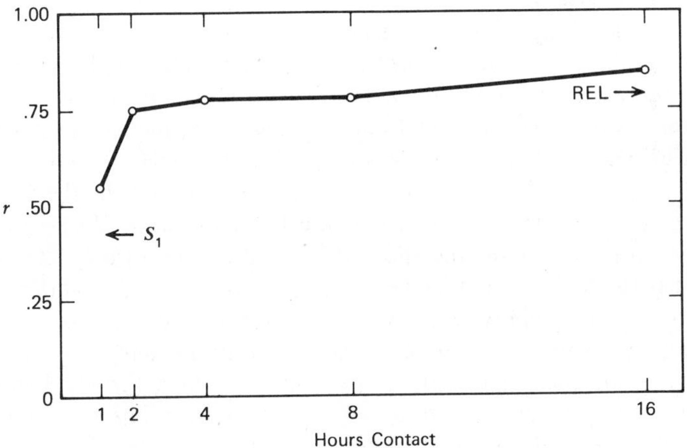

Figure 1. Q correlation between therapist's sort at 24 contacts and earlier sorts. (Phenotypic pool; $N = 182$ items; Stopol).

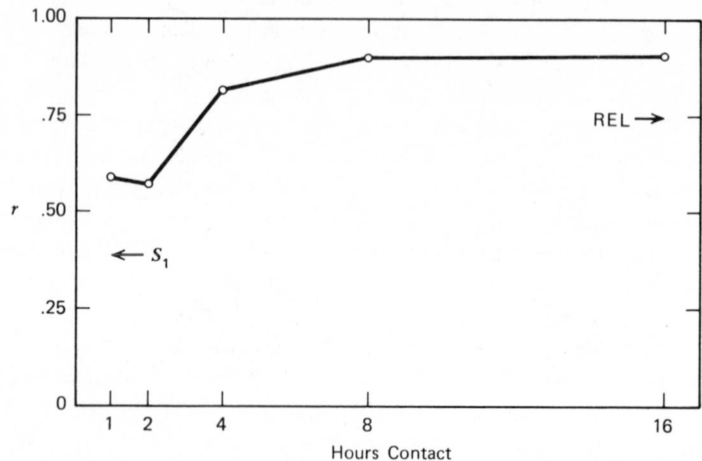

Figure.2. Q correlations between therapist's sort at 24 contacts and earlier sorts. (Genotypic pool; N = 113 items; Stopol).

Now this state of affairs presents any psychological test with a difficult task. If, after two to four hours of therapeutic interviewing, the therapist tends to arrive at a stable image of the patient which is not very different from the one he will have after 24 contacts, and if that final image is pretty accurate, the test would need to have very high validity before we could justify the expenditure of skilled psychological time in giving, scoring, interpreting, and communicating it.

When we first began this convergence study, our primary interest was in the pragmatic utility of the MMPI. One way to consider validity (which makes more practical sense than the conventional validation study) is to ask: "How long does it take the psychotherapist to find out what the test would have told him in the first place?" We were interested in plotting the Q correlation between a blind MMPI description of the patient and the successive sorts done by the therapist as he gathered more extensive samples of the latter's behavior during treatment, hoping to find that, as the therapist gets "wised up" by further interviews, he learns what the MMPI would have told him all along. This pleasant fantasy was disturbed by the rapidity with which the therapist's image of the patient converges, even before the Campbell-Fiske correlations were run. It is of some interest to plot the curve of Q correlation between a "good" blind MMPI description of the patient and the successive descriptions by the therapist (Figure 3). These results are surely nothing to write home about!

In a recent paper reporting on an empirical study of MMPI sorting behavior (Meehl 1959b) I listed six factors or circumstances which might be expected theoretically to favor the clinician's brain as a cognizing and decision making

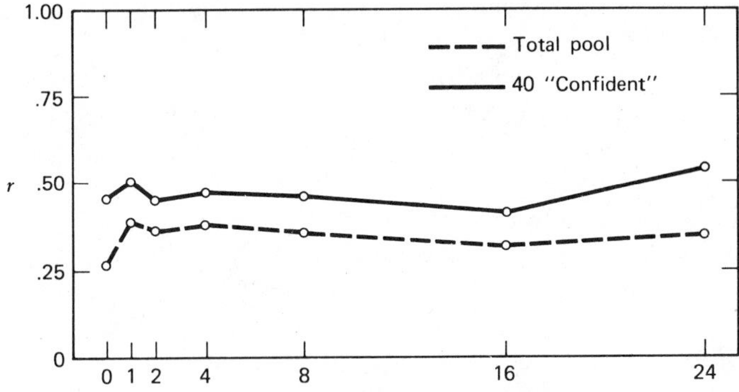

Figure 3. Q correlations between MMPI reader's sort and successive sorts by therapist. (Phenotypic pool; Meehl and Stopol).

instrument in competition with the traditional statistical methods of combining data. Among these six factors is one in which I have a particular interest, I suppose partly because it lends itself more readily to quantitative study than do some of the others. This factor is the presumed ability of the clinician to react on the basis of higher order configural relations (Meehl 1954, pp. 130-134; Horst 1954) by virtue of the fact that a system of variables can be graphically represented as a profile; and thereafter, given extensive clinical experience with a particular instrument, the clinician can respond to the visual gestalt. This he could do by *exemplifying* a complex mathematical function which neither he nor anyone else had as yet succeeded in *formulating*. The search for that function could take place in the context of studying the generalization and discrimination of complex visual forms. I recommend to your attention the recent work of Paul J. Hoffman on this subject, some of which has been reported (1958a, 1958b, 1959). Hoffman has undertaken a mathematical analysis of the rating behavior of judges who are presented with multivariable profiles, and the application of his formulas should teach us a great deal about the clinician's cognitive activity.

Comparing the impressionistic judgment of a group of Minnesota clinicians as to the amount of "psychotic tendency" revealed by MMPI profiles with six statistical methods of treating the profiles, I found that the pooled judgment of 21 clinicians was significantly better (against the diagnostic criterion) than the linear discriminant function. In fact, there was a significant tendency (although slight) for even the *individual* clinicians to do a better job than the linear discriminant function. However, the best cross-validative results displayed by any method of sorting these profiles thus far tried utilizes a very complex set of configural rules developed by Grant Dahlstrom and myself (Meehl & Dahlstrom, 1960). Table 1 shows the results of applying these rules to almost a thousand cases from eight clinics over the United States. These rules were concocted by a combination of clinical experience with statistical checking; and, while relatively crude and surely failing to extract all of the profile information, they are more efficient at this than a linear combination of scores, the pooled judgments of 29 MMPI readers, or the judgment of the best of 29. Without knowing the form and constants of the mathematical function relating probability of psychosis to the MMPI variables, we cannot answer the question: "How much of the information contained in the profile is extracted by the clinician?" One may plot probability of psychosis as a function of the clinicians' placement of profiles on an 11-step subjective scale of degree (or confidence) of psychoticism. Figure 4 shows probability of psychosis as a function of impressionistic profile placement by the best and worst clinician, and the pooled judgment of a group of 29. Figure 5 shows hit rate (whether neurotic or psychotic) as a function of the amount of consensus among 29 judges.

Table 1. Concurrent Validity of Meehl-Dahlstrom Rules in Eight Cross-Validation Samples

Sample	N	$H\%$	$M\%$	$I\%$	$\frac{H}{H+M}$	P
A[a]	92	55	16	28	.77	$<.001$
B[a]	77	45	29	26	.61	$<.05$
C	103	49	16	35	.75	$<.001$
D	42	40	21	38	.65	nonsig.
E[a]	181	45	18	36	.71	$<.001$
F	166	47	20	33	.70	$<.001$
G	273	63	12	25	.84	$<.001$
K[a]	54	78	5	17	.93	no test
Total	988	53	17	30	.76	.001

[a]Essentially uncontaminated samples.

While our data do indicate that the clinician's judging behavior with respect to the psychoticism variable is significantly configural, the *amount* of departure from a linear, additive model does not appear to be very great. For many years, skeptical statisticians have been pointing out to us clinicians that there is more conversation about nonlinear functions than there is actual demonstration of such and, anyway, that the value of departures from linearity and additivity involved in clinical judgments is likely to be attenuated, if not completely washed out, by the clinician's assignment of nonoptimal weights and the unreliability invariably involved in the impressionistic use of multivariate data.

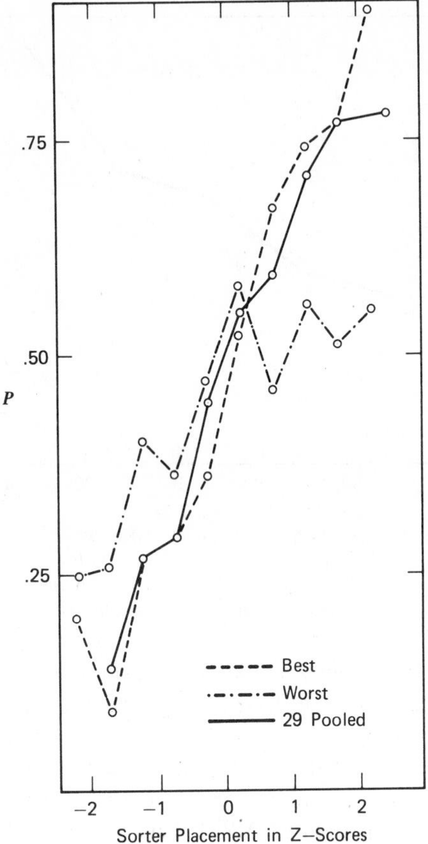

Figure 4. Probability of psychosis as function of MMPI profile placement by sorters.

Lykken, Hoffman, and I plan to utilize some of the MMPI psychoticism data for the kinds of analysis the latter has suggested, but in the meantime I have applied one of Hoffman's formulas to a portion of these data. He suggests that, if we treat the clinician's quantitative sorting as the dependent variable, the multiple R of this variable upon the profile scores should differ from unity only because of the clinician's unreliability, provided his sorting behavior follows a linear model. The multiple R of the 11-step psychoticism ratings for my four best clinicians, when divided by the square root of their reliabilities (Hoffman's "complexity" formula), varies from .871 to .975, with a mean of .942, indicating that the departure of their judging behavior from a linear model is small. It is also interesting that the *inter*sorter reliability (Horst's generalized coefficient) reaches .994 for the four best sorters and .987 for the four worst. Whatever these MMPI readers are doing when asked to judge psychoticism from the profile, they seem to be doing it in very much the same way.

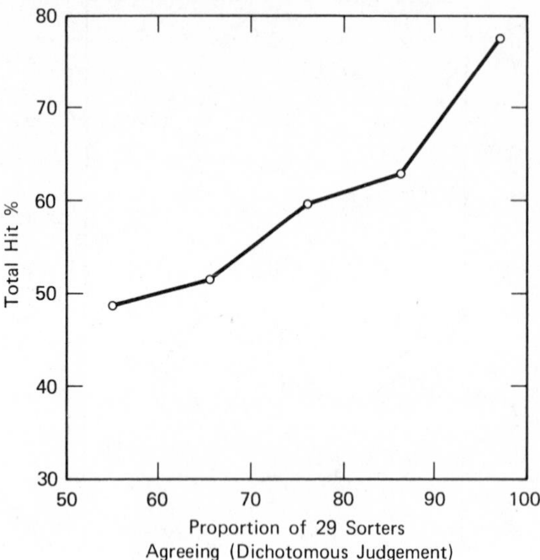

Figure 5. Hit rate as function of MMPI sorter consensus. (neurosis-psychosis)

Let me turn next to a brief account of an exploratory study which was a dismal failure and which I am still trying to figure out. All told, there now exist almost 200 different scoring keys for the MMPI item pool, ranging all the way from "dependency" to "baseball talent" and derived by a variety of methods (including factor analysis, face validity, and criterion keying). I thought it might be interesting to treat the patient's MMPI behavior more like the psychoanalyst than like the factor analyst: namely, to overdetermine the psychology of the patient by scoring him on a large number of these scales, in spite of their redundancy. Imagine two patients who produce identical profiles when scored on a very large number of partially overlapping but distinguishable variables. One might hope, except for the intrinsic defects of *coverage* in the MMPI item pool, that such a pair of individuals would be, so to speak, pinpointed in personality space as very close together. In practice it is impossible to find identical (or even nearly identical) profiles as the number of scored dimensions is increased, but perhaps one could get an estimate of this extreme by extrapolating interpatient similarities from lesser degrees of profile resemblance.

Selecting a sample of 20 females outpatients rated by staff psychiatrists or psychologists in connection with a study on the new ataraxic Mellaril (Fleeson, Glueck, Heistad, King, Lykken, Meehl, & Mena, 1958), we calculated the interviewer rating Q correlations for all possible pairs, thus generating an interpatient resemblance matrix of 190 elements. Turning then to the MMPI (by which the clinical raters were, of course, uncontaminated) and eliminating scales of fewer than 10 or more than 80 items, we set up random sets of 10 scales after defining the first set of 10 as the basic profile of clinical scales commonly used. The Cronbach-Gleser distance measure was then computed on the MMPI profiles for the same 190 pairs. Thus we had a matrix of interpatient resemblances as clinically described by skilled interviewers through Q sorts and a corresponding matrix of MMPI profile similarity indices. A *series* of matrices of this latter kind was then generated by progressively extending the profile, adding successive blocks of 10 randomly chosen scales. Thus, the first MMPI matrix was based upon the interpatient distance measures for the usual 10 scores, the second one upon 20 scores (the usual 10 plus 10 randomly chosen), the third one on 30 scores, and so forth up to a profile of 160 variables! The idea, of course, was that through this procedure we would be squeezing all of the blood out of the psychometric turnip and that a second order correlation (apologies to the statisticians) between the corresponding elements of the two matrices would show a steady rise.

It would have been very nice had the asymptote of this intermatrix coefficient, when plotted as a function of the number of MMPI variables entering into the distance measure, approached a very high value. That is, if you measure—however unreliably and redundantly—a huge mass of variables (schizoid trend, recidivism, dominance, defensiveness, baseball talent, dependency, control, ego strength, use of repression, tendency to homesickness, academic potential, etc.), then the psychological resemblance between two patients will be closely related to their profile similarity on this extended list of MMPI scores. It turned out that there was no problem of curve fitting, for the simple reason that the intermatrix resemblances began at zero for the first 10 scales and remained at zero, without the slightest tendency to increase as we included further blocks of scales in computing the distance measures. We know from a good deal of evidence that neither the MMPI nor the clinical Q sorts are quite *that* bad, and I am at a loss to understand these results. My suspicion is that they arise from inadequacies of the distance measure itself, and further analysis of the data is being undertaken with this hypothesis in mind. I still think that it was an interesting idea.

Leaving profile pattern interpretation, I should like to consider one more topic briefly. One of the most important problems in clinical psychology is deciding what kind of language communicates the largest amount of information about a patient. Most clinical practice today is predicated upon the assumption that useful statements about the patient can best be formulated (or at least inferentially mediated) by a theoretical language. The power of theoretical discourse in the other sciences makes this predilection understandable, and the characteristic Allport-Vernon-Lindzey profiles of clinical psychologists reflect strong theoretical interest. However, we learn in undergraduate physics that in order to apply theoretical constructs to the solution of practical problems (specifically, to predict the subsequent course of a particular physical system), one must fulfill two conditions. First, he must possess a reasonably well developed theory. That is, he must know the laws that systems of the given kind obey. Secondly, he must have a technology, a set of measuring instruments, for determining the initial and boundary conditions of the particular system under study. To the extent that either, or both, of these conditions are not fulfilled, predictions arrived at by theoretical inference will be untrustworthy. I do not see how anyone taking an objective view of the enterprise could claim that we fulfill *either,* let alone both, of these conditions in clinical psychology today. For this reason, in spite of my own personal interest in theoretical questions, I remain among that minority who persist in skepticism as to the pragmatic utility of theoretical constructions in daily clinical decision making.

Suppose, however, that some kind of theoretical discourse is to be used; which of the several kinds of theoretical sublanguages is most economical? As a pilot study in connection with a Ford Foundation project now going on at Minnesota, I collected some preliminary data which you may find of interest. Twenty psychotherapists were asked to describe a patient whom they had had in treatment for at least 25 hours, using the 182-item phenotypic pool which generated the curves previously shown. They also described the patient in terms of the 113-item genotypic pool. Although the latter pool was not constructed in any systematic way with respect to theoretical orientation, having been built for a different purpose, one can identify five relatively homogeneous subsets of genotypic items as follows: 25 Murray needs, 14 areas of conflict, 13 mechanisms of defense, 10 value-orientation components, and 7 items referring to dimensions of psychiatric nosology. After calculating the 190 interpatient Q correlations based upon each of these subpools, we may ask how well the pattern of interpatient resemblances in the phenotype is reproduced by the genotypic matrix. Unfortunately, I have not been able to find a statistician who will tell me how to do a significance test on such data, but the coefficients obtained are shown in Table 2. It is remarkable, I think, that the 13 defense mechanisms do about as well in reproducing the 182-item phenotypic matrix as does the entire genotypic pool consisting of almost 10 times as many items. We hope that with a more systematic coverage of the domain the Ford project will give us some definite information about this question.

I have presented some samples of research currently in progress at Minnesota which, while somewhat heterogeneous and difficult to pull together, all treat of what we see as pragmatically important aspects of the clinician's cognitive activity. In order to place any confidence in either the theoretical constructs we employ in discussing patients, or in the instrument-interpreter combinations we use to assess them, studies of convergent and discriminative validity must be carried out. The Campbell-Fiske multitrait-multimethod matrix, or the multiperson-multimethod variant of it, should be useful for this purpose. It seems obvious that even adequate and sophisticated studies of construct validity

Table 2. Correlations Between Interpatient *P* Matrix and *G* Matrices Based on Various Subpools

Variables	r
P (182 items) vs. entire G pool (113 items)	.59
P vs. 13 defense mechanisms	.52
P vs. 25 Murray needs	.22
P vs. 7 nosological components	.22
P vs. 10 value dimensions	.03
P vs. 14 conflict areas	−.03
P vs. all 69 G items in above subpools	.45

Note. ${}_{20}C_2$ patients rated; N = 190 coefficients.

must be supplemented by data upon the *rate* at which the clinician acquires information from various sources. Since the commonest justification for expenditure of psychometric time is the utility to the therapist of "advance knowledge" (especially of the genotype), the skepticism expressed by our sample of psychotherapists, taken in combination with the convergence curves for the therapist's perception of his patient, put this widely held belief badly in need of experimental support. An important aspect of such data, presumably rather specific to various populations and clinical instruments, is that of differential convergence rates among items. There are probably certain attributes for which a test's validity is insufficient to justify a marked departure from the base rates or mean rating of the given clinical population, and others for which the therapist tends to be in error early in the game and to converge to the truth rather slowly in contrast to the test. I would predict that an example of this is MMPI Scale 6, which is a rather weak scale when used as an exclusion test, but which, when elevated, turns out almost invariably to be right. I have had patients in treatment whose paranoid potential did not manifest itself until 50 or 75 sessions, by which time I had concluded (erroneously) that the MMPI was giving me a false positive.

As has been pointed out by many clinicians, lacking adequate clinical cookbooks (Meehl 1956) we have in practice to treat our instruments as instrument-interpreter combinations. I believe we can say upon present evidence that no one interpreter succeeds in extracting all of the information contained in a profile and that the development of objective configural methods of profile analysis (of which the Meehl-Dahlstrom rules are a primitive example) is a task of great importance. David Lykken and I are currently engaged in a study comparing more complex functions—such as a second degree polynomial having squares and cross-products—with clinical judgment and the Meehl-Dahlstrom Rules. I am betting on the lastnamed, because—while nonoptimally weighted—they do at least tap configural effects involving interactions up to the sixth order.

Finally the question of what is the most economical language to employ in describing a patient remains open, although it appears that there are many practitioners who are not sufficiently aware that this problem exists.

I look forward to the next decade of research in clinical psychology with a certain ambivalence. We are asking more sensible questions and being more critical of our procedures; and several research techniques are now available, and in wide use, which should give us some pretty clear answers. The reason for my ambivalence (and I regret that in the role of prophet I have to sound like Jeremiah) is that the evidence already available suggests that the outcomes will look pretty gloomy. My advice to fledgling clinical psychologists is to construct their self-concept mainly around "I am a researcher" or "I am a psychotherapist," because one whose self-concept is mainly "I am a (test oriented) psychodiagnostician" may have to maintain his professional security over the next few years by not reading the research literature, a maneuver which has apparently proved quite successful already for some clinicians. Personally, I find the cultural lag between what the published research shows and what clinicians persist in claiming to do with their favorite devices even more disheartening than the adverse evidence itself.

Psychologists cannot administer shock treatment or pass out tranquilizers, and I do not know of any evidence that we are better psychotherapists than our psychiatric colleagues. If there is anything that justifies our existence—other than the fact that we come cheaper—it is that we think scientifically about human behavior and that we come from a long tradition, going way back to the very origins of experimental psychology in the study of human error, of being critical of ourselves as cognizing organisms and of applying quantitative methods to the outcomes of our cognitive activity. If this methodological commitment is not strong enough to compete with the commitments clinicians have to particular diagnostic instruments, the unique contribution of our discipline will have been lost. I can mobilize some enthusiasm for the next 10 years within the field: while I expect discouraging findings at the level of practice, from the standpoint of the sociology of professions and the history of ideas, the developments should be very interesting to watch.

3. SIMPLE MODELS OR SIMPLE PROCESSES? SOME RESEARCH ON CLINICAL JUDGMENTS[1]

Lewis R. Goldberg

Imagine the following situation: You are sitting unobserved in a physician's office watching a week of his professional activities. During the course of the week, some 100 patients come to his office, each telling him of his symptoms, which you record; after each patient leaves the office, and any requested laboratory findings have arrived, the physician records his diagnosis for that patient. At the end of the week you have collected a set of 100 symptom configurations, one for each patient, and a set of 100 corresponding diagnoses.

Alternatively, you are sitting unobserved in the office of a personnel officer of a large manufacturing concern. He has 100 folders on his desk, each containing information about a different applicant for 50 sales positions with his company. He spends his week carefully looking through the application materials for each applicant—examining the applicant's test scores, the ratings made by each of the company's three initial interviewers, and the reference forms from each of the applicant's past employers. When he has completed examining the materials for each applicant in turn, he records his selection decision. At the end of the week each of the 100 folders of application data has a corresponding personnel recommendation associated with it.

Again alternatively, you are watching a clinical psychologist function over the course of a month at a busy outpatient psychiatric clinic. Most of his day he spends administering tests and interviewing patients. But, for a few hours at the

SOURCE. Lewis R. Goldberg, Professor of Psychology at the University of Oregon, is also a senior research associate at the Oregon Research Institute and was a field selection officer for the Peace Corps. He has written a number of articles on the assessment of personality and the nature of clinical judgment. This article originally appeared in the *American Psychologist,* 1968, **23**, 483-496. Reprinted by permission of the American Psychological Association and the author.

[1]This is a revised version of an invited address presented at the meeting of The Netherlands Psychological Association, April 14, 1967, in Nijmegen, The Netherlands. An earlier version has been published in the Dutch journal, *Gawein.* The address was prepared while the author was serving as Fulbright Professor of Psychology at the University of Nijmegen (Psychologisch Laboratorium der Katholieke Universiteit, Nijmegen), during the 1966-67 academic year. The author is deeply indebted to the staff of the Oregon Research Institute, especially Paul J. Hoffman, Leonard G. Rorer, and Paul Slovic, for their help in formulating some of these ideas, for their stimulation and encouragement of the author's research, and for their own research efforts—many of which are discussed in this paper. Most of the Oregon Research Institute judgmental studies have been funded by Research Grants MH-04439, MH-10822, or MH-08160 from the National Institute of Mental Health, United States Public Health Service. While this paper is not intended as a comprehensive review of all studies of the clinical judgment process, a more complete bibliography is available from the author.

end of every day he gathers together all of the information he has collected on one patient, examines it all carefully, and proceeds to write a report of his findings. In this report he includes some descriptive statements about the patient and his problems, the patient's diagnosis, and some predictions of the likelihood of certain important consequences for the clinic (e.g., the probability of the patient committing suicide, his probable response to treatment, etc.). The data collected from the patient (test scores, interview notes, etc.) are stored in one folder; the resulting reports are sent elsewhere in the clinic. At the end of the month, you can gather together 100 patient folders, plus the 100 corresponding psychological reports.

Each of these three professional activities has as its central core a reliance upon what the practitioner might call "clinical wisdom," but which in psychology is more modestly called "clinical judgment." Each is an important human cognitive activity, typically carried out by a professional person, aimed at the prediction of significant outcomes in the life of another individual. When the same type of prediction is made repeatedly by the same judge, using the same type of information as a basis for his judgments, then the process becomes amenable to scientific study. And, not surprisingly, over the past 20 years the clinical judgment process has begun to be studied intensively by investigators all over the world.

The Focus on Accuracy

Historically, the earliest research efforts centered on the accuracy of such clinical judgments. And, since World War II had sparked the emergence of clinical psychology as an applied speciality area (in which, at least at first, clinicians spent a good deal of their professional time making diagnostic judgments), it was natural that the first major focus of accuracy research was upon the diagnostic acumen of clinical psychologists themselves. Over the past 20 years, a flurry of such studies has appeared, the most dramatic and influential being the early ones reported by Kelly and Fiske (1951) and Holtzman and Sells (1954).

Studies of the accuracy of these sorts of judgments have yielded rather discouraging conclusions. For example, one surprising finding—that the amount of professional training and experience of the judge does not relate to his judgmental accuracy—has appeared in a number of studies (e.g., Goldberg, 1959; Hiler & Nesvig, 1965; Johnston & McNeal, 1967; Levy & Ulman, 1967; Luft, 1950; Oskamp, 1962, 1967; Schaeffer, 1964; Silverman, 1959; Stricker, 1967). Equally disheartening, there is now a host of studies demonstrating that the amount of information available to the judge is not related to the accuracy of his resulting inferences (e.g., Borke & Fiske, 1957; Giedt, 1955; Golden, 1964;

Grant, Ives, & Ranzoni, 1952; Grigg, 1958; Hunt & Walker, 1966; Jones, 1959; Kostlan, 1954; Luft, 1951; Marks, 1961; Schwartz, 1967; Sines, 1959; Soskin, 1959; Winch & More, 1956). Let us look at Oskamp's (1965) study as one example of some of these findings.

Oskamp had 32 judges, including 8 experienced clinical psychologists, read background information about a published case, divided into four sections. After reading each section of the case in turn, and thus before seeing any other information, each judge answered a set of 25 questions about the personality of the target (questions for which the correct answers were known to the investigator). For each question, the judge also indicated his confidence in the accuracy of his prediction by indicating the percentage of questions answered with that much confidence that he would expect to answer correctly. Oskamp found that as the amount of information about the target increased, accuracy remained at about the same level, while confidence increased dramatically. In general, the average judge was slightly overconfident when he had only one-fourth of the total amount of data available to him (he estimated that he would be correct on 33% of the questions, while he was actually correct on 26%); by the time he had seen all of the information, however, he was extremely overconfident (53% estimated correct versus 28% actually correct). Oskamp (1965) concluded:

> the judges' confidence ratings show that *they become convinced of their own increasing understanding of the case.* As they received more information their confidence soared. Furthermore, their certainty about their decisions became entirely out of proportion to the actual correctness of those decisions (p. 264).

For another demonstration of this same phenomenon, see Ryback (1967).

Such findings relative to the validity of clinical judgments obviously raise questions as to their reliability. Within the judgment domain, we can distinguish at least three different types of inferential reliability (Goldberg & Werts, 1966): (*a*) *stability,* or reliability across time (for the same judge using the same data); (*b*) *consensus,* or reliability across judges (for the same data and the same occasion); and (*c*) *convergence,* or reliability across data sources (administered on the same occasion and interpreted by the same judge). While the relatively few investigations of judgmental stability have concluded that judges may show substantial consistency in their judgments over time, the vast majority of reliability studies have focused upon judgmental consensus and have come to widely disparate conclusions. Findings have ranged from extremely high consensus on some judgmental tasks (e.g., Bryan, Hunt, & Walker, 1966; Goldberg, 1966; Hunt & Jones, 1958a, 1958b; Hunt, Jones, & Hunt, 1957; Hunt, Walker, & Jones, 1960; Weitman, 1962; Winslow & Rapersand, 1964) to virtually no consensus on other tasks (e.g., Brodie, 1964; Grosz & Grossman, 1964; Gunderson, 1965a, 1965b; Howard, 1963; Marks, 1961; Ringuette & Kennedy, 1966; Watley, 1967; Watson, 1967).

The classic study of the convergence among clinical inferences was carried out by Little and Shneidman (1959), who concluded that the reliability of clinicians' judgments leaves "much to be desired" (a most dramatic understatement if one examines their important findings). In a more recent study, Goldberg and Werts (1966) concluded that "an experienced clinican's judgments from one data source do *not* correlate with another clinician's judgments from another data source, even though both clinicians are diagnosing the very same patient on—ostensibly—the very same trait (p. 205)." Most of the other studies of judgmental convergence (e.g., Howard, 1962, 1963; Phelan, 1964, 1965; Vandenberg, Rosenzweig, Moore, & Dukay, 1964; Wallach & Schooff, 1965) have tended to confirm this somewhat dismal general picture.

If one considers the rather typical findings that clinical judgments tend to be (*a*) rather unreliable (in at least two of the three senses of that term), (*b*) only minimally related to the confidence and to the amount of experience of the judge, (*c*) relatively unaffected by the amount of information available to the judge, and (*d*) rather low in validity on an absolute basis, it should come as no great surprise that such judgments are increasingly under attack by those who wish to substitute actuarial prediction systems for the human judge in many applied settings. Since I assume that virtually all psychologists are acquainted with what has come to be known as the "clinical versus statistical prediction controversy" (e.g., Gough, 1962; Meehl, 1954, 1956, 1957, 1959, 1960; Sawyer, 1966), I can summarize this ever-growing body of literature by pointing out that over a rather large array of clinical judgment tasks (including by now some which were specifically selected to show the clinician at his best and the actuary at his worst), rather simple actuarial formulae typically can be constructed to perform at a level of validity no lower than that of the clinical expert.

The Focus on The Judgment Process

As a consequence of these sorts of findings, the research focus among judgmental investigators has begun to turn from validity studies to investigations of the process of clinical inference, the aim of which is to "represent" (or "simulate" or "model") the hidden cognitive processes of the clinician as he makes his judgmental decisions (Hoffman, 1960). Hopefully, by understanding this process more completely than we do today, clinical training programs can be made more effective and judgmental accuracy can thereby be increased.

An investigator of the clinical judgment process might express his aims through the following questions: By what psychological model can one best depict the cognitive activities of a judge? More specifically, what model allows one to use the same data available to the judge and combine these data so as to simulate most accurately the judgments he actually makes? To return to the three illustrative examples described at the beginning of this paper, these questions could be reformulated, respectively:

1. By what model can the 100 symptom configurations from each of the 100 patients be combined so as to generate most accurately the physician's resulting diagnoses?
2. By what model can the information extracted from the 100 applicant folders be combined so as to produce the most accurate prediction of the personnel officer's selection decisions?
3. By what model can the information from the psychological folders of the 100 psychiatric patients be combined so as to most accurately reproduce the material found in the 100 psychological reports?

All of these questions have some common elements, namely, (*a*) a search for some formal (i.e., specificable) model, which (*b*) uses as its "input" the information (data, cues, symptoms, etc.) initially presented to the judge, and (*c*) combines the data in some optimal manner, so as to (*d*) produce as accurate as possible a copy of the responses of the judge—(*e*) regardless of the actual validity of those judgments themselves. Note that such a model is always an intra-individual one; that is, it is intended as a representation of the cognitive activities of a single judge. Moreover, the test of the model is not how well it works as a representation of the state of the world (e.g., how well it predicts who will or will not be a successful employee), but rather how well it predicts the inferential products of the judge himself.

In mathematical terms, one begins with a cue matrix of size $M \times N$, where M = the number of variables presented to the judge and N = the number of targets for which the judge is asked to predict. One wishes to discover some combinatorial model which will reproduce as accurately as possible the vector of N responses produced by the judge to the same cue matrix. For this process to be amenable to mathematical analyses, the original cue matrix and the terminal judgmental response vector should be in a quantified format (or in a format easily transformable into a set of numbers). While it is fashionable to lament about the difficulty of transforming "behavioral" data into quantitative form, this difficulty may be more apparent than real. For if the cues (and resulting judgments) can be represented in even so simple a form as a binary digit (e.g., the patient has characteristic X versus the patient does not have this characteristic), then quantification is straightforward (e.g., $X = 0$; non-$X = 1$). Since a good deal of the data available to many clinicians is already in quantitative form (e.g., test scores, laboratory findings) or can be easily transformed quantitatively with no apparent loss of information (e.g., trait ratings), it is typical for most judgmental investigators to simply present the data to the judge and ask for the judgmental responses in a previously quantified format.

What sort of judgmental model should one try? Since introspective accounts describe the clinical judgment process as curvilinear, configural, and sequential (e.g., McArthur, 1954; Meehl, 1954, 1960; Parker, 1958), one possible strategy is to begin with fairly complex representations, perhaps with an eye to seeing how they may eventually be simplified. For example, Kleinmuntz (1963a, 1963b, 1963c) had a clinician "think aloud" into a tape recorder as he made judgments about the adjustment of college students on the basis of their MMPI profiles. Kleinmuntz then used these introspections to construct a computer program simulating the clinician's thought processes. The resulting program was a complex sequential (e.g., hierarchical or "tree") representation of the clinician's verbal reports.

The research of investigators at two major centers for research on clinical inference–Oregon Research Institute and the Behavior Research Laboratory of the University of Colorado–has proceeded from a diametrically opposite strategy (see Hammond, Hursch, & Todd, 1964; Hoffman, 1960), namely, to start with an extremely simple model and then to proceed to introduce complications only so far as is necessary to reproduce the inferential responses of a particular judge. Rather than beginning with a model which is already complex (e.g., curvilinear, configural, sequential) as Kleinmuntz did, we have opted to start with what is perhaps the simplest of all models: a linear, additive, regression model (of the sort now used rather universally for a host of applied prediction problems). That is, we begin with the hopefully naive assumption that the responses of a person in a judgment task can be reproduced by a mathematical model of the form:

$$Z = b_1X_1 + b_2X_2 \dots + b_kX_k$$

where Z is the vector of judgmental responses, $X_1 \dots X_k$ are the values of the matrix of K cues by N targets presented to the judge, and $b_1 \dots b_k$ are constants representing the "weight" of each cue in the judgmental model. In practice, the X values (the $N \times K$ matrix of cues) are known to the investigators (they are the stimulus or input variables presented to the judge) and the Z values are produced by the judge during the course of the experiment. The b values (regression weights) are found from one subset of the judge's responses by a standard linear regression analysis, and the "accuracy" of this linear model can then be ascertained by cross-validating these regression weights on the other subset of the judge's responses. The resulting correlation coefficient (R_a) represents the extent of agreement between the linear model and the inferential products of the judge.

Since we routinely ask each judge to make his judgments on two occasions (typically these "retest" protocols are sandwiched among the original protocols so that the judge is unaware of the fact that he is ever judging the exact same protocol twice), it is possible to compute a reliability coefficient (r_{tt}) to represent the stability of the judge's responses (or, alternatively, the extent to which one can predict his judgments from his own previous judgments of the same stimuli). This reliability coefficient can be viewed as the upper limit to the predictability of any model which we might construct. To the extent that the value of R_a approaches the value of r_{tt}, the model can be seen as representing the cognitive processes of the judge. When R_a and r_{tt} are identical for a particular judge, we have a perfect "paramorphic representation" of his judgment processes. Hoffman (1960) introduced this term to indicate that we do not pretend to be mapping any mind in an "isomorphic" fashion, but are merely seeking to discover some model which accurately generates the judgmental responses themselves.

Since clinicians generally describe their cognitive processes as complex ones involving the curvilinear, configural, and sequential utilization of cues, one might expect that the linear additive model would provide a rather poor representation of their judgments. Consequently, we might anticipate the need to introduce into the model mathematical expressions to represent these more complex processes. For example, if the judge is using a particular cue (X) in a curvilinear fashion (e.g., a personnel officer may feel that applicants who score in the middle range of a standardized intelligence test will be more successful salesmen than those who score at either extreme), then we may be able to approximate this judgmental process by adding to the model terms like X^2, or X^3, X^4, etc. That is, we can represent curvilinear cue utilization generally by introducing into the more basic equation terms of the form bX^a, where X represents the cue value, a is a power constant reflecting the particular curvilinear use of that cue by the judge, and b is once again the weight of the entire term in the overall judgmental model.

While clinicians frequently attest that they use cues in a curvilinear fashion, even more commonly do they call attention to their use of cues in a configural (or interactive) manner. What they mean is that their judgments are not simply dependent on the value of a particular cue, but rather that the relationship between cue X_1 and their response is dependent upon (i.e., interacts with) the value of a second cue, X_2. For example, a physician might feel that body temperature is positively related to the likelihood of some disease if a patient has symptom Y, while temperature has no relevance for this diagnosis if the patient does not have symptom Y. Therefore, once again we must find mathematical expressions which approximate such configural cue usage. One way to express the interactive use of two cues, X_1 and X_2, is by the product term, $X_1 \cdot X_2$. Higher order interactions could be introduced into the basic equation by using even more complex cross-products (e.g., $X_1 \cdot X_2 \cdot X_3$, a term analogous to the three-way interaction line in the classical analysis of variance).

What should be clear from these examples is that we can systematically begin to introduce more complex terms into the basic multiple regression model and see whether the new models are more adequate representations of the judge's mental processes than was the original linear one. In general, we can introduce curvilinearity in cue utilization, for example,

$$\sum_{i=1}^{k} b_i X_i^{a_i}$$

configurality, for example,

$$\sum_{i=1}^{k-1} \sum_{j=2}^{k} b_{ij} X_i \cdot X_j \qquad (i<j)$$

and, of course, much more complex sets of terms, for example,

$$\sum_{i=1}^{k-1} \sum_{j=2}^{k} b_{ij} X_i^{a_i} \cdot X_j^{a_j} \qquad (i<j)$$

While the introduction of additional terms into the model can never serve to decrease its accuracy in the sample of judgments used to derive the *b* weights, these extra terms may simply serve to explain chance characteristics of the particular judgments from the derivation sample and thus can severely attenuate the accuracy of the resulting model upon its cross-validation in another sample of judgments. However, when the judge is actually using the cues in a curvilinear or in a configural manner, then the introduction of the mathematical approximations of these processes should serve to improve the model.

While the preceding discussion has focused primarily on the use of multiple regression techniques, it could just as easily have been formulated in terms of the fixed-model analysis of variance (ANOVA), both systems simply being alternative formulations of a general linear model. Since the structural elements underlying both the multiple regression and the ANOVA model are formally equivalent, it is often possible to use the latter in judgment studies–thereby capitalizing on the well-known descriptive and inferential properties of ANOVA (Hoffman, Slovic, & Rorer, 1968). However, the ANOVA model imposes two important restrictions on the cue values to be used in judgment research: (*a*) the cues must be treated as categorical rather than continuous variables; and (*b*) the cues must be orthogonal (uncorrelated). While these restrictions make the ANOVA model less suitable for some real life judgment situations (for example, differential diagnosis from the profile of highly correlated MMPI scale scores), there are many real situations–plus a host of contrived situations–where the restrictions are not too severe. In some of these cases, it is possible to use a completely crossed experimental design (all possible combinations of each of the cue levels), provided that neither the number of cues nor the number of levels per cue is too large.

When judgments are analyzed in terms of the ANOVA model, a significant main effect for cue X_1 implies that the judge's responses varied systematically with X_1 as the levels of the other cues were held constant. Provided sufficient levels of the factor were included in the design, the main effect may be divided into effects due to linear, quadratic, and cubic (i.e., curvilinear) trends. Similarly, a significant interaction between cues X_1 and X_2 implies that the judge was responding to particular patterns of those cues (i.e., the configural effect of variation of cue X_1 upon judgment differed as a function of the corresponding level taken by cue X_2). Moreover, it is possible to calculate an index of the importance of individual or configural use of a cue, relative to the importance of other cues. The index ω^2, described by Hays (1963), provides a rough estimate of the proportion of the total variation in a person's judgments which can be predicted from a knowledge of the particular levels of a given cue or of a configural pattern of cues. An alternative technique for expressing the extent of configural cue usage in the judgment process has been proposed by Hammond *et al.* (1964).

The Search for Configural Judges

With this technical digression now out of the way, let us return to some empirical studies of the clinical judgment process. You will recall that while our research strategy forces us to begin with a simple linear additive model, this model should soon give way to more complex ones, as configural and curvilinear terms are added to fit the judgmental processes of each particular judge. However, in study after study our initial hopes went unrealized; the accuracy of the linear model was almost always at approximately the same level as the reliability of the judgments themselves, and—no doubt because of this—the introduction of more complex terms into the basic equation rarely served to significantly increase the cross-validity of the new model. Hammond and Summers (1965) have reviewed a series of studies in which the same general finding has emerged: for a number of different judgment tasks and across a considerable range of judges, the simple linear model appreared to characterize quite adequately the judgmental processes involved—in spite of the reports of the judges that they were using cues in a highly configural manner.

Three possible hypotheses spring to mind to account for these findings: (*a*) human judges behave in fact remarkably like linear data processors, but somehow they believe that they are more complex than they really are; (*b*) human judges behave in fact in a rather configural fashion, but the power of the linear regression model is so great that it serves to obscure the real configural processes in judgment;[2] (*c*) human judges behave in fact in a decidedly linear fashion on most judgmental tasks (their reports notwithstanding), but for some kinds of tasks they use more complex judgmental processes.

During the past few years, my colleagues at Oregon Research Institute and I have been systematically experimenting to see which of these three hypotheses is the most plausible. Our general goals have been (*a*) to discover and use some alternative judgmental models which allow more rigorous checks on the process of cue utilization (e.g., Hoffman, 1967), and (*b*) to discover and study some new judgmental tasks—tasks where configural cue utilization is most likely to be necessary for making accurate inference and therefore where configural judgmental processes are most likely to be found. The remainder of this paper will focus primarily on our efforts to achieve this latter goal.

The search for inherently configural tasks has led to three major fields: physical medicine, psychiatry, and clinical psychology. Subject matter experts in each of these fields were consulted in search of diagnostic decisions of clearly configural nature, and three judgmental tasks—one from each field—were finally selected for intensive study. Experienced medical gastroenterologists chose the first purportedly highly configural task: the differential diagnosis of a benign versus malignant gastric ulcer from the signs which are visible on a stomach X ray. The staff of a large psychiatric hospital provided a second important clinical judgment task: the decision to permit temporary liberty for a chronic patient committed to a psychiatric hospital. And finally, Paul Meehl (1959) chose the third purportedly highly configural judgment task: the differential diagnosis of psychosis versus neurosis from a patient's MMPI profile.

Let us begin with the problem from medicine, the diagnosis of benign versus malignant gastric ulcers (Hoffman *et al.*, 1968). Physicians have assured us that there are seven major signs which can be seen in X rays of gastric ulcer patients and that this diagnostic problem can be assessed only by the configural (interactive) use of these seven cues. The seven cues are either present or absent in a given X ray, and one of the cues can only occur when another one is present; consequently, two of the seven cues can be combined into one variable having three levels, while each of the other five cues has two levels (absent versus present). There are thus 3×2^5, or 96, possible combinations of all seven cues. Nine judges, six experienced radiologists and three radiology residents, were asked to make differential diagnoses for 192 presumably real, but actually hypothetical, patients (two administrations of each of the 96 possible cue combinations). The judges made their diagnoses on a seven-point scale, from

[2]In the same way, a straight line can provide an excellent approximation of many curved lines, exemplified by the fact that we often use a straight line to navigate between two cities even though the real route is along a curved arc. For an excellent discussion of this point, see Ghiselli (1964, pp. 3-7). For a more complete treatment of this topic in judgment research, see Hoffman (1968).

"definitely benign," through "uncertain," to "definitely malignant." The inferences of each judge were analyzed by the ANOVA model to ascertain the main effects (i.e., linear use of the cues), each of the 15 possible two-way interactions, each of the 20 possible three-way interactions, each of the 15 possible four-way interactions, each of the 6 possible five-way interactions, and the 1 six-way interaction.

The major finding was that the largest of the 57 possible interactions, for the most configural judge, accounted for but 3% of the variance of his responses. In the investigators' own words (Hoffman *et al.*, 1968):

> the largest main effect usually accounted for 10 to 40 times as much of the total variance in the judgments as the largest interaction. On the average, roughly 90% of a judge's reliable variation of response could be predicted by a simple formula combining only individual symptoms in an additive fashion and completely ignoring interactions (pp. 343-344).
>
> it should be noted that the performance of the judges in this study was rather adequately accounted for in terms of linear effects, in spite of the fact that a deliberate attempt had been made to select a task in which persons would combine cues configurally (p. 347).

While these findings may be disheartening to judgment researchers, another finding could be more generally terrifying. When one examines the degree of agreement between physicians for this diagnostic problem, these interjudge correlations were distressingly low. Of the 36 coefficients of consensus, 3 were negative—the median correlation being only .38. The intrajudge test-retest correlations were reasonably high (ranging .60–.92, *Mdn* = .80), and the task itself was certainly not seen as an impossibly difficult one. Yet, these findings suggest that diagnostic agreement in clinical medicine may not be much greater than that found in clinical psychology—some food for thought during your next visit to the family doctor.[3]

Let us turn now to some ANOVA analyses of another judgmental task, the decision whether or not to grant temporary liberty to a psychiatric patient (Rorer, Hoffman, Dickman, & Slovic, 1967). The six presumably most relevant variables for making this decision were used in this study. With two levels of each variable (e.g., "Does the patient have a problem with drinking?" "Yes" versus "No"), there were thus 2^6, or 64, possible cue combinations. Twenty-four members of the professional staff of a psychiatric hospital—6 physicians, 12 nurses, 3 clinical psychologists, and 3 psychiatric social workers—served as judges. Each of them decided whether 128 presumably real, but actually hypothetical, patients (two administrations of each of the 64 possible cue

[3]For some intriguing corroborative evidence concerning this seemingly subversive statement see Garland (1959, 1960).

configurations) should be granted the privilege of leaving the hospital for 8 hours on a weekend. Again, as in the previous study, the judgments from each judge were analyzed individually to ascertain the proportion of his response variance which was associated with each of the six main effects and each of the possible two-way, three-way, four-way, five-way, and six-way interactions.

The results were, unfortunately, remarkably similar to those from the previous study. On the average, less than 2% of the variance of these judgments was associated with the largest interaction term, these percentages ranging across the 24 judges from virtually zero to less than 6%. And again, one of the most striking findings was the great diversity—the startling lack of interjudge agreement—among clinicians for this judgment task.

Let us now turn to the third purportedly configural judgment task, the differential diagnosis of neurotic from psychotic patients by means of their MMPI profiles. Paul Meehl (1959) initially focused research on this task on the grounds that: "the differences between psychotic and neurotic profiles are considered in MMPI lore to be highly configural in character, so that an atomistic treatment by combining single scales linearly should theoretically be a very poor substitute for a configural approach (p. 104)." Meehl collected 861 MMPI profiles from seven hospitals and clinics throughout the United States; each of these profiles was produced from the MMPI responses of a psychiatric patient who had been diagnosed by the psychiatric staff as being rather clearly either psychotic or neurotic—the total sample containing approximately equal numbers of both diagnostic groups. Twenty-nine clinicians (13 PhD clinical psychologists, plus 16 advanced graduate students in clinical psychology) attempted to diagnose each of the 861 patients from their MMPI profiles; the 29 judges rated each profile on an 11-step forced-normal distribution from least to most psychotic. After making some preliminary comparisons of the validity of the clinicians' judgments with the validities achieved by various actuarial techniques (Meehl, 1959), Meehl generously turned over these valuable data to Oregon Research Institute for further analyses.

An extensive investigation of the validity of the clinicians' judgments, as compared to that of numerous MMPI signs and indexes, has already been published (Goldberg, 1965). As in many previous judgment studies, accuracy on this task was not associated with the amount of professional experience of the judge; the average PhD psychologist achieved a validity coefficient identical to that of the average graduate student. Moreover, an unweighted composite of five MMPI scale scores ($L + Pa + Sc - Hy - Pt$) achieved a validity coefficient ($r = .44$) greater than that of the average judge ($r = .28$), greater than that of the pooled ratings of all 29 clinicians ($r = .35$), and even greater than that of the single most accurate judge ($r = .39$). Moreover, I recently discovered a moderator for the above index, namely another unweighted linear composite ($D + Pd + Sc - F - Hs - Pa$); when some 1,248 patients were divided into three subsamples on the basis of their scores on the moderator variable (i.e., high versus medium versus low moderator scores), the validity coefficients for the three groups were .27, .42, and .58, respectively.

When one turns from analyses of validity to those focused on the judgment process, conclusions become more difficult. For unlike the two previously described judgmental tasks, this one has some serious limitations. Two of these problems are inherent to the task, while a third stems from Meehl's (1959) experimental procedures: (*a*) the 11 MMPI scale scores presented to the judges are not orthogonal (the 55 intercorrelations range up to almost .80–for example, *Hs* versus *Hy*–8 of them being higher than .50); (*b*) each scale score is a relatively continuous variable covering a considerable range of scale values; and (*c*) the 29 clinicans in Meehl's original study judged each of the 861 profiles only once (i.e., no repeated profiles were presented). For reasons *a* and *b* the ANOVA model is inappropriate for these data, and for reason *c* it is impossible to ascertain to what extent various judgment models approach the reliability of the judges' responses, since these reliability values are not known. Nonetheless, it has been possible to make some estimates about the nature of these clinical judgments (Wiggins & Hoffman, 1968).

Wiggins and Hoffman (1968) compared–as representations of the cognitive processes of each of the 29 clinicians–the following three models: (*a*) the standard linear regression model; (*b*) a quadratic model, which added to the first model all squared terms (e.g., $X_1{}^2$) and cross-product terms (e.g., $X_1 \cdot X_2$); and (*c*) a "sign" model, which included a set of 70 MMPI diagnostic signs from the psychometric literature. While Wiggins and Hoffman (1968) interpreted their findings as indicating that, for some judges, one of the non-linear models provided a slightly better representation of their judgments than the linear model, nonetheless, the most overwhelming finding from this study was how much of the variance in clinicians' judgments could be represented by the linear model. For example, if one compares the judgment correlations produced by the linear model with those from each of the two configural models (see Wiggins & Hoffman, 1968, Table 3), one finds that (*a*) the linear model was equal to, or superior to, the quadratic model for 23 of the 29 judges (and at best, for the most configural judge, the quadratic model produced a correlation with his judgments which was only .03 greater than that of the linear model); and (*b*) the linear model was equal to, or superior to, the sign model for 17 judges (the superiority of the sign model being but .04 for the single most configural judge). In the authors' own words,

> A note of caution should be added to the discussion of differences between linear and configural judges. Though the differences appear reliable, their magnitude is not large; the judgments of even the most seemingly configural clinicians can often be estimated with good precision by a linear model (pp. 76-77).

Once again, the linear model provided an excellent representation of the judgments of most of these clinicians, even for a task which they believed to be a highly configural one.

The point of this discussion is *not* to assert that clinicians, including the many clinicians studied in the experiments already described, cannot and do not use cue relationships more complex than simple linear ones. In the first two of these studies, for example, there were one or more statistically significant interactions in the judgment models of at least some of the clinicians, and in the third study there were clinicians whose judgments were at least slightly better represented by a model other than the linear one. Moreover, Paul Slovic (1968) has recently demonstrated that the judgments of each of two professional stockbrokers, asked to predict future stock prices from 11 dichotomized indexes, showed significant interactions which are explainable in terms of the theoretical orientations of the brokers themselves. And, in a number of other judgmental studies (e.g., Slovic, 1966), evidence of configural cue utilization has been uncovered. Clearly, clinical judgments *can* involve the configural utilization of cues. What are, then, the implications from these judgmental investigations?

First of all, it is important to realize that the very power of the linear regression model to predict observations generated by a large class of nonlinear processes can serve to obscure our understanding of all but the more gross types of configural judgments. Yntema and Torgerson (1961) and Rorer (1967) have both demonstrated rather dramatically how observations generated by nonlinear processes can become interpreted as linear ones when analyzed by standard regression and ANOVA methodology; Hoffman *et al.* (1968) and Hoffman (1968) provide an excellent discussion of this problem as it applies to the judgment process. If we return once again to the three competing hypotheses which provided the framework for launching these judgmental investigations, I would now assert that our original hypothesis (*b*)–that judges can process information in a configural fashion, but that the general linear model is powerful enough to reproduce most of these judgments with very small error–is, at this point, certainly the most compelling one.

Consequently, if one's sole purpose is to reproduce the responses of most clinical judges, then a simple linear model will normally permit the reproduction of 90%–100% of their reliable judgmental variance, probably in most–if not all–clinical judgment tasks. While Meehl (1959) has suggested that one potential superiority of the clinician over the actuary lies in the human's ability to process cues in a configural fashion, it is important to realize that this is neither an inherent advantage of the human judge (i.e., the actuary can include nonlinear terms in his equations), nor is this attribute–in any case–likely to be the clinician's "ace in the hole." If the clinician does have a long suit–and the numerous clinical versus statistical studies have not yet demonstrated that he has–it is extremely unlikely that it will stem from his alleged ability to process information in a complex configural manner.

Learning Clinical Inference

If "clinical wisdom" results in linearly reproducible judgments of rather low validity, it becomes sensible to ask whether these judgments could not be improved through training. Leonard G. Rorer and I reasoned that the major cause of the low validity coefficients reported for the judgments of practicing clinicians is the fact that in most, if not all, clinical settings there is no realistic opportunity for the clinician to improve his predictive accuracy. For learning to occur, some systematic feedback regarding the accuracy of the judgmental response must be linked to the particular cue configuration which led the clinician to make that judgment. But, in clinical practice feedback is virtually nonexistent, and in the relatively rare cases when feedback does occur the long interval of time which elapses between the prediction and the feedback serves to ensure that the initial cue configuration leading to the prediction has disappeared from the clinician's memory. As an example, say a clinician infers the prognosis "high suicide potential" from the MMPI profile of Patient A and writes in his report a statement like "Patient A has a high risk of committing suicide and therefore should be carefully watched." In most cases Patient A eventually returns to the community or moves to another hospital, and the clinician does not know whether the patient ever attempted suicide (accurate inference) or not (inaccurate inference). And if in 3 years the clinician happens to read in the newspaper that Patient A committed suicide, he is unlikely to be able to recall the particular MMPI profile configuration which initially led to this (successful) prediction, with the result that the "cue configuration→suicide inference" link is in no way strengthened.[4]

What is necessary for clinical inference to be learned, Rorer and I reasoned, is that the clinician obtain immediate feedback concerning the accuracy of his judgments–ideally feedback which occurs after the judgmental response has been formulated but before the removal of the cue configuration which led the clinician to that response. Moreover, if the cues are related to the criterion in some curvilinear and/or configural manner, then the clinician should be able to learn these more complex relationships, modify his own judgmental processes to incorporate such configural elements, and thereby begin to make judgments for which the best representation is a more complex model than the linear one.

To test this hypothesis, Rorer and I designed a study in which judges were given immediate feedback on the same task previously described, namely, the differential diagnosis of psychosis versus neurosis from MMPI profiles. Three

[4]B. F. Skinner (1968) has made much the same point in rebutting the belief in the accumulated wisdom of the classroom teacher: "It is actually very difficult for teachers to profit from experience. They almost never learn about their long-term successes or failures, and their short-term effects are not easily traced to the practices from which they presumably arose (pp.112-113)."

groups of judges—termed expert, middle, and naive—were studied. The expert group was composed of three clinical psychologists who had had extensive MMPI experience. The naive group was composed of 10 nonpsychologists who were unfamiliar with the MMPI and who were told only that their task was to learn to differentiate "N" from "P" profiles. The middle group was composed of 10 psychology graduate students who had at least a passing familiarity with the MMPI and some idea of the difference between a neurotic and a psychotic patient.

The judges received alternate weeks of training and testing. Five sets of 60 training profiles, each of which contained the criterion diagnosis on the back of the profile sheet, were assembled from 300 profiles drawn at random from one hospital sample. Thirty of these profiles in each set were repeated so that there was a total of 90 profiles in each training set. Ten testing sets were constructed, each set including profiles from a different clinical sample (one of which was the same as that used in the training set). Whenever possible, the testing set was composed of 100 profiles, 50 of which were then repeated, so that there was typically a total of 150 profiles in each testing set. Judges were instructed to diagnose the profiles from one set per day for 5 days per week. The judges were asked to classify each profile in turn and also to indicate their confidence in each of their judgments.

While all of the analyses of these data have not been completed, some preliminary results are available (Goldberg & Rorer, 1965; Rorer & Slovic, 1966). Let us first look at the levels of accuracy achieved after 9 weeks of daily training and 8 alternate weeks of daily testing. By this point, the judges had already received 90 training profiles per day (450 per week) for a total of over 4,000 training profiles (each followed by immediate feedback), plus another 6,000 testing profiles—over 10,000 profiles in all. But, while all three groups of judges manifested some learning on the training profiles, only the naive group showed *any* generalization of this training in improving their accuracy on the testing profiles. The average naive judge was correct about 52% of the time at the beginning, and after 17 weeks he had increased his accuracy to about 58%. The middle and expert judges were virtually indistinguishable, both groups achieving an average accuracy percentage around 65% at the beginning of training and the same figure after 17 weeks. Thus, even after 4,000 training profiles, the average accuracy percentage for the naive judges was still substantially below that manifested by the expert and middle judges. For the expert and middle judges, training on this task turned out to almost completely sample specific; there was virtually no cross-sample generalization of learning as a result of intensive training on over 4,000 MMPI profiles!

Faced with these startling findings, a number of experimental variations in the training procedures were introduced in an effort to increase judgmental accuracy. Two naive and two middle subjects were assigned to each of the following five subgroups:

Standard condition. These subjects continued what they had been doing all along. They were therefore a control group for the other four experimental variations.

Group Training. Two subjects worked together and agreed on a response. There was one naive pair and one middle pair. They were tested both individually and as a pair.

Generalization Training. Subjects in the generalization training group were given training on previously unused profiles from those installations on which the judges had achieved their poorest results.

Formula Training. These subjects were given the formula ($L + Pa + Sc - Hy - Pt$) and told that it would increase the accuracy of their judgments. They were encouraged to use the formula as a guide to indicate the scales to which they might profitably attend.

Value Training. The judges in this group, including all three experts, were given the numerical value of the formula for each profile and the optimum cutting score. They were told that this formula would achieve approximately 70% accuracy and that it would be more accurate for extreme values than for values close to the cutting score. They were free simply to report the formula diagnosis for every profile (a procedure which in every case would have allowed them to increase their judgmental accuracy), though they were encouraged to try to find ways in which they might improve on the formula decision.

After 8 more weeks (4 of training and 4 of testing), we found that those groups given value training (including all of the experts) had, on the average, increased their accuracy to a bit below 70% correct. But, none of the other experimental groups showed any substantial learning. Giving judges the optimal formula (formula training) resulted in a rapid increase in diagnostic accuracy (especially for the naive group), but this effect gradually wore away over time. By the end of the study formula training groups were again achieving approximately the same level of accuracy as the standard training control groups. On the other hand, giving judges the actual values of the optimal formula for each profile (value training) did result in a stable increase in diagnostic accuracy, though the accuracy of these judges' diagnoses was not as high as would have been achieved by simply using the formula itself.

The thousands of judgments collected during those months of intensive training should yield many more nuggets than these few which I have scraped off the top. But, I doubt whether the conclusions we can already draw will have to be drastically changed. It now appears that our initial formulation of the problem of learning clinical inference was far too simple—that a good deal more than outcome feedback is necessary for judges to learn a task as difficult as the present one. The research of Chapman and Chapman (1967) serves to reinforce this belief by providing an even more stunning example of the pitfalls of relying solely upon feedback to improve the accuracy of clinical inferences.

In what is perhaps the most ingenious series of studies of clinical judgment ever carried out, Chapman and Chapman (1967) have demonstrated how prior expectations of the relationships between cues and criteria can lead to faulty observation and inference, even under seemingly excellent conditions for learning. The Chapmans exposed subjects to human figure drawings, each of which was paired with two criterion statements concerning the characteristics of the patients who allegedly drew the figures. Though these training materials were constructed so that there was no relationship between the cues and the criterion statements, most subjects erroneously "learned" the cue-criterion links which they had expected to see. In fact, the "illusory correlation" phenomena demonstrated by the Chapmans was such a powerful one that many subjects trained on materials where the cue-criterion relationships were constructed to be the opposite of those expected still persisted in "learning" the erroneous relationships! For further documentation of this pervasive source of bias in the learning of clinical (and other) types of inference see Chapman (1967).

The intriguing research of the Chapmans illustrates the ease with which one can "learn" relationships which do *not* exist. Our own MMPI learning research, plus that of others (e.g., Crow, 1957; Sechrest, Gallimore, & Hersch, 1967; Soskin, 1954), demonstrates the problems which can be encountered in learning those relationships which *do* exist. What now seems clear is that at least three conditions–all of which are missing from the typical clinical setting–must hold if more complex clinical inferences are to be learned. First of all, some form of feedback (e.g., Skinner, 1968: Todd & Hammond, 1965) is a necessary, though not necessarily a sufficient, condition for learning to occur. Second, at least for problems of the complexity of many encountered in clinical practice, it may be necessary to be able to disturb the natural sequence of cue presentations–to rearrange the order of cases–so that one's hypotheses can be immediately verified or discounted. It does little good to formulate a rule for profile Type A, only to have to wait for another 100 profiles before an additional manifestation of Type A appears; what one must do is group together all Type A profiles in order to be able to verify one's initial inference. In the clinical setting this means studying those patients who manifest some particular cue configuration of interest, rather than taking patients as they come in the door. Finally, as the Chapmans' (1967) clever research so vividly demonstrates, it may often be necessary to *tally* the accuracy of one's hypotheses, thereby letting some variant of a paper-and-pencil boxscore substitute for the more emphemeral storage capacitites of the unaided human brain.

But, what do we call that process which is characterized by a disruption of the naturally occurring order of observations, plus immediate feedback on cue-criterion links, followed by some concrete form of tallying the accuracy of one's hypotheses? We call it RESEARCH.

4. EFFECTS OF RULE RELAXATION AND SYSTEM COMBINATION ON CLASSIFICATION RATES IN TWO MMPI "COOKBOOK" SYSTEMS

Frank D. Payne and Jerry S. Wiggins

There are presently two highly configural MMPI profile classification systems in clinical diagnostic use: the Marks and Seeman (1963) and the Gilberstadt and Duker (1965) schemes. Although the latter authors made no claim for high rates of classification, Marks and Seeman (1963) reported a classification rate of 80% in the application of their rules to the original derivation population. Subsequent applications have resulted in sharply reduced rates of classification. Huff (1965) applied the Marks-Seeman scheme to a sample of 149 male and female inpatients and obtained a 28% classification rate. An even lower classification rate of 17.2% was reported by Sines (1966) in the application of the Marks-Seeman rules to 1102 male and female patients at a Missouri medical center. Klett and Vestre (1967) applied the Gilberstadt-Duker rules to a Veterans Administration psychiatric hospital sample and obtained a 28% classification rate.

Until now, no attempt has been made to investigate the effects of the joint application of the Marks-Seeman and Gilberstadt-Duker systems within the same sample. Since there are only six profile types that are identical in their high-point codes, and even these differ in detail, it appears reasonable to assume that the overlap in patients classified by the two systems is not large. The possibility thus exists that the overall percentage of classified patients could be sizably increased by including patient profiles which can be fitted into a category of either system. There is, in addition, a second way in which the number of patients classified by these cookbook systems might be augmented. The respective authors of the two systems have indicated that, with a certain risk, profile rules may be relaxed in order to achieve tentative classification of patients almost fitting profile specifications. If some method were available for minor relaxation of profile rules, it might be possible to increase substantially the percentage of patients classified. The present study seeks to investigate the effects on classification rate of the joint application of cookbook systems and of provision for some minor flexibility in the classification process itself.

SOURCE. Frank D. Payne was a graduate student in psychology at the University of Illinois when this article was published. Jerry S. Wiggins is Professor of Psychology at that university, and is a consultant in psychology both to the Veterans Administration and to the Kankakee State Hospital. Dr. Wiggins has been an active researcher in personality assessment. This article originally appeared in the *Journal of Consulting and Clinical Psychology*, 1968, **32**, 734-736. Reprinted by permission of the American Psychological Association and the authors.

Method

Subjects. Patients at a large Illinois state mental hospital for whom recent and complete MMPI protocols were available were selected for study. Staff diagnoses for the 541 inpatients (294 males and 247 females) indicated a wide variety of psychopathology.

Test Materials. MMPI admission protocols were scored for the standard clinical and validity scales (Hathaway & McKinley, 1951). Raw scale scores were *K* corrected and converted to *T* scores by means of the Minnesota norms provided by Hathaway and Briggs (1957).

Classification Procedures. All MMPI protocols were processed by means of the Gilberstadt and Duker (1965) and Marks and Seeman (1963) systems of profile analysis. Profile rules were converted in exact form to MAD (Michigan Algorithm Decoder) computer language. Following certain initial checks on validity scale elevations specified by the cookbook authors, classification proceeded by testing a patient's profile against each successive set of rules. Contrary to usual clinical practice, therefore, testing began with the first set of rules within a cookbook and ended with the last set of rules.

Rule Relaxation. Relaxation of cookbook rules was achieved in a straightforward manner emphasizing ease of application. In all cases the first rule of each profile type, the one responsible for the type's high-point code name, was retained. Any other rule within the set of rules for the profile type could be violated for the "one rule relaxed" condition, or any two rules for the "two rules relaxed" condition, and so forth up to the maximum number of rules for each of the profile types.

Results

Profile Classification Rates

The number of patients in the total sample classified under each profile type within the Gilberstadt-Duker system is listed in the second column of Table 1. A similar listing is given in Column 2 of Table 2 for the Marks-Seeman classification system. It is notable that even though the profile types for these systems were selected somewhat on the basis of frequency of occurrence in psychiatric populations, many profile types were responsible for negligible percentages of classification. In the Gilberstadt-Duker system only seven profile types classified five or more patients; five profile types did this well in the Marks-Seeman system. It should be recognized, however, that the unproductive profile types in the present sample might prove useful in classifying patients in other samples.

Listed at the bottom of the second columns of Table 1 and of Table 2, respectively, are the total percentages of patients classified by the two cookbook

Table 1. Classification Rates for the Gilberstadt and Duker Rules

Profile type	No rules relaxed	One rule relaxed	Two rules relaxed
1-2-3	0	1	1
1-2-3-4	3	3	3
1-2-3-7	2	7	7
1-3-2	0	2	2
1-3-7	0	0	1
1-3-8	0	1	2
1-3-9	0	0	1
2-7	0	4	6
2-7-4	3	14	14
2-7-8	9	20	20
4	56	153	153
4-3	6	6	6
4-9	4	4	4
7-8	11	16	17
8-1-2-3	0	1	1
8-2-4	3	3	3
8-6	30	32	32
8-9	15	17	17
9	16	26	29
Total percentage classified	29	57	59

Note. $N = 541$.

Table 2. Classification Rates for the Marks and Seeman Rules

Profile type	No rules relaxed	One rule relaxed	Two rules relaxed
2-3-1	5	6	7
2-7	0	2	3
2-7-4	3	11	15
2-7-8	2	5	5
2-8	9	15	18
3-1	0	1	1
3-2-1	3	7	10
4-6	1	3	10
4-6-2	2	2	3
4-8-2	7	15	17
4-9	2	15	21
8-3	1	6	6
8-6	4	6	6
8-9	36	56	60
9-6	0	1	1
K+	70	100	135
Total percentage classified	27	47	59

Note. $N = 541$.

systems. The overall classification rate of 27% for the Marks-Seeman system is just slightly less than the 28% reported by Huff (1965), but considerably greater than the 17.2% reported by Sines (1966). The total system percentage of 29% for the Gilberstadt-Duker scheme is comparable to that previously reported by Klett and Vestre (1967). In the present sample, 37 patients were jointly classified within both the Marks-Seeman and Gilberstadt-Duker systems. The overall classification rate for the two systems combined was therefore 49%. This represents a considerable increase over either system applied alone.

Effects of Rule Relaxation

The third and fourth columns of Table 1 list the effects of rule relaxation on the number of patients classified under each profile type for the Gilberstadt-Duker system. Table 2 contains a comparable listing for the Marks-Seeman system. For any given profile type, Column 3 contains the total number of patients classified by that type with any one of its rules relaxed except for the important first rule. Therefore, the increment in the number classified by relaxing one rule may be calculated by subtracting the second column from the third. The fourth column lists the number of patients classified with any two rules relaxed other than the important first rule.

Relaxation of one rule resulted in a large additional percentage of classified patients in both systems: 28% for Gilberstadt and Duker and 20% for Marks and Seeman. Violation of two rules produced a 12% additional increment in the Marks-Seeman system, but only a 2% increase in the Gilberstadt-Duker system. Relaxation of more than two rules resulted in very small additional increases in the number of patients classified by either system. It should be noted that even with the relaxation of two rules certain profile types still failed to occur with any great frequency. The total percentage of patients classified by the two systems combined, with one rule relaxed, was 74%. The "two rules relaxed" condition resulted in an additional increment of 8%, or a total classification rate of 82%, for the combined systems.

Discussion

The results of the present study have clear implications for utilization of the Marks-Seeman and Gilberstadt-Duker systems in clinical practice. Whereas application of either system alone resulted in a classification rate of 27% and 29%, respectively, joint application increased the percentage classified to 49%. Relaxation of one rule resulted in a joint classification rate of 74%; two rules relaxed produced a combined rate of 82%. These results should be considerably more encouraging to practicing clinicians than those previously reported for single system application. The regular increase in the percentage of patients classified up to and including relaxation of one rule indicates the worth of implementing such a procedure in clinical practice.

Relaxation of two rules per profile type does not appear justified. In the first place, such relaxation results in a joint increment of only 8%. But in addition, it is probable that for many profile types, relaxation of two rules effectively destroys a great deal of the integrity of the configural type. The very small increase in classification rate does not appear to justify the indeterminable loss in homogeneity of patients within a profile type. The 25% increment in classification resulting from the relaxation of one rule per profile type does appear to justify this more conservative procedure.

The increase in classification rate resulting from relaxation of one rule is not bought without some cost, however. Aside from the perhaps minor distortion which occurs, it is apparent that certain configural types occur with undesirable frequency. The Gilberstadt-Duker Profile Type 4 and the Marks-Seeman *K*+ category are responsible for such large percentages of classification that it seems doubtful the underlying dimensions of similarity among patients could be very great. However, the degree of distortion produced by rule relaxation in these types, as well as in the 33 others, is an empirical matter yet to be fully investigated. In the meantime, it would appear that relaxation of one rule is a moderately conservative policy which provides tentative classification for a sizable portion of a clinical population.

5. THE RELATIVE CONTRIBUTION OF FOUR KINDS OF DATA TO ACCURACY IN PERSONALITY ASSESSMENT[1]

Lloyd K. Sines

Does the information available to the clinical psychologist through his tests and other resources, as in the psychodiagnostic process, provide him with a

SOURCE. Lloyd K. Sines received his doctoral degree at the University of Minnesota. He is presently Associate Professor at the University of Minnesota Medical School. Dr. Sines' special areas of clinical interest are objective personality assessment, the teaching of clinical technique, and behavioral research. This article originally appeared in the *Journal of Consulting Psychology,* 1959, **23,** 483-492. Reprinted by permission of the American Psychological Association and the author.

[1]This paper is based upon the doctoral dissertation of the author at the University of Minnesota. He wishes to thank William Schofield for his invaluable assistance and encouragement in planning and completing the study. Also, the services of the trainees and staff at the VA Mental Hygiene Clinic, Fort Snelling, Minnesota, were indispensable and especially appreciated.

significant amount of understanding of the patients about whom he is asked to make judgments, descriptive and diagnostic statements, and for whom he is asked to make decisions? This question implies others: (*a*) if significant insights into patients are possible via the information available to the psychologist, which kinds of data contribute most to an adequate level of understanding, (*b*) what is the relationship between the amount of data available to the clinician and the degree of insight he achieves, and (*c*) is it possible to identify most efficient batteries of tests and/or other data. More precisely, we see that it is not only the data themselves in which we are interested but the data as they are used by the psychologist. As Kelly (1954) has noted, the introduction of the human element into the assessment process means that the techniques of assessment (tests, data) have validity which is not independent of the assessor. The problem is, then, one of evaluation of interaction between data and user.

Hypotheses

1. Clinicians are able, on the basis of psychological test, history, and interview data, to describe psychiatric patients more accurately than does a stereotyped personality description obtained by reference to the prevailing conceptions of the typical or "average" psychiatric patient.

2. (*a*) Psychological test, history, and interview data are not of equal value in terms of their contribution to diagnostic and descriptive accuracy.

(*b*) Of the psychological tests used, that which is designed to tap the inner, unconscious, and genotypic facets of personality yields a greater degree of insight into patients, and a higher level of accuracy of judgments.

3. There is a positive relationship between the amount of data available about a patient and the accuracy with which judgments, inferences, and diagnostic statements can be made about him. The information conveyed about a patient by each kind of data is additive, each succeeding datum increasing the accuracy of judgments.

4. Although there are differences among the kinds of data with respect to their usefulness or "validity," clinicians differ with respect to their success with the available techniques or data.

5. Because psychodiagnostic techniques (especially psychological tests) reveal the covert, often unconscious aspects of personality, the judgments and inferences made about patients' personality characteristics by psychodiagnosticians will agree more closely with psychotherapists' perceptions of those patients after more extended therapeutic contact with them than with the therapists' impressions after only a moderate amount of such contact.

Method

Patients and Instruments. Applicants[2] to a Veterans Administration mental hygiene clinic were screened during the intake process for (*a*) judged "stay-ability" in individual psychotherapy, and (*b*) availability for a psychological evaluation of approximately six hours in length. The psychological examination consisted of the following procedures: each patient completed a four-page Biographical Data Sheet (BDS) and the booklet form of the Minnesota Multi-phasic Personality Inventory (MMPI). He was also interviewed and given a Rorschach test by the clinical psychologist who was the "diagnostician" and who performed the subsequent clinical Q sorts.

The data were made available to the clinician sequentially, and he performed a Q sort of 97 items describing phenotypic and genotypic personality and behavioral characteristics after considering each of the four major groups or kinds of data. The biographical data were uniformly made available to the clinician as the first group of data, and the initial Q sort was performed on that basis alone. Six sequences of data were possible with the remaining three kinds of data, and in order to exhaust the number of sequences each of the (five) diagnosticians examined six patients, each patient being studied by a different sequence of data. The sequence followed in a given clinician's first case was assigned by random selection, and each subsequent sequence by random selection from among the remaining (unused) sequences. It was understood that the four Q sorts in each instance would not represent interpretations of the specific data which immediately preceded them, but a summation of all the data which has been made available to the clinician up to that point in the diagnostic process. Thus, the fourth (final) clinical sort represented the clinician's integration of all the data included in the battery, rather than his interpretations of the data which were made available after the third Q sort had been performed. An 11-category quasi-normal forced distribution was used in performing the Q sorts.

After the patient had been seen for a total of 10 interviews,[3] his therapist[4] performed a (criterion) Q sort of the 97 items used by the diagnostician in describing the patient. Comparisons between the diagnosticians' four clinical

[2]The patients ranged in age from 24 to 47 years (median 32.5) and in education from 6 to 19 years (median 12.0). Approximately two thirds had disability ratings for a psycho-neurotic condition and about one fifth for a psychotic condition. The degree of impairment ranged from 0% to 100% (median 10%).

[3]In three cases the therapist's Q sort was obtained after the eighth therapeutic interview because of the conclusion of the study.

[4]Thirteen therapists drawn from each of the three major disciplines in the clinic (7 clinical psychologists, 4 psychiatrists, and 2 social workers) were involved in the study. About one half of the patients were seen for therapy by psychologists.

sorts and the therapists' 10th-hour Q sort descriptions of the patients constitute the major data of the study. In addition, for those patients who remained in therapy for 15 or more interviews, an additional Q sort description of them by their therapist was obtained at the time the study was terminated. The range of therapy interviews in this group was from 15 to 49. Comparisons between Q sort descriptions obtained at that time and the 10th-hour Q sorts as well as between the former and the diagnosticians' four clinical sorts were made. As a further methodological consideration, in 10 of the 30 cases a re-sort from the therapist was obtained between the 10th and 11th therapy interviews or after the terminal Q sort was obtained in those cases remaining in therapy beyond 15 interviews. The correlations between the 10th hour Q sorts and the re-sort, and between the terminal Q sort and its re-sort, are considered a measure of reliability.

Five clinical psychologist trainees comprised the group of diagnosticians (hereafter referred to as clinicians). They were at different levels of training (within the limits of the doctoral training program), but had all been employed by the VA as trainees for at least one year.

Selection of the Q Sort Item Pool. The item pool finally selected for use in the present study was obtained from a larger pool[5] consisting of 295 items gathered from a variety of sources, including the studies by Halbower (1955), Block and Bailey (1953), and others. Further, each of the Murray (1938) needs was included as a separate item, as were the psychoanalytic defense mechanisms. Various of the diagnostic categories found in the *Diagnostic and Statistical Manual* (American Psychiatric Association, 1952) were represented by items, as were the personality and behavioral characteristics associated with the more common MMPI code types described by Hathaway and Meehl (1951).

Each of 11 psychology trainees performed a Q sort describing their conception of the typical MHC patient (referred to psychology for testing). These sorts were summed to form a composite from which was derived a Mean Average Patient (MAP) description. The MAP description was given to each of the five clinicians in the study who dichotomized the distribution at the point where he felt that the items became, by and large, *false* with respect to the typical MHC patient. (This procedure was also employed by the clinicians when performing the fouth clinical sort for each patient.) The stereotype (MAP) description was compared with the criterion (therapist) Q sort for each patient. The average level of agreement between the two over the sample of 30 patients was considered the baseline (chance, or expected level) against which the clinical sorts were evaluated.

[5]This pool was made available to the author by P. E. Meehl. The 97 items used in this study may be made available upon request.

The method and results of the Q sort item selection were as follows: four pairs of judges (one pair for each of the four data groups included in the diagnostic battery) rated each of the 295 items in the original pool. Each item was judged as "suitable," "of questionable suitability," or "unsuitable" to rating, on the basis of the information conveyed by the specific kind of data. The judges' ratings were arbitrarily assigned weights of 2, 1, or 0, respectively, so that each item had a possible score of 0 to 4 for each data group, and from 0 to 16 as an over-all rating. Since it was desirable that the items finally selected have relevance to each of the kinds of data utilized by the clinicians, items were selected from the larger pool on the basis of (*a*) a high total rating score, and (*b*) specific pertinence (judged suitability) to one or more of the four types of data to be used by the diagnosticians as the basis for their subsequent sortings. A total of 94 items was so selected, and two of the items were modified and expanded into five separate items, thus comprising the final 97-item pool used in the study proper. An attempt was made to equate the final pool with items judged to have particular pertinence to each specific kind of data. The extent to which an equating of the pool for items pertinent to each data type was accomplished is indicated by the data in Table 1. From Table 1 it may be seen that the Interview, MMPI, and Rorschach were roughly comparable in terms of their item representation in the Q pool, while the BDS was distinctly under-represented by items judged to have pertinence to that source of data.

Table 1. Judges' Ratings of the 94 Q Sort Items Originally Selected from the Larger Pool in Terms of Their "Suitability" to Rating from the Specific Types of Data Utilized by the Clinicians

	Sum of the Two Judges' Ratings						
Kind of Data	4	3	2	1	0	Sum X Frequency	%
Interview	44	29	16	4	1	299	28.8
MMPI	45	22	16	5	6	283	27.3
Rorschach	43	25	10	12	4	279	26.9
BDS	15	16	20	25	17	176	17.0

As a further measure of the representation in the item pool of items relevant to each of the data types, the subsamples of items contained in the final pool which were rated by each of the two judges as "suitable" to a specific data type may be compared with the total pool in terms of item placements (means and variances) in the stereotype (MAP) sort. The 97-item Q sort distribution utilized in the final sortings yielded a mean of 6.0 and a variance of 4.54. The means of the four subsamples of items were as follows: Interview, 5.52; MMPI, 5.36; Rorschach, 5.61; and BDS, 7.53. The variances were: 5.06, 4.28, 5.56, 5.05, respectively. An analysis of variance of these values yields an F of 3.76, which indicates statistically significant differences among the item subsample means. By t test analyses it was shown that the BDS item subsample differed from the remaining three samples in the mean placement of items in the MAP sort. It would appear then, that the 97-item Q pool was underrepresented with items inferable from the BDS, and further, that the small sample of items "suitable" to rating from the BDS which was included in the total pool could not be considered a random sample from the total item pool, but rather, contained items which tended to be placed toward the less descriptive end of the Q sort continuum in the MAP sort.

Results and Discussion

Reliability of the Q Sort. The reliability sorts were performed by the therapists on different days, and were not separated in time by a therapeutic interview with the patient. The number of days between initial sort and re-sort for the 10 cases ranged from 1 to 42, with a median of three days. The two sorts were correlated and yielded a range of reliability coefficients from .795 to .936 (median .858, mean .866). There was little apparent relationship between the magnitude of the reliability coefficient and the length of the time interval between sorts, perhaps because of the small dispersion of the latter. These data are interpreted as indicating satisfactory reliability of the Q sort.

Results of Testing Hypothesis 1. (*a*) In 21 of the 30 cases the correlation between the final clinical sort and the therapist's criterion description for that patient exceeded numerically the correlation between the MAP description and the latter. The sign test indicates that this proportion would arise on the basis of chance alone in less than 5 out of 100 instances. (*b*) In 15 of the above 21 cases the observed differences between correlations were statistically reliable ($p < .05$). (*c*) In 9 of the 30 cases the MAP (stereotype) description exceeded the validity of the final clinical sort. Four of the nine differences were statistically reliable. (*d*) In 21 of the 30 cases the number of items agreed upon by clinician and therapist on the true–false dichotomy exceeded the comparable figure in the case of the MAP description/therapist comparison. Again, the sign test yields a probability of less than .05, which indicates a significant difference in favor of the clinical sorts over the MAP description. (*e*) The average percentage of the 97 items agreed upon (over the 30 cases) by clinician and therapist was 66.0, whereas the comparable figure in the case of the MAP description/therapist comparisons was 60.0. The difference between these two means is statistically reliable ($p < .05$). (*f*) For the entire sample of 30 cases the average validity coefficient of the final clinical sort was .480, while the average validity coefficient of the MAP (stereotype) description was .340. The difference between these mean values is statistically reliable ($p < .01$).

In each of the above analyses, evidence of the superiority of the clinical sorts over the stereotype description is observed. Although the final clinical sort (which represented a clinician's integration of all the available data on a patient) did not *always* result in better than chance descriptive accuracy, it did so in a majority of the cases, and in one half of the cases the greater accuracy of the clinical description was statistically reliable. Hypothesis 1 is accepted.

Results of Testing Hypothesis 2. The validity coefficients of six batteries or subgroups of data are reported in Table 2. The data indicate that although the subsamples of patients seemed to be roughly comparable in terms of the degree to which their BDS contributed to descriptive accuracy, and they were not markedly dissimilar with respect to their "typicalness" (MAP validity), quite different validities accrued from the data (MMPI, Rorschach, or Interview) which were considered by the clinicians following the BDS sorts. None of the BDS *plus* MMPI or BDS *plus* Rorschach validity coefficients equaled or exceeded the median coefficient obtained in the BDS *plus* Interview group. Further, the mean validity in the latter group (.566) was significantly greater than the mean in either of the other two groups ($p < .05$). Also, only the BDS *plus* Interview mean validity was reliably greater than the average validity of the MAP description for that subgroup ($p < .01$) and, in addition, significantly greater than the average validity of the BDS alone for the 10 cases in the subgroup. Further, considerable differences were observed at the point of the third clinical sort, depending on which kind of data was omitted from the battery. In only one case from each of the Battery *minus* Interview and Battery *minus* MMPI groups did the validity coefficient equal or exceed the median coefficient in the Battery *minus* Rorschach group. Further, although the average validity coefficient in each of the three groups exceeded the average validity coefficient of the MAP description for the 10 cases in that group, in only the Battery *minus* Rorschach sample was the observed difference statistically reliable ($p < .01$). Finally, the mean Battery *minus* Rorschach validity coefficient (.595) was significantly greater than the mean validity coefficient in either of the other two groups ($p < .05$). In view of these facts, and (as may be seen from Table 2) since the average validity coefficient of the BDS *plus* Rorschach did not exceed the average validity coefficient of the BDS *plus* MMPI, Hypothesis 2b, which implies the greater validity of the Rorschach relative to the MMPI, is not confirmed.

A further method of elucidating the relative power or usefulness of the data used in the diagnostic process is reflected in Table 3. The frequency with which each of the kinds of data immediately preceded the Q sort which yielded the highest validity coefficient of the four obtained during the diagnostic process was tabulated. In addition to the four kinds of clinical information, the MAP description is included in the tabulations. Finally, the ranks of one through five are given (inverse) weights and, when multiplied by the observed frequencies and summed, the data are ranked in terms of their contribution to the maximum validity obtained during the diagnostic process.

Table 2. Validity Coefficients of Six Subgroups of Data

	Biographical Data Sheet *plus**			Complete Battery *minus**		
	Interv.	MMPI	Rorsch.	Interv.	MMPI	Rorsch.
Mean validity of the stereotype	.272	.384	.347	.343	.348	.294
Mean validity of the BDS alone	.381	.385	.411	.402	.403	.366
Validity of the data subgroup						
Range	.282 to .734	.120 to .539	.016 to .550	.016 to .627	.220 to .607	.341 to .698
Median	.610	.410	.395	.456	.453	.604
Mean	.566	.378	.368	.403	.450	.595

* $N = 10$ different cases in each subgroup, thus exhausting the total sample of 30 patients.

Table 3. The Frequency with which Each of the Kinds of Data, and the Stereotype, Immediately Preceded the Highest to Lowest Validity Coefficients in Each of the 30 Diagnostic Cases

Magnitude of Validity Coefficient	Weight	Interv.	MMPI	Rorsch.	BDS	MAP
Highest	4	12.0	5.0	1.0	4.0	8.0
2nd	3	8.0	7.0	8.0	5.0	2.0
3rd	2	5.5	8.0	13.0	3.5	0.0
4th	1	1.5	7.0	6.0	10.5	5.0
Lowest	0	3.0	3.0	2.0	7.0	15.0
Sum of Weight X Frequency		84.5	64.0	60.0	48.5	43.0

Note. $\chi^2 = 58.39$; $df = 16$; $P < .01$.

Several important trends may be observed in the data reported in Table 3. First, the frequency with which the Interview yielded the greatest agreement with the therapist (40% of the cases) is striking. In addition to a possible explanation in terms of the similarity between this data type and the criterion (the fact that diagnosticians' interview impressions were correlated with therapists' interview impressions), the possibility is suggested that the diagnostic interview was in itself a quite useful technique which contributed at least as much to the diagnostic process as the best available "test" in the conventional sense. A second important fact reflected in Table 3 is the distribution of the MAP validities. It would appear that the stereotype description tended either to fit the patient very well (better than the tests) or to miss him almost completely, so that any specific test or history data about him afforded a more accurate description than did the stereotype. In 27% of the cases no single test or combination of data led to a more accurate description of the patient than was afforded by the stereotype. That the latter did not obtain by virtue of the tests' failure to describe the patients well, but rather, was due to the absolute accuracy of the stereotype description in many instances was attested to as follows. In the eight cases where the latter yielded the highest validity coefficient, the correlations ranged from .368 to .705 with a mean of .550, which is just about as good as even the best test batteries did in a given series. There appeared then, to be a subpopulation of patients for whom the MAP description was quite accurate, and for whom little further data were needed in order that they be described as adequately as the psychologist was able to do on the basis of an extended workup. On the other hand, there was a larger subgroup which was quite unlike the MAP description, and for whom additional data were needed in order that they be accurately described or diagnosed.

The data presented in this section, plus several of the compairsons discussed in the previous section, may be summarized by means of a ranking of the batteries reviewed above in terms of their average validity coefficients (Table 4). The average validity of the MAP description may be construed as the baseline or chance level of accuracy.

Table 4. Average Validity Coefficients of the Several "Batteries" of Data

Battery (Basis of Q Sort)	*N*	Average Validity Coefficient
Battery *minus* Rorschach	10	.595
BDS *plus* Interview	10	.566
Complete Battery	30	.480
Battery *minus* MMPI	10	.450
Battery *minus* Interview	10	.403
BDS alone	30	.396
BDS *plus* MMPI	10	.378
BDS *plus* Rorschach	10	.368
Stereotype (MAP)	30	.340

From the preceding, it may be seen that the kinds of data used by the clinician differed with respect to their contribution to diagnostic accuracy. By way of summarizing the relationships among the kinds of data used it would appear that (*a*) the superior batteries (in terms of agreement with the therapist) were those which included the Interview, (*b*) omitting the Rorschach test from the battery was associated with higher validity of personality descriptions than when it was included, and (*c*) heavy reliance on the Rorschach was associated with no better than chance accuracy of personality descriptions. Hypothesis 2a, which postulates differences among the data in their contribution to accuracy in personality description, is accepted.

Results of Testing Hypothesis 3. Hypothesis 3 implies that as data are added during the course of the diagnostic process the accuracy of judgments about the individuals studied increases. Further, it was hypothesized that each kind of data used in the study increases the validity of the subsequent Q sort over that of the previous Q sorts as it is added to the battery.

From Table 5 there does appear, over the entire sample, to be a consistent positive relationship between the amount of data concerning patients that clinicians had on which to base their judgments and the accuracy of such judgments. However, in spite of the consistent trend toward increments in validity as a function of the amount of data available, the absolute improvement from initial (BDS) to final clinical sort was quite small. While, on the average, the BDS sorts accounted for about 15% of the criterion variance, the sorts on the basis of the entire battery accounted for less than 25% of that variance—an absolute gain of less than 10% fewer errors in judgments (accuracy of description).

Table 5. The Relationship between the Ordinal Position of the Q Sorts and Their Average Validity Coefficients (*N* = 30)

Q Sort	Mean Validity Coefficient
Individual clinician's "average patient" sort	.289
MAP description	.340
Clinical sorts	
1st	.396
2nd	.446
3rd	.477
4th	.480

Although the actual gains in validity with additions of data were minimal, there is very good evidence that clinicians' perceptions of patients rapidly crystalize as a function of the amount of data (Table 6).

Table 6 shows clearly that the clinicians changed their impressions of a patient less and less with further increments to the available data. While they

Table 6. Average Intercorrelation of Successive Q Sorts by the Diagnosticians

Q Sort	Mean Intercorrelation
Clinician's "average patient" sort vs. his 1st clinical sort	.459
1st clinical sort vs. 2nd clinical sort	.698
2nd clinical sort vs. 3rd clinical sort	.805
3rd clinical sort vs. 4th clinical sort	.850*

*Approximates the median reliability coefficient of the Q sort.

may have changed from their "average patient" conception on the basis of a patient's BDS, they were unwilling to greatly alter their statements after they had considered two or three kinds of data about a patient. In view of the rapid crystalization of clinicians' perception of patients, and only slight improvement in validity as a function of increments in the amount of data available, Dailey's (1952) finding, that clinicians in this type of enterprise begin to interpret their early inferences as *facts* as they are required to make further judgments, appears altogether plausible.

By way of further analysis, the number of times the addition of the MMPI, Interview, and Rorschach, respectively increased or decreased the validity of the clinicians' judgments may be interpreted as evidence of their contribution to the diagnostic battery. Considering the absolute numerical value of the validity coefficients as the basis of comparison, it may be seen that a given Q sort validity should either exceed or be less than the validity of the preceding Q sort in an equal number of cases if there were no differential value of the specific data class in the battery. The chance frequency with which each data class should yield a higher or lower validity coefficient than the immediately preceding sort is 15. Tabulation of the actual frequencies shows that the Rorschach Q sort yielded a (numerically) higher validity coefficient than the Q sort immediately preceding it in 10 cases, the MMPI in 13, and the Interview in 25. According to the sign test of significance, only the last value is reliably different from the expected value of 15. These data indicate that whether or not the data class added to the validity of an existing battery depended on the nature of the data. In this analysis, only in the case of the Interview did an increase in validity over that obtained on the basis of previously considered data accrue in a significant number of cases.[6]

Finally, although the Interview tended to add to the accuracy of judgments made on the basis of test and other data, the extent to which it contributed

[6]It should be noted that sequence or ordinal position in the series was equated for all groups, since the values were computed on the bases of all 30 cases. Each data type, then, appeared as the second, third, and fourth group an equal number of times.

depended upon how much data about the patient had already been made available to the clinican. That is, if the Interview was held early in the diagnostic process a much greater contribution to the validity of the clinician's judgments was made than if the Interview was held later, or was the last procedure employed. Since there is evidence indicating that clinicians tended to crystalize their thinking about patients early in the diagnostic process regardless of the specific data on which their judgments were made, it appeared that if the Interview was a part of the early body of data on which closure was based, a relatively high level of validity obtained, not only at that point, but also at the completion of the diagnostic process. However, though the Interview was a powerful diagnostic technique, it could not overcome the false leads obtained early in the diagnostic process on the basis of the less valid measures or techniques. Table 7 contains the data on which these conclusions are based.

Table 7. Validity Coefficients of the Interview when it was the Second, Third, and Fourth Data Group Considered in the Diagnostic Process

($N = 10$ in each sample)

Ordinal Position of Interview	Average Validity Coefficient of Sort	Average Validity Coefficient of Final Sort
2nd	.566	.542
3rd	.480	.477
4th	.412	.412

In summary, the relationship between the amount of data available to clinicians and the accuracy of their judgments appeared to be complex rather than as simply stated in the hypothesis. When all cases and all data groups were considered, there appeared to be a consistent trend toward increased accuracy (validity) as further increments to the data were made. However, the above relationship is seen to depend largely on the nature of the data which were added to the battery. In the case of the Rorschach, decrements in validity were as frequently observed as were increments when that test was added to the battery, while the Interview almost invariably added to the accuracy of the diagnostic judgments, the degree of the latter being related to the point in the diagnostic process at which it occurred.

Results of Testing Hypothesis 4. Hypothesis 4 states that individual differences would be observed among the clinicians in terms of their success with the kinds of data utilized. The analysis in this connection is a rather straightforward one, namely the tabulation of the frequency with which each clinician's highest validity coefficient in each of his six diagnostic cases followed the introduction of each of the four data types. Table 8 contains the pertinent data.

First, it should be noted that with the exception of the BDS, which was routinely analyzed first and without benefit of other test data being available, sequence or ordinal position in the diagnostic process is not a significant factor in the distribution of validity scores, since the figures were computed on the basis of the entire sample of 30 cases, which indicates that each of the MMPI, Rorschach, and Interview was second, third, and fourth an equal number of times (10) in the sequence.

The cell frequencies in Table 8 may be evaluated for significance by means of a nonparametric test. Since, for each clinician, there were six trials (patients) and four data-types, the mean expected frequency per cell is 1.5. Further, the probability that a specific data group (test) would yield the highest validity coefficient in a given case is one in four (.25), of the same data group being highest in any two cases (.0625) (15) = .9375, in any three cases (.015625) (10) = .156, in any four cases (.00390625) (10) = .039, in any five cases (.0009765625) (4) = .004, and in all six cases .0002. From these facts it may be said with statistical confidence that clinicians B and D were more successful with the Interview, relative to their use of the other data, than were clinicians A and C, relative to the latter's use of the other data. Although these relationships are quite clear from a descriptive point of view, it is not possible from the data to explain the relationships, or to make inferences to over-all diagnostic (or even interview) ability. It may be seen in this connection that the fact that clinician D obtained his greatest validity on the basis of the Interview in each instance could have come about as readily from lack of skill with the other data as from some unique interview acumen.[7]

Table 8. The Frequency with which Each of the Data Groups Produced the Highest Validity Coefficient in the Six Cases Studied by Each Clinician

Clinician	VA Training Classification (year)	Highest Validity Coefficient			
		BDS	MMPI	Rorschach	Interview
A	IV	1	3	2	0
B	III	2	0	0	4
C	III	2	2	1	1
D	III	0	0	0	6
E	II	2	1	0	3
Total		7	6	3	14

A further matter relating to individual differences among the clinicians concerns their over-all level of accuracy in the diagnostic enterprise. An evaluation of this factor was accomplished as follows: the 30 validity coefficients

[7]A further interesting possibility is suggested by the data in Table 8, namely, that a trend indicating a relationship between the amount of experience (level of training) of the clinician and his degree of success with psychological tests may exist. Though the range of experience among the clinicians was relatively small, it is interesting to note that only in the case of the most advanced trainee were the tests used to particular advantage.

obtained by the five clinicians were ranked in terms of their magnitude, and each clinician's distribution of six coefficients was obtained. An analysis of variance was applied to the five distributions of validity coefficient ranks, and yielded an F of 12.8 indicating a probability of less than .001 that the distributions of ranks represented random samples from a common source. A t test analysis of the individual distributions of ranks indicated that clinician E produced validity coefficients significantly lower than those of the other four clinicians. Further, only two of clinician E's six validity coefficients exceeded the lowest median coefficient obtained by any of the other clinicians. Although it would have been desirable to relate the degree of experience and the level of the clinicians' training to their relative success in the diagnostic enterprise, the range of experience (training) among the five was quite restricted. However, as indicated in Table 9, the fourth year trainee had the highest median validity coefficient, while the second year trainee had the lowest coefficients. Ideally, of course, a critical evaluation of the relative power or usefulness of various kinds of data, and a definitive statement of the relationships between amount of experience (or level of training) and diagnostic accuracy, would require study or a group of thoroughly trained, broadly experienced clinicians, rather than persons at the initial phases of their training such as were represented in this study.

Table 9. Validity Coefficients of the Five Clinicians' Q Sort Diagnostic Judgments

Clinician	VA Training Classification (year)	Validity Coefficients		
		Range	Mean	Median
A	IV	.361 to .659	.531	.533
B	III	.327 to .652	.475	.460
C	III	.293 to .705	.535	.523
D	III	.125 to .627	.458	.528
E	II	.123 to .466	.387	.429

Results of Testing Hypothesis 5. Hypothesis 5 states that the agreement between diagnosticians' judgments about patients and those made by the patients' psychotherapists would increase as a function of the amount of therapeutic contact the latter had with the patients.

For 10 of the 30 patients, criterion Q sorts were obtained from the therapists at a point in therapy well beyond the 10th hour, the point at which the original criterion Q sorts were routinely obtained. The number of therapy interviews which had taken place at the time of the terminal Q sort ranged from 15 to 49 (median of 23). In each case the clinician's final sort was correlated with the terminal criterion sort of the therapist and the distribution of such coefficients was obtained. The coefficients obtained between the clinical sorts and the 10th-hour sorts for the 10 cases were also noted and a comparison between the two sets of data is interpreted as reflecting the relationship between amount of therapeutic contact and therapist/diagnostician agreement.[8] The data in this analysis do not support the hypothesis as stated. The average of the validity coefficients of the clinicians' Q sorts was the same when compared with therapists' judgments based upon more extended therapeutic contact, as when compared with therapists' sorts based upon only 10 interviews.

Summary and Conclusions

The relative contribution of four commonly used kinds of clinical information to the description of the personality characteristics of male veteran psychiatric outpatients was studied.

Five clinicians studied the group of patients from a psychodiagnostic point of view, and performed four Q sorts of items describing the patients' personality characteristics and current psychiatric status. Increasing amounts of test and other relevant data concerning the patient were made available to the clinicians sequentially. The data considered by the clinicians included (*a*) a four-page Biographical Data Sheet (BDS), (*b*) the patient's MMPI profile, (*c*) a Rorschach protocol (administered, scored, and interpreted by the clinician who performed the four Q sorts), and (*d*) a diagnostic interview conducted by the clinician. In each case, the sequence in which the clinican obtained and considered each of the above four kinds of data was specified. Although the BDS was always the first data-group considered and Q sorted, the other three kinds of data were arranged in the six possible sequences and each sequence was followed in one, and only one, diagnostic case per each of the five clinicians. A Q sort was performed after the clinician considered each kind of data, and the final sort represented the clinician's integration and interpretation of all the available data concerning the patient under consideration.

Each patient was assigned to a psychotherapist in the usual clinic manner, with the exception that the psychological test results and the usual written report were not made available to the therapist. After the patient had been seen by the therapist for 10 interviews (in three cases for only eight interviews) the therapist performed a criterion Q sort, describing the patient as he saw him on the basis of his therapeutic contact and whatever record material was available on him.

[8]The therapists' terminal criterion sorts were also compared with the corresponding 10th-hour criterion sorts. The resulting correlation coefficients ranged from .580 to .850 (median .734), which suggests that the therapists did not markedly alter their impressions of their patients (as reflected by the Q sort) between the 10th hour of therapy and the point at which the terminal sort was performed.

On the basis of the comparisons between the diagnosticians' and therapists' Q sort descriptions of patients, the following conclusions were drawn:

1. Although in some instances a stereotype personality description was the most accurate description of the patient obtained, bettering even the clinician's judgments made on the basis of any or all of the available test, history, and interview data, clinicians were generally able to describe psychiatric patients more accurately than did a single stereotyped description obtained by reference to the prevailing conceptions of the typical psychiatric patient seen in that setting.
2. Significant differences among the kinds of data were observed in terms of their contribution to accurate personality descriptions.
3. The diagnostic interview was consistently observed to contribute to greater accuracy of judgments about the personality characteristics of the patients. The interview was most useful when it was held early in the diagnostic sequence.
4. Neither the Rorschach nor the MMPI appeared to increase the validity of previous judgments in a significant number of cases (more frequently than they detracted from previously established validity of judgments).
5. Biographical data appeared to be a promising source of information in accurately assessing the personality characteristics of psychiatric patients. The BDS at least "held its own" relative to the other data even though under-represented in the item pool and routinely considered without collateral information or data about the patients.
6. The relationship between the amount of information available to the diagnostician and the accuracy of his judgments is complex rather than linear, and varies according to the particular type (or kind) of data made available to the clinician.
7. Clinicians differ among themselves with respect to their over-all diagnostic accuracy, and also in terms of their success with the various tests or kinds of data utilized in the diagnostic process.
8. There was little difference in the degree of agreement between diagnosticians and therapists as a function of the amount of therapeutic contact (over a certain minimal amount) the latter had with specific patients.
9. The over-all agreement between diagnosticians and therapists was rather modest (mean r = .48), suggesting that somewhat different frames of reference were emphasized by each.

Chapter 9

Criticisms of Personality Assessment

Psychological testing, especially personality assessment, has always been subject to criticism. Lately this criticism has taken two distinct forms: responsible concern involving substantive issues and emotional, public outcries with consequent political pressures. This latter form of reaction seemingly reached a crescendo in 1965 when there were two Congressional hearings, primarily to investigate the routine use of personality tests in the selection of federal employees. These hearings, however, also served the important purpose of giving many different people an opportunity to voice a broad range of dissatisfactions with both current psychological test technology and with current test usage. These hearings apparently resulted in forcing psychologists to face a variety of issues implicit in their then current testing strategy that heretofore had been ignored or minimized. Thus public outcries and political pressures had served as a spur to reconsideration and reform in some important aspects of psychological testing.

A number of attempts were made at that time, and subsequently, to analyze the substantive issues underlying these criticisms and most of them involve two major themes or areas of concern: that the tests are *inaccurate* or invalid and/or that the tests are *immoral,* for instance, tests invade the respondent's privacy. Our position is that some uses of psychological tests, including personality assessment devices, have been both inaccurate and immoral but that it is these inaccuracies and immoralities that need to be eliminated rather than testing *per se.*

One major, popular critic who has taken the extreme view that testing ought to be abolished was Martin Gross. His best-selling book, *The Brain Watchers* (Gross, 1962), in its criticism of personality assessment in personnel selection, strongly suggests that there are no legitimate uses of psychological tests.

In our first article, Garlie Forehand attempts to deal with the most salient point made by Gross, namely, that testing should not be used in personnel practice. As a basis for evaluating the legitimacy of testing, Forehand identifies two situations in which tests have achieved widely acknowledged usefulness: (1) the use of abilities tests for routine selection in situations where clear-cut criteria exist; and (2) clinical assessment in mental health situations. Forehand acknowledges that neither of these situations are exactly similar to personnel selection—the focus of Gross's attack. However, he sees four options open to personnel workers: (1) the "dog fight" strategy—competition until the best man wins; (2) intuitive judgment; (3) random selection; and (4) systematic observation of behavior through testing. Emphasizing the need for professional responsibility and caution, Forehand argues that the fourth strategy—testing—is still the most desirable, provided the ultimate decision is clearly made by an individual and not a test.

The second article, by MMPI author Starke R. Hathaway, attempts to deal with the complex pros and cons of using a clinically derived test, such as the MMPI, for personnel selection practices. Writing in the context of the responsible use of testing by adequately trained professional persons, Hathaway makes a number of points that are basic to the sophisticated use of the MMPI and any complex personality assessment device. First, certain "objectionable" items (such as those pertaining to religion) may be necessary for an adequate clinical assessment, in order to identify certain well-known patterns of psychological distortion, such as "religiosity." Second, the use of a mental health screening device constitutes a reasonable personnel practice, and this is particularly important in the selection of persons for critical social roles such as policemen, who have great power in the community. Third, absolute reliance is not placed on the content of the person's responses, but, in the empirical tradition, they are considered simply as bits of verbal behavior for which nontest correlates are known. Fourth, it is possible to have a person's responses machine-scored and printed in summary profile form, after which the individual item responses are destroyed, so that the individual content of the responses is permanently protected. Fifth, Hathaway defends any use of the MMPI that falls within the context of ethical professional practice, and he believes that no harm could be done to a respondent by taking it in such circumstances.

The first two articles primarily deal with criticisms of the use of personality tests outside the context of personality assessment in mental health settings. The third paper, by Louis Breger, analyzes a more widespread issue—the appropriateness or usefulness of routine psychological testing in clinical situations. Breger regards this tradition as stemming from the similarity of mental health practice with medical practice in which formal diagnosis traditionally precedes treatment, and also to the need of clinical psychologists to feel that they have their own unique area of expertise in the mental health enterprise. A third influence might also be psychologists' long and traditional identification with the mental testing movement and its emphasis on formal evaluation and prediction procedures.

Breger argues, however, that there are two legitimate uses for psychological testing in clinical settings: (1) where it might be possible to provide practical information concerning the best kind of treatment to employ; and (2) where knowledge obtained from testing might be useful to a therapist during the course of treatment. Unfortunately, there is so little known about the selection of mental health treatment procedures that it is impossible to utilize testing for this purpose; and it is by no means clear what prior knowledge about a patient aids the therapist. On the other hand, one danger of testing before treatment is that the patient's initial commitment to treatment may be diminished; also, it may give the patient inappropriate expectations about the patient-therapist relationship. Thus, clinicians should carefully consider the negative consequences before testing patients.

Researchers in personality assessment have long been puzzled by the high reliance that clinicians place on many common personality devices, despite the continued lack of research evidence for their validity. The explanations offered for this phenomenon have argued that the research designs employed have not involved the sophistication required to capture the complexity of the clinical use of these instruments. Recently, however, an entirely different kind of explanation has been offered for this paradox. In a paper written especially for this volume, Loren and Jean Chapman summarize the research that has led them to propose that much of the test usage *is* basically invalid, and that continued use is a function of an associative artifact which the Chapmans have termed "illusory correlation." This term refers to the common acceptance of a relationship between two classes of events that in reality are not related, and it is seen as analogous to common visual illusions such as the Müller-Lyer illusion. The Chapmans began their work with a series of basic studies in verbal learning which showed that words were likely to be (erroneously) reported as having occurred together if they had a high associative connection (e.g., bacon–

eggs). Their research continued using a series of human figure drawings and a variety of personality-related statements which might be made about them. Their results have strongly suggested that commonly used "signs" (such as the inference of suspiciousness from the drawing of atypical eyes) are simply a product of associations that are held by psychologists and nonpsychologists alike, and cannot necessarily be supported by empirical findings. The Chapmans extended their work to the study of homosexual signs on the Rorschach, a situation in which both valid and invalid test signs could be simultaneously investigated. It will be of interest to see what effect their work will have on the future use of personality assessment procedures which are open to the distorting influence of illusory correlation.

The last two articles in this chapter deal directly with moral issues in personality assessment. In one, Victor Lovell presents a carefully reasoned proposal concerning the ethical use of personality tests. Rather than restricting the *content* of personality tests, as is commonly proposed, Lovell argues for restricting their *function.* He draws an important distinction, also made by other writers, between the *personnel* or selection function of tests, where there is a potential conflict of interest between the assessor and the respondent, and the *client* or counseling function, where the assessor's interests are the same as those of the client. He then presents a number of arguments as to why tests of character (personality tests), as distinct from ability tests, should be used only for client functions, and not for any kind of personnel function. First, Lovell sees the latter uses as questionable from an ethical point of view. Second, from a scientific viewpoint, he argues that whenever response dissimulation may be a significant factor, the validity of the information provided by the test is always suspect. And finally, he believes that psychologists will be serving neither their own best interests nor those of the community if personality tests are used in situations where a conflict of interest may be possible.

The last article contains Gwynn Nettler's terse and startling report of the action of a school board which, in an emotional response to complaints from an unknown number of parents, burned the answer sheets to a battery of psychological tests which had been administered to some 5000 of their ninth-grade students. That emotionality rather than democratic decision making was involved is indicated by the fact that when, in a neighboring school district, parents were given an opportunity to request the deletion of their own children's test responses, only about one percent did so.

Of major significance for our present discussion is the explosiveness of the situation described by Nettler. The event, which took place in 1959, can be viewed as a forerunner to the heated controversies of the 1960s, and it is of interest to note that the lessons that Nettler drew from this local incident were illustrated time and time again during the heat of the national dispute.

1. COMMENTS ON COMMENTS ON TESTING[1]

Garlie A. Forehand

The field of psychological testing appears to have joined advertising, television, bureaucracy, and public school systems as an object for the crusades of socially righteous authors. The charges brought against testing have ranged from sensible to ridiculous. Even the more vituperative criticisms, however, can serve the valuable function of revealing perspectives otherwise hidden from the practitioner deeply involved in his craft. The use of tests in personnel decisions has been most vehemently and widely criticized by Martin L. Gross (1962). The remarks in this paper result from an attempt to sort out and evaluate some of his criticisms, and to examine their implications for the practice of testing.

Many of Gross' comments on the theory and practice of testing neither require nor deserve rebuttal—certainly not in a professional forum. He has simplified a complex set of issues concerning the assessment of human performance—issues of which the technical problems of testing are only a subset; and for this simplified problem he offers a simple solution: the abolition of the practice of testing. He solicits support for this solution by painting the practice of testing in the sombre colors of anxiety. The individual, or as Gross suggests, the victim, is projected into a frightening situation where his livelihood depends on the whims of some shadowy institutional decision-maker poring over his test protocols, while his children, under the watchful eyes of schoolteachers, are recording his intimate family habits on test blanks. The anxious mood is intensified by mordant remarks and rhetorical questions about the motives and competence of testers and the content of assorted discomforting items. To alleviate the state of anxiety thus so carefully nourished, Gross offers a scapegoat: the sinister figure of the brainwatcher.

The brainwatcher is both a varied and a versatile species. His ranks include executives, personnel officers, school administrators, teachers, and psychologists—

SOURCE. Garlie A. Forehand is Professor of Psychology at Carnegie-Mellon University. Dr. Forehand specializes in the psychological investigation of executive performance, intellectual and cognitive processes, and statistical and research design. This article originally appeared in *Educational and Psychological Measurement,* 1964, **24,** 853-859. Reprinted by permission of Duke University Press and the author.

[1] Based on remarks presented in a symposium on "The Use and Misuse of Tests" at the annual meeting of the Pennsylvania Psychological Association, Lancaster, Pa., May 10, 1963. The principal speaker was Martin L. Gross. Discussants were Zigmunt A. Piotrowski and G. A. Forehand. The symposium was arranged and chaired by Richard Teevan.

psychologists who use and make tests, and those who criticize them. The latter either have their eyes diverted momentarily from the cash box, or are engaging in shameless fratricidal backbiting. The traits of the brainwatcher are also varied; the major distinguishing characteristic is the somewhat awesome ability to select, systematically and efficiently, the colorless, other-directed individual for influential positions in our society, while ruthlessly excluding the creative individualist—all by means of invalid tests.

One of the most unfortunate effects of all of this rhetoric is the camouflage of a number of thoughtful, valuable points that Gross has to make. He questions the validity of present personality tests for executive selection—or indeed any selection. He criticizes the theoretical poverty of the trait-names attached to personality scales. He describes intolerable abuses; and while one may doubt the implied typicality of the abuses, they sound plausible as incidents. All of these, and other of Gross' points, have been stated repeatedly, and often less eloquently, by responsible psychologists.

We can certainly grant a number of specific, vexing problems in personality testing, particularly in applications thereof. We can also grant the appropriateness of a concern for the rights of the individuals who undergo such testing. Does personality testing, then, have a legitimate, defensible place in the personnel decisions made in our society?

It is not difficult to find motives for the testing movement that are at once more fundamental and more commendable than those posited by Mr. Gross. The question of what persons in a society are to fill what roles is, as Gardner (1961) has pointed out, an old and important one. A functioning society demands a wide range and diversity of talent, and it demands that its roles be taken by persons who have both the relevant talents and the personal qualities necessary for the appropriate, effective exercise of those talents. Such a range and diversity exists among the members of a society, but individuals are not neatly labeled as to the qualities they possess. If we grant such diversities, and if our society rejects a solution based upon hereditary or other *a prior* stratification, then the matching of persons and roles becomes a gigantic casting process—a process in which auditions will occur, human behavior will be assessed wisely or unwisely, validly or invalidly, with or without the complicity of tests. The fairness of the auditions and their relevance to the performance are reasonable concerns of both the professional psychologist and the aspiring actor.

What function can and should psychological tests serve in the casting? There are circumstances in which testing has achieved widely acknowledged usefulness. I suggest that there are two sets of conditions under which tests have been shown to be effective, both of them understood only after long and laborious experience. They provide a needed context for the consideration of more controversial applications.

The first set of conditions are those in which abilities tests can be used most effectively. Selection of college students is a good example, and there are many others. Ideally, many persons are being selected for a task whose performance is to be evaluated in terms of relatively homogeneous expectations. A quantitative criterion exists, and can be understood in terms of abilities and skills that can be abstracted and mirrored in test items. Under such conditions, a combination of ability (aptitude, achievement, proficiency, etc.) tests, while not eliminating "mistakes," will probably provide the fairest and best economically feasible basis for making decisions. The conditions are approximated sufficiently well and sufficiently often to establish for the abilities test a strategic importance in personnel decisions.

The second set of conditions under which the usefulness of testing is acknowledged is found in the clinic. Here, again stating the conditions ideally, the test is used as one source of information about the emotional and intellectual characteristics of an individual. It is evaluated in the context of professional judgment, based upon observation from several professional perspectives. The decisions that stem from the tests are made for the welfare of the patient. They are not fixed and absolute, but rather are modifiable, and often, if need be, reversible as further information is accumulated. Thus, the information provided by tests is continuously re-evaluated by persons who have the responsibility of being alert to circumstances requiring new interpretation.

There exist other circumstances in which human behavior is assessed—with or without the aid of tests—circumstances not characterized by either of the above sets of ideal conditions. Good examples are executive and professional selection. Here, a meaningful quantitative criterion is lacking; the behaviors that lead to achievement are expected to be individualistic rather than common; within the limited population from which selections are made, variation in ability seems generally unrelated to achievement. At the same time, the decision is not made for the individual's personal welfare, is not evaluated in the context of a diagnostic conference, and is not readily tested and modified as a continuous process. These problems thus are characterized by the ideal conditions for neither the application of abilities tests nor the application of diagnostic clinical judgment. Both approaches have been tried in this area. The regression equations of abilities testers have been computed, often with farfetched variables as predictors, and usually with questionable measures serving as criteria. Clinical judgment applied to test protocols has produced personality analyses of candidates, and, in turn, recommendations based upon clinicians' assumptions about the traits relevant to personnel decisions. Both approaches have been disappointing; and it is in this shadowland that Gross finds his greatest cause for complaint.

Gross carries his criticism of personality testing in these situations further. He believes that personality testing is both unscientific and immoral. Unscientific because of faulty statistical claims, nonreplication of results, and the general atmosphere of hucksterism that surrounds it; immoral because its false predictions produce human misfortune, and because it results in discrimination on the basis of personality traits, which Gross sees as akin to discrimination on the basis of race or religion.

But in rejecting a solution, the critic has left us with the dilemma—the casting dilemma. How shall we select and place individuals in positions assuring fairness to the individual, and a reasonable expectation of competent performance of the roles? The question is a relevant one, both for psychologists and their critics.

Suppose we have the responsibility for filling a few positions from a sample of many applicants. The applicants all have the experience and educational requisites and all have demonstrated sufficient ability on the best set of ability tests we can assemble. It seems to me that we have four alternative strategies for solving our problem. The first might be called a "dog fight" strategy: permit applicants to compete for a position until the best man wins. A second would be to leave the decisions to the intuitive judgment of a person or persons with that assigned responsibility. A third would be to assign applicants randomly to the available positions. And finally, the fourth strategy is to make further systematic observations of the behavior of the applicants, in short to use tests in some form.[2]

The first strategy—the dog fight—would, I believe, be considered unacceptable and unworkable both by psychologists and their critics, except, perhaps, in limited conditions in which several employees are being considered for a single promotion.

The second—the intuitive judgment strategy—carries with it the familiar problems of lack of control over competence of the judges, the limited range of available information, and the dangers of personal bias, favoritism, even nepotism. Even if the bias problem could be eliminated, it seems doubtful that the procedure could avoid the scientific defects attributed by Gross to personality tests; and his moral objection to discriminating on the basis of personality characteristics would apply as much to this strategy as to tests—perhaps more.

The third alternative—random selection—has the merit of impartiality. If we do not select according to relevant characteristics, at least we do not reject according to irrelevant ones. Some such strategy is posited by utility theory as a baseline against which to evaluate strategies involving tests or other additional information (Cronbach and Gleser, 1957).

If we adopt the random selection strategy as a fixed one rather than as a baseline, we are assuming that no further observations of personal characteristics will contribute to the values of the selection situation. Those values include those of the employers and thus refer to the validity or utility of a strategy from the employers' point of view. But they include individual and social values as

[2]Another set of alternatives would involve changing the position to fit the persons. The need for and problems in evaluating behavior would be essentially the same as those discussed here.

well. If a person's interests, motives, and other personal characteristics are relevant to the satisfaction he will get from a particular job and to the likelihood of his using his abilities maximally, then information about these qualities may contribute to the achievement of his own values.

The fourth strategy, testing, rests upon two postulates: that whether a person can or will exercise his abilities in a given situation depends at least in part upon personal characteristics, and that these personal characteristics can be inferred from observations of behavior in standard situations. The question that our critics have raised—and answered with a premature negative—is whether these postulates provide a workable basis for the establishment of conditions under which personality testing can be effective aids to decision. The question has both short-range and long-range facets.

In evaluating the reasonableness of using tests at the present and in the immediate future, irresponsibility and abuse are troublesome problems, but they are not matters of issue between psychologists and their critics. All parties agree that irresponsibility is intolerable, and that measures can and should be taken to control it. But clearly not all psychologists and executives who use tests are irresponsible. The point of issue is whether there is a valid basis for the *responsible* use of tests. Accumulated research findings do not lend encouragement to confident routine application of test results to executive and professional selection (Tagiuri, 1961). As we have noted, these areas of application are not well adapted to the testing models that we can apply most confidently. The rationale for using tests at present that I find most convincing can be stated something like this: a person, not a test, is responsible for a personnel decision. A psychologist or executive who accepts that responsibility ought to use all available sources of information, personality tests included, that in his judgment help him make a fair and useful decision. Such a formulation places the responsibility for a decision clearly upon the individual. And evaluation of a decision is an evaluation of the individual who makes it; the individual cannot blame tests for his failures, and need not credit them with his success.

The long range question is this: can research and experience provide a rationale for testing that is more viable than the personal judgment of the decision maker? The question is clearly not one that can be answered by one or a few investigators in one or a few years. The assumption that existing models can be readily applied to these refractory areas has probably hindered the research needed to provide answers to it. The attempt to answer it will not commit us to existing tests, existing methods, existing concepts, or indeed to existing definitions of the roles to be filled. Recent developments may enable us to foresee some of the directions that the inquiry is likely to take. The "criterion problem" will probably have to be tackled by separating observations of behavior from evaluation of behavior in performance appraisal. Assessment systems will probably include systematic appraisal of environmental characteristics among the data to be collected. The usefulness of decisions based on tests will probably be evaluated against decisions that could be made without the tests. The implementation of these suggestions—all found in recent personnel psychology literature—as well as the invention of new procedures, will require ingenuity at least equal to that of the developers of the earliest ability tests. The effort can result in extensive new values—both practical and social—for psychological tests.

2. MMPI: PROFESSIONAL USE BY PROFESSIONAL PEOPLE

Starke R. Hathaway

This long letter was prompted by a courteous inquiry that I received. The inquiry referred to the use of the MMPI as an aid in the selection of policemen from among applicants. It was pointed out that there are laws against inquiry about religious affiliation and the specific issue was the presence in the MMPI of items relating to religion.

Letter to Mr. R.

First I would like to express my appreciation of your reasonably expressed inquiry about the MMPI as possibly offensive in the statements that relate to religious activities and which might provide personal information on which discriminatory acts might be based. Because of sporadic public antagonism to psychological testing, and in view of our mutual concern for our civil liberties, I am going to answer you at considerable length and with unusual care. I shall send copies of this answer to the Psychological Corporation and to others who may be concerned. Let me assure you at the outset that I believe I am proceeding from a considered position rather than from a defensive attitude that could lead me to irrationally protect the MMPI, other such tests, or psychologists in general. I believe that I would be among the first to criticize some of the uses to

SOURCE. Starke R. Hathaway is Professor and Head of the Division of Clinical Psychology at the University of Minnesota Medical School. Dr. Hathaway, the co-developer (with J. C. McKinley) of the Minnesota Multiphasic Personality Inventory, has published many articles on the MMPI, on the efficiency of clinical assessment, and on the development of the profession of clinical psychology. This article originally appeared in the *American Psychologist,* 1964, **19,** 204-210. Reprinted by permission of the American Psychological Association and the author.

which tests are put, and some of those who use them improperly. I must also immediately make it clear that I am antagonistic to ignorant attacks upon tests. Tests are not offensive elements; the offensive elements, if any, come with the misuse of tests. To attack tests is, to a certain extent, comparable to an attack upon knives. Both good and bad use of knives occurs because they are sharp instruments. To eliminate knives would, of course, have a limiting effect upon the occurrence of certain hostile acts, but it would also greatly limit the activities of surgeons. I simply discriminate between the instrument and the objectives and applications of the persons who wield it. I am calling attention to the difference between a switchblade knife, which is good for nothing but attack, and a scalpel knife, good for healing purposes but which can also be used as a weapon. I hope that no one will think that any test was devised in the same spirit that switchblade knives were devised. It is absurd if someone holds the belief that psychologists malignantly developed instruments such as the MMPI for use against the welfare of man, including of course man's personal liberties and rights. But if the MMPI and such tests have origins analogous to the scalpel, and are really perversely used to man's disadvantage, we are properly concerned. Let me turn to a history of the MMPI items about which you have inquired.

I should begin with an account of the origin of the MMPI itself. I believe I am competent to do this, and I hope you will see that its origins were motivated toward virtue as I have suggested above. In about 1937, J.C. McKinley, then head of the Department of Neuropsychiatry of the Medical School at the University of Minnesota, supported me in a venture which grew out of a current problem in our psychopathic hospital. The problem lay in the fact that insulin therapy as a treatment method for certain forms of mental disease had just become a widespread method of treatment. Different clinics were finding highly varied values. Some reported the treatment to be exceedingly effective; others said it was ineffective. The treatment was somewhat dangerous to patients, and it was exceedingly expensive in terms of hospitalization and nursing care. McKinley happened to be one of the neuropsychiatrists of the time who felt that more careful investigation should be undertaken before such treatments were applied, and in particular before we used them on our patients.

It occurred to us that the difficulty in evaluation of insulin treatment lay largely in the fact that there was no good way to be assured that the patients treated by this method in one clinic were like those treated in another clinic. This was due to the fact that the estimations of the nature of a person's mental illness and of its severity were based upon professional judgment, and could vary with the training background of the particular psychiatrist as well as with his personal experiences. Obviously, if the patients treated at one center were not like those treated at another center, the outcome of treatment might be different. At that time there was no psychological test available that would have helped to remove the diagnostic decisions on the patients in two clinics from the personal biases of the local staffs. There was no way that our hospital staff could select a group of patients for the new treatment who would be surely comparable in diagnosis and severity of illness to those from some other setting. It became an obvious possibility that one might devise a personality test which, like intelligence tests, would somewhat stabilize the identification of the illness and provide an estimate of its severity. Toward this problem the MMPI research was initiated.

I have established that decisions about the kind and severity of mental illness depend upon the psychological examinations of the psychiatrists and other professional persons. The items upon which the judgments are based constitute the symptoms of mental maladjustment or illness. Such symptoms have for many, many years been listed in the textbooks of psychiatry and clinical psychology that treat with mental disorder. These symptoms are verbal statements from or about the patient. The simplest and most obvious form of these symptoms are statements that confess feelings of unhappiness, depression, and the like. The statements may also be less personal, as in complaints about one's lot in life and about the inability to find employment or the mistreatment by others.

In summary, the symptoms of mental illness and unhappiness are represented in verbal complaints or statements that relate to personal feelings or personal experiences or reactions to job and home. It should be immediately apparent that unlike most physical illnesses, these verbally presented complaints or symptoms usually do not permit direct observation by others. If a patient reports a painful nodule or abdominal pain, the reported pain can usually be observed by some physical or nonverbal means that lends credence to the complaint. Many symptoms of mental illness are contrastingly difficult to observe by nonverbal means. It is almost impossible to establish that the person presenting the symptom is actually suffering from a distortion of his psychologically healthy mental state by some psychological complex. There is much arbitrariness even in the statement, "I am unhappy." Frequently no physical observation can be brought to bear upon the statement. The complainant may look unhappy and may even add that he is suicidal, yet friends and the examiner can agree that he is, "just asking for sympathy, is no worse off than the average." There is no way of solidly deciding what the words really mean. This point is crucial to what I am writing. If it is not clear at this point, reference books on semantics should be consulted. S. I. Hayakawa would be a good source.

I know of no method which will permit us to absolutely assess unhappiness or mental illness, either as to kind or severity, unless we start from inescapable symptoms that are verbally expressed and subject to the vagaries in the personal connotations of words and phrases. In initiating the research upon what was to produce the MMPI, we collected as many as we could find of the symptomatic statements recognized by authorities as indicative of unhappiness and mental illness. There were hundreds of these statements. We had at one time well over a thousand of them. Every one of these symptomatic statements had already been written into the literature or had been used as a practical bit of clinical evidence in the attempt to understand patients. I repeat this because I want to thoroughly emphasize that every item in the MMPI came from assumed relationships to the assessment of human beings for better diagnosis and treatment of possible mental illness.

Now with all this preamble I am prepared to discuss the particular items that you have highlighted in your letter. It happens that, among the many items collected and finally selected to make up the MMPI, there were at least 19 relating to religion in one way or another (Table 1).

Table 1

	Male		Female	
	True	No Answer	True	No Answer
I am very religious (more than most people).	8	9	11	9
Religion gives me no worry.	83	4	70	4
I go to church almost every week.	42	3	52	4
I pray several times every week.	50	3	83	2
I read in the Bible several times a week.	21	5	30	3
I feel sure that there is only one true religion.	49	8	51	11
I have no patience with people who believe there is only one true religion.	56	4	47	10
I believe there is a God.	92	5	96	2
I believe there is a devil and a hell in afterlife.	63	14	67	14
I believe in a life hereafter.	76	12	87	7
I believe in the second coming of Christ.	57	18	68	12
Christ performed miracles such as changing water into wine.	69	16	77	15
The only miracles I know of are simply tricks that people play on one another.	37	10	27	14
A minister can cure disease by praying and putting his hand on your head.	4	10	5	11
Everything is turning out just like the prophets of the Bible said it would.	52	29	54	32
My soul sometimes leaves my body.	8	18	5	12
I am a special agent of God.	14	13	16	21
I have had some very unusual religious experiences.	20	5	13	2
I have been inspired to a program of life based on duty which I have since carefully followed.	42	14	50	15

I have listed these items to remind you again of the ones you cited, and I have added others that may further illustrate what I am saying. Now you have asked why we included these statements on religion among the possible symptoms of psychological maladjustment. Why should these items still appear in the MMPI?

In the first instance, the subject matter evidenced in the symptoms of depressed or otherwise mentally disturbed persons often largely centers in religion. There is a well-recognized pattern of psychological distortion to which we apply the term religiosity. When we use the word "religiosity," we indicate a symptomatic pattern wherein the process of an intercurrent psychological maladjustment is evidenced by extremes of religious expression that are out of the usual context for even the deeply religious person. A bishop friend of mine once illustrated the problem he sometimes had in this connection by his account of a parishioner who had routinely given a tithe as his offering toward support of the church, but who, within a few weeks, had increased the amount he gave until it was necessary for him to embezzle money for his weekly offering. Surely, my friend said, there is more here than ordinary devotion; there is something which should be considered from another frame of reference. In this anecdote there is an element of the symptomatic pattern, religiosity. But, as is true of nearly every other aspect of human personality to which the MMPI refers, no one item will ordinarily establish this distortion of the ordinarily meaningful position of religion. And no one item can be used to detect the problem as it occurs in various persons. Two persons rarely express even their usual religious feelings in identical ways.

It never occurred to us in selecting these items for the MMPI that we were asking anything relative to the particular religion of our patients. It obviously did not occur to us that there were other than the Christian orientation wherein religiosity might be observed. Because of this oversight on our part, several of our MMPI symptoms that we assumed were indicative of religiosity happen to be obviously related to the Christian religion, although we find that most persons simply translate to their own orientation if it is different. I should hasten to add that although these symptoms were hoped to be specific to persons who suffer from religiosity, they have not all turned out that way. Not every aspect of religion is at times a symptom of mental illness. Certainly it is obvious that there is nothing symptomatic in admitting to one's personal acceptance or rejection of several of the items. The point at which a group of items becomes consistent in suggesting symptoms is subtle to distinguish. As my bishop friend's story illustrated, it is not unusual that one contributes to religious work even though there exists a doubtful extreme. As I will show below, all these items are endorsed or rejected by some ordinary, normal people. If any of the items have value toward clinical assessment, the value comes in combination with other items which probably will not seem to relate to religion.

The MMPI, which started out so small and inconspicuously, has become a world-known and -used instrument. We did not expect this outcome. If I were to select new items, I would again include items that related to religiosity. I would this time, of course, try to avoid the implication that the religiosity occurred only among adherents to the Christian faith. I am obviously unhappy about the limited applicability of these items, but I am, in the same sense, unhappy about other items in the MMPI. A considerable number of the items have been challenged by other groups from other standpoints. By this I mean only to remind those concerned about these religiosity items that there are frankly stated items on sex, there are items on body functions, there are items on certain occupations; in fact, there are items on most every aspect of psychological life that can be symptomatic of maladjustment and unhappiness. If the psychologist cannot use these personal items to aid in the assessment of people, he suffers as did the Victorian physician who had to examine his female patients by feeling the pulse in the delicate hand thrust from behind a screen. I shall come back to this point later, but it is obvious that if we were making a new MMPI, we would again be faced either with being offensive to subgroupings of people by personal items they object to or, if we did not include personal items and were inoffensive, we would have lost the aim of the instrument.

One may protest that the MMPI is intended for the patient, the mentally ill person, not applicants to schools, high-school children, or to those being considered for jobs. I cannot give a general defense of every such use, but this is a time when preventive health is being emphasized. We urge everyone to get chest X rays and to take immunizing shots. We are now beginning to advocate general surveys with such psychological instruments as the MMPI. The basic justification is the same. We hope to identify potential mental breakdown or delinquency in the school child before he must be dragged before us by desperate parents or by other authority. We hope to hire police, who are given great power over us, with assurance that those we put on the rolls should have good personal qualities for the job. This is not merely to protect us, this also is preventive mental health, since modern job stability can trap unwary workers into placements that leave them increasingly unhappy and otherwise maladjusted. If the personality of an applicant is not appropriate to the job, neither employer nor applicant should go ahead. We have always recognized the employer's use of this principle in his right to personal interview with applicants. Since the items and responses are on record, the MMPI and such devices could be considered to be a more fair method of estimation than the personal interview, and, when they are machine scored, they make possible much greater protection from arbitrary personal judgments and the open ended questions that are standard for personal interviews.

It seems to me that the MMPI examination can be rather comparable to the physical examination for selection of persons. One would not wish to hire a person with a bad heart when the job required behavior that was dangerous to him. I think it would be equally bad to hire a person as a policeman whose psychological traits were inappropriate and then expect him to do dangerous things or shoot to kill as a policeman is expected to do. There is, from physical and psychological examinations, a protection to the person being hired as well as to those hiring him. This is not meant as an argument for the use of the MMPI in every placement that requires special skills or special personality traits. I am arguing a general point.

I would next like to take up MMPI items to bring out a new line of evidence which, I am sorry to say, is not familiar to some psychologists, but which is of importance in giving you an answer to your questions. Turn again to the above items, particularly to the "True" response frequencies. We will look at implications about the people taking the MMPI as we interpret the True frequencies of response for these items.

Before we do so, we should consider the source of the frequency figures. The males and females who provided these standard data, which are the basis for all MMPI standards, were persons who came to the University Hospitals bringing patients or who were around the hospitals at the time when we were collecting data. Only those were tested who were not under a doctor's care and who could be reasonably assumed to be normal in mind and body. These persons, whom we call the normal adult cross-section group, came from all over Minnesota, from every socioeconomic and educational level; there is reason to believe that they are a proper representation of the rank and file people of Minnesota. It is probably well known that, in the main, Minnesota population was drawn from North European stock, is largely Christian in background, and has a rather small number in the several minority groups. Certainly, it can hardly be said that this population is unduly weighted with extremists in the direction of overemphasis upon religion or in atheism or in other belief characteristics. Probably one would expect this population to be rather more religious than the average for all the states. Finally, the majority of the persons who provided these basic norms were married persons and most were parents. Data given in the table can be found in the fundamental book on the MMPI, *An MMPI Handbook* by Dahlstrom and Welsh (1960).

But now consider the items. Let us assume, as is often naively assumed, that when one answers an item one tells the truth about oneself. Of course, there is no requirement that those who take the MMPI should tell the truth, and this is a very important point. Also, I have tried to establish that truth is a very complicated semantic concept. But let us assume for the moment that people do tell the truth as they see it. Take the item, "I go to church almost every week." According to the data given, 42% of the men and 52% of the women go to church almost every week. Now these data are representative of the whole state. I am sure that ministers of the state would be gratified if all these people were reporting accurately. Parenthetically, I suppose that "church" was read as "synagogue" or "temple" without much trouble. But I do not know what percentage of people are actually estimated to go to some church almost every week. At any rate I cannot conceive that 42% of the men of the state of Minnesota are in church nearly every week even if 52% of the women are. I even cannot conceive that half of the men in Minnesota and 83% of the women actually pray several times a week. I might imagine that 21% of the men and 30% of the women would read in the Bible several times a week. This would represent about one-fifth of all the men and about one-third of all the women. My real impression is that people simply do not know that much about the Bible. However, take the next item. Here it says that one feels sure there is only one true religion. To this about half of the men and half of the women answered True. Perhaps these might be considered bigoted, but what of the ones who have obviously answered false? There seems to be a great deal of religious tolerance here; about half of the persons of Minnesota do not even express a belief that there is only one true religion.

It is true that a high percentage say they believe there is a God. This seems to be a noncommittal item, since most people are aware that God has many meanings. The item which follows it, however, which permits denying or accepting a belief in a devil and hell in afterlife, is quite interesting. Twenty-three percent of men and 19% of women reject this belief. By contrast, a life hereafter is denied by 24% of men and by 13% of women. The second coming of Christ is expected by only 57% of men and 68% of women if we accept what these figures seem to say. Again, with reversal, Christ as a miracle worker is doubted by 31% of men and by 23% of women. Stated more directly, 37% of men and 27% of women come straight out and say that miracles were not performed. The item apparently includes Old and New Testament sources among others. On down in the list, one finds that only 14% of men and 16% of women believe themselves to be special agents of God.

I think I have gone over enough of these items to provide a suggestion of what I am going to next point out. But I would like to add two more MMPI items in sharper illustration of the point. These two additional items have nothing obvious to do with religion. The first of them is, "I almost never dream," and the second is, "I dream frequently." One of the first things we found in the early studies of MMPI items was that the same person frequently answered True to both these items. When asked about the seeming contradiction, such a person would respond, among other possibilities, by saying to the first item that surely he had very few dreams. But, coming to the next item, he changed his viewpoint to say that he dreamed frequently as compared to some of the people he knew. This shift of emphasis led us to recognize that, in addition to the general semantic problem developed above, when people respond to items, they also do not usually respond with the connotations we expect. Apparently even if the people are telling a truth of some kind, one would need an interview with them to know what they really intend to report by answering True or False. I suppose this is similar to the problem of the oath of allegiance over which some people are so concerned. One may state that he is loyal to the United States, for example, yet really mean that he is deeply convinced that its government should be overthrown and that, with great loyalty to his country, he believes revolution to be the only salvation for the country. However much we might object to it, this belief would permit a person to swear to his loyalty in complete honesty. I think most everyone is aware of this problem about oaths, and it is a routine one with MMPI item responses.

In summary of all this, if one wished to persecute those who by their answers to these items seemed inconsistent with some religious or atheistic pattern of beliefs, there would be an embarrassingly large number of ordinary people in Minnesota who would be open to suspicion both ways. In reality, the responses made to these items have many variations in truth and meaning. And it would betray considerable ignorance of the practical psychology of communication if any absolute reliance were placed on responses.

As a final but most significant point relative to these items, I should point out that administration of the MMPI requires that those who are taking the test be clearly informed that they may omit any item they do not wish to answer for whatever purpose. I have never seen any studies that have drawn conclusions from the omission of particular items by a particular person. We found that items among these that are being considered were unusually frequently omitted. You may notice this in the No Answer columns. One-third of all the respondents failed to answer the item relative to the Bible and the prophets, for example. This is a basic fact about the MMPI and such tests, and I cannot see why this freedom will not permit to each person the latitude to preserve his privacy if he is afraid. Still again I would add that, in many settings, possibly nearly every setting, where the MMPI is used in group administration, those who take it are permitted to refuse the whole test. I admit that this might seem prejudicial, and I suspect that if any one chooses to protect himself, he will do it by omitting items rather than by not taking the test at all. Is refusal to take the test any different from refusing to subject oneself to an employment or admission interview by a skilled interviewer? I think that some people who have been writing about the dangers of testing must have an almost magical belief in tests. Sometimes, when I feel so at a loss in attempting to help someone with a psychological problem, I wish that personality tests were really that subtle and powerful.

Groups of items called scales, formed into patterns called profiles, are the useful product of tests like the MMPI. I note that in your inquiry you show an awareness that the MMPI is usually scored by computers. The scales that are used for most interpretation include 10 "clinical" scales. These are the ones that carry most of the information. Several other scales indicate whether the subject understood and followed the directions. No one of these main scales has less than 30 items in it and most of them have many more than 30. The scores from the machine come back not only anonymously indicating the number of items answered in a way that counts on the scale, but the scores are usually already transformed into what we call *T* or standard scores. These *T* scores are still more remote from the particular items that make up a scale. The graphic array of *T* scores for the scales are finally printed into the profile.

In this connection, there is a very pretty possibility offered by the development of computer scoring. If we wish to take advantage of the presumed advantages of the use of tests, yet be assured that particular item responses shall not be considered, then we only need to be assured that those using the test do not score it, must send it straightway to the computer center, and, in the end, receive back only the profiles which are all that should be used in any case. The original test may be destroyed.

The scales of the profile were not arbitrarily set up. The MMPI is an experimentally derived instrument. If an item counts on a scale, I want to make it very clear that that item counts, not because some clinician or somebody thought that the item was significant for measuring something about human personality, but it counts because in the final analysis well-diagnosed groups of maladjusted, sometimes mentally ill persons answered the item with an average frequency differing from the average frequency of the normative group that I have used for the above illustrative data. This is an exceedingly significant point and is probably least often understood by those who have not had psychometric training. No one read or composed these items to decide what it meant if one of them were answered True or False. The meanings of the items came from the fact that persons with a certain kind of difficulty answered in an average way different from the "normal" standard. For example, the item "I go to church almost every week" is counted on a scale for estimating the amount of depression. We did not just decide that going to church was related to depression. We had the response frequencies from men who complained that they were depressed. They answered True with a frequency of only 20%. You will note that the normals answered True with a frequency of 42%–22% more often. Now this difference also turned up for women who were depressed. We adopted a False response to this item as a count on the depression scale of the MMPI. We do not even now know why depressed people say they go to church less often. Note that you are not depressed if you say False to this one item. Actually, 55% of the normals answered False. Use of the item for an MMPI scale depended on the fact that even more of the depressed persons answered False and so if you say False you have added one item more in common with depressed people than with the normals despite the fact that more than half the normals answered as you did.

Even psychologists very familiar with the MMPI cannot tell to which scale or scales an item belongs without looking it up. People often ask for a copy of a test so they can cite their objections to items they think objectionable, and they assume that the meaning of the item is obvious and that they can tell how it is interpreted. I am often asked what specified items mean. I do not know because the scoring of the scales has become so abstracted that I have no contact with items.

One more point along this line. Only 6 of the above 19 items are counted on one of the regular scales that are mostly used for personality evaluation. Four more are used on a measure that is only interpreted in estimation of the ability of the subject to follow directions and to read well enough. In fact, about 200 of the whole set of items did not end up on any one of the regularly used scales. But, of course, many of these 200 other items occur on one or another of the many experimental MMPI scales that have been published.

We cannot change or leave out any items or we lose an invaluable heritage of research in mental health. To change even a comma in an item may change its meaning. I would change the words of some items, omit some, and add new ones if I could. A new test should be devised, but its cost would be on the order of a $100,000 and we are not at this time advanced enough so that the new one would be enough better to compensate for the loss of the research and diagnostic value of the present MMPI even in view of its manifest weaknesses.

The subject of professional training brings me to my next line of response. It is appropriate that the public should be aware of the uses of such tests as the MMPI, but I have repeatedly pointed out that it is far more important that the public should be aware of the persons who are using the test and of the uses to which it is put. In this context, the distributor of the MMPI, the Psychological Corporation of New York City, accepts and practices the ethical principles for test distributors that have been promulgated by the American Psychological Association. These rules prohibit the sale of tests to untrained or incompetent persons. Use or possession of the MMPI by others is prohibited but, since this carries no present penalty, the distributor is helpless except for his control of the supply. Tests, as I have said above, are not like switchblade knives, designed to be used against people; they offer potential contributions to happiness. And I cannot believe that a properly accredited clinical psychologist or psychiatrist or physician who may use the MMPI would under any circumstances use it to the disadvantage of the persons being tested. If he does so, he is subject to the intraprofessional ethical-practice controls that are explicit and carry sanctions against those of us who transgress. The MMPI provides data which, like certain medical data, are considered by many to be helpful in guidance and analysis and understanding of people. Of course, in the making of this point, I am aware that there is no absolute meaning to what is ethical. What one group may think should be done about a certain medical-examination disclosure may be considered by another group to be against the patient's interest. I cannot do more than extend this ubiquitous ethical dilemma to the use of the personality test.

The essential point is that such tests should not be used except in professional circles by professional people and that the data it provides should be held confidential and be protected within the lawful practice of ethics. When these requirements are not met, there is reason for complaint. I hope I have made it clear that it is also my conviction that the MMPI will hurt no one, adult or child, in the taking of it. Without defending all uses of it, I surely defend it, and instruments like it, when they are in proper hands and for proper purposes. Monachesi and I have tested 15,000 ninth-grade school children with the MMPI. This took us into public schools all over the state, even into some parochial schools. In all of this testing, we had no difficulties with children, parents, or teachers except for a few courteous inquiries. We are now publishing what we hope will be significant data from this work, data bearing on delinquency and school dropout. We believe that this work demonstrates that properly administered, properly explained, and properly protected tests are acceptable to the public.

At the beginning of this statement I warned that I was going to make it quite long because I felt deeply on the matter. I hope I have not sounded as though I were merely being defensive, protecting us from those who would burn tests and who for good reasons are exceedingly sensitive about psychological testing. I am apologetic if I have sounded too much like the professional scientist and have seemed to talk down to the issue or to be too minutely explicit. I have not meant to insult by being unduly simple, but I have felt that I had to expand adequately on the points. As for psychologists who are those most widely applying such tests, I am aware that the public will look with increasing seriousness upon those who are entrusted with problems of mental health and the assessment of human actions.

I will end with a repetition of my feeling that, while it is desirable for the public to require ethical practices of those using tests, the public may be reassured that the psychologists, physicians, and others who use these new tests will be even more alert to apply the intraprofessional controls that are a requisite to professional responsibility. But I must emphasize that it is not to public advantage to so limit these professional judgments that we fail to progress in mental-health research and applications from lack of freedom to use the best instruments we have and to develop better ones.

3. PSYCHOLOGICAL TESTING: TREATMENT AND RESEARCH IMPLICATIONS

Louis Breger

Psychological testing has long been the unique speciality of the clinical psychologist, a fact that stems from the particular history of the field. Recent developments bring out a number of conflicts between the assumptions of this traditional emphasis and clinical practice. For example, Meehl (1960) has reported that only 17% of psychotherapists (N = 168 drawn from a "wide spectrum of orientations") believe that the prior knowledge contributed by testing is of much value to them. While this change in emphasis has come about first at the level of practice, the recent conference on training in clinical psychology (Hoch, Ross, & Winder, 1966) indicated that a reappraisal of the role of psychological testing in teaching and clinical training programs is also in progress. In these and other ways, it seems apparent that conflict exists between the traditional emphasis on testing and current practices. An examination of the history of this conflict and of the issues involved may allow us to break free of certain outmoded assumptions and practices.

Testing should be oriented in two broad directions: first, toward the practical question of what to do about persons and their problems—what might be called treatment in the most general sense—second, toward the comprehension of the nature of problems and effects of treatment—a function which might be labeled research or theoretical understanding. Traditional models of testing have been tied to the concepts of diagnosis and selection, both of which may prove largely inappropriate to much of the data that the clinical psychologist is faced with and, more particularly, will be faced with in the future. Similarly, a good deal of the traditional research in the testing area (e.g., the innumerable Rorschach studies or the vast literature with intelligence tests directed at controversies over IQ constancy and the like) has not led to significant advances in theoretical understanding. To anticipate, it will be argued that assessment, built around the clinical-therapeutic interview, provides a more appropriate model for practice with that large group of persons referred for personality "diagnosis." First, let us consider a common justification for testing, that it constitutes an essential part of the clinical psychologist's "role."

SOURCE. Louis Breger is currently Associate Professor of Psychiatry and Visiting Associate Professor of Psychology at the University of California, Berkeley. After receiving his doctoral degree from Ohio State University, Dr. Breger was on the faculty of the University of Oregon and on the staff of the Langley Porter Neuropsychiatric Institute. This article originally appeared in the *Journal of Consulting and Clinical Psychology*, 1968, **32**, 176-181 and is reprinted by permission of the American Psychological Association and the author.

Testing as Part of the Psychologist's Professional Role

Deciding how best to help persons can be a very stress-producing affair, particularly when the state of understanding about persons, problems, and treatments is so far from complete. Clinical psychologists, along with their psychiatric and social-work colleagues, are, nevertheless, expected to function as experts in dealing with the persons and problems that face them in mental hospitals, outpatient clinics, counseling centers, and the like. Since it is almost impossible for anyone to continually question everything in his day-to-day functioning, psychologists and others react to this stressful state of affairs by falling back on some generally defined professional role which dictates in what areas they are experts, what kind of activities they will perform, what kind of language they will speak, how their relationships with other professionals will be structured, and other similar considerations. This is inevitable, though the pressure for it is probably greater in situations where there is much uncertainty about how to function ("treat" patients) and about who can function best. In this respect, we find psychiatrists falling back on certain historically established aspects of the physician role. (Physicians treat the sick—hence, they are the ones who must treat the "mentally ill"; physicians have the final responsibility—hence, they must be in charge of the ward or the "psychiatric team.") Similarly, we find clinical psychologists relying on certain historically established role characteristics in defining their functions and their areas of expertness vis-à-vis other professionals.

Psychological testing becomes especially valued in this regard because it is an area in which the psychologist is the unquestioned expert, as contrasted with an activity such as interviewing, where he must compete with psychiatrists, social workers, and others. Thus, testing becomes a key activity in defining the clinical psychologist's role in a way that gives him a sense of expertise in a distinctly outlined area with its own jargon, research literature, and special prerogatives.

Certainly not all, or even most, clinical psychologists use psychological testing solely as a rationalization for their lesser status or to gain security by reliance on a clearly defined set of routines, but these factors do enter to some degree in the functioning of many. More to the point is the inappropriateness of professional role considerations as a justification for psychological testing. To say that psychologists should test because this is their professional role makes little sense; it is like saying that barbers should bleed people because this is their professional role or that psychiatrists should give lobotomies because this is their role. Obviously this is a line of reasoning that can be used to perpetuate any existing form of practice, no matter how inappropriate or harmful. Psychological testing, like any other technique, must be evaluated in terms of the adequacy of its basic assumptions, its helpfulness to persons seeking treatment, and its contributions to actual decision making about patients, problems, and treatments. It makes little sense for the psychologist to perpetuate his role as tester in a state hospital where all patients receive the same treatment (or lack of treatment), regardless of what the psychological tests reveal, or in a situation where the individuals making decisions about treatment do not read the psychological report until after they have made their decisions. Testing may also be inappropriate when sources of information that may be more directly related to the decisions to be made can be quickly obtained (e.g., age, job history, length and number of previous hospitalizations).

Historical Antecedents

Beginning with Freud and continuing through the variety of psychotherapies that have branched out from psychoanalysis, there has been a merger of diagnosis with treatment. The psychoanalytic method of therapy is the method of personality "diagnosis." Sullivan's psychiatric interview is both "diagnosis" and "treatment." (Roger's client-centered approach, arising outside the medical framework, has never stressed the need for "diagnosis" before treatment.) The notion of separating treatment and diagnosis derives from different historical sources, as Gill, Newman, and Redlich (1954) point out, and cannot be justified within the frameworks of the major therapies themselves. Two such historical influences may be discerned: *(a)* a belief in the necessity of diagnosing patients before treating them, essentially a reassertion, following the psychodynamic trend begun by Freud, of the medical identification of psychiatry[1]; and *(b)* a belief in the value of accurate "selection," derived from the mental testing movement within psychology.

The medical diagnostic position is identified with workers such as Schafer (1948) and Rapaport (1954), who used tests to generate descriptions of personality or psychological functioning. Their identification with medical psychoanalysis has led many in this tradition to advocate complete psychological assessment as a part of the comprehensive diagnostic work-up. But, as Szasz (1965) points out, such a commitment to "diagnosis" is logically inconsistent with the basic premises of psychoanalytic therapy.

The belief in the value of selection springs from the mental testing movement, so prominent in clinical psychology's past, as typified by work with the MMPI and the value placed on accurate prediction (whether clinical or actuarial). The confluence of these traditions has reinforced a belief in the value of testing prior

[1]A parallel reassertion is represented by the insistence of the orthodox psychoanalytic institutes that their candidates have medical training despite the almost wholly nonmedical nature of both psychoanalytic training and therapy (see Eissler, 1965).

to treatment, a belief which begs the central questions concerning test usefulness and validity.

Testing, whether personality descriptive or selection oriented, is wasteful and may even be harmful insofar as it is separated from, and makes no practical contribution to, treatment. Many persons are most in need of, as well as most receptive to, treatment when they make their initial contact with a treating agency. A diagnostic enterprise that is separated from treatment may function as a roadblock at this stage. Commitments to "diagnosis" before treatment or to "selection" both reinforce the fixed position or status of existing treatments. This is inappropriate in a field where little solid knowledge about the relationship between patient-treatment interactions exists. These commitments further the illusion that once a patient is diagnosed or selected, differential treatment will be forthcoming. An honest look at clinical practice reveals that in most instances differential treatment does not follow from differential categorization based on psychological tests. The main reason that testing is not integrally related to treatment is that the central implicit assumption underlying testing—that one will know what to do with the patient, how to "treat" him, once he has been "diagnosed" or assessed—is not true. The basic question of what sort of treatments (insight psychotherapy, group psychotherapy, family therapy, help in getting a divorce, help in changing jobs, etc.) work with what sort of people and with what effects or outcomes remains the central unanswered research question in the clinical assessment area. These points may be illuminated by a consideration of their implications for treatment and research.

Treatment

The following discussion is directed at those persons who voluntarily seek psychological help. Their disturbances may range from mild adjustment problems to severe psychosis, and their attitudes towards treatment may be resolute or conflicted; yet in a basic sense these voluntary patients differ from persons who are referred because someone other than themselves—whether parent, friend, or social agency—has decided that they have "psychological problems." Voluntary patients compose the bulk of the population which applies to outpatient clinics, counseling centers, private practitioners, and community mental health programs. What is done with such persons at the time of their initial contact is frequently of great importance. Erikson (1964) directs his attention to what he terms "the problem of the lost momentum of initial commitment." He states:

> Hospitalized patients, having been committed, are often ready to commit themselves. They expect "to go to work," both on themselves and on whatever task they may be asked to do. But too often

> they are met by a laborious process of diagnosis and initiation which emphasizes the absolute distance of patienthood from active life. Thus literally, "insult is added to injury" in that the uprooted one, already considered expendable or abnormal by his previous group of affiliations, finds himself categorized and judged by those who were expected to show him the way through a meaningful moratorium. Many a man acquires the irreversible identity of being a lifelong patient and client not on the basis of what he "is," but on the basis of what is first done about him [p. 97].

The importance of not obstructing the individual's initial attempts to seek help holds equally with the less disturbed nonhospitalized person. Since psychological testing, like history taking and other diagnostic procedures, may obstruct the individual's initial help-seeking attempts, if and when one does test one should have very good reasons for doing so. Most clinician-testers would probably agree that the taking of tests themselves is of no great help to the patient; in fact the process may be harmful insofar as it reinforces his expectations of expert or magical cure and structures the future patient-therapist relationship in an inappropriate way. And as was pointed out above, when one tests during the initial contact, the opportunity to initiate treatment, whether psychotherapy or whatever, at the precise time when the patient is most receptive may be lost.

What reasons can be advanced in favor of testing? Essentially, the reasons are: first, testing can provide valuable information which aids in the decision about what kind of treatment is most appropriate; second, the information from testing is useful to the therapist if and when treatment is begun. Consider the following examples: (*a*) A patient may be tested to determine if he has sufficient resources (ego-strength) and assets to warrant psychoanalytic treatment, as opposed to brief less intensive psychotherapy[2]; (*b*) a patient may be tested to determine if he could be more suitably treated as an in- or outpatient.

Examples of how testing could provide useful information to the therapist are: (*a*) Tests can detect psychotic or suicidal potential that might not become apparent to the therapist for some time and, hence, alert him; (*b*) it might be argued that the therapist is generally aided by prior knowledge of personality dynamics.

Each of these reasons raises its own important questions. First, can the testing procedures actually indicate which sorts of personalities are suitable for which sorts of treatment? Second, is the personality data supplied by testing useful in treatment? Clear-cut answers do not exist for either of these important questions at this time. In fact, the question of patient-treatment interaction, what sorts of treatments have effects with what sorts of patients, should be the central

[2]Such considerations are very likely to be irrelevant in most clinics where staff availability is the overriding concern.

research concern of anyone working with this material. Unfortunately, a commitment to diagnosis before treatment leads many to bypass this crucial issue.

Assuming that the patient somehow gets placed in treatment, whether group psychotherapy, individual psychotherapy, or whatever, one may again ask whether a knowledge of history and diagnosis is helpful in treatment. Again, there is no clear-cut answer; there are advantages and disadvantages. First, a foreknowledge of personality dynamics may alert the therapist to key conflict areas, key defensive operations, and the like and, hence, increase his sensitivity in responding to these areas. On the other hand, the same foreknowledge may give the therapist a set for certain areas or topics which leads him to overlook or miss the importance of other things the patient is saying. Another consideration regards the effect of foreknowledge on the therapist's conception of himself—does it make him feel like an expert with secret wisdom to impart? If so, how does this affect his relationship with the patient? Many of the difficulties that stem from the untenable assumptions underlying diagnosis and assessment as prerequisites for treatment disappear when treatment is seen primarily as something which the patient himself must seek out and become involved in. Intake or first contact with voluntary patients may be viewed as the initial phase of treatment in which therapist and patient together explore the patient's difficulties and desires. The therapist acts as a therapist, giving the patient an opportunity to sample, first-hand, therapy as a way of coping with his problems. On the basis of this sample, the patient and therapist can work toward a decision about further treatment. Approaching the initial contact in this way is consistent with the assumptions of a variety of therapies—psychoanalytic, Sullivanian, Rogerian, etc. Furthermore, it makes good sense in terms of the assessment literature on predicting performance in complex situations. Experience here has shown that the best predictions stem from situations that most closely approximate the criterion situation itself. The best way for both therapist and patient to reach a decision on how the latter will perform in psychotherapy (or whether he wants to try it further) is to sample this criterion situation.

It should be stressed that the question of whether knowledge about personality dynamics is useful for treatment is a very open one that may ultimately depend on the kind of treatment, the kind of personality, and future improvements in both treatment techniques and testing instruments. For the present, it would seem that there are many ways in which testing is unrelated to treatment and may hinder it as well as help. One wonders whether many psychologists resort to tests rather than a direct engagement of the patient in an intake interview, which may be both diagnosis and treatment, for irrelevant professional role considerations. Hopefully, psychologists are beyond the point where they need feel they are infringing on the prerogatives of psychiatry when they interview rather than test. After all, what is medical about an interview?

An altogether different set of problems is presented by the chronic institutionalized populations found in many large state and veterans hospitals. Here, the basic treatment goal is to get the patient to the point where he can maintain a minimal level of functioning outside the hospital. In most cases, little in the way of internal psychological change can be accomplished, and treatment becomes oriented primarily to changing the syndrome of institutionalization. Programs in which the patients are formed into semiautonomous groups where they are forced to take charge of their own fates seem much more effective than many traditional forms of treatment (Fairweather, 1964). More recent modifications in this social-psychological approach to treatment include the establishment of patient-managed work centers in the community to facilitate the patient's reintegration in society. Traditional assessment and psychological testing activities have little use in these programs; rather, the psychologist turns his attention to the creation of experimental social groups and the evaluation of their effects.

Research

From the preceding discussion it should be clear that it is the use of tests in the clinical setting that is being considered and not their use for a variety of other research purposes (e.g., work in personality, child development, studies of stress, and the like). Still, within the clinical framework a number of research questions remain. The previous discussion indicated that psychological testing, like other diagnostic procedures, may obstruct the persons' initial effort to do something about his difficulties. In fact, the actual effects of psychological tests on the person's subsequent response to treatment may be directly investigated. In a related form of research, Frank (1965) and his co-workers (Frank, Gliedman, Imber, Stone, & Nash, 1959; Frank, Nash, Stone, & Imber, 1963) have been studying the interaction of patient expectations and response to treatment. They find that patients with the most accurate expectations (i.e., those who were told what to expect in terms of their own and the therapist's behavior, including typical therapy phenomena such as resistance) exhibited the most favorable responses to the therapy. Insofar as testing and other diagnostic activities foster erroneous expectations (which they may do when no differential treatment follows diagnosis or when the therapist never "tells" the person what deep knowledge he has gleaned from the tests), they may be antitherapeutic.

While many persons voluntarily seek what amounts to therapy, there are others who voluntarily seek diagnosis or assessment. Along with these is a sizable group who are referred by others, including young children referred by parents or schools, cases of possible organic involvement, and similar problems. In all these cases, clinical assessment using psychological tests may be quite appropriate. In fact, because they lend themselves to standardized administration and scoring and, hence, may be more readily objectified, tests are superior to the interview for these purposes. Continuing research into the validity of tests for such specific assessment work is, of course, a necessity. There has been a tendency within the field towards identification with single instruments such as the Rorschach or with single approaches such as projective techniques, which really makes little sense when the goal should be the development of valid assessment procedures with respect to some specific goal such as identifying types of organic pathology. One would expect a process of on-going validation to result in the continual modification of the specific tests used in such a procedure. The fact that this has rarely taken place is probably the result of the confounding of two contradictory purposes—the "diagnosis of personality" and the assessment of specific problems such as organic brain damage. While the latter represents a legitimate use of tests in the clinical setting—it may be justified on both clinical and scientific grounds—the former is an unjustified carryover of certain historical assumptions.

Perhaps, by recognizing these different purposes, clinical psychologists may give up, with a clear conscience, the testing of persons who voluntarily seek psychological help and, instead, use tests in those cases where they may make a valid contribution to specific decisions. Such a shift in emphasis has already occurred at the level of practice, but without a clear rationale the clinical psychologist is likely to feel guilty about not fulfilling his professional role. This guilt then tends to perpetuate the traditional emphasis on testing in training programs, an emphasis that may take training time away from more important skills. It is skills such as the sensitive use of the initial contact as both treatment and assessment and the continuing research refinement of assessment procedures with respect to specific and answerable diagnostic questions that seem more suited to the future roles of the clinical psychologist.

4. ASSOCIATIVELY BASED ILLUSORY CORRELATION AS A SOURCE OF PSYCHODIAGNOSTIC FOLKLORE[1]

Loren J. Chapman and Jean P. Chapman

Practicing psychodiagnosticians share a considerable number of beliefs concerning the kinds of test responses that are made by patients who have various kinds of symptoms. For example, clinicians who use the Draw-a-Person Test (DAP) often report observing that those patients who clinically show paranoid behavior draw figures of people with unusually elaborate eye details. Many clinicians who use the Rorschach report observing that male homosexuals see, in the Rorschach ink blots, percepts of people whose gender is unclear to them. Such a percept might be, "I see a person here, but I'm not sure if it's a man or a woman."

These beliefs of clinicians are stated as reports of observations of correlations between patients' symptoms and their test responses. As will be shown in this paper, the same correlations are reported by many different clinicians and, hence, are supported by consensual validation, a highly regarded criterion of truth. A large body of consensually validated observations of this type have been passed from clinician to clinician, have been continually revalidated by new observation, and have come to constitute a massive professional folklore of psychodiagnostic principles.

Many of the correlations contained in this psychodiagnostic folklore have been discredited by experimental evidence. Experimental evidence simply consists of a counting of the relevant phenomena, for example, counting the number of paranoid and nonparanoid patients who elaborate the eye, or counting the number of homosexual and heterosexual males who report sexual uncertainty in their Rorschach percepts. For example, the report that patients who show paranoid behavior draw human figures with unusual elaboration of the eye has been tested by four separate studies, all of which have failed to substantiate the observation (Fisher & Fisher, 1950; Holzberg & Wexler, 1950; Reznikoff &

SOURCE. Loren J. Chapman is currently Professor of Psychology at the University of Wisconsin. He previously taught at the University of Chicago, Southern Illinois University, and the University of Kentucky. Dr. Chapman's interests include experimental psychopathology, personality, and cognitive processes. This manuscript, especially prepared for this volume, was written in collaboration with Dr. Jean Chapman, Lecturer in Psychology at the University of Wisconsin and wife of the first author.

[1]This paper is based on studies by Chapman (1967), Chapman and Chapman (1967), Chapman and Chapman (1969) and Chapman, Chapman and Miller (in preparation). All these studies were supported by Research Grant #MH-07987-01 from the National Institute of Mental Health, United States Public Health Service. The authors are indebted to the American Psychological Association and to Academic Press for permission to reproduce extensive portions of the first three of these articles.

Nicholas, 1958; Ribler, 1957). A possible exception to these uniformly negative findings is provided by a study of Griffith and Peyman (1959) who selected from the drawings of 745 patients the extreme 5% on elaboration of either the eye or ear, or both. This extreme group differed significantly from an unselected group of patients on ideas of reference.

The observation that male homosexuals express sexual uncertainty in their Rorschach percepts more than heterosexual males has been tested by a number of studies, none of which found a significant difference (Wheeler, 1949; Davids, Joelson & McArthur, 1956; Hooker, 1958; Reitzell, 1949).

Much psychodiagnostic folklore is not readily susceptible to experimental test. This is because much of the folklore consists of statements concerning emotional states or impulses that cannot readily be observed. Consider, for example, the common belief that patients who are concerned about their intellectual functioning produce DAP drawings of people with large or elaborated heads. Everyone is to some extent concerned about his intellectual functioning, and there is no clear criterion by which one may rank-order different individuals on this concern. The investigator cannot make a definitive test of the hypothesis. One might also observe that the clinician similarly lacks a clear criterion for his clinical observation of this correlation.

Insofar as there is evidence concerning the correlation between characteristics of patients and popular psychodiagnostic test signs, that evidence has been largely disconfirming. Swensen (1957) reviewed the DAP research literature concerned with the validity of Machover's (1949) principles of DAP interpretation and reached that conclusion. In his more recent review, Swensen (1968) concluded that only overall goodness of drawing, and other qualities of drawings that reflect overall quality, are clearly related to the absence of pathology. He found minimal support for relationships between specific content and specific characteristics of patients. Roback (1968) reviewed much of the same evidence and concluded, somewhat more generously, "Although the studies reviewed in this manuscript generally failed to support Machover's (1949) hypotheses, there is still an insufficient number of well-designed investigations." Evidence for the clinical usefulness of Rorschach interpretations is only slightly more positive. Many of the more popular observational reports of relationships between Rorschach sign and personality characteristic are either absent or are much weaker than the observers believe (Harris, 1960; Jensen, 1964).

In addition, research has shown that clinicians using projective tests are much less able to make valid statements about patients than they commonly believe. An outstanding paper that provides such evidence is the exhaustive study of Little and Shneidman (1959). These investigators found that prominent clinicians, each using his favorite psychodiagnostic test, were able to make valid statements about patients with an accuracy only slightly better than chance. Other similar studies have been reviewed by Jensen (1964).

This conflict between the two sources of evidence, that is, between clinical observation and research findings, is one of the most puzzling and distressing problems that confronts clinical psychology today. It is a conflict that generates much ill will and mutual disrespect and suspicion among psychologists. Research-oriented psychologists often suggest that psychodiagnosticians show a peculiar lack of responsivity to scientific evidence. Meehl (1960) has commented,

> Personally, I find the cultural lag between what the published research shows and what clinicians persist in claiming to do with their favorite devices even more disheartening than the adverse evidence itself.

Much stronger views are often expressed privately by experimental psychologists who contend that clinicians are inferior as scientists because they are unresponsive to evidence. Clinical psychologists, on the other hand, usually reject research findings that conflict with their clinical observations. It is hard for the clinician to accept research findings that cast doubt on the accuracy of observations that he has made repeatedly throughout years of clinical practice, and which have been consensually validated by other experienced clinical observers. The clinician also usually attacks the adequacy of the research studies that are offered as tests of the validity of their observations. It is clear, however, that the clinicians' real basis for rejecting the research findings is that they and their colleagues have observed contrary phenomena. Their stance is not surprising. Most of us accept the evidence of our own senses.

In the light of the massive negative experimental evidence, how can one account for the consistent agreement between different clinicians as to the clinical correlates of invalid test signs. The highly reliable but invalid nature of such observations clearly suggests a systematic error. In fact, systematic error is defined as a reliable inaccuracy. The present writers offer an explanation in terms of a systematic error in the report of correlations between two classes of events. The error is systematic in the sense that instead of being random it has a consistent direction and is, moreover, shared by different observers. We suggest the term "illusory correlation" for the report by an observer of a correlation between two classes of events which, in reality, (*a*) are not correlated, or (*b*) are correlated to a lesser extent than reported, or (*c*) are correlated in the opposite direction than that which is reported. We see this illusion as analogous to the well-known visual illusions, such as the Müller-Lyer illusion. Like the visual illusions, illusory correlation is a systematic error of observation that is shared by different observers and is not dependent on the observers having some exceptional prior experience or training. As will be seen below, one massive source of illusory correlation is a strong verbal associative connection between the events that are seen as correlated.

Illusory Correlation in Everyday Life

Illusory correlation is, of course, not limited to psychodiagnosticians. Analogous errors have been studied by psychologists and by anthropologists and have been given a variety of names. By examining some of these examples, we may get some impression as to how common is this type of error. We may also derive, from examination of such examples, hypotheses as to the sources of illusory correlation.

Illusory correlation includes phenomena from a variety of areas. These include the observational errors necessary to sustain most superstitions and folklore (e.g., the report that one's luck is better when carrying a rabbit's foot), as well as beliefs in magic (e.g., the report that it is more likely to rain after a rain dance). Prejudice is in part an illusory correlation between race or religion and negatively valued traits, while "halo effect" (Thorndike, 1920) is a term usually used for a report of an illusory correlation between positively valued traits.

The literature on primitive magic, superstition, and folklore indicates that similarity is a powerful variable in producing illusory correlation. Many omens and all imitative magic are predicated on a correlation in the frequency of occurrence of similar events, as described at great length by Frazer (1935) and as discussed by Freud (1938). Sometimes the stimulus dimension is one of physical similarity. In the use of voodoo dolls, a doll resembling one's enemy is injured and the practitioners report observing a correlation between injury to the doll and injury to the victim. Frazer (1935, Vol. I) has described similar rituals that are found in dozens of societies.

In other magical practices the similarity is more one of analogy between events. For example, natives of both Java and Central America have intercourse in the fields in order to stimulate growth of the crops (Frazer, 1935, Vol. II, p. 98). In many rain-producing rituals, rain is imitated in order to produce rain. For all such magical practices, the practitioners report observing a correlation between their ritual and the desired event.

These examples indicate that there is often agreement among observers in erroneously reporting the same correlations. This suggests that some systematic principles are operating to distort the observational report. It seems likely that the same principles may account for illusory correlation regardless of differences in the subject matter being observed. One probable genesis of such erroneous observations is from the characteristics of the stimulus events that are erroneously perceived as correlated.

Illusory Correlation in the Observation of Word Pairs

We have performed a number of laboratory investigations of illusory correlation. Our first such study used words as stimuli. The purpose of this investigation was to produce illusory correlation in the laboratory and to study some of the stimulus variables that influence it. Several pilot studies had indicated that illusory correlations could be effectively studied using a series of pairs of words visually presented. These preliminary results also suggested that illusory correlation occurs between words that are similar in meaning and associatively related. Other results indicated that it occurs between words that are longer than other words in a list. The investigation reported below was designed to test the effects on illusory correlation of (*a*) associative strength, (*b*) distinctiveness of atypically long words, (*c*) the length of the series of word pairs, and (*d*) the number of successive testings on such series.

Method

Apparatus. *S*s were presented with three series of pairs of words projected on a screen. At each stimulus presentation, a single pair was shown, one word on the left and one on the right. The film was moved through the projector by an automatic transport connected with an automatic timer. The word pairs were changed every 2 sec. The length of time required by the apparatus for changing word pairs was measured by a photoelectric cell with a timer and found to be 0.1 sec. Therefore, the exposure time for each word pair was 1.9 sec.

Materials. The words on the left and on the right-hand sides of the screen for the three series were as follows: Series A on left–*boat, lion, bacon, blossoms,* and on right–*tiger, eggs, notebook;* Series B on left–*door, hat, knife, building;* and on right–*head, fork, magazine;* Series C on left–*clock, bread, hand, envelope;* and on right–*butter, foot, sidewalk.* All 12 possible pairings of the four left-hand words with the three right-hand words appeared equally often.

As seen above, for 2 of the 12 word pairs of each series the right-hand word was a strong associate to the left-hand word. The other 10 pairs had minimal associative connections. Also, one word used on the left and one word used on the right were three or four letters longer than any of the other words. In addition, one word used on the left in each series was a filler word (*boat, door,* and *clock*) in that it neither was of atypical length nor had a high strength associate on the right. The word pairs with high strength association were selected so as to be of low or medium similarity of meaning. The 6 high associative pairs and the 3 pairs of atypically long words are shown in Table 1.

Strength of associative connection between words was judged by a group of 33 students in an undergraduate course. They were asked to rate the word pairs on a six-point scale for the strength of the tendency of the first word to call to mind the second word, with "1" representing highest associative strength. The six pairs of words with high associative connection ranged from 1.36 to 2.73.

Similarity of meaning was rated by a second group of 36 students on a five-point scale, with a rating of "1" representing highest similarity. The mean similarity ratings of the six pairs of words with high associative connection ranged from 3.42 to 4.61.

The 3 pairs of long words and the remaining 27 pairs were very low on both variables. Mean rated similarity ranged from 4.89 to 5.00 with a composite mean of 4.99 for these 30 pairs. Mean rated strength of associative connection ranged from 5.45 to 6.00 with a composite mean of 5.90.

Each of the three series was prepared in three different lengths consisting of 48, 120, and 240 pairings.

Subjects. The *S*s were 163 students from a large introductory psychology course, divided into three groups of 55, 49, and 59.

Procedure. The *S*s were told before viewing the word pairs that their task was to observe and report how often each word was paired with each other word.

Each group received three successive testings within a single hour, and received in its three testings all three series and all three lengths of series. The order of presentation of the three series and the three lengths of series were counterbalanced across the three groups of *S*s. Thus, each of the three series appeared equally often in the three ordinal testings (i.e., first, second, or third testing) and each was presented once for each of the three lengths of series. Also, each of the three lengths of series appeared once in each of the three testings.

Measure of Illusory Correlation. After each series, the *S* was given a questionnaire on which he was asked about the co-occurrence of the words he had just observed. It contained four items, each of which named one left-hand word and all three right-hand words, and asked for an estimate of the percentage of the total occurrences of the left-hand word in which it was paired with each of the three right-hand words. The correct co-occurrence in each case was, of course, 33 1/3%. It was predicted that for the six high associative pairs and the three pairs of long words, the reported co-occurrence would be higher than this value. This excess over the correct value is the measure of illusory correlation.

Results and Discussion

Presence of Illusory Correlation. Table 1 shows the mean reported co-occurrence at each of the three testings for the nine word pairs for which illusory correlation was predicted. As seen there, Series A, B, and C were fairly comparable on these values.

For each of the nine word pairs for which illusory correlation was predicted the reported co-occurrence was compared with the correct value of 33 1/3% by means of a double-tailed large sample *t*-test, pooling the three testings.

Table 1. The Mean Reported Co-occurrence at Each of the Three Testings for the Nine Pairs of Words for which Illusory Correlation Was Predicted

	First Testing	Second Testing	Third Testing
Series A			
lion–tiger	41.3	37.4	33.8
bacon–eggs	46.7	37.0	35.8
blossoms–notebook	47.0	45.9	43.6
Series B			
hat–head	43.7	36.3	37.9
knife–fork	40.2	34.2	35.8
building–magazine	44.8	43.6	39.0
Series C			
bread–butter	43.3	40.8	36.4
hand–foot	39.1	39.3	34.2
envelope–sidewalk	41.5	40.0	37.3

The difference was significant for each of the six pairs with high associative connection, $z = 3.45$ or larger, $p < .001$ in each case. The reported co-occurrence of each of the other two right-hand words with each of the left-hand associate words was, in every case, less than the objectively correct value of 33 1/3%. This is not surprising because of the restriction that the percentage values for the three right-hand words total 100% in each case. The mean co-occurrence between the left-hand filler words and the right-hand associative words was 32.5, close to the correct value of 33 1/3%.

Since several of these pairs of words with high associative connection had low similarity of meaning, these findings clearly demonstrate that the occurrence of illusory correlation on the basis of associative connection is not dependent on similarity. It would be difficult to investigate the converse possibility that illusory correlation occurs in response to semantic similarity independent of associative connection, because high similarity of meaning is usually accompanied by strong association (Bastian, 1961; Haagen, 1949).

For each of the three pairs of atypically long words, the mean reported co-occurrence was also higher than the correct value of 33 1/3%, $z = 5.40$ or larger, $p < .001$ in each case. This is interpreted as occurring on the basis of the distinctiveness of the long words.

However, one might suspect that the high reported co-occurrence of the pair of atypically long words in each series arose as the result of an erroneous observation that the long word on the right-hand side occurred more often than the other two right-hand words, regardless of which word appeared on the left. This would result if distinctive stimuli are seen as occurring more often than non-distinctive stimuli. This possibility was investigated by examining the reported co-occurrence of the long right-hand word in each series with the left-hand filler word. The mean values, pooling the three testings, were "boat–notebook," 32.6; "door–magazine," 35.9; and "clock–sidewalk," 36.7. These values differed significantly from 33 1/3% for "door–magazine," $z = 2.33$, $p < .05$, and for "clock–sidewalk," $z = 2.78$, $p < .01$. This indicates that the erroneously high reported co-occurrence of the pairs of long words may have been inflated by an error of seeing each long right-hand word as having a heightened frequency. In order to determine whether the long pairs showed illusory correlation beyond that which might be attributed to such an effect, the reported co-occurrence of each of the long right-hand words with the long left-hand words was compared with the reported co-occurrence of the long right-hand word with the left-hand filler word, by means of a direct difference t-test. It was found that the reported co-occurrence was significantly greater for "blossoms–notebook" than for "boat–notebook," $z = 8.25$, $p < .001$, was greater for "building–magazine" than for "door–magazine," $z = 4.26$, $p < .001$, and tended to be greater for "envelope–sidewalk" than for "clock–sidewalk," $z = 1.85$, $p < .07$. These results indicate that illusory correlation occurred for the pairs of long words to a degree beyond that which might be attributed to the *S*s' attributing excessive frequency to each alone.

Effect of Length of Series. There was a small but significant variation in illusory correlation for the high-associate pairs between the three lengths of series. The mean reported co-occurrence for the three lengths of series were 38.35 (short), 40.16 (medium) and 37.09 (long). The three values differed significantly, $F\ (2,324) = 3.33$, $p < .05$. For the pairs of long words, the values were 42.91 (short), 41.79 (medium) and 42.89 (long), and they did not differ significantly, $F\ (2,324) = .31$, $p > .05$.

Effect of Successive Testings. As seen in Table 1, the amount of illusory correlation declined across successive testings. Combining word pairs from the three series, the mean reported co-occurrence for the high-associate pairs was found to have dropped from the first testing (42.30) to the second (37.66) and from the second to the third testing (35.64). This decline was significant, $F\ (2,324) = 17.65$, $p < .01$.

Similarly, the mean reported co-occurrence of the long words declined across successively presented series. The values here for the first, second, and third testings were 44.35, 43.09 and 40.15, respectively, $F\ (2,324) = 3.56$, $p < .05$. The reason for these declines is unknown. However, they may indicate that some *S*s "caught on" to the nature of the experiment as they progressed through the three series, or they may be attributable to fatigue and lowered attention. It is also possible that these declines represent a genuine improvement in handling the task as a function of practice.

Comment

Associative connection between two events and the distinctiveness of the events were effective in producing illusory correlation. Therefore, it seems likely that these two variables are also influential in the development of illusory correlations in situations outside the laboratory. It seems particularly important to investigate the role that these variables may play in clinical psychodiagnostic practice, in the frequently reported observations of disconfirmed correlations between patients' symptoms and performance on diagnostic tests.

Illusory Correlation in the Genesis of Popular Invalid Psychodiagnostic Observations

We will next present seven studies that attempted to produce laboratory replicas of the situation in which a beginning clinician observes the responses of patients to a test and seeks to discover which kinds of test responses are made by patients with each of several different kinds of symptoms. The purpose of these studies was to determine the extent of illusory correlation in such observations, to investigate the basis of such errors, and the conditions under which they occur. The DAP was chosen for these studies because it appears to lack validity and is a widely used test, second only to the Rorschach in frequency of usage (Sundberg, 1961).

Machover (1949) described the clinical meaning of the DAP almost entirely in terms of clinical correlates of various drawing characteristics. She also mentioned that the patients' verbalizations about the drawings may be useful, but she regarded such data as "of only supplemental significance [p. 29]." The present studies are concerned with illusory correlation between patients' symptoms and their drawings and are not concerned with the patients' verbalizations.

The method of the present studies was to present to naive observers a series of DAP drawings, each drawing being arbitrarily paired with contrived statements about the symptoms of the alleged patient who drew it. Six different statements of symptoms were used and each was attached to several different drawings. The observers were asked to inspect the drawings and the symptom statements describing the patients in order to discover what kinds of drawings were made by patients with each symptom. In looking through the paired drawings and symptom statements, the observers were accumulating "clinical experience" as to the meanings of various aspects of DAP performance. However, in all but one of these experiments (Experiment IV), the drawings and the symptom statements were paired in such a way that there was no relationship between the occurrence of any symptom and any drawing characteristic that is viewed as its correlate in conventional clinical practice.

The hypothesis was that the naive observers would "rediscover" in the drawings the widely accepted correlates of the six symptoms despite the fact that these relationships did not exist in the task materials. If many of the naive observers report the same correlates, one must infer shared systematic errors. If these should be the same correlates that clinicians commonly report on the basis of their clinical practice, one might suspect that the clinicians also show these same systematic errors.

Subjects Used in the Seven Studies. All of the *S*s were students in an introductory psychology course, except for Experiment V, in which 23 of the 41 *S*s were from more advanced undergraduate psychology courses. No *S* served in more than one study.

All *S*s were naive concerning the DAP. In order to be certain of this, each *S* was given a brief questionnaire that asked whether or not he "had heard" of the DAP before, and if he had, to list one drawing characteristic together with its interpretation. The *S*s who showed any indication of prior acquaintance with the DAP were dropped from the sample; this was necessary for a total of 18 *S*s in the seven studies.

Experiment I

Method

Six symptom statements were used for pairing with drawings. The six symptom statements were:

1. "He is worried about how manly he is."
2. "He is suspicious of other people."
3. "He is worried about how intelligent he is."
4. "He is concerned with being fed and taken care of by other people."
5. "He has had problems of sexual impotence."
6. "He is very worried that people are saying bad things about him."

Preliminary Survey of Practicing Psychodiagnosticians. Before testing naive observers, it was first necessary to learn the characteristics of the drawings that practicing psychodiagnosticians report that they have observed to be correlated with each of the six symptoms. A questionnaire for clinicians was prepared to elicit this information. For each of the six symptoms or emotional problems, the questionnaire presented an item of the following form:

He is worried about how manly he is.

The pictures drawn by such men would more often be characterized by

1. ....
2. ....

The clinician was instructed to assume in each case that the patient was a man who drew a picture of a man.

The reactions of practicing clinicians to the first attempts to obtain responses to this questionnaire indicated that many psychodiagnosticians were reluctant to expose themselves in this manner. Therefore, the questionnaire was made anonymous. It did not ask for the clinician's name, but it asked for his academic degrees and the year each was obtained, the number of years of his psychodiagnostic experience, and the extent to which he uses the DAP. It also asked the clinician if he finds the test useful for discovering the emotional problems of patients.

The questionnaire was circulated primarily by mailing several copies, with return envelopes, to each of a number of clinical psychologists who were interested in psychodiagnosis and who worked with other clinical psychologists. The recipients were asked to distribute the questionnaire with return envelope to each of their colleagues who were active in diagnostic testing. The institutions of the recipients were eight Veterans Administration hospitals or Veterans Administration clinics, eight medical schools, six academic departments, and four others. Almost all recipients were in widely known departments that have large psychology training programs, either in the form of intern training or graduate teaching. Of 110 questionnaires sent out, 67 were returned. Only three respondents added that they based their interpretations on inquiry data as well as on characteristics of the drawings. (This figure may be low since the questionnaire did not specifically ask about the use of inquiry.) Of the 67 respondents, 44 answered the questions fully and also said that they found the test useful. Only these 44 are included in the present analysis. Most of them said that they used the DAP regularly as part of a larger battery of tests. The highest academic degrees of these clinicians were Ph.D, 34; M.A or M.S, 8; B.A, 2. Most of the non-Ph.D clinicians were currently active Ph.D candidates. The mean years of psychodiagnostic experience reported by the group of 44 clinicians was 8.4.

The clinicians' responses concerning the drawing characteristics that are correlates of each of the six symptoms were tabulated, combining similar statements of drawing characteristics. For example, a single category was used for muscular, broad-shouldered, manly, or athletic builds. About 35 such categories were used.

The choice of how many of these categories of drawing characteristics to report is a somewhat arbitrary one. The decision here is to report all those that were listed by 15% or more of the clinicians as a correlate of at least one symptom statement. A total of 14 drawing characteristics met this criterion, and 6 of these 14 met the criterion for two different symptom statements. For example, "broad-shouldered, muscular figures" met the criterion for the symptoms of both impotence (25%) and worry about manliness (80%). These 14 drawing characteristics may be found in Table 2 (the first 14 characteristics

Table 2. Percentage of Clinicians and Naive Observers Reporting Various Drawing Characteristics as Accompanying the 6 Symptom Statements

Drawing	Manliness		Suspiciousness		Intelligence		Fed and Cared for		Impotence		Say Bad Things	
	Clinician	Observer	Clinician	Observer	Clinician	Observer	Clinician	Observer	Clinician	Observer	Clinician	Observer
Characteristic												
1. Broad shoulders, muscular, manly	80	76	0	6	0	8	0	12	25	31	0	6
2. Feminine, child-like	23	22	7	12	2	11	32	39	23	25	11	13
3. Hair distinctive	23	13	2	2	2	8	0	1	11	6	0	3
4. Eyes atypical	0	0	91	58	0	6	0	3	2	2	43	26
5. Ears atypical	0	0	55	6	0	3	0	0	2	0	64	7
6. Facial expression atypical	0	17	18	44	2	21	2	21	2	14	18	52
7. Head large or emphasized	0	5	0	13	82	55	2	7	0	3	9	10
8. Detailed drawing	20	8	2	6	34	13	0	3	7	3	2	6
9. Mouth emphasis	0	0	7	5	0	1	68	8	2	1	5	5
10. Passive posture, outstretched arms	5	4	2	8	0	2	36	21	2	2	0	8
11. Buttons	0	0	0	0	0	0	23	1	0	0	0	0
12. Sexual area elaborated	14	5	0	0	0	0	0	0	55	8	0	0
13. Sexual area deemphasized	0	0	0	0	0	0	0	0	18	27	0	0
14. Phallic nose, limbs	9	0	0	0	0	0	0	0	23	2	0	0
15. Fat	0	2	0	1	0	0	7	16	0	4	0	1

listed there), together with the percentage of the clinicians who gave each one for each symptom statement. In order to determine whether the drawing characteristics were distributed among the six symptoms in a nonchance pattern, Cochran's Q statistic was computed for each drawing characteristic. The six symptoms were found to differ in their frequency for each of the 14 drawing characteristics ($p < .01$ in each case). This demonstrates that the clinicians agreed with one another beyond chance as to which drawing characteristics were correlates of each symptom. Most, if not all, of these correlates are either specifically listed by Machover (1949) or are consistent with the principles of interpretation that she advances.

One of the purposes of this research was to compare these reports, made by clinicians on the basis of their clinical practice, with similar observations by naive observers who were shown randomly paired drawings and symptom statements. The expectation was that the naive judges would erroneously report observing, in such contrived clinical materials, the same relationships between drawing characteristics and symptoms that clinicians reported observing in their diagnostic practice.

Construction of Task Material. Drawings were collected from psychotic patients at a state hospital and from graduate students in clinical psychology. Extremely simple drawings, such as stick figures, were eliminated. The final collection consisted of 45 drawings, of which 35 were drawn by psychotics and 10 by nonpsychotics.

High-quality Xerox reproductions of each drawing were obtained in order to produce multiple sets of the stimulus materials. Each Xerox reproduction was backed by cardboard and covered with a clear plastic sheet in order to protect it from damage.

Printed on the same sheet of paper as each drawing was a pair of statements concerning the alleged symptoms of the patient who made the drawing, for example,

The man who drew this

1. is suspicious of other people.
2. is worried about how manly he is.

These pairs of symptom statements were taken from the six symptoms for which the practicing psychodiagnosticians had listed DAP correlates. The pairs of symptom statements were assigned to the drawings so that each symptom statement appeared once with each of 15 drawings.

Three parallel forms (Forms A, B, and C) of the task were constructed, using the same drawings and symptom statements, by systematically reassigning the symptom statements among the drawings. This was done in such a way that, pooling the three forms, each of the six symptom statements appeared only once with each of the 45 drawings. Thus it followed that each drawing characteristic occurred as often with one symptom statement as another.

In addition, it was desirable to prevent, within each form, any differential relationship between the occurrence of each symptom and any drawing characteristic that clinicians reported as its correlate. In order to do this, an attempt was made to rank order the drawings on the 14 characteristics listed by at least 15% of the clinicians for at least one symptom. A meaningful rank ordering was found to be feasible for nine of the drawing characteristics (Nos. 1, 2, 3, 4, 5, 7, 8, 9, and 14 of Table 2), but the remaining five either occurred rarely in the drawings or were of such a subjective character that they were impossible to judge. Even some of these nine characteristics appeared to a detectable degree only in a portion of the drawings. For example, the drawings were rank ordered on muscularity, although about half of the pictures showed no muscular development at all. Therefore, the reliability of each rank ordering was examined only for the dichotomization of the drawings into the 22 that were high on the variable, versus the 23 that were low. The percentage agreement between two judges on the dichotomizations ranged from 82 to 100%.

The drawings having the characteristics that occurred too infrequently to be rank ordered were also identified. Then the results of the rank orderings on the nine characteristics, as well as the identification of the drawings with infrequent characteristics, were used to assign symptom statements to drawings. This was done in such a way that within each form no systematic relationship existed between the occurrences of a symptom and any drawing characteristic that 15% of the clinicians had reported as its correlate. This was done by pairing the symptom statement equally often with the drawings having each of various degrees of possession of the drawing characteristic. For example, the symptom statement, "He is worried about how intelligent he is" was paired as often with drawings having small heads as with large or medium-sized heads. As will be discussed later, the design provided a convenient internal check on any possible inadequacy of this balancing which would account for any of the reports by observers, concerning correlates of symptoms. This could be checked simply by comparing the three forms as to the content of these reports. This comparison showed that the balancing was successful.

Procedure

There were 108 *S*s divided into three groups (*N*s = 34, 38, and 36), each of which received a different one of the three forms of the task.

The *S*s were tested in groups. The experimenter (*E*) first presented a brief description of the DAP and its clinical use, explaining that psychologists make interpretations about patients' emotional problems from the nature of their drawings. However, no examples of relevant drawing characteristics were offered.

The *E* then instructed *S*s as follows:

> Now we want to test your powers of judgment and observation. I'm going to show you some drawings made by men with various emotional problems. Together with each drawing you will find two statements that describe the emotional problems of the man who made the drawing. Many of the men have some of the same problems. Please study the pictures and the statements carefully because when you are through I am going to ask you about the characteristics of the drawings that were made by men with each kind of problem.

Each *S* was handed one drawing, face down. At prearranged signals, *S*s looked at the drawings and then passed them in a pattern such that each *S* saw each of the 45 drawings only once. The signals were timed so that each *S* had 30 seconds to examine each drawing together with the two symptom statements that accompanied it.

After all of the *S*s had seen all 45 pictures, they were given questionnaires that contained items of the following format:

Some of the pictures were drawn by men with the following problem:

He is worried about how manly he is.

The pictures drawn by these men were more often characterized by

1. ....
2. ....
3. ....

Five additional items of a format identical to the above were built around the other five symptom statements.

Results

The responses of *S*s receiving each of the three forms of the task were tabulated and were found, as expected, to be highly comparable. (The comparability of the three forms will be discussed in greater detail below.) Therefore, they were combined for purposes of the main analysis of results. Eight of the drawing characteristics were listed by as many as 15% of the sample as a correlate of at least one symptom. These may be found in Table 2, together with the drawing characteristics that were listed by at least 15% of the clinicians. As seen there, seven of the eight characteristics that met this criterion for the experimental *S*s had also met it for the clinicians.

In all, there are 15 drawing characteristics listed in Table 2, although two of them ("buttons" and "phallic nose or limbs") seldom occurred for the experimental *S*s. For each of the remaining 13, a Cochran's *Q* analysis was used to determine whether each drawing characteristic was distributed randomly among the six symptoms by the experimental *S*s. The distribution was found to be nonrandom for each of the 13 drawing characteristics ($p < .01$ in each case). This indicates that the reported correlates were not based on the erroneous perception that one drawing characteristic occurred more often than other drawing characteristics with all symptoms. If this were the case, the drawing characteristics would be randomly distributed across different symptoms. Instead, these results show that *S*s saw each drawing characteristic as systematically occurring with one symptom more than others and that the different *S*s agreed on which symptom occurred with each drawing characteristic.

The central interest of this paper is in the degree of similarity between the clinicians and experimental *S*s in the drawing characteristics that were listed as correlates of each symptom. It is seen in Table 2 that for each of the 15 drawing characteristics, the symptom for which the clinicians most often reported it as a correlate was the same symptom for which the naive observers most often reported it (with the exception of a single tie). For example, both the clinicians and naive observers reported broad-shouldered, muscular figures more often as a correlate of the symptom "He is worried about how manly he is" than for any other of the six symptoms, and both groups reported drawings with atypical eyes more often for the symptom "He is suspicious of other people" than for any other symptom.

One may also examine the data of Table 2 from the opposite starting point; that is, taking one symptom at a time, one may compare the clinicians and experimental *S*s as to which drawing characteristic they most often reported as a correlate of that symptom. From this point of view, the agreement was again impressive, although imperfect. For three of the six symptoms (Nos. 1, 2, and 3) the two groups listed most often the same one of the 15 drawing characteristics. For each of the six symptoms the two groups had in common two of the three drawing characteristics that they listed most frequently as its correlate.

It is clear that the experimental *S*s showed massive illusory correlation and that the illusory correlates that they reported showed a remarkable similarity to the correlates that clinicians reported from their clinical practice.

Comparability of Forms. As mentioned above, the design made it possible to rule out true relationships as a source of the correlates reported, simply by comparing these reports for the three forms. If any relationship were a true one for one form, it would necessarily follow that the opposite relationship would exist for at least one of the other two forms. This follows from the fact that, pooling the three forms, each drawing was paired with each statement one time. For example, if in one of the three forms the more muscular figures were more often paired with the symptom statement, "He is worried about how manly he is," it would necessarily follow that for another form the less muscular figures, rather than the more muscular ones, would be paired with this statement. Hence, if a drawing characteristic was reported as a correlate on the basis of a true relationship for one form, it would not be reported for one of the others. This means that if a drawing characteristic is reported as a strong correlate of the same symptom on all three forms, this report cannot be based on a true relationship.

In order to investigate this, the three forms were compared as to the drawing characteristic listed most often for each symptom. For four of the symptoms (Nos. 1, 2, 3, and 6) the same drawing characteristic was reported most often for each of the three forms. For the other two symptoms (Nos. 4 and 5) there was not perfect agreement. These are the two symptoms for which, as seen in Table 2, there was more than one drawing characteristic frequently reported as a correlate. Nevertheless, each drawing characteristic that was most frequently reported for one of the symptoms on one form was always within 11 percentage points of being most frequent on each of the other two forms, and was always within the top four drawing characteristics of the other two. One would expect a negative, not a positive, relationship to be reported for one of the forms if the reports were based on true relationships. It is clear, therefore, that the correlates reported could not have been objectively present, but were instead illusory.

Table 3 shows comparative data for the three forms in Experiment I. The table is limited to the most commonly reported drawing characteristic for each of the six symptoms. (Five drawing characteristics are listed instead of six since one is listed for two symptoms.) For each of the three forms separately, Cochran's Q was employed in the same manner as reported above for the three forms combined. This was done in order to determine if the five drawing characteristics were randomly distributed among the six symptoms. Of the 15 analyses, 14 showed significant departure from randomness ($p < .01$ in each case). (The single nonsignificant finding was for "distinctive facial expression" in Form A.) This shows that the agreement of *S*s as to the symptom with which the drawing characteristics were most often paired was not a chance phenomenon for the individual forms.

The Associative Basis of This Illusory Correlation

An examination of the data of Table 2 indicates the possibility that the most commonly reported illusory correlates are drawing characteristics with highest-strength associative connection to the symptom statements. For example, it seems likely that suspiciousness tends to call to mind the eye more often than other parts of the body, and problems concerning intelligence tend to call to mind the head. In order to provide more objective evidence on this, a questionnaire was constructed for measuring the associative strength between the problem area of each symptom statement and the parts of the body that are referred to in the various drawing characteristics. The decision was made to limit these ratings to body parts alone and not the other aspects of the drawings. This was done for two reasons. The drawing characteristics of Table 2 are summary

Table 3. Percentage of Subjects Reporting the Most Popular Illusory Correlate of Each Symptom Statement

Symptom and Drawing Characteristic	Experiment I			Experiment II			Experiment III	Experiment V	Experiment VI
	Forms			Testings					
	A $N = 34$	B $N = 38$	C $N = 36$	First $N = 56$	Second $N = 56$	Third $N = 56$	$N = 44$	$N = 41$	$N = 42$
1. Worry about manliness Manly, muscular	74	79	75	71	73	77	91	85	45
2. Suspicious Eyes atypical	59	53	77	52	50	48	55	56	36
3. Worry about intelligence Head emphasized	50	47	77	41	48	46	33	56	19
4. Need to be fed and cared for Feminine or childlike	50	45	27	21	21	23	45	44	24
5. Impotence Manly, muscular	44	29	27	25	27	30	34	27	10
6. Say bad things Facial expression atypical	26	63	77	50	50	48	45	63	45

statements of a fairly wide range of responses by the various observers. The choice of any single brief phrase, other than body parts, would be arbitrary and subjective and would entail the risk of obtaining a biased associative rating. In addition, some of the drawing characteristics could not be communicated without mentioning drawings, which would negate the purpose of the associative ratings.

The problem areas of the symptom statements were each summarized as follows: "manliness," "suspiciousness," "intelligence," "being fed and cared for," "sexual impotence," and "bad things being said about one's self." The parts of the body with which association was measured for each of these were: shoulders and muscles, hair, eyes, head, mouth, genital organs, and ears. The six problem areas and seven body parts yielded 42 pairs, for each of which an item was constructed in the following format:

The tendency for SUSPICIOUSNESS to call to mind HEAD is

a. very strong
b. strong
c. moderate
d. slight
e. very slight
f. no tendency at all

The questionnaire was given to a group of 45 undergraduate students who had not participated in the other studies reported in this paper.

The six associative ratings from (a) to (f) were assigned values of 6 to 1, and a mean was computed for each item. Table 4 reports the mean rated associative strength for the 42 pairs. For each of the six symptoms the highest-strength associate was compared with the second highest by means of a direct difference t test. The difference was found to be significant ($p < .001$) for the first five symptoms, but not for the sixth ($t = 1.28; p = .20$).

Table 4. Mean Rated Associative Connection Between Problem Areas and Body Parts

Body Part	Manliness	Suspiciousness	Intelligence	Fed and Cared for	Impotence	Say Bad Things
Shoulders and muscles	4.8	1.3	1.7	1.8	1.8	1.3
Hair	2.4	1.2	1.3	1.6	1.5	1.5
Eyes	2.0	3.8	2.5	1.5	1.2	1.9
Head	2.3	1.8	4.3	1.6	1.5	1.8
Mouth	2.0	1.9	2.1	3.9	1.5	3.2
Genital organs	4.2	1.3	1.2	1.5	5.4	1.6
Ears	1.3	2.5	1.4	1.2	1.0	2.9

The relationship of illusory correlation to associative strength can be seen by comparing the naive observers' responses in Table 2 with the associative ratings of Table 4. Taking one body part at a time, one finds, for all seven body parts, agreement between the two measures as to the symptom with which the body part has the strongest relationship. For example, it is seen in Table 4 that "eyes" are a stronger associate to "suspiciousness" than to any other symptom, and it is seen in Table 2 that drawing characteristics mentioning "eyes" were listed as an illusory correlate of that same symptom more often than any other symptom.

The data of the two tables may also be compared from the opposite starting point. Taking one symptom at a time, one may determine which of the seven body parts has the strongest relationship to it. Using this comparison, the agreement was again impressive but not perfect. For four of the six symptoms (Nos. 1, 2, 3, and 5) the body part that was the strongest associate of the symptom was also the one most commonly reported in the drawing characteristics that were their illusory correlates.

It is of interest to note that, for almost all of these comparisons, the correlates reported by the clinical psychologists were even more frequently the highest-strength associate than was the case for the naive observers.

This finding that associative connection produces illusory correlation is congruent with the similar finding of our earlier laboratory study which used only pairs of words as stimuli. The present results do not show that associative connection is the only source of illusory correlation in the DAP, but they do indicate that it is a major source.

Experiment II

The *S*s in Experiment I had much less opportunity to observe the DAP protocols and the accompanying symptoms than do clinicians who interpret the DAP in clinical practice. One might wonder whether the experimental *S*s would continue to show these same errors if given repeated opportunity to view the stimulus materials. Experiment II was designed to investigate this. Naive observers were given repeated experience with one of the three forms of the task used in Experiment I.

Procedure

The *S*s (N = 56) were shown the drawings and the symptom statements, followed by a questionnaire at each of three sessions on consecutive days. The experimental procedure was substantially the same as in Experiment I. The instructions on the first session were identical to those of Experiment I, but on the second and third days they were shortened by eliminating the introductory material. Form A of the task was used on all three occasions.

Results

The responses at all three sessions were substantially the same as those in Experiment I, and there was little change with repeated testings. At all three testings the most frequently reported drawing characteristic for each of the six symptoms was the same as that of Experiment I. Table 3 shows the drawing characteristic most often reported for each of the six symptoms and the percentage of *S*s who reported it. As seen in Table 3, these percentages remained highly stable across the three testings. A Cochran's *Q* analysis was used to determine whether any of the changes in percentage were significant. None approached the 5% level.

From this we conclude that with stimulus materials of this type, repeated exposure does not reduce errors of illusory correlation.

Experiment III

The observers in Experiments I and II showed massive illusory correlation that appeared to be produced in large part by associative connection between the symptom statements and certain drawing characteristics. This suggests the possibility that the observers' illusory correlates may correspond to their prior expectations as to which stimuli are correlated in their occurrence. Many high-strength associates are names of objects that tend to co-occur in everyone's daily experiences, for example, butter-bread and table-chair. The observers might be extending this principle to the DAP so that they expect symptoms and drawing characteristics that have an associative connection to be correlated in their occurrence. Experiment III was designed to test this possibility by asking *S*s to guess the kinds of drawings made by men with each problem.

Procedure

The *S*s (N = 44) were told about the DAP in the same manner as *S*s in Experiment I, but they were not shown any stimulus materials. They were then given the following instructions.

> Now we want to see what you can guess about this test. We have gathered a group of drawings by men with various emotional problems. In each case, we asked the patient to draw a picture of a man.

The *S*s were then given a questionnaire that listed an item in the following format for each of the six symptom statements.

He is worried about how manly he is.

The pictures drawn by such men would more often be characterized by

1. ....

2. ....
3. ....

Results

The responses were found to resemble closely those of the naive observers in Experiments I and II. The most frequently guessed drawing characteristic for each of the six symptoms was the same as the one most frequently reported by *S*s of those two studies. Table 3 lists the percentage of *S*s who guessed each of these six relationships. A Cochran's Q analysis was used to determine if each of these drawing characteristics was guessed more often with some symptoms than with others. The difference was significant for each of the five drawing characteristics ($p < .01$ in each case). This indicates that *S*s tended to agree as to their guesses.

The similarity of the guesses to the reports of illusory correlates in the first two studies indicates that the illusory correlates corresponded to the observers' expectations. This also leads one to suspect that the similar observations by practicing psychodiagnosticians may also be based on the same prior expectations.

Experiment IV

The finding of Experiment III that the blind guesses of naive *S*s closely resemble their observational reports might lead one to speculate that the illusory correlates reported by *S*s in Experiments I and II might be attributable to their failing to perceive the stimulus materials. This might result either through lack of motivation to attend to the task or insufficient opportunity to do so in the time allotted. Actually, *S*s seemed to be interested in the material and highly motivated to discover the relationships between the symptoms and the drawings. Also, no one complained about lack of time for determining the correct answers. Nevertheless, it seemed necessary to attempt to rule out these interpretations by means of appropriate experiments. The first such study was Experiment IV.

In Experiment IV, the task materials of Experiments I and II were altered so as to introduce true correlations between certain symptom statements and drawing characteristics. The expectation was that if *S*s were truly attending to the task, their responses to these altered materials would differ from the responses made in Experiments I and II.

Procedure

The same drawings and symptom statements were used as in Experiments I and II, but the pattern of assignment of the symptom statements to the various drawings was altered. They were assigned so that for each of five symptoms there was a strong negative correlation between the occurrence of the symptom statement and one drawing characteristic which had often been reported as occurring with it in the earlier studies. For example, in both studies it was reported that the symptom statement of worry about intelligence was most often accompanied by a drawing of a figure with a head that was either large or emphasized in some other way. Therefore, in the present study the 15 presentations of the statement "He is worried about how intelligent he is" were not paired with any of the figures with large heads, but were instead paired only with the smallest heads. A similar negative correlation was built in between four other symptom statements and drawing characteristics. These symptoms and drawing characteristics are listed in Table 5. Note that the categories of drawing characteristics are more narrowly defined than the categories used in Tables 2 and 3. The categories were chosen so that the true negative relationships could be built in unambiguously. For example, the category "large eyes" was used instead of "atypical eyes" which included not only large eyes, but eyes that were staring, slanted, beady, etc.

Table 5. Percentage of Subjects Who Reported Each of 5 Illusory Correlates in Experiment I and Experiment IV

Symptom and Drawing Characteristics[a]	Experiment I (N = 108)	Experiment IV (N = 38)	p
1. Worry about manliness Manly, muscular	76	50	.01
2. Suspicious Large or elaborate eyes	28	8	.02
3. Worry about intelligence Large heads	44	16	.01
4. Need to be fed and cared for Childlike figures	25	3	.01
5. Impotence Manly, muscular	31	21	ns
	—	—	—
Mean percentage	41	20	

[a]Note that the drawing characteristics are more narrowly defined for Symptoms 2, 3, and 4 than in Table 3.

This task was presented to the *S*s (N = 38) in the same manner as in Experiment I. The prediction was that *S*s would respond to these true negative correlations by reducing the number of erroneous reports of the contrary positive illusory correlates.

Results

The responses were tabulated in the same manner as in the previous studies. Table 5 lists the percentage of *S*s who reported observing the five illusory positive correlates. In each case, the illusory correlate is in the direction opposite to that which is objectively present. As seen in Table 5, these five illusory correlates were reported only about half as often as in Experiment I. Chi-square analysis indicated that the reduction in frequency of report was significant for four of the five.

It is clear, therefore, that *S*s were attending to the materials much of the time and that the illusory correlation found in Experiments I and II cannot be attributed solely to *S*s failing to attend. Nevertheless, the data of Table 5 reveal that the illusory correlates show surprisingly strong survival in the face of negative evidence. Is this residual illusory correlation attributable to the strength of the error, or might it instead be attributable to insufficient time or low motivation of some of the *S*s? The next study, Experiment V, was designed to test these possibilities more directly.

Experiment V

The *S*s ($N = 41$) in Experiment V were tested under circumstances designed to maximize both their motivation to observe accurately and their opportunity to do so. The task materials were Form A from Experiment I, in which there was no true correlation between symptom statements and drawing characteristics. As in Experiments I, II, and IV, *S*s were told that their task was to observe what kinds of drawings were made by men with each kind of problem. However, a prize of $20 was offered for the *S* who was most accurate in his observations. Also, unlike the earlier studies, *S*s were tested individually and were permitted to look at each drawing and its symptom statements as long as they wished. However, they were not permitted to look at more than one drawing at a time and were required to look at them in a prearranged random order. They were not permitted to return to a picture after they had once put it down.

In order to make the contest more realistic, the questionnaire was modified to request an additional bit of information. The *S*s were asked to list, for each drawing characteristic that they reported as drawn by patients with a given symptom, the percentage of such patients who showed it. However, these latter data were not analyzed.

Results

Surprisingly, the observational reports made under these conditions were quite similar to those of Experiments I, II, and III. For each of the six symptoms, the drawing characteristic most often listed as its correlate was the same as in those studies. Table 3 shows the percentage of *S*s who reported each of these correlates. Chi-square analysis indicated that none of the percentages was significantly different from those of Experiment I.

Since the illusory correlation was not reduced by the prospect of a $20 prize for accuracy of observation combined with unlimited viewing time, one concludes that it is not attributable either to lack of motivation or lack of time to view the stimulus materials.

Experiment VI

The findings of Experiment V led to the question of what are the conditions of observation that might reduce the incidence of report of these illusory correlates. In Experiment VI, *S*s were tested under conditions designed to facilitate greatly their accuracy so that they might discover that the illusory correlates were unwarranted.

The task materials were again Form A and the questionnaire also was the same as in Experiment V. The *S*s were given the questionnaire together with the stack of cards, as well as scratch paper, a ruler, and a pencil. Again, a $20 prize was offered for the *S* who was most accurate. Unlike Experiment V, *S*s were allowed to shuffle the cards, rearrange them, compare groups of cards, and return to any card as often as they wished. Thus, *S*s could, if they wished, sort the cards with a given symptom into one pile and those with a second symptom into another pile, spread out the two piles of pictures and compare them. However, not all *S*s went to this much effort. Table 3 shows the percentage of *S*s who reported each of the illusory correlates that in the previous studies had been most often reported for each of the six symptoms.

As seen in Table 3, there was a drop from Experiment I in the percentage of *S*s reporting these six illusory correlates. The drop was significant ($p < .05$) for Symptoms 1, 2, 3, and 5, but it fell short of significance for the other two. The mean of the six percentages was 52% in Experiment I and 30% in the present study.

Although the frequency of report of these illusory correlates dropped under these conditions, the most striking aspect of the findings is the resistance of the error to the influence of reality.

Experiment VII

Consensual Pseudo-Validation in Psychodiagnostic Observation

The contrived laboratory situations of these studies differed in one important respect from the real-life clinical situation. The observers in these studies, unlike psychodiagnosticians in clinical practice, were not allowed to communicate with one another. Clinicians commonly discuss their observations with one another and, as a result, are reassured of their accuracy, because they find that their colleagues observe the same test correlates of symptoms as they observe. However, the findings of the studies summarized above indicate that such shared observations may often be shared error rather than shared accuracy. If this is the case, one might describe their agreement with one another as producing a consensual "pseudo-validation." The observers would be strengthened in their conviction that the correlations are valid, despite the fact that the correlations are illusory.

The purpose of Experiment VII was to study, using psychodiagnostic test materials, the enhancement of illusory correlation by consensual pseudo-validation. This enhancement of illusory correlation was studied both in terms of increased frequency of report of popular illusory correlates, and of increased confidence in the accuracy of the erroneous observations.

The task materials were identical to those of Form A, Experiment I. After all of the *S*s ($N = 43$) had seen all 45 pictures, they were given questionnaires containing items of the following format:

He is worried about how manly he is.

The pictures drawn by these men were more often characterized by	How confident are you of your observation?
1.	1.___Extremely confident 2.___Very much confidence 3.___Much confidence 4.___Fairly confident 5.___Little confidence 6.___Very little confidence 7.___No confidence at all
2.	1.___Extremely confident 2.___Very much confidence 3.___Much confidence 4.___Fairly confident 5.___Little confidence 6.___Very little confidence 7.___No confidence at all

Five additional items identical in format to the above were built around the other five symptom statements.

After the *S*s had observed the materials and filled out the questionnaire, they were divided into groups of eight or nine subjects each, so that they might compare and discuss their responses. They were instructed to discuss one symptom statement at a time, to take turns reading the drawing characteristics that each member had recorded as correlates of that symptom, to discuss the extent to which they agreed or did not agree with one another, and to attempt to arrive at a consensus as to the true correlate of the symptom. They were not allowed, however, to alter their written protocols after the discussion began.

The *S*s returned for a second testing the next day. At this session the *S*s viewed the identical task materials as at their first testing, and they filled out the identical questionnaire. However, they did not discuss their observations after recording them. A control group was provided by the *S*s of Experiment II in which *S*s were tested on repeated occasions without provision for comparison of their responses.

The observations of the first and second testings were compared as to the frequency of report of the three most popular illusory correlates. These three correlates were (1) broad shoulders, muscular or manly—for worry about manliness, (2) head, large or emphasized—for worry about intelligence, and (3) atypical eyes—for suspiciousness. The frequency of report of these most popular illusory correlates was found to increase between the first and second testings ($t = 2.16$, $d.f. = 42$, $p < .05$), as shown by a direct difference t-test. The subjects' ratings of their confidence in their observations also increased from the first to the second testing ($t = 4.46$, $d.f. = 30$, $p < .005$).

These findings are in striking contrast to the results of Experiment II in which subjects were tested on three successive occasions without being provided with systematic opportunity to discuss their observations with one another. In this experiment, it was found that the subjects did not change the frequency of report of the popular illusory correlates with repeated testings.

Illusory Correlation in the Presence of Valid Psychodiagnostic Signs

A clinician who believes strongly in the validity of the DAP signs used in these studies might offer the following objection. Perhaps the signs are all truly valid. It may be that test responses that have a verbal associative connection to a symptom are truly produced more often by patients who have that symptom, and perhaps our clinically naive observers guessed this truth and then believed that they observed such relationships in the task materials of the experiments.

This reinterpretation of these studies would not appear relevant to our first study, in which words were used as stimuli. Nevertheless, such an alternative interpretation of our studies of psychodiagnostic observation cannot be completely dismissed without further evidence. The validity of most of the signs used in these studies has not been investigated. Therefore, we conducted a series of additional studies to determine whether observers would report associatively based illusory correlates of symptoms even when competing valid test signs are present. We will summarize these studies more briefly than the previous studies.

The design required a choice of a symptom and a test for which valid signs exist, but invalid signs have been reported by clinical observers. Male homosexuality and Rorschach content analysis were chosen because they appear to fulfill these criteria. Wheeler (1949) offered 20 Rorschach content signs of male homosexuality. Clinicians commonly report several of these signs as substantiated by their own clinical experience, but research evidence strongly supports only two of the signs. Three studies by different investigators (Davids, Joelson & McArthur, 1956; Hooker, 1958; Wheeler, 1949) have reported statistically interpretable evidence on the validity of all 20 Wheeler Rorschach signs, and these studies show some agreement.

Wheeler Signs 7 and 8 were both found to distinguish homosexual from heterosexual groups at the 5% level (using a one-tailed test) by two of the three studies (Sign 7 by Wheeler and by Davids et al., Sign 8 by Davids et al. and by Hooker). Wheeler Sign 7 is a response on Card IV of "human or animal—contorted, monstrous, or threatening," and Wheeler Sign 8 is a response on Card V, W or Center D, of a "human, or humanized animal." Signs 10, 17, 19, and 20 were each found to distinguish the groups in one study but were tested and not found valid in the other two studies. A finding by chance alone, of a significant difference in a study for one or two signs out of 20 is not unexpected. Therefore, for purposes of the present paper, Signs 7 and 8 will be considered the only clinically valid signs. This conclusion tends to be supported by Reitzell (1949) who reported Signs 7, 8, and 16 as the most discriminating of the 20 Wheeler signs. (Unfortunately, her data are presented in a form not amenable to computation of tests of signficance).

A series of studies were performed closely analogous to those that we have previously reported for the Draw-a-Person Test. First, a group of clinicians were surveyed as to the kinds of content that they have observed in the Rorschach responses of male homosexuals. The hypothesis was that the popularity of signs among the practicing psychodiagnosticians would have little relationship to the objective clinical validity of the signs as indicated by research evidence, but that the most popular signs would, instead, be the ones with the strongest verbal associative connection to the symptom of male homosexuality. This prediction was confirmed. None of the clinicians (N = 32) who responded to the survey reported observing either of the two clinically valid signs (Signs 7 and 8) as a correlate of male homosexuality. The clinicians most frequently reported observing (in order of frequency) Wheeler Sign 16 (human or animal anal content), Sign 20 (feminine clothing), Sign 19 (male or female genitalia), Sign 4 (humans with sex confused), and Sign 5 (humans with sex uncertain).

The hypothesis that popularity of signs was based on associative connection was tested by obtaining ratings of strength of associative connection of homosexuality to each of the five popular invalid signs as listed above, as well as to each of the two unpopular valid signs. The ratings were done by college students in the same manner as previously described for the DAP.

The predictions were confirmed. All five of the popular invalid signs were found to have a stronger associative connection to male homosexuality than either of the two unpopular clinically valid signs.

A series of laboratory studies were designed to determine whether naive observers, when presented with contrived statements of patients' symptoms and their Rorschach responses, would make the same errors of observation that the clinicians appear to have made in their observational reports. The demonstration in the laboratory of these same errors of observation would lend strong additional support to the contention that the clinicians' reports reflected illusory correlation based on associative connection.

An experiment was designed to determine if the invalid signs that were found to be popular with the clinicians are also reported by naive observers when no valid relationship is present between any category of percepts and the symptom of male homosexuality.

Clinical materials were fabricated to be shown to naive observers, in much the same fashion as previously described for the DAP. The materials consisted of 30 Rorschach cards, on each of which one percept (or response) was paired with two statements of the emotional problems of the patient who was alleged to have given the response. Rorschach percepts were indicated by circling an area of the card and pasting on it a typed statement of the response. For example, for one of the 30 Rorschach responses, the center area of Card V (Beck's area D-7) was circled and labeled "Bugs Bunny." In a corner of the card appeared the statement:

> The man who said this
> 1. has sexual feelings toward other men.
> 2. feels sad and depressed much of the time.

The two statements of emotional problems or symptoms listed on the cards were drawn from a pool of four such statements. These were:

1. He has sexual feelings toward other men.
2. He believes other people are plotting against him.
3. He feels sad and depressed much of the time.
4. He has strong feelings of inferiority.

The statements of symptoms and Rorschach percepts were paired on the 30 cards so that there was no relationship between the occurrence of any one symptom and any one category of response.

Each *S* viewed each of the 30 cards for 60 seconds. He was then given a questionnaire that presented items in the following format.

> Some of the things in the ink blots were seen by men who have the following problem:
> *He has sexual feelings toward other men.*
> Did you notice any general kind of thing that was seen most often by men with this problem? Yes__No__. If your answer is yes, name that kind of thing, and give one example of that kind of thing.
> Kind of thing____
> Example____

Results. Only 11% of the *S*s indicated that they could find no relationship between the percepts and the symptoms. In each condition, the *S*s reported, as predicted, that they observed the hypothesized illusory correlate as accompanying homosexual problems more often than any other category of percept. Associatively based illusory correlates were reported by 44% of the observers. The clinically valid signs were reported as a correlate of homosexuality by an average of 8% of the observers for each class of percepts, despite the fact that objectively they occurred equally often as the associatively based percepts. One may conclude, therefore, that the observations of popular invalid Rorschach signs of male homosexuality were reproduced in the laboratory as associatively based illusory correlates.

*S*s were tested in an additional series of conditions to determine if the illusory correlates would be reported by naive observers even if the clinically valid signs have contrived validity in the experimental task materials. The design was identical to that of the previous study except that the clinically valid Wheeler Signs 7 and 8 were paired with the symptom statement of homosexuality more often than with the other symptoms.

Three degrees of contrived validity were investigated: one in which the symptom statement of homosexuality occurred with 2/3 of the percepts of each of the two valid signs, one in which it occurred with 5/6 of them, and one in which it occurred with all of them. Each of the four symptom statements accompanied 50% of each of the other categories of percepts.

Some Additional Results. The illusory correlates based on associative connection proved to be impervious to the contrary influence of valid correlations. For all three degrees of contrived validity, the clinically popular invalid sign was the most frequently reported correlate of the symptom statement. The clinically popular invalid signs were reported as a correlate of homosexuality by an average of 47% of the observers, as compared to an average of 15% apiece for the two valid signs.

These findings might lead one to wonder if the infrequent detection of valid signs on these tasks is due to the distracting influence of illusory correlates or if instead the valid signs are inherently difficult to discover. One might also wonder whether associatively based illusory correlation occurs only because the detection of valid signs is very difficult even without the presence of associatively based illusory correlates. A further study was designed to give evidence on this question. The stimulus materials were almost identical to those of the two conditions of the previous study in which the symptom statement of homosexuality accompanied 5/6 of the percepts of the two clinically valid signs (Signs 7 & 8) and 50% of each of the other categories of percepts. The only change from the previous study was that there was no popular invalid sign (illusory correlate) presented.

In these conditions, the two clinically valid signs were the most frequently reported categories of percepts. (One was reported by 27% of the observers, and the other by 38%.) These values were about double the percentages reported in the comparable conditions in which associatively based illusory correlates were present, and the increases in accuracy were significant.

Discussion

These findings demonstrate that when naive *S*s observe test responses paired with statements concerning the symptoms of the alleged patients who made the responses, they tend to agree with one another by reporting that they observe the same illusory correlates of the symptom statements. The correlates that they erroneously report correspond to associative connections between symptoms and test responses. These systematic errors persist both under repeated exposure to the stimulus materials and under conditions designed to maximize motivation and opportunity to observe accurately. They persist even in the presence of competing valid correlates of the symptoms. Moreover, these associatively based illusory correlates are markedly similar to popular invalid clinical observations by practicing psychodiagnosticians of the kinds of test responses made by patients with these symptoms. This striking similarity leads one to suspect that many clinical observations have their genesis in illusory correlation arising from associative connection.

The *S*s in the present studies observed the stimulus materials under conditions far more amenable to accuracy of observation than the conventional clinical situation. In all of these studies, *S*s observed the various symptom statements and drawings in close temporal proximity. In clinical practice such observations are often separated by a period of days or even weeks, thus allowing selective forgetting. In these experiments, the number of symptoms stated for each alleged patient was limited to two, while in the clinical situation it is usually many more, which greatly complicates the clinician's task. Moreover, the clinician usually has considerable latitude in deciding which of the symptoms he sees as most important for a given patient, while in these experiments the symptoms were unambiguously stated.

Consensual pseudo-validation enhanced the frequency of the report of illusory correlates in Experiment VII on the DAP despite the fact that the observers communicated on only one brief occasion during the experimental sessions. It seems likely that in clinical practice the observer is repeatedly reassured as to the accuracy of his observation of illusory correlates, because of the reports of his fellow clinicians who themselves are subject to the same illusions. Such consensual validation, especially among experts, is usually regarded as evidence of truth.

The present findings indicate that illusory correlates reported by clinicians do not reflect personal defects of the clinicians as much as difficulties inherent in the clinician's task. The errors are ones to which most, or perhaps all, people are prone. By analogy, if the members of some profession had as their task the estimation of the length of lines, the practitioners would surely not be regarded as inferior if most members of the profession were subject to the Müller-Lyer illusion.

What is the solution to this problem? One partial solution might be to attempt to reduce the tendency toward forming illusory correlations by special training. Each graduate student in clinical psychology could be asked to serve, during his training, as an observer in a task like those used in the present studies, and he could be shown the source of the illusory correlates that he reports. He would then probably have a keener awareness of the difficulties of making such observations, and he would be better able to guard against them in his future clinical practice. Hopefully, as a result of such training, he would also be more receptive to relevant research evidence, and would be less inclined to rely solely on his own clinical observations. He would also be aware that "consensual validation" may reflect shared systematic error rather than shared accuracy.

Such training, however, would not solve the more basic problem that the psychodiagnostician's cognitive task often apparently exceeds the capacity of the human intellect. The ultimate solution, as suggested by Meehl (1960), may lie in at least a partial replacement of clinical psychodiagnostic methods by actuarial prediction.

5. THE HUMAN USE OF PERSONALITY TESTS: A DISSENTING VIEW

Victor R. Lovell[1]

During the past 10 years, public resentment of personality testing has become increasingly evident (Amrine, 1965; Dailey, 1963; Gross, 1962; Hoffman, 1962; Packard, 1964; Whyte, 1956). Testimony has been given on the abuse of personality tests before the Senate Subcommittee on Constitutional Rights (1965) and the House Special Subcommittee on Invasion of Privacy of the Committee on Government Operations (1965). It seems evident that unless psychologists concerned with personality assessment voluntarily restrict their own activities in some fashion, they will soon be subject to legal restrictions. At this writing, one bill to set up such restrictions has already been introduced into the House of Representatives (Doctor, 1966).

The response of psychologists to this outcry has usually been to attribute it to public ignorance or political extremism (Amrine, 1965; Dailey, 1963; Vance, 1965). I think we have been somewhat fatuous in this matter. In my opinion, the protests we have heard, however ill informed and inarticulate they have been, are directed at misuses of psychology which are quite real and very serious, to which our vested interests have blinded us.

Fundamentally, I think the issue is one of reconciling three divergent interests: (*a*) the public's right to privacy; (*b*) the social scientist's freedom of inquiry; and (*c*) the personnel worker's right to determine fitness for employment. Solutions, insofar as they have been proposed, have usually taken the direction of *restricting test content.* I do not think this tack can ever lead to any resolution of the basic conflicts involved.

The problem with restricting content is twofold. First, as is always the case with censorship, one does not know how to go about laying down concrete guidelines. Second, to do so will not offer adequate protection to the public, nor to the social scientist, nor to the personnel worker. Even if items dealing with sex, politics, and religion are deleted from personality inventories, the respondent's private thoughts are still likely to be probed. *Any* restriction of

SOURCE. Victor R. Lovell is Director of the Institute for Group and Family Studies, Palo Alto, California. He was formerly on the staffs of Stanford University and San Francisco State College. Dr. Lovell's fields of research specialization are personality inventories, higher education, and psychotherapy. This article originally appeared in the *American Psychologist,* 1967, **22**, 383-393 and is reprinted by permission of the American Psychological Association and the author.

[1]I am indebted to my colleague, Norman S. Ciddan, for the benefit of numerous clarifying discussions on the problems with which this paper is concerned.

content is clearly an incursion on freedom of inquiry. Finally, determination of job qualifications may require the use of threatening stimuli, as, for example, when candidates for work in hospitals are given concept-formation tests involving pictures of horrible wounds.

An alternative to restricting content is to *restrict function.* Specifically, I am going to propose that certain kinds of tests should not be used in certain ways. I will lay down concrete guidelines for this proposal by arguing that certain kinds of "contracts" between assessors and respondents should be outlawed.

Basically, personality testing is used for two very different purposes, which I shall call the *personnel function* and the *client function.* I define the former as applying to situations where there is a potential conflict of interest between assessor and respondent, and the latter as applying to situations where there is not. The personnel function usually involves decisions about hiring, promotion, and termination. The client function usually involves providing services to the respondent. There are, however, important exceptions to these generalizations.

Where testing is purely for research purposes, we have the client function, except in situations where research subjects are coerced, deceived, or when their test results are not considered to be confidential, in which case we have the personnel function. The latter would include all research enterprises where participation by subjects is not voluntary. Testing serves a personnel function in all service situations where the respondent is not free to accept or reject services (as when he is committed to a mental hospital), or where he must qualify for them in some way other than by being able to pay for them (as when he is applying for welfare benefits).

Three Test Contracts

Whether a particular assessment situation involves the client function or the personnel function becomes apparent when we examine the test contract involved. By "test contract," I mean whatever is understood between assessor and respondent. This involves some extension of the sense of "contract," since the term is usually restricted to voluntary agreements, and assessment often involves involuntary elements.

Suppose we should administer a personality inventory to a group of incoming freshmen at a college or university, and suppose the following message were to appear printed on the first inside page of the booklet which contains the test items:

> *To the Respondent:*
>
> We are asking you these questions because we really want to know what you think, and how you feel, and because we are convinced that it will

contribute to your education in some small way for you to ask them of yourself.

The information we are asking you to give will be used in one or both of two ways. First, it may contribute to our research on the process of higher education and the character of youth in our contemporary world. Second, it may be used to help provide you with psychological services during your college career, if you should decide that you require them. It will not be used by others to make decisions about you although it may contribute to helping you make your own decisions more effectively.

If you take this inventory, the information you give us will be held in the strictest confidence. It will not be made available without your express permission (written, signed, and in our judgment uncoerced) to administrators, faculty members, parents, prospective employers, or anyone else except those on your campus whose primary obligation is to provide you with mental health or counseling services, or to do unbiased research in the social sciences.

When you take the inventory, we would like you to enter into a contract with us: *You don't try to fool us and we don't try to fool you.* The appropriate response to an item in this inventory is the one which you feel in your heart to be honest; the inappropriate one is the one which you know is not. If you do not feel that you can accept these terms, we would prefer that you did not take the inventory, for without this contract you will be wasting both your time and ours.

Since the inventory contains material which is personal and controversial, you should think carefully before deciding to take it. If you should decide not to, we shall understand and respect your decision.

If you do decide to take the inventory, we wish you a pleasant and provocative exercise in self-discovery. We hope that this experience will move you a little closer to that intimate self-knowledge which has always been one of the primary goals of higher education.

Good luck!

Signed,
(the test authors)

We shall call this message the *client contract.*

Now suppose instead this message appears:

To the Respondent:

Because of the complexity of the technical considerations involved, and the limited space available here, it is not possible for us to explain to you the nature of this psychological assessment. We assure you that it is being done for sound reasons, and that nothing is being demanded of you capriciously.

The information you give us will be used in many very important ways. It will become a part of your permanent academic record. It may influence critical decisions which others will have to make about your career. It will be made available in various forms to administrators, faculty members, parents, prospective employers, and others who have a vital interest in your character and your welfare.

Make your test responses as honestly as you can. It will not be in your best interest to do otherwise. If you should try to slant your answers so as to make a more favorable impression than is justified, this will become apparent to us when we score your test, and will reflect badly upon you.

Be conscientious and be careful!

Signed,
(the test authors)

We shall call this message the *strong personnel contract.*

Finally, consider a third message:

To the Respondent:

Because of the complexity of the technical considerations involved, the limited space available here, and the uses to which the material is to be put, it is not possible for us to explain to you the nature of this psychological assessment. We assure you that it is being done for sound reasons, and that nothing is being demanded of your capriciously.

The information which we will gain from this test will be used in many very important ways. It will become a part of your permanent academic record. It may influence critical decisions which others will have to make about your career. It will be made available in various forms to administrators, faculty members, prospective employers, parents, and others who have a vital interest in your character and your welfare.

You may try to slant your test answers so as to create a favorable impression. We will take this into consideration when we score your test. Your ability to create a favorable impression is of great interest to us, for it is likely to contribute much to your success or failure in a great many life situations. If you don't want to play this game with us, you can probably get away with refusing to take this test, if you really want to push it. We will try to make it as hard as possible for you to do so, because our boss wants you tested, and we work for him, and not for you.

We have to live too!

Signed,
(the test authors)

We shall call this message the *weak personnel contract.*

Test Contracts and Test Standardization

The three examples given above represent the major alternatives available to the psychologist when he administers a personality assessment program. For the sake of brevity, the research contract and the counseling contract have been fused into one. It should be clear that current practice seldom involves making the nature of the situation explicit to the respondent. Typically, in the kind of situation alluded to above, the freshman class would be herded into an auditorium at some time during a crowded "orientation week," handed the test materials, and told to follow the simple instructions printed thereon. If someone should object, it is likely to be communicated to him that he is a trouble maker who has no business questioning the wisdom of professional people who obviously have only his best interests at heart.

The first point I should like to make is that, both as individuals involved in the administration of assessment programs, and I am convinced, eventually as a profession, we must choose between the alternatives suggested above, and we must make them explicit to the respondent. If we do not, we shall not be able to validate our assessment instruments in any very broad and profound fashion, because we shall not be able to maintain standard and uniform testing conditions. No matter what validation data we may have about our hypothetical personality inventory, if these data have been gathered under the client contract, we shall have difficulty making valid inferences about the meaning of test scores acquired under conditions where a personnel contract was involved. Further, if the testing actually serves a personnel function, the effect of personnel decisions will probably be a feeding back of information into the respondent population, which will alter the relationship of test variables with critical nontest variables; that is to say, people will become test wise and validity will vanish. For a discussion of the relationship between test validity and test situations, see Sarason (1950).

It has traditionally been argued that where the message making explicit the testing contract (or lack of such) is withheld, the respondent will make his own idiosyncratic interpretation of the situation, and that this interpretation, as manifested in his responses, will be indicative of broad and enduring traits of character in which the assessor is interested. While this argument is based on what is perhaps one of the most profound ideas in psychological assessment, its specific application to the *assessment contract* is naïve and wrongheaded. This is because most situations in which personality tests are administered are in fact highly structured. The respondent may be expected to infer the rules and goals of the game from the context in which it is played, even if they are not articulated by the assessors. In other words, variance due to interpretation of the test contract is probably mostly situational, rather than individual, in its determination.

If a man is applying for a job, and we give him a test, he does not need to be told that the success of his application is contingent on his responses (although present ethical standards state that he should be). He reasonably assumes that we would not do it if it were not good business, and he knows that the task at hand is to decide whether or not to hire him. If we in fact tested the job applicant for some other purpose, such as to decide where in the organization he might best be placed, we would run some danger of defeating ourselves, for our validity data would probably be based on the responses of men already placed, rather than on job applicants.

In the freshman testing situation described above, the respondent has spent a good deal of time during the past weeks providing information for various administrative records. Further, he has just spent the past year providing information to admissions officers, on the basis of which various critical decisions about his life have been made. It is unlikely to make much difference if a client contract is in fact the intention of the assessors. Even if independent psychological services exist on the campus, he will not come to the conclusion that they do, and he will infer a personnel contract.

I hold that eventually we must choose among the client contract, the strong personnel contract, and the weak personnel contract, not only for specific instruments and specific assessment programs, but also as a profession, for all "personality tests." This is because each time any one of us administers a personality test, he is participating in the creation of a cultural institution. Which test contract is understood by the respondent depends not only upon what cues are present in the testing situation, nor upon the immediate institutional context which surrounds it, but also upon the respondent's general understanding of the legitimate functions of personality assessment in his society. If one looks at what is said about personality tests, one gets the impression that, outside the private practice of psychology, with individual clients, the weak personnel contract is fast becoming normative, both from the point of view of the lay public, and from the point of view of professional psychologists. If we do not make the decision, it will be made for us as a result of the institutional processes in which we are involved. I am concerned lest it be already too late for a rational and considered choice to be possible.

If the reader has followed the argument thus far, three questions are likely to come to mind. First, what sort of contract with the respondent is most consistent with the ethical practice of psychology? Second, what sort of contract is most likely to lead in the long run to the valid measurement of personality? And third, what contract will allow us to offer the community the broadest range of psychological services?

In the remainder of this essay, I shall argue for a client contract on all three counts. I shall further take the view that our three questions cannot ultimately be considered independently from one another, because ethics, science, and services are all outcomes of a single activity, and this activity is one of many interdependent components of a unitary social process. One cannot do something ethically, if one cannot do it at all. We cannot use our personality tests to provide psychological services if we are unable to construct valid measures. And, as I have already tried to suggest comparing sample contracts, the validity of our tests is not independent of our ethics, because our ethics supply the social context in which our tests are administered, and in which they are validated.

Test Contracts and Ethics

In its public manifestos, the profession of psychology is firmly committed to political democracy, civil liberties, and the dignity of the individual. In practice, we sometimes violate these commitments, on behalf of bureaucratic or commercial interests. I do not believe that the strong personnel contract has any place in a free society, and I think that its occasional appearance is psychology's unique contribution to creeping totalitarianism in our times.

The strong personnel contract flatly denies the respondent's right to privacy. It proposes that kind of total surveillance of the individual which is characteristic of police states. Further, the strong personnel contract reeks with paternalism. It suggests total supervision as well as total surveillance. Finally, it creates the conditions for mutual suspicion and distrust among men. It invokes the possibility that deceit, if successful, may be richly rewarded, while at the same time threatening dire consequences if it is not.

The weak personnel contract might be considered ethically marginal. It is not a clear-cut invasion of privacy. It neither demands truth, nor threatens falsehood. Surveillance is more limited to that which is directly relevant, for to the degree to which the goal of the respondent's task is made clear, the test could be considered a work sample. Like the strong personnel contract, however, it is paternalistic (perhaps "maternalistic" would be more exact). It implies that those in positions of authority need not account to the public for their actions, and that their decisions must be taken on faith. Finally, the weak personnel contract, if received sufficiently often, will contribute in some small part to undermining the foundations of democratic process, for the efficacy of that process depends upon the authentic confrontation by the citizenry of each other, in order that their collective will may be determined. Since the weak personnel contract promises to reward conformity, it may discourage the articulation of loyal opposition, if it is true that what is learned in social situations is widely generalized.

The client contract protects the right to privacy, for it guarantees confidentiality, specifies the limits of confidence, and invites the respondent to decline to take the test if this is not satisfactory. It leaves him in a good position to make his decision, since it states the nature of the assessment, and indicates the possible benefits of making the choice to participate. Finally, it attempts to promote the kind of human relationships which contribute to harmonious living in a free and open community.

Although Messick (1965) suggests that, "We should be especially careful not to let it be inferred that any change in our standards for psychological assessment necessarily reflects a general admission of past guilt [p. 137]," both the strong and the weak personnel contracts are quite permissible under present APA (1963) Ethical Standards, which simply state that:

> The psychologist who asks that an individual reveal personal information in the course of interviewing, testing, or evaluation, or who allows such information to be divulged to him, does so only after making certain that the responsible person is fully aware of the purpose of the interview, testing or evaluation and of the ways in which the information may be used [Principle 7d, p. 57].

This is analogous to the legal principle which demands that the accused be informed that anything he says may be held against him, but the analogy is not carried out consistently. The accused may not decline to testify against himself. His psychological interrogator need obtain no search warrant in order to examine his psyche.

Privacy and Duplicity

Two related ethical themes arise when the proper use of personality tests is considered: *privacy* and *duplicity*. If the assessor is bound by no constraints in his invasions of the former, then the respondent is sure to react with the latter, and the assessor must outwit him by the use of *counterduplicity*. This is a particularly messy business, because the respondent is not typically asked to testify as to objective matters of fact, but rather to the status of his attitudes, impulses, memories, emotions, and so forth. Because of this, his testimony cannot be independently corroborated. It may be examined for its internal consistency, but this is not relevant in the way that it would be, say in a legal situation, because consistency is not necessarily a property of attitudes, impulses, memories, emotions, etc.

It is sometimes suggested that this impasse may be resolved scientifically, rather than ethically. We need only investigate duplicity as a behavioral phenomenon, and when we have come to understand it, our subjects will not be able to deceive us. This line of thought springs from the notion that social science can function outside the social contract, without reference to moral concepts. All experimenters have moral commitments, however, just as all experimenters are either male or female, and I think it reasonable to expect the former to be as much involved in determining the behavior of subjects as the latter.

Once the respondent and the assessor have entered into a contract which permits them to deceive each other, it is difficult to see how any operational meaning can be given to the notion of duplicity. In order to investigate duplicity, the assessor must have some way of determining its presence or absence, but this requires that the declarations of the respondent be in some way corroborated, and we have seen that it is not clear how this is to be done. Even if the responses of the subject are recorded under conditions where it is believed that he is not aware of being observed, the authenticity of his behavior will be hard to establish, because this belief may be mistaken, and the observer is involved in a social game which leaves him no way to check up on himself.

However, even though duplicity is neither observed nor understood, administration of personality tests accompanied by a personnel contract might make it possible to validly predict some very critical events in which someone had a legitimate interest. The question of whether it is likely that this *can* be done will be taken up at a later point. The question at hand is whether it *should* be done.

Those who think it should often espouse what might be called the "hired-gun ethic." Duplicity in human relations, particularly in the presentation of one's own character to others, seems to be a common and pervasive characteristic of human society in general and personnel situations in particular. As long as this sort of thing is going to go on, the game might as well be played as well as possible by all concerned. It is not the business of professional psychologists either to rebel against the human condition, or to make policy for their employers. A similar defense is usually given by scientists and technicians involved in the design and production of war machines intended for the destruction of human property and human life.

Another kind of cold war could result. Some psychologists will make it their business to devise ever more complex and subtle ways of tricking their unwilling victims into revealing themselves. Others will offer their services as coaches to the respondent, to help him outwit the assessor. It is difficult to see how the enterprise of measuring individual differences could survive such a social holocaust, or how the individual would retain a voice in the conduct of his society. Actually, the orthodox version of the hired-gun ethic usually assumes that it is ethical for the psychologist to help the personnel worker to deceive the respondent, but not vice versa. The reasons for this bias are commercial, not ethical. So far, respondent coaching has been by nonpsychologists (Alex, 1965; Whyte, 1956).

In a nation where private enterprise is the dominant form of economic organization, it may be argued that while public agencies may be restricted, private institutions should be allowed to handle their personnel problems as they see fit, and therefore that professional psychologists who are employed by them should feel free to help them do so. A little thought should convince one that this is not so. Under our present system, hiring and firing practices are regulated by ethics and by legislation, just as working conditions are. To deny that this is as it should be would be to argue, for example, that personnel workers should be able to tap the telephone lines of job applicants, or inject them with truth serums.

Ethics, Prejudice, and Paternalism

It is sometimes argued that the use of personality tests in selection is equalitarian in effect, if not libertarian in method. The advent of abilities tests as selection devices contributed a great deal to the leveling of barriers to social mobility in our society. It tended to make advancement more dependent on merit, and less on privilege. It has been claimed that personality tests, if used in the same fashion, may do the same. I think it is more likely that they will have the opposite effect. The correlation between personality traits and demographic variables such as social class, caste, and religious persuasion is well known.

Suppose a personality inventory contained the following item:

I am a Negro. (T) (F)

As social scientists, we know that this item would be a valid predictor of all sorts of critical social outcomes in which the personnel worker has a legitimate interest, such as whether or not the respondent's conduct is likely to be criminal. However, we also know that the validity of the item would depend upon the operation of social forces the existence of which most of us deplore. Few of us would use this item if we could, because we would recognize that to do so would help perpetuate those social forces. Our prediction would be self-fulfilling, and contribute to the maintenance of barriers to social mobility. Yet it is probable that whenever we use personality tests in selection, we capitalize upon, and perpetuate, all sorts of prejudices, more subtle, less well understood, and perhaps more profound and in the very long run even more destructive than those regarding race. No matter how inclined we might be to use brute empiricism with our prediction problems, Federal law would prohibit us from using the item above. However, for the most part, the choice of what test content to use for what assessment purpose is presently left to our own discretion, as well as the use we make of such. I suggest that we should exercise discretion, before this choice is taken away from us by a justifiably resentful public.

It is often pointed out that effective selection may protect the respondent from being put in a situation where he will fail, or where he will be uncomfortable. If the information necessary to do this must be extracted from him without his consent, is it not doing him a service to extract it? The trouble with this view is that it presupposes a paternalistic view of society which seems hardly compatible with the democratic values to which we are committed. In order to afford the respondent this kind of "protection," someone else has to decide what is good for him. In some areas, it makes sense to do this. A doctor does not usually feel the need to ask permission to save a patient's life; he assumes that the patient wants to live. But in the area of physical well-being there are norms with which it can be safely assumed that almost everyone will agree. In the area of emotional well-being there are no such norms.

Test Contracts and Test Validity

Our grandiosity in assuming that we can measure people who we can safely assume do not wish to be measured barely conceals our manifest failure, at least up to now, to measure nonintellective personality traits at all. I suspect that there is some kind of connection between the two. Would a physiologist attempt to measure basal metabolism without the cooperation of his subject? Why should we think we can do better?

The public seems well informed of the basic principles underlying the use of personality tests in personnel work, including the rather crude devices presently in existence for the detection of faking (Alex, 1965). This has been true for some time now (Whyte, 1956). I think it likely, as Whyte suggests, that the general nature of the game is understood intuitively even by unsophisticated respondents. The vast body of "hard data" in existence on dissimulation is probably irrelevant here, since almost all of it has been collected in totally artificial situations.

What is ethical is usually what is practical when one takes a broad view of things. We guarantee complete confidentiality to our clients in psychotherapy because we know that if we did not do so, they would not trust us and we would not obtain the kind of communication from them which we require in order to effectively provide this service. I believe that something of this sort applies to the relationship between validity and contract in personality testing.

What kind of test contract will tend to maximize overall validity? This, of course, is an "empirical question," but if it is approached in the hammer-and-tongs fashion which the term often implies when used by psychologists, the results could well be disastrous. If we gave our hypothetical personality inventory to three different groups of freshmen from the same class, each with a different one of our three contracts printed in the test booklet, we might then proceed to examine its validity under the three conditions, relative to various prediction problems. However, even if our consciences permitted us to conduct such an experiment, and we were able to obtain administrative approval for it, we might run some danger of precipitating a student revolt. In any case, we would create an atmosphere on the campus which would make validity data collected there subsequently somewhat difficult to interpret.

Nevertheless, let us suppose that as a profession we embark on a program of research of the sort alluded to above. I doubt that after 10 or 15 years of this sort of thing we will be much closer to resolving the issue on so-called empirical grounds than we are right now. We will have accumulated another one of those vast and diffuse bodies of literature which have become so common, of late. Even those of us working in the immediate area will not have time to read it all. Everyone who has taken a stand on the issue will find ways to produce results consistent with his position. Everyone who has not will be unable to digest the data and make up his mind.

Investigations of this kind are fruitless because they rest on an outmoded and wrongheaded notion of what validity is. They are addressed to no legitimate theoretical issue. They proliferate, not because one finding leads to others which can be reconciled with it in more general terms, but because one finding provokes the production of others which are interesting only because they can be made to appear inconsistent with it, or with each other. The proper dialectic of science is not advanced. Such research programs regard validity solely in terms of predictive power, without taking predictive scope into consideration.

To decide the issue at hand in light of the outcome of some set of particular predictive ventures would be to make the implausible assumption that there exists some general solution which would be true for all test variables, all criterion variables, all populations, and all combinations thereof. It would be to treat a methodological bias as if it were a theoretical model. Moreover, the decision would have to be based on investigations limited by the marginal level of validity characteristic of most existent personality measures.

If the empirical question be approached in a less concretistic fashion, I believe that there are good empirical grounds for choosing the client contract, in order to facilitate the development of valid procedures for personality assessment. All of our psychological theories contain propositions, well supported by empirical evidence, to the effect that when an organism is in danger, its behavior becomes less variable and less complex. Such behavior may not lend itself to the enterprise of differentiating between organisms.

Learning theory tells us that when organisms are placed on a reinforcement schedule their behavior becomes less variable. Cognitive theory informs us that when an organism is exposed to the threat of punishment or to induced conflict, dedifferentiation of the cognitive structure and isolation of its components is the result. Social psychology tells us that when the status of human beings is in jeopardy, their behavior will be characterized by rigid and pervasive conformity to norms which are perceived as associated with its maintenance. Psychoanalytic theory holds that the threat of ego damage evokes anxiety, and that anxiety produces repression and constriction, which prevent expression and articulation of the whole personality. All of these propositions seem to suggest that the threat and coercion involved in personnel contracts will tend to mitigate against the measurement of individual differences, where honesty is required of the subject.

Good psychological theory therefore, would seem to predict that under many conditions, with many variables, the effect of test administration involving personnel contracts will be to restrict the dispersion of the test variables, while at the same time increasing their intercorrelation, an effect which we would expect in general to render them less useful in the prediction of external criteria. To specify for which test variables, which criterion variables, and under exactly what conditions this will be so is the task of the theorist. Because this task is part of a process which is never complete, the issue at hand can never be summarily "settled" empirically, although it may always be further investigated, if other considerations do not dictate otherwise.

In terms of common sense, what is being suggested here is that we will obtain more information from people if we trust them and they trust us. This thesis is in good accord with the accumulated wisdom of the Judeo-Christian heritage. To hold that it will be true for all people, all situations, and all kinds of information would indeed be naïve. It is both normative and descriptive in intent, for as a prediction, it is likely to be self-fulfilling. I do not think it naïve to suggest that, for our profession, there is a presumption that it is the most viable game, both scientifically and socially.

Those who do personality research are often concerned lest if the option to refuse to take a personality test is made explicit and available, and is as a result often accepted, the generality of their findings will suffer. Potential respondents who decline to be tested will surely be different from those who do not, in ways that are important to us as scientists. I do not think that the truth of this can be disputed, but I think that it is often felt to have implications which it does not, namely, that opportunity for empirical inquiry is seriously diminished. Offering potential respondents the option of refusing to be tested will enable us to record and search for correlates of this behavior. An imaginative investigator who has a clear understanding of the theoretical questions and practical applications to which he has addressed himself will be able to use the data to achieve his goals. The loss involved in making the population tested more highly selected may not seem so great when we recall that most of the populations we test are already highly selected. Furthermore, we will now administer an additional "test," namely the acceptance or rejection of the assessment itself. We psychologists sometimes involve ourselves in an interesting paradox: On one hand we claim that our understanding of human nature will contribute to the "control" of human behavior, while on the other we demand that the control of human behavior be handed over to us in order that we may accomplish our ends.

A New Ethical Standard

It should be clear from what has already been said that I am proposing a considerable restriction of the uses to which certain kinds of mental tests may be put. The client contract is clearly appropriate to different assessment goals from those of the personnel contract. What will be the effect of this restriction on our capacity to provide psychological services? In order to discuss this question it is necessary to specify exactly what restrictions I advocate.

Up to now I have used the term "personality test." Although this more or less accords with popular usage, it is a misnomer, because all mental tests are properly speaking tests of personality. The kinds of tests I mean this discussion to refer to might best be called tests of character, virtue, psychopathology, and the like. The kinds of tests I do not mean to include under this rubric are tests of ability, aptitude, achievement, proficiency, and their ilk, where what is assessed is a work capacity or a work sample. In the remainder of this paper, I shall refer to the former as *tests of character,* and to the latter as *tests of capacity*.

A test of capacity is one for which there are criteria for deciding which responses are correct and which responses are incorrect, which are independent of the respondent, and of which the respondent is properly informed. By "correct responses" I mean those which will be rewarded; by "incorrect responses" those which will be punished. In testing for capacity, the respondent is told that he is to be evaluated, given an understanding of what is to constitute success and what failure, and success and failure are determined by norms which are external to him, be they subjective, as in an essay examination, or objective, as in an intelligence test. A test of character is one for which there are no criteria for deciding which responses are correct and which responses are not, or one for which the criteria of "correctness" are norms which are relative to the respondent, i.e., when the respondent is told that the "correct" answer is the "honest" one. Tests of character involve the recording of behavior under conditions where the assessor has not defined success and failure for the respondent, or under conditions where the assessor has defined success and failure for the respondent only in terms of the authenticity of self-report.

Personality inventories and projective techniques usually involve tests of character. Tests of capacity are most often concerned with ability, skills, problem solving, learning, the production of specified mechanical outputs, and so forth. But none of this is necessarily so, because the definition given above is independent of the nature of the test stimuli. A personality inventory becomes a test of capacity if the respondent is instructed to give the responses which will make a good impression on some particular class of people, and his protocol is scored for its correspondence with some reasonable determination of what responses do in fact make a good impression on this class. An intelligence test becomes a test of character if the respondent is asked not to solve problems but rather to indicate which kinds of problems he prefers and which he does not. It is still a test of character if the respondent is asked to solve problems, but his protocol is scored for his style of problem solving, rather than for the merit of his solutions. A person perception test is a test of capacity if it is scored for accuracy; if it is scored in terms of preferences for certain response categories, regardless of the appropriateness of these categories to actual persons, it is a test of character. Whether a test involves character or capacity depends upon what the respondent is told to do, and upon how response categories are defined by the assessor when he scores the test protocol.

Tests of *social stimulus value,* in which the respondent is not identical with the person assessed, fall into a third category. Letters of recommendation, ratings of others, sociometric data, and so forth, are neither tests of capacity nor tests of character with respect to the person recommended, rated, or chosen. *With respect to the respondent,* they may be either tests of capacity or of character, depending upon the nature of his contract with the assessor.

One may determine whether a test is one of character or of capacity by asking if the respondent can "fake good." The notion of representing oneself as *better than one is* is never applicable to tests of capacity, but always applicable to tests of character. The latter are motivationally labile in a way that the former are not.

A moment's reflection should reveal that this distinction is independent not only of test content, but also of the construct which is measured. If intelligence is measured by the success of problem-solving activity, as it usually is, we have a test of capacity. But if it is measured, as it occasionally is, by the tendency to claim attitudes characteristic of successful problem solvers, then we have a test of character. If flexibility is measured by some kind of self-report device, then it is measured by a test of character. But if it is measured by success in a problem-solving situation, then it is measured by a test of capacity.

If the administration of a personality inventory involves the client contract or the strong personnel contract, as given earlier, the inventory is a test of character, because the respondent is asked to give an honest self-report. The interesting thing about the weak personnel contract is that it is a mixed bag. In terms of the distinction between character and capacity it is neither fish nor fowl. The question of whether a correct response is to be defined in terms of internal or external norms is left ambiguous. The accused is properly informed that what he says may be used against him, but he does not know how. If the task assigned the respondent were solely to make a good impression, and the persons to be impressed were indicated, and the scoring of the test were based in some way on the actual attitudes of these persons towards the test items, then we would have a *pure* test of capacity; otherwise we would not.

It may be objected that the categories of character and capacity may not be mutually exclusive. The weak personnel contract may make the inventory *both* a test of character and of capacity, since it is suggested that a correct response may be defined either with reference to internal or to external norms. The nature of the situation where the categories seem to overlap is perplexing, because the distinction involves what the respondent is asked to do, and it is not clear what he is being asked to do when he is told that his responses will be evaluated in terms of potentially conflicting norms. My inclination is to argue that under such conditions, we have a test of character, rather than of capacity, because if it is not clear what the respondent has been asked to do, then he has not been asked to do anything in particular.

The distinction between tests of character and tests of capacity is similar to that made by Cronbach (1960) between *tests of typical performance* and *tests of maximal performance,* and to that made by Wallace (1966) between *response predisposition* and *response capability.* The principal difference is that the categories used here are based solely on the nature of the test instructions and the test scoring, while those used by Cronbach and Wallace have reference also to theoretical constructs.

My position is that tests of character should never be used for any kind of personnel function, whether it be selection or placement. They should be used only for unbiased research, subject to the restrictions implicit in the client function, and to provide psychological services in situations where the assessor's first professional loyalty is to the respondent. I have argued this position on ethical grounds and on scientific grounds. I shall now consider what effect its implementation might have on the marketing of psychological services.

Ethics and Psychological Services

I should first like to reemphasize a point which has already been made. Our capacity to provide assessment services cannot be discussed independently of the validity, present and future, of our assessment procedures, nor of the ethical standards which are to be applied to these procedures. We cannot provide services with invalid instruments. It is likely that we shall not be allowed to offer services if our ethics offend the public. Bills to restrict the activity of psychological testing have been appearing in our state legislatures for some time. They appeal to a variety of political groups for a variety of reasons, and are capable of attracting widespread support.

I have tried to define the sort of assessment procedure which must be restricted as narrowly as possible. In principle, the personnel psychologist is not to be enjoined from measuring any construct, nor from using any kind of test content. Essentially, all that must be given up is the demand for a certain kind of contract with the respondent, one which I doubt that much sense can be made of anyway, either in a legalistic or a scientific way. In practice, the personnel psychologist will not be able to measure constructs involving the notions of self-report or spontaneous behavior. I doubt that this is a real limitation; I think that the logic of such constructs dictates that they cannot be measured in personnel settings anyway, because of the likelihood that spontaneous or authentic behavior may be penalized. Many writers on the subject have reached similar conclusions. Cronbach (1960), for example, says:

> Complete frankness cannot be anticipated in any situation where the subject will be rewarded or punished for his response. Some degree of reward and punishment is implicit in any institutional use of tests, such as clinical diagnosis or employee selection. Honest self-examination can be hoped for only when the tester is helping the subject solve his own problems, and even then the subject may have a goal for which he wishes the support of the counselor's authority, which biases his response [p. 454].

I would not go so far as to endorse the suspicion, suggested by the last phrase, that the notion of "honest self-examination" can have no place at all in our psychological constructs. Rather, my position is that the only way to escape from this dilemma is to make it clear in our testing contracts whether or not we intend to reward and punish, and if we do so intend, to indicate which response classes are to be rewarded and which punished, and then to try to the best of our ability to keep the contract, and that the only way to do this is to uniformly confront our potential respondents as a profession with some simple and broad ethical commitment. I think that if we do this we can become involved with constructs in which the concept of authenticity plays a part, while if we do not we shall of necessity close off many possible areas of research and service. I do not mean that we can produce interpersonal processes in which self-deception and the need to deceive others will not play a part; dynamic psychology dictates otherwise. I mean that we can only give operational value to such notions as authenticity and honest self-examination by creating situations where the integrity of interpersonal processes is protected by a particular kind of ethical structure, such as we have with regard to the processes of counseling and psychotherapy.

By restricting the activities of the personnel psychologist and in some cases those of the research psychologist, I believe we will act to protect the integrity of a variety of other psychological services, such as counseling and psychodiagnosis. These enterprises are simpler and more profound if we have the trust of our clients. Service-oriented research will also be facilitated if psychological assessors are trusted by their subjects. The counseling service might even be extended. Institutions which formerly depended only upon the personnel process to assign persons to places might employ private counseling psychologists who would report only to the candidate, and who would guarantee complete confidentiality to him. Self-selection and self-placement could then contribute to personnel decisions at the option of the candidate.

6. TEST BURNING IN TEXAS

Gwynn Nettler

By a 5–1 vote the governing board of the Houston Independent School District, one of the largest in the nation, in June 1959 ordered burned the answer sheets to six sociopsychometrics administered to some 5,000 ninth graders. Four of these instruments were taken from a pilot study of the National Talent Project to be administered by the University of Pittsburgh and the American Institute for Research in 1960; the remaining instruments were added by local psychologists interested in forecasting the realization of talent and in the assessment of psychological health.

The board also instructed the assistant superintendent in charge of special services, whose office had served as repository for tests administered in other school systems within the county, to return several thousand additional answer sheets to a dozen participating districts that they might reconsider submission of these results.

The action of the Houston trustees destroyed the labors of responsible school personnel and social scientists. It countermanded the administrative decision of its own school executives to participate in such a study and challenged the thoughtfulness of all the other school officials who, at a March meeting of the County Superintendent's Association, had agreed to take part in this project guided by its own members and subsidized by the Hogg Foundation for Mental Health of the University of Texas. The board's public action, and the response of the metropolitan press, exposed a prevailing misunderstanding of the nature of a psychometric and suspicion of the good sense of psychologists.

The instruments that had been used included a Vocabulary-Information Profile Test, an Interest Blank, a High School Personality Test, a Student Information Blank that included self-evaluating items on health, a sociometric rating device, and the Youth Attitude Scales. These last measures, which contained most of the troublesome items, concern students' perceptions of

SOURCE. Gwynn Nettler received her doctoral degree at Stanford University and has served as senior clinical psychologist at the Reno Mental Health Center of the Nevada State Department of Health. Dr. Nettler is presently Professor of Sociology at the University of Alberta and has worked in the areas of attitude measurement and determination, psychotherapy, and behavior deviation. This article originally appeared in the *American Psychologist,* 1959, **14**, 682-683. Reprinted by permission of the American Psychological Association and the author.

themselves and their relations with their families, teachers, and peers. These scales are not part of the National Talent Project but were adapted from questionnaires used in the 1956 Texas Cooperative Youth Study that had been administered to more than 13,000 children in 169 schools throughout the state without parental objection.[1]

The Houston test burning came as a result of a few telephone calls (no one knows how many) from parents complaining, at the outset, to two of the seven trustees concerning the content and purpose of the tests. The metropolitan press was alerted and published stories in advance of the school board meeting promising a ruckus (board meetings are televised) under such headlines as PARENTS PROTEST TEST QUESTIONS, PARENTS STILL BOILING OVER THOSE "TALENT HUNT" QUESTIONS, and DR. MC FARLAND [the superintendent] FACES TOUGH MONDAY NIGHT.

According to newspaper accounts parents were objecting to having their children respond to such items as:

> I enjoy soaking in the bathtub.
> A girl who gets into trouble on a date has no one to blame but herself.
> If you don't drink in our gang, they make you feel like a sissy.
> Sometimes I tell dirty jokes when I would rather not.
> Dad always seems too busy to pal around with me.

Houston school board members, with one exception, seconded the allegation of some parents that these and similar questions (*a*) could serve no useful function in a talent search or in the guidance of children ("If you can show me one iota of value to these tests," one trustee is quoted as saying, "I'll quit the board.") and that (*b*) such questions might undermine a child's moral character. One board member saw the tests as an additional symptom of the encroachment of "outside agencies" upon local school systems.

News items and exchanges in the letters-to-the-editor columns continued for at least two weeks after the Houston board's decision. Within 24 hours of the televised meeting one citizen prepared an application for a court order restraining officials from burning test results only to learn that the answer sheets had been destroyed earlier in the day.

The clamor spread to the suburban Spring Branch school district where the superintendent was called upon for an explanation in a meeting at which it was announced, incidentally, that the DAR was interested in the possible subversive uses of psychological instruments and that it had prepared a list of proscribed tests. A spokesman for the antitest group also suggested that answers to some of

[1] Preliminary findings of the Texas Cooperative Youth Study are reported by Bernice M. Moore and Wayne H. Holtzman, "What Texas Knows About Youth," in the *National Parent-Teacher,* September 1958, pages 22-24. A detailed report will be published in 1960 by the University of Texas Press.

the questions–as, for example, those on family income, family size, and home ownership–would be of value to communists. The Spring Branch board decided that, rather than destroy the answer sheets of all students for all tests, parents who objected to the inclusion of their child's responses would be given the opportunity to request deletion. As of this writing, some six weeks after this decision, 11 parents of a possible 750 have made this request.

Social scientists and interested citizens, concerned that the Houston board action not go unprotested, conferred informally to discuss measures that might effectively indicate to the community the questionable wisdom of the board's decision (Once the tests had been administered, why destroy the *results?* And why without a hearing? And why the results of *all* tests of *all* students?). As a result of these telephonic and luncheon conclaves, it was apparent that no organized civic or professional body felt justified in making further remonstrance and that, pragmatically, any continued debate with the school board and its supporters aired in the press would probably result in victory for the board with possible harmful consequences for other phases of school testing programs.

Each man will read his own lessons from the events outlined above; I should like to suggest these:

1. In general, the public relations of psychometricians is in a sad state and in need of repairs.

   a. There are national bodies interested in attacking psychology and psychologists as potential instruments of state control, *ergo,* of communism.

   b. We have not been able to explain the role of tests in personnel selection procedures to a wide audience.

   c. The press, with few exceptions, is a dubious factor in the fair reporting of our case if only because the rationale of testing is difficult to explain to editors and reporters.

2. It seems advisable that future large-scale testing programs be preceded by a public "warm up" explaining to as broad a segment of the public as possible the purposes and methods of such research. For example, effort spent in the education of PTAs and boards of education in advance of such surveys may prevent such loss as Houston has suffered.

3. Psychologists are behaving "ethnocentrically" in assuming that their ethic is shared by the people they study. The statement of "Ethical Standards of Psychologists" carried in the June issue of the *American Psychologist* holds:

> As a scientist, the psychologist believes that society will be best served when he investigates where his judgment indicates investigation is needed . . . (page 279).
>
> The psychologist in the practice of his profession shows sensible regard for the social codes and moral expectations of the community in which he works . . . (page 279).

When the student of behavior works in a xenophobic and individualistic community, he cannot assume that his scientifically honorable intentions will be considered morally justifiable by those whom he seeks to help. Even though the scientist says, in effect, "I am studying you, and asking you these questions, for your own good," his subject may respond, "It is part of my 'good' that you desist from your intrusion of my privacy."

As with all such conflicts in ethics (in ultimate values), facts are irrelevant—and consequences too.

Chapter 10

New Directions in Personality Assessment

The conclusion that there are rather serious problems and difficulties confronting the field of personality assessment will not come as any surprise to the reader of the first nine chapters of this volume, or to any serious student of the area. Given both the magnitude of these issues and the uncertainties involved, it might seem foolhardy to attempt to either predict or influence the future course of work in this field. Nevertheless, this is the task that we have set for ourselves in this final chapter. From our vantage point it appears that changes in our field are possible on at least three different levels: (1) theoretical or conceptual approaches to personality assessment; (2) practical procedures involved in assessment; and (3) statistical or psychometric aspects of the assessment process.

One new conceptual approach to personality assessment that has become important in the last few years is derived from social learning theory and emphasizes the laboratory approach to the generation of new knowledge, an elemental as opposed to a holistic view of behavior, and a relatively empirical attitude, in which explanatory concepts and structures are kept at as low a level of abstraction as possible. Related to this behavioral approach is the point of view that the existence of generalized and long-lasting personality characteristics is questionable, and that complex interpersonal behavior in any given situation is determined, to a much greater degree than typically supposed, by cues that are specific to that situation rather than by the person's general response predisposition or personality.

The implications of this viewpoint for personality assessment are far-reaching. One important area that has already been affected by this stance is clinical assessment and psychiatric evaluations. As noted in the previous chapter, the traditional procedures stem from medical practice and seek to identify, or diagnose, or label, the patient's illness as a necessary prerequisite to treatment. The behavioral approach, on the other hand, holds that a thorough and complete behavioral analysis of the patient's responses (and of his environment) is a necessary and sufficient process for initiating and continuing the treatment process.

In our first reading, Kanfer and Saslow examine the traditional approaches to psychodiagnosis and classification of patients in some detail and conclude that these systems are limited by the lack of predictive validity, so that it is difficult to make meaningful predictions about differential patient responses to varying kinds of psychiatric treatments or therapeutic milieus. In contrast, the behavioral system proposed by Kanfer and Saslow is oriented toward action, since it attempts to define a patient's problems in such a manner as to suggest which particular treatment operations should be adopted. Other important aspects of their formulation include its emphasis on discovery of the environmental variables that are the most strongly related to the patient's current behavioral excesses or deficits, and its relatively concrete descriptions of behavior rather than higher-order levels of abstraction.

John Wallace's paper, the second in this section, is addressed to a related theoretical assumption, the utility of traditional personality concepts such as needs, traits, and other general response *predispositions.* Instead of such concepts he argues for the conceptualization of personality in terms of *abilities* or skills. He suggests two central concepts for this view of personality: response capability, which refers to whether or not the person is capable of making the response, and response performance, which specifies the conditions necessary for the individual to make the response in question. Wallace goes on to discuss the implications that this approach holds for both personality assessment and personality change.

In our third reading, Wernimont and Campbell propose that a more behavioral approach be used in the applied field of personnel assessment. As an alternative to the traditional procedure of employing empirically based test signs as evidence of certain underlying response predispositions, from which potential job behaviors are then predicted, the authors propose that appropriate samples of past and present behavior be directly used as predictors of future behavior. The procedure would involve a thorough job analysis oriented toward defining the specific behaviors required, followed by an analysis of the individual's previous behavioral background to determine which of these behaviors were exhibited in the past. This approach, in which consistencies are sought between job behaviors and preemployment behaviors, would avoid the present tendency toward an overemphasis on *generalized* statements of skills and abilities. In addition, the authors believe that the traditional problems of selecting appropriate criteria would be simplified, response distortions would pose less of a problem, and other difficulties such as invasion of privacy and unfair discriminatory practices would be minimized.

A second area in which change is obviously underway in personality assessment is the use of computers and other automated data-handling procedures. Although it is too early to determine precisely the impact that computers will have on assessment, it is likely that the most important changes will be qualitative—that is, innovations in the kinds and quality of the work that can be performed. As yet, the major changes seen have been quantitative—increases in the volume of work output that is possible. To clear up a popular misconception in this field, the notion that computers have made personality assessment more objective is erroneous. The use of objective rules and signs, discussed in Chapter 8, preceded the use of computers; however, it is true that the essential aspects of assessment must be made objective before the computer can be usefully employed.

Perhaps the most ambitious effort in the application of computers to personality assessment is that of Zygmunt Piotrowski in his work with the Rorschach, which is reported in our fourth reading. Although written several years earlier, Piotrowski's article gives the essential details of his computer system and of his general philosophy of computer technology. This work, which has extended over a number of years, is an attempt to objectify what Piotrowski as a Rorschach expert knows about Rorschach interpretation, so that this expertise can be made easily and widely available. The reader will readily appreciate the many problems inherent in any attempt to objectify such discursive and idiosyncratic material as Rorschach responses. In attempting to meet these problems, Piotrowski has based his work to a greater extent on the formal scoring categories of the Rorschach rather than upon its content, and has devised a system which, according to a recent communication, now identifies more than 800 response components and nearly a thousand interpretive rules. One difficulty yet unsolved is the considerable length of time required to code each Rorschach protocol in preparation for computer processing.

In our next paper, which was especially prepared for this volume, Raymond Fowler deals with some of the generic problems of using computers in personality assessment and interpretation. To reduce the complexities involved in using Rorschach responses, Fowler has used the responses to the MMPI for developing an automated scoring and interpretative schema for personality assessment. In Fowler's system the computer output consists of the MMPI profile, a sheet containing the various MMPI scores and "critical items," and a narrative interpretative report. The system was evolved in a clinical setting, and underwent continuous modification over a number of years as more and more cases became available in the data pool and the mechanically produced reports were evaluated and modified by the professionally trained staff.

Among the statistical and psychometric aspects of personality assessment that may well receive more attention in the future is the use of the kind of *decision making* model initially introduced in David Rimm's article in Chapter 6. In our sixth reading, A. Z. Arthur gives a more detailed account of this approach, after first enumerating the limitations of traditional diagnostic procedures and discussing two other possible frameworks for assessment: the *behavioral* model, which we discussed above, and the *experimental* model, described as a direct application of the scientific method to the problems of a single person. The decision-making model approaches assessment by focusing specifically on the alternative courses of action that are available, and weighs each according to a criterion of *utility*—the cost or value of making each particular decision, all things considered. One of the current limitations of the decision-making approach involves the determination of these costs. These costs are much broader than simple monetary values, since they include the intangible but very real values of a social, interpersonal, and community nature. Arthur also introduces the operations-research model, in which the decision-making approach is taken to its logical extreme and is applied holistically to the total endeavor of the clinic or institution. Well developed in certain industrial contexts, operations research is seen as a powerful tool for increasing the over-all efficiency of an operation, though its uses in the context of personality assessment have not yet been explored.

Another statistical development with considerable promise for the future is the use of *moderator variables.* Put simply, a moderator is a bit of information that can be used to predict the accuracy of another predictor. For example, if engineering grades can be more accurately predicted from intelligence test scores for students with a high engineering interest than for those whose interest in engineering is low, then a measure of engineering interest would be said to moderate the prediction of engineering grades from intelligence test scores. Moderator effects are also possible with respect to reliability, since it can be shown that some types of individuals are more reliably assessed than others. In our final reading, Edwin Ghiselli explains the concept of moderators—their history, techniques for discovering or developing them, and possible explanations of their effects.

1. BEHAVIORAL ANALYSIS: AN ALTERNATIVE TO DIAGNOSTIC CLASSIFICATION

Frederick H. Kanfer and George Saslow

During the past decade attacks on conventional psychiatric diagnosis have been so widespread that many clinicians now use diagnostic labels sparingly and apologetically. The continued adherence to the nosological terms of the traditional classificatory scheme suggests some utility of the present categorization of behavior disorders, despite its apparently low reliability (Ash, 1949; Rotter, 1954); its limited prognostic value (Freedman, 1958; Windle, 1952); and its multiple feebly related assumptive supports. In a recent study of this problem, the symptom patterns of carefully diagnosed paranoid schizophrenics were compared. Katz, Cole, and Lowery (1964) found considerable divergence among patients with the same diagnosis and concluded that "diagnostic systems which are more circumscribed in their intent, for example, based on manifest behavior alone, rather than systems which attempt to comprehend etiology, symptom patterns and prognosis, may be more directly applicable to current problems in psychiatric research (p. 202)."

We propose here to examine some sources of dissatisfaction with the present approach to diagnosis, to describe a framework for a behavioral analysis of individual patients which implies both suggestions for treatment and outcome criteria for the single case, and to indicate the conditions for collecting the data for such an analysis.

I. Problems in Current Diagnostic Systems

Numerous criticisms deal with the internal consistency, the explicitness, the precision, and the reliability of psychiatric classifications. It seems to us that the more important fault lies in our lack of sufficient knowledge to categorize behavior along those pertinent dimensions which permit prediction of responses to social stresses, life crises, or psychiatric treatment. This limitation obviates anything but a crude and tentative approximation to a taxonomy of effective individual behaviors.

SOURCE. Frederick H. Kanfer is Professor of Psychology at the University of Cincinnati. George Saslow is Professor and Head of the Department of Psychiatry at the University of Oregon Medical School. Both authors have contributed many publications to the professional literature on clinical research, personality theory, and psychotherapy. This article originally appeared in the *Archives of General Psychiatry,* 1965, **12,** 529-538. Reprinted by permission of the American Medical Association and the authors.

Zigler and Phillips (1961), in discussing the requirement for an adequate system of classification, suggest that an etiologically-oriented closed system of diagnosis is premature. Instead, they believe that an empirical attack is needed, using "symptoms broadly defined as meaningful and discernible behaviors, as the basis of the classificatory system" (p. 616). But symptoms as a class of responses are defined after all only by their nuisance value to the patient's social environment or to himself as a social being. They are also notoriously unreliable in predicting the patient's particular etiological history or his response to treatment. An alternate approach lies in an attempt to identify classes of dependent variables in human behavior which would allow inferences about the particular controlling factors, the social stimuli, the physiological stimuli, and the reinforcing stimuli, of which they are a function. In the present early stage of the art of psychological prognostication, it appears most reasonable to develop a program of analysis which is closely related to subsequent treatment. A classification scheme which implies a program for behavioral change is one which has not only utility but the potential for experimental validation.

The task of assessment and prognosis can therefore be reduced to efforts which answer the following three questions: (a) which specific behavior patterns require change in their frequency of occurrence, their intensity, their duration, or in the conditions under which they occur, (b) what are the best practical means which can produce the desired changes in this individual (manipulation of the environment, of the behavior, or the self-attitudes of the patient), and (c) what factors are currently maintaining it and what are the conditions under which this behavior was acquired. The investigation of the history of the problematic behavior is mainly of academic interest, except as it contributes information about the probable efficacy of a specific treatment method.

Expectations of Current Diagnostic Systems

In traditional medicine, a diagnostic statement about a patient has often been viewed as an essential prerequisite to treatment because a diagnosis suggests that the physician has some knowledge of the origin and future course of the illness. Further, in medicine, diagnosis frequently brings together the accumulated knowledge about the pathological process which leads to the manifestation of the symptoms, and the experiences which others have had in the past in treating patients with such a disease process. Modern medicine recognizes that any particular disease need not have a single cause or even a small number of antecedent conditions. Nevertheless, the diagnostic label attempts to define at least the necessary conditions which are most relevant in considering a treatment program. Some diagnostic classification system is also invaluable as a basis for many social decisions involving entire populations. For example, planning for treatment facilities, research efforts and educational programs take into account the distribution frequencies of specified syndromes in the general population.

Ledley and Lusted (1959) give an excellent conception of the traditional model in medicine by their analysis of the reasoning underlying it. The authors differentiate between a disease complex and a symptom complex. While the former describes known pathological processes and their correlated signs, the latter represents particular signs present in a particular patient. The bridge between disease and symptom complexes is provided by available medical knowledge and the final diagnosis is tantamount to labeling the disease complex. However, the current gaps in medical knowledge necessitate the use of probability statements when relating disease to symptoms, admitting that there is some possibility for error in the diagnosis. Once the diagnosis is established, decisions about treatment still depend on many other factors including social, moral, and economic conditions. Ledley and Lusted (1959) thus separate the clinical diagnosis into a two-step process. A statistical procedure is suggested to facilitate the primary or diagnostic labeling process. However, the choice of treatment depends not only on the diagnosis proper. Treatment decisions are also influenced by the moral, ethical, social, and economic conditions of the individual patient, his family, and the society in which he lives. The proper assignment of the weight to be given to each of these values must in the last analysis be left to the physician's judgment (Ledley and Lusted, 1959).

The Ledley and Lusted model presumes available methods for the observation of relevant behavior (the symptom complex), and some scientific knowledge relating it to known antecedents or correlates (the disease process). Contemporary theories of behavior pathology do not yet provide adequate guidelines for the observer to suggest what is to be observed. In fact, Szasz (1960) has expressed the view that the medical model may be totally inadequate because psychiatry should be concerned with problems of living and not with diseases of the brain or other biological organs. Szasz (1960) argues that "mental illness is a myth, whose function it is to disguise and thus render more potable the bitter pill of moral conflict in human relations" (p. 118).

The attack against use of the medical model in psychiatry comes from many quarters. Scheflen (1958) describes a model of somatic psychiatry which is very similar to the traditional medical model of disease. A pathological process results in onset of an illness; the symptoms are correlated with a pathological state and represent our evidence of "mental disease." Treatment consists of removal of the pathogen, and the state of health is restored. Scheflen suggests that this traditional medical model is used in psychiatry not on the basis of its adequacy but because of its emotional appeal.

The limitations of the somatic model have been discussed even in some areas of medicine for which the model seems most appropriate. For example, in the nomenclature for diagnosis of disease of the heart and blood vessels, the criteria committee of the New York Heart Association (1953) suggests the use of multiple criteria for cardiovascular diseases, including a statement of the patient's functional capacity. The committee suggests that the functional capacity be "... estimated by appraising the patient's ability to perform physical activity" (p. 80), and decided largely by inference from his history. Further, (New York Heart Association, 1953) "... (it) should not be influenced by the character of the structural lesion or by an opinion as to treatment or prognosis" (p. 81). This approach makes it clear that a comprehensive assessment of a patient, regardless of the physical disease which he suffers, must also take into account his social effectiveness and the particular ways in which physiological, anatomical, and psychological factors interact to produce a particular behavior pattern in an individual patient.

Multiple Diagnosis

A widely used practical solution and circumvention of the difficulty inherent in the application of the medical model to psychiatric diagnosis is offered by Noyes and Kolb (1963). They suggest that the clinician construct a diagnostic formulation consisting of three parts: (1) A *genetic* diagnosis incorporating the constitutional, somatic, and historical-traumatic factors representing the primary sources or determinants of the mental illness; (2) A *dynamic* diagnosis which describes the mechanisms and techniques unconsciously used by the individual to manage anxiety, enhance self-esteem, i.e., that traces the psychopathological processes; and (3) A *clinical* diagnosis which conveys useful connotations concerning the reaction syndrome, the probable course of the disorder, and the methods of treatment which will most probably prove beneficial. Noyes' and Kolb's multiple criteria (1963) can be arranged along three simpler dimensions of diagnosis which may have some practical value to the clinician: (1) etiological, (2) behavioral, and (3) predictive. The kind of information which is conveyed by each type of diagnostic label is somewhat different and specifically adapted to the purpose for which the diagnosis is used. The triple-label approach attempts to counter the criticism aimed at use of any single classificatory system. Confusion in a single system is due in part to the fact that a diagnostic formulation intended to describe current behavior, for example, may be found useless in an attempt to predict the response to specific treatment, or to postdict the patient's personal history and development, or to permit collection of frequency data on hospital populations.

Classification by Etiology

The Kraepelinian system and portions of the 1952 APA classification emphasize etiological factors. They share the assumption that common etiological factors lead to similar symptoms and respond to similar treatment. This dimension of diagnosis is considerably more fruitful when dealing with behavior disorders which are mainly under control of some biological condition. When a patient is known to suffer from excessive intake of alcohol his halucinatory behavior, lack of motor coordination, poor judgment, and other behavioral evidence of disorganization can often be related directly to some antecedent condition such as the toxic effect of alcohol on the central nervous system, liver, etc. For these cases, classification by etiology also has some implications for prognosis and treatment. Acute hallucinations and other disorganized behavior due to alcohol usually clear up when the alcohol level in the blood stream falls. Similar examples can be drawn from any class of behavior disorders in which a change in behavior is associated primarily or exclusively with a single, *particular* antecedent factor. Under these conditions this factor can be called a pathogen and the situation closely approximates the condition described by the traditional medical model.

Utilization of this dimension as a basis for psychiatric diagnosis, however, has many problems apart from the rarity with which a specified condition can be shown to have a direct "causal" relationship to a pathogen. Among the current areas of ignorance in the fields of psychology and psychiatry, the etiology of most common disturbances probably takes first place. No specific family environment, no dramatic traumatic experience, or known constitutional abnormality has yet been found which results in the same pattern of disordered behavior. While current research efforts have aimed at investigating family patterns of schizophrenic patients, and several studies suggest a relationship between the mother's behavior and a schizophrenic process in the child, (Jackson, 1960) it is not at all clear why the presence of these same factors in other families fails to yield a similar incidence of schizophrenia. Further, patients may exhibit behavior diagnosed as schizophrenic when there is no evidence of the postulated mother-child relationship.

In a recent paper Meehl (1962) postulates schizophrenia as a neurological disease, with learned content and a dispositional basis. With this array of interactive etiological factors, it is clear that the etiological dimension for classification would at best result in an extremely cumbersome system, at worst in a useless one.

Classification by Symptoms

A clinical diagnosis often is a summarizing statement about the way in which a person behaves. On the assumption that a variety of behaviors are correlated and consistent in any given individual, it becomes more economical to assign the individual to a class of persons than to list and categorize all of his behaviors. The utility of such a system rests heavily on the availability of empirical evidence concerning correlations among various behaviors (response-response relationships), and the further assumption that the frequency of occurrence of such behaviors is relatively independent of specific stimulus conditions and of specific reinforcement. There are two major limitations to such a system. The first is that diagnosis by symptoms, as we have indicated in an earlier section, is often misleading because it implies common etiological factors. Freedman (1958) gives an excellent illustration of the differences both in probable antecedent factors and subsequent treatment response among three cases diagnosed as schizophrenics. Freedman's patients were diagnosed by at least two psychiatrists, and one would expect that the traditional approach should result in whatever treatment of schizophrenia is practiced in the locale where the patients are seen. The first patient eventually gave increasing evidence of an endocrinopathy, and when this was recognized and treated, the psychotic symptoms went into remission. The second case had a definite history of seizures and appropriate anticonvulsant medication was effective in relieving his symptoms. In the third case, treatment directed at an uncovering analysis of the patient's adaptive techniques resulted in considerable improvement in the patient's behavior and subsequent relief from psychotic episodes. Freedman (1958) suggests that schizophrenia is not a disease entity in the sense that it has a unique etiology, pathogenesis, etc., but that it represents the evocation of a final common pathway in the same sense as do headache, epilepsy, sore throat, or indeed any other symptom complex. It is further suggested that the term "schizophrenia has outlived its usefulness and should be discarded" (p. 5). Opler (1957; 1963) has further shown the importance of cultural factors in the divergence of symptoms observed in patients collectively labeled as schizophrenic.

Descriptive classification is not always this deceptive, however. Assessment of intellectual performance sometimes results in a diagnostic statement which has predictive value for the patient's behavior in school or on a job. To date, there seem to be very few general statements about individual characteristics, which have as much predictive utility as the IQ.

A second limitation is that the current approach to diagnosis by symptoms tends to center on a group of behaviors which is often irrelevant with regard to the patient's total life pattern. These behaviors may be of interest only because they are popularly associated with deviancy and disorder. For example, occasional mild delusions interfere little or not at all with the social or occupational effectiveness of many ambulatory patients. Nevertheless, admission of their occurrence is often sufficient for a diagnosis of psychosis. Refinement of such an approach beyond current usage appears possible, as shown for example by Lorr, Klett, and McNair (1963) but this does not remove the above limitations.

Utilization of a symptom-descriptive approach frequently focuses attention on by-products of larger behavior patterns, and results in attempted treatment of behaviors (symptoms) which may be simple consequences of other important aspects of the patient's life. Emphasis on the patient's subjective complaints, moods and feelings tends to encourage use of a syndrome-oriented classification. It also results frequently in efforts to change the feelings, anxieties, and moods (or at least the patient's report about them), rather than to investigate the life conditions, interpersonal reactions, and environmental factors which produce and maintain these habitual response patterns.

Classification by Prognosis

To date, the least effort has been devoted to construction of a classification system which assigns patients to the same category on the basis of their similar response to specific treatments. The proper question raised for such a classification system consists of the manner in which a patient will react to treatments, regardless of his current behavior, or his past history. The numerous studies attempting to establish prognostic signs from projective personality tests or somatic tests represent efforts to categorize the patients on this dimension.

Windle (1952) has called attention to the low degree of predictability afforded by personality (projective) test scores, and has pointed out the difficulties encountered in evaluating research in this area due to the inadequate description of the population sampled and of the improvement criteria. In a later review Fulkerson and Barry (1961) came to the similar conclusion that psychological test performance is a poor predictor of outcome in mental illness. They suggest that demographic variables such as severity, duration, acuteness of onset, degree of precipitating stress, etc., appear to have stronger relationships to outcome than test data. The lack of reliable relationships between diagnostic categories, test data, demographic variables, or other measures taken on the patient on the one hand, and duration of illness, response to specific treatment, or degree of recovery, on the other hand, precludes the construction of a simple empiric framework for a diagnostic-prognostic classification system based only on an array of symptoms.

None of the currently used dimensions for diagnosis is directly related to methods of modification of a patient's behavior, attitudes, response patterns, and interpersonal actions. Since the etiological model clearly stresses causative factors, it is much more compatible with a personality theory which strongly emphasizes genetic-developmental factors. The classification by symptoms facilitates social-administrative decisions about patients by providing some basis for judging the degree of deviation from social and ethical norms. Such a classification is compatible with a personality theory founded on the normal curve hypothesis and concerned with characterization by comparison with a fictitious average. The prognostic-predictive approach appears to have the most direct practical applicability. If continued research were to support certain early findings, it would be indeed comforting to be able to predict outcome of mental illness from a patient's premorbid social competence score, (Zigler and Phillips, 1961) or from the patient's score on an ego-strength scale, (Barron, 1953) or from many of the other signs and single variables which have been shown to have some predictive powers. It is unfortunate that these powers are frequently dissipated in cross validation. As Fulkerson and Barry have indicated (1961) single predictors have not yet shown much success.

II. A Functional (Behavioral-Analytic) Approach

The growing literature on behavior modification procedures derived from learning theory (Bandura, 1961; Ferster, 1965; Kanfer, 1961; Krasner, 1962; Wolpe, 1958) suggests that an effective diagnostic procedure would be one in which the eventual therapeutic methods can be directly related to the information obtained from a continuing assessment of the patient's current behaviors and their controlling stimuli. Ferster (1965) has said " . . . a functional analysis of behavior has the advantage that it specifies the causes of behavior in the form of explicit environmental events which can be objectively identified and which are potentially manipulable" (p. 3). Such a diagnostic undertaking makes the assumption that a description of the problematic behavior, its controlling factors, and the means by which it can be changed are the most appropriate "explanations." It further makes the assumption that a diagnostic evaluation is never complete. It implies that additional information about the circumstances of the patient's life pattern, relationships among his behaviors, and controlling stimuli in his social milieu and his private experience is obtained continuously until it proves sufficient to effect a noticeable change in the patient's behavior, thus resolving "the problem." In a functional approach it is necessary to continue evaluation of the patient's life pattern and its controlling factors, concurrent with attempted manipulation of these variables by reinforcement, direct intervention, or other means until the resultant change in the patient's behavior permits restoration of more efficient life experiences.

The present approach shares with some psychological theories the assumption that psychotherapy is *not* an effort aimed at removal of intrapsychic conflicts, nor at a change in the personality structure by therapeutic interactions of intense nonverbal nature (e.g., transference, self-actualization, etc.). We adopt the assumption instead that the job of psychological treatment involves the utilization of a variety of methods to devise a program which controls the patient's environment, his behavior, and the consequences of his behavior in such a way that the presenting problem is resolved. We hypothesize that the essential ingredients of a psychotherapeutic endeavor usually involve two separate stages: (1) a change in the perceptual discriminations of a patient, i.e., in his approach to perceiving, classifying, and organizing sensory events, including perception of himself, and (2) changes in the response patterns which he has established in relation to social objects and to himself over the years (Kanfer, 1961). In addition, the clinician's task may involve direct intervention in the patient's environmental circumstances, modification of the behavior of other people significant in his life, and control of reinforcing stimuli which are available either through self-administration, or by contingency upon the behavior of others. These latter procedures complement the verbal interactions of traditional psychotherapy. They require that the clinician, at the invitation of the patient or his family, participate more fully in planning the total life pattern of the patient outside the clinician's office.

It is necessary to indicate what the theoretical view here presented does *not* espouse in order to understand the differences from other procedures. It does *not* rest upon the assumption that (a) insight is a sine qua non of psychotherapy, (b) changes in thoughts or ideas inevitably lead to ultimate change in actions, (c) verbal therapeutic sessions serve as replications of and equivalents for actual life situations, and (d) a symptom can be removed only by uprooting its cause or origin. In the absence of these assumptions it becomes unnecessary to conceptualize behavior disorder in etiological terms, in psychodynamic terms, or in terms of a specifiable disease process. While psychotherapy by verbal means may be sufficient in some instances, the combination of behavior modification in life situations as well as in verbal interactions serves to extend the armamentarium of the therapist. Therefore verbal psychotherapy is seen as an *adjunct* in the implementation of therapeutic behavior changes in the patient's total life pattern, not as an end in itself, nor as the sole vehicle for increasing psychological effectiveness.

In embracing this view of behavior modification, there is a further commitment to a constant interplay between assessment and therapeutic strategies. An initial diagnostic formulation seeks to ascertain the major variables which can be directly controlled or modified during treatment. During successive treatment stages additional information is collected about the patient's behavior repertoire, his reinforcement history, the pertinent controlling stimuli in his social and physical environment, and the sociological limitations within which both patient and therapist have to operate. Therefore, the initial formulation will constantly be enlarged or changed, resulting either in confirmation of the previous therapeutic strategy or in its change.

A Guide to a Functional Analysis Of Individual Behavior

In order to help the clinician in the collection and organization of information for a behavioral analysis, we have constructed an outline which aims to provide a working model of the patient's behavior at a relatively low level of abstraction. A series of questions are so organized as to yield immediate implications for treatment. This outline has been found useful both in clinical practice and in teaching. Following is a brief summary of the categories in the outline.[1]

[1] A limited supply of the full outline is available and copies can be obtained upon request from us.

1. *Analysis of a Problem Situation.*[2] The patient's major complaints are categorized into classes of behavioral excesses and deficits. For each excess or deficit the dimensions of frequency, intensity, duration, appropriateness of form, and stimulus conditions are described. In content, the response classes represent the major targets of the therapeutic intervention. As an additional indispensable feature, the behavioral assests of the patient are listed for utilization in a therapy program.

2. *Clarification of the Problem Situation.* Here we consider the people and circumstances which tend to maintain the problem behaviors, and the consequences of these behaviors to the patient and to others in his environment. Attention is given also to the consequences of changes in these behaviors which may result from psychiatric intervention.

3. *Motivational Analysis.* Since reinforcing stimuli are idiosyncratic and depend for their effect on a number of unique parameters for each person, a hierarchy of particular persons, events, and objects which serve as reinforcers is established for each patient. Included in this hierarchy are those reinforcing events which facilitate approach behaviors as well as those which, because of their aversiveness, prompt avoidance responses. This information has as its purpose to lay plans for utilization of various reinforcers in prescription of a specific behavior therapy program for the patient, and to permit utilization of appropriate reinforcing behaviors by the therapist and significant others in the patient's social environment.

4. *Developmental Analysis.* Questions are asked about the patient's biological equipment, his sociocultural experiences, and his characteristic behavioral development. They are phrased in such a way as (a) to evoke descriptions of his habitual behavior at various chronological stages of his life, (b) to relate specific new stimulus conditions to noticeable changes from his habitual behavior, and (c) to relate such altered behavior and other residuals of biological and sociocultural events to the present problem.

5. *Analysis of Self-Control.* This section examines both the methods and the degree of self-control exercised by the patient in his daily life. Persons, events, or institutions which have successfully reinforced self-controlling be-

[2]For each patient a detailed analysis is required. For example, a list of behavioral excesses may include specific aggressive acts, hallucinatory behaviors, crying, submission to others in social situations, etc. It is recognized that some behaviors can be viewed as excesses or deficits depending on the vantage point from which the imbalance is observed. For instance, excessive withdrawal and deficient social responsiveness, or excessive social autonomy (nonconformity) and deficient self-inhibitory behavior may be complementary. The particular view taken is of consequence because of its impact on a treatment plan. Regarding certain behavior as excessively aggressive, to be reduced by constraints, clearly differs from regarding the same behavior as a deficit in self-control, subject to increase by training and treatment.

haviors are considered. The deficits or excesses of self-control are evaluated in relation to their importance as therapeutic targets and to their utilization in a therapeutic program.

6. *Analysis of Social Relationships.* Examination of the patient's social network is carried out to evaluate the significance of people in the patient's environment who have some influence over the problematic behaviors, or who in turn are influenced by the patient for his own satisfactions. These interpersonal relationships are reviewed in order to plan the potential participation of significant others in a treatment program, based on the principles of behavior modification. The review also helps the therapist to consider the range of actual social relationships in which the patient needs to function.

7. *Analysis of the Social-Cultural-Physical Environment.* In this section we add to the preceding analysis of the patient's behavior as an individual, consideration of the norms in his environment. Agreements and discrepancies between the patient's idiosyncratic life patterns and the norms in his environment are defined so that the importance of these factors can be decided in formulating treatment goals which allow as explicitly for the patient's needs as for the pressures of his social environment.

The preceding outline has as its purpose to achieve definition of a patient's problem in a manner which suggests specific treatment operations, or that none are feasible, and specific behaviors as targets for modification. Therefore, the formulation is *action oriented.* It can be used as a guide for the initial collection of information, as a device for organizing available data, or as a design for treatment.

The formulation of a treatment plan follows from this type of analysis because knowledge of the reinforcing conditions suggests the motivational controls at the disposal of the clinician for the modification of the patient's behavior. The analysis of specific problem behaviors also provides a series of goals for psychotherapy or other treatment, and for the evaluation of treatment progress. Knowledge of the patient's biological, social, and cultural conditions should help to determine what resources can be used, and what limitations must be considered in a treatment plan.

The various categories attempt to call attention to important variables affecting the patient's *current* behavior. Therefore, they aim to elicit descriptions of low-level abstraction. Answers to these specific questions are best phrased by describing classes of events reported by the patient, observed by others, or by critical incidents described by an informant. The analysis does not exclude description of the patient's habitual verbal-symbolic behaviors. However, in using verbal behaviors as the basis for this analysis, one should be cautious not to "explain" verbal processes in terms of postulated internal mechanisms without adequate supportive evidence, nor should inference be made about nonobserved processes or events without corroborative evidence. The analysis includes many items which are not known or not applicable for a given patient. Lack of information on some items does not necessarily indicate incompleteness of the analysis. These lacks must be noted nevertheless because they often contribute to the better understanding of what the patient needs to learn to become an autonomous person. Just as important is an inventory of his existing socially effective behavioral repertoire which can be put in the service of any treatment procedure.

This analysis is consistent with our earlier formulations of the principles of comprehensive medicine (Guze, Matarazzo, and Saslow, 1953; Saslow, 1952) which emphasized the joint operation of biological, social, and psychological factors in psychiatric disorders. The language and orientation of the proposed approach are rooted in contemporary learning theory. The conceptual framework is consonant with the view that the course of psychiatric disorders can be modified by systematic application of scientific principles from the fields of psychology and medicine to the patient's habitual mode of living.

This approach is not a substitute for assignment of the patient to traditional diagnostic categories. Such labeling may be desirable for statistical, administrative, or research purposes. But the current analysis is intended to replace other diagnostic formulations purporting to serve as a basis for making decisions about specific therapeutic interventions.

III. Methods of Data Collection For a Functional Analysis

Traditional diagnostic approaches have utilized as the main sources of information the patient's verbal report, his nonverbal behavior during an interview, and his performance on psychological tests. These observations are sufficient if one regards behavior problems only as a property of the patient's particular pattern of associations or his personality structure. A mental disorder would be expected to reveal itself by stylistic characteristics in the patient's behavior reportoire. However, if one views behavior disorders as sets of response patterns which are learned under particular conditions and maintained by definable environmental and internal stimuli, an assessment of the patient's behavior output is insufficient unless it also describes the conditions under which it occurs. This view requires an expansion of the clinician's sources of observation to include the stimulation fields in which the patient lives, and the variations of patient behavior as a function of exposure to these various stimulational variables. Therefore, the resourceful clinician need not limit himself to test findings, interview observations in the clinician's office, or referral histories alone in the formulation of the specific case. Nor need he regard himself as hopelessly handicapped when the patient has little observational or communicative skill in verbally reconstructing his life experiences for the clinician. Regardless of the patient's communicative skills the data must consist of a description of the patient's behavior *in relationship* to varying environmental conditions.

A behavioral analysis excludes no data relating to a patient's past or present experiences as irrelevant. However, the relative merit of any information (as, e.g., growing up in a broken home or having had homosexual experiences) lies in its relation to the independent variables which can be identified as controlling the current problematic behavior. The observation that a patient has hallucinated on occasions may be important only if it has bearing on his present problem. If looked upon in isolation, a report about hallucinations may be misleading, resulting in emphasis on classification rather than treatment.

In the *psychiatric interview* a behavioral-analytic approach opposes acceptance of the content of the verbal self-report as equivalent to actual events or experiences. However, verbal reports provide information concerning the patient's verbal construction of his environment and of his person, his recall of past experiences, and his fantasies about them. While these self-descriptions do not represent data about events which actually occur internally, they do represent current behaviors of the patient and indicate the verbal chains and repertoires which the patient has built up. Therefore, the verbal behavior may be useful for description of a patient's thinking processes. To make the most of such an approach, variations on traditional interview procedures may be obtained by such techniques as role playing, discussion, and interpretation of current life events, or controlled free association. Since there is little experimental evidence of specific relationships between the patient's verbal statements and his nonverbal behavioral acts, the verbal report alone remains insufficient for a complete analysis and for prediction of his daily behavior. Further, it is well known that a person responds to environmental conditions and to internal cues which he cannot describe adequately. Therefore, any verbal report may miss or mask the most important aspects of a behavioral analysis, i.e., the description of the relationship between antecedent conditions and subsequent behavior.

In addition to the use of the clinician's own person as a controlled stimulus object in interview situations, *observations of interaction with significant others* can be used for the analysis of variations in frequency of various behaviors as a function of the person with whom the patient interacts. For example, use of prescribed standard roles for nurses and attendants, utilization of members of the patient's family or his friends, may be made to obtain data relevant to the patient's habitual interpersonal response pattern. Such observations are especially useful if in a later interview the patient is asked to describe and discuss the observed sessions. Confrontations with tape recordings for comparisons between the patient's report and the actual session as witnessed by the observer may provide information about the patient's perception of himself and others as well as his habitual behavior toward peers, authority figures, and other significant people in his life.

Except in working with children or family units, insufficient use has been made of material obtained from *other informants* in interviews about the patient. These reports can aid the observer to recognize behavioral domains in which the patient's report deviates from or agrees with the descriptions provided by others. Such information is also useful for contrasting the patient's reports about his presumptive effects on another person with the stated effects by that person. If a patient's interpersonal problems extend to areas in which social contacts are not clearly defined, contributions by informants other than the patient are essential.

It must be noted that verbal reports by other informants may be no more congruent with actual events than the patient's own reports and need to be equally related to the informant's own credibility. If such crucial figures as parents, spouses, employers can be so interviewed, they also provide the clinician with some information about those people with whom the patient must interact repeatedly and with whom interpersonal problems may have developed.

Some observation of the patient's daily *work behavior* represents an excellent source of information, if it can be made available. Observation of the patient by the clinician or his staff may be preferable to descriptions by peers or supervisors. Work observations are especially important for patients whose complaints include difficulties in their daily work activity or who describe work situations as contributing factors to their problem. While freer use of this technique may be hampered by cultural attitudes toward psychiatric treatment in the marginally adjusted, such observations may be freely accessible in hospital situations or in sheltered work situations. With use of behavior rating scales or other simple measurement devices, brief samples of patient behaviors in work situations can be obtained by minimally trained observers.

The patient himself may be asked to provide samples of his own behavior by using tape recorders for the recording of segments of interactions in his family, at work, or in other situations during his everyday life. A television monitoring system for the patient's behavior is an excellent technique from a theoretical viewpoint but it is extremely cumbersome and expensive. Use of recordings for diagnostic and therapeutic purposes has been reported by some investigators (Bach, 1963; Cameron, 1964; Slack, 1960). Playback of the recordings and a recording of the patient's reactions to the playback can be used further in interviews to clarify the patient's behavior toward others and his reaction to himself as a social stimulus.

Psychological tests represent problems to be solved under specified interactional conditions. Between the highly standardized intelligence tests and the unstructured and ambiguous projective tests lies a dimension of structure along which more and more responsibility for providing appropriate responses falls on the patient. By comparison with interview procedures, most psychological tests provide a relatively greater standardization of stimulus conditons. But, in addition to the specific answers given on intelligence tests or on projective tests, these tests also provide a behavioral sample of the patient's reaction to a problem situation in a relatively stressful interpersonal setting. Therefore, psychological tests can provide not only quantitative scores but they can also be treated as a miniature life experience, yielding information about the patient's interpersonal behavior and variations in his behavior as a function of the nature of the stimulus conditions.

In this section we have mentioned only some of the numerous life situations which can be evaluated in order to provide information about the patient. Criteria for their use lies in economy, accessibility to the clinician, and relevance to the patient's problem. While it is more convenient to gather data from a patient in an office, it may be necessary for the clinician to have first-hand information about the actual conditions under which the patient lives and works. Such familiarity may be obtained either by utilization of informants or by the clinician's entry into the home, the job situation, or the social environment in which the patient lives. Under all these conditions the clinician is effective only if it is possible for him to maintain a nonparticipating, objective, and observational role with no untoward consequences for the patient or the treatment relationship.

The methods of data collecting for a functional analysis described here differ from traditional psychiatric approaches only in that they require inclusion of the physical and social stimulus field in which the patient actually operates. Only a full appraisal of the patient's living and working conditions and his way of life allow a description of the actual problems which the patient faces and the specification of steps to be taken for altering the problematic situation.

2. WHAT UNITS SHALL WE EMPLOY? ALLPORT'S QUESTION REVISITED

John Wallace

Despite the existence of a substantial body of theory and data, the problems which face the psychologist interested in personality theory, measurement, and assessment continue to appear formidable. The search for stable and enduring individual difference variables (other than intellective ones) which would permit

SOURCE. John Wallace, who received his doctorate from Northwestern University, is Associate Professor of Psychology at the University of California (Irvine). Dr. Wallace's fields of research inquiry include personality, and cognitive and social psychological processes. This article originally appeared in the *Journal of Consulting Psychology,* 1967, **31,** 56-64. Reprinted by permission of the American Psychological Association and the author.

prediction of behavior across varied stimulus situations has yielded considerably less than modest successes. One is increasingly tempted to argue that the time has come to vary our strategies in personality research. Further data collection along traditional lines may very well prove inadequate for the task at hand. Our current problems in personality appear to constitute matters of conceptualization rather than further data collection. The present paper is an attempt to develop an alternative strategy for the psychologist interested in personality in both research and applied settings.

Viewed in historical perspective, it would not be unfair to characterize our efforts in personality research and theory as a search for viable units of study. In a provocative paper, Allport (1958) raised the question: "What units shall we employ?" As we examine personality research in historical perspective, it seems clear that much of our effort has been devoted to finding an answer to this question. While much has been learned, both methodological and substantive, from efforts to view human behavior and thought through templates such as need, drive, trait, type, instinct, and habit, it is entirely possible that units of potentially greater utility are now available.

Structure of Personality: Limited Utility Of Dispositional Units

The majority of our structural units in the study of personality have centered about the focal concept of response predisposition. Concepts such as instinct, need, drive, and trait are considered energy units as well as structural units and, as such, possess clear motivational implications. For example, Allport (1937) argued that "trait" is both a motivational concept as well as a structural concept. For Allport, a "gregarious" person is not only in evidence in social situations but such a person frequently arranges such situations in order that trait-related behaviors might become manifest. Similarly, a "need-related response" to a Thematic Apperception Test card is thought to have implications beyond the mere presence of the "need" in the personality structure of the individual giving such a response. It is frequently assumed that the individual characterized by given needs will act to bring about homeostatic balance.

If a response dispositional concept were taken to mean nothing more than a statement of the probability of a given response in a well-defined stimulus situation, one would have little with which to quarrel. Thus, for example, while scores on various measures of "intelligence" predict academic grades with moderate success, few persons, if any, would argue that intelligent persons are predisposed to behave intelligently. While nonintellective factors may very well contribute to the demonstrated realtionship between measured intelligence and academic achievement, to explain this relationship entirely in motivational terms would appear absurd. In this instance, a statement of probability concerning the prediction of certain events suffices.

But as we have noted, dispositional units in the study of personality go far beyond statements of response probability. Traits and needs are assumed to operate as motivational determinants of behavior across varied stimulus situations. The problem for the personologist interested in assessing personality within the framework of trait or need theory has been one of laying bare the structural aspects of personality and, hence, the response tendencies which presumably reside in the individual. The equation is as follows: structure = predisposition = response probability. While a theory of generalized response predispositions which operate across varied stimulus situations is appealing and elegant in its simplicity, it suffers from at least two major flaws.

First, the attempt to devise relatively pure measures of response dispositions has posed serious methodological, operational, and conceptual difficulties which appear formidable. Elsewhere, this writer (Wallace, 1966) has argued that typical measures of response predisposition are very likely confounded by a neglected but highly important response property, response capability. For example, a "hostile" response to a projective stimulus may suggest nothing more than the individual giving such a response is capable of a verbal response of this nature in this particular context. However, to assume that such an individual is predisposed to respond with hostility in other situations and through response modes other than verbal ones is clearly unwarranted. Continued problems in the attempt to assess dispositional units raise serious questions about the ultimate utility of such units.

Aside from problems of measurement, the loose equivalence of structure, disposition, and response probability constitutes the second major weakness. As recent research in trait theory has indicated, efforts to predict behavior from measures of personality structure have yielded considerably less than modest successes (e.g., Brim, Glass, Lavin, & Goodman, 1962; Endler, Hunt, & Rosenstein, 1962; Hilgard, 1965; Peterson, 1965; Rorer, 1965). While a more sophisticated trait model such as that employed by Kogan and Wallach (1964) may result in increased prediction, it appears likely that our failures to predict behavior from measures of personality structure are attributable in large part to neglect of psychosocial variables in the assessment situation itself as well as in the criterion situation to which predictions are made.

Response Capability and Response Performance as Focal Concepts

As alternatives to dispositional units in the study of personality, the strategy presented here involves the two focal concepts of response capability and response performance. The task of the personologist interested in assessment is inescapably twofold. First, an analysis of the structure of personality should center about the extant response repertoire, that is, the response capabilities of the individual. Stated quite simply, if one wishes to get a person to perform a given response, one must first determine whether or not the person is capable of performing the response. Second, one must specify the conditions necessary for performance of the response. Statements about the structural aspects of personality are, in and of themselves, meaningless unless one can specify the conditions under which the individual can demonstrate his capabilities. Obviously, questions concerning response capability and response performance are related considerations. It would appear impossible to assess response capability without making some statement about conditions controlling response performance. As researchers in personality have come to appreciate, observations are always gathered in some situational context (e.g., Masling, 1960; Murstein, 1963; Rotter, 1960).

Construing personality in terms of response capability rather than response disposition leads one quite naturally to a definition of personality structure in terms of abilities. Accustomed to dispositional concepts, the personologist may think it odd indeed to consider such things as "hostility," "gregariousness," "nurturance," "assertiveness," "dependence," etc., as skills rather than dispositions. However, a moment's reflection would readily suggest that it is not only possible but possibly fruitful to construe psychological phenomena such as these in this manner. Thus, for example, when observers are in agreement that a particular individual has performed a sequence of responses that can be labeled "aggressive," it would appear reasonable to assert that the individual is capable of assuming an aggressive role. And the student who seeks assistance from others before a given examination can be described as possessing the skill of dependency.

At first blush, it might appear that a capabilities conception of personality as presented here amounts to little more than a play upon words. However, our choice of units of study in personality is a matter of far greater significance than is immediately apparent. A skills conception of personality structure posseses vastly differing implications for the problems of personality measurement and change than those indicated by various dispositional conceptions. As this writer has shown (Wallace, 1966), an abilities conception of personality leads one to measurement operations which are quite at odds with those demanded by dispositional conceptions. And as will be developed shortly, the implications for personality change which stem from an abilities conception are strikingly different from those which obtain within dispositional concepts. In addition to differing implications for both measurement and change, an abilities conception of structure permits one to avoid the persistent epistemological quandaries inherent in dispositional conceptions. How does one, for example, decide upon the level at which the real dispositions of the person (whatever that may mean) can be found? And when faced with the inevitably incompatible evidence, how does one decide upon the stimulus situations in which such dispositions can be expected to appear in behavior?

In contrast to dispositional descriptions of structure, response-capability descriptions do not comprise statements of response probability. While the description of personality structure in terms of capabilities has implications for response performance, factors other than capability enter into the prediction of response performance. Obviously, while an individual cannot perform a response which is not in his repertoire of responses, the mere fact that it is does not guarantee that the response will be performed. In other words, the factors which control response performance do not inhere in response capability.

Recent research on social learning by Bandura (1965a) demonstrates that capabilities cannot be expected to eventuate in actual behavior until appropriate incentive conditions are introduced. In Bandura's research, children observed a film-mediated model engage in highly novel, aggressive responses. The model's aggressive behavior was punished, rewarded, or left without consequences in three experimental conditons. Postexposure tests revealed that response consequences for the model resulted in differential amounts of imitative behavior of the novel aggressive responses. Children who had observed the model being punished for aggressive responses displayed significantly less imitative behavior than children who had observed the models rewarded or left without consequences. However, when reinforcements contingent upon reproduction of the model's responses were offered directly to the children, differences in performance were totally eliminated. In short, while the children in all conditions were capable of reproducing the model's behavior, appropriate incentives had to be introduced before response performance could be obtained. Bandura's research suggests that discrepancies between response capability and response performance can be expected under conditions of negative sanctions.

While some personologists have chosen to view situational factors as matters best left to the social psychologist or experimental psychologist, it seems to be the case that situational determinants of behavior are as much the legitimate domain of the individual differences psychologist as they are of the psychologist searching for general stimulus-response laws. Moreover, an examination of situational determinants of behavior, as we shall see, can prove most congruent with the interests of the personologist. In the following discussion, three sets of situational factors are presented as follows: reinforcement conditions, situational specific hypotheses, and formal properties of situations themselves.

Reinforcement Conditions

In considering situational factors, our attention is immediately drawn to individual differences in response to various conditions of reinforcement. The old adage that "one man's meat is another man's poison" holds true for reinforcement. Even the most casual observation of human beings suggests that various classes of incentives do not have equal appeal. Examination of recent research in behavioral modification (e.g., Krasner & Ullmann, 1965) indicates clearly that the assessment of persons in clinical settings might well include procedures for determining the effectiveness and appropriateness of various classes of reinforcing stimuli.

Staats and Staats (1963) convincingly argue that differences in social learning histories can be expected to produce differences in preferences for given classes of reinforcements. Social learning theorists have long been concerned with the concept of reinforcement value. Rotter (1954), in his social learning theory, assigned an important role to the concept of reinforcement value. More recently, Homans (1961) has equated reinforcement value with the economic theoretical construct of utility. In short, the fact that human values range over an extraordinary span of events should alert the individual differences psychologist to the importance of including procedures for the assessment of such matters.

General statements concerning the effectiveness of given classes of reinforcers should be qualified by considerations of temporal matters. The personologist should also concern himself with the important question of the effectiveness of given reinforcers over time. It may well prove to be the case that, for given individuals, reinforcers who maintain behavior for short intervals will prove to be ineffective for long term behavioral maintenance.

In additon to questions concerning the effectiveness of given classes of reinforcing stimuli, the assessment of individual differences might very well take into account other reinforcement conditions. The scheduling of reinforcements seems an additional matter of importance. For different persons, behavioral maintenance may be enhanced by different schedules of reinforcement. A number of researches by Mischel and his colleagues (e.g., Mischel, 1961a, 1961b; Mischel & Metzner, 1962) indicate clearly that differences can be expected in the ability of persons to sustain delay of noncontingent reinforcement. And closely related to individual differences in ability to tolerate delay in noncontingent reinforcement is the matter of persistence of behavior in the absence of immediate contingent reinforcement. Even the most casual observation of persons suggests that differences in behavioral persistence can be expected under varying conditions of delayed contingent reinforcement. Thus, an important assessment question might center around the ability of the individual to sustain effort over temporal intervals of various lengths prior to receipt of reinforcement.

A further consideration in the examination of individual differences in response to reinforcement conditions centers about the patterning of reinforcements (Crandall, 1963). The individual can be expected to respond differently to nonreward embedded in a series of rewards as opposed to nonreward embedded in a series of punishments. And as is the case with other reinforcement conditions, one may very well expect to find differences among individuals in responsiveness to such patterning of reinforcing stimuli.

Situational Specific Hypotheses

Conditions of reinforcement constitute only one set of situational factors of interest to the individual differences psychologist. Situational specific hypotheses of the individual are a second important class of variables. While it might appear odd to discuss hypotheses of the individual in situational rather than structural terms, there is some logic in this approach. It would certainly appear to be the case that individuals develop hypotheses concerning themselves, others, and events in which they are involved. And the possibility that such hypotheses are important in the mediation of behavior cannot be overlooked. However, the generality of various subjective hypotheses of the individual remains open to question. As with other constructs, one would expect to find that the predictive utility of subjective hypotheses would decrease as specificity is sacrificed to more general statement. Thus, for example, when we ask a subject in personality research to describe himself on a trait dimension such as hostility, we are asking the subject for a rather complex inference, that is, a hypothesis concerning himself. To the extent that the subject attempts to answer such a question in the abstract, that is, without reference to his behavior in actual situations, we would expect him to experience increasing degrees of uncertainty in arriving at a conclusion concerning himself. In essence, self-report inventories frequently require the subject to engage in rather complex inferential processes. In arriving at tenable hypotheses concerning himself, other things being equal, the subject will be in a position to reduce uncertainty in direct proportion to the availability of relevant validating information. Some evidence from studies of self-prediction of performance supports this line of reasoning. Mischel (1968) demonstrated that when subjects were permitted increased knowledge of a specific situation, the utility of their hypotheses concerning future performance, that is, self-predictions, increased as well.

It would appear to be the case, then, that hypotheses concerning oneself, others, and events in which one is involved, gain in predictive utility to the extent that such hypotheses are tied to specific situations. Hence, it would appear appropriate to consider such hypotheses in situational terms rather than as structural aspects of the personality.

Individual differences in expectancies concerning success or failure in specific situational contexts constitute one set of hypotheses of individuals worthy of the attentions of the personologist. As with other hypotheses of the individual, the question of the predictive utility of generalized expectancies is an open one. Rotter (1954) argued that any expectancy is composed of two components, generalized expectancy (GE) and expectancy specific to the task at hand (E'). However, a number of researches suggest that expectancies are clearly influenced by situational factors (e.g., James & Rotter, 1958; Phares, 1957; Rotter, Liverant, & Crowne, 1961; Rychlak & Lerner, 1965). Moreover, recent research by Mischel and Staub (1965) suggests that when response outcomes are fairly clearly defined by success-failure information in specific situations, the effects of generalized expectancies are minimal. Generalized expectancies, in the research by Mischel and Staub, affected delay of reinforcement choices only when the subjects were confronted with a situation in which no information relevant to success probability was provided. In Atkinson's (1958) achievement-motivation model, expectancy is tied directly to situational manipulations with some success in the prediction of behavior. These findings suggest that E' is likely of greater predictive utility than GE.

In addition to situation specific hypotheses concerning success-failure, individual differences in hypotheses concerning noncontingent reinforcing stimuli from social agents in the individual's environment constitute another important assessment question for the personologist. Without question persons can and do develop hypotheses about probabilities of noncontingent reinforcements from other persons in their social environments. That is, individuals come to think of specific persons in their interpersonal worlds as predisposed to behave toward them with "hostility" or "warmth" or "indifference," etc., irrespective of the justification for such behaviors. Whether or not the other person is, in fact, predisposed to behave in certain ways toward the individual is not of importance here. However, the fact that the person being assessed has developed subjective probabilities of noncontingent reinforcement from specific others is obviously of considerable importance.

Situation specific hypotheses involving success-failure and probabilities of noncontingent reinforcements from specific others are illustrative of situational concerns of importance to the individual differences psychologist. Additional variables of importance which involve subjective hypotheses can be developed for particular assessments.

Formal Properties of Situations

A third class of situational variables controlling response performance involves differences in situations themselves in terms of their formal properties. While the assessment of persons should never proceed without reference to some stimulus situation, it is unfortunately the case that assessments which do take account of situations are the exception rather than the rule. The attempt to predict to unknown situations is fraught with difficulty.

The multifarious dimensions along which situations vary must, of necessity, render the discussion presented here suggestive rather than exhaustive. However, examination of several important formal attributes of situations themselves is illustrative. For example, social situations vary considerably in the range of behaviors considered acceptable and desirable. Relative freedom versus constraint for various forms of behavior in given social contexts can and does exert powerful influences over behavior. A very large portion of both individual and group behavior is predictable from knowledge of role appropriate and inappropriate behaviors in given social contexts.

Social environments differ in terms of the availability and accesibility of social reinforcers of various kinds. An exploratory study by the author (Wallace, 1963) revealed that teachers in elementary schools varied remarkably in terms of their properties as "reinforcement machines." One teacher administered verbal rewards and punishments in an approximate ratio of twenty rewards to a single punishment. Another teacher showed the reverse, administering approximately twenty verbal punishments to each reward! Striking differences in the behavior of the children in these two classes were apparent.

Finally, recent research on social learning (Bandura & Walters, 1963) indicates clearly that the personologist interested in behavior prediction must examine vicarious response-reinforcement contingencies which obtain in the individual's social environment. Without question, the performance of social behaviors is importantly influenced by observation of reinforcement outcomes experienced by others. Thus, for example, if one wished to predict the occurrence of "deviant" behaviors for a given individual, one might well be advised to concentrate upon the frequency with which such behaviors are displayed by significant group members and the consequences for such behaviors.

Obviously, the attempt to relate personality characteristics of any kind to behavior cannot proceed with any degree of success in the absence of detailed information about given social contexts. Rotter (1960) has so effectively argued the need to examine the situation carefully in personality assessment that it would appear redundant to pursue the matter in detail here.

Despite arguments to the contrary, examination of situational factors controlling response performance can be viewed as most congruent with the interests of the personologist. Murray (1938), in his analysis of presses as well as needs, called attention to the necessity to consider the individual in some environment. It would appear that in their search for a consistent man personologists have confused rather strikingly the two concepts of consistency and generality. While a man's behavior may prove remarkably consistent under given sets of stimulus conditions, it is quite another matter to expect him to show generality of such behavior across markedly different conditions. To the extent that he does show invariant behavior across varied stimulus situations, one might be tempted to suggest that something is quite wrong with him. After all, one might best define psychotic behavior as behavior unaffected by stimulus variations, that is, behavior under inappropriate stimulus control or in the absence of stimulus control.

A capabilities conception of personality has implications for decision making in assessment situations. Once answers have been obtained to questions concerning the conditions under which the individual can demonstrate his capabilities, cost-decision considerations could center about two important questions. First, in cases where environmental flexibility permits, one would attempt to assess the costs involved in manipulating situations so as to provide optimal conditions necessary for maximum performance. In essence, concern with the costs involved in "fitting the right situation to the man" would be uppermost in this case. Secondly, in cases where environmental flexibility does not obtain, cost-decision considerations would center about the costs involved in developing necessary response repertoires in given individuals in order to meet situational demands. Approaching personality from this perspective would permit the personologist to engage more directly the growing concern with human potentialities.

Implications for Personality Change

The implications for change which have stemmed from dispositional concepts of personality structure have proven most problematic. When the structure of personality is construed in terms of stable and enduring response dispositions which have reached full development early in the developmental history of the individual, the possibility of change seems limited. Moreover, conceiving of personality structure in terms of various energy units poses serious difficulties for alteration of such structure. How does one, for example, modify an instinct? Similarly, other than providing for temporary satiation of given needs, how does one go about altering the patterning of an individual's needs in some fundamental sense? In recognition of the fact that it is difficult to modify energy directly, dispositional theorists have approached the problem of personality change through various tactics. Redistribution of energy (sublimation), release (catharsis), and control through uncovering of unconscious determinants (insight) have constituted three important tactics of change.

Within recent years, each of these tactics for producing behavioral change has been challenged sharply. London (1964) has examined critically the assumption that insight into putative unconscious behavioral dispositions is of value in producing behavioral change. Recent well-controlled research by Bandura (1965b) appropriately calls into question the validity of the catharsis notion. As Bandura appropriately points out, the expression of socially unacceptable behaviors such as hostility would appear to lead to an increase in the probability of further expression rather than a decrease. Furthermore, one would expect such expression to be further enhanced if it eventuates in positive reinforcement, and also, if inhibitory factors over further expression are eliminated. Redistribution of energy tactics are based upon questionable assumptions such as "symptom subsituation." It is frequently assumed that one cannot change a single aspect of the personality without giving rise to the expression of various other compensatory symptoms. Hence, if one were to treat a phobia successfully by direct means without addressing oneself to the putative "underlying conflict" upon which the phobia is based, the patient would be expected to display some other symptom. Recent evidence from a wide variety of behavioral modification settings (e.g., Krasner & Ullmann, 1965; Wolpe, 1958) suggests that symptom substitution not only does not occur, but one may expect generalization of positive effects in the successful treatment of isolated symptomatic behaviors.

While the implications for personality change inherent in disposition conceptions have proven most problematic, those stemming from a capability conception of structure are straightforward indeed. When the structure of personality is construed in terms of units of skill, the problem of personality change is seen as one involving the development of response repertoires in conjunction with the selection and maintenance of situations which will enhance performance. Significant strides along these lines have already been made in behavioral modification procedures involving positive reinforcement (e.g., Bandura & Walters, 1963; Ferster, 1961; Krasner & Ullmann, 1965), assertive behavior training (Wolpe, 1958), fixed-role therapy (Kelly, 1955), and vicarious learning through use of behavior models (Bandura, 1965c).

It should not be assumed that procedures for enlarging response capabilities must, of necessity, be restricted to small behavior units. Kelly's (1955) fixed-role therapy demonstrates the feasibility of working with large and complex units in developing response repertoires. And interest is developing in the possibility of employing role theoretical constructs as units of change in positive reinforcement settings (Krasner & Ullmann, 1965). Moreover, the use of modeling procedures can provide the means through which very large behavioral sequences can be transmitted to an observer. Nor should it be assumed that increasing the individual's capabilities is restricted entirely to behavioral or action units. It is entirely conceivable that cognitive strategies of various kinds can be taught directly to individuals in efforts to increase their capabilities. Thus, for example, a portion of the psychotherapist's time might well be devoted to teaching the patient appropriate decision-making strategies and tactics. Similarly, direct tuition of the patient in strategies for seeking, assimilating, and utilizing information necessary for the validation of hypotheses he develops concerning himself, others, and events in which he is involved can be seen as an integral part of psychotherapy and other behavioral modification settings. An approach to the problems of human adjustment in terms of tactics and strategies as an alternative to the classical approach of defenses has been developed fully elsewhere (Sechrest & Wallace, 1967).

This, then, has been an attempt to take seriously the important question raised by Allport (1958), "What units shall we employ?" Construing personality in terms of the two central foci of response capability and response performance leads one to concern with units not suggested by dispositional concepts. A psychology of personality in which we choose to search for that of which man is capable would appear to have important implications. Moreover, these implications would appear to be meaningful and relevant to the scientific investigation of personality, whether we choose to work at the level of theory and research or that of application.

3. SIGNS, SAMPLES, AND CRITERIA

Paul F. Wernimont and John P. Campbell

Many writers (e.g., Dunnette, 1963; Ghiselli & Haire, 1960; Guion, 1965; Wallace, 1965) have expressed concern about the difficulties encountered in trying to predict job performance, and in establishing the validity of tests for this purpose. In general, their misgivings center around the low validities obtained and misapplications of the so-called "classic validity model." To help ameliorate these difficulties it is proposed here that the concept of validity be altered as it is now applied to predictive and concurrent situations and introduce the notion of "behavioral consistency." By consistency of behavior is meant little more than that familiar bit of conventional wisdom, "The best indicator of future performance is past performance." Surprisingly few data seem to exist to either support or refute this generalization. It deserves considerably more attention.

Some History

It is perhaps not too difficult to trace the steps by which applied psychologists arrived at their present situation. During both World War I and II general intelligence and aptitude tests were effectively applied to military personnel problems. Largely as the result of these successes, the techniques developed in the armed services were transported to the industrial situation and applied to the personnel problems of the business organization. From a concentration on global measures of mental ability, validation efforts branched out to include measures of specific aptitudes, interests, and personality dimensions. The process is perhaps most clearly illustrated by the efforts of the United States Employment

SOURCE. Paul F. Wernimont is now personnel research advisor for the 3M Company. He has been a research fellow at the Management Development Laboratory at the University of Minnesota and a senior staff specialist at the General Motors Institute. John P. Campbell is Associate Professor of Psychology at the University of Minnesota. Both Drs. Wernimont and Campbell have specialized in the fields of personnel and managerial selection. This article originally appeared in the *Journal of Applied Psychology,* 1968, **52,** 372-376 and is reprinted by permission of the American Psychological Association and the authors.

Service to validate the General Aptitude Test Battery across a wide range of jobs and occupations. In general, testing seemed to be a quick, economical, and easy way of obtaining useful information which removed the necessity for putting an individual on the job and observing his performance over a trial period.

It was in the context of the above efforts that an unfortunate marriage occurred, namely, the union of the classic validity model with the use of tests as signs, or indicators, of predispositions to behave in certain ways (Cronbach, 1960, p. 457), rather than as samples of the characteristic behavior of individuals. An all too frequent procedure was to feed as many signs as possible into the classic validity framework in hopes that the model itself would somehow uncover something useful. The argument here is that it will be much more fruitful to focus on meaningful samples of behavior, rather than signs of predispositions, as predictors of later performance.

The Consistency Model

To further illustrate the point, consider a hypothetical prediction situation in which the following five measures are available:

1. Scores on a mental ability test;
2. School grade-point average (GPA);
3. Job-performance criterion at Time 1;
4. Job-performance criterion at Time 2;
5. Job-performance criterion at Time 3.

Obviously, a number of prediction opportunities are possible. Test scores could be correlated with GPA; school achievement could be correlated with first-year job success; or the test scores and GPA could be combined in some fashion and the composite used to predict first-, second-, or third-year job performance. All of these correlations would be labeled validity coefficients and all would conform to the classic validity model. It is less clear what label should be attached to the correlation between two different measures of job performance. Few would call it validity; many would probably refer to it as reliability. There seems to be a tendency among applied psychologists to withhold the term validity from correlations between measures of essentially the same behavior, even if they were obtained at two different points in time. That is, the subtleties of the concept of reliability and the ingredients of the classic validity model seem to have ingrained the notion that validity is a correlation between a predictor and a criterion and the two should somehow be dissimilar.

However, each of the 10 correlations that one could compute from the above situation represents the degree of common variation between the two variables, given the appropriateness of the linear correlation model. After all, that is what correlation is all about. In this sense there is no logical reason for saying that some of the coefficients represent validity and others reliability, although there certainly may be in other contexts. An implicit or explicit insistence on the predictor being "different" seems self-defeating. Rather one should really be trying to obtain measures that are as similar to the criterion or criteria as possible. This notion appears to be at least implicit in much of the work on prediction with biographical data where many of the items represent an attempt to assess previous achievement on similar types of activities. Behavior sampling is also the basis on which simulation exercises are built for use in managerial assessment programs.

At this point it should be emphasized that for the consistency notion to be consistent, the measures to be predicted must also be measures of behavior. For example, it would be something less than consistent to use a behavior sample to predict such criteria as salary progression, organizational level achieved, or subunit production. The individual does not always have substantial control over such variables, and, even with the more obvious biasing influences accounted for, they place a ceiling on the maximum predictive efficiency to be expected. Furthermore, they are several steps removed from actual job behavior. In this respect, the authors are very much in accord with Dunnette (1966) who argues strongly for the measurement of observable job behavior in terms of its effect on meaningful dimensions of performance effectivenss. A recently developed method for accomplishing this aim is the behavior retranslation technique of Smith and Kendall (1964). The applied psychologist should reaffirm his mandate and return to the measurement of behavior. Only then will one learn by what means, and to what extent, an individual has influenced his rate of promotion, salary increases, or work group's production.

In general terms, what might the selection or prediction procedure look like if one tried to apply a consistency model? First, a comprehensive study of the job would be made. The results of this effort would be in the form of dimensions of job performance well defined by a broad range of specific behavior incidents which in turn have been scaled with respect to their "criticalness" for effective or ineffective performance.

Next, a thorough search of each applicant's previous work experience and educational history would be carried out to determine if any of the relevant behaviors or outcomes have been required of him or have been exhibited in the past. Items and rating methods would be developed to facilitate judging the frequency of such behaviors, the intensity with which they were manifested, the similarity of their context to the job situation, and the likelihood that they will show up again. These judgments can then be related to similar judgments concerning significant and consistent aspects of an individual's job behavior.

Such a procedure places considerable emphasis on background data and is similar in form to the "selection by objectives" concept of Odiorne and Miller

(1966). However, the aim is to be considerably more systematic and to focus on job behavior and not summary "objectives."

After the analysis of background data it might be found that the required job behaviors have not been a part of the applicant's past repertoire and it would be necessary to look for the likelihood of that job behavior in a variety of work-sample tests or simulation exercises. A number of such behavior measures are already being used in various management assessment programs.

Finally, individual performance measures of psychological variables would be given wider use where appropriate. For example, the Wechsler Adult Intelligence Scale (Wechsler, 1955) might be used to assess certain cognitive functions. Notice that such a measure is a step closer to actual performance sampling than are the usual kinds of group intelligence tests.

How does the above procedure compare to conventional practice? The authors hope they are not beating at a straw man if the usual selection procedure is described as follows. First, a thorough job analysis is made to discover the types of skills and abilities necessary for effective performance. This is similar to the consistency approach except that the objective seems to be to jump very quickly to a generalized statement of skills and abilities rather than remaining on the behavioral level. The conventional approach next entails a search for possible predictors to try out against possible criteria. Based on knowledge of the personnel selection and individual differences literature, personal experience, and "best guesses," some decisions are made concerning what predictors to include in the initial battery. It is the authors' contention that the classic validity model has forced an undue amount of attention on test and inventory measures at this stage. Witness the large amount of space devoted to a discussion of "test validation" in most books dealing with the selection problem. Again, signs seem to take precedence over samples. Lastly, one or more criterion measures are chosen. Too often the choice seems to be made with little reference to the previous job analysis and is based on a consideration of "objectivity" and relevance to the "ultimate" criterion. Unfortunately, even a slight misuse of these considerations can lead to criteria which are poorly understood. In contrast, working within the framework of a consistency model requires consideration of dimensions of actual job behavior.

It might be added that the above characterization of the conventional approach is meant to be somewhat idealized. Certain departures from the ideal might reinforce the use of signs to an even greater extent. For example, there is always the clear and present danger that the skill requirements will be stated in terms of "traits" (e.g., loyalty, resourcefulness, initiative) and thus lead even more directly to criteria and predictors which are oriented toward underlying predispositions.

Relationship to Other Issues

The consistency notion has direct relevance for a number of research issues that appear frequently in the selection and prediction literature. One important implication is that selection research should focus on individuals to a much greater extent than it has. That is, there should be more emphasis on intra-individual consistency of behavior. In their insightful discussion of the criterion problem, Ghiselli and Haire (1960) point out that intraindividual criterion performance sometimes varies appreciably over time, that is, is "dynamic." They give two examples of this phenomenon. However, after an exhaustive review of the literature, Ronan and Prien (1966) concluded that a general answer to the question, "Is job performance reliable?" is not really possible with present data. They go on to say that previous research has not adequately considered the relevant dimensions that contribute to job performance and very few studies have actually used the same criterion measure to assess performance at two or more points in time. In the absence of much knowledge concerning the stability of relevant job behaviors it seems a bit dangerous to apply the classic validation model and attempt to generalize from a one-time criterion measure to an appreciable time span of job behavior. Utilizing the consistency notion confronts the problem directly and forces a consideration of what job behaviors are recurring contributors to effective performance (and therefore predictable) and which are not.

In addition, the adoption of signs as predictors in the context of the classic model has undoubtedly been a major factor contributing to the lack of longitudinal research. It makes it far too easy to rely on concurrent studies, and an enormous amount of effort has been expended in that direction. Emphasis on behavior samples and behavior consistency requires that a good deal more attention be devoted to the former, along with very explicit consideration of the crucial parameters of a longitudinal study.

The moderator or subgrouping concept also seems an integral part of the consistency approach. The basic research aim is to find subgroups of people in a particular job family for whom behavior on a particular performance dimension is consistent. Subgrouping may be by individual or situational characteristics but the necessity is clear and inescapable. Only within such subgroups is longitudinal prediction possible.

Lastly, the process the authors are advocating demands a great deal in terms of being able to specify the contextual or situational factors that influence performance. It is extremely important to have some knowledge of the stimulus conditions under which the job behavior is emitted such that a more precise comparison to the predictor behavior sample can be made. Because of present difficulties in specifying the stimulus conditions in an organization (e.g., Sells, 1964), this may be the weakest link in the entire procedure. However, it is also a severe problem for any other prediction scheme, but is usually not made explicit.

It is important to note that the authors' notion of a consistency model does not rest on a simple deterministic philosophy and is not meant to preclude taking account of so-called "emergent" behaviors. Relative to "creativity," for example, the question becomes whether or not the individual has ever exhibited in similar contexts the particular kind of creative behavior under consideration. If a similar context never existed, the research must investigate creative performance and outputs obtained in a test situation which simulates the contextual limitations and requirements in the job situation.

An additional advantage of the consistency approach is that a number of old or persistent problems fortunately appear to dissipate, or at least become significantly diminished. Consider the following:

1. Faking and response sets—Since the emphasis would be on behavior samples and not on self-reports of attitudes, beliefs, and interests, these kinds of response bias would seem to be less of a problem.

2. Discrimination in testing—According to Doppelt and Bennett (1967) two general charges are often leveled at tests as being discriminatory devices:

(*a*) Lack of relevance—It is charged that test items are often not related to the work required on the job for which the applicant is being considered, and that even where relationships can be shown between test scores and job success there is no need to eliminate low-scoring disadvantaged people since they can be taught the necessary skills and knowledge in a training period after hiring.

(*b*) Unfairness of content—It is further maintained that most existing tests, especially verbal measures, emphasize middle-class concepts and information and are, therefore, unfair to those who have not been exposed to middle-class cultural and educational influences. Consequently, the low test scores which are earned are not indicative of the "true" abilities of the disadvantaged. Predictions of job success made from such scores are therefore held to be inaccurate.

The examination of past behaviors similar in nature to desired future behavior, along with their contextual ramifications, plus the added techniques of work samples and simulation devices encompassing desired future behavior, should markedly reduce both the real and imagined severity of problems of unfairness in prediction.

3. Invasion of privacy—The very nature of the consistency approach would seem to almost entirely eliminate this problem. The link between the preemployment or prepromotion behavior and job behavior is direct and obvious for all to see.

Concluding Comments

The preceding discussion is meant to be critical of the concepts of predictive and concurrent validity. Nothing that has been said here should be construed as an attack on construct validity, although Campbell (1960) has pointed out that reliability and validity are also frequently confused within this concept. Neither do the authors mean to give the impression that a full-scale application of the consistency model would be without difficulty. Using available criteria and signs of assumed underlying determinants within the framework of the classic model is certainly easier; however, for long-term gains and the eventual understanding of job performance, focusing on the measurement of *behavior* would almost certainly pay a higher return on investment.

Some time ago, Goodenough (1949) dichotomized this distinction by referring to signs versus samples as indicators of future behavior. Between Hull's (1928) early statement of test validities and Ghiselli's (1966) more recent review, almost all research and development efforts have been directed at signs. Relatively small benefits seem to have resulted. In contrast, some recent research efforts directed at samples seem to hold out more promise. The AT&T studies, which used ratings of behavior in simulated exercises (Bray & Grant, 1966), and the In-basket studies reported by Lopez (1965) are successful examples of employing behavior samples with management and administrative personnel. Frederiksen (1966) has reported considerable data contributing to the construct validity of the In-basket. In addition, Ghiselli (1966) has demonstrated that an interview rating based on discussion of specific aspects of an individual's previous work and educational history had reasonably high validity, even under very unfavorable circumstances. In a nonbusiness setting, Gordon (1967) found that a work sample yielded relatively high validities for predicting final selection into the Peace Corps and seemed to be largely independent of the tests that were also included as predictors.

Hopefully, these first few attempts are the beginning of a whole new technology of behavior sampling and measurement, in both real and simulated situations. If this technology can be realized and the consistencies of various relevant behavior dimensions mapped out, the selection literature can cease being apologetic and the prediction of performance will have begun to be understood.

4. DIGITAL-COMPUTER INTERPRETATION OF INKBLOT TEST DATA

Zygmunt A. Piotrowski

Automatic, machine interpretation of visual images elicited by inkblots is now a reality. The interpretive program, which is not yet completed, consists of about 450 test components (parameters or variables) and nearly 600 rules in which the test components appear in varying combinations and proportions. The program will ultimately consist of at least 1,000 rules and over 500 components or parameters.

Reasons for Digital-Computer Program

Many considerations entered into the decision to prepare inkblot percept-analytic test data for digital computer interpretation. While some of these considerations were of a non-essential nature, others were most compelling, particularly if the inkblot test were to attain scientific stature and grow into an even more desirable method of personality analysis than it is at present. Among the non-essential reasons are convenience, speed, facilitation of the process of interpretation, and reduction of personal responsibility for the test interpretation. Convenience, that is, the saving of time and effort, and the decrease of personal involvement are by far the most frequent motives for writing digital-computer programs. Most of the tasks performed by digital computers, especially in medicine and psychology, are primarily time and labor saving.

The essential considerations responsible for the computer program relate to functions which no human being can perform even under optimal conditions, but which a digital computer can easily perform well. These functions are necessary if interpretation of the inkblot test data is to be raised to a high level of objectivity and validity, and if there is to be a continuous improvement in the scope and meaningfulness of the information produced by the inkblot personality test.

One of these essential reasons is the limited mental grasp of even the best trained and most experienced psychologist. It is simply impossible to interpret many Rorschach records with exactly the same high degree of reliability in each.

SOURCE. Zygmunt A. Piotrowski, Professor of Psychology at Jefferson Medical College, has frequently contributed to the professional literature on personality, projective tests, and clinical prognosis. In previous articles, Dr. Piotrowski has examined the interpretation of responses to projective tests and the assumptions underlying projective measures. This article originally appeared in *Psychiatric Quarterly,* 1964, **38,** 1-26. Reprinted by permission of State Hospitals Press and the author.

This is true even of relatively brief test records, not to mention records which contain many and greatly diverse test responses. The interpretation of an inkblot-test record requires keeping track of so many test components and so many different rules of interpretation of these components in their innumerable interrelations that it takes an unusual psychologist to produce regularly interpretations of equal comprehensiveness and of uniformly very high reliability. The psychologist of necessity overlooks, forgets, and misapplies some of the rules, simply because of his limited mental grasp. Sometimes he is even led astray, either by a wish to modify his interpretive rules, or by an interesting and original response which may unduly influence the interpretation of the entire record. The computer, on the other hand, does not tire and has no emotions. It always applies the same rules regardless of the content of the test records. Thus, the foremost essential purpose of the digital-computer program is perfect reliability. For the first time in psychology, it is now possible to have an unlimited number of inkblot test records interpreted with that perfect reliability. This is an important gain, advancing the objectivity of the test.

The wish to facilitate and speed up the validation of the inkblot test was another serious reason for the digital-computer program. The usual validating procedures have failed because of the great complexity of the test. Complexity defeats accuracy if one wishes to see all the test components at once in their innumerable combinations. Therefore, it has been customary to tackle one, or at best a few, components at a time. The difficulty with this part-approach is that many components taken singly do not have the same meaning as in the context of the entire test. Failure to differentiate between the two meanings (the unconditional or nuclear, and the conditional or amplified) (Piotrowski, 1957) is responsible for poor results. It is, of course, very difficult to assign a meaning to a test component which will hold true regardless of the type of test record in which the component appears. Besides, while nearly all investigators have used the original set of Rorschach inkblots, they have differed significantly in the manner in which they interpreted the test data. Thus, there is, not one Rorschach Test, but a vast number of varieties of the test, a situation which often makes a direct comparison of different investigations meaningless. Since it is impossible to validate anything that is measured unreliably, the perfect digital-computer reliability of the test interpretation is a very important step toward the process of validation. The program has been written in such a way that the rules contain various combinations of components in various proportions. The degree of validity of each rule can be determined independently of that of any other rule.

A third essential reason for the digital-computer program is the impossibility of assuring a rapid and systematic development of the test (broadening its scope and raising its validity) without the aid of the digital computer. Once a body of well worked-up cases has been collected, it will be used to check any theory of the test and any new interpretive rule. This rapid and adequate checkup on the value of any new idea applied to the test opens the road to inventiveness, making us less dependent on the slow accumulation of experience. This is perhaps the most significant function of the digital computer in any field–that it stimulates inventiveness by providing rapid and adequate means to calculate the validity of creative ideas.

Thus, the digital computer interpretation of inkblot test data is not only a technical advance, but is an important step toward making the test more objective, more valid, and capable of continuous progress. Such an improvement in the test would be impossible without the digital computer. With time and increasing experience with this program, it will be possible to remove, improve or replace rules found to have an unsatisfactory degree of validity.

The program will always be deficient in one respect. It will not be able to foresee the unique responses which are sometimes obtained. The unique and original[1] responses in any record provide extremely significant material concerning the individual who produced these responses. However, two comments are in order.

In the first place, we can gradually build up a library of original responses, since the computers are displaying an increasingly wider memory capacity. Over the years it will also be possible to build into the program very rare responses for use in the event another record contains some of the very same responses. Thus, time will decrease the lack, which will characterize the program in the beginning, of interpretation of unique or original responses.

In the second place, we do not know enough about the meaning of original responses. We do know that "statistically unique" responses contain a great deal of important information about the individual. This is based on the fact that patients who are in prolonged and intensive psychotherapy regularly bring up material which clarifies the meaning of these unusual, unique inkblot reactions. However, while we can by statistical means identify a meaningful response, we cannot always tell, for lack of evidence, what that response may mean, for the number of patients in intensive and prolonged psychotherapy is a very small one. Thus, the objection that unique or original responses will be underestimated is actually not a serious objection. There should be one final comment about original answers. There will be nothing to prevent the psychologist who uses the digital computer from adding his own interpretation of his subject's original responses.

[1]Unique (here) = an extremely unusual response; original = (Rorschach's definition) a response found less frequently than in 2 per cent of healthy subjects' records.

Validation of the Digital-Computer Program

In its present form the digital-computer program is not final. It is not a standardization, to end all changes, but rather marks a new era, the beginning of an incisive process of validation and of a systematic development of the test. This process will be lengthy, difficult and complicated. Functioning somewhat like a psychological microscope, the test is not easily validated. Adequate independent criteria are not readily available to check the test results. The diagnostic rules of the program are the part most easily accessible to verification. Dependable and valid neuropsychiatric diagnoses are not so hard to obtain as are dependable, quantitative assessments of many specific personality traits such as motives, frustrations, intensity and quality of emotions, anxieties, strength and persistence of drive, unrealized potentialities and so on. Prolonged and intensive psychotherapy offers the best opportunity to assess such traits. Careful and repeated observations of the subjects' overt behavior supplement these assessments. Unfortunately, the obstacles in collecting such vital information are many. For this reason alone, the validation of the digital computer program will require a number of years.

The digital-computer program contains over 20 rules for diagnosing schizophrenia. None of these rules cover all cases. In fact, some are incompatible: If one of these incompatibles applies, some of the others cannot. At most, no more than about 10 of the rules are applicable in any individual test record. Neuropsychiatric diagnoses made after a first, short-term observation and examination of patients are hardly a standard by which the computer-test diagnoses are to be judged, because, roughly, only two of three short-term diagnoses are retained after second neuropsychiatric examinations by new examiners.

Long-term neuropsychiatric diagnoses are much more trustworthy. Long-term follow-up diagnoses made three to six years after the onset of the first serious mental disorder, are based on much more information than is the case when the patients are first seen. Moreover, there is a very relevant psychological reason for the higher degree of reliability of follow-up diagnoses of schizophrenia and of mental conditions spuriously resembling schizophrenia. That reason is simply that the mental conditions of the vast majority of mental patients become chronic within the first three to six years after the onset of psychoses; sudden, great, and unexpected changes in behavior and personality then become rare.

To determine the diagnostic power of the digital-computer diagnoses in their present form, 100 schizophrenics, neurotics and some organic cerebral cases, all of whom had been re-diagnosed on a follow-up by Nolan D. C. Lewis, M. D. were selected. The earliest pre-follow-up inkblot test records of these patients were re-scored to fit the requirements of the digital computer program (the input data). The diagnoses made by the digital computer were then compared with the post-follow-up clinical diagnoses. The results were encouraging. The computer diagnoses agreed with the clinical follow-up neuropsychiatric diagnoses in 86 per cent of the 100 patients. As the program improves, the percentage of correct computer diagnoses can also be expected to improve. Incidentally, it is noteworthy that the agreement between the digital-computer diagnoses and the first admission, clinical, discharge-diagnoses was lower than the agreement between the computer and follow-up neuropsychiatric diagnoses. In any case, "diagnosis ex machina" (Piotrowski, 1959) is now a fact.

The validation of the main and largest part of the digital computer program, the part which describes the relationship of the subject with his human environment, has not yet begun in earnest. At present only 10 records processed by machine have been subjected to verification. Inasmuch as more than three out of four of the nondiagnostic-report statements were confirmed (some with minor qualifications), there is justification for anticipating satisfactory results with any future test record—particularly when the program is improved.

History of the Digital-Computer Program

We desire before we will. The thoughts and procedures for the creation of a digital-computer method of inkblot-test interpretation were outlined in "The Methodological Aspects of the Rorschach Personality Method" by Piotrowski in 1936, which sought "to present a manner of looking at the method which may aid to clarify its problems and their logical interrelationships." "Clearly formulated principles which determine the process of analyzing the empirical data obtained in a clearly prescribed procedure" were emphasized. The two following ideas also influenced the digital-computer program: "Everything that is original and essential in the Rorschach seems to refer merely to the manner in which personality is projected into the inkblot interpretations (the subject's responses). It is a method, not a theory"; and, "We can apply any psychological principles (taken from any theory of personality) to the Rorschach conclusions in order to increase the usefulness of the method; always, however, a clear distinction must be made between the proper Rorschach personality description and additions to it made by applying general psychological principles."

In all his subsequent work, the writer has persistently differentiated between the theory of the inkblot test and theories of personality. His effort at formalizing the test has also been persistent and consistent. It is apparent in the signs for the diagnosis of organic cerebral disorders, (Piotrowski, 1937) in the epileptic signs, (Piotrowski, 1947) in the so-called alpha formula, (Piotrowski and Lewis, 1950) in the short-term and long-term prognostic signs, (Piotrowski, 1938; Piotrowski and Bricklin, 1958) and most prominently in *Perceptanalysis*

(Piotrowski, 1957). All the changes introduced by the writer into the scoring or definitions of the inkblot test components were deliberately made to advance a more objective and more valid interpretation of the inkblot test. It is but natural that these efforts should result in a digital-computer program. It is an old hope, expressed years ago, and gradually realized: "When this process (of tidying up and tightening) will have been completed one day, we shall be able to feed the Rorschach data, scored, classified, and counted according to objective rules, into a machine which will take the drudgery out of thinking consistently in terms of many variables and which will make the interpretation of the scored test data perfectly reliable." (Piotrowski, 1957, p-x).

The most extensive set of interpretive rules, one most nearly resembling a digital-computer program, was published in 1943 under the title: "Tentative Rorschach Formulae for Educational and Vocational Guidance in Adolescents" (Piotrowski, 1943). The rules were distributed under eight headings according to which vocationally important trait they measured. The headings were: (1) drive for planned and significant personal achievement; (2) attitude toward the world and conception of one's role in the world; (3) performance level, its quality and evenness; (4) persistence of effort and purpose; (5) relations with superiors in authority; (6) attitude toward own age group; (7) sense of responsibility for tasks undertaken, and (8) initiative or self-reliance in new undertakings.

As can be seen, the digital computer program was not a product of a moment's fancy. It has grown slowly for a long time, animated by an old wish.

Plans for the Future

It is the author's immediate purpose to submit the digital-computer program to a systematic evaluation by raters who are thoroughly acquainted with the subjects whose test records they will assess. These raters will have the choice of one of six reactions to every statement in every digital-computer report. These six reactions are: (1) I agree; (2) I agree with a qualification; (3) I have no evidence to pass judgment on the statement's adequacy; (4) I disagree with a qualification; (5) I disagree because I have evidence which proves the opposite; and (6) I am not sure I understand what you mean.

The plan also calls for the machine to interpret the inkblot-test records of subjects completely unknown to the investigators. After the re-scoring of the records and their interpretation by digital computer the reports will be returned for an assessment by those who had studied the subjects. This "double-blind" technique will guarantee objectivity, raising the value of the validation of the digital-computer program.

Rorschach's original set of inkblots and most of his ideas are used in this program. However, a number of his concepts have been updated or replaced with new ones. The main effort at improving the test centered around the percept-analytic features of the subject's responses. Whenever possible, preference was given to the formal or non-anecdotal aspects of the visual images. It is true that the anecdotal content and the formal features of the blot responses are intimately interrelated. Nevertheless, it is frequently possible to disregard the anecdotal content and obtain meaningful conclusions with a satisfactory degree of reliability and validity solely from the formal features of the response. As a result, the Rorschach test has been greatly revised, both in the scoring and in the meaning ascribed to the scoring categories (especially as regards shading, color and movement). One can find most of these revisions and the beginnings of a theory of the test in *Perceptanalysis.*

More information can be extracted with the aid of appropriate personality theories. While a theory of the test explains how the test succeeds in revealing the personality traits which it does disclose and measure, a theory of personality offers an explanation of how the individual has developed the personality traits which show up on a test or under any other conditions. The test-personality description can be interpreted in accordance with one or several personality theories. As the comprehensiveness and validity of a theory improves, it contributes increasingly valuable knowledge about the subject. Psychoanalysis and its insights into the human personality, Jungian symbolism, cultural and anthropological generalizations, in fact, any relevant cultural or physical principle, including medical and clinical psychiatric observations, can be fruitfully used to gain a deeper and more penetrating understanding of a subject's personality. So far, only a modest beginning has been made in theory application to inkblot-test findings.

Other tests, particularly projective personality tests like the Thematic Apperception Test or the free drawings of human figures, can also be programmed and added to the digital-computer personality description. Biographical data, psychiatric symptoms, psychiatric opinions and diagnoses will be added eventually to increase the practical-treatment usefulness of the computer program.

The expression of inkblot-test conclusions in generally understandable terms is a problem of its own. One soon becomes aware of its importance in working with the computer program. Since each rule's interpretation appears in exactly the same verbal form in every report to which that rule applies, it must be free of overgeneralization, understatement, praise, criticism, and unnecessary elaborations. The reason for this restraint is the effect of the whole report (all other interpreted rules) upon the understanding of each single rule. The psychologist, who writes a report, consciously (or unwittingly) qualifies each statement in the report by reference to the statements which precede or by reference to his over-all evaluation of the subject about which he writes. In this manner he can obtain a much higher degree of inner consistency and thus can also avoid exaggerations or understatements by changing his text. The digital computer is not flexible. Its perfect reliability and objectivity—admirable assets that they are—prevent flexibility and qualifications.

On the other hand, by trying to write a logically consistent and smooth report under the influence of a premature etiological formula (as is frequently the case), the psychologist is running the risk of becoming unreliable by understating the patient's inconsistencies and irrationalities. The digital computer is forcing us to phrase our conclusions in clear, universally-understandable language. This is a gain. It is obvious even now that the program requires a degree of precision which is above that usually encountered now in inkblot-test records or in other types of analysis of inner attitudes and external behavior.

The rearrangement of the sequence of the rules as they appear in a report will be an improvement, although it is not essential and can wait until we know more about the degree of validity of each rule.

It is much easier to learn how to prepare the input data sheets for the processing of test records by the digital computer than it is to learn how to apply the entire system of interpretive rules with a high degree of reliability. Since the machine performs the difficult job of manipulating the input data to write a report, the fact that it is so much easier to identify and list the input advances the objectivity of the test.

At some future date, the author will try to make the test still more objective by greatly reducing the human handling of the input data: The digital computer will be made to score and classify the subject's responses. The construction of such a scoring and classification program will be a long, complicated and difficult task and it had, therefore, better wait. However, here is an area in which marked technical improvements can be made which will increase the objectivity of the test. The present program requires many more components (parameters) and a much more detailed scoring system than any system evolved to date. As a matter of fact, the program in its present form contains more than 15 times as many components as Rorschach's own.

Finally, the program can be improved by appropriate statistical and logical procedures. The digital computer facilitates the generation of new hypotheses or new interpretive rules, and the grouping of the rules according to degrees of affinity of meaning. An attempt will be made to see if the program can be simplified and still yield the same vital information. With mounting validating evidence, it will be possible to revise the quantification of the components (to correct the critical points at which a continuous distribution can best be divided into several subgroups). Undoubtedly there is room here too for improvement.

The digital computer program is a major breakthrough, providing a solid frame within which all corrections can be made, not only with greater ease, but also with more telling effectiveness. Without the program, the conceptual and empirical aspects of the inkblot test would remain indeterminate.

The Computer and The Psychologist

The computer will not take the place of a thoughtful, thorough and diligent psychologist. The machine may seem a threat to the impressionistic psychologist who relies mainly on his free associations to test data collected haphazardly. Since there can be no artificial brains without live brains, the psychologist is needed to make the artificial brains work well. Instead of becoming a clerk, the psychologist will rise to the level of a master, making effective use of the artificial thinking machine.

The psychologist will always retain the right and duty to pass judgment on everything within his competence. This obviously includes reports written by digital computers—which he should submit to criticism. Any changes in the machine report—be they deletions, corrections or additions—will become his responsibility.

The psychologist will also be free to try his hand at something difficult and rarely done though extremely helpful to the understanding and treatment of patients: a synthesis of relevant information, based not only on the tests, but on everything he knows about the patient. Rarely in clinical practice is information from all sources fully utilized. This information should be properly correlated and its implications made explicit systematically. There are many helpful possible conclusions which remain dormant because the psychologist does not have the time to investigate all the available data. By saving hours of work, the computer will enable the psychologist to find time to perform the difficult task of synthesizing all his information and thereby raising the value of his professional contribution.

There is little doubt that the digital computer will change the psychologist's outlook just as the microscope changed that of the biologist. Human personality is most complex; but it is a complexity which is highly organized in areas vital to the individual and which maintains its system of organization (except in many psychotics) for many long years. As psychologists, we cannot isolate our variables or personality traits (action tendencies and action patterns) the way the physicists and even biologists (biochemists) isolate their variables. This fact heightens the value of the computer to psychologists, whose science has developed much more through the formulation of abstract speculations, later subjected to verification, than by the inductive elaboration of numerous little facts. The digital computer is the proper instrument for adequate and rapid verification of abstract principles applicable to concrete empirical observations. A close association with computers, and the mental discipline they require make one keenly aware of the difference between thought and reality. The purpose of science is more than a confrontation of the two: It is a striving toward the reconciliation of the two.

The computer program demands complete and accurate test records. In time, this demand will improve the taking of test records. We shall have to be more definite about many test reactions which at present are left indeterminate, that is, capable of being interpreted in a variety of ways with equal plausibility. A response like "two people" is insufficient. A careful inquiry must be made to determine whether this is a movement or merely a form response. "Two people facing each other" also is insufficient. We need to know what the "facing" is meant to imply, curiosity, friendliness, hostility, and so on, and so on. The inkblots elicit visual images in a specific way and are not directly (without qualification) comparable even to the same visual images of a single person, occurring at another time under different conditions. For this reason, careful inkblot testing is an important requirement for success. Clever and detailed interpretation can never substitute for carefully gathered empirical test data. Visual images are essential to life, as well as to personality research: We could not function without them. They must be taken seriously and differentiated carefully from one another. The computer will provide much of the precision the psychologist needs to be exact, valid and meaningful.

Conclusion

This digital computer program for the interpretation of visual images elicited by the Rorschach set of inkblots has a deeper foundation than mere descriptive statistics. It does not consist of the comparison of an individual's test profile with the average profiles of a number of subject groups, on the assumption that the individual is likely to possess personality traits typical of the group of people whose average test performance the individual's own test record approaches most. The computer program rests on a theory of the test, and its interpretive rules apply to any adult past the age of 16 (a program for children remains to be written). Each component (or specific reaction to the test) and each component combination is assigned the function of a measure of a specific personality trait (action tendency, latent; action tendency, overt; emotional attitude; anxiety and the handling of it; drive for personal achievement; level and quality of thought processes; and so on). The degree of validity of each interpretive rule of the program will be ascertained by counting the number of times the psychological conclusion of the rule is verified or contradicted (either unqualifiedly or qualifiedly) by pertinent and valid independent criteria in a large number of individuals and not by agreement with estimates of group averages.

Preliminary validation of a limited number of individual test records has been satisfactory. The author hopes to complete the computer program and validate it within the next several years. One point has already been demonstrated: It is that—with the aid of an appropriate theory of the inkblot test—it is possible to translate the clinical psychologist's experience and intuition into digital-computer language. The computer program greatly reduces subjectivism; there is only a small (and temporary) loss in meaningfulness. The program provides an excellent opportunity to submit the very complex inkblot test to a thorough, convenient and adequate validation. Moreover, it provides the additional opportunity to broaden the test's comprehensiveness, thus increasing its application in depth as a sort of psychological microscope.

In these respects, the program is a major breakthrough. Digital computers mark the beginning of a new and significant era in human thought. They increase the power of human thought, enabling us to make quick and meaningful use of even limited amounts of personal experience. The significance of the new and powerful "thinking machines" will probably be as great as was the introduction of the zero and Arabic numerals into mathematics.

Type of Patient–Case History Excerpts

(Digital Computer Cases–Case 1)

MALE C.A. = 15 yrs. IQ = 125. (Schizophrenic.)
MALE C.A. = 21 yrs. IQ = 131. (Schizophrenic.)

At the age of 15, the patient was hospitalized for the first time because of debilitating and excessive compulsiveness. He washed his hands for hours at a time in a ritual that required absolute silence. He often behaved bizarrely, dressing as Rembrandt or in other peculiar costumes, sewing his socks to his pants legs, wearing pajamas over his street clothes. He produced sudden displays of hostility and talked a great deal about "symbols." One of his favorite phrases was: "I get so many impressions." He was extremely stubborn and retrenched. He was exposed to insulin coma and electric shock treatments. At times he cooked his own food, being unable to eat food prepared by others. He was bright and planned to become a nuclear physicist. None of the treatments helped and the condition gradually became worse, disabling the patient to such a degree that he became completely dependent on others (whose help he often refused to accept).

At the age of 21, a frontal bilateral transorbital lobotomy was performed. The second Rorschach record was taken two months after this operation. A follow-up three years after the lobotomy reveals improvement in the sense that the patient was less irritable and was able to get along better with his family. He still was unable to organize his life activities. Insight became poorer, reducing anxiety. In his own words: "I have stopped thinking about a lot of things." Constant supervision was still required.

MALE C.A. = 15 yrs, IQ = 125.

Schizophrenia: five yrs. later, worse, and then had transorbital lobotomy.

Machine Interpretation

024 Needs additional stimulation and continuous encouragement to perform satisfactorily on a job which is more than simple routine and requires some initiative and inventiveness.

050 Is hesitant and neurotically ambivalent about handling personally vital matters in accordance with own life roles.

055 Has an immature outlook on life. Is mentally or intellectually dependent. Has an underdeveloped personal scale of values, and a meager inner life. Is a much greater conformist than would be expected or found in persons of similar intelligence and education.

056 Not sensitive. Can tolerate a great deal of discomfort without much bother.

063 Unimaginative: inhibited fantasy. Down-to-earth type. Only practical problems arouse subject's interest. Motivation limited chiefly to gratification of basic needs for food, shelter and security. Has an uncomplicated outlook on human motives, human nature and interhuman relations.

102 Intermittent doubt and indecisiveness concerning the value and desirability of own ideas and plans for action. Changes them quickly with a feeling of finality—at least for a while until the next change comes.

145 Has limited genuine interest in sharing emotional experiences with others. Both his hates and loves are weak.

146 Needs a long warming-up period before responding emotionally to others.

147 Is capable of making an easy and adequate social adjustment of a conventional kind in new but nonchallenging social situations.

163 Has a weak or mild need to share intense pleasurable experiences with others.

210 Prefers to sacrifice (abandon, postpone, or modify) important goals of external achievement in order to appear noncompetitive and nonassertive. Subject values relations with the environment too much to jeopardize the respect, affection and protection which others can give. If necessary, surrenders part of own personality rather than antagonize others.

211 Places an over-all damper on activities concerned with matters which cause him anxiety and activate his fears, especially if he believes that he might fail in their pursuit.

239 Spontaneous emotional interest in people is not as strong as in most people of superior intellectual ability.

243 Is considerate of others as a result of training but puts little genuine feeling or emotional warmth in his relations with others.

264 Makes adequate adjustment to others in conventional social situations.

277 Displays less than average emotional interest in others for a person of his intellectual level.

291 Possibility of schizophrenia should be investigated.

292 Uses strength defensively.

1001 Has insufficient awareness of the relation of own endeavors to the activities, interests, and goals of others. Not interested in improving own position in life through planned and persistent personal effort. Relaxed about own work and responsibilities. Not interested in being a great success.

1005 Fails to participate in common, social endeavors. Pursues own spontaneous interests mildly.

1026 Apparently has had no conflict over attitude to any authoritarian male figure.

1027 The presence of others slows subject down markedly. Emotions interfere with efficiency.

1028 Caution and reserve determined by anxiety rather than depression.

1035 Very little zeal. Practically no diligence.

1046 Occasionally uses definite denial as a defense against anxiety. At times feels dissociated, out of joint.

1067 Shares very few common ideas with others. Shares common interests only in a moderate degree.

1070 Conspicuously obsessive. Seriously handicapped by obsessive-compulsive symptoms.

1073 Marked obsessiveness, especially afraid of making definite inferences.

1090 Poor concentration. Inferior conscious control over thinking. Poor direction of thoughts. Much deviant thinking.

1105 Extremely poor self-control as regards conscious voluntary attention, thought processes, and overt motor behavior. Conspicuously inadequate in thought and action.

1108 Insufficient and very inferior capacity for conscious and deliberate control over outward manifestation of emotions, other actions and thinking.

1124 Occasionally jumps at unwarranted conclusions in an attempt to size up a situation on insufficient evidence. At times lacks patience to carefully think matters through, wishing reality would conform with personal expectations to a degree which unfavorably affects judgment.

1126 A scatterbrain.

1131 Has confidence in no one because of acute anxiety. Will not easily enter into any emotionally close relationship with any other person.

1156 Afraid of failure, of losing out in competition with others. Worried.

1166 Does not give priority to any specific interest which would overshadow all others and give a firm and lasting direction to creative intellectual work. Lacks adequate mental concentration. Keeps away from intellectual activities that might interest him.

1173 A model student type. Knows the correct answers without a real understanding of the problems. Strong tendency to avoid intellectual competition and to repeat clichés and generally accepted ideas.

1181 Possibility of schizophrenia should be investigated.

1217 Sometimes the emotional desires are not definite in their intent. They are blurred and inhibited even when they arise. When aroused, a definite emotional attitude also stimulates anxiety. Subject feels very uncomfortable having the emotion, let alone acting in accordance with it.

1232 A decompensating obsessive compulsive psychoneurosis. Schizophrenia.

1234 Schizophrenia.

1245 Schizophrenia.

1257 Schizophrenia.

1262 Schizophrenia.

1266 Schizophrenia.

1267 Schizophrenia.

1269 Schizophrenia.

1271 There is a keen awareness of anxiety whenever a genuine feeling (positive or negative) is aroused. The patient has the habit of deliberately controlling the strength and the outward manifestations of this anxiety.

MALE C.A. = 21 yrs. IQ = 131.

Schizophrenic. Two months after transorbital lobotomy.

Machine Interpretation

0008 Has about average interest in becoming conscious of psychosocial relations between self and others; the subject has some intermittent insight into the manner in which others relate to him and in which the subject relates to them.

0069 Subject is assertive in personally vital matters; he likes to take responsibility for his own actions and to be independent. This self-confident assertiveness probably developed in early childhood and was shaped by relations with his father.

0072 Basic attitudes determining interhuman relationships are likely to remain wishes and to be expressed rarely in overt motor behavior.

0144 Emotionally flat.

0145 Has a limited genuine interest in sharing emotional experiences with others. Both his hates and loves are weak.

0248 Above average intelligence.

0259 Emotionally flat. Apathetic. Pathologically indifferent. Not interested in an emotional give-and-take with others.

0274 Shows no interest in others as potential partners in emotional relationships but is somewhat anxious and is capable of some superficial affect.

0277 Displays less than average emotional interest in others for a person of his intellectual level.

1001 Has insufficient awareness of the relation of own endeavors to the activities, interests, and goals of others. Not interested in improving own position in life through planned and persistent personal effort. Relaxed about own work and responsibilities. Not interested in being a great success.

1005 Fails to do share in common, social endeavors. Pursues mildly own spontaneous interests.

1026 Apparently has had no conflict over attitude to any authoritarian male figure.

1028 Caution and reserve determined by anxiety rather than depression.

1030 Weak personality structure. Frequently at a loss to know how to handle situations. Largely ineffectual.

1031 Intermittent depressive moods which are not conspicuous in overt social behavior. However, once in a while makes a sudden move which in the eyes of others looks unnecessarily hostile and aggressive. When feeling anxious is strongly inclined to actively do something to lower anxiety, even if this might incur the opposition or hostility of others. Feels increase in energy when anxiety increases and answers challenges better than when in a state of relaxation. Avoids pain less than do others.

1035 Very little zeal. Practically no diligence.

1050 Dissimulates fear.

1081 Probably shows initiative in leading others.

1121 Does not care to occupy an administrative position of power and responsibility. Not interested in managing others.

1124 Occasionally jumps at unwarranted conclusions in an attempt to size up a situation on insufficient evidence. At times lacks patience to carefully think matters through, wishing reality would conform to personal expectations to a degree which unfavorably affects judgment.

1151 Tries to dissimulate his real traits and appear different from true self.
1163 The degree of variety of ideas produced is within statistically normal limits.
1165 Exaggerated interest in the psychology of others, in their motives and goals, probably because of fear that some of their actions might be dangerous to subject.
1197 Is internally ready to be himself when dealing with others in personally vital matters. Accepts himself.
1203 Insecure and secretive with respect to a good part of own inner life. Dislikes self-analysis. Does not like to display own true feelings and attitudes.
1224 Very likely was overprotected by mother.
1250 Schizophrenia.
1257 Schizophrenia.
1258 Schizophrenia.
1269 Schizophrenia.

Case 2

FEMALE C.A. = 19. IQ = 101. (Schizophrenic.)

This patient was admitted to a psychiatric hospital for the first time because she had for several years experienced intervals during which she became depressed, irritable, hostile. During these intervals, which could last for months at a time, she gained a great deal of weight (as much as 50 pounds). She told untruths, engaged in petty thefts. At times she was boisterous and gregarious. There were periods of euphoria. At other times she became out of touch with reality: "I do not seem to have the passions others feel." The patient was very promiscuous.

Four years later the patient was admitted in a state of excitement following the birth of an illegitimate child—for which she refused all responsibility and which eventually was placed in a foster home. Two years later (six years after the initial testing) she became overactive, incapable of working, and began to forge checks. She seemed to have no insight into the fact that her behavior was abnormal—feeling no one understood her. She was repeatedly diagnosed as psychotic (always with an unfavorable prognosis).

FEMALE C.A. =19. IQ =101.

Schizophrenia: four yrs. later much worse (committed).

Machine Interpretation

0008 Has about average interest in becoming conscious of psychosocial relations between self and others; subject has some intermittent insight into the manner in which others relate to her and in which subject relates to them.

0012 Aggressive competitiveness characterizes the subject's adjustment to others in personally vital matters most of the time.

0085 Anxiety or tension symptoms are likely to be somatic (neuromuscular); conversion, compulsive habits, muscular weakness, or rigidity, rather than ideational (phobias, obsessive thoughts).

0094 Very responsive to environmental stimulation. The immediate environment easily influences subject's feelings, and to a lesser extent overt actions.

0107 Cannot work efficiently unless emotionally comfortable. Whenever feels not fully accepted by others, subject's capacity for work drops markedly.

0113 Has need for self-reliance. Likes to prove self through actions that confidence in self is justified. Loves to initiate activities and consistently pursues personal goals without dependence on others. When challenged is likely to intensify efforts to demonstrate to others as well to own self capacity to handle problems independently and successfully. Would like to leave an imprint of own personality on fellow-men. May arouse dislike because of independent manner.

0136 Convinced one has to fight directly and compete with others in order to survive socio-economically, if not physically.

0147 Is capable of making an easy and adequate social adjustment of a conventional kind in new but nonchallenging social situations.

0150 Habitually makes an adequate adjustment of a conventional sort to usual social situations, showing proper type of interest in and attention to others. The emotional reactions tend to be determined by social norms rather than by genuine personal emotions and are of a mild intensity. Is polite and pleasant though emotional relations may lack depth. Overdrilling in childhood discouraged pursuit of emotional gratifications.

0152 Constitutionally very strong. Can stand a great deal of emotional strain without breakdown.

0154 Immature emotionally. Has problem controlling impulses to act in an inconsiderate, demanding and imprudent manner, disregarding the rights, wishes and powers of others.

0165 From time to time feels like getting away from people because subject feels uncomfortable in their company.

0166 Is easily stimulated emotionally by others and experiences very frequently a desire to contact others for the purpose of sharing pleasurable experiences with them.

0191 Emotionally lively, at least inwardly. Great interest in emotional ties with others. Experiences powerful emotions.

0197 Has insufficient self-regulating or automatic self-control over outward manifestations of emotions, especially in states of fatigue or when an emotionally stimulating situation has been lasting for some time.

0199 Is rather restless in motor behavior. Moods and emotions readily show in overt behavior. Fears losing self-control, resulting in impulsive behavior.

0234 Displays more than average emotional interest in others.

0279 Likes to be active. Does not tire easily. Moves about swiftly. Looks younger than own age.

1011 At times thinking is definitely akin to that of a child in the sense that conclusions are reached in an inconsistently free manner; arrives sometimes at some conclusions as if they were by accident and shows then some degree of surprise at the conclusion. Inadequate intellectual discipline.

1028 Caution and reserve determined by anxiety rather than depression.

1031 Has intermittent depressive moods which are not conspicuous in overt social behavior. However, once in a while makes a sudden move which in the eyes of others looks unnecessarily hostile and aggressive. When feeling anxious is strongly inclined to do something actively to lower anxiety, even if this might incur the opposition or hostility of others. Feels increase in energy when anxiety increases and answers challenges better than when in a state of relaxation. Avoids pain less than do others.

1046 Occasionally uses definite denial as a defense against anxiety. At times feels dissociated. Out of joint.

1047 Very much preoccupied with personality growth. In fact too much so. Apparently fears to be left behind in the competitive world.

1065 Lack of genuine interest in others. Lack of psychological interest in what makes people tick, probably because of hostility toward people.

1067 Shares very few common ideas with others. Shares common interests only in a moderate degree.

1087 Possibility of schizophrenia should be investigated.

1105 Extremely poor self-control as regards conscious voluntary attention, thought processes and overt motor behavior. Conspicuously inadequate in thought and action.

1108 Insufficient and very inferior capacity for conscious and deliberate control over outward manifestation of emotions, other actions and thinking.

1124 Occasionally jumps at unwarranted conclusions in an attempt to size up a situation on insufficient evidence. At times lacks patience to think matters through carefully, wishing reality would conform to personal expectations to a degree which unfavorably affects judgment.

1138 Conspicuously slow pace of thought. Subjectively feels seriously mentally disturbed.
1139 Reaction formations against anxiety are pleasantly toned.
1156 Afraid of failure, of losing out in competition with others. Worried.
1167 Preoccupied with sex problems which she tries to hide from the observation of others. Unresolved sexual tension.
1170 A model pupil type.
1190 Can easily withdraw from meaningful overt relations but can also be pulled in relatively easily.
1211 Generally moody and dissatisfied, critical of self and others. Anticipates difficulties.
1217 Sometimes the emotional desires are not definite in their intent. They are blurred and inhibited, even when they arise. When aroused, a definite emotional attitude also stimulates anxiety. Subject feels very uncomfortable having the emotion, let alone acting in accordance with it.
1223 Has been unaccepted by mother. In childhood was persistently criticized and punished by her.
1229 The patient experiences the psychosis as something senseless and inpulsive, as a disease which is passing over her like a storm. Easily outwardly manifests own inner experiences.
1240 Schizophrenia.
1249 Schizophrenia.
1250 Schizophrenia.
1258 Schizophrenia.
1260 Schizophrenia.

Case 3

FEMALE C.A. = 22. IQ = 103. (Psychoneurotic.)

The subject was hospitalized with a variety of somatic complaints (chiefly anorexia and hemi-blindness). She became a great problem to her family, and was confined to bed. The onset was sudden, occurring while the patient was caring for her mother, who was ill with pneumonia. At five, the patient vomited when she was told of the sudden death of an older sister. There were nine siblings. The patient was extremely attached to a brother who was one year her senior. Though somewhat shy, the patient was sociable and particularly demonstrative in her affection for her father. However, she sided with her mother in family quarrels. At one time she developed a great fear of death and unreality: "I don't know how people felt their thoughts." She also made such statements as: "I am dead"; "I can't see"; "Everything is a dream." However, there were no ideas of suicide expressed.

Aside from these rarely made, unusual statements the patient's reasoning ability was not affected. She was able to say: "My family, what seems stupid to them is real to me"; "A millionaire I'm not but I got a millionaire's sickness." Her voice was always firm and friendly. She was in excellent contact with her environment.

Seven years later she had little social life—few dates. She became the cook for her large family, including the mates of her siblings, when they jointly occupied the entire floor of an apartment building. From time to time the patient experienced agoraphobia and was unable to leave the house unless in the company of her favored brother. The brother attempted in vain to find the patient a husband. She was said to perform her household duties efficiently despite her obsessiveness. She developed an obsession about the number "4," refusing to use the fourth sheet of paper; the fourth card in a series, and refusing to wear a dress for the fourth time, etc.

FEMALE C.A. = 22. IQ = 103.

PN (Anx. Hyst.): 7 yrs. later impr.

Machine Interpretation

050 Is hesitant and neurotically ambivalent about handling personally vital matters in accordance with own life roles.

055 Has an immature outlook on life. Is mentally or intellectually dependent. Has an underdeveloped personal scale of values, and a meager inner life. Is a much greater conformist than would be expected or found in persons of similar intelligence and education.

063 Unimaginative: Inhibited fantasy. Down-to-earth type. Only practical problems arouse subject's interest. Motivation limited chiefly to gratification of basic needs for food, shelter and security. Has an uncomplicated outlook on human motives, human nature and interhuman relations.

071 As a child felt rejected and neglected by parents and incapable of influencing parents' (especially mother's) attitudes toward self. Has an infantile or immature outlook on life.

146 Needs a long warming-up period before responding emotionally to others.

147 Is capable of making an easy and adequate social adjustment of a conventional kind in new but non-challenging social situations.

155 Now and then experiences an urge to behave in an impulsive and inconsiderate manner, oblivious of consequences.

228 Displays about average amount of emotional interest in others.

231 Emotionally lively; feelings easily aroused.

240 Spontaneous emotional interest in people is about average.

264 Makes adequate adjustment to others in conventional social situations.

1026 Apparently has had no conflict over attitude to any authoritarian male figure.

1030 Weak personality structure. Frequently at a loss on how to handle situations. Largely ineffectual.

1031 Has intermittent depressive moods which are not conspicuous in overt social behavior. However, once in a while makes a sudden move which in the eyes of others looks unnecessarily hostile and aggressive. When feeling anxious, is strongly inclined to actively do something to lower anxiety, even if this might incur the opposition or hostility of others. Feels increase in energy when anxiety increases and answers challenges better than when in a state of relaxation. Avoids pain less than do others.

1047 Very much preoccupied with personality growth. In fact too much so. Apparently fears to be left behind in the competitive world.

1071 Obsessive-compulsive.

1136 Neurotic ambivalence regarding the manner of relating to others in personally vital matters. Avoids thinking about interhuman relations. Feels increase in anxiety when has to face a serious life situation involving those who are close to her. It is possible that rather strong latent homosexual tendencies are in part responsible for this ambivalence.

1139 Reaction formations against anxiety are pleasantly toned.

1147 May feel that she is losing conscious control over her thought processes.

1169 Normal, average amount of interest in what makes others tick, in their motives and goals, and in the possible effects of the action of others upon her own life and future.

1170 A model pupil type.

1175 Possesses a high degree of conscious and voluntary control over conscious thought processes and overt manifestation of action tendencies. Can control self well even in very irritating situations at least for a limited time. General behavior in usual social situations is adequate.

1177 Alert, adaptable, capable of steady and good but routine work.

1184 Systematic, disciplined thinking, good capacity for prolonged voluntary attention. Methodical approach to problems.

1271 There is keen awareness of anxiety whenever a genuine feeling (positive or negative) is aroused. The patient has the habit of deliberately controlling the strength and the outward manifestations of this anxiety.

Sample Input Data Sheets PAGE 6

0	5	0	1	IRT (longest) = plate ( )
1	5	0	2	IRT (longest) = ( ) seconds
2	5	0	5	IRT (shortest) = plate ( )
3	5	0	6	IRT (shortest) = ( ) seconds
4	5	0	3	IRT (2nd longest) = plate ( )
5	5	0	4	IRT (2nd longest) = ( ) seconds
6	3	5	2	ΣM-
7	3	4	1	ΣM (I)
8	3	4	2	ΣM (II)
9	3	4	3	ΣM (III)
0	3	4	4	ΣM (IV)
1	3	4	5	ΣM (V)
2	3	4	6	ΣM (VI)
3	3	4	7	ΣM (VII)
4	3	4	8	ΣM (VIII)
5	3	4	9	ΣM (IX)
6	3	5	0	ΣM (X)
7	3	8	0	M: alternative
8	3	8	9	ΣMa + ΣMad
9	3	5	3	ΣM-assert
0	3	6	1	ΣM (assert-aggressive)
1	3	6	8	ΣM (assert-animal)
2	3	5	4	ΣM-assertcompl.
3	3	7	1	ΣM-assertcompl. (animal)
4	3	7	0	ΣM-assertcompl. (female)
5	3	6	9	ΣM-assertcompl. (male)
6	5	8	4	ΣM-(assert-competitive)
7	3	6	7	ΣM-assert (female)
8	3	6	6	ΣM-assert (male)
9	3	6	2	ΣM (assert-overt)
0	3	6	3	ΣM (assert-pose)
1	3	5	5	ΣM-blocked
2	3	7	4	ΣM-blocked (animal)
3	3	6	4	ΣM-blocked (confined)
4	3	7	3	ΣM-blocked (female)
5	3	7	2	ΣM-blocked (male)
6	3	9	0	Mc
7	5	7	3	Mc
8	3	5	7	ΣM-compl.
9	3	7	9	ΣM-compl. (animal)

NAME ______________________ PAGE 10

0	6	3	1	Fit inadequate, irrel. corr.
1	6	3	0	Thought control lost
2	6	2	9	F cont: religion
3	6	2	8	Proportions unrealistic
4	6	2	0	Percept overlapping
5	6	0	8	Percept lingering
6	6	0	7	Percept delayed
7	9	0	0	Rpt. (3 succes. plates) (12)
8	6	0	6	Vagueness, percept., meaning
9	6	0	5	Breakdown interpret. attitude
0	6	0	4	Invalidity, physical
1	6	0	3	Invalidity, logical
2	9	0	0	Rpt. (VIII-X) (11)
3	6	0	0	d Orig.-
4	5	9	9	d inside Orig.-
5	5	9	8	cont: "split," etc.
6	9	0	0	R in <4 words, 90% (10)
7	9	0	0	Rpt. (multiple) (8)
8	9	0	0	Doubt, "split," refl, etc. (7)
9	9	0	0	Doubt R with pri. th. d. (6)
0	5	9	5	CR cont: disease, infect.
1	5	9	7	Affect inappropriate
2	9	0	0	Cut-off small areas etc. (5)
3	5	8	2	M cont: killing, destroying
4	9	0	0	Ontological mixup (4)
5	5	8	1	M orig. +
6	5	7	9	dM-
7	5	6	8	F+% (VIII-X)
8	6	3	2	ΣM hd
9	6	4	7	Color shock verbalized
2	9	0	1	Succession rigid (4)
3	6	3	3	ΣM (orig.)
4	6	4	8	Cw shock
5	6	8	2	d cont: large animals
6	6	6	1	Asoc, sec, loosen, intermittent
7	6	8	1	W cont: small creature
8	6	3	4	S orig.-
9	7	0	9	Σ (C earthy)

5. THE INTERPRETATION OF PERSONALITY TESTS BY COMPUTER: THE MINNESOTA MULTIPHASIC PERSONALITY INVENTORY

Raymond D. Fowler, Jr.

The acute shortage of manpower in the mental health professions has given rise to a number of strategies to make the use of existing personnel more efficient. The most common approach has involved the training of subprofessionals or technicians to operate in areas previously reserved for highly trained professionals. In some cases, these "new professionals" have made a substantial contribution to mental health services, and have freed members of the professional staff to perform those specialized functions for which they are uniquely trained. In other cases, the introduction of partially trained personnel has resulted in a degrading of the quality of services available and to public confusion as to who is qualified to provide services.

Another strategy of more recent origin is the use of computers to amplify professional time. The purpose of this paper is to describe a method by which the computer has been programmed to carry out some of the functions traditionally performed by the clinical psychologist.

Although computers have been extensively used in the standardization of psychological tests and the analysis of data derived from such tests, it is only recently that they have been used to "interpret" the meaning of test responses and to generate psychological test reports.

Tests vary in the degree to which they are *structured.* Some have few specified rules, and the interpreter must rely heavily upon his clinical experience and intuition to assess the meaning of a response. Others are highly structured in administration and scoring, and the rules for the attribution of meaning are specified. In the realm of personality tests, the Rorschach and the other projective techniques lie toward the unstructured end of the continuum and the personality inventories lie toward the structured end. Since the computer requires a structured input, it is not surprising that most of the progress in computer interpretation of personality tests has been with the objective personality inventories. Much of this work has been with the MMPI, since (1) it is

SOURCE. Raymond D. Fowler, Jr., is Professor and Chairman of the Department of Psychology at the University of Alabama. Dr. Fowler is also research consultant to the Alabama Department of Health's Division of Alcoholism and a consultant to the Roche Psychiatric Service Institute. Dr. Fowler has been interested in the development of computer interpretation of psychological tests. This original article is based upon "Computer interpretation of personality tests: the automated psychologist" which originally appeared in *Comprehensive Psychiatry,* 1967, **8**, 455-467. The permission of the author and of Grune & Stratton, Inc., are gratefully acknowledged.

the most widely used objective personality test, (2) there is a large research literature available, and (3) the traditions of the MMPI have emphasized an empirical approach to interpretation.

The MMPI[1]

The Minnesota Multiphasic Personality Inventory was developed at the University of Minnesota in the early 1940's by Starke R. Hathaway, a psychologist, and J. C. McKinley, a neuropsychiatrist. Insulin therapy as a treatment method with mental patients was just becoming widespread, and the reports of its results were highly variable from one clinical setting to another. Since the treatment was both expensive and somewhat dangerous, Hathaway and McKinley set about to develop an objective means of assessment so that patients in one setting could be compared with patients in another. As Hathaway states (1964):

> Obviously, if the patients treated at one center were not like those treated at another center, the outcome of treatment might be different. At that time there was no psychological test available that would have helped to remove the diagnostic decisions on the patients in two clinics from the personal biases of the local staffs. There was no way that our hospital staff could select a group of patients for the new treatment who would be surely compatible in diagnosis and severity of illness to those from other settings. It became an obvious possibility that one might devise a personality test, which like intelligence tests, would somewhat stabilize the identification of the illness and provide an estimate of its severity. Toward this problem the MMPI research was initiated (p. 205).

Despite the modestly expressed goals of the developers, the MMPI rapidly gained acceptance in the United States for clinical and research use. As a clinical instrument, it is the most widely used objective personality test in this country (Sundberg, 1961), and it is increasingly used in other countries as acceptable translations become available (Tellegen, 1964). Its use as a research instrument has increased each year. By 1959, there were over 1000 publications relating to the MMPI, and a current bibliography contains almost twice that number of references.

The rationale for computer interpretation of the MMPI was well stated by Hathaway (1967):

> A high rate of research reporting of MMPI experience is continually adding to the available stock of these profile signs in associate clinical items. By

[1]The Minnesota Multiphasic Personality Inventory (MMPI) is published by the Psychological Corporation, New York, copyright 1943, 1965, University of Minnesota.

today, the accumulated data that may be used to interpret a given profile may have become much too voluminous for even an experienced worker to remember. It is fortunate that at this stage, computer technology has been developed to supplement the clinician's experience.

Computers and Psychological Tests

The affinity of psychometricians for computers is not surprising, since this particular group has always been among the most quantitatively oriented psychologists. A rapprochement between clinical psychologists and computers is less predictable, and the existence of such an unlikely realtionship may require some explanation.

The proliferation of psychological testing in education, industry and mental health required the development of methods of scoring which were more rapid and economical than manual scoring. Several devices were designed and used to score tests by responding to the presence or absence of electrographic pencil marks on special answer sheets. Of more recent development is the optical scanner, which "reads" the answer sheet and tabulates the responses in patterns for which it previously has been programmed. It is possible to take advantage of the speed and efficiency of the computer by connecting the "eyes" of the optical scanner to the "brain" of the computer. For several years this principle has been utilized in the scoring of large volumes of tests by several commercial test scoring services.

Obviously, the availability of a practical method of input for psychological test data made it possible to use the computer's data processing ability for tasks more demanding than simple scoring. It introduced the feasibility of using the computer to analyze complex configurations of scores and report the results.

Developments in Computerized Test Interpretation

Because of the rapid developments in the area, it is difficult if not impossible, to give a complete account of the current status of computer interpretation of personality test data. There are probably a number of systems under development which have not yet been reported through professional channels. Although automated systems have been developed for the Rorschach (Piotrowski, 1964) and for the 16 PF (Eber, 1964), most of the work in this area has centered on the MMPI. Some of the existing MMPI programs will be referred to briefly, followed by a more detailed presentation of the system developed by this writer.

The first operational system for the MMPI was developed at the Mayo Clinic (Rome, *et al.,* 1962). With the goal of providing a brief personality outline for the medical staff, the Mayo group developed an operational system which provided an efficient means of screening the large number of medical patients at the Clinic. The Mayo system deals principally with the absolute elevation of single scales, although some configural branches are also included.

Glueck and Reznikoff (1965) developed a modification of the Mayo program for use with a psychiatric population. Marks & Seeman (1963) developed a program which made use of previously collected descriptive data to print out reports on 16 empirically defined code types. His system was also programmed to print out the Mayo report on cases which did not fit the rules for any of his types.

Finney (1966) reports progress in developing a program which will produce a report several pages in length. His system utilizes a number of special scales which he developed and several alternative print-outs are available depending upon the use to which the report will be put. Caldwell (1970) has developed a highly configural, partially automated MMPI interpretation system for clinical use and Gilberstadt (1970) has designed a system with particular application to a Veteran's Administration Hospital population.

The program developed by Fowler (1964, 1965) was designed to be used by psychiatrists and psychologists as a part of a total diagnostic evaluation. The goal was to produce a valid and clinically useful report in an easy to read narrative style. A description of the system follows.

The Interpretation System

The scoring of the MMPI yields 4 validity scale scores and 10 clinical scale scores. In addition, there is a large number of scales designed for special purposes or specific populations.

The validity scales are used to determine whether the test subject responded relevantly and honestly to the questions. The scales are sensitive to efforts on the part of the subject to exaggerate or minimize his problems, and to failure of the subject to give an interpretable test protocol because of insufficient responses, misinterpretation of the questions, confusion, or other factors.

In the interpretation system, the computer, after scoring the test, is instructed to inspect the various patterns of the validity scales. If any of the patterns which identify tests of questionable validity are found, the computer selects from the statement library a paragraph which informs the reader that the validity is doubtful and how this has affected the patient's test results.

The clinical scales, singly and in combinations, are the principal source of interpretive inferences for any method of interpreting the MMPI. Most interpreters use a configural (pattern) approach rather than single scale elevations. The most common pattern used is the two-point code; that is, the highest two scales. Other scale elevations may modify or add to the two-point code interpretation.

The computer is programmed to list the scales in order to identify the two-point code, or in some cases the three-point code, and to locate the appropriate interpretive statement in the statement library. For each possible two-point code there is a number of alternative statements depending upon the elevation of the highest two scales, the presence of other scale elevations, and such factors as sex, age, and marital status.

Since other profile elevations may contribute to the clinical picture, additional statements were prepared for elevated scales not already accounted for in the two-point configuration, and for several of the special scales which appear to contribute useful information to the interpretation system. In addition, the computer is programmed to calculate several actuarial "decision rules" which take a number of scale relationships into account and help in making decisions about the present status of the patient and predictions about future developments.

For each of the statements, there is a set of rules specifying the conditions under which the statement is to be included in the final report. The statement library and the interpretive rules were converted into a functional computer program by translating them into Fortran IV.[2]

The Report

The output from the computer is a three-page print-out. The first page is the narrative report which is a compilation of the paragraphs which the computer has selected according to instructions. The second page is a technical sheet. The top half contains the raw scores and the T scores (standard scores which permit the scores on each scale to be compared with scores on the others) on 4 validity scales, 10 clinical scales and 14 special scales. The bottom half of the page is a print-out of the Critical Items. These are a selection of 38 MMPI items which bear on serious symptoms, impulses or experiences (Grayson, 1951). Only items answered in the deviant direction are printed. The items may be used to alert the clinician to serious psychopathology or to areas which should be discussed in subsequent interviews.

The third page is a profile sheet which contains a print-out of the validity and clinical scales in graphic form.

An example of an automated report follows:

[2]The Fortran IV version of the program was prepared by Guy Marlowe, who was assisted by Joel Gilbert. The scoring routine was prepared by Betty Whitten.

MMPI CASE HISTORY
THE PSYCHOSOMATIC PATIENT

The practicing physician often refers, for psychological and psychiatric evaluation, patients for whose persistent physical symptoms no organic basis can be found and none of the traditional therapies is effective. He may also refer patients who have physical conditions with a known organic basis if he feels that emotional and personal factors are intensifying the symptoms or preventing adequate response to treatment.

These patients may pose a difficult diagnostic problem since (a) the physical symptoms may be both the "result" and the "cause" of emotional difficulties, (b) the physical symptoms may preoccupy the attention of the patient and interfere with his willingness to discuss his personal situation and (c) the consequences of the physical symptoms may mask the evidence of underlying conflict which activates or causes the physical symptoms.

The following case history describes a psychosomatic patient who was referred by a gynecologist to a psychiatric clinic for evaluation. As a part of the evaluation, an MMPI was administered and sent by the clinic for computer interpretation.

Mrs. L, a 41-year-old married woman with a fourteen-year-old son, was referred to a psychiatric outpatient clinic for evaluation. Mrs. L, according to the referring physician, suffers from a " . . . mild rheumatoid arthritis, but she also has innumerable complaints for which no organic cause can be found." He described her as a rigid, opinionated person who generally dominated those around her and was always sure she knew what was best for everyone. He stated that she was bitterly resentful toward her husband because of his "inability to satisfy her sexually" and toward her son because of his failure to do well in school.

Administration of Test

The MMPI was administered to Mrs. L in the waiting room of the clinic. The test was completed within approximately one hour. The computerized MMPI report follows (Figs. 1, 2, 3).

Comments on Computerized MMPI Report

The first paragraph of the report describes Mrs. L's test-taking attitude. Although adjustment for deviant test-taking attitudes is built into a computer-

ROCHE PSYCHIATRIC SERVICE INSTITUTE

MMPI REPORT

CASE NO: 90028 RPSI NO: 0
AGE 41 FEMALE MAR. 29, 1970

THE TEST RESULTS OF THIS PATIENT APPEAR TO BE VALID. SHE SEEMS TO HAVE MADE AN EFFORT TO ANSWER THE ITEMS TRUTHFULLY AND TO FOLLOW THE INSTRUCTIONS ACCURATELY. TO SOME EXTENT THIS MAY BE REGARDED AS A FAVORABLE PROGNOSTIC SIGN SINCE IT INDICATES THAT SHE IS CAPABLE OF FOLLOWING INSTRUCTIONS AND ABLE TO RESPOND RELEVANTLY AND TRUTHFULLY TO PERSONAL INQUIRY.

THIS PATIENT MAY EXHIBIT A VARIETY OF PHYSICAL SYMPTOMS WITH AN ABSENCE OF OVERT ANXIETY AND DEPRESSION. IT APPEARS THAT THE PATIENT IS FOCUSING HER ATTENTION AND CONCERN ON BODILY FUNCTIONS AND SHOWING EXTREME DENIAL OF EMOTIONAL PROBLEMS. FREQUENT SYMPTOMS ARE PAIN, ESPECIALLY IN THE HEAD, CHEST OR STOMACH, PROBLEMS IN EATING SUCH AS LOSS OF APPETITE OR OVER-EATING, AND INSOMNIA. SUCH PATIENTS LACK INSIGHT AND HAVE DIFFICULTY ESTABLISHING MATURE INTERPERSONAL RELATIONS. ALTHOUGH HER PROGNOSIS IN PSYCHOTHERAPY MIGHT BE FAIRLY GOOD, CONSIDERABLE DIFFICULTY IN MOTIVATING THIS PATIENT FOR TREATMENT MAY BE ANTICIPATED.

SHE HAS SOME DIFFICULTY IN DEALING WITH HOSTILE FEELINGS. TO THE EXTENT THAT SHE CONTROLS THE DIRECT EXPRESSION OF THESE FEELINGS. SHE MAY BE A BITTER, RESENTFUL AND PERHAPS SOMEWHAT IRRESPONSIBLE PERSON. WHERE CONTROL FACTORS ARE NOT PRESENT, HOWEVER, THE HOSTILITY MAY BE EXPRESSED IN DIRECT ANTISOCIAL BEHAVIOR. IN ANY EVENT, SHE IS LIKELY TO HAVE PROBLEMS IN ESTABLISHING CLOSE PERSONAL RELATIONSHIPS, AND SHE MAY BE UNDEPENDABLE IN TREATMENT.

SHE IS A RIGID PERSON WHO MAY EXPRESS HER ANXIETY IN FEARS, COMPULSIVE BEHAVIOR AND RUMINATION. SHE MAY BE CHRONICALLY WORRIED AND TENSE, WITH MARKED RESISTANCE TO TREATMENT DESPITE OBVIOUS DISTRESS.

IN THE FACE OF EMOTIONAL STRESS AND PRESSURES, THIS PATIENT MAY TEND TO DEVELOP SOMATIC SYMPTOMS. IF PHYSICAL COMPLAINTS EXIST FOR WHICH NO MEDICAL BASIS CAN CAN BE DETERMINED, ATTENTION SHOULD BE FOCUSSED ON THE RELIEF OF HER EMOTIONAL PROBLEMS.

THIS PATIENT'S CONDITION APPEARS TO FALL WITHIN THE NEUROTIC RANGE. SHE IS USING NEUROTIC DEFENSES IN AN EFFORT TO CONTROL HER ANXIETY.

NOTE: ALTHOUGH NOT A SUBSTITUTE FOR THE CLINICIAN'S PROFESSIONAL JUDGMENT AND SKILL, THE MMPI CAN BE A USEFUL ADJUNCT IN THE EVALUATION AND MANAGEMENT OF EMOTIONAL DISORDERS. THE REPORT IS FOR PROFESSIONAL USE ONLY AND SHOULD NOT BE SHOWN OR RELEASED TO THE PATIENT.

Figure 1. Page 1 of MMPI Computer Interpretation.

ROCHE PSYCHIATRIC SERVICE INSTITUTE

SCALE SCORES FOR MMPI

CASE NO: 90028 RPSI NO: 0
AGE 41 FEMALE MAR. 29, 1970

SCALE	?	L	F	K	HS	D	HY	PD	MF	PA	PT	SC	MA	SI
RAW	5	2	1	15	18	22	34	19	41	10	17	14	18	24
K-C	5	2	1	15	26	22	34	25	41	10	32	29	21	24
T-C	OK	44	46	55	76	55	77	64	41	56	61	60	60	49

SCALE	A	R	ES	LB	CA	DY	DO	RE	PR	ST	CN	AT	SO-R	MT
RAW	9	15	37	10	17	19	17	24	8	21	25	25	31	22
T-C	43	44	45	53	60	44	56	57	43	58	48		42	79

CRITICAL ITEMS

THESE TEST ITEMS, WHICH WERE ANSWERED IN THE DIRECTION INDICATED, MAY REQUIRE FURTHER INVESTIGATION BY THE CLINICIAN. THE CLINICIAN IS CAUTIONED, HOWEVER, AGAINST OVERINTERPRETATION OF ISOLATED RESPONSES.

334 PECULIAR ODORS COME TO ME AT TIMES. (TRUE)

69 I AM STRONGLY ATTRACTED BY MEMBERS OF MY OWN SEX. (TRUE)
133 I HAVE NEVER INDULGED IN ANY UNUSUAL SEX PRACTICES. (FALSE)

114 OFTEN I FEEL AS IF THERE WERE A TIGHT BAND ABOUT MY HEAD. (TRUE)

Figure 2. Page 2 of MMPI Computer Interpretation.

ized report, it is also important to know whether the patient cooperated with the clinician's test instructions or whether, consciously or unconsciously, an attempt was made to exaggerate or minimize. In this case, it appears that the patient attempted to cooperate.

The second paragraph carries the important information that Mrs. L's symptoms are predictable from, and related to, her personality characteristics. This helps corroborate the physician's clinical impression regarding the psychogenic nature of her "innumerable complaints." Indications of low insight and resistance to treatment forewarn the clinician that careful preparation will be required if she is to be introduced into treatment for her personality problems, since these problems are largely outside of her awareness. The estimate of "fair" prognosis suggests that, even if persuaded to enter treatment, she is not likely to make major changes in her personality.

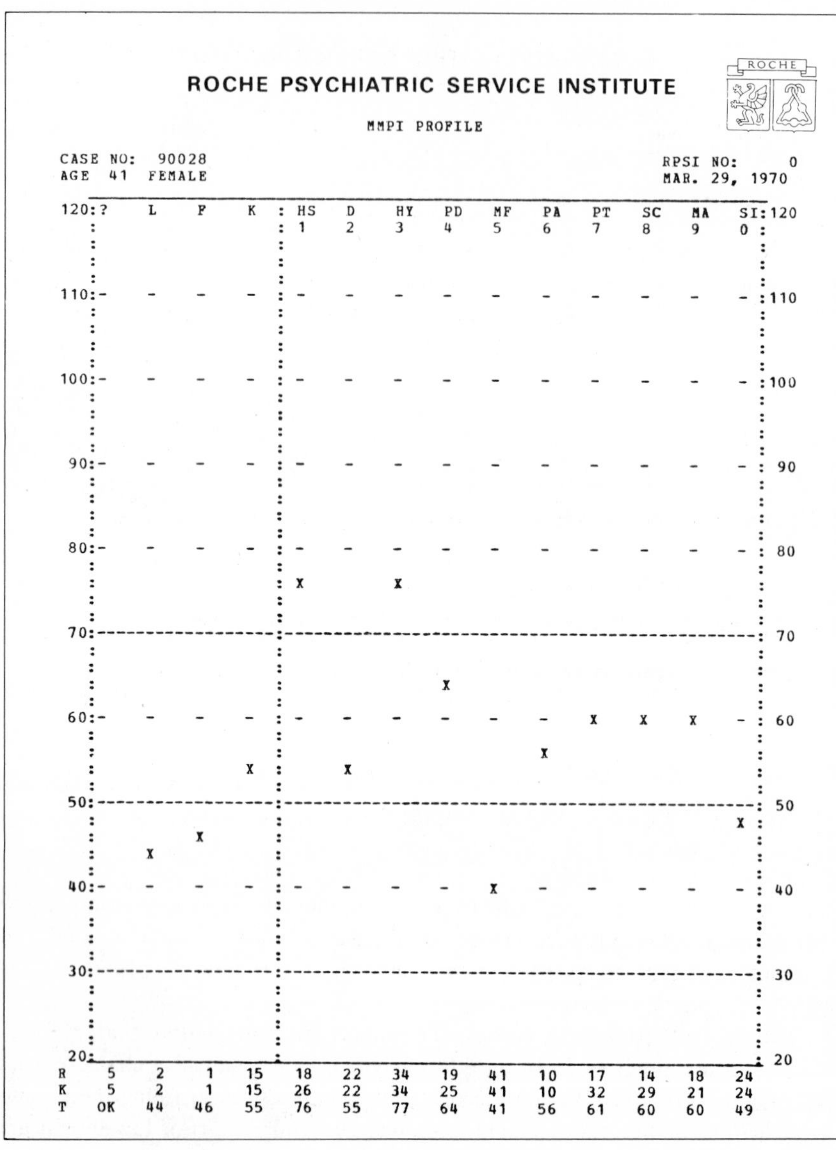

ROCHE PSYCHIATRIC SERVICE INSTITUTE

MMPI PROFILE

CASE NO: 90028 RPSI NO: 0
AGE 41 FEMALE MAR. 29, 1970

	?	L	F	K	HS 1	D 2	HY 3	PD 4	MF 5	PA 6	PT 7	SC 8	MA 9	SI 0
R	5	2	1	15	18	22	34	19	41	10	17	14	18	24
K	5	2	1	15	26	22	34	25	41	10	32	29	21	24
T	OK	44	46	55	76	55	77	64	41	56	61	60	60	49

Figure 3. Page 3 of MMPI Computer Interpretation.

The fifth and sixth paragraph propose a general diagnostic formulation. The patient appears to convert emotional stress into physical symptoms. Her diagnostic category is likely to be neurotic; certainly, she is utilizing neurotic defenses.

Postevaluation of the Psychological Report

A follow-up with the referring physician one year later revealed the following additional information. The physician stated that Mrs. L had made numerous visits over the years regarding her physical complaints. He confirmed the variety of physical complaints, her tension and rigidity, and his impression that her condition was a neurotic one.

Although Mrs. L had been referred to the clinic for psychotherapy, the referring physician stated that while he had not discussed her treatment with her, he could see no evidence in his subsequent medical contacts with Mrs. L that she had made any improvement as a result of her therapy.

A follow-up with the clinic revealed that Mrs. L had never entered treatment at all. Instead, after one visit to the clinic she brought both her husband and her son to the clinic, expressing the opinion that they were the ones with the problems. She did not keep any subsequent appointments. Through an error, the referring physician had not been informed.

In summary, the MMPI administered to Mrs. L in a psychiatric clinic and interpreted by computer supported her physician's impression that her physical symptoms were, at least in part, psychogenic in nature. Although she has thus far avoided treatment for her emotional problems, her physician, working in conjunction with the psychiatric clinic, can help Mrs. L understand her need for psychotherapeutic as well as medical assistance.

Clinical Evaluation Of the Reports

Throughout the development of the interpretation system, the goal was to produce a psychological report which would provide the professional user with valid, clinically useful information in a style and format which he would find readable and understandable. From the beginning, the system evolved in a clinical context. The author, serving as a consultant to five outpatient mental health and alcoholism clinics, initiated the use of the automated system in those clinics in the early stages of its development. During a period of four years, the system underwent continuous modification and sharpening on the basis of clinical use. On each case which was evaluated, background data including case histories, medical reports, and psychiatric summaries were available. Each mechanically generated report was subjected to the scrutiny of the professional clinic staff, and differences in interpretation and emphasis were examined. The assistance and patience of these psychiatrists, psychologists, and social workers played an important part in the steady evolution of the interpretation system.

Approximately 2000 clinic cases were evaluated during the developmental period. In order to prevent excessive specificity of the interpretations, MMPI protocols and background data were also obtained from the following sources; psychiatrists and clinical psychologists in private practice, a military prison, a state prison, state, federal and private psychiatric hospitals, and psychiatric, medical, and surgical services in a university medical center.

In the early stages of clinical application, the reports served only as a modest adjunct to the usual clinical interpretation of the MMPI. As the system was modified and improved, the reports began to be used as an increasingly independent source of input in the total evaluation process.

At the conclusion of the four-year developmental period, the computer-generated reports were being used routinely in a number of settings. Roche Laboratories expressed interest in sponsoring a pilot test to evaluate clinicians' responses to automated reports.

As a first step, the Roche Psychiatric Service Institute (RPSI) was established, and a Professional Advisory Committee[3] was formed to provide continuous counsel with respect to the ethical, scientific, and professional aspects of the services to be provided.

The Pilot Test

A three-part pilot study was designed to evaluate the feasibility of offering a professional scoring and interpretation service on a national basis.

a. The first phase of the study was a series on interviews with psychiatrists and psychologists in various parts of the country to determine their reaction to a computerized scoring and interpretation service. Practicing clinicians were interviewed as well as officers and representatives of the professional associations. In the opinion of the respondents, such a service would be accepted in concept by the professions and would be widely used.

b. On the basis of these interviews, a decision was made to conduct a small-scale pilot test of the service. Before such a test could be conducted it was necessary to establish, in miniature, the same organization that would be re-

[3] Dr. B. C. Glueck, the Chairman of the Professional Advisory Committee is research Director of the Institute of Living and officially represents the American Psychiatric Association on the Advisory Committee. Dr. Grant Dahlstrom, author of the principal resource book on the MMPI entitled *An MMPI Handbook* (1960) is Professor of Psychology and Psychiatry at the University of North Carolina. Dr. R. D. Fowler, who developed the MMPI program and serves as principal consultant in its application, is Professor and Chairman of the Department of Psychology at the University of Alabama. Mr. Marvin L. Miller is the Director of the Roche Psychiatric Service Institute, and serves as coordinator of its services.

quired for a national service. The principal components were: (1) a computer network with input and output terminals, (2) a processing center to receive the completed answer sheets, process them, and return the completed report, and (3) a control system to assure the appropriate professional use of the service.

A decision was made to choose a single suburban county in New Jersey for the initial pilot test. Prior to contacting the prospective participants in the test area, the following controls were adopted to assure appropriate professional use of the service.

(1) The service is limited to psychiatrists and psychologists who meet the standards of their respective professions. The qualifications established Psychiatrists: (a) Member, American Psychiatric Association, (b) Full time psychiatric practice; Psychologists: (a) Member, American Psychological Association, (b) Ph.D. in Psychology (or state license/certification, or Diplomate, ABEPP).

(2) Each answer sheet sent in must be identified by the clinician's identification number and his signature. Reports are sent only to the clinician's office address.

(3) To assure the patient's anonymity, the answer sheets do not contain the patient's name. They are identified by a code number which only the clinician can identify with a specific patient.

A list was prepared of all of the psychiatrists and clinical psychologists in private practice in the county who met the criteria established. A letter, and material describing the service, was sent to each, with an invitation to participate in the service for a small fee. Those who elected to participate received a kit with the necessary testing materials, and an instruction manual for the administration of the test and use of the reports.

The purpose of the small-scale prepilot test was to evaluate the response to the letter and to the educational material, to establish a smooth work flow in the processing center and to test, in actual operation, the computer network.

For practical reasons, it was necessary to locate the processing center at some distance from the computer center. For this reason the network which evolved was more complex than would have been required for an in-house operation. Personnel involved in the operation of the computer and the control and modification of the computer program were located in Alabama. The facilities for receiving and handling the test material were located at Roche Laboratories in Nutley, New Jersey. The following system was developed:

(1) The answer sheet which was mailed by the clinician is received at the RPSI processing center in New Jersey, scanned by a 1232 optical scanner, and read into a 1004 terminal.

(2) The data is transmitted, by Dataphone, to a 1004 terminal at the computer center in Alabama.

(3) The data is read-in from the terminal to a Univac 1107 computer.

(4) The computer scores the test, and selects the appropriate interpretive paragraphs from the statement library according to the programmed decision rules.

(5) The results of the computer's analysis, which takes 2.5 seconds, is transmitted to the terminal in the processing center.

(6) The remote terminal prints the final reports on 8 X 11 paper.

(7) The final report is assembled and mailed to the referring clinician.

The prepilot test operated smoothly, and the response was favorable. The third phase was a large-scale pilot test of the service in various areas of the country (Fowler and Miller, 1969). One large city and its surrounding metropolitan area was chosen from each of the following sections: Pacific Northwest, Middle West, Middle Atlantic, and North Central. The initial mailing went to all of the practicing psychiatrists and clinical psychologists in the four areas who met the criteria for eligibility.

The purpose of the large-scale pilot test was to determine the need, usefulness, and acceptability of the service, and to estimate the extent to which the service would be used on a national basis. The pilot test also provided an opportunity to determine whether the control procedures assured that the service would be consistent with professional and ethical standards.

In the initial contact by mail, material describing the service was sent to 352 psychiatrists and 54 clinical psychologists in the test areas. A letter was sent to each prospective participant, along with descriptive literature and a return envelope. To participate in the service, the recipient sent $2 for a testing kit which included all testing materials necessary for utilizing the service, instructions and a manual, *The MMPI Notebook: A Guide to the Clinical Use of the Automated MMPI* (Fowler, 1966).

In response to the initial mailing, 40% of the psychiatrists and 19% of the psychologists ordered the testing kits. Because of the relatively small number of psychologists in the sample, they were not included in the subsequent survey.

Several months after the service became available in these areas a survey questionnaire was sent to 64 psychiatrists who had received a test kit and who had used the service one or more times. The 50 psychiatrists who returned the questionnaires (78%) comprised the survey sample on which the following analysis was based.

The results of the survey are presented in detail elsewhere (Fowler and Miller, 1969). In general, most of the respondents were satisfied with the testing kit (96%), the manual (94%), the price (100%) and the adequacy of the controls to assure appropriate professional use (98%).

In response to the question "Were the reports easy to understand?", 100% responded yes. Almost all of the users felt that the reports expanded and/or confirmed their impressions of the patient (98%). To the question "How has this service affected your referrals to psychologists?" the responses of 94% were classified as "no effect"; and the remainder stated that it slightly decreased their referrals or decreased referrals for MMPI interpretations only.

In response to an open-ended question "How would you sum up the value of this service to you?" the responses were overwhelmingly favorable (97%). In response to the final question "Should this service be continued?" the users showed an unusual unanimity: 100% answered yes.

On the basis of the favorable responses elicited from the respondents, a national service was initiated in October 1967 through the Roche Psychiatric Service Institute. The initial response of the psychiatrists and psychologists contacted followed the response in the test areas quite closely.

After a year of national availability, 30% of private practicing psychiatrists and several hundred psychiatric institutions were subscribing to the service.

Validation of the Interpretation System

The initial survey following the pilot test was designed to determine the general reaction of the clinicians in the test area to the availability of the service and to the quality of the reports and the instructional materials. After the RPSI service was made nationally available, a series of studies was designed to examine, in more detail, the clinical usefulness and validity of the reports. Although the literature is replete with validation studies of various tests and test scales, there is a lack of studies designed to assess the validity of psychological reports. Since psychologists write several million reports each year, it is somewhat surprising that no methodology has been developed for systematically evaluating their accuracy. Tallent (1963) in an extensive study of the reactions of psychiatrists, psychologists, and social workers to psychological reports, found that the responses were often quite critical and that the reports often were not highly regarded by the users for whom they were prepared. Other studies (Tallent, 1958; Patterson, 1951) have demonstrated that a single report, written to express bland and trivial truisms, will be willingly endorsed by subjects as being highly descriptive of themselves. This phenomenon, known as the "Barnum" or "Aunt Fanny" effect, doubtless occurs to some extent in many psychological reports prepared for professional use.

In the initial validation studies, an attempt was made to determine, on a large number of users, the extent to which the reports agreed with clinical impressions based on interviews. The studies focused on the following variables: (a) the degree to which reports were clear and understandable to the rater and internally consistent. (b) the accuracy with which the reports described symptoms and behaviors of the patient, as seen by the interviewer; (c) the degree to which the reports omitted important information, or included useless trivial or stereotyped or contradictory information; (d) the extent to which the reports provided information useful in working with the patient and (e) how the computerized reports fared when compared with psychological reports prepared in the usual manner.

To examine these aspects of the computerized reports, a 16-item, five-point report rating scale (RRS) was devised. In a series of studies, the RRS was completed by judges with varied professional backgrounds and degree of familiarity with the patients being rated. Studies I, II, and III (Webb, Miller and Fowler, 1970) used 18 raters. Group I consisted of three clinical psychologists at a state hospital, each rating reports on six patients seen professionally for at least two hours. Group II consisted of four psychiatric social workers in a community mental health clinic, each rating approximately 10 outpatients. Group III consisted of four clinical psychologists and four psychiatrists in private practice, each judge rating an average of three reports. The results of these preliminary studies were consistent with the results of studies IV and V and therefore will not be presented here.

In study IV (Webb, Miller and Fowler, 1969) the RRS was completed by 697 users of the RPSI service, with each judge rating only one patient. Patients had been seen by the raters (14% psychologists, 76% psychiatrists, and 10% "other") a median of 4 hours, with a range of 1 to 400 hours. Seventy-eight percent of the raters indicated that they knew their patients "very well," "well," or "moderately," and 22% knew the patients "somewhat" or "scarcely at all."

In study V (Webb, 1970), 158 Veteran's Administration patients were rated at 16 different VA facilities in various parts of the country. The patients rated had been seen professionally a median of 15 hours (range 1 to 250 hours) and 96% of the raters (71% psychologists, 11% M. D., 18% "other") indicated they knew their patients "very well," "well," or "moderately."

Despite the difference in training of the raters and the difference in the number of hours the patients had been seen, the ratings were, in general, remarkably similar. Significant differences between the groups were found on four items, but an inspection of the data suggests that the differences, while significant, are not large in absolute terms except on one item. In the following discussion, the "neutral" ratings have been omitted, since their meaning may be ambiguous, and the comparisons are made on the revised percentages. Because of the similarity of the two studies, the discussion will focus on Group IV (national survey) with the results of Group V introduced only when they are significantly different.

(a) Clarity and Internal Consistency

In the development of the computerized interpretation system, a major aim was "to program the computer to simulate, as nearly as possible, the interpretation and report-writing functions of the psychologist and to produce a report similar in style and content to a report written by a clinician" (Fowler, 1969).

To assess the subjective dimension of "style" Item 1: "The report is well organized and clear" was included. Ninety-five percent of the reports in the national rating scale sample (Group IV) were judged to have met that criterion. Another critical aspect in the acceptance of reports by clinicians is the absence of statements which are contradictory or mutually inconsistent within a single report. In the national sample, 15% of the reports were judged to contain contradictions. In the VA study, a significantly higher percent (35%) were judged to have contradictions ($p < .01$).

(b) Accuracy of Descriptions

In the national sample, 87% of the reports were rated as giving valid overall descriptions of the patients (Item 2), significantly higher than the 77% rating obtained in the VA study ($p<.01$). In 88% of the reports in the national sample, the symptoms that were reported were accurate (Item 8).

The behaviors described (Item 3) were rated accurate in 90% of the reports in the national sample and 84% of the VA sample ($p<.05$), and the mood and feelings of the patients (Item 6) were correctly portrayed in 87% of the reports. Interpersonal relationships (Item 7) were correctly portrayed in 78% of the cases, and the description of psychosomatic complaints in the reports (Item 5) were judged to have been overemphasized in 37% of the cases.

Predictions of response to therapy (Item 14) contained in the reports were considered accurate in 75% of the cases, and severity of the personality disorder (Item 12) was judged to have been overemphasized in 20% of the cases.

(c) Pertinence of Information

In order to examine for the "Barnum" effect in the computerized reports, the raters' attention was drawn to this possibility by Item 13: "Unimportant or trivial information was included." Ninety-one percent of the reports in the national sample were judged not to contain any such information. Further evidence of the lack of stereotypy in the computerized reports can be inferred from the response to Item 11: "I could find little useful in this report." In the national sample, this statement was disagreed with 91% of the time.

Since the judges in both the national sample and the VA sample had had a considerable number of hours of professional contact with their patients, it is not surprising that both groups of raters found that some major symptoms had been omitted in the reports. Major symptoms were judged to have been omitted in 40% of the national sample reports and 52% of the VA reports.

(d) Usefulness in Working with Patients

In view of the considerable contact which the judges had had with their patients prior to receiving the RPSI report, it is interesting that the reports were judged to be helpful (Item 9) in planning treatment (89%).

In addition, the judges felt that the reports would, in some cases, help them make more efficient use of their time with the patient (national sample 81%).

(e) General Evaluation

At the conclusion of the rating scale (Item 15), the rater was asked to compare the reports with "most non-computerized psychological reports" they had seen. The degree of familiarity of the raters in the national sample with standard psychological reports is unknown, but the majority of the judges in the VA study were psychologists who had had considerable experience with non-computerized reports. In the national sample, 38% of the reports were judged to be equal, 27% better and 13% much better (VA 39%, 24%, and 9%).

The studies described above were designed as a part of the overall assessment of the RPSI service and as an initial step in the validation of the content of the reports. Another study, independently conducted by Bachrach (1970), focuses upon the attitudes developed toward the RPSI reports by psychiatrists in training in a university hospital. Over a two-year period, all psychiatric residents (N=25) utilized the RPSI service. A 30-item questionnaire was administered to all of the residents at the end of their six-month tenure on a particular service, and also to five senior staff members using the RPSI service. Bachrach found that "there is substantial agreement that the reports provide new and useful information, are diagnostically accurate, distinguish one patient from another, raise important questions and that they often confirm one's own understanding." The users were satisfied with the system of administration and the cost, and did not feel that the testing interfered with the treatment relationship. They did not feel that the reports provide "all of the information necessary for disposition," or that the reports "go about as far as one can go with psychological testing," but they felt that they could "agree with 90% of what the reports state." The raters were more neutral (that is, they neither agreed nor disagreed) on statements that the reports influenced their treatment of patients, that they made for a better use of clinical time, or that they would, if in private practice, "use MMPI on all patients." Not surprisingly, the reports were seen more helpful and useful to the residents than to their more experienced supervisors. Bachrach concluded that "these results do seem to warrant a recommendation that the present system be experimentally adopted by other clinical centers because of its potential for training, service and research." Bachrach's results seem to be in close agreement with the RPSI studies, and provide some external validation.

A recent study by Anderson, Marks and Smeltzer (1970) gives some additional information in this regard. These investigators compared the utility of narrative reports (RPSI) with MMPI profile analysis. Twenty-four well-known MMPI "experts" were asked to rate patients on 12 personality variables (i.e., ego strength; motivation for psychotherapy). On some patients the judge received the profile; on others, he received the RPSI narrative report. The results showed that the ratings based on the narrative reports correlated significantly better with the criterion (therapist ratings) than did the ratings based on profile interpretation.

The validity studies completed thus far provide some reassurance that the reports are providing information which is satisfactory to the user and that the information contained in the reports agrees with the clinical impressions gained from interviews. However, with the exception of Anderson *et al.*, they represent only an indirect validation of the accuracy of the statements as they pertain to the patient. The ratings of reports could have been inflated by a desire on the part of the rater to please the investigator, a justification by the user for his use of the reports or from a generalized "halo effect," although the variety of the patients, raters, and investigators make it doubtful that any or all of these factors could account for the strongly favorable general evaluation, or for the high degree of consistency among the studies. Nevertheless, it would be most informative to have evidence that the patients' behavior, observed and rated independently of the MMPI report, bears a consistent relationship to the descriptive statements in the MMPI reports.

A series of studies currently underway was designed for this purpose. As a first step, the statement library was analyzed and every word or phrase describing personality traits, symptoms, behavior, or response potentials was extracted. These were condensed into a 105-item Personality Checklist. Although the items were drawn from the statement library, in order to expedite comparisons, it is not a restricted list. It covers a range of symptoms and traits comparable to other checklists which have been used in personality studies.

With the Personality Checklist, it is possible to ask a clinician to complete the checklist at the time he administers the MMPI and the computer can be programmed to compare the clinician's responses to the patient with the statements contained in the report in a variety of ways. At the time of this writing, the first studies have just begun, but the prospect of having a systematic method of assessing the accuracy of narrative reports is encouraging.

It is also anticipated that the checklist will provide a rich source of material for the development of actuarial cookbooks. The results of thousands of such checklists can be related to MMPI three point codes or other configurations to produce an actuarial atlas of descriptive terms. With the large volume of cases regularly processed by RPSI, such a goal becomes a matter of routine procedure rather than a monumental research project.

At the present time, initial studies are underway to determine the applicability of the MMPI computer interpretation system in various European countries. Under the direction of Peter Blaser, at the University of Basel (Switzerland), a small group of psychologists from several European countries began to consider the formidable problems associated with such a project. Psychologists, psychiatrists and others in various countries were contacted to determine the status of the MMPI in terms of how extensively it was used, how it was viewed by the clinicians, and the adequacy of the translation and standardization. The preliminary survey indicated that the MMPI was gaining rapidly in popularity, that it was at least as widely used as any other personality inventory in Europe, and that good translations existed in several languages. Clinicians using the MMPI evidenced considerable enthusiasm for it and there was a clear, although subjective, feeling on the part of most of them that the existing interpretive literature applied quite well to their patients.

The statement library has been translated into German, Dutch, and Italian, and validation studies are in progress in Germany, Switzerland, Italy, Belgium, Holland, England, Scotland, and Australia. Although the technical difficulties in such a project should not be underestimated, the potential utility of a valid clinical instrument with equivalent meaning across languages justifies the effort.

Concluding Remarks

The computer system described is capable of generating rapidly and economically psychological reports which can be useful in the clinical evaluation of patients. Although developed largely on an outpatient clinic population, the system has been used successfully in a wide variety of clinical situations. The "ideal" patient is the voluntary admission who is cooperative and relatively intact. However, clinically useful reports are obtained on patients who differ greatly from this ideal. For instance, the ratio of invalid and uninterpretable tests on military and civil prisoners has been quite low, and there have been very few refusals to cooperate with the testing procedures.

Similarly, although the reports are particularly directed to the initial evaluation phase of the treatment process, they are often used to provide a measure of therapeutic progress or condition on termination as well.

One limitation of the MMPI, and thus of the automated MMPI, is that it requires approximately a sixth-grade level of reading and comprehension. Thus, agencies which deal largely with semi-literate, or culturally deprived patients may not be able to use the system successfully.

The use of mechanically generated reports may, as Meehl (1956) says, "take some of the 'fun' out of psychodiagnostic activity." But, as he continues, "If all of the thousands of hours currently being expended in concocting clever and flowery personality sketches from test data could be devoted instead to scientific investigation, . . . it would probably mean a marked improvement in our net social contribution."

It should be apparent that an automated interpretation system does not in any sense replace the psychologist. The computer provides a means of making one type of psychological service more efficient and readily available, thus freeing valuable professional time for other functions.

6. DIAGNOSTIC TESTING AND THE NEW ALTERNATIVES

A. Z. Arthur

Psychologists have become concerned about the status of the psychodiagnostic or assessment function of clinical psychology (Carson, 1958; Holt, 1967). Breger (1968) has even argued that there is no need for diagnostic testing. However, surveys indicate that diagnostic testing remains the most frequently demanded function in hospitals (Swenson, 1965; Wellner, 1968).

Psychologists and clinicians seldom discuss the nature of diagnosis. It seems to be such an established part of clinical practice that few clinicians stop to consider what is meant by it and whether it is an essential prerequisite to medical practice (Engle & Davis, 1963). The introduction of behavioral techniques into the clinic and other developments in psychology and in the field of scientific decision making have resulted in the appearance of several new models for psychological assessment which challenge the diagnostic model. They are the experimental, the behavioral, the decision-making, and the operations-research models. These are discussed in turn in the present paper.

Diagnostic Model

This model is well known and only a brief summary is here offered. The medical diagnostic model might be characterized as the determination of the illness, disease, or dysfunction which accounts for the symptoms, signs, complaints, or behavior deemed to be an aspect of ill health. One must always add that the aim of this process is treatment. Thus Engle and Davis (1963) defined diagnosis as the art, science, or act of recognizing disease from signs, symptoms, or laboratory data, and also as the decision reached. Thorne (1947) listed nine objectives of diagnosis: (*a*) to demonstrate the etiological factors, (*b*) to differentiate between organic and functional disorders, (*c*) to discover the personality reaction of the organism to its disability, (*d*) to discover the extent of organic damage with resulting functional disability, (*e*) to estimate the extensity or intensity of the morbid process in relation to actuarial data concerning type and severity, (*f*) to determine the prognosis or probable course, (*g*) to

SOURCE. Artur Z. Arthur is presently Associate Professor of Psychology at Queen's University (Ontario, Canada). He was previously clinical psychologist at Maudsley & Bethlehem Royal Hospitals, London, and Lecturer in Psychology at the University of Canterbury in New Zealand. Dr. Arthur is interested in the study of word association and meaning, response sets, and methodology in clinical psychology. This article originally appeared in the *Psychological Bulletin,* 1969, **52,** 372-376. Reprinted by permission of the American Psychological Association and the author.

provide a rational basis for specific psychotherapy, (*h*) to provide a rational basis for discussing the case with the patients and relatives, (*i*) to provide a scientific basis for classification and statistical analysis of data.

Some psychologists (Greening & Bugental, 1962) distinguish psychodiagnosis from diagnosis. Psychodiagnosis is the total study of the individual as opposed to a description of the symptoms of the individual. It includes a description of current functioning of an individual, of his functioning prior to any intervention of accident or disorder, and of what his functioning may reasonably be expected to be if remedial or therapeutic measures are instituted.

Clinical versus Statistical Diagnosis

There are two variants of the diagnostic model: the clinical and the statistical. Those who espouse the clinical method tend to appropriate the term psychodiagnosis for their own use exclusively. According to Breger (1968), sometimes a single test, the Rorschach, or projective techniques alone are identified with diagnosis. For example, on careful reading of the article by Holt (1967), it becomes apparent that he takes it for granted that diagnostic testing is the skillful use of a few techniques such as the Rorschach and the Wechsler. Similarly, Harrower (1965) finds it hard to conceive of anyone in the field of clinical psychology reaching the postdoctoral level without being thoroughly well versed in the Rorschach. She also adds that some form of personal analysis or insight-giving therapy is desirable for a psychodiagnostician. This subtype of the diagnostic model is thus psychodynamically oriented and is intuitive. It aims at describing the "whole personality" of an individual in an ad hoc or a theoretically conceived framework of human behavior.

The statistical diagnostic model is not based on any particular theoretical framework of human behavior but on empirical evidence, usually on evidence of association between predictor (present characteristic of an individual) and criterion (aim of treatment, diagnosis, prognosis).

While the psychodynamic model is identified with the use of the Rorschach and other projective techniques and the statistical with the use of objective tests, Meehl (1954) attempted to distinguish between them not in terms of aims, theories, and data preferred by either but by the differences in the logic of *combination* of data and the *methods of inference.* According to Meehl (1954), in the clinical method the clinician develops a structural-dynamic model of an individual and makes deductions from the model. He has complete freedom from constraint in combining data. In the statistical method, only a classification of the individual according to prior rules is required, since inferences about behavior follow automatically from the individual's membership in a class. Meehl's (1954) distinction between the two models has received wide acceptance (Gough, 1962; Helmstadter, 1964, pp. 30-31; McArthur, 1955) but it contains some defects. The formulation of a structural-dynamic hypothesis about an individual belongs to the context of research and discovery, not to prediction. Any hypothesis or theory has to be validated by means of objective procedures before any degree of confidence may be placed in the predictions derived from it. The process of validation may in fact be statistical (Sarbin, 1944). Hence, statistical data and method are sequentially a result of a "clinical" hypothesis and are not alternatives to it. In addition, Meehl (1954) did not demonstrate how predictions are made by the clinical method; he merely assumed, intuitively, that they are made on the basis of an ad hoc model of behavior. As Gauron and Dickinson (1966) indicated, clinicians seem to use many different methods in diagnosis.

Despite Meehl's (1954) stress on the logic of the combination of data, major differences exist between the practitioners of clinical and statistical models in their formulations of aims and behavior to be predicted, in the use of types of predictor data, and in processing data and making inferences (Holt, 1958; Sarbin, Taft, & Bailey, 1960).

Evaluation of the Diagnostic Model

Holt (1967) listed the following reasons for the apparent neglect of diagnostic testing: decline in the quality of the clinical psychological apprenticeship, due mainly to the tremendous expansion in the numbers of clinical psychologists in training; the rise of statistical prediction; objections to the passivity of the diagnostic role of psychologists (cf. Rosenwald, 1963); objections to the authoritarian nature of apprenticeship; deficiencies of diagnostic success; hostility by laymen toward testing; and the erosion of the medical model in clinical psychology and in psychiatry. Some of these reasons are objections to the clinical diagnostic model, but others are relevant to the diagnostic model as a whole. They can be grouped under four headings: (*a*) evidence on the unreliability of psychiatric diagnosis, (*b*) objections to the concept of mental illness, (*c*) the limitations of diagnosis, and (*d*) development of alternative approaches.

Psychiatric Diagnosis

This is a well-known area summarized by Kreitman (1961), Zigler and Phillips (1961a), Beck (1962), and many others. It should be emphasized, however, that the shortcomings of psychiatric diagnosis do not relate to labeling alone. There are deficiencies in the whole process of diagnosis. The findings can be summarized as follows: Psychiatrists and clinicians tend to arrive at different diagnostic labels when either the diagnosticians or the occasions vary; the agreement between different diagnosticians, using four major categories, is about 63%;

diagnosis is more reliable for organic states than for major psychoses but is least reliable for personality disorders; equally unsatisfactory is the reliability of detecting symptoms or of agreeing on their importance (Kreitman, Sainsbury, Morrisey, Towers, & Scrivener, 1961); the most reliable symptoms are at the same time the least differentiating, for example, insomnia and headaches (Freudenberg & Robertson, 1957); there is evidence of independence of diagnosis from symptoms (Zigler & Phillips, 1961b) and from treatment (Bannister, Salmon, & Leiberman, 1964); a similar degree of disagreement exists for the selection of treatment as for diagnosis (Kreitman *et al.,* 1961). Ward, Beck, Mendelson, Mock, and Erbaugh (1962) suggested that disagreement in diagnosis is engendered by nosological inadequacies, excessively fine distinctions, forced choice (cf. Katz, Cole, & Lowery, 1964), or ambiguous criteria. They found that only 5% of disagreements were attributed to patient inconstancy, 33% to diagnostician variation, and 62% to nosological inadequacies.

Objections to the Concept of Mental Illness

The unsatisfactoriness of the concepts of mental and physical health and illness is discussed by Scott (1958), Smith (1961), Engle (1963), and many others. Retention of the concept of mental illness is defended by Ausubel (1961) and Ellis (1967). The defects of the illness orientation are widely recognized. First, health and illness are ambiguous concepts (Engle, 1963). Second, disease is not an entity (Stainbrook, 1953) mainly because of independence of symptoms from single causes and from specific treatments. Third, independent criteria for mental illness are absent, especially for functional and neurotic illnesses. In this connection, Sarbin (1967, 1968) and Szasz (1961) discussed the tendency in psychology and psychiatry to invent labels for ill-defined and even non-existent phenomena. Fourth, conception of psychological problems in terms of mental illness prevents a variety of other possible approaches. The most influential alternative approach is that many psychological disturbances are aspects of learning (Eysenck, 1960; Krumboltz, 1966). Other conceptualizations of problems of behavior are rule following, game playing, problems in living (Szasz, 1960), sin (Mowrer, 1960), and residual deviance (Scheff, 1966).

Limitations of Diagnosis

In addition to the defects of the current diagnostic system and of the illness approach, it is necessary to consider the diagnostic orientation as a whole. It is generally taken for granted that diagnosis in the sense of an attempt to understand an individual is useful. Yet it is possible that the difficulties discussed so far actually represent a failure of the descriptive and explanatory orientation, since such an orientation is not designed to serve the purposes of determining optimum treatment from the beginning.

First of all, the explanation and understanding of behavioral problems has proved itself to be a difficult task. In view of the wide agreement that current explanations of human behavior and disorders are inadequate, it seems illogical to attempt to explain routinely the behavior of individuals who come to the clinic. This leads to the second criticism, namely, that diagnostic explanations tend to be formulated in terms of a single conceptualization of the nature of a behavior disorder. The kind of information one seeks is determined partly by this conceptualization and only partly by the aims of treatment. Cameron (1953) recognized explicitly that a diagnosis must reflect what one considers possible to do in the light of one's current understanding of causes. The unsatisfactoriness of explanation is clearly brought out in cases where there are a number of alternative explanations (Arthur, 1968). For example, in the consulting room, there are the approaches of Rogers, Freud, Ellis, or Wolpe. A scientist cannot arbitrarily choose the approach he prefers. He must choose the objectively best approach. If this is impossible to determine, there is only one strategy remaining. As Arthur (1968) pointed out, the strategy that is available right from the beginning of the diagnostic process is to concentrate, instead, on the aims of treatment and how to achieve them optimally. The clinician can then use the full range of his scientific knowledge and technology, as well as his capacity for invention, to obtain optimal treatment results without being unduly affected by the defects of the prevailing notions of the causes of the disorders.

Third, descriptive or explanatory diagnosis may often be unnecessary (Arthur, 1966; Breger, 1968; Saslow, 1965). If the problem is one of improvement of average performance there is nothing to diagnose. In any case, both behavior therapists and psychotherapists in practice begin treatment without initial diagnosis. Saslow (1965) argued against the necessity of understanding and explanation on the basis that present function may be independent of much past historical information, disability may be modified without a person attaining insight and without examination of its origin, and much of human behavior may be independent of particular clinical disorganization.

The fourth limitation of diagnosis is that it is not sufficient for decisions about treatment (Arthur, 1968; Bijou, 1966; Krumboltz, 1966). In the process of diagnosis, information is not collected which permits one to decide on the *best* treatment (Krumboltz, 1966; Lindsley, 1964) nor indeed between any alternative treatments. In more practical terms, the role of clinical psychologists as assessment consultants is very limited indeed unless they know exactly what treatments and dispositions for management and discharge are contemplated for each patient. Knowledge of specific decisions permits them to gather the most relevant information.

Finally, the fifth limitation is that, as Medawar (1957) pointed out, diagnosis is merely a hypothesis, not a certainty. Arthur (1966) argued that therefore treatment cannot be derived directly from diagnosis. All other possible diagnoses have to be borne in mind constantly, and treatment must be selected not on the basis of one diagnosis but on the basis of an overall consideration of expected effects of treatments should the patient belong to any one of the probable diagnoses.

Alternative Approaches

Experimental Model

Shapiro (1951) put forward four rules for the description of individual psychiatric patients: standardization–use of standardized methods of observation; validity–use of as far as possible only methods which have already been shown valid for each purpose; calibration–use of precise measures which allow estimation of error; and scientific testing of inferences–any theory or hypothesis made about an individual has to be, if possible, tested using the usual scientific principles of experimental inference (cf. Meehl's 1954, structural-dynamic hypothesis making, and clinical inferences, which are presumably only "clinically" tested). This approach was also discussed by Payne (1957), Jones (1960), and Shapiro (1951, 1967). The experimental method is to be used only when existing standard techniques of prediction and measurement prove inadequate. Instead of turning to human judgment and clinical opinion, Shapiro (1951) advocated the carrying out of a full research investigation. The method involves three phases. In the first phase, the investigator formulates exactly the observation which is to be explained or studied. This is usually some behavior abnormality. Which particular aspect of behavior will be studied depends on its importance for the patient as well as on the practical possibilities of research. In the next phase, one formulates an explanation of the phenomenon. The explanation which is favored is one that accounts for the greatest amount of clinical data and that has the most important implications for treatment. Sometimes an easily testable explanation may be tackled first to get it out of the way. Finally, an explanation must be preferred which is most adequately rooted in the current knowledge of psychology and for which techniques of investigation are available. The third phase involves deduction and testing of hypotheses rigorously derived from the explanation. If they are not confirmed, the explanation has to be rejected and a new explanation formulated. Jones (1960) suggested that such experimental investigations can be carried out at any one of six stages of a psychiatric procedure, for example, collection of data, evaluation of data, carrying out of additional checks, diagnostic and treatment decision making, treatment itself, and assessment of the effects of treatment. In the stage of collection of data, no standard validated tests may be available for some purposes. Bartlett and Shapiro (1956) reported an investigation of a 10-year-old child with severe psychiatric symptoms who also showed a reading difficulty in spite of average intelligence. As no validated tests were available, two experimental investigations were carried out to define the reading difficulty using control subjects. The results showed that the child had initial learning difficulties which applied to visual material but not to auditory material. Other descriptive single-case investigations were reported by Metcalfe (1956) and by Beech and Parboosingh (1962). The early applications of the experimental model to treatment were described by Jones (1956), Meyer (1957), and Yates (1958). Jones (1960) provided examples of the method in other stages of psychiatric and psychological procedure. The experimental model represents the application of the scientific method to the problems encountered in the clinic. Observations are made, a theory is formulated, and hypotheses are deduced and tested using the usual canons of scientific procedure. The model does not accept any particular diagnostic or theoretical framework as correct and useful. Shapiro (1951) and Payne (1957) stressed that this is the truly alternative role for the clinical psychologist who works as a scientist and makes his own unique contributions to the solution of problems in the clinic.

Hamilton (1964) criticized the experimental model on the grounds that it is inefficient–it is time consuming, would demand much manpower to become applicable to everyday cases, and it delays treatment; it is too restrictive–by insisting on the use of validated techniques alone, the clinical psychologist might have to withdraw from the whole area of psychiatric decision making which is presumably based on personal experience, skill, belief, and opinion; it may lead to the investigation of irrelevant behavior, since it permits the most available scientific knowledge and techniques to affect the choice of investigation.

Behavioral Model

The origin of this approach is in the behavioristic psychology of Pavlov, Watson, Dunlap, Hull, and Skinner. Its application to the problems of diagnosis and assessment is recent and mainly associated with behavior-modification techniques. Kanfer and Saslow (1965, 1969) characterized diagnosis as an endeavor to ascertain the explicit environmental and historical variables which control the observed behaviors. The aim of assessment is to decide or to find which specific behavior patterns require change, what are the means for producing the change, and what factors currently maintain the behavior or under what conditions it was acquired.

Diagnostic information is sought only if it can be shown that such data serve to advance some specific aspect of the clinical process (Bijou, 1966; Kanfer & Saslow, 1965, 1969). According to Bijou (1966), classification of persons in terms of current diagnostic procedures, usually in terms of traits, fails to give information which is of direct use for treatment purposes. The full implications of this approach are truly revolutionary, according to Krumboltz (1966). One of the changes implied is that therapeutic intervention may be directed at persons or objects other than the patient or client himself–it may consist of modification of the patient's physical or social environment (Kanfer & Saslow, 1969). Lindsley (1964) recommended the design of what he called prosthetic environments for old people to restore competent performance rather than treatment which concentrates on the individual. Ferster (1965), indeed, advocated that a diagnostic system be established which is based on the analysis of the environment. After the establishment of the practices, contingencies, etc., of the environment, an individual's repertoire of behavior can be classified by comparing it with the behavioral potential of the milieu.

Diagnostic information in the behavioral model includes not only the interview and tests but also observation of patient's work behavior; tape recordings of patient's interactions at home, at work, and other situations; and possibly actual attempts at conditioning on an exploratory basis.

For Krumboltz (1966), the advantages of the learning approach to behavioral problems lie in the principles that there is much evidence and knowledge on the problems of learning, that learning is integrated with the enterprise of modification, that the goals of learning can be defined and reached better than those of other techniques, that learning focuses more on action than on problems, and that patients can be expected to face an increased sense of responsibility for their actions when they become aware that they can learn effective ways of dealing with their problems.

Shoben (1966) criticized the behavioral approach on the grounds that it fails to deal with human aims and values. Behavior-control methods do not reveal the normative ends toward which conduct may be directed. Wrenn (1966) pointed out that a patient may require help in formulating his problem within a pattern of living that is recognizable as his own. By its concentration on explicit manipulable behavior, the behavioral approach neglects to deal with the purely ideational, human, and probably complex and not easily formulated needs or dissatisfactions. Moreover there is evidence that behavior is not only a function of current stimulation but also of growth, modelling, and insight.

Further, it neglects such everyday clinical considerations as the value of treatment to the patient, in addition to its payoff, the relative efficienty of alternative treatments, and the general question of the method of selecting *optimal* treatment. The approach leaves the decision about specific treatments to individual clinicians. Again, it ignores knowledge on behavioral decisions by means of testing and classification. In terms of Cronbach's (1957) distinction between the two disciplines of psychology, it is an experimental approach and it has developed in total disregard of the correlational evidence. Finally, for a fruitful application of the method, one needs clinical personnel who will actually use the information to modify the behavior of patients. In the absence of such personnel or when it is in short supply, the behavioral model cannot be brought to full fruition.

Decision-Making Model

Hamilton (1966) pointed out that the trouble with explanatory and predictive diagnostic models for clinicians is that they do not represent the complexity of decisions that are taken in the clinic. Typically, the clinician is constantly involved in sequential decisions, asking for more information whenever he needs it, and verifying his diagnosis or the choice of treatment in the light of current available information and his expectations at that time. Neither the experimental nor the behavioral model takes account of this *process of making decisions* itself. Moreover, the models discussed so far assume that the particular procedures, aims, information, and treatment that are decided upon or collected are best—that the clinicians will make the best decisions, in fact. The decision-making model attempts to take the guesswork out of the process and to replace it with explicit rules and strategies. It is thus basic to all models discussed so far and can accommodate them as aspects of decision making. In brief, the model does not depend on the understanding or on any particular conceptualization of a disorder—psychiatric, dynamic, or behavioral. It is a direct attempt to find a course of action to achieve an aim. Information that is available at any time is used to find the optimal course of action. Only if a clear decision is impossible or if the expected outcome falls short of the aim is further information, research, or understanding sought. Although this looks like a common sense approach, the crucial point is that the process is made explicit and definite rules are adopted including the use of figures.

One advantage of the model is that decision making is a focus of interest of mathematicians and other methodologists and has developed into a science or technology of decision making (Edwards, Lindman, & Phillips, 1965). Problem solving and diagnostic decision making in general are discussed by Ledley and Lusted (1959), Shelly (1964), and Edwards *et al.* (1965). It is not possible to do full justice to the ideas in this area in the present review. There are five essential elements or steps in every decision (or problem): (*a*) identification of the decision maker and his aim(s); (*b*) determination of all possible courses of action (treatments); (*c*) determination of all possible outcomes of actions, including "no treatment" action; (*d*) estimation of the probabilities of outcomes for each action; and (*e*) determination of the values of all outcomes. Simple arithmetic is then used to determine which action is likely to produce the outcome with the highest value and thus which action is optimal. Arthur (1966) stresses other advantages of the decision-making model: It deals with the probabilistic nature of diagnosis by taking account of all possible states of the patient; it makes decision making explicit and permits science to bring its full resources to bear upon improving it; it takes account of human and other values; and it specifies at the outset what information is required without permitting superfluous categorizations (Cole & Magnussen, 1966).

The decision-making model accommodates the research function of psychology by indicating that research on any one of the five essential elements of a decision should be undertaken whenever the expected value of better informed decision outweighs the costs. Large scale and expensive projects for single problems may be justifiable if the expected payoff warrants them. Current hospital orientations do not provide for this possibility.

The stress on the *value* of psychological endeavor and on *optimization* of outcomes in place of *success* and *accuracy* of prediction puts clinical psychology into the action center of the clinic, which is intended to provide service rather than predictions. The role of the psychologist does not stop at a single assessment of a patient, which is then used for all kinds of decisions. His role must include decisions on all aspects of management, treatment, disposal, and follow-up after discharge. Therefore, to bring the decision-making approach to full fruition, again, the psychologist must participate more intimately in everyday decisions concerning the patient than he does at present.

There are at present few examples of the application of decision making to clinical psychology. Cronbach and Gleser (1957) discussed the impact of decision theory on the utilization of psychological tests in the context of decision making. Darlington and Stauffer (1966) showed how to evaluate the usefulness of discrete test information. Arthur (1966) demonstrated the applicability of the approach to everyday decisions in the clinic. Cole and Magnussen (1966) stressed the action-oriented nature of decision making; in this sense, it is similar to the behavioral approach. Arthur (1967) applied its concepts toward resolving the conflict between behavioral and psychotherapeutic approaches to treatment.

Criticisms of decision theory are reviewed by Churchman (1961). First, optimization of decisions may be an unrealistic requirement in practical settings since to get all the relevant information may be too costly. Simon (1957) suggested that in these circumstances, it is better to adopt the criterion of satisfying—satisfying the decision maker—rather than optimizing. Presumably, in clinical psychology the problems of information gathering would soon be overcome if the decisions were repetitive and it proved possible to classify patients in terms of what aims they want to achieve. Another difficulty is to get the whole organization or institution to move along the path which is recommended by the decision-theory analysis. Third, optimization may be impossible to estimate and to attain since the effect of actions runs off into infinity in time and space. Hitch (1953) suggested the use of the principle of suboptimization rather than optimization. Presumably, for example, the therapist may use the immediate consequences of a treatment for the patient, for his family and friends, and for his work situation as the assessment criterion rather than *all* of the possible consequences.

Objections have been made to decision making on the grounds of lack of information about probabilities of outcomes and about values of outcomes.

They must be countered by the charge that unless they can be at least estimated, defensible decisions are impossible under any model. The decision-making model actually points out that indefensible decisions are being made in the diagnostic and other approaches whenever values are ignored.

Operations-Research Model

The operations-research model is an extension of the decision-making model to optimize the total endeavor of the clinic rather than of single decisions. Several considerations dictate the necessity to take the structure and processes of institutions into account to optimize decisions. First, every decision can always be improved, at least in principle, by further research. But the total treatment resources are scarce and likely to remain scarce with respect to what is possible to do. Hence it is necessary to relate the values and costs of single assessments to the total treatment endeavor. The second consideration is that since behavior is determined by a vast number of variables, and there are accordingly a number of independent disciplines that can help to make decisions, a multidisciplinary team is necessary for decision making. Finally, a clinic or institution must be aware of the ways in which its own structure and process of hospitalization affects the type and quality of information available, decisions taken, and treatment carried out.

Churchman, Ackoff, and Arnoff (1957) define operations research as the application of scientific methods, techniques, and tools to problems involving the operations of a system so as to provide those in control of the system with optimum solutions to the problems. It seems to be in fact the only way in which the total treatment effort of an institution may be improved by the use of scientific procedures.

There are as yet few examples of the application of operations research by psychologists to their activities. One possible example is the analysis by Sarason, Levine, Goldenberg, Cherbin, and Bennett (1966) of the considerations that led a group of psychologists to adopt a teacher-consultation role in preference to a child-assessment or treatment role. In spite of the development of the science of organizations and of the study of organizational behavior, psychologists have not contributed anything significant to the organization of the clinics. Zagorski (1955) also pointed out the conspicuous absence of psychologically oriented disciplines in the field of operations research itself. If mental hospitals and clinics wish to evaluate the efficiency with which they carry out their functions, the new sciences of organizational behavior (Cooper, Leavitt, & Shelly, 1964), systems engineering (e.g., Gagne, 1962), and operations research have much to offer. For optimal functioning, large organizations need more than a single appraisal and the solution is to have a continuous reappraisal by a team of experts in institutional values, procedures, and efficiency.

Conclusion

New and exciting prospects are opening up in the area of assessment which tend to replace the old test-oriented and test-centered function of clinical psychology. Diagnostic testing will continue to be essential, but the new conceptualizations pose a stronge challenge to the popular techniques which lack evidence of utility. For the behavioral, decision-making, and operations-research models are all based on explicitness, utility, and clearly demonstrable value in the treatment endeavor and not in the abstract area of description and understanding, where the assessment criterion is accuracy or correctness. Diagnostic testing, unintegrated with action and treatment, seems to be under strong attack on all sides. This represents new responsibilities, and new opportunities for clinical psychologists to participate in decisions of management, treatment, and disposal to an extent never before possible.

7. MODERATING EFFECTS AND DIFFERENTIAL RELIABILITY AND VALIDITY

Edwin E. Ghiselli

For more than half a century the notions of Yule and Spearman have dominated theoretical formulations in psychometrics. Pursuant to these classical notions errors are taken to be random and scores are combined additively. The possibility of interactive effects among variables is not recognized. Because in the linear combination of variables their weights are the same for all individuals, it is presumed that the psychological structure of all individuals is precisely the same.

On any one administration of a test, error scores are taken to vary from individual to individual. Hence for some individuals the error of measurement is smaller and for others it is larger. However, over many parallel tests the standard deviation of the errors is taken to be the same for all individuals. More correctly it should be said that as the number of parallel tests increases without limit the

SOURCE. Edwin E. Ghiselli is Professor of Psychology at the University of California, Berkeley. He has had considerable experience as a consultant in personnel selection and evaluation for business and industry. A frequent contributor to the professional literature on industrial psychology and psychological measurement, he is now concerned with the use of moderator variables in personality assessment. This article originally appeared in the *Journal of Applied Psychology,* 1963, **47**, 81-86 and is reprinted by permission of the American Psychological Association and the author.

standard error of measurement approaches the same value for all individuals. Hence it is concluded that for a given test all individuals are measured with the same degree of reliability.

Similarly, for any one administration of a given criterion and a test the error with which the test predicts the criterion is taken to vary from individual to individual. Hence for some individuals the error of prediction is smaller and for others it is larger. However, over many parallel criteria and tests the standard deviation of the errors is taken to be the same for all individuals. Again, more correctly it should be said that as the number of parallel criteria and tests increases without limit the standard error of prediction approaches the same value for all individuals. Hence it is concluded that for a given criterion and test all individuals are measured with the same degree of validity.

Because it is held that errors are random and equal for all individuals, and scores are additive with no interactive effects, it follows that neither reliability nor validity can be improved by selecting out from the total group those individuals for whom error is smaller. Reliability can be improved only by increasing the number of measurements, elimination of elements of lesser reliability, or better "house-keeping" procedures designed to reduce random error. Validity can be improved only by increasing the reliability of the criterion and predictor, or adding other predictors which cover aspects of the criterion not measured by the original predictor or aspects of the original predictor which are independent of the criterion.

Classic psychometric theory deals with a large number of sets of measurements, but let us concern ourselves only with two as we ordinarily do in the practical situation. Consider the bivariate distribution of scores on two variables where the relationship is less than unity. The two variables can be either two parallel tests or a criterion and a predictor. Running from the upper right hand to the lower left hand of the bivariate distribution chart is a group of individuals for whom scores are highly related. For this group the differences, regardless of sign, between standard scores on the two variables and the error of measurement or of prediction are small. For the remainder of the individuals the differences between the two standard scores are greater and hence the error is greater. If it could be demonstrated that these differences, or some other measure of error such as the standard error or the correlation coefficient, were related to another variable then some modification of classic psychometric theory would appear to be in order. Ghiselli (1960b) has called this other variable a predictability variable, but Saunders (1956) has better termed it a moderator thus drawing attention to the interactive effects.

Fisk and Rice (1955) have summarized early evidence indicating that individual error of measurement may be predicted by a moderator. More recent demonstrations are provided by Fisk (1957a) and Berdie (1961). Stagner (1933), Abelson (1952), Hoyt and Norman (1954), Holtzman, Brown, and Farquhar

(1954), Fredericksen and Melville (1954), Saunders (1956), Ghiselli (1956), Fredericksen and Gilbert (1960), and Ghiselli (1960b), among others, have shown that the error of prediction itself may be predicted by a moderator.

Using the procedure he employed to study moderating effects on validity (Ghiselli, 1960b), the present author further examined moderating effects in reliability of measurement. Two parallel forms of a complex reactions test were administered to 775 semi-skilled workers, 517 of whom were used as an experimental group and 258 as a cross-validation group. Each person took both forms of the test on the same occasion. For each member of the experimental group the difference, regardless of sign, between standard scores on the two forms was determined. It was found that age, education, and scores on a tapping and dotting test were related to these differences. A combination of scores on these variables was taken to form a moderator. The reliability coefficient, the correlation between the two parallel forms, was .92 for the entire group, whereas for the 9% of subjects earning the lowest moderator scores it was only .82 and for the 15% earning the highest moderator scores it was .97.

Three other instances of moderating effects in validity also may be described. A 64-item forced-choice inventory was administered to 96 factory workers on whom criterion scores in the form of supervisors' ratings were available. Seventeen of the items were used in a scale designed to measure "Sociometric Popularity." Half of the workers were used as an experimental group and half as a cross-validation group. For the experimental group the differences, regardless of sign, were determined for each individual between standard criterion and standard test scores. For the 47 items not used in the predictor scale an item analysis was performed against these differences. Response to 15 of these items were found to be significantly related to the differences and were formed into a moderator to be applied to the cross-validation group. For the entire cross-validation group the validity of the scale as given by the Pearsonian coefficient was −.01, whereas for the 19% earning the lowest moderator scores the validity was −.47 and for the 32% earning the highest scores it was .39.

A group of 144 foremen and a group of 154 executives were rated by their superiors who divided them into two groups, the more and the less successful. Forty percent of the foremen and 42% of the executives were placed in the upper category. All men took the 64-item forced-choice inventory, 24 items of which were scored in a supervisory ability scale. Critical test scores had been set for the two groups such that the scores of 43% of the foremen fell above their critical score and 39% of the executives fell above theirs. In both groups half of the men were placed in an experimental group and the other half in a cross-validation group. Each of the two experimental groups were further subdivided into two groups, one consisting of those individuals who were either high or low on both variables, the "on quadrant" cases, and those who were high on one variable and low on the other, the "off quadrant" cases. An item analysis was performed using the 40 nonscored items. For the foremen, 9 items, and for the executives, 13 items, were found to differentiate significantly between the on quadrant and off quadrant cases, and they were formed into two moderators to be applied to the cross-validation groups. Only three items were common to both moderators. For the entire cross-validation group of foremen the phi coefficient between the criterion and predictor was .26, whereas for the 17% earning the lowest moderator scores the coefficient was .10 and for the highest it was .41. For the entire group of executives the phi coefficient between the criterion and predictor was .41, whereas for the 21% earning the lowest moderator scores the coefficient was .10 and for the 26% earning the highest scores it was .68.

There is, then, a substantial body of evidence indicating that it is possible to predict individual error of measurement and error of prediction. Clearly those individuals for whom a test has a greater degree of reliability or validity can be systematically differentiated from those for whom it has a lesser degree. The higher the cutting score on the moderator is set the higher is the reliability or validity of the test for those individuals who fall above it. The choice of a cutting score is a matter of how many individuals one is willing to eliminate in order to achieve a higher degree of reliability or validity.

Even recognizing that it is possible to differentiate within a group those individuals whose scores are more reliable from those whose scores are less reliable, the practical value of such a differentiation might well be questioned. However, purely for descriptive purposes it might be desirable to know how reliably an individual is measured. Thus if administrative decisions are to be made on the basis of some test or other measuring device, it would be very helpful in borderline cases to have some indication of whether a given individual is measured with a small or large error. Furthermore, with a lower error of measurement validity should be enhanced. Classic psychometric theory itself teaches this, and Berdie (1961) has given an empirical demonstration. Finally, in some situations it might be highly desirable to be able to predict the extent of intraindividual variability in performance. In personnel selection ordinarily the aim is to pick out those individuals whose performance is high. But for planning purposes or to insure the smooth flow of work it might be equally important to select individuals whose rate of work does not vary greatly from one period to another, that is, has a high degree of self-consistency or reliability.

The case for validity is much clearer since a reduction in error means more accurate prediction and hence the selection of higher performing individuals. But even here the use of moderators might be criticized on the grounds that it necessitates the elimination of a substantial proportion of cases from the appraisal procedures which in turn eliminates even more. However, this is not necessarily the case. Ghiselli (1956) has shown that if a given percentage of individuals is to be selected and the rest eliminated, selecting that given percentage on the combined basis of their moderator and test scores yields a substantially superior group of individuals than that selected on the basis of test scores alone.

Furthermore, in some instances, especially those where the validity for the total group is low or zero, for those individuals who earn low scores on the moderator and who might therefore be eliminated from the appraisal, the validity coefficient may be of respectable magnitude and negative. For example, with the factory workers mentioned earlier the validity of the predictor for the 32% earning the highest moderator scores was .39. But in addition, for the 19% who earned the lowest moderator scores the validity coefficient was −.47. So for these latter individuals high predictor scores were associated with low criterion scores. Consequently for half of the total group, the 32% earning high moderator scores and 19% earning low moderator scores, the validity of the predictor is of the order of .40. It may seem peculiar, but a given score on a test may indicate the promise of success for some individuals, whereas for others it may indicate the likelihood of failure.

Another way to use a moderator, and a way which permits an assessment of all individuals, is to determine which of two predictors to use in selection. Ghiselli (1960a) accomplished this by determining for each individual the difference between his standard criterion score on Predictor 1, and also the difference between his standard criterion score and his standard score on Predictor 2. These differences were taken regardless of sign. Thus for each individual the difference between the two differences was determined. For a given individual a positive difference indicates that the one test gives the better prediction and a negative difference that the other is better. Moderators were then developed which were related to these differences and could be applied to cross-validation groups. For some individuals the moderator selects Predictor 1 and for the others it selects Predictor 2, but the standard scores for all individuals are thrown together regardless of predictor.

Ghiselli presents three instances where this proved to be an effective procedure. In one the validity coefficients for two predictors for a particular criterion were .02 and .20, and using predictors selected by the moderator the coefficient was .33. In another instance the validity coefficients of the two predictors were .55 and .61, with predictors selected by the moderator having a validity of .73. Finally, in an instance where the two validity coefficients were .17 and .51, using a moderator to select the better predictor for each individual gave a coefficient of .73.

Obviously the nature of the traits which function as moderators is a matter of considerable importance. Clearly it would be most helpful if all moderators had characteristics in common. Some of the research does suggest that "undesirable" traits such as a lack of personality integration and low motivation are associated with larger error. But certainly many of the traits which have been found to be effective as moderators are of quite a different sort such as age, education, type of interest, and manual dexterity. In a number of Ghiselli's studies moderators were developed through item analyses of the same inventory so that similarity of items which form different moderators can be examined. His results indicate that there is a high degree of specificity. With two different tests predicting the same criterion for a given group, and with the same test predicting different though similar criteria for two different groups, the items which form the moderators are quite different. While moderator variables are by no means as elusive as suppressor variables, since so many investigators have been able to find or develop them, they do seem to be just as specific. It would therefore appear to be impossible to state any general principles about the nature of the traits which act as moderators. Of course when the bivariate distribution of criterion and test scores is heteroscedastic then test scores themselves serve as a moderator because they are related to error of prediction (Kahneman & Ghiselli, 1962).

Some of the findings indicate that the relationships between moderator scores and scores both on criteria and predictors are quite low. Therefore, they do not add to prediction in a multiple correlation sense. The contribution of moderators is of an entirely different order, differentiating those individuals for whom error is smaller from those for whom it is larger. Their contribution, then, is unique.

As has been seen, there is a substantial body of empirical evidence indicating that moderator effects do occur. Convincing though these findings may be, one would be much more persuaded of moderating effects if some theoretical foundation of them were provided. It could be, as Saunders (1956) and Berdie (1961) have suggested, that moderators operate by sorting a heterogeneous aggregation of individuals into homogeneous groups. The magnitude and pattern of intercorrelations among variables, and hence reliability and validity, vary from group to group. Heterogeneity would be indicated by systematic variation of error from individual to individual whereas homogeneity would be indicated by all individuals having the same error. This notion permits retention of the classic psychometric concepts of randomness of errors and the linear combination of variables. What it adds is the admission that the magnitude of error and the differential weights carried by the components in a composite, the psychological structure, may vary from group to group. However, within a group the error of measurement and of prediction, and the relative weights carried by a set of tests in predicting a criterion are the same for all individuals.

Thus, women might be less distracted than men by environmental changes during a testing session and hence be more reliably measured. In this case, sex would moderate error of measurement. Intelligence might be more related to grades in engineering school for those students who have substantial interest in engineering than for those whose interest is low. Engineering interest, then, moderates error of prediction. For younger factory workers finger dexterity might be more important than spatial ability in predicting rate of production on the job, and the reverse might be true for older workers. So age would function to moderate the relative weights finger dexterity and spatial ability have in predicting rate of production.

This notion that moderators sort heterogeneous aggregations of individuals into homogeneous groups is a very useful way of conceptualizing moderator effects. It focuses attention on the kinds of differences which exist among individuals who in some given respect are homogeneous thereby suggesting types of moderators. Furthermore, it does little violence to classic psychometric theory. However, it presumes individuals can be divided into clear and distinct classes. Yet in actual practice moderators distribute individuals along a continuum. Individuals are not sorted into separate classe. and a "group" is merely those individuals who fall at the same point on the continuum.

Another possible explanation of moderator effects is that the common elements which account for the correlation between two variables differ from individual to individual rather than just from group to group. What in the first point of view were considered as classes are now thought of as class intervals. Interactions among variables of the sort proposed by Lee (1961) are involved.

Error of measurement would be taken as varying from being quite small for some individuals to being quite large for others. Consequently error scores would carry less weight in determining fallible scores for some individuals than for others. Obviously a necessary condition is that individual differences in error scores possess some consistency or reliability over parallel tests. Evidence supporting this is provided by Fisk and Rice (1955), Fisk (1957b), and Berdie (1961). Such a position would not require that all variation commonly termed error of measurement is predictable by the moderator, but only a portion of it. The remainder would still be thought of as being random error. The reliability coefficient, then, would be an average description of precision of measurement.

The importance of a given trait in determining performance on some criterion is taken to differ among individuals. The trait varies from being of prime importance in determining criterion performance for some individuals to being of little or no importance for others. At the one extreme, then, error of prediction is smaller and test validity higher and at the other error is larger and test validity lower. Consequently the weight a test carries in prediction varies from individual to individual. Ghiselli's (1961) demonstration that two tests can be differentiated in terms of the accuracy with which they predict a criterion for a given individual is evidence of this effect. In effect Ghiselli weighted one test 1 and the other 0 for some individuals and the reverse for the remaining. Applying the optimally predicted pattern of weights for each individual accounted for a greater proportion of criterion variance. Pursuant to this position validity coefficients are average descriptions of predictive accuracy and multiple regression weights indicators of the average relative importance of the different predictors.

With respect to validity, the function of the moderator is to predict for a given individual the weight a test carries in determining criterion performance. It is not necessary that the moderator account for all criterion variance unpredicted by the tests, since some of this variance can be due to unreliability and the rest to unmeasured but important traits. The individuals' weights might be unrelated both to their criterion and test scores, or related to one or both. But nothing in this concept indicates what such correlations should be. Perhaps the correlations between the weights and the criterion and test differ from situation to situation.

Moderators are most attractive since they promise significant improvements in reliability and especially in predictive validity. However, that other subtle variable, the suppressor, also promises much in adding to prediction but in practice seldom makes much of a contribution nor holds up well from sample to sample. Hence some counsel of caution might be in order. It is quite possible that the time and effort required to develop moderators might be more fruitfully spent in seeking improvements in reliability and validity of the sort that follow from classic psychometric theory (Ghiselli, 1960). Furthermore, since the indications are that moderators are rather specific it might be that they, like suppressors, do not hold up well from sample to sample.

References

Abelson, R. P. Sex differences in predictability of college grades. *Educational and Psychological Measurement,* 1952, **12**, 638-644.

Abrams, E. N. A comparative factor analysis study of normal and neurotic veterans: A statistical investigation of the interrelationships of intellectual and emotional factors as disclosed in the Primary Mental Abilities Examination and the Minnesota Multiphasic Personality Inventory. Unpublished doctoral dissertation, New York University, 1950.

Abramson, L. S. The influence of a set for area on the Rorschach test results. *Journal of Consulting Psychology,* 1951, **15**, 337-342.

Adams, H. E. Statistical rigidity in schizophrenic and normal groups measured with auditory and visual stimuli. *Psychological Reports,* 1960, **7**, 119-122.

Adler, A. Individual psychology. In C. Murchison (Ed.), *Psychologies of 1930.* Worcester, Mass.: Clark University Press, 1930.

Albee, G. W., & Hamlin, R. M. Judgment of adjustment from drawings: The applicability of rating scale methods. *Journal of Clinical Psychology,* 1950, **6**, 363-365.

Albee, G. W., Lane, E. A., & Reuter, J. Childhood intelligence of future schizophrenics and neighborhood peers. *Journal of Psychology,* 1964, **58**, 141-144.

Alex, C. *How to beat personality tests.* New York: Arc, 1965.

Allport, F. H. Teleonomic description in the study of personality. *Character & Personality,* 1937, **6**, 202-214.

Allport, G. W. *Personality: A psychological interpretation.* New York: Holt, 1937.

Allport, G. W. *The use of personal documents in psychological science.* New York: Social Science Research Council, 1942.

Allport, G. W. What units shall we employ? In G. Lindzey (Ed.), *The assessment of motives.* New York: Rinehart, 1958.

Allport, G. W. The trend in motivational theory. In G. W. Allport (Ed.), *Personality and social encounter.* Boston: Beacon, 1960.

Allport, G. W. Comment. In R. May (Ed.), *Existential psychology.* New York: Random House, 1961. (a)

Allport, G. W. *Pattern and growth in personality.* New York: Holt, Rinehart & Winston, 1961. (b)

Allport, G. W. The general and the unique in psychological science. *Journal of Personality,* 1962, **30**, 405-422. (a)

Allport, G. W. Das Allgemeine und das Eigenartige in der psychologischen Praxis. *Psychologische Beitrage,* 1962, 630-650. (b)

Allport, G. W., & Postman, L. P. *The psychology of rumor.* New York: Holt, 1947.

Allport, G. W., & Vernon, P. E. *The study of values.* New York: Houghton Mifflin, 1931.

Allport, G. W., Vernon, P. E., & Lindzey, G. *A study of values.* (3rd ed.) Boston: Houghton Mifflin, 1960.

American Board of Professional Standards in Vocational Counseling, Inc. *Directory of Vocational Counseling Services,* 1959-60. Washington, D. C.: APGA, 1958.

American Council on Education: The Cooperative Test Service. *A booklet on norms.* New York: 1938.

American Psychiatric Association. Committee on Nomenclature and Statistics. *Diagnostic and statistical manual.* Washington, D. C.: American Psychiatric Association Mental Hospital Services, 1952.

American Psychological Association Committee on Psychological Tests. *Technical recommendations for psychological tests and diagnostic techniques.* Washington, D. C.: APA, 1954. (Reprinted from: *Psychological Bulletin Supplement,* 1954, **51**, 619-629.)

American Psychological Association. Ethical standards of psychologists. *American Psychologist,* 1959, **14**, 279-282. (a)

American Psychological Association. *1959 Directory.* Washington, D. C.: APA, 1959. (b)

American Psychological Association. Ethical standards of psychologists. *American Psychologist,* 1963, **18**, 56-60.

Amrine, M. The 1965 Congressional inquiry into testing: A commentary. *American Psychologist, 1965,* **20**, 859-870.

Anastasi, A. *Psychological testing.* New York: Macmillan, 1954.

Anderson, B., Marks, P., and Smeltzer, D. The utility of the MMPI in a private psychiatric hospital setting. Unpublished manuscript, 1970.

Anderson, S. B. Estimating grade reliability. *Journal of Applied Psychology,* 1953, **37**, 461-464.

Apfeldorf, M., Randolph, J. J., & Whitman, G. Figure drawing correlates of furlough utilization in an aged institutionalized population. *Journal of Projective Techniques,* 1966, **30**, 467-470.

Arbit, J., Lakin, M., & Mathis, A. G. Clinical psychologists' diagnostic utilization of human figure drawings. *Journal of Clinical Psychology,* 1959, **15,** 325-327.

Armon, V. Some personality variables in overt female homosexuality. *Journal of Projective Techniques,* 1960, **24,** 292-309.

Armstrong, R. G., & Hauck, P. A. Sexual identification and the first figure drawn. *Journal of Consulting Psychology,* 1961, **25,** 51-54.

Arnold, F. C., & Walter, V. A. The relationship between a self- and other-reference sentence completion test. *Journal of Counseling Psychology,* 1957, **4,** 65-70.

Arthur, A. Z. A decision-making approach to psychological assessment in the clinic. *Journal of Consulting Psychology,* 1966, **30,** 435-438.

Arthur, A. Z. Behaviour therapy versus psychotherapy and applied science. *Canadian Psychologist,* 1967, **8,** 105-113.

Arthur, A. Z. Is diagnosis really necessary? *Ontario Psychological Association Quarterly,* 1968, **21,** 12-16.

Asch, S. E. Forming impressions of personality. *Journal of Abnormal and Social Psychology,* 1946, **41,** 258-290.

Ash, P. Reliability of psychiatric diagnosis. *Journal of Abnormal and Social Psychology,* 1949, **44,** 272-277.

Atkinson, J. W. (Ed.) *Motives in fantasy, action, and society.* Princeton, N.J.: Van Nostrand, 1958. (a)

Atkinson, J. W. Towards experimental analysis of human motivation in terms of motives, expectancies, and incentives. In J. W. Atkinson (Ed.), *Motives in fantasy, action, and society.* New York: Van Nostrand, 1958. (b)

Auerback, A. (Ed.) *Schizophrenia: An integrated approach.* New York: Ronald Press, 1959.

Auld, F., Jr., & Eron, L. The use of Rorschach scores to predict whether patients will continue psychotherapy. *Journal of Consulting Psychology,* 1953, **17,** 104-109.

Ausubel, D. P. Personality disorder is disease. *American Psychologist,* 1961, **16,** 69-74.

Bach, G. Quoted in S. Alexander, Fight promoter for battle of sexes. *Life,* 1963, **54,** 102-108.

Bachrach, H. Psychiatrists' attitudes toward the Roche MMPI system. Unpublished manuscript, 1970.

Baldwin, A. L. Personal structure analysis: A statistical method for investigation of the single personality. *Journal of Abnormal and Social Psychology,* 1942, **37,** 163-183.

Baldwin, I. T. The head-body ratio in human figure drawings of schizophrenic and normal adults. *Journal of Projective Techniques,* 1964, **28,** 393-396.

Bales, R. F. *Interaction process analysis.* Cambridge: Addison-Wesley, 1950.

Bandura, A. Psychotherapy as learning process. *Psychological Bulletin,* 1961, **58,** 143-159.

Bandura, A. Influence of models' reinforcement contingencies on the acquisition of imitative responses. *Journal of Personality and Social Psychology,* 1965, **1,** 589-595. (a)

Bandura, A. Psychotherapeutic applications of modeling procedures. Paper read at *American Association for the Advancement of Science,* Berkeley, 1965. (b)

Bandura, A. Vicarious processes: A case of no-trial learning. In L. Berkowitz (Ed.), *Advances in experimental social psychology,* Vol. 2. New York: Academic Press, 1965. (c)

Bandura, A., & Walters, R. H. *Social learning and personality development.* New York: Holt, Rinehart & Winston, 1963.

Bannister, D., Salmon, P., & Leiberman, D. M. Diagnosis-treatment relationships in psychiatry: A statistical analysis. *British Journal of Psychiatry,* 1964, **110,** 726-732.

Barker, R. G., & Wright, H. F. *Midwest and its children.* Evanston, Ill.: Row, Peterson, 1954.

Barnes, E. H. The relationship of biased test responses to psychopathology. *Journal of Abnormal and Social Psychology,* 1955, **51,** 286-290.

Barnes, E. H. Factors, response bias, and the MMPI. *Journal of Consulting Psychology,* 1956, **20,** 419-421.

Barron, F. Some test correlates of response to psychotherapy. *Journal of Consulting Psychology,* 1953, **17,** 235-241. (a)

Barron, F. Ego strength scale which predicts response to psychotherapy. *Journal of Consulting Psychology,* 1953, **17,** 327-333. (b)

Barron, F. Personal soundness in university graduate students. Unpublished manuscript, University of California, Berkeley, 1954.

Barry, J. R. The relation of verbal reactions to adjustment levels. *Journal of Abnormal and Social Psychology,* 1950, **46,** 647-658.

Barthel, C. E., & Crowne, D. P. The need for approval, task categorization, and perceptual defense. *Journal of Consulting Psychology,* 1962, **26,** 547-555.

Barthell, C. N., & Holmes, D. S. High school yearbooks: A nonreactive measure of social isolation in graduates who later become schizophrenic. *Journal of Abnormal Psychology,* 1968, **73,** 313-316.

Bartlett, D., & Shapiro, M. B. Investigation and treatment of a reading disability in a dull child with severe psychiatric disturbances. *British Journal of Educational Psychology,* 1956, **26,** 180-190.

Bartlett, F. C. *Remembering.* New York: Cambridge University Press, 1932.

Bartlett, M. S. The use of transformations. *Biometrics,* 1947, **3,** 39-52.

Bass, B. M. Development and evaluation of a scale for measuring social acquiescence. *Journal of Abnormal and Social Psychology,* 1956, **53,** 296-299.

Bastian, J. Associative factors in verbal transfer. *Journal of Experimental Psychology,* 1961, **62,** 70-79.

Bechtoldt, H. P. Construct validity: A critique. *American Psychologist, 1959,* **14**, 619-629.

Beck, A. T. Reliability of psychiatric diagnoses: I. A critique of systematic studies. *American Journal of Psychiatry,* 1962, **119**, 210-216.

Beck, S. *Rorschach's test.* Vol. I. *Basic processes.* (3rd ed.) New York: Grune & Stratton, 1961.

Beech, H. R., & Parboosingh, P. C. An experimental investigation of disordered motor expression in a catatonic schizophrenic patient. *British Journal of Social and Clinical Psychology,* 1962, **1**, 222-227.

Bellak, L. On the problems of the concept of projection. In L. E. Abt & L. Bellak (Eds.), *Projective psychology.* New York: Knopf, 1950.

Bellak, L., & Parcell, B. The pre-psychotic personality in dementia praecox. *Psychiatric Quarterly,* 1946, **20**, 627-637.

Bellak, L., & Smith, M. B. An experimental exploration of the psychoanalytic process: Exemplification of a method. *Psychoanalytic Quarterly,* 1956, **25**, 385-414.

Bendig, A. W. The reliability of letter grades. *Educational and Psychological Measurement,* 1953, **13**, 311-321.

Benjamin, J. D., & Ebaugh, F. G. The diagnostic validity of the Rorschach test. *American Journal of Psychiatry,* 1938, **94**, 1163-1178.

Bennett, V. Does size of figure drawing reflect self concept? *Journal of Consulting Psychology,* 1964, **28**, 285-286.

Bennett, V. Combinations of figure drawing characteristics related to drawer's self concept. *Journal of Projective Techniques,* 1966, **30**, 192-196.

Benton, A. L., Windle, C. D., & Erdice, E. *SUI Sentence Completions.* Unpublished monograph, 1952.

Benton, A. L., Windle, C. D., & Erdice, E. *A review of sentence completion techniques.* Project NR 151-075. Washington, D. C.: Office of Naval Research, 1957.

Berdie, R. F. Intra-individual variability and predictability. *Educational and Psychological Measurement,* 1961, **21**, 663-676.

Berg, I. A. Response bias and personality: The deviation hypothesis. *Journal of Psychology,* 1955, **40**, 60-71.

Berg, I. A. Deviant responses and deviant people: The formulation of the deviation hypothesis. *Journal of Counseling Psychology,* 1957, **4**, 154-161.

Berg, I. A. The unimportance of test item content. In B. M. Bass & I. A. Berg (Eds.), *Objective approaches to personality assessment.* New York: Van Nostrand, 1959.

Berg, I. A. Measuring deviant behavior by means of deviant response sets. In I. A. Berg & B. M. Bass (Eds.), *Conformity and deviation.* New York: Harper, 1961.

Berger, I. L., & Sutker, A. R. The relationship of emotional adjustment and intellectual capacity to academic achievement of college students. *Mental Hygiene,* 1956, **40**, 65-77.

Bergmann, G. The contribution of John B. Watson. *Psychological Review,* 1956, **63**, 265-276.

Berkeley, M. H. *A comparison between the empirical and rational approaches for keying a heterogeneous test.* Research Bulletin No. 53-24, 1953, United States Air Force, Air Research and Development Command, Human Resources Research Center.

Bernardin, A., & Jessor, R. A construct validation of the Edwards Personal Preference Schedule with respect to dependency. *Journal of Consulting Psychology,* 1957, **21**, 63-67.

Bernstein, L. The examiner as an inhibiting factor in clinical testing. *Journal of Consulting Psychology,* 1956, **20**, 287-290.

Berryman, E. The self-portrait: A suggested extension of the HTP. *Perceptual and Motor Skills,* 1959, **9**, 411-414.

Bieliauskas, V. J. Sexual identification in children's drawings of human figure. *Journal of Clinical Psychology,* 1960, **16**, 42-44.

Bieliauskas, V. J., & Bristow, R. B. The effect of formal art training upon the quantitative scores of the H-T-P. *Journal of Clinical Psychology,* 1959, **15**, 57-59.

Bieliauskas, V. J., & Heffron, A. Differences in performance on the chromatic vs. achromatic H-T-P drawings. *Journal of Clinical Psychology,* 1960, **16**, 334-335.

Bieliauskas, V. J., & Kirkham, S. An evaluation of the "organic sign" in the H-T-P drawings. *Journal of Clinical Psychology,* 1958, **14**, 50-54.

Bieliauskas, V. J., & Moens, J. An investigation of the H-T-P as an intelligence test for children. *Journal of Clinical Psychology,* 1961, **17**, 178-180.

Bieri, J., Blacharsky, E., & Reid, J. W. Predictive behavior and personal adjustment. *Journal of Consulting Psychology,* 1955, **19**, 351-360.

Bijou, S. W. (Ed.) The psychological program in AAF convalescent hospitals. *AAF Aviation Psychology Research Report No. 15.* Washington, D. C.: U. S. Government Printing Office, 1947.

Bijou, S. W. Implications of behavioral science for counseling and guidance. In J. D. Krumboltz (Ed.), *Revolution in counseling.* Boston: Houghton Mifflin, 1966.

Blake, R. R., & Ramsey, G. V. *Perception: An approach to personality.* New York: Ronald Press, 1951.

Blenkner, M. Predictive factors in the initial interview in family casework. *Social Service Review,* 1954, **28**, 65-73.

Block, J. Some differences between the concepts of social desirability adjustment. *Journal of Consulting Psychology,* 1962, **26**, 527-530.

Block, J., & Bailey, D. *Q-sort item analyses of a number of MMPI scales scored on an Air Force officer sample.* Berkeley: University of California Institute of Personality Assessment Research, 1953.

Block, J., Levine, L., & McNemar, Q. Testing for the existence of psychometric patterns. *Journal of Abnormal and Social Psychology,* 1951, **46**, 356-359.

Bloom, R. F., & Brundage, E. G. Prediction of success in elementary schools for enlisted personnel. In D. B. Stuit (Ed.), *Personnel research and test development in the Bureau of Naval Personnel.* Princeton, N. J.: Princeton University Press, 1947.

Blum, R. H. *Police selection.* Springfield, Ill. Charles C Thomas, 1964.

Bobbitt, J. M., & Newman, S. H. Psychological activities at the United States Coast Guard Academy. *Psychological Bulletin,* 1944, **41**, 568-579.

Bodwin, R. R., & Bruck, M. The adaptation and validation of the Draw-A-Person test as a measure of self concept. *Journal of Clinical Psychology,* 1960, **16**, 427-429.

Boneau, C. A. The effects of violations of assumptions underlying the *t* test. *Psychological Bulletin,* 1960, **57**, 49-64.

Boozer, D. G. Response sets as indicators of senescence and of psychopathology in old age. Unpublished doctoral dissertation, Louisiana State University, 1961.

Borden, H. G. Factors for predicting parole success. *Journal of the American Institute of Criminal Law and Criminology,* 1928, **19**, 328-336.

Bordin, E. S. A theory of vocational interests as dynamic phenomena. *Educational and Psychological Measurement,* 1943, **3**, 49-66.

Borislow, B. The Edwards Personal Preference Schedule (EPPS) and fakability. *Journal of Applied Psychology,* 1958, **42**, 22-27.

Borke, H., & Fiske, D. W. Factors influencing the prediction of behavior from a diagnostic interview. *Journal of Consulting Psychology,* 1957, **21**, 78-80.

Bower, E. M., Shellhamer, T. A., & Daily, J. M. School characteristics of male adolescents who later became schizophrenic. *American Journal of Orthopsychiatry,* 1960, **30**, 712-729.

Bradfield, R. H. The predictive validity of children's drawings. *California Journal of Educational Research,* 1964, **15**, 166-174.

Bradshaw, D. H. A study of group consistencies on the Draw-A-Person test in relation to personality projection. Unpublished master's thesis, Catholic University, 1952.

Bray, D. W., & Grant, D. L. The assessment center in the measurement of potential for business management. *Psychological Monographs,* 1966, **80** (17, Whole No. 625).

Breger, L. Psychological testing: Treatment and research implications. *Journal of Consulting Psychology,* 1968, **32**, 176-181.

Brim, O. G., Jr., Glass, D. C., Lavin, D. E., & Goodman, N. *Personality and decision processes.* Stanford: Stanford University Press, 1962.

Brodie, C. M. Clinical prediction of personality traits displayed in specific situations. *Journal of Clinical Psychology,* 1964, **20**, 459-461.

Broverman, D. M. Cognitive style and intra-individual variation in abilities. *Journal of Personality,* 1960, **28**, 240-256.

Brown, D. G., & Tolor, A. Human figure drawings as indicators of sexual identification and inversion. *Perceptual and Motor Skills,* 1957, **7**, 199-211.

Brown, W. P. Conceptions of perceptual defence. *British Journal of Psychology Monograph Supplements,* 1961, No. 35.

Brozek, J., & Erickson, N. K. Item analysis of the psychoneurotic scales of the Minnesota Multiphasic Personality Inventory in experimental semi-starvation. *Journal of Counsulting Psychology,* 1948, **12**, 403-411.

Brown, S. W. The use of an incomplete sentences test for the study of attitudes towards Negroes. Unpublished doctoral dissertation, Ohio State University, 1950.

Bruck, M., & Bodwin, R. F. Age differences between SCS-DAP test results and GPA. *Journal of Clinical Psychology,* 1963, **19**, 315-316.

Bruner, J. S., Shapiro, D., & Tagiuri, R. The meaning of traits in isolation and in combination. In R. Tagiuri & L. Petrullo (Eds.), *Person perception and interpersonal behavior.* Stanford University Press, 1958.

Bryan, J. H., Hunt, W. A., & Walker, R. E. Reliability of estimating intellectual ability from transcribed interviews. *Journal of Clinical Psychology,* 1966, **22**, 360.

Buchwald, A. M. Verbal utterances as data. In H. Feigl & G. Maxwell (Eds.), *Current issues in the philosophy of science: Symposium of scientists and philosophers.* (A.A.A.S. Section on History and Philosophy of Science; Proceedings of Section L, 1959), New York: Holt, Rinehart & Winston, 1961.

Burdock, E. I., Fleiss, J., & Hardesty, A. S. A new view of interobserver agreement. *Personnel Psychology,* 1963, **16**, 373-384.

Burdock, E. I., Hakerem, G., Hardesty, A. S., & Zubin, J. A ward behavior rating scale for mental hospital patients. *Journal of Clinical Psychology,* 1960, **16**, 246-247.

Burdock, E. I., & Hardesty, A. S. Structured clinical interview and inventory. Paper presented at a meeting of the Eastern Psychological Association, Atlantic City, May, 1962.

Burdock, E. I., & Hardesty, A. S. Quantitative techniques for the evaluation of psychiatric treatment. In P. H. Hoch & J. Zubin (Eds.), *The evaluation of psychiatric treatment.* New York: Grune & Stratton, 1964.

Burdock, E. I., & Hardesty, A. S. Contrasting behavior of normals and mental patients on a screening interview. *Proceedings of the 73rd annual convention of the American Psychological Association,* Washington, D. C.: APA, 1965.

Burdock, E. I., & Hardesty, A. S. Behavior patterns of chronic schizophrenics. In P. H. Hoch & J. Zubin (Eds.), *Psychopathology of schizophrenia.* New York: Grune & Stratton, 1966.

Burgess, E. W. Factors determining success or failure on parole. In A. A. Bruce (Ed.), *The workings of the indeterminate sentence law and the parole system in Illinois.* Springfield: State of Illinois, 1928.

Burgess, E. W. An experiment in the standardization of the case-study method. *Sociometry,* 1941, **4**, 329-348.

Burgess, E. W., & Wallin, P. *Engagement and marriage.* Philadelphia: Lippincott, 1953.

Burks, B. S., & Jones, M. C. Personality development in childhood: A survey of problems, methods, and experimental findings. *Monographs of the Society for Research in Child Development,* 1936, **1**, 1-205.

Buros, O. K. (Ed.) *The fourth mental measurements yearbook.* Highland Park, N. J.: Gryphon, 1953.

Buros, O. K. (Ed.) *The fifth mental measurements yearbook.* Highland Park, N. J.: Gryphon, 1959.

Burwen, L. S., Campbell, D. T., & Kidd, J. The use of a sentence completion test in measuring attitudes toward superiors and subordinates. *Journal of Applied Psychology,* 1956, **40**, 248-250.

Butler, J. M. The use of a psychological model in personality testing. *Educational and Psychological Measurement,* 1954, **14**, 77-80.

Butler, R. L., & Marcuse, F. L. Sex identification at different ages using the Draw-A-Person test. *Journal of Projective Techniques,* 1959, **23**, 299-302.

Caldwell, A. Recent advances in automated interpretation of the MMPI. Paper presented to the fifth annual symposium on Recent Developments in the Use of the MMPI, Mexico City, 1970.

Cameron, D. E. A theory of diagnosis. In P. H. Hoch & J. Zubin (Eds.), *Current problems in psychiatric diagnosis.* New York: Grune & Stratton, 1953.

Cameron, D. E., *et al.* Automation of psychotherapy. *Comprehensive Psychiatry,* 1964, **5**, 1-14.

Cameron, N. Reasoning, regression, and communication in schizophrenia. *Psychological Monographs,* 1938, **50**, 1-34. (a)

Cameron, N. A study of thinking in senile deterioration and schizophrenic disorganization. *American Journal of Psychology,* 1938, **51**, 650-664. (b)

Cameron, N., & Margaret, A. Experimental studies in thinking: I. Scattered speech in the responses of normal subjects to incomplete sentences. *Journal of Experimental Psychology,* 1949, **39**, 617-627.

Cameron, N., & Margaret, A. Correlates of scattered speech in the responses of normal subjects to incomplete sentences. *Journal of General Psychology,* 1950, **43**, 77-84.

Campbell, D. T. The indirect assessment of social attitudes. *Psychological Bulletin,* 1950, **47**, 15-38.

Campbell, D. T. A typology of tests, projective and otherwise. *Journal of Consulting Psychology,* 1957, **21**, 207-210.

Campbell, D. T. Lectures in social psychology. Unpublished manuscript, 1959.

Campbell, D. T. Recommendations for APA test standards regarding construct, trait, or discriminant validity. *American Psychologist,* 1960, **15**, 546-553.

Campbell, D. T., & Fiske, D. W. Convergent and discriminant validation by the multitrait-multimethod matrix. *Psychological Bulletin,* 1959, **56**, 81-105.

Cantril, H. Perception and interpersonal relations. *American Journal of Psychiatry,* 1957, **114**, 119-126.

Carp, A., & Shavzin, A. The susceptibility to falsification of the Rorschach Psychodiagnostic Technique. *Journal of Consulting Psychology,* 1950, 14, 230-233.

Carr, A. C. Intra-individual consistency in response to tests of varying degrees of ambiguity. *Journal of Consulting Psychology,* 1954, **18**, 251-258.

Carr, A. C. The relation of certain Rorschach variables to expression of affect in the TAT and SCT. *Journal of Projective Techniques,* 1956, **20**, 137-142.

Carr, A. C. The psychodiagnostic test battery: Rationale and methodology. In D. Brower & L. E. Abt (Eds.), *Progress in clinical psychology.* Vol. II. New York: Grune & Stratton, 1958.

Carroll, J. B. Ratings on traits measured by a factored personality inventory. *Journal of Abnormal and Social Psychology,* 1952, **47**, 626-632.

Carson, R. The status of diagnostic testing. *American Psychologist,* 1958, **13**, 79.

Carter, H. L. J. A combined projective and psychogalvanic response technique for investigating certain affective processes. *Journal of Consulting Psychology,* 1947, **11**, 270-275.

Cass, L. K. An investigation of parent-child relationships in terms of awareness, identification, projection and control. *American Journal of Orthopsychiatry,* 1952, 22, 305-313. (a)

Cass, L. K. Parent-child relationships and delinquency. *Journal of Abnormal and Social Psychology,* 1952, **47**, 101-104. (b)

Cassel, R. H., Johnson, A., & Burns, W. H. Examiner, ego defense, and the H-T-P Test. *Journal of Clinical Psychology,* 1958, **14**, 157-160.

Cattell, R. B. *The description and measurement of personality.* New York: World Book, 1946.

Cattell, R. B. *Personality: A systematic theoretical and factual study.* New York: McGraw-Hill, 1950.

Cattell, R. B. Principles of design in "projective" or misperception tests of personality. In H. H. Anderson & L. Anderson (Eds.), *Projective Techniques.* New York: Prentice-Hall, 1951.

Cattell, R. B. *Personality and motivation structure and measurement.* New York: World Book, 1957.

Cavan, R. S., Hauser, P. M., & Stouffer, S. A. Note on the statistical treatment of life history material. *Social Forces,* 1930, **9**, 200-203.

Centers, L., & Centers R. A comparison of the body images of amputee and non-amputee children as revealed in figure drawings. *Journal of Projective Techniques,* 1963, **27**, 158-165.

Chance, J. E. Adjustment and prediction of others' behavior. *Journal of Consulting Psychology,* 1958, **22**, 191-194.

Chapman, L. J. Illusory correlation in observational report. *Journal of Verbal Learning and Verbal Behavior,* 1967, **6**, 151-155.

Chapman, L. J., & Chapman, J. P. The genesis of popular but erroneous psychodiagnostic observations. *Journal of Abnormal Psychology,* 1967, **72**, 193-204.

Chauncey, H. Personal communication. Reported by P. E. Meehl in *Clinical vs. statistical prediction.* Minneapolis: University of Minnesota Press, 1954.

Chenoweth, J. H. Situational tests—a new attempt at assessing police candidates. *Journal of Criminal Law, Criminology, & Police Science,* 1961, **52**, 232-238.

Churchill, R., & Crandall, V. J. The reliability and validity of the Rotter Incomplete Sentences Test. *Journal of Consulting Psychology,* 1955, **19**, 345-350.

Churchman, C. W. Decision and value theory. In R. L. Ackoff (Ed.), *Progress in operations research.* Vol. 1. New York: Wiley, 1961.

Churchman, C. W., Ackoff, R. L., & Arnoff, E. L. *Introduction to operations research.* New York: Wiley, 1957.

Cieutat, L. G. Deviant responses as a function of mental deficiency. Unpublished doctoral dissertation, Louisiana State University, 1960.

Clark, E. T., & Degenhardt, F. J. Ability of females to draw sexually undifferentiated figures. *Perceptual and Motor Skills,* 1965, **20**, 60.

Cleckley, H. *The mask of sanity.* St. Louis: Mosby, 1941.

Cliff, R. Validation of selection procedures in enlisted-to-officer programs. *USN Bureau of Naval Personnel Technical Bulletin,* 1958, No. 58-11.

Cofer, C. N., Chance, J., & Judson, A. J. A study of malingering on the MMPI. *Journal of Psychology,* 1949, **27**, 491-499.

Cohen, H. Psychological test findings in adolescents having ovarian dysgenesis. *Psychosomatic Medicine,* 1962, **24**, 249-256.

Cohen, R. A., & Cohen, M. D. Research in psychotherapy: A preliminary report. *Psychiatry,* 1961, **24**, 46-61.

Colby, K. M. Experiment on the effects of an observer's presence on the imago system during psychoanalytic free-association. *Behavioral Science,* 1960, **5**, 215-232.

Cole, J. D. Evaluation of drug treatments in psychiatry. In P. H. Hoch & J. Zubin (Eds.), *The evaluation of psychiatric treatment.* New York: Grune & Stratton, 1964.

Cole, J. K., & Magnussen, M. G. Where the action is. *Journal of Consulting Psychology,* 1966, **30**, 539-543.

Conners, T., Walkon, G. H., Haefner, D. P., & Stotsky, B. A. Outcome of post-hospital rehabilitative treatment of mental patients as a function of ego strength. *Journal of Counseling Psychology,* 1960, **7**, 278-282.

Conrad, H. S. The validity of personality ratings of preschool children. *Journal of Educational Psychology,* 1932, **23**, 671-680.

Conrad, H. S., & Satter, G. A. Use of test scores and quality classification ratings in predicting success in electrician's mates school. In D. B. Stuit (Ed.), *Personnel research and test development in the Bureau of Naval Personnel.* Princeton, N. J.: Princeton University Press, 1947.

Conrad, H. S. Information which should be provided by test publishers and testing agencies on the validity and use of their tests. In *Proceedings 1949 invitational conference on testing problems.* Princeton, N. J.: Educational Testing Service, 1950.

Cook, E. B., & Wherry, R. J. A factor analysis of the MMPI and aptitude test data. *Journal of Applied Psychology,* 1950, **34**, 260-265.

Coombs, C. M. A theory of data. *Psychological Review,* 1960, **67**, 143-159.

Coon, G. P., & Raymond, A. F. *A review of the psychoneuroses at Stockbridge.* Stockbridge, Massachusetts: Austen Riggs Foundation, 1940.

Cooper, W. W., Leavitt, H. J., & Shelly, M. W. *New perspectives in organizational research.* New York: Wiley, 1964.

Copple, G. E. Effective intelligence as measured by an unstructured sentence-completion technique. *Journal of Consulting Psychology,* 1956, **20**, 357-360.

Corah, N. L., Feldman, M. J., Cohen, I. S., Gruen, A. W., & Ringwall, E. A. Social desirability as a variable in the Edwards Personal Preference Schedule. *Journal of Consulting Psychology,* 1958, **22**, 70-72.

Costin, F., & Eiserer, P. E. Students' attitudes toward school life as revealed by a sentence completion test. *American Psychologist,* 1949, **4**, 289.

Cottle, W. C. A factorial study of the Multiphasic, Strong, Kuder, and Bell inventories using a population of adult males. *Psychometrika,* 1950, **15**, 25-47.

Cowen, E. L., Davol, S. H., Reimanis, G., & Stiller, A. The social desirability of trait-descriptive terms: Two geriatric samples. *Journal of Social Psychology,* 1962, **56**, 217-225.

Cowen, E. L., & Frankel, G. The social desirability of trait-descriptive terms: Applications to a French sample. *Journal of Social Psychology,* 1964, **63**, 233-239.

Cowen, E. L., Staiman, M. G., & Wolitzky, D. L. The social desirability of trait-descriptive terms: Applications to a schizophrenic sample. *Journal of Social Psychology,* 1961, **54**, 37-45.

Cowen, E. L., & Stricker, G. The social desirability of trait-descriptive terms: A sample of sexual offenders. *Journal of Social Psychology,* 1963, **59**, 307-315.

Cowen, E. L., & Tongas, P. The social desirability of trait-descriptive terms: Applications to a self-concept inventory. *Journal of Consulting Psychology,* 1959, **23,** 361-365.

Craddick, R. A. Draw-A-Person characteristics of psychopathic prisoners and college students. *Perceptual and Motor Skills,* 1962, **15,** 11-13.

Craddick, R. A. The self-image in the Draw-A-Person Test and self-portrait drawings. *Journal of Projective Techniques and Personality Assessment,* 1963, **27,** 288-291.

Craddick, R. A., Leipold, W. D., & Cacavas, P. D. The relationship of shading on the Draw-A-Person Test to Manifest Anxiety scores. *Journal of Consulting Psychology,* 1962, **25,** 193.

Crandall, V. C. The reinforcement effects of adult reactions and nonreactions on children's achievement expectations. *Child Development,* 1963, **34,** 335-354.

Crider, B. A study of a character analyst. *Journal of Social Psychology,* 1944, **20,** 315-318.

Cromwell, R. L., & Lundy, R. M. Productivity of clinical hypotheses on a sentence completion test. *Journal of Consulting Psychology,* 1954, **18,** 421-424.

Cronbach, L. J. Response sets and test validity. *Educational and Psychological Measurement,* 1946, **6,** 475-494.

Cronbach, L. J. A validation design for qualitative studies of personality. *Journal of Consulting Psychology,* 1948, **12,** 365-374.

Cronbach, L. J. *Essentials of psychological testing.* New York: Harper & Bros., 1949.

Cronbach, L. J. Further evidence of response sets and test design. *Educational and Psychological Measurement,* 1950, **10,** 3-31.

Cronbach, L. J. Assessment of individual differences. In *Annual Review of Psychology.* Stanford: Annual Reviews, 1956.

Cronbach, L. J. The two disciplines of scientific psychology. *American Psychologist,* 1957, **12,** 671-684.

Cronbach, L. J. *Essentials of psychological testing.* (2nd ed.) New York: Harper, 1960.

Cronbach, L. J., & Gleser, G. *Psychological tests and personnel decisions.* Urbana: University of Illinois Press, 1957.

Cronbach, L. J., & Meehl, P. E. Construct validity in psychological tests. *Psychological Bulletin,* 1955, **52,** 281-302.

Crovitz, H. F. On direction in drawing a person. *Journal of Consulting Psychology,* 1963, **26,** 196.

Crow, W. J. The effect of training upon accuracy and variability in interpersonal perception. *Journal of Abnormal and Social Psychology,* 1957, **55,** 355-359.

Crow, W. J., & Hammond, K. R. The generality of accuracy and response sets in interpersonal perception. *Journal of Abnormal and Social Psychology,* 1957, **54,** 384-390.

Crowne, D. P., & Liverant, S. Conformity under varying conditions of personal commitment. *Journal of Abnormal and Social Psychology,* 1963, **66,** 547-555.

Crowne, D. P., & Marlowe, D. A new scale of social desirability independent of psychopathology. *Journal of Consulting Psychology,* 1960, **24,** 349-354.

Crowne, D. P., & Strickland, B. The conditioning of verbal behavior as a function of the need for social approval. *Journal of Abnormal and Social Psychology,* 1961, **63,** 395-401.

Crumpton, E. The influence of color on the Rorschach test. *Journal of Projective Techniques,* 1956, **20,** 150-158.

Cruse, D. B. Socially desirable responses in relation to grade level. *Child Development,* 1963, **34,** 777-789.

Crutchfield, R. S. Conformity and character. *American Psychologist,* 1955, **10,** 191-198.

Dahlstrom, W. G., & Craven, D. The Minnesota Multiphasic Personality Inventory and the stuttering phenomenon in young adults. *American Psychologist,* 1952, **7,** 341 (abstract).

Dahlstrom, W. G., & Welsh, G. S. *An MMPI handbook: A guide to use in clinical practice and research.* Minneapolis: University of Minnesota Press, 1960.

Daily, C. A. The effects of premature conclusions upon the acquisition of understanding of a person. *Journal of Psychology,* 1952, **33,** 133-152.

Dailey, J. T. Emotional criticisms of testing. Paper read at American Educational Research Association and National Council on Measurement in Education (joint meeting), Chicago, February, 1963.

Darley, J. G., & Marquis, D. G. Veterans' guidance centers: A survey of their problems and activities. *Journal of Clinical Psychology,* 1946, **2,** 109-116.

Darlington, R. B., & Stauffer, G. F. Use of evaluation of discrete test information in decision making. *Journal of Applied Psychology,* 1966, **50,** 125-129.

Davids, A., & De Vault, S. Use of the TAT and human figure drawings in research on personality, pregnancy and perception. *Journal of Projective Techniques,* 1960, **24,** 362-365.

Davids, A., Joelson, M., & McArthur, C. Rorschach and TAT indices of homosexuality in overt homosexuals, neurotics, and normal males. *Journal of Abnormal and Social Psychology,* 1956, **53,** 161-172.

Dawson, J. G., Jr. A comparative investigation of three diagnostic indicators of brain damage. Unpublished doctoral dissertation, University of Chicago, 1949.

Dean, S. I. Adjustment testing and personality factors of the blind. *Journal of Consulting Psychology,* 1957, **21,** 171-177.

DeGroot, A. D. Via clinical to statistical prediction. *Acta Psychologica,* 1961, **18,** 274-284.

Denenberg, V. H. The relationship between a measure of kinesthesis and two indices of adjustment. *Journal of General Psychology,* 1960, **62,** 43-52.

Denker, P. G. The prognosis of insured neurotics. *New York State Journal of Medicine,* 1939, **39,** 238-247.

Dennis, W. Handwriting conventions as determinants of human figure drawing. *Journal of Consulting Psychology,* 1958, **22,** 293-295.

Dennis, W., & Raskin, E. Further evidence concerning the effect of handwriting habits upon the location of drawings. *Journal of Consulting Psychology,* 1960, **24,** 548-549.

DeVore, I. (Ed.) *Primate behavior: Field studies of monkeys and apes.* New York: Holt, Rinehart & Winston, 1965.

Dicken, C. Good impression, social desirability, and acquiescence as suppressor variables. *Educational and Psychological Measurement,* 1963, **23,** 699-720.

Dilworth, T. A comparison of the Edwards Personal Preference Schedule variables with some aspects of the TAT. *Journal of Consulting Psychology,* 1958, **22,** 486.

Dixon, W. J. (Ed.) *Biomedical computer programs* (Rev. ed.). Health Sciences Computing Facility, Health, School of Medicine, University of California, Los Angeles, September, 1965.

Doctor, R. F. Testing: The heat is on in Congress. *California State Psychologist,* 1966, **7,** 3.

Dole, A. A. The Vocational Sentence Completion Blank in counseling. *Journal of Counseling Psychology,* 1958, **5,** 200-205.

Dole, A. A., & Fletcher, F. M., Jr. Some principles in the construction of incomplete sentences. *Educational and Psychological Measurement,* 1955, **15,** 101-110.

Doleys, E. J., & Renzaglia, G. A. Accuracy of student prediction of college grades. *Personnel and Guidance Journal,* 1963, **41,** 528-530.

Doll, E. A. *Measurement of social competence.* Darien, Conn.: Educational Publishers, Educational Test Bureau, 1953.

Dollard, J., & Miller, N. E. *Personality and psychotherapy.* New York: McGraw-Hill, 1950.

Doppelt, J. P., & Bennett, G. K. Testing job applicants from disadvantaged groups. *Test Service Bulletin* (No. 57). New York: Psychological Corporation, 1967.

Dorris, R. J., Levinson, D. J., & Hanfmann, E. Authoritarian personality studied by a new variation of the sentence completion technique. *Journal of Abnormal and Social Psychology,* 1954, **49,** 99-108.

Drake, L. E., & Oetting, E. R. *MMPI codebook for counselors.* Minneapolis: University of Minnesota Press. 1959.

Dublin, L. I., & Benzel, B. *To be or not to be: A study of suicide.* New York: Harrison Smith & Robert Haas, 1933.

DuBois, C., & Oberholzer, E. Rorschach tests and native personality in Alor, Dutch East Indies. *Transactions of the New York Academy of Science,* 1942, **4**, 168-170.

DuBois, P. H. On relationships between numbers and behavior. *Psychometrika,* 1962, **27**, 323-333.

Duff, F. L. Item sublety in personality inventory scales. *Journal of Consulting Psychology,* 1965, **29**, 565-570.

Duncan, O. D., Ohlin, L. E., Reiss, A. J., & Stanton, H. R. Formal devices for making selection decisions. *American Journal of Sociology,* 1953, **58**, 573-584.

Dunham, H. W., & Meltzer, B. N. Predicting length of hospitalization of mental patients. *American Journal of Sociology,* 1946, **52**, 123-131.

Dunlap, J. W., & Wantman, M. J. An investigation of the interview as a technique for selecting aircraft pilots. Washington, D. C.: Civil Aeronautics Administration, 1944 (Report No. 33).

Dunnette, M. D. A modified model for test validation and research. *Journal of Applied Psychology,* 1963, **47**, 317-323.

Dunnette, M. D. *Personnel selection and placement.* Belmont, California: Wadsworth, 1966.

Dunnette, M. D., & Maetzold, J. Use of a weighted application blank in hiring seasonal employees. *Journal of Applied Psychology,* 1955, **39**, 308-310.

Durost-Walter Word Mastery Test. Yonkers-on-Hudson, N. Y.: World Book Company, 1950.

Ebbinghaus, H. Ueber eine neue methode zur prufung geistiger fahigkeiten und ihre anwendung bei schulkinders. *Zeitschrift fur Psychologie und Physiologie der Sinnersorgane,* 1897, **13**, 401-459.

Ebel, R. L. Must all tests be valid? *American Psychologist,* 1961, **16**, 640-647.

Eber, H. W. Computer reporting of 16 PF data. Paper presented to the American Psychological Association, Los Angeles, 1964.

Ebner, E., & Shaw, F. J. An investigation of modes and responses to contradictions. *Psychological Reports,* 1960, **6**, 206.

Edwards, A. L. The relationship between the judged desirability of a trait and the probability that the trait will be endorsed. *Journal of Applied Psychology,* 1953, **37**, 90-93.

Edwards, A. L. Social desirability and probability of endorsement of items in the Interpersonal Check List. *Journal of Abnormal and Social Psychology,* 1957, **55**, 394-395. (a)

Edwards, A. L. *The social desirability variable in personality assessment and research.* New York: Dryden, 1957. (b)

Edwards, A. L. *Manual for the Edwards Personal Preference Schedule.* New York: Psychological Corporation, 1959. (a)

Edwards, A. L. Social desirability and the description of others. *Journal of Abnormal and Social Psychology,* 1959, **59**, 434-436. (b)

Edwards, A. L. Social desirability or acquiescence in the MMPI? A case study with the SD scale. *Journal of Abnormal and Social Psychology,* 1961, **63**, 351-359.

Edwards, A. L. A factor analysis of experimental social desirability and response set scales. *Journal of Applied Psychology,* 1963, **47**, 308-316.

Edwards, A. L. The objective assessment of human motives. In D. Levine (Ed.), *Nebraska symposium on motivation.* Lincoln: University of Nebraska Press, 1964.

Edwards, A. L., & Diers, C. J. Social desirability and the factorial interpretation of the MMPI. *Educational and Psychological Measurement,* 1962, **22**, 501-509.

Edwards, A. L., & Diers, C. J. Neutral items as a measure of acquiescence. *Educational and Psychological Measurement,* 1963, **23**, 687-698.

Edwards, A. L., Diers, C. J., & Walker, J. N. Response sets and factor loadings on sixty-one personality scales. *Journal of Applied Psychology,* 1962, **46**, 220-225.

Edwards, A. L., & Heathers, L. B. The first factor of the MMPI: Social desirability or ego strength? *Journal of Consulting Psychology,* 1962, **26**, 99-100.

Edwards, A. L., Heathers, L. B., & Fordyce, W. B. Correlations of new MMPI scales with Edwards SD scale. *Journal of Clinical Psychology,* 1960, **16**, 26-29.

Edwards, A. L., & Walker, J. N. A short form of the MMPI: The SD scale. *Psychological Reports,* 1961, **8**, 485-486. (a)

Edwards, A. L., & Walker, J. N. Social desirability and agreement response set. *Journal of Abnormal and Social Psychology,* 1961, **62**, 180-183. (b)

Edwards, A. L., & Walsh, J. A. The relationship between the intensity of the social desirability keying of a scale and the correlation of the scale with Edwards' SD scale and the first factor loading of the scale. *Journal of Clinical Psychology,* 1963, **19**, 200-203. (a)

Edwards, A. L., & Walsh, J. A. Relationships between various psychometric properties of personality items. *Educational and Psychological Measurement,* 1963, **23**, 227-238. (b)

Edwards, A. L., & Walsh, J. A. Response sets in standard and experimental personality scales. *American Educational Research Journal,* 1964, **1**, 52-61.

Edwards, A. L., Walsh, J. A., & Diers, C. J. The relationship between social desirability and internal consistency of personality scales. *Journal of Applied Psychology,* 1963, **47**, 255-259.

Edwards, W., Lindman, H., & Phillips, L. D. Emerging technologies for making decisions. In F. Barron (Ed.), *New Directions in Psychology,* Vol. 2. New York: Holt, Rinehart & Winston, 1965.

Effron, H. V. An attempt to employ a sentence completion test for the detection of psychiatric patients with suicidal ideas. *Journal of Consulting Psychology,* 1960, **24**,156-160.

Eissler, K. R. *Medical orthodoxy and the future of psychoanalysis.* New York: International Universities Press, 1965.

Elizur, A. Content analysis of the Rorschach with regard to anxiety and hostility. *Rorschach Research Exchange,* 1949, **13**, 247-284.

Ellis, A. The validity of personality questionnaires. *Psychological Bulletin,* 1946, **43**, 385-440.

Ellis, A. Should some people be labelled mentally ill? *Journal of Consulting Psychology,* 1967, **31**, 435-446.

Ellis, A., & Conrad, H. S. The validity of personality inventories in military practice. *Psychological Bulletin,* 1948, **45**, 385-426.

Ellsworth, R. B. The regression of schizophrenic language. *Journal of Consulting Psychology,* 1951, **15**, 387-391.

Endler, N. S., Hunt, J. M., & Rosenstein, A. J. An S-R inventory of anxiousness. *Psychological Monographs,* 1962, **76** (17, Whole No. 536).

Engen, E. P. Response set of pulmonary tuberculosis patients. Unpublished doctoral dissertation, Louisiana State University, 1959.

England, G. W. *Development and use of weighted application blanks.* Dubuque, Iowa: William C. Brown, 1961.

Engle, R. L., Jr. Medical diagnosis: Present, past and future, II. *Archives of Internal Medicine,* 1963, **112**, 520-529.

Engle, R. L., Jr., & Davis, R. J. Medical diagnosis: Present, past and future, I. *Archives of Internal Medicine,* 1963, **112**, 512-519.

Epstein, S. The measurement of drive and conflict in humans: Theory and experiment. In M. R. Jones (Ed.), *Nebraska symposium on motivation: 1962.* Lincoln: University of Nebraska Press, 1962.

Erikson, E. Identity and uprootedness in our time. In E. Erikson (Ed.), *Insight and responsibility.* New York: Norton, 1964.

Eron, L. D. Frequencies of themes and identifications in the stories of schizophrenic patients and non-hospitalized college students. *Journal of Consulting Psychology,* 1948, **12**, 387-395.

Eron, L. D. A normative study of the Thematic Apperception Test. *Psychological Monographs,* 1950, **64** (9, Whole No. 315).

Eron, L. D. Responses of women to the Thematic Apperception Test. *Journal of Consulting Psychology,* 1953, **17**, 269-282.

Eron, L. D., Terry, D., & Callahan, R. The use of rating scales for emotional tone of TAT stories. *Journal of Consulting Psychology,* 1950, **14**, 473-478.

Estes, W. K. Of models and men. *American Psychologist,* 1957, **12**, 609-617.

Evans, F. J., & Schneidler, D. Inter-judge reliability of human figure drawing measures of field dependence. *Perceptual and Motor Skills,* 1966, **22**, 630.

Eysenck, H. J. *Dimensions of personality.* London: Kegan Paul, 1947.

Eysenck, H. J. *The scientific study of personality.* London: Routledge and Kegan Paul, 1952.

Eysenck, H. J. *Behavior therapy and the neuroses.* New York: Pergamon, 1960.

Exner, J. E. A comparison of human figure drawings of psychoneurotics, character disturbances, normals and subjects experiencing experimentally induced fear. *Journal of Projective Techniques,* 1962, **26,** 392-397.

Fairweather, G. W. (Ed.) *Social psychology in treating mental illness: An experimental approach.* New York: Wiley, 1964.

Farago, O., & Gittler, L. F. (Eds.) *German psychological warfare: Survey and bibliography.* New York: Committee for National Morale, 1941.

Farber, I. E., Harlow, H. F., & West, L. J. Brainwashing, conditioning and DDD (debility, dependency, and dread). *Sociometry,* 1957, **20,** 271-285.

Farber, M. L. English and Americans: A study in national character. *Journal of Psychology,* 1951, **13,** 241-249.

Farberow, N. L. Personality patterns of suicidal mental hospital patients. *Genetic Psychology Monographs,* 1950, **42,** 3-79.

Feldman, M., & Graley, J. The effects of an experimental set to stimulate abnormality on group Rorschach performance. *Journal of Projective Techniques,* 1954, **18,** 326-334.

Feldman, M. J., & Hunt, R. G. The relation of difficulty in drawing to ratings of adjustment based on human figure drawings. *Journal of Consulting Psychology,* 1958, **22,** 217-219.

Fenichel, O. *Psychoanalytic theory of neurosis.* New York: Norton, 1945.

Ferster, C. B. Positive reinforcement and behavior deficits in autistic children. *Child Development,* 1961, **32,** 437-456.

Ferster, C. B. Classification of behavior pathology. In L. Krasner & L. P. Ullmann (Eds.), *Research in behavior modification.* New York: Holt, Rinehart & Winston, 1965.

Finney, J. C. A programmed interpretation of the MMPI and CPI. *Archives of General Psychiatry,* 1966, **15,** 75-81.

Fisher, G. M. Nudity in human figure drawings. *Journal of Clinical Psychology,* 1961, **17,** 307-308.

Fisher, S. Body reactivity gradients and figure drawing variables. *Journal of Consulting Psychology,* 1959, **23,** 54-59.

Fisher, S., & Fisher, R. Test of certain assumptions regarding figure drawing analysis. *Journal of Abnormal and Social Psychology,* 1950, **45,** 727-732.

Fiske, D. W. The constraints of intra-individual variability in test response. *Educational and Psychological Measurement,* 1957, **17,** 317-337. (a)

Fiske, D. W. An intensive study of variability scores. *Educational and Psychological Measurement,* 1957, **17,** 453-465. (b)

Fiske, D. W., & Butler, J. M. The experimental conditions for measuring individual differences. *Educational and Psychological Measurement,* 1963, **23**, 249-266.

Fiske, D. W., & Rice, L. Intra-individual response variability. *Psychological Bulletin,* 1955, **52**, 217-250.

Fiske, D. W., & Van Buskirk, C. The stability of interpretations of sentence completion tests. *Journal of Consulting Psychology,* 1959, **23**, 177-180.

Fitzgerald, B. J. Some relationships among projective test, interview, and sociometric measures of dependent behavior. *Journal of Abnormal and Social Psychology,* 1958, **56**, 199-203.

Flanagan, J. C. (Ed.) *The Aviation Psychology Program in the AAF. Aviation Psychology Research Report No. 1.* Washington, D. C.: U. S. Government Printing Office, 1947.

Flanagan, J. C. The use of comprehensive rationales in test development. *Educational and Psychological Measurement,* 1951, **11**, 151-155.

Fleeson, W., Glueck, B., Heistad, G., King, J., Lykken, D., Meehl, P., & Mena, A. The ataraxic effect of two phenothiazine drugs on an outpatient population. *University of Minnesota Medical Bulletin,* 1958, **29**, 274-286.

Ford, A. H. Prediction of academic success in three schools of nursing. *Journal of Applied Psychology,* 1950, **34**, 186-189.

Fordyce, W. E. Social desirability in the MMPI. *Journal of Consulting Psychology,* 1956, **20**, 171-175.

Forer, B. R. A structured sentence completion test. *Journal of Projective Techniques,* 1950, **14**, 15-29.

Forer, B. R. Research with projective techniques: Some trends. *Journal of Projective Techniques,* 1957, **21**, 358-361.

Forer, B. R. Word association and sentence completion methods. In A. I. Rabin & M. R. Haworth (Eds.), *Projective techniques with children.* New York: Grune & Straton, 1960. (a)

Forer, B. R. Sentence completion. In A. C. Carr (Ed.), *The prediction of overt behavior through the use of projective techniques.* Springfield, Ill.: Charles C Thomas, 1960. (b)

Forer, B. R., & Tolman, R. S. Some characteristics of clinical judgment. *Journal of Consulting Psychology,* 1952, **16**, 347-352.

Fosberg, I. Rorschach reactions under varied instructions. *Rorschach Research Exchange,* 1938, **3**, 12-30.

Fosberg, I. An experimental study of the reliability of the Rorschach psychodiagnostic technique. *Rorschach Research Exchange,* 1941, **5**, 72-84.

Fosberg, I. How do subjects attempt to fake results on the Rorschach test? *Rorschach Research Exchange,* 1943, **7**, 119-121.

Fowler, R. D. Computer processing and reporting of personality test data. Paper presented to the American Psychological Association, Los Angeles, 1964.

Fowler, R. D. Purposes and usefulness of the Alabama program for the automatic interpretation of the MMPI. Paper presented to the American Psychological Association, Chicago, 1965.

Fowler, R. D. *The MMPI notebook: A guide to the clinical use of the automated MMPI.* Nutley, N. J.: Roche Psychiatric Service Institute, 1966.

Fowler, R. D. Automated interpretation of personality test data. In J. Butcher (Ed.), *MMPI: Research Developments and Clinical Applications.* New York: McGraw-Hill, 1969.

Fowler, R. D. and Miller, M. L. Computer interpretation of the MMPI: Its use in clinical practice. *Archives of General Psychiatry,* 1969, **21**, 502-508.

Frank, J. D. Discussion of H. J. Eysenck, "The effects of psychotherapy." *International Journal of Psychiatry,* 1965, **1**, 288-290.

Frank, J. D., Gliedman, L. H., Imber, S. D., Stone, A. R., & Nash, E. H. Patient's expectancies and relearning as factors determining improvement in psychotherapy. *American Journal of Psychiatry,* 1959, **115**, 961-968.

Frank, L. K. Comments on the proposed standardization of the Rorschach method. *Rorschach Research Exchange,* 1939, **3**, 19-27. (a)

Frank, L. K. Projective methods for the study of personality. *Journal of Psychology,* 1939, **8**, 289-413. (b)

Frank, L. K. *Projective methods.* Springfield, Ill.: Charles C Thomas, 1948.

Frederiksen, N. Validation of a simulation technique. *Organizational Behavior and Human Performance,* 1966, **1**, 87-109.

Frederiksen, N., & Gilbert, A. C. F. Replication of differential predictability. *Educational and Psychological Measurement,* 1960, **10**, 759-767.

Frederiksen, N., & Melville, S. D. Differential predictability in the use of the test scores. *Educational and Psychological Measurement,* 1954, **14**, 647-656.

Frederiksen, N., & Messick, S. Response set as a measure of personality. *Educational and Psychological Measurement,* 1958, **19**, 137-157.

Freedman, D. A. Various etiologies of schizophrenic syndrome. *Diseases of the Nervous System,* 1958, **19**, 1-6.

Frenkel-Brunswik, E. Intolerance of ambiguity as an emotional and perceptual personality variable. *Journal of Personality,* 1949, **18**, 108-143.

Freud, S. *The ego and the id.* London: Hogarth Press, 1927.

Freudenberg, R. K., & Robertson, J. P. S. Symptoms in relation to psychiatric diagnosis and treatment. *Archives of Neurology and Psychiatry,* 1956, **76**, 14-22.

Freyd, M. The statistical viewpoint in vocational selection. *Journal of Applied Psychology,* 1925, **9**, 349-356.

Fricke, B. G. Subtle and obvious test items and response set. *Journal of Consulting Psychology,* 1957, **21**, 250-252.

Friesen, E. P. The incomplete sentences technique as a measure of employee attitudes. *Personnel Psychology,* 1952, **5**, 329-345.

From, F. Perception of human action. In H. David and J. C. Brenglemann (Eds.), *Perspectives in personality research.* London: Crosby Lockwood, 1960.

Fruchter, B. *Introduction to factor analysis.* Princeton, N. J.: Van Nostrand, 1954.

Fujita, B. Applicability of the Edwards Personal Preference Schedule to Nisei. *Psychological Report,* 1957, **3**, 518-519.

Fulkerson, J., & Barry, J. R. Methodology and research on the prognostic use of psychological tests. *Psychological Bulletin,* 1961, **58**, 117-204.

Gage, N. L. Explorations in the understanding of others. *Educational and Psychological Measurement,* 1953, **13**, 14-26.

Gage, N. L., Leavitt, G. S., & Stone, G. C. The psychological meaning of acquiescence set for authoritarianism. *Journal of Abnormal and Social Psychology,* 1957, **55**, 98-103.

Gagne, R. M. (Ed.) *Psychological principles in system development.* New York: Holt, Rinehart & Winston, 1962.

Gardner, J. W. *Excellence: Can we be equal and excellent too?* New York: Harper, 1961.

Garfield, S. *Introductory clinical psychology.* New York: MacMillan, 1957.

Garland, L. H. Studies of the accuracy of diagnostic procedures. *American Journal of Roentgenology, Radium Therapy, and Nuclear Medicine,* 1959, **82**, 25-38.

Garland, L. H. The problem of observer error. *Bulletin of the New York Academy of Medicine,* 1960, **36**, 569-584.

Gaudet, F. J., & Kulick. W. Who comes to a vocational guidance center? *Personnel and Guidance Journal,* 1954, **33**, 211-214.

Gauron, E. F., & Dickinson, J. K. Diagnostic decision making in psychiatry. II. Diagnostic styles. *Archives of General Psychiatry,* 1966, **14**, 233-237.

Gee, H. H. A comparison of empirical and homogeneous keys in interest measurement. Unpublished doctoral dissertation, University of Minnesota, 1955.

Getzels, J. W., & Jackson, P. W. Occupational choice and cognitive functioning. *Journal of Abnormal and Social Psychology,* 1960, **61**, 119-123.

Ghiselli, E. E. Differentiation of individuals in terms of their predictability. *Journal of Applied Psychology,* 1956, **40**, 374-377.

Ghiselli, E. E. Differentiation of tests in terms of the accuracy with which they predict for a given individual. *Educational and Psychological Measurement,* 1960, **20**, 675-684. (a)

Ghiselli, E. E. The prediction of predictability. *Educational and Psychological Measurement,* 1960, **20**, 3-8. (b)

Ghiselli, E. E. *Theory of psychological measurement.* New York: McGraw-Hill, 1964.

Ghiselli, E. E. *The validity of occupational aptitude tests.* New York: Wiley, 1966.

Ghiselli, E. E., & Haire, M. The validation of selection tests in the light of the dynamic character of criteria. *Personnel Psychology,* 1960, **13,** 225-231.

Gibson, J. J. Theories of perception. In W. Dennis (Ed.), *Current trends in psychological theory.* Pittsburgh: University of Pittsburgh Press, 1951.

Giedt, F. H. Comparison of visual, content, and auditory cues in interviewing. *Journal of Consulting Psychology,* 1955, **19,** 407-416.

Gilberstadt, H. *Comprehensive MMPI codebook for males.* Minneapolis: Veterans Administration Hospital, 1970.

Gilberstadt, H., & Duker, J. *A handbook for clinical and actuarial MMPI interpretation.* Philadelphia: Saunders, 1965.

Gilbert, J., & Hall, M. R. Changes with age in human figure drawing. *Journal of Gerontology,* 1962, **17,** 397-404.

Gill, M., Newman, R., & Redlich, F. C. *The initial interview in psychiatric practice.* New York: International Universities Press, 1954.

Gisvold, D. A validity study of the autonomy and deference subscales of the Edwards Personal Preference Schedule. *Journal of Consulting Psychology,* 1958, **22,** 445-447.

Glaser, D. A reconsideration of some parole prediction factors. *American Sociological Review,* 1954, **19,** 335-341.

Glaser, D., & Hangren, R. F. Predicting the adjustment of federal probationers. *National Probation and Parole Association Journal,* 1958, **4,** 258-267.

Glaser, R., & Schwarz, P. A., & Flanagan, J. C. The contribution of interview and situational performance procedures to the selection of supervisory personnel. *Journal of Applied Psychology,* 1958, **42,** 60-73.

Glatter, A. M., & Hauch, P. Sexual symbolism in line qualities. *Journal of Psychology,* 1958, **14,** 168-169.

Glueck, B. C., Jr., & Reznikoff, M. Comparison of computer derived personality profile and projective psychological test findings. *American Journal of Psychiatry,* 1965, **121,** 1156-1161.

Goffman, E. *The presentation of self in everyday life.* University of Edinburgh: Social Science Research Center, Monograph No. 2, 1956.

Goldberg, L. R. The effectiveness of clinicians' judgments: The diagnosis of organic brain damage from the Bender-Gestalt test. *Journal of Consulting Psychology,* 1959, **23,** 25-33.

Goldberg, L. R. A model of item ambiguity in personality assessment. *Educational and Psychological Measurement,* 1963, **23,** 467-492. (a)

Goldberg, L. R. Test-retest item statistics for the Oregon Instructional Preference Inventory. *Oregon Research Institute Monograph,* 1963, **3** (Whole No. 4). (b)

Goldberg, L. R. Diagnosticians vs. diagnostic signs: The diagnosis of psychosis vs. neurosis from the MMPI. *Psychological Monographs,* 1965, **79** (9, Whole No. 602).

Goldberg, L. R. Reliability of Peace Corps selection boards: A study of interjudge agreement before and after board discussions. *Journal of Applied Psychology,* 1966, **50**, 400-408.

Goldberg, L. R., & Rorer, L. G. Learning clinical inference: The results of intensive training on clinicians' ability to diagnose psychosis versus neurosis from the MMPI. Paper presented at the meeting of the Western Psychological Association, Honolulu, June, 1965.

Goldberg, L. R., & Rorer, L. G. The use of two different response modes and repeated testings to predict social conformity. *Journal of Personality and Social Psychology,* 1966, **3**, 28-37.

Goldberg, L. R., & Werts, C. E. The reliability of clinicians' judgments: A multitrait-multimethod approach. *Journal of Consulting Psychology,* 1966, **30**, 199-206.

Golde, P., & Kogan, N. A sentence completion procedure for assessing attitudes toward old people. *Journal of Gerontology,* 1959, **14**, 355-360.

Golden, M. Some effects of combining psychological tests on clinical inferences. *Journal of Consulting Psychology,* 1964, **28**, 440-446.

Goldstein, A. P., & Rawn, M. L. The validity of interpretative signs of aggression in the human figure. *Journal of Clinical Psychology,* 1957, **13**, 169-171.

Goodenough, F. *Mental testing: Its history, principles, and applications.* New York: Holt, Rinehart & Winston, 1949.

Goodstein, L. D., & Heilbrun, A. B. The relationship between personal and social desirability values of the Edwards Personal Preference Schedule. *Journal of Consulting Psychology,* 1959, **23**, 183.

Gordon, L. V. Clinical, psychometric, and work sample approaches in the prediction of success in Peace Corps training. *Journal of Applied Psychology,* 1967, **51**, 111-119.

Gottschalk, L. A., & Auerbach, A. H. (Eds.), *Methods of research in psychotherapy.* New York: Appleton-Century-Crofts, 1966.

Gough, H. G. Simulated patterns on the Minnesota Multiphasic Personality Inventory. *Journal of Abnormal and Social Psychology,* 1947, **42**, 215-225.

Gough, H. G. The F minus K dissimulation index for the MMPI. *Journal of Consulting Psychology,* 1950, **14**, 408-413.

Gough, H. G. On making a good impression. *Journal of Educational Research,* 1952, **46**, 33-42.

Gough, H. G. The construction of a personality scale to predict scholastic achievement. *Journal of Applied Psychology,* 1953, **37**, 361-366.

Gough, H. G. Some common misconceptions about neuroticism. *Journal of Consulting Psychology,* 1954, **18**, 287-292.

Gough, H. G. *Manual for the California Psychological Inventory.* Palo Alto: Consulting Psychologists Press, 1957.

Gough, H. G. Clinical vs. statistical prediction in psychology. In L. Postman (Ed.), *Psychology in the making.* New York: Knopf, 1962.

Gough, H. G. Academic achievement in high school as predicted from the California Psychological Inventory, *Journal of Educational Psychology,* 1964, **55**, 174-180.

Gough, H. G., & Fink, M. B. Scholastic achievement among students of average ability, as predicted from the California Psychological Inventory. *Psychology in the Schools,* 1964, **1**, 375-380.

Gough, H. G., & Hall, W. B. Prediction of performance in medical school from the California Psychological Inventory. *Journal of Applied Psychology,* 1964, **48**, 218-226.

Gough, H. G., & Heilbrun, A. B. *Joint manual for the Adjective Check List and the ACL Need Scales.* Palo Alto, Calif.: Consulting Psychologists Press, 1965.

Grams, A., & Rinder, L. Signs of homosexuality in human figure drawings. *Journal of Consulting Psychology,* 1958, **22**, 394.

Granick, S. Comparative performance of normal and psychoneurotic children on the Draw-A-Person test. *Journal of Germantown Hospital,* 1963, **4**, 17-22.

Grant, M., Ives, V., & Ranzoni, J. Reliability and validity of judges' ratings of adjustment on the Rorschach. *Psychological Monographs,* 1952, **66** (2, Whole No. 334).

Graumann, C. F. Eigenschaften als Persönlichkeits-Forschung. In P. Lersch & H. Thomae (Eds.), *Persönlichkeitsforschung und Persönlichkeitstheorie.* Gottingen: Hogrefe, 1960.

Gravitz, M. A. Normal adult differentiation patterns on the figure drawing test. *Journal of Projective Techniques,* 1966, **30**, 471-473.

Gray, D. M., & Pepitone, A. Effect of self-esteem on drawings of the human figure. *Journal of Consulting Psychology,* 1964, **28**, 452-455.

Grayson, H. M. *A psychological admissions testing program and manual.* Los Angeles: Veterans Administrative Center, Neuropsychiatric Hospital, 1951.

Grayson, H. M., & Olinger, L. B. Simulation of "normalcy" by psychiatric patients on the MMPI. *Journal of Consulting Psychology,* 1957, **21**, 73-77.

Grebstein, L. Relative accuracy of actuarial prediction, experienced clinicians, and graduate students in a clinical judgment test. *Journal of Consulting Psychology,* 1963, **37**, 127-132.

Greening, T., & Bugental, J. F. T. Psychologists in clinics. In W. B. Webb (Ed.), *The profession of psychology.* New York: Holt, 1962.

Gregory, E. Evaluation of selection procedures for women naval officers. *USN Bureau of Naval Personnel Technical Bulletin,* 1956, No. 56-11.

Griffin, M. L., & Flaharty, M. R. Correlation of CPI traits with academic achievement. *Educational and Psychological Measurement,* 1964, **24**, 369-372.

Griffith, A. V., & Peyman, P. A. R. Eye-ear emphasis in the DAP as indicating ideas of reference. *Journal of Consulting Psychology,* 1959, **23,** 560.

Grigg, A. E. Experience of clinicians, and speech characteristics and statements of clients as variables in clinical judgment. *Journal of Consulting Psychology,* 1958, **22,** 315-319.

Grigg, A. E., & Kelley, H. P. A scale for self-description. *Journal of Clinical Psychology,* 1960, **16,** 153-158.

Gross, M. L. *The brainwatchers.* New York: Random House, 1962.

Grosz, H. J., & Grossman, K. G. The sources of observer variation and bias in clinical judgment: I. The item of psychiatric history. *Journal of Nervous and Mental Disease,* 1964, **138,** 105-113.

Guertin, W. H. An analysis of gross errors on a sentence completion test. *Journal of Clinical Psychology,* 1959, **15,** 414-416.

Guilford, J. P. *Psychometric methods.* New York: McGraw-Hill, 1954.

Guinan, J. F., & Hurley, J. R. An investigation of the reliability of human figure drawings. *Journal of Projective Techniques,* 1965, **29,** 300-304.

Guion, R. M. Synthetic validity in a small company: A demonstration. *Personnel Psychology,* 1965, **18,** 49-65.

Gunderson, E. K. E. Determinants of reliability in personality ratings. *Journal of Clinical Psychology,* 1965, **21,** 164-169. (a)

Gunderson, E. K. E. The reliability of personality ratings under varied assessment conditions. *Journal of Clinical Psychology,* 1965, **21,** 161-164. (b)

Gunderson, E. K., & Lehner, G. F. J. Reliability in a projective test (the Draw-A-Person). *American Psychologist,* 1949, **4,** 387.

Guze, S. B., Matarazzo, J. D., & Saslow, G. Formulation of principles of comprehensive medicine with special reference to learning theory. *Journal of Clinical Psychology,* 1953, **9,** 127-136.

Haagen, C. H. Synonymity, vividness, familiarity, and association value ratings of 400 pairs of common adjectives. *Journal of Psychology,* 1949, **27,** 453-463.

Hadley, J. M., & Kennedy, V. E. A comparison between performance on a sentence completion test and academic success. *Educational and Psychological Measurement,* 1949, **9,** 649-670.

Hafner, A. J., & Kaplan, A. M. Hostility content analysis of the Rorschach and TAT. *Journal of Projective Techniques and Personality Assessment,* 1960, **24,** 137-143.

Haggard, E. A., Hiken, J. R., & Isaacs, K. S. Some effects of recording and filming on the psychotherapeutic process. *Psychiatry,* 1965, **28,** 169-191.

Haire, M., & Grunes, W. F. Perceptual defenses; processes protecting an organized perception of another personality. *Human Relations,* 1950, **3,** 403-412.

Halbower, C. C. A comparison of actuarial versus clinical prediction to classes discriminated by the Minnesota Multiphasic Personality Inventory. Unpublished doctoral dissertation, University of Minnesota, 1955.

Hall, C. S., & Lindzey, G. *Theories of personality.* New York: Wiley, 1957.

Hallowell, A. I. The Rorschach technique in personality and culture studies. In B. Klopfer, *et al.*, (Eds.), *Developments in the Rorschach technique.* Vol. II. *Fields of application.* Yonkers-on-Hudson, N. Y.: World Book Co., 1956.

Hamilton, M. *Clinicians and decisions.* Leeds: Leeds University Press, 1966.

Hamilton, V. Techniques and methods in psychological assessment. *Bulletin of the British Psychological Society,* 1964, **17**, 27-36.

Hamlin, R. Predictability of institutional adjustment of reformatory inmates. *Journal of Juvenile Research,* 1934, **18**, 179-184.

Hammer, E. F. *The clinical application of projective drawings.* Springfield, Ill.: Charles C Thomas, 1958.

Hammer, M., & Kaplan, A. M. The reliability of profile and front-facing directions in children's drawings. *Child Development,* 1964, **35**, 973-977. (a)

Hammer, M., & Kaplan, A. M. The reliability of sex of first drawn figure by children. *Journal of Clinical Psychology,* 1964, **20**, 251-252. (b)

Hammer, M., & Kaplan, A. M. The reliability of size of children's drawings. *Journal of Clinical Psychology, 1964,* **20**, 121-122. (c)

Hammer, M., & Kaplan, A. M. The reliability of children's human figure drawings. *Journal of Clinical Psychology,* 1966, **22**, 316-319.

Hammond, K. R., Hursch, C. J., & Todd, F. J. Analyzing the components of clinical inference. *Psychological Review,* 1964, **71**, 438-456.

Hammond, K. R., & Summers, D. A. Cognitive dependence on linear and nonlinear cues. *Psychological Review,* 1965, **72**, 215-224.

Handler, L., & Reyher, J. The effects of stress on the Draw-A-Person Test. *Journal of Consulting Psychology,* 1964, **28**, 259-264.

Handler, L., & Reyher, J. Figure drawing anxiety indices: A review of the literature. *Journal of Projective Techniques,* 1965, **29**, 305-313.

Handler, L., & Reyher, J. Relationship between GSR and anxiety indexes in projective drawings. *Journal of Consulting Psychology,* 1966, **30**, 60-67.

Hanfmann, E. Projective techniques in the assessment program of the Office of Strategic Services. In *Exploring individual differences.* Washington, D. C.: American Council on Education, 1947.

Hanfmann, E., & Getzels, J. W. Studies of the sentence completion test. *Journal of Projective Techniques,* 1953, **17**, 280-294.

Hanley, C. Social desirability and responses to items from three MMPI scales: D, Sc, and K. *Journal of Applied Psychology,* 1956, **40**, 324-328.

Hanley, C. Deriving a measure of test-taking defensiveness. *Journal of Consulting Psychology,* 1957, **21**, 391-397.

Hardt, R. H., & Feinhandler, S. J. Social class and mental hospital prognosis. *American Sociological Review,* 1959, **29**, 815-821.

Hardy, V. T. Relations of dominance to non-directiveness in counseling. *Journal of Clinical Psychology,* 1948, **4**, 300-303.

Harlow, R. G. Masculine inadequacy and compensatory development of physique. *Journal of Personality,* 1951, **19**, 312-323.

Harper, F. B. W. The California Psychological Inventory as a predictor of yielding behavior in women. *Journal of Psychology,* 1964, **58**, 187-190.

Harris, D. B., & Tseng, S. C. Children's attitudes toward peers and parents as revealed by sentence completions. *Child Development,* 1957, **28**, 401-411.

Harris, H. *The group approach to leadership testing.* London: Kegan Paul, 1959.

Harris, J. G. Validity: The search for a constant in a universe of variables. In M. A. Rickers-Ovsiankina (Ed.), *Rorschach psychology.* New York: Wiley, 1960.

Harris, J. G. Judgmental versus mathematical prediction: An investigation by analogy of the clinical versus statistical controversy. *Behavioral Science,* 1963, **8**, 324-335.

Harris, J. L. Deviant response frequency in relation to severity of schizophrenic reaction. Unpublished master's thesis, Louisiana State University, 1958.

Harrower, M. Differential diagnosis. In B. B. Wolman (Ed.), *Handbook of clinical psychology.* New York: McGraw-Hill, 1965.

Hartshorne, H., May, M. A., & Shuttleworth, F. K. *Nature of character. III. Studies in the organization of character.* New York: Macmillan, 1930.

Harvey, O. J., Hunt, D. E., & Schroder, H. M. *Conceptual systems and personality organization.* New York: Wiley, 1961.

Hase, H. D. The predictive validity of different methods of deriving personality inventory scales. Unpublished doctoral dissertation, University of Oregon, 1965.

Hase, H. D., & Goldberg, L. R. The comparative validity of different strategies of deriving personality inventory scales. *Psychological Bulletin,* 1967, **67**, 231-248.

Hastorf, A. H., & Piper, G. W. A note on the effect of explicit instructions on prestige suggestions. *Journal of Social Psychology,* 1951, **33**, 289-293.

Hathaway, S. R. Foreword. In W. G. Dahlstrom & G. S. Welsh, *An MMPI handbook: A guide to use in clinical practice and research.* Minneapolis: University of Minnesota Press, 1960.

Hathaway, S. R. MMPI: Professional use by professional people. *American Psychologist,* 1964, **19**, 204-210.

Hathaway, S. R. Introduction. In R. D. Fowler, *The MMPI notebook: A guide to the clinical use of the automated MMPI.* Nutley, N. J.: Roche Psychiatric Service Institute, 1967.

Hathaway, S. R., & Briggs, P. F. Some normative data on new MMPI scales. *Journal of Clinical Psychology,* 1957, **13**, 364-368.

Hathaway, S. R., & McKinley, J. C. A multiphasic personality schedule (Minnesota): I. Construction of the schedule. *Journal of Psychology,* 1940, **10**, 249-254.

Hathaway, S. R., & McKinley, J. C. *The Minnesota Multiphasic Personality Inventory manual* (Rev.). New York: Psychological Corporation, 1951.

Hathaway, S. R., & McKinley, J. C. Scales 5 (masculinity-femininity), 6 (paranoia), and 8 (schizophrenia). In G. S. Welsh & W. G. Dahlstrom (Eds.), *Basic readings on the MMPI in psychology and medicine.* Minneapolis: University of Minnesota Press, 1956.

Hathaway, S. R., & Meehl, P. E. The Minnesota Multiphasic Personality Inventory. *U. S. Departments of Army and Air Force, Military Clinical Psychological Report,* 1951, TM 8-242, AFM 160-45.

Hawkins, W. A. Deviant responses, response variability, and paired associate learning. Unpublished doctoral dissertation, Louisiana State University, 1960.

Haworth, M., & Normington, C. A sexual differentiation scale for the D-A-P Test. *Journal of Projective Techniques,* 1961, **25**, 441-450.

Hays, W. L. *Statistics for psychologists.* New York: Holt, Rinehart & Winston, 1963.

Hearnshaw, L. S. Presidential address. *Bulletin of British Psychological Society,* 1956, **1**, No. 36.

Hebb, D. O. Emotion in man and animal: An analysis of the intuitive processes of recognition. *Psychological Review,* 1946, **53**, 88-106.

Heider, F. *The psychology of interpersonal relationships.* New York: Wiley, 1958.

Heider, F., & Simmel, M. An experimental study of apparent behavior. *American Journal of Psychology,* 1944, **57**, 243-259.

Heilbrun, A. B. Personality differences between adjusted and maladjusted college students. *Journal of Applied Psychology,* 1960, **44**, 341-346.

Heilbrun, A. B. The psychological significance of the MMPI K scale in a normal population. *Journal of Consulting Psychology,* 1961, **25**, 486-491.

Heilbrun, A. B. A comparison of empirical derivation and rational derivation of an affiliation scale. *Journal of Clinical Psychology,* 1962, **18**, 101-102. (a)

Heilbrun, A. B. Social desirability and the relative validities of achievement scales. *Journal of Consulting Psychology,* 1962, **26**, 383-386. (b)

Heilbrun, A. B. Revision of the MMPI K correction procedure for improved detection of maladjustment in a normal population. *Journal of Consulting Psychology,* 1963, **27**, 161-165.

Heilbrun, A. B., & Goodstein, L. D. Social desirability response set: Error or predictor variable? *Journal of Psychology,* 1961, **51**, 321-329.

Heineman, C. E. A forced-choice form of the Taylor anxiety scale. Unpublished doctoral dissertation, University of Iowa, 1952.

Helmstadter, G. C. *Principles of psychological measurement.* New York: Appleton-Century-Crofts, 1964.

Henry, E., & Rotter, J. Situational influences on Rorschach responses. *Journal of Consulting Psychology,* 1956, **20**, 457-462.

Hesterly, S. O. Deviant response patterns as a function of chronological age. Unpublished doctoral dissertation, Louisiana State University, 1960.

Hesterly, S. O., & Berg, I. A. Deviant responses as indicators of immaturity and schizophrenia. *Journal of Consulting Psychology,* 1958, **22**, 389-393.

Hiler, E. W. The sentence completion test as a predictor of continuation in psychotherapy. *Journal of Consulting Psychology,* 1959, **23**, 544-549.

Hiler, E. W., & Nesvig, D. An evaluation of criteria used by clinicians to infer pathology from figure drawings. *Journal of Consulting Psychology,* 1965, **29**, 520-529.

Hilgard, E. R. *Hypnotic susceptibility.* New York: Harcourt, 1965.

Hills, J. R. Prediction of college grades for all public colleges in a state. *Journal of Educational Measurement,* 1964, **2**, 155-160.

Himmelstein, P., Eschenbach, A., & Carp. A. Interrelationships among three measures of need achievement. *Journal of Consulting Psychology,* 1958, **22**, 451-452.

Hitch, C. Sub-optimization in operations research problems. *Journal of the Operations Research Society of America,* 1953, **1**, 87-99.

Hoch, E. L., Ross, A. O., & Winder, C. L. Conference on the professional preparation of clinical psychologists: A summary. *American Psychologist,* 1966, **21**, 42-51.

Hoffman, B. *The tyranny of testing.* New York: Crowell-Collier, 1962.

Hoffman, P. J. Criteria of human judgment ability: I. The "clinical" assessment of intelligence and personality. *American Psychologist,* 1958, **13**, 388. (Abstract) (a)

Hoffman, P. J. Human judgment as a decision process. *American Psychologist,* 1958, **13**, 368. (Abstract) (b)

Hoffman, P. J. The prediction of clinical prediction. *American Psychologist,* 1959, **14**, 356. (Abstract)

Hoffman, P. J. The paramorphic representation of clinical judgment. *Psychological Bulletin,* 1960, **57**, 116-131.

Hoffman, P. J. Non-shrinkable, wrinkle-resistant configural prediction. Paper presented at the meeting of the American Psychological Association, Washington, D. C., September, 1967.

Hoffman, P. J. Cue-consistency and configurality in human judgment. In B. Kleinmuntz (Ed.), *Formal representation of human judgment.* New York: Wiley, 1968.

Hoffman, P. J., Slovic, P., & Rorer, L. G. An analysis of variance model for the assessment of configural cue utilization in clinical judgment. *Psychological Bulletin,* 1968, **69**, 338-349.

Holland, J. L. The prediction of college grades from the California Psychological Inventory and the Scholastic Aptitude Test. *Journal of Educational Psychology,* 1959, **50**, 135-142.

Holsopple, J. Q., & Miale, F. R. *Sentence completion: A projective method for the study of personality.* Springfield, Ill.: Charles C Thomas, 1954.

Holt, R. R. Clinical and statistical prediction: A reformulation and some new data. *Journal of Abnormal and Social Psychology,* 1958, **56**, 1-12.

Holt, R. R. Diagnostic testing: Present status and future prospects. *Journal of Nervous and Mental Disease,* 1967, **144**, 444-465.

Holt, R. R., & Luborsky, L. *Personality patterns of psychiatrists.* Vol. 1. *A study of methods for selecting residents.* New York: Basic Books, 1958. (a)

Holt, R. R., & Luborsky, L. *Personality patterns of psychiatrists.* Vol. 2. *Supplementary and supporting data.* Topeka: Menninger Foundation, 1958. (b)

Holt, W. L., Jr., & Holt, W. M. Long-term prognosis in mental illness: A thirty-year follow-up of 141 mental patients. *American Journal of Psychiatry,* 1952, **108**, 735-739.

Holtzman, W. H., Brown, W. F., & Farquhar, W. G. The survey of study habits and attitudes: A new instrument for the prediction of academic success. *Educational and Psychological Measurement,* 1954, **14**, 726-732.

Holtzman, W. H., & Sells, S. B. Prediction of flying success by clinical analysis of test protocols. *Journal of Abnormal and Social Psychology,* 1954, **49**, 485-490.

Holzberg, J. D., & Wexler, M. The validity of human form drawings as a measure of personality deviation. *Journal of Projective Techniques,* 1950, **14**, 343-361.

Holzberg, J., Teichner, A., & Taylor, J. L. Contributions of clinical psychology to military neuropsychiatry in an army psychiatric hospital. *Journal of Clinical Psychology,* 1947, **3**, 84-95.

Homans, G. C. *Social behavior: Its elementary forms.* New York: Harcourt, 1961.

Hooker, E. Male homosexuality in the Rorschach. *Journal of Projective Techniques,* 1958, **22**, 33-54.

Horowitz, M. F. A study of clinicians' judgments from projective test protocols. *Journal of Consulting Psychology,* 1962, **26**, 251-256.

Horowitz, R., & Murphy, L. B. Projective methods in the psychological study of children. *Journal of Experimental Education,* 1938, **7**, 133-140.

Horst, P., *et al. The prediction of personal adjustment.* New York: Social Science Research Council, 1941. (Bulletin 48)

Horst, P. Pattern analysis and configural scoring. *Journal of Clinical Psychology,* 1954, **10**, 3-11.

Horst, P. *Factor analysis of data matrices.* New York: Holt, Rinehart & Winston, 1965.

House, C. W. Response bias as a measure of emotional disturbance in children. Unpublished doctoral dissertation, Louisiana State University, 1960.

Hovey, H. B., & Stauffacher, J. C. Intuitive versus objective prediction from a test. *Journal of Clinical Psychology,* 1953, **9**, 349-351.

Howard, K. I. The convergent and discriminant validation of ipsative ratings from three projective instruments. *Journal of Clinical Psychology,* 1962, **18**, 183-188.

Howard, K. I. Ratings of projective test protocols as a function of degree of inference. *Educational and Psychological Measurement,* 1963, **23**, 267-275.

Howard, R. C., & Berkowitz, L. Reactions to the evaluators of one's performance. *Journal of Personality,* 1958, **26**, 494-507.

Hoyt, D. P., & Norman, W. T. Adjustment and academic predictability. *Journal of Counseling Psychology,* 1954, **1**, 96-99.

Hoyt, T. E., & Baron, M. R. Anxiety indices in same sex drawings of psychiatric patients with high and low MAS scores. *Journal of Consulting Psychology,* 1958, **23**, 448-452.

Huff, F. W. Use of actuarial description of personality in a mental hospital. *Psychological Reports,* 1965, **17**, 224.

Hull, C. L. *Aptitude testing.* New York: Harcourt, Brace & World, 1928.

Humm, D. G., Storment, R. C., & Iorns, M. E. Combination scores for the Humm-Wadsworth temperament scale: With consideration of the effects of subject's response bias. *Journal of Psychology,* 1939, **7**, 227-253.

Hunt, H. F. The effect of deliberate deception on MMPI performance. *Journal of Consulting Psychology,* 1948, **12**, 396-402.

Hunt, H. F. Clinical methods: Psychodiagnostics. *Annual Review of Psychology,* 1950, **1**, 207-220.

Hunt, R. G., & Feldman, M. J. Body image and ratings of adjustment on human figure drawings. *Journal of Clinical Psychology,* 1960, **16**, 35-38.

Hunt, W. A., & Jones, N. F. Clinical judgment of some aspects of schizophrenic thinking. *Journal of Clinical Psychology,* 1958, **14**, 235-239. (a)

Hunt, W. A., & Jones, N. F. The reliability of clinical judgments of asocial tendency. *Journal of Clinical Psychology,* 1958, **14**, 233-235. (b)

Hunt, W. A., Jones, N. F., & Hunt, E. B. Reliability of clinical judgment as a function of clinical experience. *Journal of Clinical Psychology,* 1957, **13**, 377-378.

Hunt, W. A., & Walker, R. E. Validity of diagnostic judgments as a function of amount of test information. *Journal of Clinical Psychology,* 1966, **22**, 154-155.

Hunt, W. A., Walker, R. E., & Jones, N. F. The validity of clinical ratings for estimating severity of schizophrenia. *Journal of Clinical Psychology,* 1960, **16**, 391-393.

Huntley, C. W. Judgments of self based upon records of expressive behavior. *Journal of Abnormal and Social Psychology,* 1940, **35**, 398-427.

Husen, T. La validite des interviews par rapport a l'age au sexe a la formation des interviewers. *Travail Humain,* 1954, **17**, 60-67.

Hutt, M. L. The use of projective methods of personality measurement in army medical installations. *Journal of Clinical Psychology,* 1945, **1**, 134-140.

Hutt, M. L., Gibby, R., Milton, E. O., & Pottharst, K. The effect of varied experimental "sets" upon Rorschach test performance. *Journal of Projective Techniques,* 1950, **14**, 181-187.

Ichheiser, G. Misunderstandings in human relations. *American Journal of Sociology,* 1949, **55**, No. 2, Pt. ii.

Ittelson, W. H., & Slack, C. W. The perception of persons as visual objects. In R. Tagiuri & L. Petrullo (Eds.), *Person perception and interpersonal behavior.* Stanford, Calif.: Stanford University Press, 1958.

Iwawaki, S., & Cowen, E. L. The social desirability of trait-descriptive terms: Applications to a Japanese sample. *Journal of Social Psychology,* 1964, **63**, 199-205.

Izard, C. E., Rosenberg, N., Bair, J. T., & Maag, C. Construction and validation of a multiple-choice sentence completion test: an interim report. *U. S. Naval School of Aviation Medical Research Report,* 1953.

Jackson, D. D. A. *Etiology of schizophrenia.* New York: Basic Books, 1960.

Jackson, D. N. Stylistic response determinants in the California Psychological Inventory. *Educational and Psychological Measurement,* 1960, **20**, 339-346.

Jackson, D. N. Desirability judgments as a method of personality assessment. *Educational and Psychological Measurement,* 1964, **24**, 223-238.

Jackson, D. N., & Messick, S. Content and style in personality assessment. *Psychological Bulletin,* 1958, **55**, 243-252.

Jackson, D. N., & Messick, S. Acquiescence and desirability as response determinants in the MMPI. *Educational and Psychological Measurement,* 1961, **21**, 771-790.

Jackson, D. N., & Messick, S. Response style on the MMPI: Comparison of clinical and normal samples. *Journal of Abnormal and Social Psychology,* 1962, **65**, 285-299.

Jackson, D. N., & Pacine, L. Response styles and academic achievement. *Educational and Psychological Measurement,* 1961, **21**, 1015-1028.

Jahoda, M. Toward a social psychology of mental health. In A. M. Rose (Ed.), *Mental health and mental disorder.* New York: Norton, 1955.

James, W. *Memories and studies.* New York: Longmans, Green, 1912.

James, W. *Psychology: The briefer course.* G. W. Allport (Ed.) New York: Harper Torchbooks, 1961.

James, W. H., & Rotter, J. B. Partial and 100% reinforcement under chance and skill conditions. *Journal of Experimental Psychology,* 1958, **55**, 397-403.

Jenkin, N. Affective processes in perception. *Psychological Bulletin,* 1957, **54**, 100-127.

Jenkins, R. L. Quantitative aspects of sentence completion in the study of the improvement of schizophrenic patients. *Journal of Projective Techniques,* 1961, **25**, 303-311.

Jenkins, R. L., & Blodgett, E. Prediction of success or failure of delinquent boys from sentence completion. *American Journal of Orthopsychiatry,* 1960, **30**, 741-756.

Jensen, A. R. The Rorschach technique: A re-evaluation. *Acta Psychologica,* 1964, **22**, 60-77.

Jessor, R., & Hammond, K. R. Construct validity and the Taylor anxiety scale. *Psychological Bulletin,* 1957, **54**, 161-170.

Jessor, R. N., & Hess, H. F. Levels of aspiration behavior and general adjustment: An appraisal of some negative findings. *Psychological Reports,* 1958, **4**, 335-339.

Johnson, A. G., & Wawaszek, F. Psychologists' judgments of physical handicap from H-T-P drawings. *Journal of Consulting Psychology,* 1961, **25**, 284-287.

Johnston, R., & McNeal, B. F. Statistical versus clinical prediction: Length of neuropsychiatric hospital stay. *Journal of Abnormal Psychology,* 1967, **72**, 335-340.

Jones, E. E., & Thibaut, J. W. In R. Tagiuri & L. Petrullo (Eds.), *Person perception and interpersonal behavior.* Stanford, Calif: Stanford University Press, 1958.

Jones, H. G. The application of conditioning and learning techniques to the treatment of a psychiatric patient. *Journal of Abnormal and Social Psychology,* 1956, **52**, 414-419.

Jones, H. G. Applied abnormal psychology: The experimental approach. In H. J. Eysenck (Ed.), *Handbook of abnormal psychology.* London: Pitman Medical, 1960.

Jones, N. F., Jr. The validity of clinical judgments of schizophrenic pathology based on verbal responses to intelligence test items. *Journal of Clinical Psychology,* 1959, **15**, 396-400.

Judson, A. J., & MacCasland, B. W. A. A note on the influence of the season on tree drawings. *Journal of Clinical Psychology,* 1960, **16**, 171-173.

Kahn, M. W. Psychological test study of a mass murderer. *Journal of Projective Techniques,* 1960, **24**, 148-160.

Kahn, M. W., & Jones, N. F. Human figure drawings as predictors of admission to a psychiatric hospital. *Journal of Projective Techniques,* 1965, **29**, 319-322.

Kahn, R. L., & Cannell, C. F. *The dynamics of interviewing.* New York: Wiley, 1957.

Kahneman, D., & Ghiselli, E. E. Validity and non-linear heteroscedastic models. *Personnel Psychology,* 1962, **15**, 1-11.

Kamano, D. K. An investigation of the meaning of human figure drawings. *Journal of Clinical Psychology,* 1960, **16**, 429-430.

Kanfer, F. H. Comments on learning in psychotherapy. *Psychological Reports,* 1961, **9**, 681-699.

Kanfer, F. H., & Saslow, G. Behavioral analysis. *Archieves of General Psychiatry,* 1965, **12**, 529-539.

Kanfer, F. H., & Saslow, G. Behavioral diagnosis. In C. Franks (Ed.), *Assessment and status of the behavioral therapies and associated developments.* New York: McGraw-Hill, 1969.

Karen, R. L. A method for rating sentence completion test responses. *Journal of Projective Techniques,* 1961, **25**, 312-314.

Kassebaum, G. G., Couch, A. S., & Slater, P. E. The factorial dimensions of the MMPI. *Journal of Consulting Psychology,* 1959, **23**, 226-236.

Katz, M. M., Cole, J. O., & Lowery, M. A. Non-specificity of diagnosis of paranoid schizophrenia. *Archives of General Psychiatry,* 1964, **11**, 197-202.

Kelley, H. H. The warm-cold variable in first impressions of persons. *Journal of Personality,* 1950, **18**, 431-439.

Kelley, T. L. Individual testing with completion test exercises. *Teachers College Record,* 1917, **18**, 371-382.

Kelley, T. L. *Interpretation of educational measurements.* New York: World Book Co., 1927.

Kelly, E. L. Theory and techniques of assessment. *Annual Review of Psychology,* 1954, **5**, 281-310.

Kelly, E. L. Multiple criteria of medical education and their implications for selection. In *The Appraisal of Applicants to Medical Schools.* Rep. of Fourth Teaching Institute. Evanston: Association of American Medical Colleges, 1957.

Kelly, E. L., & Fiske, D. W. The prediction of success in the V. A. training program in clinical psychology. *American Psychologist,* 1950, **5**, 395-406.

Kelly, E. L., & Fiske, D. W. *The prediction of performance in clinical psychology.* Ann Arbor: University of Michigan Press, 1951.

Kelly, E. L., Miles, C., & Terman, L. M. Ability to influence one's score on a typical pencil-and-paper test of personality. *Character & Personality,* 1935, **4**, 206-215.

Kelly, G. A. *The psychology of personal constructs.* New York: Norton, 1955.

Kelly, H. H., & Thibaut, J. W. Experimental studies of group problem-solving and process. In G. Lindzey (Ed.), *Handbook of Social Psychology.* Vol. 2. Cambridge, Mass.: Addison-Wesley, 1954.

Kenny, D. T. The influence of social desirability on discrepancy measures between real self and ideal self. *Journal of Consulting Psychology,* 1956, **20**, 315-318.

Kidd, A., & Cherymisin, D. Figure reversal as related to specific personality variables. *Perceptual and Motor Skills,* 1965, **20**, 1175-1176.

Kilpatrick, F. P., & Cantril, H. Self-anchoring scale: A measure of the individual's unique reality world. *Journal of Individual Psychology,* 1960, **16**, 158-170.

Kimball, B. The sentence-completion technique in a study of scholastic underachievement. *Journal of Consulting Psychology,* 1952, **16,** 353-358.

Kimber, J. A. M. The insight of college students into the items on a personality test. *Educational and Psychological Measurement,* 1947, **7,** 411-420.

King, F. W. A normative note on sentence completion cross-sex identification responses. *Journal of Consulting Psychology,* 1958, **22,** 63-64.

Kirk, B. A. Evaluation of in-service counselor training. *Educational and Psychological Measurement,* 1956, **16,** 527-535.

Kjenaas, N. K., & Brozek, J. Personality in experimental semistarvation. *Psychosomatic Medicine,* 1952, **14,** 115-128.

Kleinmuntz, B. MMPI decision rules for the identification of college maladjustment: A digital computer approach. *Psychological Monographs,* 1963, **77** (14, Whole No. 577). (a)

Kleinmuntz, B. Personality test interpretation by digital computer. *Science,* 1963, **139,** 416-418. (b)

Kleinmuntz, B. Profile analysis revisited: A heuristic approach. *Journal of Counseling Psychology,* 1963, **10,** 315-324. (c)

Klett, C. J. The social desirability stereotype in a hospital population. *Journal of Consulting Psychology,* 1957, **21,** 419-421. (a)

Klett, C. J. The stability of the social desirability scale values in the Edwards Personal Preference Schedule. *Journal of Consulting Psychology,* 1957, **21,** 183-185. (b)

Klett, C. J., & Yaukey, D. W. A cross-cultural comparison of judgments of social desirability. *Journal of Social Psychology,* 1959, **49,** 19-26.

Klett, W. G., & Vestre, N. D. Demographic and prognostic characteristics of psychiatric patients classified by gross MMPI measures. *American Psychologist,* 1967, **22,** 562. (Abstract)

Klopfer, B., & Spiegelman, M. Methodological research problems. In B. Klopfer, *et al.* (Eds.), *Developments in the Rorschach technique.* Vol. II. *Fields of application.* Yonkers-on-Hudson, N. Y.: World Book Co., 1956.

Kluckhohn, C. M., Murray, H. A., & Schneider, D. M. (Eds.) *Personality in nature, society, and culture.* New York: Knopf, 1953.

Klugman, S. F. Group and individual judgments for anticipated events. *Journal of Social Psychology,* 1947, **26,** 21-28.

Koch, S. Behavior as "intrinsically" regulated: Work notes towards a pretheory of phenomena called "motivational." In M. R. Jones (Ed.), *Nebraska symposium on motivation.* Lincoln, Neb.: University of Nebraska Press, 1956.

Kogan, N., & Wallach, M. A. *Risk taking: A study in cognition and personality.* New York: Holt, Rinehart & Winston, 1964.

Kohn, M. L., & Clausen, J. A. Social isolation and schizophrenia. *American Sociological Review,* 1955, **20,** 265-273.

Koppitz, E. Emotional indicators on human figure drawings and school achievement of first and second graders. *Journal of Clinical Psychology,* 1966, **22,** 481-483. (a)

Koppitz, E. Emotional indicators on human figure drawings of children: A validation study. *Journal of Clinical Psychology,* 1966, **22,** 313-315. (b)

Koppitz, E. Emotional indicators on human figure drawings of shy and aggressive children. *Journal of Clinical Psychology,* 1966, **22,** 466-469. (c)

Koppitz, E., Sullivan, J., Blyth, D. D., & Shelton, J. Prediction of first grade school achievement with the Bender Gestalt Test and human figure drawings. *Journal of Clinical Psychology,* 1959, **15,** 164-168.

Kostlan, A. A method for the empirical study of psychodiagnosis. *Journal of Consulting Psychology,* 1954, **18,** 83-88.

Kramer, C. Extension of multiple range test to group means with unequal numbers of replications. *Biometrics,* 1956, **12,** 307-310.

Krasner, L. The therapist as social reinforcement machine. In H. Strupp & L. Luborsky (Eds.), *Research in psychotherapy.* Washington, D. C.: American Psychological Association, 1962.

Krasner, L., & Ullmann, L. P. (Eds.), *Research in behavior modification.* New York: Holt, Rinehart & Winston, 1965.

Kreitman, N. The reliability of psychiatric diagnosis. *Journal of Mental Science,* 1961, **107,** 876-886.

Kreitman, N., Sainsbury, P. P., Morrisey, J., Towers, J., & Schrivener, J. The reliability of psychiatric assessment: An analysis. *Journal of Mental Science,* 1961, **107,** 887-908.

Krugman, J. A clinical validation of the Rorschach with problem children. *Rorschach Research Exchange,* 1942, **6,** 61-70.

Krumboltz, J. D. Promoting adaptive behavior: New answers to familiar questions. In J. D. Krumboltz (Ed.), *Revolution in counseling.* Boston: Houghton Mifflin, 1966.

Kurtzberg, R. L., Cavior, N., & Lipton, D. S. Sex drawn first and sex drawn larger by opiate addict and non-addict inmates on the Draw-a-Person Test. *Journal of Projective Techniques,* 1966, **30,** 55-58.

Lair, C. V., & Trapp, E. P. Performance decrement on the H-T-P Test as a function of adjustment level. *Journal of Clinical Psychology,* 1960, **16,** 431.

Laird, J. T. A comparison of female normals, psychiatric patients, and alcoholics for sex drawn first. *Journal of Clinical Psychology,* 1962, **18,** 473. (a)

Laird, J. T. A comparison of male normals, psychiatric patients and alcoholics for sex drawn first. *Journal of Clinical Psychology,* 1962, **18,** 302. (b)

Lakin, M. Formal characteristics of human figure drawings by institutionalized and non-institutionalized aged. *Journal of Gerontology,* 1960, **15,** 76-78.

Lamb, R., & Mahl, G. F. Manifest reactions of patients and interviewers to the use of sound recording in the psychiatric interview. *American Journal of Psychiatry,* 1956, **112,** 731-737.

Lawton, M., & Sechrest, L. Figure drawings by young boys from father-present and father-absent homes. *Journal of Clinical Psychology,* 1962, **18,** 304-305.

Lazarus, R. S. *Adjustment and personality.* New York: McGraw-Hill, 1961.

Lazarus, R. S., Ericksen, C. W., & Fonda, C. P. Personality dynamics and auditory perceptual recognition. *Journal of Personality,* 1951, **19,** 471-482.

Ledley, R. S., & Lusted, L. B. Reasoning foundations of medical diagnosis. *Science,* 1959, **130,** 9-21.

Lee, M. C. Interactions, configurations, and non-additive models. *Educational and Psychological Measurement,* 1961, **21,** 797-805.

Lepley, W. M., & Hadley, H. T. In J. P. Guilford (Ed.), *Printed classification tests.* (Army Air Force Aviation Psychology Program Research Report No. 5). Washington, D. C.: United States Government Printing Office, 1947.

Lesser, G. S. Conflict analysis of fantasy aggression. *Journal of Personality,* 1958, **26,** 29-41.

Leuba, C. J., & Lucas, W. B. Effects of attitudes on descriptions of pictures. *Journal of Experimental Psychology,* 1945, **35,** 517-524.

Levy, B. I., & Ulman, E. Judging psychopathology from painting. *Journal of Abnormal Psychology,* 1967, **72,** 182-187.

Levy, L. H., & Orr, T. R. The social psychology of Rorschach validity research. *Journal of Abnormal and Social Psychology,* 1959, **58,** 79-83.

Levy, S., & Southcombe, R. Suicide in a state hospital for the mentally ill. *Journal of Nervous and Mental Diseases,* 1953, **117,** 504-514.

Lewinsohn, P. M. Relationship between height of figure drawings and depression in psychiatric patients. *Journal of Consulting Psychology,* 1964, **28,** 380-381.

Lewinsohn, P. M. Psychological correlates of overall quality of figure drawings. *Journal of Consulting Psychology,* 1965, **29,** 504-512.

Lewis, E. C., & MacKinney, A. C. Counselor versus statistical predictions of job satisfaction in engineering. *Journal of Counseling Psychology,* 1961, **8,** 224-229.

Liccione, J. V. The changing family relationships of adolescent girls. *Journal of Abnormal and Social Psychology,* 1955, **51,** 421-426.

Lindgren, H. C. The use of a sentence completion test in measuring attitudinal changes among college freshmen. *Journal of Social Psychology,* 1954, **40,** 79-92.

Lindner, R. M. Content analysis in Rorschach work. *Rorschach Research Exchange,* 1946, **10,** 121-129.

Lindner, R. M. Analysis of the Rorschach test by content. *Journal of Clinical Psychopathology,* 1947, **8,** 707-719.

Lindner, R. M. The content analysis of the Rorschach protocol. In L. E. Abt & L. Bellak (Eds.), *Projective psychology.* New York: Knopf, 1950.

Lindquist, E. F. Goodness of fit of trend curves and significance of trend differences. *Psychometrika,* 1947, **12,** 65-68.

Lindquist, E. F. *Design and analysis of experiments in psychology and education.* Boston: Houghton-Mifflin, 1953.

Lindsley, O. R. Geriatric behavioral prosthetics. In R. Kastenbaum (Ed.), *New thoughts on old age.* New York: Springer, 1964.

Lindzey, G. On the classification of projective techniques. *Psychological Bulletin,* 1959, **56,** 158-168.

Lindzey, G. Seer versus sign. *Journal of Experimental Research in Personality,* 1965, **1,** 17-26.

Litt, S., & Margolies, A. Sex-change in successive Draw-A-Person Tests. *Journal of Clinical Psychology,* 1965, **29,** 504-512.

Little, J. W. An analysis of the Minnesota Multiphasic Personality Inventory. Unpublished master's thesis, University of North Carolina, 1949.

Little, K. B., & Shneidman, E. S. Congruencies among interpretations of psychological test and anamnestic data. *Psychological Monographs,* 1959, **73** (6, Whole No. 473).

Locke, B. Comparison of naval offenders with nonoffenders on a projective sentence completion test. *U. S. Armed Forces Medical Journal,* 1957, **8,** 1825-1828.

Loevinger, J. Some principles of personality measurement. *Educational and Psychological Measurement,* 1955, **14,** 3-17.

Loevinger, J. Objective tests as instruments of psychological theory. *Psychological Reports,* 1957, **3,** 635-694.

Loevinger, J. Theory and techniques of assessment. *Annual Review of Psychology,* 1959, **10,** 287-316.

Loevinger, J., Glesser, G., & DuBois, P. H. Maximizing the discriminating power of a multiple score test. *Psychometrika,* 1953, **18,** 309-317.

London, P. *The modes and morals of psychotherapy.* New York: Holt, Rinehart & Winston, 1964.

Longstaff, H. P. Fakability of the Strong Vocational Interest Blank and the Kuder Preference Record. *Journal of Applied Psychology,* 1948, **32,** 360-369.

Lopez, F. M., Jr. *Evaluating executive decision making: The in-basket technique.* New York: American Management Association, 1965.

Lorge, I., Tuckman, J., & Dunn, M. B. Human figure drawings by younger and older adults. *Journal of Clinical Psychology,* 1958, **14,** 54-56.

Lorr, M., Klett, C. J., & McNair, D. M. *Syndromes of psychosis.* New York: Macmillan, 1963.

Lourenso, S., Greenberg, J., & Davidson, H. Personality characteristics in drawings of deprived children who differ in school achievement. *Journal of Educational Research,* 1965, **59,** 63-67.

Louttit, C. M., & Browne, C. G. Psychometric instruments in psychological clinics. *Journal of Consulting Psychology,* 1947, **11**, 49-54.

Lovaas, O. I. Social desirability ratings of personality variables by Norwegian and American college students. *Journal of Abnormal and Social Psychology,* 1958, **57**, 124-125.

Lovell, V. R. Components of variance in two personality inventories. Unpublished doctoral dissertation, Stanford University, 1964.

Lubin, A., & Osborn, H. G. A theory of pattern analysis for the prediction of a quantitative criterion. *Psychometrika,* 1957, **22**, 63-73.

Lubin, B. Some effects of set and stimulus properties on TAT stories and resulting clinical judgment. *Dissertation Abstracts,* 1958, **19**, 181-182.

Lubin, B. Differentiation of overtly stable and unstable psychiatric aides by means of the DAP Test. *Psychological Reports,* 1959, **5**, 26.

Luborsky, L., & Holt, R. F. The selection of candidates for psychoanalytic training. *Journal of Clinical and Experimental Psychopathology,* 1957, **18**, 166-176.

Luchins, A. S. Forming impressions of personality: A critique. *Journal of Abnormal and Social Psychology,* 1948, **43**, 318-325.

Luft, J. Implicit hypotheses and clinical predictions. *Journal of Abnormal and Social Psychology,* 1950, **45**, 756-760.

Luft, J. Differences in prediction based on hearing versus reading verbatim clinical interviews. *Journal of Consulting Psychology,* 1951, **15**, 115-119.

Luft, J., Wishan, W., & Moody, H. A projective technique to measure adjustment to hospital environment. *Journal of General Psychology,* 1953, **49**, 209-219.

Mabry, M. Serial projectives drawings in a patient with a malignant brain tumor. *Journal of Projective Techniques,* 1964, **28**, 206-209.

MacBrayer, C. T. Differences in perception of the opposite sex by males and females. *Journal of Social Psychology,* 1960, **52**, 309-314.

Macfarlane, J. W., & Tuddenham, R. D. Problems in the validation of projective techniques. In H. H. Anderson and G. L. Anderson (Eds.), *An introduction to projective techniques.* Englewood Cliffs, N. J.: Prentice-Hall, 1951.

Machover, K. *Personality projection in the drawing of the human figure.* Springfield, Ill.: Charles C Thomas, 1949.

MacKinnon, D. W. The effects of increased observation upon the accuracy of prediction. *American Psychologist,* 1951, **6**, 311. (Abstract)

MacLeod, R. B. Person perception: A commentary. In H. David & J. C. Brengelmann (Eds.), *Perspectives in personality research.* London: Crosby Lockwood, 1960.

Marais, H. C., & Strumpfer, D. J. W. DAP body-image disturbance scale and quality of drawing. *Perceptual and Motor Skills,* 1965, **21**, 196.

Marks, P. A. An assessment of the diagnostic process in a child guidance setting. *Psychological Monographs,* 1961, **75**, (3, Whole No. 507).

Marks, P. A., & Seeman, W. *The actuarial description of abnormal personality.* Baltimore: Williams & Wilkins, 1963.

Marlowe, D., & Crowne, D. P. Social desirability and response to perceived situational demands. *Journal of Consulting Psychology,* 1961, **25**, 109-115.

Masling, J. M. The effects of warm and cold interaction on the interpretation of a projective protocol. *Journal of Projective Techniques,* 1957, **21**, 377-383.

Masling, J. M. The influence of situational and interpersonal variables in projective testing. *Psychological Bulletin,* 1960, **57**, 65-85.

Matarazzo, J. D., Allen, B. V., Saslow, G., & Wiens, A. Characteristics of successful policeman and firemen applicants. *Journal of Applied Psychology,* 1964, **48**, 123-133.

Medawar, P. B. *The uniqueness of the individual.* New York: Basic Books, 1957.

Mednick, S. A., & McNeil, T. F. Current methodology in research on the etiology of schizophrenia. Serious difficulties which suggest the use of the high-risk group method. *Psychological Bulletin,* 1968, **70**, 681-693.

Meehl, P. E. The dynamics of "structured" personality tests. *Journal of Clinical Psychology,* 1945, **1**, 296-303.

Meehl, P. E. Configural scoring. *Journal of Consulting Psychology,* 1950, **14**, 165-171.

Meehl, P. E. *Clinical versus statistical prediction: A theoretical analysis and a review of the evidence.* Minneapolis: University of Minnesota Press, 1954. (a)

Meehl, P. E. Comment on C. C. McArthur. Analyzing the clinical process. *Journal of Counseling Psychology,* 1954, **1**, 207-208. (b)

Meehl, P. E. Clinical versus actuarial prediction. *Proceedings, 1955 Invitational Conference on Testing Problems.* Princeton, N.J.: Educational Testing Service, 1956. (a)

Meehl, P. E. Wanted—A good cookbook. *American Psychologist,* 1956, **11**, 263-272. (b)

Meehl, P. E. When shall we use our heads instead of a formula? *Journal of Counseling Psychology,* 1957, **4**, 268-273.

Meehl, P. E. A comparison of clinicians with five statistical methods of identifying psychotic MMPI profiles. *Journal of Counseling Psychology,* 1959, **6**, 102-109. (a)

Meehl, P. E. Some ruminations on the validation of clinical procedures. *Canadian Journal of Psychology,* 1959, **13**, 102-128. (b)

Meehl, P. E. The cognitive activity of the clinician. *American Psychologist,* 1960, **15**, 19-27.

Meehl, P. E. Schizotaxia, schizotypy, schizophrenia. *American Psychologist,* 1962, **17**, 827-838.

Meehl, P. E. Seer over sign: The first good example. *Journal of Experimental Research in Personality,* 1965, **1**, 27-32.

Meehl, P. E., & Dahlstrom, W.G. Objective configural rules for discriminating psychotic from neurotic MMPI profiles. *Journal of Consulting Psychology,* 1960, **24**, 375-387.

Meehl, P. E., & Hathaway, S. R. The K factor as a suppressor variable in the MMPI. *Journal of Applied Psychology,* 1946, **30**, 525-564.

Meehl, P. E., & Rosen, A. Antecedent probability and the efficiency of signs, patterns, or cutting scores. *Psychological Bulletin,* 1955, **52**, 194-216.

Mehlman, B., & Rand, M. E. Face validity of the MMPI. *Journal of General Psychology,* 1960, **63**, 171-178.

Melton, R. S. A comparison of clinical and actuarial methods of prediction with an assessment of the relative accuracy of different clinicians. Unpublished doctoral dissertation, University of Minnesota, 1952.

Meltzoff, J. The effect of mental set and item structure upon response to a projective test. *Journal of Abnormal and Social Psychology,* 1951, **46**, 177-189.

Messick, S. Personality measurement and the ethics of assessment. *American Psychologist,* 1965, **20**, 136-142.

Messick, S., & Jackson, D. N. Authoritarianism or acquiescence in Bass's data. *Journal of Abnormal and Social Psychology,* 1957, **54**, 424-426.

Messick, S., & Jackson, D. N. Acquiescence and the factorial interpretation of the MMPI. *Psychological Bulletin,* 1961, **58**, 299-304. (a)

Messick, S., & Jackson, D. N. Desirability scale values and dispersions for MMPI items. *Psychological Reports,* 1961, **8**, 409-414. (b)

Metcalfe, M. Demonstration of a psychosomatic relationship. *British Journal of Medical Psychology,* 1956, **29**, 63-66.

Meyer, M. M., & Tolman, R. S. Parental figures in sentence completion test, in TAT, and in therapeutic interviews. *Journal of Consulting Psychology,* 1955, **19**, 170.

Meyer, V. The treatment of two phobic patients on the basis of learning principles. *Journal of Abnormal and Social Psychology,* 1957, **55**, 261-266.

Michael, C. M., Morris, D. P., & Soroker, E. Follow-up studies of shy, withdrawn children—II. Relative incidence of schizophrenia. *American Journal of Orthopsychiatry,* 1957, **24**, 331-337.

Michotte, A. E. *La perception de la causalite.* Paris: J. Vrin, 1946.

Miller, N., & Gekoski, N. Employee Preference Inventory: A forced-choice measure of employee attitude. *Engineering and Industrial Psychology,* 1959, **1**, 83-90.

Mills, R. B., McDevitt, R. J., Tonkin, S. Selection of Metropolitan Police Officers. Paper presented in symposium, *Psychological factors in selection of police personnel* at American Psychological Association convention, Los Angeles, September, 1964.

Mischel, W. Preference for delayed reinforcement and social responsibility. *Journal of Abnormal and Social Psychology,* 1961, **62,** 1-7. (a)

Mischel, W. Father-absence and delay of gratification: Cross cultural comparisons. *Journal of Abnormal and Social Psychology,* 1961, **63,** 116-124. (b)

Mischel, W. *Personality and assessment.* New York: Wiley, 1968.

Mischel, W., & Metzner, R. Preference for delayed reward as a function of age, intelligence, and length of delay interval. *Journal of Abnormal and Social Psychology,* 1962, **64,** 425-431.

Mischel, W., & Staub, E. Effects of expectancy on working and waiting for larger rewards. *Journal of Personality and Social Psychology,* 1965, **2,** 625-633.

Mishler, E. G. A scalogram analysis of the Sentence Completion Test. *Educational and Psychological Measurement,* 1958, **18,** 75-90.

Mogar, R. E. Anxiety indices in human figure drawings. *Journal of Consulting Psychology,* 1962, **26,** 108.

Mooney, R. L., & Gordon, L. V. *Manual: The Mooney Problem Check Lists.* New York: Psychological Corporation, 1950.

Moore, B. V. Educational facilities and financial assistance for graduate students in psychology, 1959-60. *American Psychologist,* 1958, **13,** 741-760.

Morris, B. S. Officer selection in the British Army, 1942-1945. *Occupational Psychology,* 1949, **23,** 219-234.

Morris, D. P., Soroker, E., & Burrus, G. Follow-up studies of shy, withdrawn children—I. Evaluation of later adjustment. *American Journal of Orthopsychiatry,* 1954, **24,** 743-753.

Morton, R. A controlled experiment in psychotherapy based on Rotter's social learning theory of personality. Unpublished doctoral dissertation, Ohio State University, 1949.

Mosier, C. I. Problems and designs of cross-validation. *Educational and Psychological Measurement,* 1951, **11,** 5-28.

Mowrer, O. H. Learning theory and the neurotic paradox. *American Journal of Orthopsychiatry,* 1948, **18,** 571-610.

Mowrer, O. H. "Sin": The lesser of two evils. *American Psychologist,* 1960, **15,** 301-304.

Murphy, G. *Personality.* New York: Harper & Brothers, 1947.

Murphy, M. Sexual differentiation of male and female job applicants on the Draw-A-Person Test. *Journal of Clinical Psychology,* 1957, **13,** 87-88.

Murray, D. C., & Deabler, H. L. Drawings, diagnoses, and the clinician's learning curve. *Journal of Projective Techniques,* 1958, **22,** 415-420.

Murray, E. J. Conflict and repression during sleep deprivation. *Journal of Abnormal and Social Psychology,* 1959, **59,** 95-101.

Murray, H. A. The effect of fear upon estimates of the maliciousness of other personalities. *Journal of Social Psychology,* 1933, **4,** 310-329.

Murray, H. A. *Explorations in personality.* New York: Oxford University Press, 1938.

Murray, H. A., & MacKinnon, D. W. Assessment of OSS personnel. *Journal of Consulting Psychology,* 1946, **10,** 76-80.

Murray, H. A., & Stein, M. Note on the selection of combat officers. *Psychosomatic Medicine,* 1943, **4,** 386-391.

Murray, H. A., Skinner, B. F., Maslow, A. H., Rogers, C. R., Frank, L. K., Rapaport, A., & Hoffman, H. Cultural evolution as viewed by psychologists. *Daedalus,* 1961, **90,** 570-586.

Murstein, B. I. The projection of hostility on the Rorschach as a result of ego-threat. *Journal of Projective Techniques and Personality Assessment,* 1956, **20,** 418-428.

Murstein, B. I. The effect of long-term illness of children on the emotional adjustment of parents. *Child Development,* 1960, **31,** 157-171.

Murstein, B. I. The relationship of the possession of the trait of hostility to the accuracy of perception of hostility in others. *Journal of Abnormal and Social Psychology,* 1961, **62,** 216-220.

Murstein, B. I. *Theory and research in projective techniques.* New York: Wiley, 1963.

Murstein, B. I. Projection of hostility on the TAT as a function of stimulus, background, and personality variables. *Journal of Consulting Psychology,* 1965, **29,** 43-48.

Murstein, B. I., David, D., Fisher, D., & Furth, H. The scaling of the TAT for hostility by a variety of scaling methods. *Journal of Consulting Psychology,* 1961, **25,** 497-504.

Murstein, B. I., & Pryer, R. S. The concept of projection: A review. *Psychological Bulletin,* 1959, **56,** 353-374.

Mussen, P. H., Conger, J. J., & Kagan, J. *Child development and personality.* New York: Harper & Row, 1963.

McArthur, C. Analyzing the clinical process. *Journal of Counseling Psychology,* 1954, **1,** 203-208.

McArthur, C. Clinical versus actuarial prediction. In *Proceedings of the 1955 invitational conference on testing problems.* Princeton, N. J.: Educational Testing Service, 1956.

McArthur, C. C., Meehl, P. E., & Tiedeman, D. V. Symposium on clinical and statistical prediction. *Journal of Counseling Psychology,* 1956, **3,** 163-173.

McCall, R. J. Psychometric evaluation of Rorschach records in brain-operated patients. Unpublished doctoral dissertation, Columbia University, 1951.

McCall, R. J. Face validity in the D scale of the MMPI. *Journal of Clinical Psychology,* 1958, **15,** 77-80.

McGee, R. K. The relationship between response style and personality variables: I. The measurement of response acquiescence. *Journal of Abnormal and Social Psychology,* 1962, **64,** 229-233. (a)

McGee, R. K. The relationship between response style and personality variables: II. The prediction of independent conforming behavior. *Journal of Abnormal and Social Psychology,* 1962, **65**, 347-351. (b)

McGee, R. K. Response style as a personality variable: By what criterion? *Psychological Bulletin,* 1962, **59**, 284-295. (c)

McGreevy, J. C. Interlevel disparity and predictive efficiency. *Journal of Projective Techniques,* 1962, **26**, 80-87.

McHugh, A. H-T-P proportion and perspective in Negro, Puerto Rican, and white children. *Journal of Clinical Psychology,* 1963, **19**, 312-314. (a)

McHugh, A. Sexual identification, size, and associations in children's figure drawings. *Journal of Clinical Psychology,* 1963, **19**, 381-382. (b)

McHugh, A. Age associations in children's figure drawings. *Journal of Clinical Psychology,* 1965, **21**, 429-431.

McHugh, A. Children's figure drawings in neurotic and conduct disturbances. *Journal of Clinical Psychology,* 1966, **22**, 219-221.

McKinley, J. C., & Hathaway, S. R. The Minnesota Multiphasic Personality Inventory: V. Hysteria, hypomania, and psychopathic deviate. *Journal of Applied Psychology,* 1944, **28**, 153-174.

Narrol, H. G., & Levitt, E. E. Formal assessment procedures in police selection. *Psychological Reports,* 1963, **12**, 691-694.

Nash, H. Incomplete sentences tests in personality research. *Educational and Psychological Measurement,* 1958, **18**, 569-581.

National Association for Mental Health, Inc. *1954-55 Directory of outpatient clinics and other mental health resources in the United States and territories.* New York: NAMH, 1955.

Neilson, G. C. The effects of repeated testing upon the validity of a structured personality inventory. Unpublished master's thesis, University of Oregon, 1965.

Newton, R. L. The clinician as judge: Total Rorschach and clinical case material. *Journal of Consulting Psychology,* 1954, **18**, 248-250.

New York Heart Association. *Nomenclature and criteria for diagnosis of diseases of the heart and blood vessels.* New York: New York Heart Association, 1953.

Nichols, R. C., & Strumpfer, D. J. W. A factor analysis of Draw-A-Person test scores. *Journal of Consulting Psychology,* 1962, **26**, 156-161.

Norman, W. T. Personality measurement, faking, and detection: An assessment method for use in personnel selection. *Journal of Applied Psychology,* 1963, **47**, 225-241. (a)

Norman, W. T. Relative importance of test item content. *Journal of Consulting Psychology,* 1963, **27**, 166-174. (b)

Noyes, A. P., & Kolb, L. C. *Modern clinical psychiatry.* Philadelphia: Saunders, 1963.

Nunnally, J. C. An investigation of some propositions of self-conception: The case of Miss Sun. *Journal of Abnormal and Social Psychology,* 1955, **50,** 87-92.

Nunnally, J. C. *Tests and measurements.* New York: McGraw-Hill, 1959.

Nunnally, J. C., & Husek, T. R. The phony language examination: An approach to the measurement of response bias. *Educational and Psychological Measurement,* 1958, **18,** 275-282.

Odiore, G. S., & Miller, E. L. Selection by objectives: A new approach to managerial selection. *Management of Personnel Quarterly,* 1966, **5,** 2-10.

Office of Strategic Services, Assessment Staff. *Assessment of men: Selection of personnel for the Office of Strategic Services.* New York: Rinehart, 1948.

Oldfield, R. C. *The psychology of the interview.* (3rd ed.) London: Methuen, 1947.

Opler, M. K. Schizophrenia and culture. *Scientific American,* 1957, **197,** 103-112.

Opler, M. K. Need for new diagnostic categories in psychiatry. *Journal of the National Medical Association,* 1963, **55,** 133-137.

Orgel, R. The relationship of the H-T-P to a sociometric evaluation of a group of primary grade school children in determining the degree of social acceptance. *Journal of Clinical Psychology,* 1959, **15,** 222-223.

Osburn, H. G., & Lubin, A. The use of configural analysis for the evaluation of test scoring methods. *Psychometrika,* 1957, **22,** 359-371.

Osgood, C. E. Studies on the generality of affective meaning systems. *American Psychologist,* 1962, **17,** 10-28.

Osgood, C. E., Suci, G. J., & Tannenbaum, P. H. *The measurement of meaning.* Urbana, Ill.: University of Illinois Press, 1957.

Oskamp, S. The relationship of clinical experience and training methods to several criteria of clinical prediction. *Psychological Monographs,* 1962, **76** (28, Whole No. 547).

Oskamp, S. Overconfidence in case-study judgments. *Journal of Consulting Psychology,* 1965, **29,** 261-265.

Oskamp, S. Clinical judgment from the MMPI: Simple or complex? *Journal of Clinical Psychology,* 1967, **23,** 411-415.

Osterweil, J., & Fiske, D. W. Intra-individual variability in sentence completion responses. *Journal of Abnormal and Social Psychology,* 1956, **52,** 195-199.

Packard, V. *The naked society.* New York: McKay, 1964.

Parker, C. A. As a clinician thinks.... *Journal of Counseling Psychology,* 1958, **5,** 253-262.

Parrish, J. A., Klieger, W. A., & Drucker, A. J. A self description blank for officer candidate school applicants. *USA Personnel Research Branch Report,* 1954, No. 1091. Summarized in A. J. Drucker, Predicting leadership ratings in the United States Army. *Educational and Psychological Measurement,* 1957, **17,** 240-263.

Pascal, G. R., & Suttell, B. Testing the claims of a graphologist. *Journal of Personality,* 1947, **16**, 192-197.

Patterson, D. G. Character reading at sight of Mr. X according to the system of Mr. P. T. Barnum. Unpublished manuscript, University of Minnesota, 1951.

Payne, A. F. *Sentence completions.* New York: New York Guidance Clinic, 1928.

Payne, R. W. Experimental method in clinical psychological practice. *Journal of Mental Science,* 1957, **103**, 189-196.

Peak, H. Problems of objective observation. In L. Festinger & D. Katz (Eds.), *Research methods in the behavioral sciences.* New York: Dryden Press, 1953.

Peck, R. F., & McGuire, C. Measuring changes in mental health with the sentence completion technique. *Psychological Reports,* 1959, **5**, 151-160.

Peskin, H. Unity of science begins at home: A study of regional factionalism in clinical psychology. *American Psychologist,* 1963, **18**, 96-100.

Peterson, D. R. Scope and generality of verbally defined personality factors. *Psychological Review,* 1965, **72**, 48-59.

Phares, E. J. Expectancy changes in skill and chance situations. *Journal of Abnormal and Social Psychology,* 1957, **54**, 339-342.

Phelan, H. The incidence and possible significance of the drawing of female figures by sixth-grade boys in response to the Draw-A-Person Test. *Psychiatric Quarterly,* 1964, **38**, 488-503.

Phelan, J. G. Rationale employed by clinical psychologists in diagnostic judgment. *Journal of Clinical Psychology,* 1964, **20**, 454-458.

Phelan, J. G. Use of matching method in measuring reliability of individual clinician's diagnostic judgment. *Psychological Reports,* 1965, **16**, 491-497.

Phillips, L., & Cowitz, B. Social attainment and reactions to stress. *Journal of Personality,* 1953, **22**, 270-283.

Pierson, L. R. High school teacher prediction of college success. *Personnel and Guidance Journal,* 1958, **37**, 142-145.

Piltz, R. J. Problems in validity for the Copple Sentence Completion Test as a measure of "effective intelligence" with Air Force personnel. *Dissertation Abstracts,* 1957, **17**, 1914-1915.

Piotrowski, Z. A. The methodological aspects of the Rorschach personality method. *Rorschach Research Exchange,* 1936, **1**, 23-39.

Piotrowski, Z. A. The Rorschach inkblot method in organic disturbances of the central nervous system. *Journal of Nervous and Mental Diseases,* 1937, **86**, 525-527.

Piotrowski, Z. A. The prognostic possibilities of the Rorschach method in insulin treatment. *Psychiatric Quarterly,* 1938, **12**, 679-689.

Piotrowski, Z. A. Tentative Rorschach formulae for educational and vocational guidance in adolescents. *Rorschach Research Exchange,* 1943, **7**, 16-27.

Piotrowski, Z. A. The personality of the epileptic. In P. Hoch and R. Knight (Eds.), *Epilepsy.* New York: Grune & Stratton, 1947.

Piotrowski, Z. A. *Perceptanalysis: A fundamentally reworked, expanded, and systematized Rorschach method.* New York: Macmillan, 1957.

Piotrowski, Z. A. Diagnosis ex machina. *Psychiatric Quarterly,* 1959, **33,** 765-766.

Piotrowski, Z. A. Digital-computer interpretation of inkblot test data. *Psychiatric Quarterly,* 1964, **38,** 1-26.

Piotrowski, Z. A., & Bricklin, B. A long-term prognostic criterion for schizophrenics based on Rorschach data. *Psychiatric Quarterly Supplement,* 1958, **32,** 315-329.

Piotrowski, Z. A., & Lewis, N. D. C. An experimental Rorschach diagnostic aid for some forms of schizophrenia. *American Journal of Psychiatry,* 1950, **107,** 360-366.

Polansky, N. How shall a life-history be written? *Character and Personality,* 1941, **9,** 188-207.

Pollit, E., Hirsch, S., & Money, J. Priapism, impotence and human figure drawing. *Journal of Nervous and Mental Disease,* 1964, **139,** 161-168.

Ponzo, E. An experimental variation of the Draw-A-Person technique. *Journal of Projective Techniques,* 1957, **21,** 278-285.

Pounian, C. A. Recent studies of patrolman examinations. Paper read at International Conference, Public Personnel Association, San Francisco, October, 1959.

Purcell, K. The TAT and antisocial behavior. *Journal of Consulting Psychology,* 1956, **20,** 449-456.

Purcell, K., & Brady, K. Adaptations to the invasion of privacy: Monitoring behavior with a miniature radio transmitter. *Merrill-Palmer Quarterly,* 1966, **12,** 242-254.

Rabin, A. I., & Limuaco, J. Sexual differentiation of American and Filipino children as reflected in the Draw-A-Person Test. *Journal of Social Psychology,* 1959, **50,** 207-211.

Rapaport, D. The theoretical implications of diagnostic testing procedures. In R. P. Knight & C. R. Friedman (Eds.), *Psychoanalytic psychiatry and psychology.* New York: International Universities Press, 1954.

Reichenbach, H. *Experience and prediction.* Chicago: University of Chicago Press, 1938.

Reitzell, J. M. A comparative study of hysterics, homosexuals and alcoholics using content analysis of Rorschach responses. *Rorschach Research Exchange,* 1949, **13,** 127-141.

Reznikoff, M., & Nicholas, A. L. An evaluation of human figure drawing indicators of paranoid pathology. *Journal of Consulting Psychology,* 1958, **22,** 395-397.

Ribler, R. I. Diagnostic prediction from emphasis on the eye and the ear in human figure drawings. *Journal of Consulting Psychology,* 1957, **21,** 223-225.

Richey, M. Qualitative superiority of the "self" figure in children's drawings. *Journal of Clinical Psychology,* 1965, **21,** 59-61.

Ries, H. A., Johnson, M. H., Armstrong, H. E., & Holmes, D. S. The Draw-A-Person Test and process-reactive schizophrenia. *Journal of Projective Techniques,* 1966, **30,** 184-186.

Ringuette, E. L., & Kennedy, T. An experimental study of the double bind hypothesis. *Journal of Abnormal Psychology,* 1966, **71,** 136-141.

Roback, H. B. Human figure drawings: Their utility in the clinical psychologist's armamentarium for personality assessment. *Psychological Bulletin,* 1968, **70,** 1-19.

Roberts, R., & Renzaglia, G. The influence of tape recording on counseling. *Journal of Counseling Psychology,* 1965, **12,** 10-16.

Rogers, C. R. A theory of therapy, personality, and interpersonal relationships as developed in the client-centered framework. In S. Koch (Ed.), *Psychology: A study of a science.* Vol. III. *Formulations of the person and the social context.* New York: McGraw-Hill, 1959.

Rohde, A. R. Explorations in personality by the sentence completion method. *Journal of Applied Psychology,* 1946, **30,** 169-181.

Rohde, A. R. A note regarding the use of the Sentence Completion Test in military installations since the beginning of World War II. *Journal of Consulting Psychology,* 1948, **12,** 190-193.

Rohde, A. R. *The sentence completion method: Its diagnostic and clinical application to mental disorders.* New York: Ronald Press Co., 1957.

Roitzsch, J. C., & Berg, I. A. Deviant responses as indicators of immaturity and neuroticism. *Journal of Clinical Psychology,* 1959, **15,** 417-419.

Rome, H.P., Swenson, W. M., Mataya, P., McCarthy, C. E., Pearson, J. S., & Keating, R. F. Symposium on automation techniques in personality assessment. *Proceedings of the Mayo Clinic,* 1962, **37,** 61-82.

Rommetviet, R. *Selectivity, intuition and halo effects in social perception.* Oslo: Oslo University Press, 1960.

Ronan, W. W., & Prien, E. P. *Toward a criterion theory: A review and analysis of research and opinion.* Greensboro, N. C.: Richardson Foundation, 1966.

Roose, L. J. The influence of psychosomatic research on the psychoanalytic process. *American Psychoanalytic Association Journal,* 1960, **8,** 317-334.

Rorer, L. G. The great response-style myth. *Psychological Bulletin,* 1965, **63,** 129-156.

Rorer, L. G. Conditions facilitating discovery of moderators. Paper presented at the meeting of the American Psychological Association, Washington, D. C., September, 1967.

Rorer, L. G., & Goldberg, L. R. Acquiescence and the vanishing variance component. *Journal of Applied Psychology,* 1965, **49**, 422-430. (a)

Rorer, L. G., & Goldberg, L. R. Acquiescence in the MMPI? *Educational and Psychological Measurement,* 1965, **25**, 801-817. (b)

Rorer, L. G., Hoffman, P. J., Dickman, H. D., & Slovic, P. Configural judgments revealed. *Proceedings of the 75th Annual Convention of the American Psychological Association,* 1967, **2**, 195-196.

Rorer, L. G., & Slovic, P. The measurement of changes in judgmental strategy. *American Psychologist,* 1966, **21**, 641-642. (Abstract)

Rosen, A., Hales, W. M., & Simon, W. Classification of "suicidal" patients. *Journal of Consulting Psychology,* 1954, **18**, 359-362.

Rosen, E. Self-appraisal, personal desirability, and perceived social desirability of personality traits. *Journal of Abnormal and Social Psychology,* 1956, **52**, 151-158.

Rosen, N. A., & Van Horn, J. W. Selection of college scholarship students: Statistical versus clinical methods. *Personnel and Guidance Journal,* 1961, **40**, 150-154.

Rosenberg, L. A. Rapid changes in overt behavior reflected in the Draw-A-Person: A case report. *Journal of Projective Techniques,* 1965, **29**, 348-351.

Rosenberg, S. Some relationships between attitudes expressed toward the parent in a sentence completion test and case history data. *Journal of Projective Techniques,* 1950, **14**, 188-193.

Rosenwald, G. C. Psychodiagnostics and its discontents. *Psychiatry,* 1963, **26**, 222-240.

Rosenzweig, S. An outline of frustration theory. In J. McV. Hunt (Ed.), *Personality and the behavior disorders.* New York: Ronald Press, 1944.

Rosenzweig, S. The picture-association method and its application in a study of reactions to frustration. *Journal of Personality,* 1945, **14**, 3-23.

Ross, T. A. *An inquiry into prognosis in the neuroses.* London: Cambridge University Press, 1936.

Rotter, J. B. The incomplete sentence test as a method of studying personality. *American Psychologist,* 1946, **1**, 286.

Rotter, J. B. Word association and sentence completion methods. In H. H. Anderson & G. H. Anderson (Eds.), *An introduction to projective techniques.* Englewood Cliffs, N. J.: Prentice-Hall, 1951.

Rotter, J. B. *Social learning and clinical psychology.* Englewood Cliffs, N. J.: Prentice-Hall, 1954.

Rotter, J. B. Some implications of a social learning theory for the prediction of goal directed behavior from testing procedures. *Psychological Review,* 1960, **67**, 301-316.

Rotter, J. B., Liverant, S., & Crowne, D. P. The growth and extinction of expectancies in chance and skilled tasks. *Journal of Psychology,* 1961, **52**, 161-177.

Rotter, J. B., & Rafferty, J. E. *Manual: The Rotter Incomplete Sentences Blank.* New York: Psychological Corporation, 1950.

Rotter, J. B., & Rafferty, J. E. Rotter Incomplete Sentences Blank. In A. Weider (Ed.), *Contributions toward medical psychology: Theory and psychodiagnostic methods.* New York: Ronald Press, 1953.

Rotter, J. B., Rafferty, J. E., & Lotsof, A. B. The validity of the Rotter Incomplete Sentences Blank: High school form. *Journal of Consulting Psychology,* 1954, **18,** 105-111.

Rotter, J. B., Rafferty, J. E., & Schachtitz. E. Validation of the Rotter Incomplete Sentences Blank for college screening. *Journal of Consulting Psychology,* 1949, **13,** 348-356.

Rotter, J. S., & Willerman, B. The incomplete sentence test. *Journal of Consulting Psychology,* 1947, **11,** 43-48.

Rozynko, V. V. Social desirability in the sentence completion test. *Journal of Consulting Psychology,* 1959, **23,** 280.

Rusmore, J. T. An experimental comparison of the composite and jury methods of obtaining group judgments. Unpublished doctoral dissertation, University of California, 1944.

Ryback, D. Confidence and accuracy as a function of experience in judgment-making in the absence of systematic feedback. *Perceptual and Motor Skills,* 1967, **24,** 331-334.

Rychlak, J. F., & Guinouard, D. Rorschach content, personality and popularity. *Journal of Projective Techniques,* 1960, **24,** 322-332.

Rychlak, J. F., & Lerner, J. J. An expectancy interpretation of manifest anxiety. *Journal of Personality and Social Psychology,* 1965, **2,** 677-684.

Rychlak, J. F., Mussen, P. H., & Bennett, J. W. An example of the use of the incomplete sentence test in applied anthropological research. *Human Organization,* 1957, **16,** 25-29.

Sacks, J. M. The relative effect upon projective responses of stimuli referring to the subject and of stimuli referring to other persons. *Journal of Consulting Psychology,* 1949, **13,** 12-20.

Sacks, J. M., & Levy, S. The Sentence Completion Test. In L. E. Abt & L. Bellak (Eds.), *Projective psychology.* New York: Knopf, 1950.

Samuels, H. The validity of personality-trait ratings based upon projective techniques. *Psychological Monographs,* 1952, **66** (5, Whole No. 337).

Sandler, J., & Ackner, B. Rorschach content analysis: An experimental investigation. *British Journal of Medical Psychology,* 1951, **24,** 180-201.

Sanford, N., McArthur, C. C., Zubin, J., Humphreys, L. G., & Meehl, P. E. Panel discussion: Clinical versus actuarial prediction. *Proceedings 1955 invitational conference on testing problems.* Princeton, N. J.: Educational Testing Service, 1956.

Santorum, A. A cross validation of the House-Tree-Person drawing indices predicting hospital discharge of tuberculosis patients. *Journal of Consulting Psychology,* 1960, **24,** 400-402.

Sarason, B. R., & Sarason, I. C. The effect of type of administration and sex of subject on emotional tone and outcome ratings of TAT stories. *Journal of Projective Techniques,* 1958, **22**, 333-337.

Sarason, S. B. The test-situation and the problems of prediction. *Journal of Clinical Psychology,* 1950, **6**, 387-392.

Sarason, S. B. *The clinical interaction.* New York: Harper, 1954.

Sarason, S. B., Levine, M., Goldenberg, I. L., Cherbin, D. L., & Bennett, E. M. *Psychology in community settings.* New York: Wiley, 1966.

Sarbin, T. R. A contribution to the study of actuarial and individual methods of prediction. *American Journal of Sociology,* 1943, **48**, 593-602.

Sarbin, T. The logic of prediction in psychology. *Psychological Review,* 1944, **51**, 210-228.

Sarbin, T. On the futility of the proposition that some people be labelled mentally ill. *Journal of Consulting Psychology,* 1967, **31**, 447-453.

Sarbin, T. Ontology recapitulates philology: The mythic nature of anxiety. *American Psychologist,* 1968, **23**, 411-418.

Sarbin, T. R., Taft, R., & Bailey, D. E. *Clinical inference and cognitive theory.* New York: Holt, Rinehart & Winston, 1960.

Saslow, G. On the concept of comprehensive medicine. *Bulletin of the Menninger Clinic,* 1952, **16**, 57-65.

Saslow, G. A case history of attempted behavior manipulation in a psychiatric ward. In L. Krasner & L. P. Ullmann (Eds.), *Research in behavior modification.* New York: Holt, Rinehart & Winston, 1965.

Saunders, D. R. Moderator variables in prediction. *Educational and Psychological Measurement,* 1956, **16**, 209-222.

Sawyer, J. Measurement *and* prediction, clinical *and* statistical. *Psychological Bulletin,* 1966, **66**, 178-200.

Schaeffer, R. W. Clinical psychologists' ability to use the Draw-A-Person Test as an indicator of personality adjustment. *Journal of Consulting Psychology,* 1964, **28**, 383.

Schafer, R. *The clinical application of psychological tests.* New York: International Universities Press, 1948.

Schafer, R. Psychological tests in clinical research. *Journal of Consulting Psychology,* 1949, **13**, 328-334.

Schafer, R. *Psychoanalytic interpretation in Rorschach testing.* New York: Grune & Stratton, 1954.

Scheff, T. J. *Being mentally ill: A sociological theory.* Chicago: Aldine, 1966.

Scheflen, A. E. Analysis of thought model which persists in psychiatry. *Psychosomatic Medicine,* 1958, **20**, 235-241.

Schiedt, R. *Ein Beitrag zum Problem der Ruckfallsprongnose.* Munich: Muchner-Zeitungs-Verlag, 1936.

Schmidt, H. O. Notes on the MMPI: The K factor. *Journal of Consulting Psychology,* 1948, **12**, 337-342.

Schneider, A. J. N., Lagrone, C. W., Glueck, E. T., & Glueck, S. Prediction of behavior of civilian delinquents in the Armed Forces. *Mental Hygiene,* 1944, **28,** 456-475.

Schofield, W., & Balian, L. A comparative study of the personal histories of schizophrenic and nonpsychiatric patients. *Journal of Abnormal and Social Psychology,* 1959, **59,** 216-225.

Schumacher, C. F. A comparison of three methods for keying interest and personality inventories. Unpublished doctoral dissertation, University of Minnesota, 1959.

Schwartz, M. L. Validity and reliability in clinical judgments of C-V-S protocols as a function of amount of information and diagnostic category. *Psychological Reports,* 1967, **20,** 767-774.

Scott, R. D. Using the weighted application blank in determining the factors associated with job turnover. Unpublished master's thesis, University of Massachusetts, 1966.

Scott, W. A. Research definitions of mental health and mental illness. *Psychological Bulletin,* 1958, **55,** 29-45.

Sechehay, M. *A new psychotherapy for schizophrenia.* New York: Grune & Stratton, 1956.

Sechrest, L., Gallimore, R., & Hersch, P. D. Feedback and accuracy of clinical predictions. *Journal of Consulting Psychology,* 1967, **31,** 1-11.

Sechrest, L. B., & Hemphill, J. K. Motivational variables in the assuming of combat obligation. *Journal of Consulting Psychology,* 1954, **18,** 113-118.

Sechrest, L. B., & Jackson, D. N. Deviant response tendencies: Their measurement and interpretation. *Educational and Psychological Measurement,* 1963, **23,** 33-53.

Sechrest, L., & Wallace, J. *The psychology and human problems.* Columbus: Merrill, 1967.

Seeman, W. "Subtlety" in structured personality tests. *Journal of Consulting Psychology,* 1952, **16,** 278-283.

Sells, S. B. Toward a taxonomy of organizations. In W. W. Cooper, H. J. Leavitt, & W. W. Shelly, II (Eds.), *New perspectives in organization research.* New York: Wiley, 1964.

Sen, A. A statistical study of the Rorschach test. *British Journal of Psychology: Statistical Section,* 1950, **3,** 21-39.

Shaffer, L. F. Information which should be provided by test publishers and testing agencies on the validity and use of their tests. In *Proceedings 1949 invitational conference on testing problems.* Princeton, N.J.: Educational Testing Service, 1950.

Shakow, D. The recorded psychoanalytic interview as an objective approach to research in psychoanalysis. *Psychoanalytic Quarterly,* 1960, **29,** 82-97.

Shanan, J. Intraindividual response variability in figure drawing tasks. *Journal of Projective Techniques,* 1962, **26,** 105-111.

Shapiro, M. B. An experimental approach to diagnostic psychological testing. *Journal of Mental Science,* 1951, **97**, 748-764.

Shapiro, M. B. The single case in fundamental clinical psychological research. *British Journal of Medical Psychology,* 1961, **34**, 255-262.

Shapiro, M. B. Clinical psychology as an applied science. *British Journal of Psychiatry,* 1967, **113**, 1039-1042.

Shay, M. M. The construction of a multiple-choice sentence completion test. Unpublished master's thesis, Purdue University, 1950.

Shelly, M. W. II, & Bryan, G. L. Judgments and the language of decisions. In M. W. Shelly, II, & G. L. Bryan (Eds.), *Human judgments and optimality.* New York: Wiley, 1964.

Sherman, L. J. The influence of artistic quality on judgments of patient and non-patient status from human figure drawings. *Journal of Projective Techniques,* 1958, **22**, 338-340. (a)

Sherman, L. J. Sexual differentiation or artistic ability? *Journal of Clinical Psychology,* 1958, **14**, 170-171. (b)

Shiman, E. S. The comparative validity of different strategies of predicting college achievement. Unpublished master's thesis, University of Oregon, 1966.

Shoben, E. J. Personal worth in education and counseling. In J. D. Krumboltz (Ed.), *Revolution in counseling.* Boston: Houghton Mifflin, 1966.

Shor, J. Report on a verbal projective technique. *Journal of Clinical Psychology,* 1946, **2**, 279-282.

Shry, S. A. Relative size of same and opposite sex drawings on the DAP as an index of dominance-submissiveness. *Journal of Consulting Psychology,* 1966, **30**, 568.

Siegel, S. *Nonparametric statistics for the behavioral sciences.* New York: McGraw-Hill, 1956.

Silverman, L. H. A Q-sort study of the validity of evaluations made from projective techniques. *Psychological Monographs,* 1959, **73** (7, Whole No. 477).

Silverstein, A. B. Anxiety and quality of human figure drawings. *American Journal of Mental Deficiency,* 1966, **70**, 607-608.

Silverstein, A. B., & Robinson, H. A. The representation of physique in children's figure drawings. *Journal of Consulting Psychology,* 1961, **25**, 146-148.

Simon, H. A. *Models of man.* New York: Wiley, 1957.

Simpson, G. G. *The meaning of evolution.* New Haven: Yale University Press, 1950.

Sines, J. O. Actuarial methods in personality assessment. In B. A. Maher (Ed.), *Progress in experimental personality research.* Vol. 3. New York: Academic Press, 1966.

Sines, L. K. The relative contribution of four kinds of data to accuracy in personality assessment. *Journal of Consulting Psychology,* 1959, **23,** 483-492.

Skinner, B. F. *Science and human behavior.* New York: Macmillan, 1953.

Skinner, B. F. Freedom and the control of men. *American Scholar,* 1955-56, **25,** 47-65.

Skinner, B. F. The design of cultures. *Daedalus,* 1961, **90,** 534-546.

Skinner, B. F. *The technology of teaching.* New York: Appleton-Century-Crofts, 1968.

Slack, C. W. Experimenter-subject psychotherapy: A new method of introducing intensive office treatment for unreachable cases. *Mental Hygiene,* 1960, **44,** 238-256.

Slovic, P. Cue consistency and cue utilization in judgment. *American Journal of Psychology,* 1966, **79,** 427-434.

Slovic, P. Analyzing the expert judge: A descriptive study of a stockbroker's decision processes. Paper presented at the meeting of the Western Psychological Association, San Diego, March 1968.

Smith, E. E. Defensiveness, insight, and the K scale. *Journal of Consulting Psychology,* 1959, **23,** 275-277.

Smith, M. B. Group judgment in the field of personality traits. *Journal of Experimental Psychology,* 1932, **14,** 562-565.

Smith, M. B. "Mental health" reconsidered: A special case of the problem of values in psychology. *American Psychologist,* 1961, **16,** 299-306.

Smith, P. C., & Kendall, L. M. Retranslation of expectations: An approach to the construction of unambiguous anchors for rating scales. *Journal of Applied Psychology,* 1963, **47,** 149-155.

Smith, W. E. A comparison of the responses of stutterers and non-stutterers in a college population on the Rotter Incomplete Sentence Blank. Unpublished master's thesis, Bowling Green State University, 1952.

Soskin, W. F. Bias in post-diction from projective tests. *Journal of Abnormal and Social Psychology,* 1954, **49,** 69-74.

Soskin, W. F. Influence of four types of data on diagnostic conceptualization in psychological testing. *Journal of Abnormal and Social Psychology,* 1959, **58,** 69-78.

Soskin, W. F., & John, V. P. The study of spontaneous talk. In R. G. Barker (Ed.), *The stream of behavior.* New York: Appleton-Century-Crofts, 1963.

Souelem, O. Mental patients' attitudes toward mental hospitals. *Journal of Clinical Psychology,* 1955, **11,** 181-185.

Staats, A. W., & Staats, C. K. *Complex human behavior.* New York: Holt, Rinehart & Winston, 1963.

Stagner, D. R. The relation of personality to academic aptitude and achievement. *Journal of Educational Research,* 1933, **26,** 648-660.

Stagner, R. *Psychology of personality.* New York: McGraw-Hill, 1937.

Stainbrook, E. Some historical determinants of contemporary diagnostic and etiological thinking in psychiatry. In P. H. Hoch & J. Zubin (Eds.), *Current problems in psychiatric diagnosis.* New York: Grune & Stratton, 1953.

Stanton, F., & Baker, K. H. Interviewer-bias and the recall of incomplete learned materials. *Sociometry,* 1942, **5,** 123-134.

Starr, S., & Marcues, F. L. Reliability in the Draw-A-Person Test. *Journal of Projective Techniques,* 1959, **23,** 83-86.

Stein, M. I. The use of a sentence completion test for the diagnosis of personality. *Journal of Clinical Psychology,* 1947, **3,** 46-56.

Stein, M. I. The record and a sentence completion test. *Journal of Consulting Psychology,* 1949, **13,** 448-449.

Stephens, M. W. The Incomplete Sentences Blank: Sources of variance in retest reliability. *Journal of Clinical Psychology,* 1960, **3,** 331-333.

Stephenson, W. *The study of behavior.* Chicago: University of Chicago Press, 1953.

Stern, G. G., Stein, M. I., & Bloom, B. S. *Methods in personality assessment.* Glencoe, Ill.: Free Press, 1956.

Sternberg, R. S., Chapman, J., & Shakow, D. Psychotherapy research and the problem of intrusions on privacy. *Psychiatry,* 1958, **21,** 195-203.

Stoltz, R. E., & Coltharp, F. C. Clinical judgments and the Draw-A-Person Test. *Journal of Consulting Psychology,* 1961, **25,** 43-45.

Stone, H. K. TAT aggressive content scale. *Journal of Projective Techniques and Personality Assessment,* 1956, **20,** 445-452.

Stone, H. K., & Dellis, N. P. An exploratory investigation into the levels hypothesis. *Journal of Projective Techniques,* 1960, **24,** 333-340.

Stone, L. A. Subtle and obvious response on the MMPI. *Psychological Reports,* 1964, **15,** 721-722.

Stone, L. A. Subtle and obvious response on the MMPI as a function of acquiescence response style. *Psychological Reports,* 1965, **16,** 803-804.

Stotsky, B. A. Comparison of normals and schizophrenics on a work-oriented projective technique. *Journal of Counseling Psychology,* 1957, **13,** 406-408.

Stotsky, B. A., & Weinberg, H. The prediction of the psychiatric patient's work adjustment. *Journal of Counseling Psychology,* 1956, **3,** 3-7.

Stouffer, S. A. An experimental comparison of statistical and case history methods of attitude research. Unpublished doctoral dissertation, University of Chicago, 1930.

Stouffer, S. A. Notes on the case study and the unique case. *Sociometry,* 1941, **4,** 349-357.

Stouffer, S. A., Borgatta, E. F., Hays, D. G., & Henry, A. F. A technique for improving cumulative scales. *Public Opinion Quarterly,* 1952, **16,** 273-291.

Stout, M. An analysis of the structure of the Minnesota Multiphasic Personality Inventory. Unpublished master's thesis, Pennsylvania State College, 1949.

Stricker, G. Actuarial, naive clinical, and sophisticated clinical prediction of pathology from figure drawings. *Journal of Consulting Psychology,* 1967, **31**, 492-494.

Strickland, B., & Crowne, D. P. Conformity under conditions of simulated group pressure as a function of need for social approval. *Journal of Social Psychology,* 1962, **58**, 171-181.

Strumpfer, D. J.,W. The relation of Draw-A-Person Test variables to age and chronicity in psychotic groups. *Journal of Clinical Psychology,* 1963, **19**, 208-211.

Strumpfer, D. J. W., & Nichols, R. C. A study of some communicable measures for the evaluation of Human Figure Drawings. *Journal of Projective Techniques,* 1962, **26**, 342-353.

Summerwell, H., Campbell, M., & Sarason, I. The effect of differential motivating instructions on the emotional tone and outcome of TAT stories. *Journal of Consulting Psychology,* 1958, **22**, 385-388.

Sundberg, N. D. A note concerning the history of testing. *American Psychologist,* 1954, **9**, 150-151.

Sundberg, N. D. The practice of psychological testing in clinical services in the United States. *American Psychologist,* 1961, **16**, 79-83.

Sundberg, N. D., & Bachelis, W. D. The fakability of two measures of prejudice: The California F scale and Gough's Pr scale. *Journal of Abnormal and Social Psychology,* 1956, **52**, 140-142.

Sweetland, A. Hypnotic neurosis: Hypochondriasis and depression. *Journal of General Psychology,* 1948, **39**, 91-105.

Swensen, C. H., Jr. Sexual differentiation on the Draw-A-Person Test. *Journal of Clinical Psychology,* 1955, **11**, 37-40.

Swenson, C. H., Jr. Empirical evaluations of human figure drawings. *Psychological Bulletin,* 1957, **54**, 431-466.

Swenson, C. H., Jr. Some data on clinical training programs. *Journal of Clinical Psychology,* 1965, **21**, 332-333.

Swenson, C. H., Jr. Empirical evaluations of human figure drawings: 1957-1966. *Psychological Bulletin,* 1968, **70**, 20-44.

Swenson, W. M., & Lindgren, E. The use of psychological tests in industry. *Personnel Psychology,* 1952, **5**, 19-23.

Sydiaha, D. On the equivalence of clinical and statistical methods. *Journal of Applied Psychology,* 1959, **43**, 395-401.

Szasz, T. S. The myth of mental illness. *American Psychologist,* 1960, **15**, 113-118.

Szasz, T. S. The uses of naming and the origin of the myth of mental illness. *American Psychologist,* 1961, **16**, 59-65.

Szasz, T. S. *The ethics of psychoanalysis.* New York: Basic Books, 1965.

Taft, R. The ability to judge people. *Psychological Bulletin,* 1955, **52**, 1-28.

Taft, R. Judgment and judging in person cognition. In H. David & J. C. Brengelmann (Eds.), *Perspectives in personality research.* London: Crosby Lockwood, 1960.

Tagiuri, R. (Ed.). *Research needs in executive selection.* Boston: Graduate School of Business Administration, Harvard University. 1961.

Tallard, G. A. A review of J. Q. Hosopple & F. R. Miale. *Sentence completion: A projective method for the study of personality.* In O. Buros (Ed.), *Fifth mental measurements yearbook.* New Jersey: Gryphon Press, 1959.

Tallent, N. On individualizing the psychologist's clinical evaluation. *Journal of Clinical Psychology,* 1958, **14**, 243-244.

Tallent, N. *Clinical psychological consultation: A rationale and guide to team practice.* Englewood Cliffs, N.J.: Prentice Hall, 1963.

Taylor, D. W. The analysis of predictions of delinquency based on case studies. *Journal of Abnormal and Social Psychology,* 1947, **42**, 45-56.

Taylor, J. B. Social desirability and MMPI performance: The individual case. *Journal of Consulting Psychology,* 1959, **23**, 514-517.

Taylor, R. E. Figure location in student and patient samples. *Journal of Clinical Psychology,* 1960, **16**, 169-171.

Tellegen, A. The Minnesota Multiphasic Personality Inventory. In L.E. Abt & B. F. Reiss (Eds.), *Progress in clinical psychology.* Vol. 6. New York: Grune & Stratton, 1964.

Tendler, A. D. A preliminary report on a test for emotional insight. *Journal of Applied Psychology,* 1930, **14**, 123-136.

Testimony before the House Special Subcommittee on Invasion of Privacy of the Committee on Government Operations. *American Psychologist,* 1965, **20**, 955-988.

Testimony before the Senate Subcommittee on Constitutional Rights of the Committee on the Judiciary. *American Psychologist,* 1965, **20**, 888-954.

Thorndike, E. L. Fundamental theorems in judging men. *Journal of Applied Psychology,* 1918, **2**, 67-76.

Thorndike, E. L. A constant error in psychological ratings. *Journal of Applied Psychology,* 1920, **4**, 25-29.

Thorndike, R. L. *Personnel selection.* New York: Wiley, 1949.

Thorne, F. C. The clinical method in science. *American Psychologist,* 1947, **2**, 159-166.

Todd, F. J., & Hammond, K. R. Differential feedback in two multiple-cue probability learning tasks. *Behavioral Science,* 1965, **10**, 429-435.

Touchstone, F. V. A comparative study of Negro and white college students' aggressiveness by means of sentence completion. *Dissertation Abstracts,* 1957, **17**, 1588-1589.

Trankell, A. Erfarenheter av en metod for uttagning av piloter till Scandinavian Airlines System. *Meddelanded fran Flyg-och Navalmedincinska Namnden,* 1956, No. 1.

Traube, M. R. Completion-test language scales. *Contributions to education,* No. 77. New York: Bureau of Publications, Teachers College, Columbia University, 1916.

Travers, R. M. W. A study in judging the opinions of groups. *Archives of Psychology,* New York, 1941, No. 266, 1-73.

Travers, R. M. W. Rational hypotheses in the construction of tests. *Educational and Psychological Measurement,* 1951, **11**, 128-137.

Trites, D. K. Psychiatric screening of flying personnel: Evaluation of assumptions underlying interpretation of sentence completion tests. *U.S.A.F. School Aviation Medical Report,* 1955, No. 55-33.

Trites, D. K. Evaluation of assumptions underlying interpretation of sentence completion tests. *Journal of Consulting Psychology,* 1956, **20**, 8.

Trites, D. K., Holtzman, W. H., Templeton, R. C., & Sells, S. B. *Research on the SAM sentence completion test.* San Antonio, Texas: USAF School of Aviation Medicine, Randolph Field, July, 1953. (Project No. 21-0202-0007, Project Report No. 3).

Truesdell, A. B., & Bath, J. A. Clinical and actuarial predictions of academic survival and attrition. *Journal of Counseling Psychology,* 1956, **3**, 50-53.

Tryon, R. C. The component programs of the BC TRY system. Unpublished manuscript, University of California, Berkeley, 1964.

Tryon, R. C., & Bailey, D. E. The BC TRY computer system of cluster and factor analysis. *Multivariate Behavioral Research,* 1966, **1**, 95-111.

Tucker, L. R. A suggested alternative formulation in the developments by Hursch, Hammond, and Hursch, and by Hammond, Hursch, and Todd. *Psychological Review,* 1964, **71**, 528-530.

Tuddenham, R. D. Correlates of yielding to a distorted group norm. *Journal of Personality,* 1959, **27**, 272-284.

Tyler, F. T. A factorial analysis of fifteen MMPI scales. *Journal of Consulting Psychology,* 1951, **15**, 451-456.

Tyler, F. T., & Michaelis, J. U. K-scores applied to MMPI scales for college women. *Educational and Psychological Measurement,* 1953, **13**, 459-466.

U. S. Department of Commerce, Bureau of the Census. *Statistical abstract of the United States.* Washington: U. S. Government Printing Office, 1953.

Vance, F. L. Work on the APA Committee on Psychological Assessment in relation to public concern about testing. *American Psychologist,* 1965, **20**, 873-874.

Vandenberg, S. G., Rosenzweig, N., Moore, K. R., & Dukay, A. F. Diagnostic agreements among psychiatrists and "blind" Rorschach raters on the education of an interdisciplinary research team. *Psychological Reports,* 1964, **15**, 211-224.

Vane, J., & Eisen, V. The Goodenough Draw-A-Man Test and signs of maladjustment in kindergarten children. *Journal of Clinical Psychology,* 1962, **18**, 276-279.

Van Lennep, D. J., & Houwink, R. H. Projection tests and overt behavior. *Acta Psychologia,* 1953, **9**, 240-253.

Vernon, M. D. *A further study of visual perception.* New York: Cambridge University Press, 1952.

Vernon, M. D. The functions of schemata in perceiving. *Psychological Review,* 1955, **62**, 180-192.

Vernon, P. E. The validation of civil service selection board procedures. *Occupational Psychology,* 1950, **24**, 75-95.

Vernon, P. E., & Allport, G. W. A test for personal values. *Journal of Abnormal and Social Psychology,* 1931, **26**, 231-248.

Viteles, M. S. The clinical viewpoint in vocational selection. *Journal of Applied Psychology,* 1925, **9**, 131-138.

Wagner, M. E., & Schubert, H. J. P. *D.A.P. quality scale for late adolescents and young adults.* Kenmore, N. Y.: Delaware Letter Shop, 1955.

Walker, H. M., & Lev, J. *Statistical inference.* New York: Holt, Rinehart & Winston, 1953.

Wallace, J. Cognitive complexity and teachers' reinforcement behavior. Unpublished manuscript, Stanford University, 1963.

Wallace, J. An abilities conception of personality: Some implications for personality measurement. *American Psychologist,* 1966, **21**, 132-138.

Wallace, S. R. Criteria for what? *American Psychologist,* 1965, **20**, 411-417.

Wallace, W. L. The prediction of grades in specific college courses. *Journal of Educational Research,* 1951, **44**, 587-595.

Wallach, M. S., & Schooff, K. Reliability of degree of disturbance ratings. *Journal of Clinical Psychology,* 1965, **21**, 273-275.

Wallin, P. The prediction of individual behavior from case studies. In P. Horst, *et al. (Eds.), The prediction of personal adjustment.* New York: Social Science Research Council, 1941.

Walter, V. A., & Jones, A. W. An incomplete sentence test and the attitudes of manual arts therapy patients. *Journal of Counseling Psychology,* 1956, **3**, 140-144.

Ward, C. H., Beck, A. T., Mendelson, M., Mock, J. E., & Erbaugh, J. K. The psychiatric nomenclature: Reasons for diagnostic disagreement. *Archives of General Psychiatry,* 1962, **13**, 198-205.

Watkins, J. G., & Stauffacher, J. C. An index of pathological thinking in the Rorschach. *Journal of Projective Techniques,* 1952, **16**, 276-286.

Watley, D. J. Counselor predictive skill and differential judgments of occupational suitability. *Journal of Counseling Psychology,* 1967, **14**, 309-313.

Watley, D. J., & Vance, F. L. Clinical versus actuarial prediction of college achievement and leadership activity. United States Office of Education Cooperative Research Project No. 2202, September, 1964, University of Minnesota.

Watson, C. G. Relationship of distortion to DAP diagnostic accuracy among psychologists at three levels of sophistication. *Journal of Consulting Psychology,* 1967, **31**, 142-146.

Watts, A. F. *The language and mental development of children.* London: Harrap, 1944.

Wawrzaszek, F., Johnson, O. G., & Sciera, J. L. A comparison of H-T-P responses of handicapped and non-handicapped children. *Journal of Clinical Psychology,* 1958, **14**, 160-62.

Waxenberg, S. E. Psychosomatic patients and other physically ill persons: A comparative study. *Journal of Consulting Psychology,* 1955, **19**, 163-169.

Webb, E. J., Campbell, D. T., Schwartz, R. D., & Sechrest, L. *Unobtrusive measures: Nonreactive research in the social sciences.* Chicago: Rand McNally, 1966.

Webb, J.T. Validity and utility of computer produced MMPI reports with V.A. psychiatric populations. Paper presented to the American Psychological Association, Miami, 1970.

Webb, J.T., Miller, M.L., and Fowler, R.D. Validation of a computerized MMPI interpretation system. *Proceedings,* 77th Annual Convention of the American Psychological Association, 1969.

Webb, J.T., Miller, M.L., and Fowler, R.D. Extending professional time: A computerized MMPI interpretation service. *Journal of Clinical Psychology,* 1970, **26**, 210-214.

Wechsler, D. *Manual for the Wechsler Adult Intelligence Scale.* New York: Psychological Corporation, 1955.

Weick, K.E. Systematic observational methods. In G. Lindzey & E. Aronson (Eds.), *Handbook of social psychology* (Rev. ed). Reading, Mass.: Addison-Wesley, 1968.

Weiner, I. B. Three Rorschach scores indicative of schizophrenia. *Journal of Consulting Psychology,* 1961, **25**, 436-439.

Weisskopf, E.A., & Dieppa, J.J. Experimentally induced faking of TAT responses. *Journal of Consulting Psychology,* 1951, **13**, 469-474.

Weitman, M. Some variables related to bias in clinical judgment. *Journal of Clinical Psychology,* 1962, **18**, 504-506.

Wellner, A.M. Survey of psychology services in state mental hospitals. *American Psychologist,* 1968, **23**, 377-380.

Welsh, G.S. Factor dimensions A and R. In G.S. Welsh & W.G. Dahlstrom (Eds.), *Basic readings on the MMPI in psychology and medicine.* Minneapolis: University of Minneapolis Press, 1956.

Wesman, A.G. Faking personality test scores in a simulated employment situation. *Journal of Applied Psychology,* 1952, **36**, 112-113.

West, J.T. An investigation of the constructs "Effective intelligence" and "social competence" with the Copple Sentence Completion Test utilizing a school of social work population. *Dissertation Abstracts,* 1958, **19**, 1121.

West, J. V., Baugh, V. S., & Baugh, A. P. Rorschach and Draw-A-Person responses of hypnotized and non-hypnotized subjects. *Psychiatric Quarterly,* 1963, **37**, 123-127.

Westoff, C. F., Sagi, P. C., & Kelly, E. L. Fertility through twenty years of marriage: A study in predictive possibilities. *American Sociological Review,* 1958, **23**, 549-556.

Wheeler, W. M. An analysis of Rorschach indices of male homosexuality. *Rorschach Research Exchange,* 1949, **13**, 97-126.

Wheeler, W. M., Little, K. B., & Lehner, G. F. J. The internal structure of the MMPI. *Journal of Consulting Psychology,* 1951, **15**, 134-141.

Whitaker, L. The use of an extended Draw-A-Person Test to identify homosexual and effeminate men. *Journal of Consulting Psychology,* 1961, **25**, 482-485.

White, Mary A. A study of schizophrenic language. *Journal of Abnormal and Social Psychology,* 1949, **44**, 61-74.

White, R. W. *The abnormal personality.* New York: Ronald Press, 1956.

Whitmyre, J. W. The significance of artistic excellence in the judgment of adjustment inferred from human figure drawings. *Journal of Consulting Psychology,* 1953, **17**, 421-422.

Whyte, W. H., Jr. *The organization man.* New York: Simon & Schuster, 1956.

Wiener, D. N. Subtle and obvious keys for the MMPI. *Journal of Consulting Psychology,* 1948, **12**, 164-170.

Wiener, M., Blumberg, A., Segman, S., & Cooper, A. Judgment of adjustment by psychologists, psychiatric social workers, and college students, and its relationship to social desirability. *Journal of Abnormal and Social Psychology,* 1959, **59**, 315-321.

Wiggins, J. S. Interrelationships among MMPI measures of dissimulation under standard and social desirability instructions. *Journal of Consulting Psychology,* 1959, **23**, 419-427.

Wiggins, J. S. Content dimensions in the MMPI. In J. N. Butcher (Ed.), *MMPI: Research developments and clinical applications.* New York: McGraw-Hill, 1969.

Wiggins, J. S., & Rumrill, C. Social desirability in the MMPI and Welsh's factor scales A and R. *Journal of Consulting Psychology,* 1959, **23**, 100-106.

Wiggins, N., & Hoffman, P. J. Three models of clinical judgment. *Journal of Abnormal Psychology,* 1968, **73**, 70-77.

Wildman, R. W. The relationship between knee and arm joints on human figure drawings and paranoid trends. *Journal of Clinical Psychology,* 1963, **19**, 460-461.

Willingham, W. W. The sentence-completion test as a measure of moral. *USN School of Aviation Medical Research Report,* 1958, Project No. N. M. 16 01 11, Sub. 4, No. 4, iii, 6, A-9.

Willoughby, R. P., & Morse, M. E. Spontaneous reactions to a personality inventory. *American Journal of Orthopsychiatry,* 1936, **6**, 562-575.

Wilson, I. The use of a sentence completion test in differentiating between well-adjusted and maladjusted secondary school pupils. *Journal of Consulting Psychology,* 1949, **13**, 400-402.

Wilson, N. A. B. Interviewing candidates for technical appointments or training. *Occupational Psychology,* 1945, **19**, 161-179.

Winch, R. F., & More, D. M. Does TAT add information to interviews? Statistical analysis of the increments. *Journal of Clinical Psychology,* 1956, **12**, 316-321.

Windle, C. Psychological tests in psychopathological prognosis. *Psychological Bulletin,* 1952, **49**, 451-482.

Winne, J. F. The factorial composition of normal and neurotic responses to an adaptation of the Minnesota Multiphasic Personality Inventory. Unpublished doctoral dissertation, University of Pennsylvania, 1950.

Winslow, C. N., & Rapersand, I. Postdiction of the outcome of somatic therapy from the Rorschach records of schizophrenic patients. *Journal of Consulting Psychology,* 1964, **28**, 243-247.

Wirt, R. O. Actuarial prediction. *Journal of Consulting Psychology,* 1956, **20**, 123-124.

Wishner, J. Reanalysis of "Impressions of Personality." *Psychological Review,* 1960, **67**, 96-112.

Wisotsky, M. A note on the order of figure drawing among incarcerated alcoholics. *Journal of Clinical Psychology,* 1959, **15**, 65.

Witkin, H. A., Lewis, H. B., Hertzman, M., Machover, K., Meissner, P. B., & Wapner, S. *Personality through perception: An experimental and clinical study.* New York: Harper, 1954.

Wittman, M. P. A scale for measuring prognosis in schizophrenic patients. *Elgin Papers,* 1941, **4**, 20-33.

Wittman, M. P., & Steinberg, L. Follow-up of an objective evaluation of prognosis in dementia praecox and manic-depressive psychoses. *Elgin Papers,* 1944, **5**, 216-227.

Wolff, W. *Expression of personality.* New York: Harper, 1943.

Wolman, B. B. (Ed.) *Handbook of clinical psychology.* New York: McGraw-Hill, 1965.

Wolpe, J. *Psychotherapy by reciprocal inhibition.* Stanford, Calif.: Stanford University Press, 1958.

Wrenn, C. G. Two psychological worlds: An attempted rapprochement. In J. D. Krumboltz (Ed.), *Revolution in counseling.* Boston: Houghton Mifflin, 1966.

Wylie, R. C. *The self concept: A critical survey of pertinent research literature.* Lincoln: University of Nebraska Press, 1961.

Wysocki, B. A., & Whitney, E. Body image of crippled children as seen in Draw-A-Person Test behavior. *Perceptual and Motor Skills,* 1965, **21**, 499-504.

Yates, A. J. The application of learning theory to the treatment of tics. *Journal of Abnormal and Social Psychology,* 1958, **56**, 175-182.

Yntema, D. B., & Torgerson, W. S. Man-computer co-operation in decisions requiring common sense. *IRE Transactions of the Professional Group on Human Factors in Electronics,* 1961, **2**, 20-26.

Zagorski, H. J. A "science of complex judgment." *American Psychologist,* 1955, **10**, 250-251.

Zamansky, H. S., & Goldman, A. E. A comparison of two methods of analyzing Rorschach data in assessing therapeutic change. *Journal of Projective Techniques,* 1960, **24**, 75-82.

Zax, M., Cowen, E. L., Budin, W., & Biggs, C. F. The social desirability of trait descriptive terms: Applications to an alcoholic sample. *Journal of Social Psychology,* 1962, **56**, 21-27.

Zax, M., Cowen, E. L., & Peter, Sister Mary. A comparative study of novice nuns and college females using the response set approach. *Journal of Abnormal and Social Psychology,* 1963, **66**, 369-375.

Zigler, E., & Phillips, L. Psychiatric diagnosis: A critique. *Journal of Abnormal and Social Psychology,* 1961, **63**, 600-618. (a)

Zigler, E., & Phillips, L. Psychiatric diagnosis and symptomatology. *Journal of Abnormal and Social Psychology,* 1961, **63**, 69-75. (b)

Zimmer, H. Prediction by means of two projective tests of personality evaluations made by peers. *Journal of Clinical Psychology,* 1955, **11**, 352-356.

Zimmer, H. Validity of sentence completion and human figure drawings. In D. Brower & L. E. Abt (Eds.), *Progress in clinical psychology,* Vol. II. New York: Grune & Stratton, 1958.

Zinner, L. The consistency of human behavior in various situations: A methodological application of functional ecological psychology. Unpublished doctoral dissertation, University of Houston, 1963.

Zubin, J. Failures of the Rorschach technique. *Journal of Projective Techniques,* 1954, **18**, 303-315.

Zubin, J., Eron, L. D., & Schumer, F. *An experimental approach to projective techniques.* New York: Wiley, 1965.

Zuckerman, M. The validity of the Edwards Personal Preference Schedule in the measurement of dependency–rebelliousness. *Journal of Clinical Psychology,* 1958, **14**, 379-382.

Zuckerman, M., & Grosz, H. Suggestibility and dependency. *Journal of Consulting Psychology,* 1958, **22**, 328.

Zuckerman, M., & Monashkin, I. Self-acceptance and psychopathology. *Journal of Consulting Psychology,* 1957, **21**, 145-148.

Zuk, G. H. Relation of mental age to size of figures on the Draw-A-Person Test. *Perceptual and Motor Skills,* 1962, **14**, 410.

Author Index

Subject Index